James B. Finch Julius Caesar

Caesar Completely Parsed: Completely Parsed Caesar's Gallic War

Book I With Interlinear and Marginal Translations

James B. Finch Julius Caesar

Caesar Completely Parsed: Completely Parsed Caesar's Gallic War
Book I With Interlinear and Marginal Translations

ISBN/EAN: 9783743607972

Printed in Europe, USA, Canada, Australia, Japan

Cover: Foto ©ninafisch / pixelio.de

Manufactured and distributed by brebook publishing software (www.brebook.com)

James B. Finch Julius Caesar

Caesar Completely Parsed: Completely Parsed Caesar's Gallic War

Completely Parsed Classics

CAESAR'S GALLIC WAR

BOOK I.

*Being the Latin Text in the Original Order;
with a Literal Interlinear Translation; and with an Elegant
Translation in the Margin;*

AND

FOOTNOTES IN WHICH EVERY WORD IS COMPLETELY PARSED, THE CON
STRUCTIONS AND CONTEXT EXPLAINED, WITH REFERENCES TO
THE REVISED GRAMMARS OF ALLEN & GREENOUGH,
BINGHAM, GILDERSLEEVE, AND HARKNESS

BY

Rev. JAMES B. FINCH, M.A., D.D.

COPYRIGHT, 1898, BY HINDS & NOBLE

HINDS & NOBLE, Publishers
4–5–6–12–13–14 COOPER INSTITUTE, NEW YORK CITY
Schoolbooks of all publishers at one store

WE ARE ACTING

As the Agents of numerous Educational Institutions, large and small, throughout the country, for the purchase and forwarding of all Text-books used therein. Our exceptional facilities enable us to attend to this line of business with the utmost promptness, and we save our customers the delay and uncertainty of correspondence and dealings with numerous publishers, express companies, etc.

We can present no better testimony as to the success of our efforts in this direction, than the cordial approval of our old patrons, who are constantly sending us new customers.

We have purchased the stock and goodwill of the New York School Book Clearing House, which firm retires from business.

HINDS· & NOBLE,

4-5-13-14 Cooper Institute, N. Y. City.

TYPOGRAPHY OF
LANGUAGES PRINTING COMPANY
114 FIFTH AVENUE
NEW YORK

PREFACE.

WITH this book *anyone* can learn not only *about* the Latin language, but can learn *the language itself*.

I have designed it as an aid to three classes of learners, and it is my confident belief that *they* will find it in practice to be of really invaluable service — first, *teachers*, both those rusty in Latin who nevertheless find themselves called upon to teach Caesar without much time for preparation; and also those who are "up" in Caesar but still may benefit greatly, at the first, by having at their elbow a model for teaching and drilling which, like this, sets forth to the most minute detail each step in the parsing and the translation of every word in the text — then *clergymen* whose opportunities may not have permitted the acquisition of the Latin, but who yet desire to possess themselves rapidly of so much of this language as a minister really needs for etymological and philological and literary purposes, as well as for the simple satisfaction of emerging from a state of ignorance regarding a language so familiar to the educated — then *students*, both those who are not so situated as to have an instructor, but are still ambitious enough to study Latin without a teacher, and also students who, though members of a class, yet need the help of a complete model for translation and analysis, to be used, of course, under wise guidance. Again it is not wholly unlikely that the perfectly competent teacher of Latin will prize this book — not because of any need for assistance, but because of the advantage of comparing one's own ways and opinions with the methods and views of another competent teacher, particularly if that other's ideas are not always in accord with one's own.

The following suggestions are made to aid any learner who may wish to use this book as A BEGINNER'S LATIN BOOK: Take any one of the Latin grammars referred to in the preface; learn from it to distinguish and to decline the five Latin declensions of nouns; the first, the second, and the third declension of adjectives; learn also how to distinguish the four conjugations of the verbs, and how to inflect the verbs; read attentively Latin Syntax, especially the coarse print portion of it. With this equipment, turn to any nude text of the First Book of Caesar's Gallic War — Harper's for instance, or the Tutorial, or any other. Read a line, or sentence or paragraph, noting carefully the cases and numbers of the nouns and adjectives, and the persons and numbers of the verbs. If without knowledge of the *meaning* of the words, turn to the interlined translation in this volume, using it *now* as a vocabulary; and then turning from this back to the nude text, *translate* the line, sentence, or paragraph — always in the Latin order of the words. Compare your version with the interlinear translation. After this transpose your line, sentence or paragraph into the English order of the words, making as good English as possible, and then, not till then, compare your perfected whole with the English *translation in the margin*. Finally, look up the grammatical references as given in the footnotes, and examine the synonyms carefully and thus develop a critical scholarship. Not only will rapid progress be made in the facility to translate Latin, but a certain degree of culture will be attained as the outcome of the process.

As to the Latin text, this FIRST BOOK OF CAESAR'S GALLIC WAR is substantially that of Kraner; yet Kraner's Grecisms and other peculiarities in orthography, especially in that of proper names, have not been adopted; in these respects, the common lection is retained.

The text is accompanied by a rigidly literal interlinear translation according to the Latin order of the words, and a passably literal translation in the English order of the words in the margin. These translations are entirely new, having been made by me from the Latin text word by word, line by line, paragraph by paragraph.

The footnotes are both explanatory and critical. Every word of the text is parsed; and when the construction seems to require it, references are made to the Latin grammars of Allen and Greenough's Revised Edition, Bingham revised by McCabe, Gildersleeve revised by Lodge, and Harkness's Standard Edition. Caesar's *formal* indirect speeches throughout this FIRST BOOK OF THE GALLIC WAR have been put, at stated intervals in the notes, into the *direct* form by way of illustration and contrast; and for the same reason his *informal* indirect discourses may generally be found there, put into the direct form.

Latin synonyms have been noted and sharply discriminated wherever they occur; and thus hints as to critical word study are given on almost every page. Grammatical references, and occasionally the synonyms, are repeated, especially in the first part of the book, in order that principles grammatical and philological may be kept continually before the reader's eye.

As to pronunciation, the Roman method may be used from the start if desired, as the long vowels are marked (thus ¯) and all vowels not so marked are to be considered short vowels. If some other than the Roman pronunciation is preferred, Allen and Greenough's grammar explains the English method as well as the Roman; Harkness's, both these methods, and also the Continental; Bingham's and Gildersleeve's confining themselves to the Roman.

JAMES B. FINCH.

ABBREVIATIONS.

abl.	= ablative.		*impers.*	= impersonal.
abs. or *absol.*	= absolute.		*ind.*	= indicative.
acc.	= accusative.		*indecl.*	= indeclinable.
act.	= active.		*indef.*	= indefinite.
adj.	= adjective.		*infin.*	= infinitive.
adv.	= adverb.		*interrog.*	= interrogative.
A. & G.	= Allen & Greenough's Latin Grammar, Revised Edition.		*intrans.*	= intransitive.
			l.	= line.
			ll.	= lines.
			m.	= masculine.
B.	= Bingham's Latin Grammar, Rev. by McCabe.		*n.* or *neut.*	= neuter.
			neg.	= negative.
			nom.	= nominative.
cf. (cōnfer)	= compare.		*num.*	= numeral.
comp.	= compound.		*obj.*	= object.
conj.	= conjunction.		*p.*	= page.
dat.	= dative.		*pp.*	= pages.
decl.	= declension.		*part.*	= participle.
dem.	= demonstrative.		*pass.*	= passive.
dep.	= deponent.		*perf.*	= perfect.
disc.	= discourse.		*pers.*	= personal.
distrib.	= distributive.		*poss.*	= possessive.
=	= equals, equivalent to, or denotes.		*pred.*	= predicate.
			prep.	= preposition.
e.g. (exemplī grātiā)	= for example.		*pres.*	= present.
			pron.	= pronoun.
etc. (et caetera)	= and so forth.		*rel.*	= relative.
f. or *fem.*	= feminine.		*sc. (scīlicet)*	= that is to say; sometimes = supply.
ff.	= following.			
fr.	= from.			
fut.	= future.		*sing.*	= singular.
G.	= Gildersleeve's Latin Gram., Revised Ed.		*subj.*	= subject.
			subst.	= substantive.
			superl.	= superlative.
gen.	= genitive.		*trans.*	= transitive.
H.	= Harkness's Latin Grammar, Rev. Stand. Edit.		*viz. (vidēlicet)*	= namely.
			1, 2, 3, 4 with verbs	= 1st, 2d, 3d, 4th conjugation.
i.e. (id est)	= that is.			
imperf.	= imperfect.			

[LINES 1-3.] BOOK I. **1**

1 I. Gallia	est	omnis	dīvīsa	in	partēs	I. Gaul, as a whole, is divided into three parts: the Belgae inhabit one of these; the Aquitani another; and those who in their own language are call-
Gaul	*is*	*all*	*divided*	*into*	*parts*	
2 trēs,	quārum	ūnam	incolunt		Belgae,	
three,	*of which*	*one*	*inhabit*		*the Belgae,*	
3 aliam	Aquitānī,	tertiam		quī	ipsōrum	
the other	*the Aquitani,*	*the third*	*(those) who*		*of themselves*	

LINE 1. **Gallia, -ae,** nom. sing. f., subj. of *est dīvīsa* (*dīvīsa est*); the generic term for the three divisions — Belgica, Celtica and Aquitania — conceived as a totality. The Greek equivalent is Γαλατία. —— **est,** 3d pers. sing. pres. ind. of the irr. verb *sum, esse, fuī, futūrus,* no supine; compare A.S. is, GER. ist, GK. ἐστί ; *est* in the text may be taken as the copula, or as a part of the compound *dīvīsa est*, perf. pass., 3d pers. sing. of *dīvidō, -ere, -vīsī, -vīsum*, 3. Thus the Greek paraphrast regarded it, and translated *est dīvīsa* by διῄρηται. —— **omnis, -e,** an adj. of two endings, an *ī*-stem; agrees with *Gallia*, but seems to have here the force of an adv., and = *as a whole*. Consult A. & G. 191; B. 128, REM. 10; G. 325, 6; H. 443. —— **dīvīsa,** see *est*, above. —— **in,** prep. with acc. or abl.: with acc. after verbs of motion = *into*; with abl. after verbs of rest = *in*, or *on*, or *among*. —— **partēs,** acc. plur. of *pars, partis,* f.; acc. after *in*. See *In*, A. & G. 153, I, 2; B. 120, I, 2, 3; G. 418, I, 2; H. 435, I.

LINE 2. **trēs,** acc. plur. of numeral adj. *trēs, tria,* an *ī*-stem, declined regularly like the plur. of *levis;* agrees with *partēs*. Of the cardinals up to *centum*, only *ūnus, duo* and *trēs* are declinable. —— **quārum,** gen. plur. f. of *quī, quae, quod,* rel. pron. in use both as subst. and adj.; in the text it refers to *partēs* as antecedent; it might also be taken as modifying *partium*, to be supplied; it is a partitive gen. after *ūnam*. A. & G. 216, *a*, 2; B. 134; G. 370; H. 397, 2. —— **ūnam,** acc. sing. f.; supply *partem*, which is the direct obj. of *incolunt*. Note that *ūnus, -a, -um* is one of the adjectives that have the gen. in *-īus*, and dat. in *-ī*. For list of these, see A. & G. 83; B. 56, 3, 4; G. 76, I, 2; H. 151. —— **incolunt,** 3d pers. plur. pres. ind. act. of *incolō, -ere, -uī, -cultum*, 3. —— **Belgae, -ārum,** nom. plur. m., subj. of *incolunt*. Note the gender from the signification rather than the declension. The Belgae were a mixed race, partly Germanic and partly Celtic in origin; they inhabited northern Gaul, or the region bounded by the Marne, the Seine, the Rhine and the ocean.

LINE 3. **aliam,** supply *partem;* acc. sing. f. of adj. *alius, -ia, -iud;* lit. = *other, another,* but in the text = *alteram*, i.e. *the second* (*partem* if supplied would be direct obj. of *incolunt*. For decl., see A. & G. 83; B. 56 and REM. I; G. 76 and REM. I; H. 151. —— **Aquitānī,** nom. plur. m. of the adj. *Aquitānus, -a, -um*, used substantively; as subj. of *incolunt* understood. They were the inhabitants of south-western Gaul. —— **tertiam,** supply *partem;* acc. sing. f. of the ordinal adj. *tertius, -a, -um* (*partem* if supplied would be direct obj. of *incolunt*). —— **quī,** nom. plur. m. of rel. pron. *quī, quae, quod;* subj. of *appellantur;* its antecedent is *eī* understood, which latter is subj. of *incolunt*, to be supplied. The antecedent of a rel. pron. is often omitted if indefinite, or if naturally implied from the context. —— **ipsōrum,** gen. plur. m. of the pron. *ipse, -sa -sum,* gen. *-īus*, dat. *-ī;* lit. *of themselves;* more emphatic than *suā,* and sometimes used in connection with the latter. A. & G. 197, *e*; B. 85, REM. 2, and 128, REM. 8; G. 311, 321, 2; H. 398, 3, and 452. With ellipses supplied, the text would read here: *quārum partium ūnam partem incolunt Belgae, aliam partem Aquitānī incolunt, tertiam partem eī incolunt quī,* etc.

ed Celtae, in ours Galli, inhabit the third. All these peoplediffer from one another in language, customs and laws. The Garumna river separates the Galli from the Aquitani; the Matrona and the Sequana	linguā *in the language* Hī omnēs *These all* sē *themselves* Garumna *the Garonne*	Celtae, *Celts,* linguā, *in language,* differunt. *differ.* flūmen, *river,*	nostrā *in ours* īnstitūtīs, *in customs,* Gallōs *The Gauls* ā *from*	Gallī *Gauls* lēgibus *in laws* ab *from* Belgīs *the Belgae*	appellantur. 4 *are called.* inter 5 among Aquitānīs 6 *the Aquitani* Matrona et 7 *the Marne and*

LINE 4. **linguā**, sing., abl. of manner of *lingua, -ae,* f. A. & G. 248; B. 168; G. 399; H. 419, III. —— **Celtae, -ārum**, nom. plur. m., the people of central Gaul; GK. Κέλτοι; *appellantur Celtae = are called Celts.* See *appellantur*, just below. —— **nostrā**, abl. sing. of poss. pron. *noster, -tra, -trum;* supply *lingud.* —— **Gallī**, nom. plur. m. of adj. *Gallus, -a, -um,* used as a subst. See *appellantur,* just below. —— **ap(ad)pellantur,** 3d pers. plur. pres. ind. pass. of *appello, -āre, -āvi, -ātum,* 1. Observe that in this clause ending with the passive verb, *Celtae* and *Gallī* are predicate-nominatives; the subject-nom. is *quī.* A. & G. 176, *a;* B. 130, 3; G. 206; H. 362, 2, 2).

LINE 5. **Hī**, nom. plur. m. of dem. pron. *hīc, haec, hōc = those just mentioned;* expressed for emphasis; used here substantively. A. & G. 195, 1; B. 84, 1; G. 305, 5; H. 450, 1. —— **omnēs**, nom. plur. m. of the adj. *omnis, -e,* an adj. of two endings; an *ī*-stem as shown by the gen. plur. *omnium; omnēs* modifies *hī.* As *omnēs* includes the whole, it takes a case in agreement, and does not admit of the partitive construction. Hence, as in the text, *hī omnēs,* and not *hōrum omnēs.* A. & G. 216, *e;* B. 134, REM. 4; G. 370, 2; H. 397, NOTE. —— **linguā**, sing., abl. of specification of *lingua, -ae,* f. A. & G. 253; B. 162; G. 397; H. 424. —— **īnstitūtīs**, plur., abl. of specification of *īnstitūtum, -ī,* n. —— **lēgibus**, plur., abl. of specification of *lēx, lēgis,* f. Observe that in a series of words either no conjunction is used, or it is repeated between the words. The enclitic *-que,* however, may be appended to the last word of a series. A. & G. 208, 3, and 346, *c;* B. 123, REM. 6; G. 474, NOTE; H. 554, 6. —— **inter,** prep. with acc.; lit. = *between.*

LINE 6. **sē,** acc. plur. of *suī,* reflexive pron. of the 3d pers., obj. of *inter.* Observe that the phrase *inter sē* indicates a reciprocal relation, and see A. & G. 196, *f;* B. 78, REM. 4; G. 221; H. 448, NOTE. —— **differunt,** 3d pers. plur. pres. ind. act. of *differō, -ferre, distulī, dīlātum* (dis + ferre) = lit. *to bear apart;* hence, *to differ.* —— **Gallōs,** acc. plur., direct obj. of *dīvidit.* For decl., see *Gallī,* l. 4, above. —— **ab,** compare *ā,* l. 7, below; *d* is used before consonants only; *ab,* before vowels or consonants; prep. with the abl. A. & G. 152, *b;* B. 120, 2; G. 417; H. 434. —— **Aquitānīs,** plur., abl. after *ab.* For decl., etc., see *Aquitānī,* l. 3, above.

LINE 7. **Garumna,** nom. sing., appositive; *Garumna, -ae,* m.; rivers, winds and months are masculine; this river forms the boundary between Aquitania and Celtica. —— **flūmen, -inis,** nom. sing. n. (*fluere,* to flow; hence lit. *flūmen = the flowing*); subj. of *dīvidit,* to be supplied from the following clause of this, in fact, compound sentence. —— **ā,** see *ab,* l. 6, above. —— **Belgīs,** plur., abl. after prep. *ā.* For decl., etc., see l. 2, above. —— **Matrona, -ae,** nom. sing. m., appositive = *the Marne; flūmen* to be supplied. —— **et,** cop. conj., joins words of equal importance.

[LINES 8-11.] BOOK I. 3

						rivers separate them from the Belgae. The bravest of all these people are the Belgae, because they are very remote from the civilization and refinement of our province, and the traders do not
Sēquana	dīvidit.	Hōrum	omnium	fortissimī		
the Seine	*divides.*	*Of these*	*all*	*the bravest*		
sunt	Belgae,	proptereā	quod		ū	
are	*the Belgae,*	*on this account*	*because*		*from*	
cultū	atque	hūmānitāte		prōvinciae		
the civilization	*and*	*refinement*		*of the province*		
longissimē	absunt,	minimēque		ad	eōs	
very far	*are they distant,*	*least and,*		*to*	*them*	

LINE 8. **Sēquana**, -ae, nom. sing. m. = *the Seine;* in apposition with *flūmen* understood, which latter is the subj. of *dīvidit.* —— **dīvidit**, 3d pers. sing. pres. ind. act. For principal parts, see l. 1, above. The verb agrees with its subj. *flūmen* understood. The clauses fully constructed are : *Gallōs ab Aquitānīs Garumna flūmen dīvidit, et Gallōs ā Belgīs Matrona et Sēquana dīvidunt.* The sing. verb, however, may be explained by A. & G. 205, *b;* B. 126, REM. 2; G. 285, EXC. 1, end; H. 463, II. 3; the two rivers being conceived as forming a single boundary. —— **Hōrum**, gen. plur. m. of dem. pron. *hīc, haec, hōc;* partitive gen. after *fortissimī; hōrum* is here used substantively, and is modified by *omnium.* A. & G. 216, *a,* 2; B. 134, and for *omnium*, REM. 4; G. 372; H. 397, 3. —— **omnium**, gen. plur. m. of *omnis, -e.* For decl., etc., see note on *hī omnēs*, l. 5, above. Note carefully that *omnium* here is not a partitive gen., but simply an attributive of *hōrum.* —— **fortissimī**, adj. plur. m., superl. degree of *fortis, -ior, -issimus, -a, -um;* predicate-adj. with *sunt.*

LINE 9. **sunt**, 3d pers. plur. of *sum, esse, fuī, futūrus; sunt* is here the copula; the subj. is *Belgae.* —— **Belgae**, for decl., see l. 2, above. —— **proptereā** (propter + eā), adv.; lit. *on account of. proptereā* here is simply the herald, so to speak, of the *quod*-clause following, and, in such use, it may, usually, be omitted in the translation. —— **quod**, conj., but originally an adv. of specification; acc. n. of *quī, quae, quod.* —— **ā**, see note on *ab*, l. 6, above.

LINE 10. **cultū**, abl. of *cultūs, -ūs*, m.; abl. after prep. *ā.* A. & G. 152, *b;* B. 120, 2; G. 417; H. 434. (Derived from *colere,* lit. *to cultivate,* orig. *pertaining to the culture of the fields;* compare stem κολ as seen in βουκολέω.) —— **atque** (ad + que), abridged = *āc;* it adds sometimes a more important notion = *and also; atque* is used before vowels and consonants, especially before vowels; *āc* is used before consonants only, in classic Latin. —— **hūmānitāte**, abl. of *hūmānitās, -ātis,* m., connected by *atque* to *cultū,* and governed by *ā.* Note that *hūmānitās* is derived from adj. *hūmānus,* and this from *homō;* hence = lit. *humanly, humanity.* To explain *cultū atque hūmānitāte* as an hendiadys (ἓν διὰ δυοῖν), see A. & G. 385, I; B. 310, 2, (*b*); G. 698; H. 636, III. 2. As thus explained, the words = *a refined mode of life.* —— **prōvinciae**, gen. of *prōvincia, -ae*, f.; as a gen. it limits the two immediately preceding substantives. Here *prōvinciae* = the Roman Province in the south-east part of *Gallia omnis.*

LINE 11. **longissimē**, adv., modifies *absunt,* superl. degree; positive *longē* or *longiter;* comparative *longius.* As to the formation of adverbs from adjectives, see A. & G. 148, *a, b, c, d;* B. 117, 5, 6; G. 91, 2, *b, c, d, e;* H. 304. As to the signification, see A. & G. 93, *b;* B. 68, REM. 4; G. 302, 303; H. 444, 1. —— **absunt**, 3d pers. plur. pres. ind. of *absum, abesse, ab(ā)fuī, ab(ā)futūrus, -a, -um;* irr. intrans. verb; its subj. is the pron. *eī* understood, referring to *Belgae,* l. 9, above. —— **minimēque**

very often visit them and import such things as tend to enervate the mind; and besides, they are next to the Germans who dwell across the Rhine,	mercātōrēs *the merchants* ad efféminandōs *to* proximīque *nearest*	saepe *often* animōs *enervate* sunt *and,*	commeant *go to and fro* pertinent, *minds* Germānīs, *are they to the Germans,*	atque *and* *tend,* quī *who*	ea, *those things* important, *do they bring in,* trāns *across*	quae 12 *which* 13 Rhēnum 14 *the Rhine*

(minimē + que). The enclitic is always appended to some word, and it joins a word or sentence closely to another. The adv. *minimē* is compared thus: positive *parum* or *parvē* (rare), comparative *minus*, superl. *minimē*. This superl. = lit. *least;* often it = *not at all.* See A. & G. 92, end, 209, *e*; B. 119, REM. 2; G. 93; H. 552, 3. *minimē* modifies *saepe*, and the two words taken together = *very rarely.* —— **ad**, prep. with the acc., lit. = *toward*, with verbs of motion = *to.* —— **eōs**, acc. plur. m. of dem. pron. *is, ea, id*, here used substantively as a personal pron. of the 3d person. A. & G. 98, *a*, 102, *d*, middle; B. 83, 1; G. 102; H. 451; *eōs* is the acc. after *ad*. A. & G. 258; B. 141, REM. 1; G. 345, REM. 2, end; H. 380, I, and 384, 3, 1).

LINE 12. **mercātōrēs**, nom. plur. of *mercātor, -ōris*, m., subj. of *commeant*. —— **saepe**, adv., comparative *saepius* (compare GER. öfter), superl. *saepissimē*. See observation on *minimē*, l. 11, above. *saepe* modifies *commeant*. —— **commeant**, 3d pers. plur. pres. ind. act. of *commeō, -āre, -āvī, -ātum*, 1 (con + meāre = *to go together with a view to return;* hence = *to go to and fro*). The subj. of *commeant* is the pron. *eī* understood, referring to *Belgae*, l. 9, above. —— atque, see note on this particle, l. 10, above. —— **ea**, acc. plur. n. of the dem. pron. *is, ea, id;* direct obj. of *important.* —— **quae**, nom. plur. n. of the pron. *quī, quae, quod;* refers to *ea;* is subj. of *pertinent*.

LINE 13. **ad**, see note on *ad*, l. 11, above; it is followed here by the acc. of the gerundive construction. —— **efféminandōs**, limits *animōs* and is acc. plur. gerundive of the verb *effēminō, -āre, -āvī, -ātum*, 1 (ex + fēmina) = *to change one's nature, to make a woman out of it.* —— **animōs** is acc. plur. of *animus, -ī*, m., after *ad*. The better translation of this so-called gerundive construction is to translate it as if it were a gerund with a direct object. See A. & G. 296, 300; B. 184; G. 430, 432; H. 543. The gerundive is merely the fut. pass. participle. —— **pertinent**, 3d pers. plur. pres. ind. act. of *pertineō, -ēre, -uī*, no supine, 2, intrans. (per + tenēre); it agrees with the subj. *quae*. —— **important**, 3d pers. plur. of *importō, -āre, -āvī, -ātum*, 1; its subj. is *mercātōrēs*, i.e. *important* is connected by *atque* with *commeant*, and has the same subj. as the latter. *importāre* is compounded of in + portāre. *n* becomes *m* before *p* by assimilation. A. & G. 11, *f*, 3, NOTE; B. 122; G. 9, 4, middle; H. 33, 3.

LINE 14. **proximīque** (proximī + que). As to the enclitic, see note on *-que*, l. 11, above. *proximī* is nom. plur. m. of *proximus, -a, -um*, superl. of the comparative *propior*, no positive, though the comparative is formed from the stem of the adv. *prope*.. There are some every-day adjectives that lack the positive. See A. & G. 91, *a*; B. 74, 1; G. 87, 8; H. 166. *proximī* is predicate-adj. after *sunt*. —— **sunt**, for principal parts, see l. 9, above; its subj. is *Belgae*, to be supplied. —— **Germānīs**, dat. plur. m. of *Germānī, -ōrum*, the eastern neighbors of the Gauls. Occasionally the sing. *Germānus, -ī*, m., occurs. The word is probably of Celtic origin. Some derive it from *Wehr-Mann*, war-man. *Germānīs* is dat. after *proximī*, a word of nearness. See A. & G. 234, *a*; B. 144, REM. 4; G. 359; H. 391, I. —— **quī**, nom. plur. m. of *quī, quae, quod*, refers to *Germānīs*, and is the subject-nom. of *incolunt*. For grammatical

LINES 15-17.] BOOK I. 5

15 incolunt, quibuscum continenter bellum gerunt. | with whom they
   dwell,   *whom with,*   *continually*   *war they wage.* | are incessantly waging war: for
16 Quā dē causā Helvētiī quoque reliquōs | which reason the Helvetii also ex-
   Which for,   *cause*   *the Helvetii*   *also*   *the remaining* | cel the rest of the Gauls in valor, be-
17 Gallōs virtūte praecēdunt, quod ferē cotīdiānīs | cause they fight
   Gauls   *in valor*   *surpass,*   *because almost*   *in daily* | with the Germans

usage of the rel. pron., see note on *quārum*, l. 2, above. —— **trāns**, prep. with the acc. —— **Rhēnum**, acc. of *Rhēnus, -ī*, and follows the prep. *trāns*. This prep. is used after verbs of motion and verbs of rest. See *Trāns*, A. & G. 153, *a, b*; B. 120, 1; G. 416, 26; H. 433. The Rhine is a general boundary between Gaul and Germany.

LINE 15. **incolunt**, 3d pers. plur. of *incolō, -ere, -uī, -cultum*, 3; its subject-nom. is *quī*. —— **quibuscum** (quibus+cum) = *with whom. quibus* is the abl. plur. of the rel. *quī, quae, quod;* it refers to *Germānīs*, and is governed by the prep. *cum* that is appended to it. The prep. *cum*, as an enclitic, is appended to all forms of the abl. of *quī*. See A. & G. 104, *e*; B. 87, 4, REM. 2; G. 413, REM. 1; H. 187, 2. —— **continenter**, adv. (*continēns* from con + tenēre = *to hang together*, hence =) *connectedly, continuously.* —— **bellum**, acc. sing. of *bellum, -ī*, n.; direct obj. of *gerunt*. The original form was *duellum (duo)*, denoting a conflict in which two parties were striving for the mastery. Compare English *duel*. —— **gerunt**, 3d pers. plur. pres. ind. of *gerō, -ere, gessī, gestum*, 3; its subj. is the pron. *eī*, referring to *Belgae*, l. 9, above.

LINE 16. **Quā dē causā**. In this phrase *quā* is used adjectively, and agrees with the noun *causā;* it refers both to what is stated in the last clause of the preceding sentence and to what follows. The phrase as such is the herald of the following *quod*-clause. When a relative thus begins a sentence, it is best translated by a demonstrative with the conjunction *and* or *but*. Consult A. & G. 180, *f*; B. 129, REM. 9; G. 610, REM. 1; H. 453. —— **dē**. A monosyllabic prep. is often thus placed between a noun and its modifier. See A. & G. 345, *a*; B. 58. 2; G. 413, REM. 1; H. 569, II. 1. —— **causā**, abl. of *causa, -ae*, f.; it is in the abl. after the prep. *dē*. Observe its idiomatic use in the phrase, and consult A. & G. 153 under *dē, c;* B. 120, 2; G. 408, NOTE 4, and 417, 5; II. 434, and 434 under *dē*, 6. *dē*, lit. in the phrase = *from;* but the best English for this phrase, standing at the head of the sentence, is: *and for this reason.* —— **Helvētiī**, nom. plur. m. of the adj. *Helvētius, -a, -um*, used substantively, subj. of *praecēdunt*. The Helvetii were a Celtic people whose territory was bounded by Mount Jura, Lake Geneva, the Rhone and the Rhine. —— **quoque**, adv.; some regard it as a conj.; its position is after one or more words. See A. & G. 345, *b*; B. 123, REM. 5; G. 479; H. 569, III. —— **reliquōs**, acc. plur. m. of adj. *reliquus, -a, -um;* it limits *Gallōs*.

LINE 17. **Gallōs**, acc. plur. of *Gallī, -ōrum*, m.; see l. 4, above; it is the direct obj. of *praecēdunt*. —— **virtūte**, abl. of *virtus, -ūtis*, f.; abl. of specification. See note on *linguā*, l. 5, above. *virtus* is derived from *vir;* hence = *manliness*. —— **praecēdunt**, 3d pers. plur. pres. ind. act. of *praecēdō, -ere, -cēssī, -cēssum*, 3; here transitive, but sometimes intransitive (prae + caedere = lit. *to go before*). —— **quod**, conj., but see note on *quod*, l. 9, above. —— **ferē**, adv., modifies *cotīdiānīs* (derived from *ferō*, and denotes that which is brought near a thing; hence = *within a little, almost*). —— **cotīdiānīs**, abl. plur. n. of *cotīdiānus, -a, -um;* another orthography is *quotīdiānus*, from *quotīdiē* (quot + diēs); *cotīdiānīs* modifies *proeliīs*.

in almost daily battles, while they are keeping them from their own borders, or themselves are waging war in their confines. One part	proeliīs *battles*	cum *with*	Germānīs *the Germans*	contendunt, *they contend,*	cum *when*	18
	aut *either (from)*	suīs *their own*	fīnibus *territory*	eōs *them*	prohibent, *they keep off,*	aut *or*	19
	ipsī *themselves*	in *in*	eōrum *their*	fīnibus *territory*	bellum *war*	gerunt. *they wage.*	20

LINE 18. **proeliīs**, abl. plur. of *proelium, -ī*; abl. of manner. For grammatical references, see *linguā*, l. 4, above. (prae + īre = *to go forward in a hostile manner.*) Synonyms: *proelium* is the occasional action or skirmish between two forces; it sometimes, however, denotes a general contest. But *pūgna* is the usual word to designate, in a general sense, any sort of contest, from fisticuffs to a pitched battle. —— **cum**, prep. with the abl. This word in its present position is to be carefully discriminated from *cum*, a conjunction meaning *when*, or *as*, or *since*. The discrimination can only be made by sharply noting the construction. *cum* meaning *with*, and *cum* meaning *when* or *since* are in form precisely alike; but as *cum*, in the text, is in a clause which has its own connective *quod*, the inference, quick as thought, is that the *cum* of the text is a preposition. —— **Germānīs**, abl. plur. of manner of *Germānī, -ōrum*. A. & G. 248; B. 168; G. 392, REM. 1; H. 419, III. Note that *Germānīs* is not from the adj., used as a noun, *germānus, -a, -um*, but from *Germānī*, GK. Γερμάνοι, *the Germans*, a people occupying the territory between the Rhine, the Danube and the Vistula, the modern Weichsel. —— **contendunt**, 3d pers. plur. pres. ind. act. of *contendō, -ere, contendī, contentum*, 3; its subject-nom. is *eī*, i.e. *Helvētiī*. (con + tendere = (*a*) *to stretch eagerly*, (*b*) *to go hastily*, (*c*) *to strive*, i.e. with weapons, (*d*) *to fight*.) —— **cum**, conj.; in narration denoting *time when*, it takes the imperf. and pluperf. subj.; in the other tenses, the ind. A. & G. 325; B. 220; G. 580; H. 521, I. *cum* here is a conjunction, because it introduces a clause (consisting of a verb, a direct object and a remote object) which requires a connective.

LINE 19. **aut . . . aut**, correlative conjunctions = *either . . . or*. These particles, thus used, generally denote that the difference is exclusive; if the difference is neither important nor exclusive, *vel . . . vel* are used. —— **suīs**, abl. plur. of the reflexive pron. *suus, -a, -um*; it agrees with *fīnibus*; it refers to the Helvetii, the subject of the principal clause. Consult A. & G. 196; B. 80, REM. 2 and 3; G. 309; H. 449. —— **fīnibus**, abl. plur. of *fīnis, -is*, m.; abl. after *prohibent*, a verb of separation. A. & G. 243; B. 160; G. 390, NOTE 3; H. 414. —— **eōs**, acc. plur. of dem. pron. *is, ea, id*, used as a pron. of the 3d pers.; it refers to the Germans, and is the direct obj. of *prohibent*. —— **prohibent**, 3d pers. plur. pres. ind. act. of *prohibeō, -ēre, -uī, -itum*, 2 (pro + habēre, lit. *to hold before* or *off*).

LINE 20. **ipsī**, i.e. *Helvētiī*; nom. plur. of *ipse, -a, -um*, subj. of *gerunt*; it is here an emphatic pron. of the 3d pers. Consult A. & G. 195, *g*; B. 85, REM. 1; G. 311, 2; H. 452. As to the declension of this pron., see grammatical references to *ipsōrum*, l. 3, above. —— **in**, here takes the abl. plur. *fīnibus*. See A. & G. 153, on prep. *In*, 2; B. 120, 2; G. 418, *b*; H. 435, 1, end. —— **eōrum**, gen. plur. of dem. pron. *is, ea, id*, used as a pers. pron. of the 3d person. Note that, in this use, it corresponds to *their*, the possessive case, plur. of the pron. *he*. As to the position of *eōrum* between the prep. and its case, see A. & G. 344, *g*; B. 43, 2; G. 678, 4; H. 569, II. 3. —— **fīnibus**, abl. plur. after *in*; for decl., see l. 19, above. —— **bellum**, acc. of *bellum, -ī*, n.; direct obj. of *gerunt*. See note on this word, l. 15, above. —— **gerunt**, 3d pers. plur. pres. ind. act. of *gero*; its subj. is *ipsī*, i.e. *Helvētiī*. For principal parts of *gero*, see l. 15, above.

21 Eōrum	ūna	pars,	quam	Gallōs	obtinēre	of this country, which we have said the Gauls occupy, begins at the Rhone river; it is bounded by the Garonne river, the ocean and the territory of the Belgae; on the side of the Sequani and the Helvetii it also reaches to the Rhine river;
Of these	*one*	*part,*	*which*	*the Gauls*	*to occupy,*	
22 dictum est,		initium	capit	ā	flūmine	
it was said,		*the beginning*	*takes*	*from*	*the river*	
23 Rhodanō;	continētur	Garumnā	flūmine,		Ōceanō,	
Rhone;	*it is bounded*	*by the Garonne*	*river,*		*by the ocean,*	
24 fīnibus		Belgārum;	attingit	etiam	ab	
by the territory		*of the Belgae;*	*it touches*	*also*	*on the side of*	
25 Sēquanīs	et Helvētiīs	flūmen	Rhēnum;	vergit		
of the Sequani and	*Helvetii*	*the river*	*Rhine;*	*it slopes*		

LINE 21. **Eōrum**, see note, l. 20, above; partitive gen. after *pars*. Consult A. & G. 216, *a*, 1; B. 134; G. 368; H. 396, IV. Observe that the people are put by metonymy for the country. —— **ūna**, nom. sing. f. of the adj. *ūnus, -a, -um*; it agrees with *pars*. For decl., see note, l. 2, above. —— **pars,** *partis*, f., subject-nom. of *capit*, l. 22, below. —— **quam**, rel. pron., acc. sing. f. of *qui, quae, quod*; it refers to *pars*, and is the direct obj. of *obtinēre*. —— **Gallōs**, for the decl. of the word, and a description of the Gallī, see note, l. 4, above; *Gallōs* is subject-acc. of *obtinēre*. —— **obtinēre**, pres. inf. act. of *obtineō, -ēre, -uī, -tentum,* 2 (ob + tenēre, lit. *to hold to something*).

LINE 22. **dictum est,** 3d pers. sing. perf. ind. pass. of *dīcō, -ere, dīxī, dictum,* 3; it is here used impersonally; or, strictly, the object-clause *quam Gallōs obtinēre* is the subject. Consult A. & G. 330, *a*, 2; B. 180, REM. 1; G. 535; H. 538. Supply *ā mē* as the abl. of the agent. For what Caesar said in regard to the matter, see the first few lines, at the beginning of the chapter. —— **initium**, acc. sing. of *initium, -ī*, n. (in + ire); direct obj. of *capit*. —— **capit**, 3d pers. sing. pres. ind. act. of *capiō, -ere, cēpī, captum,* 3; its subj. is *pars*, above. —— **ā**, see note on *ab*, l. 6, above. —— **flūmine**, n., abl. after the prep. *ā*. For decl., see l. 7, above.

LINE 23. **Rhodanō,** abl. of *Rhodanus, -ī,* m.; in apposition with *flūmine*. See A. & G. 183, 184; B. 36, 127; G. 321; H. 359, NOTE 2. —— **continētur,** 3d pers. sing. pres. ind. pass. of *contineō, -ēre, -uī, -tentum,* 2 (con + tenēre, lit. *to hold together*; hence, passive, *to be held together, to be bounded*); its subj. is *pars*, to be supplied. —— **Garumnā,** abl. of *Garumna, -ae,* m., an appositive. This river formed the boundary between Aquitania and Celtica. *Garumna = the modern Garonne*. —— **flūmine,** see l. 7, above; abl. of means. —— **Ōceanō,** abl. of *Ōceanus, -ī,* m.; in the same grammatical construction as *flūmine*.

LINE 24. **fīnibus,** see l. 19, above; abl. of means. Note the omission of the conjunctions — *asyndeton* — and compare remarks and grammatical references on *linguā, institūtīs, lēgibus,* l. 5, above. —— **Belgārum,** gen. plur. of *Belgae;* for decl., and an account of this people, see note on *Belgae,* l. 2, above; *Belgārum* limits *fīnibus,* as poss. gen. A. & G. 214, 1; B. 131, REM. 1; G. 362; H. 396, I. —— **attingit,** 3d pers. sing. pres. ind. act. of *attingō, -ere, -tigī, -tactum,* 3 (ad + tangere); its subj. is *pars* or *Gallia*. —— **etiam,** usually taken as a conjunction (et + iam); it serves to add a notion = *and also*. But sometimes it has an adverbial force and = *even*. —— **ab**, here = *on the side of*. See note on *ab*, l. 6, above.

LINE 25. **Sēquanīs,** abl. plur. of *Sēquanī, -ōrum,* m.; a Gallic clan occupying the territory between the river Arar and Mount Jura; abl. after the prep. *ab*. ——

it slopes toward the north. The territory of the Belgae begins at the farthest boundaries of Celtic Gaul; it extends to the lower part of the Rhine river; it faces northeast. Aquitania	ad septentriōnēs. Belgae ab extrēmīs Galliae 26 *toward the north. The Belgae from the farthest of Gaul* fīnibus oriuntur; pertinent ad īnferiōrem 27 *boundaries arise; they extend to the lower* partem flūminis Rhēnī; spectant in septentriōnem 28 *part of the river Rhine; they look to the north* et orientem sōlem. Aquitānia ā Garumnā 2 *and the rising sun. Aquitania from the Garonne*

et, see note on *et*, l. 7, above. —— **Helvētiīs**, abl. plur. connected by *et* with *Sēquanīs*, and in the same grammatical construction. See note on *Helvētiī*, l. 16, above. —— **flūmen**, acc. sing. of *flūmen, -inis*, n., direct obj. of *attingit*. —— **Rhēnum**, acc. of *Rhēnus, -ī*, m., an appositive. The river Rhine is, in general, a boundary between Gaul and Germany. —— **vergit**, 3d pers. sing. pres. ind. act. of *vergō, -ere;* perf. *versī* according to some critics; its subject is either *pars* or *Gallia*, to be supplied. *vergit = verges*, or *slopes*, i.e. the rivers generally flow in a northerly direction from the point of view of the Cevennes mountains.

LINE 26. **ad**, prep. with the acc. = *toward*. See note on *ad*, l. 11, above. —— **septentriōnēs**, acc. plur. of *septentriō, -ōnis*, m.; acc. after the prep. *ad* (septem + triō, *the seven plow-oxen*) = the stars in the Great Bear constellation, i.e. = *the north*. The word is found in the lexicons in the plur., but often occurs in the sing. See l. 28, below. Frequently the parts of the compound are separated by *tmēsis*. —— **Belgae**, see note, l. 2, above. —— **ab**, see note, l. 6, above. —— **extrēmīs**, adj. abl. plur. of *exterus, exterior, extrēmus (extimus)*. The positive is rare, and generally is used in the plur. as a substantive, as e.g. *exterī = foreigners*. The adj. *extrēmīs* limits *fīnibus*. —— **Galliae**, gen. sing. of *Gallia, -ae*, f.; it, also, limits *fīnibus*. The Gaul here referred to is Celtic Gaul. Note the position of the gen. between the adj. and the noun it modifies; the usual order when a noun limited by a gen. has an adj. with it.

LINE 27. **fīnibus**, abl. plur. after the prep. *ab*. See note, l. 20, above. —— **oriuntur**, 3d pers. plur. pres. tense of the deponent *orior, orīrī, ortus*, 4. —— **pertinent**, 3d pers. plur. of *pertineō, -ēre, -uī*, 2; see note on *pertinent*, l. 13, above; its subj. is *Belgae* understood. —— **ad**, see note on *ad*, l. 11, above. —— **īnferiōrem**, acc. sing. f. of the comparative *īnferior*. The adj. is thus compared: *īnferus, īnferior, īnfimus (-īmus); īnferiōrem* modifies *partem*.

LINE 28. **partem**, acc. sing. of the noun *pars, partis*, f.; it follows the prep. *ad*. —— **flūminis**, gen. sing. of *flūmen, -inis*, n.; it limits *partem*. —— **Rhēnī**, gen. sing. of *Rhēnus, -ī*, m.; see note on *Rhēnum*, l. 14, above; *Rhēnī* is in apposition with *flūminis*. —— **spectant**, 3d pers. plur. pres. ind. act. of *spectō, -āre, -āvī, -ātum*, 1; its subj. is *Belgae*, to be supplied. —— **in**, prep., here with the acc. With *spectant* the prep. = *toward;* i.e. the territories of the Belgae from their southern boundary, or from the Province, look or lie toward the north and the rising sun, i.e. the east. —— **septentriōnem**, acc. sing. of *septentriō, -ōnis*, m.; the acc. follows *in*. See note on *septentriōnēs*, l. 26, above.

LINE 29. **et**, see note on *et*, l. 7, above. —— **orientem**, acc. sing. m. of the pres. participle *oriēns* of the deponent verb *orior, orīrī, ortus*, 4; the participle here limits *sōlem*. Observe that deponent verbs have the participles of both

LINES 30-32.]   BOOK I.   9

30 flūmine   ad   Pyrēnaeōs   montēs   et   eam   partem
    river   to the Pyrenean mountains and that   part
31 Ōceanī,   quae   est   ad   Hispāniam,   pertinet;
  of the ocean which is   near   Spain   extends;
32 spectat   inter   occāsum   sōlis   et   septentriōnēs.
  it looks between the setting of the sun and   the north.
	extends from the Garonne river to the Pyrenean mountains, and that part of the ocean which is near Spain; it faces north-west.

voices. Consult A. & G. 135, *a*; B. 109, 2; G. 128; H. 231, 1. Observe further that the Belgian rivers, generally, flow north-east. See maps, and note the direction of *Sabis flūmen*, and other streams. —— **sōlem**, acc. sing. of *sōl, sōlis,* m.; connected by *et* with *septentriōnem,* and governed by *in.* With *sōl* compare the GK. ἥλιος, m., and GER. *Sonne*, f., and the English *sun*, m.; and observe that the ancient classic languages, and most of the modern languages in imitation of these languages, conceive of the sun as masculine from the notion of the greatness or power displayed; whereas the German conception must have arisen from the notion of the sun as a mother-source of being and life. —— **Aquitānia, -ae,** f., subject-nom. of *pertinet,* l. 31, below. *Aquitania* = that part of *Gallia omnis* that lies between the *Garumna flūmen* and the Pyrenees. —— **ā,** see note on *ab,* l. 6, above; the prep. here governs *flūmine*. —— **Garumnā,** abl. of *Garumna, -ae,* f.; see note on *Garumna,* l. 7, above. *Garumnā* is here an appositive.

LINE 30. **flūmine,** abl. after *ā.* For decl., see note on *flūmen,* l. 7, above; for case references, see those on *ab Aquitānīs,* l. 6, above. —— **ad,** takes the acc. *montēs* after it. See note on *ad,* l. 11, above. —— **Pyrēnaeōs,** adj. acc. plur. of *Pyrēnaeus, -a, -um;* it modifies *montēs.* —— **montēs,** acc. plur. of *mōns, montis,* m.; acc. after *ad;* twenty-six prepositions take the acc. Observe that the first vowel in the stem of this word — *montĭ* — is short; that it is only to be conceived as long in the nom. and voc. cases. Consult A. & G. 18, *f*; G. 12, REM. 1, and 3, REM.; H. 16, I. 2. —— **et,** conj., see l. 7, above. —— **eam,** dem. adj. pron., acc. sing. f. of *is, ea, id;* it limits *partem*. —— **partem,** acc. sing. of *pars, partis,* f.; and is connected by *et* with *montēs,* and, like *montēs,* is governed by *ad.*

LINE 31. **Ōceanī,** gen. sing. of *Ōceanus, -ī,* m.; it limits *partem*. —— **quae,** rel. pron., nom. sing. f. of *quī, quae, quod;* it refers to *partem* as its antecedent, and is subj. of *est.* —— **est,** 3d pers. sing. pres. ind. of *sum, esse, fuī,* fut. participle *futūrus;* its subj. is *quae*. —— **ad,** prep. with acc. —— **Hispāniam,** acc. of *Hispānia, -ae,* f.; in the text it is the acc. after the prep. *ad* which here = *near*, i.e. the Bay of Biscay. The phrase here is adjectival and predicative. For meaning of *ad* in such construction, see A. & G. 258, *c*, 2, NOTE 1; B. 173, 1; G. 337, 4; H. 380, I. —— **pertinet,** 3d pers. sing. pres. ind. act. of *pertineō, -ēre, -uī,* 2 (l. 13, above); its subject-nom. is *Aquitānia,* l. 29, above.

LINE 32. **spectat,** see *spectant,* l. 28, above; the subj. is *Aquitānia* understood. —— **inter,** prep. with the acc. —— **occāsum,** acc. of *occāsus, -ūs,* m. (ob + *cadere, to fall down;* hence lit. the noun = *a falling down*); *occāsum* is in the acc. after the prep. *inter.* A. & G. 152, *a*; B. 120, 1; G. 416, 13; H. 433. —— **sōlis,** gen. of *sōl,* m., limiting the noun *occāsum*. See *sōlem,* l. 29, above. —— **et,** see note on *et,* l. 7, above. —— **septentriōnēs,** acc. plur. of *septentriō, -ōnis,* m., connected by *et* with *occāsum,* and governed by *inter.* See note on *septentriōnēs,* l. 26, above. The reader will note that the point of observation is the *Cevenna Mōns,* the north-western boundary of the Roman Province. From this mountain-range the rivers rise, and flow in a north-westerly direction.

10 · CAESAR'S GALLIC WAR [CHAP. II.

II. Among the Helvetii, Orgetorix was by far the noblest-born and the richest man. He, in the consulship of Marcus Messala and Marcus Piso, influ-

II. Apud Helvētiōs longē nōbilissimus fuit 1
Among   the Helvetii   by far   the noblest   was
et dītissimus Orgetorix.   Is,   M. Messālā et 2
and   the richest   Orgetorix.   He,   Marcus Messala and
M. Pīsōne cōnsulibus,   rēgnī   cupiditāte 3
Marcus Piso being the consuls, of the sovereignty by a desire

LINE 1. **Apud**, prep. with the acc. instead of the partitive gen. after the adj. *nōbilissimus*. See A. & G. 153; B. 134, REM. 2; G. 372, REM. 2; H. 397, NOTE 3. —— **Helvētiōs**, see note on *Helvetii*, l. 16, Chap. I. —— **longē**, adv., positive degree, comparative *longius*, superl. *longissimē*. As to formation of adverbs from adjectives, see l. 11, Chap. I. *longē* modifies and strengthens the superl. *nōbilissimus*. Consult A. & G. 93, *b*, middle; B. 68, REM. 4; G. 303; H. 170, 2, (2). —— **nōbilissimus** is the superl. degree of *nōbilis, -ior,.-issimus* (derived from *nōscere*, to know; hence *nōbilis* = *known, noted*); predicate-adj. after *fuit*. —— **fuit**, 3d pers. sing. perf. ind. act. of irr. verb *sum*. For parts, see l. 1, Chap. I; its subj. is *Orgetorix*.

LINE 2. **et**, cop. conj., joins words of equal importance. —— **dītissimus**, adj., superl. degree; positive *dīves*; comparative *dīvitior*, or *dītior*; connected by *et* with *nōbilissimus*, and in the same grammatical construction. —— **Orgetorix, -torīgis**, m., an Helvetian chief. *Orgetorix* is subject-nom. of *fuit*. Observe its emphatic position, and consult A. & G. p. 389, REM.; B. 22. 6; G. 673, (*a*); H. 561, II. The unemphatic order of the words is: *Orgetorix fuit vir apud Helvētiōs longē nōbilissimus et dītissimus*. —— Is, expressed for emphasis and rhetorical effect; it is subject-nom. of *fēcit*, below. —— **M.**, an abbreviation for the praenōmen *Marcus*. Here, of course, the form is *Marcō*, abl. —— **Messālā**, abl. sing. of *Messāla, -ae*, m. The full name was Marcus Valerius Messāla: Marcus, the praenōmen, Valerius, the nōmen, and Messāla, the cōgnōmen. Messāla was consul 61 B.C. The grammatical construction is the abl. absolute with *cōnsulibus*, which see, l. 3, below. —— **et** connects *Marcō Messālā* with *Marcō Pīsōne*.

LINE 3. **M. Pīsōne** is in the same grammatical construction as *M. Messālā*, i.e. both the names are in the abl. absolute with *cōnsulibus*. The full name of *Pīsō, -ōnis*, m., was Marcus Papius Pīsō Calpurniānus. Calpurniānus denotes the gēns. —— **cōnsulibus**, abl. plur. of *cōnsul, -is*, m. The construction is abl. absolute with *M. Messālā et M. Pīsō*, denoting time. Consult A. & G. 255, *a*; B. 192, REM. 1; G. 409; H. 431, 4. In this construction, the noun and participle, or adj. or other noun form an essentially predicative proposition. If *ēns* were in use, as the present participle of *sum*, the form of the sentence would be: *M. Messālā et M. Pīsōne entibus cōnsulibus* = lit. *M. Messāla and M. Pīsō* BEING *the consuls*. *cōnsulibus* is in the plural because referring to two nouns. See A. & G. 185, *b*; B. 67. 3, REM. 1; G. 285; H. 362, 3, and 364, end. Observe (1) that predicate-nouns are sometimes used without a verb, or without even a participle. Observe (2) that the consuls were the two presidents of the Roman state, elected annually by the Roman people; and (3) that their names are given to indicate the date of an event. Orgetorix's conspiracy, accordingly, occurred in 61 B.C.; or, which is the same thing, in A.U.C. 693; for 754 — 693 = 61. On reckoning time, see A. & G. p. 425; G. p. 492. —— **rēgnī**, objective gen. sing. of *rēgnum, -ī*, n. (*rēx*, king); it limits *cupiditāte*. —— **cupiditāte**, abl. sing. of *cupiditās, -ātis*, f.; abl. of cause. A. & G. 245, and *b*; B. 165, and REM. 4; G. 408, NOTE 2; H. 416, NOTE 1.

[LINES 4-6.]   BOOK I.   11

4 inductus	coniūrātiōnem	nōbilitātis	fēcit	et	enced by an excessive zeal for royal power, formed a conspiracy of the nobles, and persuaded the citizens to migrate from their territory with all their
being led,	*a conspiracy*	*of the nobility*	*made*	*and*	
5 cīvitātī	persuāsit,	ut dē	fīnibus	suīs	cum
the state	*persuaded,*	*that from*	*boundaries*	*their,*	*with*
6 omnibus	cōpiīs	exīrent:	perfacile		esse,
all	*resources*	*they should go out:*	*very easy*		*to be,*

LINE 4. **inductus**, perf. pass. participle of *indūco, -ere, -dūxī, -ductum*, 3; it limits the subj. *is*, l. 2, above. —— **coniūrātiōnem**, acc. sing. of *coniūrātiō, -ōnis*, f. (con + iūrāre = *to swear together*). —— **nōbilitātis**, gen. sing. of *nōbilitās, -ātis*, f. (*nōbilis*, from *nōscere*, see l. 1, above). Here the abstract is used for the concrete: *nōbilitātis* = *nōbilium*, i.e. he formed a conspiracy *of the nobles*. —— **fēcit**, 3d pers. sing. perf. ind. act. of *faciō, -ere, fēcī, factum*, 3; its subj. is *is*, l. 2, above.

LINE 5. **cīvitātī**, dat. sing. of *cīvitās, -ātis*. Here too the abstract is for the concrete; *cīvitātī* = *cīvibus*. For the dat. case after *persuāsit*, see A. & G. 227, and NOTE 1; B. 142; G. 346, REM. 2; H. 385, II. —— **persuāsit**, 3d pers. sing. perf. ind. act. of *persuādeō, -ēre, -suāsī, -suāsum*, 2 (per + suādēre = lit. *to advise thoroughly;* the *per* is merely intensive). *persuāsit* is connected by *et* with *fēcit*, and has the same subject. —— **ut**, conj. = *that* in a subjunctive-clause; but a *purpose*-clause is, ordinarily, best rendered into English by the infinitive. —— **dē**, prep. with the abl. —— **fīnibus**, abl. plur. of *fīnis, -is*, m.; abl. after prep. *dē*. —— **suīs**, abl. plur. of the reflexive pron. *suus, -a, -um*; it agrees with *fīnibus*; it refers to *eī* understood, i.e. *Helvētiī* = the omitted subject of the subordinate clause — *ut . . . exīrent.* —— **cum**, prep. with the abl. *omnibus*.

LINE 6. **omnibus**, abl. of the adj. *omnis, -e*, see note on *omnis*, l. 1, Chap. I; *omnibus* limits *cōpiīs*. —— **cōpiīs**, abl. plur. of *cōpia, -ae*, f. (con + ops; compare *inops*); in the sing. it = *plenty*; in the plur. = *resources, troops. cōpiīs* is an abl. of accompaniment with *cum*. A. & G. 248, *a*; B. 168, REM. 4; G. 392, REM. 1; H. 419, I, and III. 1, 1). In military phrases *cum* is generally omitted if the noun has a modifier, but not always. —— **exīrent**, 3d pers. plur. imperf. subjunct. act. of *exeō, -īre, -īvī (-iī), -itum*, irr.; it agrees with *Helvētiī* understood; subjunctive of purpose after *ut*. A. & G. 331; B. 200, REM. 2; G. 546, and NOTE 1; H. 498, I. Observe (1) that the noun-clause, *ut . . . exīrent*, is the direct obj. of *persuāsit*; (2) that *exīrent* (ex + īre) here takes after it *dē* with the abl., but also admits of the abl. with *ab* or *ex*, and even the abl. alone, Caesar himself being the voucher. —— **perfacile**, acc. n. of the adj. *perfacilis, -e* (per, intensive = *very* + facilis); predicate after *esse*. Observe here the change from direct into indirect discourse. In the direct form, the main clause would be: *perfacile est, cum virtūte omnibus praestēmus, tōtīus Galliae imperiō potīrī*. But note carefully that when the thought takes the indirect form, or is put in the *ōrātiō oblīqua*, the infinitive clause *perfacile esse* depends on *persuāsit*, or on *dīxit* (= verb of *saying*) implied in *persuāsit*, and that, therefore, *praestēmus* in direct discourse is changed in the indirect discourse into the imperfect subjunctive by the law of sequence of tenses. Consult A. & G. 336, and 336. B; B. 245. 1, (*a*), (*b*); G. 508, 2, and 654; H. 522, 525. —— **esse**, for principal parts, see under *est*, l. 1, Chap. I.

Note. — Indirect discourse is reporting what one has himself thought, or what another has thought, in a species of noun-clause; e.g. *dīcit montem ab hostibus tenērī*.

12   CAESAR'S GALLIC WAR   [CHAP. II.

| effects. He said that it was very easy, since they surpassed all the Gauls in valor, to win the sovereignty of entire Gaul. He persuaded them to this migration the more easily, because the Helvetii are hemmed | cum   virtūte   omnibus   praestārent,   tōtīus 7
since in valor all (the Gauls) they excelled, of entire
Galliae   imperiō   potīrī.   Id   hōc 8
Gaul   the supreme power to win. That   by this
facilius   eīs   persuāsit,   quod   undique 9
the more easily them he persuaded, because on every side
locī   nātūrā   Helvētiī continentur: ūnā 10
of the place by nature, the Helvetii are hemmed in: one |

LINE 7. **cum**, conj. — causal — and hence followed by the subjunctive. A. & G. 326; B. 198, (c); G. 579, II. (b); H. 517. —— **virtūte**, abl. sing. of *virtus, -tūtis,* f.; abl. of specification. A. & G. 253; B. 162; G. 397; H. 424. —— **omnibus**, dat. plur. m.; it limits *Gallīs* understood. *Gallīs*, if expressed, would be dat. after the *prae* in the compound *praestārent.* —— **praestārent**, 3d pers. plur. imperf. subjunctive act. of *praestō, -stāre, -stitī, -stitum* and *-stātum,* 1 (prae + stāre = lit. *to stand before,* i.e. *to be superior to*). —— **tōtīus**, gen. sing. f. of the adj. *tōtus, -a, -um.* *tōtīus* modifies *Galliae.* For list of words having the gen. in *-īus* and dat. in *-ī,* see grammatical references to *ūnum,* l. 2, Chap. I. Synonyms: *tōtus* = an original whole that may be resolved into parts; whereas *omnis* = a whole formed of original parts.
    LINE 8. **Galliae**, gen. sing. of *Gallia, -ae,* f.; see note, l. 1, Chap. I. *Galliae* limits *imperiō.* —— **imperiō**, abl. sing. of *imperium, -ī,* n.; abl. after *potīrī.* A. & G. 249; B. 167, 1; G. 407; H. 421, I. Observe that *potīrī* is followed sometimes by the gen., and sometimes (rarely) by the acc. With the abl., as in the text with *imperiō,* it means *to get possession of the sovereignty;* with the gen. the meaning would be: *to gain the mastery of.* Consult A. & G. 223, *a*; B. 167, 1, REM.; G. 407, NOTE 2, (*d*); II. 410, V. 3. —— **potīrī**, pres. inf. of deponent *potior, -īrī, -ītus,* 4. This inf. with its modifiers is the subject-acc. of *esse.* A. & G. 329; B. 86; G. 422; H. 538. Note that while this inf. is the subject-acc. of *esse,* if the discourse had been direct, the same inf. would have been the subject-nom. of *est.* —— **Id**, a colorless pron. referring to the thought contained in the clause *ut . . . exīrent; id* is the direct obj. of *persuāsit.* A. & G. 227, *f*; B. 150, REM. 2; G. 344; H. 384, II. —— **hōc**, abl., measure of difference after *facilius.* *hōc* is the herald of the following *quod-*clause. Consult A. & G. 102, *f*, and 250, NOTE; B. 84, REM. 3, and 164; G. 403; H. 423. The older grammars regard *hōc* in such construction as an abl. of cause.
    LINE 9. **facilius**, adv., comparative degree of *facile,* superl. *facillimē.* For the formation of adverbs from adjectives, see A. & G. 148; B. 117. 6; G. 91, (*c*); H. 306. —— **eīs**, dat. plur. of the dem. pron. *is, ea, id,* used as a personal pron. of the 3d person. *eīs* is dat. after *persuāsit.* A. & G. 227, and NOTE 1; B. 142; G. 346, REM. 2; H. 385, II. —— **persuāsit**, for parts, see l. 5, above. —— **quod**, conj. (really an acc. of effect of rel. pron. *quī, quae, quod*), but in use here as a conj. and = *because,* introducing a statement or a fact. The *quod-*clause is an adverbial modifier of *persuāsit.* —— **undique**, adv. (unde + que = *wheresoever*) = as used here, *on all sides.*
    LINE 10. **locī**, gen. sing. of *locus, -ī,* m. in the sing., but m. or n. in the plur., but with difference of meaning: *locī* in the plur. = *single places; loca* = *connected places — regions; locī* in the text is gen. sing., and limits *nātūrā.* —— **nātūrā**, abl. sing. of *nātūra, -ae,* f.; *nātūrā* is the abl. of cause (derived from *nāscor, nātus,* 3).

11 ex	parte	flūmine	Rhēnō	lātissimō	atque	in, on all sides, by the nature of their country: on one side, by the Rhine river very broad and very deep, which separates the Helvetian territory from the Germans; on the second side, by the very lofty Jura
on,	*side*	*by the river*	*Rhine*	*very broad*	*and also*	
12 altissimō,	quī	agrum	Helvētium	ā	Germānīs	
very deep,	*which*	*the territory*	*Helvetian*	*from the Germans*		
13 dīvidit,	alterā	ex	parte	monte	Iūrā	
separates;	*the second*	*on,*	*side*	*by Mount*	*Jura*	
14 altissimō,	quī	est	inter	Sēquanōs	et	
very high,	*which*	*is*	*between*	*the Sequani*	*and*	

Note that in nouns of the first declension the ultima of the abl. is always long; in the nom. and voc. it is short. —— **Helvētiī**, nom. plur. m., subj. of *continentur*. See note on *Helvētiī*, l. 16, Chap. I. —— **continentur**, 3d pers. plur. of *contineō*, *-ēre*, *-uī*, *-tentum*, 2 (con + tenēre). Note that here this verb in the pass. voice denotes that the *people* are held together, i.e. *are hemmed in;* while in l. 23, Chap. I, the same verb indicates that the *territory* is held together, i.e. *is bounded*. —— **ūnā**, abl. sing. of *unus*, *-a*, *-um;* for decl., see *ūnām*, l. 2, Chap. I; *ūnā* limits *parte*.

LINE 11. **ex**, prep. with the abl.; it has the form *ē* which is only used before consonants, whereas *ex* is used before either vowels or consonants. A monosyllabic prep. is often thus placed between a noun and its modifier. A. & G. 345, *a*, 2; B. 58. 2; G. 413, REM. 1; H. 569, II. 1. —— **parte**, abl. sing. of *pars*, *partis*, f.; it is in the abl. after the prep. *ex*. (*ūnā ex parte:* compare *quā dē causā*, l. 16, Chap. I.) —— **flūmine**, abl. sing. of *flūmen*, *-inis*, n.; abl. of means. —— **Rhēnō**, abl. of *Rhenus*, *-ī*, m.; in apposition with *flūmine*. —— **lātissimō**, abl. sing. of the adj. *lātissimus*, *-a -um;* superl. degree of *lātus*, *-ior*, *-issimus;* superl. of eminence. See A. & G. 93, *b*; B. 68, REM. 4; G. 302; H. 444, 1. —— **atque**, conj., see note on this particle, l. 10, Chap. I.

LINE 12. **altissimō**, abl. sing. of the adj. *altissimus*, *-a*, *-um;* superl. degree of *altus*, *-ior*, *-issimus*. *altissimō* is connected by *atque* with *lātissimō*, and is in the same grammatical construction. Note that *altus* = *high* or *low*, according to the conception of the point of observation. —— **quī**, rel pron., nom. sing. m., refers to the appositive *Rhēnō* rather than to *flūmine;* *quī* is subject-nom. of *dīvidit*. —— **agrum**, acc. sing. of *ager*, *agrī*, m., direct obj. of *dīvidit* *ager* denotes the *open country* — *the fields;* whereas *fīnis* in the sing. = *a boundary*, in the plur. = *boundaries*, i.e. territory with limits. —— **Helvētium**, acc. sing. m. of the adj. *Helvētius*, *-a*, *-um;* it limits *agrum*. —— **ā**, prep. with the abl. See note on *ab*, l. 6, Chap. I. —— **Germānīs**, abl. plur. after prep. *ā*. See note on *Germānīs*, l. 18, Chap. I.

LINE 13. **dīvidit**, 3d pers. sing. pres. ind. act. of *dīvidō*, *-ere*, *-vīsī*, *-vīsum*, 3; it agrees with its subject-nom. *quī*. —— **alterā**, abl. sing. f. of *alter*, *altera*, *alterum*, gen. *alterīus*, dat. *alterī*. The gen. *alterīus* is usually accented on the antepenult. *alterā* modifies *parte*. Synonyms: *alter* = *the one*, the other of two; whereas *alius* = *other, another*, of an indefinite number. —— **ex**, prep. with the abl. See note on *ex parte*, l. 11, above. —— **monte**, abl. sing. of *mōns*, *montis*, m. *monte* is the abl. of means after *continentur*, l. 10, above. —— **Iūrā**, abl. sing. of *Iūra*, *-ae*, m. *Iūrā* is in apposition with *monte*. The Iūra is a mountain-range, extending from the Rhine to the Rhone.

LINE 14. **altissimō**, see note on *altissimō*, l. 12, above. —— **quī**, nom. sing. m. of the rel. pron.; its antecedent is *monte*, and *quī* is the subject-nom. of *est*. See

mountain-range, which lies between the Sequani and the Helvetii; on the third side, by Lake Geneva and the Rhone river, which separates our province from the Helvetii. From this state of things,	Helvētiōs, *the Helvetii;* flūmine *the river* ab *from* fīēbat, *it came to pass*	tertiā *on the third (side) by Lake* Rhodanō, *Rhone,* Helvētiīs *the Helvetii* ut *that*	lacū qui *which* dīvidit. *separates.* et *both*	Lemannō *Leman* prōvinciam *province* His *Because of these* minus lātē *less widely*	et 15 and nostram 16 our, rēbus 17 things, vagārentur 18 they roamed

note on *est*, l. 1, Chap. I. —— **inter**, prep. with the acc. *Sēquanōs*. —— **Sēquanōs**, acc. pl. of *Sēquanī*, *-ōrum*, m.; acc. after the prep. *inter*. The Sēquanī were a Gallic clan occupying the territory between the river Arar — the modern Saône — and Mount Jura.

LINE 15. **Helvētiōs**, acc. plur. of *Helvētiī*, *-ōrum*, m., connected by *et* with *Sēquanōs*, and in the same grammatical construction. See note on *Helvētiōs*, l. 1, above. —— **tertiā**, abl. sing. f. of ordinal-adj. *tertius*, *-a*, *-um*; supply *ex parte*. *tertiā* agrees with *parte* thus supplied; and *parte* thus supplied is governed by the prep. *ex* understood. —— **lacū**, abl. sing. of *lacus*, *-ūs*, m. *lacū* is an abl. of means after *continentur*, l. 10, above. —— **Lemannō**, abl. sing. of *Lemannus*, *-ī*, m. *Lemannō* is an appositive. The Leman Lake here mentioned is the modern Lake Geneva situated between Switzerland and the recently acquired territories of France; its length in crescent-form is rather more than fifty miles; its greatest breadth eight miles.

LINE 16. **flūmine**, abl. of *flūmen*, *-inis*, n.; connected by *et* with *lacū*, and in the same grammatical construction. —— **Rhodanō**, see note on *Rhodanō*, l. 23, Chap. I. —— **quī**, rel. pron., refers to the appositive *Rhodanō* as its antecedent, and is the subject-nom. of *dīvidit*. —— **prōvinciam**, acc. sing. of *prōvincia*, *-ae*, f.; it is the direct obj. of *dīvidit*. The reference is to the Roman Province in the south-east part of *Gallia omnis*. —— **nostram**, acc. sing. f. of the poss. pron. *noster*, *-tra*, *-trum*; it limits *prōvinciam*.

LINE 17. **ab**, prep. with the abl. See note on *ab*, l. 6, Chap. I. —— **Helvētiīs**, abl. plur. of the adj. *Helvētius*, *-a*, *-um*, used substantively. *Helvētiīs* is in the abl. after the prep. *ab*. For description, see note on *Helvētiī*, l. 16, Chap. I. —— **dīvidit**, 3d pers. sing. pres. ind. act. of *dīvidō*, *-ere*, *-vīsī*, *-vīsum*, 3. —— **hīs**, abl. plur. f. of the dem. pron. *hīc*, *haec*, *hōc*; it modifies *rēbus*. —— **rēbus** is the abl. plur. of *rēs*, *reī*, f. *rēbus* is abl. of cause. See A. & G. 245; B. 165; G. 408; H. 416.

LINE 18. **fīēbat**, 3d pers. sing. of the imperf. ind. of *fīō*, *fierī*, *factus*, used as pass. of *faciō*. *fīēbat* is used impersonally, or, strictly, the following *ut . . . possent* is the subject. —— **ut**, conj. = *that*. —— **et** . . . **et** = strictly, *both . . . and;* it is often the better way to omit the first *et* in the translation. —— **minus**, adv., comparative degree of *parum*, superl. *minimē*. *minus* modifies *lātē*. —— **lātē**, adv. (*lātus*, wide); it modifies *vagārentur*. —— **vagārentur**, 3d pers. plur. imperf. subjunctive of *vagor*, *-ārī*, *-ātus*, deponent; its subject-nom. is *eī*, i.e. *Helvētiī*. *vagārentur* is subjunctive of result after *ut;* i.e. the clause *ut . . . vagārentur* is a noun-clause, and subj. of *fīēbat*. Consult A. & G. 332, *a*, 2; B. 201, REM. 1, (*c*); G. 553, 3; H. 501, I.

LINES 19-21.] BOOK I. 15

19 et	minus	facile	finitimīs	bellum	inferre	it resulted that they wandered the less widely, and could the less easily bring war upon the neighboring clans; in which respect these men so fond of wag-
and	less	easily	upon the neighbors	war	to bring	
20 possent;	quā	ex	parte	hominēs	bellandī	
were they able;	which	on,	ground	men	of warring	
21 cupidī	māgnō	dolōre	afficiēbantur.		Prō	
eager,	with great	grief	were affected.		For	

LINE 19. **minus**, adv.; it modifies *facile*. —— **facile**, adv., comparative *facilius*, superl. *facillimē*. For formation of adverbs from adjectives, see A. & G. 148; B. 117. 6; G. 91, (c); H. 306. *facile* modifies *inferre*. —— **finitimīs**, dat. plur. m. of the adj. *finitimus, -a, -um* (derived from *finis*); in the plur. used as a subst. *finitimīs* is dat. plur. after the *in* in the compound *inferre*. A. & G. 228; B. 143; G. 347; H. 386, 1. —— **bellum**, acc. sing. of *bellum, -ī,* n.; *bellum* is the acc. of the direct obj. of *inferre*. Observe that the dat. after this verb depends on the prepositional part of the compound, and the acc. upon the strictly verbal part — *ferre*. —— **inferre**, pres. inf. act. of *inferō, -ferre, -tulī, ill-* or *in-lātum*. *inferre* is a complementary inf. depending on *possent*. Consult A. & G. 271, and NOTE; B. 181; G. 423; H. 533, 2.

LINE 20. **possent** is 3d pers. plur. imperf. subjunctive of *possum, posse, potuī* (potis + sum); it is connected by *et* with *vagārentur*, and in the subjunctive for the same reason. —— **quā**, at the beginning of a sentence = *et eā*. See A. & G. 180, *f*; B. 129, REM. 9; G. 610, REM. 1; H. 453. *quā* limits *parte*. —— **ex**, prep. with the abl. (*ē* before consonants only; *ex* before vowels and consonants). —— **parte**, abl. sing. of *pars, partis*, f.; *parte* is in the abl. after *ex*. See note on *quā dē causā*, l. 16, Chap. I. *quā ex parte* = lit. *on which part* or *side*; more freely the phrase = *and in this respect*. The older reading here is: *quā dē causā*. The phrase *quā ex parte* is a *locātiō vexātīva*. The text and context show it is to be explained by what immediately follows, and = *in which respect* — being men fond of war — they had great vexation. —— **hominēs**, nom. plur. of *homō, -inis*, m. and f. *hominēs* is the subject-nom. of *afficiēbantur*; or, better perhaps, taken as an appositive to *eī*, the subject; i.e. *they as men*. Synonyms: *homō* is the generic term for *man; vir* is the special designation = *the man of courage, the hero*. —— **bellandī**, gen. of the gerund *bellandum, -dī, -dō, -dum, -dō*. This neuter verbal noun occurs only in the gen., dat., acc. and abl. cases. This gerund is formed from the first stem of *bellō, -āre, -āvī, -ātum*, 1, thus: bella + ndī, -ndō, -ndum, -ndō. *bellandī* is objective gen. after the adj. *cupidī*. A. & G. 298; B. 184, REM. 4, 1; G. 428; H. 542, 1. The adjectives that take the gen. of the gerund denote desire, knowledge, recollection, and their contraries.

LINE 21. **cupidī**, nom. plur. m. of the adj. *cupidus, -a, -um* (*cupere*, to desire). *cupidī* is an attributive of *hominēs*, but = the relative predicative clause: *who were desirous*. —— **māgnō**, abl. sing. m. of the adj. *māgnus, -a, -um*; comparative *māior*, superl. *māximus*. *māgnō* modifies *dolōre*. —— **dolōre** is the abl. sing. of *dolor, -ōris*, m.; it is an abl. of manner. A. & G. 248; B. 168, REM. 1; G. 399; H. 419, III. —— **afficiēbantur**, 3d pers. plur. imperf. ind. pass. of *af(d)ficiō, -ere, -fēcī, -fectum*, 3 (ad + facere, lit. *to do to* one something, i.e. to affect him in some way). —— **Prō**, prep. with the abl. = *for, in view of*.

ing war were affected with great discontent. Moreover, considering their large number of men and their reputation for prowess in war, they thought that they had too narrow limits which extended	multitūdine *the large number,* bellī *of war* fīnēs *boundaries* longitūdinem *length*	atque *and* habēre *to have* mīlia *thousands*	autem *moreover,* fortitūdinis *of bravery* arbitrābantur, *they thought,* passuum *of paces*	hominum *of men* angustōs *narrow* ducenta *two hundred*	et *and* quī *which*	prō *for* sē *themselves* in *in* et *and*	glōriā *the glory*	22 23 24 25

LINE 22. **multitūdine**, abl. sing. of *multitūdō, -inis*, f. (*multus*); abl. after *prō*. —— **autem**, a weak adversative conj., usually = *but*. Here, however, it = *moreover*. —— **hominum**, gen. plur. of *homō, -inis*, m.; it limits *multitūdine*. —— **et**, cop. conj., here joins the phrases as if of equal importance. —— **prō**, note how the notions are kept quite distinct by the repetition of the prep. —— **gloriā**, abl. sing. of *gloria, -ae*, f.; abl. after *prō*.

LINE 23. **bellī**, gen. poss. of *bellum, -ī*, n.; it limits *gloria*. The phrase *prō gloriā bellī* = lit. *for war's glory*. —— **atque**, adds a more important notion = *and also*. —— **fortitūdinis**, gen. sing. of *fortitūdō, -inis*, f. Observe that *bellī atque fortitūdinis* = *bellicae fortitūdinis* (hendiadys). See note on *hūmānitāte*, l. 10, Chap. I. —— **angustōs**, acc. plur. m. of the adj. *angustus, -a, -um; angustōs* is an attributive of *fīnēs*. —— **sē**, acc. plur. of pron. *suī, sibi, sē, sē; sē* is here the subject-acc. of *habēre*.

LINE 24. **fīnēs**, acc. plur. of *fīnis, -is*, m. *fīnēs* is the direct obj. of *habēre*. —— **habēre** is the pres. inf. act. of *habeō, -ēre, -uī, -itum*, 2. —— **arbitrābantur**, 3d pers. plur. imperf. ind. of deponent *arbitror, -ārī, -ātus*, 1; its subject-nom. is the pron. *eī*, i.e. *Helvētiī*. Note that the positive *angustos* in l. 23, above, with the preceding *prō* phrases expresses disproportion; i.e. indicates limits too narrow for their number. Vide Gildersleeve's Lat. Gram. § 289, REM. The direct form of the acc.-clause is: *angustōs nōs fīnēs habēmus*. —— **quī**, rel. pron., nom. plur. m.; it refers to *fīnēs*, the obj. of *habēre*, as its antecedent, and is the subject-nom. of *patēbant*, l. 27, below. Here the pron. seems to = *since*. Causal propositions indeed generally take the subjunctive, but a statement viewed as fact admits of the indicative with *quī*. Consult A. & G. NOTE immediately preceding 321, under the caption 5. *Causal Clauses;* B. 198, REM. 2; G. 626; H. 517, 2. —— **in**, prep. with acc. and abl.; here with the acc. See grammatical references, l. 1, Chap. I, end.

LINE 25. **longitūdinem**, acc. sing. of *longitūdō, -inis*, f. (*longus*); acc. after *in*. —— **mīlia**, acc. plur. of adj. *mille*, indeclinable in the sing., but in the plur. it is declinable, and used as a neuter noun. *mīlia* is here an acc. of extent of space. A. & G. 257; B. 153; G. 335; H. 379. Observe that the form *millia* is used in some editions instead of *mīlia*. —— **passuum**, gen. plur. of *passus, -ūs*, m.; partitive gen. after *mīlia*. A. & G. 216, a, 2; B. 134; G. 370; H. 397, 2. *mīlia passuum* = lit. *thousands of paces;* i.e. about four hundred feet less than an English mile. The phrase may be elegantly rendered into English by our word *mile*, although it should be borne in mind that one Roman mile = ten-elevenths of an English mile. —— **ducenta** (duo + centum), acc. plur. n. of *ducentī, -ae, -a*; it agrees with *mīlia*. —— **et**, cop. conj., connects the two cardinals. In some texts, this numeral is expressed by CC.

LINES 20-27.]   BOOK I.   17

26 quadrāgintā,	in	lātitūdinem	centum	et
forty	*in*	*breadth*	*a hundred*	*and*
27 octōgintā	patēbant.			
eighty	*extended.*			

merely two hundred and forty miles in length, and one hundred and eighty in breadth.

1 III.	Hīs	rēbus	adductī	et	auctōritāte
	By these	*things*	*led*	*and*	*by the counsel*
2 Orgetorigis	permōtī	cōnstituērunt		ea,
of Orgetorix	*moved*	*they determined*		*those things*

III. Influenced by these considerations, and persuaded by the counsel of Orgetorix, the Hel-

---

LINE 26. **quadrāgintā,** indecl. num. adj.; it is connected by *et* with *ducenta,* and limits *mīlia* also. *quadrāgintā* is sometimes expressed by XL. Observe that of the cardinals, *ūnus, duo* and *trēs* are declined; but that from *quattuor* to *centum* the cardinals are indeclinable. —— **in,** prep. with acc.; for grammatical references, see l. 1, Chap. I. —— **lātitūdinem,** acc. sing. of *latitūdō, -inis,* f. *(lātus,* wide); acc. after prep. *in.* —— **centum,** an indecl. num. adj.; sometimes represented by C.

LINE 27. **octōgintā,** an indecl. num. adj.; sometimes represented by LXXX. These adjectives limit *mīlia,* to be supplied. —— **patēbant,** 3d pers. plur. imperf. ind. act. of *pateō, -ēre, -uī,* 2, intrans.; it agrees with its subject-nom. *quī,* l. 24, above.

Note. — Let the reader bear in mind that (a) this multitude was, according to Chap. XXIX, about 263,000 of those *quī arma ferre possent;* (b) that the boundaries of Helvetia extended *in longitūdinem* from the Jura range of mountains to Lake Constance; (c) that the boundaries extended *in latitūdinem* from Basle to the Lepontine Alps.

LINE 1. **Hīs,** abl. plur. f. of the dem. pron. *hīc, haec, hōc. Hīs* is an attributive of *rēbus.* —— **rēbus,** abl. plur. of *rēs, reī,* f. *rēbus* is an abl. of cause. A. & G. 245, and 2. *b*; B. 165, and REM. 4; G. 408, and NOTE 2; H. 416, and NOTE 1. So far as the form goes, *rēbus* might be in the dat. case, but we infer that it is in the abl. of cause, because we know that intrans. and pass. verbs, and pass. participles of emotion usually take the cause in the abl. case. —— **adductī,** perf. pass. participle of *addūcō, -ere, -dūxī, -ductum,* 3 = *having been led,* or *being led,* or simply *led. adductī* agrees with *Helvētiī,* the omitted subj. of *cōnstituērunt.* —— **et,** cop. conj., connects *adductī* and *permōtī.* —— **auctōritāte,** abl. of subjective cause after *permōtī.*

LINE 2. **Orgetorigis,** gen. sing. of *Orgetorix, -igis,* m.; limits *auctōritāte.* Orgetorix was an Helvetian nobleman. Observe that the nom. case *Orgetorix* is formed by adding *s* to the stem *Orgetorig;* the final *g,* a palatal, uniting with *s* forms *x.* Compare *rēx,* stem *reg,* and consult A. & G. 44; B. 46, II, 1; G. 50 and 52; H. 30, and 59, 1, 3). —— **permōtī,** nom. plur. m. of perf. pass. participle *permōtus, -a, -um,* of the verb *permoveō, -ēre, -mōvī, -mōtum,* 2 (per, intensive = *very +* movēre). *permōtī* agrees with *Helvētiī,* the omitted subj. of *cōnstituērunt.* —— **cōnstituērunt,** 3d pers. plur. perf. ind. act. of *cōnstituō, -ere, -stituī, -stitūtum,* 3. Observe that the pres. stem and the perf. stem of this verb are alike. —— **ea,** acc. neuter plur. of the dem. pron. *is, ea, id;* direct obj. of *comparāre; ea* agrees with the word for *things* to be supplied; or, in other words, the pron. is used substantively. See A. & G. 189, *b*; B. 60, REM.; G. 204, NOTE 2; H. 441, 1.

vetii determined to provide such things as were necessary for the expedition: to buy as large a number as possible of horses and carts; to sow as many fields as possible, in order that they might	quae *which*	ad *to*	proficīscendum *going forth*	pertinērent, *pertained,*	comparāre, 3 *to prepare,*
	iūmentōrum *of beasts of burden*		et carrōrum *and of carts*	quam *as much as*	maximum 4 *the greatest*
	numerum *number*	coëmere, *to purchase,*	sēmentēs *sowings*	quam *as much as*	maximās 5 *the greatest*
	facere, *to make,*	ut *that*	in itinere *on the journey*	cōpia *a plenty*	frūmentī 6 *of corn*

LINE 3. **quae**, nom. plur. n. of the rel. pron. *quī, quae, quod;* it agrees with its antecedent in gender and number, but not in case. *quae* is subject-nom. of *pertinērent*. —— **ad**, prep. with the acc. —— **proficīscendum**, acc. of the gerund of the verb *proficīscor, -ī, profectus*, deponent, 3; the gerund is in the acc. after the prep. *ad*. Consult A. & G. 300; B. 184, REM. 4, III ; G. 432; H. 542, III. *ad proficīscendum* = lit. *to the going forth*. —— **pertinērent**, 3d pers. plur. imperf. subjunctive act. of *pertineō, -ēre, -uī* (per + tenēre = lit. *to stretch through to a place;* hence *pertinēre = to reach, to extend, to pertain to anything*). *pertinērent* is in the subjunctive mode, because it expresses the thought of the *Helvētiī*, not Caesar's thought. Consult A. & G. 341, *d*; B. 235; G. 628; H. 528, 1. *quae ad proficīscendum pertinērent* = *which things* (they said) *pertained to their departure*. This is a good example of what is styled informal indirect discourse. —— **comparāre**, pres. inf. complementary of *comparō*, 1. *comparāre* completes the meaning of *cōnstituērunt* without a subject-acc. See A. & G. 271 ; B. 86. 2 ; G. 423, 1 and 2 ; H. 533.

LINE 4. **iūmentōrum**, gen. plur. of *iūmentum, -ī*, n.; it limits *numerum*. (Contracted from *iūgumentum* = iūgum + mentum.) —— **carrōrum**, gen. plur. of either *carrus, -ī*, m., or of *carrum, -ī*, n.; connected by *et* with *iūmentōrum*, and in the same grammatical construction. Note that this noun of two genders is called a heterogeneous noun. See A. & G. 78. 2; B. 50, 1; G. 67; II. 144. —— **quam**, adv., modifies *maximum;* quam is really an acc. of specification of the rel. *quī, quae, quod = in what way, how*. Further, in the use of *quam* with the superl., it is a correlative to *tam*. The full expression is : *tam māgnum quam maximum numerum = so great as the greatest number;* i.e. as great as possible. —— **maximum**, acc. sing. m. of adj. *maximus, -a, -um*. *maximum* is superl. degree of *māgnus*, comparative *māior;* it limits *numerum*.

LINE 5: **numerum** is acc. sing. of *numerus, -ī*, m.; direct obj. of *coëmere*. —— **coëmere** is pres. inf. act. of *coëmō, coëmere, -ēmī, -ēmptum*, 3 (con, intensive + emere = lit. *to buy up*). The diaeresis shows that the vowels do not coalesce as a diphthong. *coëmere* is also a complementary inf. depending on *cōnstituērunt*. —— **sēmentēs**, acc. plur. of *sēmentis, -is*, f. (*sēmen*, seed). Some editions have here *sēmentīs*, another form of the acc. plur. of *ī*-stems. *sēmentēs* is the direct obj. of *facere*. —— **quam**, see *quam*, l. 4, above. —— **maximās**, acc. plur.; agrees with *sēmentēs;* see *maximum*, l. 4, above.

LINE 6. **facere**, pres. inf. act. of *faciō, -ere, -fēcī, -factum*, 3; complementary, and depends on *cōnstituērunt*. —— **ut**, conj. = *that*. —— **in**, prep. with acc. and abl. ; here it takes the abl. —— **itinere**, abl. sing. of *iter, itineris*, n.; abl. after prep. *in*. The nom. *iter* is formed from the stem *itiner*, without *s*, by dropping *i* and *n* from

BOOK I.

7 suppeteret,	cum	proximīs	cīvitātibus	pācem	have a plenty of corn during the journey; and to establish peace and friendship with the nearest states. They thought that a period of two years was suffi-
might be in store,	*with*	*the nearest*	*states*	*peace*	
8 et	amīcitiam	cōnfīrmāre.	Ad	eās	rēs
and	*friendship*	*to confirm.*	*For*	*these*	*things*
9 cōnficiendās	biennium		sibi	satis	esse
to be done	*the space of two years*		*for them*	*enough*	*to be*

the middle of the stem. —— **cōpia, -ae,** f., subject-nom. of *suppeteret. cōpiae* in the plur. = *resources, troops.* —— **frūmentī,** gen. sing. of *frūmentum, -ī,* n.; it limits *cōpia.* (Contracted from frūgī [stem of *frūx, frūgis*] + mentum.)

LINE 7. **suppeteret,** 3d pers. sing. imperf. subjunctive of *suppetō, -ere, -tīvī (-iī), -fitum,* 3, n. (sub + petere = lit. *to go to one;* hence, *to be near*). *suppeteret* is a neuter verb; supply *eīs,* dat. of possessor. A. & G. 231; B. 146; G. 349; H. 387. The dat. of the possessor occurs after *abest, deëst, dēfit, fore* and *suppetit;* it is in the subjunctive of purpose after *ut.* A. & G. 317; B. 200, (*b*); G. 544; H. 497, II. —— **cum,** prep. with the abl. —— **proximīs,** abl. plur. f., adj., superl. of the comparative *propior;* it agrees with *cīvitātibus.* The comparative degree is derived from stem *prope=near,* not used as adj. The positive degree is wanting. See A. & G. 91; B. 74, 1; G. 87. 8; H. 166. This list of every-day adjectives should be memorized. —— **cīvitātibus,** abl. plur. of *cīvitās, -ātis,* f.; abl. of manner with prep. *cum.* A. & G. 248; B. 168, REM. 1; G. 399; H. 419, III. (*cīvitās* is derived from cīvis + the ending tās, forming an abstract noun = *citizenship.*) —— **pācem,** acc. sing. of *pāx, pācis,* f.; direct obj. of *cōnfīrmāre. pāx* is from the root *pac,* as seen in *pacīscor, pactus,* 3; hence = *a thing agreed to,* and, as a result, *peace.*

LINE 8. **et,** conj.; observe how it joins here words of equal importance. —— **amīcitiam,** acc. sing. of *amīcitia, -ae,* f.; direct obj. of *cōnfīrmāre.* (*amīcus* = *that loves,* from *amāre.*) —— **cōnfīrmāre,** also complementary inf. of *cōnfīrmō,* 1, and depends on *cōnstituērunt,* l. 2, above. Observe the omission of the conjunction before the complementary infinitives *facere* and *cōnfīrmāre* (asyndeton). —— **Ad,** prep. with the acc. —— **eās,** acc. plur. of the dem. pron. *is, ea, id;* it is the attributive of *rēs;* it refers to the particulars mentioned in the preceding sentence. —— **rēs** is the acc. plur. of *rēs, reī,* f., and follows the prep. *ad.*

LINE 9. **cōnficiendās,** gerundive or fut. pass. participle of *cōnficiō, -ere, -fēcī, -fectum,* 3; it agrees in gender, number and case with *rēs.* The construction as a whole denotes purpose. Consult A. & G. 300; B. 184, REM. 4, III; G. 432; H. 544, and NOTE 2. The phrase *ad eās rēs cōnficiendās* = lit. *for those things to be accomplished.* This construction is often best rendered by a participle in *-ing* with a direct obj. The gerundive phrase thus = *for accomplishing these things.* Compare note on *effēminandōs,* l. 13, Chap. I. —— **biennium,** acc. sing. of *biennium, -ī,* n.; subject-acc. of *esse.* (bis + annus.) —— **sibi,** dat. plur. of the reflexive pron. *suī, sibi, sē, sē. sibi* is dat. of reference. A. & G. 235; B. 145; G. 352; II. 384, II, 1, 2). This dat. is usually called dat. of advantage or disadvantage (*dat. com. aut incom.*). —— **satis,** usually an adv.; here it is an adj. in predicate-acc. after *esse.* —— **esse,** pres. inf. of *sum, esse, fuī,* fut. participle *futūrus.* Observe that the infinitive-clause is the direct obj. of *dūxērunt.* This is an example of implied indirect discourse. What they thought, expressed in direct form, is: *biennium nōbīs satis est.*

| cient for them to accomplish these things, and, accordingly, they established by law their migration for the third year. Orgetorix was chosen to consummate these plans. He took upon himself an | dūxērunt;
they thought;
lēge cōnfīrmant.
by law they establish.
Orgetorix dēligitur.
Orgetorix is chosen.
ad cīvitātēs suscēpit.
to the states took. | in tertium annum
for the third year
Ad eās rēs
For these things
Is sibi
He upon himself
In eō
On that | profectiōnem 10
the departure
cōnficiendās 11
to be accomplished
lēgātiōnem 12
a legation
itinere 13
journey |

LINE 10. **dūxērunt**, 3d pers. plur. perf. ind. act. of *dūcō, -ere, dūxī, ductum*, 3. Its subj. is, of course, *Helvētiī* to be supplied. *dūcere* = lit. (*a*) *to lead*, in the widest sense; (*b*) to lead in regard to one's will, hence, *to influence*; (*c*) to lead one in regard to time, *to protract, put off;* and (*d*) to lead or control one's own thought, *to reckon, to think*. —— **in**, prep. with acc. and abl.; here with the acc. in an idiomatic phrase =*for*. —— **tertium**, acc. sing. m. of the ordinal-adj. *tertius, -a, -um;* it limits *annum*. —— **annum**, acc. sing. of *annus, -ī*, m.; the object of the prep. *in*. The phrase *in tertium annum* =*for the third year*. See A. & G. 259, *b*; B. 120. 3; G. 418. 1; H. 435, I, 2. —— **profectiōnem**, acc. of *profectiō, -ōnis*, f.; direct obj. of *cōnfīrmant*. (Derived from *profectus*, the participle of *proficīscor, -ī*, 3, deponent; hence lit. = *a going away*.)

LINE 11. **lēge**, abl. of *lēx, lēgis*, f.; abl. of means. *By law* here means by a resolution of an assembly of the people. —— **cōnfīrmant**, 3d pers. plur. pres. ind. act. of *cōnfīrmō, -āre, -āvī, -ātum*, 1; its subject-nom. is *Helvētiī* understood. —— **Ad eās rēs cōnficiendās**, see the phrase explained lines 8 and 9, above.

LINE 12. **Orgetorix, -origis**, m.; subject-nom. of *dēligitur*. —— **dēligitur**, 3d pers. sing. pres. ind. pass. of *dēligō, -ere, -lēgī, -lectum*, 3 (dē + legere = lit. *to choose from*). Observe that *dēligitur* is an historical pres.; so also *cōnfīrmant*, l. 11, above; while the very next sentence has the perfect. This use of the historical pres. for the historical perf. is common enough in all languages; it conduces to vivacity, but is at the expense of stateliness and dignity of historical narration. *Caution:* Do not confound *dēligō*, 3 = *I choose*, with *dēligō*, 1 = *I find*. —— **Is**, dem. pron. = lit. *this*, or *that*, but, often, as here used, as a personal pron. of the 3d person. *is* is a weaker demonstrative than *hīc, ille* and *iste;* it frequently refers to an object just mentioned, as in the text it refers to Orgetorix; but *is* is emphatic when it stands at the head of a principal sentence. *Is* is the subject-nom. of *suscēpit*. For special directions, as to the use of this pron., see A. & G. 102, *d*; B. 87, B. 7; G. 308; H. 451. —— **sibi**, dat. of the indirect obj. after the compound *suscēpit*. A. & G. 227, *f*, and 228; B. 143; G. 345, 347; H. 384, 386, 1. —— **lēgātiōnem**, acc. sing. of *lēgātiō, -ōnis*, f.; direct obj. of *suscēpit. lēgātiō* is a verbal abstract noun formed from the verb-stem lēga (of *lēgere*, to despatch) + tiō = lit. *a despatching*.

LINE 13. **cīvitātēs**, acc. plur. after *ad;* for other particulars, see *cīvitātibus*, l. 7, above. —— **suscēpit**, 3d pers. sing. of *suscipiō, -ere, -cēpī, -ceptum*, 3 (sub + capere = lit. *to take from beneath;* hence = *to undertake*). *suscēpit* agrees with its subject-nom. *is*. —— **In**, prep. with acc. and abl.; here it takes the abl. —— **eō**, abl. sing. n. of dem. pron. *is, ea, id;* it agrees with *itinere*, but it refers to his embassy. Here *in eō itinere* = *in eā lēgātiōne*, but might be freely rendered as if the text were *in suō itinere*. The design of Orgetorix's tour to the Sēquanī, Aeduī, etc., was to arouse

LINES 14-17.] BOOK I. 21

14 persuādet	Casticō,		Catamantaloedis	fīliō,	embassy to the states. In the course of that progress he prevailed on Casticus, son of Catamantaloedes, a Sequanian, whose father had held the royal power among the Sequani for many
he persuades	*Casticus,*		*Catamantaloedes's*	*son,*	
15 Sēquanō,	cūius	pater	rēgnum	in	
a Sequanian,	*whose*	*father*	*the sovereignty*	*among*	
16 Sēquanīs	multōs	annōs	obtinuerat	et	
the Sequani	*many*	*years*	*had held*	*and*	
17 ā senātū		populī	Rōmānī	amīcus	
by the senate		*of the people*	*Roman,*	*friend*	

the various clans to make some sort of united effort to secure the sovereignty of entire Gaul. The number of clans throughout Gaul was about sixty. —— **itinere,** see *itinere,* l. 6, above.

LINE 14. **persuādet,** 3d pers. sing. pres. ind. act. of *persuadeō, -ēre, -suāsī, -suāsum,* 2 (per + suādēre = lit. *to advise thoroughly*). Note that *persuādet* is an historical pres., and see remarks on *dēligitur,* l. 12, above. —— **Casticō,** dat. of the proper noun *Casticus, -ī,* m.; dat. after the intrans. verb *persuādet.* A. & G. 227; B. 142; G. 346, REM. 2; H. 385, II. The student will observe that, in such constructions, many intrans. verbs in Latin have a transitive meaning in English, and are to be rendered into English as such; i.e. just as if they took the acc. of the direct obj. Casticus was an influential Sequanian. —— **Catamantaloedis,** gen. sing. of *Catamantaloedēs, -is,* m.; it limits *fīliō.* Often spelled *Catamantalēdēs;* he was a nobleman among the Sēquanī. —— **fīliō,** dat. sing. of *fīlius, -ī,* m., an appositive.

LINE 15. **Sēquanō,** dat. sing. of the noun *Sēquanus, -ī,* m.; an appositive; both *fīliō* and *Sēquanō* are in apposition with *Casticō.* Consult A. & G. 184; B. 127; G. 321; H. 363. The territory of the Sēquanī was bounded by Mount Jura and the river Doubs. —— **cūius,** gen. sing. m. of *quī, quae, quod;* it limits *pater.* *cūius pater* = lit. *father of whom;* the rel. refers to *Casticō.* —— **pater,** nom. sing. of *pater, patris,* m.; *pater* is subject-nom. of *obtinuerat.* The stem of *pater* is regarded by some as *patr,* as seen in the gen. *patris.* But compare GK. πατήρ, gen. πατέρος, syncopated form πατρός. Comparative grammar thus favors *pater* as the true stem. —— **rēgnum,** acc. sing. of *rēgnum, -ī,* n.; direct obj. of *obtinuerat.* *rēgnum* here denotes the dominion of which the old kings had been dispossessed. —— **in,** prep. with acc. and abl.; here with the abl. = *among.*

LINE 16. **multōs,** acc. plur. m. of the adj. *multus, -a, -um;* comparative *plūs,* superl. *plūrimus.* *multōs* is an attribute of *annōs.* —— **annōs,** acc. plur. of *annus, -ī,* m.; acc. of *time how long.* A. & G. 256, 2; B. 153; G. 336; H. 379. —— **obtinuerat,** 3d pers. sing. pluperf. ind. act. of *obtineō, -ēre, -uī, -tentum,* 2; it agrees with its subject-nom. *pater.* —— **et,** cop. conj., connects the verbs.

LINE 17. **ā,** prep. with the abl. *ā* before consonants, *ab* before either vowels or consonants. —— **senātū,** abl. sing. of *senātus, -ūs,* m.; abl. of the agent with prep. *ā.* Consult A. & G. 246; B. 166; G. 401; H. 415, I. —— **populī,** gen. sing. of *populus, -ī,* m.; *populī* limits *senātū.* —— **Rōmānī,** gen. sing. m. of the adj. *Rōmānus, -a, -um;* it modifies *populī.* Synonyms: *populus* = *the people* collectively, including the senate; whereas *plēbs* or *plēbēs* = *the common people* opposed to senators and knights. —— **amīcus, -ī,** m.; here predicate-nom. after *appellātus erat.* *amīcus* is here the designation of a mere title, conferred by the Roman senate with the design of attaching the barbarians to Roman interests.

22 CAESAR'S GALLIC WAR [CHAP. III.

years, and who had been called *friend* by the senate of the Roman people, to seize the sovereignty in his own state, which his father had held previously. And he also prevailed on Dumnorix the Aeduan, brother	ap(d)pellātus erat, *had been called,* suā *his own,* habuerat; *had held;* Dīvitiācī, *of Divitiacus,*	ut *that* occupāret, *he might seize,* itemque *also and,* quī *who*	rēgnum *the sovereignty* quod *which* Dumnorīgī *Dumnorix* eō *at that*	in *in* pater *his father* Aeduō, *an Aeduan,* tempore *time*	cīvitāte 18 *state* ante 19 *before* frātrī 20 *a brother* prīncipātum 21 *the first position*

LINE 18. **appellātus erat**, 3d pers. sing. pluperf. pass. of *appello, -āre, -āvī, -ātum*, 1; it is connected by the conj. *et* with *obtinuerat*, and has the same subj.: *pater.* —— **ut**, telic conj. here. —— **rēgnum**, -ī, n.; direct obj. of *occupāret*. See note on *rēgnum*, l. 15, above. —— **in**, prep. with acc. and abl.; here it takes the abl. —— **cīvitāte**, abl. sing. of *cīvitās, -ātis*, f.; abl. after prep. *in*.

LINE 19. **suā**, abl. sing. f. of poss. pron. *suus, -a, -um*; it modifies *cīvitāte*. —— **occupāret**, 3d pers. sing. imperf. subjunctive of *occupō, -āre, -āvī, -ātum*, 1; its subject-nom. is *Casticus*, to be supplied; subjunctive of purpose after *ut*. A. & G. 317, 1; B. 200, (*b*); G. 552, 553; H. 497, II. The tense is imperf., because *persuādet* is the historical pres. which admits the secondary sequence. Consult A. & G. 287, *e*; B. 190, REM. 1; G. 511; H. 495, II. —— **quod**, acc. sing. n. of rel. pron. *quī, quae, quod*; its antecedent is *rēgnum*; it is the direct obj. of *habuerat*. —— **pater, patris**, m.; subject-nom. of *habuerat*. —— **ante**, adv., here = *previously;* it is oftener a prep. with the acc.

LINE 20. **habuerat**, 3d pers. sing. pluperf. ind. act. of *habeō, -ēre, -uī, -itum*, 2. —— **itemque** = item + que. *item*, adv. (*is*). Synonyms: *etiam* (et + iam) serves to add a notion to a statement = *and also*; whereas *item* indicates that one statement is made *after the same manner* as another = *also. etiam* alone often = item + que. —— **Dumnorīgī**, dat. of *Dumnorix, -igis*, m.; dat. after *persuādet*, l. 24, below. See A. & G. 227; B. 142; G. 346, REM. 2; H. 385, II. See also note on *Casticō*, l. 14, above. Dumnorix was a younger brother of Divitiacus, a devotee of the old aristocratic order of things among the Aeduī. He was intensely hostile to the Roman party in his clan. —— **Aeduō**, dat. sing. of *Aeduus, -ī*, m.; here used as a noun from the adj. *Aeduus, -a, -um. Aeduō* is in opposition with *Dumnorīgī*. The Aeduī were a Gallic clan living, at the time of Caesar's invasion of Gaul, in the territory between the Loire and the Saône. —— **frātrī**, dat. sing. of *frāter, frātris*, m.; appositive of *Dumnorīgī*.

LINE 21. **Dīvitiācī**, gen. sing. of *Dīvitiācus, -ī*, m.; it limits *frātrī*. —— **quī**, rel. pron., nom. sing. m., refers to *Dīvitiācī*; it is subject-nom. of *obtinēbat.* —— **eō**, abl. n. of dem. pron. *is, ea, id;* it limits *tempore*. —— **tempore**, abl. case of *tempus, -oris*, n.; abl. of *time when*. See A. & G. 256, I; B. 171; G. 393; H. 429. The root of *tempus* is *tem*, as seen in the GK. τέμνω, to cut; hence = *a section* or *division*, in particular, of time. The time referred to is that of Orgetorix's journey. —— **prīncipātum**, acc. sing. of *prīncipātus, -ūs*, m.; direct obj. of *obtinēbat. prīncipātus* is derived from *prīnceps* (prīmus + capere); hence = *the foremost position* or *the most influential position* in the state.

22 in cīvitāte	obtinēbat	āc	māximē		plēbī	of Divitiacus, who at that time was holding a very influential position in his state, and was very acceptable to the common people, to make a like attempt, and he gave him his daughter in mar-
in the state	*was holding*	*and*	*especially*	*to the common people*		
23 acceptus	erat,	ut	idem		cōnārētur,	
acceptable	*was,*	*that*	*the same*		*he might attempt,*	
24 persuādet	eīque		fīliam	suam	in	
he persuades,	*him and,*		*daughter*	*his*	*in* (into)	
25 mātrimōnium	dat.	Perfacile		factū	esse	
marriage	*he gives.*	*Very easy*	*in the doing*		*to be* (it is)	

LINE 22. in cīvitāte, see note on this phrase, l. 18, above. —— obtinēbat, 3d pers. sing. of *obtineō, -ēre, -uī, -tentum*, 3 (ob + tenēre = lit. *to hold by* or *against anything*); it agrees with its subject-nom. *quī*. —— āc, see note on *atque*, l. 10, Chap. I. —— māximē, adv., superl. degree of the comparative *magis*; *multum* (*multō*) is sometimes used as an irr. positive. *māximē* qualifies the adj. *acceptus*. —— plēbī, dat. sing. of *plēbs, -is*, f.; dat. after the adj. *acceptus*. A. & G. 234; B. 144; G. 359; H. 391, I.

LINE 23. acceptus, a participial adj.; predicate after *erat*. This participle is from the verb *accipiō, -ere, -cēpī, -ceptum*, 3 (ad + capere = lit. *to take to one's self*; hence in participle = *acceptable*). Synonyms: *grātus* is the proper epithet to bestow upon one who is *dear, beloved*; it has reference to the feelings; whereas *acceptus* refers to the expression of the feelings; in other words, *acceptus* is related to *grātus* as effect to cause: he who is *grātus*, for that very reason is *acceptus*. —— erat, 3d pers. sing. imperf. ind. of the intrans. verb *sum, esse, fuī*, fut. participle *futūrus*; connected by *āc* with *obtinēbat*, and has the same subj. *quī*. —— ut, telic conj. here. —— idem, acc. sing. n. of the dem. pron. *īdem, eadem, idem* (from root *i*, whence *is*, and the demonstrative suffix *-dem*); cognate acc. after *cōnārētur*. A. & G. 238, *b*; B. 150, REM. 2; G. 333, I; H. 371, II. Observe that the cognate acc. is used with both trans. and intrans. verbs. —— cōnārētur, 3d pers. sing. imperf. subjunctive of the deponent verb *cōnor, -ārī, -ātus*, 1; subjunctive of purpose after *ut*. Note that *ut idem cōnārētur* is a noun-clause of purpose, the direct obj. of *persuādet*. Consult A. & G. 331; B. 200, and REM. 2; G. 546; H. 498. *cōnārētur* is in the imperf. tense, because it depends on an historical pres., which admits of either the primary or secondary sequence, more commonly the latter.

LINE 24. persuādet, see note on this verb, l. 14, above; historical pres. —— eīque = eī + que; *eī* is dat. sing. of the dem. pron. *is, ea, id*; dat. of the indirect obj. after *dat*. Observe how closely the clauses are connected by the enclitic *-que*. —— fīliam, acc. sing. of *fīlia, -ae*, f.; direct obj. of *dat*. Let the student remember that *dea* and *fīlia*, though nouns of the first declension, yet have the dat. and abl. plur. in *-ābus*, by exception. The exception is taken in order to avoid confusion with the dat. plur. of *deus* and *fīlius*. —— suam, acc. sing. f. of the poss. adj. pron. *suus, -a, -um*; it refers to the subj. of *dat*, but agrees in gender and number with *fīliam*. This is the usual construction; *fīliam suī* would be inadmissible. —— in, prep. with acc. and abl.; here used idiomatically with the acc. after *dat*, as if *dat* were a verb of motion: he gives *into* marriage; the English idiom is: he gives *in* marriage.

LINE 25. mātrimōnium, acc. sing. of *mātrimōnium, -ī*, n.; the obj. of the prep. *in* (from stem mātrī + mónium = *state of motherhood*). —— dat, 3d pers. sing. of *dō*,

24   CAESAR'S GALLIC WAR   [CHAP. III.

riage. He showed them how easy it would be to accomplish the venture, as he personally was about to seize the supreme power in his own state;	illīs to them	probat he proves	cōnāta attempts	perficere, to accomplish,	proptereā 26 for this reason
	quod because	ipse he himself	suae of his own	cīvitātis state	imperium 27 the military power
	obtentūrus about to acquire		esset; was;	nōn not	esse dubium, 28 to be (it is) doubtful,

dare, dĕdi, dătum, 1; but observe that by exception the *a* before -*re* in the pres. inf. act. is short; *dăt*, like *persuādĕt*, in the preceding line, agrees with *Orgetorix* understood as subject-nom. —— **Perfacile**, acc. sing. n. of the adj. *perfacilis, -e*, predicate-acc. after *esse* (per + facilis). —— **factū**, a latter supine of *faciō, -ere, fēcī, factum*, 3; in fact, it is a noun of the fourth decl., in the abl. case of specification. Consult A. & G. 253, *a*; B. 186 (B); G. 397, 436; H. 545, NOTE 1. —— **esse**, its subject-acc. is the inf. phrase *cōnāta perficere*.

LINE 26. **illīs**, i.e. Casticus and Dumnorix; dat. of the indirect obj. after *probat*. —— **probat**, 3d pers. sing. pres. ind. act. of *probō, -āre, -āvi, -ātum*, 1 (*probus*, good); an historical present-conative. Consult A. & G. 276, *d*; G. 227, 2; H. 467, 6. —— **cōnāta**, acc. plur. of noun *cōnātum, -ī*, n.; it is the direct obj. of *perficere*. *cōnātā* is properly a participle, acc. n. plur. of *cōnātus, -a, -um* (from *cōnor*, 1), used substantively. —— **perficere**, pres. inf. act. of *perficiō, -ere, fēcī, -fectum*, 3; it is here used with its direct obj. as the subject-acc. of *esse*. Consult A. & G. 270, 3, *a*; B. 86. 1; G. 422; H. 538. —— **proptereā**, adv., herald of the following *quod*-clause; see note on *proptereā*, l. 9, Chap. I.

LINE 27. **quod**, a conj. = *because*; but see note on *quod*, l. 9, Chap. I. —— **ipse**, nom. sing., dem. pron. = *he himself*; more emphatic than *is*, as subject-nom. in l. 12, above; *ipse* is subject-nom. of *obtentūrus esset*. Observe that *ipse* is the only dem. pron. that from its signification admits of the voc. case. —— **suae**, gen. sing. of the poss. adj. pron. *suus, -a, -um*; it is reflexive in meaning = *of his own*; it limits *cīvitātis*. —— **cīvitātis**, gen. sing. of *cīvitās, -ātis*, f.; it limits *imperium*. —— **imperium**, acc. sing. of *imperium, -ī*, n.; direct obj. of *obtentūrus esset*. Synonyms: *imperium* = *supreme military power*; whereas *potestās* = *the civil power*. Caesar, however, seems to use *rēgnum, prīncipātus* and *imperium*, with very little difference in meaning, in this chapter. If there is any difference, *rēgnum* = sovereignty as one's hereditary right, though now dispossessed of it; *prīncipātus* = the sovereignty which one exercises on account of his wealth or popularity; and *imperium* = the sovereignty that is the outcome of military power.

LINE 28. **obtentūrus esset**, 3d pers. sing. imperf. subjunctive, first periphrastic conjugation, formed of the fut. act. participle of *obtineō, -ēre, -uī, -tentum*, 2, and *esset*, 3d pers. sing. imperf. subjunctive of *sum, esse, fuī*. It is in the subjunctive mode, because it is in a subordinate clause in the *ōrātiō oblīqua*; it is in the imperf. tense, because *probat* is an historical pres.; in other words, the tense-sequence is secondary. —— **nōn**, adv., modifies adj. *dubium*. —— **esse**, pres. inf. of *sum, esse, fuī, futūrus*, an intrans. verb; the grammatical subj. of *esse* is the following *quīn*-clause used as a noun in the acc. case. —— **dubium**, acc. sing. n. of the adj. *dubius, -a, -um*; predicate after *esse*. *Ōrātiō rēcta* of lines 25-28: perfacile factū *vōbīs est* cōnāta perficere, proptereā quod *ego* ipse *meae* cīvitātis imperium *obtinēbō*.

[LINES 29-32.] BOOK I. 25

29	quīn	tōtīus	Galliae	plūrimum	Helvētiī	and he said that there was no doubt that the Helvetii were the most powerful of all the Gauls, and he declared that he would win for them the royal power with his own resources and with his own
	that	*of entire*	*Gaul*	*most*	*the Helvetii*	
30	possent;	sē	suīs	cōpiīs	suōque	
	were able;	*himself*	*with his*	*resources*	*with his and,*	
31	exercitū	illīs	rēgna		conciliātūrum	
	army	*for them*	*the royal powers*		*to be about to secure,*	
32	cōnfirmat.	Hāc	ōrātiōne	adductī	inter	sē
	he affirms.	*By this*	*oration*	*led*	*among themselves*	

LINE 29. quīn, conj. (quī + nē, or nōn); after a negative *quīn = that.* —— tōtīus, gen. sing. f. of the adj. *tōtus, -a, -um;* it agrees with *Galliae.* For list of the adjectives whose gen. end in *-īus*, dat. in *-ī*, see A. & G. 83; B. 56; G. 76, and REMS.; H. 151, 175. —— Galliae, gen. sing. of *Gallia, -ae*, f.; partitive gen. after *plūrimum.* Consult A. & G. 216, 4; B. 134; G. 372; H. 397, 3. —— plūrimum, adj., cognate acc. of *plūrimus, -a, -um,* superl.; positive *multus,* comparative *plūs.* As to cognate acc. with adverbial force, see A. & G. 240; B. 150, REM. 2; G. 333, 338, 2; H. 371, II. —— Helvētiī, nom. plur. of adj. *Helvētius, -a, -um,* used substantively; subject-nom. of *possent.*

LINE 30. possent, 3d pers. plur. of *possum, posse, potuī;* imperf. subjunctive after *quīn*, a clause of result. A. & G. 319, *d*; B. 201, REM. 3; G. 555, 2; H. 504, 3, 2). The *quīn*-clause of the text is equivalent to: *quīn omnium Gallorum Helvētiī potentissimī essent.* It will be noticed that the Helvetians here are classed with the Gauls. —— sē, acc. sing. of the reflexive pron. *suī, sibi, sē, sē; sē* is subject-acc. of *conciliātūrum,* supply *esse.* —— suīs, abl. sing. f. of poss. pron. *suus, -a, -um;* it refers to Orgetorix, but agrees with *cōpiīs.* —— cōpiīs, abl. plur. of *cōpia, -ae,* f.; in the sing. = *plenty;* in the plur. = *resources,* sometimes = *troops. cōpiīs* is an abl. of means. —— suōque (suō + que); *suō* is abl. sing. m. of *suus, -a, -um;* it is the attributive of *exercitū. que,* note how closely the phrase *suō exercitū* is connected with *cōpiīs* by this enclitic.

LINE 31. exercitū, abl. sing. of *exercitus, -ūs,* m.; abl. of means. Synonyms: *aciēs* = *an army in battle-array; āgmen* = *an army in motion* or *on the march* (*agere*); but *exercitus* = *an exercised* or *disciplined army* (*exercēre*, to train). —— illīs, i.e. Casticus and Dumnorix; dat. of reference or advantage. A. & G. 235; B. 145; G. 352; H. 384, II, 1, 2). Observe that *illīs* in direct discourse is changed into *vōbīs.* —— rēgna, acc. plur. of *rēgnum, -ī,* n.; direct obj. of *conciliātūrum* (*esse*); it is in the plur. as denoting the three powers. —— conciliātūrum (esse), fut. inf. act. of *conciliō, -āre, -āvī, -ātum,* 1; its subject-acc. is the personal pron. *sē,* preceding line.

LINE 32. cōnfirmat, 3d pers. sing. of *cōnfirmō, -āre, -āvī, -ātum,* 1; historical pres.; its subject-nom. is a pron. of the 3d pers. referring to Orgetorix. The above speech which Caesar reports in lines 28–31, above, in the *ōrātiō rēcta* would have this form: nōn *est* dubium, quīn tōtīus Galliae plūrimum Helvētiī *possint;* egō meīs cōpiīs meōque exercitū *vōbīs* rēgna *conciliābō.* —— Hāc, abl. sing. f. of the dem. pron. *hīc, haec, hōc;* it modifies *ōrātiōne.* —— ōrātiōne is the abl. sing. of *ōrātiō, -ōnis,* f.; abl. of cause. A. & G. 245, and 2. *b;* B. 165, and REM. 4; G. 408, and NOTE 2; H. 416, and NOTE 1. —— adductī, nom. plur. m. of the perf. pass. participle of *addūcō, -ere, -dūxī, -ductum,* 3; it agrees with *eī* understood, referring to the trio, Orgetorix, Casticus and Dumnorix; the subject-nom. of *dant,* l. 33, below. —— inter sē, a reciprocal phrase; see note on the phrase, l. 6, Chap. I.

army. Influenced by this speech, they gave to one another the pledge of an oath, and hoped that, when they had seized the sovereignty in their own states, they could, by means of three very influential and very powerful peoples, gain the mastery of entire Gaul.	fidem *a pledge* rēgnō *the sovereignty* potentissimōs *very powerful* Galliae *of Gaul* spērant. *they hope.*	et *and* ac *and* sēsē *themselves*	iūs iūrandum *an oath* occupātō, *having been seized,* firmissimōs *very strong* potīrī *to gain the mastery,*	dant *they give* per *through* populōs *peoples* posse *to be able,*	et, 33 *and,* trēs 34 *three* tōtīus 35 *of the whole* 36 37

LINE 33. **fidem**, acc. sing. of *fidēs, -ei*, f., stem *fidē;* direct obj. of *dant*. —— **iūs iūrandum** (iūs + iūrandum), a compound noun in which both parts are declined; *iūs* is a neuter noun of the third decl., and *iūrandum* is a neuter noun of the second decl. But in the plur., the gen., dat. and abl. are wanting. The two nouns connected by *et = a pledge confirmed by an oath*, hendiadys (ἓν διὰ δυοῖν) — the use of two nouns connected by a conj. instead of a single noun with a modifier. Consult A. & G. 385; B. 310, 2, (*b*); G. 698; H. 636, III, 2. —— **dant**, 3d pers. plur. pres. ind. act. of *dō, dare, dēdī, datum*, 1. See note on *dat*, l. 25, above. —— **et**, cop. conj.; connects *dant* with *spērant*, l. 37, below.

LINE 34. **rēgnō**, abl. sing. of *rēgnum, -ī,* n.; abl. absolute with *occupātō*, denoting *time when*. A. & G. 255; B. 172, 192; G. 409, 410; H. 431, 1 and 2. —— **occupātō,** abl. sing. n. of perf. pass. participle of *occupō*, 1; abl. absolute with *rēgnō*. Supply *ab eīs*, as abl. of the voluntary agent. —— **per**, prep. with the acc. = *through, by means of*. —— **trēs**, acc. plur. of num. adj. *trēs, tria;* an *ī*-stem, and declined like the plur. of *levis*. The first three cardinals, *ūnus, duo* and *trēs*, are declined; from *quattuor* to *centum* the cardinals are indeclinable; *trēs* is an attributive of *populōs*.

LINE 35. **potentissimōs**, acc. plur. m. of the adj. *potentissimus, -a, -um*, superl. degree of *potēns*, comparative *potentior* (properly a participle of *possum*); the adj. qualifies *populōs*. —— **ac**, stronger than *et*, see note on *atque*, l. 10, Chap. I. —— **firmissimōs**, acc. plur. m. of the superl. degree of *firmus*, comparative *firmior*; this adj. also qualifies *populōs*. —— **populōs**, acc. plur. of *populus, -ī,* m.; acc. after *per* denoting the persons *through* whom   Consult A. & G. 246, *b*; B. 166, REM. 1; G. 401; H. 415, NOTE 1. —— **tōtīus**, see note on *tōtīus*, l. 29, above.

LINE 36. **Galliae**, gen. sing. of *Gallia, -ae,* f.; gen. case after *potīrī*. A. & G. 249, *a*; B. 167, 1, REM.; G. 407, NOTE 2, (*d*); H. 410, V, 3. *potīrī* usually takes the abl. —— **sēsē**, acc. plur., a reduplication of the reflexive pron. *sē; sēsē* is subject-acc. of *posse*. —— **potīrī**, pres. inf. of *potior, -īrī, -itus,* 4, deponent; it completes the meaning of *posse*. —— **posse**, in form a pres. inf. of *possum, posse, potuī,* irr. (potis + sum); in use here, it = the fut. inf. After verbs of *hoping, promising* and *undertaking*, the fut. inf. usually occurs, but *possum* has no fut. inf., and hence there often occurs the pres. *posse* as equivalent to the periphrase *fore ut possint*. Consult A. & G. 288, *f*; B. 245, 4, (3); G. 248, REM., and 656, REM.; H. 537, 3, and NOTE 1.

LINE 37. **spērant**, 3d pers. plur. pres. ind. act. of *spēro, -āre, -āvī, -ātum,* 1; it agrees with *ei*, a pron. representing Orgetorix, Casticus and Dumnorix.

						IV. This con-
1 IV.	Ea	rēs	est	Helvētiīs	per	spiracy was dis-
	This	*thing*	*is*	*to the Helvetii*	*through*	closed to the Hel-
2 indicium		ēnūntiāta.		Mōribus	suīs	vetii by an in- former; and they
information		*made known.*		*According to customs*	*their,*	compelled Orge-
3 Orgetorigem		ex	vinclīs	causam	dīcere	torix, according to their custom,
Orgetorix		*from*	*chains*	*(his) case*	*to plead*	to plead his case
4 coēgērunt;			damnātum	poenam	sequī	in chains. The punishment of be-
they compelled;			*(him) condemned*	*punishment*	*to overtake*	ing burned with

LINE 1. **Ea**, nom. sing. f. of the dem. pron. *is, ea, id*; it is an attributive of *rēs*. —— **rēs**, nom. sing. of *rēs, reī*, f., subj. of *est ēnūntiāta* (*ēnūntiāta est*). Observe: that the phrase *ea rēs* is descriptive of the plot referred to in the preceding chapter; that *haec rēs* might have been used as indicating nearness of time or place; but that *ea rēs* denotes *that* conspiracy of three years ago, B.C. 61, *is* denoting *this* or *that*, according to the connection; and that *rēs* is a word of very elastic meaning. —— **est**, 3d pers. sing. of *sum, esse, fuī*, but here used as part of the compound perf. pass. tense *ēnūntiāta est*. Note the insertion of *Helvētiīs per indicium* between the parts, by which the entire group of words is made emphatic. —— **Helvētiīs**, dat. plur. m. of the adj. *Helvētius, -a, -um*, used as a noun; indirect obj. of *est ēnūntiāta*. For description, see note on *Helvētiī*, l. 16, Chap. I. —— **per**, prep. with the acc.

LINE 2. **indicium**, acc. sing. of *indicium, -ī*, n.; the agent considered as means is denoted by *per* with the acc. See A. & G. 246, *b*; B. 166, REM. 1; G. 401; H. 415, I, 1, NOTE 1. Observe that *indicium* = lit. *information*, but here the abstract is put for the concrete, and *indicium* = *an informer*. —— **est ēnūntiāta** (*ēnūntiāta est*), 3d pers. sing. perf. pass. ind. of *ēnūntiō, -āre, -āvī, -ātum,* 1; it agrees with its subject-nom. *rēs*; *ēnūntiāre* (ē + nūntius) = lit. *to speak out*, especially what ought to be kept secret. —— **Mōribus**, abl. plur. of the noun *mōs, mōris*, m.; may be taken as an abl. of cause, A. & G. 245; B. 165; G. 408; H. 416; or as an abl. of specification, A. & G. 253, NOTE; B. 162; G. 397; H. 424. —— **suīs**, abl. plur. m. of poss. pron. *suus, -a, -um*; it agrees with *mōribus*, but refers to the subj. of the proposition. A. & G. 196; B. 80, REM. 2; G. 309, I; H. 449.

LINE 3. **Orgetorigem**, acc. sing. of *Orgetorix, -igis*, m.; subject-acc. of *dīcere*. See note on *Orgetorix*, l. 2, Chap. II. —— **ex**, prep. with the abl.; the form *ē* before consonants only, *ex* before vowels and consonants. —— **vinclīs**, abl. plur. of *vinclum, -ī*, n.; abl. after prep. *ex*. See A. & G. 152, *b*; B. 120. 2; G. 417; H. 434. The common editions read *vinculīs* instead of the syncopated *vinclīs*. The phrase *ex vinclīs* = lit. *out of chains*, in the sense of *under arrest*. The critics tell us the phrase = *in chains*. Does it not rather mean that Orgetorix was compelled to defend himself, although he was not formally imprisoned? —— **causam**, acc. sing. of *causa, -ae*, f.; direct obj. of *dīcere*. —— **dīcere**, pres. inf. act. of *dīcō, -ere, dīxī, dictum,* 3; its subject-acc. is *Orgetorigem*. Note that the acc. infinitive-clause, as a whole, is the direct obj. of *coēgērunt*.

LINE 4. **coēgērunt**, 3d pers. plur. perf. ind. act. of *cōgō, cōgere, coēgī, coāctum,* 3 (con + agere = lit. *to drive together*; hence *cōgere* = *to urge, to compel*). The subject-nom. is pron. *eī*, i.e. *Helvētiī* understood. —— **damnātum**, perf. pass. participle of *damnō, -āre, -āvī, -ātum,* 1; it agrees with *eum*, to be supplied, which latter pron. is the

fire must needs overtake him if condemned. On the day appointed for pleading his case, Orgetorix assembled at the place of trial, from all quarters, all his vassals, about ten thousand people, and	oportēbat, *it must needs be,* cōnstitūtā *appointed of (for)* ad iūdicium *near the court* hominum *of human beings*	ut *that* causae *(his) case's* omnem *all* mīlia *thousands*	īgnī *with fire* dictiōnis *pleading* suam *his* decem, *ten,*	cremārētur. *he be burned.* Orgetorix *Orgetorix* familiam, *household,* undique *from every side*	Diē 5 *On the day* Orgetorix 6 *Orgetorix* ad 7 *about* coēgit 8 *collected,*

direct obj. of *sequī*. The participle here denotes condition. See A. & G. 292; B. 204, REM. 6; G. 667; H. 549, 2. —— **poenam**, acc. sing. of *poena*, *-ae*, f.; subject-acc. of *sequī*. Consult A. & G. 270, *b*, 272, *a*, I; B. 194, REM. 2, (*e*); G. 535; H. 538. Observe that the acc.-clause *damnātum (eum) poenam sequī* is the subj. of *oportēbat*. —— **sequī**, pres. inf. of the deponent *sēquor*, *-ī*, *secūtus*, 3; its subject-acc. is *poenam*.

LINE 5. **oportēbat**, 3d pers. sing. imperf. ind. of *oportet*, *-ēre*, *-uit*, impersonal (*opus*, need). Synonyms: *oportet = it behooves*, i.e. expresses duty in general; whereas *debēre* denotes the obligation of a particular person; *dē + habēre = to have from a person*, hence = *to owe him*. —— **ut**, conj., ecbatic. —— **īgnī**, abl. sing. of *īgnis*, *-is*, m. The more common form of the abl. is *īgne*, though the regular form of an *i*-stem, in the abl. sing. is *-ī*. But see A. & G. 57, *b*; B. 46, IV, Class II, near the end; G. 57. 2; H. 62; *īgnī* is an abl. of means. A. & G. 248, *c*, 1; B. 167; G. 401; H. 420. —— **cremārētur**, 3d pers. sing. imperf. subjunctive of *cremō*, *-āre*, *-āvī*, *-ātum*, 1; its subject-nom. is a personal pron: implied in the ending, and referring to the pron. *eum*, the omitted obj. of *sequī*. Note that the clause *ut . . . cremārētur* is a result-clause in apposition with, and explanatory of, *poenam*; and consult A. & G. 332, *f*; B. 201, REM. 3, NOTE; G. 557; H. 501, III. Synonyms: *cremāre = to consume by fire*; whereas *urere = to burn*, simply, though sometimes = *to burn up*. —— **Diē**, abl. sing. of *diēs*, *-ēī*, m. and f. in the sing.; always m. in the plur.; *diē* is abl. of *time at which*. A. & G. 256; B. 171; G. 393; H. 429. *diēs* is f. usually when it denotes a set time; see A. & G. 73; B. 49, REM. 2; G. 64; H. 123.

LINE 6. **cōnstitūtā**, abl. sing. f. of the perf. pass. participle of *cōnstituō*, *-ere*, *-uī*, *-ūtum*, 3; used here as an adj. agreeing with *diē*. —— **causae**, gen. sing. of *causa*, *-ae*, f.; objective gen. limiting *dictiōnis*; see A. & G. 217; B. 131, REM. 2; G. 363, 2; H. 396, III. —— **dictiōnis**, gen. sing. of *dictiō*, *-ōnis*, f. (*dīcere*); compare English *diction*; it limits *diē*. —— **Orgetorix**, see note on this word, l. 2, Chap. II; *Orgetorix* is subject-nom. of *coēgit*, l. 8, below.

LINE 7. **ad**, prep. with the acc. —— **iūdicium**, acc. sing. of *iūdicium*, *-ī*, n. (*iūs + dicere*, through *iūdicāre*); *iūdicium* is the obj. of the prep. *ad*. —— **omnem**, acc. sing. f. of adj. *omnis*, *-e*; it limits *familiam*. —— **suam**, acc. sing. f. of poss. pron. *suus*, *-a*, *-um*; it modifies *familiam*, but refers to *Orgetorix*, the subj. of the proposition. A. & G. 196; B. 80, REM. 2; G. 309, 1; H. 449. —— **familiam**, acc. sing. of *familia*, *-ae*, f.; direct obj. of *coēgit*. This word here = *serfs*. —— **ad**, here an adv. denoting an approximation = *about*; compare GK. ὡς.

LINE 8. **hominum**, gen. plur. of *homō*, *-inis*, m. and f.; partitive gen. after *mīlia*. A. & G. 216, 3; B. 134; G. 293; H. 397. 2. —— **mīlia**, acc. plur. n. of indecl. adj. *mille* in the sing.; in the plur. it is a decl. noun; *mīlia* is an appositive, an explanatory modifier

9 et	omnēs	clientēs	obaerātōsque		suōs,	conducted to the same place all his clients and debtors, of whom he had a large number; and through their instrumentality he saved himself from the necessity of pleading his case.
and	all	retainers	debtors and,		his,	
10 quōrum	māgnum		numerum		habēbat,	
of whom	a great		number		he had,	
11 eōdem		condūxit;	per	eōs,	nē	
to the same place		he brought;	through	them,	that not	
12 causam	dīceret,		sē	ēripuit.	Cum	
(his) case	he might plead,		himself	he rescued.	When	

of *familiam*. —— **decem**, indecl. num. adj., cardinal; it modifies *mīlia*. —— **undique**, (unde + que) = lit. *whencesoever;* and indef. adv. The enclitic *-que* gives to the word a tone of universality. —— **coēgit**, 3d pers. sing. perf. ind. act. of *cōgo, -ere, coēgi, coāctum*, 3; its subject-nom. is *Orgetorix*.

LINE 9. **et**, cop. conj., connects *coēgit* with *condūxit*, l. 11, below. —— **omnēs**, acc. plur. of the adj. *omnis, -e;* it limits *clientēs*. —— **clientēs**, acc. plur. of *cliēns, -entis*, m. and f. (*cluēns* from *cluēre*, to hear); hence = *one who hears, a protégé, clientēs* is the direct obj. of *condūxit*. —— **obaerātōsque** (obaerātōs + que); *obaerātōs* is an acc. plur. m. of the adj. *obaerātus, -a, -um*, used substantively, connected with *clientēs* by the enclitic *-que*, and in the same grammatical construction. This word is derived from *oberārius* (ob + aes); and hence = *debtors*, those that must work out their debts. The vassals and retainers were intensely devoted to their chiefs. They shared with them prosperity and adversity. If the chiefs suffered violent deaths, the vassals shared a like fate; and if they would not meet death with them in battle, they often committed suicide. —— **suōs**, acc. plur. m. of the poss. pron. *suus, -a, -um;* it agrees with *obaerātōs*, but refers to *Orgetorix*.

LINE 10. **quōrum**, gen. plur. m. of the rel. *quī, quae, quod;* it refers to *obaerātōs* as its antecedent, but, as a gen., limits *numerum*. —— **māgnum**, acc. sing. m. of the adj. *māgnus, māior, māximus;* it modifies *numerum*. —— **numerum**, acc. sing. of *numerus, -ī*, m.; direct obj. of *habēbat*. —— **habēbat**, 3d pers. sing. imperf. ind. act. of *habeō, -ēre, -uī, -itum*, 2; it agrees with a subject-nom. implied in the ending, referring to *Orgetorix*.

LINE 11. **eōdem**, an adv., strictly, an old dat. of *īdem;* sc. *locō;* as an adv. *eōdem* modifies *condūxit*. The place referred to, of course, is that denoted by *iūdicium*, l. 7, above. —— **condūxit**, 3d pers. sing. perf. ind. act. of *condūcō, -ere, -dūxī, -ductum*, 3; its subj. is *Orgetorix* understood. —— **per**, prep. with the acc. —— **eōs**, acc. plur. m. of the dem. pron. *is, ea, id*, used as a personal pron. of the 3d pers.; acc. of the agent as means after *per*. See A. & G. 246, *b*; B. 166, REM. 1; G. 401; H. 415, I, 1, NOTE 1. —— **nē**, conj. adv. = *that not*, telic; if the construction were ecbatic, *ut nōn* would be used.

LINE 12. **causam**, acc. sing. of *causa, -ae*, f.; direct obj. of *dīceret*. —— **dīceret**, 3d pers. sing. imperf. subjunctive of *dīcō, -ere, dīxī, dictum*, 3; subjunctive of purpose after *nē*. Consult A. & G. 317; B. 200, (*b*); G. 545, 3, end; H. 497, II. Observe that the purpose-clause *nē causam dīceret* depends on *sē ēripuit*. —— **sē**, acc. sing. of the reflexive pron. *suī, sibi, sē, sē;* direct obj. of *ēripuit*. —— **ēripuit**, 3d pers. sing. perf. ind. act. of *ēripiō, -ere, -uī, -reptum*, 3 (ē + rapere, *to snatch away*). —— **Cum**, conj. = *when*, or *while*, or *as*, or *since;* here it = *when*, and is used *to describe* the time of the main-clause: *Orgetorix mortuus est*.

CAESAR'S GALLIC WAR [CHAP. IV.

When the state, incensed at such action, attempted to secure its own rights by arms, and the magistrates were collecting a large number of men from the country, Orgetorix died;	cīvitās *the state* iūs *right* hominum *of men* Orgetorix *Orgetorix*	ob *on account of* suum *its own* ex *from* mortuus *died;*	eam *this* exsequī *to enforce* agrīs *the fields* est;	rem *thing* cōnārētur, *attempted,* magistrātūs *the magistrates* neque *not and,*	incitāta *aroused,* multitūdinemque *a great number and,* cōgerent, *were collecting,* abest *is wanting*	armīs 13 14 15 16

LINE 13. **cīvitās, -ātis,** nom. sing. f.; used by metonymy for *cīvēs cīvitātis*; subj. of *cōnārētur*. —— **ob,** prep. with the acc. —— **eam,** acc. sing. f. of the dem. pron. *is, ea, id*; it is an attributive of *rem*. —— **rem,** acc. sing. of *rēs, reī*, f.; obj. of the prep. *ob*. Observe that the objective cause is thus expressed by *ob*, or *per* with the acc. If the cause-subjective were to be indicated, the abl. of cause would be the construction. Consult A. & G. 245, *b*; B. 165, REM. 4; G. 408, NOTE 3; H. 416, I, 2). The thing referred to is the conduct of Orgetorix. —— **incitāta,** perf. pass. participle of *incitō, -āre, -āvī, -ātum,* 1; it agrees with *cīvitās*. —— **armīs,** abl. plur. of *arma, -ōrum,* n.; abl. of means after *exsequī*. Synonyms: *arma* = arms used in close contest. *tēla* = those used in contests at a distance.

LINE 14. **iūs,** acc. sing. of *iūs, iūris,* n.; direct obj. of *exsequī*. —— **suum,** acc. sing. n., poss. reflexive adj. pron.; it qualifies *iūs*, but refers to *cīvitās*, the grammatical subj. of the sentence. —— **exsequī,** pres. inf. of the deponent verb *exsequor, -ī, -cūtus,* 3; complementary inf.; it completes the meaning of *cōnārētur*. A. & G. 271; B. 181; G. 423; H. 533. Observe the force of the prep. in the compound = to follow *out* to the end, i.e. with *iūs* = *to enforce*. —— **cōnārētur,** 3d pers. sing. imperf. subjunctive of the deponent verb *cōnor, -ārī, -ātus,* 1; subjunctive after the conj. *cum*, relative time; i.e. the temporal clause defines the time of the principal action. A. & G. 323; B. 222; G. 585; H. 521, II, 2. —— **multitūdinemque** (multitūdinem + que); *multitūdinem* is acc. sing. of *multitūdō, -inis,* f. (*multus*); acc. of the direct obj. after *cōgerent*.

LINE 15. **hominum,** gen. plur. of *homō, -inis,* m. and f.; it limits *multitūdinem*. —— **ex,** prep. with the abl. —— **agrīs,** abl. plur. of *ager, agrī,* m. Synonyms: *agrī* = *the fields, the open country; rūs* = *the country* in opposition to the town. —— **magistrātūs,** nom. plur. of *magistrātus, -ūs,* m., subj. of the verb *cōgerent*. *magistrātus* (*magister*, root *mag,* whence *māgnus*) in contradistinction from *imperia* is used of civil offices at Rome; *imperia*, of the authority of the officials in the provinces. But in Rome there were two species of civil offices — the *magistrātūs extraordināriī* and *ordināriī*. The former were the dictators and other extraordinary rulers; the latter consisted of the consuls, praetors and censors, and some other minor officers. There were also *magistrātūs patriciī* and *magistrātūs plēbiī*. —— **cōgerent,** 3d pers. plur. imperf. subjunctive act. of *cōgō, -ere, coēgī, coāctum,* 3; connected by the enclitic conj. *-que* with *cōnārētur*, and still under the influence of *cum*.

LINE 16. **Orgetorix, -igis,** m., subject-nom. of *mortuus est*. —— **mortuus est,** 3d pers. sing. perf. ind. act. of the deponent verb *morior, morī, mortuus,* 3; it agrees with its subject-nom. *Orgetorix*. —— **neque** (nē + que) = lit. *and not;* but *neque ... neque* = *neither ... nor*. —— **abest,** 3d pers. sing. pres. ind. of *absum, -esse, ab(ā)fuī, ab(ā)futūrus;* it agrees with the subject-nom. *suspīciō*.

BOOK I.   31

17	suspīciō,	ut	Helvētiī	arbitrantur,	quīn	and there is no doubt, as the Helvetii think, that he committed suicide.
	the suspicion,	*as*	*the Helvetii*	*think*	*that*	
18	ipse	sibi	mortem	cōnscīverit.		
	he himself	*to himself*	*death*	*decreed.*		

1	V. Post	ēius	mortem	nihilō	minus	V. After Orgetorix's death, the Helvetii nevertheless attempted to do as they had purposed — to emigrate from their borders.
	After	*his*	*death*	*in nothing*	*the less*	
2	Helvētiī	id,	quod	cōnstituerant,	facere	
	the Helvetii	*that,*	*which*	*they had resolved on,*	*to do*	
3	cōnantur,	ut	ē	fīnibus	suīs	exeant.
	they attempt	*that*	*from*	*limits*	*their own,*	*they may go forth.*

LINE 17. **suspīciō, -ōnis,** f., sometimes written *suspītiō;* it is subject-nom. of *abest*. Observe that *suspīciō* is derived from sub + *specere, to look at secretly* or *askance;* hence (*effectus prō causā*) = *to mistrust*. —— **ut,** adv. = *as*. —— **Helvētiī,** nom. plur. m. of the adj. *Helvētius, -a, -um,* used as a noun, and subject-nom. of *arbitrantur*. —— **arbitrantur,** 3d pers. plur. pres. ind. of the deponent verb *arbitror, -ārī, -ātus,* 1 (*arbiter,* a witness); it agrees with its subject-nom. *Helvētiī*. —— **quīn** (quī + nē) = lit. *who* or *which not;* but after negations and negative phrases = *that*.

LINE 18. **ipse,** intensive pron. expressed for emphasis, subject-nom. of *cōnscīverit;* or *ipse* may be taken as an appositive of the omitted subj. of the verb. —— **sibi,** dat. of the reflexive pron. *suī, sibi, sē, sē;* dat. of the indirect obj. after *cōnscīverit*. —— **mortem,** acc. sing. of *mors, mortis,* f.; the direct obj. of *cōnscīverit*. —— **cōnscīverit,** 3d pers. sing. perf. subjunctive act. of *cōnscīscō, -ere, -scīvī, -scītum,* 3; subjunctive of result after *quīn*. Note carefully that the result-clause: *quīn sibi mortem cōnscīverit,* is in apposition with *suspīciō*. See A. & G. 332, *f*; B. 201, REM. 3; G. 555, 2; H. 501, III. Observe that the perf. subjunctive is used after a primary tense to denote any past action. Here it represents an historical perfect. The direct statement is: *sibi mortem cōnscīvit*.

LINE 1. **Post,** prep. with the acc. —— **ēius,** gen. sing. m. of dem. pron. *is, ea, id,* used substantively, i.e. as a personal pron.; in the gen. = Engl. poss. case *his*. —— **mortem,** acc. sing. of *mors, mortis,* f.; the obj. of the prep. *post*. —— **nihilō,** abl. of *nihilum, -ī,* n.; abl. of degree of difference after the comparative *minus*. See A. & G. 250; B. 164; G. 403; H. 423. The word is sometimes written with *minus* thus: *nihilōminus*. —— **minus,** adv., comparative degree of *parum* (*parvē,* rare), superl. *minimē;* minus modifies *cōnantur*.

LINE 2. **Helvētiī,** nom. plur. m. of the adj. *Helvētius, -a, -um,* used as a noun; subject-nom. of *cōnantur*. For description, see note on *Helvētiī,* l. 16, Chap. I. —— **id,** acc. sing. n. of the dem. pron. *is, ea, id;* direct obj. of *facere*. —— **quod,** acc. sing. n. of the rel. pron. *quī, quae, quod;* it refers to *id* as its antecedent, and is the direct obj. of *cōnstituerant*. —— **cōnstituerant,** 3d pers. plur. pluperf. ind. act. of *cōnstituō, -ere, -uī, -ūtum,* 3; it agrees with a pron. implied in the ending *-ēī,* i.e. *Helvētiī*. —— **facere,** pres. inf. act. of *faciō, -ere, fēcī, factum,* 3; complementary of *cōnantur*. See A. & G. 271, and NOTE; B. 181; G. 423; H. 533, 2.

LINE 3. **cōnantur,** 3d pers. plur. pres. ind. of deponent verb *cōnor, -ārī, -ātus,* 1; it agrees with its subject-nom. *Helvētiī*. —— **ut,** ecbatic conj. —— **ē,** prep. with the

When at length they thought they were ready for the undertaking, they set fire to all their towns about twelve in number, to their villages about four hundred, and to the remaining private	Ubi *When* esse *to be* numerō *in number* quadringentōs, *four hundred,*	iam *already* arbitrātī *they* ad *about*	sē *themselves* sunt, *thought,* duodecim, *twelve,* reliqua *the remaining*	ad *for* oppida *towns*	eam *that* sua *their own,* vīcōs *villages* prīvāta *private*	rem *thing* omnia, *all,*	parātōs 4 *prepared* omnia, 5 *all,* ad 6 *about* aedificia 7 *buildings*

abl. (*ē* before consonants; *ex* before vowels and consonants). —— **finibus**, abl. plur. of *fīnis, -is*, m.; abl. after prep. *ē*. —— **suīs**, abl. plur. of the poss. pron. *suus, -a, -um;* it modifies *fīnibus*, but refers to *Helvētiī* of the principal clause — indirect reflexive. —— **exeant**, 3d pers. plur. pres. subjunctive of the verb *exeō, -īre, -īvī (-iī), -itum;* subjunctive of result after *ut;* but note that this clause is explanatory of, and in apposition with, the dem. pron. *id.* See A. & G. 332, *f*; B. 201, REM. 3, NOTE; G. 557, and REM., end; H. 501, III, and NOTE.

LINE 4. **Ubi**, adv. (quī + ending bi) = (*a*) *in what place;* (*b*) of time = *whenever*. —— **iam**, adv. = *now*, of any time present, past or future; whereas *nunc* = *now*, of the present. —— **sē**, acc. plur. of the reflexive pron. *suī, sibi, sē, sē;* subject-acc. of *esse*. —— **ad**, prep. with the acc.; with verbs of motion = *to* or *toward;* with verbs of rest = *to, at, for*. —— **eam**, acc. sing. f. of dem. pron. *is, ea, id;* it modifies *rem*. —— **rem**, acc. sing. of noun *rēs, reī*, f.; it follows the prep. *ad*. The phrase *ad eam rem* = *for that thing*, i.e. the emigration. —— **parātōs**, acc. plur. of the participial adj. *parātus, -a, -um*, from the verb *parō*, 1; predicate after *esse*.

LINE 5. **esse**, pres. inf. of the verb *sum, fuī, futūrus;* its subject-acc. is the pron. *sē*. —— **arbitrātī sunt**, 3d pers. plur. perf. ind. of the deponent verb *arbitror, -ārī, -ātus*, 1; its subject-nom. is *Helvētiī* understood. —— **oppida**, acc. plur. of *oppidum, -ī*, n.; direct obj. of *incendunt*. —— **sua**, acc. plur. n. of poss. pron. *suus, -a, -um;* it qualifies *oppida*. —— **omnia**, acc. plur. n. of the adj. *omnis, -ē;* it also qualifies *oppida*.

LINE 6. **numerō**, abl. of specification. See A. & G. 253; B. 162; G. 397; H. 424. —— **ad**, usually a prep., but here an adv. = *about;* it modifies *duodecim*. —— **duodecim**, cardinal num. adj. (duo + decim). —— **vīcōs**, acc. plur. of *vīcus, -ī*, m.; direct obj. of *incendunt*. —— **ad**, here *too*, an adv.

LINE 7. **quadringentōs** (quattuor + centum), acc. plur. m. of the adj. *quadringentī, -ae, -a*, num. adj., modifies *vīcōs*. Observe that the num. adjectives *in the hundreds* are declined like the plur. of *bonus: bonī, -ae, -a*. —— **reliqua**, acc. plur. n. of adj. *reliquus, -a, -um;* it modifies *aedificia*. Synonyms: *reliquī* = *the rest*, the remainder that completes the whole; whereas *cēterī (caeterī)* = *others* in opposition to those first mentioned; compare GK. οἱ ἄλλοι; and *aliī* = *others* as merely differentiated from those mentioned. —— **prīvāta**, acc. plur. n. of participial adj. *prīvātus, -a, -um*, from the verb *prīvō, -āre, -āvī, -ātum*, 1. —— **aedificia**, acc. plur. of the noun *aedificium, -ī*, n.; direct obj. of *incendunt*. Note the omission of the conjunctions between the direct obj. phrases preceding *incendunt* — asyndeton. See note on *lēgibus*, l. 5, Chap. I; and especially A. & G. 346, *c*; B. 123, REM. 6; G. 474, NOTE; H. 636, I, 1. Synonyms: *aedificium* = the general word for *a building of any kind; domus* = *the dwelling-house, the family home*.

8 incendunt;	frūmentum	omne,		praeterquam	edifices; and they burned up all their grain except what they had purposed to carry along with them, in order that, all hope of returning home being taken away, they might be the more ready to endure all per-
they set fire to;	*the grain*	*all,*		*further than*	
9 quod	sēcum	portātūrī erant,		combūrunt,	
what	*themselves with,*	*about to carry they were,*		*they burn up,*	
10 ut	domum	reditiōnis	spē	sublātā,	
that	*home,*	*of return*	*the hope being taken away,*		
11 parātiōrēs	ad	omnia	perīcula	subeunda	
more prepared	*for*	*all*	*dangers*	*to be endured*	

LINE 8. **incendunt**, 3d pers. plur. pres. ind. act. of *incendō, -ere, -cendī, -cēnsum,* 3; it agrees with its subject-nom. *Helvētiī,* to be supplied. Synonyms: *incendere = to burn; combūrere = to burn up.* —— **frūmentum,** acc. sing. of *frūmentum, -ī,* n.; direct obj. of *combūrunt,* l. 9, below. Note that *frūmentum,* sing. = *the grain,* while *frūmenta,* the plur. = *the growing crop.* —— **omne,** acc. sing. n., an attributive of *frūmentum.* —— **praeterquam,** adv. (praeter + quam). Note that *quam,* which is sometimes separated from *praeter* by tmesis, merely adds intensiveness to the *beyond-*notion involved in *praeter* (prae + ter) = motion beyond somewhat.

LINE 9. **quod,** acc. sing. n. of the rel. pron. *quī, quae, quod;* it refers to *frūmentum,* as its antecedent, and is the direct obj. of *portātūrī erant.* —— **sēcum** (sē + cum). *sē,* abl. plur. of the reflexive pron. *suī, sibi, sē, sē;* it is in the abl. after the prep. *cum,* which is here enclitic. Consult A. & G. 99, *e;* B. 79. 2; G. 413, REM. 1; H. 184, 6. —— **portātūrī erant,** 3d pers. plur. imperf. ind. of the first periphrastic conjugation of *portō, -āre, -āvī, -ātum,* 1. Consult A. & G. 129; B. 106, II; G. 247; H. 233; and observe that verbs in the act. periphrastic conjugation denote purpose. —— **combūrunt,** 3d pers. plur. pres. ind. act. of *combūrō, -ere, -ūssī, -ūstum,* 3 (con + būrō). Observe that *b* is rejected in *-ūrō,* but retained in *combūrō; combūrunt* agrees with its subject-nom. *Helvētiī,* to be supplied.

LINE 10. **ut,** telic conj. —— **domum,** acc. of *domus, -ūs* or *-ī,* f.; end of motion after the verbal noun *reditiōnis,* as if the latter were a gerund — *redeundī.* Consult A. & G. 258, *b;* B. 174; G. 337; H. 380, II, 2, 1). —— **reditiōnis,** gen. sing. of the verbal noun *reditiō, -ōnis,* f. (red + īre) = lit. *to go back;* hence the noun = *return; reditiōnis* limits *spē.* —— **spē,** abl. of *spēs, eī,* f., absolute with *sublātā,* denoting cause. A. & G. 255. 2; B. 192; G. 409, 410; H. 431. —— **sublātā,** abl. f. perf. pass. participle of *tollō, -ere, sustulī, sublātum,* irr.; abl. absolute with *spē.*

LINE 11. **parātiōrēs,** nom. plur. m. of the participial adj., comparative degree, *parātior, -ius;* positive *parātus,* comparative *-ior,* superl. *-issimus; parātiōrēs* is predicate-adj. after *essent.* —— **ad,** prep. with the acc. —— **omnia,** acc. plur. n. of adj. *omnis, -e;* it is an attributive of *perīcula.* —— **perīcula,** acc. plur. of *perīculum, -ī,* n.; obj. of the prep. *ad.* —— **subeunda,** acc. plur. n. of the gerundive *subeundus, -a, -um,* of the verb *subeō, -īre, -īvī (-iī), -itum* (sub + īre). Observe that *perīcula* is the acc. after *ad,* and that the gerundive agrees with the noun. The literal translation of the complete gerundive phrase is: *with respect to all the perils to be undergone.* Observe again that in the third and fourth conjugations the gerund and the gerundive frequently end in *-undum* and *-undus,* instead of *-endum* and *-endus.*

34 CAESAR'S GALLIC WAR [CHAP. V.

ils; they ordered each one to carry for himself from home meal supplies for three months. They prevailed on the Raurici, the Tulingi and the Latovici their neighbors to adopt	essent; *they might be;*	trium *three*	mēnsum *months'*	molita *ground-meal*	cibāria *supply*	12
	sibi *for himself*	quemque *each*	domō *from home*	efferre *to carry*	iubent. *they order.*	13
	Persuādent *They persuade*		Rauricīs *the Raurici*	et *and*	Tulingīs *the Tulingi*	et 14 *and*
	Latovīcīs *the Latovici (their)*		finitimīs, *neighbors,*	utī *that*	eōdem *the same,*	ūsī 15 *using,*

LINE 12. **essent**, 3d pers. plur. imperf. subjunctive of *sum, esse, fuī, futūrus;* subjunctive of purpose after *ut*. Consult A. & G. 317, I; B. 200, (*b*); G. 544, I; H. 497, II. —— **trium**, gen. plur. m. of the num. adj. *trēs, trium;* it is an attributive of *mēnsum*. Of the cardinals up to *centum*, only *ūnus, duo* and *trēs* are declined; *trēs* is an *ī*-stem, and is declined like the plur. of *levis*. —— **mēnsum**, gen. plur. of *mēnsis, -is,* m.; gen. of measure. See A. & G. 215, *b*; B. 132; G. 365, 2; H. 396, V. Note that the regular gen. plur. of *mēnsis* is *mēnsium*, showing that this noun is properly an *ī*-stem; in fact, most editions read *mēnsium* in this text; *mēnsum*, however, occurs. But see A. & G. 59; B. 46, IV, gen. plur. class II, end; G. 57, 3, middle; H. 62, V, and especially foot-note 3. —— **molita**, acc. plur. n. of participial adj. *molitus, -a, -um;* in form a perf. pass. participle of *molō, -ere, -uī, -itum,* 3; it modifies *cibāria*. —— **cibāria**, acc. plur. n. of the adj. *cibārius, -a, -um,* used as a noun; it is the direct obj. of *efferre*.

LINE 13. **sibi**, dat. sing. of the reflexive pron. *suī, sibi, sē, sē;* dat. of reference or advantage. A. & G. 235; B. 145; G. 352; H. 384, II, 1, 2). —— **quemque**, acc. sing. of the indef. pron. *quisque, quaeque, quodque, quidque* or *quicque; quidque* and *quicque* are substantive forms; *quemque* is subject-acc. of *efferre*. —— **domō**, abl. of *domus, -ūs,* or loc. *-ī,* f.; abl. of *place from which*. A. & G. 258, *a*; B. 175; G. 390, 2; H. 412, II, 1. —— **efferre**, pres. inf. act. of *efferō, efferre, extulī, ēlātum*. —— **iubent**, 3d pers. plur. pres. ind. act. of *iubeō, -ēre, iūssī, iūssum,* 2. Note that the regular construction after this verb is the acc. with the inf. The subject-nom. of *iubent* is a pron. implied in the ending referring to *Helvētiī*.

LINE 14. **Persuādent**, 3d pers. plur. pres. ind. act. of *persuādeō -ēre, -suāsī, -suāsum,* 2 (per, intensive + suādēre, *to advise*); supply *eī,* as subject-nom. —— **Rauricīs**, dat. of the noun *Rauricī, -ōrum,* m.; dat. after *persuādent*. A. & G. 227; B. 142; G. 346, REM. 2; H. 385, II; sometimes spelled *Rauracī*. These people were a Celtic tribe on the upper Rhine. —— **Tulingīs**, dat. plur. of *Tulingī, -ōrum,* m., connected by *et* with *Rauricīs,* and in the same grammatical construction. The *Tulingī* were a German tribe east of the *Rauricī*.

LINE 15. **Latovīcīs**, dat. plur. of *Latovīcī, -ōrum,* m.; in the same grammatical construction as *Tulingīs*. The *Latovīcī* dwelt north of the *Tulingī;* they were a German clan. Some texts read *Latobrigīs,* instead of *Latovīcīs*. —— **finitimīs**, dat. plur. of the adj. *finitimus, -a, -um,* in the plur. used as a noun; it is in apposition with the three preceding nouns. —— **utī**, the original form of the more common conj. and adv. *ut*. —— **eōdem**, abl. n. of the dem. adj. pron. *idem, eadem, idem;* it modifies *cōnsiliō*. —— **ūsī**, nom. plur. of the participle *ūsus, -a, -um,* of the deponent verb *ūtor, -ī, ūsus,* 3; it agrees with *eī,* the omitted subj. of *proficīscantur,* l. 17, below. Note that, as a deponent participle, it is used in an act. sense.

						their plan — to
16 cōnsiliō	oppidīs	suīs	vīcīsque		exūstīs,	burn their towns
plan	*towns*	*their own,*	*villages and,*		*being burned,*	and villages, and
17 ūna	cum	eīs	proficīscantur;		Bōiōsque,	to emigrate along with them; and
together	*with*	*them*	*they may set out;*		*the Boii and,*	the Boii, who had
18 quī	trāns	Rhēnum	incoluerant	et	in	dwelt across the
who	*across*	*the Rhine*	*had dwelt*	*and*	*into*	Rhine and had crossed into the
19 agrum	Nōricum	trānsierant		Nōrēiamque		Norican country
the country	*Norican*	*had crossed*		*Noreia and,*		and had stormed

LINE 16. cōnsiliō, abl sing. of *cōnsilium*, *-ī*, n.; abl. after *ūsī* — participles are followed by the same cases as their verbs. A. & G. 289; B. 98, 1; G. 112. 5, I; H. 548. For *ūsī* as followed by the abl., see A. & G. 249; B. 167, 1; G. 407; H. 421. —— oppidīs, abl. plur. of *oppidum*, *-ī*, n.; abl. absolute with the perf. pass. participle *exūstīs*. See A. & G. 255; B. 192; G. 409, 410; H. 431. —— suīs, abl. plur. of the poss. pron. *suus*, *-a*, *-um;* it agrees with *oppidīs*. —— vīcīsque (vīcīs + que). *vīcīs*, abl. plur. of *vīcus*, *-ī*, m., connected by the enclitic *-que* with *oppidīs*, and it is in the same grammatical construction. —— exūstīs, perf. pass. participle, abl. plur. of *exūstus*, *-a*, *-um*, from *exūrō*, *-ere*, *-ūssī*, *ūstum*, 3; abl. absolute with *oppidīs* and *vīcīs*. Observe that this construction is made necessary, because there is no perf. act. participle of *ūrō*.

LINE 17. ūna, adv. modifying the prep. *cum*. Note that the adv. *ūna* is derived from the adj. *ūnus*, *-a*, *-um*, and hence with *cum* = *together with*, a prepositional phrase = *closely with*. —— cum, prep. with the abl. *eīs*. —— eīs, abl. plur. of the dem. pron. *is*, *ea*, *id*, used as a personal pron. of the 3d pers; it is the obj. of the prep. *cum*. Instead of the three words *ūna cum eīs*, Caesar might have used simply *sēcum*, an indirect reflexive. —— proficīscantur, 3d pers. plur. pres. subjunctive of *proficīscor*, *-ī*, *profectus*, 3; subjunctive of purpose after *utī*, l. 15, above. Consult A. & G. 331; B. 200, (*b*), and REM. 2; G. 546, 1, and NOTE 1; II. 498, I. Observe that *utī* ... *proficīscantur* as a noun-clause is the direct obj. of *persuādent*, l. 14, above. —— Bōiōsque (Bōiōs + enclitic que). *Bōiōs*, acc. plur. of *Bōii*, *-ōrum*, m., direct obj. of *adscīscunt*, l. 21, below. The Boii were a people of Celtic Gaul; a part of them migrated to Germany, a part settled in Pannonia, and a part federated in some sort with the Helvetii, and migrated with them.

LINE 18. quī, nom. plur. of rel. pron. *quī*, *quae*, *quod;* it refers to *Bōiōs* as its antecedent, and is subject-nom. of *incoluerant*. —— trāns, prep. with acc. *Rhēnum*. —— Rhēnum, acc. sing. of *Rhēnus*, *-ī*, m.; an appositive of *flūmen* understood, which latter is the obj. of the prep. *trāns*. —— incoluerant, 3d pers. plur. pluperf. ind. of *incolō*, *-ere*, *-uī*, *-cultum*, 3; it agrees with its subject-nom. *quī*. —— in, prep. with the acc. or abl.; here it takes the acc. For use, see note on *in*, l. 1, Chap. I, end.

LINE 19. agrum, acc. sing. of *ager*, *agrī*, m.; obj. of the prep. *in*. —— Nōricum, acc. m. of the adj. *Nōricus*, *-a* *-um;* it modifies *agrum*. The adj. = *of* or *belonging to Noricum*, a region of Germany, which had the Danube on the north, the Alps on the south, upper Romania on the east and Rhetia on the west. —— trānsierant, 3d pers. plur. pluperf. ind. act. of *trānseō*, *-īre*, *-īvī* (*-iī*), *-itum;* syncopated form for *trānssīverant*. See A. & G. 128. I, 2; B. 251; G. 131. 1; H. 235. *trānsierant* is connected by the conj. *et* with *incoluerant*, and agrees with the same subject-nom. *quī*. —— Nōrēiamque (Nōrēiam + que). *Nōrēiam* is acc. sing. of *Nōrēia*, *-ae*, f.; direct obj. of *oppūgnārant*. Noreia was a town of Noricum.

| Noreia, they received to their number and united to themselves as allies. | oppūgnārant, *had stormed,* | receptōs *having been received* | ad *to* | sē *themselves,* | sociōs *as allies* 20 |
| | sibi *to themselves* | adscīscunt. *they unite.* | | | 21 |

| VI. There were but two routes, by which the Helvetii could leave home. One route | VI. Erant *There were* | omnīnō *in all* | itinera *routes* | duo, *two,* | quibus *by which* 1 |
| | itineribus *routes* | domō *from home* | exīre *to go forth* | possent; *they were able;* | ūnum *one (route)* 2 |

LINE 20. **oppūgnārant**, 3d pers. plur. pluperf. ind. act. of *oppūgnō, -āre, -āvī, -ātum*, 1; connected by the conj. *que* with *trānsierant*, and in the same grammatical construction. —— **receptōs**, acc. plur. of perf. pass. participle *receptus, -a, -um* of the verb *recipiō, -ere, -cēpī, -ceptum*, 3; it agrees with the noun *Bōiōs*, l. 17; but is best translated by a coördinate clause. Consult A. & G. 292, and REM.; B. 191; G. 664, REM. 1; H. 549. 5. —— **ad**, prep. with the acc. —— **sē**, acc. plur. of the reflexive pron. *suī, sibi, sē, sē*; it is the obj. of the prep. *ad*. —— **sociōs**, predicate-acc. See A. & G. 239, 1, *a*; B. 151, (*b*); G. 340, (*b*); H. 373, 1.

LINE 21. **sibi**, dat. plur. of the indirect obj. —— **adscīscunt**, 3d pers. plur. pres. ind. act. of *adscīscō, -ere, -scīvī, -scītum*, 3; it agrees with its subject-nom. *Helvētiī*, to be supplied. Observe the strictly literal translation of the last line: *they admit as allies to themselves the Boii having been received to themselves.*

LINE 1. **Erant**, 3d pers. plur. imperf. indicative of *sum, esse, fuī, futūrus;* its subject-nom. is *itinera*. *erant* here makes a complete predicate in itself; and hence as thus used is called a substantive-verb, and as such usually stands first in the sentence. Consult A. & G. 172, NOTE, end, and 344, *c*. —— **omnīnō**, adv. (*omnis*) = *in all*, i.e. *alone, only*. —— **itinera**, nom. plur. of *iter, itineris*, n., subject-nom. of *erant*. Synonyms: *via* (digammated from *i* in *īre* thus: ϝi + a = *via* or *wia*) = the ordinary travelled way; whereas *iter*, in a concrete sense = the way direct to a particular point, whether travelled or not. But both *iter* and *via* are used in an abstract sense, and = *journey, march*, without any particular difference in meaning. —— **duo**, nom. plur. n. of the num. adj. *duo, duae, duo*. See note on *trēs*, l. 2, Chap. I. *duo* modifies *itinera*. —— **quibus**, abl. plur. n. of the rel. pron. *quī, quae, quod;* it refers to *itinera* as its antecedent, but is here used adjectively, and agrees with *itineribus*. Observe the repetition of the antecedent in the relative clause, and consult A. & G. 200, *a*; B. 129, REM. 1, (*b*); G. 615; H. 445. 8.

LINE 2. **itineribus**, abl. plur. of *iter, itineris*, n.; abl. of *the way by which*. See A. & G. 258, *g*; B. 170, REM. 4; G. 389; H. 425, II, 1). —— **domō**, abl. sing. of the noun *domus, -ūs*, or loc. *-ī*, f.; abl. of *the place from which*. A. & G. 258, *a*; B. 175; G. 390, 2; H. 412, II, 1. —— **exīre**, pres. inf. act. of *exeō, -īre, -īvī (-iī), -itum;* complementary inf., depends on *possent*. Consult A. & G. 271, and NOTE; B. 181; G. 423; H. 533, I, 2. —— **possent**, 3d pers. plur. imperf. subjunctive of *possum, posse, potuī* (potis + sum); subjunctive, because it is a *clause of characteristic*. See A. & G. 320; B. 234, 1; G. 631; H. 503, I. —— **ūnum**, nom. sing. n. of the adj. *ūnus, -a -um;* supply *iter;* the latter is an explanatory appositive of *itinera;* or *erat* may be supplied, of which *iter* would be subject-nom.

3 per Sēquanōs, angustum et difficile, inter *through the Sequani, narrow and difficult, between* 4 montem Iūram et flūmen Rhodanum, vix *Mount Jura and the river Rhone, scarcely* 5 quā singulī carrī dūcerentur; mōns *where one by one waggons could be dragged; a mountain* 6 autem altissimus impendēbat, ut facile *moreover very high was overhanging, so that easily* 7 perpaucī prohibēre possent; alterum *a very few to hold (the pass) were able; a second (way was)*	was through the Sequani, between Mount Jura and the river Rhone, narrow and difficult, along which in single file carts could with difficulty be drawn. Moreover, a high beetling mountain was near it, so that a very few men could easily impede the

LINE 3. **per**, prep. with the acc. —— **Sēquanōs**, acc. plur. of *Sēquanī, -ōrum*, m.; it follows the prep. *per*. As to this clan, see note on *Sēquanīs*, l. 25, Chap. I. —— **angustum**, nom. sing. n. of the adj. *angustus, -a, -um (angere*, to press together); *angustum* is an attributive of *iter* understood. —— **difficile**, nom. sing. n. of the adj. *difficilis, -e;* connected by the conj. *et* with *angustum*, and in the same grammatical construction (dis + facilis); the *s* is assimilated; *dis* denotes privation; and hence *difficilis = not easy, difficult.* —— **inter**, prep. with the acc.

LINE 4. **montem**, acc. sing. of *mōns, montis*, m.; acc. after the prep. *inter*. —— **Iūram**, acc. sing. *Iūra, -ae*, m.; it is in apposition with *montem*. For description, see note on *Iūrā*, l. 13, end, Chap. II. —— **flūmen**, acc. sing. n. of *flūmen, -inis*, n.; connected by the conj. *et* with *montem*, and in the same grammatical construction. —— **Rhodanum**, acc. sing. of *Rhodanus, -ī*, m.; an appositive. —— **vix**, adv.; it modifies *dūcerentur*. Observe how emphatic it becomes by being placed at the beginning of the clause.

LINE 5. **quā**, adv.; strictly, an abl. of the pron. *quī, quae, quod*, used adjectively, and agreeing with *parte* understood; and hence = *in which direction, where*. —— **singulī**, nom. plur. of the distributive num. adj. *-ī, -ae, -a;* declined like the plur. of *bonus*. See A. & G. 95, *a*; B. 63, *c*; G. 97; H. 174, 2; it agrees with *carrī*. —— **carrī**, nom. plur. of *carrus, -ī*, m.; it is the subject of *dūcerentur*. —— **dūcerentur**, 3d pers. plur. imperf. subjunctive pass. of *dūcō, -ere, dūxī, ductum*, 3; its subject is *carrī;* subjunctive, because a clause of characteristic. For grammatical references, see note on *possent*, l. 2, above. —— **mōns**, nom. sing., and subj. of *impendēbat*. Note that the vowel *o* is conceived to be *naturally* long only in the nom. and voc. sing.; in the other cases it is conceived to be short.

LINE 6. **autem**, conj., a weak adversative particle; here = *moreover*. —— **altissimus**, superl. degree of the adj. *altus*, comparative *altior;* it is an attributive of *mōns;* the superl. of *eminence*. A. & G. 93, *b*; B. 68, REM. 4; G. 302; H. 444, 1. —— **impendēbat**, 3d pers. sing. imperf. ind. act. of *impendeō, -ēre* (no perf. or supine); in + pendēre = *to hang on or over*. This verb is in use sometimes t.ans., and sometimes intrans.; it is here to be taken as intrans. = *was overhanging*. —— **ut**, ecbatic conj. = *so that*. —— **facile**, adv., modifying *prohibēre;* the neuter acc. of the adj. is often used as an adv. See A. & G. 148, *d*; B. 117, 6; G. 91, 1, (*c*); H. 304, 1, 3, 1).

LINE 7. **perpaucī**, nom. plur. of the adj. *perpaucus, -a, -um*, used substantively; it is subject-nom. of *possent*. —— **prohibēre**, pres. inf. act. of *prohibeō, -ēre, -uī, itum*, 2

passage. The other route was through our province; it was much easier and quicker, because the Rhone flows between the territories of the Helvetii and the Allobroges, who had lately been sub-	per *through* atque *and* fīnēs *the boundaries* nūper *lately*	prōvinciam *province* expedītius, *expeditious* Helvētiōrum *of the Helvetii* pācātī *pacified*	nostram, *our,* proptereā *on this account,* et *and* erant, *were,*	multō *much* quod *because* Allobrogum, *the Allobroges,* Rhodanus *the Rhone*	facilius *more easy* inter *between* quī *who* fluit, *flows,*	8 9 10 isque 11 this and,

---

(pro + habēre = lit. *to hold forth* or *from*); complementary inf. See note on *exīre*, l. 2, above. The pron. *id*, i.e. *iter*, may be here supplied as the direct obj. of *prohibēre*; or, if preferred, *eōs exīre* may be supplied, giving a little different turn to the meaning. —— **possent**, 3d pers. plur. imperf. subjunctive of *possum;* see *possent*, l. 2, above; here, however, *possent* is subjunctive of result. A. & G. 319, 1; B. 201; G. 552, 1; H. 500, II. —— **alterum**, nom. sing. n. of adj. *alter, -era, -erum* = *the one, the other of two;* as a numeral it = *secundus, -a, -um;* supply here *iter*, of which *alterum* is a modifier. *iter* thus supplied may be put in apposition with *itinera*, l. 1, above; or it may be taken as subject-nom. to *erat*, to be supplied. The route intended is the southern route.

LINE 8. **per**, prep. with the acc. —— **prōvinciam**, acc. sing. of *prōvincia, -ae*, f.; it is the obj. of the prep. *per*. —— **nostram**, acc. sing. f. of the poss. pron. *noster, -tra, -trum;* it modifies *prōvinciam;* it refers to the Roman province. See note on *prōvinciae*, l. 10, Chap. I. —— **multō**, abl. n. of the adj. *multus, -a, -um;* abl. of degree of difference after the comparative *facilius;* it may, however, be taken as an adv. But consult A. & G. 250; B. 164; G. 403; H. 423. —— **facilius**, nom. sing. n. of the comparative degree *facilior, -ius;* positive *facilis*, superl. *facillimus; facilius* modifies *iter*, already supplied, and with which *alterum*, in the preceding line, agrees.

LINE 9. **atque**, see note on this particle, l. 10, Chap. I. —— **expedītius**, nom. sing. n. of the participial adj. *expedītus*, comparative degree *expedītior*, superl. *expedītissimus; expedītius* is connected by the conj. *atque* with *facilius*, and is in the same grammatical construction. Observe (*a*) that the verb from which this participle comes is *expediō, -īre, -īvī (-iī), -ītum*, 4; and (*b*) that it is derived from ex + pēs = lit. *to get the foot out of the snare;* hence *expedīre* = *to extricate*. —— **propterea quod**, see notes on these particles, l. 9, Chap. I. —— **inter**, prep. with the acc.

LINE 10. **fīnēs**, acc. plur. of *fīnis, -is*, m.; it is the obj. of the prep. *inter*. For synonyms, see note on *agrum*, l. 12, Chap. II. —— **Helvētiōrum**, gen. plur. of *Helvētiī, -ōrum*, m.; it limits *fīnēs*. For description, see note on *Helvētiī*, l. 16, Chap. I. —— **Allobrogum**, gen. plur. of *Allobrogēs, -um*, m., connected by the conj. *et* with *Helvētiōrum*, and in the same grammatical construction. The Allobroges occupied the country near the junction of the Saône and the Rhone. —— **quī**, nom. plur. m. of the rel. pron. *quī, quae, quod;* it is the subject-nom. of *pācātī erant*.

LINE 11. **nūper**, adv. (for *noviper* from *novus*) = *newly;* it modifies *pācātī erant*. —— **pācātī erant**, 3d pers. plur. pluperf. ind. pass. of *pācō, -āre, -āvī, -ātum*, 1; the subject-nom. is the rel. pron. *quī*. The Allobroges were "pacified" by Caius Pomptinus 61 B.C., after a desperate struggle. —— **Rhodanus, -ī**, m.; subject-nom. of

BOOK I.

12 nōnnūllīs	locīs	vadō	trānsītur.	Extrēmum	dued; and this river can be forded in some places.
in some	*places*	*by a ford*	*is crossed.*	*The most distant*	
13 oppidum	Allobrogum	est		proximumque	Geneva was the furthermost town of the Allobroges,
town	*of the Allobroges*	*is,*		*nearest and,*	
14 Helvētiōrum	fīnibus	Genūva.	Ex	eō oppidō	and was very near to the territory
to the Helvetian	*boundaries,*	*Geneva.*	*From*	*this town*	of the Helvetii.
15 pōns	ad	Helvētiōs	pertinet.	Allobrogibus	From this town a bridge reached across to the Hel-
a bridge	*to*	*the Helvetii*	*extends.*	*The Allobroges,*	

fluit. —— **fluit,** 3d pers. sing. pres. ind. act. of *fluō, -ere, flūxī, fluctum,* 3; it agrees with its subj. *Rhodanus.* —— **īsque** (is + que). *is,* a dem. pron., *is, ea, id;* it points to *Rhodanus* as its antecedent; is expressed for emphasis, and is the subject-nom. of *trānsītur.* Observe that the enclitic *-que* connects the clauses very closely.

LINE 12. **nōnnūllīs,** abl. plur. of the adj. *nōnnūllus, -a, -um;* it is an attributive of *locīs.* Observe that the position of *nōn,* as either before or after *nūllus,* and some other words, changes the meaning: thus *nōnnūllī = some;* whereas *nūllus nōn = every.* Consult A. & G. 150, *a* and *b*; B. 117. 10; G. 449, 4; H. 553, I. —— **locīs,** locative abl. of *locus, -ī,* m., plur. *locī,* m., or *loca,* n., gen. *locōrum.* For definition of meaning, see note on *locī,* l. 10, Chap. II. *locīs* is locative abl. by A. & G. 258, *f;* B. 170, REM. 3; G. 385, NOTE 1; H. 425, II, 2. —— **vadō,** abl. sing. of *vadum, -ī,* n.; abl. of the *way by which,* i.e. *means.* —— **trānsītur,** 3d pers. sing. pres. ind. pass. of *trānseō, -īre, -īvī (-iī), -itum;* it agrees with its subject-nom. *is.* —— **Extrēmum,** nom. sing. n. of the superl. degree of the adj. *exterus, -rior, extrēmus* or *extimus; extrēmum* modifies *oppidum.*

LINE 13. **oppidum,** *-ī,* n.; predicate-nom. after *est.* —— **Allobrogum,** gen. plur. of *Allobrogēs, -um,* m.; it limits *oppidum.* —— **est,** 3d pers. sing. of the intrans. verb *sum, esse, fuī, futūrus;* it agrees with its subject-nom. *Genāva.* —— **proximumque** (proximum + que). *proximum,* nom. sing. n. of the superl. degree of the adj. *proximus, -a, -um,* comparative *propior;* the positive is wanting; closely connected by the enclitic *-que* with the adj. *extrēmum,* and in the same grammatical construction.

LINE 14. **Helvētiōrum,** gen. plur. of *Helvētiī, -ōrum,* m.; it limits *fīnibus.* —— **fīnibus,** dat. plur. of *fīnis, -is,* m.; it is dat. after the adj. *proximum.* See A. & G. 234, *a*; B. 144, REM. 4; G. 359; H. 391, I. —— **Genāva,** nom. sing. of *Genāva, -ae,* f.; subject-nom. of *est.* *Genāva* was a town of the Allobroges; it is sometimes written *Geneva,* and also *Genua;* compare the GER. *Genf,* and the GK. Γεvoύα, of the Greek paraphrase. The reader will note the emphasis indicated by the order of the words. The natural Latin order is: *Genāva est extrēmum Allobrogum oppidum proximumque Helvētiōrum fīnibus.* —— **Ex,** prep. with the abl. (*ē* before consonants only, *ex* before vowels or consonants). —— **eō,** abl. sing. n. of the dem. adj. pron. *is, ea, id;* it is an attributive of *oppidō.* —— **oppidō,** abl. sing. of the noun *oppidum, -ī,* n., after the prep. *ex.*

LINE 15. **pōns,** nom. sing. of *pōns, pontis,* m.; it is subject-nom. of *pertinet.* —— **ad,** prep. with the acc. —— **Helvētiōs,** acc. plur. of *Helvētiī, -ōrum,* m.; it is the obj. of the prep. *ad.* —— **pertinet,** 3d pers. sing. pres. ind. act. of *pertineō, -ēre, -uī, -tentum,* 3; it agrees with its subject-nom. *pōns.* —— **Allobrogibus,** dat. plur. of

40 CAESAR'S GALLIC WAR [CHAP. VI.

vetii. The latter thought that they could either persuade the Allobroges, inasmuch as they did not as yet seem to be well-disposed toward the Roman people, or they could force them, to allow them to go through their

sēsē vel persuāsūrōs, quod nōndum 16
themselves either to be about to persuade, because not yet
bonō animō in populum Rōmānum vidērentur, 17
of good mind to the people Roman they seemed,
exīstimābant, vel vī coāctūrōs 18
they thought, or by force to be about to compel (them)
ut per suōs fīnēs eōs īre paterentur. 19
that through their boundaries them to go they might permit.

Allobrogĕs, -um, m.; dat. after *persuāsūrōs (esse)*. Consult A. & G. 227, and NOTE 1; B. 142; G. 346, and REM. 2; H. 385, II.

LINE 16. **sēsē**, acc. plur. of *suī, sibi, sē, sē;* reduplicated reflexive pron. for the simple *sē*, but more emphatic; subject-acc. of *persuāsūrōs (esse)*. —— **vel . . . vel** = *either . . . or.* Synonyms: *vel*, imperative of *volō*, gives a choice between the alternatives; whereas *aut* excludes the alternative. This distinction is not always observed. —— **persuāsūrōs (esse)**, fut. inf. act. of *persuādeō, -dĕre, -suāsī, -suāsum*, 2 (per, intensive + *suādēre* = *to advise thoroughly*); its subject-acc. is the pron. *sēsē*. —— **quod**, conj. = *because*. —— **nōndum**, adv. (nōn + dum); it modifies *vidērentur*.

LINE 17. **bonō**, abl. sing. m. of the adj. *bonus, -a, -um;* comparative *melior*, superl. *optimus; bonō* is the attributive of *animō*. —— **animō**, abl. of quality with the adj. *bonō*. See A. & G. 251; B. 169; G. 400; H. 419, II. Observe that the abl. of quality is essentially a predicative construction. —— **in**, prep. with the acc. and abl.; here it takes the acc. and = *to* or *toward*. —— **populum**, acc. sing. of *populus, -ī*, m.; it is the obj. of the prep. *in*. —— **Rōmānum**, acc. sing. m. of the adj. *Rōmānus, -a, -um;* it is an attributive of *populum*. Synonyms: *populus* = *the people* in their civil capacity; *plēbs* = *the common people* in distinction from the patricians; and *vulgus* = *the crowd, the rabble*. —— **vidērentur**, 3d pers. plur. imperf. subjunctive of *videō, -ēre, vīdī, vīsum*, 2; in the pass., *vidērī* = lit. *to be looked up to* or *regarded*; hence = *to seem, to appear*. *vidērentur* is in the subjunctive, because the statement is made on the authority of the Helvetii, not on that of Caesar. Consult A. & G. 341; B. 245, 1, (*b*); G. 663, I; H. 516, II, and 528, 3.

LINE 18. **exīstimābant**, 3d pers. plur. imperf. ind. act. of *exīstimō, -āre, -āvī, -ātum*, 1; its subject-nom. is *Helvētiī* understood. Note (1) that the construction here is that of informal indirect discourse. What the Helvetii thought in direct form is: *Allobrogibus persuādēbimus, quod nōndum bonō animō in populum Rōmānum videntur*. Note (2) that a few years before the time of this narrative, the ambassadors of the Allobroges had been tampered with by Catiline's agents. Compare Cic., *ōrātiō III in Cat.*, Sec. II. —— **vel**, see *vel*, l. 16, above. —— **vī**, abl. of *vīs, vīs*, f.; nom. plur. *virēs; vī* is an abl. of means. —— **coāctūrōs (esse)**, fut. inf. act. of *cōgō, -ĕre, coēgī, coāctum;* its subject-acc. is *sēsē*, to be supplied; supply also *eōs*, as direct obj. What the Helvetii said in direct form is: *vī (eōs) cōgēmus, ut per suōs fīnēs nōs īre patiantur.*

LINE 19. **ut**, telic conj. = lit. *that*, but often best rendered in connection with its verb in the subjunctive by the English *to*, with the verb-stem. —— **per**, prep. with

20 Omnibus rēbus ad profectiōnem comparātīs, country. Now when all things
   All   things for the expedition having been prepared, were ready for the migration,
21 diem dīcunt, quā diē ad rīpam Rhodanī they appointed a day on which all
   a day they name, on which day near the bank of the Rhone were to assemble at the margin of
22 omnēs conveniant; is diēs erat ante diem the river Rhone;
   all   should assemble; this day was before, day, and this day was

the acc. —— suōs, acc. plur. m. of the poss. pron. *suus, -a, -um;* it agrees with *fīnēs*, but refers to the Allobroges. —— fīnēs, acc. plur. of *fīnis, -is,* m.; obj. of the prep. *per.* —— eōs, acc. plur. m. of the dem. pron. *is, ea, id,* used as a personal pron. of the 3d pers.; it is subject-acc. of *īre;* it refers to the Helvetii. Observe that the pronouns are not used according to the rules. If Caesar had written leisurely he would probably have written here: *per eōrum fīnēs sē īre.* —— īre, pres. inf. act. of *eō, īre, īvī (iī), itum;* its subject-acc. is *eōs.* —— paterentur, 3d pers. plur. imperf. subjunctive of *patior, patī, passus,* 3, deponent; subjunctive of purpose after *ut.* A. & G. 331, and foot-note 2; B. 200, REM. 2; G. 546, I; H. 498, II.

LINE 20. **Omnibus**, abl. plur. f. of adj. *omnis, -e;* see note on *omnis,* l. 1, Chap. I; *omnibus* is an attributive of *rēbus.* —— rēbus, abl. plur. of *rēs, reī,* f.; abl. absolute with the participle *comparātīs,* denoting *time when.* See A. & G. 255, *d*, 1; B. 172, 192; G. 409, 410; H. 431, and 2. (3). —— ad, prep. with the acc.; it is here used with the acc. to denote purpose, and may be rendered *for.* —— profectiōnem, acc. sing. of *profectiō, -ōnis,* f.; it is in the acc. after the prep. *ad.* —— comparātīs, abl. plur. f. of *comparātus, -a, -um,* perf. pass. participle of the verb *comparō, -āre, -āvī, -ātum,* 1; abl. absolute with the noun *rēbus.*

LINE 21. **diem**, acc. sing. of *diēs, -ēī,* f. here, denoting *fixed time,* as indicated by the following *quā diē;* but m. next line, as describing the time. Consult A. & G. 73; B. 49, REM. 2; G. 64; H. 123. *diem* is the direct obj. of *dīcunt.* —— dīcunt, 3d pers. plur. pres. ind. act. of *dīcō, -ere, dīxī, dictum,* 3; its subject-nom. is *Helvetiī,* to be supplied. —— quā, abl. sing. f. of the rel. pron. *quī, quae, quod;* it is used here both relatively and adjectively; as a rel. it refers to *diem;* as an adj. it agrees with *diē.* See note on *itineribus,* l. 2, above. —— diē, abl. sing. f., denoting *time when.* See A. & G. 256, 1; B. 171; G. 393; H. 429. —— ad, prep. with the acc.; here it = *near;* not *on;* the latter notion would be indicated by *in rīpā.* —— rīpam, acc. sing. of *rīpa, -ae,* f.; it is the obj. of the prep. *ad.* —— Rhodanī, gen. sing. of *Rhodanus, ī,* m.; it limits the noun *rīpam.*

LINE 22. **omnēs**, nom. plur. m. and f. of *omnis, -e;* used here substantively as the subject-nom. of *conveniant,* or may be taken as an adj. modifying *Helvētiī* understood. —— conveniant, 3d pers. plur. pres. subjunctive act. of *conveniō, -īre, -vēnī, -ventum,* 4; subjunctive denoting *purpose.* Observe that the phrase *quā diē = ut eā diē,* and consult A. & G. 317, 2, and NOTE; B. 200, (*b*), 233, 1; G. 630; H. 497, I. —— **is**, dem. pron.; it is an attributive of *diēs,* and is here a pure demonstrative. —— diēs, subject-nom. of *erat.* —— erat, 3d pers. sing. imperf. ind. of the intrans. verb *sum, esse, fuī, futūrus;* it agrees with its subject-nom. *diēs.* —— ante, prep. with the acc. —— diem, acc. sing. of *diēs, -ēī,* m.; acc. after prep. *ante.* Observe that *ante* is both a prep. and an adv., like its opposite *post.* The archaic form of this particle is *anti,* whence *antideā* and *antihāc;* kindred with the GK. ἀντί.

the fifth before the April Kalends (March 28th), in the consulship of Lucius Piso and Aulus Gabinius.	quīntum *the fifth,*	Kalendās *Kalends*	Aprīlēs, *April,*	Lūciō *Lucius*	Pīsōne, 23 *Piso, (and)*
	Aulō *Aulus*	Gabīniō *Gabinius*	cōnsulibus. *being the consuls.*		24

VII. When the report was made to Caesar that the Helvetii were attempting to	VII.	Caesarī *To Caesar*	cum *when*	id *this*	nūntiātum esset, 1 *had been announced,*
	eōs *them*	(that they)	per *through*	prōvinciam *province*	nostram iter 2 *our a journey*

LINE 23. **quīntum**, acc. sing. m. of the ordinal adj. *quīntus, -a, -um;* it agrees with *diem.* But observe carefully (1) that the complex phrase *ante diem quīntum Kalendās Aprīlēs* is the predicate-nom. after *erat.* Observe (2) that the phrase *ante diem* by itself is used as an indecl. noun, and may take an acc. after it; that the grammatical form would be strictly: *diē quīntō ante Kalendās Aprīlēs;* or (3) that the phrase takes, sometimes, the prep. *in* or *ex* before it. On the Roman method of designating dates, the reader may consult A. & G. 259, *e,* and 376; B. 261. 5; G. pp. 491, 492; H. 642, 3. —— **Kalendās,** acc. plur. of *Kalendae, -ārum,* f.; anomalous acc. after the phrase *ante diem quīntum;* see specifications (1) and (2), immediately preceding. —— **Aprīlēs,** acc. plur. f. of the adj. *Aprīlis, -e;* it agrees with *Kalendās.* Observe that the Latin names of months are adjectives. —— **Lūciō,** abl. sing. of the praenōmen *Lūcius, -ī,* m., praenōmen of Pīsō. —— **Pīsōne,** abl. sing. of *Pīsō, -ōnis,* m.; abl. absolute with *cōnsulibus.*

LINE 24. **Aulō,** abl. sing. of the praenōmen *Aulus, -ī,* m., praenōmen of Gabīnius. —— **Gabīniō,** abl. of *Gabīnius, -ī,* m.; abl. absolute with *cōnsulibus.* Gabīnius was consul with Pīsō, 58 B.C. For the construction here, see note on *M. Messāla et M. Pīsōne,* l. 3, Chap. II. Observe (1) that the names of the consuls put in the abl. absolute with *cōnsulibus* — often without a conj. — denote the year in the narrative of Roman historic events. Observe (2) that the complex phrase *ante diem quīntum Kalendās Aprīlēs* is sometimes abbreviated thus: *a. d. V. Kal. Apr.* Observe (3) that this phrase = in our method of designating the time of the month, the 28th of March. The process of transmutation is thus represented: *V. Kal. Apr.* (33 — 5) = *March 28th.* See A. & G. 376, *a, b, c, d;* B. 261, 7, (*b*); G. p. 492; H. 644, II. —— **cōnsulibus,** see l. 3, Chap. II.

LINE 1. **Caesarī,** dat. of *Caesar, -aris,* m.; indirect obj. of *nūntiātum esset.* A. & G. 224; B. 140; G. 344; H. 384, I. —— **cum,** conj., temporal. —— **id,** nom. sing. n. of the dem. pron. *is, ea, id;* used here as a n. personal pron. of the 3d pers., and = *it;* it is subject-nom. of *nūntiātum esset.* Note that *id* — i.e. the following statement — is the herald of the following infinitive-clause *eōs . . . cōnārī,* and is in apposition with it. That is to say, the infinitive-clause is the real subj. of *nūntiātum esset.* —— **nūntiātum esset,** 3d pers. sing. pluperf. subjunctive of *nūntiō* (sometimes written *nūnciō*), *-āre, -āvī, -ātum,* 1; subjunctive after *cum,* temporal. Consult A. & G. 325; B. 220; G. 585; H. 521, and II, 2. Observe that the participle-part of this tense is neuter, because the subject-nom. is neuter.

LINE 2. **eōs,** acc. plur. m. of the dem. pron. *is, ea, id,* used as a personal pron. of the 3d pers.; it refers to the Helvetii, and is subject-acc. of *cōnārī.* —— **per,** prep. with the acc. —— **prōvinciam,** acc. sing. of *prōvincia, -ae,* f.; it is the obj. of the

BOOK I.

3 facere	cōnārī,	mātūrat	ab	urbe	march through our province, he made haste to leave the city, — Rome, — and with all possible speed he pressed on into ulterior Gaul, and arrived at Geneva. He
to make	*to attempt* (attempt),	*he hastens*	*from*	*the city*	
4 proficīscī	et,	quam	māximīs	potest	
to set out	*and*	*by as much as*	*the greatest,*	*he is able,*	
5 itineribus,	in	Galliam	ūlteriōrem	contendit	
marches,	*into*	*Gaul*	*farther*	*he presses on*	
6 et	ad	Genāvam	pervenit.	Prōvinciae	
and	*at*	*Geneva*	*he arrives.*	*To the province*	

---

prep. *per.* —— **nostram**, acc. sing. f. of the poss. pron. *noster*, *-tra*, *-trum*; it is an attributive of *prŏvinciam*. The allusion is to the Roman province, south of *Celtica* and east of *Aquitania*. —— **iter**, acc. sing. of *iter, itineris*, n.; direct obj. of *facere*.

LINE 3. **facere**, pres. inf. act. of *faciō, -ere, fēci, factum*, 3; complementary inf., and depends on *cōnārī*. Consult A. & G. 271, and NOTE; B. 181; G. 423; H. 533, 2. —— **cōnārī**, pres. inf. of deponent verb *cōnor, -ārī, -ātus*, 1; its subject-acc. is the pron. *eōs*. —— **mātūrat**, 3d pers. sing. pres. ind. act. of *mātūrō, -āre, -āvī, -ātum*, 1; its subject-nom. is Caesar understood. *mātūrāre* is derived from the adj. *mātūrus* = *ripe*; hence lit. the verb = *to ripen*; then of events *mātūrāre* = those that ripen or come to pass speedily; hence tropically the verb = *hasten*. Observe that *mātūrat* is the historical pres. which admits of the primary or secondary sequence. Consult A. & G. 276, *d*, 287, *e*, NOTE; B. 190, REM. 1; G. 511, REM. 1; H. 495, II. —— **ab**, prep. with the abl. —— **urbe**, abl. sing. of *urbs, urbis*, f.; abl. after the prep. *ab*. Note that *ab*, not *ex*, is used, because Caesar was *near*, not *in* the city. Caesar was consul 59 B.C. He became pro-consul in 58, and the provinces of Cis- and Trans-Alpine Gaul and Illyricum were assigned him for five years. As pro-consul he held the military power — *imperium* — and was not permitted to enter the city.

LINE 4. **proficīscī**, pres. inf. of the deponent verb *proficīscor, -ī, profectus*, 3; complementary infinitive, depending on *mātūrat*. Consult A. & G. 271, and NOTE; B. 181; G. 423; H. 533, I. 1. —— **quam**, adv., modifies *māximīs*. —— **māximīs**, abl. plur. n. of *māximus, -a, -um*; superl. of *magnus*, comparative *māior*; it modifies *itineribus*. —— **potest**, 3d pers. sing. pres. ind. of *possum, posse, potuī*; it agrees with its subject-nom. *is*, referring to Caesar understood.

LINE 5. **itineribus**, abl. plur. of *iter, itineris*, n.; abl. of means. Note the ellipses, and supply as follows: *tam māgnīs quam māximīs mātūrāre potest itineribus*; i.e. *by so great as the greatest marches he can hasten*. Caesar is said to have travelled 100 miles a day, and to have reached the Rhone in a week, after leaving Rome. —— **in**, prep. with the acc. or abl.; here it takes the acc. after a verb of motion. —— **Galliam**, acc. sing. of *Gallia, -ae*, f.; acc. after the prep. *in*. See note on *Gallia*, l. 1, Chap. I. —— **ūlteriōrem**, acc. sing. f. of the adj. *ūlterior, -ius*, comparative degree, no positive; it modifies *Galliam*. The reference is to Gaul beyond the Alps; i.e. from Rome it was *trāns*-Alpine in distinction from *cis*-Alpine Gaul. —— **contendit**, 3d pers. sing. pres. ind. act. of *contendō, -ere, -tendī, -tentum*, 3; its subject-nom. is Caesar understood; *con* + *tendere* = *to stretch out*; hence, to hasten one's course eagerly in a certain direction — *to press on*. See note on *contendunt*, l. 18, Chap. I.

LINE 6. **ad**, prep. with the acc.; after verb of motion = *toward*. —— **Genāvam**, acc. sing. of *Genāva, -ae*, f.; acc. after the prep. *ad*. —— **pervenit**, 3d pers. sing.

made requisition upon the entire province for as large a number of soldiers as possible — there was but one legion in ulterior Gaul — and he ordered the bridge which was near Geneva	tōtī *entire* in *in* quī *which*	quam *as much as* Galliā *Gaul* erat *was*	māximum *the greatest* ulteriōre *farther* ad *near*	potest *he is able,* legiō *legion* Genāvam *Geneva*	mīlitum *of soldiers* ūna; *one;* iubet *he orders*	7
	numerum *the number (to be levied)*		imperat *he gives orders*	— *—*	erat *there was*	8
					omnīnō *in all*	
					pontem *— the bridge*	9
					rescindī. *to be broken down.*	10

pres. ind. act. of *perveniō, -īre, -vēnī, -ventum*, 4; connected by the conj. *et* with *contendit*, and in the same grammatical construction. Observe that the finite verbs in this sentence, with the exception of *nūntiātum esset*, are historical presents. —— **Prōvinciae**, dat. of the indirect obj. after *imperat*.

LINE 7. **tōtī**, dat. sing. f. of the adj. *tōtus, -a, -um*, gen. *tōtīus; tōtī* is the attributive of *prōvinciae*. The province referred to here is transalpine Gaul. —— **quam māximum potest**, see notes on these words, l. 4, above, and note on the entire phrase, l. 4, Chap. III. *potest*, 3d pers. sing. pres. ind. of *possum, posse, potuī* (potis + sum); its subject-nom. is *ea*, i.e. *provincia* understood. —— **mīlitum**, gen. plur. of *mīles, -itis*, m.; it limits *numerum*.

LINE 8. **numerum**, acc. sing. of *numerus, -ī*, m.; direct obj. of *imperat*. Observe that some verbs have both the direct and indirect obj. Consult A. & G. 227, *f*; B. 141; G. 345; H. 384, II. Observe that this construction may be fully analyzed by supplying *cōgendum*, the gerundive agreeing with *numerum*. —— **imperat**, 3d pers. sing. pres. ind. act. of *imperō*, 1; it agrees with a pron. as subject-nom. implied in the ending, referring to Caesar. —— **erat**, 3d pers. sing. imperf. ind. of *sum, esse, fuī*, fut. participle *futūrus*; it is here a verb of complete predication, and agrees with its subject-nom. *legiō*. —— **omnīnō**, adv. (*omnis*) = lit. *in all*; it modifies *erat*.

LINE 9. **in**, prep. with the acc. or abl.; here it takes the abl. —— **Galliā**, abl. of *Gallia, -ae*, f.; abl. after prep. *in*. —— **ulteriōre**, abl. sing. f. of the adj. *ulterior, -ius*. See note on *ulteriōrem*, l. 5, above. —— **legiō**, nom. sing. of *legiō, -ōnis*, f.; subject-nom. of *erat*. This was the tenth legion — Caesar's favorite. —— **ūna**, nom. sing. f. of the num. adj. *ūnus, -a, -um*, gen. *ūnīus*, dat. *ūnī; ūna* is an attributive of *legiō*. For a description of the Roman legion, see the article *Legion* in any of the Encyclopedias. —— **pontem**, acc. sing. of *pōns, pontis*, m.; subject-acc. of *rescindī*.

LINE 10. **quī**, nom. sing. of the rel. pron. *quī, quae, quod*; it refers to *pontem* as its antecedent; and is the subject-nom. of *erat*. —— **erat**, see *erat*, l. 7, above. —— **ad**, prep. with the acc.; here = *near* or *at*. —— **Genāvam**, acc. sing. of *Genāva, -ae*, f.; obj. of the prep. *ad*. Some copies here read *Genuam*, and others read *Genēvam*. —— **iubet**, 3d pers. sing. pres. ind. act. of *iubeō, -ēre, -iūssī, -iūssum*, 2; it agrees with a pron., referring to Caesar, implied in the ending. —— **rescindī**, pres. inf. pass. of *rescindō, -ere, -scidī, -scissum*, 3; its subject-acc. is *pontem*. This construction follows *iubet*. Observe that *verba sentiendī et dēclārandī* have the acc. and inf. after them.

11 Ubi	dē	ēius	adventū	Helvētiī	certiōrēs	to be destroyed. When the Helvetii were informed of his arrival, they sent to him ambassadors of the highest rank in the state—and of this embassy Nammeius and Verudoctius were
When	*of*	*his*	*arrival*	*the Helvetii*	*more certain*	
12 factī sunt,		lēgātōs	ad	eum	mittunt	
were made,		*legates*	*to*	*him*	*they send,*	
13 nōbilissimōs		cīvitātis,		cūius	lēgātiōnis	
the noblest		*of the state,*		*of which*	*legation*	
14 Nammēius	et	Vĕrudoctius		prīncipem	locum	
Nammeius	*and*	*Verudoctius*		*the chief*	*place*	

LINE 11. **Ubi,** adv. (supposed to be from quō + bi, a locative form = *in what place*); transf., most frequently of time = *when*. Sometimes, colloquially, it is used as referring to things and persons, and = *with which, with whom*. —— **dē,** prep. with the abl. —— **ēius,** gen. sing. m. of the dem. pron. *is, ea, id,* used as a personal pron. of the 3d pers.; it limits *adventū;* it refers to Caesar. —— **adventū,** abl. sing. of *adventus, -ūs,* m. (ad + venīre); abl. after the prep. *dē.* —— **Helvētiī,** nom. plur. m. of *Helvētiī, -ōrum,* m.; subject-nom. of *factī sunt;* see note on *Helvētiī,* l. 16, Chap. I. —— **certiōrēs,** nom. plur. m. of the adj. comparative degree *certior, -ius;* positive *certus* (originally a participle of *.cernō,* 3); superl. *certissimus; certiōrēs* is predicate-adj. after *factī sunt.*

LINE 12. **factī sunt,** 3d pers. plur. perf. ind. of *fīō, fierī, factus,* 3; used as a pass. of *faciō, -ere, fēcī, factum,* 3; it agrees with its subject-nom. *Helvētiī.* —— **lēgātōs,** acc. plur. of *lēgātus, -ī,* m.; an appositive of *virōs* understood, which is the direct obj. of *mittunt.* —— **ad,** prep. with the acc. after verb of motion. —— **eum,** acc. sing. m. of the dem. pron. *is, ea, id,* used as a personal pron. of the 3d pers.; it is the object of the prep. *ad.* —— **mittunt,** 3d pers. plur. pres. ind. act. of *mittō, -ere, mīsī, missum,* 3; it agrees with the pron. *eī,* i.e. *Helvētiī* understood, as its subject-nom.

LINE 13. **nōbilissimōs,** acc. plur. m. of the adj. *nōbilissimus, -a -um;* superl. degree; positive *nōbilis,* comparative *nōbilior. nōbilissimōs* modifies *verōs* understood, which is the direct obj. of *mittunt.* For derivation, see note on *nōbilissimōs,* l. 2, Chap. II. —— **cīvitātis,** gen. sing. of *cīvitās, -ātis,* f. *(cīvēs);* it limits *virōs* understood; *cīvitātis* might be taken as a partitive gen. after *nōbilissimōs.* See note on *hōrum,* l. 8, Chap. I. —— **cūius,** gen. sing. of the rel. pron. *quī, quae, quod,* used adjectively; it limits *lēgātiōnis.* —— **lēgātiōnis,** gen. sing. of *lēgātiō, -ōnis,* f.; it limits *locum.*

LINE 14. **Nammēius, -ī,** m.; subject-nom. of *obtinēbant.* —— **Verudoctius, -ī,** m.; connected by the conj. *et* with *Nammēius,* and in the same grammatical construction. These men were Helvetian nobles. Some copies have *Verucloetius* instead of *Verudoctius.* We suggest that *Verucloetius* is an orthography based on worn Latin type used in the printing of some early copy of MS. text. The Greek paraphrast has Βεροδοξίον in the gen. absolute construction; the nom. is Βεροδόξιος. Worn type might make *doc* look like *cloe.* —— **prīncipem,** acc. sing. m. of the adj. *prīnceps, -ipis;* it is an attributive of the noun *locum. prīnceps* is often used as a subst. As such, it often denotes *the first, the chief, the most noble.* Compare Cic.: *Eudoxus in astrologiā facile prīnceps.* —— **locum,** acc. sing. of *locus, -ī,* m. in the sing., but m. or n. in the plur.; see note on *locī,* l. 10, Chap. II; *locum* is the direct obj. of *obtinēbant.*

holding the chief place — to say that they purposed without doing any damage to march through the province because they had no other route. They requested that it might be	obtinēbant, *were holding,* in animō *in mind* prōvinciam *the province* iter *route*	quī *who* sine *without* facere, *to make,* habērent *they had*	dīcerent, *should say* ūllō *any* propterea *for this reason* nūllum: *none:*	sibi *to themselves* maleficiō *harm* quod *because* rogāre, *to ask*	esse 15 *to be* (it is) iter per 16 *a journey through* aliud 17 *another* ut ēius 18 (they ask), *that with his*

LINE 15. **obtinēbant**, 3d pers. plur. imperf. ind. act. of *obtineō, -ēre, -uī, -tentum*, 2 (ob + tenēre) = lit. *to hold against;* hence = *to retain, to possess. obtinēbant* is plur., because it has two sing. subjects connected by *et.* Consult A. & G. 205; B. 126, REM. 1; G. 285; H. 463, II. —— **quī**, nom. plur. of the rel. pron. *quī, quae, quod;* it refers to *Nammēius et Verudoctius* as its antecedents, and is subject-nom. of *dīcerent; quī* here = *ut eī.* —— **dīcerent**, 3d pers. plur. imperf. subjunctive of *dīcō, -ere, dīxī, dictum*, 3; it agrees with its subj. *quī;* it is in the subjunctive mode, because it is a rel.-clause denoting *purpose.* See A. & G. 317, and NOTE 2; B. 233, and 1; G. 545, 1, and 630; H. 497, I; and note that *quī* in this construction = *ut eī.* —— **sibi**, dat. plur. of the reflexive pron. *suī, sibi, sē, sē;* dat. possessor after *esse.* Consult A. & G. 231; B. 146; G. 349; H. 387. —— **esse**, pres. inf. of *sum, esse, fuī, futūrus;* it is here used impersonally; strictly, however, *iter facere* is its subject.

LINE 16. **in**, prep. with the acc. or abl.; here it takes the abl. —— **animō**, abl. sing. of *animus, -ī*, m.; it is in the abl. after the prep. *in.* Synonyms: *anima* = *the soul*, the principle of animal life like the GK. ψυχή; *mēns* denotes the *intellectual* or *thinking faculty;* whereas *animus* = *the soul* including all its faculties. —— **sine**, prep. with the abl. —— **ūllō**, abl. sing. n. of the adj. *ūllus, -a, -um,* gen. *ūllīus,* dat. *ūllī* (contracted from *ūnulus,* diminutive adj. of *ūnus); ūllō* is an attributive of *maleficiō.* —— **maleficiō**, abl. sing. of *maleficium, -ī,* n. (malum + facere); it is in the abl. after the prep. *sine.* —— **iter**, acc. sing. of *iter, itineris,* n.; direct obj. of *facere.* —— **per**, prep. with the acc.

LINE 17. **prōvinciam**, acc. sing. of *prōvincia, -ae,* f.; it is the obj. of the prep. *per.* —— **facere**, pres. inf. of *faciō, -ere, fēcī, fāctum; facere* with its modifiers is subject-acc. of *esse.* —— **propterea quod**, see note on these words, l. 9, Chap. I. —— **aliud**, acc. sing. n. of the adj. *alius, -a, -ud,* gen. *alīus,* dat. *aliī; aliud* is an attributive of *iter.*

LINE 18. **iter**, acc. sing. of *iter, itineris,* n.; direct obj. of *habērent.* —— **habērent**, 3d pers. plur. imperf. subjunctive act. of *habeō, -ēre, -uī, -itum,* 2; it agrees with the pron. *eī,* i.e. *Helvētiī,* implied in its ending as subject-nom. It is in the subjunctive mode, because it is in a dependent clause in the *ōrātiō oblīqua.* Consult A. & G. 336, 2; B. 245, 1, (*b*); G. 650; H. 524. —— **nūllum**, acc. sing. n. of the adj. *nūllus, -a, -um* (nē + ūllus); it is an attributive of *iter.* Observe its very emphatic position. —— **rogāre**, pres. inf. act. of *rogō, -āre, -āvī, -ātum,* 1; supply *sē,* i.e. *Helvētiōs,* as subject-acc. For the inf. in indirect discourse, see A. & G. 336; B. 245, 1; G. 650; H. 523, I. —— **ut**, telic conj. —— **ēius**, gen. sing. of the dem. pron. *is, ea, id,* used as a personal pron. of the 3d pers.; it refers to Caesar; it limits *voluntāte.*

BOOK I.

19 voluntāte	id	sibi	facere		liceat.	allowed them to do so with his permission. Cae-
permission	this	for themselves	to do	it might be lawful.	
20 Caesar,	quod	memoriā	tenēbat,	L. Cassium	sar, as he remem- bered the fact that Lucius Cas-
Caesar,	because	in memory	he held,	Lucius Cassius	
21 cōnsulem	occīsum	exercitumque	ēius	ab	sius the consul had been slain and his army had
the consul	to have been slain,	army	and,	of him	by the
22 Helvētiīs	pulsum	et	sub	iugum	been sent under the yoke by the
Helvetii	to have been routed	and	under	the yoke	

LINE 19. **voluntāte**, abl. sing. of *voluntās, -tātis*, f.; abl. of *in accordance with*. A. & G. 253, NOTE; B. 162, and REM. 3; G. 397; H. 416. Synonyms: *voluntās* (*velle*, to wish) = an act of the will whose impulse is *good-will;* whereas *sponte* = an act of the will whose impulse is *freedom* in opposition to fate or chance. —— **id**, acc. sing. of the dem. pron. *is, ea, id*, used substantively; direct obj. of *facere;* it refers to the idea of making a march through the Roman province. —— **sibi**, dat. plur. of the reflexive pron. *suī, sibi, sē, sē;* it refers to the Helvetii; it is dat. after the impersonal verb *liceat.* Consult A. & G. 227, *e;* B. 142; G. 346; H. 384. Observe that strictly *id facere* is the subj. of *liceat.* —— **liceat**, 3d pers. sing. pres. subjunctive of *licet, -ēre, licuit* or *lictum est*, 2; an impersonal verb; it is in the subjunctive, because it expresses with *ut* the purpose of *rogāre.* Consult A. & G. 331; B. 200; G. 546; H. 498. Note particularly that the entire clause *ut . . . liceat*, as such, is the direct obj. of *rogāre.* What the Helvetians said in lines 15-19, in direct form, was: *nōbīs est in animō sine ūllō maleficiō iter per prōvinciam facere, proptereā quod aliud iter habēmus* nūllum: *rogāmus*, ut *tuā* voluntāte *hōc nōbīs* facere liceat.

LINE 20. **Caesar**, -aris, m.; subject-nom. of *putābat*, l. 23, below. —— **quod**, conj. = *because.* —— **memoriā**, abl. sing. of *memoria, -ae*, f. (*memor*); abl. of means. —— **tenēbat**, 3d pers. sing. imperf. ind. act. of *teneō, -ēre, -uī, tentum*, 2; it agrees with a pron. implied in the ending as its subject-nom., referring to Caesar. Observe that *memoriā tenēbat* = *he remembered*, and hence is followed by the inf. with the acc. —— **L.**, an abbreviation for *Lūcium* here; acc. sing. of *Lūcius, -ī*, m., the prae- nōmen. —— **Cassium**, acc. sing. of *Cassius, -ī*, m., the nōmen; subject-acc. of *occīsum* (*esse*). This was that Lucius Cassius whose cōgnōmen was *Longīnus;* he was consul 107 B.C.; was slain in battle by the Tigurini, in his province Gallia Narbonensis.

LINE 21. **cōnsulem**, acc. sing. of *cōnsul, -ulis*, m.; an appositive of *Cassium*, and in the same grammatical construction. —— **occīsum** (*esse*), perf. inf. pass. of *occīdō, -ere, -cīdī, -cīsum*, 3 (ob + *caedere*) = lit. *to strike down.* Not to be confounded with *occīdō* (ob + *cadere*) = lit. *to fall down.* Note the difference in the quantity of the penults. —— **exercitumque** (exercitum + que). *exercitum*, acc. sing. of *exercitus, -ūs*, m.; subject-acc. of *pulsum* (*esse*) and *missum* (*esse*). For synonyms, see note on *exercitū*, l. 31, Chap. III. —— **ēius**, gen. sing. of the dem. pron. *is, ea, id*, used sub- stantively; it is an attributive of *exercitum;* it refers to Cassius. —— **ab**, prep. with the abl.

LINE 22. **Helvētiīs**, abl. plur. of *Helvētiī, -ōrum*, m.; abl. of the agent with *ab*. A. & G. 246; B. 166; G. 401; H. 415, I. —— **pulsum** (**esse**), perf. inf. pass. of *pellō, -ere, pepulī, pulsum*, 3; it agrees with its subject-acc. *exercitum.* —— **et**, conj., con- nects *pulsum* (*esse*) with *missum* (*esse*). —— **sub**, prep. with the acc. and abl.; here

48   CAESAR'S GALLIC WAR   [CHAP. VII.

| Helvetii, did not think that the request ought to be granted; nor did he think that men of hostile disposition, if the privilege of marching through the province were granted, would refrain from outrage and wrong-doing. And | missum, *to have been sent,* neque homines *not and,   men* facultāte *the opportunity* faciundī, *to be made,* et maleficiō *and   outrage,* | concēdendum *it to be conceded* inimīcō animō, *of hostile   mind* per prōvinciam *through   the province* temperātūrōs *to be about* (themselves) *to restrain* exīstimābat. *he thought.* | nōn *did not* having *of a journey* ab *from* Tamen, *Yet* | putābat; 23 *think;* datā 24 *been given* itineris 25 iniūriā 26 *wrong* ut 27 *that* |

it takes the acc. after a verb of motion. —— **iugum**, acc. sing. of *iugum, -ī*, n. (compare *iungere*, to join); acc. after the prep. *sub*.

LINE 23. **missum (esse)**, perf. inf. pass. of *mittō, -ere, mīsī, missum*, 3; connected by *et* with *pulsum*, and in the same grammatical construction. With the phrase *sub iugum* compare the English word *subjugate*. Observe, as explaining the language of the text, that a species of arch was formed by sticking two spears into the ground, and by placing another horizontally across them. Under this arch, in token of their defeat, conquered armies were compelled to go. —— **concēdendum** **(esse)**, pres. inf. pass. of *concēdō, -ere, -cessī, -cessum*, 3; used impersonally; second periphrastic conjugation. See A. & G. 113, *d*; B. 106, II, middle; G. 251; H. 234. —— **nōn**, negative adv.; observe that it has here its normal place in a Latin sentence. —— **putābat**, 3d pers. sing. imperf. ind. act. of *putō, -are, -āvī, -ātum*, 1; it agrees with a subject-nom. implied in the ending, i.e. *Caesar*.

LINE 24. **neque** (nē + que = lit. *and not*), a conjunctive adv. here; as a conj., it connects the sentences; as an adv., it modifies *exīstimābat*, l. 27, below. —— **hominēs**, acc. plur. of *homō, -inis*, m. and f.; subject-acc. of *temperātūrōs (esse)*. —— **inimīcō**, abl. of the adj. *inimīcus, -a, -um* (in, *not* + amīcus); it modifies *animō*. —— **animō**, abl. of *animus, -ī*, m.; abl. of quality with the adj. *inimīco*. Consult A. & G. 251; B. 169; G. 400; II. 419, II. —— **datā**, perf. pass. participle of *dō, dare, dedī, datum*, 1; abl. absolute with *facultāte*.

LINE 25. **facultāte**, abl. sing. of *facultās, -ātis*, f.; abl. absolute with *datā*, denoting condition. A. & G. 255, *d*, 4; B. 172; G. 409; H. 431, 2, (3). —— **per**, prep. with the acc. —— **prōvinciam**, acc. sing. of *prōvincia, -ae*, f.; acc. after the prep. *per*. —— **itineris**, gen. sing. of *iter, itineris*, n.; it limits *facultāte*.

LINE 26. **faciundī**, gen. of the gerundive *faciundus, -a, -um*, of the verb *faciō, -ere, fēcī, factum*, 3; the gerundive is an attributive of *itineris*. Observe that *-undī* for *-endī* is the usual orthography of the gerund and gerundive in verbs of the third and fourth conjugations, especially after *i*. —— **temperātūrōs (esse)**, fut. inf. act. of *temperō*, 1; it agrees with its subject-acc. *hominēs*. Note that the participial form of this compound is in the acc. plur., conforming thus in case with its subj. Note further that *esse* is oftener omitted than expressed in such compounds. —— **ab**, prep. with the abl. —— **iniūriā**, abl. of *iniūria, -ae*, f.; abl. after *ab*.

LINE 27. **maleficiō**, abl. of *maleficium, -ī*, n. (malum + facere = lit. *to do evil*); hence *maleficium = a deed of evil*. Observe that in general usage *maleficium* denotes

[LINES 28-31.] BOOK I. 49

28 spatium	intercēdere	posset,	dum	mīlitēs,	yet that length of time might intervene, until the
space of time	*to intervene*	*might be,*	*until*	*the soldiers*	
29 quōs	imperāverat,			convenīrent,	soldiers whom he had ordered to be levied might
whom	*he had ordered to be levied*			*might come together,*	
30 lēgātīs	respondit,		diem	sē	assemble, he replied to the ambassadors that
to the legates	*he replied :*		*a day*	*himself*	
31 ad	dēlīberandum	sūmptūrum ;			sī he would take
for	*deliberating*	*to be (ho is) about to take ;*			*if* time for deliber-

a deed of evil intent that deserves punishment; while *iniūria* (in + iūs) = any act or deed contrary to right. *maleficiō* is connected by *et* with *iniūriā*, and is in the same grammatical construction. —— **existimābat**, 3d pers. sing. imperf. ind. act. of *exīstimō*, 1; its subject-nom. is a pron. implied in the ending, referring to Caesar. Synonyms : *exīstimāre* (ex + aestimāre) = *to think* or *judge after examination; arbitrārī* = *to think as an arbiter*, i.e. *to consider; putāre* = *to think as a reckoning process;* and *cōgitāre* (con + agitāre) = *to pursue something in the mind.* —— **Tamen**, conjunctive adv., a particle that introduces a thought in contrast with some preceding concession expressed or implied. —— **ut**, telic conj.

LINE 28. **spatium**, nom. sing. of *spatium, -iī*, n.; subj. of *posset. spatium* here = *time.* —— **intercēdere**, pres. inf. act. of *intercēdō, -ere, -cessī, -cessum*, 3; complementary inf. A. & G. 271, and NOTE; B. 181; G. 423; H. 533, I, 2; it depends on *posset.* —— **posset**, 3d pers. sing. imperf. subjunctive of *possum, posse, potuī* (potis + sum); subjunctive of purpose after *ut. posset* agrees with its subject-nom. *spatium.* —— **dum**, conj., synonymous with *dōnec*, and = *as long as, until.* —— **mīlitēs**, nom. plur. of *mīles, -itis*, m.; subject-nom. of *convenīrent.*

LINE 29. **quōs**, acc. plur. m. of the rel. pron. *quī, quae, quod;* it refers to *mīlitēs;* it is the direct obj. of *imperāverat.* —— **imperāverat**, 3d pers. sing. pluperf. ind. act. of *imperō*, 1. Supply the *lacūna* in the construction thus: *quōs cōgendōs imperāverat;* if the ellipsis be thus filled, *quōs* is the obj. of *imperāverat,* with which the gerundive will agree. Consult A. & G. 294, *d*; B. 184, REM. 4, III, *a*; G. 430; H. 544. —— **convenīrent**, 3d pers. plur. imperf. subjunctive of *conveniō, -īre, -vēnī, -ventum*, 4 (con, *together* + venīre); imperf. subjunctive after *dum* signifying futurity. Consult A. & G. 328; B. 229, (2); G. 572; H. 519, II, 2.

LINE 30. **lēgātīs**, dat. plur. of *lēgātus, -ī*, m.; indirect obj. after *respondit.* —— **respondit**, 3d pers. sing. perf. ind. act. of *respondeō, -ēre, -spondī, -spōnsum*, 2; it agrees with a subject-nom. implied in the ending, referring to Caesar. —— **diem**, acc. sing. of *diēs, -ēī*, m. or f. in sing., always m. in the plur.; *diem* is the direct obj. of *sūmptūrum (esse).* Observe that *diem* here denotes time in general. —— **sē**, acc. sing. of the reflexive pron. *suī, sibi, sē, sē;* subject-acc. of *sūmptūrum (esse).*

LINE 31. **ad**, prep. with the acc. —— **dēlīberandum**, acc. of the gerund of *dēlīberō*, 1 (dē + lībra); hence *dēlīberāre* denotes that what is spoken is weighed; *dēlīberandum* is the acc. of the gerund after the prep. *ad,* denoting purpose. See A. & G. 300; B. 184, REM. 4, III; G. 432; H. 542, III. —— **sūmptūrum (esse)**, fut. act. inf. of *sūmō, -ere, sūmpsī, sūmptum*, 3; it agrees with its subject-acc. *sē.* —— **sī**, conditional conj.

ation; if they wished anything, let them return on the thirteenth of April.	quid *anything*	vellent, *they wanted,*	ad *at*	Īdūs *the Ides*	Aprīlēs *of April*	32
	reverterentur. *let them return.*					33

VIII. Meanwhile Caesar, with the aid of the legion that he had with him and the sol-	VIII.	Intereā *Meantime*	eā *with that*	legiōne *legion*	quam *which*	1
	sēcum *himself with,*	habēbat *he had*	mīlitibusque, *with the soldiers and,*		quī *who*	ex *from*	2

LINE 32. **quid**, acc. sing. n. of indef. adj.-pron. *quis, quae, quid;* direct obj. of *vellent.* Sometimes the conj. and pron. are combined, and written as one word: *sīquis*, etc. But note that after *sī, nisi* and *num* the f. sing. and the n. plur. have *quae* or *qua*. On the indef. pronouns, consult A. & G. 104, 105, *d*; B. 89, 1; G. 315; H. 190. —— **vellent**, 3d pers. plur. imperf. subjunctive of *volō, velle, voluī;* subjunctive, because in the condition after *sī;* it is in the imperf. tense, because the verb of saying —— *respondit* —— is an historic perf. —— **ad**, prep. with the acc.; it here = *at* or *on*. The common text reads here: *ante diem Īdūs*. —— **Īdūs**, acc. plur. of *Īdūs, -uum,* f., plur.; the obj. of the prep. *ad.* Observe that the Ides fell on the 15th of March, May, July and October, and on the 13th of the other months. According to the text, they were directed to return on the 13th of April. According to the common lection —— *ante diem Īdūs* —— they were directed to return on the 12th of April. —— **Aprīlēs**, acc. plur. of the adj. *Aprīlis, -le;* it agrees with the noun *Īdūs*. Note that the month-designations in Latin are adjectives, and also that *Īdūs Aprīlēs* are sometimes abbreviated *Id. Apr.*

LINE 33. **reverterentur**, 3d pers. plur. imperf. subjunctive of the deponent verb *revertor, -ī, -versus,* 3; subjunctive, because the discourse is indirect. *reverterentur* is for the 2d pers. plur. imperative in *ōrātiō rēcta.* See A. & G. 339; B. 45, 2; G. 652; H. 523, III. The *ōrātiō rēcta* of lines 30–33 is: *diem egō ad dēlīberandum sūmam; sī quid vultis, ad Īdūs Aprīlēs revertiminī.*

LINE 1. **Intereā**, adv. (inter + ea) = lit. *between these things,* i.e. *meanwhile*. The long ultima in this and some other words similarly compounded is anomalous. —— **eā**, abl. sing. f. of *is, ea, id,* dem. pron.; it is an attributive of *legiōne*. —— **legiōne**, abl. sing. of *legiō, -ōnis,* f.; abl. of *means;* not *agent*, because not voluntary. The legion referred to is the tenth, see note on *legiō*, l. 9, Chap. VII. —— **quam**, acc. sing. f. of the rel. pron. *quī, quae, quod;* it refers to *legiōne* as its antecedent; it is the direct obj. of *habēbat*.

LINE 2. **sēcum** (sē + cum); *sē* is the abl. sing. of the reflexive pron. *suī, sibi, sē, sē;* it is the obj. of the enclitic prep. *cum.* For the prep. *cum* as enclitic with pronouns, see A. & G. 99, *e*; B. 79, 2; G. 413, REM. 1; H. 184, 6. —— **habēbat**, 3d pers. sing. imperf. ind. act. of *habeō, -ēre, -uī, -itum,* 2; it agrees with a pron. as subject-nom. implied in the ending, referring to Caesar. —— **mīlitibusque** (mīlitibus + que). *mīlitibus*, abl. plur. of *mīles, -itis,* m.; connected by the enclitic conj. *-que* with *legiōne*, and in the same grammatical construction. —— **quī**, nom. plur. m. of the rel. pron *quī, quae, quod;* it refers to *mīlitibus*, as its antecedent, and is the subject-nom. of *convēnerant*. —— **ex**, prep. with the abl.

BOOK I.   51

3 prōvinciā	convēnerant,	ā	lacū	Lemannō,	diers that had been collected from the province, constructed a wall sixteen feet high, and a ditch nineteen miles in length, from Lake Geneva which flows into the river Rhone, to Mount Jura which separates the country of the Sequani from that	
the province	*had assembled,*	*from*	*Lake*	*Leman,*		
4 quī	in	flūmen	Rhodanum	īnfluit,	ad	
which	*into*	*the river*	*Rhone*	*flows,*	*to*	
5 montem	Iūram,	quī	fīnēs	Sēquanōrum		
Mount	*Jura,*	*which*	*the borders*	*of the Sequani*		
6 ab	Helvētiīs	dīvidit,	mīlia	passuum		
from	*the Helvetii*	*,divides,*	*thousands*	*of paces*		
7 decem	novem	mūrum	in	altitūdinem	pedum	
nineteen,		*a wall*	*to*	*the height*	*of feet*	

LINE 3. prōvinciā, abl. sing. of *prōvincia, -ae*, f.; it is the obj. of the prep. *ex*. —— convēnerant, 3d pers. plur. pluperf. ind. act. of *conveniō, -īre, -vēnī, -ventum*, 4 (con + venīre) = *to come together;* it agrees with its subject-nom. *quī*. —— ā, prep. with the abl. *ā* before consonants, *ab* before vowels or consonants. —— lacū, abl. sing. of *lacus, -ūs*, m.; it is in the abl. after the prep. *ā*. —— Lemannō, abl. of *Lemannus, -ī*, m.; in apposition with *lacū*. See note on *Lemannō*, l. 15, Chap. II.

LINE 4. quī, nom. sing. m. of the rel. pron.; it refers to *lacū*, as its antecedent, and is the subject-nom. of *īnfluit*. —— in, prep. with acc. or abl.; here it takes the acc. See note on *in*, l. 1, Chap. I. —— flūmen, acc. sing. of *flūmen, -inis*, n.; it is the obj. of the prep. *in*. —— Rhodanum, acc. sing. of *Rhodanus, -ī*, m.; it is in apposition with *flūmen*. —— īnfluit, 3d pers. sing. pres. ind. act. of *īnfluō, -ere, -flūxī, -fluxum*, 3 (in + fluere); it agrees with its subject-nom. *quī*. Observe that when the idea of motion is distinct, the noun with a prep. is used, instead of a dat. after verbs compounded with certain prepositions; in other words, the prep. which enters into the compound is repeated with its appropriate case, instead of the dat. construction. —— ad, prep. with the acc.

LINE 5. montem, acc. sing. of *mōns, montis*, m.; *montem* is the obj. of the prep. *ad*. —— Iūram, acc. sing. of *Jūra, -ae*, m.; an appositive. See note on *Jūrā*, l. 13, Chap. II. —— quī, nom. sing. m. of the rel. pron. *quī, quae, quod;* it refers to *montem*, as its antecedent, and is the subject-nom. of *dīvidit*. —— fīnēs, acc. plur. of *fīnis, -is*, m.; direct obj. of *dīvidit*. For synonyms, see *agrum*, l. 12, Chap. II. —— Sēquanōrum, gen. plur. of *Sēquanī, -ōrum*, m.; as a gen. it limits *fīnēs*. For description of this clan, see note on *Sēquanīs*, l. 25, Chap. I.

LINE 6. ab, prep. with the abl. —— Helvētiīs, abl. plur. of *Helvētiī, -ōrum*, m.; abl. after the prep. *ab*. See note on *Helvētiī*, l. 16, Chap. I. —— dīvidit, 3d pers. sing. of *dīvidō, -ere, -vīsī, -vīsum*, 3; it agrees with its subject-nom. *quī*. —— mīlia, acc. plur. of adj. *mille;* in the sing. indecl.; in the plur. used as a n. subst. and decl. throughout. *mīlia* is an acc. of extent of space. A. & G. 257; B. 153; G. 335; H. 379. —— passuum, gen. plur. of noun *passus, -ūs*, m.; gen. partitive after *mīlia*. A. & G. 216, 2; B. 134; G. 370; H. 397, 2.

LINE 7. decem, num. adj. cardinal; an attributive of *mīlia*. —— novem, num. adj. cardinal; also an attributive of *mīlia*. Observe the various forms in which the

of the Helvetii.	sēdecim	fossamque	perdūcit.	Eō	opere	8
After completing this work, he stationed garrisons and intrenched redoubts at intervals, in order that, should the Helvetii attempt	*sixteen*	*moat and,*	*he extends.*	*This*	*work*	
	perfectō,	praesidia	dispōnit,		castella	9
	being finished,	*garrisons*	*he places apart,*		*redoubts*	
	commūnit,	quō	facilius,	sī	sē	10
	he fortifies,	*that*	*the more easily,*	*if*	*himself*	

equivalent of *nineteen* in English may be expressed in Latin: by *XVIIII*, by *novendecim*, by *undēvīgintī*, and by *decem novem*, as in our text. The distance here indicated = about 17½ English miles. —— **mūrum**, acc. sing. of *mūrus, -i*, m.; direct obj. of *perdūcit*. Synonyms: *mūrus = any sort of wall; moenia = city walls, ramparts*. —— **in**, prep. with the acc. here; it sometimes takes the abl. See note on *in*, l. 1, Chap. I. *in* here = *to;* it is followed by *altitūdinem*. —— **altitūdinem**, acc. sing. of *altitūdō, -inis*, f. (*altus*, high); it is in the acc. after *in*. —— **pedum**, gen. plur. of *pēs, pedis*, m. (compare GK. τούς, ποδός); quality gen. of measure with the adj. *sēdecim*. Consult A. & G. 215, *b*; B. 132; G. 365, 2; H. 395, V, and NOTE 1. We might take *pedum* as a partitive gen. after *sēdecim, sēdecim* agreeing with *mūrum*, and the phrase *in altitūdinem* as an adjective-phrase equivalent to *altum*. The lit. English of the whole of which would be: *a wall sixteen of feet in height.* The construction is to be preferred, however, that takes *in altitūdinem* as denoting the limit reached after the verb *perdūcit*.

LINE 8. **sēdecim** (sex + decem); sometimes written *sexdecim;* it is an attributive of *pedum*. —— **fossamque** (fossam + que). *fossam*, acc. sing. of *fossa, -ae*, f. (compare perf. participle f. of *fodere*). Note how closely *fossam* is connected by the enclitic with *mūrum*, and is in the same grammatical construction. —— **perdūcit**, 3d pers. sing. pres. ind. act. of *perdūcō, -dūxī, -ductum*, 3 (per + dūcere). The reader is not to understand that the wall and the ditch were continuous, but that a line of forts and moats were constructed where needed at the fordable places on the southeast bank of the Rhone between Lake Geneva and Pas de l'Ecluse. —— **Eō**, abl. sing. n. of the dem. pron. *is, ea, id;* it is an attributive of *opere*. —— **opere**, abl. sing. of *opus, -eris*, n.; abl. absolute with *perfectō*, denoting *time when*. Consult A. & G. 255; B. 192; G. 409, 410; H. 431.

LINE 9. **perfectō**, abl. sing. n. of the perf. pass. participle *perfectus, -a, -um*, of the verb *perficiō, -ere, -fēcī, -fectum*, 3; abl. absolute with *opere*. —— **praesidia**, acc. plur. of *praesidium, -ī*, n.; direct obj. of *dispōnit*. —— **dispōnit**, 3d pers. sing. pres. ind. act. of *dispōnō, -pōnere, -posuī, -positum*, 3 (dis + pōnere) = lit. *to place apart*. —— **castella**, acc. plur. of *castellum, -ī*, n. (diminutive of *castrum*, compare English *castle*); direct obj. of *commūnit*.

LINE 10. **commūnit**, 3d pers. sing. pres. ind. act. of *commūniō, -īre, -īvī (-iī), -ītum*, 4 (con, *intensive* + mūnīre) = lit. *to fortify strongly*. —— **quō**, strictly an abl. of the rel. *quī;* but in use in clauses containing an adv. in the comparative degree, *quō = ut, in order that;* hence in this construction *quō* is a conj. —— **facilius**, comparative degree of adv. *facile* or *faciliter*, superl. *facillimē*. *facilius* as an adv. modifies *prohibēre*. As to the formation of this adv., see A. & G. 148, *d*; B. 117. 6; G. 91, I, (*c*); H. 304, I, 3, 1). —— **sī** (original form *sei*, sibilated from GK. *ei*), conditional conj. = *if*. —— **sē**, abl. sing. of the reflexive pron. *suī, sibi, sē, sē;* it refers to Caesar, and is in the abl. absolute with *invītō*. See A. & G. 255, *a*; B. 192, REM. I; G. 409; H. 431, 4.

11 invītō	trānsīre			cōnārentur,		the passage without his permission, he might
being unwilling	*to cross over*			*they should attempt,*		
12 prohibēre	possit.		Ubi	ea	diēs	the more easily oppose them.
(them) to prohibit	*he may be able.*		*When*	*that*	*day*	When the day which he had appointed for meeting the ambassadors came, and the ambassadors had returned to
13 quam	cōnstitūerat	cum	lēgātīs	vēnit,	et	
which	*he had agreed on*	*with*	*the legates*	*came,*	*and*	
14 lēgātī	ad	eum	revertērunt,	negat	sē	
the legates	*to*	*him*	*returned,*	*he denies*	*himself*	

LINE 11. **invītō**, abl. sing. m. of the adj. *invītus, -a, -um;* abl. absolute with the pron. *sē.* The phrase *sē invītō* = lit. *he himself (being) unwilling.* —— **trānsīre**, pres. inf. act. of *trānseō, -īre, -īvī (-iī), -itum,* 4, but somewhat irr.; complementary inf. depending on *cōnārentur.* Consult A. & G. 271, and NOTE; B. 181; G. 423; H. 533, I, 1. —— **cōnārentur**, 3d pers. plur. imperf. subjunctive of deponent verb *cōnor, -ārī, -ātus,* 1; subjunctive, because the conditional clause is an *essential* part of the sentence. Consult A. & G. 342; B. 235, REM. 1; G. 629; H. 529, II. Observe the shifting of the point of view as indicated by the imperf. tense. And observe also that *cōnārentur* is subjunctive by attraction of mode, as if *sī cōnārentur* were = *quī cōnārentur.*

LINE 12. **prohibēre**, pres. inf. act. of *prohibeō, -ēre, -uī, -itum,* 2 (pro + habēre). *prohibēre* = lit. *to hold from;* supply *eōs* as direct obj. —— **possit**, 3d pers. sing: pres. subjunctive of *possum, posse, potuī* (potis + sum); subjunctive after the conj. *quō,* denoting purpose. See A. & G. 317, *b*; B. 233, 1; G. 545, 2; H. 497, II, 2. Note carefully that the historic presents *dispōnit* and *commūnit* take, as we have seen in the preceding lines, the secondary sequence in the conditional clause, and the primary sequence in the purpose-clause; and consult A. & G. 287, *e*; B. 190, REM. 1; G. 511, REMS. 1 and 2; H. 495, II. —— **Ubi**, conjunctive adv. here (quī + ending bi); see note on *ubi,* l. 4, Chap. V. —— **ea**, nom. sing. f. of the dem. pron. *is, ea, id;* it is an attributive of *diēs.* —— **diēs**, nom. sing. of *diēs, -ēī,* m. and f. in the sing.; always m. in the plur.; it here denotes a fixed time; hence it is in the f. For time referred to, see note on *diem,* l. 30, Chap. VII; *diēs* is subject-nom. of *vēnit.*

LINE 13. **quam**, acc. sing. f. of the rel. pron. *quī, quae, quod;* it refers to *diēs,* as its antecedent, but is the direct obj. of *cōnstitūerat.* —— **cōnstitūerat**, 3d pers. sing. pluperf. ind. of *cōnstituō, -ere, -stituī, -stitūtum,* 3 (con + statuere); its subject-nom. is a pron. implied in the ending, referring to Caesar. —— **cum**, prep. with the abl.; original form *com;* with the abl. it usually designates accompaniment, or the connection of one obj. with another. It is known here to be the prep., and not the conj. *cum,* not merely because it is followed by a noun in a case-form which may possibly be the abl., but because it occurs in a clause that has its own connective — *ubi.* —— **lēgātīs**, abl. plur. of *lēgātus, -ī,* m. (*lēgere,* to delegate); abl. after prep. *cum.* —— **vēnit**, 3d pers. sing. perf. ind. act. of *veniō, -īre, vēnī, ventum,* 4; it agrees with its subject-nom. *diēs.* Observe that *vēnit* has long *ē* in the penult; if it were the pres. tense, the *e* would be short.

LINE 14. **lēgātī**, nom. plur. of *lēgātus, -ī,* m.; subj. of *revertērunt.* —— **ad**, prep. with the acc. —— **eum**, acc. sing. m. of the dem. pron. *is, ea, id,* used as a personal pron. of the 3d pers.; it is the obj. of the prep. *ad.* —— **revertērunt** (re + vertere = lit. *to turn back*), 3d pers. plur. of *revertō, -ere, -vertī;* it agrees with its subject-nom.

him, he told them that he could not, according to the usages and precedents of the Roman people, give any one the right of way through the province; and he explicitly declared that, if they attempted to use	mōre *by the custom* posse *to be able* dare, *to give,* prohibitūrum *to be about to stop*	et *and* iter *a journey* et, *and,*	exemplō *example* ūllī *to any one* sī *if* (them) he	populī *of the people* per *through* vim *violence* ostendit. *shows.*	Rōmānī 15 *Roman* prōvinciam 16 *the province* facere cōnentur, 17 *to make they attempt,* / Helvētiī eā 18 *The Helvetii from this*

---

lēgātī; a deponent form, *revertor, -ī, -versus,* frequently occurs in the imperf. tenses. —— **negat**, 3d pers. sing. pres. ind. act. of *negō, -āre, -āvī, -ātum,* 1 (nĕ + āiō). *negat* = lit. *he denies, he says ... not.* The English idiom of *negat sē posse* would be indicated by the Latin: *dīcit sē nōn posse.* —— **sē**, acc. sing. of the reflexive pron. *suī, sibi, sē, sē; sē* is subject-acc. of *posse.*

LINE 15. **mōre**, abl. of *mōs, mōris,* m.; abl. of *accordance with*. A. & G. 253, and NOTE; B. 162; G. 397; H. 416. It will be observed that the first three references make this construction an abl. of specification; while Professor Harkness makes it an abl. of cause. The true principle appears to be *subjective cause.* —— **exemplō**, abl. sing. of *exemplum, -ī,* n.; connected by *et* with *mōre*, and in the same grammatical construction. —— **populī**, gen. sing. of *populus, -ī,* m.; it limits *mōre et exemplō.* —— **Rōmānī**, gen. sing. m. of the adj. *Rōmānus, -a, -um;* it is an attributive of *populī.* Synonyms: *populus = the people* in their civil capacity; *plēbs = the common people* in distinction from the patricians; whereas *vulgus = the crowd, the rabble.*

LINE 16. **posse**, pres. inf. of *possum, potuī* (potis + sum); its subject-acc. is the pron. *sē.* —— **iter**, acc. sing. of *iter, itineris,* n.; direct obj. of *dare.* —— **ūllī**, dat. sing. m. of the adj. *ūllus, -a, -um,* gen. *ūllīus;* used here substantively = *cuiquam;* indirect obj. of *dare.* Note that *ūllus* and *quisquam* are chiefly used in negative sentences. —— **per**, prep. with the acc. —— **prōvinciam**, acc. sing. of *prōvincia, -ae,* f.; *prōvinciam* is the obj. of the prep. *per.*

LINE 17. **dare**, pres. inf. act. of *dō, dare, dedī, datum,* 1; complementary inf.; it depends on *posse.* See A. & G. 271, and NOTE; B. 181; G. 423; H. 533, I, 2. —— **et**, conj.; connects *negat* with *ostendit.* —— **sī**, conditional conj. See note on *sī,* l. 10, above. —— **vim**, acc. sing. of *vīs, vīs* (digammated from GK. *ἴς*); *vim* is the direct obj. of *facere.* —— **facere**, pres. inf. act. of *faciō, -ere, fēcī, factum,* 3; complementary inf., and depends on *conentur.* See note on *trānsīre,* l. 11, above. —— **cōnentur**, 3d pers. plur. pres. subjunctive of *cōnor, -ārī, -ātus,* deponent, 1; it agrees with a pron. implied in the ending, referring to the Helvetii. *cōnentur* is in the subjunctive mode, because the conditional clause is an integral part of the sentence. See note on *cōnārentur,* l. 11, above.

LINE 18. **prohibitūrum** (esse), fut. inf. act. of *prohibeō, -ēre, -uī, -itum,* 2; its subject-acc. is the pron. *sē*, to be supplied, referring to Caesar; supply also *eōs,* as direct obj. —— **ostendit**, 3d pers. sing. pres. ind. act. of *ostendō, -ere, -tendī, -tentum,* 3 (ob + tendere); *ostendere = to stretch out;* hence, *to expose to view, to show.* *ostendit*

[LINES 19-22.]   BOOK I.   55

19 spē	dēiectī,	nāvibus	iūnctīs	ratibusque	force, he would resist them, The Helvetii, disappointed in this hopè, tried, sometimes by day, oftener by night, to see whether they could force a passage; some, on a bridge formed by uniting boats and numerous
hope	cast down,	boats	being joined together,	rafts and	
20 complūribus	factīs,	aliī	vadīs	Rhodanī,	
very many	being made,	others	by the fords	of the Rhone,	
21 quā	minima	altitūdō	flūminis	erat,	
where	least	the depth	of the river	was,	
22 nōnnumquam		interdiū,	saepius	noctū,	
sometimes		by day,	oftener	by night,	

agrees with a subject-nom. implied in the ending, referring to Caesar. —— **Helvētiī**, nom. plur. of the adj. *Helvētius, -a, -um,* used as a substantive; it is subject-nom. of *dēstitērunt,* l. 26, below. The *ōrātiō rēcta* of lines 14-18 is: *ĕgŏ,* mōre et exemplō populī Rōmānī, *nōn possum* iter ūllī per prōvinciam dare et, sī vim facere *cōnābimini*, *prohibēbō.* —— **eā,** abl. sing. f. of the dem. pron. *is, ea, id;* it is an attributive of the noun *spē.* Note the long vowel *ā* in the ultima of the abl., and compare it with the short *a* in the nom. f., as seen in *ea,* l. 12, above.

LINE 19. **spē,** abl. sing. of *spēs, speī,* f.; abl. of separation after *dēiectī.* A. & G. 243; B. 160; G. 390, I, 2, and NOTE 3; II. 414, I. —— **dēiectī,** nom. plur. of the perf. pass. participle *dēiectus, -a, -um* of the verb *dēiciō, -ere, -iēci, -iectum,* 3 (dē + iacere); hence *dēicere* = lit. *to hurl down.* *dēiectī* as a participle agrees with the noun *Helvētiī.* —— **nāvibus,** abl. plur. of *nāvis, -is,* f.; abl. absolute with the participle *iūnctīs,* denoting the means. See A. & G. 255; B. 192; G. 410; H. 431. —— **iūnctīs,** abl. plur. f. of the perf. pass. participle *iūnctus, -a, -um* of the verb *iūngō, -ere, iūnxī, iūnctum,* 3; abl. absolute with the noun *nāvibus.* —— **ratibusque** (ratibus + que). *ratibus,* abl. plur. of *ratis, -is,* f.; abl. absolute with *factīs.*

LINE 20. **complūribus,** abl. plur. f. of the adj. *complūrēs, -a* (com, *intensive* + plūs). *complūribus* is an attributive of *ratibus.* —— **factīs,** abl. plur. of the perf. pass. participle *factus, -a, -um,* of the verb *faciō, -ere, fēcī, factum,* 3; it is in the abl. absolute with the noun *ratibus,* denoting the means. The boats thus joined formed a species of bridge. —— **aliī,** nom. plur. m. of the adjective-pron. *alius, -a -um,* used substantively, and in apposition with *Helvētiī.* In translating, supply another *aliī* before *ratibus,* with which the *aliī* of the text is contrasted. —— **vadīs,** abl. plur. of the noun *vadum, -ī,* n.; abl. of means. —— **Rhodanī,** gen. sing. of *Rhodanus, -ī,* m.; it limits *vadīs.*

LINE 21. **quā,** adv. = *where;* may, however, be taken as a rel. adj. by supplying *viā,* which latter would be an abl. of the *way by which.* —— **minima,** nom. sing. f. of the superl. adj. *minimus, -a, -um;* the adj. is thus compared: *parvus, minor, minimus;* predicate-adj. after *erat.* —— **altitūdō, -inis,** f. (*altus,* high or low, according to the *ā quō* of the mental conception). *altitūdō* is subject-nom. of *erat.* —— **flūminis,** gen. sing. of *flūmen, -inis,* n.; it limits *altitūdō.* —— **erat,** 3d pers. sing. imperf. ind. of *sum, esse, fuī, futūrus.*

LINE 22. **nōnnumquam,** negative adv. (nōn + num[n]quam) = lit. *not never,* i.e. *sometimes;* as in English, two negatives in Latin are equivalent to a positive. Con-

rafts; others, at the fords of the Rhone where the depth of the river was least; but, on being repulsed by the strength of our fortifications and the onsets and the missiles of our soldiers, they desisted from the attempt.	sī *whether*	perrumpere *to break through*	possent, *they might be able,*	cōnātī, 23 *attempting,*
	operis *by the work's*	mūnītiōne *intrenchment*	et mīlitum *and the soldiers'*	concursū 24 *attack*
	et *and*	tēlīs *weapons*	repulsī *being repulsed,* hōc *from this*	cōnātū 25 *attempt*
	dēstitērunt. *desisted.*			26

sult A. & G. 150, and *a;* B. 117. 10; G. 449, 4; H. 553, 1. —— **interdiū**, adv. (inter + diū). Observe that *diū* is an old form of *diē*, used only in connection with *noctū*. —— **saepius**, adv., comparative of *saepe*, superl. *saepissimē*. —— **noctū**, adv.; strictly an old form of the abl. of *nox*. Note that the forms *nox*, *nocte* and *noctū* all occur as adverbs. In such use of the abl., compare GK. gen. νυκτός, denoting *time within which.*

LINE 23. **sī**, conj., usually means *if*, but here it = *whether*. —— **perrumpere**, pres. inf. act. of *perrumpō*, *-ere*, *-rūpī*, *-ruptum*, 3 (per + rumpere); complementary inf., depending on *possent*. Consult A. & G. 271, and NOTE; B. 181; G. 423; H. 533, 1, 2. —— **possent**, 3d pers. plur. imperf. subjunctive of *possum, posse, potuī* (potis + sum); it agrees with a subj. implied in the ending, referring to *Helvētiī*; it is in the subjunctive, because an *indirect* question. Consult A. & G. 334, *f*; B. 242, 2; G. 460, *b*; H. 529, II, 1, NOTE 1. —— **cōnātī**, nom. plur. m. of the perf. pass. participle *cōnātus, -a, -um* of the deponent verb *cōnor, -ārī, -ātus,* 1; *cōnātī* as a participle agrees with *Helvētiī*, l. 18, above; but might be translated as if it were *cōnātī sunt.*

LINE 24. **operis**, gen. sing. of *opus, operis,* n.; it limits *mūnītiōne*. —— **mūnītiōne**, abl. sing. of *mūnītiō, -ōnis,* f.; abl. of means. Observe that *operis mūnītiōne* = lit. *by the fortification of the work*, i.e. *by the fortified works* — the redoubts and the moat. —— **et**, conj., connects *mūnītiōne* and *concursū*. —— **mīlitum**, gen. plur. of *mīles, -itis,* m.; it limits *concursū*. —— **concursū**, abl. sing. of *concursus, -ūs,* m. (con + cursus = *a running together*); *concursū* is also an abl. of means.

LINE 25. **tēlīs**, abl. plur. of noun *tēlum, -ī,* n.; abl. of means after *repulsī*. For synonyms, see note on *armīs*, l. 13, Chap. IV. —— **repulsī**, nom. plur. of the perf. pass. participle *repulsus, -a, -um* of the verb *repellō, -ere, reppulī* or *repulī, repulsum,* 3. Note that in this long and somewhat involved sentence *dēiectī, cōnātī* and *repulsī* are all participles, and limit *Helvētiī*, at the beginning of the sentence. In the translation it will be the better way to render some of the participles as if they were principal verbs, supplying conjunctions where needed, in order to make good English. —— **hōc**, abl. sing. m. of the dem. pron. *hīc, haec, hōc; hōc* limits *cōnātū*. —— **cōnātū**, abl. of the noun *cōnātus, -ūs,* m.; abl. of separation. See grammatical references to *spē*, l. 19, above.

LINE 26. **dēstitērunt**, 3d pers. plur. perf. ind. act. of *dēsistō, -ere, -stitī, -stitum,* 3 (dē + sistere, lit. *to stand off*). *dēstitērunt* agrees with *Helvētiī* as its subject-nom., l. 18, above.

BOOK I.

					IX. The route through the Sequani alone remained, by which, without their permission, the Helvetii could not go, on account of the narrow pass. Since, by their own influence, they could not prevail on them,
1 IX.	Relinquēbātur	ūna	per	Sēquanōs	
	There was left	*one,*	*through*	*the Sequani,*	
2 via,	quā	Sēquanīs	invītīs	propter	
way	*by which,*	*the Sequani*	*being unwilling,*	*on account of*	
3 angustiās	īre	nōn poterant.		Hīs cum	
the narrow pass	*to go*	*not they were able.*		*Them, since*	
4 suā	sponte	persuādēre		nōn possent,	
by their own	*will*	*to persuade,*		*not they were able,*	

LINE 1. **Relinquēbātur**, 3d pers. sing. imperf. ind. pass. of *relinquō, -ere, -līquī, -līctum*, 3 (re + linquere); it agrees with its subject-nom. *via*. —— **ūna**, nom. sing. f. of the adj. *ūnus, -a, -um; ūna* is an attributive of *via*. For grammatical references as to the peculiarities of this adj., see note on *ūnam*, l. 2, Chap. I. —— **per**, prep. with the acc. —— **Sēquanōs**, acc. plur. of the adj. *Sēquanus, -a, -um*, used substantively here, and is the obj. of the prep. *per*. Observe that the phrase *per Sēquanōs* is an adjectival modifier of *via*. As to this way, see lines 2 and 3, Chap. VI.

LINE 2. **via, -ae**, nom. sing. f., subj. of *relinquēbātur* (digammated from *ī* in *īre*). Synonyms: *via* = the ordinary travelled way, compare GK. ὁδός; whereas *iter*, in a *concrete* sense = the way direct to a particular point, whether travelled or not. But both *via* and *iter* are sometimes used in an abstract sense without any particular difference in meaning, and = *a journey*, *a march*. —— **quā**, abl. sing. f. of the rel. pron. *quī, quae, quod*; it agrees with *via*, to be supplied; and *via* supplied is in the abl. of the *way by which*. See A. & G. 258, *g*; B. 170, REM. 4; G. 389; H. 425, II, 1, 1). *viā* is, in fact, an abl. of means as well as place. —— **Sēquanīs**, abl. plur of *Sēquanī, -ōrum*, m.; abl. absolute with the adj. *invītīs*, denoting condition. See A. & G. 255, *a*, and *d*. 4; B. 192, REM. 1; G. 409; H. 431, 4. —— **invītīs**, abl. plur. m. of the adj. *invītus, -a, -um* (derivation dubious); abl. absolute with the noun *Sēquanīs*. —— **propter**, prep. with the acc. (prope + ter); sometimes an adv.

LINE 3. **angustiās**, acc. plur. of the noun *angustiae, -ārum*, f.; sometimes used in the sing., *angustia, -ae*, f. (*angustus* from *angere*, to press together). Observe that *propter* with the acc. here denotes the objective cause. See A. & G. 245, *b*; B. 165, REM. 4; G. 408, NOTE 3; H. 416, I, 2). —— **īre**, pres. inf. act. of *eō, īre, īvī (iī), itum*, irr.; complementary inf. depending on *poterant*. Consult A. & G. 271, and NOTE; B. 181; G. 423; H. 533, I, 2. —— **nōn** (nē + ūnum, apocopated); observe its normal Latin position, immediately before the word it modifies. —— **poterant**, 3d pers. plur. imperf. ind. of *possum, posse, potuī* (potis + sum); it agrees with a pron. implied in its ending as its subject-nom., referring to *Helvētiī*. —— **Hīs**, dat. plur. of the dem. pron. *hīc, haec, hōc*, used as a personal pron. of the 3d pers.; dat. after *persuādēre*. A. & G. 227; B. 142; G. 346; H. 385, II. —— **cum**, conj., denoting here both time and cause; also written *quum, quom* and (rarely) *qum* (an old adverbial acc. n. of *quī*). It is known to be the conj. and not the prep., because it is seen to introduce a dependent clause which requires a connective. Observe that particular emphasis is put upon the pron. *hīs* by its position before *cum;* that, sometimes, several words precede the conj. when the subordinate precedes the main clause.

LINE 4. **suā**, abl. sing. f. of the poss. adj. pron. *suus, -a, -um;* it is an attributive of *sponte*. —— **sponte**, abl. sing. of a supposed theme *spōns, spontis,* f.; used only in

58 CAESAR'S GALLIC WAR [CHAP. IX.

they sent ambassadors to Dumnorix, the Aeduan, that, through his mediation, they might obtain from the Sequani their request. Dumnorix through his	lēgātōs *deputies* ut, *that,* impetrārent. *privilege)*	ad *to* eō ·	Dumnorigem *Dumnorix,* dēprecātōre, *he being the intercessor,* they might obtain.	Aeduum *the Aeduan,* ā *from* Dumnorix	mittunt, *they send,* Sēquanīs *the Sequani (this* grātiā *Dumnorix through his popularity*	5 6 7

the gen. and abl.; *sponte* is in the abl. of means. The phrase *suā sponte* here = *by their influence*, a rare meaning of the phrase, but classical; usually it = *of their own accord*. Synonyms: *sponte* usually = an act of the will, whose impulse is choice, in opposition to fate or chance; whereas *voluntās* = an act of the will, whose impulse is a background of willingness, good-will (*velle*, to wish). —— **persuādēre**, pres. inf. act. of *persuādeō, -ēre, -suāsī, -suāsum*, 2; complementary inf., depending on *possent*. See grammatical references to *īre*, l. 3, above. —— **nōn**, adv. negative (contracted from nē + oenum or ūnum); there is an archaic form *nēnum*. Observe its normal position immediately before the word it modifies; it is very often made emphatic by being put in an abnormal position. —— **possent**, 3d pers. plur. imperf. subjunctive of *possum, posse, potuī* (potis + sum); subjunctive after *cum* causal. A. & G. 326; B. 198, *c*, and 223; G. 586; H. 517.

LINE 5. **lēgātōs**, acc. plur. of *lēgātus, -ī* (*legere*, to despatch); direct obj. of *mittunt*. —— **ad**, prep. with the acc.; the usual construction after a verb of motion. —— **Dumnorigem**, acc. sing. of *Dumnorix, -igis*, m.; the obj. of the prep. *ad*. For historical description, see note on *Dumnorigī*, l. 20, Chap. III. —— **Aeduum**, acc. sing. m. of the adj. *Aeduus, -a, -um*; but here used as a noun in apposition with *Dumnorigem*. —— **mittunt**, 3d pers. plur. pres. ind. act. of *mittō, -ere, mīsī, missum*, 3; historical pres.; its subject-nom. is the pron. *eī*, i.e. *Helvētiī*.

LINE 6. **ut**, telic conj., original form *utī*. —— **eō**, abl. sing. m. of the dem. pron. *is, ea, id*, used as a personal pron. of the 3d person; it refers to *Dumnorigem*. —— **dēprecātōre**, abl. of *dēprecātor, -ōris*, m. (dē + precārī = *to pray against*); abl. absolute with the pron. *eō*. Observe that here we have a noun and pron. in this construction; in l. 2, above, we have a noun and an adj.; in Chap. VI, end, we have two nouns in the abl. absolute construction. Observe, further, that the abl. absolute construction here denotes the means; i.e. *eō dēprecātōre* = lit. *he being the intercessor* = *by his intercession*. Observe again that nouns in -*tor* appended to the first verb-stem denote the agent or doer. —— **ā**, prep. with the abl. (*ā* used before consonants only, *ab* before vowels or consonants). —— **Sēquanīs**, abl. plur. of *Sēquanī, -ōrum*, m.; abl. after the prep. *ā*, denoting *the source*. A. & G. 244, 1; B. 120. 2; G. 417, I; H. 413.

LINE 7. **impetrārent**, 3d pers. plur. imperf. subjunctive act. of *impetrō, -āre, -āvī, -ātum*, 1; its subject-nom. is a pron. implied in the ending; i.e. *eī*, referring to *Helvētiī*. As this verb is transitive, supply *voluntātem* as direct obj. *impetrārent* is subjunctive, because it is in a purpose-clause after *ut*; the clause expresses the purpose of *mittunt*. —— **Dumnorix, -igis**, m., subject-nom. of *poterat*; see note on *Dumnorigem*, l. 5, above. —— **grātiā**, abl. sing. of *grātia, -ae*, f.; abl. of cause. A. & G. 245; B. 165; G. 408; H. 416.

BOOK I.

8 et	largītiōne	apud	Sēquanōs	plūrimum		grace and gifts had very great influence with the Sequani, and besides he was friendly to the Helvetii, because from that state he had taken in marriage Orgetorix's daughter; and too, influenced by an ex-
and	liberality	among	the Sequani	very much		
9 poterat	et	Helvētiīs	erat	amīcus,	quod	
was able,	and	to the Helvetii	was	friendly,	because	
10 ex	eā	cīvitāte	Orgetorigis	filiam	in	
from	that	state	Orgetorix's	daughter	into	
11 mātrimōnium		dūxerat;		et	cupiditāte	
marriage		he had led;		and	through lust	

LINE 8. **largītiōne**, abl. sing. of *largītiō, -ōnis*, f. (*largīre*, to give bountifully); connected by *et* with *grātiā*, and in the same grammatical construction. —— **apud**, prep. with the acc. = *at, by, among*. —— **Sēquanōs**, acc. plur. of the adj. *Sēquanus, -a, -um*, used as a subst.; it is the obj. of the prep. *apud*. For description of this clan, see note on *Sēquanīs*, l. 25, Chap. I. —— **plūrimum**, adverbial acc. n. of the superl. degree of adj. *plūrimus, -a, -um;* positive degree *multum*, comparative *plūs;* cognate acc. See A. & G. 238, *b*; B. 150, REM. 2; G. 333, 2; H. 371, II, (2).

LINE 9. **poterat**, 3d pers. sing. imperf. ind. of *possum, posse, potuī* (*potis* + *sum*); it agrees with its subject-nom. *Dumnorix*. Observe that *poterat* here is a verb of complete predication, and = *valēbat*. See note on *possent*, l. 4, above. —— **et**, cop. conj., connects *poterat* with *erat*. —— **Helvētiīs**, dat. of the adj. *Helvētius, -a, -um*, used as a subst.; dat. after the adj. *amīcus*. Consult A. & G. 234, a; B. 144; G. 359; H. 391, I. For description of the clan, see note on *Helvētiī*, l. 16, Chap. I. —— **erat**, 3d pers. sing. imperf. ind. of *sum, esse, fuī, futūrus;* connected by *et* with *poterat*, and in the same grammatical construction. —— **amīcus**, nom. sing. m. of the adj. *amīcus, -a -um;* sometimes used as a noun; and may be here rendered as such; but it is here, strictly, an adj., and as such is followed by the dat. —— **quod**, conj.

LINE 10. **ex**, prep. with the abl. (*ē* before consonants, *ex* before vowels and consonants). —— **eā**, abl. sing. f. of the dem. pron. *is, ea, id;* it is an attributive of *cīvitāte*. —— **cīvitāte**, abl. sing. of *cīvitas, -ātis*, f. (*cīves*). By metonymy *ex eā cīvitāte* is put for *ex cīvibus cīvitātis*. Note that Caesar by the use of the prep. *ex* indicates that he took his wife from *within* the borders of that state; if he had used the prep. *ab*, he would indicate that he took his wife from the border-line of the state, not from *within* it. —— **Orgetorigis**, gen. sing. of *Orgetorix, -igis*, m.; as a gen. it limits *fīliam*. For description, see note on *Orgetorix*, l. 2, Chap. II. —— **fīliam**, acc. sing. of the noun *fīlia, -ae;* direct obj. of *dūxerat*. Observe that the dat. and abl. plur. of *fīlia* ends in *-ābus;* so also *dea*, a goddess. —— **in**, prep. with the acc. or abl.; here it takes the acc., and = (after the verb of motion *dūxerat*) *in* or *into;* i.e. he led her to his house. The phrase *dūcere in mātrimōnium* is descriptive of the man's act. The woman is said to vail herself for her husband: *nūbere sē virō*.

LINE 11. **mātrimōnium** (*matri* + *mōnium* = *motherhood*), acc. sing. of *mātrimōnium, -ī*, n.; acc. after the prep. *in*. —— **dūxerat**, 3d pers. sing. pluperf. ind. act. of *dūcō, -ere, dūxī, ductum*, 3; it agrees with a pron. implied in the ending, referring to *Dumnorix*. —— **et**, cop. conj.; it connects the sentences. —— **cupiditāte**, abl.

60   CAESAR'S GALLIC WAR   [CHAP. IX.

| cessive zeal for royal power, he was plotting a revolution in his own state, and wished to have as many states as possible attached to him for his kindness. Accordingly, he undertook the | rēgnī *of sovereignty* et *and* beneficiō *favor* rem *the affair* | adductus, *being led,* quam *as much as* habēre obstrictās *to have put under obligation* suscipit *he undertakes* | novīs *of new* plūrimās *the most* et *and* | rēbus *things* cīvitātēs *states* volēbat. *he wished.* ā *from* | studēbat 12 *was desirous,* suō 13 *by his* Itaque 14 *Therefore* Sēquanīs 15 *the Sequani* |

sing. of *cupiditās, -tātis,* f. (*cupidus,* desirous); abl. of *subjective cause* after *adductus.* Consult A. & G. 245, and 2, *b*; B. 165, and REM. 4; G. 408, and NOTE 2; H. 416, and NOTE 1.

LINE 12. **rēgnī**, gen. sing. of the noun *rēgnum, -ī,* n. (*rēx*); it limits *cupiditāte.* —— **adductus**, perf. pass. participle of the verb *addūco, -ere, -dūxī, -ductum,* 3 (*addūcere* = lit. *to draw to*); *adductus,* as a participle, agrees with the subj. of the proposition in which it stands, i.e. with *Dumnorix* understood. —— **novīs**, dat. plur. f. of the adj. *novus, -a, um;* it is an attributive of *rēbus.* —— **rēbus**, dat. plur. of the noun *rēs, reī,* f.; it is in the dat. after the verb *studēbat.* Consult A. & G. 227, and foot-note; B. 142; G. 346; H. 385, 1. —— **studēbat**, 3d pers. sing. imperf. ind. act. of *studeō, -ēre, -uī,* 2 (rare perf. *studīvī,* kindred with GK. σπουδάζειν, to hasten).

LINE 13. **et**, cop. conj., connects *studēbat* and *volēbat.* —— **quam**, adv., modifies *plūrimās.* Note that *quam* is here a correlative to *tam* understood. The complete expression is: *tam multās quam plūrimās cīvitātēs.* Compare note on *quam,* l. 4, Chap. III. —— **plūrimās**, acc. plur. f. of the superl. adj. *plūrimus, -a, -um;* positive *multus,* comparative *plūs. plūrimās* modifies *cīvitātēs.* —— **cīvitātēs**, acc. plur. of noun *cīvitas, -ātis,* f.; direct obj. of *habēre.* —— **suō**, abl. sing. n. of the poss. reflexive pron. *suus, -a, -um;* it agrees with *beneficiō,* but refers to *Dumnorix.*

LINE 14. **beneficiō**, abl. of the noun *beneficium, -ī,* n. (*bene* + *facere*); hence the noun = lit. *well-doing;* abl. of cause. —— **habēre**, pres. inf. act. of *habeō, -ēre, -uī, -itum,* 2; complementary inf. depending on *volēbat.* A. & G. 271, and NOTE; B. 181; G. 423; H. 533, I, 1. —— **obstrictās**, perf. pass. participle, acc. plur. f. of the verb *obstringō, -ere, -strīnxī, -strictum,* 3; *obstrictās* agrees with the noun *cīvitātēs* in gender, number and case; but forms with *habēre* a sort of periphrase nearly = *obstrīnxisse;* but the periphrase emphasizes the maintenance of the result. Consult A. & G. 292, *c*; B. 191, 3, (*d*); G. 238; H. 388, 1, NOTE. —— **volēbat**, 3d pers. sing. imperf. ind. of the irr. verb *volō, velle, voluī;* it agrees with *Dumnorix,* to be supplied. —— **Itaque** (ita + que), conjunctive adv. Observe that when an enclitic is appended to the ultima of any dissyllabic or polysyllabic word, whether that ultima be naturally long or short, it takes the ictus. In the interest of uniform pronunciation, there should be no difference of pronunciation on account of the different meanings of a word; e.g. *itáque* (*and . . . so*) should not be discriminated in pronunciation from *itáque* (*therefore*). Enclitics *invariably* lean upon the ultima of the word to which they are appended.

LINE 15. **rem**, acc. sing. of *rēs, reī,* f.; the direct obj. of *suscipit.* The matter alluded to here is *the consent of the Sequani.* —— **suscipit**, 3d pers. sing. pres. ind.

16 impetrat	ut	per	fīnēs	suōs	negotiation, and obtained from the Sequani permission for the Helvetii to go through the country, and arranged that they should exchange hostages : the Sequani, not to prevent the Helvetii from making
obtains	*that*	*through*	*borders*	*their*	
17 Helvētiōs	īre	patiantur,	obsidēsque	utī	
the Helvetii	*to go*	*they allow,*	*hostages and,*	*that*	
18 inter	sēsē	dent,	perficit:	Sēquanī,	
among	*themselves*	*they give*	*he effects :*	*the Sequani,*	
19 nē		itinere	Helvētiōs	prohibeant;	
that not		*from the route*	*the Helvetii*	*they will keep ;*	

act. of *suscipiō, -ere, -cēpī, -ceptum*, 3 (sub + capere); hence *suscipere = to take up*, i.e. from beneath. *suscipit* agrees with *Dumnorix* understood as its subject-nom. —— **et**, cop. conj., connects *suscipit* with *impetrat*. —— **ā**, prep. with the abl. —— **Sēquanīs**, abl. of *Sēquanī, -ōrum*, m.; abl. of the source after the prep. *ā*. For grammatical references, see note on *Sēquanīs*, l. 6, above; for description of this clan, see note on *Sēquanīs*, l. 25, Chap. I.

LINE 16. **impetrat**, 3d pers. sing. pres. ind. act. of *impetrō*, 1; it agrees with its subject-nom. *Dumnorix* understood; its direct obj. here is the following *ut*-clause. —— **ut**, ecbatic conj. —— **per**, prep. with the acc. *fīnēs*. —— **fīnēs**, acc. plur. of the noun *fīnis, -is*, m.; obj. of the prep. *per*. For synonyms, see note on *agrum*, l. 12, Chap. II. —— **suōs**, acc. plur. of the poss. pron. *suus, -a, -um*; it agrees with *fīnēs*, but refers to *Sēquanīs*.

LINE 17. **Helvētiōs**, acc. plur. of *Helvētiī, -ōrum*, m.; subject-acc. of the verb *īre*. For description of this clan, see note on *Helvētiī*, l. 16, Chap. I. —— **īre**, pres. inf. act. of *eō, īre, īvī (iī), itum*; it, with its subject-acc. *Helvētiōs*, depends on *patiantur*. —— **patiantur**, 3d pers. plur. pres. subjunctive of the deponent verb *patior, -ī, passus*, 3; subjunctive of result after *ut*, as an object-clause. See A. & G. 332; B. 201; G. 553; H. 501, II. —— **obsidēsque** (obsidēs + que). *obsidēs*, acc. plur. of *obses, -idis*, m. and f.; direct obj. of *dent*. *que*, enclitic conj., connects the clauses very closely. —— **utī**, the original form of the adv. and conj. *ut*; ecbatic conj.

LINE 18. **inter**, prep. with the acc. —— **sēsē**, acc. plur. of the reflexive pron. *suī, sibi, sē, sē*; reduplicated; the obj. of the prep. *inter*. The phrase *inter sēsē* denotes a reciprocal relation. See A. & G. 196, *f*; B. 78, REM. 4; G. 221; H. 448, NOTE. —— **dent**, 3d pers. plur. pres. subjunctive act. of verb *dō, dare, dedī, datum*, 1 (a short before -*re* in the pres. inf. act. in a verb of the first conjugation by exception); subjunctive of result after *utī*; an object-clause like *ut . . . patiantur*, lines 16 and 17, above. See the grammatical references on *patiantur*. Note that the subj. of *dent* is a pronoun, referring to both *Sēquanī* and *Helvētiī*. —— **perficit**, 3d pers. sing. pres. ind. act. of *perficiō, -ere, -fēcī, -factum*, 3; it agrees with *Dumnorix* understood. —— **Sēquanī**, nom. plur. of the adj. *Sēquanus, -a, -um*, used substantively, and subject-nom. of *dant*, to be supplied. The complete lacuna here is: *obsidēs dant*.

LINE 19. **nē**, conjunctive adv. = *that not*; telic; if the construction were ecbatic, *ut non* would be used. —— **itinere**, abl. sing. of the noun *iter, itineris*, n.; abl. of separation of *prohibeant*. See A. & G. 243; B. 160; G. 390, I, 2, and NOTE 3; H. 414, I. —— **Helvētiōs**, acc. plur. of *Helvētiī, -ōrum*, m.; direct obj. of *prohibeant*. For description of the clan, see L 16, Chap. I. —— **prohibeant**, 3d pers. plur. pres.

use of this route; the Helvetii, to pass through the country without damage or outrage.	Helvētiī,	ut	sine	maleficiō	et	iniūriā	20
	the Helvetii,	*that*	*without*	*harm*	*and*	*injury*	
	trānseant.						21
	they will cross.						

X. Word was brought to Caesar by his scouts that the Helvetii were purposing to march through the country of the Sequani and the Aedui to the border	X. Caesarī	renūntiātur,	Helvētiīs		esse	1
	To Caesar	*it is reported,*	*to the Helvetii*		*to be (it is)*	
	in animō,	per	agrum	Sēquanōrum	et	2
	in mind,	*through*	*the territory*	*of the Sequani*	*and*	
	Aeduōrum	iter	in	Santonum	fīnēs	3
	of the Aedui	*a journey*	*into*	*the Santones'*	*borders*	

subjunctive act. of *prohibeō, -ēre, -uī, -itum,* 2; it agrees with a pron. implied in the ending, referring to *Sēquanī;* it is subjunctive, because negative purpose after *nē.* Consult A. & G. 317; B. 200, and (*b*); G. 545, 3; H. 497, II.

LINE 20. **Helvētiī,** supply *obsidēs dant* from the preceding *obsidēs inter sēsē dent; Helvētiī* is subject-nom. of *dant* understood. —— ut, telic conj. —— **sine,** prep. with the abl. *maleficiō.* —— **maleficiō,** abl. sing. of the noun *maleficium, -ī,* n. (malum + facere); hence *maleficium* = lit. *evil-doing;* it is the obj. of the prep. *sine.* —— **et,** cop. conj.; it connects words of equal importance. —— **iniūriā,** abl. sing. of the noun *iniūria, -ae,* f. (in, *negative* + iūs); *iniūriā* is connected with *maleficiō* by the conj. *et,* and is in the same grammatical construction.

LINE 21. **trānseant,** 3d pers. sing. pres. subjunctive of the verb *trānseō, -īre, -īvī (-iī), -itum,* 4, irr. (trāns + īre) = lit. *to go across;* subjunctive of purpose after the conjunctive particle *ut.* Vide grammatical references to *prohibeant,* l. 19, above.

LINE 1. **Caesarī,** dat. sing. of the proper noun *Caesar, -aris,* m.; dat. of the indirect obj. after *renūntiātur.* A. & G. 225, 3, *e*; B. 140; G. 344; H. 384, I. —— **renūntiātur,** 3d pers. sing. pres. ind. pass. of *renūntiō (-ciō), -āre, -āvī, -ātum,* 1; pass. parts: *renūntior, -ārī, -ātus; renūntiātur* is here used impersonally and = lit. *it is reported;* or more exactly, its subject is the entire clause: *Helvētiīs esse in animō, per agrum . . . iter . . . facere.* —— **Helvētiīs,** dat. plur. of the adj. *Helvētius, -a, -um,* used as a noun; dat. of possessor after *esse.* See A. & G. 231; B. 146; G. 349; H. 387. —— **esse,** pres. inf. of the intrans. verb *sum, esse, fuī, futūrus;* it, too, is here used impersonally; strictly, however, *per agrum . . . iter . . . facere* is its subject-acc.

LINE 2. **in,** prep. with the acc. and abl.; here it takes the abl. *animō.* —— **animō,** abl. sing. of *animus, -ī,* m.; abl. after the prep. *in.* Synonyms: *anima* = the soul as the principle of animal life; *animus* = the human soul with all its faculties; while *mēns* = the soul as rational or reflective faculty. —— **per,** prep. with the acc. —— **agrum,** acc. sing. of *ager, agrī,* m.; the obj. of the prep. *per.* For synonyms, see note on *agrum,* l. 12, Chap. II. —— **Sēquanōrum,** gen. plur. of *Sēquanī, -ōrum,* m.; it limits *agrum.* For description of this clan, see note on *Sēquanīs,* l. 25, Chap. I.

LINE 3. **Aeduōrum,** gen. plur. of *Aeduī, -ōrum,* m.; connected by the conj. *et* with *Sēquanōrum,* and in the same grammatical construction. For description, see note on *Aeduō,* l. 20, Chap. III. —— **iter,** acc. sing. of the noun *iter, itineris,* n.; direct obj. of *facere.* —— **in,** prep. with acc. and abl.; here it takes the acc. *fīnēs.*

[LINES 4-7.]   BOOK I.   63

4 facere,	quī	nōn	longē	ā	Tolōsātium	ders of the San-
to make,	which	not	far	from	the Tolosates'	tones, which were not very far from
5 fīnibus	absunt,		quae	cīvitās	est in	the frontier of the Tolosates, a peo-
borders	are distant,		which	state	is in	ple who were liv-
6 prōvinciā.	Id	sī		fieret,	intellegēbat	ing in the province. Should this
the province.	That,	if,		should be done,	he saw	be done, Caesar perceived that it
7 māgnō	cum	perīculō	prōvinciae		futūrum,	would be attend-
great	with,	peril	of the province		(it) about to be	ed with great dan-

—— **Santonum**, gen. plur. of *Santonēs, -um*, m.; gen. limiting *fīnēs*. Sometimes the forms *Santonī, -ōrum* are given. The country of the Santones lay between the Loire and the Garonne. —— **fīnēs**, acc. plur. of the noun *fīnis, -is*, m.; the obj. of the prep. *in*. For the position of the obj. after a prep. if modified by a gen., etc., see A. & G. 344, *g*; B. 43; G. 413, REM. 3, and 678, REM. 4; H. 569, II, 3.

LINE 4. **facere**, pres. inf. act. of *faciō, facere, fēcī, factum*, 3; it with its modifiers is the subject-acc. of *esse*. —— **quī**, nom. plur. m. of the rel. *quī, quae, quod*; it refers to *Santonum*, as its antecedent, and is the subject-nom. of *absunt*. —— **nōn**, adv., qualifying adv. *longē*. —— **longē** (*longus*), comparative *longius*, superl. *longissimē*; it modifies *absunt*. —— **ā**, prep. with the abl. (*ā* before consonants, *ab* before either vowels or consonants). —— **Tolōsātium**, gen. plur. of the proper noun *Tolōsātēs, -ium*, m.; it, as a gen., limits *fīnibus*. These were a people of *Tolōsa*, modern Toulouse, in the department Haute-Garonne of modern France.

LINE 5. **fīnibus**, abl. plur. of *fīnis, -is*, m.; abl. after the prep. *ā*. —— **absunt**, 3d pers. plur. of the intrans. verb *absum, abesse, ab(ā)fuī, ab(ā)futūrus* (ab + sum); it agrees with its subject-nom. *quī*. —— **quae**, rel. pron., nom. sing. f.; it logically refers to *Tolōsātium*; it grammatically agrees with *cīvitās* in gender, number and case; in other words, it is subject-nom. of *est*. —— **cīvitās, -ātis**, f.; predicate-nom. after *est*. This species of attraction is a common Latin idiom. Consult A. & G. 199; B. 129, REM. 5; G. 616, 2; H. 445, 4. —— **est**, 3d pers. sing. pres. ind. of the intrans. verb *sum, esse, fuī, futūrus*; it agrees with its subject-nom. *quae*. —— **in**, prep. with the acc. and abl.; here it takes the abl.

LINE 6. **prōvinciā**, abl. of *prōvincia, -ae*, f.; it is the obj. of the prep. *in*. The Romans had a military colony at *Tolōsa*; but it is not strictly accurate to say that the tribe of the Tolosates were in the province. —— **Id**, nom. sing. n. of the dem. pron. *is, ea, id*, used substantively, and subj. of the verb *fieret*. The *id* = the purpose of the Helvetii to settle among the Santones. —— **sī**, conditional conj.; archaic form *seī*, sibilated from GK. εἰ. —— **fieret**, 3d pers. sing. imperf. subjunctive of *fīō, fīerī, factus*, used as pass. of *faciō*; it agrees with its subject-nom. *id*; is in the subjunctive after *sī* in the protasis. —— **intellegēbat**, 3d pers. sing. imperf. ind. act. of *intellego, -ere, -lēxī, -lēctum*, 3 (inter + legere) = lit. *to choose* or *select between*; it agrees with a pron. implied in the ending as its subject-nom., referring to Caesar.

LINE 7. **māgnō**, abl. sing. n. of adj. *māgnus, -a, -um*, comparative *māior*, superl. *māximus*; it is the attributive of *perīculō*. —— **cum**, prep. with the abl. —— **perīculō**, abl. of the noun *perīculum, -ī*, n.; abl. after the prep. *cum*. Observe, as to the position of the prep., that a monosyllabic prep. is often thus placed. See A. & G. 345, *a*; B. 58. 2; G. 413, REM. 2. —— **prōvinciae**, gen. sing. of *prōvincia, -ae*, f.;

ger to the prov-	ut	hominēs	bellicōsōs,	populī	Rōmānī 8
ince to have war-	*that*	*men*	*bellicose,*	*of the people*	*Roman*
like men and en-					
emies of the Ro-	inimīcōs,	locīs	patentibus		māximēque 9
man people as	*enemies,*	*in places*	*lying open*		*most and,*
neighbors, in an					
open country and	frūmentāriīs		finitimōs	habēret.	Ob 10
in a district espe-	*productive in grain*		*as neighbors (it) would have.*		*For*
cially fruitful in					
grain. For these	eās	causās	eī	mūnitiōnī,	quam fēcerat, 11
reasons he put	*these*	*reasons*	*over that*	*fortification*	*which he had made,*
Titus Labienus,					

---

gen. objective, limiting *perīculō*. Consult A. & G. 217; B. 131, REM. 2; G. 363, 2; H. 396, III. —— **futūrum (esse)**, fut. inf. of the intrans. verb *sum*, *esse*, *fuī*, fut. participle *futūrus*; it is used here impersonally; but strictly its subject-acc. is the result-clause *ut . . . habēret*. Consult A. & G. 329, and NOTE; B. 201, and REM. 1, (*c*); G. 506; H. 501, I, 1.

LINE 8. **ut**, ecbatic conj. —— **hominēs**, acc. plur. of *homō*, *-inis*, m. and f.; direct obj. of *habēret*, l. 10, below. Synonyms: *homō* = man in the generic sense, including woman; whereas *vir* (digammated from the GK. pron. *Ϝε* = *he*) denotes the male person, the man of valor, GK. ἀνήρ. —— **bellicōsōs**, acc. plur. m. of the adj. *bellicōsus*, *-a*, *-um* (*bellicus*, bellum + ōsus). Note that words ending in *-ōsus* and *-ōsus* denote fulness. *bellicōsōs* is an attributive of *hominēs*. —— **populī**, gen. sing. of *populus*, *-ī*, m.; gen. objective after *inimīcōs*. Consult A. & G. 234, *d*, 1; B. 144, REM. 3; G. 359, REM. 1; H. 391, II, 4. For synonyms, see note on *populum*, l. 17, Chap. VI. —— **Rōmānī**, gen. sing. m. of the adj. *Rōmānus*, *-a*, *-um*; it is an attributive of *populī*.

LINE 9. **inimīcōs**, acc. plur. m. of the adj. *inimīcus*, *-a -um* (in, *not* + amīcus, *friendly*); used here as a subst. in apposition with, and an explanatory modifier, of *hominēs*. Observe that, as an adj., *inimīcus* takes the dat. —— **locīs**, abl. plur. of *locus*, *-ī*, m. in the sing., but m. or n. in the plur.; i.e. either *locī* or *loca*. See note on *locī*, l. 10, Chap. II. *locīs* is locative abl. Consult A. & G. 258, *f*, 1; B. 170, REM. 3; G. 385, NOTE 1; H. 425, II, 2. —— **patentibus**, abl. plur. of the pres. participle *patēns*, used as an adj., of the verb *pateō*, *-ēre*, *-uī*, no supine, 2; as an adj. it modifies *locīs*. —— **māximēque** (māximē + que). *māximē* is the superl. of the comparative *magis*; *multum* is sometimes used as the positive. *māximē* modifies the adj. *frūmentāriīs*. Observe that adjectives in *-us* preceded by a vowel are usually compared by prefixing the adverbs *magis*, more, and *māximē*, most. See A. & G. 89, *d*; B. 74, 4; G. 87. 6; H. 170.

LINE 10. **frūmentāriīs**, abl. plur. of the adj. *frūmentārius*, *-a*, *-um* (*frūmentum*, grain); connected by the enclitic conj. *-que* with *patentibus*, and in the same grammatical construction. —— **finitimōs**, acc. plur. m. of the adj. *finitimus*, *-a*, *-um* (*finis*, border); used here as a subst., and is predicate-acc. after *habēret*. See A. & G. 239, 1; B. 151, (*b*); G. 340, (*b*), and REM. 1; H. 373, 1, and NOTE 1. —— **habēret**, 3d pers. sing. imperf. subjunctive act. of *habeō*, *-ēre*, *-uī*, *-itum*, 2; its subject-nom. is *prōvincia*, to be supplied; subjunctive of result after *ut*, l. 8, above. —— **Ob**, prep. with the acc.

LINE 11. **eās**, acc. plur. f. of the dem. pron. *is*, *ea*, *id*; it is an attributive of the noun *causās*. —— **causās**, acc. plur. of *causa*, *-ae*, f.; obj. of the prep. *ob*. Observe

						his lieutenant, in
12 T. Labiēnum	lēgātum	praefēcit;		ipse	in	command of the
Titus Labienus,	*lieutenant,*	*he placed;*		*he himself*	*into*	line of fortifica-
13 Italiam	māgnīs	itineribus	contendit	duāsque		tions that he had constructed,
Italy	*by great*	*marches*	*hastens,*	*two and,*		while he him-

that the reference in the phrase *ob eās causās* is to the considerations specified in the preceding sentence; and that *ob* with the acc. is used instead of the abl. of cause, because the *object* exciting the feeling is thus expressed. See A. & G. 245, 2, *b*; B. 165, REM. 4; G. 408, 3; H. 416, I, 2). *Ōrātiō rēcta* of lines 6–10, above: Id sī *fīet* māgnō cum perīculō prōvinciae *erit* ut . . . (prōvincia) *habeat.* Observe that as this conditional sentence depends on *intellegēbat*, a past tense, the periphrastic fut. is carried into the past. The fut. tense in the protasis becomes the imperf. subjunctive; and the pres. subjunctive in the result-clause is also changed to the imperf. subjunctive. Consult A. & G. 288, *f*; B. 196, (*b*); G. 248; H. 537, 3. —— ei, dat. f. of the dem. pron. *is, ea, id;* it is an attributive of *mūnitiōnī*. —— mūnitiōnī, dat. sing. of *mūnitiō, -ōnis,* f. (*mūnīre,* to fortify); dat. after *prae* in *praefēcit.* See A. & G. 228; B. 143; G. 347; H. 386. For description of this fortification, read again Chap. VIII. —— quam, acc. sing. f. of the rel. pron. *quī, quae, quod;* it refers to *mūnitiōnī* as its antecedent, but it is the direct obj. of *fēcerat.* —— fēcerat, 3d pers. sing. pluperf. ind. act. of *faciō, -ere, fēcī, factum,* 3; it agrees with a pron. implied in its ending as its subject-nom., referring to Caesar.

LINE 12. T., an abbreviation for *Titum,* acc. sing. of *Titus, -ī,* m.; praenōmen of *Labiēnum,* and in the same grammatical construction. —— Labiēnum, acc. sing. of *Labiēnus, -ī,* m. (cōgnōmen); direct obj. of *praefēcit.* Observe that trans. compounds have the direct obj. as well as the dat. depending on the prep. in the compound. See A. & G. 228, NOTE 1, end; B. 143, end; G. 347, immediately after the list of prepositions; H. 386, 1. Titus Attius Labienus was Caesar's most trusted legatus in the Gallic War. He subsequently, however, in the Civil War sided with Pompey, and was slain at Munda, 45 B.C. Among Caesar's other legates in the Gallic War were Sabīnus, C. Trēbōnius and Quīntus Cicero. The reader will observe that *lēgātus* is a word of somewhat flexible meaning. At one time *lēgātus* = *a leader of an army-corps;* at another it = *an ambassador.* The context must give the clew to its meaning. —— lēgātum, acc. sing. of *lēgātus, -ī,* m.; predicate-acc. See grammatical references to *fīnitimōs,* l. 10, above. —— praefēcit, 3d pers. sing. perf. ind. act. of *praeficiō, -ere, -fēcī, -fectum,* 3; it agrees with Caesar understood as subject-nom. —— ipse, intensive dem. pron. (is + pse) = *self;* it refers to Caesar, and is subject-nom. of *contendit.* —— in, prep. with the acc. and abl.; here it takes the acc. after a verb of motion.

LINE 13. Italiam, acc. sing. of *Italia, -ae,* f., and is the obj. of the prep. *in.* Sometimes in Caesar's Commentaries *in Italiam* = *in Galliam Cisalpīnam,* the plain of the Po, northern Italy. Cisalpine Gaul was one of the provinces given to Caesar by the senate and Roman people; the other provinces given him were Transalpine Gaul and Illyricum. —— māgnīs, abl. plur. n. of the adj. *māgnus, -a, -um;* comparative *māior,* superl. *māximus; māgnīs* modifies *itineribus.* —— itineribus, abl. plur. of *iter, itineris,* n.; abl. of manner. See A. & G. 248; B. 168; G. 399; H. 419, III. The Roman army's ordinary day's march was fifteen miles; the extraordinary, twenty or twenty-five. —— contendit, 3d pers. sing. pres. ind. act. of *contendō, -ere, -tendī, -tentum,* 3; it agrees with its subject-nom. *ipse.* For etymolog-

self hastened in-	ibi	legiōnēs	cōnscrībit	et	trēs,	quae	14
to Italy by forced marches,	*there,*	*legions*	*levies*	*and*	*three,*	*which*	
and there enrolled two legions; and led	circum	Aquilēiam		hiemābant,		ex	15
out of their winter-quarters the	*around*	*Aquileia*		*were wintering*		*from*	
three legions that had been passing	hībernīs		ēdūcit,	et,	quā	proximum	16
the winter near Aquileia, and	*winter-quarters*		*leads out,*	*and*	*where*	*nearest*	
marched quickly	iter	in	ūlteriōrem		Galliam	per	17
	the route	*into*	*ulterior*		*Gaul*	*through*	

ical and different meaning, see note on *contendunt*, l. 18, Chap. I. —— **duāsque** (duās + que). *duās*, acc. plur. f. of cardinal num. *duo, -ae, -o ;* it is an attributive of *legiōnēs*. Note that of the cardinals up to *centum*, only *ūnus, duo* and *trēs* are declined.

LINE 14. **ibi**, adv., modifies *cōnscrībit*. Observe that *ibi* is formed thus: i + bi; i.e. by adding the locative case-form *bi* to *i*, the root of *is*; hence *ibi* = *in that place*, *there*. —— **legiōnēs**, acc. plur. of *legiō, -ōnis*, f.; direct obj. of *cōnscrībit*. As to the Roman legion, consult the article under *Legion* in any of the encyclopedias. —— **cōnscrībit**, 3d pers. sing. pres. ind. act. of *cōnscrībō, -ere, -scrīpsī, -scrīptum*, 3; connected by the enclitic *-que* with *contendit*, and in the same grammatical construction. —— **trēs**, num. adj. cardinal, acc. plur.; it modifies *legiōnēs* understood, which latter, as understood, is the direct obj. of *ēdūcit*. These three legions were the seventh, eighth and ninth. —— **quae**, nom. plur. f. of the rel. pron. *quī, quae, quod;* it refers to *legiōnēs* understood, and is subject-nom. of *hiemābant*.

LINE 15. **circum**, prep. and adv.; here a prep. with the acc. —— **Aquilēiam**, acc. sing. of *Aquilēia, -ae*, f.; the obj. of the prep. *circum*. Aquileia was a colony in Venetia, at the head of the Adriatic gulf, not far from the modern Trieste. —— **hiemābant**, 3d pers. plur. imperf. ind. act. of *hiemō, -āre, -āvī, -ātum*, 1 (*hiems;* compare GK. χεῖμα, χειμών); it agrees with its subject-nom. *quae*. —— **ex**, prep. with the abl. (*ē* before consonants only, *ex* before vowels and consonants).

LINE 16. **hībernīs**, abl. plur. n. of the adj. *hibernus, -a, -um;* supply *castrīs*, of which *hībernīs* is an attributive. —— **ēdūcit**, 3d pers. sing. pres. ind. act. of *ēdūcō, -ere, -dūxī, -ductum*, 3 (ē + dūcere); *ēdūcit* agrees with its subj. implied in the ending, referring to Caesar. —— **et**, cop. conj., connects the verbs *ēdūcit* and *contendit*, l. 19, below. Caesar led these legions up the Po valley by way of Turin and Mount Genèvre through to the Rhone. —— **quā**, adv., strictly an abl. f. of the rel. pron. *quī, quae, quod;* supply *viā*. Consult A. & G. 148, *e*; B. 117. 6, end; G. 91, 2, (*e*); H. 304, II, 2, and foot-note 10. —— **proximum**, nom. sing. n. of the adj. *proximus, -a, -um:* comparative *propior*, no positive; *proximum* is predicate-adj. after *erat;* it = lit. *nearest*.

LINE 17. **iter**, nom. sing. n.; subj. of *erat*. For synonyms, see note on *itinera*, l. 1, Chap. VI. —— **in**, prep. with the acc. and abl.; here it takes the acc. —— **ūlteriōrem**, acc. sing. f. of the comparative *ūlterior, -us;* no positive; superl. *ūltimus; ūlteriōrem* is an attributive of *Galliam*. —— **Galliam**, acc. sing. of *Gallia, -ae*, f.; it is the obj. of the prep. *in*. Observe that *ūlterior Gallia* = *Gallia Trānsalpīna*, with Rome as the *ā quō terminus*. —— **per**, prep. with the acc.

						with these five legions by the shortest route through the Alps into farther Gaul. On this march the Ceutrones, the Graioceli and the Caturiges seized the higher places and attempted to keep our
18 Alpēs	erat,	cum	his	quīnque	legiōnibus	
the Alps	*was,*	*with*	*these*	*five*	*legions*	
19 īre	contendit.	Ibi	Ceutrōnēs	et	Grāiocelī	
to go	*hastens.*	*There*	*the Ceutrones*	*and*	*the Graioceli*	
20 et	Caturigēs,	locīs	superiōribus		occupātīs,	
and	*the Caturiges,*	*places*	*higher*		*having been seized,*	
21 itinere		exercitum	prohibēre		cōnantur.	
from the route		*the army*	*to prohibit*		*attempt.*	

LINE 18. **Alpēs**, acc. plur. of *Alpēs, -ium*, f.; sometimes used in the sing. *Alpis, -is; Alpēs* is here the obj. of the prep. *per.* The derivation of *Alpēs*, GK. Ἄλπεις from the Latin adj. *albus*, white, because of the perpetual snow on their summits, is plausible. —— **erat**, 3d pers. sing. imperf. ind. of *sum, esse, fuī, futūrus*; it agrees with its subject-nom. *iter.* —— **cum**, prep. with the abl. *his.* —— **his**, abl. plur. f. of the dem. pron. *hīc, haec, hōc;* it is an attributive of *legiōnibus.* Observe that *his* denotes that the legions have just been mentioned. Consult A. & G. 102, *a* and *f;* B. 84, 1; G. 305; H. 450, 1. —— **quīnque**, num. adj. cardinal; it modifies *legiōnibus.* —— **legiōnibus**, abl. plur. of the noun *legiō, -ōnis*, f.; abl. of accompaniment. See A. & G. 248, *a*; B. 168, REM. 4; G. 392; H. 419, I.

LINE 19. **īre**, pres. inf. act. of *eō, īre, īvī (iī), itum;* complementary inf. A. & G. 271, and NOTE; B. 181; G. 423; H. 533, I, 1. —— **contendit**, 3d pers. sing. pres. ind. act. of *contendō, -ere, -tendī, -tentum*, 3; it agrees with a pron. implied in its ending as its subject-nom., referring to Caesar. For composition and various meanings, see note on *contendunt*, l. 18, Chap. I. —— **Ibi**, adv. = *there;* it points to the region of modern Savoy and Provence, the home of the Alpine clans *Ceutrōnēs*, *Caturigēs* and *Grāiocelī.* —— **Ceutrōnēs**, -um, nom. plur. m., subj. of *cōnantur.* —— **Grāiocelī**, -ōrum, nom. plur. m., connected by *et* with *Ceutrōnēs*, and in the same grammatical construction.

LINE 20. **Caturigēs**, -um, nom. plur. m., connected by *et* with *Grāiocelī*, and disposed of in the same way. —— **locīs**, abl. plur. of *locus, -ī*, m., plur. *locī*, m., or *loca*, n. See note on *locī*, l. 10, Chap. II. *locīs* is in the abl. absolute with the perf. pass. participle *occupātīs.* —— **superiōribus**, abl. plur. of the comparative adj. *superior, -us;* superl. *suprēmus* or *summus.* A positive *posterus* is used generally as a noun in the plur. meaning *posterity. superiōribus* modifies *locīs.* —— **occupātīs**, abl. plur. of the perf. pass. participle *occupātus, -a, -um* of the verb *occupō, -āre, -āvī, -ātum*, 1 (ob + capere, lit. = *to lay hold of*); hence *occupāre* = *to seize, to occupy* a thing. *occupātīs* is in the abl. absolute with the noun *locīs.* See A. & G. 255; B. 192; G. 409; H. 431.

LINE 21. **itinere**, abl. sing. of the noun *iter, itineris*, n.; abl. of separation after *prohibēre.* See A. & G. 243; B. 160; G. 390, 2; H. 414, I. —— **exercitum**, acc. sing. of *exercitus, -ūs*, m.; direct obj. of *prohibēre.* For synonyms, see note on *exercitū*, l. 31, Chap. III. —— **prohibēre**, pres. inf. act. of *prohibeō, -ēre, -uī, -itum*, 2 (pro + habēre), lit. = *to hold off* or *from; prohibēre* is a complementary inf. depending on *cōnantur.* A. & G. 271, and NOTE; B. 181; G. 423; H. 533, I, 1. —— **cōnantur**, 3d pers. plur. pres. ind. of the deponent verb *cōnor -ārī, -ātus*, 1; it agrees with its subjects *Ceutrōnēs* and *Grāiocelī* and *Caturigēs.*

68 CAESAR'S GALLIC WAR [CHAP. X.

army from the road. After routing these people in several skirmishes, Caesar reached the frontier of the Vocontii in the farther province on the seventh day from Ocelum, which is the furthermost	Complūribus *In very many,*	hīs *these,*	proeliīs *battles,*	pulsīs, *having been routed,*	ab 23 *from*
	Ocelō, *Ocelum,*	quod *which*	est *is*	citeriōris *of the citerior*	prōvinciae 23 *province*
	extrēmum, *the farthest (town),*	in *to*		fīnēs *the borders*	Vocontiōrum 24 *of the Vocontii*
	ulteriōris *of the ulterior*		prōvinciae *province,*	diē *on day*	septimō 25 *the seventh*

LINE 22. **Complūribus,** abl. plur. n. of *complūres, -plūra* (-*ia*) (con, *intensive* + *plūs*); it agrees with *proeliīs.* —— **hīs,** abl. plur. m. of the dem. pron. *hīc, haec, hōc,* used substantively as a personal pron. of the 3d pers.; abl. absolute with the perf. pass. participle *pulsīs.* —— **proeliīs,** abl. plur. of *proelium, -ī,* n.; locative abl., really an abl. of means. But see A. & G. 254, *a*; B. 170, REM. 4; G. 389; H. 425, II, 1, 1). Note the synchysis or confusion in the order of the words: *hīs,* which is connected with *pulsīs* in the abl. absolute construction, being inserted between *proeliīs* and its attributive *complūribus.* —— **pulsīs,** abl. plur. of the perf. pass. participle *pulsus, -a, -um* of the verb *pellō, -ere, pepulī, pulsum,* 3; abl. absolute with the pron. *hīs.* —— **ab,** prep. with the abl. (*ā* before consonants, *ab* before vowels or consonants).

LINE 23. **Ocelō,** abl. sing. of *Ocelum, -ī,* n. Ocelum was an Alpine town in *Gallia citerior,* southwest of Turin. —— **quod,** nom. sing. n. of the rel. pron. *quī, quae, quod;* it relates to *Ocelō* as its antecedent, but is subject-nom. of *est.* —— **est,** 3d pers. sing. pres. ind. of the intrans. verb *sum, esse, fuī, futūrus;* it agrees with its subject-nom. *quod.* —— **citeriōris,** gen. sing. f. of the adj. *citerior, -us,* comparative degree; superl. *citimus. citeriōris* is an attributive of *prōvinciae.* For the list of five every-day adjectives that want the positive, see A. & G. 91, *a*; B. 74, 1; G. 87. 8; H. 166. —— **prōvinciae,** gen. sing. of *prōvincia, -ae,* f.; it limits *oppidum,* to be supplied.

LINE 24. **extrēmum,** nom. sing. n. of the adj. *extrēmus, -a, -um;* it modifies *oppidum* understood, which latter is the predicate-noun after *est. extrēmum* is the superl. degree of the positive *exterus,* comparative *exterior,* superl. *extrēmus* or *extimus.* Consult A. & G. 91, *b*; B. 72, 4; G. 87, 2 and 7; H. 163, 3. Ocelum was the extreme western town in *Gallia Cisalpīna,* from Rome as the *terminus ā quō.* —— **in,** prep. with the acc. or abl.; here it takes the acc. —— **fīnēs,** acc. plur. of the noun *fīnis, -is,* m.; it is the obj. of the prep. *in.* For synonyms, see note on *agrum,* l. 12, Chap. II. —— **Vocontiōrum,** gen. plur. of *Vocontiī, -ōrum,* m.; it limits, as a gen., *fīnēs.* The Vocontii were a people of Gaul, living east of the Rhine river, and about a hundred miles from its mouth. Their principal town was Dea, now Die.

LINE 25. **ulteriōris,** gen. sing. f. of the comparative adj. *ulterior, -us,* superl. *ultimus;* it wants the positive. But the comparative and superl. are from the adv. *ultrā,* beyond. See grammatical references to *citeriōris,* l. 23, above; *ulteriōris* modifies *prōvinciae.* —— **prōvinciae,** gen. sing. of *prōvincia, -ae,* f.; it, as a gen., limits *Vicontiōrum.* The ulterior province is the Roman province or *Gallia Trānsalpīna.* —— **diē,** abl. sing. m. of *diēs, diēī;* abl. of *time when.* See A. & G. 256, 1; B. 171; G. 393; H. 429. —— **septimō,** abl. sing. of the ordinal num. adj. *septimus, -a, -um;* it agrees with the noun *diē.*

26 pervenit;	inde	in	Allobrogum		fīnēs,	town from Rome in the hither province. Thence he led his army into the country of the Allobroges, and from the Allobroges to the country of the Segusiavi. These are the first people beyond the province across the Rhone.
he arrives;	*thence*	*into*	*the Allobroges'*		*territory,*	
27 ab	Allobrogibus		in		Segusiāvōs	
from	*the Allobroges*		*into*		*the Segusiavi*	
28 exercitum	dūcit.		Hī	sunt	extrā	
the army	*he leads.*		*These*	*are*	*outside*	
29 prōvinciam	trāns		Rhodanum	prīmī.		
of the province,	*across*		*the Rhone,*	*the first (people).*		

LINE 26. **pervenit**, 3d pers. sing. pres. ind. act. of *perveniō, -īre, -vēnī, -ventum*, 4 (per + venīre). *pervenīre* = lit. *to come through. pervenit* is an historical pres.; it agrees with Caesar understood as its subject-nom. — **inde** (derived from is + adverbial termination de); hence = lit. *from that place.* — **in**, prep. with the acc. and abl.; here it takes the acc. — **Allobrogum**, gen. plur. of the proper noun *Allobrogès, -um*, m.; as a gen. it limits *fīnēs*. Observe that *Allobrogum* is embodied in the phrase, and consult A. & G. 344, *g*; B. 43; G. 413, REM. 3, and 678, REM. 4; H. 569, II, 3. — **fīnēs**, acc. plur. of the noun *fīnis, -is*, m.; obj. of the prep. *in*. But note that the phrase *in Allobrogum fīnēs* is an adverbial modifier of *dūcit*, which with its direct obj. is to be supplied from the following line; in other words, with this *terminus ad quem* phrase supply *exercitum dūcit*. As to the Allobroges, see note on *Allobrogum*, l. 10, Chap. VI.

LINE 27. **ab**, prep. with the abl. (*ā* before consonants, *ab* before vowels or consonants, *abs* before pron. *tē* and the enclitic conj. *-que*). Observe the omission of the cop. conj. between the clauses (asyndeton); and consult A. & G. 346, *c*; B. 123, REM. 6; G. 474, NOTE; H. 636, I, 1. — **Allobrogibus**, abl. plur. of *Allobrogès, -um*; abl. after the prep. *ab*. — **in**, prep. with the acc. or abl.; here it takes the acc. after a verb of motion, and = *into*. — **Segusiāvōs**, acc. plur. of *Segusiāvī, -ōrum*, m.; obj. of the prep. *in*. The *Segusiāvī* were a clan whose territory lay west of the Rhone, and whose principal town was *Lugdūnum*, the modern Lyons.

LINE 28. **exercitum**, acc. sing. of *exercitus, -ūs*, m.; direct obj. of *dūcit*. For synonyms, see note on *exercitū*, l. 31, Chap. III. — **dūcit**, 3d pers. sing. pres. ind. act. of *dūcō, -ere, dūxī, ductum*, 3; it agrees with its subject-nom. *Caesar*, to be supplied. — **Hī**, nom. plur. m. of the dem. pron. *hīc, haec, hōc*; used substantively expressed for emphasis, and also to indicate that the reference is to the last mentioned people. Consult A. & G. 102, *a* and *f*; B. 84, 1; G. 305; H. 450, 1. *Hī* is the subject-nom. of *sunt*. — **sunt**, 3d pers. plur. pres. ind. of the neuter or intrans. verb *sum, esse, fuī, futūrus*; it agrees with its subject-nom. *Hī*. — **extrā**, prep. with the acc.; sometimes an adv. (contracted from *exterā*, abl. of the adj. *exter*).

LINE 29. **prōvinciam**, acc. sing. of the noun *prōvincia, -ae*, f.; it is the obj. of the prep. *extrā*. — **trāns**, prep. with the acc. — **Rhodanum**, acc. sing. of *Rhodanus, -ī*, m.; obj. of the prep. *trāns*. Caesar's purpose was to confront the Helvetii, who were advancing westward, and had already reached the territory of the Aedui. *trāns Rhodanum* = towards the west, as the Rhone at Lyons turns to the south. — **prīmī**, nom. plur. m. of the adj. *prīmus, -a, -um*; supply *populī*, as predicate-nom. after *sunt*, with which *prīmī* agrees.

XI. The Helvetii had already led their forces through the narrow pass and the country of the Sequani, and had arrived at the borders of the Aedui, and were ravaging their	XI. Helvētiī *The Helvetii* fīnēs *the territory* et *and* eōrumque *of them and,*	iam *now* Sēquanōrum *of the Sequani* in *into* agrōs *the fields*	per *through* suās *their* Aeduōrum *the Aeduan* populābantur. *were laying waste.*	angustiās *the narrow pass* cōpiās *forces* fīnēs *territory*	et 1 *and* trādūxerant 2 *had led* pervēnerant 3 *had arrived* Aeduī, 4 *The Aedui,*

LINE 1. **Helvētiī**, nom. plur. m. of the adj. *Helvētius, -a, -um*, used as a subst., and subj. of *trādūxerant*. For description of the clan, see note on *Helvētiī*, l. 16, Chap. I. —— **iam**, adv. = *now*, of any action pres., past or fut.; whereas *nunc* emphasizes the present time. —— **per**, prep. with the acc. —— **angustiās**, acc. plur. of noun *angustiae, -ārum*, f.; it is the obj. of the prep. *per*. The pass referred to is the Pas de l'Ecluse.

LINE 2. **fīnēs**, acc. plur. of noun *fīnis, -is*, m.; it is connected by the conj. *et* with *angustiās*, and is in the same grammatical construction. For synonyms, see note on *agrum*, l. 12, Chap. II. —— **Sēquanōrum**, gen. plur. of *Sēquanī, -ōrum*, m.; it limits *fīnēs*. For description, see note on *Sēquanīs*, l. 25, Chap. I. —— **suās**, acc. plur. f. of the poss. and direct-reflexive pron. *suus, -a, -um*; it agrees with *cōpiās*, but refers to the subj. *Helvētiī*. —— **cōpiās**, acc. plur. of the noun *cōpia, -ae*, f.; direct obj. of *trādūxerant*. Observe that *cōpia* in the sing. = *plenty;* in the plur., *resources* or *troops*. —— **trādūxerant**, 3d pers. plur. pluperf. ind. act. of *trādūco, -ere, -dūxī, -ductum*, 3 (trāns + dūcere); it agrees with its subject-nom. *Helvētiī*.

LINE 3. **in**, prep. with the acc. or abl.; here it takes the acc.; after verbs of motion *in* with the acc. = *into*. See note on *in*, l. 1, end, Chap. I. —— **Aeduōrum**, gen. plur. of *Aeduī, -ōrum*, m.; as a gen. it limits *fīnēs*. For its position, between the prep. and its obj., see A. & G. 344, *g*; B. 43; G. 413, REM. 3, and 678, REM. 4; H. 569, II, 3. —— **fīnēs**, acc. plur. of *fīnis, -is*, m.; obj. of the prep. *in*. —— **pervēnerant**, 3d pers. plur. pluperf. ind. act. of *perveniō, -īre, -vēnī, -ventum*, 4 (per + venīre); connected by the conj. *et* with *trādūxerant*, and in the same grammatical construction.

LINE 4. **eōrumque** (eōrum + que). *eōrum*, gen. plur. of the dem. pron. *is, ea, id*, used as a personal pron. of the 3d pers. *eōrum* refers to *Aeduōrum*, but limits *agrōs*. *que*, enclitic conj.; connects very closely the clauses. —— **agrōs**, acc. plur. of the noun *ager, agrī*, m.; direct obj. of the deponent verb *populābantur*. For synonyms, see note on *agrum*, l. 12, Chap. II. —— **populābantur**, 3d pers. plur. imperf. ind. of *populor, -ārī, -ātus*, 1 (derived from *populus*), hence *populārī* = to spread out in a multitude over a place; and so, transf. = *to ravage*, etc. Observe that the act. form *populō, -āre* is sometimes used. *populābantur* is connected by the enclitic conj. *que* with *pervēnerant*, and also agrees with *Helvētiī*, as its subject-nom. The Helvetii were devastating the fields of the Aedui, because the latter were allies of Rome. —— **Aeduī**, nom. plur. of the adj. *Aeduus, -a, -um*, used as a subst.; subj. of *mittunt*, l. 6, below. Compare GK. Ἔδουοι, and Αἴδουοι, and especially Ἐδουεῖς, of the paraphrast; and observe the aspirate, from which comes the form *Hedui*, occurring in some editions. For description of this clan, see note on *Aeduō*, l. 20, Chap. III. Note the emphatic position of *Aeduī*, as it precedes the conj. *cum*.

5 cum	sē	suaque	ab	eīs	dēfendere	fields. The Ae-
since	*themselves*	*their own and,*	*from*	*them*	*to defend*	dui, inasmuch as they could not de-
6 nōn possent,	lēgātōs	ad·	Caesarem		mittunt	fend themselves and their proper-
not were able,	*delegates*	*to*	*Caesar*		*send*	ty, sent ambassa- dors to Caesar to
7 rogātum	auxilium:		Ita	sē·	omnī	ask for help, who
to solicit	*aid:*		*So*	*themselves*	*at every*	said: they had, on every occasion,
8 tempore	dē	populō	Rōmānō	meritōs esse,		so served the
time	*from*	*the people*	*Roman*	*to have deserved,*		interests of the

LINE 5. **cum**, conj., denoting here both time and cause. —— **sē**, acc. plur. of the reflexive pron. *suī, sibi, sē, sē,* the same case-forms occurring in both sing. and plur.; the number to be determined by the context; here *sē* is direct obj. of *dēfendere.* —— **suaque** (sua + que). *sua,* acc. plur. n. of poss. pron. *suus, -a, -um,* used substantively, or the English word *things* may be supplied. Consult A. & G. 189, *b*; B. 59, REM.; G. 204, NOTE 2; H. 441. *sua* is connected with the pron. *sē* by the enclitic conj. *-que,* and is also a direct obj. of *dēfendere.* —— **ab**, prep. with the abl. (*ab* before vowels or consonants, *ā* before consonants only). —— **eīs**, abl. plur. of the dem. pron. *is, ea, id,* used as a personal pron. of the 3d pers.; it is the obj. of the prep. *ab;* it refers to the Helvetii. —— **dēfendere**, pres. inf. act. of *dēfendō, -ere, -fendī, -fēnsum,* 3 (dē + fendere, a prim. word, used only in compounds); hence *dēfendere = to ward off. dēfendere* is here a complementary inf., depending on *possent.* See A. & G. 271, and NOTE; B. 181; G. 423; H. 533, I, 2.

LINE 6. **nōn**, adv. (nĕ + oenum or ūnum); observe its natural Latin position: immediately before the word it modifies. —— **possent**, 3d pers. plur. imperf. sub- junctive of *possum, posse, potuī* (potis, *able* + sum); its subject-nom. is *eī* understood, referring to the Aedui; subjunctive after *cum* denoting both time and cause. A. & G. 326; B. 223; G. 586; H. 517. —— **lēgātōs**, acc. plur. of *lēgātus, -ī,* m. (*legere,* to despatch); direct obj. of *mittunt.* —— **ad**, prep. with the acc., used after a verb of motion. —— **Caesarem**, acc. sing. of *Caesar, -aris,* m.; obj. of the prep. *ad.* —— **mittunt**, 3d pers. plur. pres. ind. act. of *mittere, mīsī, missum,* 3; it agrees with *Aeduī,* l. 4, above.

LINE 7. **rogātum**, former supine of the verb *rogō, -āre, -āvī, -ātum,* 1, denoting purpose. Consult A. & G. 302; B. 186 (A); G. 435; H. 546. Observe that the supine in *-um* is used after verbs of motion. —— **auxilium**, acc. of *auxilium, -ī,* n.; direct obj. of the supine *rogātum.* Observe that supines in *-um* are followed by the same case as their verbs. —— **Ita**, adv. (radical *i,* whence is + ta); correlate of the conj. *ut,* l. 9, below. —— **sē**, acc. plur. of the reflexive pron. *suī, sibi, sē, sē;* subject- acc. of *meritōs esse.* Observe that *ita sē* introduces the indirect form of discourse here, which, as principal clause, depends on *dīcentēs,* to be supplied from *mittunt rogātum.* —— **omnī**, abl. sing. n. of the adj. *omnis, -e;* it is an attributive of *tempore.*

LINE 8. **tempore**, abl. sing. of *tempus, -oris,* n.; abl. of *time when.* Consult A. & G. 256, 1; B. 171; G. 393; H. 429. For derivation, see note on *tempore,* l. 21, Chap. III. —— **dē**, prep. with the abl. —— **populō**, abl. sing. of the noun *populus, -ī,* m.; obj. of the prep. *dē.* —— **Rōmānō**, abl. sing. m. of the adj. *Rōmānus, -a, -um;* it is an attributive of *populō.* —— **meritōs esse**, perf. inf. of the deponent verb *mereor, merērī, meritus,* 2; it agrees with its subject-acc. *sē,* l. 7, above. Observe

Roman people, that their fields ought not to be laid waste, their children led into captivity, and their towns taken by storm almost within sight of our army. At the same time the Ambarri, in-	ut *that*	paene *almost*	in *in*	cōnspectū *sight*	exercitūs *of army*	nostrī *our,*	9
	agrī *fields*	vāstārī, *to be laid waste,*		līberī *children*	eōrum *of them*	in servitūtem *into slavery*	10
	abdūcī, *to be led,*	oppida *towns*		expūgnārī *to be stormed*		nōn dēbuerint. *not ought.*	11
	Eōdem *At the same*	tempore *time*		Ambarri, *the Ambarri,*	necessāriī *close friends*	et *and*	12

that the participial form of this compound is in the acc. plur. m., agreeing thus with its subject-acc. in gender, number and case.

LINE 9. **ut**, ecbatic conj. here. —— **paene**, adv., comparative wanting, superl. *paenissimē*; this adv. here seems to modify the phrase *in cōnspectū.* —— **in**, prep. with the acc. or abl.; here it takes the abl. —— **cōnspectū**, abl. sing. of the noun *cōnspectus, -ūs*, m.; it is the obj. of the prep. *in.* Synonyms: *cōnspectus* = *the sight of*; *adspectus* = the act of *seeing*; in other words: *cōnspectus* has a passive meaning, *adspectus*, an active. —— **exercitūs**, gen. sing. of *exercitus, -ūs*, m.; it limits *cōnspectū.* For synonyms, see note on *exercitū*, l. 31, Chap. III. —— **nostrī**, gen. sing. m. of the poss. pron. *noster, -tra, -trum*; it is an attributive of *exercitūs.* Caesar, as the reporter of the Aeduan ambassadors' words, should have written *tuī* or *vestrī*, i.e. your army, the Roman army. Possibly, however, as the Aedui were the allies of the Romans, they might call the Roman army *our* army.

LINE 10. **agrī**, nom. plur. of the noun *ager, agrī*, m.; subj. of *dēbuerint*, l. 11, below. —— **vāstārī**, pres. inf. pass. of *vāstō, -āre, -āvī, -ātum*, 1; complementary, depending on *dēbuerint*, l. 11, below. —— **līberī**, nom. plur. of the adj. *līber, -era, -erum*, used substantively; subject-nom. of *dēbuerint*, to be supplied. Observe that *līberī* = *children*, in contrast with *servī*, the domestics. —— **eōrum**, gen. plur. of the dem. pron. *is, ea, id*, used as a personal pron. of the 3d pers.; as a gen. it limits *līberī.* —— **in**, prep. with the acc. or abl.; here it takes the acc. —— **servitūtem**, acc. sing. of the noun *servitūs, -ūtis*, f. (*servus*); it is the obj. of the prep. *in.*

LINE 11. **abdūcī**, pres. inf. pass. of *abdūcō, -ere, -dūxī, -ductum*, 3; complementary inf., depending on *dēbuerint* understood. —— **oppida**, nom. plur. of *oppidum, -ī*, n.; subj. of *dēbuerint* understood. —— **expūgnārī**, pres. inf. pass. of *expūgnō, -āre, -āvī, -ātum*, 1; complementary inf., depending on *dēbuerint* understood. —— **nōn**, adv. neg., modifying *dēbuerint.* Note that *nōn dēbuerint* are expressed only with the first dependent clause, and that they are to be supplied with the remaining dependent clauses. —— **dēbuerint**, 3d pers. plur. perf. subjunctive of *dēbeō, -ēre, -uī, -itum*, 2 (dē + habēre); hence *dēbēre* = *to have from* a person, and so owe him something. *dēbuerint* is subjunctive of result after *ut*, referring to *ita.* A. & G. 319, 1, and REM.; B. 201, (*b*), and REM. 1, (*a*); G. 552; H. 500, II. As to tense-sequence, see A. & G. 287, *c*; B. 190, REM. 1; G. 513; H. 495, VI. *Orātiō rēcta* of lines 7-11: Ita *nōs . . . meritō sumus, . . . exercitūs Rōmānī agrī vāstārī, līberī nostrī . . . dēbuerint.*

LINE 12. **Eōdem**, abl. sing. n. of *īdem, eadem, idem* (from root *i*, whence is + the suffix dem); iterative pron.; it modifies *tempore.* —— **tempore**, abl. of *tempus, -oris*, n.; abl. of *time when* or *at which*; see note on *tempore*, l. 8, above. —— **Ambarrī, -ōrum**, nom. plur. m. (compare Gk. οἱ 'Αμβάρροι = according to some, ἀμφ' 'Αραριν). These people were clients of the Aedui, and occupied the territory

[LINES 13-15.] BOOK I. 73

13 cōnsanguineī	Aeduōrum,	Caesarem	certiōrem	timate friends and relatives of the Aedui, informed Caesar that, since their fields had been devastated, they were with difficulty keeping the
relations	of the Aedui,	Caesar	more certain	
14 faciunt,	sēsē	dēpopulātīs	agrīs	
make,	themselves,	having been laid waste	(their) fields,	
15 nōn	facile	ab oppidīs	vim hostium	
not	easily	from the towns	the force of the enemy	

between the Arar (Saône) and the Rhone. Many editions read here *Aeduī Ambarrī* or *Haeduī Ambarrī*. See note on *Aeduī*, l. 4, above. *Ambarrī* is subject-nom. of *faciunt*, l. 14, below. —— **necessāriī**, nom. plur. of the adj, *necessārius, -a, -um*, used as a noun, in apposition with *Ambarrī*. *necessāriī* = those friends or clients to whom offices of kindness are necessarily due.

LINE 13. **cōnsanguineī**, nom. plur. of the adj. *cōnsanguineus, -a, -um* (con + sanguineus, sanguis); hence = lit. *blood-relations;* connected by the conj. *et* with *necessāriī*, and in the same grammatical construction. —— **Aeduōrum**, gen. plur. of *Aeduī, -ōrum*, m.; it limits, as a gen., *necessāriī* et *cōnsanguineī*. As to the Aeduan clan, see note on *Aeduō*, l. 20, Chap. III. —— **Caesarem**, acc. sing. of *Caesar, -aris,* m.; direct obj. of *faciunt.* —— **certiōrem**, acc. sing. m. of the adj. *certior, -us*, comparative degree of *certus*, a participle by metathesis for *crētus* from the verb *cernō, -ere, crēvī, crētum,* 3; superl. *certissimus.* Observe that the adj. as predicate is in the same case as the direct obj. A complete analysis requires the copula *esse* between *Caesarem* and *certiorem. certiorem* is predicate-acc. Consult A. & G. 239, *a*, and NOTE 1; B. 151, (*b*); G. 340; H. 373, 1, and NOTE 2. Observe that the phrase *aliquem facere certiōrem* is followed by the acc. with the inf., or by a relative-clause. Sometimes, however, the phrase is used absolutely.

LINE 14. **faciunt**, 3d pers. plur. of *faciō, -ere, fēcī, factum,* 3; it agrees with its subject-nom. *Ambarrī,* l. 12, above. —— **sēsē**, acc. plur. of the reflexive pron. *suī, sibi, sē, sē,* reduplicated *sēsē;* it is subject-acc. of *prohibēre.* Observe that the tenses are the historic pres. If the participial phrase be taken as a preliminary, and not as a coördinate expression, the necessity of rendering the inf. *prohibēre*, as if it depended on *posse*, will not be felt. —— **dēpopulātīs**, perf. participle of the deponent verb *dēpopulor, -ārī, -ātus,* 1. Sometimes the perf. participle of a deponent verb has a pass. signification; abl. absolute with *agrīs*, denoting cause. Consult A. & G. 135, *b*; B. 109, 2; G. 220, NOTE 1; H. 231, 2. —— **agrīs**, abl. plur. of the noun *ager, agrī,* m.; abl. absolute with the participle *dēpopulātīs*. See A. & G. 255; B. 192; G. 409; H. 431. Between the villages there were, usually, long stretches of forests and fields, which were some sort of defense. The Helvetii were laying these waste; hence it was difficult to keep the enemy from the towns.

LINE 15. **nōn**, adv. (nōn + ūnum); modifies the adv. *facile.* —— **facile**, adv. (*facilis*). See A. & G. 148, *d*; B. 117. 6; G. 91, (*c*); H. 304, I, 3, 1); *facile* modifies *prohibēre.* —— **ab**, prep. with the abl. (*ā* before consonants, *ab* before vowels or consonants). —— **oppidīs**, abl. plur. of *oppidum, -ī,* n.; it is the obj. of the prep. *ab.* —— **vim**, acc. sing. of the noun *vīs, vīs,* f.; direct obj. of *prohibēre.* —— **hostium**, gen. plur. of *hostis, -is,* m. and f.; it limits *vim.* Synonyms: *hostis* = lit. *a stranger;* hence, because of distrust of strangers, *an enemy;* oftener *hostēs,* plur., than *hostis;* it generally denotes a public enemy; whereas *inimīcus* = *a private foe. Ōrātiō rēcta* of lines 14-16: *nōs dēpopulātīs agrīs nōn facile ab oppidīs vim hostium prohibēmus.*

violence of the enemy from their towns. The Allobroges, also, who had villages and possessions across the Rhone, fled to Caesar and informed him that they had nothing left except their country's soil.	prohibēre. *to restrain.*	Item *Likewise*	Allobrogēs, *the Allobroges,*	quī *who*	trāns *across*	16
	Rhodanum *the Rhone*	vīcōs *villages*	possessionēsque *possessions and,*		habēbant, *had,*	17
	fugā *in flight*	sē *themselves*	ad *to*	Caesarem *Caesar*	recipiunt *betake*	et *and*	18
	dēmōnstrant, *show,*	sibi *to themselves*		praeter *except*	agrī *of land*	solum *the soil,*	19

LINE 16. **prohibēre**, pres. inf. act. of *prohibeō, -ēre, -uī, -itum*, 2; complementary inf. depending on *posse* understood; or *sēsē . . . prohibēre* may be taken as an acc. and infinitive-clause depending immediately on *Caesarem certiōrem faciunt*. See observation on *prohibēre*, l. 14, above. —— **Item**, adv. (formed from the radical *i* as seen in pron. is + adverbial accusative-suffix tem; = in *that* way, also). For synonyms, see note on *itemque*, l. 20, Chap. III. —— **Allobrogēs**, nom. plur. of *Allobrox, -ogis*, m.; but in Caesar in the plur. *Allobrogēs, -gum*, m.; subject-nom. of *recipiunt* and *dēmōnstrant*. The word *Allobrogēs* is said to mean *highlanders*. These people, who in Caesar's time were living in *Gallia Narbōnensis*, on the east side of the Rhone and to the north of what is now Savoy, had been already subdued by Caius Pomptinus, the praetor, and their territory, of course, was considered Roman. —— **quī**, nom. plur. of the rel. pron. *quī, quae, quod*; it refers to *Allobrogēs*, but is subject-nom. of *habēbant*. —— **trāns**, prep. with the acc.; used with verbs of motion.

LINE 17. **Rhodanum**, acc. sing. of *Rhodanus, -ī*, m.; it is the obj. of the prep. *trāns*. —— **vīcōs**, acc. plur. of *vīcus, -ī*, m. (digammated from GK. οἶκος); direct obj. of *habēbant*. —— **possessionēsque** (possessionēs + que). *possessionēs*, acc. plur. of *possessiō, -ōnis*, f. (*possidēre* = *to have* and *to hold*); connected by the enclitic conj. *-que* with *vīcōs*, and in the same grammatical construction. —— **habēbant**, 3d pers. plur. imperf. ind. act. of *habeō, -ēre, -uī, -itum*, 2; it agrees with its subject-nom. *Allobrogēs*.

LINE 18. **fugā**, abl. sing. of the noun *fuga, -ae*, f. (compare GK. φυγή); abl. of manner; compare *vid* and *iniūriā*, and consult A. & G. 248, REM.; B. 168, REM. 2, (*e*); G. 399, NOTE I; H. 419, III, NOTE 2. But *fugā* might be taken as an abl. of means. —— **sē**, acc. plur. of the reflexive pron. *suī, sibi, sē, sē*; direct obj. of *recipiunt*. —— **ad**, prep. with the acc. denoting *to* or *towards*. —— **Caesarem**, acc. sing. of *Caesar, -aris*, m.; it is the obj. of the prep. *ad*, after a verb of motion. —— **recipiunt**, 3d pers. plur. pres. ind. act. of *recipiō, -ere, -cēpī, -ceptum*, 3 (re + capere, *to take back*); it agrees with its subject-nom. *Allobrogēs*.

LINE 19. **dēmōnstrant**, 3d pers. plur. pres. ind. act. of *dēmōnstrō, -āre, -āvī, -ātum*, 1 (dē, *out* + mōnstrāre, *to point*); connected by the conj. *et* with *recipiunt*, and has the same grammatical construction. —— **sibi**, dat. plur. of reflexive pron. *suī, sibi, sē, sē*, the same forms in the plur.; dat. of possessor after *esse*. See A. & G. 231; B. 146; G. 349; H. 387. —— **praeter**, adv. and prep.; here prep. with the acc. —— **agrī**, gen. sing. of the noun *ager, agrī*, m.; as a gen. it limits the noun *solum*. Note its position, and consult A. & G. 344, *g*; B. 43; G. 413, REM. 3, and 678, REM. 4; H. 569, II, 3. —— **solum**, acc. sing. of *solum, -ī*, n.; obj. of the prep. *praeter*. *solum* is to be carefully discriminated from *sōlum*, adv. Observe the difference in

20 nihil	esse	reliquī.	Quibus	rēbus
nothing	to be (there is)	of remainder.	By which	things
21 adductus	Caesar	nōn exspectandum		sibi
led	Caesar	not it ought to be awaited		by himself
22 statuit,	dum	omnibus	fortūnīs	sociōrum
determined,	until	all	the fortunes	of the allies
23 cōnsūmptīs	in	Santonōs Helvētiī pervenīrent.		
being destroyed,	among	the Santoni the Helvetii should arrive.		

Influenced by these representations, Caesar did not think that he ought to wait until the Helvetii, after destroying all the resources of his allies, should reach the country of the Santoni.

the length of the vowels in the penultimate syllables. The phrase *praeter agrī solum* = freely, *except the bare soil*.

LINE 20. **nihil**, acc. sing. of the indecl. noun *nihil*, which is only used in the nom. and acc. cases; *nihil* is subject-acc. of *esse*. Observe that the indecl. *nihil* = *nihilum*, -ī, n., contracted from *nil* and *nilum* (nē + hilum = *not the least*); observe also that *nihil* is sometimes an adverbial acc. = an emphatic *nōn*. —— **esse**, pres. inf. act. of the intrans. verb *sum*, *esse*, *fuī*, fut. participle *futūrus*; *esse* is a verb of complete predication here, and agrees with its subject-acc. *nihil*. —— **reliquī**, gen. sing. n. of the adj. *reliquus*, *-a*, *-um*, used as a noun, and in the partitive gen. construction after *nihil*; the phrase *nihil reliquī* = lit. *nothing of remainder*. For the partitive construction, consult A. & G. 216, 3, and REM.; B. 134; G. 369, REM. 2; H. 397, 1. *Ōrātiō rēcta*, lines 19 and 20: *nōbīs praeter agrī solum nihil est reliquī*. —— **Quibus**, acc. plur. f. of the rel. pron. *quī*, *quae*, *quod*, used here adjectively as an attributive of *rēbus*. At the beginning of a sentence the rel. is rendered in the best manner by a dem. with a connective. Consult A. & G. 180, *f*; B. 129, REM. 9; G. 610; H. 453. —— **rēbus**, abl. plur. of *rēs*, *reī*, f. (stem *rē*, but vowel shortened in the gen. and dat. sing.); abl. of cause after the perf. pass. participle *adductus*. See A. & G. 245, and 2, *b*; B. 165, and REM. 4; G. 408, and NOTE 2; H. 416, and NOTE 1.

LINE 21. **adductus**, nom. sing. m. of the perf. pass. participle of the act. verb *addūcō*, *-ere*, *-dūxī*, *-ductum*, 3 (ad + dūcere); as a participle it agrees with the noun *Caesar*. —— **Caesar**, nom. of *Caesar*, *-aris*, m.; subj. of *statuit*. —— **nōn**, negative adv.; it modifies *exspectandum* (*esse*). —— **exspectandum** (**esse**), pres. inf. of the 2d periphrastic conjugation of *exspectō*, *-āre*, *-āvī*, *-ātum* (ex + spectāre = lit. *to look out for*); *exspectandum* (*esse*) is here used impersonally. See A. & G. 330, *c*; B. 185; G. 427, NOTE 4; H. 234. —— **sibi**, dat. sing. of the reflexive pron. *suī*, *sibi*, *sē*, *sē*; it refers to *Caesar*, but is dat. of the agent after the gerundive. Consult A. & G. 232; B. 148; G. 355; H. 388.

LINE 22. **statuit**, 3d pers. sing. perf. ind. act. of *statuō*, *-ere*, *-uī*, *-ūtum*, 3 (derived from *status* and this from *stāre*); hence *statuere* = lit. *to cause to stand*. —— **dum**, conj.; here = *until*. —— **omnibus**, abl. plur. f. of the adj. *omnis*, *-e*; it is an attributive of *fortūnīs*. —— **fortūnīs**, abl. plur. of *fortūna*, *-ae*, f. (compare *fors*, chance, from *ferō*); abl. absolute with the participle *cōnsūmptīs*. —— **sociōrum**, gen. plur. of *socius*, *-ī*, m.; poss. gen. limiting *fortūnīs*.

LINE 23. **cōnsūmptīs**, perf. pass. participle *cōnsūmptus*, *-a*, *-um* of the verb *cōnsūmō*, *-ere*, *-sūmpsī*, *-sūmptum*, 3 (con + sūmere); hence = lit. *to take together*. *cōnsūmptīs* is in the abl. absolute with *fortūnīs*. See A. & G. 255; B. 192; G. 409; H. 431. —— **in**, prep. with the acc. or abl.; here it takes the acc. —— **Santonōs**, acc. plur. of *Santonī*, *-ōrum*, m. (sometimes *Santonēs*, *-um*); *Santonōs* is the obj. of

XII. There is a river, Arar (Saône), which flows through the territories of the Aedui and the Sequani with such wonderful smoothness, that it cannot be determined by the eye in which di-	XII.	Flūmen	est	Arar,	quod	per	1
		A river	is	the Arar,	which	through	
	fīnēs	Aeduōrum	et	Sēquanōrum	in	2
	the boundaries	of the Aedui	and	the Sequani	into	
	Rhodanum	īnfluit,	incrēdibilī	lēnitāte,	ita	3
	the Rhone	inflows,	of incredible	smoothness,	so	
	ut	oculīs,	in	utram	partem	fluat,	4
	that	with the eyes,	in	what	direction	it flows,

the prep. *in*. For historic description, see note on *Santonum*, l. 3, Chap. X. —— **Helvētiī**, nom. plur. m. of the adj. *Helvētius*, *-a, -um*, used substantively; subj. of *pervenīrent*. —— **pervenīrent**, 3d pers. plur. imperf. subjunctive act. of *perveniō, -īre, -vēnī, -ventum*, 4; subjunctive after *dum*, implying futurity. Consult A. & G. 328; B. 229, (2); G. 572; H. 519, II, 2.

LINE 1. **Flūmen**, predicate-nom. after *est* of *flūmen, -inis*, n. —— **est**, 3d pers. sing. of the intrans. verb *sum, esse, fuī*, fut. participle *futūrus*; often a copula, as here. —— **Arar**, nom. sing. of *Arar, -aris*, m.; subj. of *est*; acc., usually, in *-im*, and abl. in *-ī*. See A. & G. 56, *a*, 1, and 57, *a*, 1; B. 33, REM. 2; G. 57, REM. 2; H. 62, III, 1. The river Arar is the modern Saône (English pron. Sōne). —— **quod**, nom. sing. n. of the rel. pron. *quī, quae, quod*; it refers to the predicate-nom. *flūmen*, and agrees with it in gender; in such construction, with nouns of different genders, the rel. may agree with either. For voucher, compare *flūmine Rhodanō, quī*, l. 16, Chap. II. —— **per**, prep. with the acc.

LINE 2. **fīnēs**, acc. plur. of the noun *fīnis, -is*, m.; it is the obj. of the prep. *per*. For synonyms, see note on *agrum*, l. 12, Chap. II. —— **Aeduōrum**, gen. plur. of *Aeduī, -ōrum*, m.; it limits *fīnēs*. For further particulars, see note on *Aeduō*, l. 20, Chap. III. —— **Sēquanōrum**, gen. plur. of *Sēquanī, -ōrum*, m.; connected by the conj. *et* with *Aeduōrum*, and in the same grammatical construction. For description of the clan, see note on *Sēquanīs*, l. 25, Chap. I. —— **in**, prep. with the acc. after *īnfluit*, a verb of motion.

LINE 3. **Rhodanum**, acc. sing. of *Rhodanus, -ī*, m.; obj. of the prep. *in*. Note the repetition of the prep. *in* with the acc. after *īnfluit*, instead of the dat. construction, and see A. & G. 228, *c*; B. 143, REM. 1; G. 347, REM. 1; H. 386, 3. —— **īnfluit**, 3d pers. sing. pres. ind. act. of *īnfluō, -ere, -flūxī, fluxum*, 3; it agrees with its subject-nom. *quod*. —— **incrēdibilī**, abl. sing. f. of the adj. *incrēdibilis, -e* (in, *negative* + *crēdibilis* = lit. *unworthy of belief*); *incrēdibilī* is an attributive of *lēnitāte*. —— **lēnitāte**, abl. sing. of *lēnitās, -ātis*, f.; abl. of manner. Consult A. & G. 248; B. 168; G. 399; H. 419, III. —— **ita**, adv., correlate of the conj. *ut*.

LINE 4. **ut**, ecbatic conj. —— **oculīs**, abl. plur. of *oculus, -ī*, m.; abl. of means. See A. & G. 248, *c*; B. 167; G. 401; H. 420. —— **in**, prep. with the acc. or abl.; here it takes the acc. with a verb of motion. —— **utram**, acc. sing. f. of the pron. *uter, -tra, -trum*, gen. *utrīus* = lit. *which* (of two); *utram* is an attributive of *partem*. For declension, see A. & G. 83; B. 56; G. 76; H. 151, and 1. —— **partem**, acc. sing. of the noun *pars, partis*, f.; it is the obj. of the prep. *in*. For grammatical references, see note on *in*, l. 1, end, Chap. I. —— **fluat**, 3d pers. sing. pres. subjunctive act. of *fluō, -ere, flūxī, fluxum*, 3; subjunctive, because it is an *indirect question*. Consult A. & G. 334; B. 242; G. 467; H. 529, I.

5 iūdicārī	nōn possit.		Id	Helvētiī	ratibus	rection it flows; at length it empties into the Rhone. The Helvetii were crossing this stream on rafts and canoes joined. When Caesar was informed by scouts that the Helvetii had already led
to be judged	*is not able.*		*This*	*the Helvetii*	*by rafts*	
6 āc	lintribus	iūnctīs		trānsībant.	Ubi	
and	*boats*	*joined together*		*were crossing.*	*When*	
7 per	explōrātōrēs	Caesar	certior		factus est,	
through	*scouts*	*Caesar*	*more certain*		*was made,*	
8 trēs	iam	partēs	cōpiārum		Helvētiōs	
three	*already*	*parts*	*of forces*		*the Helvetii*	

LINE 5. **iūdicārī**, pres. inf. pass. of *iūdicō, -āre, -āvī, -ātum*, 1 ; pass. parts: *iūdicor, -cārī, -cātus*, 1 ; complementary inf., depending on *possit*. See A. & G. 271, and NOTE; B. 181; G. 423; H. 533, I, 2. —— **nōn**, adv. (nĕ + ūnum); observe its position: immediately before the word it modifies. —— **possit**, 3d pers. sing. pres. subjunctive of *possum, posse, potuī* (potis + sum); subjunctive of result after *ut*, referring to the adv. *ita*. A. & G. 319, and REM.; B. 201, and REM. I, (*a*); G. 552; H. 500, II. Observe that *possit* is used here impersonally; but, strictly, the indirect question *in utram partem fluat*, as a noun-clause, is the subj. of *possit*. —— **Id**, acc. sing. n. of the dem. pron. *is, ea, id*, used substantively; it refers to *flūmen*, and is the direct obj. of *trānsībant;* or *id* may be taken as an attributive of *flūmen* understood, which latter would be the direct obj. Observe how emphatic *id* becomes by being placed at the beginning of the sentence. —— **Helvētiī**, nom. plur. m. of the adj. *Helvētius, -a, -um*, used substantively; and is the subject-nom. of *trānsībant*. For description of the clan, see note on *Helvētiī*, l. 16, Chap. I. —— **ratibus**, abl. plur. of *ratis, -is*, f.; abl. absolute with the participle *iūnctīs*, denoting means. A. & G. 255; B. 192; G. 409; H. 431.

LINE 6. **āc**, cop. conj. here; see note on *atque*, l. 10, Chap. I. —— **lintribus**, abl. plur. of *linter, -tris*, f.; connected by the conj. *āc* with *ratibus*, and in the same grammatical construction. —— **iūnctīs**, abl. plur. f. of the perf. pass. participle *iūnctus, -a, -um* of the verb *iungō, -ere, iūnxī, iūnctum*, 3 ; abl. absolute with *ratibus āc lintribus*. —— **trānsībant**, 3d pers. plur. imperf. ind. act. of *trānseō, -īre, -īvī (-iī), -itum* (trāns + īre); it agrees with its subject-nom. *Helvētiī*. Observe the force of the imperf. tense — continued action. —— **Ubi**, locative adv. (quō, old dat. of *quī* + bi) = *where*, but more frequent transf., of time = *when*.

LINE 7. **per**, prep. with the acc. —— **explōrātōrēs**, acc. plur. of *explōrātor, -ōris*, m.; acc. after *per*, denoting the agent as means. Consult A. & G. 246, *b*; B. 166, REM. 1 ; G. 401; H. 415, I, 1, NOTE 1. An *explōrātor* (*explōrāre*, to reconnoitre) = *a scout*, a cavalryman sent to get information concerning the enemy; whereas *speculātor* (*speculārī*, to spy) = etymologically at least, *a spy*. —— **Caesar**, **-aris**, m., subject-nom. of *factus est*. —— **certior**, comparative adj. of positive *certus*, formed by metathesis from *crctus*, perf. pass. participle of *cernō, -ere, crēvī, -crētum*, 3 ; *certior* is predicate-adj. after the pass. *factus est*. See A. & G. 176, *a*; B. 128; G. 205, 206; H. 362, 2, 2), 438, 2. —— **factus est**, 3d pers. sing. perf. ind. pass. of *fīō, fierī, factus*, 3 ; used as pass. of *faciō, -ere, fēcī, factum*, 3.

LINE 8. **trēs, -ia**, num. adj., acc. plur. f.; it is an attributive of *partēs;* compare note on *trēs*, l. 2, Chap. I. —— **iam**, adv.; it modifies *trāduxisse*. Observe that *iam* = *now* in reference to the past, pres. or future; while *nunc* puts emphasis on the pres. —— **partēs**, acc. plur. of *pars, partis*, f.; direct obj. of *trāduxisse*. ——

78 CAESAR'S GALLIC WAR [CHAP. XII.

| three quarters of their forces across this stream, but that nearly one quarter of them remained on this side, he went forth out of his camp, during the third watch, with three legions, and overtook that divi- | id flūmen trādūxisse, *across that river to have led,* citrā flūmen *on this side the river* tertiā vigiliā *the third watch* castrīs profectus *the camp setting out* | quartam *the fourth* Ararim *Arar* cum *with* ad *to* | ferē *nearly* reliquam *left* legiōnibus *legions* eam *that* | partem *part* esse, *to be,* tribus *three* partem *part* | 9 dē 10 *from* ē 11 *from* pervēnit, 12 *he came,* |

cōpiārum, gen. plur. of *cōpia, -ae,* f.; as a gen. it limits *partēs*. Note that *cōpia*, in sing. = *plenty;* in the plural, *resources, troops*. —— Helvētiōs, acc. plur. of *Helvētiī, -ōrum*, m.; subject-acc. of *trādūxisse*.

LINE 9. id, acc. sing. n. of the dem. pron. *is, ea, id;* it is an attributive of *flūmen*. —— flūmen, acc. sing. of *flūmen, -inis,* n.; acc. depending on the prep. *trāns* in composition. Consult A. & G. 239, 2, *b;* B. 152, REM. 2; G. 331, REM. 1; H. 376. —— trādūxisse, perf. inf. act. of *trādūcō, -ere, -dūxī, -ductum,* 3 (trāns, *across* + dūcere, *to lead);* its subject-acc. is *Helvētiōs*. —— quartam, acc. sing. f. of the ordinal adj. *quartus, -a -um;* it is an attributive of *partem*. —— ferē, adv.; it modifies the ordinal adj. *quartam*. —— partem, acc. sing. of *pars, partis,* f.; subject-acc. of *esse*.

LINE 10. citrā, adv., and prep. with the acc. = *this side,* i.e. toward Italy. —— flūmen, acc. sing. of *flūmen, -inis,* n.; obj. of the prep. *citrā*. —— Ararim, acc. sing. of noun *Arar, -aris,* m.; in apposition with *flūmen*. As to the accusative-ending *-im,* see A. & G. 56, *a* and *b;* B. 33, REM. 2 and 3; G. 57, REM. 1; H. 62, III, 1. —— reliquam, acc. sing. of the adj. *reliquus, -a, -um;* predicate-acc. after *esse*. —— esse, pres. inf. of the intrans. verb *sum, esse, fuī, futūrus*. Observe that *reliquus* in the predicate after *esse* has the force of a participle; here *reliquam* = *relictam*. —— dē, prep. with the abl.; *dē* followed by *tertiā vigiliā* = *in the course of;* see lexicon under *dē*. This phrase appears to have the same meaning as *tertiā vigiliā,* — time within which, — which Caesar himself uses in Chap. XXXIII, Book II.

LINE 11. tertiā, abl. sing. f. of the ordinal adj. *tertius, -a, -um;* it is an attributive of *vigiliā*. —— vigiliā, abl. sing. of *vigilia, -ae,* f.; it is the obj. of the prep. *dē*. The night by the Romans was divided into four watches; the third watch began at midnight. —— cum, prep. with the abl. *legiōnibus*. —— legiōnibus, abl. plur. of *legiō, -ōnis,* f. (*legere,* to choose); hence *legiō* = lit. *a chosen number; legiōnibus* is abl. of accompaniment with the prep. *cum*. For description of the Roman legion, see any good encyclopedia under *Legion*. —— tribus, abl. sing. f. of the num. adj. *trēs, tria*. See note on *trēs,* l. 2, Chap. I. *tribus* is an attributive of *legiōnibus*. —— ē, prep. with the abl. (*ē* before consonants, *ex* before either vowels or consonants).

LINE 12. castrīs, abl. plur. of *castrum, -ī,* n.; it is the obj. of the prep. *ē*. Observe that *castrum,* sing. = *a fort;* in the plur. *castra* = *a camp;* i.e. the plur. denotes that several soldiers' huts or tents were located near each other. Among the Romans the camp was generally square; sometimes, in imitation of the Greeks, circular; it was surrounded by a ditch and rampart or wall; it had front, back, and side gates. —— profectus, perf. participle of the deponent verb *proficīscor, -ī, -fectus,* 3; it agrees with a pron. understood, referring to *Caesar,* l. 7, above, which pron. is subject-nom. of *pervēnit*. —— ad, prep. with the acc. after a verb of motion. —— eam, acc. sing. f. of the dem. pron *is, ea, id;* it is the attributive of *partem*. —— partem,

BOOK I.

13 quae	nōndum	flūmen	trānsierat.	Eōs	sion that had not yet crossed the river. Attacking these forces encumbered with baggage, and off their guard, he slaughtered a great part of them; the rest fled, and hid in the nearest
which	*not yet*	*the river*	*had crossed.*	*Them*	
14 impedītōs	et	inopīnantēs	aggressus	māgnam	
impeded	*and*	*unawares*	*he assailing*	*a great,*	
15 eōrum	partem	concīdit;	reliquī	sēsē	
of them,	*part*	*cut to pieces;*	*the rest*	*themselves*	
16 fugae	mandārunt	atque	in	proximās	silvās
to flight	*committed*	*and*	*in*	*the nearest*	*woods*

acc. sing. of *pars, partis,* f.; it is the obj. of the prep. *ad.* —— **pervēnit,** 3d pers. sing. of *perveniō, -īre, -vēnī, -ventum,* 4; it agrees with a subj. implied in the ending, referring to Caesar.

LINE 13. **quae,** nom. sing. f. of the rel. pron. *quī, quae, quod;* it refers to *partem* as its antecedent, but is the subject-nom. of *trānsierat.* —— **nōndum,** adv. (nōn + dum); it modifies *trānsierat.* —— **flūmen,** acc. sing. of the noun *flūmen, -inis,* n.; direct obj. of *trānsierat.* —— **trānsierat,** 3d pers. sing. pluperf. ind. act., for *trānsīverat;* observe that *v* is syncopated without contraction. The reader will note that the reference is to that part of the enemy's forces still on the east side of the Saône. —— **Eōs,** acc. plur. m. of the dem. pron. *is, ea, id,* used as a personal pron. of the 3d pers.; acc. of the direct obj. after the deponent participle *aggressus.*

LINE 14. **impedītōs,** acc. plur. m. of the perf. pass. participle *impedītus, -a, -um* of *impediō, -īre, -īvī (-iī), -ītum,* 4 (in + pēs, *the foot in it*); hence *impedīre = to entangle the feet.* —— **inopīnantēs,** acc. plur. m. of the adj. *inopīnāns, -antis;* connected by the conj. *et* with *impedītōs,* and in the same grammatical construction. These modifiers of *eōs* indicate that Caesar attacked them while impeded by their packs, or by the river, and also while off their guard. —— **aggressus,** perf. participle of the deponent verb *ag(d)gredior, aggredī, aggressus* (ad + gradī); *aggressus,* as a participle, agrees with *is* or *ille,* the omitted subject-nom. of *concīdit.* —— **māgnam,** acc. sing. f. of the adj. *māgnus, -a, -um,* positive *māior,* superl. *māximus;* **māgnam** is an attributive of *partem.*

LINE 15. **eōrum,** gen. plur. of the dem. pron. *is, ea, id,* used as a personal pron. of the 3d pers.; as a gen. it limits *partem.* Observe the natural Latin order of the words, when the limited noun has an adj. with it: adj., gen., noun; observe also that some copies read here: *māgnam partem eōrum.* —— **concīdit,** 3d pers. sing. perf. ind. act. of *concīdō, -ere, concīdī, concīsum,* 3 (con + caedere, *to cut*); it agrees with a subj. implied in the ending, referring to Caesar. This verb should be carefully discriminated from *concidō, -ere, -cidī,* 3 (con + cadere, *to fall*). —— **reliquī,** nom. plur. m. of the adj. *reliquus, -a, -um,* used substantively; subj. of *mandārunt* and *abdidērunt.* Synonyms: *cēterī,* sometimes written *caeterī,* nom. pl. of the adj. *cēterus, -a, -um* (in Caesar only used in the plur.) = *others,* in opposition to those first mentioned; compare GK. οἱ ἄλλοι; but *aliī = others* as merely differential from those mentioned; and *reliquī = the rest,* the remainder that completes the whole. —— **sēsē,** acc. plur. of the reflexive pron. *suī, sibi, sē, sē,* reduplicated form; direct obj. of *mandārunt.*

LINE 16. **fugae,** dat. of the noun *fuga, -ae,* f.; indirect obj. —— **mandārunt,** 3d pers. plur. perf. ind. act. of *mandō,* 1 (manus + dare = *to commit to one's hands*); for *mandāvērunt;* it agrees with its subject-nom. *reliquī.* As to syncopation and

woods. This canton was called Tigurinus; for the entire Helvetian state is divided into four cantons. This single canton having left home, in the recollection of our fathers, (to engage in pred-	abdidērunt. *hid.*	Is *This*	pāgus *district*	appellābātur *was called*	Tigurīnus; 17 *Tigurinus;*
	nam *for*	omnis *every*	cīvitās *state*	Helvētia *Helvetian*	in quattuor 18 *into four*
	pāgōs *districts*	dīvīsa est. *was divided.*	Hīc *This*	pāgus *district*	ūnus, cum 19 *alone, when*
	domō *from home*		exīsset *it had gone forth*	patrum *in fathers'*	nostrōrum 20 *our*

contraction, see A. & G. 128, *a*; B. 251; G. 131, 1; H. 235. —— **atque** (ad + que), conj., usually adds a more important notion; see note on this particle, l. 10, Chap. I. —— **in**, prep. with either the acc. or abl.; here it takes the acc.; with this case it usually = *to* or *into;* but by a difference of idiom after *abdidere* it = in the English idiom simply *in* with the acc.; that is, the construction after *abdidere* is *as if* it were a verb of motion. —— **proximās**, acc. plur. of the superl. degree *proximus, -a, -um;* comparative *propior;* positive wanting; *proximās* modifies *silvās*. —— **silvās**, acc. plur. of *silva, -ae* (sibilated from GK. ὕλη); obj. of the prep. *in.*

LINE 17. **abdidērunt**, 3d pers. plur. perf. ind. act. of *abdō, -ere, -didi, -ditum,* 3 (ab + dare) = lit. *to give away. abdidērunt* is connected by the conj. *atque* with *mandārunt*, and in the same grammatical construction. —— **Is**, nom. sing. m. of the dem. pron. *is, ea, id;* it is an attributive of *pāgus*. —— **pāgus, -ī,** m.; subject-nom. of *ap(d)pellābātur.* Observe (1) that *is pāgus* refers to the *fourth part* mentioned in l. 9, above; (2) that *pāgus* here = a division of the *cīvitās*. —— **ap(d)pellābātur,** 3d pers. sing. imperf. ind. pass. of *appellō, -āre, -āvī, -ātum,* 1. —— **Tigurīnus, -ī,** m.; predicate-noun after the pass. verb. *Tigurīnus* was, probably, the district round about the modern Zürich in Switzerland.

LINE 18. **nam**, conj., introduces an objective reason; *enim*, a subjective. —— **omnis**, nom. sing. f. of the adj. *omnis, -e;* it is an attributive of *cīvitās*. —— **cīvitās, -ātis,** f. (*cīvēs*), subject-nom. of *dīvīsa est.* —— **Helvētia**, nom. sing. f. of the adj. *Helvētius, -a, -um;* it, too, is an attributive of *cīvitās*. —— **in**, prep. with the acc. or abl.; here it takes the acc. —— **quattuor**, indecl. num. adj.; here, of course, in the acc. plur., modifying *pāgōs*.

LINE 19. **pāgōs**, acc. plur. of *pāgus, -ī,* m.; obj. of the prep. *in.* —— **dīvīsa est**, 3d pers. sing. perf. ind. pass. of *dīvidō, -ere, dīvīsī, dīvīsum,* 3; or *dīvīsa* may be taken as a predicate-adj. after *est.* See note on *dīvīsa est*, l. 1, Chap. I. —— **Hīc**, nom. sing. m. of the dem. pron.; it is an attributive of *pāgus; hīc* indicates that the obj. is near in space: the *hīc pāgus* explains the *is pāgus* of l. 17, above, conceived to be near; whereas the *is pāgus* designates the object *quartam partem*, l. 9, above, conceived to be remote. —— **pāgus, -ī,** m.; subject-nom. of *interfēcerat*, l. 21, below. —— **ūnus**, num. adj., gen. *ūnīus,* dat. *ūnī;* an attributive of *pāgus;* it here = *alone, peculiar.* Observe that *pāgus* here is put by metonymy for the people of the canton. —— **cum**, conj., temporal; known to be such, because it is seen, at a glance, to introduce a clause subordinate to the main proposition.

LINE 20. **domō**, abl. sing. of *domus, -ūs,* or *-ī* locative; abl. denoting whence the motion proceeds after *exīsset.* Consult A. & G. 258, 2, *a*; B. 175; G. 390, 2; H. 412, II, 1. —— **exīsset**, 3d pers. sing. pluperf. subjunctive act. of *exeō, -īre, -īvī (-iī), -itum,* for the syncopated and contracted form *exīvisset;* as to the form, see A. & G. 128,

LINES 21-24.] BOOK I. 81

21 memoriā,	L. Cassium	cōnsulem	interfēcerat	atory war,) had ambushed Lucius Cassius, the consul; he was slain, and his army was sent under the yoke. Thus, whether by chance or by the purpose of the immortal gods, that part of the Helve-
memory,	*Lucius Cassius,*	*the consul,*	*had slain*	
22 et	ēius	exercitum	sub	iugum	mīserat.	
and	*his*	*army*	*under*	*the yoke*	*had sent.*	
23 Ita	sīve	cāsū	sīve	cōnsiliō	deōrum	
So,	*whether*	*by chance*	*or*	*by design*	*of the gods*	
24 immortālium,	quae	pars	cīvitātis	Helvētiae	
immortal,	*what*	*part*	*of the state*	*Helvetian*	

a, 2; B. 251; G. 131, 1; H. 235, 1; as to the subjunctive mode after *cum* temporal, see A. & G. 325; B. 222; G. 585; H. 521, II, 2. —— **patrum,** gen. plur. of the noun *pater, patris,* m.; as a gen. it limits *memoriā.* —— **nostrōrum,** gen. plur. of the poss. pron. *noster, -tra, -trum;* it is an attributive of *patrum.*

LINE 21. **memoriā,** abl. sing. of *memoria, -ae,* f.; abl. of *time when.* See A. & G. 256, 1; B. 171; G. 393; H. 429. —— **L.,** an abbreviation for the acc. sing. of *Lūcius, -ī,* m., a Roman praenōmen. —— **Cassium,** acc. sing. of *Cassius, -ī,* m.; the nōmen, the name of the *gēns; Cassium* is here an appositive. The allusion is to Lucius Cassius Longinus, consul 107 B.C.; he was slain by the Tigurini. —— **cōnsulem,** acc. sing. of *cōnsul, -ulis,* m.; direct obj. of *interfēcerat.* —— **interfēcerat,** 3d pers. sing. pluperf. ind. of *interficiō, -ere, -fēcī, -fectum,* 3 (inter + facere) = lit. *to put between, to make away with;* hence *to destroy. interfēcerat* agrees with its subj. *pāgus.*

LINE 22. **et,** cop. conj.; connects *interfēcerat* with *mīserat.* —— **ēius,** gen. sing. m. of the dem. pron. *is, ea, id,* used as a personal pron. of the 3d pers.; it refers to *Cassium,* but, as a gen., limits *exercitum.* —— **exercitum,** acc. sing. of *exercitus, -ūs,* m.; direct obj. of *mīserat.* For synonyms, see note on *exercitū,* l. 31, Chap. III. —— **sub,** prep. with the acc. or abl.; here it takes the acc. *sub* when followed by the acc. denotes *motion to,* when followed by the abl. it denotes *rest in,* a place. —— **iugum,** acc. sing. of *iugum, -ī,* n.; it is the obj. of the prep. *sub.* —— **mīserat,** 3d pers. sing. pluperf. ind. act. of *mittō, -ere, -mīsī, -mīssum,* 3; connected by *et* with *interfēcerat,* and in the same grammatical construction.

LINE 23. **Ita,** adv. (radical *i,* whence is + ta). —— **sīve** (sī + ve), conj.; *sīve . . . sīve* = *whether . . . or.* —— **cāsū,** abl. sing. of *cāsus, -ūs,* m. (*cadere,* to fall); abl. of cause. Consult A. & G. 245; B. 165; G. 408; H. 416. —— **cōnsiliō,** abl. sing. of *cōnsilium, -ī,* n.; connected by *sīve* with *cāsū,* and in the same grammatical construction. —— **deōrum,** gen. plur. of *deus, -ī,* m.; as a gen. it limits *cōnsiliō.* For declension of *deus,* which is irr. in the plur., see A. & G. 40, *f*; B. 24, REM. 3; G. 33, REM. 6; H. 51, 6.

LINE 24. **immortālium,** gen. plur. m. of the adj. *immortālis, -le* (in, *negative* + *mortālis*). —— **quae,** nom. sing. f. of the rel. pron. *quī, quae, quod,* used here adjectively, agreeing with the noun *pars,* which is logically its antecedent. —— **pars,** nom. sing. of *pars, partis,* f.; subj. of *intulerat.* Observe carefully that the relative clause precedes the antecedent clause; that in such constructions the antecedent noun appears in the relative clause, a species of attraction, *quae pars . . . ea = ea pars . . . quae.* Consult A. & G. 200, *b,* NOTE, EXAMPLE 2; B. 129, REM. 1, (*a*); G. 620; H. 445, 9. —— **cīvitātis,** gen. sing. of *cīvitās, -ātis,* f. (*cīvēs*); as a gen. it limits *pars.* —— **Helvētiae,** gen. sing. f. of the adj. *Helvētius, -a, -um;* it is an attributive of *cīvitātis.*

tian state, which had brought signal calamity on the Roman people, was the first to suffer punishment. In this affair, Caesar not only avenged the wrongs of the state, but even his own private	īnsīgnem *a remarkable*	calamitātem *calamity*	populō *upon the people*	Rōmānō *Roman* 25
	intulerat, *had brought,*	ea *that (part)*	prīnceps poenās *the first, punishment*	persolvit. 26 *suffered.*
	Quā *Which*	in *in,*	rē Caesar *affair Caesar*	nōn sōlum 27 *not only*
	pūblicās, *public,*	sed *but*	etiam *also*	prīvātās iniūriās 28 *private wrongs*

LINE 25. īnsīgnem, acc. sing. f. of the adj. *īnsīgnis, -e* (in + sīgnum, compare GK. εἰκών); hence *īnsīgnis* = lit. *inmarked*, distinguished by a mark. *Īnsīgnem* modifies *calamitātem*. —— calamitātem, acc. sing. of the noun *calamitās, -ātis,* f.; direct obj. of *intulerat*. —— populō, dat. sing. of *populus, -ī,* m.; indirect obj. of *intulerat*. The rigidly exact statement is: *calamitātem* is the direct obj. of *tulerat*, the latter part of the compound, and *populō* is the dat. after *in*, the former part of it. —— Rōmānō, dat. sing. m. of the adj. *Rōmānus, -a, -um; Rōmānō* is an attributive of *populō*. For synonyms of *populus,* see note on *populum,* l. 17, Chap. VI.

LINE 26. intulerat, 3d pers. sing. pluperf. ind. act. of *īnferō, -ferre, intulī, il(n)lātum;* it agrees with its subject-nom. *pars*. —— ea, nom. sing. f. of the dem. pron. *is, ea, id; ea* is an attributive of *pars,* to be supplied; which *pars* is subject-nom. of *persolvit*. —— prīnceps, adj. (primus + capere, *to take the first place*); here the adj. = the adv. *prīnum*. For the adverbial use of the adj., see A. & G. 191; B. 117. 6; G. 325, REM. 6; H. 443. *prīnceps,* however, might be taken here as a subst. and an appositive, and = *as the first one*. —— poenās, acc. plur. of *poena, -ae,* f. (GK. ποινή) = *puit-noney, fine*). *poenās* is the direct obj. of *persolvit*. —— persolvit, 3d pers. sing. perf. ind. act. of *persolvō, -ere, -solvī, -solūtum,* 3 (per + solvere); hence *persolvere* = lit. *to discharge completely*. Among the ancients, punishment was a fine or penalty to be paid, and not suffering to be inflicted except as an incident of the difficulty of raising the wherewith to pay the fine.

LINE 27. Quā, abl. sing. f. of the rel. pron. *quī, quae, quod;* used here adjectively, agreeing with *rē*. As to the use and translation of the relative, at the beginning of a sentence, see A. & G. 180, *f*; B. 129, REM. 9; G. 610; H. 453. —— in, prep. with the acc. or abl.; here it takes the abl. Note the position of the prep. *in:* between a modifier and a noun; modified monosyllabic prepositions are frequently thus placed. —— rē, abl. sing. of the noun *rēs, reī,* f.; it is the obj. of the prep. *in*. Caesar, -aris, m.; subject-nom. of *ultus est*. —— nōn, adv., modifies the adv. *sōlum*. —— sōlum, adv. (*sōlus,* only); it modifies the adj. *pūblicās*. Observe that in the adv. the penult is long; while in the noun *solum,* soil, the penult is short.

LINE 28. pūblicās, acc. plur. of the adj. *pūblicus, -a, -um* (contraction for *populicus* from *populus*). *pūblicās* modifies *iniūriās*. —— sed, conj., adversative; stronger than *autem*. —— etiam, adv. (et + iam). Observe that the phrases *nōn sōlum . . . sed etiam* are the equivalents of two copulatives; but when thus used, prominence is given to the second word or clause; that *nōn modo* or *nōn tantum* sometimes take the place of *nōn sōlum;* and *vērum etiam* sometimes take the place of *sed etiam,* with no particular difference of meaning. —— prīvātās, acc. plur. f. of the adj. *prīvātus, -a, -um* (really a participial adj. of *prīvō, -āre, -āvī, -ātum,* 1); *prīvātās* is an attrib-

29 ultus est;	quod	ēius		socerī	wrongs; because the Tigurini, in the same battle in which they had slain Cassius, had also slain his lieutenant Lucius Piso, grandfather of Lucius Piso, Caesar's father-in-law.
avenged;	because	his		father-in-law (was)	
30 L. Pīsōnis		avum,	L. Pīsōnem	lēgātum,	
Lucius Piso, (whose) grandfather Lucius Piso, the lieutenant,					
31 Tigurīnī	eōdem		proeliō	quō Cassium	
the Tigurini	in the same		battle	as Cassius	
32 interfēcerant.					
had slain.					

1 XIII.	Hōc	proeliō	factō,	reliquās
	This	battle	being done,	the remaining

XIII. When this battle was ended, Caesar

utive of *iniūriās*. —— **iniūriās**, acc. plur. of *iniūria, -ae*, f. (*iniūrius*, in + *iūs*); direct obj. of *ultus est*.

LINE 29. **ultus est**, 3d pers. sing. perf. ind. of the deponent *ulcīscor, -ī, ultus, 3*; it agrees with its subject-nom. *Caesar*. —— **quod**, conj. = *because*. —— **ēius**, gen. sing. m. of the dem. pron. *is, ea, id*, used as a personal pron. of the 3d pers.; it is an attributive of *socerī*, but refers to Caesar. —— **socerī**, gen. sing. of *socer, socerī*, m.; as a gen. it limits *avum*.

LINE 30. **L.**, an abbreviation of *Lūciī*, gen. sing. of *Lūcius, -ī*, m., the praenōmen of *Pīsōnis*. —— **Pīsōnis**, gen. sing. of *Pīsō, -ōnis*, m. *Pīsōnis* is in apposition with *socerī*. The allusion is to Lucius Calpurnius Piso, whose daughter Calpurnia Caesar married in 59 B.C. Calpurnia was the great-granddaughter of the defeated lieutenant. —— **avum**, acc. sing. of *avus, -ī*, m.; direct obj. of *interfēcerant*. —— **L.**, abbreviation for *Lūcium*, praenōmen. —— **Pīsōnem**, acc. sing. of *Pīsō, -ōnis*, m.; appositive of *avum*. —— **lēgātum**, acc. sing. of *lēgātus, -ī*, m. (*legere*, to delegate); in apposition with *L. Pīsōnem*.

LINE 31. **Tigurīnī**, nom. plur. of *Tigurīnus, -ī*, m.; subj. of *interfēcerant*. See note on *Tigurīnus*, l. 17, above. —— **eōdem**, abl. sing. n. of dem. pron. *idem, eadem, idem*; it is an attributive of *proeliō*. —— **proeliō**, abl. sing. n. of *proelium, -ī*, n.; locative abl. viewed as means. A. & G. 258, *f*, 1; B. 170, REM. 4; G. 389; H. 425, II, 1, 1). —— **quō**, abl. sing. n. of the rel. pron. *quī, quae, quod*; it refers to *proeliō* as its antecedent, and agrees with *proeliō* understood, which latter is to be conceived to be in the locative abl. like the abl. *proeliō* expressed in the text. —— **Cassium**, acc. sing. of *Cassius, -ī*, m.; direct obj. of *interfēcerant*, to be supplied. For historical explanation, see note on *L. Cassium*, l. 21, above.

LINE 32. **interfēcerant**, 3d pers. plur. pluperf. ind. act. of the verb *interficiō, -ere, -fēcī, -fectum*, 3 (inter + facere); it agrees with its subject-nom. *Tigurīnī*.

LINE 1. **Hōc**, abl. sing. n. of the dem. pron. *hīc, haec, hōc*; it is an attributive of *proeliō*. —— **proeliō**, abl. sing. of the noun *proelium, -ī*, n. (prō + īre, i.e. *to go forth* or *advance* in a hostile manner); *proeliō* is abl. absolute with the perf. pass. participle *factō*, denoting *time when*. See A. & G. 255; B. 192; G. 409; H. 431. —— **factō**, abl. sing. n. of the perf. pass. participle *factus, -a, -um* of *fīō, fierī, factus*, used as the pass. of *faciō, -ere, fēcī, factum, 3*; abl. absolute with the noun *proeliō*. —— **reliquās**, acc. plur. f. of the adj. *reliquus, -a, -um*; it modifies *cōpiās*.

84   CAESAR'S GALLIC WAR   [CHAP. XIII.

had a bridge built over the Arar, and thus he led his army across, in order that he might overtake the rest of the Helvetian forces. The Helvetii were alarmed at his sudden approach, and when	cōpiās Helvētiōrum ut cōnsequī posset, *forces of the Helvetii that to overtake he might be able,* pontem in Ararī faciendum cūrat atque *a bridge on the Arar to be made he cares for and* ita exercitum trādūcit. Helvētiī repentīnō *so the army he leads across. The Helvetii at the sudden* ēius adventū commōtī, cum id, quod *of him coming agitated, when that, which*	2 3 4 5

Synonyms: *reliquī* = *the rest, the remainder* that completes the whole; whereas *cēterī* (*caeterī*) = *the others* in opposition to those first mentioned; compare GK. ἄλλοι; and *aliī* = *others* as merely differentiated from those mentioned.

LINE 2. **cōpiās,** acc. plur. of *cōpia, -ae,* f.; direct obj. of *cōnsequī.* Observe that *cōpia* in the sing. = *plenty*; in the plur., *resources, troops.* —— **Helvētiōrum,** gen. plur. of *Helvētiī, -ōrum,* m.; it limits *cōpiās.* —— **ut,** telic conj.; it generally stands at the head of its clause; its normal position in this case is immediately before *reliquās;* observe how the group of words immediately preceding it are made emphatic by its abnormal position. —— **cōnsequī,** pres. inf. of the deponent verb *cōnsequor, -sequī, secūtus* (con, *intensive* + sequī; compare the GK. ἔπεσθαι); *cōnsequī* is a complementary inf. See A. & G. 271; B. 181; G. 423; H. 533, I, 2. —— **posset,** 3d pers. sing. imperf. subjunctive of *possum, posse, potuī* (potis + sum); subjunctive of purpose after *ut.* Consult A. & G. 317, 1; B. 200, (*b*); G. 545, 1; H. 497, II.

LINE 3. **pontem,** acc. sing. of the noun *pōns, pontis,* m.; acc. with the gerundive denoting purpose. —— **in,** prep. with the acc. or abl.; here it takes the abl. —— **Ararī,** abl. sing. of the noun *Arar, -aris,* m. (the Saône); it has the acc. *-im* or *-em,* abl. *-ī* or *-e; Ararī* is the obj. of the prep. *in,* which here = *on.* The bridge built on the Arar was, probably, a pontoon bridge. —— **faciendum,** acc. of the gerundive *faciendus, -a, -um* of *fīō, fierī, factus,* 3; the gerundive with the obj. is used to denote purpose. See A. & G. 294, *d*; B. 184, REM. 4, III, (*a*); G. 430; H. 544, NOTE 2. —— **cūrat,** 3d pers. sing. pres. ind. act. of *cūrō, -āre, -āvō, -ātum,* 1; it agrees with its subj. implied in the ending, referring to Caesar. —— **atque,** conj.; it adds, usually, a more important notion; see note on this particle, l. 10, Chap. I.

LINE 4. **ita,** adv. (radical *i,* whence is + ta); hence = *in this manner, thus.* —— **exercitum,** acc. sing. of *exercitus, -ūs,* m.; direct obj. of *trādūcit.* For synonyms, see note on *exercitū,* l. 31, Chap. III. —— **trādūcit,** 3d pers. sing. pres. ind. act. of *trādūcō, -ere, -dūxī, -ductum,* 3 (trāns + dūcere); it is connected by *atque* with *cūrat,* and is in the same grammatical construction. —— **Helvētiī,** nom. plur. of *Helvētiī, -ōrum,* m.; subj. of *mittunt,* l. 9, below. —— **repentīnō,** abl. sing. m. of the adj. *repentīnus, -a, -um;* it modifies *adventū.*

LINE 5. **ēius,** gen. sing. of the dem. pron. *is, ea, id,* used as a personal pron. of the 3d pers.; as a gen. it limits *adventū.* —— **adventū,** abl. sing. of the noun *adventus, -ūs,* m.; abl. of cause after *commōtī.* · See A. & G. 245, and 2, *b*; B. 165, and REM. 4; G. 408, and NOTE 2; H. 416, and NOTE 1. —— **commōtī,** nom. plur. of the perf. pass. participle *commōtus, -a, -um* of the verb *commoneō, -ēre, -mōvī, -mōtum,* 2; it agrees with *Helvētiī.* —— **cum,** conj., temporal. —— **id,** acc. sing. n. of the dem.

LINES 6-9.]   BOOK I.   85

6	ipsī *themselves*	diēbus *in days*	vīgintī *twenty*	aegerrimē *with very great trouble*	they saw that he had actualized in a single day what
7	cōnfēcerant, *had accomplished,*	ut *that*	flūmen *the river*	trānsīrent, *they might cross,*	illum *him,*	they had, with the greatest difficulty, accomplished in twenty
8	ūnō *in one*	diē *day*	fēcisse *to have done,*	intellegerent, *they perceived,*	lēgātōs *delegates*	ad *to*	days, namely, the crossing of the
9	eum *him*	mittunt; *they send;*	cūius *of which*	lēgātiōnis *delegation*	Divicō *Divico*	river, they sent ambassadors to him. Of this

pron. *is, ea, id,* used as a personal pron. of the 3d pers., and the direct obj. of *fēcisse*, l. 8, below. —— **quod,** acc. sing. n. of the rel. pron. *quī, quae, quod;* it refers to *id* as its antecedent, but is the direct obj. of *cōnfēcerant.* Observe that the reference, logically, is to the noun-clause *ut flūmen trānsīrent,* which is in apposition with *id;* that, when the reference is thus to a group of words, *id quod* or *quae rēs* is used instead of the simple *quod.* Consult A. & G. 200, *e*; B. 129, REM. 8; G. 614, REM. 2; H. 445, 7.

LINE 6. **ipsī,** nom. plur. of the intensive dem. pron. *ipse, -sa, -sum;* it refers to *Helvētiī;* is expressed for emphasis, and is the subject-nom. of *cōnfēcerant.* —— **diēbus,** abl. plur. of *diēs, -ēī,* m. and f. in the sing.; always m. in the plur.; abl. of *time within which.* A. & G. 256, 1; B. 171; G. 393; H. 429. —— **vīgintī,** num. adj. cardinal, modifies *diēbus.* —— **aegerrimē,** adv., superl. degree; positive degree *aegrē.* comparative *aegrius. aegrē = vix,* GK. μόλις. *aegerrimē* modifies *cōnfēcerant.*

LINE 7. **cōnfēcerant,** 3d pers. plur. pluperf. ind. act. of *cōnficiō, -ere, -fēcī, -fectum,* 3; it agrees with its subject-nom. *ipsī.* —— **ut,** ecbatic conj. —— **flūmen,** acc. sing. of the noun *flūmen, -inis,* n. (*fluere,* to flow); hence the noun = *a flowing;* direct obj. of *trānsīrent.* —— **trānsīrent,** 3d pers. plur. imperf. subjunctive of *trānseō, -īre, -īvī (-iī), -itum;* it agrees with a subject implied in the ending, referring to *Helvētiī;* it is in the subjunctive mode, because it is in a subst.-clause of result, referring to the pron. *id,* and with which it is, grammatically, in apposition. Consult A. & G. 332, *f*; B. 201, REM. 1, (*b*); G. 553, 1, and 557; H. 501, II, 1, and III. —— **illum,** acc. sing. m. of the dem. pron. *ille, -la, -lud,* gen. *illīus,* dat. *illī. illum* is the subject-acc. of *fēcisse;* it refers to Caesar; it is expressed to indicate the contrast between Caesar and the Helvetii; compare *ipsī,* preceding line.

LINE 8. **ūnō,** abl. sing. m. of the num. adj. *ūnus, -a, -um,* gen. *ūnīus,* dat. *ūnī;* it modifies *diē.* —— **diē,** abl. sing. of *diēs, diēī;* abl. of *time in which.* See note and grammatical references on *diēbus,* l. 6, above. —— **fēcisse,** perf. inf. act. of *faciō, -ere, fēcī, factum,* 3; it agrees with its subject-acc. *illum;* and the acc. and inf. depend on *intellegerent.* —— **intellegerent,** 3d pers. plur. imperf. subjunctive act. of *intellegō, -ere, -lēxī, -lēctum,* 3 (inter + legere); hence *interlegere* = lit. *to select between.* Note that this verb is often written *intelligō. intellegerent* is in the subjunctive after *cum,* temporal, l. 5, above. Consult A. & G. 325; B. 222; G. 585; H. 521, II, 2. —— **lēgātōs,** acc. plur. of *lēgātus, -ī,* m. (*lēgere,* to despatch); direct obj. of *mittunt.* —— **ad,** prep. with the acc.

LINE 9. **eum,** acc. sing. m. of the dem. pron. *is, ea, id,* used as a personal pron. of the 3d pers.; it is the obj. of the prep. *ad;* it refers to Caesar. Observe that the prep. with the acc. is used with verbs of motion. —— **mittunt,** 3d pers. plur. pres.

embassy Divico, who had been the leader of the Helvetii in the war with Cassius, was the chief. He thus addressed Caesar: If the Roman people	prīnceps *chief*	fuit, *was,*	quī *who*	bellō *in the war*	Cassiānō *with Cassius*	dux *leader*	10
	Helvētiōrum *of the Helvetii*		fuerat. *had been.*	Is *He*	ita *thus*	cum *with*	Caesare *Caesar*	11
	ēgit: *treated:*	Sī *If*	pācem *peace*	populus *the people*	Rōmānus *Roman*	cum *with*	12

ind. act. of *mittō, -ere, mīsī, mīssum,* 3; historical pres.; it agrees with the subject-nom. *Helvētiī*, expressed in l. 4, above. The reader will note that Caesar uses the historic present, here and elsewhere, frequently, while the sequence of the tenses in the subordinate clauses is secondary. —— **cūius,** gen. sing. f. of the rel. pron. *quī, quae, quod;* as a rel., it refers to *lēgātōs*, but is here used adjectively, and agrees in gender, number and case with *lēgātiōnis.* The reader will recall that a rel. pron. at the beginning of a sentence is, often, best rendered into English by a dem. pron. with the conj. *and* or *but.* Consult A. & G. 180, *f*; B. 129, REM. 9; G. 610; H. 453. —— **lēgātiōnis,** gen. sing. of the noun *lēgātiō, -ōnis,* f.; it limits *prīnceps*, which is here used as a predicate-noun after *fuit.* —— **Divicō, -ōnis,** m., proper noun, subject-nom. of *fuit. Divicō* was an influential chief among the Helvetii.

LINE 10. **prīnceps, -ipis,** usually an adj.; here used substantively, and in the predicate. —— **fuit,** 3d pers. sing. perf. ind. of the irr. intrans. verb *sum, esse, fuī,* fut. participle *futūrus;* it is here the perf. indef. and the copula. —— **quī,** nom. sing. m. of the rel. pron. *quī, quae, quod;* it refers to *Divicō* as its antecedent, and is subject-nom. of *fuerat.* —— **bellō,** abl. sing. of the noun *bellum, -ī,* n.; locative abl. Consult A. & G. 258, *f*, 1; B. 170, REM. 4; G. 389; H. 425, II, 1, 1). As to the original form of *bellum,* consult note on this word, l. 15, Chap. I. —— **Cassiānō,** abl. sing. n. of the adj. *Cassiānus, -a, -um;* it is an attributive of *bellō.* The adj. is derived from the proper noun *Cassius,* and = *of Cassius, Cassianian.* The allusion is to the battle in which Lucius Cassius was slain by the Tigurini. See note on *Cassium,* l. 20, Chap. VII. —— **dux, ducis,** m. and f. (compare *dūcere,* to lead); predicate-noun after *fuerat.*

LINE 11. **Helvētiōrum,** gen. plur. of *Helvētiī, -ōrum,* m.; poss. gen., limiting *dux.* —— **fuerat,** 3d pers. sing. pluperf. ind. of *sum, esse, fuī, futūrus;* it agrees with its subject-nom. *quī.* —— **Is,** nom. sing. m. of the dem. pron. *is, ea, id;* it is here used as a personal pron. of the 3d pers.; it refers to *Divicō;* it is subject-nom. of *ēgit;* expressed for emphasis, but is the weakest of all the dem. pronouns. —— **ita,** adv. (radical *i,* whence is + ending ta) = lit. *in this manner;* as an adv. *ita* modifies *ēgit,* but refers to what follows. —— **cum,** prep. with the abl. —— **Caesare,** abl. sing. of *Caesar, -aris,* m.; it is the obj. of the prep. *cum.*

LINE 12. **ēgit,** 3d pers. sing. perf. ind. act. of *agō, -ere, ēgī, actum,* 3; it agrees with its subject-nom. *is;* i.e. *Divicō.* The reader will observe that the remainder of this chapter is in the *ōrātiō oblīqua.* Consult A. & G. 336, 1, 2, to 340; B. 244, 245, entire; G. 650-61; H. 520-30. —— **Sī** (archaic form *seī,* sibilated from the GK. *ei*), conditional particle, introducing the protasis of the sentence. —— **pācem,** acc. sing. of the noun *pāx, pācis,* f. (compare *pācāre,* to pacify); direct obj. of *faceret.* —— **populus,** nom. sing. of *populus, -ī,* m.; subject-nom. of *faceret.* For synonyms, see note on *populus,* l. 17, Chap. VI. —— **Rōmānus,** nom. sing. m. of the adj. *Rōmānus, -a, -um;* it is the attributive of *populus.* —— **cum,** prep. with the abl. *Helvētiīs.* Instead of *cum Helvētiīs, nōbīscum* might be used in the direct form.

13 Helvētiīs	faceret,	in	eam	partem		would make peace with the Helvetii, they would go in such direction, and remain in such a place as Caesar would appoint or wish; but if he persisted in pursuing them with war, let him re-
the Helvetii	*would make,*	*in*	*that*	*part*		
14 itūrōs	atque	ibi	futūrōs	Helvētiōs,		
to be about to go	*and*	*there*	*to be about to be*	*the Helvetii,*		
15 ubi	eōs	Caesar	cōnstituisset	atque	esse	
where	*them*	*Caesar*	*had determined,*	*and*	*to be*	
16 voluisset;	sīn	bellō	persequī	perseverāret,		
had wished;	*but if with*	*war*	*to follow up*	*he persevered,*		

LINE 13. **Helvētiīs**, abl. plur. of the adj. *Helvētius, -a, -um*, used substantively; abl. after the prep. *cum*. For historical information, see note on *Helvētii*, l. 16, Chap. I. —— **faceret**, 3d pers. sing. imperf. subjunctive act. of *faciō, -ere, fēcī, factum*, 3; it agrees with its subject-nom. *populus Rōmānus*; it is in the subjunctive, because it represents the fut. ind. in the more vivid conditional form after *sī* in the *ōrātio recta*. Consult A. & G. 336, 2; B. 245, (*b*); G. 650; H. 524; it is in the imperf. tense, because the secondary sequence is required after the secondary *ēgit*, on which the entire speech, logically, depends. Mark now that the protasis, as the subordinate clause, is always in the subjunctive in the *ōrātio oblīqua*. —— **in**, prep. with the acc. or abl., but with difference of signification; here it takes the acc. For meaning of *in* with the acc., see note on *in*, l. 1, end, Chap. I. —— **eam**, acc. sing. f. of the dem. pron. *is, ea, id;* it is an attributive of *partem*. —— **partem**, acc. sing. of *pars, partis*, f.; it is the obj. of the prep. *in*.

LINE 14. **itūrōs (esse)**, fut. inf. act. of *eō, īre, īvī (iī), itum;* its subject-acc. is *Helvētiōs*. Observe that *itūros (esse)* is for *ībunt* of direct discourse; and consult A. & G. 336, 2; B. 245, 1, (*a*); G. 527; H. 523, I. —— **atque** (ad + que), conj.; see note on this particle, l. 10, Chap. I; it connects *itūrōs (esse)* and *futūrōs (esse)*. —— **ibi**, adv. (from the radical *i*, whence is + locative ending bi); hence = in *that* place, *there*. *ibi* modifies *futūrōs (esse)*. —— **futūrōs (esse)**, fut. inf. of *sum, esse, fuī;* connected by the conj. *atque* with *itūrōs (esse)*, and in the same grammatical construction. *futūrōs (esse)* is for *erunt* of direct discourse. —— **Helvētiōs**, acc. plur. of the adj. *Helvētius, -a, -um*, used substantively, and is subject-acc. of both *itūrōs (esse)* and *futūrōs (esse)*.

LINE 15. **ubi** (quō + locative ending bi) = of place, *where;* of time, *when;* here as correlative of *ibi* it = *where*. As an adv. it modifies *cōnstituisset*. —— **eōs**, acc. plur. m. of the dem. pron. *is, ea, id*, used as a personal pron. of the 3d pers.; it is the direct obj. of *cōnstituisset;* it refers to the Helvetii. —— **Caesar**, -**aris**, m., subject-nom. of *cōnstituisset*. —— **cōnstituisset**, 3d pers. sing. pluperf. subjunctive of *cōnstituō, -ere, -stituī, -stitūtum*, 3; it agrees with its subject-nom. *Caesar*, and is in the subjunctive mode, because it is in a dependent clause in *ōrātiō oblīqua*. This pluperf. subjunctive is for the fut. perf. *cōnstitūeris* in the *ōrātiō recta*. —— **atque**, see note on this particle, l. 14, above. —— **esse**, pres. inf. of the intrans. verb *sum*, perf. ind. *fuī*, fut. participle *futūrus;* its subject-acc. is *eōs*, to be supplied; the infinitive-clause *eōs esse* is the direct obj. of *voluisset*.

LINE 16. **voluisset**, 3d pers. sing. pluperf. subjunctive of *volo, velle, voluī;* connected by the conj. *atque* with *cōnstituisset*, and in the subjunctive mode for the same reason. —— **sīn** (sī + nē, apocopated) = *but if*. —— **bellō**, abl. of *bellum, -ī*, n.; abl.

member both the ancient disaster to the Roman people, and the former valor of the Helvetii. As to his having suddenly attacked the people of a single canton, while those who had crossed the	reminīscerētur	et	veteris	incommodī	populī 17
	he should remember	*both*	*the old*	*disaster*	*of the people*
	Rōmānī	et	prīstinae	virtūtis	Helvētiōrum. 18
	Roman	*and*	*the former*	*valor*	*of the Helvetii.*
	Quod		imprōvīsō	ūnum	pāgum 19
	As to the fact that he		*suddenly*	*one*	*canton*
	adortus esset,	cum	eī,	quī	flūmen 20
	had attacked,	*when*	*those,*	*who*	*the river*

of means. A. & G. 248, *c*, 1; B. 167; G. 401; H. 420. —— **persequī**, pres. inf. of the deponent verb *persequor, -sequī, -secūtus,* 3; complementary inf. Consult A. & G. 271; B. 181; G. 423; H. 533, I, 1. —— **persevērāret**, 3d pers. sing. imperf. subjunctive of *persevēro, -āre, -āvī, -ātum,* 1; imperf. subjunctive in condition in *ōrātiō oblīqua* for the fut., *persevērābis* in *ōrātiō rēcta.* Observe the difference of idiom. Latin: if he should persist *to follow;* English: if he should persist *in following.*

LINE 17. **reminīscerētur**, 3d pers. sing. imperf. subjunctive of the deponent verb *reminīscor, -ī (mēns,* mind), 3; hortatory subjunctive for the imperative *reminīscere,* of direct discourse. As to the hortatory subjunctive, consult A. & G. 266, *e*; B. 189, I, (*b*); G. 263, 2; H. 484, II. As to the subjunctive in indirect discourse, for the imperative in direct, consult A. & G. 339; B. 245, 2; G. 652; H. 523, III. —— et . . . et = *both . . . and.* —— **veteris**, gen. sing. n. of the adj. *vetus, veteris;* comparative *veterior;* superl. *veterrimus.* —— **incommodī**, gen. sing. of the noun *incommodum, -ī,* n. (in, *negative* + *commodum*); gen. after *reminīscerētur,* a verb of *remembering.* Consult A. & G. 219; B. 135, (*b*); G. 376; H. 406, II. The allusion is to the defeat of Cassius. —— **populī**, gen. of *populus, -ī,* m.; gen. objective; it limits *incommodī.* For synonyms, see note on *populum,* l. 17, Chap. VI.

LINE 18. **Rōmānī**, gen. sing. m. of the adj. *Rōmānus, -a, -um;* it is an attributive of *populī.* —— **prīstinae**, gen. sing. f. of the adj. *prīstinus, -a, -um* (from obsolete *pris,* whence *prīscus* and *prior*); it modifies *virtūtis.* —— **virtūtis**, gen. sing. of the noun *virtus, -tūtis,* f.; connected by the conj. *et* with *incommodī,* and in the same grammatical construction. —— **Helvētiōrum**, gen. plur. of the adj. *Helvētius, -a, -um,* used as a noun; poss. gen.; it limits *virtūtis.*

LINE 19. **Quod**, acc. sing. n. of the rel. *quī, quae, quod;* acc. of specification = *as to the fact that.* Observe that the clause *Quod . . . adortus esset* is an adverbial modifier of the principal clause in the sentence. —— **imprōvīsō**, adv.; really an abl. of the adj. *imprōvīsus, -a, -um,* used as an adv.; it modifies *adortus esset.* —— **ūnum**, acc. sing. m. of the adj. *ūnus, -a -um;* it is an attributive of *pāgum.* —— **pāgum**, acc. of *pāgus, -ī,* m.; direct obj. of deponent *adortus esset. Ōrātiō rēcta* of lines 12–18: Sī pācem populus Rōmānus cum Helvētiīs *faciet,* in eam partem *ībunt* atque ibi *erunt Helvētiī,* ubi eōs *tū cōnstitueris* atque esse *volueris;* sīn bellō persequī *persevērābis, reminīscere* et veteris incommodī populī Rōmānī, et prīstinae virtūtis Helvētiōrum.

LINE 20. **adortus esset**, 3d pers. sing. pluperf. subjunctive of *adorior, -orīrī, -ortus,* 4, deponent; subjunctive, because it is a verb in a subordinate clause in the *ōrātiō oblīqua.* The form in *ōrātiō rēcta* is *adortus es.* For *quod = as to the fact that* with the subjunctive, see A. & G. 333, *a,* and 341, *a,* and REM.; B. 123, REM. 21, and 198, REM. 1; G. 525, 2 and 3; H. 516, II, and especially the NOTE. —— **cum**, conj.,

[LINES 21-23.]   BOOK I.   89

21 trānsīssent,	suīs		auxilium	ferre	nōn
had crossed,	*to their (friends)*		*aid*	*to bring*	*not*
22 possent,	nē	ob	eam	rem	aut	suae
were able,	*not*	*on account of*	*that*	*thing*	*either to his own,*
23 māgnō	opere	virtūtī	tribueret	aut	ipsōs
with great labor,		*valor should he ascribe,*	*or*	*themselves*

river could not bring aid to their friends, let him not on this account attribute too much to his own valor, or despise them. For

---

temporal. —— eī, nom. plur. m. of the dem. pron. *is, ea, id*, used substantively, and is the subject-nom. of *possent*. —— quī, nom. plur. m. of the rel. pron. *quī, quae, quod;* it refers to *eī* as its antecedent, but is the subject-nom. of *trānsīssent*. —— flūmen, acc. sing. of the noun *flūmen, -inis*, n.; direct obj. of *trānsīssent*.

LINE 21. trānsīssent, 3d pers. plur. pluperf. subjunctive of *trānseō, -īre, -īvī (-iī), -itum;* syncopated and contracted for *trānsīvissent*. As to syncopation and contraction, see A. & G. 128, 2; B. 251; G. 131, 1; H. 235. *trānsīssent* is subjunctive, because it is in a subordinate clause in the *ōrātiō oblīqua*. The proper form in the *ōrātiō rēcta* is the pluperf. ind. *trānsierant*, syncopated for *trānsīverant* —— suīs, dat. plur. m. of the poss. adjective-pron. *suus, -a, -um;* in the m. plur. used substantively to designate *persons;* in the n. plur., to designate *things*. See A. & G. 190, *a*; B. 60, REM.; G. 204, NOTE 1, *b*; H. 441, 1. *suīs* is dat. of the indirect obj. after *ferre*. —— auxilium, acc. sing. of *auxilium, -ī*, n. (*augēre*, to increase); direct obj. of *ferre*. —— ferre, pres. inf. of the verb *ferō, ferre, tulī, lātum; ferre* is a complementary inf., depending on *possent*. —— nōn, adv. (nē + ūnum, apocopated); observe its position: immediately before the word it modifies.

LINE 22. possent, 3d pers. plur. imperf. subjunctive of *possum, posse, potuī* (potis + sum); it agrees with its subject-nom. *eī;* it is in the subjunctive, after *cum*, denoting both *time* and *cause*. —— nē, negative adv., the particle used with the hortatory subjunctive. —— ob, prep. with the acc. = lit. *to* or *toward*, compare GK. ἐπί; transf., it indicates the cause = *for*. —— eam, acc. sing. f. of the dem. pron. *is, ea, id;* it is an attributive of *rem*. —— rem, acc. sing. of the noun *rēs, reī*, f.; stem *rē*, which is shortened in the gen. and dat. sing.; *rem* is the obj. of the prep. *ob*. —— aut ... aut = *either ... or*. These particles, thus used, denote that the difference is exclusive; but see note on them, l. 19, Chap. I. —— suae, dat. sing. f. of the poss. pron. *suus, -a, -um;* it refers to Caesar, the subj. of the proposition, but agrees, in gender, number and case, with *virtūtī*.

LINE 23. māgnō, abl. sing. n. of the adj. *māgnus, -a, -um;* comparative *māior*, superl. *māximus; māgnō* modifies *opere*. —— opere, abl. sing. of *opus, operis*, n.; with *māgnō* it is an abl. of manner = lit. *with great labor;* hence = adv. *greatly;* the words as one word are frequently written *māgnopere*. —— virtūtī, dat. of the noun *virtūs, virtūtis*, f.; dat. of the indirect obj. after *tribueret;* supply *quicquam* as direct obj. —— tribueret, 3d pers. sing. imperf. subjunctive act. of *tribuō, -ere, -uī, -ūtum*, 3 (compare *tribus*, a division); it agrees with a subj. implied in the ending, referring to Caesar. Observe that the subjunctive here in the *ōrātiō oblīqua* is the hortatory subjunctive for the 2d pers. sing. of the perf. subjunctive with *nē* in the direct form *nē tribueris*, which latter is for the imperative; and indeed *nōlī tribuere* might be used in the direct form, as an elegant equivalent for *nē tribueret* of the indirect form. Consult A. & G. 269, *a*, 1 and 2; B. 189, REM. 1; G. 270, 2; H. 489. —— aut, see note on this particle, preceding line. —— ipsōs, acc. plur. m. of the dem. pron. *ipse, -sa, -sum*, gen. *ipsīus*, dat. *ipsī* (is + pse); *ipse* = *self;* it belongs to the emphatic word. *ipsōs* refers to the Helvetii, and is the direct obj. of *dēspiceret*.

90   CAESAR'S GALLIC WAR   [CHAP. XIII.

the Helvetii had been so instructed by their fathers and ancestors, that they waged war relying more on valor than on artifice or stratagem. Wherefore, let him not cause	dēspiceret. should he despise.	Sē Themselves	ita so	ā from	patribus the fathers	24
	māiōribusque ancestors	suīs and, their own	dīdicisse, to have learned,		ut that	magis more	25
	virtūte by valor	contenderent they fought,	quam than		dolō on treachery	aut or	26
	insidiīs ambuscades	nīterentur. they relied.	Quārē Wherefore,	nē not should	committeret he bring to pass		27

LINE 24. dēspiceret, 3d pers. sing. imperf. subjunctive act. of *dēspiciō, -ere, -spexī, -spectum,* 3 (dē + spicere); hence *dēspicere* = lit. *to look down* on one. The subjunctive hortatory is for the imperative, or its equivalent, in direct discourse. See note on *tribueret,* preceding line. —— Sē, acc. plur. of the reflexive pron. *suī, sibi, sē, sē,* same form in both numbers; subject-acc. of *didicisse. sē* is for *nōs* in the *ōrātiō rēcta.* —— ita, adv. (radical *i,* whence is + ta) = *in this way,* i.e. *thus.* —— ā, prep. with the abl. (*ā* before consonants, *ab* before vowels or consonants). —— patribus, abl. plur. of the noun *pater, patris,* m.; abl. of the source after the prep. *ā.*

LINE 25. māiōribusque (māiōribus + que). *māiōribus,* abl. plur. m. of the adj. *māior, -ius,* used substantively; *māiōribus* may, or may not, be followed by *nātū;* it is connected by the enclitic *-que* with *patribus,* and is in the same grammatical construction. *Ōrātiō rēcta* of lines 19–24: Quod imprōvīsō ūnum pāgum *adortus es,* cum eī, quī flūmen *trānsierant,* suīs auxilium ferre nōn possent, nē ob *hanc* rem aut *tuae* māgnō opere virtūtī *tribueris,* aut *nōs dēspēxeris.* —— suīs, abl. plur. of the poss. reflexive pron. *suus, -a, -um;* it is an attributive of *patribus māiōribusque.* —— didicisse, perf. inf. act. of *discō, -ere, didicī,* 3. This inf. is for *didicimus* in the *ōrātiō rēcta.* —— ut, ecbatic conj. —— magis, adv., comparative degree; positive *multum;* superl. *māximē.*

LINE 26. virtūte, abl. sing. of *virtūs, -ūtis,* f.; abl. of means. —— contenderent, 3d pers. plur. imperf. subjunctive of *contendō, -ere, -tendī, -tentum,* 3; subjunctive, because in a result-clause after *ut,* referring to the adv. *ita.* See A. & G. 319; B. 201.; G. 552; H. 500, II. —— quam, conj., following *magis;* after comparatives or words of comparison *quam* = *than.* —— dolō, abl. of the noun *dolus, -ī. dolō* is an abl. of means. —— aut, see note on this particle, l. 22, above.

LINE 27. insidiīs, abl. plur. of *īnsidiae, -ārum,* f.; the sing. *īnsidia, -ae,* f., is rare. *īnsidiīs* is connected by the disjunctive conj. *aut* with *dolō,* and is in the abl. for the same reason. Observe that Latin *dolus* = GK. δόλος; compare GK. τέχνη and English *craft;* hence *dolus* = originally, *artifice.* But in later usage, either with or without the attributive *malus, dolus* = *guile, deception;* whereas *īnsidiae* = lit. *an ambush;* metaphorically = *stratagem.* For the peculiarity of the grammatical construction of *dolō* and *īnsidiīs* with *nīterentur,* see A. & G. 254, *b;* B. 167, 5; G. 401, REM. 6; H. 425, II, 1, 1), and NOTE. But this abl. is, in fact, an abl. of means or instrument. —— nīterentur, 3d pers. plur. imperf. subjunctive of the deponent verb *nītor, -ī, nīsus* or *nīxus,* 3; it is connected by the conj. *quam* with *contenderent,* and in the subjunctive for the same reason. —— Quārē, adv. (quā + rē) = lit. *by which thing.* —— nē, see note on *nē* with *tribueret,* l. 22, above. —— committeret, 3d pers. sing. imperf. subjunctive act.; subjunctive for imperative in direct discourse. For explanations and grammatical references, see note on *tribueret,* l. 23, above.

BOOK I.   91

28 ut is locus, ubi cōnstitissent, ex calamitāte	this place where they stood to take its name or transmit a tradition from the defeat of the Roman people and the destruction of an army.
that that place, where they had stood, from the loss	
29 populī Rōmānī et interneciōne exercitūs	
of the people Roman and the utter destruction of an army	
30 nōmen caperet, aut memoriam prōderet.	
(its) name should take or the memory hand down.	

LINE 28. **ut**, ecbatic conj. Observe that *committere ut* with the subjunctive following often form a periphrasis for a simple verb. Consult A. & G. 332, *e*; B. 201, REM. 1, (*b*); G. 533, I, 1; H. 501, II, 1, compare 498, II, NOTE 2. —— **is**, nom. sing. m. of the dem. pron. *is, ea, id*; *is* is an attributive of *locus*. Observe that *is* is the weakest of all the Latin demonstratives, and that, accordingly, the Latin phrase *is locus* is scarcely more definite than the English *the place*. —— **locus**, nom. sing. of the noun, *locus, -ī*, m. in the sing.; m. or n. in the plur., but with difference of meaning. See note on *loci*, l. 10, Chap. II. *locus* is subject-nom. of *caperet* and *prōderet*, l. 30, below. —— **ubi** (quō + bi) = of place, *where*; transf. of time = *when*. —— **cōnstitissent**, 3d pers. plur. pluperf. subjunctive of *cōnsistō, -ere, -stitī*, 3 (con + sistere); subjunctive, because in a subordinate clause in the *ōrātiō oblīqua*; it is for the perf. ind. *cōnstitimus* in the *ōrātiō rēcta*. —— **ex**, prep. with the abl. (*ē* before consonants, *ex* before vowels or consonants). —— **calamitāte**, abl. sing. of *calamitās, -ātis*, f. (derived, according to some, from *calamus*); originally it designated *mutilation of crops*; hence *calamitās = loss, misfortune*. *calamitāte* is in the abl. after the prep. *ex* denoting cause. A. & G. 245; B. 120, 2; G. 408, NOTE 3; H. 416, I, 1).

LINE 29. **populī**, gen. sing. of *populus, -ī*, m.; it, as a gen., limits *calamitāte*. For synonyms, see note on *populus Rōmānus*, l. 17, Chap. VI. —— **Rōmānī**, gen. sing. of the adj. *Rōmānus, -a, -um*; it is an attributive of *populī*. —— **interneciōne**, abl. sing. of the noun *interneciō, -ōnis*, f. (inter, intensive + necāre); as *necāre = to kill, internecare = to murder*; hence *interneciō = utter destruction*. *interneciōne* is connected by *et* with *calamitāte*, and is in the same grammatical construction. —— **exercitūs**, gen. sing. of the noun *exercitus, -ūs*, m.; as a gen., *exercitūs* limits *interneciōne*. For synonyms, see note on *exercitū*, l. 31, Chap. III.

LINE 30. **nōmen**, acc. sing. of the noun *nōmen, -inis*, n. (for *gnōmen* from stem *gnō*, GK. γνόω, archaic Latin form *gnōscō*). *nōmen* is the direct obj. of *caperet*. —— **caperet**, 3d pers. sing. imperf. subjunctive of *capiō, -ere, cēpī, captum*, 3; it agrees with its subject-nom. *locus* and is subjunctive *of result* after *ut*. —— **aut**, see note on this particle, l. 22, above. —— **memoriam**, acc. sing. of the noun *memoria, -ae*, f. (*memor*); it is the direct obj. of *prōderet*. —— **prōderet**, 3d pers. sing. imperf. subjunctive of *prōdō, -ere, -idī, -itum*, 3 (prō + dare); connected by the conj. *aut* with *caperet*, and in the same grammatical construction; i.e. agrees with *locus* as its subject-nom., and is the subjunctive *of result* after *ut*. *Ōrātiō rēcta* of lines 24-30: *Nōs ita ā patribus māiōribusque nostrīs didicimus, ut magis virtūte contendāmus quam dolō aut insidiīs nītāmur. Quārē nē commīseris* (nōlī committere), *ut hīc locus, ubi cōnstitimus, ex calamitāte populī Rōmānī et interneciōne exercitūs nōmen capiat, aut memoriam prōdat.* Observe that *cōnstitissent*, l. 28, above, of the text, stands for the perf. ind. *cōnstitimus* in the *ōrātiō rēcta*. See *adortus esset*, l. 20, above = *adortus es*, in direct discourse.

XIV. To these ambassadors Caesar replied thus: He had the less hesitation in regard to his conduct, because he remembered the incidents which the Helvetian envoys had mentioned—	XIV.	Hīs *To these (envoys)* Eō *On this account* quod *because* commemorāssent *had mentioned,*	Caesar *Caesar* sibi *to himself* eās *those*	ita *thus* minus *less* rēs *things* memoriā *in memory*	respondit: *replied:* dubitātiōnis *of doubt* quās *which* tenēret, *he held,*	1 darī, *to be given,* 2 lēgātī *the envoys* Helvētiī *Helvetian* atque *and* 3 4

LINE 1. **Hīs**, dat. plur. m. of the dem. pron. *hĭc, haec, hōc;* used as a personal pron. of the 3d pers.; indirect obj. of the verb *respondit;* the allusion is to the ambassadors, of whom Divico was the leader and spokesman. —— **Caesar, -aris,** m.; subject-nom. of *respondit.* —— **ita,** adv. (from radical *i,* whence is + ta) = lit. *in this manner,* i.e. *thus.* —— **respondit,** 3d pers. sing. perf. ind. act. of *respondeō, -ēre, -spondī, -spōnsum,* 2 (re + spondēre) = originally, to promise something in return for something; hence transf. = *to answer. respondit* agrees with its subject-nom. *Caesar.* The reader will observe that from this point the self-reported speech of Caesar continues to *esse factūrum,* l. 34, below; that it is reported just as formally as it would have been if it were a speech of another, and not Caesar's.

LINE 2. **Eō,** abl. sing. n. of the dem. pron. *is, ea, id;* abl. of degree of difference after *minus.* Consult A. & G. 250, and NOTE; B. 164, REM. 1; G. 403; H. 423. The older grammars explain this construction as an abl. of cause; it appears to be the herald here of the following *quod*-clause. —— **sibi,** dat. sing. m. of the reflexive pron. *suī, sibi, sē, sē,* same form in both numbers; dat. of the indirect obj. after the pass. verb *darī.* —— **minus,** acc. sing. n. of the comparative adj. *minor, -us;* positive *parvus,* superl. *minimus. minus* is used substantively, and is the subject-acc. of the pass. inf. *darī.* —— **dubitātiōnis,** gen. sing. of *dubitātiō, -ōnis,* f.; partitive after *minus.* See A. & G. 216, 2; B. 134; G. 372; H. 397, 3. —— **darī,** pres. inf. pass. of the act. *dō, dare, dedī, datum,* 3; pass. parts: *dor, darī, datus.* Observe that, by exception to the rule, *a* is short before -*re* in the pres. inf. act. *darī* agrees with its subject-acc. *minus,* used as a noun. Let the reader recall that in the *ōrātiō oblīqua* the main clause of a declaratory sentence is put in the inf. with subject-acc. *darī,* accordingly, is for *datur* in *ōrātiō rēcta.*

LINE 3. **quod,** conj. = *because. quod,* which is in fact an adverbial acc. sing. n. of *quī,* attained its causal meaning from the original signification of *in what respect, in that.* —— **eās,** acc. plur. f. of the dem. pron. *is, ea, id;* it is an attributive of *rēs.* —— **rēs,** acc. plur. of *rēs, reī,* f.; the direct obj. of *tenēret.* —— **quās,** acc. plur. f. of the rel. pron. *quī, quae, quod;* it refers to *rēs* as its antecedent, but is the direct obj. of *commemorāssent.* —— **lēgātī,** nom. plur. of the noun *lēgātus, -ī,* m. (*lēgere,* to delegate); subject-nom. of *commemorāssent.* —— **Helvētiī,** nom. plur. m. of the adj. *Helvētius, -a, -um. Helvētiī* is an attributive of *lēgātī.*

LINE 4. **commemorāssent,** 3d pers. plur. pluperf. subjunctive of *commemorō, -āre, -āvī, -ātum,* 1, for the uncontracted form *commemorāvissent;* it agrees with its subject-nom. *lēgātī.* As to syncopation and contraction, see A. & G. 128, 2; B. 251; G. 131, 1; H. 235. *commemorāssent* is in the subjunctive, because it is in a subordinate clause in *ōrātiō oblīqua.* Consult A. & G. 336, 2; B. 245, 1, (*b*); G. 650; H. 524. —— **memoriā,** abl. sing. of the noun *memoriă -ae,* f.; abl. of means, a

BOOK I.   93

5 eō	gravius	ferre,	quō	tioned, and was the more indignant at them, the less they had occurred in accordance with the deserts of the Roman people. If they had been
by so much	*the more heavily*	*to bear (them), by how much*		
6 minus	meritō	populī	Rōmānī	
the less	*according to the merit*	*of the people*	*Roman*	
7 accidissent;	quī	sī	alicūius	iniūriae	
they had happened;	*who*	*if*	*of any*	*wrong*	

species of locative. Consult A. & G. 248, *c*; B. 167; G. 401; H. 420. —— **tenēret**, 3d pers. sing. imperf. subjunctive act. of *teneō, -ēre, -uī, tentum*, 2; it agrees with a pron. as subj. implied in the ending, referring to *Caesar;* it is in the subjunctive mode, because it is in the *quod* (a subordinate) clause in *ōrātiō oblīqua*. —— **atque** (ad + que), conj.; adds a more important notion, often = *and also*.

LINE 5. **eō**, abl. sing. n. of the dem. pron. *is, ea, id*, used substantively, or the noun *thing* may be supplied with which *eō* may agree; abl. of degree of difference after the comparative *gravius*. Consult A. & G. 106, *c*; B. 164, REM. 1; G. 403; H. 423. —— **gravius**, adv., comparative degree; positive *graviter* (from the adj. *gravis* thus: stem *gravi* + ter); superl. *gravissimē*. *gravius* as an adv. modifies *ferre*. —— **ferre**, pres. inf. act. of irr. verb *ferō, ferre, tulī, lātum;* the subject-acc. of *ferre* is the pron. *sē*, to be supplied, referring to *Caesar*. —— **quō**, abl. sing. n. of the rel. pron. *quī, quae, quod;* abl. of degree of difference after *minus*. Observe that *eō* and *quō*, in this line, are used as correlatives, and that the literal translation of *eō gravius ferre, quō minus* is: *by that* he bears these things more heavily, *by which* the less, etc.; rendered into English by the pronominal adv. *the . . . the*. Observe also that *rēs* is to be supplied from the preceding as the direct obj. of *ferre*.

LINE 6. **minus**, adv., comparative degree; see note on *minus*, l. 2, above. *minus* modifies *accidissent*. —— **meritō**, abl. sing. of the noun *meritum, -ī*, n. (from *meritus*, participle of *merēre*, to merit). *meritō* is an abl. of *in accordance with*. See A. & G. 253, and NOTE; B. 162; G. 397; H. 416. But see also note on *more*, l. 15, Chap. VIII. —— **populī**, gen. sing. of *populus, -ī*, m.; it limits the noun *meritō*. For synonyms, see note on *populum*, l. 17, Chap. VI. —— **Rōmānī**, gen. sing. m. of the adj. *Rōmānus, -a, -um;* it is an attributive of *populī*. Note that the adj. always follows the noun in this phrase.

LINE 7. **accidissent**, 3d pers. plur. pluperf. subjunctive act. of *accidō, -ere, -cidī*, no supine, 3 (ad + *cadere, to fall*); subjunctive, because in a subordinate clause in *ōrātiō rēcta. Ōrātiō rēcta* of lines 2-7: *Hōc mihi* minus dubitātiōnis *datur*, quod eās rēs quās *vōs, Helvētiī lēgātī, commemorāvistis* memoriā *teneō*, atque *hōc* gravius *ferō*, quō minus meritō populī Rōmānī *accidērunt*. —— **quī**, nom. sing. m. of the rel. pron. *quī, quae, quod;* subject-nom. of *fuisset*. *quī* here = *populus Rōmānus*. As to the proper translation of a rel. pron. beginning a sentence, consult A. & G. 180, *f*; B. 129, REM. 9; G. 610; H. 453. —— **sī**, conditional conj.; archaic form *seī*, sibilated from the Gk. particle *εἰ*. Observe that the normal position for a conj. is at the beginning of the clause, but it may sometimes follow a relative or emphatic word, or even words; see the position of *ut*, l. 2, Chap. XIII. —— **alicūius**, gen. sing. f. of the indef. pron. *aliquis, aliqua (-ae), aliquid* or *-quod;* the forms *aliquī, -qua, -quod* are adjectives; *-quis, -quae, -quid* are substantives. *alicūius* is an attributive of *iniūriae*. —— **iniūriae**, gen. sing. of *iniūria, -ae*, f. (in + *iūs*); objective gen. after *cōnscius*. Consult A. & G. 218, *a*; B. 135, *a*; G. 374; H. 399, 2.

conscious of any wrong against the Helvetii, it would not have been difficult to take precaution against them; but they had been misled in this respect, because they were	sibi *to themselves* difficile *difficult* dēceptum, *(they) were deceived,* commīssum *to have been done*	cōnscius *conscious* cavēre; *to be cautious;* ā *by*	fuisset, *had been,* sed *but* quod *because* sē *themselves*	nōn *not* neque *neither (anything)* intellegeret *did they perceive*	fuisse 8 *it was* eō 9 *on this account* neque 10 quārē 11 *why*

LINE 8. **sibi**, dat. after *cōnscius*. See A. & G. 234; B. 144; G. 359; H. 391. Observe that the dat. is here expletive; it might have been omitted; but it is oftener expressed by classical writers in such constructions than omitted. —— **cōnscius**, nom. sing. m. of the adj. *cōnscius, -a, -um* (con + scīre) = lit. *to know within;* hence *cōnscius* = *known to one's self*. *cōnscius* is predicate-adj. after *fuisset*. —— **fuisset**, 3d pers. sing. pluperf. subjunctive of the intrans. verb *sum, esse, fuī, futūrus;* subjunctive, because in the condition after *sī*, protasis. Consult A. & G. 304, *a;* B. 204, 2; G. 590, and NOTE 1; H. 507, III, and 511, I, remembering that the ind. in the conclusion in the *ōrātiō rēcta* becomes the inf. in the *ōrātiō oblīqua*. —— **nōn**, adv. (nē + oe[ū]num, apocopated). *nōn* modifies *fuisse*. —— **fuisse**, perf. inf. of the irr. intrans. verb *sum, esse, fuī;* it is for *fuit* in direct discourse. *fuisse* is here used impersonally, or rather the inf. *cavēre* as a neuter noun is its subj., and *difficile* is predicate-adj. after *fuisse*.

LINE 9. **difficile**, acc. sing. n. of the adj. *difficilis, -e* (dis + facilis). Observe the assimilation of *s* to *f* in the compound, and that the inseparable prep. has a privative force; hence *difficilis* = *not easy to do* or *bear*. —— **cavēre**, pres. inf. of *caveō, -ēre, cāvī, cautum*, 2; it is subject-acc. of *fuisse*. Observe that if this were direct discourse, *cavēre* would be the subject-nom. of *fuit*. —— **sed**, conj.; the strongest of the adversatives. —— **eō**, abl. sing. n. of the dem. pron. *is, ea, id*, used substantively; *eō* is an abl. of cause. A. & G. 245; B. 165; G. 408; H. 416; it is, so to speak, the herald of the following *quod*-clause.

LINE 10. **dēceptum (esse)**, perf. inf. pass. of *dēcipiō, -ere, -cēpī, -ceptum*, 3 (dē + capere); hence *dēcipere* = to snatch away the will-power, i.e. *to deceive*. Supply here *populum Rōmānum* as subject-acc. of *dēceptum (esse)*. —— **quod**, conj.; etymologically an adverbial acc. sing. n. of *quī*, meaning *in what respect, in that;* hence as a conj. = *because*. —— **neque** (nē + que = *and not, nor);* but *neque* . . . *neque* = *neither* . . . *nor*.

LINE 11. **commīssum (esse)**, perf. inf. pass. of *committō, -ere, -mīsī, -mīssum*, 3; supply the indef. pron. *aliquid* as its subject-acc. —— **ā**, prep., takes the abl. (*ā* before consonants, *ab* before either vowels or consonants). —— **sē**, abl. sing. of the reflexive pron. *suī, sibi, sē, sē*, same form in both sing. and plur.; it refers to *populum Rōmānum*, the omitted subject-acc. of *dēceptum (esse)*, but it is the obj. of the prep. *ā*. Note particularly that the pron. *sē* with the prep. *ā* is abl. of the agent, and consult A. & G. 246; B. 166; G. 401; H. 415, I. —— **intellegeret**, 3d pers. sing. imperf. subjunctive of *intellegō, -ere, -lēxī, -lēctum*, 3; subjunctive, because in a dependent clause in the *ōrātiō oblīqua*. —— **quārē** (quā + rē) = lit. *by which thing*.

12 timēret,	neque	sine	causā	timendum	not aware of having done any‑ thing of which
they should fear,	*nor*	*without*	*cause (anything)*	*to be feared*	
13 putāret.	Quod	sī	veteris	contumēliae	to be afraid, and they did not think they ought, with‑ out cause, to be afraid. But if he
did they think.	*But*	*if*	*the ancient*	*disgrace*	
14 oblīvīscī	vellet,	num	etiam	recentium	
to forget	*he wished,*		*also*	*of recent*	

LINE 12. **timēret**, 3d pers. sing. imperf. subjunctive of *timeō, -ēre, -uī,* 2; subjunctive, because the question is indirect. As an indirect question it would be in the subjunctive mode in direct discourse. See A. & G. 334; B. 242; G. 467; H. 529, I. The subject-nom. of *timēret* is a pron. implied in the ending, referring to *populum Rōmānum*, the supplied subject-acc. of *dēceptum (esse).* Synonyms: *timēre = to fear,* as the result of some external cause; *metuere = to fear,* because one reflects; the fear is a rational impulse, the outcome of reflection on the consequences of limitations and dangers; whereas *verērī = to fear,* as an emotion arising from apprehension of the venerable or apprehension of disgrace. —— **neque,** see note on *neque,* l. 10, above. —— **sine,** prep. with the abl. —— **causā,** abl. sing. of the noun *causa, -ae,* f.; it is the obj. of the prep. *sine.* —— **timendum (esse),** pres. inf. of the 2d periphrastic conjugation of *timeō* (see the beginning of the line for principal parts); supply *aliquid* as subject-acc. just as *aliquid* was supplied before *commissum (esse);* or regard the construction as impersonal, supplying *ā sē* as the abl. of the voluntary agent.

LINE 13. **putāret,** 3d pers. sing. imperf. subjunctive of *putō, -āre, -āvī, -ātum,* 1. The subject-nom. is a pron. implied in the ending, referring to the Roman people. *putāret* is connected by the conj. *neque* to *intellegeret,* and is in the subjunctive mode for the same reason. Synonyms: *opīnārī, putāre* and *rērī = to think,* as a mere subjective process; whereas *arbitrārī, cēnsēre, iūdicārī = to think* objectively, as when an *arbiter,* or *censor,* or *judge* gives an official opinion. —— **Quod,** strictly an adverbial acc. of *quī, quae, quod = as to which;* if it be taken as a relative, its antecedent is the previous sentence; in transitions, however, it *= but* or *now.* Consult A. & G. 240, *b*; B. 123, REM. 22, and 155; G. 333, 1, and 610, REM. 2; H. 453, 6. —— **veteris,** gen. f. of the adj. *vetus, veteris;* comparative *vetior;* superl. *veterrimus. veteris* is an attributive of *contumēliae.* —— **contumēliae,** gen. sing. of *contumēlia, -ae,* f.; gen. after *oblīvīscī,* a verb of forgetting. Consult A. & G. 219; B. 135, (*b*); G. 376; H. 406, II.

LINE 14. **oblīvīscī,** pres. inf. of the deponent verb *oblīvīscor, -ī, oblītus,* 3; complementary inf. A. & G. 271; B. 181; G. 423; H. 533, I, 1. *Ōrātiō rēcta* of lines 7-13: *quī sī alicūius iniūriae sibi cōnscius fuisset, nōn fuit difficile cavēre; sed eō dēceptus, quod neque commissum ā sē intellegēbat quārē timēret, neque sine causā timendum putābat.* —— **vellet,** 3d pers. sing. imperf. subjunctive of *volō, velle, voluī,* irr. verb; it agrees with *ipse,* i.e. *Caesar* as its subject-nom.; it is subjunctive, because in the condition after the conj. *sī.* Consult grammatical references to *fuisset,* l. 8, above. —— **num,** adv., interrogative particle; questions introduced with *num* imply a negative answer. See A. & G. 210, *e,* end; B. 81, 3; G. 456; H. 351, NOTE 3. In direct questions, *num* is untranslatable; in indirect questions it *= whether.* Consult A. & G. 210, *f,* REM., end; B. 242, 1; G. 460, (*a*); H. 529, II, NOTE 3. —— **etiam** (et + iam), conjunctive adv., serves to add a notion to that already expressed. —— **recentium,** gen. plur. of the adj. *recēns, recentis,* abl. sing. regularly *recentī* (etymology dubious). *recentium* is an attributive of *iniūriārum.*

wished to forget the old affront, could he also lay aside the remembrance of recent wrongs? that, against his will, they had forcefully attempted to march through our province?	iniūriārum, *wrongs,*	quod *because,*	eō *he (being)*	invītō *unwilling,*	iter 15 *a journey*
	per *through*	prōvinciam *the province*	per *through*	vim *violence*	temptāssent, 16 *they had attempted,*
	quod *because*	Aeduōs, *the Aedui,*	quod *because*	Ambarrōs, *the Ambarri,*	quod 17 *because*
	Allobrogas *the Allobroges*		vēxāssent, *they had harassed,*	memoriam *the memory*	dēpōnere 18 *to lay aside*

LINE 15. **iniūriārum,** gen. plur. of *iniūria, -ae,* f.; it limits *memoriam,* l. 18, below. —— **quod,** conj. = *that;* it introduces the *quod*-clause *quod . . . temptāssent,* which, as an explanatory noun-clause, is in apposition with *iniūriārum;* so also the three immediately following *quod*-clauses. —— **eō,** abl. sing. m. of the dem. pron. *is, ea, id,* used as a personal pron. of the 3d pers.; it refers to *Caesar,* and is in the abl. absolute construction with *invītō.* Observe that *eō* is m. here and in the abl. absolute, while *eō,* l. 5, above, is n., and is the abl. of degree of difference, and that *eō,* l. 9, above, is n., and an abl. of cause. —— **invītō,** abl. sing. m. of the adj. *invītus, -a, -um;* abl. absolute with the pron. *eō.* —— **iter,** acc. sing. of *iter, itineris,* n.; direct obj. of *temptāssent.* For synonyms, see note on *via,* l. 2, Chap. IX.

LINE 16. **per,** prep. with the acc. —— **prōvinciam,** acc. sing. of the noun *prōvincia, -ae,* f.; it is the obj. of the prep. *per.* —— **per,** prep. like GK. διά, denotes, lit., motion *through* space; then transf. it indicates the means or instrument *through* which anything is done, or the *manner* of the action. —— **vim,** acc. sing. of the noun *vīs, vīs,* f.; obj. of the prep. *per,* denoting here the manner. Consult A. & G. 153, under *per, c* and *d;* B. 166, REM. 1, end; G. 399, NOTE 1, end; H. 419, III, NOTE 3. —— **temptāssent,** 3d pers. plur. pluperf. subjunctive of *temptō, -āre, -āvī, -ātum;* it agrees with a pron. implied in the ending as its subject-nom., referring to the Helvetii. *temptāssent* is syncopated and contracted for *temptāvissent.* For the law thereof, see A. & G. 128, 2; B. 251; G. 131, 1; H. 235. Note carefully that a *quod*-clause is a clause expressing fact in direct discourse, and has the ind. mode; that the *quod*-clause here has the subjunctive, because the discourse is indirect. Consult A. & G. 333; B. 198 and 235, (*b*); G. 524, and 525, 3; H. 516, II. Note again that in some of the lexicons *temptō* is written *tentō* (freq. of *tendō,* compare GK. τείνω = *grasp at repeatedly*); hence *temptāre* or *tentāre* = *to grasp, feel, touch, test.*

LINE 17. **quod,** conj. like *quod,* l. 15, above; it introduces the clause *quod Aeduōs vēxāssent,* which also is explanatory of *iniūriārum.* —— **Aeduōs,** acc. plur. of the adj. *Aeduus, -a, -um,* used substantively, and is the direct obj. of *vēxāssent,* to be supplied from a following clause. —— **quod,** observe again that each of these noun-clauses is explanatory of, and in apposition with *iniūriārum,* l. 15, above. —— **Ambarrōs,** acc. plur. of *Ambarrī, -ōrum,* m.; direct obj. of *vēxāssent,* to be supplied. These people are supposed to have been clients of the Aedui; their territory was near the junction of the Saône and the Rhone. —— **quod,** see notes on the *quod*-clauses, immediately preceding.

LINE 18. **Allobrogas,** acc. plur. of the proper noun *Allobrogēs, -um,* m. Note that *Allobrogas* is the Greek acc. plur., with the short vowel *a* in the ultima, instead of the long vowel *ē,* as seen in the Latin form of the acc. plur. *Allobrogēs.* See declension of Greek nouns, A. & G. 64; B. 248; G. 66, and NOTE 4; H. 68. *Allobrogas*

[LINES 19-21.]   BOOK I.   97

19	posse?		Quod	suā	vīctōriā	tam	and had been har-
	(himself) to be able?		*As to what*	*in their*	*victory*	*so*	assing the Aedui, the Ambarri and
20	īnsolenter	glōriārentur		quodque	tam	diū	the Allobroges? As to their boast-
	insolently	*they gloried,*		*as to what and,*	*so*	*long*	ing so insolently of their victory,
21	sē		impūnē	iniūriās		tulisse	and as to their
	themselves		*with impunity*	*wrongs*		*to have borne,*	wondering that

---

is the direct obj. of *vēxāssent*. As to the Aedui, see l. 20, Chap. III; the Ambarri, l. 12, Chap. XI; the Allobroges, l. 10, Chap. VI. —— **vēxāssent**, 3d pers. plur. of *vēxō, -āre, -āvī, -ātum,* 1, pluperf. subjunctive for the uncontracted form *vēxāvissent.* See note on *temptāssent,* l. 16, above; the subject-nom., of course, is *Helvētiī;* subjunctive for the same reason as *temptāssent;* see grammatical references to the latter word. —— **memoriam**, acc. sing. of *memoria, -ae,* f.; direct obj. of *dēponere.* —— **dēponere**, pres. inf. act. of *dēpōnō, -ere, -posuī, -positum,* 3; complementary inf. See A. & G. 271; B. 181; G. 423; H. 533, I, 2.

LINE 19. **posse**, pres. inf. of *possum, posse potuī* (potis + sum); its subject-acc. is the pron. *sē,* i.e. *Caesarem,* to be supplied. Observe that the question is rhetorical, and the form of the indirect discourse is the inf. instead of the subjunctive. Consult A. & G. 338; B. 245, 3, REM. 1; G. 651, REM. 1; H. 523, II, 2. —— **Quod**, acc. sing. of the rel. pron. *quī, quae, quod;* it differs from the preceding *quods* only in not having any noun to explain; it is an adverbial accusative; see A. & G. 333, *a*, B. 123, REM. 21; G. 525, 2; H. 516, II, and NOTE, end. Observe critically the different uses of *quod* in lines 3, 10, 13, 15, 17 and 19. In lines 3 and 10 it is a mere clause-connective and = *because;* in lines 13, 15 and 17 it = *ut,* and = *that;* in l. 19 it is an acc. of specification and = *whereas.* —— **suā**, abl. sing. of the poss. and reflexive pron. *suus, -a, -um;* it refers to the Helvetii, but is an attributive of *vīctōriā.* —— **vīctōriā**, abl. sing. of *vīctōria, -ae,* f.; abl. of cause. See A. & G. 245; B. 165; G. 408; H. 413. A. & G.'s grammar makes this construction after *glōrior* a species of abl. locative; see A. & G. 254, *b.* —— **tam**, adv.; it modifies *īnsolenter.* *Ōrātiō rēcta* of lines 13-19: Quod sī veteris contumēliae oblīvīscī *volō,* num etiam recentium iniūriārum, quod *mē* invītō iter per prōvinciam per vim *temptāvistis,* quod Aeduōs, quod Ambarrōs, quod Allobrogas *vēxāvistis,* memoriam dēponere *possum?*

LINE 20. **īnsolenter**, adv. (in, *negative* + solēns = *unwonted*); it modifies *glōriārentur.* —— **glōriārentur**, 3d pers. plur. imperf. subjunctive of the deponent verb *glōrior, -ārī, -ātus,* 1; it agrees with *Helvētiī,* to be supplied, as its subject-nom. —— **quodque** (quod + que), adverbial acc., see *quod,* preceding line. —— **tam**, adv., an accusative form analogous to adv. *quam,* a particle denoting comparison in degree = lit. *in so far; tam* modifies the adv. *diū.* —— **diū**, adv. (derived from *diēs*); comparative degree *diūtius,* superl. *diūtissimē; diū* modifies *tulisse.*

LINE 21. **sē**, acc. plur. of the reflexive pron. *suī, sibi, sē, sē,* the same form in both numbers; *sē* is subject-acc. of *tulisse.* —— **impūnē**, adv. (in, *negative* + poena, through the adj. *impūnis, -e*); it, too, modifies *tulisse.* —— **iniūriās**, acc. plur. of the noun *inūria, -ae,* f.; it is the direct object of *tulisse.* —— **tulisse**, perf. inf. act. of *ferō, ferre, tulī, lātum;* its subject-acc. is the pron. *sē.* The acc.-clause: *sē impūnē iniūriās tulisse* = *that they had inflicted wrongs with impunity. tulisse* here appears to be used in the sense of *intulisse.*

they had committed outrages so long without punishment tended to the same result. For the immortal gods are wont, at times, to grant a somewhat lengthy impunity to such as	admīrārentur, *they wondered,* Cōnsuēsse *To have been wont* gravius *the more heavily* rērum *of things*	*(these conceits)* enim *for,* hominēs *men* doleant, *they may grieve,*	eōdem *to the same thing* deōs *the gods* ex *from* quōs *whom*	pertinēre. 22 *to tend.* immortālēs, *immortal,* prō *for*	quō 23 *that* commūtātiōne 24 *a change* scelere eōrum 25 *guilt their,*

Line 22. **admīrārentur**, 3d pers. plur. imperf. subjunctive of the deponent verb *admīror, -ārī, -ātus,* 1 (ad + mīrārī = *to wonder at*); its subject-nom. is *Helvētiī*, to be supplied; it is in the subjunctive mode, because it is in a subordinate clause in the *ōrātiō oblīqua*. Observe that the two immediately preceding *quod*-clauses are noun-clauses, and as such are subject-accusatives of *pertinēre*. —— **eōdem**, adv. (old dat. of idem + locō); as an adv. it modifies *pertinēre*. —— **pertinēre**, pres. inf. of *pertineō, -ēre, -uī,* no supine, 2; its subject-accusatives are the two immediately preceding *quod*-clauses. The meaning appears to be that both the vanity and presumption of the Helvetians alike show their ignorance of the punishment that awaits them.

Line 23. **Cōnsuēsse**, contracted perf. act. inf. for *cōnsuēvisse* of the verb *cōnsuēscō, -ere, -suēvī, -suētum,* 3. For the syncopation and contraction, see A. & G. 128, 2; B. 251; G. 131, 1; H. 235. —— **enim**, conj., always postpositive, and denotes merely a subjective reason; whereas *nam* indicates an objective reason. —— **deōs**, acc. plur. of *deus, -ī,* m. *deōs* is subject-acc. of the verb *cōnsuēsse*. For the declension of *deus*, which is irregular in the plur., see A. & G. 40, *f*; B. 24, REM. 3; G. 33, REM. 6; H. 51, 6. With *deus* compare the GK. θεός, noticing especially that both words begin with a lingual mute. —— **immortālēs**, acc. plur. m. of the adj. *immortālis, -e* (in, *negative* + *mortālis*); *immortālēs* is an attributive of the noun *deōs*. —— **quō**, here a conj., and usually when an adj. of the comparative degree is in a clause; it = *ut eō*; consult A. & G. 317, *b*; B. 200, (*b*); G. 545, 2; H. 497, II, 2.

Line 24. **gravius**, adv. in the comparative degree; positive *graviter*, superl. *gravissimē*. *gravius* modifies *doleant*. —— **hominēs**, nom. plur. of the noun *homō, -inis,* m. and f.; it is subject-nom. of *doleant*. Synonyms: *homō* is the generic term denoting *man* or *woman*, and is accordingly of the common gender; whereas *vir* (digammated from *ις*) = *a male person* and, in a pregnant sense, *a man of courage, a hero*. —— **ex**, prep. with the abl. (*ē* before consonants, *ex* before vowels or consonants). —— **commūtātiōne**, abl. of *commūtātiō, -ōnis,* f. (com, *intensive* + mūtāre); it is the obj. of the prep. *ex*.

Line 25. **rērum**, gen. plur. of the noun *rēs, reī,* f.; stem *rĕ*, with vowel shortened in the gen. and dat. sing. *rērum* is objective gen. limiting *commūtātiōne*. —— **doleant**, 3d pers. plur. pres. subjunctive of *doleō, -ēre, -uī, -itum,* 2; its subject-nom. is *hominēs*; it is subjunctive of purpose after *quō* = *ut eō*. —— **quōs**, acc. plur. of the rel. pron. *quī, quae, quod*; it refers to *hīs* in the following clause, but is the direct obj. of *ulcīscī*. Observe that the relative clause here, as often, precedes the demonstrative; and consult A. & G. 201, *c*; B. 129, REM. 1; G. 620; H. 572, II, NOTE. —— **prō**, prep. with the abl.; compare GK. πρός. —— **scelere**, abl. sing. of the noun *scelus, -eris,* n.; abl. after *prō*. Synonyms: *facinus* = any *bold, daring crime*; *flāgitium* = an offense against one's self — *moral pollution*; whereas *scelus* = an offense against

[LINES 26-29.]   BOOK I.   99

26 ulcīscī	velint,	hīs	secundiōrēs		interdum	they purpose to punish for their guilt, that they may the more severely suffer from a change of fortune. Although these things were so, yet if they would give him hostages, that he
to punish,	*they wish,*	*to them*	*more favorable,*		*sometimes*	
27 rēs	et	diūturniōrem	impūnitātem		concēdere.	
things and		*a longer*	*impunity*		*to concede.*	
28 Cum	ea	ita	sint,	tamen,	sī obsidēs	
Though	*these (things)*	*thus*	*are,*	*yet*	*if hostages*	
29 ab	eīs	sibi	dentur,	utī ea,	quae	
by	*them*	*to himself*	*are given,*	*that those (things)*	*which*	

individuals or society — *robbery, murder* and *sedition.* —— **eōrum**, gen. plur. of the dem. pron. *is, ea, id,* used as a personal pron. of the 3d pers., like the English poss. case = *their;* as a gen. it limits *scelere.*

LINE 26. **ulcīscī**, pres. inf. of the deponent verb *ulcīscor, -ī, ultus,* 3; complementary inf. depending on *velint.* See A. & G. 271; B. 181; G. 423; H. 533, I, 1. —— **velint**, 3d pers. plur. pres. subjunctive of the irr. verb *volō, velle, voluī;* subjunctive, because in a dependent clause in the *ōrātiō oblīqua.* Observe that the primary sequence obtains in the rest of the speech, because, probably, general truths are, for the most part, stated. —— **hīs**, dat. plur. of the dem. pron. *hīc, haec, hōc,* used substantively; indirect obj. after *concēdere.* —— **secundiōrēs**, acc. plur. f. of the comparative adj. *secundior, -us;* positive degree *secundus, -a, -um (sequī,* to follow); hence *secundus = favorable,* a notion derived from winds following ships to their destination. *secundiōrēs* is an attributive of *rēs.* —— **interdum**, adv. (inter + dum); it modifies the verb *concēdere.* Note its emphatic position.

LINE 27. **rēs**, acc. plur. of *rēs, reī,* f.; direct obj. of *concēdere.* Observe that the phrase *secundiōrēs rēs* = lit. *more favorable things.* —— **diūturniōrem**, acc. sing. f. of the comparative degree of *diūturnus (diū);* the superl. is not in use. *diūturniōrem* is an attributive of *impūnitātem.* —— **impūnitātem**, acc. sing. of the noun *impūnitās, -ātis,* f.; it is connected by the conj. *et* with *rēs,* and is in the same grammatical construction. —— **concēdere**, pres. inf. of *concēdō, -ere, -cessī, -cessum,* 3 (con, *intensive* + cēdere); lit. = *to go from;* then *to go out of the way for one, to submit, yield, grant.* *Ōrātiō rēcta* of lines 19-27: Quod vestrā victōriā tam insolenter glōriāminī, quodque tam diū vōs impūne iniūriās tulisse admīrāminī, eōdem pertinet. Cōnsuēvērunt enim dī immortālēs, quō gravius hominēs ex commūtātiōne rērum doleant, quōs prō scelere eōrum ulcīscī volunt, hīs secundiōrēs interdum rēs et diūturniōrem impūnitātem concēdere.

LINE 28. **Cum**, concessive conj., here = *although;* known to be such, because it is followed by the correlative *tamen.* —— **ea**, nom. plur. n. of the dem. pron. *is, ea, id,* used substantively, and as a noun the subject-nom. of *sint.* The things referred to are the specifications in the last sentence. —— **ita**, adv., modifies *sint.* —— **sint**, 3d pers. plur. pres. subjunctive of the intrans. verb *sum, esse, fuī, futūrus;* it agrees with its subject-nom. *ea;* it is in the subjunctive after *cum* concessive. Consult A. & G. 326; B. 210; G. 587; H. 515, III. —— **tamen** (etymology dubious), conjunctive adv. —— **sī** (archaic form *seī,* sibilated from GK. *eī*), conditional conj. —— **obsidēs**, nom. plur. of *obses, -idis,* m. and f.; subject-nom. of *dentur.*

LINE 29. **ab**, prep. with the abl. (*ā* before consonants, *ab* before vowels or consonants); compare GK. ἀπό and English *off.* —— **eīs**, abl. plur. of the dem. pron. *is, ea, id,* used as a personal pron. of the 3d pers.; abl. of the agent after the pass. verb

might feel con-	polliceantur,	factūrōs	intellegat,	et	sī 30
vinced that they would fulfill their	they promise,	(they) will do,	he may know;	and	if
promises; if they would give satis-	Aeduīs	dē	iniūriīs,	quās	ipsīs 31
faction to the	to the Aedui	for	wrongs	which	on themselves
Aedui for the wrongs they had	sociīsque	eōrum	intulerint,	item	sī 32
inflicted on them	allies and,	of them	they have brought,	also	if

dentur. Consult A. & G. 246; B. 96, REM. 1, and 166; G. 401; H. 415, I. —— **sibi**, dat. sing. of the reflexive pron. *suī, sibi, sē, sē;* it is dat. of the indirect obj. after *dentur;* it refers to Caesar. —— **dentur**, 3d pers. plur. pres. subjunctive passive of *dō, dare, dedī, datum,* 1 (*a* is short before -*re* in pres. inf. act., contrary to rule); pass. parts: *dor, darī, datus;* pres. subjunctive in the protasis after *sī,* for the fut. in direct discourse. —— **utī**, telic conj.; the shorter *ut* is more common, though the form *utī* is not rare. —— **ea**, acc. plur. n. of the dem. pron. *is, ea, id,* used substantively, and as a noun the direct obj. of *factūrōs (esse).* —— **quae**, acc. plur. n. of the rel. pron. *quī, quae, quod;* it refers to *ea* as its antecedent, but it is the direct obj. of *polliceantur.*

LINE 30. **polliceantur**, 3d pers. plur. pres. subjunctive of the deponent verb *polliceor, -ērī, -licitus,* 2 (pote, neuter of *potis,* as an adv. + *licērī*) = lit. *to bid largely;* hence *to offer, promise.* *polliceantur* agrees with a pron. implied in the ending as its subject-nom., referring to the Helvetii; it is in the subjunctive, because it occurs in a subordinate clause in *ōrātiō oblīqua.* Synonyms: *pollicērī* = *to promise* of one's own free will; hence only used of "free and gracious promises"; whereas *promittere* = *to give forth,* and is the general word for promising, especially of promising that which has been requested. —— **factūrōs (esse)**, fut. inf. of the intrans. verb *sum, esse, fuī, futūrus;* its subject-acc. is *sē* understood, referring to the Helvetii. —— **intellegat**, 3d pers. sing. pres. subjunctive act. of *intellegō, -ere, -lēxī, -lēctum,* 3 (inter + legere, *to choose between);* hence *intellegere* = *to choose between, to perceive, to know,* etc. This verb is often spelled *intelligō.* *intellegat* is the subjunctive of purpose after *utī.* See A. & G. 317; B. 200; G. 544, I; H. 497, II. —— **et**, conj., connects the conditional clauses. —— **sī**, see note on *sī,* l. 28, above.

LINE 31. **Aeduīs**, dat. plur. of *Aeduī, -ōrum,* m.; dat. after *satisfaciant,* to be supplied from l. 33, below. Consult in reference to this dat. A. & G. 227, *e,* 2; B. 142; G. 346; H. 384, II, 4, NOTE 1. —— **dē**, prep. with the abl. —— **iniūriīs**, abl. of the noun *iniūria, -ae,* f.; it is the obj. of the prep. *dē.* —— **quās**, acc. plur. f. of the rel. pron. *quī, quae, quod;* it refers in gender and number to its antecedent *iniūriīs,* but it is the direct obj. of *intulerint.* —— **ipsīs**, dat. plur. of the intensive pron. *ipse, -sa, -sum,* gen. *ipsīus,* dat. *ipsī;* it refers to the Aedui; it is the dat. after *in* in *intulerint.* See A. & G. 228; B. 143; G. 347; H. 386, and 1.

LINE 32. **sociīsque** (sociīs + que). *sociīs,* dat. plur. of *socius, -ī,* m.; connected closely with *ipsīs* by the enclitic conj. *-que,* and in the same grammatical construction. —— **eōrum**, gen. plur. of the dem. pron. *is, ea, id,* used as a personal pron. of the 3d pers.; the allusion is to their allies, i.e. the allies of the Aedui; if *suīs* had been used, the reference would have been to the allies of the Helvetii. —— **intulerint**, 3d pers. plur. perf. subjunctive act. of *īnferō, īnferre, intulī, il(n)lātum;* its subject-nom. is a pron. implied in the ending, referring to the Helvetii; it is in the subjunctive, because it is in a subordinate clause in indirect discourse. —— **item**, adv. (from

						and their allies;
33 Allobrogibus	satisfaciant,		sēsē	cum	eīs	if, too, they would
for the Allobroges	*they shall do enough,*		*himself*	*with*	*them*	give satisfaction to the Allobroges,
34 pācem	esse	factūrum.	Divicō		respondit:	he would make
peace	*to be about*	*to make.*	*Divico*		*replied:*	peace with them. Divico replied:
35 Ita	Helvētiōs	ā	maiōribus		suīs	The Helvetii
So	*the Helvetii*	*by*	*ancestors*		*their,*	have been so

radical *i*, whence is + tem) = lit. *in this manner;* hence *thus, also;* different from *etiam* (et + iam), which adds a notion = *and also.* —— **sī**, conditional particle; see note on *sī*, l. 28, above.

LINE 33. **Allobrogibus**, dat. plur. of *Allobrogēs, -um,* m., after *satisfaciant;* see grammatical references to *Aeduīs*, l. 31, above. —— **satisfaciant**, 3d pers. plur. pres. subjunctive act. of *satisfacio, -ere, -fēcī, -factum,* 3 (satis + facere); hence *satisfacere* = lit. *to do enough. satisfaciant* is the pres. subjunctive after *sī* in the protasis. This subjunctive is for the more vivid fut. ind. in the *ōrātiō rēcta.* —— **sēsē**, acc. sing. of the reduplicated reflexive pron. for the less emphatic *sē*. This reflexive is declined thus: *suī, sibi, sē, sē;* the same form is used in both numbers; whether the pron. is sing. or plur. must be determined from the context. *sēsē* is here the acc. sing., referring to Caesar, and subject-acc. of *esse factūrum (factūrum esse).* —— **cum**, prep. with the abl.; it is known to be the prep., not merely because there is a possible abl. case after it; so far as the form of the pron. *eīs* goes, it might be the dat.; but because it is seen at a glance that there is no finite verb either in the ind. or subjunctive with which *cum* as a conj. could form a subordinate clause. —— **eīs**, abl. plur. of the dem. pron. *is, ea, id,* used as a personal pron. of the 3d pers.; it is the obj. of the prep. *cum.*

LINE 34. **pācem**, acc. sing. of the noun *pāx, pācis,* f.; direct obj. of *esse factūrum (factūrum esse).* —— **esse factūrum**, fut. inf. act. of *faciō, -ere, fēcī, factum,* 3; its subject-acc. is the reduplicated personal pron. *sēsē.* —— **Divicō, -ōnis,** m.; subject-nom. of *respondit.* For description of *Divicō*, see l. 9, Chap. XIII. —— **respondit**, 3d pers. sing. perf. ind. act. of *respondeō, -ēre, respondī, respōnsum,* 2; it agrees with its subject-nom. *Divicō. Ōrātiō rēcta* of lines 28–34: Cum *haec* ita sint, tamen, sī obsidēs *ā vōbīs mihi dabuntur,* utī *haec,* quae *pollicēminī,* factūrōs *intellegam,* et sī Aeduīs dē iniūriīs, quās ipsīs sociīsque eorum *intulistis,* item sī Allobrogibus *satisfaciētis, ego vōbīscum* pācem *faciam.*

LINE 35. **Ita**, adv. (from radical *i*, whence is + ta) = *in this way, thus;* correlative of the conj. *utī,* next line, below. —— **Helvētiōs**, acc. plur. of *Helvētiī, -ōrum,* m.; subject-acc. of *institūtōs esse.* For description of this people, see note on *Helvētiī,* l. 16, Chap. I. —— **ā**, prep. with the abl. (*ā* before consonants only, *ab* before vowels or consonants). —— **maiōribus**, in form the abl. plur. of the comparative adj. *māior;* the comparative and superl. are used as substantives, either with or without *nātū* = greater in respect to birth, i.e. *elder, ancestor.* The superl. *māximus* is also thus used. The reader will observe that the positive *māgnus* is derived from a radical *mag,* which is common to *māgnus* and the GK. μέγας. *māiōribus* as a noun is the obj. of the prep. *ā*; it is here, in fact, the abl. of the agent after the pass. verb *īnstitūtōs esse.* Consult A. & G. 246; B. 166; G. 401: H. 415, I. —— **suīs**, abl. plur. m. of the poss. and reflexive pron. *suus, -a, -um;* it refers to the Helvetii, but is an attributive of *māiōribus.*

102   CAESAR'S GALLIC WAR   [CHAP. XV.

| trained by their ancestors, that they were accustomed to receive, not to give hostages; of this fact the Roman people were witnesses. After giving this reply, he withdrew. | īnstitūtōs esse, *to have been instructed,* dare *to give* Rōmānum *Roman* datō *having been given,* | cōnsuērint; *they have been wont;* esse *to be* discessit. *he left.* | utī *that* | obsidēs *hostages* eius *of that* testem. *witness.* | accipere, *to receive,* reī *thing* Hōc *This* | nōn *not* populum *the people* respōnsō *reply* | 36 37 38 39 |

LINE 36. īnstitūtōs esse, perf. inf. pass. of the act. *īnstituō, -ere, -stituī, -stitūtum*, 3; its subject-acc. is the noun *Helvētiōs*. Observe that the participial part of this inf. corresponds in case with the subject-acc. —— utī, ecbatic conj., the original form; the more common form is *ut*; in use, like the GK. ὡς. —— obsidēs, acc. plur. of the noun *obses, -idis*, m. and f.; the direct obj. of *accipere*. —— accipere, pres. inf. act. of *accipiō, -ere, -cēpī, -ceptum*, 3 (ad + capere); hence *accipere* = lit. *to take to one's self, to receive*. *accipere* is a complementary inf. —— nōn, negative adv. (nē + oenum [ūnum], apocopated); *nōn* modifies the inf. *dare*.

LINE 37. dare, pres. inf. act. of *dō, dare, dedī, datum*, 1 (short *a* before *-re*, in pres. inf. act. by exception); inf. complementary; supply *eōs* as direct obj. —— cōnsuērint, 3d pers. plur. perf. subjunctive of *cōnsuēscō, -ere, -suēvī, -suētum*, 3; subjunctive of result after the conj. *utī*. Consult A. & G. 319, 3, and REM.; B. 201, REM. 1, (a); G. 552; H. 500, II. Observe that *cōnsuērint* is syncopated and contracted for *cōnsuēverint*. See A. & G. 128, 2; B. 251; G. 131, 1; H. 235. —— eius, gen. sing. f. of the dem. pron. *is, ea, id;* it is an attributive of *reī*. —— reī, gen. sing. of *rēs, reī,* f.; as a gen. it limits *testem*. —— populum, acc. sing. of the noun *populus, -ī*, m. *populum* is subject-acc. of *esse*. For synonyms, see note on *populum*, l. 17, Chap. VI; and observe, further, that *gēns* and *nātiō* = *a people* in a physical sense without reference to civilization, *gēns* being more compressive than *nātiō;* whereas *cīvitās* = *a people* in a political sense, a society formed by compact, civilized society.

LINE 38. Rōmānum, acc. sing. m. of the adj. *Rōmānus, -a, -um;* it is an attributive of *populum*. —— esse, pres. inf. of the intrans. verb *sum, esse, fuī, futūrus;* its subject-acc. is *populum*. —— testem, acc. sing. of the noun *testis, -is*, m. and f.; predicate-acc. after *esse*. Observe that the construction from *Dīvicō respondit* is that of indirect discourse, in which the main clauses are put in the inf. with subject-acc., while the subordinate clause takes the subjunctive. —— Hōc, abl. sing. n. of the dem. pron. *hīc, haec, hōc;* it is an attributive of *respōnsō*. —— respōnsō, abl. sing. of the noun *respōnsum, -ī,* n.; it is in the abl. absolute with *datō*, denoting *time when*. Consult A. & G. 255, *d,* 1; B. 172; G. 409, 410; H. 431, 2, 3). *Ōrātiō rēcta* of lines 35–38: Ita *Helvētiī* ā māiōribus suīs *īnstitūtī sunt*, utī obsidēs accipere, nōn dare cōnsuērint; *hūius* reī *populus Rōmānus est testis.*

LINE 39. datō, perf. pass. participle of the act. verb *dō, dare, dedī, datum;* pass. parts.: *dor, darī, datus*. The construction is explained by the remarks on *respōnsō*. —— discessit, 3d pers. sing. perf. ind. act. of *discēdō, -ere, -cēssī, -cessum* (dis + cēdere, *to go apart*), 3; it agrees with a pron. implied in the ending, referring to Dīvicō, as the subject-nom.

LINES 1-4.]   BOOK I.   103

1 XV. Posterō diē castra ex eō locō | XV. On the following day the Helvetii moved
   The next   day the camp from that place
2 movent. Idem facit Caesar equitātumque | their camp. Caesar did the same; and sent in advance all the cavalry which he had collected from the entire province and the
   they move. The same does Caesar the cavalry and,
3 omnem   ad numerum quattuor mīlium,
   all   to the number of four thousands,
4 quem ex omnī prōvinciā et Aeduīs
   which from all the province and the Aedui

LINE 1. **Posterō**, abl. sing. m. of the adj. *posterus, -a, -um (post);* comparative *posterior,* superl. *postrēmus* or *postumus; posterō* is an attributive of the noun *diē.* —— **diē**, abl. sing. of *diēs, diēī,* m. or f. in the sing., always m. in the plur.; abl. of *time when.* Consult A. & G. 256, 1; B. 171; G. 393; H. 429. —— **castra**, acc. plur. of noun *castrum, -ī,* n. (sometimes, though rare, *castra, -ae,* f.); in the sing. =*fortress;* in the plural = several soldiers' tents or huts collected together, i.e. = *a camp. castra* in our text is the direct obj. of *movent.* —— **ex**, prep. with the abl. (*ē* before consonants only, *ex* before vowels or consonants). —— **eō**, abl. sing. m. of the dem. pron. *is, ea, id; eō* is an attributive of *locō.* —— **locō**, abl. sing. of the noun *locus, -ī,* m.; in the plur. *locī* or *loca;* compare note on *locī,* l. 10, Chap. II; *locō* is the obj. of the prep. *ex.* The Helvetian camp was on the right bank of the Saône, a little south of Matisco. See Chap. XII, at the beginning, and also consult map.

LINE 2. **movent**, 3d pers. plur. pres. ind. act. of *moveō, -ēre, mōvī, mōtum,* 2; historical present; supply *Helvētiī* as its subject-nom. —— **Idem**, acc. sing. n. of the iterative pron. *īdem, eadem, idem;* it is here used substantively; or after it supply the English word *thing. idem* is the direct obj. of *facit.* —— **facit**, 3d pers. sing. pres. ind. acc. of *faciō, -ēre, fēcī, factum,* 3; it agrees with its subject-nom. *Caesar.* —— **Caesar, -aris,** m. (*caesariē,* some say, i.e. from his dark hair); subject-nom. of *facit.* —— **equitātumque** (equitātum + que). *equitātum,* acc. sing. of *equitātus, -ūs,* m. (compare *equitāre* from *equus); equitātum* is the direct obj. of *praemittit,* l. 6, below. The body of cavalry consisted (*a*) of a permanent force; and (*b*) of a contingent furnished by the allies of Rome at the opening of the campagne. *equitēs,* the plur. of *eques,* a horseman, is frequently used in the same sense as *equitātus;* see *equitibus* and *equitum,* lines 12 and 13, below; but *equitēs* is often, in classic writers, used to denote the equestrian order — the knights — an order among the Romans, holding a middle rank between senators and plebeians. After 102 B.C. the knights became the administrators of justice.

LINE 3. **omnem**, acc. sing. m. of the adj. *omnis, -e;* it is an attributive of *equitātum.* —— **ad**, prep. with the acc. —— **numerum**, acc. sing. of the noun *numerus, -ī,* m.; it is the obj. of the prep. *ad.* —— **quattuor**, num. adj., cardinal, indecl., i.e. it is in any case, according to the requirements of the construction; here it is in the gen. plur., modifying *mīlium.* —— **mīlium**, gen. plur. of the adj. *mille,* indecl. in the sing.; in the plur., *mīlia, -um,* it is used as a noun. Consult A. & G. 94, *e*; B. 64, REM. 9; G. 95, REM. 3; H. 178. *mīlium,* as a gen., limits *numerum.* But observe that the phrase *ad numerum quattuor mīlium,* as well as the following relative-clause are adjective-modifiers of *equitātum.*

LINE 4. **quem**, acc. sing. m. of the rel. pron. *quī, quae, quod;* it refers to *equitātum,* but is the direct obj. of *habēbat.* —— **ex**, prep. with the abl.; see note on *ex,*

104   CAESAR'S GALLIC WAR   [CHAP. XV.

| Aedui and their allies to the number of four thousand, to see in what direction the enemy were marching. And these forces press- | atque *and* praemittit, *he sends forward,* hostēs *the enemy* | eōrum *their* quī *who* iter *a march* | sociīs *allies* videant, *might see,* faciant. *are making.* | coāctum *having been collected* quās *what* Quī *Who* | habēbat, 5 *he had,* in partēs 6 *into parts* cupidius 7 *too eagerly* |

l. 1, above. —— **omnī**, abl. sing. f. of the adj. *omnis, -e*, an *i*-stem, with the abl. regularly ending in *-ī; omnī* is an attributive of *prōvinciā*. —— **prōvinciā**, abl. sing. of the noun *prōvincia, -ae*, f.; it is the obj. of the prep. *ex*. —— **Aeduīs**, abl. plur. of *Aeduī, -ōrum*, m.; connected by the conj. *et* with *prōvinciā*, and in the abl. after the prep. *ex*.

LINE 5. **atque** (ad + que), differs from *et* in that it adds a notion = *and also*. —— **eōrum**, gen. plur. of the dem. pron. *is, ea, id;* used as a personal pron. of the 3d pers. The allusion is to the allies of the Aedui. —— **sociīs**, abl. plur. of *socius, -ī*, m. (compare *sequī*, to follow); connected by *atque* with *Aeduīs*, and in the same grammatical construction. —— **coāctum**, acc. sing. m. of the perf. pass. participle of *cōgō, -ere, -coēgī, coāctum*, 3 (cum + agere); *coāctum*, as a participle, agrees with the pron. *quem;* hence *quem . . . coāctum habēbat* = lit. *which having been collected he had*. It is thus seen that the phrase *coāctum habēbat* = *coēgerat*, nearly. Consult A. & G. 292, *c*; B. 191, 3, (*d*); G. 238; H. 388, I, NOTE; also compare note on *habēre obstrictās*, l. 14, Chap. IX. —— **habēbat**, 3d pers. sing. imperf. ind. act. of *habeō, -ēre, -uī, -itum*, 2. *habēbat* agrees with a pron. implied in the ending as its subject-nom., referring to *Caesar*.

LINE 6. **praemittit**, 3d pers. sing. historical pres. ind. act. of *praemittō, -ere, mīsī, missum*, 3; connected by the conj. *-que*, appended to *equitātum*, with *facit*, and has the same subject-nom., *Caesar*. Observe the force of the *prae* in composition = *in advance*. —— **quī**, nom. plur. m. of the rel. pron. *quī, quae, quod;* it refers to *equitātum* as its antecedent, a noun which *in idea* is plur.; *quī* here = *ut eī*, and is the subject-nom. of *videant*. —— **videant**, 3d pers. plur. pres. subjunctive act. of *videō, -ēre, vīdī, vīsum*, 2 (digammated from the GK. radical *ἰδ*, as seen in the 2d aorist participle *ἰδών*). *videant* is subjunctive of *purpose* after *quī* = *ut eī*, and *quī videant* = *in order that they might see*. Consult A. & G. 317, 2; B. 233, and I; G. 630; H. 497, I. —— **quās**, acc. plur. f. of the pron. *quī, quae, quod;* used here adjectively, agreeing with the noun *partēs*. —— **in**, prep. with the acc. or abl.; here it takes the acc. For its meaning with the acc., see note on *in*, l. 1, end, Chap. I. Observe that a monosyllabic prep. is often placed between a noun and its modifier. Consult A. & G. 345, *a*; B. 58. 2; G. 413, REM. 1; H. 569, II, 1. —— **partēs**, acc. plur. of the noun *pars, partis*, f. *partēs* is the obj. of the prep. *in*.

LINE 7. **hostēs**, nom. plur. of the noun *hostis, -is*, m. and f.; it is subject-nom. of *faciant*. —— **iter**, acc. sing. of the noun *iter, itineris*, n.; *iter* is the direct obj. of *faciant*. —— **faciant**, 3d pers. plur. pres. subjunctive act. of *faciō, -ere, fēcī, factum*, 3; it agrees with its subject-nom. *hostēs*, and is subjunctive, because the question is *indirect*. Consult A. & G. 334; B. 242; G. 467; H. 529, I. —— **Quī**, nom. plur. of the rel. pron. *quī, quae, quod;* it refers to *equitātum*, l. 2, above, but is the subject-nom. of *committunt*, l. 10, below. Observe that *quī* here introduces an independent sentence, and = *et hī* or *eī*. See A. & G. 180, *f*; B. 129, REM. 9; G. 610; H. 453. —— **cupidius**, adv., comparative degree of *cupidē*, superl. *cupidissimē*. The compar-

8 novissimum	agmen	insecūtī	aliēnō	locō	ing too eagerly the enemy's rear, joined battle with the cavalry of the Helvetii in an unfavorable place, and a few of our soldiers fell. The Helvetii, elated at the issue of this skirmish, be-
the newest	*line*	*pursuing*	*in a strange*	*place*	
9 cum	equitātū	Helvētiōrum		proelium	
with	*the cavalry*	*of the Helvetii*		*a battle*	
10 committunt;	et	paucī dē	nostrīs	cadunt.	
join;	*and*	*a few of*	*ours*	*fall.*	
11 Quō	proeliō	sublātī	Helvētiī,	quod	
By which	*battle*	*being elated*	*the Helvetii,*	*because*	

ative degree is here to be rendered *too* or *rather*. Consult A. & G. 93, *a*; B. 163, REM. 6; G. 297, 2; H. 444, 1.

LINE 8. **novissimum**, acc. of the superl. degree of *novus* (kindred with the GK. νέος); it is an attributive of the noun *ăgmen*. —— **ăgmen**, acc. sing. of the noun *ăgmen, -inis*, n.; direct obj. of the participle *insecūtī*. Observe that *ăgmen (agere)* = *an army in motion;* whereas *exercitus* = *a disciplined army*, and *aciēs* = *an army in battle array*. Observe also that *novissimum ăgmen* = *the newest* or *nearest part of the army* to a pursuing enemy, i.e. nearest in this case to the Roman cavalry; *novissimum ăgmen* therefore = *the rear*. —— **insecūtī**, nom. plur. m. of the participle *insecūtus, -a, -um* of the verb *insequor, -sequī, -secūtus*, deponent, 3; it agrees with *quī*, the subj. of the sentence. —— **aliēnō**, abl. sing. m. of the adjective pron. *aliēnus, -a, -um (alius)* = lit. *another's;* here it = *unfavorable*, opposed to *suō* or *opportūnō;* it is an attributive of *locō*. —— **locō**, abl. sing. of the noun *locus, -ī*, m.; locative abl. Consult A. & G. 258, *f*, 1 and 2; B. 176, NOTE 2; G. 385, NOTE 1, middle; H. 425, II, 2.

LINE 9. **cum**, prep.; known to be such both from its position and the nature of the clause in which it stands; *cum* takes the abl. —— **equitātū**, abl. of the noun *equitātus, -ūs*, m.; abl. after *cum;* *cum* is thus used with words of contention. See A. & G. 248, *b;* B. 168; G. 399; H. 419, III, 1, 2). —— **Helvētiōrum**, gen. plur. of *Helvētiī, -ōrum*, m.; it limits, as a gen., *equitātū*. As to this clan, see note on *Helvētiī*, l. 16, Chap. I. —— **proelium**, acc. sing. of the noun *proelium, -ī*, n. (prō or prae + īre) = *to go forward;* direct obj. of *committunt*. For synonyms, see note on *proeliīs*, l. 18, Chap. I.

LINE 10. **committunt**, 3d pers. plur. historic pres. ind. act. of *committō, -ere, -mīsī, -missum*, 3 (con + mittere) = lit. *to bring together;* transf. *to arrange* or *commence a battle*. *committunt* agrees with its subject-nom. *quī*, l. 7, above. —— **et**, conj.; joins the sentences. —— **paucī**, nom. plur. m. of the adj. *paucus, -a, -um*, used substantively, and subject-nom. of the verb *cadunt;* as an adj. thus compared: comparative *paucior*, superl. *paucissimus*. —— **dē**, prep. with the abl. —— **nostrīs**, abl. plur. m. of the poss. adjective pron. *noster, -tra, -trum;* used substantively; or, if preferred, supply *mīlitibus*. *nostrīs* is in the abl. with prep. *dē*, instead of the partitive construction. Consult A. & G. 216, *c;* B. 134, REM. 2; G. 372, REM. 2; H. 397, 3, NOTE 3. —— **cadunt**, 3d pers. plur. historic pres. ind. of *cadō, -ere, cecidī, cāsum*, 3; it agrees with its subject-nom. *paucī*.

LINE 11. **Quō**, abl. sing. n. of the rel. pron. *quī, quae, quod;* it refers to *proelium* as its antecedent, and as an adj. it agrees with *proeliō*. For exposition of the relative at the beginning of a sentence, see grammatical references to *quī*, l. 7, above. —— **proeliō**, abl. of the noun *proelium, -ī*, n.; abl. of cause after the perf. pass. participle *sublātī*. Consult A. & G. 245; B. 165; G. 408; H. 416. —— **sublātī**, nom.

106   CAESAR'S GALLIC WAR   [CHAP. XV.

| cause they had put to route so large a number of horse with five hundred cavalry, began to make a bolder stand, and with their rearguard to provoke our men to battle. But Caesar re- | quīngentīs *with five hundred* equitum *of horsemen* nōnnunquam *sometimes* nostrōs *ours* | equitibus *horsemen* prōpulerant, *they had put to flight,* et *and* lacēssere *to exasperate* | tantam *so great* audācius *more boldly* novissimō *with the newest* coepērunt. *began.* | multitūdinem *a multitude* subsistere *to halt* āgmine *line* Caesar *Caesar* | 12 13 proeliō 14 *by battle* suōs 15 *his own* |

plur. m. of the perf. pass. participle *sublātus, -a, -um* of the verb *tollō, tollere, sustulī, sublātum;* it agrees with *Helvētiī.* Observe that *tollō* has as its root *tol,* whence *tulī,* compare GK. τολμάω, and = *to lift up,* hence *to take heart,* and rarely in the perf. pass. participle = *elated.* —— **Helvētiī,** nom. plur. m. of the adj. *Helvētius, -a, -um,* used substantively, and subject-nom. of *coepērunt,* l. 15, below. As to this clan, see note on *Helvētiī,* l. 16, Chap. I. —— **quod,** conj. = *because.*

LINE 12. **quīngentīs,** abl. plur. m. of the num. adj. *quīngentī, -ae, -a* (quīnque + centum); it is an attributive of *equitibus.* Observe that hundreds are regularly declined like the plural of *bonus.* —— **equitibus,** abl. plur. of *eques, -itis,* m.; abl. of means. See A. & G. 248, 8, *c*; B. 167; G. 401; H. 420. Compare note on *equitātum,* l. 2, above. —— **tantam,** acc. sing. f. of the adj. *tantus, -a, -um* (tam + tus) = *so much,* as compared with some standard either expressed or understood. *tantam* modifies *multitūdinem.* —— **multitūdinem,** acc. sing. of the noun *multitūdō, -inis,* f. (*multus*); it is the direct obj. of *prōpulerant.*

LINE 13. **equitum,** gen. plur. of *eques, -itis,* m.; it limits *multitūdinem.* See note on *equitātum,* l. 2, above. Observe that *eques* is a lingual-mute stem — *equit;* the nom. is formed by adding *s,* thus: equit + s; the lingual is suppressed, and the vowel preceding the formative *s* is changed to *e.* If the stem of *eques* were *equiti,* i.e. an *ī*-stem, the gen. plur. would be *equitium.* —— **prōpulerant,** 3d pers. plur. pluperf. ind. act. of *prōpellō, -ere, -pulī, -pulsum,* 3 (prō + pellere, *to drive forward*); it agrees with a pron. implied in the ending, referring to *Helvētiī.* —— **audācius,** adv., comparative degree of *audācter;* superl. *audācissimē* (adj. *audax,* bold). *audācius* modifies *subsistere.* —— **subsistere,** pres. inf. act. of *subsistō, -ere, -stitī,* 3 (sub + sistere) = lit. *to stand a little, to halt;* but *subsistere* = *to remain, to subsist;* it has the lit. meaning in our text. *subsistere* is a complementary inf., and depends on *coepērunt.* See A. & G. 271; B. 181; G. 423; H. 533, I, 1.

LINE 14. **nōnnunquam** (nōn + num[n]quam) = lit. *not never,* i.e. *sometimes;* as in English, two negatives in Latin = a positive. See A. & G. 150, and *a*; B. 117. 10; G. 449, 4; H. 553, I. —— **et,** cop. conj.; it here connects *subsistere* and *lacēssere.* —— **novissimō,** abl. sing. n. of the adj. *novissimus, -a, -um;* superl. degree of the positive *novus;* it modifies *āgmine.* —— **āgmine,** abl. of *āgmen, -inis,* n.; abl. of manner. See A. & G. 248; B. 168; G. 399; H. 419, III. —— **proeliō,** abl. of the noun *proelium, -ī,* n.; abl. of means. A. & G. 248, *c,* 1; B. 167; G. 401; H. 420. A possible construction of *proeliō* is the locative abl.; see H. 425, II, 1, 2); but even thus the idea of means is dominant.

LINE 15. **nostrōs,** acc. plur. of the poss. adjective pron. *noster, -tra, -trum;* used substantively; or, in analyzing, supply *mīlitēs.* —— **lacēssere,** pres. inf. act. of *lacēssō, -ere, -īvī (-iī), -ītum,* 3; complementary inf.; depends on *coepērunt.* —— **coepērunt,**

BOOK I.

16 ā   proeliō   continēbat   āc   satis   habēbat | strained his men from fighting, thinking it to be sufficient for the present to keep the enemy from rapine, foraging and pil-
   from *battle* *held in check* *and* *enough* *he held (it to be)*
17 in   praesentiā   hostem   rapīnīs,   pābulātiōnibus
   for *the present* *the enemy* *from robberies,*   *foragings*
18 populātiōnibusque   prohibēre.   Ita   diēs
   devastations   *and,*   *to restrain.*   *Thus* *for days*

3d pers. plur. of the defective preteritive verb *coepī, coepisse*, fut. participle *coeptūrus*, perf. pass. participle *coeptus, coepērunt* agrees with its subject-nom. *Helvētiī*, l. 11, above. As to inflection and use of this verb, see A. & G. 143, *a*; B. 113; G. 175, 5, *a*; H. 297, I. and 1. —— **Caesar, -aris**, m.; subject-nom. of *continēbat*. As to a possible derivation of *Caesar*, see note, l. 2, above. —— **suōs**, acc. plur. m. of the poss. adjective pron. *suus, -a, -um*; used substantively; or *hominēs*, or *mīlitēs* may be supplied. The later grammarians, however, object to the supposition of an ellipsis. See A. & G. 197, *d*, and NOTE; B. 60, REM.; G. 204, NOTES 1, (*a*), (*b*), and 2; H. 441, 1. But no rigid analysis can be made without such supposition. *suōs* is the direct obj. of *continēbat*.

LINE 16. **ā**, prep. with the abl. (*ā* before consonants only, *ab* before vowels or consonants). —— **proeliō**, abl. of *proelium, -ī*, n.; abl. after the prep. *ā*. For synonyms, see note on *proeliīs*, l. 18, Chap. I. —— **continēbat**, 3d pers. sing. imperf. ind. act. of *continēō, -ēre, -uī, -tentum*, 2 (con + tenēre) = lit. *to hold together*. *continēbat* agrees with its subject-nom. *Caesar*. —— **āc**, conj., contracted from *atque*; see note on *atque*, l. 10, Chap. I. —— **satis**, adv. sometimes; sometimes, as here, an indecl. adj.; here it is a predicate-adj.; acc. after *esse*, to be supplied; of which *esse*, *prohibēre* with its modifiers is the subject-acc. —— **habēbat**, 3d pers. sing. imperf. ind. act. of *habeō, -ēre, -uī, -itum*, 2; it is connected by the conj. *āc* with *continēbat*, and has the same subject-nom. The reader will bear in mind that *habēre* = *to have*, in the widest sense, and that *to have* in one's mind = *to think*.

LINE 17. **in**, prep. with either the acc. or abl., but with different significations; compare note on *in*, l. 1, Chap. I. —— **praesentiā**, abl. sing. of the noun *praesentia*, *-ae*, f. (*praesēns*, participial adj. of *praesum*) = lit. that which *is before* one. *praesentiā* is the obj. of the prep. *in*. —— **hostem**, acc. sing. of the noun *hostis, -is*, m. and f.; it is the direct obj. of *prohibēre*. Note that the plur. form is oftener used, in Caesar, than the sing. Synonyms: *hostis*, originally = *a stranger*; transf. *a public enemy*; whereas, in contrast, *inimīcus* = *a private foe*. —— **rapīnīs**, abl. plur. of the noun *rapīna, -ae*, f. (compare *rapere*, to pillage); abl. of separation after *prohibēre*. Consult A. & G. 243; B. 160; G. 390, 2, and NOTE 3, end; H. 414. —— **pābulātiōnibus**, abl. plur. of the noun *pābulātiō, -ōnis*, f.; in the same construction as *rapīnīs*, the conj. being omitted.

LINE 18. **populātiōnibusque** (populātiōnibus + que). *populātiōnibus*, abl. plur. of the noun *populātiō, -ōnis*, f.; connected by the enclitic *-que* with *pābulātiōnibus*, and in the same grammatical construction. Note that in a series either no conj. is used, or it is repeated between the words. But the enclitic *-que*, as shown in our text, may be appended to the last word of the series. See A. & G. 208, 3, and 346, *e*; B. 123, REMS. 2 and 6; G. 474, NOTE; H. 554, 6. —— **prohibēre**, pres. inf. act. of the verb *prohibeō, -ēre, -uī, -itum*, 2 (pro + habēre); hence *prohibēre* = lit. *to hold in front*, i.e. *to keep in check, restrain*. *prohibēre*, as we have seen, is the subject-acc. of *esse*, to be supplied, of which the adj. *satis* is predicate-acc. —— **Ita**, adv. (derived from

CAESAR'S GALLIC WAR [CHAP. XVI.

| laging. Both armies marched for about fifteen days in such a manner, that not more than five or six miles' space intervened between the enemy's rearguard and our van. | circiter
about
inter
between
nostrum
our
sēnīs
six | quīndecim
fifteen
novissimum
the newest
prīmum
first,
mīlibus
thousands | iter
a march
hostium
enemy's
nōn
not
passuum
of paces | fēcērunt,
they made,
āgmen
line
amplius
more than
interesset.
intervened. | utī 19
so that
et 20
and
aut 21
or
22 |

radical *i*, whence is + suffix ta) = lit. *in this manner. ita* modifies *fēcērunt*. —— diēs, acc. plur. of the noun *diēs, -ēi,* m. and f. in the sing.; always m. in the plur. *diēs* is the acc. of *extent* of time. See A. & G. 256, 2; B. 153; G. 336; H. 379.

LINE 19. circiter, prep. and adv.; here an adv., and modifies the num. adj. *quīndecim. circiter* is derived from *circus,* whence *circum.* —— quīndecim (quīnque + decem), an indecl. num. adj.; it is an attributive of the noun *diēs.* —— iter, acc. sing. of the noun *iter, itineris,* n.; direct obj. of *fēcērunt.* —— fēcērunt, 3d pers. plur. perf. ind. act. of the verb *faciō, -ere, fēcī, factum,* 3; it agrees with the subject-nom. *mīliēs,* to be supplied. —— utī, ecbatic conj., here for the more common and shorter *ut.*

LINE 20. inter, prep. with the acc.; derived from in + the adverbial suffix ter; sometimes, though rarely and poetically, an adv. —— novissimum, acc. of superl. degree of the positive *novus;* see note on *novissimum,* l. 8, above. *novissimum* modifies *āgmen.* —— hostium, gen. plur. of the noun *hostis, -is,* m. and f.; an *i-*stem; *hostium* limits the noun *āgmen.* For synonyms, see note on *hostem,* l. 17, above. —— āgmen, acc. sing. of the noun *āgmen, -inis,* n.; obj. of the prep. *inter.* For derivation and synonyms, see note on *āgmen,* l. 8, above. —— et, cop. conj., connecting the phrases.

LINE 21. nostrum, acc. sing. n. of the poss. adjective pron. *noster, -tra, -trum;* it is an attributive of *prīmum,* which latter is here used as a noun. —— prīmum, in form an acc. sing. n. of the adj. *prīmus, -a, -um;* in use here it is a noun, connected by the conj. *et* with *āgmen,* and in the same grammatical construction; in other words, *prīmum* is also the obj. of the prep. *inter;* or *āgmen* may be supplied and *prīmum* may be taken as an adjective-modifier of *āgmen* thus understood, and the latter would be the obj. of the prep. *inter.* —— nōn, negative adv. (ne + oenum [ūnum], apocopated). *nōn* modifies *interesset.* —— amplius, nom. n. of the comparative *amplior, -us,* used as a subst.; positive *amplus,* superl. *amplissimus. amplus* as a noun is here the subject-nom. of *interesset.* —— quīnīs, abl. plur. n. of the distributive num. adj. *quīnī, -ae, -a;* it is an attributive of *mīlibus.* —— aut, conj.; it usually excludes an alternative; see note on *aut,* l. 19, Chap. I.

LINE 22. sēnīs, abl. plur. of the distributive adj. *sēnī, -ae, -a;* connected by the disjunctive conj. *aut* with *quīnīs,* and in the same grammatical construction, i.e. it, too, is an attributive of the noun *mīlibus.* Observe that the distributives indicate that the same interval was maintained *each* day. —— mīlibus, abl. plur. n. of the adj. *mīlia,* used substantively; abl. after the comparative degree *quam* being omitted. Consult A. & G. 247; B. 163; G. 398; H. 417. —— passuum, gen. plur. of *passus, -ūs,* m.; partitive after *mīlibus;* consult A. & G. 216, *a,* 2; B. 134; G. 370; H. 397, 2. For the exact literal and the best rendering into English of this construction, see

BOOK I.

1	XVI.	Interim	cotīdiē	Caesar		Aeduōs	XVI. Mean-
		Meantime	*daily*	*Caesar*		*from the Aedui*	while Caesar kept daily de-
2	frūmentum	quod	essent		pūblicē	pollicitī	manding from the Aedui the
	grain	*which*	*they had*		*officially*	*promised*	grain which they had promised in
3	flāgitāre.		Nam	propter		frīgora,	the name of the state. For on ac-
	to demand (began).		*For*	*on account of the times*		*of cold,*	count of the cold

note on *passuum*, l. 25, Chap. I. —— **interesset**, 3d pers. sing. imperf. subjunctive of the verb *intersum*, *-esse*, *-fuī*, fut. participle *-futūrus;* it agrees with its subject-nom. *amplius*, an adj. used as a noun; it is the subjunctive of *result* after the conj. *ut*. Observe (1) the composition of the verb (inter + esse) = lit. *to be between;* then (a) impersonally it = *it concerns;* (b) *there is a difference*. But observe (2) that in the text the grammatical subject is the colorless adj. *amplius*, used substantively; while the logical subject of *interesset* is the entire complex phrase: *nōn amplius quīnīs aut sēnīs mīlibus passuum*.

LINE 1. **Interim**, adv. (inter + im for *eum*) = *interea* (inter + ea) in significa-tion. —— **cotīdiē**, adv. (quot + diē) = lit. *every day*. These adverbs modify the historical inf. *flāgitāre*, which, in use, is the main verb in the sentence. —— **Caesar, -aris**, m., subject-nom. of the historic inf. *flāgitāre*, which is said by the grammarians to be = *flāgitābat*. —— **Aeduōs**, acc. of *the person* of the noun *Aeduī*, *-ōrum*, m., after *flāgitāre*. As to the Aedui, see note on *Aeduō*, l. 20, Chap. III.

LINE 2. **frūmentum**, acc. of *the thing* of the noun *frūmentum, -ī,* n., after *flāgi-tāre*, a verb of demanding which takes two accusatives. Consult A. & G. 239, *c;* B. 151; G. 339; H. 374. —— **quod**, acc. sing. n. of the rel. pron. *quī, quae, quod;* it refers to *frūmentum* as its antecedent, but is the direct obj. of the deponent verb *essent pollicitī*. —— **pūblicē**, adv. (*pūblicus*, public). As to the formation of this adv. from the adj., see A. & G. 148, *a;* B. 117. 5; G. 91, 2, (*b*); H. 304, II, 2, end. Observe the emphatic position of the adv., between the parts of the compound formation of the pluperf. tense. —— **essent pollicitī** (*pollicitī essent*), 3d pers. plur. pluperf. subjunctive of the deponent *polliceor, -ērī, -licitus,* 2; it agrees with a pron. implied in the ending as its subject-nom., referring to *Aeduōs;* it is in the subjunc-tive, because in a *quod*-clause expressing a reason of the speaker's own thoughts under other conditions — informal indirect discourse. See A. & G. 341, *d*, and REM.; B. 198, (*b*); G. 539, REM., and 628; H. 528, 1. Synonyms: *prōmittere = to promise*, as the general word, especially in response to a request; *pollicērī = to promise*, as a free and gracious act.

LINE 3. **flāgitāre**, historical pres. inf. of *flāgitō, -āre, -āvī, -ātum,* 1. For its use in narrating vivid historic events, see A. & G. 275; B. 182; G. 647; H. 536, 1. Prob-ably in such use there is an ellipsis of *coepit* or *coepērunt*. Consult G. 647, NOTE 1. Synonyms: *postulāre = to demand*, as a simple request; *poscere = to demand* energetic-ally, because one has a consciousness of right; whereas *flāgitāre* (strongest of all verbs of demanding) = *to demand* eagerly and importunately. —— **Nam**, conj.; it introduces an objective reason, while *enim* introduces a subjective, and is post-positive. —— **propter**, prep. with the acc. —— **frīgora**, acc. plur. of *frīgus, -oris,* n. (diagammated from ῥῑγος); it is the obj. of the prep. *propter*. The plur. here = *the times of cold*. See A. & G. 75, 3, *c*, end; G. 204, NOTE 5.

weather, since Gaul lies toward the north — as we have before said — the standing grain was not only unripe in the fields, but not even a sufficient quantity of for-	quod *Gallia* sub septentriōnibus, ut ante 4 *because* *Gaul* *under* *the north,* *as* *before* dictum est, posita est, nōn modo frūmenta 5 *it has been said,* *was situated,* *not* *only* *the crops* in agrīs mātūra nōn erant, sed nē 6 *in* *the fields* *ripe* *not* *were,* *but* *not* pābulī quidem satis māgna cōpia 7 *of fodder* *even* *a sufficiently* *great* *abundance*

LINE 4. **quod**, conj. = *because;* note that the *quod*-clause is explanatory of *frigora*. —— **Gallia**, nom. sing. of *Gallia, -ae,* f.; subj. of *posita est.* Caesar is comparing the climate of Gaul with that of Italy. —— **sub** (sibilated and apocopated from the GK. *ὑπό*); prep. with either the acc. or abl.; here it takes the abl. —— **septentriōnibus**, abl. plur. of the noun *septentriō, -ōnis,* m. (septem + triō); abl. after the prep. *sub.* The phrase gives the idea of the situation of that part of Gaul that seems to be *under* the stars in the Great Bear constellation. See note on *septentriōnēs,* l. 26, Chap. I. —— **ut**, adv., and usually such in a parenthetical clause. —— **ante**, adv. See lines 21-26, Chap. I.

LINE 5. **dictum est**, 3d pers. sing. perf. ind. pass. of *dīcō, -ere, -dīxī, -dictum,* 3; it is here used impersonally; supply *mihi,* as dat. of the agent, and we have the equivalent of the personal construction = *dīxī*. —— **posita**, participle as predicate after *est,* forming a species of periphrastic conjugation; it agrees in gender and number with *Gallia*. —— **est**, 3d pers. sing. pres. ind. of the verb *sum, esse, fuī, futūrus;* it agrees with its subject-nom. *Gallia.* —— **nōn** (nē + ūnum), adv., modifies *modo.* But observe that *nōn modo ... sed etiam* are conjunctive adverbial phrases, and that when *nōn modo ... nōn* are followed, as in our text, by *sed nē ... quidem,* this phraseology indicates a rising to a more emphatic negative in the second clause. —— **frūmenta**, nom. plur. of the noun *frūmentum, -ī,* n. (frūgi + mentum), subj. of the verb *erant.* Observe (*a*) that *fructus* usually denotes *tree-fruit,* but *frūmentum* = *grain;* (*b*) that *frūmenta,* in Caesar's commentaries = *standing grain,* while the sing. *frūmentum* = *the grain gathered;* in other words, it = *pābulum,* forage.

LINE 6. **in**, prep. with the acc. and abl.; here it takes the abl. On the meaning of *in,* according to the case, see note on *in,* l. 1, Chap. I. —— **agrīs**, abl. plur. of the noun *ager, agrī,* m.; *agrīs* is the obj. of the prep. *in.* —— **mātūra**, nom. plur. n. of the adj. *mātūrus, -a, -um;* comparative *mātūrior,* superl. *mātūrissimus,* less frequently *mātūrrimus.* *mātūra* is predicate-adj. after *erant.* —— **nōn**, adv. (nē + oe[ū]num), modifies the adj. *mātūra.* —— **erant**, 3d pers. plur. imperf. ind. of the intrans. verb *sum, esse, fuī, futūrus;* it agrees with its subject-nom. *frūmenta.* —— **sed**, conj.; a particle of limitation — a stronger adversative than either *at* or *autem.* —— **nē**, adv., here modifying *quidem;* sometimes a conj., and the two particles *nē ... quidem* may be taken as conjunctions here, connecting the clauses. Archaic form *neī* (*nī*); the primary Latin negative.

LINE 7. **pābulī**, gen. sing. of the noun *pābulum, -ī,* n.; it, as a gen., limits *cōpia.* —— **quidem**, conjunctive adv. Observe that the emphatic word is inserted between *nē* and *quidem.* See A. & G. 345, *b*; G. 679; H. 569, III. —— **satis**, adv., modifying *māgna;* comparative *satius* = *more satisfying,* i.e. *better.* Synonyms: *satis* = *enough,* objectively, so that one needs no more; but *affatim* = *enough,* subjectively, so that

8 suppetēbat;	eō	autem	frūmentō,	quod	age was at hand.
was in store;	*that,*	*moreover,*	*grain*	*which*	Moreover, the grain which Cae-
9 flūmine	Ararī	nāvibus	subvēxerat,	proptereā	sar had brought
on the river Arar	*by ships*	*he had conveyed,*	*for this reason*		by boats on the river Saône, he
10 minus	ūtī	poterat,	quod	iter	could not use,
the less (easily)	*to use*	*he was able,*	*because*	*the route*	because the Hel- vetii had turned
11 ab	Ararī	Helvētiī	āverterant,	ā	their course from
from	*the Arar*	*the Helvetii*	*had turned aside,*	*from*	the river, and

one wishes for no more. Doedl. *Synonyms.* —— **māgna**, nom. sing. f. of the adj. *māgnus, māior, māximus.* *māgna* is an attributive of *cōpia.* —— **cōpia**, nom. sing. of *cōpia, -ae,* f.; subj. of *suppetēbat.* Note that in the sing. *cōpia = abundance;* in the plur., *troops.*

LINE 8. **suppetēbat**, 3d pers. sing. imperf. ind. of *sup(b)petō, -ere, -īvī (-iī), -ītum*, 3, n. (sub + petere); hence *suppetere* = lit. *to seek* for that which is *near.* *suppetēbat* agrees with its subject-nom. *cōpia.* —— **eō**, abl. sing. n. of the dem. pron. *is, ea, id;* it is an attributive of the noun *frūmentō.* —— **autem**, conj., postpositive; a weak adversative; often simply marks the transition. —— **frūmentō**, abl. sing. of *frūmentum, -ī,* n. See note on *frūmenta,* l. 5, above. *frūmentō* is in the abl. after the verb *ūtī,* l. 10, below. Consult A. & G. 249; B. 167, 1; G. 407; H. 421, I. —— **quod**, acc. sing. n. of the rel. pron. *quī, quae, quod;* it refers to *frūmentō* as its antecedent, but is the direct obj. of *subvēxerat. quod* is known to be a rel. pron. in the acc., because *subvēxerat* is a trans. verb and requires a direct obj.

LINE 9. **flūmine**, abl. sing. of the noun *flūmen, -inis,* n. (*fluere,* to flow); hence *flūmen* = lit. *a flowing.* *flūmine* is in the abl. of the *way by which.* See A. & G. 258, *g;* B. 167, 5, (*b*); G. 389; H. 420, 1, 3). —— **Ararī**, abl. sing. of the noun *Arar* or *Araris,* m., acc. in *-im;* an appositive. The form *Arare,* abl., sometimes occurs. The Arar is the modern Saône; it rises in the Vosges mountains, and empties into the Rhone. —— **nāvibus**, abl. plur. of the noun *nāvis, -is,* f. (GK. ναῦς); abl. of means. A. & G. 248, *c;* B. 167, 2; H. 420. —— **subvēxerat**, 3d pers. sing. pluperf. ind. act. of *subvehō, -ere, -vēxī, -vēctum,* 3; it agrees with a pron. implied in the ending, referring to Caesar. —— **proptereā** (propter + eā), adv.; the herald of the following *quod*-clause.

LINE 10. **minus**, adv., comparative of *parum (not enough),* superl. *minimē;* it modifies the verb *ūtī.* *minus* = lit. *less,* but may be frequently rendered as if it were *nōn.* —— **ūtī**, pres. inf. of the deponent verb *ūtor, ūtī, ūsus,* 3; inf. complementary, and depends on *poterat.* See A. & G. 271; B. 181; G. 423; H. 533, I, 2. —— **poterat**, 3d pers. sing. imperf. ind. of *possum, posse, potuī* (potis + sum); it agrees with a subject-nom. implied in the ending, referring to Caesar. —— **quod**, conj., connects the clauses; known to be a conj. not merely because there is no noun immediately preceding as an antecedent, but because *āverterant,* as a plur. trans. verb, has its obj. *iter; quod,* accordingly, could neither be the subj. nor obj. —— **iter**, acc. sing. of the noun *iter, itineris,* n.; the direct obj. of *āverterant.* For synonyms, see note on *via,* l. 2, Chap. IX.

LINE 11. **ab**, prep. with the abl. (*ā* before consonants only, *ab* before either vowels or consonants); compare GK. ἀπό, English *off.* —— **Ararī**, abl. sing. of *Arar, -aris,* m.; acc. in *-im;* another form of the abl. is *Arare;* abl. after the prep. *ab.* ——

| he was unwilling to withdraw from them. The Aedui kept putting him off day after day, saying that the grain was being collected, brought in, and was near | quibus
whom

diē
day

cōnferrī,
to be brought together, | discēdere
to leave

dūcere
to put him off

comportārī,
to be collected, | nolēbat.
he was unwilling.

(began)

adesse
to be near, | Diem ex 12
Day after

Aeduī: 13
the Aedui: (the grain)

dīcere. 14
to say |

Helvētiī, nom. plur. of the adj. *Helvētius, -a, -um*, used substantively, and as such the subject-nom. of *āverterant*. For description of this clan, see note on *Helvētiī*, l. 16, Chap. I. —— **āverterant**, 3d pers. plur. pluperf. ind. act. of *āvertō, -ere, āvertī, āversum*, 3 (ab + vertere); hence *āvertere* = lit. *to turn away. āverterant* agrees with its subject-nom. *Helvētiī*. —— **ā**, see *ab*, immediately above.

LINE 12. **quibus**, abl. plur. m. of the rel. pron. *quī, quae, quod*; as a rel. it refers to *Helvētiī* as its antecedent, but it is the obj. of the prep. *ā*. —— **discēdere**, pres. inf. of *discēdō, -ere, -cessī, -cessum*, 3; complementary, depending on *nolēbat*. —— **nolēbat**, 3d pers. sing. imperf. ind. of *nōlō, nōlle, nōluī* (nē + volo); it agrees with a pron. implied in its ending as subject-nom., referring to Caesar. Note that, after crossing the Saône, the Helvetii had turned in a westerly direction, in order to cross the Cevenne mountains at their least altitude. Their destination, it will be recalled, was the country of the Santoni. —— **Diem**, acc. of the noun *diēs, -ēī*, m. or f. in sing., always m. in the plur. *diem* is here acc. of *extent of time*. Consult A. & G. 256, 2; B. 153; G. 336; H. 379. —— **ex**, prep. with the abl. (*ē* before consonants only, *ex* before vowels or consonants).

LINE 13. **diē**, abl. of *diēs, -ēī*, after the prep. *ex*, which latter here = *after*. —— **dūcere**, historical pres. inf. of *dūcō, -ere, dūxī, ductum*, 3, for *dūcēbant*. As *dūcere* is a trans. verb, supply *eum*, i.e. *Caesarem*, as direct obj. As to the use of the historic inf., and for grammatical references, see note on *flāgitāre*, l. 3, above. As to its signification, *dūcere* = (*a*) *to lead*, in its widest sense; then, of course, (*b*) *to lead a person in regard to his will*; then, (*c*), in reference to time, it = *to prolong*; and (*d*), in reference to persons, it = *to put off*, as in our text. But sometimes (*e*) it = *to lead* or *control* one's own thoughts, *to reckon*. Compare note on *dūxērunt*, l. 10, Chap. III. —— **Aeduī**, nom. plur. of the adj. *Aeduus, -a, -um*, used substantively, and here subject-nom. of the historical inf. *dūcere*. For historical description of the clan, see note on *Aeduō*, l. 20, Chap. III.

LINE 14. **cōnferrī**, pres. inf. pass. of *cōnferō, -ferre, contulī, col*(*n*)*lātum* (con + ferō); supply *frūmentum* as subject-acc. —— **comportārī**, pres. inf. pass. of *comportō, -āre, -āvī, -ātum*; *comportārī* is in the same grammatical construction as *cōnferrī*; its subject-acc. is the pron. *id*, representing *frūmentum*. Note the omission of the conj. between these infinitives (asyndeton). Note also that, as *ferrī* is used of what is borne by a servant on his own body, and *portārī* is used in reference to that which is borne on a beast or wagon; so *cōnferrī*, in our text, would have reference to the contributions of menial Aeduans to their officials, and *comportārī* would denote the official delivery of the grain to Caesar. Or *comportārī* may be taken as merely epexegetical of *cōnferrī*. —— **adesse**, pres. inf. of the intrans. *ad*(*as*)*sum, -esse, ad*(*af*)*fuī, ad*(*af*)*futūrus*. *adesse* is in the same grammatical construction as the two immediately preceding infinitives; i.e. its subject-acc. is the pron. *id*, referring to *frūmentum*. Observe that these three infinitives with their subject-accusatives depend on *dīcere*. —— **dīcere**, historical pres. inf. of *dīcō, -ere, dīxī, dictum*, 3; it

15	Ubi	sē	diūtius	dūcī	at hand. When Caesar saw that
	(began they).	When	himself	too long	to be put off	he was put off
16	intellēxit	et	diem	īnstāre,	quō	diē	too long, and that the day was
	he perceived	and	the day	to be near	on which	day	near when he
17	frūmentum	mīlitibus		mētīrī	oportēret,	must distribute grain to his sol-
	(himself) grain	to the soldiers		to measure out	it behooved,	diers, summoning
18	convocātīs	eōrum	prīncipibus,	quōrum	the Helvetian
	having been summoned	their	chiefs,	of whom	chiefs, of whom

---

stands for *dīcēbant*, in ordinary discourse, and agrees with the pron. *eī*, i.e. *Aeduī*, to be supplied, as the subject-nom. For grammatical references, see note on *flāgitāre*, l. 3, above.

LINE 15. **Ubi** (quō + bi), adv. = lit. *in which place, where;* sometimes used of time, and = *whenever* or *when*. —— **sē**, acc. sing. of the reflexive pron. *suī, sibi, sē, sē*, same form in both numbers; subject-acc. of the verb *dūcī*. —— **diūtius**, adv., comparative of *diū* (*diēs*); superl. *diūtissimē*. For the omission of the standard of comparison, see A. & G. 93, *a*; B. 163, REM. 6; G. 297, 2; H. 444, 1. *diūtius* modifies the verb *dūcī*. —— **dūcī**, pres. inf. pass. of *dūcō, -ere, dūxī, ductum*, 3; it, with its subject-acc., forms a noun-clause which is the direct obj. of *intellēxit*. *dūcī* is known to be the pres. inf. pass. of *dūcor*, and not the dat. of *dux, ducis, ducī*, to the novice by noticing that the vowel in the penult in *dux* is short; to the experienced Latinist, by the observation that the construction cannot be satisfactorily analyzed in any other way than by making *dūcī* a pass. inf. But note that *dūcī* here = *to be put off*, and compare *dūcere*, l. 13, above.

LINE 16. **intellēxit**, 3d pers. sing. perf. ind. act. of *intellegō, -ere, -lēxī, -lēctum*, 3 (inter + legere); hence *intellegere* = *to select between, to discriminate, to know*. *intellēxit* agrees with a pron. implied in the ending as subject-nom., referring to Caesar. —— **diem**, acc. sing. of the noun *diēs, -ēī*, m. and f. in sing., always m. in the plur.; *diem* is subject-acc. of the verb *īnstāre*. —— **īnstāre**, pres. inf. of *īnstō, -stāre, -stitī,* fut. participle *-statūrus*, 1 (in + stāre); hence *īnstāre* = lit. *to stand on* or *near*, i.e. *to press on, be urgent*. —— **quō**, abl. sing. m. of the rel. pron. *qui, quae, quod;* as a rel. it refers to *diem*, but it has here an adjective force, and is the attributive of the noun *diē*, repeated from *diem*. As to the repetition of the antecedent in the relative-clause, consult A. & G. 200, *a*; B. 129, REM. 1, (*b*); G. 615; H. 445, 8. —— **diē**, abl. of *time at which*, from *diēs, -ēī;* see *diem*, immediately above. For grammatical references, see A. & G. 256, I; B. 171; G. 393; H. 429.

LINE 17. **frūmentum**, acc. sing. of *frūmentum, -ī,* n.; direct obj. of the deponent verb *mētīrī*, of which verb supply the pron. *sē* as subject-acc. —— **mīlitibus**, dat. plur. of the noun *mīles, -itis*, m.; dat. of the indirect obj. after *mētīrī*. See A. & G. 225, 3, *d*; B. 141; G. 345; H. 384, II. —— **mētīrī**, pres. inf. of the deponent verb *mētior, -īrī, mēnsus*, postclassic *mētītus*, 4. Note that the infinitive-clause *frūmentum* (*sē*) *mīlitibus mētīrī* is the subject of the so-called impersonal verb *oportēret*. —— **oportēret**, 3d pers. sing. imperf. subjunctive of the impersonal verb *oportet, -ēre, -uit*, 2; subjunctive, because in a dependent clause in implied *ōrātiō oblīqua*. Consult A. & G. 342; B. 245, (*b*); G. 663; H. 529, II, NOTE 1, 1).

LINE 18. **convocātīs**, abl. plur. m. of the perf. pass. participle *convocātus, -a, -um* of the verb *convocō, -āre, -āvī, -ātum*, 1; abl. absolute with the noun *prīncipibus*. ——

114   CAESAR'S GALLIC WAR   [CHAP. XVI.

he had a large number in the camp — among them Divitiacus and Liscus, the latter the ruling chief, whom the Aedui call Vergobretus, who is	māgnam cōpiam in castrīs habēbat — in *a great plenty in camp he had — among* hīs Divitiacō et Liscō, quī summō *them Divitiacus and Liscus, who of the supreme* magistrātuī praeërat, quem Vergobretum *body of officers was the leader, whom as Vergobretus*	19 20 21

eōrum, gen. plur. m. of the dem. pron. *is, ea, id*, used as a personal pron. of the 3d pers.; it limits the noun *prīncipibus*. —— prīncipibus, abl. plur. of *prīnceps, -cipis*, m. (prīmum + capere); primarily an adj.; here a noun, and in the abl. absolute with the perf. pass. participle *convocātīs*, denoting *time when*. Consult A. & G. 255, *d*, 1; B. 172; G. 409, 410; H. 431. —— quōrum, gen. plur. of the rel. pron. *quī, quae, quod*; it refers to *prīncipibus* as its antecedent, but, as a gen., it limits *cōpiam*.

LINE 19. māgnam, acc. sing. f. of the adj. *māgnus, -a, -um*; comparative *māior*; superl. degree *māximus*; *māgnam* is an attributive of *cōpiam*. —— cōpiam, acc. sing. of the noun *cōpia, -ae*, f. (con + ops); here *cōpiam* = *multitūdinem*. *cōpiam* is the direct obj. of *habēbat*. —— in, prep. with the acc. or abl.; here it takes the abl. For definition of meaning when followed by either the acc. or abl., see note on *in*, l. 1, end, Chap. I. —— castrīs, abl. plur. of *castrum, -ī*, m.; in the sing. = *a redoubt*; in the plur. = *a camp*. *castrīs* is the obj. of the prep. *in*. —— habēbat, 3d pers. sing. imperf. ind. act. of *habeō, -ēre, -uī, -itum*, 2; it agrees with a pron. implied in the ending as its subject-nom., referring to Caesar. —— in, see note on *in*, immediately before *castrīs*, above.

LINE 20. hīs, abl. plur. m. of the dem. pron. *hīc, haec, hōc*, used as a personal pron. of the 3d person. *hīs* refers to the Aeduans, and is used, because they had just been alluded to. *hīs* is the obj. of the prep. *in*, which here = *among*. —— Divitiacō, abl. sing. of *Divitiacus, -ī*, m.; abl. absolute with the participle *convocātīs*, to be supplied. Divitiacus was an Aeduan chief, brother of Dumnorix, and a friend of the Roman people. —— et, cop. conj.; it connects objects of equal importance; *atque* (ad + que), a cop. conj., but adds a notion of greater importance; while -*que* (enclitic) merely appends a notion, and is adjunctive rather than copulative. In our text, *et* couples *Divitiacō* and *Liscō*. —— Liscō, abl. sing. of the proper noun *Liscus, -ī*, m.; it, too, is in the abl. absolute with *convocātīs*, supplied. Observe that the participle is plur., because it is in the abl. absolute construction with two nouns connected by the conj. *et*. It appears that Liscus was an Aeduan chief magistrate. —— quī, nom. sing. m. of the rel. pron. *quī, quae, quod*; it refers to Liscus, but is subject-nom. of *praeërat*. —— summō, dat. sing. m. of the adj., superl. degree, *summus, -a, -um*; one of the forms of the superl. of the adj. *superus*, comparative *superior*, superl. *suprēmus* or *summus*; *summō* is an attributive of *magistrātuī*.

LINE 21. magistrātuī, dat. sing. of the noun *magistrātus, -ūs*, m.; a contracted form *magistrātū* is read in some editions. *magistrātuī* is dat. after *prae* in composition in *praeërat*. Consult A. & G. 228; B. 143; G. 347; H. 386. —— praeërat, 3d pers. sing. imperf. ind. act. of the intrans. verb *praesum, praeësse, praefuī* (prae + esse) = lit. *to b: before*; hence *praeësse* = *to be over, to be in command of*. —— quem, acc. sing. m. of the rel. *quī, quae, quod*; its antecedent is *magistrātuī*, and *quem* is the direct obj. of *appellant*; or the clause may be taken as = *sed eum quī summō magistrātuī praeërat, Vergobretum appellant Aeduī*. —— Vergobretum, acc. sing. of *Vergobretus, -ī*, m.; predicate-

²²appellant	Aeduī,	quī	creātur	annuus	et	elected annually, and has the power of life and death among his own people — he censured them severely for not aiding him, as grain
address	*the Aedui,*	*who*	*is elected*	*an annual*	*and*	
²³vītae	necisque	in	suōs	habet	potestātem —	
of life	*death and,*	*among*	*his own*	*he has*	*the power —*	
²⁴graviter	eōs	accūsat,	quod,	cum	neque	
sharply	*them*	*he rebukes,*	*because,*	*when*	*(grain) neither*	

acc. For the two accusatives after *appellant*, see A. & G. 239, 1, *a*; B. 151, (*h*); G. 340; H. 373. With *Vergobretus* compare the GK. Βεργόβρετος. The word is Celtic in origin, and said to mean *vir ad iūdicium = a man for trying cases.* See Dr. Anthon's note in *loc.* As it evidently denotes a very important man or office, the word is entitled to a capital initial, as the older editions give it.

LINE 22. appellant, 3d pers. plur. pres. ind. act. of *ap(d)pellō, -āre, -āvī, -ātum,* 1; it agrees with its subject-nom. *Aeduī.* —— Aeduī, nom. plur. of the adj. *Aeduus, -a, -um,* used substantively; as a noun it is subject-nom. of *appellant.* As to this clan, see note on *Aeduō,* l. 20, Chap. III. —— quī, nom. sing. m. of the rel. pron. *qui, quae, quod;* it refers to *magistrātuī,* but is the subject-nom. of *creātur.* —— creātur, 3d pers. sing. pres. ind. pass. of the act. verb *creō, -āre, -āvī, -ātum;* pass. parts: *creor, creārī, creātus,* 1. —— annuus, nom. sing. m. of the adj. *annuus, -a, -um* (*annus,* a year); predicate after a copulative verb. Consult A. & G. 176, *a*, end; B. 128, B; G. 206; H. 360, NOTE I. Observe that the rigidly literal translation of *quī creātur annuus* is: *who is elected an annual;* and that the adj. here is = the adv. in the English idiom. —— et, cop. conj.; it connects the clauses.

LINE 23. vītae, gen. sing. of the noun *vīta, -ae,* f. (derived from *vīcta,* perf. participle of *vīvō*). *vītae,* as a gen., limits *potestātem.* —— necisque (necis + que). *necis,* gen. sing. of the noun *nex, necis,* f. (compare GK. νέκυς). *necis* is connected by the enclitic conj. *-que* with *vītae,* and is in the same grammatical construction. —— in, prep. with the acc. or abl.; here it takes the acc. —— suōs, acc. plur. m. of the poss. and reflexive pron. *suus, -a, -um,* used substantively. See A. & G. 190, *a*; B. 60, REM.; G. 204, NOTE I, *b*; H. 441, 1. If one prefer, he may supply *populōs* here. *suōs* as a subst. is the obj. of the prep. *in.* —— habet, 3d pers. sing. pres. ind. of the verb *habeō, -ēre, -uī, -itum,* 2; connected by the conj. *et* with *creātur,* and has the same subject-nom. *quī.* —— potestātem, acc. sing. of the noun *potestās, -ātis,* f. (*posse*); the direct obj. of *habet.*

LINE 24. graviter, adv. (*gravis*); it modifies *accūsat.* Note that adverbs are regularly formed from adjectives by the addition of *-ter* to the stem. As *gravis* is an *ī*-stem, the adv. is formed thus: gravī + ter. —— eōs, acc. plur. of the dem. pron. *is, ea, id,* used as a personal pron. of the 3d pers.; it refers to *prīncipibus,* but is the direct obj. of *accūsat.* —— accūsat, 3d pers. sing. pres. ind. act. of the verb *accūsō, -āre, -āvī, -ātum,* 1 (ad + causa); hence *accūsāre = lit. to call one to account,* i.e. = *ad causam vocāre. accūsat* agrees with a subject-nom. implied in the ending, referring to Caesar. —— quod, conj.; known to be such, because it is seen to introduce a clause, *quod . . . sublevētur,* giving a reason for the statement made in the main proposition. —— cum, conj., known to be such, because it is seen to introduce a time-clause, *cum . . . posset.* —— neque (nē + que) = lit. *and not;* but *neque . . . neque = neither . . . nor.*

could neither be	emī	neque	ex	agrīs	sūmī 25
bought nor taken	to be bought	nor	from	the fields	to be taken
from the fields; as the time was critical and the	posset, was possible,	tam at so	necessāriō necessary	tempore, a time,	tam 26 with so
enemy near; especially, as, influenced in great measure, by their	propīnquīs near	hostibus enemies	ab by	eīs them	nōn sublevētur; 27 he not was assisted;
	praesertim especially	cum since	māgnā great	ex from (in)	parte part eōrum 28 by their

LINE 25. **emī**, pres. inf. pass. of the verb *emō, -ere, ēmī, ēmptum*, 3; complementary inf. depending on *posset*. Consult A. & G. 271; B. 181; G. 423; H. 533, I, 2. —— **neque**, see *neque*, preceding line. —— **ex**, prep. with the abl. (*ē* before consonants only, *ex* before vowels or consonants). —— **agrīs**, abl. plur. of the noun *ager, agrī*, m.; abl. after the prep. *ex*. —— **sūmī**, pres. inf. pass. of *sūmō, -ere, sūmpsī, sūmptum*, 3; it is also a complementary inf., depending on *posset*.

LINE 26. **posset**, 3d pers. sing. imperf. subjunctive of *possum, posse, potuī* (potis + sum); imperf. subjunctive after *cum*, denoting both time and cause. See A. & G. 326; B. 223; G. 586; H. 517. *posset* agrees with *frūmentum*, to be supplied, as subject-nom. —— **tam**, adv. (an accusative-form; compare the correlative form *quam*); it modifies the adj. *necessāriō*. —— **necessāriō**, abl. sing. of the adj. *necessārius, -a, -um* (*necesse* [nē + cēdere]); *necessāriō* is an attributive of *tempore*. —— **tempore**, abl. of the noun *tempus, -oris*, n. (GK. τέμνειν, *to cut*); hence *tempus* = a *section* of duration. *tempore* is the abl. of *time at which*. Consult A. & G. 256, 1; B. 171; G. 393; H. 429. —— **tam**, adv.; modifies the adj. *propīnquīs*.

LINE 27. **propīnquīs**, abl. plur. of the adj. *propīnquus, -a, -um* (*prope*, near); it is a modifier of *hostibus*. —— **hostibus**, abl. plur. of the noun *hostis, hostis*, m. and f. (originally *a stranger*; transf. *an enemy*); abl. of manner. See A. & G. 248; B. 168; G. 399; H. 419, III. Another possible construction is the abl. absolute. —— **ab**, prep. with the abl. (*ā* before consonants only, *ab* before vowels or consonants); with *ab* compare GK. ἀπό, elided ἀπ' and ἀφ, and English *off*. —— **eīs**, abl. plur. of the dem. pron. *is, ea, id*, used as a personal pron. of the 3d pers.; *eīs* is the obj. of the prep. *ab*, and is the abl. of the agent. A. & O. 246; B. 166; G. 401; H. 415, I. —— **nōn** (nē + oenum or ūnum, apocopated); observe its normal Latin position immediately before the word it modifies. —— **sublevētur**, 3d pers. sing. pres. subjunctive pass. of *sublevō, -āre, -āvī, -ātum*, 1; it agrees with a pron. implied in the ending, referring to Caesar as its subject-nom. *sublevētur* is in the subjunctive mode in the *quod*-clause, because the reason is given on the authority of Caesar the general, rather than on Caesar the historian. Note that Caesar the historian is a little dubious in his statements as to Caesar the general, whose acts military necessity sometimes seemed to control. But consult A. & G. 321; B. 198, (*b*); G. 541, 663; H. 516, II.

LINE 28. **praesertim**, adv. (prae + serere) = lit. *to join before*, i.e. the adv. = *foremost, especially*. Observe (*a*) that *praesertim* is in form like an adverbial acc. *statim*; it is made by annexing the adverbial ending *tim* to the stem *ser* thus: praeser + tim. Observe (*b*) that the clause introduced by *praesertim cum . . . suscēperit* merely elaborates and gives special emphasis to the preceding *quod . . . sublevētur*-clause. —— **cum**, conj., causal. —— **māgnā**, abl. sing. f. of the adj. *māgnus, -a, -um*; comparative *māior*, superl. *māximus*. *māgnā* modifies the noun *parte*. —— **ex**, prep.

29 precibus	adductus	bellum	suscēperit,	prayers he had undertaken the
prayers	*being led*	*war*	*he has undertaken,*	war, even the
30 multō etiam	gravius,	quod	sit dēstitūtus,	more bitterly he complained of
much even	*more severely,*	*because*	*he has been abandoned,*	their desertion.
31 queritur.				
does he complain.				

| 1 XVII. | Tum | dēmum | Liscus | ōrātiōne | XVII. Then at length Liscus, |
| | *Then* | *at length* | *Liscus* | *by the oration* | influenced by |

with the abl. (*ē* before consonants only, *ex* before either vowels or consonants). For the position of the monosyllabic prep. between a noun and its modifier, see A. & G. 345, *a*; B. 58. 2; G. 413, REM. 1; H. 569, II, 1. —— **parte**, abl. sing. of the noun *pars, partis*, f.; it is the obj. of the prep. *ex*. Observe that the phrase *māgnā ex parte* = lit. *of* or *from a great part*, denoting the *source* or *measure* = *in great measure*, according to the English idiom. —— **eōrum**, gen. plur. m. of the dem. pron. *is, ea, id*, used as a personal pron. of the 3d pers.; as a gen. it limits *precibus*.

LINE 29. **precibus**, abl. plur. of the noun *prex, precis*, f.; used in the sing. only in the abl. *precibus* is an abl. of cause after the perf. pass. participle *adductus*. Consult A. & G. 245, and *b*; B. 165, and REM. 4; G. 408, NOTE 2; H. 416, NOTE 1. —— **adductus**, perf. pass. participle of the verb *addūcō, -ere, -dūxī, -ductum*, 3; as a participle it agrees with *Caesar* understood. —— **bellum**, acc. sing. of the noun *bellum, -ī*, n.; it is the direct obj. of *suscēperit*. As to the original form of the word and its derivation, see note on *bellum*, l. 15, Chap. I. —— **suscēperit**, 3d pers. sing. perf. subjunctive act. of *suscipiō, -ere, -cēpī, -ceptum*, 3 (sub + capere); subjunctive after *cum* causal; see grammatical references to *posset*, l. 26, above.

LINE 30. **multō**, may be taken as adv. modifying *gravius*; or may be taken as abl. of *degree of difference* after the same adv. —— **etiam**, adv. (et + iam), modifies *multō*. —— **gravius**, adv., comparative degree of *graviter*, superl. *gravissimē*. Observe that he complains even more severely than he did as indicated by *graviter eōs accūsat*, l. 24, above. —— **quod**, conj. = *because*. —— **sit dēstitūtus** (*dēstitūtus sit*), 3d pers. sing. perf. subjunctive pass. of *dēstituō, -ere, -stituī, -stitūtum*, 3 (dē + statuere); subjunctive, because the reason is given on the authority of Caesar the diplomatist, rather than on that of Caesar the historian. See note on *sublevētur*, l. 27, above, and the grammatical references there given.

LINE 31. **queritur**, 3d pers. sing. pres. ind. of the deponent verb *queror, -ī, questus*, 3; it agrees with a pron. implied in the ending, referring to Caesar as the subject-nom. *Ōrātiō rēcta* of lines 24–31: *Egō graviter vōs accūsō, quod, cum neque emī neque ex agrīs sūmī possit, tam necessāriō tempore, tam propīnquīs hostibus ā vōbīs nōn sublevor; praesertim cum māgnā ex parte vestrīs precibus adductus bellum suscēperim; multō etiam gravius, quod sum dēstitūtus, queror*.

LINE 1. **Tum**, adv., a correlative particle denoting coincident or sequent time, connected with *cum, ubi* and *postquam*; compare GK. τότε. —— **dēmum**, adv.; enclitically connected with the preceding *tum* to give emphasis to the idea of restriction = *at length;* compare GK. δήποτε. —— **Liscus, -ī**, m., subject-nom. of *prō-*

118 CAESAR'S GALLIC WAR [CHAP. XVII.

| Caesar's speech, disclosed what he had previously concealed. He said there were some whose authority with the common people was very great, and who, in a private capacity, | Caesaris *of Caesar* prōpōnit: *he sets forth:* auctōritās *influence* quī *who* | adductus, led, esse to be (there are) apud with prīvātim privately | quod (that) which plēbem the populace plūs more | anteā before he had concealed, nōnnūllōs, some, plūrimum most possint are able | tacuerat, quōrum whose valeat, has weight, quam than | [2] [3] [4] ipsī the very [5] |

pōnit; he was the chief magistrate among the *Aeduī.* —— **ōrātiōne,** abl. sing. of *ōrātiō, -ōnis,* f.; abl. of *cause* subjective after *adductus.* Consult A. & G. 245, and 2, *b*; B. 165, and REM. 4; G. 408, and NOTE 2; H. 416, and NOTE 1. Synonyms: *sermō = conversation* or *a conversational speech;* whereas *ōrātiō = the premeditated* and *prepared speech.*

LINE 2. **Caesaris,** gen. sing. of the noun *Caesar, -aris,* m.; as a gen. it limits *ōrātiōne.* —— **adductus,** nom. of the perf. pass. participle of the verb *addūcō, -ere, -dūxī, -ductum,* 3 (ad + dūcere); pass.: *addūcor, -ī, -ductus;* as a participle it agrees with the proper noun *Liscus.* —— **quod,** acc. sing. n. of the rel. pron. *quī, quae, quod;* its antecedent is *id,* to be supplied, which *id* is the direct obj. of *prōpōnit;* but *quod* is the direct obj. of *tacuerat,* which is here used transitively. To refer to an idea, *id quod* or *quae res,* as phrases, are generally used, though *quod* alone sometimes occurs. See A. & G. 200, *e,* and NOTE; B. 129, REM. 8; G. 614, REM. 2; H. 445, 7. —— **anteā,** adv. (ante + ea); it modifies *tacuerat.* —— **tacuerat,** 3d pers. sing. pluperf. ind. of *taceō, -ēre, -uī, -itum,* 2; it agrees with a pron. implied in the ending, referring to *Liscus* as its subject-nom.

LINE 3. **prōpōnit,** 3d pers. sing. pres. ind. act. of *prōpōnō, -ere, -posuī, -positum,* 3 (prō + pōnere) = lit. *to place* or *put forward;* hence = *to display* or *expose;* it agrees with *Liscus* as subject-nom. —— **esse,** pres. inf. of the intrans. verb *sum, fuī,* fut. participle *futūrus.* Observe (*a*) that *esse* is for *sunt* in the *ōrātiō rēcta;* (*b*) that the rest of this chapter is in the *ōrātiō oblīqua* from the speaker's point of view — *representātiō;* in other words, *prōpōnit* controls the sequence of tenses in the oblique narrative. —— **nōnnūllōs,** acc. plur. m. of the adj. pron. *nōnnūllus, -a, -um* (nōn + nūllus) = *some; nōnnūllī,* plur. = *some few;* i.e. the two negatives = an indefinite affirmative. Consult A. & G. 150, *a*; B. 117. 10; G. 449; H. 553, 1. Observe particularly that *esse nōnnūllōs* in indirect discourse = *sunt nōnnūllī* in direct discourse; and that *esse* in indirect, or *sunt* in direct, discourse is a verb of complete predication. —— **quōrum,** gen. plur. m. of the rel. pron. *quī, quae, quod;* it refers to *nōnnūllōs* as its antecedent, but as a gen. it limits *auctōritās.*

LINE 4. **auctōritās, -ātis,** nom. sing. f.; subj. of the verb *valeat.* —— **apud,** prep. with the acc. —— **plēbem,** acc. sing. of the noun *plēbs, plēbis,* f.; nom. *plēbēs* sometimes occurs; *plēbem* is the obj. of the prep. *apud.* For synonyms, see note on *populum,* l. 17, Chap. VI. —— **plūrimum,** adv., superl. of *multum;* comparative *plūs; plūrimum* modifies *valeat. plūrimum* might be taken as an adj., a cognate acc.; see A. & G. 238, *b*; B. 150, REM. 2; G. 333, and 2; H. 371, II, (2). —— **valeat,** 3d pers. sing. pres. subjunctive of *valeō, -ēre, -uī, -itum,* 2; subjunctive, because it is in a dependent clause in *ōrātiō oblīqua.* Consult A. & G. 336, 2; B. 245, 1, (*b*); G. 655; H. 524.

LINE 5. **quī,** nom. plur. m. of the rel. pron. *quī, quae, quod;* it refers to *nōnnūllōs* as its antecedent, but is the subj. of *possint.* —— **prīvātim,** adv. (from the

[LINES 6-8.] BOOK I. 119

6 magistrātūs.	Hōs	sēditiōsā	atque	improbā	had more influ-
magistrates	*These*	*by mutinous*	*and*	*wicked*	ence than the magistrates
7 ōrātiōne	multitūdinem		dēterrēre	nē	themselves; that these men by
speech	*the multitude*		*to deter* (deter)	*that not*	their seditious and wicked talk
8 frūmentum	cōnferant,		quod	dēbeant:	were keeping the
the grain	*they may collect,*		*which*	*they ought:*	populace from

stem prīvā + the acc. adverbial ending tim); this stem is seen in *prīvātus*, a participle of the verb *prīvāre*, and the root *prīv* is seen in the adj. *prīvus* = *single, each*. —— plūs, adv., comparative degree of *multum*; superl. *plūrimum*. But see note on *plūrimum*, l. 4, above. The adverbs *prīvātim* and *plūs* modify the intrans. or neuter verb *possint*. —— possint, 3d pers. plur. imperf. subjunctive of *possum, posse, potuī* (potis, *able* + sum); it agrees with its subject-nom. *quī*; it is in the subjunctive, because it is in a dependent clause in *ōrātiō oblīqua*; but more accurately, because it is in a relative clause after an indefinite or general expression, which characterizes the antecedent. See A. & G. 320, *a*; B. 234, 1; G. 631, 2; H. 503, 1. —— quam, conj., connects the clauses. —— ipsī, nom. plur. m. of the intensive dem. pron. *ipse, -sa, -sum*, gen. *ipsīus*, dat. *ipsī*, same form as nom. plur.; the distinction can only be determined by considering the context; *ipsī* here adds emphasis to *magistrātūs*; together these words = *the magistrates themselves* or *the very magistrates*.

LINE 6. magistrātūs, nom. plur. of the noun *magistrātus, -ūs*, m.; it is the subject-nom. of *possint* understood. For description of the Roman magistrates, see note on *magistrātūs*, l. 15, Chap. IV. The Gallic magistrates appear to have been a body of officers who were elected annually. —— Hōs, acc. plur. m. of the dem. pron. *hīc, haec, hōc*, used substantively, referring to the private parties. *hōs* is subject-acc. of *dēterrēre*. —— sēditiōsā, abl. sing. f. of the adj. *sēditiōsus, -a, -um*; it is an attributive of *ōrātiōne*. Observe that adjectives in *-ōsus* denote *fulness*. —— atque (ad + que), conj.; usually adds a more important notion. —— improbā, abl. of the adj. *improbus, -a, -um* (in, *negative* + probus) = *not good*, in a moral point of view; it, too, is an attributive of *ōrātiōne*. *Ōrātiō rēcta* of lines 3–6: *sunt nōnnūllī, quōrum auctōritās apud plēbem plūrimum valeat, quī prīvātim plūs possint quam ipsī magistrātūs*.

LINE 7. ōrātiōne, abl. sing. of *ōrātiō, -ōnis*, f. (*ōrāre*, to speak); abl. of means. For synonyms, see note on *ōrātiōne*, l. 1, above. —— multitūdinem, acc. sing. of the noun *multitūdō, -dinis*, f. (*multus*); it is direct obj. of *dēterrēre*. —— dēterrēre, pres. inf. act. of *dēterreō, -ēre, -uī, -itum*, 2. Note that *hōs . . . dēterrēre* is the main clause of indirect discourse = *hī . . . dēterrent*, of direct discourse; compare *esse nōnnūllōs*, l. 3, above, and note also that these clauses depend on *prōpōnit*, l. 3, above, or its equivalent *dīcit*. —— nē, adv. and conj., archaic *neī* for *nī*, primitive negative; compare GK. μή; here *nē* is telic after a verb denoting *to hinder*.

LINE 8. frūmentum, acc. sing. of the noun *frūmentum, -ī*, n. (frūgī + mentum); it is the direct obj. of *cōnferant*. —— cōnferant, 3d pers. plur. pres. subjunctive of the verb *cōnferō, -ferre, contulī, col*(n)*lātum*; it agrees with a pron as its subject-nom. implied in the ending, referring to *multitūdinem*; it is subjunctive of negative purpose after *nē*. Consult A. & G. 331, *e*, 2, (1); B. 200, REM. 5; G. 548, NOTE 1; H. 505, II, 1. —— quod, acc. sing. n. of the rel. pron. *quī, quae, quod*; it refers to *frūmentum* as its antecedent, but is the direct obj. of *cōnferre*, to be supplied from *cōnferant*; and which is an inf. complementary to *dēbeant*. —— dēbeant, 3d pers. plur. of the verb *dēbeō, -ēre, -uī, -itum*, 2; its subject-nom. is a pron. implied in the ending, referring to

| bringing in the grain, as they ought; that it were better, if they could no longer hold the supremacy of Gaul, to submit to the sway of the Gauls than to that of the Romans; and | praestāre, *it to be* (it is) *preferable,* obtinēre *to maintain* Rōmānōrum *of the Romans* dubitāre *to doubt* | nōn *not* imperia *the commands* quīn, *that,* | sī iam *if now* possint, *they are able,* perferre; *to endure;* sī *if* | prīncipātum *the leadership* Gallōrum *of the Gauls* neque *nor (themselves)* Helvētiōs *to the Helvetii* | Galliae 9 *of Gaul* quam 10 *than* 11 superāverint 12 *are superior* |

multitūdinem; it is in the subjunctive, because it is a dependent clause in *ōrātiō oblīqua.* For etymology, see note on *dēbuerint,* l. 11, Chap. XI. There is a variety of readings and punctuation at this point, in our text. Most modern editions construct the text thus after *cōnferant: quod praestāre debeant: sī iam . . . praeferre, neque dubitāre.* Some editions have a bracketed [*debeant*] after *dubitāre.* The lection of Kraner, which we have given, is to be preferred.

LINE 9. **praestāre,** pres. inf. of *praestō, -āre, -stitī, -stātum* and *stitum,* 1 ; second stem irr.; *praestāre* is used impersonally = *melius esse,* it is better; strictly speaking, the inf. *perferre,* l. 11, below, with its modifiers is the subj. of *praestāre.* It will be noted that the inf. construction is the main clause of indirect discourse; that in direct discourse *praestāre* becomes *praestat.* —— **sī,** conditional particle; original form *seī,* sibilated from GK. *εἰ.* —— **iam,** adv. = *now,* of any event, past, present or future; whereas *nunc* emphasizes the present. *iam* followed by *nōn,* in the text = *no longer.* —— **prīncipātum,** acc. sing. of the noun *prīncipātus, -ūs,* m. (primus + capere); direct obj. of *obtinēre.* For synonyms, see note on *imperium,* l. 27, Chap. III. —— **Galliae,** gen. sing. of *Gallia, -ae,* f.; it limits *prīncipātum.*

LINE 10. **obtinēre,** pres. inf. of *obtineō, -ēre, -uī, -tentum,* 2 (ob + tenēre); complementary inf., depending on *possint.* See A. & G. 271 ; B. 181 ; G. 423; H. 533, I, 2. —— **nōn,** negative adv. (nē + oe[ū]num, apocopated); note its normal position; immediately before the word it modifies. —— **possint,** 3d pers. plur. pres. subjunctive of *possum, posse, potuī* (potis + sum); it agrees with a pron. implied in its ending as its subject-nom., referring to those included among the *nōnnullōs,* l. 3, above; subjunctive in the condition after the conj. *sī;* the conclusion is contained in *praestāre.* —— **Gallōrum,** gen. plur. of *Gallī, -ōrum,* m., limiting as a gen. *imperia.* —— **quam,** conj., connecting the phrases. *magis* or *potius* is to be supplied before *quam.*

LINE 11. **Rōmānōrum,** gen. plur. of the noun *Rōmānī, -ōrum,* m.; limits *ea,* i.e. *imperia* understood. —— **imperia,** acc. plur. of the noun *imperium, -ī,* n.; direct obj. of *perferre.* For synonyms, see note on *imperium,* l. 27, Chap. III. —— **perferre,** pres. inf. act. of *perferō, -ferre, -tulī, -lātum* (per + ferre) = lit. *to bear through;* hence = *to submit;* not to be confounded with *praeferre. perferre* is here used as a noun, and is the subject-acc. of *praestāre,* l. 9, above. —— **neque,** conjunctive adv. (nē + que) = lit. *and not;* as a conj. it connects the sentences, as an adv. it modifies *dubitāre.*

LINE 12. **dubitāre,** pres. inf. of *dubitō, -āre, -āvī, -ātum,* 1 (primitive form *dubō* [*duo,* two]); hence = *to vacillate between two opinions, to be dubious.* With *dubitāre* supply the pron. *sē,* acc. plur., as subject-acc.; the reference is to the Gallic patriots. —— **quīn** (quī + nē) = lit. *by which not;* after negative clause of doubt or hindrance = *ut, that* or *but that.* —— **sī,** see note on this particle, l. 9, above. —— **Helvētiōs,**

[LINES 13-15.]   BOOK I.   **121**

13 Rōmānī,	ūnā	cum	reliquā	Galliā	that they did not
the Romans,	*together*	*with*	*remaining*	*Gaul*	doubt that, if the Romans should
14 Aeduīs	lībertātem		sint ēreptūrī.	Ab	conquer the Helvetii, they would
from the Aedui	*freedom*		*they will take.*	*By*	wrest freedom from the Aedui
15 eīsdem	nostra	cōnsilia	quaeque	in	along with the
the same	*our*	*plans,*	*what (things) and,*	*in*	rest of Gaul. By

acc. plur. of *Helvētiī, -ōrum*, m.; direct obj. of *superāverint*. As to this clan, see note on *Helvētiī*, l. 16, Chap. I. —— **superāverint**, 3d pers. plur. perf. subjunctive of *superō, -āre, -āvī, -ātum*, 1 (*super*); hence *superāre* = lit. *to be over;* it agrees with its subject-nom. *Rōmānī*; subjunctive in the condition after *sī*. Consult A. & G. 304, *a*, NOTE; B. 204, 2; G. 590, and 594, II; H. 507, II.

LINE 13. **Rōmānī**, nom. plur. of the adj. *Rōmānus, -a, -um*, used substantively; it is the subject-nom. of *superāverint*. —— **ūnā**, adv. (*ūnus*) = lit. *at one and the same time;* hence, together with *cum* = *along with*. See note on *ūnā*, l. 17, Chap. V. Note that the adverbial clause *cum reliquā Galliā* modifies *sint ēreptūrī*. —— **cum**, prep. with the abl. —— **reliquā**, abl. sing. f. of the adj. *reliquus, -a, -um;* it is an attributive of *Galliā*. —— **Galliā**, abl. sing. of the proper noun *Gallia, -ae*, f.; abl. of accompaniment after the prep. *cum*. A. & G. 248, *a;* B. 168, REM. 4; G. 392; H. 419, I. For synonyms, see note on *reliquā*, l. 7, Chap. V.

LINE 14. **Aeduīs**, dat. plur. of the adj. *Aeduus, -a, -um*, used substantively; dat. instead of the abl. after *sint ēreptūrī*, a verb of separation. Consult A. & G. 229; B. 143, REM. 3; G. 345, and REM. 1; H. 386, 2. As to the Aeduan clan, see note on *Aeduō*, l. 20, Chap. III. —— **lībertātem**, acc. sing. of the noun *lībertās, -ātis*, f. (derived from adj. *līber*, free). *lībertātem* is the direct obj. of the verb *sint ēreptūrī* (*ēreptūrī sint*). —— **sint ēreptūrī**, 3d pers. plur. pres. subjunctive, first periphrastic conjugation of *ēripiō, -ere, -uī, -reptum*, 3 (ē + *rapere*) = lit. *to snatch away;* subjunctive, because a result-clause after *quīn*, following a clause of doubt. Consult A. & G. 319, *c;* B. 201, REM. 2; G. 555, 2; H. 505, 1, 1. —— **Ab**, prep. with the abl. (*ab* before vowels and consonants, *ā* before consonants only). *Ōrātiō rēcta* of lines 6-14: *Illī sēditiōsā atque improbā ōrātiōne multitūdinem dēterrent nē frūmentum cōnferant, quod dēbent: praestat, sī iam prīncipātum Galliae obtinēre nōn possint, Gallōrum quam Rōmānōrum imperia perferre; neque dubitant quīn, sī Helvētiōs superāverint Rōmānī, ūnā cum reliquā Galliā Aeduīs lībertātem sint ēreptūrī*.

LINE 15. **eīsdem**, abl. plur. of the dem. pron. *īdem, eadem, idem*, gen. *ēiusdem*, dat. *eīdem;* abl. of the agent. See A. & G. 246; B. 166; G. 401; H. 415, I. The allusion is to the *nōnnūllōs*. Liscus is reporting the sentiments of the Gallic patriots. —— **nostra**, acc. plur. of the poss. adjective pron. *noster, -tra, -trum; nostra* is an attributive of the noun *cōnsilia*. —— **cōnsilia**, acc. plur. of the noun *cōnsilium, -ī*, n.; *cōnsilia* is subject-acc. of the verb *ēnūntiārī*. Observe that, as Liscus is a friend of the Romans, he regards their plans as his; i.e. Liscus is speaking of the Roman party among the Aeduans. —— **quaeque** (*quae* + enclitic *que*). *quae* is nom. plur. n. of the rel. pron. *quī, quae, quod;* it refers to *ea* understood as its antecedent, which is an acc. plur., and as such to be conceived as subject-acc. of *ēnūntiārī* understood; but *quae* is the subject-nom. plur. of the finite verb *gerantur*. Observe how closely the main clause here in the *ōrātiō oblīqua* is connected with the relative clause by the enclitic conj. *-que*. —— **in**, prep. with the acc. or abl.; here it takes the abl.

these persons, said he, our plans and all camp activities were reported to the enemy; nor could he restrain them. Moreover, as to the fact of his	castrīs *the camp*	gerantur, *are done,*	hostibus *to the enemy*	ēnūntiārī; *to be (are) reported;*	16
	hōs *these (men)*	ā sē *by himself*	coercērī *to be coerced*	nōn posse. *not to be (are) able.*	17
	Quīn *Aye*	etiam, *indeed,*	quod *as to the fact that*	necessāriō rem *by necessity the matter,*	18

LINE 16. **castrīs**, abl. plur. of the noun *castrum, -ī,* n.; obj. of the prep. *in.* Note that *castrum* in the sing. = *fort* or *redoubt;* in the plur., *castra* = *camp.* — **gerantur**, 3d pers. plur. pres. subjunctive pass. of the verb *gerō, -ere, gessī, gestum,* 3; it agrees with its subject-nom. *quae;* it is in the subjunctive, because in a dependent clause in the *ōrātiō oblīqua.* — **hostibus**, dat. plur. of *hostis, -is,* m. and f.; dat. of the indirect obj. after *ēnūntiārī.* See A. & G. 225, 3, *e;* B. 140; G. 344; H. 384, I. — **ēnūntiārī**, pres. inf. pass. of the verb *ēnūntiō, -āre, -āvī, -ātum,* I; pass. parts: *ēnūntior, -ārī, -ātus,* 1. Observe that *nostra cōnsilia hostibus ēnūntiārī* is a main clause of indirect discourse, depending on *prōpōnit,* or its equivalent *dīcit,* l. 3, above; and that *ēnūntiārī* in direct discourse becomes *ēnūntiātur.*

LINE 17. **hōs**, acc. plur. of the dem. pron. *hīc, haec, hōc,* used as a personal pron. of the 3d pers.; it refers to *hostibus,* a word just mentioned, and is subject-acc. of *posse.* — **ā**, prep. with the abl. (*ā* before consonants only, *ab* before vowels or consonants). — **sē**, abl. sing. m. of the reflexive pron. *suī, sibi, sē, sē,* same form in both numbers; *sē* refers to Liscus, and is in the abl. after the prep. *ab;* abl. of the agent. Consult A. & G. 246; B. 166; G. 401; H. 415, I. — **coercērī**, pres. inf. poss. of *coerceō, -ēre, -cuī, -citum,* 2 (con + arcēre); hence = lit. *to enclose completely,* i.e. *to restrain;* *coercērī* is a complementary inf., depending on *posse.* See A. & G. 271; B. 181; G. 423; H. 533, I, 2. — **nōn**, negative adv. (nē + oe[ū]num); it modifies *posse.* — **posse**, pres. inf. of the intrans. verb *possum, posse, potuī* (potis, adj. = *able* + sum). *posse* agrees with its subject-acc. *hōs.*

LINE 18. **Quīn** (quī + nē) = lit. *that not;* but frequently, especially with *etiam,* used as a particle of corroboration. When thus used, the phrase *quīn etiam* = *yes indeed* or *nay indeed.* *quīn* in such use is not a conj., but an adv. — **etiam** (et + iam), conjunctive adv.; usually adds a notion to what has been already expressed. — **quod**, an adverbial acc. of the pron. *quī, quae, quod,* and = *as to the fact that;* with the subjunctive *ēnūntiārit,* because in indirect discourse. Consult A. & G. 333, *a,* and 341, *d,* and REM.; B. 123, REM. 21, and 198, REM. I; G. 525, 2 and 3; H. 516, and especially the NOTE. — **necessāriō**, adv.; really abl. n. of the adj. *necessarius, -a, -um,* used adverbially. — **rem**, acc. sing. of the noun *rēs, reī,* f.; the direct obj. of *ēnūntiārit.* The matter referred to is the opposition of the Gallic patriots among the Aeduans to the Romans, as indicated by their inertia in regard to Caesar's food supply. Some texts read (*a*) *necessāriā rē;* others (*b*) *necessāriam rem.* The literal translation of the *quod*-clause, according to the reading of our text, is: *as to the fact that, having been compelled, he has necessarily reported the matter to Caesar.* If we read (*a*), above, the literal translation of the *quod*-clause is: *as to the fact that, by a necessary matter constrained, he has reported to Caesar;* supply *rem,* as direct obj., since *ēnūntiārit* is transitive. If we read (*b*), above, the literal translation of the *quod*-clause is: *as to the fact that, having been compelled, he has reported a necessary matter.* On these different lections we make these criticisms: (*a*) *necessāriā rē coāctus ēnūntiārit* can only mean: *constrained by a necessary matter,* i.e. Caesar's lack of food supply,

19 coāctus	Caesarī	ēnūntiārit,	intellegere		having on compulsion disclosed the matter to Caesar, he said he knew with how great danger he had done it, and for this reason he had kept silent as long as he could.
having been compelled,	*to Caesar*	*he has reported,*	*to know*		
20 sēsē,	quantō	id	cum	perīculō	
himself (he knows),	*how great,*	*that,*	*with,*	*peril*	
21 fēcerit, et	ob	eam	causam,	quam-diū	
he has done, and	*for*	*that*	*reason,*	*as long as*	
22 potuerit,		tacuisse.			
he may have been able,	*(himself) to have been silent.*				

he has reported. As *ēnūntiārit* is transitive, an obj. — *rem* — must be supplied; but it is not very probable that Caesar would, even in his haste, use in the same clause different cases of *rēs* in different significations. Besides, *rem* representing the opposition of the Gallic patriots, could be no *necessary* matter. (*b*) *necessāriam rem* must be the direct obj. of *ēnūntiārit*, as the accusative construction is not probable after *coāctus*, and not possible, except as an acc. of specification. But *he has reported a necessary matter* seems to be irrelevant; for Caesar, of course, knew his own lack and *needed* no telling, and the Gallic patriots' acts were rather the impulse of their *wills* than of *necessity*. From the nature of the case, therefore, we are constrained necessarily to keep to the common lection here: *necessāriō ēnūntiārit Caesarī ēnūntiārit* — the reading of the best texts for centuries. Any idea of tautology arising from this reading vanishes the moment we reflect that *coāctus* = compulsion by an objective force; whereas *necessāriō ēnūntiārit* = a revelation whose impulse is subjective necessity, though it may have been occasioned by objective constraint.

LINE 19. **coāctus**, nom. sing. of the perf. pass. participle *coāctus, -a, -um* of *cōgō, -ere, coēgī, coāctum*, 3 (con + agere); hence = lit. *to bring together*. *coāctus* as a participle agrees with *Liscus* understood. —— **Caesarī**, dat. sing. of *Caesar, -aris*, m.; dat. of the indirect obj. after *ēnūntiārit*. —— **ēnūnt(c)iārit**, 3d pers. sing. perf. subjunctive of *ēnūnt(c)iō, -āre, -āvī, -ātum*, 1; it agrees with a pron. implied in the ending, as subject-nom., referring to *Liscus*; subjunctive, because in a dependent clause in *ōrātiō oblīqua*. Observe that *ēnūntiārit* is contracted for *ēnūntiāverit*. For syncopation and contraction, see A. & G. 128, 2; B. 251; G. 131, 1; H. 235. —— **intellegere**, pres. inf. act. of *intellegō, -ere, -lēxī, -lēctum*, 3 (inter + legere); often written *intelligō*.

LINE 20. **sēsē**, acc. sing. of the reflexive pron. *suī, sibi, sē, sē*, reduplicated *sēsē*; subject-acc. of *intellegere*. Observe that *intellegere sēsē* is the main clause of the indirect discourse, and stands for *intellegō egō* in direct discourse. —— **quantō**, abl. of the adj. *quantus, -a, -um*; it agrees with *perīculō*. —— **id**, acc. sing. n. of the dem. pron. *is, ea, id*; direct obj. of *fēcerit*; the allusion is to his report to Caesar. —— **cum**, prep. with the abl. —— **perīculō**, abl. sing. of the noun *perīculum, -ī*, n.; abl. of manner after the prep. *cum*. A. & G. 248; B. 168; G. 399; H. 419, III. Observe that the prep. is not absolutely necessary here, as the noun has a modifier.

LINE 21. **fēcerit**, 3d pers. sing. perf. subjunctive of *faciō, -ere, fēcī, factum*, 3; it agrees with a personal pron. implied in the ending, referring to *Liscus* as the subject-nom.; it is subjunctive, because in a dependent clause in *ōrātiō oblīqua*. —— **et**, cop. conj.; connects *intellegere* and *tacuisse*. —— **ob**, prep. with the acc. —— **eam**, acc. sing. f. of the dem. pron. *is, ea, id*; it is an attributive of *causam*. —— **causam**, acc. sing. of the noun *causa, -ae*, f.; it is the obj. of the prep. *ob*. —— **quam-diū**, adv. (quam + diū); often written as two words: *quam diū*; as an adv. it modifies *potuerit*.

LINE 22. **potuerit**, 3d pers. sing. perf. subjunctive of *possum, posse, potuī* (potis, *able* + sum); it agrees with *Liscus*, to be supplied, as its subject-nom.; it is in the

XVIII.

XVIII. Caesar from this speech of Liscus perceived that Dumnorix, the brother of Divitiacus, was meant; but, as he was unwilling to have these mat-	XVIII. Caesar,	Caesar *by this*	hāc *oration*	ōrātiōne *of Liscus*	Liscī 1
	Dumnorigem, *Dumnorix,*	Divitiacī *Divitiacus's*	frātrem, *brother,*	dēsīgnārī *to be pointed at,*	2
	sentiēbat; *perceived;*	sed, *but,*	quod *because*	plūribus *very many*	praesentibus 3 *being present,*

subjunctive, because in a dependent clause in indirect discourse. —— **tacuisse,** perf. inf. of *taceō, -ēre, -uī, -itum,* 2; connected by the conj. *et* with *intellegere,* and in the same grammatical construction, i.e. its subject-acc. is *sēsē.* The *ōrātiō rēcta* of lines 14-22: Ab eīsdem nostra cōnsilia quaeque in castrīs *geruntur,* hostibus *ēnūntiantur; hī ā mē* coërcērī nōn *possunt.* Quīn etiam, quod necessāriō rem coāctus *tibi* (Caesarī) *ēnūntiāvī, intellegō egō,* quantō id cum perīculō *fēcī,* et ob *hanc* causam, quam-diū *potuī, tacuī.*

LINE 1. **Caesar, -aris,** m., subject-nom. of *sentiēbat.* —— **hāc,** abl. sing. f. of the dem. pron. *hīc, haec, hōc;* it is an attributive of *ōrātiōne;* its use indicates that the reference is to the speech just delivered. A. & G. 102, *a;* B. 84, 1; G. 305, and 3; H. 450, 1. —— **ōrātiōne,** abl. sing. of *ōrātiō, -ōnis,* f.; abl. of means after *sentiēbat.* Synonyms : *ōrātiō* = the finished speech — premeditated and prepared; *sermō* is the conversationally delivered speech — a species of extemporaneous harangue. —— **Liscī,** gen. sing. of the proper noun *Liscus, -ī,* m.; as a gen. it limits *ōrātiōne.* Liscus was a chief magistrate of the Aedui.

LINE 2. **Dumnorigem,** acc. sing. of *Dumnorix, -igis,* m.; subject-acc. of *dēsīgnārī.* Dumnorix was a leader of the Gallic patriotic party among the Aedui, while his brother Divitiacus remained loyal to the Romans. —— **Divitiacī,** gen. sing. of the noun *Divitiacus, -ī,* m.; as a gen. it limits *frātrem.* —— **frātrem,** acc. sing. of *frāter, -ris,* m. (kindred with GK. φράτρα, which = *brotherhood*); an appositive. —— **dēsīgnārī,** pres. inf. pass. of the act. *dēsīgnō, -āre, -āvī, -ātum,* 1; pass. parts: *dēsīgnor, -ārī, -ātus,* 1 (dē + sīgnāre [*sīgnum*]); hence = lit. *to mark out.* The subject-acc. of *dēsīgnārī* is *Dumnorigem,* and the acc. and inf. is an object-clause of *sentiēbat.*

LINE 3. **sentiēbat,** 3d pers. sing. imperf. ind. act. of *sentiō, -īre, sēnsī, sēnsum,* 4; it agrees with its subject-nom. *Caesar.* Synonyms : *sentīre* = *to know* through the feelings; *intellege* = *to know* through reflection; and *cōgnōscere* = *to know* through the senses, or by tradition. —— **sed,** conj., the strongest of all the adversative particles; *autem* and *at* are much weaker; but *vērum* = *sed,* nearly. —— **quod,** conj. = *because;* introduces a statement of fact. Consult A. & G. 321; B. 198; G. 540; H. 516, I. —— **plūribus,** abl. plur. m. of the comparative adj. *plūs, plūris;* declined in the sing. only in the neuter, with the dat. wanting ; the plur. declined regularly as an *ī*-stem : *plūrēs, plūra,* gen. *plūrium,* etc. *plūribus,* in our text, is used substantively, and as a subst. it is in the abl. absolute with the adj. *praesentibus.* For declension, see A. & G. 86; B. 72, 7; G. 89, REMS. 2, 3; H. 165, NOTE I. —— **praesentibus,** abl. plur. m. of the adj. *praesēns, -entis* (participle of *praesum, -esse, -fuī*); in the abl. sing., of persons usually *praesente;* of things, *praesentī. praesentibus* is in the abl. absolute construction with *plūribus* used as a noun; the construction as such denotes the *time when.* Consult A. & G. 255, *a;* B. 192, REM. I; G. 409; H. 431, 4.

BOOK I.   125

4 eās	rēs	iactārī	nōlēbat,	celeriter	ters discussed in the presence of a crowd, he speedily dismissed the council, yet detained Liscus. He inquired of him alone about the matters that he had mentioned at the conven-
these	*things*	*to be talked about*	*he was unwilling,*	*quickly*	
5 concilium	dīmittit,	Liscum		retinet.	
the council	*he breaks up,*	*Liscus*		*he keeps back.*	
6 Quaerit		ex	sōlō	eā,	
He (Caesar) *inquires*		*from* (him)	*alone*	*as to those* (things)	
7 quae	in	conventū	dīxerat.	Dīcit	
which	*in*	*the assembly*	*he had said.*	*He* (Liscus) *speaks*	

LINE 4. eās, acc. plur. of the dem. pron. *is, ea, id; eās* is an attributive of the noun *rēs.* —— rēs, acc. plur. of *rēs, reī,* f.; stem *rĕ,* shortened in the gen. and dat. sing.; subject-acc. of the inf. *iactārī.* The things alluded to are those that Liscus had disclosed. —— iactārī, pres. inf. pass. of *iactō, -āre, -āvī, -ātum,* 1 (freq. of *iacere,* to hurl). Observe that frequentative verbs are usually of the first conjugation, whatever may be the conjugation of the verbs from which they are derived. —— nōlēbat, 3d pers. sing. imperf. ind. of the irr. verb *nōlō, nōlle, nōluī* (nē + volō); it agrees with a pron. implied in the ending as its subject-nom., referring to Caesar. Observe, in the formation of the compound, that *v* is suppressed, and then the *ĕ* and *o* are contracted in *ō.* Thus: *nĕ + volō* become *nĕ 'olō* = *nōlō.* —— celeriter, adv. (adj. *celer,* swift); adv. formed by adding *-ter* to the adj. stem *celeri. celeriter* modifies the verb *dīmittit.*

LINE 5. concilium, acc. sing. of the noun *concilium, -ī,* n.; the direct obj. of *dīmittit.* This word is not to be confounded with *cōnsilium,* counsel; though it frequently is thus confounded by Latin writers in all eras. *concilium,* by careful writers = an assembly for consultation — *a council;* whereas *cōnsilium* = *the counsel* that is taken in such assembly. But, as already intimated, the significations are often confused. —— dīmittit, 3d pers. sing. pres. ind. act. of *dīmittō, -ere; -mīsī, -missum,* 3 (dĭs + mittere, *to send apart);* it agrees with a pron. implied in the ending, referring to Caesar. —— Liscum, acc. sing. of *Liscus, -ī,* m.; direct obj. of *retinet.* Note the asyndeton here between the clauses, and consult A. & G. 346, *c*; B. 310, 1, (*a*); G. 483, NOTE; H. 636, I, 1. —— retinet, 3d pers. sing. pres. ind. act. of *retineō, -ēre, -tenuī, -tentum,* 2 (re + tenēre, *to hold back);* it agrees with a pron. implied in the ending as subject-nom., referring to Caesar.

LINE 6. Quaerit, 3d pers. sing. pres. ind. act. of the verb *quaerō, -ere, -sīvī (-iī), -ītum,* 3 (irr. in 2d stem); it also agrees with *Caesar* understood. —— ex, prep. with the abl. (*ē* before consonants only, *ex* before vowels or consonants). —— sōlō, abl. sing. m. of the adj. *sōlus, -a, -um,* gen. *sōlīus,* dat. *sōlī. sōlō* is an attributive of *eō,* to be supplied, which refers to *Liscum.* Note that *quaerō* takes the abl. of the person with the prepositions *ab, dē* or *ex,* instead of the acc. of the person; it takes besides the acc. of the thing. Consult A. & G. 239, *c,* NOTE 1; B. 151, REM. 2; G. 339, REM. 1; H. 374, 2, NOTE 4, and p. 193, FOOTNOTE 1. —— eā, acc. plur. of the dem. pron. *is, ea, id,* used substantively — the acc. of the thing after *quaerit.*

LINE 7. quae, acc. plur. of the rel. pron. *quī, quae, quod;* it refers to *eā* as its antecedent, but is the direct obj. of *dīxerat.* —— in, prep. with the acc. or abl.; here it takes the abl. —— conventū, abl. sing. of *conventus, -ūs,* m. (con + venīre, *to come together);* it is the obj. of the prep. *in.* —— dīxerat, 3d pers. sing. pluperf. ind. act. of *dīcō, -ere, dīxī, dictum,* 3; it agrees with a pron. implied in the ending as its subject-nom., referring to *Liscus.* —— Dīcit, 3d pers. sing. pres. ind. act. of *dīcō,* 3; its subject-nom. is *Liscus,* to be supplied.

| tion. Liscus now spoke with a freer and bolder spirit. Caesar inquired privately of others about the same matters, and found the truth to be, that it was Dumnorix | līberius *more freely* sēcrētō *privately* esse *to be* | atque *and* ab *from* vēra: *true:* | audācius. *more boldly.* aliīs *others* Ipsum *Himself* | quaerit; *he (Caesar) inquires;* esse *to be (was)* | Eadem *About the same (things)* reperit *he finds* Dumnorigem, *Dumnorix,* | 8 9 10 |

LINE 8. līberius, adv., comparative degree of positive *līberē* (*līber*, free); the adv. modifies *dīcit*, and denotes *rather freely.* For the omission of the standard of comparison, see A. & G. 93, *a*; B. 163, REM. 6; G. 297, 2; H. 444, 1. —— atque (ad + que), conj. = *and also.* See note on this particle, l. 10, Chap. I. —— audācius, adv., comparative degree of *audācter* (*audax*, bold); superl. *audācissimē;* connected by the conj. *atque* with *līberius*, and modifies *dīcit.* —— Eadem, acc. plur. n. of the dem. pron. *īdem, eadem, idem;* used substantively, or supply the English word *things;* direct obj. of *quaerit.*

LINE 9. sēcrētō, adv., derived from the participle *sēcrētus, -a, -um* of the verb *secernō, -ere, -crēvī, -crētum,* 3 (se, inseparable prep. + cernere), hence *secernere* = lit. *to put apart, separate,* the participle *sēcrētus* = *separated* — that which is out of the way, *retired, secret.* For the formation of adverbs from the abl. neuter of adjectives, see A. & G. 148, *e*; B. 117. 6; G. 91, 2, (*c*); H. 304, II, 2. *sēcrētō* modifies *quaerit.* —— ab, prep. with the abl. (*ab* before vowels or consonants, *ā* before consonants only). —— aliīs, abl. plur. of the adj. pron. *alius, -a, -ud;* gen. *alīus;* dat. *aliī; aliīs* is in the abl. after *ab.* Observe that *quaerō* takes the abl. of the person with *ab, dē* or *ex;* and also the acc. of the thing. See grammatical references on *sōlō,* l. 6, above. For synonyms, see note on *reliqua,* l. 7, Chap. V. —— quaerit, 3d pers. sing. pres. ind.; for parts, see note on *quaerit,* l. 6, above; it agrees with a pron. implied in the ending as subject-nom., referring to Caesar. —— reperit, 3d pers. sing. pres. ind. act. of *reperiō, -īre, rep(p)erī, repertum,* 4 (re, *intensive* + parere, *to acquire*); hence *reperīre* = *to acquire again;* i.e. = *to find.*

LINE 10. esse, pres. inf. of the intrans. verb *sum,* perf. *fuī,* fut. participle *futūrus;* it is used impersonally, or, more accurately, the following speech in *ōrātiō oblīqua* is its subject-acc. We may, however, supply *illa* — referring to what follows — as the subject-acc. —— vēra, acc. n. plur. of the adj. *verus, -a, -um;* predicate after *esse.* The reader will observe that from this point to, and inclusive of, the word *dēspērāre,* l. 43, below, the discourse is indirect, depending on *reperit* (or its representative *dīcit* understood). Let the reader recall that in the *ōrātiō oblīqua* the main clause of a declarative sentence is put in the inf. with subject-acc.; that the tense of the *verb of saying* introducing this discourse determines the tense of this inf.; and that the tenses of the subjunctive are also thus determined, i.e. if the *verb of saying* is a primary tense, the sequence is primary; if secondary, the sequence is secondary. —— Ipsum, acc. sing. m. of the intensive dem. pron. *ipse, -sa, -sum. ipsum* as an adj. pron. modifies *Dumnorigem.* —— esse, pres. inf. of the neuter or intrans. verb *sum, esse, fuī, futūrus;* it is for *est* in direct discourse. —— Dumnorigem, acc. sing. of *Dumnorix, -igis,* m.; it is subject-acc. of *esse,* of which *cupidum,* l. 12, below, is the predicate-adj.

[LINES 11-14.] BOOK I. 127

11 summā	audāciā,	māgnā apud		plēbem
of the greatest	*boldness,*	*of great*	*among*	*the common people*
12 propter	līberalitātem	grātiā,	cupidum	rērum
because	*of (his) liberality,*	*favor,*	*desirous*	*of things*
13 novārum.		Complūrēs	annōs	portōria
new.		*Very many*	*years,*	*the customs*
14 reliquaque		omnia	Aeduōrum	vēctīgālia
remaining and,		*all*	*the Aedui's*	*revenues,*

himself, a man of consummate audacity, and of great influence among the people on account of his liberality, who was eager for revolution. / For many years he had farmed the

LINE 11. summā, abl. sing. f. of *summus, -a, -um*, superl. degree of the adj. *superus, superior, suprēmus* or *summus*; *summā* is an attributive of the noun *audācia*. —— audāciā, abl. sing. of *audācia, -ae*, f.; abl. of quality with the adj *summā*. Consult A. & G. 251, and *a*; B. 169; G. 400; H. 419, II. The phrase *summā audāciā* is, in fact, an adjective-modifier of *virum*, to be supplied, which latter is in apposition with *Dumnorigem*. —— māgnā, abl. sing. f. of the adj. *māgnus, māior, māximus*; *māgnā* is an attributive of *grātiā*, l. 12, below. —— apud, prep. with the acc. —— plēbem, acc. sing. of the noun *plēbs, plēbis*, f.; rare nom. *plēbes, -is*; *plēbem* is the obj. of the prep. *apud*. For synonyms, consult note on *populī*, l. 17, Chap. III.

LINE 12. propter (*prope*, near), prep. with the acc. —— līberalitātem, acc. sing. of the noun *līberalitās, -tātis*, f. (*liber*, free); it is the obj. of the prep. *propter*, immediately above. —— grātiā, abl. sing. of the noun *grātia, -ae*, f.; it is an abl. of quality with the adj. *māgnā*. Consult A. & G. 251; B. 169; G. 400; H. 419, II. —— cupidum, acc. sing. m. of the adj. *cupidus, -a, -um*, predicate-adj. after *esse*, l. 10, above. With *cupidus* compare *cupere*, to desire, and the English noun-derivative *cupid*. —— rērum, gen. plur. of the noun *rēs, reī*, f. (stem *rē*, shortened in gen. and dat.); objective gen. after the adj. *cupidum*. Consult A. & G. 218, *a*; B. 135, (*a*); G. 374; H. 399, I, 1.

LINE 13. novārum, gen. plur. f. of the adj. *novus, -a, -um*; it is an attributive of the noun *rērum*. —— Complūrēs, acc. plur. m. of the adj. *complūrēs, -a*, rarely *-ia*, gen. *-ium* (con, *intensive*, whose equivalent in this compound = English *very* + *plūrēs, many*); *complūrēs* is an attributive of *annōs*. Observe that this adj. is used only in the plural, and that in some editions the form *complūrīs* instead of *complūrēs* occurs. —— annōs, acc. plur. of the noun *annus, -ī*, m.; acc. of extent of time. See A. & G. 256, 2; B. 153; G. 336; H. 379. —— portōria, acc. plur. of noun *portōrium, -ī*, n. (compare *portāre*, to carry); hence the noun *portōrium* = lit. the condition or terms of carrying, i.e. *tax, toll*, or, as we say, *tariff*, for the *portōria* were *frontier-duties*. *portōria* is the direct obj. of *habēre*.

LINE 14. reliquaque (reliqua+que). *reliqua* is acc. n. plur. of the adj. *reliquus, -a, -um*; it is an attributive of *vēctīgālia*. For synonyms, see note on *reliqua*, l. 7, Chap. V. Observe that the enclitic *-que* connects *portōria* with *vēctīgālia*. —— omnia, acc. plur. n. of the adj. *omnis, -e*, an *ī*-stem. *omnia*, too, modifies *vēctīgālia*, or rather the phrase *reliqua vēctīgālia*. —— Aeduōrum, gen. plur. of the adj. *Aeduus, -a, -um*, used substantively; as a noun-gen. it limits *vēctīgālia*. —— vēctīgālia, acc. plur. of the noun *vēctīgal, -ālis*, n. (*vehere*, to bring); hence *vēctīgālia* = *that which is brought in*; connected by the conj. *-que* with *portōria*, and in the same grammatical construction, i.e. direct obj. of *habēre*. The *vēctīgālia* were taxes and rents put on every species of property; and both the *portōria* and *vēctīgālia* were farmed out for collection to the *publicānī*.

imports and all other taxes of the Aedui at a low rate, because when he bid, no one dared to bid in opposition. By these means	parvō *at small* propterea *for this reason* licērī *to bid*	pretiō *cost* quod *because* audeat *dares*	redēmpta *having been bought up* illō *he* nēmō. *no one.*	*to have* licente *bidding,* Hīs *By these*	habēre, 15 (he had), contrā 16 *against* (him) rēbus et suam 17 *things both his*

LINE 15. **parvō**, abl. sing. n. of the adj. *parvus, -a, -um;* comparative *minor*, superl. *minimus. parvō* is an attributive of *pretiō*. —— **pretiō**, abl. sing. of the noun *pretium, -ī,* n.; abl. of price, according to the general rule, when it is expressed by a noun. Consult A. & G. 252; B. 167, 4; G. 404; H. 422. —— **redēmpta**, acc. plur. n. of the perf. pass. participle of *redimō, -ere, -ēmī, -ēmptum*, 3; it agrees with *portōria* and *vēctīgālia*. —— **habēre**, pres. inf. act. of *habeō, -ēre, -uī, -itum,* 2; supply *sē* as subject-acc., referring to Dumnorix. The words, therefore, *redēmpta sē habēre* = lit. *having been purchased, he had.* The reader will observe that this form of expression is a periphrase = *redēmisse,* nearly. See A. & G. 292, *c*; B. 191, 3, (*d*); G. 238; H. 388, 1, NOTE. Compare note on *coēctum habēbat,* l. 5, Chap. XV.

LINE 16. **propterea**, adv. (propter + ea); herald of the *quod*-clause immediately following. —— **quod**, conj. See note on this particle, l. 9, Chap. I. —— **illō**, abl. sing. m. of the dem. pron. *ille, -la, -lud;* gen. *illīus,* dat. *illī. illō* points back to *Dumnorigem,* of whom the narrative is a description, but is in the abl. absolute construction with *licente; illō* is more emphatic than *eō,* and also indicates that Dumnorix is somewhat remote from the speaker, at least, that he is not present. —— **licente**, abl. sing. of the pres. participle *licēns, -entis* of the deponent verb *liceor, -ērī, licitus,* 2; observe that deponent verbs have the participles in both voices. *licente* is abl. absolute with *illō,* denoting *time when.* See A. & G. 255, *d,* 1; B. 192; G. 409, 410; H. 431, 2, 3). —— **contrā**, adv. (from an obsolete adjective *conterus* [*con*], in the abl. f.); might be taken as a prep., if *eum* were supplied.

LINE 17. **licērī**, pres. inf. of the deponent verb *liceor* (for principal parts, see note on *licente,* preceding line); complementary inf., depending on *audeat.* See A. & G. 271; B. 181; G. 423; H. 533, I, 1. —— **audeat**, 3d pers. sing. pres. subjunctive of *audeō, -ēre, ausus,* neuter pass. or semi-deponent verb; it agrees with a pron. implied in the ending as subject-nom., referring to Dumnorix; it is in the subjunctive mode, because in a dependent clause in an *ōrātiō oblīqua.* —— **nēmō** (nē + homō), noun, m. and f., acc. *nēminem;* the gen. *nēminis,* and the abl. *nēmine* are not used, except, occasionally, *nēmine* with the abl. perf. participle; instead of *nēminis, nullīus,* and instead of *nēmine, nūllō* are used. Observe the emphatic position of *nēmō;* its normal and unemphatic position would be immediately after *quod.* —— **Hīs**, abl. plur. f. of the dem. pron. *hīc, haec, hōc;* it is the attributive of the noun *rēbus.* —— **rēbus**, abl. plur. of the noun *rēs, reī,* f.; abl. of means. A. & G. 248, *c,* I; B. 167; G. 401; H. 420. —— **et**, cop. conj.; *et ... et* = *both ... and.* —— **suam**, acc. sing. f. of the poss. pron. *suus, -a, -um;* it is an attributive of *rem,* but refers to Dumnorix. The *ōrātiō rēcta* of lines 10-17: *Ipse est Dumnorix,* summā audāciā, magnā apud plēbem propter līberalitātem grātiā, *cupidus* rērum novārum. Complūrēs annōs portōria reliquaque omnia Aeduōrum vēctīgālia parvō pretiō redēmpta *habet,* propterea quod illō licente contrā licērī *audet* nēmō.

18 rem	familiārem	auxisse	et	he had increased
property	*personal*	*to have (he has) increased*	*and*	both his own private property,
19 facultātēs	ad	largiendum	māgnās	and had acquired
resources	*for*	*bribery*	*great,*	large resources for bribery. He
20 comparāsse;		māgnum	numerum	always supported
to have (he has) acquired;		*a large*	*number*	and kept near his person a large
21 equitātūs	suō	sūmptū	semper	number of cavalry at his own
of cavalry	*at his own*	*expense*	*always*	expense; and at home not to say,
22 alere		et	circum	sē
to maintain (he maintains)		*and*	*around*	*himself*	but even among

LINE 18. **rem**, acc. sing. of *rēs, reī*, f.; it is the direct obj. of *auxisse*. —— **familiārem**, acc. sing. f. of the adj. *familiāris, -e*, abl. sing. regularly *familiārī; familiārem* modifies *rem*. The phrase *suam rem familiārem = his private property*. —— **auxisse**, perf. inf. act. of *augeō, -ēre, auxī, auctum*, 2; supply the pron. *sē* as subject-acc., referring to Dumnorix. With *augeō* compare GK. root αυγ, as seen in αὔξω and αὐξάνω. —— **et**, conj., connects *auxisse* and *comparāsse*.

LINE 19. **facultātēs**, acc. plur. of *facultās, -ātis*, f. (*facilis*, archaic form of the adv. *facul*); hence the noun = lit. the capacity of doing anything *easily;* and hence, further, as faculty used brings increase, *facultās*, transf. = *cōpia* or *plenty*, and the plur. *facultātēs = riches*. *facultātēs* is the direct obj. of *comparāsse*. —— **ad**, prep. with the acc. —— **largiendum**, gerund of the verb *largior, -gīrī, -gītis*, 4, deponent (adj. *largus*, large); acc. of the gerund with *ad*, denoting purpose. See A. & G. 300; B. 184, REM. 4, III; G. 432; H. 542, III. The phrase *ad largiendum* accordingly *= for giving largesses*. —— **māgnās**, acc. plur. f. of the adj. *māgnus, -a, -um;* comparative degree *māior;* superl. *māximus*. *māgnās* is the attributive of *facultātēs*.

LINE 20. **comparāsse**, perf. inf. act. of the verb *comparō, -āre, -āvī, -ātum*, 1; for the uncontracted *comparāvisse*. For the rules as to syncopation and contraction, see A. & G. 128, 2; B. 251; G. 131, 1; H. 235. *comparāsse* is connected by the conj. *et* with *auxisse*, and has the same subject-acc., namely *sē* understood. The reader remembers that here is another main clause of the indirect discourse, depending on *reperit*, l. 9, above. —— **māgnum**, acc. sing. of the adj. *māgnus;* see note on *māgnās*, preceding line; an attributive of *numerum*. —— **numerum**, acc. sing. of the noun *numerus, -ī,* m.; direct obj. of *alere*.

LINE 21. **equitātūs**, gen. sing. of the noun *equitātus, -ūs*, m. (*equitāre* from *equus*); hence = lit. *a riding;* concretely = *cavalry; equitātūs* as a gen. limits *numerum*. Observe that the ultima of *equitātus* is short in the nom. and voc., but is long in the other cases. —— **suō**, abl. sing. m. of the poss. reflexive pron. *suus, -a, -um;* it is an attributive of *sūmptū*, but refers to Dumnorix. —— **sūmptū**, abl. of the noun *sūmptus, -ūs,* m. (compare *sūmere*, to take, expend); abl. of means. —— **semper**, adv., modifies *alere*.

LINE 22. **alere**, pres. inf. act. of *alō, -ēre, aluī, alitum*, 3; supply *sēsē*, referring to *Dumnorigem*, l. 10, above, as subject-acc. —— **et**, conj., connects *alere* and *habēre*. —— **circum**, prep. with the acc. *sē*. —— **sē**, acc. sing. of the reflexive pron. *suī, sibi, sē, sē;* same form in both numbers. *sē* is the obj. of the prep. *circum;* it refers to Dumnorix.

| the neighboring states he had great influence; and to keep this influence, he had given his mother in marriage to a man of the highest rank and greatest favor in the country of | habēre, *to have* (he has), apud *among* posse; *to be* (he is) *able;* mātrem *of (his) mother* | neque *not and,* fīnitimās *the neighboring* atque *and* in *among* | sōlum *only* cīvitātēs *states* huius *this* Biturigibus *the Bituriges* | domī, *at home,* potentiae *power* | sed *but* largiter *largely* causā *for the sake* hominī *to a man* | etiam *even* 23 24 25 26 |

LINE 23. **habēre**, pres. inf. act. of *habeō, -ēre, -uī, -itum*, 2; its subject-acc. is a pron., to be supplied, referring to Dumnorix. —— **neque**, conjunctive adv. (nē + que); here it = *et nōn*. —— **sōlum**, adv.; but with *neque* followed by *sed etiam*, the particles have a conjunctive force. —— **domī**, locative of the noun *domus, -ūs*, or loc. *domī*, f. As to this case, see A. & G. 258, *d*; B. 176; G. 411. 2; H. 426, 2. —— **sed**, conjunctive adversative, stronger than *autem* or *at*. —— **etiam** (et + iam), adv.; but with *sed*, in contrast with *nōn sōlum*, the phrase gives prominence to the second clause. Consult A. & G. 151, *a*, 154, *a*, 155, *b*; B. 123, 3; G. 482. 5; H. 554, 5.

LINE 24. **apud**, prep. with the acc.; with reference to persons = *among;* sometimes *apud aliquem* = *at one's house*. —— **fīnitimās**, acc. plur. f. of the adj. *fīnitimus, -a, um* (*fīnis*, border); *fīnitimās* is the attributive of *cīvitātēs*. —— **cīvitātēs** (*cīvēs*), acc. plur. of *cīvitās, -ātis*, f. *cīvitātēs* is the obj. of the prep. *apud*. —— **largiter**, adv. (adj. *largus*, poetic and late Latin). *largiter* modifies *posse*. The adv. has three forms: *largē, largiter* and *largitus*. The form *largē* is classic; *largiter* is rare in classic prose; comparative degree *largius;* superl. *largissimē*.

LINE 25. **posse**, pres. inf. of the intrans. verb *possum, posse, potuī* (potis + sum); supply here *sē* as the subject-acc. As here *posse* is a verb of complete predication, the clause *sē largiter posse* = lit. *he is abundantly able*, i.e. *he has great influence*. —— **atque** (ad + que), conj. (*atque* before vowels or consonants, *āc* before consonants only). *atque* = *and also;* though sometimes it has the meaning only of the simple copulative *et* or *-que*. —— **huius**, gen. sing. f. of the dem. pron. *hīc, haec, hōc; huius* is an attributive of *potentiae*. —— **potentiae**, gen sing. of the noun *potentia, -ae*, f. (*potēns*, participle of *possum*). *potentiae* is a gen. limiting *causā*. Synonyms: *potentia* = *power* as a personal quality; *potestās* = *power* in execution and plan of action; *imperium* = *military power*. —— **causā**, abl. sing. of the noun *causa, -ae*, f. *causā* is strictly an abl. of cause; but in use = a prepositional substantive usually following the gen. depending on it. Consult A. & G. 245, *c*; B. 165, REM. 3; G. 373, REM. 1; H. 416, and FOOTNOTE 2. The *ōrātiō oblīqua* of lines 17–25: His rēbus et suam rem familiārem *auxit* et facultātēs ad largiendum māgnās *comparāvit;* māgnum numerum equitātūs suō sūmptū semper *alit* et circum sē *habet*, neque *sōlum* domī, sed etiam apud fīnitimās cīvitātēs largiter *potest*.

LINE 26. **mātrem**, acc. sing. of the noun *māter, -tris*, f.; direct obj. of *col(n)-locāsse*, l. 28, below. Observe that the stem is properly *māter*, in which the *e* is syncopated in all the cases except the nom. and voc. sing. Some authorities hold the stem of *māter* to be *mātr*, and of *pater* to be *patr*, yet concede that the stem originally ended in *-ter*. Consult A. & G. 48, *c*, and FOOTNOTE 4; B. 38, REM. 1; G. 44, 1, middle; H. 77, 2. —— **in**, prep. with the acc. or abl.; here it takes the abl. —— **Biturigibus**, abl. plur. of *Biturigēs, -um*, m.; *Biturigibus* is the obj. of the prep.

27 illīc	nōbilissimō	āc	potentissimō	the Bituriges; that he had himself taken a wife from the Helvetii, and had given his half-sister and near relations in marriage, in other states.
there	*of the highest rank*	*and*	*very powerful*	
28 collocāsse,		ipsum	ex	
to have (he has) given (in marriage),		*himself*	*from*	
29 Helvētiīs	uxōrem	habēre,	sorōrem	
the Helvetii	*a wife*	*to have (he has),*	*a sister*	
30 ex	mātre	et	propinquās	suās
from	*(his) mother*	*and*	*female relations*	*his own*

in. The Bituriges were a Celtic tribe located near modern Bourges in France. —— **hominī**, dat. of the noun *homō, -inis*, m. here, as determined by the context. *hominī* is indirect obj. of *col(n)locāsse*. A. & G. 225; B. 141; G. 344; H. 384, II.

LINE 27. **illīc**, adv. (ille + ce); hence = *in that place*. —— **nōbilissimō**, dat. sing. m. of the adj. *nōbilissimus, -a, -um ;* positive *nōbilis (nōscere,* to know); comparative degree *nōbilior.* **nōbilissimō** is a modifier of the noun *hominī*. —— **āc**, conj., contracted from *atque* (*āc* before consonants only, *atque* before both vowels and consonants). *āc* or *atque* usually adds a notion of importance, while *et* connects equally important notions. —— **potentissimō**, dat. sing. m. of the adj. *potentissimus, -a, -um*, superl. degree; positive *potēns* (participle of *possum*); comparative *potentior*. *potentissimō* is connected by the conj. *āc* with *nōbilissimō*, and is in the same grammatical construction, i.e. it agrees with *hominī*.

LINE 28. **col(n)locāsse**, perf. inf. act. of *col(n)locō, -āre, -āvī, -ātum*, 1 (con, intensive + locāre); hence = lit. *to place* a person or thing somewhere, i.e. *to establish, to give*, etc.; supply *sē* as subject-acc., referring to Dumnorix; for a complete analysis, supply also the supine *nūptum*, which is expressed in l. 31, below. Observe that the uncontracted form of the inf. is *collocāvisse*. For the suppression of *v*, and the subsequent contraction of the vowels, see A. & G. 128, 2; B. 251; G. 131, 1; H. 235. —— **ipsum**, acc. sing. m. of the intensive dem. pron. *ipse, -sa, -sum*, gen. *ipsīus*, dat. *ipsī. ipsum* = *he himself*, and is subject-acc. of *habēre*. —— **ex**, prep. with the abl. (*ē* before consonants only, *ex* before vowels or consonants).

LINE 29. **Helvētiīs**, abl. plur. of the adj. *Helvētius, -a, -um*, used substantively, and is the obj. of the prep. *ex*. —— **uxōrem**, acc. sing. of *uxor, -ōris*, f.; direct obj. of *habēre*. Synonyms: *uxor* is the common word = *the married woman* as helpmeet for the man — man's inferior. *cōniunx (coniungere)*, m. and f., sometimes = *the husband*, more frequently = *the wife*, that is the man's equal (compare *cōnsors*); whereas *marīta* is the poetic and postclassic word for *wife*. —— **habēre**, pres. inf. act. of *habeō, -ēre, -uī, -itum*, 2; its subject-acc. is the pron. *ipsum*. —— **sorōrem**, acc. sing. of the noun *soror, -ōris*, f.; direct obj. of *col(n)locāsse*, line 32, below.

LINE 30. **ex**, prep. with the abl.; see note on *ex*, l. 28, above. —— **mātre**, abl. sing. of *māter, -tris*, f.; see note on *mātrem*, l. 26, above. *mātre* is the obj. of the prep. *ex*. *ex mātre* = lit. *from the mother*, i.e. *on the mother's side* = Dumnorix's half-sister. —— **et**, cop. conj.; connects *sorōrem* and *propinquās*. —— **propinquās**, acc. plur. f. of the adj. *propinquus, -a, -um (prope)*, used as a noun; direct obj. of *collocāsse*. —— **suās**, acc. plur. f. of the poss. and reflexive pron. *suus, -a, -um ;* it is an attributive of *propinquās*, but refers to Dumnorix.

He favored and	nūptum	in	aliās	cīvitātēs 31
wished well to	to veil (themselves)	in	other	states
the Helvetii on				
account of this	collocāsse.		Favēre	et 32
relationship; he	to have (he has) contracted.		To favor (he favors)	and
hated even on				
his own account	cupere	Helvētiīs	propter	eam 33
Caesar and the	to be (he is) zealous	for the Helvetii	because	of this
Romans, because				
by their com-	affīnitātem,	ōdisse	etiam	suō nōnine 34
ing his own	affinity,	to hate (he hates)	even	in his own name

LINE 31. **nūptum**, supine in *-um* of the verb *nūbō, -ere, nūpsī, nūptum*. The supine in *-um* usually follows verbs of motion to express the purpose; but in some cases after verbs which do not express motion, as in our text. Consult A. & G. 302; B. 186, (A); G. 435; H. 546, 1. Observe that *nūbere* = lit. *to cover, to veil*, i.e. as a woman's act, to veil herself for her husband; and therefore a complete analysis requires us to supply thus: *sē virō nūptum — sē* referring to *sorōrem*, or rather to both *sorōrem* and *propīnquās*. The veil alluded to in this expression is the *flammeum* or the flame-colored veil, worn by the bride at the wedding. —— **in**, prep. with the acc. or abl.; here it takes the acc. After verbs of motion *in* = *into*; after verbs of rest = *in*, or *on*, or *among*. See *In*, A. & G. 153, 1, 2; B. 120, 1, 2, 3; G. 418, I, 2; H. 435, I. Observe that *collocāsse* is not strictly a verb of motion; yet it is followed by *in* with the acc. as if it were such. Probably this usage arose from the formula *in mātrimōnium dūcere* — the phraseology used of a man who marries. —— **aliās**, acc. plur. f. of the adj. *alius, -ia, -iud*, gen. *alīus*, dat. *aliī;* the plur. is regular, like that of *bonus*. *aliās* is an attributive of *cīvitātēs*. Observe that *alius* = *another, other*, of an indefinite number; whereas *alter* = *the one, the other* of two. —— **cīvitātēs**, acc. plur. of the noun *cīvitās, -ātis*, f. (*cīvēs*). *cīvitātēs* is the obj. of the prep. *in*. Synonyms: *cīvitās*, abstractly = the condition of a citizen, hence = *citizenship*. *cīvitās*, concretely = *the citizens* of a city or cities, united in a district, forming a body-politic — *the state*. *urbs* = *a city*, whose district is coterminous with the dwellings of the citizens; but sometimes by metonymy *cīvitās* = *urbs*. *rēspūblica* = *the commonwealth* — *the state* conceived to be formed by the concessions of all for the common weal.

LINE 32. **collocāsse**, see note on this word, l. 28, above. —— **Favēre**, pres. inf. act. of *faveō, -ēre, fāvī, fautem*, 2; supply *sē* as subject-acc., referring to Dumnorix. —— **et**, cop. conj., connects words and clauses of equal importance. The *ōrātiō rēcta* of lines 25–32: atque hūius potentiae causā mātrem in Biturigibus hominī illīc nōbilissimō āc potentissimō *collocāvit, ipse* (Dumnorix) ex Helvētiīs uxōrem *habet*, sorōrem ex mātre et propīnquās suās nūptum in aliās cīvitātēs *collocavit*.

LINE 33. **cupere**, pres. inf. act. of the verb *cupiō, -ere, cupīvī (-iī), cupītum*, 3; connected by *et* with *favere*, and in the same grammatical construction, i.e. *sē* understood is its subject-acc. —— **Helvētiīs**, dat. plur. of *Helvētiī, -ōrum*, m.; dat. after the verbs *favēre* and *cupere* — words of favoring. Consult A. & G. 227; B. 142; G. 346; H. 385, I. —— **propter**, prep. with the acc. —— **eam**, acc. sing. f. of the dem. pron. *is, ea, id; eam* is an attributive of *af(d)fīnitātem*.

LINE 34. **affīnitātem**, acc. sing. of *affīnitās, -tātis*, f. (ad + fīnis); it is the obj. of the prep. *propter*. Observe that *affīnitās* = *affinity* by marriage, not by blood;

[LINES 35-37.] BOOK I. 133

35 Caesarem	et	Rōmānōs,	quod	eōrum	power was di-
Caesar	*and*	*the Romans,*	*because*	*at their*	minished, and his brother Divitia-
36 adventū	potentia	ēius	dēminūta,	et	cus was restored
coming	*the power*	*of him*	*was diminished,*	*and*	to his old position of popu-
37 Divitiacus	frāter	in	antīquum	locum	larity and honor.
Divitiacus,	*the brother,*	*to (his)*	*former*	*place*	If any disaster

affinity by blood is denoted by *cōnsanguinitās.* —— **ōdisse,** perf. inf. in form, but pres. in meaning of the preteritive verb *ōdī, ōdisse;* supply *sē* or *ipsum,* referring to Dumnorix as the subject-acc. —— **etiam** (et + iam), a conjunctive adv. here of restrictive force. —— **suō,** abl. sing. n. of the poss. and reflexive pron. *suus, -a, -um;* it agrees with *nōmine,* but refers to Dumnorix. —— **nōmine,** abl. sing. of the noun *nōmen, -inis,* n. (compare *nōscere* and the GK. γιγνώσκω); it is thus seen that *nōmen* = that by which a person or thing is known. *nōmine* is an abl. of manner. A. & G. 248; B. 168; G. 399; H. 419, III. The phrase *suō nōmine* = *on his own account,* i.e. *for personal reasons.*

LINE 35. **Caesarem,** acc. of the proper noun *Caesar, -aris,* m.; direct obj. of *ōdisse.* —— **et,** conj.; it connects *Caesarem* and *Rōmānōs.* —— **Rōmānōs,** acc. plur. of the adj. *Rōmānus, -a, -um,* used substantively; connected by *et* with *Caesarem,* and in the same grammatical construction. —— **quod,** conj. = *because;* the *quod-* clause gives the reason of Dumnorix's hatred of Caesar and the Romans. —— **eōrum,** gen. plur. of the dem. pron. *is, ea, id,* used as a personal pron. of the 3d pers.; English poss. case; it refers to Caesar and the Romans; but as a gen. it limits *adventū.*

LINE 36. **adventū,** abl. sing. of the noun *adventus, -ūs,* m. (ad + venīre); abl. of *time at which.* See A. & G. 256, 1; B. 171, REM. 3; G. 393; H. 429. —— **potentia, -ae,** f.; subject-nom. of *dēminūta (sit).* Synonyms: *potentia (potēns)* = the objective *power* by which men move men. *potestās (possum)* = lawful *power* that men exercise in courts of law, and under an ethical impulse; compare GK. ἐξουσία; whereas *vīs* (GK. ἴς) = the *power* that men use both in attacking and in restraining others. —— **ēius,** gen. sing. m. of the dem. pron. *is, ea, id,* used as a personal pron. of the 3d pers.; as a gen. *ēius* limits *potentia,* but it refers to Dumnorix. —— **dēminūta,** supply *sit,* 3d pers. sing. perf. pass. subjunctive of the verb *dēminuō, -ere, -minuī, -minūtum,* 3 (dē, *intensive* + minuere [*minus*]); *dēminūta sit* agrees with its subject-nom. *potentia;* it is in the subjunctive, because in a dependent clause in *ōrātiō oblīqua.* —— **et,** cop. conj.; it connects the subordinate clauses.

LINE 37. **Divitiacus, -ī,** m., in apposition with *frāter;* he was an Aeduan chief, brother of Dumnorix, and a friend of the Romans. —— **frāter,** nom. sing. of *frāter, -tris,* m.; subject-nom. of *sit restitūtus (restitūtus sit).* The allusion is to Dumnorix; he, too, was an Aeduan of influence, and was a leader, in some sort, of the Gallic patriotic party, who were hostile to the Roman power. —— **in,** prep. with acc. or abl.; here it takes the acc., and = *to* or *into.* See A. & G. 153, under *In,* 1; B. 120, 3; G. 418, 1; H. 435, 1. —— **antīquum,** acc. sing. m. of the adj. *antīquus, -a, -um* (antī, i.e. *ante* + cus). *antīquum* is an attributive of *locum.* Synonyms: *vetus* = *the old* in opposition to *the recent,* i.e. in opposition to that which has not been long in existence; whereas *antīquus* = *the old* in opposition to that which has not previously existed. —— **locum,** acc. sing. of the noun *locus, -ī,* m. in the sing., m. or n. in the plur.; see note on *locī,* l. 10, Chap. II. *locum* is the obj. of the prep. *in.*

should happen to the Romans, he indulged the largest hope of obtaining sovereign power through the agency of the Helvetii; while,	grātiae *of favor*	atque *and*	honōris *of honor*	sit *was*	restitūtus. *restored.*	Sī *If*
	quid *anything*	accidat *should happen*		Rōmānīs, *to the Romans,*	summam *highest*	in *into,*
	spem *hope*	per *through*	Helvētiōs *the Helvetii*		rēgnī *of the sovereignty*	obtinendī *to be gained*

LINE 38. **grātiae,** gen. sing. of the noun *grātia, -ae,* f. (*grātus,* favor, both act. and pass.; compare *cārus,* GK. χάρις, and English *grace*). —— **atque** (ad + que), conj. that adds a more emphatic notion. See note on this particle, l. 10, Chap. I. —— **honōris,** gen. sing. of the noun *honor, -ōris,* m.; connected by *atque* with *grātiae,* and in the same grammatical construction. —— **sit restitūtus** (*restitūtus sit*), 3d pers. sing. perf. subjunctive pass. of *restituō, -ere, -uī, -ūtum,* 3 (re + statuere, *to set up again*); connected by *et* with *dēminūta* (*sit*), and the subjunctive for the same reason — namely, because in a subordinate clause in the *ōrātiō oblīqua.* —— **Sī,** conditional conj. (archaic form *seī,* sibilated from the GK. *eī*). The *ōrātiō rēcta* of lines 32–38: *Favet* et *cupit* Helvētiīs propter *hanc* affīnitātem, *ōdit* etiam suō nōmine Caesarem et Rōmānōs, quod eōrum adventū potentia ēius dēminūta, et Divitiacus frāter in antīquum locum grātiae atque honōris *est* restitūtus.

LINE 39. **quid,** nom. sing. n. of the indef. pron. *quis* (*quī*), *quae, quid* (*quod*). The forms *quis, quae, quid* are used substantively; *quī, quae, quod,* adjectively. *quid* is the subject-nom. of *accidat.* —— **accidat,** 3d pers. sing. pres. subjunctive act. of *accidō, -ere, -cidī* (ad + cadere); hence *accidere* = lit. *to fall to,* i.e. *to befall, happen;* pres. subjunctive in the condition of *sī.* Observe that *sī quid accidat* is used euphemistically for *if defeat shall happen to.* Observe, further, that the pres. infinitives and pres. subjunctives are used when the writer has no intention to express an action as prior to another, because *reperit,* on which the indirect discourse depends, is a present tense. —— **Rōmānīs,** dat. plur. of the adj. *Rōmānus, -a, -um,* used substantively, and is the indirect object of *accidat.* —— **summam,** acc. sing. f. of the adj. *summus, -a, -um,* superl. degree of the positive *superus,* comparative *superior,* superl. *suprēmus* or *summus. summam* is an attributive of the noun *spem.* —— **in,** prep. with either the acc. or abl., here it takes the acc.; note its position between the modifier and the noun modified, and see A. & G. 345, *a,* 2; B. 58. 2; G. 413, REM. 2; H. 569, II, 1.

LINE 40. **spem,** acc. sing. of the noun *spēs, -eī,* f. Observe that the final vowel of the stem is short in the gen. and dat. of *spēs;* it is short also in the gen. and dat. of the stems of *fidēs* and *rēs. spem* is the obj. of the prep. *in.* —— **per,** prep. with the acc. —— **Helvētiōs,** acc. plur. m. of the adj. *Helvētius, -a, -um,* used as a subst.; it is here the acc. of the agent, considered as means, after the prep. *per.* Consult A. & G. 246, *b;* B. 166, REM. 1; G. 401; H. 415, I, NOTE 1. —— **rēgnī,** gen. sing. of the noun *rēgnum, -ī,* n. (*rēx*). *rēgnī* as a gen. limits *spem.* —— **obtinendī,** gen. of the gerundive *obtinendus, -a, -um* of the verb *obtineō, -ēre, -uī, -tentum,* 2 (ob + tenēre). *obtinendī* as a gerundive agrees with the noun *rēgnī.* The phrase *rēgnī obtinendī* constitutes what is called the gerundive construction, and as such depends on *spem.* Consult A. & G. 298; B. 184, REM. 4, 1; G. 428; H. 544, 1. It may clarify this matter to say that the gerundive is simply the fut. pass. participle, and is the attributive, in the oblique cases, of some noun; while the gerund is a verbal noun in the active voice, and takes a direct obj. Thus *in spem rēgnī obtinendī* = lit. *into the*

41 venīre;		imperiō	populī	Rōmānī		under the sway of the Roman people, he not only despaired of the sovereignty, but even of maintaining the influence which he at that time had. As to the unsuccessful cavalry skirmish
to come (he comes);		under the power	of the people	Roman		
42 nōn	modo	dē	rēgnō,	sed	etiam	dē
not	only	of	the sovereignty,	but	even	of
43 eā,	quam	habeat,	grātiā			dēspērāre.
that,	which	he has,	popularity,			to despair (he despairs).
44 Reperiēbat		etiam	in	quaerendō		Caesar,
Ascertained,		too,	on	inquiring		Caesar,

hope of the sovereignty to be obtained, which is equivalent to: *into the hope of obtaining the sovereignty*. For the gerund construction thus: *patriam spes videndī = the hope of seeing one's fatherland.*

LINE 41. **venīre**, pres. inf. act. of the verb *veniō, -īre, vēnī, ventum,* 4; supply *eum*, referring to *Dumnorigem*, l. 10, above, as subject-acc. of *venīre*. —— **imperiō**, a lone abl. absolute, denoting both time and cause. If the pres. participle of *esse* were in use, the phraseology would be: *imperiō ente populī Rōmānī = the rule of the Roman people being*. With such a participle, the abl. absolute construction would be regular. —— **populī**, gen. sing. of the noun *populus, -ī,* m.; as a gen. it limits *imperiō*. For synonyms, see l. 17, Chap. VI. —— **Rōmānī**, gen. sing. m. of the adj. *Rōmānus, -a, -um;* it is an attributive of *populī*. Note that the adj., in this phrase, always follows the noun.

LINE 42. **nōn**, adv. (nē + ūnum); it modifies *modo*. —— **modo**, adv. (*modus*); hence *modo* = lit. *by measure,* i.e. expressing a restriction of the notion = in English *only*. —— **dē**, prep. with the abl. —— **rēgnō**, abl. of the noun *rēgnum, -ī,* n. (*rēx*). *rēgnō* is the obj. of the prep. *dē*. Observe that the phrase *dē rēgnō* follows the verb *dēspērāre*, and that the prep. *dē* in the compound is repeated with *rēgnō*. This is the common construction in Caesar, but other writers construct more frequently with the acc. —— **sed**, conj.; strongest of the adversatives. —— **etiam** (et + iam), adv. As adverbs, both *modo* and *etiam* modify *dēspērāre;* but as conjunctive phrases, *nōn modo ... sed etiam* indicate that prominence is given to the second word or clause. —— **dē**, prep. with the abl.

LINE 43. **eā**, abl. sing. f. of the dem. pron. *is, ea, id;* it is an attributive of *grātiā*. —— **quam**, acc. sing. f. of the rel. pron. *quī, quae, quod;* as a rel. it refers to *grātiā;* in grammatical construction it is the direct object of *habeat*. —— **habeat**, 3d pers. sing. pres. subjunctive of the verb *habeō, -ēre, -uī, -itum,* 2; it agrees with a pron. implied in the ending as subject-nom., referring to Dumnorix; it is in the subjunctive mode, because it is in a dependent clause in *ōrātiō oblīqua*. —— **grātiā**, sing. of the noun *grātia, -ae,* f. (*grātus,* favor; kindred with *cārus,* GK. χάρις). *grātiā* is the obj. of the prep. *dē*. —— **dēspērāre**, pres. inf. of the verb *dēspērō, -āre, -āvī, -ātum,* 1 (dē + spērāre, *to be without hope);* supply *eum* as subject-acc. of *dēspērāre*, referring to Dumnorix. The *ōrātiō rēcta* of lines 38–43: Sī quid *accidit* Rōmānīs, summam in spem per Helvētiōs rēgnī obtinendī *venit;* imperiō populī Rōmānī nōn modo dē rēgnō, sed etiam dē eā, quam *habet*, grātiā *dēspērat*.

LINE 44. **Reperiēbat**, 3d pers. sing. imperf. ind. act. of *reperiō, -īre, rep(p)erī, repertum,* 4 (re + parere, *to procure again);* it agrees with its subject-nom. *Caesar*. —— **etiam** (et + iam), adv. = *also*. —— **in**, prep. with the acc. or abl.; here it takes the abl. —— **quaerendō**, abl. of the gerund of the verb *quaerō, -ere, quaesīvī* (*-siī*),

which had taken place a few days before, Caesar also found on inquiry, that the beginning of that stampede was made by Dumnorix and his	quod *in that*	proelium *a battle*	equestre *cavalry*	adversum *unsuccessful*	paucīs *a few,* 45
	ante *before*	diēbus *days,*	esset *had been*	factum, *fought,*	initium *the beginning* ēius *of that* 46
	fugae *flight*	factum *(had been) made*	ā *by*	Dumnorige *Dumnorix*	atque *and* ēius 47 *his*

-*sĭtum*, 3; *quaerendō* as a gerund is the obj. of the prep. *in*. Consult A. & G. 301, (3); B. 184, REM. 4, IV; G. 433; H. 542, IV, (2). —— Caesar, -aris, m.; subject-nom. of *reperiēbat*. Note how both the subj. and predicate are made emphatic by exchange of positions; the natural Latin order is: *Caesar etiam in quaerendō reperiēbat.*

LINE 45. **quod**, adv.; acc. of the rel. *quī, quae, quod* = *whereas* or *in that.* Consult A. & G. 333, *a*; B. 123, REM. 21; G. 525, 2; H. 516, II, 2, NOTE. But *quod* might be taken as a rel. pron., and *fugae* as = to *proelii,* and then the following *ōrdō* might explain the construction: *initium ēius proeliī equestris adversī, quod proelium esset factum, factum (esse)*, etc. Compare *quae pars . . . ea,* l. 24, Chap. XI. —— **proelium**, nom. sing. of the noun *proelium, -ī,* n.; subject-nom. of *esset factum (factum esset).* As to derivation and synonyms, see note on *proeliīs,* l. 18, Chap. I. As to the battle, read again Chap. XV. —— **equestre**, nom. sing. n. of the adj. *equester, -tris, -tre (eques [equus]). equestre* is an attributive of *proelium.* —— **adversum**, nom. sing. n. of the adj. *adversus, -a, -um* (ad + versus, participle of *vertō*); *adversum*, too, is an attributive of *proelium.* —— **paucīs**, abl. plur. m. of the adj. *paucus, -a, -um. paucīs* modifies *diēbus.*

LINE 46. **ante**, adv. and prep.; here it is an adv. and modifies *esset factum (factum esset).* —— **diēbus**, abl. plur. of the noun *diēs, -ēī* (old form in the gen. *diē*), m. or f. in the sing.; always m. in the plur. *diēbus* is the abl. of the degree of difference. Consult A. & G. 250; B. 164, REM. 3; G. 403, NOTE 4, (*a*); H. 423, and 430, NOTE 3. Note the strictly literal translation of *paucīs ante diēbus*—*before by a few days.* —— **esset factum** (*factum esset*), 3d pers. sing. pluperf. subjunctive of *fīō, fierī, factus*; used as pass. of *faciō, -ere, fēcī, factum,* 3; *esset factum* agrees with its subject-nom. *proelium,* l. 45, above; it is in the subjunctive, because it is a subordinate clause in the *ōrātiō oblīqua.* Consult A. & G. 321, *a*; B. 245, 1, (*b*); G. 525, 3; H. 524. —— **initium**, acc. sing. of the nom. *initium, -ī,* n. (in + īre). *initium* is subject-acc. of *factum (esse).* Observe that this inf. clause is the object of, and depends on, *Reperiēbat,* l. 44, above. —— **ēius**, gen sing. f. of the dem. pron. *is, ea, id;* as a gen. it limits *fugae.*

LINE 47. **fugae**, gen. sing. of. the noun *fuga, -ae,* f.; as a gen. it limits *initium.* —— **factum (esse)**, perf. inf. of *fīō, fierī, factus,* 3; its subject-acc. is *initium.* —— **ā**, prep. with the abl. (*ā* before consonants only, *ab* before either vowels or consonants). —— **Dumnorige**, abl. sing. of the proper noun *Dumnorix, -igis,* m.; abl. of the agent after the prep. *ā.* See A. & G. 246; B. 166; G. 401; H. 415, I. See note on *Dumnorigem,* l. 10, above. —— **atque** (ad + que), conj., used before vowels and consonants, *āc* before consonants only; it usually adds a notion of greater import. —— **ēius**, gen. sing. m. of the dem. pron. *is, ea, id;* used substantively; as a personal pron. of the 3d pers. = here *his;* observe that before *fugae,* immediately preceding, it has its proper demonstrative force, and = *that.* Whether used as a dem. or as a personal pron. can only be determined by the connection. *ēius* as a gen. limits *equitibus.*

48 equitibus,	— nam	equitātuī,	quem	auxiliō	cavalry; — for Dumnorix was in command of the cavalry, which the Aedui had sent to aid Caesar; — that the rest of the cavalry had been terrified and stampeded by their flight.
cavalry,	*— for*	*the cavalry,*	*which*	*for an aid*	
49 Caesarī	Aeduī	mīserant,	Dumnorix	praeërat;	
to Caesar	*the Aedui*	*had sent,*	*Dumnorix*	*was over;*	
50 — eōrum	fugā	reliquum	esse	equitātum	
— by their	*flight*	*the rest of,*	*to be (were),*	*cavalry,*	
51 perterritum.					
terrified.					

LINE 48. **equitibus**, abl. plur of the noun *eques, -itis,* m. *(equus)*; connected by the conj. *atque* with *Dumnorige,* and in the same grammatical construction. —— **nam**, conj. = *for;* expresses an objective reason; *enim,* a subjective. —— **equitātuī** (contracted form *equitātū*), dat. of *equitātus, -ūs,* m.; after *prae* in *praeërat,* l. 49, below. See A. & G. 228; B. 143; G. 347; H. 386. —— **quem**, acc. sing. m. of the rel. pron. *quī, quae, quod;* as a rel. pron. it refers to *equitātuī,* but is the direct obj. of *mīserant.* —— **auxiliō**, dat. sing. of the noun *auxilium, -iī,* n.; dat. of the *end for which.*

LINE 49. **Caesarī**, dat. sing. of the noun *Caesar, -aris,* m.; dat. of the obj. *to which.* Observe that *mīserant* takes here a direct obj. and two datives, and consult A. & G. 233, *a*; B. 147, and REM. 1; G. 356; H. 390, II. —— **Aeduī**, nom. plur. of the adj. *Aeduus, -a, -um,* used substantively; subject-nom. of *mīserant.* As to the Aedui, consult note on *Aeduō,* l. 20, Chap. III. —— **mīserant**, 3d pers. plur. pluperf. ind. act. of the verb *mittō, -ere, mīsī, mīssum,* 3; it agrees with its subject-nom. *Aeduī.* —— **Dumnorix**, -igis, m., subject-nom. of the verb *praeërat.* See note on *Dumnorigem,* l. 10, above. —— **praeërat**, 3d pers. sing. imperf. ind. of the neuter or intrans. verb *praesum, -esse, -fuī, -futūrus;* *praeërat* agrees with its subject-nom. *Dumnorix.*

LINE 50. **eōrum**, gen. plur. of the dem. pron. *is, ea, id,* used as a personal pron. of the 3d pers.; here it = *of them* or *their;* as a gen. it limits *fugā.* —— **fugā**, abl. sing. of the noun *fuga, -ae,* f. *fugā* is an abl. of *cause.* See A. & G. 245; B. 165; G. 408; H. 416. —— **reliquum**, acc. sing. m. of the adj. *reliquus, -a, -um; reliquum* is an attributive of *equitātum.* For synonyms, see note on *reliquus,* l. 7, Chap. V. —— **esse**, pres. inf. of the intrans. verb *sum, esse, fuī, futūrus;* it is here used in the formation of the perf. pass. *esse perterritum (perterritum esse).* —— **equitātum**, acc. sing. of the noun *equitātus, -ūs,* m. *(equitāre,* to ride); hence the noun abstract = *a riding;* but in concrete, *cavalry,* in the plur. has the same meaning. But after 122 B.C. the *equitēs* became an order of Roman knights, and as such were farmers of the taxes, and administrators of justice; whereas *equitātus* very rarely designates the equestrian order. *equitātum* is subject-acc. of *esse perterritum (perterritum esse).*

LINE 51. **esse perterritum** *(perterritum esse),* perf. pass. inf. of the verb *perterreō, -ēre, -uī, -itum,* 2 (per + terrēre). Observe (*a*) the intensive force of the prep. *per* in the compound *perterrēre = to frighten thoroughly.* Observe (*b*) that the construction from *reperiēbat,* with the exception of the parenthetic clause, is informal *ōrātiō oblīqua;* the acc. sentences depending on *reperiēbat.* The direct form would be: quod proelium equestre adversum paucīs ante diēbus *erat factum,* initium ēius fugae *factum est* ā Dumnorige atque ēius equitibus . . . *hōrum* fugā *reliquus est equitātus perterritus.*

XIX.* On being thus informed, since to these suspicions the most incontestable facts were added; viz., that Dumnorix had led the Helvetii through the country of the Sequani; that he had ordered the mutual exchange of	XIX. Quibus Which ad hās suspīciōnēs to these imputations quod per fīnēs that through the territory trādūxisset, quod he had led, that	rēbus things certissimae most certain Sēquanōrum of the Sequani obsidēs hostages	cōgnitīs, having been learned, rēs accēderent, things were added, Helvētiōs the Helvetii inter among	cum 1 when 2 3 eōs 4 them

LINE 1. **Quibus,** abl. plur. f. of the rel. pron. *quī, quae, quod;* it is an attributive of *rēbus;* at the beginning of a sentence the rel. = *et eīs.* See A. & G. 180,*f*; B. 129, REM. 9; G. 610; H. 453. —— **rēbus,** abl. plur. of the noun *rēs, reī,* f. (stem *rē* shortened in the gen. and dat. sing.); abl. absolute with *cōgnitīs* denoting *time when.* Consult A. & G. 255; B. 192; G. 409; H. 431. —— **cōgnitīs,** abl. sing. of the perf. pass. participle *cōgnitus, -a, -um* of the verb *cōgnōscō, -ere, -nōvī, -nitum,* 3 (con + [g]nōscō, GK. γιγνώσκω). *cōgnitīs* is in the abl. absolute construction with *rēbus.* —— **cum,** conj.; other forms *quum* and archaic *qum (quī). cum* here denotes both time and cause.

LINE 2. **ad,** prep. with the acc. —— **hās,** acc. plur. f. of the dem. pron. *hīc, haec, hōc; hās* is an attributive of *suspīciōnēs.* —— **suspīciōnēs,** acc. plur. of the noun *suspīciō, -ōnis,* f. (*suspicārī,* to suspect); it is the obj. of the prep. *ad.* —— **certissimae,** nom. plur. f. of the adj. *certissimus, -a, -um,* superl. degree; positive *certus,* by metathesis for *crētus,* a participle of the verb *cernō, -ere, crēvī, crētum;* comparative *certior. certissimae* is an attributive of the noun *rēs.* —— **rēs,** nom. plur. of the noun *rēs, reī,* f.; subj. of the verb *accēderent.* —— **accēderent,** 3d pers. plur. imperf. subjunctive of *accēdō, -ere, -cessī, -cessum,* 4 (ad + cēdere, *to approach*); hence, as *accēdere* is a neuter verb, it = sometimes *to approach* a thing with the notion of augmentation; it therefore freq. = *to be added,* as in our text. *accēderent* is in the subjunctive after *cum* temporal or historical. A. & G. 325; B. 222; G. 585; H. 521, II, 2; it agrees with its subject-nom. *rēs.*

LINE 3. **quod,** conj. = *that;* here the function of the connective is merely to introduce the following explanatory *quod*-clauses, which are in apposition with the noun *rēs.* —— **per,** prep. with the acc. —— **fīnēs,** acc. plur. of the noun *fīnis, -is,* m. *fīnēs* is the obj. of the prep. *per.* For synonyms, see note on *agrum,* l. 12, Chap. II. —— **Sēquanōrum,** gen. plur. of the proper noun *Sēquanī, -ōrum;* as a gen. it limits *fīnēs.* For description of this clan, see note on *Aeduō,* l. 20, Chap. III. —— **Helvētiōs,** acc. plur. of the adj. *Helvētius, -a, -um,* used substantively. *Helvētiōs* is the direct obj. of *trādūxisset.* For description of the Helvetii, see note on *Helvētiī,* l. 16, Chap. I.

LINE 4. **trādūxisset,** 3d pers. sing. pluperf. subjunctive of the verb *trādūcō, -ere, -dūxī, -ductum,* 3 (trāns + dūcere); it agrees with a pron. implied in the ending as subject-nom., referring to Dumnorix; it is in the subjunctive mode, because Caesar reports his own thought, as if it were another's. Consult A. & G. 321, and 341, *d*;

* The translator thus constructs the following strictly English period: On being thus informed, Caesar thought there was sufficient reason for punishing Dumnorix, or for ordering the Aeduan state to do it, since to these suspicions the most incontestable facts were added: that Dumnorix

					hostages; that
5 dandōs	cūrāsset,	quod	ea	omnia	he had done all these things not
to be given	*he had cared for,*	*that*	*these*	*all (things)*	only without Cae-
6 nōn	modo	iniūssū	suō	et	cīvitātis,	sar's orders or
not	*only*	*without leave*	*his own,*	*and (that) of the state,*	those of the Ae-
7 sed	etiam	īnscientibus ipsīs		fēcisset,	duan state, but even without the
but	*also,*	*unaware themselves being,*		*he had done,*	knowledge of the

B. 198, (*b*); G. 525, 1, and 541; H. 516, II. —— **quod**, see *quod* at the beginning of the preceding clause. —— **obsidēs**, acc. plur. of the noun *obses, -idis*, m. and f.; direct obj. of *cūrāsset*. —— **inter**, prep. with the acc. —— **eōs**, acc. plur. m. of the dem. pron. *is, ea, id*, used as a personal pron. of the 3d pers. *eōs* is the obj of the prep. *inter*.

LINE 5. **dandōs**, gerundive, or fut. pass. participle of the verb *dō, dare, dedī, datum* (a short before -*re* in pres. inf. act. by exception). *dandōs* is the factitive obj. after *cūrāsset*. Consult A. & G. 294, *d*; B. 184, III, (*a*); G. 430; H. 544, NOTE 2. —— **cūrāsset**, 3d pers. sing. pluperf. subjunctive act. for the uncontracted form *cūrāvisset;* it agrees with a pron. implied in the ending as subject-nom., referring to Dumnorix; subjunctive mode for the same reason as *trādūxisset*, preceding line. —— **quod**, a conj. = *that.* See note on *quod*, l. 3, above. —— **ea**, acc. plur. n. of the dem. pron. *is, ea, id*, used substantively; or supply the English word *things*, and take *ea* as a dem. adj. = *these*. The things referred to were all the things to which Caesar took exception. The things just mentioned in the *quod*-clauses preceding, and in the clauses succeeding, were mere pretexts made to justify Caesar's invading the Gallic clans; his real motive for such invasion was self-glory and the glory of Rome. —— **omnia**, acc. plur. n. of the adj. *omnis, -e; omnia* is an attributive of *ea*, used as a noun.

LINE 6. **nōn**, adv. (nōn + ūnum, apocopated); it modifies the adv. *modo*. —— **modo**, adv.; as such it modifies *fēcisset*. —— **iniūssū**, abl. of the noun *iniūssus, -ūs*, m. (in + iūstus); in fact used only in the abl.; see A. & G. 71, *b*; B. 51; G. 70; H. 134. *iniūssū* is an abl. of manner. —— **suō**, abl. of the poss. pron. *suus, -a, -um;* it is an attributive of *iniūssū*, but it refers to Caesar. —— **et**, cop. conj. —— **cīvitātis**, gen. sing. of the noun *cīvitās, -ātis*, f. (*cīvēs*); as a gen. it limits *iniūssū*, to be supplied, but it refers to the state of Dumnorix — the Aeduan.

LINE 7. **sed**, conj.; the strongest of the adversatives. —— **etiam** (et + iam), adv.; as such it modifies *fēcisset*. But the reader will reflect, that while *nōn modo ... sed etiam* as phrases can be analyzed; in use they are really connectives with conjunctive force, *sed etiam* giving emphasis to the second clause. Compare GK. οὐ μόνον ... ἀλλὰ καί; or μὴ ὅτι ... ἀλλὰ καί. —— **īnscientibus**, abl. plur. of the adj. *īnsciēns, -entis* (in, *negative* + scīre); abl. absolute with *ipsīs*. —— **ipsīs**, abl. plur. m. of the intensive dem. pron. *ipse, -sa, -sum*, gen. *ipsīus*, dat. *ipsī*. *ipsīs* is abl. absolute with the adj. *īnscientibus*, but it refers to the Aedui. As to the abl. absolute construction of a noun or pron. with an adj., consult A. & G. 255, *a*; B. 192, REM. 1; G. 409; H. 431, 4. —— **fēcisset**, 3d pers. sing. pluperf. subjunctive of *faciō, -ere, fēcī, factum*, 3; subjunctive for the same reason as *trādūxisset*, l. 4, above. *fēcisset* agrees with a pron. implied in the ending as subject-nom., referring to Dumnorix.

had led the Helvetii through the country of the Sequani; that he had ordered the mutual exchange of hostages; that he had done all these things not only without Caesar's orders, or those of the Aeduan state, but even without the knowledge of the Aedui; and that, in fine, charges of sedition had been made against him by the chief magistrate of the Aedui — even Liscus himself.

Aedui; and that charges of sedition had been made against him by the chief magistrate of the Aedui, Caesar thought there was sufficient reason for punishing Dum-	quod *that*	ā *by*	magistrātū *a magistrate*	Aeduōrum *of the Aedui*	accūsārētur, *he was accused,*	8
	satis *enough*	esse *to be (it is)*	causae *of cause*	arbitrābātur, *he thought,*	quārē *wherefore*	9
	in *on*	eum *him*	aut *either*	ipse *he himself*	animadverteret *should animadvert*	aut *or*	10

LINE 8. **quod,** see note on this word, l. 3, above. —— **ā**, prep. with the abl. (*d* before consonants only, *ab* before vowels or consonants). —— **magistrātū**, abl. sing. of the noun *magistrātus, -ūs,* m.; abl. of the agent after the prep. *ā*. Consult A. & G. 246; B. 166; G. 401; H. 415, I. The allusion is to Liscus the Vergobretus. —— **Aeduōrum,** gen. plur. of the proper noun *Aeduī, -ōrum,* m.; as a gen. it limits *magistrātū*. As to this clan, see note on *Aeduō,* l. 20, Chap. III. —— **accūsārētur,** 3d pers. sing. imperf. subjunctive pass. of the act. verb *accūsō, -āre, -āvī, -ātum,* 1; it agrees with a pron. implied in the ending as subject-nom., referring to Dumnorix; it is in the subjunctive mode for the same reason as *trādūxisset,* l. 4, above. See, as to the accusation, Chapters XVII and XVIII.

LINE 9. **satis,** adv., or adj., or noun, according to the exigencies of the construction; here, with the gen. partitive, it has a substantive force, and is the subject-acc. of *esse*. —— **esse,** pres. inf. of the intrans. or neuter verb *sum,* perf. ind. *fuī,* fut. participle *futūrus;* it is here a verb of complete predication; its subject-acc. is *satis,* used as a noun. —— **causae,** gen. sing. of the noun *causa, -ae,* f.; partitive gen.; consult A. & G. 216, 4; B. 134; G. 369; H. 397, 4, and FOOTNOTE 3. —— **arbitrābātur,** 3d pers. sing. imperf. ind. of the deponent verb *arbitror, -ārī, -ātus,* 1; it agrees with a pron. implied in its ending as subject-nom., referring to Caesar. The reader will observe that *arbitrābātur* is the principal verb in this elaborate complex sentence, and carries the weight, so to speak, of all the clauses. Synonyms: *arbitrārī (arbiter)* = *to think* in a judicial way — to decide as an arbitrator; and then, generally = *to hold as true, to think,* like GK. νομίζειν. *putāre* = *to think* as an accountant — to reckon; hence, generally = *to suppose, to think.* *aestimāre* = *to think* as a process of exact estimation; whereas *existimāre* = *to think* as a moral function — to estimate a thing at its true value. —— **quārē** (quā + rē), adv., sometimes written *quā rē;* if thus written, *quā* is abl. f. of the rel. pron. *quī, quae, quod,* used adjectively, and *rē* is the abl. sing. of *rēs, reī,* f.; and the phrase *quā rē* is to be taken as an abl. of cause = *by which thing,* i.e. *wherefore*.

LINE 10. **in,** prep. with either the acc. or abl.; here it takes the acc. —— **eum,** acc. m. of the dem. pron. *is, ea, id,* used as a personal pron. of the 3d pers.; it is the obj. of the prep. *in;* it refers to Dumnorix. —— **aut,** conj., used to denote that the difference is exclusive. *aut . . . aut* = *either . . . or*. See note on this particle, as contrasted with *vel,* l. 19, Chap. I. —— **ipse,** nom. sing. of the intensive dem. pron. *ipse, -sa, -sum,* gen. *ipsīus,* dat. *ipsī;* it refers to Caesar; it is expressed for emphasis, and is the subject-nom. of *animadverteret*. —— **animadverteret,** 3d pers. sing. imperf. subjunctive of *animadvertō, -ere, -tī, -sum* (animum + ad + vertere); it agrees with its subject-nom. *ipse;* it is in the subjunctive after *quārē* — indirect question. See A. & G. 334; B. 242; G. 467; H. 529, I. Observe that *animadvertere* = lit. *to turn the mind to;* but that, as the attention to a fault usually issued in the punishment of it, this verb, especially with *in* and the acc., came to mean *to punish*. —— **aut,** see the alternate immediately before *ipse*.

[LINES 11-14.] BOOK I. 141

11 cīvitātem	animadvertere	iubēret.		Hīs	norix, or for ordering the Aeduan state to do it. One circumstance was opposed to all these considerations: that he well knew the very great devotion of Dumnorix's brother Divitiacus to the interests of the Roman people,
the state	to animadvert	he should order.		To these	
12 omnibus	rēbus	ūnum		repūgnābat,	
all	things,	one	(thing)	opposed itself,	
13 quod	Divitiacī	frātris	summum	in	
that	of Divitiacus,	the brother,	the greatest	toward	
14 populum	Rōmānum	studium,		summam	
the people	Roman,	zeal,		the greatest	

LINE 11. cīvitātem, acc. sing. of the noun cīvitās, -ātis (cīvēs); subject-acc. of animadvertere. — animadvertere, pres. inf. of animadvertō, 1; with subject-acc. depends on iubēret. See A. & G. 271, b; B. 194, REM. 2, a; G. 423, NOTE 6; H. 535, II, FOOTNOTE 1. Observe that iubēre takes the acc. and inf. instead of ut and the subjunctive. —— iubēret, 3d pers. sing. imperf. subjunctive of iubeō, -ēre, iūssī, iūssum, 2; iubēret is connected by the alternative conj. aut with animadverteret, and is in the subjunctive mode for the same reason, viz., an indirect question. —— Hīs, dat. plur. of the dem. pron. hīc, haec, hōc; it is an attributive of rēbus.

LINE 12. omnibus, dat. plur. of the adj. omnis, -e, an ī-stem; it, too, is an attributive of rēbus; strictly, however, omnibus modifies the complex idea involved in hīs rēbus. —— rēbus, dat. plur. of the noun rēs, reī, f.; dat. of the indirect obj. after repūgnābat. —— ūnum, nom. sing. n. of the adj. ūnus, -a, -um, gen. ūnīus, dat. ūnī. ūnum is here used substantively — or we may supply vērum, -ī, n., i.e. fact — and is subject-nom. of repūgnābat. —— repūgnābat, 3d pers. sing. imperf. ind. act. of repūgnō, -āre, -āvī, -ātum, 1 (re + pūgnāre); hence repūgnāre = lit. to fight back. repūgnābat agrees with its subject-nom. ūnum; and with its subj. and indirect obj. = one fact opposed itself to all these specifications.

LINE 13. quod, conj.; introduces the quod-clause quod ... cōgnōverat, which clause is explanatory of ūnum, and in apposition with it. —— Divitiacī, gen. sing. of the proper noun Divitiacus, -ī, m.; an appositive of frātris. —— frātris, gen. sing. of the noun frāter, -tris, m.; as a gen. it limits the noun studium. —— summum, acc. sing. n. of the adj. summus, -a, -um; positive superus (rare), comparative superior, superl. suprēmus or summus. summum is an attributive of studium. —— in, prep. with the acc. or abl.; here it takes the acc.

LINE 14. populum, acc. sing. of the noun populus, -ī, m.; it is the obj. of the prep. in. Observe that the phrase in populum Rōmānum is used instead of the objective gen. after studium. Compare odium in Caesarem and odium Caesaris, and consult A. & G. 217, c; B. 131, REM. 3; G. 363, REM. 1, end; H. 396, III, NOTE 1. But observe that the distinction between objective and subjective is ambiguous in the phrase odium Caesaris; while there can be no ambiguity in the phrase odium in Caesarem. —— Rōmānum, acc. sing. m. of the adj. Rōmānus, -a, -um (Roma+nus); Rōmānum is an attributive of populum. —— studium, acc. sing. of the noun studium, -ī, n. (studēre, kindred with GK. σπουδάζειν, to be zealous). studium is a direct obj. of cōgnōverat, l. 16, below. —— summam, acc. sing. of the adj. superl. degree summus, -a, -um; see note on summum, preceding line; summam is an attributive of voluntātem.

| his very great regard for Caesar, his eminent fidelity, justice and moderation; and he was afraid that by Dumnorix's punishment he might wound the feelings of | in *toward* iūstitiam, *justice,* nē *lest* | sē *himself,* temperantiam, *self-control,* ēius *by his* | voluntātem, *good-will,* cōgnōverat; *he had known;* suppliciō *punishment,* | ēgregiam *distinguished* nam, 16 *for,* Divitiacī *Divitiacus's* | fidem, 15 *fidelity,* animum 17 *soul* |

LINE 15. **in**, prep. with the acc. or abl.; here it takes the acc. —— **sē**, acc. sing. of the reflexive pron. *suī, sibi, sē, sē* — same form in both numbers; *sē* here is the obj. of the prep. *in*. Observe that the pron. *sē* refers to Caesar, and compare notes on *in* and *populum*, lines 13 and 14, above. —— **voluntātem**, acc. sing. of *voluntās, -tātis,* f. (*volō*); direct obj. of *cōgnōverat*. Observe the omission of the conjunctions between the several direct objects of *cōgnōverat* (asyndeton). Observe that in a series of words there is an entire omission of conjunctions, or they are repeated between the words or phrases. The enclitic *-que*, however, might be appended to the last word of a series. See A. & G. 208, 3, and 346, *c*; B. 123, REM. 6; G. 474, NOTE; H. 554, 6. —— **ēgregiam**, acc. sing. f. of the adj. *ēgregius, -a, -um* (ē + grex, i.e. *chosen from the herd*). *ēgregiam* is an attributive of the noun *fidem*. —— **fidem**, acc. sing. of the noun *fidēs, fideī*, f. (stem *fidē* shortened in gen., dat. and acc. sing. *fidem* is a direct obj. of *cōgnōverat*. Note that *fidēs* wants the plural.

LINE 16. **iūstitiam**, acc. sing. of the noun *iūstitia, -ae,* f. (derived from *iūs* through the adj. *iūstus*). *iūstitiam* is a direct obj. of *cōgnōverat*. —— **temperantiam**, acc. sing. of the noun *temperantia, -ae,* f. (*temperāns*, compare GK. σωφροσύνη). —— **cōgnōverat**, 3d pers. sing. pluperf. ind. act. of *cōgnōscō, -ere, -nōvī, -nitum,* 3 (con + [g]nōscere, *to know*); it agrees with the subj. implied in the ending, referring to Caesar. Observe that *cōgnōscere* in the complete tenses is sometimes used preteritively. Thus *cōgnōverat*, pluperf. in form = the perfect in sense. Consult A. & G. 279, *e*; B. 113; G. 241, REM.; H. 297, I, 2. Lit. the pluperf. = *he had learned*, i.e. *he knew*. —— **nam**, conj.; used to give a reason for the statement made in the preceding sentence. Observe that *nam* introduces a real objective reason, while *enim*, always postpositive, introduces a subjective one.

LINE 17. **nē**, conj. and adv. (the primitive Latin negative; archaic form *neī, nī*; while *nōn* is derivative). *nē* after a verb of fearing is a conj., and = *that,* because in the expression of a wish to actualize somewhat, the particle depends in the English language on the idea of fearing, and not on that of wishing. We may illustrate the idiom from our text by punctuating thus: *verēbātur; nē Divitiacī animum offenderet* (optative subjunctive) = *he was afraid; would that he might not offend the feelings of Divitiacus*. And this = *he was afraid that he would offend the feelings of Divitiacus*. Consult A. & G. 331, *f,* and FOOTNOTE; B. 200, REM. 6; G. 550, 2, and NOTE 1; H. 498, III, NOTE 1. —— **ēius**, gen. sing. m. of the dem. pron. *is, ea, id,* used as a personal pron. of the 3d pers.; *ēius* as a gen. limits *suppliciō*; it refers to Dumnorix. —— **suppliciō**, abl. sing. of the noun *supplicium, -ī,* n. (*supplex* [sub + pliō]); hence *supplicium* = *the punishment* of a suppliant; of one who *bends* or *kneels* to receive the penalty of a crime. *suppliciō* is an abl. of means. —— **Divitiacī**, gen. sing. of the proper noun *Divitiacus, -ī,* m.; as a gen. it limits the noun *animum*. —— **animum**, acc. sing. of the noun *animus, -ī,* m.; it is the direct obj. of *offenderet*. As contrasted with *mēns*, the thinking faculty, the intellect, *animus* = *the sensibility*. For complete definitions of the synonyms, see note on *animus,* l. 2, Chap. X.

18 offenderet,	verēbātur.	Itaque	prius-quam	Divitiacus. Accordingly, before attempting to exercise any discipline, he ordered Divitiacus to be summoned to his presence; and, dismissing the usual inter-
he might displease,	*he was afraid.*	*Therefore,*	*before that*	
19 quicquam	cōnārētur,	Divitiacum	ad	sē
anything	*he attempted,*	*Divitiacus*	*to*	*himself*
20 vocārī	iubet	et	cotīdiānīs	interpretibus
to be called,	*he orders,*	*and*	*the daily*	*interpreters*

LINE 18. **offenderet**, 3d pers. sing. imperf subjunctive of *offendō, -ere, -fendī, -fēnsum*, 3 (ob + fendere, *to strike against*); *offenderet* agrees with a personal pron. implied in the ending as subject-nom., referring to Caesar; it is the subjunctive of purpose after *nē*. See A. & G. 331, *f*; H. 200, REM. 6; G. 550, 1 and 2; H. 498, III. Note that the noun-clause *nē . . . offenderet* is the direct obj. of *verēbātur*. —— **verēbātur**, 3d pers. sing. imperf. ind. of the deponent verb *vereor, -ērī, veritus*, 2; it agrees with a pron. implied in the ending, referring to Caesar. Synonyms: *verērī* = *to fear* from man's innate sense of veneration — the venerable naturally inspires awe; *metuere* = *to fear* — often for a sense of shame or disgrace; while *timēre* = *to fear* impending evil as the result of reflection or caution. —— **Itaque** (ita + que), conj., illative; denotes an inference; when introducing a clause, it generally stands at the beginning. —— **prius-quam**, adv. (prius + quam); freq. written *prius quam*; often the parts are separated by tmēsis. The force of the *quam* is not obvious with the word *before* as the meaning of *prius*; but, as an illustration, if we translate *prius* with *sooner*, the force of *quam*, as a particle used in comparison, is readily seen.

LINE 19. **quicquam**, acc. sing. n. of the indef. pron. *quisquam, quaequam, quidquam* or *quicquam*; used substantively, and the direct obj. of the deponent verb *cōnārētur*. Observe that this pron. is compounded of quis + quam; that the former part of the word is declined like *quis* and *quī*, but have the *quod*-form — adj. — and the *quid*-form — subst. — in the neuter; and that this pron. is used in negative sentences, or in interrogative sentences implying a negative. —— **cōnārētur**, 3d pers. sing. imperf. subjunctive of the deponent verb *cōnor, -ārī, cōnātus*, 1. *cōnārētur* is subjunctive after *prius-quam*, temporal. Consult A. & G. 327; B. 226, REM. 1; G. 577; H. 520, 2. —— **Divitiacum**, acc. sing. of the proper noun *Divitiacus, -ī*, m.; subject-acc. of *vocārī*. —— **ad**, prep. with the acc. —— **sē**, acc. sing. of the reflexive pron. *suī, sibi, sē, sē* — the same form in both numbers; *sē* is the obj. of the prep. *ad*; it refers to Caesar.

LINE 20. **vocārī**, pres. inf. pass. of *vocō, -āre, -āvī, -ātum*, 1; pass. parts: *vocor, -ārī, -ātus*, 1; the subject-acc. of *vocārī* is the noun *Divitiacum*. —— **iubet**, 3d pers. sing. of the verb *iubeō, -ēre, iūssī, iūssum*, 2. *iubet* agrees with a pron. implied in the ending as its subject-nom., referring to Caesar. Observe that the direct obj. of *iubet* is the inf. noun-clause *Divitiacum ad sē vocārī*. Observe also that from this point to the end of the chapter the construction is affected by *repraesentātiō*, i.e. the verbs in the main clauses are in the historic pres. tense. —— **et**, cop. conj.; it connects *iubet* and *colloquitur*, l. 24, below. —— **cotīdiānīs**, abl. plur. m. of the adj. *co(quo)tīdiānus, -a, -um (co[quo]tīdiē* = quot + diē); *cotīdiānīs* is a modifier of *interpretibus*. Until recently the orthography of *cotīdiānus* was *quotīdiānus*. Who will introduce the fad of spelling *quot, cot?* —— **interpretibus**, abl. plur. of the noun *interpres, -etis*, m. and f. (inter + pres), from *pressus*, apocopated? *interpretibus* is in the abl. absolute construction with the participle *remōtīs*.

144   CAESAR'S GALLIC WAR   [CHAP. XIX.

| preters, he conversed with him through Caius Valerius Procillus, a man of influence in the Gallic province, Caesar's intimate friend, one in whom he had the greatest confidence in every | remōtīs *being removed,* prīncipem *a leading man* suum, *his own,* fidem *confidence* | per *through* Galliae *of Gaul,* cui *for whom* habēbat, *he had,* | C. Valerium Procillum, *Caius Valerius Procillus,* prōvinciae, *of the province,* summam *the highest,* cum *with* | familiārem *friend* omnium *of all* eō *him* | rērum *things,* colloquitur; *he confers;* | 21 22 23 24 |

LINE 21. remōtīs, abl. plur. of the perf. pass. participle *remōtus, a, -um* of the verb *removeō, -ēre, -mōvī, -mōtum,* 2 (re + movēre, *to move back*); abl. absolute with *interpretibus.* —— **per**, prep. with the acc. —— **C.**, an abbreviation of *Caium ;* acc. sing. of *Caius, -ī,* m., the *praenōmen.* —— **Valerium**, acc. sing. of *Valerius, -ī,* the *nōmen* — the name of the *gēns.* —— **Procillum**, acc. sing. of *Procillus, -ī,* m., the *cōgnōmen* or family name. The three names together may be taken as a complex noun-phrase, the obj. of the preposition *per,* denoting the agent as *means.* Consult A. & G. 246, *b*; B. 166, REM. 1; G. 401; H. 415, I, NOTE 1. The allusion is to Caius Valerius Procillus, a man of influence in Gaul, whose father had been made a Roman citizen; he was *facile prīnceps inter parēs.* The *cōgnōmen* is variously written in the MSS. The Greek paraphrast translates *per C. Valerium Procillum*: διὰ τοῦ Γαίου Βαληρίου Προακίλλου.

LINE 22. **prīncipem**, acc. sing. of the noun *prīnceps, -ipis,* m. (primus + capiō); an appositive of *Procillum.* —— **Galliae**, gen. sing. of the noun *Gallia, -ae,* f.; as a gen. it limits *prōvinciae.* —— **prōvinciae**, gen. sing. of the noun *prōvincia, -ae,* f.; as a gen. this noun limits *prīncipem.* The allusion is, probably, to the Roman province in Gaul, as his father had received Roman citizenship, and the son Caius, as an interpreter, must have had knowledge of the Roman tongue, which, as a resident of Celtica, he could not be supposed to have acquired. —— **familiārem**, acc. sing. of the adj. *familiāris, -re,* used substantively here, and as such in apposition with *Procillum.*

LINE 23. **suum**, acc. sing. m. of the substantive and reflexive pron. *suus, -a, -um ;* it is an attributive of the noun *familiārem,* but refers to Caesar. —— **cui**, dat. sing. of the rel. pron. *qui, quae, quod ;* it refers to *Procillum,* but is in the dat. after the phrase *fidem habēbat,* which = *cōnfīdēbat.* Consult A. & G. 227, NOTE 2; B. 142; G. 346, and 357; H. 392, I. —— **summam**, acc. sing. f. of the adj. *summus, -a, -um ;* positive *superus* (rare), comparative *superior,* superl. *suprēmus* or *summus. summam* is an attributive of *fidem.* —— **omnium**, gen. plur. f. of the adj. *omnis, -e ;* as a gen. it limits *rērum.* —— **rērum**, gen. plur. of the noun *rēs, reī,* f.; as a gen. it limits *fidem ;* gen. objective. See A. & G. 217; B. 131, REM. 2; G. 363, 2; H. 396, III.

LINE 24. **fidem**, acc. sing. of the noun *fidēs, -eī,* f. (stem *fidē,* final vowel shortened in gen. and dat. sing.). With *fidēs* compare the Latin verb *fīdō* and the GK. πείθω, root πιθ. *fidem* is the direct obj. of *habēbat.* —— **habēbat**, 3d pers. sing. imperf. ind. act. of *habeō, -ēre, -uī, -itum,* 2; it agrees with a pron. implied in the ending as subject-nom., referring to Caesar. —— **cum**, prep. with the abl.; known to be a prep., and not a conj., because it is seen at once that the verb *colloquitur* is connected immediately by *et* (l. 20, above) with *iubet,* and requires no other con-

BOOK I.   145

25 simul		commonefacit,			quae
at the same time		*he forcibly reminds (him),*			*what (things)*
26 ipsō	praesente	in	conciliō	Gallōrum	
himself	*being present,*	*in*	*the council*	*of the Gauls*	
27 dē	Dumnorige	sint	dicta,	et	ostendit,
about	*Dumnorix*	*were*	*said,*	*and*	*he shows*

respect. Caesar at once reminded Divitiacus of what, in Divitiacus's presence, had been said in the council of the Gauls concerning Dumnorix; and also

nective. —— eō, abl. sing. of the dem. pron. *is, ea, id*, used as a personal pron. of the 3d pers.; *cum eō = with him*, i.e. Divitiacus. —— col(n)loquitur, 3d pers. sing. pres. ind. of the deponent verb *colloquor, -ī, -locūtus*, 3 (con + loquī, *to speak together*). *colloquitur* agrees with a pron. implied in the termination, referring to Caesar as its subject-nom.

LINE 25. simul, adv. (kindred with the GK. ἅμα = *together with*). —— commonefacit, 3d pers. sing. pres. ind. act. of *commonefaciō, -ere, -fēcī, -factum*, 3 (commoneō + faciō) = *remind one forcibly*, hence *warn;* supply *eum* as direct obj. This verb and *ostendit*, l. 27, below, may, like verbs of teaching, take two objects — one of a person, and another of a thing. Observe that compounds of *faciō*, not prepositional, retain the ictus like the simple form. See A. & G. 19, *d*; G. 15, REM. 2; II. 18, 2, 2). —— quae, nom. plur. n. of the interrogative pron. *quis, quae, quid;* used substantively = *what things;* it is the subject-nom. of *sint dicta (dicta sint)*.

LINE 26. ipsō, abl. sing. m. of the intensive dem. pron. *ipse, -sa, -sum; ipsō* is in the abl. absolute construction with the participle *praesente;* see A. & G. 255, *a*; B. 192, REM. 1; G. 409; H. 431, 4; *ipsō* refers to Divitiacus. —— praesente, abl. sing. m. of the pres. participle *praesēns, -ntis;* abl. absolute with the pron. *ipsō*. Observe that the participle *praesēns* comes from the verb *praesum, -esse, -fuī;* and that the abl. sing., referring to *persons*, usually ends in -*e*, to *things*, in -*ī*. Our text conforms to the rule, and *praesente* is abl. absolute with *ipsō*, referring to Divitiacus. —— in, prep. with the acc. or abl.; here it takes the abl. For the meaning of *in* after verbs of motion and of rest, see note on *in* with acc. or abl., l. 1, end, Chap. I. —— conciliō, abl. sing. of the noun *concilium, -ī*, n. (*calāre*, to call); *conciliō* is the obj. of the prep. *in*. Synonyms: *concilium = an assembly* of distinguished persons for deliberation; whereas *cōnsilium = the counsel* taken in such assembly. But the meanings of the two words are often confused in the MSS. and editions. —— Gallōrum, gen. plur. of the adj. *Gallus, -a, -um*, used substantively; as a gen. it limits the noun *conciliō*.

LINE 27. dē, prep. with the abl.; lit. = *from;* here it = *about.* Observe that the prepositions *ab, dē* and *ex*, all = lit. *from*. But *dē = from*, i.e. any fixed point; *ab = from*, i.e. the external border; *ex = from*, i.e. the interior — from within a place or thing; *dē*, however, transf. to mental operations = *of, about, concerning* — the most common signification of the word; compare the GK. prep. περί. —— Dumnorige, abl. sing. of the proper noun *Dumnorix, -igis*, m.; it is the obj. of the prep. *dē*. —— sint dicta (*dicta sint*), 3d pers. plur. perf. subjunctive pass. of the verb *dīcō, -ere, -dīxī, dictum*, 3; pass. parts: *dīcor, dīcī, dīctus*, 3. *sint dicta* agrees with its subject-nom. *quae*, l. 25, above; subjunctive, because an indirect question puts its verb in the subjunctive. Consult A. & G. 334; B. 242; G. 467; A. 529, I, and 5, 1). —— et, cop. conj., connects *commonefacit* and *ostendit*. —— ostendit, 3d pers. sing. pres. ind. act. of the verb *ostendō, -ere, -tendī, -tentum*, 3 (ob + tendere, *to stretch towards*). *ostendit* agrees with a pron. implied in its ending as its subject-nom., referring to Caesar.

disclosed to him what remarks each man had privately made concerning him in Caesar's presence. Caesar begged and entreated him not to be offended, if Caesar himself	quae *what* apud *with* hortātur, *exhorts,* animī *mind's,*	(things) sē *himself* ut *that* vel *either*	sēparātim *separately* dīxerit. *had spoken.* sine *without* ipse *himself*	quisque *each one* Petit *He begs* ēius *his,* dē *about*	dē *about* atque *and also* offēnsiōne *aversion,* eō *him,*	eō 28 *him* 29 30 causā 31 *the case*

LINE 28. **quae**, acc. plur. n. of the interrogative pron. *quis, quae, quid;* direct obj. of *dīxerit.* —— **sēparātim**, adv. (*sēparāre*, to separate); as an adv. it modifies the verb *dīxerit.* —— **quisque**, nom. sing. of the indef. pron. *quisque, quaeque, quidque,* declined like the indef. *quis* with *-que* appended, which gives a notion of universality to the word. *quisque* is the subject-nom. of *dīxerit.* —— **dē**, prep. with the abl.; see note on *dē*, l. 27, above. —— **eō**, abl. sing. m. of the dem. pron. *is, ea, id,* used as a personal pron. of the 3d pers. *eō* is the obj. of the prep. *dē,* and refers to Dumnorix; in the Latin *dē eō* here = *dē Dumnorige.*

LINE 29. **apud**, prep. with the acc.; *apud* with names of persons often = *in the presence of.* —— **sē**, acc. sing. m. of the reflexive pron. *suī, sibi, sē, sē* — same form in both numbers; *sē* is the obj. of the prep. *apud;* it refers to Caesar; or in the Latin, here *apud sē* = *apud Caesarem.* —— **dīxerit**, 3d pers. sing. perf. subjunctive act. of the verb *dīcō, -ere, dīxī, dictum,* 3; it agrees with its subject-nom. *quisque* in number and person; supply *eum* as direct obj.; subjunctive, because an indirect question. We regard the construction in lines 25–29 as informal indirect discourse; the direct: quae sēparātim quisque dē eō apud *mē dīxit?* the indirect: *egō ostendō, quae,* etc.; or, as Caesar uses the 3d pers. in regard to himself — *ostendit.* As a voucher for our opinion, compare *quid cōnsiliī sit, ostendit,* l. 12, Chap. XXI. The *quae-*clauses, however, might be taken as *characteristic* subjunctive clauses. —— **Petit**, 3d pers. sing. pres. ind. act. of *petō, -ere, -īvī (-iī), -ītum,* 3; it agrees with a pron. implied in the ending, referring to Caesar as the subject-nom. —— **atque** (ad + que), conj.; usually adds a notion = *and also.* Compare note on *atque,* l. 10, Chap. I.

LINE 30. **hortātur**, 3d pers. sing. pres. ind. of the deponent verb *hortor, -tārī, -tātus,* 1 (radical *hor,* stir, urge; compare Latin *orior,* and GK. ὁρμάω); connected by the conj. *atque* with the verb *petit,* and in the same grammatical construction. —— **ut**, telic conj.; it connects the main with the subordinate clause. —— **sine** (sē + nē) = lit. *by itself;* hence *separate, without;* prep. with the abl. —— **ēius**, gen. sing. m. of the dem. pron. *is, ea, id,* used as a poss. pron. of the 3d pers.; as a gen. it is an attributive of *animī.* —— **offēnsiōne**, abl. sing. of the noun *offēnsiō, -ōnis,* f. (ob + fendere, lit. *to strike against);* hence the noun = lit. *a striking against,* i.e. *a stumbling,* and transf. *an offense. offēnsiōne* is the obj. of the prep. *sine.*

LINE 31. **animī**, gen. sing. of the noun *animus, -ī,* m.; objective gen., limiting *offēnsiōne.* The allusion is to the feelings of Divitiacus. For synonyms, see note on *animō,* l. 2, Chap. X. —— **vel** (imperative of *volō*), alternative conj. *vel . . . vel = either . . . or.* For synonyms, see note on *aut . . . aut,* l. 19, Chap. I. —— **ipse**, intensive pron.; it is expressed for emphasis, refers to Caesar, and is the subject-nom. of the verb *statuat.* —— **dē**, prep. with the abl.; see note on *dē*, l. 27, above. —— **eō**, abl. sing. m. of the dem. pron. *is, ea, id,* used as a personal pron. of the 3d

32 cōgnitā	statuat,	vel	cīvitātem	should decide the case after examination, or should order the Aeduan state to do it.
having been examined,	*should determine,*	*or*	*the state*	
33 statuere	iubeat.			
to determine,	*he should order.*			

1 XX.	Divitiacus	multīs	cum	lacrimīs	XX. Divitiacus embracing Caesar began with tears to beseech him not to pro-
	Divitiacus	*many*	*with,*	*tears*	
2 Caesarem	complexus		obsecrāre	coepit,	
Caesar	*having embraced,*		*to implore*	*began,*	

pers., referring to Dumnorix. *eō* is the obj. of the prep. *dē.* —— causā, abl. sing. of the noun *causa, -ae,* f. (sometimes *caussa;* etymology dubious); abl. absolute with *cōgnitā*.

LINE 32. **cōgnitā**, abl. f. of the perf. pass. participle *cōgnitus, -a, -um* of the verb *cōgnōscō, -ere, -nōvī, -nitum,* 3 (cum, *intensive* + [g]nōscere). *cōgnitā* is in the abl. absolute construction with *causā*, denoting time. See A. & G. 255; B. 192; G. 409; H. 431. —— **statuat**, 3d pers. sing. pres. subjunctive act. of the verb *statuō, -ere, -uī, -ūtum,* 3 (*status,* standing). *statuat* agrees with its subject-nom. *ipse;* it is in the subjunctive mode — purpose after *ut.* See A. & G. 317, 1; B. 200; G. 546; H. 498, I. —— **vel**, see note on *vel*, preceding line. —— **cīvitātem**, acc. sing. of the noun *cīvitās, -tātis,* f. (*cīvēs*); subject-acc. of *statuere.* Observe that the abstract is put for the concrete — the state for the people of the state.

LINE 33. **statuere**, pres. inf. of the verb *statuō,* 3; see parts given in preceding line; its subject-acc. is *cīvitātem.* Supply *eam,* i.e. *causam,* as direct obj. —— **iubeat**, 3d pers. sing. pres. subjunctive act. of the verb *iubeō, -ēre, iūssī, iūssum,* 2; connected by the conj. *vel* with *statuat*, and in the subjunctive for the same reason, viz., purpose after *ut.*

LINE I. **Divitiacus, -ī,** m.; an Aeduan chieftain; subject-nom. of *coepit.* —— **multīs**, abl. plur. of the adj. *multus,* comparative *plūs,* superl. *plūrimus; multīs* is an attributive of *lacrimīs.* —— **cum**, prep. with the abl. As to its position between the noun and its modifier, see A. & G. 345, *a;* B. 58. 2; G. 413, REM. 2; H. 569, II. —— **lacrimīs**, abl. plur. of *lacrima, -ae,* f.; abl. of manner with the prep. *cum.* See A. & G. 248; B. 168; G. 399; H. 419, III. Observe that the word is sometimes *lacryma* and *lachryma,* and even *lacruma;* compare GK. δάκρυμα.

LINE 2. **Caesarem**, acc. sing. of *Caesar, -aris,* m.; direct obj. of the deponent participle *complexus.* Note that participles are followed by the same cases as their verbs. —— **complexus**, perf. participle of the deponent verb *complector, -ī, -plexus* (com + plectere, GK. πλέκω, lit. *to plait together*); hence *complectī* = *to embrace. complexus,* as a participle, agrees with the noun *Divitiacus.* —— **obsecrāre**, pres. inf. act. of the verb *obsecrō, -āre, -āvī, -ātum,* 1 (ob + sacrāre [ob + sacrum]); hence *obsecrāre* = lit. *to ask for God's sake,* i.e. *to beseech.* Observe that *obsecrāre* is a complementary inf. and depends on *coepit,* and also, that it is modified by the adverb-phrase *cum lacrimīs;* and further, that it is followed by the acc. of the person *eum* understood, referring to *Caesarem* and the following subjunctive clause *nē quid . . . statueret* as the acc. of the thing. —— **coepit**, 3d pers. sing. perf. ind. of *coepī, coepisse,* fut. participle *coeptūrus,* perf. pass. participle *coeptus;* a defective verb used chiefly in the praeterite tenses. *coepit* agrees with its subject-nom. *Divitiacus.*

148   CAESAR'S GALLIC WAR   [CHAP. XX.

nounce too severe | nē   quid   gravius   in   frātrem 3
a sentence on his | *that not   anything   too severe   against (his) brother*
brother, saying
that he was aware | statueret: Scīre   sē   4
that the charges | *he might determine: To know   himself* (he knew)
made by Caesar
were true; that | illa   esse   vēra,   nec   quemquam   ex 5
no one had more | *those (things) to be   true,   not   any one   on account of*

LINE 3. **nē**, adv., primitive negative particle, archaic form *neī;* sometimes, a conj. = *lest.* —— **quid**, acc. sing. n. of the indef. pron. *quis, quae, quid;* the direct obj. of *statueret*. Observe that the indef. pron. *quis* is, usually, found in the combinations *sī quis, nē quis,* and *num quis;* and that in the older editions they are written together thus: *sīquis, nēquis, namquis.* —— **gravius**, acc. sing. n. of the adj., comparative degree *gravior, -us;* positive *gravis,* superl. *gravissimus. gravius* is a modifier of the substantive pron. *quid.* —— **in**, prep. with the acc. or abl.; here it takes the acc. For its meaning with verbs of motion and verbs of rest, see under *In*, A. & G. 153, 1, 2; B. 120, 1, 2, 3; G. 418, 1, 2; H. 435, 1. —— **frātrem**, acc. sing. of the noun *frāter, frātris,* m.; it is the obj. of the prep. *in*.

LINE 4. **statueret**, 3d pers. sing. imperf. subjunctive act. of *statuō, -ere, -uī, -ūtum,* 3; imperf. subjunctive — negative purpose after the particle *nē.* Consult A. & G. 331; B. 200, REM. 2; G. 546; H. 498, I. *statueret* agrees with a pron. implied in the ending as subject-nom., referring to *Caesarem.* Observe that if this dependent clause were expressed as an imperative sentence, it would take the perf. subjunctive — hortatory, i.e. *nē statueret* would = *nē statueritis.* See A. & G. 269, *a,* 1; B. 189, REM. 1, end; G. 263, (*b*); H. 484, IV, NOTE 1, and 489, 3); informal indirect discourse. But from this point, i.e. from *Scīre* to *āverterentur,* l. 22, the discourse is the formal *ōrātiō oblīqua*. Before entering upon its grammatical analysis, let us read again A. & G. 336–342; B. 244, 245; G. 650–661; H. 522–530; and then observe that the words *obsecrāre coepit* are equivalent to an historical perf. tense = *dīxit;* that the entire speech hangs, so to speak, thereon; that the main clauses of the declāratory sentences are in the inf. with the acc.; and that the sequence of tenses, in the subordinate clauses, is the secondary sequence. —— **Scīre**, pres. inf. act. of *sciō, scīre, scīvī (-iī), scītum,* 4; its subject-acc. is the reflexive pron. *sē.* Synonyms: *scīre* = *to know*, in the widest sense; while *vidēre* = knowledge that comes through the organ of sight, and *intellegere,* knowledge as a *rational* discernment, and *sentīre* as a *natural* discernment, especially through the sensibility, and *cōgnōscere* as an *historical* discernment — through tradition; *scīre* = *to know* in all these significations. The *ōrātiō rēcta: sciō egō.* —— **sē**, acc. sing. m. of the pron. *suī, sibi, sē, sē;* subject-acc. of the inf. *scīre.*

LINE 5. **illa**, acc. plur. n. of the dem. pron. *ille, -la, -lud,* gen. *illīus,* dat. *illī.* The reference is to the charges made against Dumnorix in the two immediately preceding chapters. This pron. is used to point in either direction, backward or forward; so is *hīc* and *is;* but *ille* is more emphatic than *hīc* or *is,* in such use, and often refers to an object as somewhat remote. *illa* is subject-acc. of *esse.* —— **esse**, pres. inf. of the neuter or intrans. verb *sum, esse, fuī, futūrus;* used here in the regular construction with the subject-acc. after a verb of *knowing.* See A. & G. 272; B. 194; G. 527; H. 535, I, 1, (2); i.e. after *verba sentiendī et dēclārandī.* But observe that the pres. inf. after an historical tense represents the imperf. tense in English. See A. & G. 288; B. 195, (*b*); G. 281, I; H. 537. —— **vēra**, acc. plur. n. of the adj. *vērus, -a, -um;* predicate-acc. after *esse.* —— **nec**, conjunctive adv.; used indiscrim-

BOOK I.

6	eō	plūs	quam	sē	dolōris	capere,	grief on his brother's account than himself; for though he could accomplish much at home and in other parts of Gaul by his influence, his brother could accomplish very little on ac-
	him	*more*	*than*	*himself,*	*of grief*	*to take,*	
7	proptereā	quod,	cum	ipse		grātiā	
	for this reason,	*because,*	*though*	*himself*	*by (his) influence*		
8	plūrimum	domī	atque		in	reliquā	
	very much,	*at home*	*and also*		*in*	*the rest*	
9	Galliā,	ille		minimum		propter	
	of Gaul,	*he*		*very little*		*on account of*	

inately with *neque* before vowels and consonants; it modifies *quemquam* as an adj. pron. —— **quemquam**, acc. sing. m. of the indef. pron. *quisquam*, subst. *quidquam* or *quicquam* (quis + quam). The compound form makes an indefinite relative; this pron. is used in negative clauses. *quemquam* is subject-acc. of *capere*. —— **ex**, prep. with the abl. (*ē* before consonants only, *ex* before either vowels or consonants).

LINE 6. **eō**, abl. sing. m. of the dem. pron. *is, ea, id*, used as a personal pron. of the 3d pers.; it is the obj. of the prep. *ex;* here *ex eō = ex Dumnorige;* the phrase indicates the source or cause of Divitiacus's grief. Some, however, make *ex eō = from that fact*, i.e. from the conduct of Dumnorix, taking *eō* as neuter gender. —— **plūs**, acc. n. of the comparative adj. *plūs, plūris;* used adverbially; superl. *plūrimum;* as an adv. it modifies *capere*. —— **quam**, conj.; with comparatives = *than*. —— **sē**, acc. sing. of the reflexive pron. *suī, sibi, sē, sē;* it is the subject-acc. of *capere*, to be supplied. —— **dolōris**, gen. sing. of the noun *dolor, -ōris*, m.; partitive gen. after *plūs*. See A. & G. 216, 2; B. 134; G. 369; H. 397, 3. —— **capere**, pres. inf. of the verb *capiō, -ere, cēpī, captum*, 3; its subject-acc. is *quemquam*.

LINE 7. **proptereā**, adv. (propter + eā) = lit. *on account of these things;* the long *ā* in this compound, and the *ā* in other words formed after its analogy are anomalies. See note on this word, l. 9, Chap. I. —— **quod**, conj.; originally an acc. of specification of the rel. pron. *quī, quae, quod;* used adverbially; but here *quod* is a conj. introducing the clause *quod . . . per sē crēvisset*. —— **cum**, concessive conj. = *although*. —— **ipse**, intensive dem. pron. *ipse, -sa, -sum*, gen. *ipsīus*, dat. *ipsī; ipse* refers to Divitiacus; is expressed for emphasis; and is subject-nom. of *posset*, to be supplied from the following clause. —— **grātiā**, abl. sing. of the noun *grātia, -ae*, f.; abl. of cause. A. & G. 245; B. 165; G. 408; H. 416.

LINE 8. **plūrimum**, adverbial acc. of the adj. *plūrimus, -a, -um;* superl. of the comparative *plūs;* it modifies *posset* understood. Consult A. & G. 240, *a;* B. 150, REM. 2; G. 334, REM. 1; H. 378, 2. —— **domī**, locative case of the noun *domus, -ūs*, or *-ī*, locative. See A. & G. 258, *d;* B. 176; G. 411, REM. 2; H. 426, 2. —— **atque** (ad + que), conj.; adds a more emphatic notion. —— **in**, prep. with the acc. or abl.; here it takes the abl. —— **reliquā**, abl. sing. f. of the adj. *reliquus, -a, -um;* it is an attributive of the noun *Galliā*. For synonyms, see note on *reliqua*, l. 7, Chap. V.

LINE 9. **Galliā**, abl. sing. of the noun *Gallia, -ae*, f.; it is the obj. of the prep. *in*. The reference is to all Gaul outside of the Aeduan country. —— **ille**, nom. sing. of the dem. adj. pron. *ille, -la, -lud*, gen. *illīus*, dat. *illī;* it is subject-nom. of the verb *posset;* it refers to Dumnorix, as somewhat removed from the place of interview; if he had been near or present, *hīc* would have been used. —— **minimum**, adverbial acc. of the adj. *minimus, -a, -um*, superl. degree of *parvus*, comparative *minor;* it modifies *posset*. See grammatical references to *plūrimum*, l. 8, above. —— **propter**, prep. with the acc.

count of his youth; yet by his means he had become influential, and was using the resources of power thus acquired for the diminution not to say, but almost for the destruc-	adolēscentiam (his) youth, crēvisset; he had become powerful; nervis power grātiam, (his) favor,	posset, was able, quibus which nōn not sed but	per through opibus influence sōlum only paene almost	sē 10 himself āc 11 and ad minuendam 12 for, to be lessened ad perniciem 13 for destruction

LINE 10. **adolēscentiam**, acc. sing. of the noun *adolēscentia, -ae,* f. (*adolēscēns*); the obj. of the prep. *propter.* Observe (*a*) that *grātiā,* l. 7, above, denoting subjective cause, is in the abl., while (*b*) the phrase *propter adolēscentiam* denotes an objective cause, i.e. that his little influence was a mere incident of his youth; and that (*c*) *adolēscentia* denotes the period between that of the *puer* and that of the *iuvenis,* i.e. between 15 and 30 years of age. —— **posset,** 3d pers. sing. imperf. subjunctive of *possum, posse, potuī* (potis, *able* + sum); it agrees with its subject-nom. *ille,* i.e. Dumnorix, in number and pers.; it is in the subjunctive mode, because in a subordinate clause in the *ōrātiō oblīqua. posset* might better be taken as in the subjunctive after *cum* concessive. See A. & G. 313, *d*; B. 211; G. 587; H. 515, III. —— **per,** prep. with the acc. = like GK. *διά,* motion *through* space, transf. = the means, the cause of an action. —— **sē,** acc. sing. of the reflexive pron. *suī, sibi sē, sē* — same form in both numbers; *sē* is the obj. of the prep. *per;* it refers to Divitiacus.

LINE 11. **crēvisset,** 3d pers. sing. pluperf. subjunctive of the verb *crēscō, -ere, crēvī, crētum,* 3; it agrees with a pron. implied in the ending as its subject-nom., referring to Dumnorix; it is in the subjunctive, because it is in the *quod* (or subordinate) clause in the *ōrātiō oblīqua.* —— **quibus,** abl. plur. of the rel. pron. *quī, quae, quod;* it refers to the ideas contained in the last three clauses, but is used here adjectively, and is an attributive of *opibus.* For the best way of translating a rel. at the beginning of a sentence, see A. & G. 180, *f*; B. 139, REM. 9; G. 610; H. 453. —— **opibus,** abl. plur. of an assumed theme *ops, opis,* f. (kindred with *opus,* compare *ops,* personification — the goddess of riches). *opibus* is in the abl. after the verb *ūterētur,* l. 14, below. Consult A. & G. 249; B. 167, 1; G. 407; H. 421, I. —— **āc,** shortened form of *atque* (ad + que). *āc* is used only before consonants. *āc* as a conj. connects *opibus* and *nervīs.*

LINE 12. **nervis,** abl. plur. of the noun *nervus, -ī,* m.; connected by the conj. *āc* with *opibus,* and in the same grammatical construction. Observe that *nervus,* sing. = *a sinew;* in the plur. = *sinews* as symbol of strength, i.e. transf. *power.* —— **nōn** (nē + oenum or ūnum, apocopated), adv., modifies *sōlum.* —— **sōlum** (*sōlus,* adj., *alone*), modifies the gerundive phrase *ad minuendam grātiam.* —— **ad,** prep. with the acc. —— **minuendam,** acc. sing. f. of the gerundive *minuendus, -a, -um* of the verb *minuō, -ere, -uī, -ūtum,* 3 (*minus,* less); the gerundive agrees with *grātiam.*

LINE 13. **grātiam,** acc. sing. of the noun *grātia, -ae,* f.; it is the obj. of the prep. *ad.* Observe that the gerundive construction following *ad* here denotes *purpose;* and consult A. & G. 300; B. 184, REM. 4, III; G. 432; H. 544, 2, NOTE 2. —— **sed,** conj., strongest of the adversatives; usually contradicts what immediately precedes. —— **paene** (*pēne*), adv. = *almost;* no comparative; superl. *pae(ē)nissimē* = *utterly. paene* modifies the adverb-phrase *ad perniciem suam.* —— **ad,** prep. with the acc.

[LINES 14-16.]   BOOK I.   151

14 suam	ūterētur.		Sēsē	tămen	et	tion of his — Divitiacus's—influence. Still love for his brother and public opinion affected him greatly. Now if Caesar should
his,	*he used.*		*Himself,*	*yet*	*both*	
15 amōre	frāternō	et	exīstimātiōne		vulgī	
by love	*fraternal*	*and*	*the opinion*		*of the people*	
16 commovērī.			Quod	sī	quid	
to be moved (he was moved).			*As to which*	*if*	*anything*	

—— perniciem, acc. sing. of the noun *perniciēs, -ēī*, f. (per, *intensive* + necō [*nex, death*]); hence *perniciēs* = lit. *utter destruction. perniciem* is the obj. of the prep. *ad.*

LINE 14. suam, acc. sing. f. of the poss. and reflexive pron. *suus, -a, -um;* it is an attributive of the noun *perniciem; suam* refers to Divitiacus. The reader will note that this noun-phrase, and the gerundive-phrase in the preceding line denote *purpose.* —— ūterētur, 3d pers. sing. imperf. subjunctive of the verb *ūtor, -ī, ūsus,* 3; it agrees with a pron. implied in the ending as subject-nom., referring to Dumnorix. *ūterētur* is in the subjunctive mode, because it is in a subordinate clause in the *ōrātiō oblīqua.* The student will observe that this member of the sentence by the phrase *quibus opibus,* which = *et eīs opibus,* is connected with *crēvisset,* and is in the subjunctive for the same reason. See note on *crēvisset,* l. 11, above. —— Sēsē, acc. sing. of the reflexive pron. *suī, sibi, sē, sē,* reduplicated; *sēsē* is the subject-acc. of *commovērī.* —— tămen, adv., introduces a thought in opposition to concession, expressed or implied. —— et ... et, conjunctions = *both ... and.* The *ōrātiō rēcta* of lines 4-14 reads: *Sciō haec esse vēra, nec quisquam ex eō plūs quam egō dolōris capit, proptereā quod, cum egō ipse grātiā plūrimum domī atque in reliquā Galliā possem, ille minimum propter adolēscentiam posset, per mē crēvit; quibus opibus āc nervīs nōn sōlum ad minuendam grātiam, sed paene ad perniciem meam ūtitur.*

LINE 15. amōre, abl. sing. of the noun *amor, -ōris,* m. (*amō*); abl. of cause after the pass. verb *commovērī.* Consult A. & G. 245; B. 165; G. 408; H. 416. Synonyms: *amor* = *love* in the most comprehensive sense, inclusive of even the affection of brutes; whereas *caritās,* denoting the impulse of affection arising from esteem and reflection, is used of men only. —— frāternō, abl. sing. m. of the adj. *frāternus, -a, -um (frāter);* it is an attributive of *amōre.* —— et, see *et* in preceding line. —— existimātiōne, abl. sing. of the noun *existimātiō, -ōnis,* f.; connected by the conjunction *et* with *amōre,* and in the same grammatical construction. Synonyms: *aestimātiō (aestimō)* = the extrinsic value of an object; whereas *existimātiō* (ex + *aestimō*) = *an opinion* after estimating the value of an object, i.e. = *an opinion* of an object because of its value. —— vulgī, gen. sing. of *vu(o)lgus, -ī,* n. (digammated from the Gk. ὄχλος); as a gen. it limits *existimātiōne.* Observe that *vu(o)lgus,* though usually neuter, is m. in *Verg.* A. 2, 99. Synonyms: *vulgus* = *the crowd, the rabble; plēbs* = *the common people* in distinction from the patricians; and *populus* = *the people* in their civil capacity.

LINE 16. commovērī, pres. inf. pass. of the verb *commoveō, -ēre, -mōvī, -mōtum,* 2; pass. parts: *commoveor, -vērī, -mōtus,* 2; its subject-acc. is *Sēsē,* l. 14, above. —— Quod, adverbial acc. n. of the rel. *quī, quae, quod* = lit. *as to which;* but in transitions with *sī* = *now if,* or *but if, and if,* according to meaning of context. —— sī, conditional particle, introducing a protasis. —— quid, nom. sing. of the indef. pron. *quis, quae, quid,* used substantively, and subject-nom. of *accidisset.*

152   CAESAR'S GALLIC WAR   [CHAP. XX.

| visit Dumnorix with severe punishment, every one would think that the punishment had been inflicted with his consent, inasmuch as he was Caesar's intimate friend; and the | eī *to him* cum *since* eum *him* (would think) | ā *from* ipse *he himself* tenēret, *held,* nōn *not* | Caesare *Caesar* eum *that* nēminem *no one* suā *by his* | gravius *too severe* locum *place* volūtāte *will* | accidisset, 17 *should happen,* amīcitiae *of friendship* exīstimātūrum 19 *to be about to think* factum; 20 *(it) to have been done;* |

LINE 17. eī, dat. sing. m. of the dem. pron. *is, ea, id,* used as a personal pron. of the 3d pers.; dat. of the indirect obj. after *accidisset. eī* refers to Dumnorix. —— ā, prep. with the abl. (*ā* before consonants, *ab* before either vowels or consonants). —— **Caesare,** abl. sing. of the proper noun *Caesar, -aris,* m.; abl. of the source or agent. The construction is somewhat anomalous: the agent usually follows pass. verbs; but *if anything should happen to him from Caesar* would = *if anything should be done to him by Caesar.* Consult A. & G. 246, and NOTE; B. 96, REM. 1, end; G. 401; H. 415, I. —— **gravius,** acc. sing. n. of the comparative adj. *gravior, -us; gravius* modifies the substantive indef. pron. *quid,* and = *too severely.* Consult A. & G. 93, *a*; B. 163, REM. 6; G. 297, 2; H. 444, 1. —— **accidisset,** 3d pers. sing. pluperf. subjunctive of *accidō, -ere, -cidī* (ad + cadere); hence *accidere* = lit. *to fall to,* i.e. *to befall. accidisset* agrees with *quid* expressed as subject-nom.; it is in the subjunctive after *sī* in the protasis for the fut. perf. in direct discourse, i.e. for *acciderit.*

LINE. 18. **cum,** conj. causal; here it = *since.* —— **ipse,** nom. sing. m. of the emphatic dem. pron. *ipse, -sa, -sum,* gen. *ipsīus,* dat. *ipsī;* it refers to Divitiacus; it is expressed for emphasis, and is the subject-nom. of the verb *tenēret.* —— **eum,** acc. sing. m. of the dem. pron. *is, ea, id;* it is an attributive of *locum.* —— **locum,** acc. sing. of the noun *locus, -ī,* m.; plur. *locī* or *loca,* i.e. m. or n., but with difference of signification; see note on *locī,* l. 10, Chap. II. *locum* is the direct obj. of *tenēret.* —— **amīcitiae,** gen. sing. of the noun *amīcitia, -ae,* f. (*amīcus*); as a gen. it limits *locum.* —— **apud,** prep. with the acc. = *among, with, before;* with names of persons it sometimes = *at the house of.*

LINE 19. **eum,** acc. sing. m. of the dem. pron. *is, ea, id,* used as a personal pron. of the 3d pers.; it here refers to Caesar; it is the obj. of the prep. *apud.* —— **tenēret,** 3d pers. sing. imperf. subjunctive of *teneō, -ere, -uī, tentum,* 2; it agrees with its subject-nom. *ipse,* expressed; it is a subjunctive after *cum* causal. See A. & G. 326; B. 198, (*c*); G. 586; H. 517. —— **nēminem,** acc. sing. of the noun *nēmō, -inis* (nē + homō); used only in the nom. and acc.; for the gen. *nūlīus* and *nulō* are used, but *nēmine* sometimes occurs with a pass. participle. *nēminem* is subject-acc. of *exīstimātūrum* (*esse*). —— **exīstimātūrum** (**esse**), fut. inf. act. of the verb *exīstimō, -āre, -āvī, -ātum,* 1 (ex + aestimō); its subject-acc. is *nēminem.*

LINE 20. **nōn,** adv. (nē + oenum or ūnum); it modifies *factum* (*esse*); but *nēminem nōn* = a general affirmative, i.e. = *every one.* —— **suā,** abl. sing. f. of the poss. pron. *suus, -a, -um;* it is an attributive of *voluntāte.* —— **voluntāte,** abl. sing. of the noun *voluntās, -ātis,* f.; abl. of *in accordance with.* See A. & G. 253, and NOTE; B. 162; G. 397; H. 416. For synonyms, see l. 19, Chap. VII. —— **factum** (**esse**), perf. inf. of *fīō, fierī, factus,* used as the pass. of *faciō, -ere, fēcī, factum,* 3. Supply *id* as subject-acc. of *factum* (*esse*), referring to *quid gravius,* lines 16 and 17, above.

21 quā	ex	rē	futūrum,	utī	tōtīus	outcome would be that the affections of all the people of Gaul would be alienated from him.
which	*from*	*thing* (it)	*to be about to be,*	*that*	*of entire*	
22 Galliae	animī	ā	sē	āverterentur.		
Gaul	*the affections*	*from*	*himself*	*would be turned.*		
23 Haec	cum	plūribus	verbīs	flēns	ā	When thus with many words he was tearfully be-
These (things) *when*	*with very many*	*words*	*weeping,*	*from*		

LINE 21. **quā**, abl. sing. of the rel. pron. *quī, quae, quod;* used here adjectively as an attributive of the noun *rē.* —— **ex**, prep. with the abl. (*ē* before consonants, *ex* before either vowels or consonants). Observe that *ex = from* within a place or thing—from the interior, while *ab = from* the external border of any place or thing; and *dē = from* any fixed point; but *dē* and *ex* with the abl. instead of the partitive gen. after cardinal numerals = *of.* —— **rē**, abl. sing. of the noun *rēs, reī,* f.; *rē* is the obj. of the prep. *ex.* The phrase *quā ex rē* refers to the notion of his ordering the punishment of Dumnorix. Observe the position of the monosyllabic prep. between the noun and its modifier; and consult A. & G. 345, *a*; B. 58. 2; G. 413, REM. 1; H. 569, II, 1. —— **futūrum** (esse), fut. inf. of the intrans. verb *sum, esse, fuī;* used impersonally; and note that *futūrum* (*esse*), *utī* . . . *āverterentur* form a periphrasis for the fut. pass. in direct discourse. See A. & G. 288, *f*; B. 195 (*b*), G. 531, PERIPHRASTIC FUTURE; H. 537, 3. —— **utī**, conj., the original form = *utī;* compare GK. ὡς. Note that the clause *utī* . . . *āverterentur* is the real subj. of *futūrum* (*esse*). See A. & G. 332, *a*, 2; B. 201, REM. 1, (*c*); G. 553, 3; H. 501, I. —— **tōtīus**, gen. sing. f. of the adj. *tōtus, -a, -um;* gen. *tōtīus,* dat. *tōtī. tōtīus* as a gen. limits *Galliae.*

LINE 22. **Galliae**, gen. sing. of the proper noun *Gallia, -ae,* f.; as a gen. it limits *animī.* —— **animī**, nom. plur. of the noun *animus, -ī,* m.; it is gen. sing.-nom. of *āverterentur.* For synonyms, see note on *animō,* l. 2, Chap. X. —— **ā**, prep. with the abl. (*ā* before consonants, *ab* before vowels or consonants). —— **sē**, abl. of the reflexive pron. *suī, sibi, sē;* — same form in both numbers; *sē* is the obj. of the prep. *ā.* Observe that actual separation after verbs compounded with a prep. requires the repetition of the prep. See A. & G. 243, *b*; B. 160, REM. 1; G. 390, 1; H. 413. —— **āverterentur**, 3d pers. plur. imperf. subjunctive pass. of *āvertō, -ere, -vertī, -versum,* 3 (ā + *vertere*); hence *āvertere* = lit. *to turn from. āverterentur* agrees with its subject-nom. *animī;* it is in the subjunctive of result after *utī.* The *ōrātiō rēcta* of lines 14–22 : Ego tamen et amōre frāternō et exīstimātiōne vulgī commoveor. Quod sī quid eī ā *tē* gravius *acciderit,* cum *egō* ipse *hunc* locum amīcitiae apud *tē teneam, nēmo exīstimābit* nōn *meā* voluntāte factum; quā ex rē tōtīus Galliae animī ā *mē āverterentur.*

LINE 23. **Haec**, acc. plur. n. of the dem. pron. *hīc, haec, hōc;* it refers to the things just mentioned; grammatically it is the direct obj. of *peteret.* —— **cum**, conj., temporal. Observe the emphasis put on *haec* by putting it before *cum.* —— **plūribus**, abl. pl. of the comparative *plūs, plūris;* positive *multus,* superl. *plūrimus. plūribus* is an attributive of *verbīs.* —— **verbīs**, abl. plur. of the noun *verbum, -ī,* n.; abl. of manner. A. & G. 248; B. 168; G. 399; H. 419, III. —— **flēns**, nom. sing. of the pres. participle *flēns, flentis* of the verb *fleō, -ēre, flēvī, flētum;* the participle as such agrees with the subj. of the verb *peteret,* to be supplied. —— **ā**, prep. with the abl. (*ā* before consonants, *ab* before either vowels or consonants).

154   CAESAR'S GALLIC WAR   [CHAP. XX.

| seeching Caesar, Caesar grasped his right hand, and cheering him, begged him to make an end of his petition. He declared that Divitiacus's influ- | Caesare *Caesar* prēndit; *takes;* faciat; *he will make;* | peteret, *he sought,* cōnsolātus *consoling (him),* tantī *of such worth,* | Caesar *Caesar* rogat, *he asks, (that)* ēius *his,* | ēius *his* fīnem *an end* apud *with* | dextram 24 *right hand* ōrandī 25 *of pleading* sē grātiam 26 *himself, influence,* |

LINE 24. **Caesare**, abl. of *Caesar, -aris,* m.; it is the obj. of the prep. *a*. The reader of Latin is aware that verbs of *asking* take a primary and a secondary obj., i.e. the acc. of the person and the acc. of the thing. But *petō* takes the acc. of the thing, and the abl. of the person, as in the text. Consult A. & G. 239, 2. *c*, and NOTE 1; B. 151, REM. 2; G. 339, REM. 1; H. 374, 2, NOTE 4. —— **peteret**, 3d pers. sing. imperf. subjunctive act. of *petō, -ere, petīvī (petiī), petītum,* 3; it agrees with a pron. implied in the ending as its subject-nom., referring to Divitiacus; it is in the subjunctive after *cum* temporal or historical. A. & G. 325; B. 222; G. 585; H. 521, II, 2. —— **Caesar, -aris,** m., subject-nom. of *prēndit*. —— **ēius**, gen. sing. m. of the dem. pron. *is, ea, id,* used as a personal pron. of the 3d pers.; it refers to Divitiacus; as a gen. it limits *dextram*. —— **dextram**, acc. sing. of the noun *dextra, -ae,* f.; really the fem. of the adj. *dexter, -tra, -trum,* used substantively; or supply *manum; dextram* is the direct obj. of *prēndit*.

LINE 25. **prēndit**, 3d pers. sing. pres. ind. act. of the verb *prēndō, -ere, prēndī, prēnsum,* 3; it agrees with a pron. implied in the ending as subject-nom., referring to Caesar. A longer form *prehendō* is in use from which *prēndo* comes by syncopation of the *h*, and the contraction of the vowels into long *ē* (prae + hendō). —— **cōnsolātus**, perf. participle of the deponent verb *cōnsolor, -ārī, -ātus,* 1. The participle is used in an active signification; supply *eum*, i.e. *Divitiacum*, as the direct obj. —— **rogat**, 3d pers. sing. pres. ind. act. of *rogō, -āre, -āvī, -ātum,* 1; it agrees with a personal pron. implied in the ending as subject-nom., referring to Caesar; historical present. —— **fīnem**, acc. sing. of the noun *fīnēs, -is,* m. and f. in the sing.; always m. in the plur. *fīnem* is the direct obj. of *faciat*. —— **ōrandī**, gen. of the gerund of the verb *ōrō, -āre, -āvī, -ātum,* 1 (*ōrō ab ōre,* abl. of *ōs, ōris,* n.). *ōrandī* as a gen. limits *fīnem*. Consult A. & G. 298; B. 184, REM. 4, 1; G. 428; H. 542, I.

LINE 26. **faciat**, 3d pers. sing. pres. subjunctive act. of the verb *faciō, -ere, fēcī, factum,* 3; it agrees with a pron. implied in the ending as its subject-nom., referring to Divitiacus; subjunctive of purpose after *ut*, to be supplied. Consult A & G. 331, and 2. REM.; B. 200, REM. 3; G. 546, REM. 2; H. 499, 2. —— **tantī**, gen. sing. n. of the adj. *tantus, -a, -um;* used substantively; or *pretiī* may be supplied. *tantī* is predicate gen. of price after *esse*. See A. & G. 252, *a*; B. 137; G. 380, REM. 1; H. 405. —— **ēius**, gen. sing. m. of the dem. pron. *is, ea, id,* used as a personal pron. of the 3d pers.; as a gen. it limits *grātiam*. —— **apud**, prep. with the acc. = *at, among, with, in the presence of;* sometimes with a personal pron. = *at the house of*. —— **sē**, acc. sing. m. of the reflexive pron. *suī, sibi, sē, sē* — same form in both numbers; *sē* is the obj. of the prep. *apud*. —— **grātiam**, acc. sing. of the noun *grātia, -ae,* f.; subject-acc. of the verb *esse*. Synonyms: *grātia* (derived from *grātus,* GK. χάρις), *favor* both subjective and objective; i.e. *grātia = the favor* one feels for another, or *the favor* in which one stands with another; whereas the Latin word *favor* has only a subjective signification; and *benevolentia* (bene + volēns) has always in it the notion of subjectivity = *love and good-will to another*.

27 esse	ostendit,	utī	et	reī-pūblicae		iniūriam
to be (is),	*he shows,*	*that*	*both*	*the republic's*		*injury*
28 et	suum	dolōrem		ēius	voluntātī	āc
and	*his own*	*vexation,*		*to his*	*wish*	*and*
29 precibus	condōnet.		Dumnorigem		ad	sē
prayers,	*he will surrender.*		*Dumnorix*		*to*	*himself*
30 vocat,	frātrem	adhibet;	quae		in	eō
he calls,	(*his*) *brother*	*he brings in;*	*what* (*things*)		*in*	*him*

ence was worth so much to him, that he would condone the wrong done to the state and the affront to himself, at his wish and prayer. He summoned Dumnorix to his presence; he brought in his brother; he dis-

LINE 27. **esse**, pres. inf. of the intrans. verb *sum, esse, fuī, futūrus.* —— **ostendit**, 3d pers. sing. pres. ind. act. of the verb *ostendō, ere, -tendī, -tentum,* 3 (ob + tendere); hence *ostendere* = lit. *to stretch toward.* *ostendit* agrees with a pron. im-. plied in its ending as subject-nom., referring to Caesar. —— **utī**, see note on this particle, l. 21, above. —— **et . . . et**, conjunctions repeated in coördinate phrases; sometimes called correlatives. —— **reī-pūblicae**, gen. of the compound noun *rēs-pūblica;* both parts of the compound are declined; objective gen.; limits *iniūriam.* —— **iniūriam**, acc. sing. of the noun *iniūria, -ae,* f. (in, *negative* + iūs); *iniūriam* is a direct obj. of *condōnet.*

LINE 28. **et**, see *et* immediately preceding. —— **suum**, acc. sing. m. of the poss. and reflexive pron. *suus, -a, -um. suum* is an attributive of *dolōrem.* —— **dolōrem**, acc. sing. of the noun *dolor, -ōris,* m.; connected by the conj. *et* with *iniūriam,* and in the same grammatical construction. —— **ēius**, gen. sing. m. of the dem. pron. *is, ea, id,* used as a personal pron. of the 3d pers.; as a gen. it limits *voluntātī;* it refers to Divitiacus. —— **voluntātī**, dat. of the noun *voluntās, -ātis,* f. (*volō*); dat. of the indirect obj. of *condōnet.* —— **āc**, conj.; see note on *atque,* l. 10, Chap. I.

LINE 29. **precibus**, dat. plur. of an assumed *prex, precis,* f.; but used in the sing. only in the abl. case. *precibus* is connected by the conj. *āc* with *voluntātī,* and is in the same grammatical construction. —— **condōnet**, 3d pers. sing. pres. subjunctive of the verb *condōnō, -āre, -āvī, ātum,* I (con +dōnāre); hence *condōnāre* = lit. *to give up. condōnet* is the subjunctive of result after *utī,* referring to *tantī.* Observe that the lit. translation is, substantially: Caesar *gives up* his indignation *to the* wish and prayers of Divitiacus; which is tantamount to saying that he pardons Dumnorix on account of Divitiacus's wish and prayers. Synonyms: *condōnāre* = *to give up;* then *to give up as a debt;* hence *to pardon;* whereas *ignōscere* = to pardon an offense by overlooking it. —— **Dumnorigem**, acc. sing. of *Dumnorix, -igis,* m.; direct obj. of *vocat.* —— **ad**, prep. with the acc. —— **sē**, acc. sing. of the reflexive pron. *suī, sibi, sē, sē* — same form in both numbers; *sē* is the obj. of the prep. *ad.*

LINE 30. **vocat**, 3d pers. sing. pres. ind. act. of the verb *vocō, -āre, -āvī, -ātum;* it agrees with a pron. implied in the ending as subject-nom., referring to Caesar. Synonyms: *appellāre, nōmenāre, vocāre; appellāre* = *to call* — to appeal to for help; *nōmenāre* = *to call* by designating the name; whereas *vocāre* = *to call* — often in the sense of *to summon,* as in the text. —— **frātrem**, acc. sing. of the noun *frāter, -tris,* m.; direct obj. of *adhibet.* —— **adhibet**, 3d pers. sing. pres. ind. act. of *adhibeō, -ēre, -uī, -itum,* 2 (ad + habēre); hence *adhibēre* = lit. *to have to,* i.e. *to bring in.* —— **quae**, acc. plur. n. of the interrogative pron. *quis, quae, quid;* used here adjectively,

156   CAESAR'S GALLIC WAR   [CHAP. XX.

closed the censurable acts of Dumnorix; he set forth his own discoveries, and the complaints of the citizens; he warned him for the future to avoid every suspicious act; he	reprehendat, *he censures,* intellegat, *knows,* proponit; *he sets forth;* tempus *time*	ostendit; *he shows;* quae *what (things)* monet, *he warns (him),* omnēs *all*	quae *what (things)* cīvitās *the state* ut in *that for* suspiciōnēs *suspicions*	ipse 31 *he himself* querātur, 32 *complains of,* reliquum 33 *the remaining* vītet; 34 *he should shun;*

agreeing with the noun *things* understood; or may be regarded as used substantively; *quae* is the direct obj. of *reprehendat*. —— **in**, prep. with either the acc. or abl., though with different significations; see note on *in*, l. 1, end, Chap. I; here *in* takes the abl. —— **eō**, abl. sing. m. of the dem. pron. *is, ea, id*, used as a personal pron. of the 3d pers. *eō* is the obj. of the prep. *in;* it refers to Dumnorix.

LINE 31. **reprehendat**, 3d pers. sing. pres. ind. act. of the verb *reprehendo, -ere, -hendī, -hēnsum*, 3 (re + prehendere); see note on *prēndit*, l. 25, above. *reprehendat* agrees with a pron. implied in the ending as its subject-nom., referring to Caesar; subjunctive, because an indirect question. See A. & G. 334; B. 242; G. 467; H. 529, I. —— **ostendit**, 3d pers. sing. pres. ind. act. of *ostendō, -ere, -tendī, -tentum*, 3 (ob + tendere); it agrees with the subject-nom. *Caesar*, to be supplied. Observe that the indirect question-clause, as a noun-clause, is the direct obj. of *ostendit*. —— **quae**, acc. plur. n. of the interrogative *quis, quae, quid;* direct obj. of *intellegat*. —— **ipse**, nom. sing. m. of the intensive dem. pron. *ipse, -sa, -sum*, gen. *ipsīus*, dat. *ipsī; ipse* is expressed for emphasis = *he himself*, and is subject-nom. of *intellegat*.

LINE 32. **intellegat**, 3d pers. sing. pres. subjunctive of the verb *intellego, -ere, -lēxī, -lēctum*, 3; it agrees with its subject-nom. *ipse*, i.e. *Caesar*, and is in the subjunctive, because an indirect question. —— **quae**, acc. plur. of the interrogative *quis, quae, quid;* direct obj. of *querātur*. See note on *quae*, preceding line. —— **cīvitās**, nom. sing. of the noun *cīvitās, -ātis*, f. (*cīves*); abs. *prō concrētō; cīvitās*, here = *cīvēs cīvitātis. cīvitās* is the subject-nom. of *querātur*. —— **querātur**, 3d pers. sing. pres. subjunctive of the deponent verb *queror, -ī, questus*, 3; it agrees with its subject-nom. *cīvitās;* it is in the subjunctive, because an indirect question.

LINE 33. **prōpōnit**, 3d pers. sing. pres. ind. of the verb *prōpōnō, -ere, -posuī, -positum*, 3 (prō + pōnere); it agrees with *Caesar*, to be supplied as subject-nom. The reader will observe that Caesar narrates from the 23d line through this chapter from the *repraesentātiō* point of view, i.e. the verbs are in the historical pres. tense. The reader will further observe the omission of the copulative conj. (asyndeton) between the two indirect question-clauses that as noun-clauses are direct objects of *prōpōnit*. —— **monet**, 3d pers. sing. pres. ind. act. of the verb *moneō, -ēre, monuī, monitum*, 2; historical pres.; it agrees with *Caesar* understood, as subject-nom. —— **ut**, telic conj. —— **in**, prep. with the acc. or abl.; here it takes the acc. and = *for*. —— **reliquum**, acc. sing. n. of the adj. *reliquus, -a, -um;* it is an attributive of *tempus*. For synonyms, see note on *reliqua*, l. 7, Chap. V.

LINE 34. **tempus**, acc. sing. of the noun *tempus, -oris*, n.; *tempus* is the obj. of the prep. *in*. As to the etymology, see note on *tempore*, l. 21, Chap. III. As to the idiomatic expression relative to *tempus*, see A. & G. 259, *b*; B. 171, REM. 5; G. 418, 1; H. 429, 2. —— **omnēs**, acc. plur. f. of the adj. *omnis, -e*, an *i*-stem.

BOOK I.   157

35 praeterita	sē	Divitiacō	frātrī	condōnāre	told him that he would condone the past for the sake of his brother Divitiacus. He appointed guards for Dumnorix that he might be informed both as to his actions and companions.
bygones,	*himself,*	*to Divitiacus*	*(his) brother*	*to give up,*	
36 dīcit.	Dumnorigī	custōdēs		pōnit,	ut,
he says.	*For Dumnorix*	*guards*		*he places,*	*that*
37 quae	agat,	quibuscum	loquātur,		scīre
what (things) he may do,		*whom with,*	*he may talk,*		*to know*
38 possit.					
he may be able.					

omnēs is an attributive of *suspiciōnēs*. —— **suspiciōnēs**, acc. plur. of the noun *suspiciō, -ōnis,* f. (*suspicārī,* to suspect). *suspiciōnēs* is the direct obj. of the verb *vītet*. —— **vītet**, 3d pers. sing. pres. subjunctive act. of the verb *vītō, -āre, -āvī, -ātum;* it agrees with a pron. implied in the ending as its subject-nom., referring to Dumnorix; subjunctive of purpose after *ut,* telic. Consult A. & G. 317, and 331; B. 200, (*b*), and REM. 2; G. 545 and 546; H. 497, II, and 498, 1.

LINE 35. **praeterita**, a participial acc. plur. of the participle *praeteritus, -a, -um* of the verb *praetereō, -īre, -īvī (-iī), -itum,* 4; used in the neuter plur. as a substantive. *praeterita* is the direct obj. of *condōnāre*. —— **sē**, acc. sing. of the reflexive pron. *suī, sibī, sē, sē;* it refers to Caesar; it is subject-acc. of *condōnāre*. —— **Divitiacō**, dat. of the proper noun *Divitiacus, -ī,* m.; dat. of the indirect obj. after *condōnāre;* see note on *voluntātī,* l. 28, above. —— **frātrī**, dat. of the noun *frāter, -tris,* m.; an appositive of *Divitiacō*. —— **condōnāre**, pres. inf. act. of the verb *condōnō, -āre, -āvī, -ātum,* 1; its subject-acc. is the pron. *sē;* and the entire construction: *praeterita sē . . . condōnāre* is a substantive construction, and as such is the direct obj. of *dīcit*.

LINE 36. **dīcit**, 3d pers. sing. pres. ind. act. of the verb *dīcō, -ere, -dīxī, -dictum,* 3; historic pres., and agrees with *Caesar,* to be supplied, as subject-nom. —— **Dumnorigī**, dat. of the proper noun *Dumnorix, -igis,* m.; dat. of the indirect obj. after the verb *pōnit*. —— **custōdēs**, acc. plur. of the noun *custōs, -ōdis,* m. and f.; acc. of the direct obj. after *pōnit*. Consult A. & G. 225; B. 141; G. 345; H. 384, II. —— **pōnit**, 3d pers. sing. pres. ind. act. of the verb *pōnō, -ere, posuī, positum,* 3; historical pres.; it agrees with Caesar, to be supplied, as subject-nom. —— **ut**, telic conj.; it introduces the telic clause *scīre possit*.

LINE 37. **quae**, acc. plur. of the interrogative pron. *quis, quae, quid;* it is the direct obj. of the verb *agat*. —— **agat**, 3d pers. sing. pres. subjunctive of the verb *agō, -ere, ēgī, actum,* 3; it agrees with a pron. implied in the ending as its subject-nom., referring to *Dumnorigī;* subjunctive, because in an indirect question. —— **quibuscum** (quibus + cum). *quibus* is the abl. plur. of the interrogative *quis, quae, quid;* it is the obj. of the enclitic *cum,* to which it is appended. As to the enclitic *cum* with pronouns, see A. & G. 99, *e*; B. 79, 2; G. 413, REM. 1; H. 184, 6. —— **loquātur**, 3d pers. sing. pres. subjunctive of the deponent verb *loquor, -ī, locūtus,* 3; it agrees with Dumnorix, to be supplied, as its subject-nom.; subjunctive, because in a clause containing an indirect question. —— **scīre**, pres. inf. act. of the verb *sciō, scīre, scīvī (-iī), scītum,* 4; complementary inf. Consult A. & G. 271; B. 181; G. 423; H. 533, I, 2. As to synonyms, see note on *scīre,* l. 4, above.

LINE 38. **possit**, 3d pers. sing. pres. subjunctive of the intrans. verb *possum, posse, potuī* (potis, *able* + sum); *possit* is subjunctive of purpose after *ut*. Consult A. & G. 317; B. 200, (*b*); G. 543, 3; H. 497, II.

158 CAESAR'S GALLIC WAR [CHAP. XXI.

XXI. On the same day as that of this interview with Divitiacus, Caesar was informed by scouts that the enemy had encamped at the foot of a mountain eight miles distant from his own camp; and he	XXI.	Eōdem	diē	ab	explōrātōribus 1
		On the	same day	by	scouts
	certior	factus	hostēs	sub	monte 2
	more certain	being made,	the enemy	under	the mountain
	cōnsēdisse		mīlia	passuum	ab ipsīus 3
	to have encamped,		thousands,	of paces	from his
	castrīs	octō,	quālis	esset	nātūrā 4
	camp,	eight,	of what sort	was	the nature

LINE 1. **Eōdem**, abl. sing. m. of the iterative dem. pron. *īdem, eadem, idem*, gen. *ēiusdem; eōdem* is an attributive of the noun *diē*. —— **diē**, abl. sing. of the noun *diēs, diēī*, m. or f. in sing.; always m. in the plur. See A. & G. 256, 1; B. 171; G. 393; H. 429. —— **ab**, prep. with the abl. (*ā* before consonants only, *ab* before either vowels or consonants). —— **explōrātōribus**, abl. plur. of *explōrātor, -ōris*, m.; it is the abl. of the agent after the prep. *ab*. Consult A. & G. 246; B. 166; G. 401; H. 415, I.

LINE 2. **certior**, nom. sing. of the adj. comparative degree *certior, -us*; positive *certus*, superl. *certissimus*. *certior* is predicate adj. after *factus*. —— **factus**, perf. participle of *fīō, fierī, factus*, used as pass. of *faciō, -ere, fēcī, factum*, 3; as a participle it agrees with Caesar, to be supplied as the subject-nom. of the verb *mīsit*. For the acc. and inf. following the phrase *certior factus*, as an expression of *telling*, see A. & G. 336, I, and FOOTNOTE (3); B. 194, 2; G. 527, 2; H. 535, 2. —— **hostēs**, acc. plur. of the noun *hostis, -is*, m. and f.; it is the subject-acc. of *cōnsēdisse*. For synonyms, see note on *hostium*, l. 15, Chap. XI. —— **sub**, prep. with either the acc. or abl.; here it takes the abl. For the meaning of the prep., see A. & G. 153, *Sub, b*; B. 120, 3; G. 418, 2, (*b*); H. 435, I, *Sub*. —— **monte**, abl. sing. of the noun *mōns, montis*, m. *monte* is the object of the prep. *sub*.

LINE 3. **cōnsēdisse**, perf. inf. act. of the verb *cōnsīdō, -ere, -sēdī, -sessum*, 3 (con, *intensive* + sēdere = lit. *to sit down*). —— **mīlia**, acc. plur. of the adj. *mille*, indeclinable in the sing., used substantively in the plur., and regularly declined like an *i*-stem — sometimes written *millia*. *mīlia* is the acc. of *extent of space*. A. & G. 257; B. 153; G. 335; H. 379. —— **passuum**, gen. plur. of the noun *passus, -ūs*, m.; partitive gen. after *mīlia*. Consult A. & G. 216, 2; B. 134; G. 370; H. 397, 2. —— **ab**, prep. with the abl.; see note on *ab*, l. 1, above. —— **ipsīus**, gen. sing. m. of the intensive dem. pron. *ipse, -sa, -sum*; it refers to Caesar; it is expressed for emphasis; as a gen. it limits *castrīs*.

LINE 4. **castrīs**, abl. plur. of the noun *castrum*, n.; in the sing. = *a fortress*; in the plur. = *a camp; castrīs* is the obj. of the prep. *ab*. —— **octō**, an indecl. num. adj.; it modifies *mīlia*. Note the phrase *ab ipsīus castrīs* embodied in the phrase *mīlia passuum . . . octō*, by which the entire group of words is made emphatic. —— **quālis**, predicate-nom. of the interrogative pron. *quālis, -e (quis)*; predicate after *esset*. —— **esset**, 3d pers. sing. imperf. subjunctive of the verb *sum, esse, fuī, futūrus*; it agrees with its subject-nom. *nātūra*; it is the subjunctive, because an *indirect question*. Consult A. & G. 334; B. 242; G. 467; H. 529, I. —— **nātūrā, -ae**, nom. sing. f. (*nāscor*, be born); hence *nātūra* = lit. *birth*, rare; transf. = *nature*, the character of a thing or person. *nātūra* is the subject-nom. of *esset*.

LINES 5-9.]   BOOK I.   159

5 montis	et	quālis	in	circuitū
of the mountain	*and*	*of what sort*	*in*	*the circuit*
6 ascēnsus	quī	cōgnōscerent,		mīsit.
the ascent	*(those) who*	*might ascertain*		*he sent.*
7 Renūntiātum est		facilem	esse.	Dē
It was reported		*easy*	*to be.*	*In the course of*
8 tertiā	vigiliā	T. Labiēnum,		lēgātum
the third	*watch*	*Titus Labienus,*		*the lieutenant*
9 prō	praetōre,	cum	duābus	legiōnibus
in the place of	*the praetor,*	*with*	*two*	*legions*

sent men to find out what kind of a mountain it was, and what sort of an ascent there might be in some roundabout way. The ascent was reported to him to be easy. He ordered his lieutenant with praetorial powers, Titus Labienus, to

LINE 5. **montis**, gen. sing. of the noun *mōns, montis*, m.; as a gen. it limits *nātūra*. —— **et**, cop. conj.; connects the clauses. —— **quālis**, interrogative pron., predicate after *esset*, to be supplied. —— **in**, prep. with the acc. or abl.; here it takes the abl. —— **circuitū**, abl. sing. of the noun *circuitus, -ūs*, m. (circum + īre); it is the obj. of the prep. *in*. The phrase *in circuitū* = lit. *in a circuit*, i.e. *all around, round about*.

LINE 6. **ascēnsus**, nom. sing. of the noun *ascēnsus, -ūs*, m. (ad + scendere = *to ascend*, opposed to *descendere*). *ascēnsus* is the subject-nom. of *esset* understood. —— **quī**, nom. plur. of the rel. pron. *quī, quae, quod*; it refers to *mīlitēs* understood as its antecedent, but is the subject-nom. of *cōgnōscerent*. The supplied antecedent to the rel. *mīlitēs* is the direct obj. of *mīsit*. —— **cōgnōscerent**, 3d pers. plur. imperf. subjunctive of the verb *cōgnōscō, -ere, -nōvī, -nitum*, 3; it agrees with its subject-nom. *quī*; it is subjunctive mode, because in a clause expressing *the purpose* of *mīsit*. Consult A. & G. 317, 2; B. 233, 1; G. 630; H. 497, I. —— **mīsit**, 3d pers. sing. perf. ind. act. of the verb *mittō, -ere, mīsī, missum*, 3; it agrees with its subject-nom. *Caesar* understood.

LINE 7. **Renūntiātum est**, 3d pers. sing. perf. pass. of *renunt(c)iō, -āre, -āvī, -ātum*, 1; it is used here impersonally; but the real subj. is the infinitive clause *facilem esse (ascēnsum). est*, 3d pers. sing. pres. ind. of *sum, esse, fuī*; here used as a part of the compound tense *renūntiātum est*. —— **facilem**, acc. sing. m. of the adj. *facilis, -e*; an *ī*-stem; predicate-acc. after *esse*. —— **esse**, pres. inf. of the intrans. verb *sum, esse, fuī, futūrus*; its subject-acc. is *ascēnsum*, to be supplied. —— **Dē**, prep. with the abl.; here = *in the course of*; see note on *dē*, l. 10, Chap. XII, and on *dē*, l. 27, Chap. XIX.

LINE 8. **tertiā**, abl. sing. f. of the ordinal adj. *tertius, -a, -um*; it is an attributive of *vigiliā*. —— **vigiliā**, abl. sing. of the noun *vigilia, -ae*, f.; it is the obj. of the prep. *dē*; see note on *vigiliā*, l. 11, Chap. XII. —— **T.**, an abbreviation for the praenōmen *Titum*. —— **Labiēnum**, acc. sing. of *Labiēnus, -ī*, m.; in apposition with *lēgātum*. *Labiēnus* is the *cōgnōmen*; the nōmen was *Attius*; for the person alluded to was Titus Attius Labienus; see note on *Labiēnum*, l. 12, Chap. X. —— **lēgātum**, acc. sing. of the noun *lēgātus, -ī*, m. (*lēgere*, to delegate). *lēgātum* is subject-acc. of *ascendere*, l. 11, below.

LINE 9. **prō**, prep. with the abl. —— **praetōre**, abl. sing. of *praetor, -ōris*, m. (prae + itor [*īre*, to go]); *praetōre* is the obj. of the prep. *prō*. Here the phrase *prō praetōre* = *with the authority of a praetor*. The *praetor* had as his own right the power to command; the *lēgātus* only was temporarily invested with the power by

ascend during the third watch the highest point of the mountain's ridge, with two legions, and with those as guides who had reconnoitred the road; he stated to him his plan; and,	et and quid what	eīs those (as) suī of his own	ducibus, guides, cōnsiliī plan	quī who sit, is,	iter the route ostendit. he shows.	cōgnōverant, 10 had discovered,	
	summum the highest	iugum ridge	montis of the mountain	ascendere to climb	iubet; 11 he orders;	
					Ipse 12 He himself	

his general. Labienus had this power in his own right by special grant. He had authority, accordingly, *in place of*, i.e. as if he were *praetor*. —— **cum**, prep. with the abl. —— **duābus**, abl. sing. f. of the num. adj. *duo, duae, duo; duābus* is an attributive of *legiōnibus*. Note that *ūnus, duo* and *trēs* are the only cardinals up to *centum* that are declinable. —— **legiōnibus**, abl. plur. of the noun *legiō, -ōnis* (*legere*, to choose); hence the noun = *a chosen number*. *legiōnibus* is abl. of accompaniment with *cum*. A. & G. 248, *a*; B. 168; G. 392, and REM. 1; H. 419, I.

LINE 10. **et**, cop. conj. —— **eīs**, abl. plur. of the dem. pron. *is, ea, id*, used as a personal pron. of the 3d pers. = *them*, connected by the conj. *et* with *legiōnibus*, and in the same grammatical construction. —— **ducibus**, abl. plur. of the noun *dux, ducis* (compare *ducere*, to lead). *ducibus* is in apposition with *eīs*, used as a pron. *cum eīs ducibus* = *with them as guides*. —— **quī**, nom. plur. m. of the rel. pron. *quī, quae, quod;* it refers to *legiōnibus* and *ducibus*, and is the subject-nom. of *cōgnōverant*. —— **iter**, acc. sing. of the noun *iter, itineris*, n.; it is the direct obj. of *cōgnōverant*. —— **cōgnōverant**, 3d pers. plur. pluperf. ind. of the verb *cōgnōscō, -ere, -nōvī, -nitum*, 3 (con + [g]nōscere, compare GK. γιγνώσκω). *cōgnōverant* agrees with its subject-nom. *quī*.

LINE 11. **summum**, acc. sing. n. of the superl. degree of the adj. *superus*, comparative *superior*, superl. *suprēmus* or *summus*. *summum* is an attributive of *iugum*. —— **iugum**, acc. sing. of the noun *iugum, -ī*, n. (*iungere*, to join); hence the noun = lit. *a yoke;* transf. = *summit*, the phrase *summum iugum* = *the top of the ridge*. —— **montis**, gen. sing. of the noun *mōns, montis*, m. (radical *min*, compare *ēminens*, a projecting); hence *mōns* = lit. *a projection*, i.e. transf. *a towering mass, a mountain*. *montis* as a gen. limits *iugum*. —— **as(d)cendere**, pres. inf. act. of the verb *ascendō, -ere, ascendī, ascēnsum*, 3 (ad + scandere); differs fron *ēscendere* (ē + scandere) in that the latter = *to ascend from a place, to reach a high object* by exertion. *ascendere* with its subject-acc. *lēgātum* depends on *iubet*. —— **iubet**, 3d pers. sing. pres. ind. of the verb *iubeō, -ēre, iūssī, iūssum*, 2; it agrees with a pron. implied in the ending as subject-nom., referring to Caesar; *iubet* is an historical present.

LINE 12. **quid**, nom. sing. n. of the interrogative pron. *quis, quae, quid;* it is the subject-nom. of the intrans. verb *sit*. —— **suī**, gen. sing. n. of the poss. and reflexive pron. *suus, -a, -um;* it refers to Caesar, but is an attributive of the noun *cōnsiliī*. —— **cōnsiliī**, gen. sing. of the noun *cōnsilium, -ī*, n. *cōnsiliī* is predicate-gen. after *sit*. Consult A. & G. 214, *c*; B. 133; G. 366, and REM. 2; H. 401, and NOTE 2. The student will note that *quid suī cōnsiliī sit* = *quid suum cōnsilium sit*, nearly. —— **sit**, 3d pers. sing. pres. subjunctive of the neuter or intrans. verb *sum, esse, fuī, futūrus;* it is in the subjunctive mode, because the question is indirect. See A. & G. 334; B. 242; G. 467; H. 529, I. Observe that this indirect question as a noun-clause is the direct obj. of *ostendit*. —— **ostendit**, 3d pers. sing. pres. ind. act.

13 dē		quartā	vigiliā	eōdem	itinere,	during the fourth watch, Caesar himself hastened toward the enemy by the same road as they had gone, sending all his cavalry in advance. Publius Consīdius, who was thought to be very expert in military affairs,
in the course of		*the fourth*	*watch*	*by the same*	*route*	
14 quō		hostēs	ierant,	ad	eōs	contendit
by which		*the enemy*	*had gone,*	*toward*	*them*	*he hastens*
15 equitātumque		omnem	ante	sē	mittit.	
cavalry and		*all*	*before*	*him*	*he sends.*	
16 P. Cōnsidius,		quī	reī		mīlitāris	
Publius Considius,		*who*	*in regard to science*		*military*	

of the verb *ostendō, -ere, ostendī, ostentum*, 3 (ob + tendere). *ostendit* agrees with a pron. implied in the ending as subject-nom., referring to Caesar. —— **Ipse**, nom. sing. m. of the intensive dem. pron. *ipse, -sa, -sum*, gen. *ipsīus*, dat. *ipsī*; it refers to Caesar; it is expressed for emphasis; and is the subject-nom. of *contendit* and *mittit*, lines 14 and 15, below.

LINE 13. **dē**, prep. with the abl. —— **quartā**, abl. sing. of the ordinal *quartus, -a, -um*; it modifies *vigiliā*. —— **vigiliā**, abl. sing. of the noun *vigilia, -ae*, f.; it is the obj. of the prep. *dē*. But see note on this phrase, l. 8, above. —— **eōdem**, abl. sing. n. of the dem. pron. *idem, eadem, idem*; it is an attributive of the noun *itinere*. —— **itinere**, abl. sing. of the noun *iter, itineris*, n.; abl. of the *way by which*. Consult A. & G. 258, *g*; B. 167, 5, (*b*); G. 389; H. 420, 1, 3). For synonyms, see note on *via*, l. 2, Chap. IX.

LINE 14. **quō**, abl. sing. n. of the rel. pron. *quī, quae, quod;* it is used both relatively and adjectively; it refers to *itinere* as a rel. pron., and is also an attributive of *itinere*, to be supplied, which is in the same grammatical construction as the preceding *itinere: way by which*. —— **hostēs**, nom. plur. of the noun *hostis, -is*, m. and f.; it is subject-nom. of the verb *ierant*. Synonyms: *hostis* = *a public enemy; inimicus* = *a private foe*. —— **ierant**, 3d pers. plur. pluperf. ind. act. of the verb *eō, īre, īvī (iī), itum;* syncopated for *iveraut;* syncopation without contraction. See A. & G. 128, 2; B. 251, end; G. 131, 2; H. 235, 1. *ierant* agrees with its subject-nom. *hostēs*. —— **ad**, prep. with the acc. after a verb of motion. —— **eōs**, acc. plur. m. of the dem. pron. *is, ea, id*, used as a personal pron. of the 3d pers.; it is the obj. of the prep. *ad*. —— **contendit**, 3d pers. sing. pres. ind. act. of the verb *contendo, -ere, -dī, -tum*, 3; it agrees with a pron. implied in the ending as subject-nom., referring to Caesar. As to different significations of this verb, see note on *contendunt*, l. 18, Chap. I.

LINE 15. **equitātumque** (equitatum + que). *equitātum* is acc. sing. of the noun *equitātus, -ūs*, m. (from *equus* through *equitāre*). *equitātum* is the direct obj. of the verb *mittit*. *que*, enclitic conj., connects *contendit* and *mittit*. —— **omnem**, acc. sing. m. of the adj. *omnis, -e*, an *i*-stem; declined like *levis* or *mītis*. *omnem* is an attributive of *equitātem*. —— **ante**, adv. or prep.; here prep. with the acc. —— **sē**, acc. sing. m. of the reflexive pron. *suī, sibi, sē, sē;* it is the obj. of the prep. *ante;* it refers to Caesar. —— **mittit**, 3d pers. sing. historical pres. ind. act. of the verb *mittō, -ere, misi, missum*, 3; it agrees with a pron. implied in the ending, referring to Caesar.

LINE 16. **P.**, an abbreviation for *Pūblius, -ī*, m., a Roman *praenōmen*. —— **Cōnsidius, -ī**, m., subject-nom. of *praemittitur*, l. 19, below. Nothing more is known

162   CAESAR'S GALLIC WAR   [CHAP. XXII.

and who had had experience in Lucius Sulla's army, and, subsequently, in that of Marcus Crassus, was sent ahead with the scouts.	perītissimus *most skilled*	habēbātur *was held*	et *both*	in *in*	exercitū *the army*	17
	L. Sullae *of Lucius Sulla*	et *and*	posteā *afterwards*	in *in (that)*	M. Crassī *of Marcus Crassus*	18
	fuerat, *had been,*	cum *with*	explōrātōribus *the scouts*	praemittitur. *is sent ahead.*		19

of Considius than that he served under Caesar in the first Gallic campaign, 58 B.C.; and that, as here intimated, Caesar supposed that he could be relied on, because of his experience under Sulla and Crassus. —— **quī**, nom. sing. m. of the rel. pron. *quī, quae, quod;* it refers to *Considius*, but is the subject-nom. of *habēbātur.* —— **reī**, objective gen. of the noun *rēs, reī* (stem *rē,* shortened in gen. and dat. sing.); as a gen. it limits the adj. *perītissimus.* Consult A. & G. 218, *a*; B. 135; G. 374; H. 399, I. —— **mīlitāris**, gen. sing. f. of the adj. *mīlitāris, -re* (*mīles*); it is an attributive of *reī.*

LINE 17. **perītissimus**, nom. sing. m. of the superl. degree of the adj., positive degree *perītus,* comparative *perītior* (radical *perī,* as seen in *experior*); hence *perītus* = lit. *tested.* *perītissimus* is predicate adj. after the pass. verb *habēbātur.* —— **habēbātur**, 3d pers. sing. imperf. pass. of the act. verb *habeō, -ēre, -uī, -itum,* 2; pass. parts: *habeor, habērī, habitus; habēbātur* agrees with its subject-nom. *quī.* —— **et**, cop. conj.; it connects the verbs *habēbātur* and *fuerat.* —— **in**, prep. with either acc. or abl.; here it takes the abl. —— **exercitū**, abl. sing. of the noun *exercitus, -ūs,* m.; it is the obj. of the prep. *in.* For synonyms, see note on *exercitū,* l. 31, Chap. III.

LINE 18. **L.**, an abbreviation for *Lūciī,* gen. sing. of the proper noun *Lūcius, -iī,* m.; *praenōmen.* —— **Sullae**, gen. sing. of the proper noun *Sulla, -ae,* m.; *cognōmen;* the nōmen was *Cornelius,* and the full name *Lūcius Cornelius Sulla. Sullae,* as a gen., limits *exercitū.* The allusion is to L. Cornelius Sulla Felix, the Roman dictator, the conqueror of Mithridates, and the celebrated opponent of Marius; a doubtful Roman patriot, who rewarded his friends with confiscated estates, and punished his enemies with death through proscriptions. —— **et**, conj., a species of correlate, as we have here *et . . . et.* —— **posteā** (post + eā), adv.; it modifies *fuerat.* —— **in**, prep. with the acc. or abl.; here it takes the abl. *exercitū,* to be supplied from the preceding phrase. Note how the notions are kept distinct by the repetition of the prep. —— **M.**, an abbreviation for *Marcī,* gen. of the proper noun *Marcus, -ī,* m.; *praenōmen.* —— **Crassī**, gen. sing. of the proper noun *Crassus, -ī,* m.; as a gen. it limits *exercitū* understood. Marcus Crassus was a commander in the civil war, 71 B.C., and fought against Spartacus. Spartacus, it will be recalled, was a native of Thrace, a shepherd, a robber-chief, and then a leader of Roman slaves in plots of insurrection in Southern Italy. He was the most distinguished leader of slave insurrections of whom history gives any account.

LINE 19. **fuerat**, 3d pers. sing. pluperf. ind. of the intrans. verb *sum, esse, fuī, futūrus;* connected by the copulatives with the verb *habēbātur,* and has the same subject-nom., viz. the rel. *quī.* —— **cum**, prep. with the abl. —— **explōrātōribus**, abl. plur. of the noun *explōrātor, -ōris,* m.; abl. of accompaniment. Consult A. & G. 248, *a*; B. 168; G. 392, and REM. 1; II. 419, I. For synonyms, see note on *explōrātōrēs,* l. 7, Chap. XII. —— **praemittitur**, 3d pers. sing. pres. ind. pass. of the verb *praemittō, -ere, -mīsī, -missum,* 3; pass. parts: *praemittor, -mittī, -missus,* 3; it agrees with *P. Considius* as its subject-nom., l. 16, above. Observe that from the 7th line the historical present is the tense of the leading verbs.

[LINES 1-4.] BOOK I. 163

1	XXII.	Prīmā	lūce,	cum	summus	XXII. At day-
		At the first	light,	when	the top	break, when the summit of the
2	mōns	ā	Labiēnō	tenērētur,	ipse	mountain was in the possession of
	of the mountain	by	Labienus	was held,	(Caesar) himself	Labienus, and
3	ab	hostium	castrīs	nōn	longius	mille	Caesar himself was not more
	from	the enemy's	camp	not	farther	than a thousand	than a mile and
4	et	quīngentīs	passibus	abesset,	neque,	ut	a half from the enemy's camp;
	and	five hundred	paces	was distant,	nor,	as	and, as he aft-

LINE 1. **Prīmā**, abl. sing. of the adj. *prīmus, -a, -um*, superl. degree; comparative *prior*. *prīmā* is an attributive of the noun *lūce*. —— **lūce**, abl. sing. of the noun *lūx, lucis*, f.; abl. of *time when*. See A. & G. 256, 1; B. 171; G. 393; H. 429. —— **cum**, conj., temporal. —— **summus**, nom. sing. m. of *summus, -a, -um;* one form of the superl. degree of the adj. *superus*, positive; comparative *superior;* superl. *suprēmus* or *summus*. *summus* is an attributive of *mōns*. Observe that the phrase *summus mōns* = *the top of the mountain*. Consult A. & G. 193; B. 68, REM. 4; G. 291, REM. 2; H. 440, 2, NOTES 1 and 2.

LINE 2. **mōns, montis**, m., subject-nom. of *tenērētur*. —— **ā**, prep. with the abl. (*ā* before consonants, *ab* before either vowels or consonants). —— **Labiēnō**, abl. sing. of the proper noun *Labiēnus, -ī*, m.; abl. of the agent after the prep. *ā*. See A. & G. 246; B. 166; G. 401; H. 415, I. As to Labienus, see note on *Labiēnum*, l. 8, Chap. XXI. —— **tenērētur**, 3d pers. sing. imperf. pass. of the verb *teneō, -ēre, -uī, tentum*, 2; pass. parts: *teneor, -ērī, tentus*, 2. *tenērētur* agrees with its subject-nom. *mōns;* it is subjunctive after *cum* temporal. A. & G. 325; B. 222; G. 585; H. 521, II, 2. —— **ipse**, nom. sing. m. of the intensive pron. *ipse, -sa, -sum*, gen. *ipsīus*, dat. *ipsī;* it refers to Caesar; it is subject-nom. of *abesset*, l. 4, below.

LINE 3. **ab**, prep. with the abl.; note its repetition after the verb *abesset*. —— **hostium**, gen. plur. of the noun *hostis, -is*, m. and f.; as a gen. it limits *castrīs*. —— **castrīs**, abl. plur. of the noun *castrum, -ī*, n.; in the sing. it = *castle, fort;* in the plur. it = *camp*. *castrīs* is the obj. of the prep. *ab*. —— **nōn** (nē + oe[ū]num, apocopated), adv.; modifies the adv. *longius*. —— **longius**, adv., comparative degree of *longē*, rare form *longiter;* superl. *longissimē*. *longius* modifies *abesset*. —— **mille**, indecl. num. adj., in the sing.; in the plur. *mīlia* or *millia;* it is regularly declined. *mille* is here, of course, in the abl. plur. case, modifying *passibus*.

LINE 4. **et**, cop. conj.; it connects the adjectives *mille* and *quīngentīs*. —— **quīngentīs**, abl. plur. of the cardinal num. adj. *quīngentī, -ae, -a;* it, too, modifies the noun *passibus*. Observe that the hundreds from *ducentī* to *nōngentī* inclusive are regularly declined like the plur. of *bonus*. —— **passibus**, abl. plur. of the noun *passus, -ūs*, m. *passibus* is the abl. after the comparative *longius*, *quam* (than) being omitted. Consult A. & G. 247; B. 70, 2; G. 398; H. 417. —— **abesset**, 3d pers. sing. imperf. subjunctive of the intrans. verb *absum, -esse, ab(ā)fuī, ab(ā)futūrus* (ab + sum). *abesset* agrees with its subject-nom. *ipse;* it is in the subjunctive, because still under the influence of *cum*. Observe the omission of the cop. conj. between the clauses (asyndeton). A. & G. 346, *c;* B. 123, REM. 6; G. 474, NOTE; H. 636, I, 1. —— **neque**, conj. and adv.; here it = *et nōn*, and connects the third clause in the series of three subordinate clauses. —— **ut**, with the ind., is a relative adv., and = *as;* with the subjunctive it is a conj., and = *that*.

erwards ascertained from the captives, neither his own arrival, nor that of Labienus was known, Considius with his horse at full speed rode up to him and said that the mountain of which he desired Labienus to get	posteā *afterwards* adventus *coming* Cōnsidius *Considius* accurrit, *runs*	ex *from* aut *or* equō *(his) horse* dīcit *(and) says*	captīvīs *prisoners* Labiēnī *(that) of Labienus* admissō *being let go* montem, *the mountain,*	comperit, *he ascertained,* cōgnitus *known* ad *towards* quem *which*	aut ipsīus 5 *either his own* esset, 6 *was,* eum 7 *him* ā Labiēnō 8 *by Labienus*

LINE 5. **posteā**, adv. (post + eā); it modifies *comperit*. —— **ex**, prep. with the abl. (*ē* before consonants, *ex* before vowels or consonants). —— **captīvīs**, abl. plur. of the noun *captīvus, -ī,* m. (*capere,* to capture). *captīvīs* is the obj. of the prep. *ex.* —— **comperit**, 3d pers. sing. perf. ind. act. of the verb *comperō, -īre, comperī, -pertum,* 4; it agrees with a pron. implied in the ending as its subject-nom., referring to Caesar. —— **aut**, conj.; *aut ... aut* = *either ... or;* see note on this particle, l. 19, Chap. I. —— **ipsīus**, gen. sing. of the intensive pron. *ipse, -sa, -sum;* it refers to Caesar; it is expressed for emphasis, and limits *adventus.*

LINE 6. **adventus**, nom. sing. of the noun *adventus, -ūs,* m. (ad + venīre); it is the subject-nom. of *cōgnitus esset.* —— **aut**, see note on *aut*, preceding line. —— **Labiēnī**, gen. sing. of *Labiēnus, -ī,* m.; as a gen. it limits *adventus*, to be supplied. —— **cōgnitus esset**, 3d pers. sing. of the pluperf. subjunctive pass. of the verb *cōgnōscō, -ere, -nōvī, -nitum,* 3; pass. parts: *cōgnōscor, cōgnōscī, cōgnitus. cōgnitus esset* is connected by the conj. *neque* with the verb *abesset,* and is in the subjunctive for the same reason; *tenērētur, abesset* and *cōgnitus esset* are under the influence, so to speak, of *cum* temporal or historical. Observe that the verbs in the subordinate clauses are put in the secondary tenses, because the verb *accurrit* of the main clause is an historical present.

LINE 7. **Cōnsidius, -ī,** m.; subject-nom. of the verb *accurrit.* See note on *Publius Cōnsidius,* l. 16, Chap. XXI. —— **equō**, abl. sing. of the noun *equus, -ī,* m.; in the abl. absolute with the participle *admissō.* —— **admissō**, abl. sing. m. of the participle *admissus, -a, -um* of the verb *admittō, -ere, -mīsī, -missum,* 3 (ad + mittere); hence the phrase *equō admissō* = lit. *the horse being sent forward,* i.e. *being given loose reins to.* But observe that this phrase is less emphatic than *equō concitātō.* —— **ad**, prep. with the acc. —— **eum**, acc. sing. m. of the dem. pron. *is, ea, id,* used as a personal pron. of the 3d pers.; *eum,* i.e. *Caesarem.*

LINE 8. **accurrit**, 3d pers. sing. pres. ind. act. of *accurrō, -ere, accucurrī (-currī), -cursum,* 3 (ad+currere). *accurrit* agrees with the proper noun *Cōnsidius* as its subject-nom. —— **dīcit**, 3d pers. sing. pres. ind. act. of the verb *dīcō, -ere, dīxī, dictum,* 3; connected by *et* understood (asyndeton) with *accurrit,* and in the same grammatical construction. As to the omission of the conj., see A. & G. 346, *c*; B. 123, REM. 6; G. 474, NOTE; H. 636, 1, 1. —— **montem**, acc. sing. of the noun *mōns, montis,* m.; *montem* is the subject-acc. of *tenērī.* —— **quem**, acc. sing. m. of the rel. pron. *quī, quae, quod;* it refers to the noun *montem;* it is the subject-acc. of *occupārī.* —— **ā**, prep. with the abl. (*ā* before consonants only, *ab* before vowels or consonants). —— **Labiēnō**, abl. sing. m. of *Labiēnus, -ī,* m.; abl. of the agent with prep. *ā* after the pass. verb *occupārī.* See A. & G. 246; B. 166; G. 401; H. 415, I. As to Labienus, see note on *Labiēnum,* l. 8, Chap. XXI.

9 occupārī	voluerit,	ab	hostibus		tenērī;	possession was held by the enemy; that he had ascertained this fact from the gleam of the Gallic arms and decorations. Caesar, accordingly, withdrew his troops to the nearest hill, and put them in battle array. La-
to be seized	*he wished,*	*by*	*the enemy*		*to be* (is) *held;*	
10 id	sē	ā	Gallicīs	armīs	atque	
this (fact)	*himself*	*from*	*the Gallic*	*arms*	*and*	
11 īnsīgnibus	cōgnōvisse.		Caesar	suās	cōpiās	
ensigns	*to have known.*		*Caesar*	*his own*	*troops*	
12 in	proximum	collem	subdūcit,		aciem	
to	*the next*	*hill*	*draws off,*		*a battle line*	

LINE 9. **occupārī** (ob + capere) = lit. *to seize upon.* —— **voluerit,** 3d pers. sing. perf. subjunctive of the irr. verb *volō, velle, voluī;* in the subjunctive mode, because in a subordinate clause in informal indirect discourse; or, perhaps better, the relative clause may be considered an *integral part* of the sentence. Consult A. & G. 342; B. 235, REM. 1; G. 629; H. 529, II, NOTE 1, 1). *voluerit* agrees with a pron. implied in the ending, referring to *Caesar* as subject-nom. —— **ab,** see note on *ā*, preceding line. —— **hostibus,** abl. plur. of the noun *hostis, hostis,* m. and f.; abl. of the agent after the prep. *ab.* See grammatical references to *Labiēnō*, preceding line. —— **tenērī,** pres. inf. pass. of the verb *teneō, -ēre, -uī, tentum,* 2; pass. parts: *teneor, -ērī, tentus,* 2. The subject-acc. of *tenērī* is *montem.*

LINE 10. **id,** acc. sing. n. of the dem. pron. *is, ea, id,* used substantively; or, one may supply the word *thing,* and still conceive of *id* as having an adj. force; *id* is the direct obj. of *cōgnōvisse.* —— **sē,** acc. sing. of the reflexive pron. *suī, sibi, sē, sē. sē* is subject-acc. of *cōgnōvisse.* —— **ā,** prep. with the abl.; see note on *ā*, preceding line. —— **Gallicīs,** abl. plur. n. of the adj. *Gallicus, -a, -um (Gallia);* it is an attributive of *armīs.* —— **armīs,** abl. plur. of the noun *arma, -ōrum;* abl. of cause with the prep. *ā.* Consult A. & G. 245; B. 165; G. 408, 3, end; H. 416, I, 1. For synonyms, see note on *armīs,* l. 13, Chap. IV. —— **atque** (ad + que), conj.; connects *armīs* and *īnsīgnibus.*

LINE 11. **īnsīgnibus,** abl. plur. of the adj. *īnsīgnis, -e,* used as a noun. *īnsīgnibus* is connected by the conj. *atque* with the noun *armīs,* and is in the same grammatical construction. —— **cōgnōvisse,** perf. inf. act. of the verb *cōgnōscō, -ere, -nōvī, -nitum,* 3; its subject-acc. is the pron. *sē.* —— **Caesar, -aris,** m.; subject-nom. of *subdūcit* and *īnstruit.* —— **suās,** acc. plur. f. of the poss. and reflexive pron. *suus, -a, -um;* it is an attributive of *cōpiās.* —— **cōpiās,** acc. plur. of the noun *cōpia, -ae,* f. (*cōpia* in the sing. = *abundance;* in the plur. = *resources, troops*). *cōpiās* is the direct obj. of the verb *subdūcit.* The student will observe that lines 8-11 are informal *ōrātiō oblīqua.* The *ōrātiō rēcta* of these lines is as follows: *mōns, quem ā Labiēnō occupārī voluistī, ab hostibus tenētur; hoc egō ā Gallicīs armīs atque īnsīgnibus cōgnōvī.*

LINE 12. **in,** prep. with the acc. or abl.; here it takes the acc. —— **proximum,** acc. sing. m. of the adj. *proximus, -a, -um,* superl. degree; comparative *propior. proximum* is the attributive of *collem.* —— **collem,** acc. sing. of the noun *collis, -is,* m. *collem* is the obj. of the prep. *in.* —— **subdūcit,** 3d pers. sing. pres. ind. act. of the verb *subdūcō, -ere, -dūxī, -ductum,* 3 (sub + dūcere); hence *subdūcere* = lit. *to lead from below. subdūcit* agrees with its subject-nom. *Caesar.* —— **aciem,** acc. sing. of the noun *aciēs, -ēī,* f., gen. sometimes *aciī* and *aciē;* compare Latin *ācer,* sharp,

bienus, as he had been directed by Caesar not to join battle unless Caesar's own forces were seen near the enemy's camp, that on all sides at one and the same time an	īnstruit. *he forms.* ā *by* ipsīus *his own* vīsae essent, *should be seen,*	Labiēnus, *Labienus,* Caesare, *Caesar,* cōpiae *troops* ut *that*	ut *as* nē *that not* prope *near* undique *on every side*	erat *was* proelium *battle* hostium *the enemy's* ūnō *at one*	eī *to him* committeret *he should join* castra *camp* tempore *time*	praeceptum 13 *ordered* nisi 14 *unless* 15 16

and GK. ákĭs, *the edge of a thing;* hence, in military language *aciēs* = *a line*. *aciem* is the direct obj. of *īnstruit*. Note the omission of the conj. between the compound predicate *subdūcit* and *īnstruit*. Synonyms: *aciēs* = *an army in battle array;* *āgmen* = *an army in motion;* whereas *exercitus* = *a disciplined army*.

LINE 13. **īnstruit**, 3d pers. sing. historical pres. ind. act. of the verb *īnstruō, -ere, -strūxī, -strūctum*, 3 (in + struere, *to build on*); connected by the omitted *et* with *subdūcit*, and agrees with the subject-nom. *Caesar*. —— **Labiēnus**, -ī, m., subject-nom. of *exspectābat* and *abstinēbat*, lines 18 and 19, below. —— **ut**, adv. = *as*. —— **erat**, 3d pers. sing. imperf. ind. of *sum, esse, fuī, futūrus*; here used in forming the compound tense, pluperf. pass. *erat praeceptum* (*praeceptum erat*). —— **eī**, dat. sing. m. of the dem. pron. *is, ea, id*, used as a personal pron. of the 3d pers.; *eī* is dat. of the indirect obj. after the pass. *erat praeceptum*. Consult A. & G. 225, *e*; B. 140; G. 344; II. 384, I. —— **praeceptum**, nom. sing. n. of the perf. pass. participle *praeceptus, -a, -um* of the verb *praecipiō, -ere, -cēpī, -ceptum*, 3; it forms with *erat* the pluperf. ind. pass., used impersonally.

LINE 14. **ā**, prep. with the abl. (*ā* before consonants only, *ab* before vowels or consonants). —— **Caesare**, abl. sing. of *Caesar, -aris*, m.; abl. of the agent after the prep. *ab*. See A. & G. 246; B. 166; G. 401; H. 415, I. —— **nē**, adv., primitive negative particle = *that not*. —— **proelium**, acc. sing. of the noun *proelium, -ī*, n.; direct obj. of *committeret*. For synonyms, see note on *proeliīs*, l. 18, Chap. I. —— **committeret**, 3d pers. sing. imperf. subjunctive of the verb *committō, -ere, -mīsī, -missum*, 3; subjunctive of *negative purpose* after *nē*. See A. & G. 317; B. 200; G. 545, 3; H. 497, II. —— **nisi** (nē + sī = lit. *not if*), conj.

LINE 15. **ipsīus**, gen. sing. of the intensive dem. pron. *ipse, -sa, -sum*; it refers to Caesar; as a gen. it limits *cōpiae*. —— **cōpiae**, nom. plur. of the noun *cōpia, -ae*, f. (co + ops); in the sing. = *plenty*; in the plur. = *troops*. *cōpiae* is the subject-nom. of *vīsae essent*. —— **prope**, adv., and prep. with the acc.; here a prep. —— **hostium**, gen. plur. of *hostis, hostis*, m. and f.; as a gen. it limits *castra*. —— Synonyms: *hostis* = lit. *a stranger;* and then *an enemy*, especially *a public enemy;* whereas *inimīcus* = *a private foe*. —— **castra**, acc. plur. of the noun *castrum, -ī*, n.; in the sing. = *a fort;* in the plur. = a number of tents or huts located near each other; hence = *a camp*. *castra* is the obj. of the prep. *prope*.

LINE 16. **vīsae essent**, 3d pers. plur. pluperf. subjunctive of *videor, -ērī, vīsus*, 2; or *vīsae* = *seen* may be taken as a participial predicate after *essent*. *essent*, 3d pers. plur. imperf. subjunctive of the intrans. verb *sum, esse, fuī, futūrus;* or it might be taken as forming a part of the compound tense — pluperf. — *vīsae essent;* it is in the subjunctive mode after *nisi* in the protasis. Consult A. & G. 315, *a;* B. 204, 2; G. 591, 2, (*b*); H. 507, III; the apodosis is involved in the purpose-

17 in	hostēs	impetus	fieret,	monte
against	*the enemy*	*an attack*	*might be made,*	*the mountain*
18 occupātō		nostrōs		exspectābat
having been seized		*ours*		*he was waiting for,*
19 proeliōque		abstinēbat.	Multō	dēnique
from the battle and,		*he was refraining.*	*Much*	*at length*
20	diē	per	explōrātōrēs	Caesar
	(being) the day,	*through*	*scouts*	*Caesar*

outset might be made against the enemy, after getting possession of the mountain was awaiting our men and holding aloof from battle. At length, Caesar, late in the day, learned from scouts that the

---

clause *nē . . . committeret*. Observe that the text from *nē*, l. 14, above, to *essent*, inclusive, l. 16, above, is the logical subj. of *erat praeceptum (praeceptum erat)*, l. 13, above. —— ut, telic conj. —— undique (unde + que); hence = lit. *whencesoever;* it modifies *fieret*. —— ūnō, abl. sing. n. of the num. adj. *ūnus, -a, -um;* gen. *ūnīus*, dat. *ūnī*. *ūnō* is an attributive of *tempore*. —— tempore, abl. sing. of the noun *tempus, -oris*, n.; abl. of *time at which*. A. & G. 256, 1; B. 171; G. 393; H. 429. For etymology of *tempus*, see note on *tempore*, l. 21, Chap. III.

LINE 17. in, prep. with the acc. or abl.; here it takes the acc. For different significations, see note on *in*, l. 1, Chap. I. —— hostēs, acc. plur. of the noun *hostis, -is*, m. and f. *hostēs* is the obj. of the prep. *in*. —— impetus, nom. sing. of the noun *impetus, -ūs*, m. (im[n] + petere); hence *impetere* = *to rush upon*, and the noun *impetus* = *an attack*. *impetus* is the subject-nom. of the pass. verb *fieret*. —— fieret, 3d pers. sing. imperf. subjunctive of *fīō, fierī, factus*, used as the pass. of *faciō, -ere, fēcī, factum*, 3; it agrees with the subject-nom. *impetus;* subjunctive of purpose after *ut*, this clause expresses the purpose of the order. —— monte, abl. sing. of the noun *mōns, montis*, m.; abl. absolute with the participle *occupātō*.

LINE 18. occupātō, abl. sing. m. of the participle *occupātus, -a, -um* of the verb *occupō, -āre, -āvī, -ātum*, 1 (ob + capere = *to seize upon*). *occupātō* is in the abl. absolute with *monte*. Consult A. & G. 255; B. 192; G. 409; H. 431. —— nostrōs, acc. plur. m. of the poss. pron. *noster, -tra, -trum;* supply *mīlitēs;* or it may be taken substantively = *ours;* yet the modified subst. may always be supplied. *nostrōs* is the direct obj. of *exspectābat*. —— exspectābat, 3d pers. sing. imperf. ind. of *exspectō, -āre, -āvī, -ātum*, 1 (ex + spectāre = *to look out for*). *exspectābat* agrees with its subject-nom. *Labiēnus*, expressed in l. 13, above.

LINE 19. proeliōque (proeliō + que). *proeliō*, abl. sing. of the noun *proelium, -ī*, n.; abl. *of separation* after *abstinēbat;* the simple abl. See A. & G. 243, *b;* B. 160; and REM. 1; G. 390, 2, NOTE 3; H. 413. *que*, note how closely the enclitic joins *abstinēbat* to *exspectābat*. As to synonyms, see note on *proeliīs*, l. 18, Chap. I. —— abstinēbat, 3d pers. sing. imperf. ind. act. of *abstineō, -ēre, -uī, -tentum*, 2 (abs + tenēre = *to hold from*), connected by the conj. *-que* with *exspectābat*, and in the same grammatical construction. —— Multō, abl. sing. m. of the adj. *multus, -a, -um;* comparative *plūs;* superl. *plūrimus*. *multō* is an attributive of the noun *diē*. —— dēnique (deinde + que), conjunctive adv.; as a conj. it connects the sentences; as an adv. it modifies *cōgnōvit*.

LINE 20. diē, abl. sing. of the noun *diēs, -ēī*, m. or f. in the sing.; always m. in the plur; abl. of *time at which*. See A. & G., 256, 1; B. 171; G. 393; H. 429; the phrase *multō diē* = *at much day*, like *prīmā lūce* which = *at first light*, i.e. *at day-*

| mountain was in the possession of his friends; that the Helvetii had broken up their camp; and that Considius, panic-stricken, had reported to him as fact a vision of his imagination. | cōgnōvit *ascertained* et *both* Cōnsidium *Considius* vīdisset, *he had seen,* | montem *the mountain* Helvētiōs *the Helvetii* timōre *by fear* prō *for* | ā *by* castra *(their) camp* perterritum *greatly terrified* vīsō *seen,* | suīs *his (men)* mōvisse *to have moved* quod *what* sibi *to himself* | tenērī 21 *to be (is) held* et 22 *and* nōn 23 *not* renūntiāsse. 24 *to have reported.* |

break. diē, however, might be taken as an abl. absolute with *multō*. The phrase *multō diē = the day being much*, i.e. = *late in the day.* —— **per**, prep. with the acc. —— **explōrātōrēs**, acc. plur. of the noun *explōrātor, -ōris,* m.; it is the obj. of the prep. *per*, i.e. the agent as means is expressed by *per* with the acc.; see A. & G. 246, *b*; B. 166, REM. 1; G. 401; H. 415, I, 1, NOTE 1. As to derivation and synonyms, see note on *explōrātōrēs*, l. 7, Chap. XII. —— **Caesar, -aris,** m., subject-nom. of the verb *cōgnōvit.*

LINE 21. **cōgnōvit,** 3d pers. sing. perf. ind. act. of *cōgnōscō, -ere, nōvī, -nitum,* 3; it agrees with its subject-nom. *Caesar.* —— **et**, cop. conj.; here *et . . . et = both . . . and.* —— **montem,** acc. sing. of the noun *mōns, montis,* m. *montem* is subject-acc. of the verb *tenērī.* —— **ā**, prep. with the abl. (*ā* before consonants only, *ab* before vowels or consonants). —— **suīs**, abl. plur. of the poss. and reflexive pron. *suus, -a, -um,* used substantively; or supply *mīlitibus. suīs,* conceived to be substantive in use, is the obj. of the prep. *ā*, i.e. an abl. of the agent. A. & G. 246; B. 166; G. 401; H. 415, I. —— **tenērī**, pres. inf. pass. of the act. *teneō, -ēre, -uī, tentum,* 2; pass. parts: *teneor, -ērī, tentus,* 2.

LINE 22. **et**, see note on *et,* preceding line. —— **Helvētiōs,** acc. plur. of the adj. *Helvētius, -a, -um,* used as a substantive. *Helvētiōs* is subject-acc. of *mōvisse.* —— **castra,** acc. plur. of the noun *castrum, -ī,* n.; in the sing. = *fort* or *redoubt;* in the plur. = *camp. castra* is the direct obj. of *mōvisse.* —— **mōvisse**, perf. inf. act. of the verb *moveō, -ēre, mōvī, mōtum,* 2; its subject-acc. is *Helvētiōs.* —— **et**, cop. conj.; connects the infinitive-clauses.

LINE 23. **Cōnsidium**, acc. sing. of the proper noun *Cōnsidius, -ī,* m. *Cōnsidium* is subject-acc. of *renūntiāsse*, l. 24, below. —— **timōre**, abl. sing. of the noun *timor, -ōris,* m. *timōre* is abl. of cause after the perf. pass. participle *perterritum.* Consult A. & G. 245, and 2, *b*; B. 165, and REM. 4; G. 408, and NOTE 2; H. 416, and NOTE 1. —— **perterritum**, acc. sing. m. of the perf pass. participle *perterritus, -a, -um* of the verb *perterreō, -ēre, uī, -itum,* 2. *perterritum* agrees with *Cōnsidius* in gender, number and case. Observe the force of *per* in composition — *perterritum = greatly terrified.* As to Considius, see note on *P. Cōnsidius,* l. 16, Chap. XXI. —— **quod**, acc. sing. n. of the rel. *quī, quae, quod;* it refers to *id,* to be supplied; i.e. the thought expressed in lines 10 and 11, above, as its antecedent; but *quod* itself is the direct obj. of *vīdisset.* Observe that in such construction *id* is generally expressed, but is sometimes omitted. Consult A. & G. 200, *e*, and NOTE; B. 129, REM. 8; G. 614, REM. 2; H. 445, 7. —— **nōn** (nĕ + ūnum, apocopated), adv.; it modifies *vīdisset.*

LINE 24. **vīdisset**, 3d pers. sing. pluperf. subjunctive of the verb *videō, -ēre, vīsī, vīsum,* 2; it agrees with a pron. implied in the ending as subject-nom., referring to *Cōnsidium;* subjunctive mode, because in informal indirect discourse. —— **prō**, prep. with the abl. —— **vīsō**, abl. sing. n. of the perf. pass. participle of the verb

BOOK I.

25 Eō	diē,	quō	cōnsuērat	intervallō,		On that day, Caesar followed the enemy at the usual distance, and pitched his camp three miles from their camp.
That	*day,*	*by which,*	*he was accustomed,*	*interval,*		
26 hostēs	sequitur	et	mīlia	passuum	tria	
the enemy	*he follows*	*and*	*thousands*	*of paces*	*three*	
27 ab	eōrum	castrīs	castra	pōnit.		
from	*their*	*camp*	*(his) camp*	*he pitches.*		

videor, vidērī, vīsus; vīsō is used substantively in the abl. n., and is the obj. of the prep. *prō. prō vīsō* = lit. *for a seen* (thing). —— *sibi*, dat. sing. m. of the reflexive personal pron. *suī, sibi, sē, sē;* dat. of the indirect obj. *sibi* = *to himself*, i.e. Caesar. —— **renūntiāsse**, perf. inf. act. of the verb *renūntiō, -āre, -āvī, -ātum,* 1 ; sometimes written *renūnciō;* contracted for *renūntiāvisse.* See A. & G. 128, 2 ; B. 251 ; G. 131, 1 ; H. 235. Note that the subject-acc. of *renūntiāsse* is *Cōnsidium,* l. 23, above. The *ōrātiō rēcta* of lines 21–24 is as follows: *mōns ā meīs tenētur* et *Helvētiī castra movērunt* et *Cōnsidius* timōre *perterritus* quod nōn *vīderat,* prō vīsō *mihi renūntiāt* (*renūntiāvit*).

LINE 25. **Eō**, abl. sing. m. of the dem. pron. *is, ea, id;* it is an attributive of the noun *diē*. —— **diē**, abl. sing. of the noun *diēs, -ēī,* m. or f. in the sing.; always m. in the plur. *diē* is abl. of *time at which.* See A. & G. 256, 1 ; B. 171; G. 393; H. 429. —— **quō**, abl sing. n. of the rel. pron. *quī, quae, quod;* used here adjectively and modifies *intervallō.* —— **cōnsuērat**, 3d pers. sing. pluperf. ind. of the verb *cōnsuēscō, -ere -suēvī, -suētum,* 3 (con + *suēscere, to become used*). *cōnsuērat* agrees with *Caesar* understood, as subject-nom. Observe (*a*) that this is a species of preteritive verb in which the perf. is as a pres., and the pluperf. as an imperf.; (*b*) that *cōnsuērat* is contracted for *cōnsuēverat.* Consult A. & G. 128, 2; B. 251; G. 131, 1; H. 235. —— **intervallō**, abl. sing. of the noun *intervallum, -ī,* n. (inter + vallum); hence the noun = *the space between two palisades;* transf. = *interval. intervallō* is an abl. of manner. See A. & G. 248; B. 168; G. 399; H. 419, III.

LINE 26. **hostēs**, acc. plur. of the noun *hostis, -is,* m. and f.; it is the direct obj. of the deponent verb *sequitur.* —— **sequitur**, 3d pers. sing. pres. ind. of the deponent verb *sequor, -ī, secūtus,* 3 (sibilated from ἕπομαι). *sequitur* agrees with a pron. implied in the ending, referring to Caesar as subject-nom. —— **et**, cop. conj.; connects the verbs *sequitur* and *pōnit.* —— **mīlia**, acc. plur. n. of the adj. *mille*, indeclinable in the sing.; regularly declined in the plur.; used here as a noun, and in the acc. of extent of space. Consult A. & G. 257, *b*; B. 153; G. 335; H. 379. —— **passuum**, gen. plur. of the noun *passus, -ūs,* m.; partitive gen. after *mīlia.* Consult A. & G. 216, 2; B. 58, 3, and 134; G. 370; H. 397, 3. —— **tria**, acc. plur. n. of the num. adj. *trēs, tria;* it is an attributive of the noun *mīlia.*

LINE 27. **ab**, prep. with the abl. (*ā* before consonants only, *ab* before vowels or consonants). —— **eōrum**, gen. plur. m. of the dem. pron. *is, ea, id,* used as a personal pron. of the 3d pers. = *their* or *of them;* as a gen. it limits *castrīs.* —— **castrīs**, abl. plur. of the noun *castrum, -ī,* n.; in the sing. = *fort;* in the plur. = *camp.* —— **castra**, acc. plur. of *castrum, -ī,* n.; direct obj. of the verb *pōnit.* —— **pōnit**, 3d pers. sing. pres. ind. act. of *pōnō, -ere, posuī, positum,* 3; connected by the conj. *et* with *sequitur,* and has the same grammatical construction, i.e. agrees with *Caesar* understood. The first part of the sentence fully expressed is: *Caesar, eō diē, eō intervallō, quō cōnsuērat, hostēs sequitur,* etc.

XXIII. Caesar, on the following day, thought that he ought to be on the lookout for a supply of provisions, as only two days remained until the time when it would be necessary for him to distribute grain to the army; and, as he was	XXIII.	Postrĭdĭē *The day after*	ēius *this*	diēī, *day,*	quod *because*	1
	omnīnō *in all*	bĭduum *the space of two days*		sŭpererat, *remained,*	cum *when*	2
	exercituī *to the army*	frūmentum *corn*	(*for him*) *to measure out*	mētīrī	oportēret, *it behooved,*	3
	et *and*	quod *because*	ā *from*	Bibracte, *Bibracte,*	oppĭdō *a town*	Aeduōrum *of the Aedui*	4
	longē *by far*	māxĭmō *the greatest*	et *and*		cōpĭōsissĭmō, *the richest,*	nōn *not*	5

LINE 1. **Postrĭdĭē** (posterī + dĭē), adv. = lit. *on the day after*. —— **ēius**, gen. sing. of the dem. pron. *is, ea, id;* as a gen. it limits *diēī*. —— **diēī**, gen. sing. of the noun *dĭēs, -ēī,* m. or f. in the sing.; always m. in the plur. This gen. depends on the noun *dĭē* contained in the adv. *postrĭdĭē.* Consult A. & G. 223, IV, *e*, and NOTE 2; B. 134; G. 372, NOTE 3; H. 398, 5. Observe that the phrase *postrĭdĭē dĭē* = lit. *on the after day of that day* (pleonasm), i.e. *on the next day.* Observe also that, though *postrĭdĭē* and *prĭdĭē* are accounted adverbs, they are, in fact, locative ablatives. —— **quod**, conj. = *because*, or *since*, or *as*.

LINE 2. **omnīnō** (*omnis*), adv. = lit. *in all.* —— **bĭduum**, nom. sing. of the noun *bĭduum, -ī,* n. (bis + dĭēs). *bĭduum* is the subject-nom. of the verb *supererat.* —— **supererat**, 3d pers. sing. imperf. ind. of the intrans. verb *supersum, -esse, -fuī, -futūrus* (super + sum); hence *superesse* = *to be over, to remain.* *supererat* agrees with its subject-nom. *bĭduum.* —— **cum**, conj. = *when*, i.e. here = *at the end of which time.*

LINE 3. **exercituī**, dat. sing. of the noun *exercitus, -ūs,* m.; dat. of the indirect obj. after *mētīrī.* —— **frūmentum**, acc. sing. of the noun *frūmentum, -ī,* n. (contracted from frugī + mentum). *frūmentum* is the direct obj. of the deponent verb *mētīrī.* —— **mētīrī**, pres. inf. of the deponent verb *mētior, -īrī, mēnsus,* 4; its subject-acc. is *eum,* i.e. *Caesarem,* omitted. —— **oportēret**, 3d pers. sing. imperf. subjunctive of *oportet, -ēre, oportuit,* 2; used impersonally, or, strictly, the infinitive-clause *exercituī frūmentum mētīrī* is the subj. *oportēret* is subjunctive after *cum* temporal. See A. & G. 325; B. 222; G. 585; H. 521, II, 2.

LINE 4. **et**, cop. conj.; connects the *quod*-clauses. —— **quod**, see *quod,* l. 1, above. —— **ā**, prep. with the abl. (*ā* before consonants only, *ab* before vowels or consonants). —— **Bibracte**, abl. sing. of the proper noun *Bibracte, -tis,* n.; abl. after the prep. *ā.* Observe that neuters in *-e* have usually the abl. in *-ī,* but names of towns in *-e* have *-e* in the abl. Observe also that Bibracte was the principal town of the Aedui; this town, possibly, developed into the modern Autun. Observe, moreover, that the prep. is required with names of towns to denote *measure of distance.* —— **oppĭdō**, abl. sing. of the noun *oppidum, -ī,* n.; an appositive. —— **Aeduōrum**, gen. plur. of the adj. *Aeduus, -a, -um,* used substantively; as a gen. it limits *oppĭdō.*

LINE 5. **longē** (*longus*), an adv., used to strengthen the superl. *māxĭmō.* Consult A. & G. 93, *d*; B. 117. 1; G. 303; H. 444, 3. —— **māxĭmō**, abl. sing. n. of the adj., superl. degree *māxĭmus, -a, -um;* positive *măgnus;* comparative *māior. māxĭmō* is an attributive of *oppĭdō.* —— **et**, conj.; connects the superlatives, as if of equal importance. —— **cōpĭōsissĭmō**, abl. sing. n. of the adj. superl. *cōpĭōsissĭmus, -a,*

6 amplius	mīlibus	passuum	octōdecim	not more than fifteen miles distant from Bibracte, by far the largest and the richest town of the Aedui, he turned his course away from the Helvetii, and marched rapidly toward Bibracte.
farther than	*thousands*	*of paces*	*eighteen*	
7 aberat,		reī	frūmentāriae	
he was distant,		*for the thing,*	*frumentary*	
8 prōspiciendum		exīstimāvit;	iter ab	
it ought to be provided for		*he thought;*	*(his) course from*	
9 Helvētiīs	āvertit	āc	Bibracte īre	
the Helvetii	*he averted*	*and*	*to Bibracte to go*	

-*um*; positive *cōpiōsus* (*cōpia*); comparative *cōpiōsior*. *cōpiōsissimō* is connected by the conj. *et* with *māximō*, and is also an attributive of *oppidō*. Observe that adjectives ending in *-ōsus* denote fulness. —— nōn (nē + oenum [ūnum]), adv., modifies the adv. *amplius*.

LINE 6. **amplius**, adv., comparative degree; positive *amplē* or *ampliter*. *amplius* modifies the verb *aberat*. —— **mīlibus**, abl. plur. n. of the indecl. adj. *mille*; declinable in the plur. n., and used as a neuter noun. *mīlibus* is an abl. of comparison after the comparative degree, *quam* (than) being omitted. Consult A. & G. 247; B. 163; G. 398; H. 417. —— **passuum**, gen. plur. of the noun *passus, -ūs*, m.; partitive gen. after *mīlia*. See A. & G. 216, 2; B. 134; G. 370; H. 397, 2. —— **octōdecim**, cardinal num. adj.; it is an attributive of *mīlibus*. Observe that the Arabic 18 may be expressed in Latin in three ways: (1) as in our text; (2) by *duodēvīgentī*; (3) by the Roman numerals *XVIII*.

LINE 7. **aberat**, 3d pers. sing. imperf. ind. of *absum, -esse, abfuī* or *āfuī, ab(ā)futūrus* (ab + sum). *aberat* agrees with a pron. implied in the ending as subject-nom., referring to Caesar. —— **reī**, dat. sing. of the noun *rēs, reī*, f. (stem *rē*, vowel shortened in the gen. and dat. sing.). *reī* is dat. after *prōspiciendum*. Consult A. & G. 227; B. 142, REM. 5; G. 346, 2; H. 385, II, 1. —— **frūmentāriae**, dat. sing. f. of the adj. *frūmentārius, -a, -um* (*frūmentum*); it is an attributive of the noun *reī*.

LINE 8. **prōspiciendum**, supply *esse*, 2d periphrastic conjugation, pres. inf. of *prōspiciō, -ere, spēxī, -spectum*; used impersonally; note that this verb is both trans. and intrans., and that as an intrans. verb it can only be used impersonally. Consult A. & G. 146, *d*; B. 142, REM. 1; G. 208, 2; H. 465, 1. Note further that the gerundive thus used denotes necessity. See A. & G. 294; B. 185; G. 251; H. 234. —— **exīstimāvit**, 3d pers. sing. perf. ind. act. of *exīstimō, -āre, -āvī, -ātum*, 1; it agrees with a pron. implied in the ending, referring to Caesar, as subject-nom. The rigidly literal translation of *reī . . . exīstimāvit* is: *he thought that it ought to be provided by himself for the thing frumentary*. Of course, *sibi* is to be supplied as dat. of the agent after the gerundive. —— **iter**, acc. sing. of the noun *iter, itineris*, n. (*īre, itum*); direct obj. of *āvertit*. For synonyms, see l. 2, Chap. IX. —— **ab**, prep. with the abl. (*ā* before consonants only, *ab* before either vowels or consonants).

LINE 9. **Helvētiīs**, abl. plur. of the adj. *Helvētius, -a, -um*, used substantively; it is the obj. of the prep. *ab*. As to this clan, see note on *Helvetiī*, l. 16, Chap. I. —— **āvertit**, 3d pers. sing. historical perf. of *āvertō, -ere, -vertī, -versum*, 3; supply *Caesar* as subject-nom. —— **āc**, abbreviated from *atque* (ad + que); it usually adds a notion with emphasis; *āc* is used before consonants only; *āc* here connects the verbs *āvertit* and *contendit*. —— **Bibracte**, acc. sing. of the proper noun *Bibracte*,

This incident was reported to the enemy by fugitives from Lucius Aemilius, a commander of the Gallic horse. The Helvetii, whether	contendit. *he hastened.* L. Aemilii, *of Lucius Aemilius,* hostibus *to the enemy*	Ea *This* decuriōnis *a decurion* nūntiātur. *is reported.*	rēs *thing* equitum *of the cavalry* Helvētiī, *The Helvetii,*	per *through* seu *whether*	fugitīvōs 10 *the deserters* Gallōrum, 11 *of the Gauls,* quod 12 *because*

-tis, n.; it is the acc. of the *limit of motion* after the verb *īre*. See A. & G. 258, *b*; B. 174; G. 337; II. 380, II; and consult note on *Bibracte*, l. 3, above. —— **īre**, pres. inf. of the verb *eō, īre, īvī* (*iī*), *itum;* complementary, depending on *contendit.* See A. & G. 271; B. 181; G. 423; H. 533, I, 1.

LINE 10. **contendit**, 3d pers. sing. perf. ind. of the verb *contendō, -ere, -tendī, -tentum,* 3; it agrees with the noun *Caesar*, to be supplied, as subject-nom.; or, better, connect it with *āvertit* by the conj. *āc*, and note that it is in the same grammatical construction. For an explanation of the various meanings of this verb, see note on *contendunt*, l. 18, Chap. I. Observe the omission of the conj. (asyndeton) before *iter*, i.e. before a clause coördinate with the preceding, and consult A. & G. 346, *c*; B. 122, REM. 6; G. 473, REM.; H. 636, I, 1. Observe, further, that, so far as form goes, *āvertit* and *contendit* might be in the pres. tense; we infer that they are historical perfects from the doctrine of coördination and connection. As we look to the next sentence which is connected logically, not grammatically, with the preceding clause, *repraesentātiō* fronts us; the verb *nūntiātur* is the historical pres. —— **Ea**, nom. sing. f. of the dem. pron. *is, ea, id. ea* is an attributive of *rēs*. —— **rēs**, nom. sing. of the noun *rēs, reī*, f. *rēs* is subject-nom. of the verb *nūntiātur;* it refers to the fact of Caesar's changing his course. —— **per**, prep. with the acc. —— **fugitīvōs**, (*fugere*, to flee), acc. plur. of the adj. *fugitīvus, -a, -um*, used substantively. *fugitīvōs* is the obj. of the prep. *per*, denoting agency as a noun. See A. & G. 246, *b*; B. 166, REM. 1; G. 401; H. 415, I, 1, NOTE 1. *fugitīvōs* = not the cavalry, but slaves. See Chap. XXVII.

LINE 11. **L.**, an abbreviation of *Lūciī*, gen. sing. of *Lūcius, -iī*, m., *praenōmen*. —— **Aemiliī**, gen. sing. of the proper noun *Aemilius, -iī*, m.; a distinguished Roman *nōmen*. But in the text, the name of Lucius Aemilius designates a Gallic cavalry officer in charge of a squad of ten men designated as *decuriō. L. Aemiliī* as a complex proper noun is a poss. gen. limiting *fugitīvōs*. —— **decuriōnis**, gen. sing. of the noun *decuriō, -ōnis*, m. (*decem* through *decuria*); an appositive of *L. Aemiliī*. A *decuriō* was originally a commander of a *decuria*: a squad of ten men; but in Caesar's time the *centuriō* commanded the *turma* or troop consisting of thirty-two horsemen. —— **equitum**, gen. plur. of the noun *eques, -itis*, m.; as a gen. it limits the noun *decuriōnis*. —— **Gallōrum**, gen. plur. of the noun *Gallī, -ōrum;* as a gen. *Gallōrum* limits *equitum*.

LINE 12. **hostibus**, dat. plur. of the noun *hostis, -is*, m. and f. *hostibus* is the indirect obj. of *nūntiātur*. A. & G. 225, *e*; B. 140; G. 345, under PASSIVE FORM; H. 384, I. —— **nūntiātur**, 3d pers. sing. pres. ind. pass. of the verb *nūntiō, -āre, -āvī, -ātum;* pass. parts: *nūntior, -ārī, -ātus*, 1. *nūntiātur* agrees with its subject-nom. *rēs*. Observe that *nūntiō* is often spelled *nūnciō*. —— **Helvētiī**, nom. plur. m. of the adj. *Helvētius, -a, -um;* used substantively. *Helvētiī* is subject-nom. of the verb *coepērunt*, l. 21, below. —— **seu** or *sīve* (sī + ve), alternative conj.; *seu . . . seu*, or *sīve . . . sīve* = *whether . . . or.* —— **quod**, causal conj.

BOOK I.

13 timōre,	perterritōs	Rōmānōs	discēdere	ā	they thought that the Romans, struck with panic, were withdrawing from them, and this all the more, because the day before, although occupying the higher position, they yet did not engage in battle, or for
by alarm	terrified	the Romans	to withdraw	from	
14 sē	existimārent,	eō	magis,	quod	
themselves	they thought,	for this reason	the more,	because	
15 prīdiē	superiōribus	locīs		occupātīs	
on the day before	the higher	places		having been occupied	
16 proelium	nōn commīsissent,	sīve		eō,	
a battle	they did not join,	or		for this reason,	

LINE 13. timŏre, abl. sing. of the noun *timor, -ōris*, m. *timōre* is an abl. of cause after the perf. pass. participle *perterritōs*. Consult A. & G. 245, and 2, *b*; B. 165, and REM. 4; G. 408, NOTE 2; H. 416, and NOTE 1. Synonyms: *timor* = *fear* that results from cowardice or weakness; whereas *metus* = *fear* that results from caution or reflection. —— **perterritōs**, acc. plur. m. of the perf. pass. participle *perterritus, -a, -um* of the verb *perterreō, -ēre, -uī, -itum*, 2; as a participle it modifies the noun *Rōmānōs*. —— **Rōmānōs**, acc. plur. of the adj. *Rōmānus, -a, -um*, used as a substantive. *Rōmānōs* is the subject-acc. of the inf. *discēdere*. —— **discēdere**, pres. inf. act. of the verb *discēdo, -ere, -cessī, -cessum*, 3 (dis + cēdere = lit. *to go apart*). —— **ā**, prep. with the abl. (*ā* before consonants only, *ab* before vowels or consonants).

LINE 14. **sē**, abl. plur. of the reflexive personal pron. *suī, sibī, sē, sē* (same form in sing. and plur.). *sē* is the obj. of the prep. *ā;* it refers to the subject-nom. of *existimārent*. —— **existimārent**, 3d pers. plur. imperf. subjunctive of the verb *existimō, -āre, -āvī, -ātum*, 1; it agrees with a pron. implied in the ending as its subject-nom., referring to *Helvetiī;* it is in the subjunctive mode, because the statement is based on Caesar's conjectures. Consult A. & G. 341, *d*, and REM.; B. 198, (*b*), and 245, (*b*); G. 541; H. 516, II, and 528, 1. Observe that when a speaker thus repeats his conjectures, as if they were of doubtful authority, the discourse is practically oblique. —— **eō**, abl. sing. n. of the dem. pron. *is, ea, id;* abl. of cause after *magis;* lit. *eō* = *on account of this* (thing). The *eō* is the herald of the following *quod*-clause. —— **magis**, adv., comparative degree; positive *multō* (*multum*); superl. *māximē*. Observe that *magis* is modified by *eō*, and that *eō* is modified by the first *quod*-clause, as a species of appositive — an explanatory modifier. —— **quod**, conj. = *because*.

LINE 15. **prīdiē**, adv. (prīs + diē). *prīdiē* modifies the verb *commīsissent*. —— **superiōribus**, abl. plur. of the comparative adj. *superior, -ōris;* positive *superus;* used in plur. as a noun — *superī* = *the gods above;* superl. *suprēmus* or *summus*. *superiōribus* is an attributive of *locīs*. —— **locīs**, abl. plur. of the noun *locus, -ī*, m. in sing.; in the plur. *locī*, m., or *loca*, n. For difference of meaning, see note on *locī*, l. 10, Chap. II. *locīs* is abl. absolute, with the perf. pass. participle denoting concession. —— **occupātīs**, abl. plur. m. of the perf. pass. participle *occupātus, -a, -um* of the verb *occupō, -āre, -āvī, -ātum*, 1; abl. absolute with *locīs*.

LINE 16. **proelium**, acc. sing. of the noun *proelium, -ī*, n.; it is the direct obj. of the verb *commīsissent*. —— **nōn** (nē + oenum [ūnum], apocopated), adv.; note its normal Latin position — immediately before the word it modifies. —— **commīsissent**, 3d pers. plur. pluperf. subjunctive of the verb *committō, -ere, -mīsī, -missum*, 3 (com + mittere = lit. *to join together*); it agrees with a pron. implied in the ending as its

174   CAESAR'S GALLIC WAR   [CHAP. XXIII.

| this reason, because they were confident that the Romans could be cut off from their supplies, the Helvetii, I say, changing their plan and altering their course, began to | quod   rē   frūmentāriā   interclūdī   posse 17 *because   for the thing frumentary   to be hindered to be able* cōnfīderent,   commūtātō   cōnsiliō   atque 18 *they trusted,   having changed   (their)   plan   and* itinere   conversō   nostrōs   ā 19 *the march   being altered,   our   (men)   on the side* |

subject-nom., referring to the Romans.   *committissent* is in the subjunctive for the same reason as *existimārent*, l. 14, above. See grammatical references there indicated. —— *sīve*, see note on *seu*, l. 12, above. —— *eō*, abl. sing. n.; abl. of cause—a herald of the following *quod*-clause.

LINE 17. **quod**, conj. = *because*. *quod*, the conj. with causal meaning, is really an adverbial acc. n. of the rel. pron. *quī*, *quae*, *quod*, and = *as to what, in that;* it is often, as a conj., preceded by *eō*, or *hōc*, or *propterea*. —— **rē**, abl. sing. of the noun *rēs*, *reī*, f. (stem *rē* shortened in the gen. and dat. sing.); abl. *of separation* after *interclūdī*. A. & G. 225, *d*; B. 160; G. 390, 2, NOTE 3; H. 384, II, 2, (2), and FOOTNOTE I. Of course, the obj. in the act. construction becomes the subj. in the pass., and the abl. *of the thing* is retained. —— **frūmentāriā**, abl. sing. f. of the adj. *frūmentārius, -a, -um* (*frūmentum*). *frūmentāriā* is an attributive of the noun *rē*. —— **interclūdī**, pres. inf. pass. of the verb *interclūdō, -ere, -clūsī, -clūsum*, 3 (inter + claudere, lit. = *to shut between*); hence *interclūdere* = *to cut off, to hinder*. *interclūdī* is a complementary inf., depending on *posse*. Consult A. & G. 271; B. 181; G. 423; H. 533, I, 2. —— **posse**, pres. inf. of the intrans. verb *possum, posse, potuī* (potis, *able* + sum); supply *eōs*, i.e. *Rōmānōs*, as subject-acc.

LINE 18. **cōnfīderent**, 3d pers. plur. imperf. subjunctive of *cōnfīdō, -ere, -fīsus*, neuter pass. or semi-deponent verb; in the subjunctive mode for the same reason as *existimārent*, l. 14, above. See in *loc*. —— **commūtātō**, abl. sing. n. of the perf. pass. participle *commūtātus, -a, -um* of the verb *commūtō, -āre, -āvī, -ātum*, 1; pass parts: *commūtor, -ārī, -ātus*, 1. *commūtātō* is in the abl. absolute with *cōnsiliō*, denoting *manner*. —— **cōnsiliō**, abl. sing. of the noun *cōnsilium, -ī*, n.; abl. absolute with the participle *commūtātō*. Synonyms: *concilium* = *an assembly* for consultation; whereas *cōnsilium* = *the counsel* taken in the assembly. There is often, however, confusion in the use of these words. —— **atque** (ad + que), conj.; it usually adds a more emphatic notion, and often = *and also*.

LINE 19. **itinere**, abl. sing. of the noun *iter, itineris*, n.   *itinere* is in the abl. absolute construction with the participle *conversō*. For synonyms, see note on *iter*, l. 2, Chap. IX. —— **conversō**, perf. pass. participle of the verb *convertō, -ere, -vertī, -versum*, 3; abl. absolute with the noun *itinere*. Consult A. & G. 255; B. 192; G. 409, 410; H. 431. Synonyms: *commūtāre* = *to change* completely by some motion in any direction; whereas *convertere* = *to change* by turning or wheeling around. But the words are often, so far as signification is concerned, used interchangeably. —— **nostrōs**, acc. plur. of the poss. pron. *noster, -tra, -trum;* used substantively; or supply *mīlitēs*. *nostrōs* as a substantive is the direct obj. of *insequī āc lacessere*. —— **ā**, prep. with the abl. (*ā* before consonants only, *ab* before either vowels or consonants).   *ā* here = *on the side of, on;* compare *ab*, l. 20, Chap. I.

20 novissimō	āgmine	īnsequī	āc	lacēssere	pursue and assail our troops in the rear.
of the newest	line	to follow on	and	to exasperate	
21 coepērunt.					
they began.					

1 XXIV.	Postquam	id	animum	XXIV. After Caesar noticed
	After that	this (thing) (his)	mind	this manoeuvre

LINE 20. **novissimō**, abl. sing. n. of the superl. degree *novissimus, -a, -um*; positive *novus*; compare GK. νέος. *novissimō* is an attributive of the noun *āgmine*. —— **āgmine**, abl. sing. of the noun *āgmen, -inis*, n. (*agere*, to set in motion); hence *āgmen* = *a moving body, an army in motion*. *āgmine* is the obj. of the prep. *ab*. Observe that the phrase *ā novissimō āgmine* = *on the newest* or *last line of an army in motion*; hence = *on the rear*, i.e. on the newest or nearest line to a pursuing enemy. Synonyms: *āgmen* as a military term = a procession of troops in a line; *cohors* usually = the tenth part of a legion, but sometimes by synecdoche is put for an entire army; *cōpiae* = *troops* consisting of several cohorts; and *exercitus* = *a disciplined army* consisting of several legions. —— **īnsequī**, pres. inf. of the deponent verb *īnsequor, -ī, -cutus*, 3 (in + *sequī* = *to follow on, to attack*). *īnsequī* is a complementary inf. and depends on *coepērunt*. —— **āc**, contracted from *atque* (ad + que), conj. See note on *atque*, l. 18, above. *āc* connects the infinitives *īnsequī* and *lacēssere*. —— **lacēssere**, pres. inf. act. of the verb *lacēssō, -ere, -īvī (-iī), -ītum,* 3 (*lacere*, to move); a form of intensive verb of the 3d conjugation, but having the perf. and supine of the 4th. *lacēssere* is also a complementary inf. See A. & G. 271; B. 181; G. 423; H. 533, I, 1.

LINE 21. **coepērunt**, 3d pers. plur. perf. ind. of the defective verb *coepī*; used only in the perf. and cognate tenses, together with the fut. participle *coeptūrus*. Observe that the pass. of this verb is used with a pass. inf. *coepērunt* agrees with its subject-nom. *Helvētiī*, l. 12, above. Note the periodic form of this long Latin sentence, and observe that the main clause of this sentence is: *Helvētiī nostrōs ā novissimō āgmine īnsequī āc lacēssere coepērunt*; that this main clause is modified (1) by the *quod . . . exīstimārent*-clause, lines 12–14, above; (2) that a lacuna is to be supplied here thus: *eōque magis id exīstimārent*; that *magis* modifies *exīstimārent*, thus supplied; (3) that *magis* is modified by *eō*; and (4) *eō* is modified by the second *quod*-clause — *quod . . . commīsissent*, lines 14–16, above — as explanatory modifier; and (5) the principal clause is further modified by *eō*, l. 16, above, which itself is modified by the *quod*-clause *quod . . . cōnfīderent*, lines 17 and 18, above; and (6) the main clause is still further modified by the abl. absolute construction: *commūtātō cōnsiliō atque itinere conversō*. And observe, in fine, that these complex and compound modifiers of the predicate of the principal clause of the sentence have an adverbial force.

LINE 1. **Postquam** (post + quam = lit. *later than*) = *after*, sometimes causal = *since*. —— **id**, acc. sing. n. of the dem. pron. *is, ea, id*, used substantively; obj. of the prep. *ad* in the compound *advertit*; *id* refers to the Helvetians' attack of Caesar's rear-line. —— **animum**, acc. sing. of the noun *animus, -ī*, m.; direct obj. of *vertit*, a part of the compound *advertit*. For the construction of *id* and *animum* after *advertit*, see A. & G. 239, 2, *b*; B. 152, REM. 2; G. 331, REM. 1; H. 376. For synonyms, see note on *animō*, l. 2, Chap. X.

176　　　　　　　　CAESAR'S GALLIC WAR　　　　　[CHAP. XXIV.

of the Helvetii,	advertit,	cōpiās	suās	Caesar	in	proximum	2
he withdrew his forces to the	he turns to,	troops	his	Caesar	to	the next	
nearest hill, and	collem	subdūcit		equitātumque,		quī	3
sent his cavalry to withstand the	hill	draws off,		cavalry and,		who	
enemy's attack.	sustinēret	hostium		impetum,		mīsit.	Ipse 4
He himself,	should sustain	the enemy's		attack,		he sent.	Himself

LINE 2. **advertit**, 3d pers. sing. pres. ind. act. of *advertō, -ere, -vertī, -versum,* 3; it agrees with a pron. implied in the ending as its subject-nom., referring to *Caesar.* —— **cōpiās**, acc. plur. of the noun *cōpia, -ae,* f. (con + ops); in the sing. = *abundance;* in the plur., *troops.* *cōpiās* is the direct obj. of the verb *subdūcit.* —— **suās**, acc. plur. f. of the poss. and reflexive pron. *suus, -a, -um;* it is an attributive of *cōpiās,* but refers to *Caesar.* —— **Caesar, -aris**, m., subject-nom. of the verb *subdūcit.* Observe the order of the words, and how the emphasis is indicated by putting the direct obj. before the subj. —— **in**, prep. with the acc. and abl.; here it takes the acc. after a verb of motion. For difference of signification, see note on *in,* l. 1, Chap. I. —— **proximum**, acc. sing. m. of the adj. superl. degree *proximus, -a, -um;* the comparative is *propior;* no positive; stem, however, is seen in the adv. *prope,* near. *proximum* is an attributive of the noun *collem.*

LINE 3. **collem**, acc. sing. of the noun *collis, -is,* m. *collem* is the obj. of the prep. *in.* Observe (*a*) that the abl. sing. of *collis* ends regularly in *-e;* that the gen. plur. is *collium;* (*b*) that *collis* (radical seen in *celsus,* participle of *cello,* which = lit. *driven to a high place*) should not be confounded with *mōns,* whose radical is seen in *minārē* and *ēminēre,* and which gives the notion *height* as the essential meaning of the word; although *collis* sometimes = *the larger hill* or *the small mountain.* If *collis* should not be confounded with *mōns,* much less should *mōns* be confounded with *collis,* and rendered *hill* in the English tongue. —— **subdūcit**, 3d pers. sing. pres. ind. act. of *subdūcō, -ere, -dūxī, -ductum* (sub + dūcere); hence *subdūcere = to lead from below.* —— **equitātumque** (equitātum + que). *equitātum,* acc. sing. of the noun *equitātus, -ūs,* m.; it is the direct obj. of the verb *mīsit. que,* enclitic conj.; it connects the verbs *subdūcit* and *mīsit.* —— **quī**, nom. sing. m. of the rel. pron. *quī, quae, quod;* it refers to *equitātum* as its antecedent, but is the subj.-nom. of *sustinēret.*

LINE 4. **sustinēret**, 3d pers. sing. imperf. subjunctive of the verb *sustineō, -ēre, -uī, -tentum,* 2 (sub + tenēre); hence *sustinēre* = lit. *to hold up from beneath. sustinēret* is in the subjunctive, because in a subordinate clause expressing *purpose* after *quī* = *is ut.* Consult A. & G. 317, 2; B. 233, 1; G. 630; H. 497, I. Observe that this relative clause expresses the purpose of *mīsit.* —— **hostium**, gen. plur. of the noun *hostis, -is,* m. and f.; poss. gen. limiting *impetum.* Synonyms: *hostis* = lit. *a stranger;* then transf. = *a public enemy;* whereas *inimīcus* (in, *negative* + amicus) = *a private foe.* —— **impetum**, acc. sing. of the noun *impetus, -ūs,* m. (in + petere, *to fall*); hence *impetus* = *the falling on one, the attack, the onset. impetum* is the direct obj. of *sustinēret.* —— **mīsit**, 3d pers. sing. perf. ind. act. of the verb *mittō, -ere, mīsī, missum,* 3; it is connected by the enclitic *-que* appended to *equitātum* with the verb *subdūcit,* and has the same subject-nom., namely *Caesar.* Observe the confusion of tenses. *repraesentātiō* gives *advertit* — probably pres. — and *subdūcit,* historical present; while there is a change in the point of view between *subdūcit* and the historical perf. This change in the point of view in the same sentence creates liveliness of expression; but such sudden change of tense sequence is not to be very frequently imitated by the modern writer of Latin prose. —— **Ipse**, nom. sing. m. of the

5 interim	in	colle	mediō	triplicem	aciem	meanwhile, marshaled, half way up the hill, a triple line, consisting of the four veteran legions; but he ordered the two legions
meantime	*in*	*the hill*	*middle of,*	*three-fold*	*line*	
6 īnstrūxit	legiōnum		quattuor		veterānārum,	
drew up	*of the legions*		*four*		*veteran,*	
7 sed	in	summō	iugō	duās	legiōnēs,	
but	*on*	*the top*	*of the ridge*	*the two*	*legions,*	

intensive pron. *ipse, -sa, -sum,* gen. *ipsīus,* dat. *ipsī;* it refers to Caesar; is expressed for emphasis; and is the subject-nom. of the verb *īnstrūxit.*

LINE 5. **interim,** adv. (inter + im for eum, i.q. *intereā*). —— **in,** prep. with the acc. and abl.; here it takes the abl. See note on *in,* l. 1, Chap. I. —— **colle,** abl. sing. of *collis, -is,* m.; it is the obj. of the prep. *in.* See note on *collem,* l. 3, above. —— **mediō,** abl. sing. m. of the adj. *medius, -a, -um; mediō* is an attributive of *colle;* but, in use, is here a species of partitive. Consult A. & G. 193; B. 128, REM. 9; G. 291, REM. 2; H. 440, NOTE 1. Observe that *colle mediō* might be used without the prep. *in;* see A. & G. 258, *f,* 2; B. 170, REM. 2; G. 388; H. 425, II, 2, NOTE 2. Observe, further, that the phrase *in colle mediō* = lit. *in the middle of the hill,* i.e. half way up the hill. —— **triplicem,** acc. sing. f. of the adj. *triplex, -icis* (trēs + plicāre, *to weave,* compare GK. πλέκω); hence *triplex* = lit. *triple-woven.* —— **aciem,** acc. sing. of the noun *aciēs, -ēī,* f. (compare GK. ἀκίς = *the edge of a thing);* transf. *aciēs* = *the edge of an army, the line of battle.* Usually, each legion was drawn up in three lines. *aciem* is the direct obj. of the verb *īnstrūxit.*

LINE 6. **īnstrūxit,** 3d pers. sing. perf. ind. act. of *īnstruō, -ere, -strūxī, -strūctum,* 3 (in + struere, *to build); hence īnstruere* = lit. *to build on. īnstrūxit* agrees with its subject-nom. *ipse.* —— **legiōnum,** gen. plur. of the noun *legiō, -ōnis,* f. (*legere,* to choose); hence *legiō* = lit. *a chosen number, a levy.* The legion, from 3000 to 6000 strong, was the unit of the Roman army organization; it was divided into ten cohorts. For further description, see the article *Legion* in any of the encyclopedias. *legiōnum* is a poss. gen. of material limiting the noun *aciem.* Consult A. & G. 214, *e;* B. 131, REM. 1; G. 368, REM.; H. 396, V. —— **quattuor,** num. adj., cardinal; it is an attributive of the noun *legiōnum.* —— **veterānārum,** gen. plur. f. of the adj. *veterānus, -a, -um* (*vetus,* digammated from ἔτος). *veterānārum* is also an attributive of *legiōnum.* These veterans were the 7th, 8th, 9th and 10th legions.

LINE 7. **sed,** the strongest of the adversative conjunctions; *at* expresses a mere contrast; and the postpositive *autem* merely adds a different notion without contradiction, and frequently merely designates a transition. —— **in,** prep. with the acc. or abl.; here it takes the abl. For various meanings, see note on *in,* l. 1, Chap. I. —— **summō,** abl. sing. n. of the adj. *summus, -a -um;* positive *superus,* comparative *superior,* superl. *suprēmus* or *summus. summō* is an attributive of the noun *iugō.* —— **iugō,** abl. sing. of the noun *iugum, -ī,* n. (*iungere,* to join). *iugō* is the obj. of the prep. *in.* Observe that *iugum* = lit. *a yoke;* but that in a transf. sense it means many things; in the text it = the highest ridge of the mountain. Most commonly, as an epithet of a mountain it has reference to breadth or range; whereas *mōns* has reference to height. —— **duās,** acc. plur. f. of the numeral adj. *duo, -ae, -o* (compare GK. δύω or δύο). Note that the first three cardinals — *ūnus, duo* and *trēs* — are declined; but that the remaining cardinals up to *centum* are indeclinable. *duās* is an attributive of the noun *legiōnēs.* These two legions were the 11th and 12th. See lines 13 and 14, Chap. X. —— **legiōnēs,** acc. plur. of the noun *legiō, -ōnis,* f. See note on *legiōnum,* l. 6, above. *legiōnēs* is subject-acc. of *collocārī,* l. 9, below.

| which he had lately levied in citerior Gaul and all the auxiliaries to be stationed on the very crest of the ridge, and the entire mountain to be covered with men, and | quās *which* cōnscrīpserat, *he had enrolled,* āc *and also* | in *in* et *and* tōtum *the entire* | Galliā *Gaul* omnia *all* montem *mountain* | citeriōre *nearer* auxilia *the auxiliaries* hominibus *with men* | proximē *last* collocārī, *to be stationed,* complērī *to be filled* | 8 9 10 |

LINE 8. **quās**, acc. plur. f. of the rel. pron. *quī, quae, quod;* it refers to *legiōnēs* as its antecedent in gender and number, but *quās* is the direct obj. of *cōnscrīpserat*. —— **in**, prep. with the acc. or abl.; here it takes the abl. —— **Galliā**, abl. sing. of the proper noun *Gallia, -ae,* f.; it is the obj. of the prep. *in*. —— **citeriōre**, abl. sing. f. of the adj. *citerior, -us,* comparative degree; superl. *citimus; citeriōre* is an attributive of *Galliā*. Observe that the phrase *in Galliā citeriōre* = *in Galliā Cisalpīnā*, i.e. Gaul on the south side of the Alps — the side nearest to Rome. Ancient Gaul was divided into two parts by the historians: *Gallia ūlterior* and *Gallia citerior*. The *ūlterior* was Gaul on the west side of the Alps. *Gallia citerior* is often referred to as *Gallia Cispadāna* and *Gallia Transpadāna*, i.e. Gaul south, or Gaul north, of the river Po. —— **proximē**, adv. (adj. *proximus);* it modifies the verb *cōnscrīpserat*. Note that adverbs are regularly formed from adjectives of the first and second declension by changing the stem-vowel to *-ē;* stem of *proximus* is *proximō*. Singularly, the adv. *proximē,* superl. in form, is itself compared thus: *proximē (proxumē),* comparative *proximius.*

LINE 9. **cōnscrīpserat**, 3d pers. sing. pluperf. ind. act. of the verb *cōnscrībō, -ere, -scrīpsī, -scrīptum,* 3 (con + scrībere); hence *cōnscrībere* = *to call together by writing, to summon, to enroll*. *cōnscrīpserat* agrees with a pron. implied in its ending as subject-nom., referring to Caesar. —— **et**, cop. conj.; it here connects the nouns *legiōnēs* and *auxilia*. —— **omnia**, acc. plur. n. of the adj. *omnis, -e;* an adj. of the third declension, an *ī*-stem, parisyllabic, and of two terminations, declined like *levis* or *mītis*. *omnia* is an attribute of the noun *auxilia*. —— **auxilia**, acc. plur. of the noun *auxilium, -iī,* n. (*augēre,* to increase). *auxilia* is connected by *et* with *legiōnēs,* and is in the same grammatical construction, i.e. it is subject-acc. of *collocārī*. Observe that *auxilia,* in military usage = *auxiliary troops,* enrolled from the Roman allies, and were light-armed; hence often used in contrast with legionary troops. —— **collocārī** or *conlocārī,* pres. inf. pass. of *col(n)locō, -āre, -āvī, -ātum,* 1; pass. parts: *collocor, -ārī, -ātus,* 1 (con + locāre = lit. *to place together).*

LINE 10. **āc**, conj.; shortened form of *atque;* adds a notion, usually, of more importance; it here connects the infinitive-clauses. —— **tōtum**, acc. sing. m. of the adj. *tōtus, -a, -um,* gen. *tōtīus,* dat. *tōtī*. *tōtum* is an attributive of *montem*. For synonyms, see note on *tōtīus,* l. 7, Chap. II. —— **montem**, acc. sing. of the noun *mōns, montis,* m. (from radical *min,* as seen in *minārī* and in *ēminēre*). See note on *collem,* l. 2, above. *montem* is subject-acc. of *complērī*. —— **hominibus**, abl. plur. of the noun *homō, hominis,* m. and f. (kindred with *humus,* GK. χαμαί, and the Hebrew *adam);* hence *homō* = etymologically, *the earth-born being;* possibly, as the Hebrew *adam* indicates, *the ruddy being*. *hominibus* is the abl. of means after *complērī*. Consult A. & G. 248, 2; B. 167, 3; G. 405; H. 421, II. —— **complērī**, pres. pass. inf. of the verb *compleō, -plēre, -plēvī, -plētum,* 2; pass. parts: *compleor, -ērī, -plētus,* 2; its subject-acc. is *montem*. Observe that the four acc. infinitive-clauses in lines 10–13 depend on the verb *iūssit,* l. 13, below.

11 et intereā sarcinās in ūnum locum	meanwhile the soldiers' personal baggage to be collected in a park, and the park to be defended by those men who were stationed in the upper line. The
and meantime (soldiers') packs into one place	
12 cōnferrī, et eum ab hīs, quī in	
to be brought and that (place) by those, who in	
13 superiōre aciē cōnstiterant, mūnīrī iūssit.	
the higher line had stood, to be protected he ordered.	

LINE 11. **et**, conj.; connects the infinitives *complēri* and *cōnferrī*. —— **intereā**, adv. (inter + eā); it modifies the verb *cōnferrī*. —— **sarcinās**, acc. plur. of the noun *sarcina, -ae,* f. (*sarcīre*, to mend); usually in the plur. *sarcinae, -ārum,* f.; *sarcinās* is the subject-acc. of the verb *cōnferrī.* Synonyms: *sarcinae* = *the baggage* of the individual soldier; whereas *impedimenta* = *the baggage* of an army — the baggage-train including the animals. —— **in**, prep. with the acc. or abl.; here it takes the acc. after a verb of motion, and = *into*. —— **ūnum**, acc. sing. m. of the cardinal adj. *ūnus, -a, -um,* gen. *ūnīus,* dat. *ūnī.* *ūnum* is an attributive of *locum*. —— **locum**, acc. sing. of the noun *locus, -ī,* m.; plur. *locī,* m., or *loca,* n., but with difference of meaning. See note on *locī,* l. 10, Chap. II.

LINE 12. **cōnferrī**, pres. inf. pass. of the verb *cōnferō, -ferre, -tulī, -col*(or *con*)-*lātum*; its subject-acc. is *sarcinās*. Observe that this infinitive-clause is connected by *et* with the preceding, and like that depends on *iūssit,* l. 13, below. —— **et**, cop. conj.; connects the infinitives *cōnferrī* and *mūnīrī,* l. 13, below. —— **eum**, acc. sing. m. of the dem. pron. *is, ea, id,* used substantively; or supply *locum,* which latter is subject-acc. of *mūnīrī,* l. 13, below. —— **ab**, prep. with the abl. (*ā* before consonants only, *ab* before vowels or consonants). This prep. usually = *from*; but after passive verbs with the abl. of the agent it = *by*. —— **hīs**, abl. plur. of the dem. pron. *hīc, haec, hōc,* used substantively. *hīs* is here the abl. of the agent with the prep. *ab,* after the passive verb *mūnīrī.* Consult A. & G. 246; H. 166; G. 401; H. 415, I. Observe that the reference in *hīs* is to *legiōnēs,* l. 7, above, i.e. the two new legions. —— **quī**, nom. plur. of the rel. pron. *quī, quae, quod;* it refers to *hīs* as its antecedent, but is subject-nom. of *cōnstiterant*. —— **in**, prep. with the acc. or abl.; here it takes the abl.

LINE 13. **superiōre**, abl. sing. f. of the adj., comparative degree *superior, -us;* positive *superus;* superl. *suprēmus* or *summus.* *superiōre* is the attributive of the noun *aciē*. —— **aciē**, abl. sing. of *aciēs, -ēi,* f.; it is the obj. of the prep. *in.* Compare *in superiōre aciē* with *in summō iugō,* l. 7, above. —— **cōnstiterant**, 3d pers. plur. pluperf. ind. act. of the verb *cōnsistō, -ere, -stitī, -stitum,* 3; it agrees with its subject-nom. *quī*. —— **mūnīrī**, pres. inf. pass. of the verb *mūniō, -īre, -īvī (-iī), -ītum,* 4 (*moenia*); hence *mūnīre* = lit. *to defend with walls.* The subject-acc. of *mūnīrī* is *eum,* l. 12, above, used as a substantive; or, better, *locum,* to be supplied, with which *eum* as an adj. agrees. —— **iūssit**, 3d pers. sing. perf. ind. act. of the verb *iubeō, -ēre, iūssī, iūssum,* 2; its subject-nom. is a pron. implied in the ending, referring to Caesar. The critical reader will observe that the text in lines 7-10, above, is different in different copies of Caesar that may come under his notice. Some copies after *veterānārum,* l. 6, above, read: *itā, suprā sē . . . collocāret:* āc tōtum, etc. Others read: veterānārum, *atque suprā eās . . .* cōnscripserat; et omnia, etc. Others still after *veterānārum* read: [*ita utī suprā*]; *sed,* etc., precisely like the reading which is given in this edition.

Helvetii follow-	Helvētiī	cum	omnibus	suīs	carrīs 14
ed with all their	The Helvetii	with	all	their	carts
carts, and park-	secūtī,		impedīmenta	in	ūnum 15
ed their imped-	having followed,		(their) heavy baggage	into	one
imenta; and the					
men themselves,	locum	contulērunt;		ipsī	cōnfertissimā 16
after repelling	place	brought;		themselves	in the closest
our cavalry and	aciē,	rēiectō	nostrō	equitātū,	phalange 17
forming a phal-	array,	having been repulsed	our	cavalry,	a phalanx

LINE 14. **Helvētiī**, nom. plur. of the adj. *Helvētius, -a, -um*, used substantively. *Helvētiī* is subject-nom. of the verb *contulērunt*. —— **cum**, prep. with the abl. of accompaniment. —— **omnibus**, abl. plur. of the adj. *omnis, -e*, an *i*-stem, declined like *levis; omnibus* is an attributive of *carrīs*. —— **suīs**, abl. plur. of the poss. and reflexive pron. *suus, -a, -um*; it also is an attributive of the noun *carrīs*; it refers to the subject of the proposition — *Helvētiī*. —— **carrīs**, abl. plur. of the noun *carrus, -ī*, m., or *carrum, -ī*, n.; abl. of accompaniment after the prep. *cum*. Consult A. & G. 248, *a*; B. 168, REM. 4; G. 392; H. 419, I. The reference in *carris* is to the heavy two-wheeled carts on which the Gallic impedimenta were carried.

LINE 15. **secūtī**, nom. plur. m. of the perf. participle of the deponent verb *sequor, -ī, secūtus*, 3 (sibilated from the GK. stem ἑπ, as seen in ἕπομαι). *secūtī*, as a participle, agrees with the noun *Helvētiī*. Observe that deponent verbs have the participles in both voices, e.g. *sequēns = following; secūtus = having followed*. —— **impedīmenta**, acc. plur. of the noun *impedīmentum, -ī*, n. (in + *pes*, through the verb *impedīre* = lit. *to entangle the feet*); hence *impedīmentum* = lit. *a hindrance*; in Caesar's use of the plur., *impedīmenta = the baggage-train*, inclusive of animals. *impedīmenta* is the direct obj. of *contulērunt*. —— **in**, prep. with either the acc. or abl.; here it takes the acc. after a verb of motion, and = *into*. For signification, compare note on *in*, l. 1, Chap. I. —— **ūnum**, acc. sing. m. of the cardinal num. adj. *ūnus, -a, -um*, gen. *ūnīus*, dat. *ūnī; ūnum* is an attributive of the noun *locum*.

LINE 16. **locum**, acc. sing. of the noun *locus, -ī*, m.; but see note on *locī*, l. 10, Chap. II. *locum* is the obj. of the prep. *in*. Compare *in ūnum locum cōnferrī*, lines 11 and 12, above. —— **contulērunt**, 3d pers. plur. perf. ind. act. of *cōnferō, -ere, contulī, col(n)lātum* (con + *ferre* = lit. *to bring together*). *contulērunt* agrees with its subject-nom. *Helvētiī*. —— **ipsī**, nom. plur. of the intensive dem. pron. *ipse, -sa, -sum*, gen. *ipsīus*, dat. *ipsī*. *ipsī* refers to the Helvetii; is expressed for emphasis; and is the subject-nom. of the verb *successērunt*. —— **cōnfertissimā**, abl. sing. of the adj., superl. degree *cōnfertissimus, -a, -um*; positive *cōnfertus*, comparative *cōnfertior*. *cōnfertus* is, in fact, a participle of the verb *cōnferciō*, no perf. act., *cōnfertum*, 4 (con + *farcēre, to cram*); hence the participle *cōnfertus* = lit. *pressed together*, i.e. *thick, close*. *cōnfertissimā* is an attributive of the noun *aciē*.

LINE 17. **aciē**, abl. sing. of the noun *aciēs, -ēī*, f. (compare *ācer*, sharp, and the GK. ἀκίς). *aciē* is an abl. of manner. Consult A. & G. 248; B. 168; G. 399; H. 419, III. Synonyms: *aciēs = an army in line of battle;* whereas *āgmen (agere) = an army in motion*, while *exercitus = a trained army*. —— **rēiectō**, abl. sing. m. of the perf. pass. participle *rēiectus, -a, -um* of the verb *rēiciō, -ere, -iēcī, -iectum*, 3 (re + *iacere* = lit. *to hurl back*). *rēiectō* is in the abl. absolute construction with the noun *equitātū*, denoting the *time when*. —— **nostrō**, abl. sing. m. of the poss. adj. pron. *noster, -tra, -trum (nōs)*; it is an attributive of the noun *equitātū*. —— **equitātū**, abl. sing. of the

18 factā,   sub   prīmam   nostram   aciem | anx, advanced to
having been formed, close to   first   our   line | our lowest line in
19 successērunt. | closest array.
they advanced.

1 XXV. Caesar   prīmum   suō,   deinde | XXV. Caesar,
        Caesar   first   his own (horse),   then, | having first sent
                                                      | out of sight his
2 omnium   ex   cōnspectū   remōtīs   equīs, | own horse, and
   of all   from   sight   being removed the horses, | next the horses
                                                      | of all his aids,

noun *equitātus, -ūs,* m. (*equus* through the verb *equitō*); it is in the abl. absolute with the perf. pass. participle *rēiectō*. —— **phalange,** abl. sing. of the noun *phalanx, -ngis,* f. (GK. φάλαγξ, -αγγος). *phalange* is in the abl. absolute construction with the perf. pass. participle *factā*. Observe that the Greek acc. plur. of *phalanx* is *phalangas,* and that *phalanx* = lit. *a line of troops,* originally, but in later usage = *troops in a solid mass.* Probably there was only a very general resemblance between the phalanx of the Greeks and that of the Gauls; from the next chapter, it would seem to be some sort of arrangement for keeping their lines unbroken by means of interlocking their shields, when they met the onsets of the heavily-armed Roman legions.

LINE 18. **factā,** perf. pass. participle, f. of the verb *fīō, fierī, factus,* used as the pass. of *faciō, -ere, fēcī, factum,* 3. *factā* is in the abl. absolute construction with the noun *phalange,* denoting the *time when.* Consult A. & G. 255, *d,* 1; B. 192; G. 409, 410; H. 431, 1. —— **sub,** prep. with the acc. or abl.; here it takes the acc. after a verb of motion, and = *close to.* —— **prīmam,** acc. sing. f. of the adj., superl. degree *prīmus, -a, -um ;* comparative *prior* (stem seen in the prep. *prae*). *prīmam* is an attributive of the noun *aciem*. As *prīmam,* lit. *the first,* was nearest to the enemy, *prīmam* here = *the lowest.* Compare the phrase *ā novissimō āgmine,* lines 19 and 20, Chap. XXIII. —— **nostram,** acc. sing. f. of the poss. adj. pron. *noster, -tra, -trum* (*nōs*). *nostram* is also an attributive of *aciem*. —— **aciem,** acc. sing. f. of the noun *aciēs, -ēī,* f. (see *aciē,* l. 17, above). *aciem* is the obj. of the prep. *sub,* denoting *motion to.* Consult A. & G. 152, *c*; B. 120. 3; G. 418, 2; H. 435, 1.

LINE 19. **successērunt,** 3d pers. plur. perf. ind. of the neuter verb *succēdō, -ere, -cessī, -cessum,* 3 (*sub* + *cēdere* = lit. *to go under*). *successērunt* agrees with its subject-nom. *ipsī,* l. 16, above. Observe that the prep. *sub* in the phrase *sub . . . aciem* merely repeats and adds some degree of emphasis to *sub* in the compound *sub(c)cessērunt*.

LINE 1. **Caesar, -aris,** m., subject-nom. of the verb *commīsit,* l. 5, below. —— **prīmum,** adv. (really, an adverbial acc. of the adj. *prīmus, -a, -um*); usually, as here, *prīmum* denotes *the first* in a series; whereas *prīmō* = *first* in a contrast. —— **suō,** abl. sing. m. of the poss. pron. *suus, -a, -um ;* it is an attributive of *equō,* to be supplied, which *equō* supplied is in the abl. absolute construction with *remōtō,* to be supplied from the following *remōtīs equīs.* As to the abl. absolute, consult A. & G. 255; B. 192; G. 409, 410; H. 431, and 2. —— **deinde,** adv. (dē + inde) = lit. *from thence ;* it indicates the second of the series.

LINE 2. **omnium,** gen. plur. m. of the adj. *omnis, -e;* an *ī*-stem; *omnium* is here used substantively; it limits the noun *equīs;* or, if preferred, *equitum* might be supplied. —— **ex,** prep. with the abl. (*ē* before consonants only, *ex* before vowels or consonants). —— **cōnspectū,** abl. sing. of the noun *cōnspectus, -ūs,* m. (*cōnspicere,*

in order that, by equalizing the danger of all, he might destroy the hope of flight, cheered his men with hopeful words and engaged in battle. His soldiers, hurling	ut aequātō omnium perīculō spem 3 *that being made equal, of all, the peril, the hope* fugae tolleret, cohortātus suōs 4 *of flight he might take away, having encouraged his (men)* proelium commīsit. Mīlitēs ē locō 5 *the battle he joined. The soldiers from the place*	

perf. pass. participle *cōnspectus = gazed at*), hence *cōnspectus*, as a noun = *sight*. *cōnspectū* is the obj. of the prep. *ex*. Synonyms: *adspectus = looking at*, act.; whereas *cōnspectus = the sight of, the appearance*, pass. —— **remōtīs**, abl. plur. m. of the perf. pass. participle of the verb *removeō*, *-ēre*, *-mōvī*, *-mōtum*, 2; abl. absolute with *equīs*. —— **equīs**, abl. plur. of the noun *equus*, *-ī*, m. (compare Gk. ἵππος). *equīs* is in the abl. absolute construction with the participle *remōtīs*.

LINE 3. **ut**, telic conj. = *in order that*. —— **aequātō**, abl. sing. n. of the perf. pass. participle *aequātus*, *-a*, *-um* of the verb *aequō*, *-āre*, *-āvī*, *-ātum*, 1 (*aequus*); abl. absolute with *perīculō*. —— **omnium**, gen. plur. of *omnis*, *-e*, used substantively; it limits the noun *perīculō*. See note on *omnium*, l. 2, above. —— **perīculō**, abl. sing. of the noun *perīculum*, *-ī*, n. (contracted *perīclum*; lit. = *trial*; transf. *danger*; for radical, see *experior*). *perīculō* is in the abl. absolute construction with *aequātō*. —— **spem**, acc. sing. of the noun *spēs*, *-eī*, f. (stem *spē*, vowel shortened in gen. and dat. sing.). *spem* is the direct obj. of the verb *tolleret*.

LINE 4. **fugae**, gen. sing. of the noun *fuga*, *-ae*, f. (Gk. φυγή); *fugae*, as a gen., limits *spem*. —— **tolleret**, 3d pers. sing. imperf. subjunctive of *tollō*, *-ere*, *sustulī*, *sublātum*. *tolleret* agrees with a pron. implied in the ending as subject-nom., referring to Caesar; it is a subjunctive of purpose after *ut*. Consult A. & G. 317; B. 200; G. 545; H. 497, II. Caesar's design was to remove all means of flight from his treacherous Gallic cavalry. —— **cohortātus**, perf. participle of the verb *cohortor*, *-ārī*, *-ātus*, 1; as a participle it is nom. sing. m., and agrees with *Caesar*, l. 1, above. —— **suōs**, acc. plur. m. of the poss. and reflexive pron. *suus*, *-a*, *-um*; it is used here substantively; or *mīlitēs* may be supplied; direct obj. of the participle *cohortātus*; participles take the same cases as their verbs; as *cohortātus* is the participle of a deponent verb, it is transitive; perf. participles of deponent verbs, however, are sometimes used in a pass. sense.

LINE 5. **proelium**, acc. sing. of the noun *proelium*, *-ī*, n.; it is the direct obj. of *commīsit*. For synonyms, see note on *proeliīs*, l. 18, Chap. I. —— **commīsit**, 3d pers. sing. perf. ind. act. of *committō*, *-ere*, *-mīsī*, *-missum*, 3. *commīsit* agrees with its subject-nom. expressed — *Caesar*, l. 1, above. —— **Mīlitēs**, nom. plur. of the noun *mīles*, *-itis*, m.; subject-nom. of the verb *perfrēgērunt*. —— **ē**, prep. with the abl. (*ē* before consonants only, *ex* before vowels or consonants). —— **locō**, abl. sing. of the noun *locus*, *-ī*, m. in the sing.; plur. *locī*, m., or *loca*, n. See note on *locī*, l. 10, Chap. II. *locō* is the obj. of the prep. *ē*. Synonyms: *locus = space* as a point; whereas *tractus = space* as an expansion; while *regiō* (*regere*, to make straight, to mark by a line) = *space* enclosed as if by a line, including the environment.

6 superiōre	pīlīs	missīs	facile	hostium		their javelins from the higher position, easily made an opening through the enemy's phalanx. When this was thrown into confusion, Caesar's men attacked the enemy with
higher,	the javelins	having been sent,	easily	the enemy's		
7 phalangem	perfrēgērunt.		Eā		disiectā	
phalanx	broke through.		This	being hurled apart,		
8 gladiīs	dēstrictīs	in	eōs	impetum		
swords	having been drawn,	against	them	an onset		

LINE 6. **superiōre**, abl. sing. m. of the adj. *superior, -ius*, gen. *superiōris*; positive *superus*; superl. degree *suprēmus* or *summus*. *superiōre* is an attributive of *locō*. —— **pīlīs**, abl. plur. of the noun *pīlum, -ī*, n. *pīlīs* is abl. absolute with the perf. pass. participle *missīs*, denoting the means. See A. & G. 255; B. 192; G. 409; H. 431. —— **missīs**, abl. plur. of the perf. pass. participle of the verb *mittō, -ere, mīsī, missum*, 3; abl. with the noun *pīlīs*. Observe that the *pīlum* was a missile weapon about six feet in length; it consisted of a shaft and shank, the former of wood, the latter of iron. The shaft was about four feet long, and the shank about two feet long which was pointed with a triangular-shaped head of steel about nine inches in length. —— **facile**, adv. (adj. *facilis*). *facile* is, in fact, an adverbial acc. n. of the adj. *facilis*. Consult A. & G. 148, *d*; B. 117. 6; G. 91, 1, (*c*); H. 304, 3, 1). *facile* modifies *perfrēgērunt*. —— **hostium**, gen. plur. of the noun *hostis, -is*, m. and f.; as a gen. it limits *phalangem*. Synonyms: *hostis* = lit. *a stranger*, and then transf. *a public enemy; inimīcus* (in, *negative* + amīcus) = *a private foe*.

LINE 7. **phalangem**, acc. sing. of the noun *phalanx, -angis*, f. (compare the GK. φάλαγξ, and the Greek acc. pl. *phalangas* which is common in Latin instead of the regular form *phalangēs*). *phalangem* is the direct obj. of the verb *perfrēgērunt*. In the phalanx order of battle the infantry stood in compact mass with their shields, vertically arranged, protecting them in front; above their heads these shields, to those who were behind the first line, were interlaced and overlapped, and formed a protection against the missiles of the foe. —— **perfrēgērunt**, 3d pers. plur. perf. ind. act. of the verb *perfringō, -ere, -frēgī, -frāctum*, 3 (per + frangere = *to break through*); with *frangere* compare the GK. ῥήγνυμι, the GER. *brechen*, and the English *break*. *perfrēgērunt* agrees with its subject-nom. *mīlitēs*, expressed l. 5, above. —— **Eā**, abl. sing. f. of the dem. pron. *is, ea, id*, used substantively, referring to *phalangem*; or supply *phalange*; abl. absolute with the pass. participle *disiectā*, denoting *time when*. —— **disiectā**, abl. sing. f. of the perf. pass. participle *disiectus, -a, -um* of the verb *disiciō, -ere, -iēcī, -iectum*, 3 (dis + iacere = lit. *to hurl apart*); the construction is abl. absolute with *eā*.

LINE 8. **gladiīs**, abl. plur. of the noun *gladius, -iī*, m.; abl. absolute with the perf. pass. participle *dēstrictīs*, denoting the manner. Synonyms: *gladius* is the usual, and *ēnsis* the poetic name for *sword*; *pugiō* = *the dagger* openly worn; whereas *sīca* = *the poniard* secretly carried. The sword of the Gauls was a long, two-edged, unwieldy affair, carried in a scabbard suspended on the right side, so as not to interfere with the shield side — the left. —— **dēstrictīs**, abl. plur. m. of the perf. pass. participle *dēstrictus, -a, -um*; in the abl. absolute construction with the noun *gladiīs*. —— **in**, prep. with the acc. or abl.; here it takes the acc., and = *against*. —— **eōs**, acc. plur. of the dem. pron. *is, ea, id*, used as a personal pron. of the 3d pers. *eōs* is the obj. of the prep. *in*. —— **impetum**, acc. sing. of the noun *impetus, -ūs*, m.; it is the direct obj. of the verb *fēcērunt*.

| drawn swords. It greatly impeded the Gauls in fighting that many of their shields were pierced through and fastened together by a single thrust of the javelins; and since the iron point of | fēcērunt, they made. pūgnam the fight, eōrum of their trānsfīxīs having been transfixed | Gallīs As the Gauls, erat was, scūtīs shields and | magnō for a great, impedīmentō, hindrance, ūnō by one et colligātīs, bound together, | ad in respect to plūribus that ictū stroke cum since | 9 10 11 12 |

LINE 9. fēcērunt, 3d pers. plur. perf. ind. act. of the verb *faciō, -ĕre, fēcī, factum*, 3; it agrees with the subject-nom. *milites* understood. Observe that, instead of using the phrase-form *in eōs impetum fēcērunt*, Caesar might with greater conciseness have written: *eōs aggressī sunt*. See *Eōs... aggressus*, lines 13 and 14, Chap. XII. —— Gallīs, dat. plur. of the adj. *Gallus, -a, -um*, used substantively. *Gallīs* is the dat. of the *object to which* after *erat*. Consult A. & G. 233; B. 147; G. 356; H. 390, I. —— magnō, dat. sing. n. of the adj. *magnus, -a, -um*; comparative *maior*; superl. *maximus*. *magnō* is an attributive of the noun *impedīmentō*. —— ad, prep. with the acc.; it = *in respect to*.

LINE 10. pūgnam, acc. sing. of the noun *pugna, -ae*, f. *pūgnam* is the obj. of the prep. *ad*. For synonyms, see note on *proeliis*, l. 18, Chap. I. —— erat, 3d pers. sing. imperf. tense, ind. mode of the intrans. verb *sum, esse, fui, futūrus*; used impersonally, or rather the following *quod*-clause is the subj. —— impedīmentō, dat. of the noun *impedīmentum, -ī*, n. (in + pēs through the verb *impediō*); hence the noun = the condition of *foot-entanglement, impediment, hindrance*. *impedīmentō* is here a dat. of service after the intrans. verb *erat*. Consult A. & G. 233, *a*; B. 147, REM. 2; G. 356; II. 390, I. The student will observe that *erat* here takes two *datives*: *Gallīs* and *impedīmentō* — the one the *object to which*, and the other the *end for which*. —— quod, conj.; here it = *that*; it introduces the clause *quod.... poterant*, which is the logical subj. of *erat*, immediately preceding. —— plūribus, abl. plur. n. of the comparative adj. *plūrēs, -a*, gen. *plurium*; the sing. *plūs* is declined only in the neuter; positive *multus*; superl. *plūrimus*. *plūribus* is an attributive of the noun *scūtīs*. For declension of *plūrēs*, see A. & G. 86, and *b*; B. 72, 7; G. 89, REMS. 1, 2, 3; H. 165, NOTE 1.

LINE 11. eōrum, gen. plur. of the dem. pron. *is, ea, id*, used as a personal pron. of the 3d pers.; as a gen. it limits *scūtīs*. —— scūtīs, abl. plur. of the noun *scūtum, -ī*, n. (σκῦτος = *tanned hide, leather*). *scūtīs* is in the abl. absolute construction with the perf. pass. participles *trānsfīxīs* and *collogātīs*, denoting *time when*. Synonyms: *scūtum* = the oblong wooden *shield*, leather-covered; whereas the *clypeus*, or *clipeus*, or *clipeum* was a round brazen *shield*. —— ūnō, abl. sing. m. of the cardinal num. adj. *ūnus, -a, -um*; gen. *ūnīus*, dat. *ūnī*. *ūnō* is an attributive of the noun *ictū*. —— ictū, abl. sing. of the noun *ictus, -ūs*, m. (*icere*, to strike). *ictū* is an abl. of manner. See A. & G. 248; B. 168; G. 399; H. 419, III. —— pīlōrum, gen. plur. of the noun *pīlum, -ī*, n. = the heavy *javelin* of the Roman infantry. *pīlōrum*, as a gen., limits the noun *ictū*.

LINE 12. trānsfīxīs, abl. plur. n. of the perf. pass. participle *trānsfīxus, -a, -um* of the verb *trānsfīgō, -ĕre, -fīxī, -fīxum*, 3 (trāns + figere = lit. *to pierce through*). *trānsfīxīs* is in the abl. absolute construction with the noun *scūtīs*. —— et, cop. conj.; connects words and phrases and clauses of equal importance. *et* here connects

13 sē	īnflēxisset,	neque	ēvellere	neque	the weapon bent itself, the Gauls could neither pull the javelin out, nor, as the left hand was encumbered with the shield, could they fight with any ease; so that	
itself	*had bent,*	*neither*	*to pluck it out*	*nor,*		
14 sinistrā	impedītā	satis	commodē			
the left hand	*being impeded,*	*enough*	*advantageously*			
15 pūgnāre	poterant,	multī	ut	diū		
to fight	*were they able,*	*many,*	*so that,*	*long*		

the two participles. —— col(n)ligātīs, abl. plur. n. of the perf. pass. participle *colligātus, -a, -um* of the verb *col(n)ligō, -āre, -āvī, -ātum,* 1 (con + ligāre = lit. *to bind together*); *colligātīs* is connected by the conj. *et* with *trānsfīxīs,* and is in the same grammatical construction. —— cum, causal conj. —— ferrum, nom. sing. of *ferrum, -ī,* n. = like GK. σίδηρος, anything made of *iron. ferrum* is the subject-nom. of the verb *īnflēxisset.*

LINE 13. sē, acc. sing. of the reflexive pron. *suī, sibi, sē, sē* — same form in both numbers; it refers to *ferrum,* and = *itself;* it is the direct obj. of the verb *īnflēxisset.* —— īnflēxisset, 3d pers. sing. pluperf. subjunctive act. of the verb *īnflectō, -ere, -flexī, -flexum,* 3 (in + flectere = lit. *to bend in);* it agrees with its subject-nom. *ferrum;* it is in the subjunctive after *cum* causal. Consult A. & G. 326; B. 223; G. 586; H. 517. Observe that *cum ... īnflēxisset* express the reason why the Gauls could not fight successfully. —— neque (nē + que = lit. *and not);* but *neque ... neque = neither ... nor;* in this use, a species of correlative conjunctions. When *neque = and not,* it is a conjunctive adv. —— ēvellere, pres. inf. act. of the verb *ēvellō, -ere, -vellī, -vulsum,* 3 (ē + vellere = *to pluck out). ēvellere* is a complementary inf., depending on *poterant,* l. 15, below. See A. & G. 271; B. 181; G. 423; H. 533, I, 2; supply *eum,* i.e. *ferrum,* as direct obj. of *ēvellere.* —— neque, see *neque,* immediately preceding.

LINE 14. sinistrā, abl. sing. f. of the adj. *sinister, -tra, -trum,* used substantively; or supply *manū. sinistrā,* as a subst., is in the abl. absolute construction with the participle *impedītā,* denoting the cause. See A. & G. 255, *d,* 2; B. 192; G. 409, 410; H. 431, 2, (3). Observe that the left hand was hampered, because the soldier wore the shield on the left arm, and one soldier's shield was fastened to the shield of another by the heavy Roman javelins that pierced it. —— impedītā, abl. sing. f. of the perf. pass. participle *impedītus, -a, -um* of the verb *impediō, -īre, -īvī (-iī), -ītum,* 4 (in + pēs) = *with the foot in it;* hence *to ensnare, impede. impedītā* is in the abl. absolute with *sinistrā,* used as a noun. —— satis, adv., comparative *satius* = lit. *more satisfying,* i.e. *better. satis* as an adv. modifies the adv. *commodē.* —— commodē, adv. (from adj. *commodus = advantageous);* it modifies the verb *pūgnāre.*

LINE 15. pūgnāre, pres. inf. act. of the verb *pūgnō, -āre, -āvī, -ātum,* 1; connected by the conj. *neque* with *ēvellere,* and in the same grammatical construction, i.e. complementary inf., and depends on *poterant.* —— poterant, 3d pers. plur. imperf. ind. of the intrans. verb *possum, posse, potuī;* and it agrees with *Gallī* understood, as the subject-nom. —— multī, nom. plur. m. of the adj. *multus, -a, -um,* used substantively; or supply *mīlitēs;* subject-nom. of the verb *praeoptārent.* Observe its emphatic position; usually the conj. *ut,* in a clause of result, stands at the head of it. —— ut, ecbatic conj. —— diū, adv. (*diēs),* comparative *diūtius,* superl. *diūtissimē. diū,* as an adv., modifies *iactātō.*

many, after tossing their arms about for a long time, preferred to throw their shields away, and fight without protection. At length, exhausted with wounds, they began to fall back, and, as there was a moun-	iactātō *having been tossed about* manū *from the hand* pūgnāre. *to fight.* pedem *the foot*	ēmittere *to throw* Tandem *At length* referre *to bear back*	brāchiō *the arm,* et *and* vulneribus *by wounds* et, *and,*	praeoptārent *preferred* nūdō *with the nude* dēfessī *worn out* quod *because*	scūtum 16 *the shield* corpore 17 *body* et 18 *both* mōns suberat 19 *a mountain was near,*

LINE 16. **iactātō**, abl. sing. n. of the perf. pass. participle *iactātus, -a, -um* of the verb *iactō, -āre, -āvī, -ātum*, 1 (frequentative of *iaciō*, 3). *iactātō* is in the abl. absolute construction with the noun *brāchiō*. —— **brāchiō**, abl. sing. of the noun *brāchium, -iī*, n. (compare GK. βραχίων). *brāchium* = lit. *the forearm*, but here it = the entire *arm*. *brāchiō* is abl. absolute with the participle *iactātō*, denoting *time when*. —— **praeoptārent**, 3d pers. plur. imperf. subjunctive of the verb *praeoptō, -āre, -āvī, -ātum*, 1 (prae + optāre); hence = lit. *to wish for one thing before another* = *to prefer*. *praeoptārent* is subjunctive of result after *ut*. Consult A. & G. 319; B. 201; G. 552, 1; H. 500, II. —— **scūtum**, acc. sing. of the noun *scūtum, -ī*, n.; it is the direct obj. of the verb *ēmittere*. As to derivation and synonyms, see note on *scūtīs*, l. 9, above.

LINE 17. **manū**, abl. sing. of the noun *manus, -ūs*, f. by exception; see A. & G. 69; B. 48, REM. 5, EXC. 1; G. 62, EXC.; H. 118, EXC. (1.). *manū* is an *abl. of separation* after the verb *ēmittere*. Consult A. & G. 243, *b*; B. 160; G. 390, 2; H. 413. —— **ēmittere**, pres. inf. act. of the verb *ēmittō, -ere, -mīsī, -mīssum*, 3 (ē + mittere = lit. *to send out*). *ēmittere* is a complementary inf., depending on *praeoptārent*. Consult A. & G. 271; B. 181; G. 423; H. 533, I, 1. —— **et**, cop. conj.; connects *ēmittere* and *pūgnāre*. —— **nūdō**, abl. sing. n. of the adj. *nūdus, -a, -um*. *nūdō*, lit. *naked*, is an attributive of the noun *corpore*. —— **corpore**, abl. of the noun *corpus, -oris*, n.; abl. of manner. See A. & G. 248; B. 168; G. 399; H. 419, III. The phrase *nūdō corpore* = with the *body unprotected* by a shield, i.e. without a shield.

LINE 18. **pūgnāre**, pres. inf. act. of the verb *pūgnō, -āre, -āvī, -ātum*, 1. *pūgnāre* is connected by *et* with *ēmittere*, and is also a complementary inf., depending on *praeoptārent*. Note that *praeoptārent* is transitive, and that the complementary infinitives, with their objects, form object-clauses, which are in the nature of direct objects. Note also the unique and, therefore, emphatic position of *praeoptārent;* its normal position in the sentence would be immediately after *pūgnāre*. —— **Tandem**, adv. (tam + dem); hence = lit. *just so far*, i.e. *at length*. *tandem* modifies *coepērunt*, l. 21, below. —— **vu(o)lneribus**, abl. plur. of *vu(o)lnus, -eris*, n.; abl. of cause. Consult A. & G. 245, and 2, *b*; B. 165, and REM. 4; G. 408, and NOTE 2; H. 416, and NOTE 1. —— **dēfessī**, nom. plur. m. of the perf. participle *dēfessus, -a, -um* of the deponent *dēfetiscor, -ī, -fessus*, 3, agreeing with *Gallī* understood — the omitted subject of *coepērunt*, l. 21, below. But note that *dēfessī* is a perf. participle of a deponent verb; it is here used in a passive sense. —— **et**, a species of correlative conj. here, followed by another *et* connecting the object-clauses.

LINE 19. **pedem**, acc. sing. of the noun *pēs, pedis*, m.; direct obj. of the verb *referre*. —— **referre**, pres. inf. act. of the verb *referō, -ferre, -tulī, -lātum*. Observe

20 circiter	mīlle	passuum	spatiō,		eō
about	*a thousand*	*of paces*	*in respect to space,*		*thither*
21 sē		recipere	coepērunt.		Captō
themselves		*to betake*	*they began.*		*Being reached*
22 monte	et	succēdentibus	nostrīs,		Bōiī
the mountain	*and*	*coming on*	*our (men),*		*the Boii*

tain near—about a mile off — they began thither to retreat. When the mountain had been reached by the enemy, and our men were approaching it in pursuit, the Boii

that this inf. with its direct obj. forms an object-clause that depends on *coepērunt*. Observe, further, that *pedem referre* = lit. *to bear the foot back*, i.e. *to retreat*; and = *terga vertere* or *terga dare*, except that *pedem referre* = *to retreat in good order*; whereas *terga vertere* or *terga dare* = generally, *to retreat in confusion*. —— et, see note on *et*, preceding line; but note that *et* here connects the object-phrases *pedem referre* and *se recipere*. —— quod, conj., causal (really an adverbial acc. of the rel. pron. *qui, quae, quod*, and = *as to which, in that, because*). —— mōns, nom. sing. of the noun *mōns, montis*, m. (from the root *min*, as seen in *minārī, ēminēre*, lit. *a projecting* object). *mōns* is the subject-nom. of the verb *suberat*. —— suberat, 3d pers. sing. imperf. ind. of the intrans. verb *subsum, -esse*, no perf., *-futūrus* (sub + sum); hence *subesse* = lit. *to be under*, i.e. *near*, or *at hand*. *suberat* agrees with its subject-nom. *mōns*.

LINE 20. circiter, adv. (*circus, circum* = *a circular line, in a ring*, compare GK. κίρκος). *circiter* modifies the adj. *mīlle*. —— mīlle, an indecl. adj. in the sing.; but sometimes used as a noun in the nom. and acc. sing., e.g. in the phrase *mille passuum*, of the text. *mille* is here an acc. of extent of space. A. & G. 257; B. 153; G. 335; H. 379. —— passuum, gen. plur. of the noun *passus, -ūs*, m. *passuum* is partitive gen. after *mille*. See A. & G. 216, 2; B. 134; G. 370; H. 397, 2. —— spatiō, abl. sing. of the noun *spatium, -iī*, n. (compare English *space*). *spatiō* is abl. of specification. Consult A. & G. 253; B. 162; G. 397; H. 424. —— eō, adv. (old dat. of the pron. *is, ea, id*); supply *locō*, and the phrase *eō locō* = *to that place, thither*. *eō* refers to *mōns*. Observe that, as often *place* by metonymy = the persons *at the place*, *eō* may sometimes in English = *on it, him* or *them*, as the context may require.

LINE 21. sē, acc. plur. of the reflexive pron. *sui, sibi, sē, sē* — same form in both numbers; *sē* refers to the subj. of the proposition, but is the direct obj. of *recipere*. —— recipere, pres. inf. act. of the verb *recipiō, -ere, -cēpī, -ceptum*, 3 (re + căpere); hence *recipere* = *to take back*; with *sē* = *to take one's self back* — *to retreat*. —— coepērunt, 3d pers. plur. of the defective verb *coepī, coepisse*, fut. participle *coeptūrus*; with the exception of the fut. act. participle used only in the perfect and cognate tenses, act. and pass.; when followed by a pass. inf. the pass. form *coeptus sum* is used instead of *coepī*. *coepērunt* agrees with its subject-nom. *Galli*, to be supplied. —— Captō, abl. sing. m. of the perf. pass. participle *captus, -a, -um* of the verb *capiō, -ere, cēpī, captum*, 3. *captō* here = *occupātō*, and is in the abl. absolute construction with the noun *monte*, denoting *time when*. See A. & G. 255, *d*, 1; B. 192; G. 409, 410; H. 431, I, 2, (3).

LINE 22. monte, abl. sing. of the noun *mōns, montis*, m.; abl. absolute with the perf. pass. participle *captō*. —— et, cop. conj.; connects the phrases. —— succēdentibus, abl. plur. m. of the pres. participle *succēdēns, -ntis* of the verb *succēdō, -ere, -cessī, -cessum*, 3 (sub + cēdere) = lit. *to go under*. *succēdentibus* is in the abl. absolute

| and Tulingi who, with about fifteen thousand men, closed the enemy's line and served as a rearguard, attacked, on the unprotected flank, our soldiers while still advancing, | et *Tulingī,* and *the Tulingi,* circiter quīndecim about *fifteen,* claudēbant et *closed,* and erant, ex itinere *were,* on *the march* | quī *who with,* āgmen *the line of march* novissimīs *to the newest* (the rear) nostrōs ā *ours* on | hominum *of men,* hostium *of the enemy* praesidiō *for a protection* latere apertō *the flank* open, | mīlibus 23 *thousands* 24 25 26 |

construction with *nostrīs,* used substantively; or supply *mīlitibus.* —— **nostrīs,** abl. plur. m. of the poss. pron. *noster, -tra, -trum;* used substantively, and abl. absolute with the pres. participle *succēdentibus,* denoting *time when.* See grammatical references to *Captō,* preceding line. —— **Bōiī, -ōrum,** m., a Celtic people, occupying a district lying between the rivers Loire and Allier; some of them settled in Cisalpine Gaul; others mīgrated to Germany; while others cast in their lot with the Helvetii, and were with them on this migration. *Bōiī* is subject-nom. of the historical inf. *circumvenīre,* l. 27, below.

LINE 23. **et,** cop. conj.; it here connects *Bōiī* and *Tulingī.* —— **Tulingī, -orum,** m., a German tribe east of the *Rauraci. Tulingī* is connected by the conj. *et* with the proper noun *Bōiī,* and is in the same grammatical construction. —— **quī,** nom. plur. m. of the rel. pron. *quī, quae, quod;* it refers to the *Bōiī et Tulingī,* and is the subj. of the verb *claudēbant.* —— **hominum,** gen. plur. of the noun *homō, -inis,* m. or f.; partitive gen. after *mīlibus.* See A & G. 216, 2; B. 134; G. 370; H. 397, 2. For synonyms, see note on *hominēs,* l. 20, Chap. I. —— **mīlibus,** abl. plur. of *mīlia, -ium,* plur. of the adj. *mīlle;* in the plur. it is used as a nenter noun. *mīlibus* is the abl. of *accompaniment* without the prep. *cum.* Consult A. & G. 248, *a,* NOTE; B. 168, REM. 4; G. 399; H. 419, III, 1, 1).

LINE 24. **circiter,** adv. *(circus, circum)* = *about; circiter* modifies the cardinal num. adj. *quīndecim.* —— **quīndecim,** num. adj. (quīnque + decem). *quīndecim* is an attributive of *mīlibus,* used as a noun. —— **āgmen,** acc. sing. of the noun *āgmen, -inis,* n. *(agere,* to agitate). *āgmen* is the direct obj. of the verb *claudēbant.* For synonyms, see note on *āgmen,* l. 9, Chap. XV. —— **hostium,** gen. plur. of the noun *hostis, hostis,* m. and f.; as a gen. it limits the noun *āgmen.* Synonyms: *hostis* = a *public enemy; inimīcus* (in + amīcus) = a *private foe.*

LINE 25. **claudēbant,** 3d pers. plur. imperf. ind. act. of the verb *claudō, -ere, clausī, clausum,* 3; it agrees with its subject-nom. *quī.* —— **et,** cop. conj.; it connects the two clauses. —— **novissimīs,** dat. plur. n. of the adj. superl. degree *novissimus, -a, -um;* positive *novus;* comparative wanting. *novissimīs* is here used substantively; or we may supply *agminis* = lit. *the newest,* i.e. *latest, last;* hence = *the rear. novissimīs* is the dat. of the obj. *to which* after *erant.* —— **praesidiō,** dat. of the noun *praesidium, -iī,* n. *(praeses). praesidiō* is the dat. of service or dat. *for which* after *erant.* Consult A. & G. 233, *a;* B. 147, REM. 2; G. 356; H. 390, I.

LINE 26. **erant,** 3d pers. plur. imperf. ind. of the intrans. verb *sum, esse, fuī, futūrus;* it is connected by the conj. *et* with the verb *claudēbant,* and has the same subject-nom. *quī.* —— **ex,** prep. with the abl. *(ē* before consonants only, *ex* before vowels or consonants). —— **itinere,** abl. sing. of the noun *iter, itineris,* n. *(īre, itum);* hence = lit. *a going. itinere* is the obj. of the prep. *ex.* —— **nostrōs,** acc. plur. of

27 aggressī	circumvenīre;		et	id
having attacked,	*to surround*	*(them tried);*	*and*	*that*
28 cōnspicātī	Helvētiī,	quī	in	montem
having seen,	*the Helvetii,*	*who*	*to*	*the mountain*
29 sēsē	recēperant,	rūrsus	īnstāre	et
themselves	*had betaken,*	*again*	*to press on*	*and*

and tried to surround them. On observing this manoeuvre, the Helvetii, who had retreated to the mountain, began again to draw near and renew

the poss. pron. *noster*, *-tra*, *-trum*, used substantively, or supply *mīlitēs*; *nostrōs* is the direct obj. of the deponent participle *ag(d)gressī*. —— **ā**, prep. with the abl. (*d* before consonants only, *ab* before vowels or consonants). *ā* here = *on*. See note on *ab*, l. 24, Chap. I. —— **latere**, abl. sing. of the noun *latus*, *-eris*, n. *latere* is the obj. of the prep. *ā*. —— **apertō**, abl. sing. n. of the participle *apertus*, *-a*, *um* of the verb *aperiō*, *-īre*, *-uī*, *-pertum*, 4 (ab + parere). *aperīre* = lit. *to bring forth* — to drop as of animals; hence in participle = *uncovered, bare*. *apertō* is an attributive of the noun *latere*.

LINE 27. **aggressī**, perf. participle of the deponent verb *ag(d)gredior*, *-gredī*, *-gressus* (ad + gradī) = lit. *to take a step toward;* hence = *to attack*. —— **circumvenīre**, pres. inf. act. of the verb *circumveniō*, *-īre*, *-vēnī*, *-ventum*, 4 (circum + veniō) = lit. *to come around;* hence = *to surround;* historical inf. having as its subject-nominatives *Bōiī* and *Tulingī*, or we may supply *cōnditī sunt*. Consult A. & G. 275; B. 182, and REM.; G. 647, and NOTE 1; H. 536, 1. Supply *eōs* as direct obj. of *circumvenīre*, and observe that the historical inf. = *circumveniēbant* — conative imperf. Some texts read here *circumvēnēre*, 3d pers. plur. perf. ind.; and some texts have not even a comma between *circumvenīre* and *et;* the inf., of course, is made in this construction to depend on *coepērunt*, l. 30, below. —— **et**, cop. conj.; it connects the sentences. —— **id**, acc. sing. n. of the dem. pron. *is*, *ea*, *id*, used substantively; the direct obj. of the deponent participle *cōnspicātī*. *id* refers to the movement of the *Bōiī* and the *Tulingī*.

LINE 28. **cōnspicātī**, nom. plur. of the perf. participle *cōnspicātus*, *-a*, *-um* of the deponent verb *cōnspicor*, *-ārī*, *-cātus*, 1; as a participle it agrees with the noun *Helvētiī* in gender, number and case. —— **Helvētiī**, nom. plur. of the adj. *Helvētius*, *-a*, *-um*, used substantively. *Helvētiī* is the subject-nom. of the verb *coepērunt*, l. 30, below. As to this clan, see note on *Helvētiī*, l. 16, Chap. I. —— **quī**, nom. plur. of the rel. pron. *quī*, *quae*, *quod;* it refers to the noun *Helvētiī;* it is the subj. of the verb *recēperant*. —— **in**, prep. with the acc. or abl.; here it takes the acc. after a verb of motion. For different significations, see note on *in*, l. 1, Chap. I. —— **montem**, acc. sing. of the noun *mōns*, *montis*, f. (root in *minārī*, and in *ēminēre);* hence lit. it = *a projecting* body. Observe that the *i* in the root *min* is short *by nature*. Query: How does the *i* which passes into *o* in the stem *mont* become, in any case, long *by nature*? *montem* is the obj. of the prep. *in*.

LINE 29. **sēsē**, acc. plur. of the pron. *sē* reduplicated; acc. plur. of the reflexive pron. *suī*, *sibi*, *sē*, *sē* — same form in both numbers. *sēsē* is the direct obj. of the verb *recēperant*. —— **recēperant**, 3d pers. plur. pluperf. ind. of the verb *recipiō*, *-ere*, *-cēpī*, *-ceptum*, 3 (re + capere); hence = lit. *to take back;* transf. = *to get back*. But lit. *sē recipere* = *to take one's self back, to withdraw, to go anywhere;* in military language, *to retreat*. *recēperant* agrees with its subject-nom. *quī*. —— **rūrsus**, adv.; another form *rūrsum* (contracted from *revorsus*, a participle of *revortor*, *-ī*, *-ver[vor]sus*, 3); hence *rūrsus* = lit. *turned back*, i.e. = *again, anew*. —— **īnstāre**, pres. inf.

190   CAESAR'S GALLIC WAR   [CHAP. XXV.

the battle. The Romans wheeled and advanced to the attack in two divisions: the first and second lines, to oppose the Helvetii who had been previously vanquished and routed;	proelium redintegrāre coepērunt. Rōmānī 30
	the battle to renew began. The Romans (then)
	conversa signa bipertītō intulērunt; 31
	turned about standards in two divisions advanced (bore in);
	prīma et secunda aciēs, ut vīctīs 32
	the first and second line, that the vanquished

of the verb *īnstō, -stāre, -stitī*, fut. participle *statūrus* (in + stāre); hence *īnstāre =* lit. *to stand on* or *near*, i.e. *to press on, be urgent. Īnstāre* is here a complementary inf., depending on *coepērunt*. Consult A. & G. 271; B. 181; G. 423; H. 533, I, 1. ——— **et**, cop. conj.; it connects the infinitives *īnstāre* and *redintegrāre*.

LINE 30. **proelium**, acc. sing. of the noun *proelium, -ī*, n.; it is the direct obj. of the verb *redintegrāre*. For synonyms, see note on *proeliīs*, l. 18, Chap. I. ——— **redintegrāre**, pres. inf. act. of the verb *redintegrō, -āre, -āvī, -ātum*, 1 (re[d] + integrāre [in + tangere], through *integer*); hence *integrāre =* lit. *to be untouched*, i.e. *sound*; and with *re- = to be whole again*; i.e. *to recover their courage — to renew the fight*. *redintegrāre* is connected by the conj. *et* with the inf. *īnstāre*, and is in the same grammatical construction; depends on *coepērunt*. ——— **coepērunt**, 3d pers. plur. of the defective verb *coepī*, which is used only in the perf. and cognate tenses. See note on *coepērunt*, l. 21, above. *coepērunt* agrees with its subject-nom. *Helvētiī*, l. 28, above. ——— **Rōmānī**, nom. plur. of the adj. *Rōmānus, -a, -um*, used substantively. *Rōmānī* is the subject-nom. of the verb *intulērunt*.

LINE 31. **conversa**, acc. plur. of the perf. pass. participle *conversus, -a, -um* of the verb *convertō, -ere, -vertī, -versum*, 3. *conversa*, as a participle, agrees with the noun *sīgna*. ——— **sīgna**, acc. plur. of the noun *sīgnum, -ī*, n. (sibilated from the GK. εἰκών, *an image, a likeness*); hence = lit. *that by which anything is known*; in military language = *the sign* of a division of an army, *a standard*. *sīgna* is the direct obj. of the verb *intulērunt*. Observe the strictly lit. translation of the phrase *conversa sīgna*; it = *the standards having been turned about.* ——— **bipertītō**, adv. (bis + partītus [*pars*]); hence *bipertītō = in bipartition*, i.e. *in two parts, ways, directions*. ——— **intulērunt**, 3d pers. plur. perf. ind. act. of the verb *īnferō, -ferre, -tulī, -lātum*. *intulērunt* agrees with its subject-nom. *Rōmānī*. Observe that the lit. translation here of *Rōmānī conversa sīgna bipertītō intulērunt = The Romans bore in the standards having been turned about in two parts*, i.e. *The Romans wheeled about and advanced in two directions.* The reader will observe that the rear, or third line, wheeled about and attacked the Boii and Tulingi who were approaching the Roman rear; while the second and third lines engaged the Helvetii who were approaching the Romans from the mountain to which they had retreated. It is interesting to note the technical military phrases in use among the Romans, in which *ferre* and compounds play a part. *sīgna ferre = to march; sīgna īnferre = to bear the standards into the fray, to advance to the attack;* while *sīgna referre = to retreat;* and *sīgna cōnferre = to engage in a conflict*.

LINE 32. **prīma**, nom. sing. f. of the ordinal adj. *prīmus, -a, -um*; superl. degree *prīmus*; comparative degree *prior, prius. prīma* is an attributive of the noun *aciēs*. ——— **et**, cop. conj.; connects the adjectives *prīma* and *secunda*. ——— **secunda**, nom. sing. f. of the adj. *secundus, -a, -um. secundus* is properly a participle of the verb

[LINES 33, 34.]   BOOK I.   191

33 āc	submōtīs	resisteret,	tertia,	ut	the third line, to withstand the shock of the Boii and Tulingi who were then approaching the Romans' unprotected flank.
and	dislodged	it might resist,	the third,	that	
34 venientēs	sustinēret.				
(those) coming	it might withstand.				

| 1 XXVI. | Ita | ancipitī | proeliō | diū | XXVI. Thus this double-fronted battle was |
| | Thus | in the two-headed | battle | long | |

---

sequor = *following;* hence = *next, second,* in time or order. *secunda* is connected by *et* with *prīma,* and has the same grammatical construction; it is an attributive of *aciēs.* ——— *aciēs,* nom. sing. of the noun *aciēs, -ēī,* f. (ἀκίς, *the edge* of a thing); in military language = *the line* of battle. *aciēs* is the subject-nom. of *intulit,* to be supplied. As the first and second lines did not wheel, but faced the enemy only, *signa intulit* fills the lacuna here. ——— *ut,* telic conj. here. ——— **vīctīs,** dat. plur. m. of the perf. pass. participle *vīctus, -a, -um* of the verb *vincō, -ere, vīcī, vīctum.* *vīctīs* is used substantively here, and is in the dat. after *resisteret* — a verb of *resistance* that takes the dat. Consult A. & G. 227; B. 142; G. 346; H.385, 1. Of course these participles here used may be regarded as such, and be made to agree with *hostibus,* to be supplied; which latter, in that case, would be datives after *resisteret.*

LINE 33. **āc,** shortened form of *atque* (ad + que); usually adds a more emphatic notion. ——— **submōtīs,** dat. plur. of the participle *submōtus, -a, -um* of the verb *submoveō, -ēre, -mōvī, -mōtum* (sub + movēre). *submōtīs* is connected by the conj. *āc* with *vīctīs,* and is in the same grammatical construction. Observe that these participles are essentially predicative, and are equivalent to a relative and a finite verb. ——— **resisteret,** 3d pers. sing. imperf. subjunctive of the verb *resistō, -ere, -stitī, -stitum,* 3; it agrees with a pron. implied in the ending as subject-nom., referring to *aciēs;* it is the subjunctive of purpose after *ut,* telic. Consult A. & G. 317; B. 200; G. 545, 3; H. 497, II. ——— **tertia,** nom. sing. f. of the ordinal adj. *tertius, -a, -um;* it is the attributive of *aciēs,* to be supplied; which latter is the subject-nom. of *intulerit,* to be supplied. Indeed, the full lacuna here to be supplied is: *tertia aciēs conversa signa intulerit,* as the *tertia aciēs* only wheeled about. ——— *ut,* telic conj.

LINE 34. **venientēs,** acc. plur. of the pres. participle *veniēns, -ntis* of the verb *veniō, -īre, vēnī, ventum,* 4; *venientēs* agrees with *eōs,* i.e. *Bōios et Tulingōs,* to be supplied. *eōs* thus supplied is the direct obj. of *sustinēret.* ——— **sustinēret,** 3d pers. sing. imperf. subjunctive of the verb *sustineō, -ēre, -uī, -tentum,* 2 (sub + tenēre); hence = lit. *to hold up from beneath,* i.e. *to sustain; sustinēret* is the subjunctive of purpose after *ut,* telic. Observe that, as to the position of the parties, the Romans fronted the west; the Helvetii, the east; while the Boii and Tulingi from a northerly direction were approaching the Romans on the right, or unprotected flank; that the Roman forces were drawn up in three parallel lines; that the first and second lines were striving to resist the renewed attack of the Helvetii, who had been previously routed and driven off; and that the third line, by wheeling to the right, were meeting the flank attack of the Boii and Tulingi.

LINE 1. **Ita,** adv. (radical *i,* whence *is* + ta); hence = *in such a manner;* here the adv. = *as thus described;* and the writer immediately repeats the idea in *ancipitī proeliō.* ——— **ancipitī,** abl. sing. n. of the adj. *anceps, ancipitis,* abl. always ending in

fought long and courageously. When the enemy was unable to endure longer the onsets of our soldiers, one party — the Helvetii — retreated to the mountain, as they had begun;	atque and	ācriter bitterly	pūgnātum est. it was fought.	Diūtius Longer	cum when	2
	sustinēre to sustain	nostrōrum our	impetūs *attacks	nōn not	possent, they were able,	3
	alterī the one	sē, themselves,	ut as	coeperant, they had begun,	in montem to the mountain	4

ī (a contraction from ambō + caput = lit. *double-headed*); hence sometimes = *doubtful*, and *double*.   ancipitī is an attributive of *proeliō*. —— proeliō, abl. sing. of the noun *proelium, -iī*, n. (prō or prae + īre); *proeliō* is an abl. of manner See A. & G. 248; B. 168; G. 399; H. 419, III.   *proelium* is often written *praelium*. For synonyms, see note on *proeliīs*, l. 18, Chap. I. —— diū (*diēs*), adv.; comparative *diūtius*.

LINE 2. atque (ad + que), conj.; adds a notion of greater importance usually; it here connects the adverbs *diū* and *ācriter*. —— ācriter, adv. (adj. *ācer*, sharp); formed by adding *-ter* to the stem *ācrī*. Observe that there are three adverbs and one adverbial phrase preceding the verb *pūgnātum est*, and modifying it. —— pūgnātum est, 3d pers. sing. perf. ind. pass. of the verb *pūgnō, -āre, -āvī, -ātum*, 1; here *pūgnātum est* is strictly an impersonal verb = *it was fought;* but as it is here a verb of complete predication with *proeliō*, it may be rendered as if *proeliō* were *proelium* — the subject-nom. For synopsis of *pūgnātum est*, as an impersonal verb, see A. & G. 145; B. 114, 115; G. 208, 2; H. 301, I. —— Diūtius, adv.; comparative degree of *diū* (*diēs*); superl. degree *diūtissimē*. *diūtius* modifies the verb *sustinēre*. —— cum, conj., historical. Observe that both *cum* and *diūtius* are made emphatic by exchange of positions.

LINE 3. sustinēre, pres. inf. act. of the verb *sustineō, -ēre, -uī, -tentum*, 2 (sub + tenēre) is a complementary inf., depending on *possent*. Consult A. & G. 271; B. 181; G. 423; H. 533, I, 2. —— nostrōrum, gen. plur. m. of the poss. pron. *noster, -tra, -trum*, used substantively, or supply *mīlitum;* as a gen. it limits *impetūs*. —— impetūs, acc. plur. of the noun *impetus, -ūs*, m. *impetūs* is the direct obj. of *sustinēre*. —— nōn (nē + oe[ū]num, apocopated), adv.; it modifies *possent*. Observe its natural position immediately before the word it modifies. —— possent, 3d pers. plur. of the intrans. verb *possum, posse, potuī* (potis, *able* + sum); it agrees with its subject-nom. *Gallī* or *hostēs* understood. *possent* is in the subjunctive after *cum*, denoting both time and cause. Consult A. & G. 325; B. 222; G. 585; H. 521, II, 2.

LINE 4. alterī, nom. plur. m. of the pron. *alter, -era, -erum*, gen. *alterīus*, dat. *alterī;* observe that *alterius* has the ictus on the antepenult. *alterī* refers to one division — the Helvetii; it is the subject-nom. of *recēpērunt*. As to synonyms, consult note on *alius*, l. 13, Chap. I. *alterī . . . alterī*, as in the text = *the one party . . . the other party.* —— sē, acc. plur. of the reflexive pron. *suī, sibi, sē, sē* — same form in both numbers. *sē* refers to the subj. of the proposition, but it is the direct obj. of the verb *recēpērunt*. —— ut, adv. = *as*, and generally when used with the ind. —— coeperant, 3d pers. plur. pluperf. ind. act. of the defective verb *coepī*, fut. participle *coeptūrus;* used in the perfect and cognate tenses; it agrees with a pron. implied in the ending as subject-nom., referring to *Gallī* or *hostēs*. —— in, prep. with either the acc. or abl.; here it takes the acc.; after a verb of motion it = *into*.

BOOK I.

5 recēpērunt,	alterī	ad	impedīmenta	et	the other party — the Boii and Tulingi — made towards the baggage and the waggons. For during this entire battle, although it lasted from one o'clock till eve-
betook,	*the other*	*near*	*the baggage-train*	*and*	
6 carrōs	suōs	sē	contulērunt.	Nam hōc	
carts	*their,*	*themselves*	*collected.*	*For in this*	
7 tōtō	proeliō,	cum	ab	hōrā septimā	
whole	*battle,*	*though*	*from*	*hour the seventh*	

For different significations of the prep., see note on *in*, l. 1, Chap. I. —— **montem,** acc. sing. of the noun *mōns, montis,* m. (root in *minārī* and *eminēre*); hence *mōns* = *a projecting* body.

LINE 5. **recēpērunt,** 3d pers. plur. perf. ind. act. of *recipiō, -ere, -cēpī, -ceptum,* 3 (re + capere); hence = *to take back;* with *sē* = *to withdraw, to retreat. recēpērunt* agrees with a pron. implied in the ending as subject-nom., referring to *Gallī* or *hostēs.* —— **alterī,** nom. plur. m. of the adj. pron. *alter;* see note on *alterī*, preceding line. *alterī* here = *Bōiī et Tulingī.* Observe that, as *alterī* in the preceding line refers to one division of the enemy, *alterī* here denotes the other division. *alterī* here is the subject-nom. of the verb *contulērunt.* —— **ad,** prep. with the acc. —— **impedīmenta,** acc. plur. of the noun *impedīmentum, -ī,* n. (in + pēs through the verb *impediō*). *impedīmenta* is the obj. of the prep. *ad.* Observe that *impedīmenta* = *the baggage* of an army, including horses and carts; whereas *sarcinae* = personal *baggage.* —— **et,** cop. conj.

LINE 6. **carrōs,** acc. plur. of the noun *carrus, -ī,* m.; sometimes the form *carrum, -ī,* n., occurs; but not in *Caesar. carrōs* is connected by the conj. *et* with *impedīmenta,* and is in the same grammatical construction. The lexicons teach us that *carrus* is a Gallic word, and denotes a species of four-wheeled waggon. A copy of notes in my possession pictures it as a two-wheeled affair. The lexicons are supposed to be true sources of information. —— **suōs,** acc. plur. of the poss. and reflexive pron. *suus, -a, -um;* it agrees, logically, with both *impedīmenta* and *carrōs,* but grammatically only with the latter. —— **sē,** acc. plur. of the reflexive pron. *suī, sibi, sē, sē* — same form in both numbers; *sē* is the direct obj. of the verb *contulērunt.* —— **contulērunt,** 3d pers. plur. perf. ind. act. of the verb *cōnferō, -ferre, -tulī, col(n)lātum. contulērunt* agrees with a pron. implied in the ending as subject-nom., representing *Gallī* or *hostēs.* Observe the words *sē recēpērunt,* lines 4 and 5, above, and compare them with *sē contulērunt.* Etymologically, *sē recēpērunt* = *they took themselves back;* while *sē contulērunt* = *they brought themselves together.* Practically, however, these forms of expression are identical in meaning, i.e. they = the English *they retreated* in an orderly manner. He uses these modes of expression to indicate that there was no disorder. If Caesar had wished to express that idea, he would have written *fūgērunt.* —— **Nam,** conj.; introduces the following statement to explain the preceding statements as to the orderly retreat. Observe that *nam* introduces an objective reason; whereas *enim* a subjective. —— **hōc,** abl. sing. n. of the dem. pron. *hīc, haec, hōc; hōc* is an attributive of the idea involved in the phrase *tōtō proeliō.*

LINE 7. **tōtō,** abl. sing. n. of the adj. *tōtus, -a, -um,* gen. *tōtīus,* dat. *tōtī. tōtō* is an attributive of the noun *proeliō.* —— **proeliō,** abl. sing. of the noun *proelium, -iī,* n. (prae or prō + īre). For derivation and synonyms, see note on *proeliīs,* l. 18, Chap. I. *proeliō* is a locative abl. of manner without a prep. See A. & G. 258, *f*, 2; B. 170, REM. 2; G. 388; H. 425, II, 1, 1), and 2. Observe that the English word *throughout* gives

ning, no one could see the back of an enemy. Till late at night, even up to the baggage, the battle raged, because the enemy	ad *to*	vesperum *evening*	pūgnātum sit, *it was fought,*	āversum 8 *turned away*
	hostem *an enemy*	vidēre *to see,*	nēmō potuit. *no one was able.*	Ad multam 9 *Till much*
	noctem *night*	etiam *even*	ad impedīmenta *to the baggage-train*	pūgnātum est 10 *it was fought,*

the idea of *tōtō* in the complex phrase: *hōc tōtō proeliō;* and that the best English for the entire phrase is: *throughout this battle.* —— **cum**, concessive conj. = *though* or *although.* Consult A. & G. 326; B. 223; G. 587; H. 515, III. Observe that the *time*-notion is involved in *cum* concessive, but it has largely faded out; so also the causal notion; the concessive notion can only be ascertained by considering the construction, and also *the sense.* Sometimes, however, we are aided in our deductions by noticing a *tamen* expressed, as an adversative, in the principal clause. —— **ab**, prep. with the abl. (*ab* before vowels or consonants, *ā* before consonants only). —— **hōrā**, abl. sing. of the noun *hora, -ae*, f. (GK. **ὥρα**). *hōrā* is the obj. of the prep. *ab.* —— **septimā**, abl. sing. of the ordinal adj. *septimus, -a, -um* (*septem*, compare GK. **ἑπτά**). *septimā* is an attributive of the noun *hōrā.* Observe that, as the day, among the Romans, was reckoned as twelve hours, from sunrise to sunset, the hours were of varying lengths, according to the season of the year; and that *ab hōrā septimā*, according to our mode of designating time = 1 h. 15 m. o'clock.

LINE 8. **ad**, prep. with the acc.; usually = *to* or *toward;* but here it = *until.* —— **vesperum**, acc. sing. of the noun *vesper, vesperis* or *vesperī*, m. (compare GK. **ἕσπερος**); abl. *vespere*, or adverbially *vesperī.* *vesperum*, as an acc., is the obj. of the prep. *ad.* —— **pūgnātum sit**, 3d pers. sing. perf. subjunctive; a verb of complete predication, used impersonally; see note on *pūgnātum est*, l. 2, above; subjunctive after *cum* concessive; see grammatical references to *cum*, preceding line. —— **āversum**, acc. sing. m. of the participle *āversus, -a, -um* of the verb *āvertō, -ere, -versī, -versum*, 3. *āversum* agrees with the noun *hostem.*

LINE 9. **hostem**, acc. sing. of the noun *hostis, hostis*, m. and f. *hostem* is the direct obj. of the verb *vidēre.* Synonyms: *hostis* = lit. *a stranger;* transf., *a public enemy;* whereas *inimīcus* (in + amīcus) = *a private enemy.* Observe that *āversum hostem* = lit. *an enemy turned away*, i.e. *in flight.* —— **vidēre**, pres. inf. act. of the verb *videō, -ēre, vīdī, vīsum*, 2 (digammated from radical *ιδ*, as seen in the 2d aorist participle *ἰδών*). *vidēre* is a complementary inf., depending on *potuit.* Consult A. & G. 271; B. 181; G. 423; H. 533, I, 2. —— **nēmō**, nom. sing. of the noun *nēmō, nēminis* (nē + homō). *nēmō* is subject-nom. of *potuit.* But observe that the gen. *nēminis* and the abl. *nēminē* are not used; instead, *nūllīus* and *nūllō* are used. —— **potuit**, 3d pers. sing. perf. ind. of the intrans. verb *possum, posse, potuī* (potis + sum). *potuit* agrees with its subject-nom. *nēmō.* —— **Ad**, prep. with the acc.; not *towards* here; that would be expressed by the prep. *sub;* as *sub vesperum* would = *toward evening;* but *ad* here, like *ad* in the phrase *ad vesperum* = *till.* —— **multam**, acc. sing. f. of the adj. *multus, -a, -um;* comparative degree *plūs;* superl. degree *plūrimus.* *multam* is an attributive of *noctem.*

LINE 10. **noctem**, acc. sing. of the noun *nox, noctis*, f. (compare GK. **νύξ, νυκτός**). *noctem* is the obj. of the prep. *ad.* Observe that the phrase *ad multam noctem* = *to* or *till much night*, i.e. *till far in the night.* —— **etiam** (et + iam), conj. adv.; here with *ad* it = *even up to.* —— **impedīmenta**, acc. plur. of *impedīmentum, -ī*, n. (in +

11 proptereā	quod	prō	vāllō	carrōs		had placed in front their wag-
for this reason	*because*	*for*	*a rampart*	*the carts*		gons as a rampart; and from
12 obiēcerant	et	ē	locō	superiōre		them, as a higher position, kept
they had opposed	*and*	*from*	*the place*	*higher*		hurling their missiles on our men,
13 in	nostrōs	venientēs	tēla	coniciēbant,		as they were coming up; and some
against	*our (men)*	*coming,*	*weapons*	*they threw,*		

pēs through the verb *impediō*); it is the obj. of the prep. *ad*. —— pūgnātum est, 3d pers. sing. perf. ind. pass. of the verb *pūgnō, -āre, -āvī, -ātum*, 1; pass. parts: *pūgnor, -ārī, -ātus*, I. See note on *pūgnātum est*, l. 2, above.

LINE 11. **proptereā** (propter + eā), adv. = lit. *on account of these things;* hence sometimes = *therefore;* the long *ā* in the ultima is anomalous. Here *proptereā* = *for this reason*, and is the herald, so to speak, of the following *quod*-clause; it is often better omitted in the translation. —— **quod**, here a conj. = *because; quod* is really an adverbial acc. sing. n. of the rel. pron. *quī, quae, quod* = *in respect to what, in that, because. quod* is frequently preceded by *hōc* and *ob hanc causam*, as well as by *proptereā*. —— **prō** (GK. πρό), prep. with the abl. —— **vāllō**, abl. sing. of the noun *vāllum, -ī*, n. *vāllō* is the obj. of the prep. *prō*. *prō vāllō* = lit. *for a defense*. Primarily *vāllum* = *a palisaded rampart;* hence = *a wall, a rampart;* compare English *wall*. —— **carrōs**, acc. plur. of the noun *carrus, -ī*, m. *carrōs* is the direct obj. of the verb *obiēcerant*. See note on *carrōs*, l. 6, above.

LINE 12. **obiēcerant**, 3d pers. plur. pluperf. ind. of *obiciō, -icere, -iēcī, -iectum*, 3 (ob + iacere); hence *obicere* = lit. *to throw* or *set against*. *obiēcerant* agrees with a pron. implied in the ending as subject-nom., referring to *Gallī* or *hostēs* understood. It will be recalled that the term *Gallī* in Caesar often includes the Helvetii and other racially allied nations or clans. —— **et**, cop. conj.; connects *obiēcerant* and *coniciēbant*, l. 13, below. —— **ē**, prep. with the abl. (*ē* before consonants only, *ex* before vowels or consonants). —— **locō**, abl. sing. of the noun *locus, -ī*, m.; plur. *locī*, m., and *loca*, n. See note on *locī*, l. 10, Chap. II. *locō* is the obj. of the prep. *ē*. —— **superiōre**, abl. sing. m. of the adj. comparative degree *superior, -ius*, gen. *-ōris;* positive *superus;* superl. *suprēmus* or *summus*. *superiōre* is an attributive of the noun *locō*.

LINE 13. **in**, prep. with the acc. or abl.; here it takes the acc., and = *against*. —— **nostrōs**, acc. plur. of the poss. pron. *noster, -tra, -trum*, used substantively; or supply *mīlitēs*. *nostrōs*, as a subst., is the obj. of the prep. *in*. —— **venientēs**, acc. plur. m. of the participle *veniēns, -ntis* of the verb *veniō, -īre, vēnī, ventum*, 4; *venientēs* agrees with the pron. *nostrōs* used as a noun, and is an attributive participle denoting the attendant circumstances. Consult A. & G. 292; B. 191, 1; G. 668; H. 549, 4. It will be observed that the participle thus used is the equivalent of a relative clause, and is essentially predicative. —— **tēla**, acc. plur. of the noun *tēlum, -ī*, n. *tēla* is the direct obj. of the verb *coniciēbant*. Observe that *tēlum* was a weapon for fighting at a distance; while *arma* = *arms* for defense or close fighting. But *arma* is a broad term denoting weapons of any kind. *arma* is usually derived from GK. ἄρω, *to fit to*, i.e. = *armor;* but transf. it = implements of war — *arms*. —— **coniciēbant**, 3d pers. plur. imperf. ind. act. of the verb *coniciō, -ere, -iēcī, -iectum*, 3; connected by *et* with *obiciēbant*, and in the same grammatical construction.

196   CAESAR'S GALLIC WAR   [CHAP. XXVI.

kept thrusting up from below their lances and javelins between the waggons and wheels, and thus kept wounding our soldiers. After fighting a long time, our men gained possession of the enemy's baggage	et *and* nōnnūllī *some* inter *between* carrōs *the carts* rotāsque *wheels and,* matarās 14 *lances*
	āc *and* trāgulās *javelins* subiciēbant, *hurled from beneath,* nostrōsque 15 *our (men) and,*
	vulnerābant. *they wounded.* Diū *For long* cum *when* esset pūgnātum, 16 *it had been fought,*
	impedīmentīs *of the baggage-train* castrīsque *camp and,* nostrī 17 *our (men)*

LINE 14. **et,** cop. conj.; connects the verbs *coniciēbant* and *subiciēbant*, l. 15, below. —— **nōnnūllī**, nom. plur. of the adj. *nōnnūllus, -a, -um* (nōn + nūllus); hence *nōnnūllus = not none*, i.e. *some*; the two negatives = a positive. *nōnnūllī* is used substantively; or *mīlitēs* may be supplied; and is the subject-nom. of the verb *subiciēbant.* —— **inter**, prep. with the acc. —— **carrōs**, acc. plur. of the noun *carrus, -ī*, m.; but see note on *carrōs*, l. 6, above. *carrōs* is here the obj. of the prep. *inter.* —— **rotāsque** (rotās + que); *rotās* is the acc. plur. of the noun *rota, -ae*, f.; connected closely by the enclitic conj. *-que* with the noun *carrōs*, and in the same grammatical construction. Observe that *rota* = lit. *a wheel*; compare the English *rotary*; sometimes *rota — pars prō tōtō — = a car.* —— **matarās**, acc. plur. of the noun *matara, -ae*, f. (a Celtic word = a species of heavy *javelin*). *matarās* is a direct obj. of the verb *subiciēbant.*

LINE 15. **āc,** shortened form of the conj. *atque* (*āc* only before consonants in classical Latin); like *atque, āc* usually adds a notion of more importance. *āc* in our text connects *matarās* with *trāgulās.* —— **trāgulās**, acc. plur. of the noun *trāgula, -ae*, f. (a Celtic word); it is connected by the conj. *āc* with *matarās*, and is also the direct obj. of *subiciēbant.* —— **subiciēbant**, 3d pers. plur. imperf. ind. act. of the verb *subiciō, -ere, -iēcī, -iectum*, 3 (sub + iacere). *subiciēbant* agrees with a pron. implied in the ending as subject-nom., referring to *Helvētiī et Bōiī et Tulingī*, i.e. *Gallī* used broadly. —— **nostrōsque** (nostrōs + que). *nostrōs*, acc. plur. of the poss. pron. *noster, -tra, -trum*, used substantively; or supply *mīlitēs*; direct obj. of *vulnerābant. que*, enclitic conj.; connects very closely the verbs *subiciēbant* and *vulnerābant.*

LINE 16. **vulnerābant**, 3d pers. plur. imperf. ind. of the verb *vulnerō, -āre, -āvī, -ātum*, I (*vulnus*, a wound); it agrees with *Gallī* or *hostēs* as subject-nom. Observe that the imperf. tenses in lines 11-16 denote repeated action. See A. & G. 277; B. 95, II; G. 231; H. 469, II. —— **Diū** (*diēs*), adv. = lit. *a space of time*; hence intensively, *a long time, long. diū*, as an adv., is compared thus: comparative *diūtius*; superl. *diūtissimē.* —— **cum**, temporal conj. Note the emphasis that is put on both *cum* and *diū* by exchange of position. *cum*, ordinarily, stands first in introducing a subordinate clause. —— **esset pūgnātum** (*pūgnātum esset*). 3d pers. sing. pluperf. subjunctive pass., used impersonally, of the verb *pūgnō, -āre, -āvī, -ātum*, 1; it is in the subjunctive mode after *cum.* Consult A. & G. 325; B. 222; G. 585; H. 521, II, 2.

LINE 17. **impedīmentīs**, abl. plur. of *impedīmentum, -i*, n.; abl. after the verb *potītī sunt.* Consult A. & G. 249; B. 167, 1; G. 407; H. 421, I. As to derivation and synonyms, see note on *impedīmenta*, l. 5, above. Observe that *potior* sometimes, though rarely, takes the gen.; see *Galliae sēsē potīrī* posse spērant, lines 36 and 37.

18 potītī sunt.		Ibi	Orgetorigis		fīlia	and camp. The daughter of Orgetorix and one of his sons were captured in this camp. About one hundred and thirty thousand men survived this battle, and during the entire
gained possession.		*There*	*Orgetorix's*		*daughter*	
19 atque	ūnus ē	fīliīs	captus est.	/ Ex	eō	
and also	*one of (his) sons*		*was captured.*	*/ After*	*that*	
20 proeliō	circiter	mīlia	hominum	centum	et	
battle	*about*	*thousands*	*of men*	*one hundred*	*and*	
21 trīgintā	superfuērunt		eāque	tōtā	nocte	
thirty	*remained,*		*in that and,*	*entire*	*night*	

Chap. III. —— **castrīsque** (castrīs + que). *castrīs* is the abl. plur. of the noun *castrum, -ī,* n.; in the sing. =*fort;* in the plur., *camp. castrīs* is closely connected by the enclitic conj. with *impedīmentīs,* and is in the same grammatical construction. —— **nostrī,** nom. plur. of the poss. pron. *noster, -tra, -trum,* used substantively; or supply *mīlitēs;* subject-nom. of the verb *potītī sunt.*

LINE 18. **potītī sunt,** 3d pers. plur. perf. ind. of the deponent verb *potior, potīrī, potītus,* 4. *potītī sunt* agrees with its subject-nom. *nostrī.* —— **Ibi** (radical *i,* whence *is* + loc. ending *bi*); hence = lit. *in that place, there;* the place alluded to is the Helvetian camp. —— **Orgetorigis,** poss. gen. of the noun *Orgetorix, -rigis,* m.; as a gen. it limits *fīlia.* Orgetorix was a Helvetian chief; see note on *Orgetorix,* l. 2, Chap. II; and read again Chapters III and IV. —— **fīlia,** nom. sing. of the noun *fīlia, -ae. fīlia* is subject-nom. of the verb *capta est,* to be supplied from the following *captus est.* Observe that by exception the dat. and abl. plur. of *fīlia* and *dea* ends in *-ābus.* Why? To distinguish between the dat. and abl. plur. of these words and the dat. and abl. plur. of *fīlius* and *deus.*

LINE 19. **atque** (ad + que), conj.; adds a notion of more importance = *and also.* —— **ūnus,** cardinal num. adj., gen. *ūnīus,* dat. *ūnī,* used substantively, and subject-nom. of the verb *captus est.* —— **ē,** prep. with the abl. (*ē* before consonants only, *ex* before vowels or consonants). —— **fīliīs,** abl. plur. of the noun *fīlius, -ī,* m.; abl. after the prep. *ē,* instead of the gen. partitive. Consult A. & G. 216, *e;* B. 134, REM. 2; G. 372, 2; H. 397, 3, NOTE 3. —— **captus est,** 3d pers. sing. perf. ind. pass. of the verb *capiō, -ere, cēpī, captum,* 3. *captus est* in fact belongs to both subjects — *fīlia* and *fīlius,* but agrees with the latter; or may be explained, as in the preceding line. —— **Ex,** prep. with the abl.; see note on *ē,* l. 12, above. —— **eō,** abl. sing. n. of the dem. pron. *is, ea, id. eō* is an attributive of the noun *proeliō.*

LINE 20. **proeliō,** abl. sing. of the noun *proelium, -ī,* n. (prae or prō + ire). *proeliō* is the obj. of the prep. *ex.* —— **circiter,** adv. (*circus, circum*); it modifies *centum et trīgintā.* —— **mīlia,** nom. plur. of the adj. *mille. mille* is indeclinable in the sing., and only used in the nom. and acc. cases; in the plur. *mīlia, -ium* is declinable throughout, and with partitives it is used substantively. *mīlia,* in our text, is the subject-nom. of the verb *superfuērunt.* —— **hominum,** gen. plur. of the noun *homō, hominis,* m. and f.; partitive gen. after *mīlia.* Consult A. & G. 216, 2; B. 134; G. 370; H. 397, 2. For synonyms, see note on *hominēs,* l. 20, Chap. II. —— **centum,** cardinal num. adj., indecl.; it is an attributive of *mīlia* which is used as a noun. —— **et,** cop. conj.

LINE 21. **trīgintā,** cardinal num. adj., indecl.; connected by the conj. *et* with *centum,* and in the same grammatical construction. —— **superfuērunt,** 3d pers. plur. perf. ind. of the intrans. verb *supersum, -esse, -fuī, -futūrus* (super + esse); hence *superesse* = lit. *to be over,* i.e. *to remain, to survive. superfuērunt* agrees with its

198   CAESAR'S GALLIC WAR   [CHAP. XXVI.

| night after it, they fled incessantly — their march ceasing during no part of the night; and they arrived at the borders of the Lingones on the fourth day; | continenter *continuously* itinere *the march* Lingonum *of the Lingones* | iērunt; *they went;* intermīssō *being intermitted* diē *on day* | nūllam *during no* quartō *the fourth* | partem *part* in *into* pervēnērunt, *they came through,* | noctis 22 *of the night* fīnēs 23 *the territory* 24 |

subject-nom. *mīlia.* —— eāque (eā + que). *eā* is abl. sing. f. of the dem. pron. *is, ea, id; eā* is an attributive of the noun *nocte*. Observe how closely the verbs *superfuērunt* and *iērunt* are connected by the enclitic conj. *-que.* —— tōtā, abl. sing. f. of the adj. *tōtus, -a, -um*, gen. *tōtīus*, dat. *tōtī. tōtā* is also an attributive of the noun *nocte.* —— nocte, abl. sing. of the noun *nox, noctis*, f. (compare GK. νύξ, νυκτός). *nocte* is an abl. here denoting the *extent of time*—rather anomalous—but the abl. is sometimes thus used. Consult A. & G. 256, *b*; B. 153, REM. 2; G. 393, REM. 2; H. 379, 1.

LINE 22. continenter, adv. (continēns [con + tenēre]); hence *continēns = a hanging together;* and the adv. *continenter =* in space or time, *close together, successively* as to space, and, in time, *continuously. continenter* modifies the verb *iērunt.* —— iērunt, 3d pers. plur. perf. ind. act. of the verb *eō, īre, īvī (iī), itum. iērunt* is connected by the enclitic *-que* with the verb *superfuērunt*, and has the same subject-nom. *mīlia.* Observe that *iērunt* is for the full form *ivērunt;* the *v* is syncopated. See A. & G. 128, 2; B. 251; G. 131, 1; H. 235, 1. —— nūllam, acc. sing. f. of the adj. *nūllus, -a, -um*, gen. *nūllīus*, dat. *nūllī* (nē + ūllus); hence = lit. *not any*, i.e. *none, no. nūllam* is an attributive of the noun *partem.* —— partem, acc. sing. of the noun *pars, partis*, f. *partem* is the acc. of time *how long*. See A. & G. 256, and 2; B. 153; G. 335; H. 379. —— noctis, gen. sing. of the noun *nox, noctis*, f. (compare GK. νύξ, νυκτός). *noctis*, as a gen., limits the noun *partem.*

LINE 23. itinere, abl. sing. of the noun *iter, itineris*, n. (from the radical *i* as seen in *īre, itum*). *itinere* is in the abl. absolute with the perf. pass. participle *intermīssō*, denoting *time*. See A. & G. 255; B. 192; G. 409, 410; H. 431. —— intermīssō, abl. sing. n. of the perf. pass. participle *intermīssus, -a, -um* of the verb *intermittō, -ere, -mīsī, -mīssum*, 3; in the abl. absolute with the noun *itinere.* —— in, prep. with the acc. and abl.; here it takes the acc. after a verb of motion. —— fīnēs, acc. plur. of the noun *fīnis, -is*, m.; it is the obj. of the prep. *in*. For synonyms, see note on *agrum*, l. 12, Chap. II.

LINE 24. Lingonum, gen. plur. of the noun *Lingonēs, -um*, m.; as a gen. it limits the noun *fīnēs*. The Lingones were a Gallic clan, dwelling in the vicinity of the Vosges mountains — the Haute-Marne department of modern France. —— diē, abl. sing. of the noun *diēs, -ēī*, m. and f. in the sing.; always m. in the plur. *diē* is the abl. of time *in which*. Consult A. & G. 256, 1; B. 171; G. 393; H. 429. —— quartō, abl. sing. m. of the ordinal adj. *quartus, -a, -um. quartō* is an attributive of the noun *diē.* —— pervēnērunt, 3d pers. plur. of the verb *perveniō, -īre, -vēnī, -ventum*, 4 (per + venīre). *pervēnērunt* agrees with a pron. implied in the ending as subject-nom., referring to *Helvētiī et Bōiī et Tulingī;* or, if preferred, make *hostēs* understood the subject-nom. Observe the force of the prep. *per* in composition. *in fīnēs Lingonum pervēnērunt =* lit. they came *through* into the territory of the Lingones.

25 cum	et	propter	vulnera	mīlitum	et	since our men, as they delayed their march for three days, to care for the wounded soldiers and to bury the slain, could not pursue them. Caesar sent letters by messengers to inform the Lingones that they were not to assist the Helvetii with
since	*both*	*because*	*of the wounds*	*of the soldiers*	*and*	
26 propter		sepultūram	occīsōrum		nostrī	
because		*of the burial*	*of the slain*		*our (men)*	
27 trīduum		morātī		eōs	sequī	
the space of three days		*having delayed,*		*them*	*to follow*	
28 nōn		potuissent.	Caesar	ad	Lingonas	
not		*had been able.*	*Caesar*	*to*	*the Lingones*	
29 litterās	nūntiōsque	mīsit,	nē	eōs	frūmentō	
letters	*messengers and,*	*sent,*	*that not*	*them*	*with grain*	

LINE 25. **cum**, conj., denoting both time and cause. —— **et** . . . **et**, a species of correlative conjunctions, repeated between co-ordinate phrases; = *both* . . . *and*. —— **propter**, prep. with the acc. —— **vulnera**, acc. plur. of the noun *vulnus, -eris*, n. *vulnera* is the obj. of the prep. *propter*. *propter vulnera* = the cause exciting the action, instead of the abl. of cause. Consult A. & G. 245, *b*; B. 165, REM. 4; G. 408, 3; H. 416, I, 2). —— **mīlitum**, gen. plur. of the noun *mīles, -itis*, m.; poss. gen., limiting the noun *vulnera*. —— **et**, see note on *et*, immediately preceding.

LINE 26. **propter**, see note on *propter*, preceding line. —— **sepultūram**, acc. sing. of the noun *sepultura, -ae*, f. (compare *sepelīre*, to bury). *sepultūram* is the obj. of the prep. *propter*. —— **occīsōrum**, gen. plur. of the participle *occīsus, -a, -um* of the verb *occīdō, -ere, -cīdī, -cīsum*, 3 (ab + caedere). *occīsōrum* is used substantively = *the slain*; as a gen., used as a noun, it limits the noun *sepultūram*; or we may supply *eōrum*, i.e. *mīlitum*. —— **nostrī**, nom. plur. of the poss. pron. *noster, -tra, -trum*, used substantively; or supply *mīlitēs*; subject-nom. of the verb *potuissent*.

LINE 27. **trīduum**, acc. sing. of the noun *trīduum, -ī*, n. (trēs + diēs). *trīduum* is the acc. of *extent of space*. Consult A. & G. 257; B. 153; G. 336; H. 379. —— **morātī**, nom. plur. m. of the perf. participle *morātus, -a, -um* of the deponent verb *moror, -ārī, -ātus*, I. *morātī* agrees with *nostrī*, conceived to be used substantively. —— **eōs**, acc. plur. m. of the dem. pron. *is, ea, id*, used as a pron. of the 3d person. *eōs* is the direct obj. of the deponent verb *sequī*. —— **sequī**, pres. inf. of the deponent verb *sequor, -ī, secūtus*, 3. *sequī* is a complementary inf., depending on *potuissent*.

LINE 28. **nōn**, adv. (nē + oe[ū]num). Observe its normal Latin position — immediately before the verb it modifies. —— **potuissent**, 3d pers. plur. pluperf. subjunctive of the intrans. verb *possum, posse, potuī* (potis + sum). *potuissent* agrees with its subject-nom. *nostrī*, and is in the subjunctive after *cum*, l. 25, above, denoting both time and cause, and especially cause. Consult A. & G. 326; B. 223; G. 586; H. 517. —— **Caesar, -aris**, m., subject-nom. of the verb *mīsit*. —— **ad**, prep. with the acc. —— **Lingonas**, Greek acc. plur. of the proper noun *Lingonēs, -um*, m., instead of the Latin form *Lingonēs*. See A. & G. 63, *f*; B. 248; G. 65, NOTE 4; H. 68. *Lingonas* is the obj. of the prep. *ad*.

LINE 29. **litterās**, acc. plur. of the noun *littera, -ae*, f. *litterās* is the direct obj. of the verb *mīsit*. Observe that *littera* in the sing. = *a letter* of the alphabet; in the plur. it = the GK. ἐπιστολή, *an epistle* as composed of words and letters. Sometimes, however, *litterae*, plur. = *letters*, i.e. *epistles*. Whether *litterae* = *one epistle* or *epistles* must be determined by the context. —— **nūntiōsque** (nūntiōs + que). *nūntiōs*, acc.

200   CAESAR'S GALLIC WAR   [CHAP. XXVI.

grain or with anything else; and if they should do so, he would regard them in the same light as the Helvetii. He in person began to	nēve *nor* iūvissent, *should have aided,* Helvētiōs, *the Helvetii,*	aliā *with another* sē *himself* habitūrum. *to be about to regard (them).*	rē *thing* eōdem *in the same*	iuvārent; *should they aid;* locō, *place,*	quī *who* quō *in which* Ipse, *He himself,*	sī 30 *if,* 31 32

plur. of the noun *nūntius, -ī,* m. (sometimes written *nūncius*). *nūnt(c)ius* (novem + tiō or ciō); hence *nūntius = one who brings news, a messenger;* but often, *abstractum prō concrētō, nūntius = the message. nūntiōs* is connected by the enclitic conj. *-que* with the noun *litterās,* and is in the same grammatical construction. —— **mīsit,** 3d pers. sing. perf. ind. act. of the verb *mittō, -ere, mīsī, missum,* 3. *mīsit* agrees with its subject-nom. *Caesar* expressed. —— **nē,** primitive negative; used with the imperative, and the subjunctive used for the imperative. —— **eōs,** acc. plur. m. of the dem. pron. *is, ea, id,* used as a pers. pron. of the 3d pers.; it stands for *Helvētiōs,* and is the direct obj. of *iuvārent.* —— **frūmentō,** abl. sing. of the noun *frūmentum, -ī,* n. (frugī, from *frux +* mentum). *frūmentō* is an abl. of means. A. & G. 248, *c,* 1; B. 167; G. 401; H. 420.

LINE 30. **nēve** or *neu* (nē + ve); hence = lit. *or not;* conjunctive adv. Observe that *nēve* or *neu* is used as a continuative after *nē,* and may be rendered either *or,* or *nor;* if *nē* in the preceding line be conceived as throwing its force on both *frūmentō* and *aliā rē, nēve* may be translated simply *or.* —— **aliā,** abl. sing. of the adj. pron. *alius, -a, -um,* gen. *alīus,* dat. *aliī. aliā* is an attributive of the noun *rē.* —— **rē,** abl. sing. of the noun *rēs, reī,* f. (stem *rē,* but shortened in gen. and dat. sing.). *rē* is an abl. of manner. Consult A. & G. 248; B. 168; G. 399; H. 419, III. —— **iuvārent,** 3d pers. plur. imperf. subjunctive act. of the verb *iuvō, -āre, iūvī, iūtum,* 1 (perf. stem formed irregularly). *iuvārent* agrees with *Lingonēs,* to be supplied, as subject-nom.; it is in the hortatory subjunctive indirect discourse representing the imperative form in direct discourse, i.e. *nē iuvārent* in *ōrātiō oblīqua = nē iuveritis —* perf. subjunctive — in *ōrātiō rēcta,* as *nē* with the 2d pers. of the perf. subjunctive is the regular form in classic prose for expressing prohibition. —— **quī,** nom. plur. of the rel. pron. *quī, quae, quod;* it refers to the Lingones, but it is the subject-nom. of the verb *iūvissent. quī,* at the beginning of the sentence = *et eī.* Consult A. & G. 180, *f;* B. 129, REM. 9; G. 610; H. 453. —— **sī** (archaic form *seī,* sibilated from the GK. *eī*); conditional conj.

LINE 31. **iūvissent,** 3d pers. plur. pluperf. subjunctive of *iuvō, -āre, iūvī, iūtum;* it agrees with its subject-nom. *quī;* it is the pluperf. subjunctive after *sī* in the protasis — *ōrātiō oblīqua,* for *sī iūveritis —* fut. perf. ind. — in *ōrātiō rēcta.* —— **sē,** acc. sing. of the reflexive pron. *suī, sibi, sē, sē —* same form in both numbers. *sē* is the subject-acc. of the verb *habitūrum (esse); sē* refers to Caesar. —— **eōdem,** abl. sing. m. of the dem. pron. *īdem, eadem, idem. eōdem* is an attributive of the noun *locō.* —— **locō,** abl. sing. of the noun *locus, -ī,* m.; *locī,* m., or *loca,* n., in the plur. See note on *locī,* l. 10, Chap. II. *locō* is a locative abl. Consult A. & G. 258, *f,* 1 and 2; B. 170, REM. 3; G. 385, NOTE 1; H. 425, II, 2. Observe that *locus* here = *position.* —— **quō,** abl. sing. of the rel. pron. *quī, quae, quod;* it refers to *locō,* as its antecedent, and agrees with *locō* understood, which latter is also a locative abl.

LINE 32. **Helvētiōs,** acc. plur. of the adj. *Helvētius, -a, -um,* used substantively. *Helvētiōs* is the direct obj. of *habeat,* to be supplied. As to this clan, see note on *Helvētiī,* l. 16, Chap. I. —— **habitūrum (esse),** fut. inf. act. of the verb *habeō, -ēre,*

33 trīduō	intermīssō,	cum follow them with all his forces after the interval of three days.
the space of three days	having been let pass,	with
34 omnibus cōpiīs eōs sequī coepit.		
all the troops them to follow began.		

1 XXVII. Helvētiī	omnium rērum inopiā	XXVII. As the Helvetii were in want of every-
The Helvetii by the	of all things scarcity	

-uī, -itum, 2; its subject-acc. is the pron. *sē* expressed; its direct obj. is the pron. *eōs*, i.e. *Lingonas*, to be supplied. The *ōrātiō rēcta* of lines 29–32 reads: nē eōs frūmentō nēve aliā rē *iūveritis; sī eōs iūveritis, egō vōs* eōdem locō, quō Helvētiōs, *habēlō*. Observe that the first clause of the above might be put into the following form: *vel eōs frūmentō vel aliā rē nōlīte iuvāre.* —— **Ipse**, nom. sing. of the intensive dem. pron. *ipse, -sa, -sum*, gen. *ipsīus*, dat. *ipsī; ipse* is subject-nom. to the verb *coepit;* it is expressed for emphasis.

LINE 33. **trīduō**, abl. sing. of the noun *trīduum, -ī*, n. (trēs + diēs). *trīduō* is in the abl. absolute construction with the perf. pass. participle *intermīssō*, denoting the *time*. Consult A. & G. 255, *d*, 1; B. 192; G. 409, 410; H. 431, and 2. —— **intermīssō**, abl. sing. n. of the perf. pass. participle *intermīssus, -a, -um* of the verb *intermittō, -ere, -mīsī, -mīssum* (inter + mittere). *intermīssō* is in the abl. absolute construction with the noun *trīduō*. Synonyms: *intermittere* (*to send between*, i.e. *to leave off, intermit*) = *to give over for a time;* but *omittere* = *to leave off altogether.* —— **cum**, prep. with the abl.

LINE 34. **omnibus**, abl. plur. f. of the adj. *omnis, -e* (an *ī*-stem; abl. sing. always *omnī*). *omnibus* is an attributive of the noun *cōpiīs*. —— **cōpiīs**, abl. plur. of the noun *cōpia, -ae*, f.; in the sing. = *plenty;* in the plur., *troops. cōpiīs* is the abl. of *accompaniment* with the prep. *cum.* Consult A. & G. 248, *a*; B. 168, REM. 4; G. 399; H. 419, I. Observe that *cum* is not absolutely necessary with words denoting military movements; it is often omitted, in such cases. —— **eōs**, acc. plur. m. of the dem. pron. *is, ea, id*, used as a personal pron. of the 3d pers. *eōs*, i.e. *Helvētiōs*, is the direct obj. of *sequī.* —— **sequī**, pres. inf. of the deponent verb *sequor, -ī, secūtus*, 3 (compare GK. ἕπομαι [GK. radical σεπ, and Latin *seq.*]). *sequī* is a complementary inf., and depends on *coepit.* Consult A. & G. 271; B. 181; G. 423; H. 533, I, 1. —— **coepit**, 3d pers. sing. of *coepī, coepisse, coepturus, coeptus* — defective preteritive verb. Consult A. & G. 143, *a*; B. 113, and REM. 1; G. 175, 5, *a*; H. 297, and 1. Observe that with pass. infinitives the pass. form *coeptus sum*, etc., is generally used, e.g. *urbs oppūgnārī coepta est.*

LINE 1. **Helvētiī**, nom. plur. of the adj. *Helvētius, -a, -um*, used substantively, and subject-nom. of the verb *mīsērunt.* —— **omnium**, gen. plur. f. of the adj. *omnis, -e*, an *ī*-stem. *omnium* is an attributive of *rērum.* —— **rērum**, gen. plur. of the noun *rēs, reī*, f. (stem *rē* shortened in the gen. and dat. sing.). *rērum* is an objective gen., limiting the noun *inopiā.* —— **inopiā**, abl. sing. of the noun *inopia, -ae*, f. (from in + opis through the adj. *inops*). *inopiā* is an abl. of cause after the perf. pass. participle *adductī.* Consult A. & G. 245, and 2, *b*; B. 165, and REM. 4; G. 408, and NOTE 2; H. 416, and NOTE 1.

adductī	lēgātōs	dē	dēditiōne	ad	eum 2
having been led	envoys	concerning	surrender	to	him
mīsērunt.	Quī	cum	eum	in	itinere 3
sent.	Who,	when	him	on	the road
convēnissent	sēque	ad	pedēs	prōiēcissent 4
had met themselves	and,	to	(his) feet	had thrown

thing, they were induced to send ambassadors to Caesar to ascertain the terms of surrender. Now when these envoys had met Caesar on the road, and had cast themselves at his feet, and,

LINE 2. **adductī**, nom. plur. m. of the perf. pass. participle *adductus, -a, -um* of the verb *addūco, -ere, -dūxī, -ductum*, 3; *adductī*, as a participle, agrees with the noun *Helvētiī* in gender, number and person. —— **lēgātōs**, acc. plur. of the noun *lēgātus, -ī*, m. (*lĕgere*, to despatch). *lēgātōs* is the direct obj. of the verb *mīsit*. —— **dē**, prep. with the abl. Synonyms: *de = from*, as if from a fixed point; *ab = from*, as if from a mere external point; while *ex = a* going forth *from* the interior of an object. —— **dēditiōne**, abl. of the noun *dēditiō, -ōnis*, f. (*dedere*, to give up). *dēditiōne* is the abl. after the prep. *dē*. —— **ad**, prep. with the acc. after a verb of motion. —— **eum**, acc. sing. m. of the dem. pron. *is, ea, id*, used as a dem. pron. of the 3d pers.; it is the obj. of the prep. *ad*.

LINE 3. **mīsērunt**, 3d pers. plur. perf. ind. act. of the verb *mittō, -ere, mīsī, missum*, 3. *mīsērunt* agrees with *Helvētiī*, expressed as subject-nom. Observe that *mīsērunt* has here the construction of a verb of motion, taking the acc. with *ad*; but this verb takes also, in connection with the direct obj., the obj. *to which*, and the end *for which*, in the dat. Compare *equitātuī, quem auxiliō Caesarī Aeduī mīserant*, lines 48 and 49, Chap. XVIII. —— **Quī**, nom. plur. m. of the rel. pron. *quī, quae, quod;* at the beginning of a sentence = *et eī*; here = *Helvētiī*; subject-nom. of the verb *convēnissent*. For the force of the relative, see A. & G. 180, *f*; B. 129, REM. 9; G. 610; H. 453. —— **cum**, conj., temporal. Observe that *quī* precedes *cum*, because the idea expressed by the relative is the emphatic notion in the writer's mind. —— **eum**, acc. sing. of the dem. pron. *is, ea, id*, used as a personal pron. of the 3d person. *eum* refers to Caesar, and is the direct obj. of the verb *convēnissent*. —— **in**, prep. with either the acc. or abl.; here it takes the abl., and = *on*. See on this prep. the grammatical references to *in*, l. 1, Chap. I. —— **itinere**, abl. sing. of the noun *iter, itineris*, n. (*īre, itum*). *itinere* is here the obj. of the prep. *in*; and the phrase *in itinere = on the march*. For synonyms, see note on *iter*, l. 2, Chap. IX.

LINE 4. **convēnissent**, 3d pers. plur. pluperf. subjunctive; it agrees with its subject-nom. *quī*; it is in the subjunctive after *cum, temporal* or *historical*. Consult A. & G. 325; B. 222; G. 585; H. 521, II, 2. —— **sēque** (sē + que). *sē*, acc. plur. of the reflexive pron. *suī, sibi, sē, sē* — same form in both numbers; it refers to the subject of the proposition, *quī*, i.e. *Helvētiī*; but it is the direct obj. of the verb *prōiēcissent*. Note how closely the verbs *convēnissent* and *prōiēcissent* are connected by the enclitic *-que*. —— **ad**, prep. with the acc.; here it = *āt*. —— **pedēs**, acc. plur. of the noun *pēs, pedis*, m. (compare GK. πούς, ποδός, radical πεδ). *pedēs* is the obj. of the prep. *ad;* of course, *ēius*, i.e. *Caesaris*, is to be supplied. —— **prōiēcissent**, 3d pers. plur. pluperf. subjunctive act. of the verb *prōiciō, -ere, -iēcī, -iectum*, 3 (prō + iacere); hence *prōicere =* lit. *to throw forward*. *prōiēcissent* is very closely connected by the enclitic *-que* with *convēnissent*, and is in the subjunctive mode for the same reason.

5 suppliciterque	locūtī	flentēs	pācem	addressing him humbly, had, in tears, begged for peace; and Caesar, through them, had ordered the Helvetian forces to await his arrival at their present halting-place,
suppliantly, and (him) having addressed		weeping	peace	
6 petīssent, atque eōs in eō locō,			quō tum	
had sought, and them in that place,			where then	
7 essent, suum adventum exspectāre			iūssisset,	
they were, his arrival		to wait for	he had ordered,	

LINE 5. **suppliciterque** (suppliciter + que). *suppliciter*, adv. (derived from the adj. *supplex* [sub + plicāre, compare GK. πλέκω]); hence, as *supplex* = lit. *bending the knees* to receive punishment; or *submission* as a *suppliant*, the adv. = *humbly*, *suppliantly*. *suppliciter*, as an adv., modifies the perf. participle *locūtī*. —— **locūtī**, nom. plur. m. of the perf. participle *locūtus*, *-a*, *-um* of the deponent verb *loquor*, *-ī*, *-cūtus*, 3; *locūtī*, as a participle, agrees with the subj. of the proposition, *quī*, i.e. *Helvētiī*. Supply *eum* as the direct obj. of the participle *locūtī*. —— **flentēs**, nom. plur. m. of the pres. participle *flēns*, *flentis* of the verb *fleō*, *flēre*, *flēvī*, *flētum*, 2. *flentēs* also agrees with the subj. of the proposition, *quī*, i.e. *Helvētiī*, and denotes the manner of the Helvetians' procedure. Observe that *locūtī*, a perf. participle of a deponent verb, is used here with *flentēs*, a pres. participle, with no appreciable difference, i.e. *locūtī* is used in the sense of a pres. participle. As to distinctions of tense in participles, see A. & G. 290 ff.; B. 98, 3, and 109, 2; G. 113, 128; H. 231, and 550, NOTE I; it agrees with the subject-nom., i.e. *Helvētiī*; its direct obj. is *sē*, i.e. *Caesarem*, to be supplied. —— **pācem**, acc. sing. of the noun *pāx*, *pācis*, f. (from radical *pac*, as seen in *pacīscī*, to covenant); here *pāx* = *peace* between parties at variance. *pacem* is the direct obj. of *petīssent*.

LINE 6. **petīssent**, 3d pers. plur. pluperf. subjunctive for *petīvissent* of the verb *petō*, *-ere*, *-īvī* (*-iī*), *-ītum*, 3. As to syncopation and contraction, see A. & G. 128, 2; B. 251; G. 131, 1; H. 235. *petīssent* is connected by the enclitic *-que* with *prōiēcissent*, and is still under the influence of *cum*, historical, and so in the subjunctive. —— **atque**, conj. (ad + que); adds a notion of more importance usually, and = *and also*. Observe that the shortened form *āc* is used only before consonants. —— **eōs**, acc. plur. of the dem. pron. *is*, *ea*, *id*, used as a personal pron. of the 3d pers.; it is the subject-acc. of *exspectāre*; it refers to the entire body of the Helvetii, and not merely to the Helvetian ambassadors. —— **in**, prep. either with the acc. or abl.; here it takes the abl. See note on *in*, l. 1, Chap. I. —— **eō**, abl. sing. m. of the dem. pron. *is*, *ea*, *id*; it is an attributive of *locō*. —— **locō**, abl. sing. of the noun *locus*, *-ī*, m. in the sing.; in the plur. *locī*, m., or *loca*, n. See note on *locī*, l. 10, Chap. II. *locō* is the obj. of the prep. *in*. —— **quō**, abl. sing. of the rel. pron. *quī*, *quae*, *quod*, used here both relatively and adjectively; as a rel. it refers to *locō*; as an adj. it is an attributive of *locō*, to be supplied, which latter is in the abl. locative case; or the prep. *in* might be regarded as understood. —— **tum**, adv.; it modifies the verb *essent*.

LINE 7. **essent**, 3d pers. plur. imperf. subjunctive of the intrans. verb *sum*, *esse*, *fuī*, *futūrus*: its subject-nom. is *Helvētiī* understood; it is in the subjunctive, because it is in a subordinate clause in informal indirect discourse. But note that this clause is an *essential part* of the sentence, and consult A. & G. 342; B. 245, (*b*); G. 629; H. 529, II, NOTE I, 1). —— **suum**, acc. sing. m. of the reflexive pron. *suus*, *-a*, *-um*; it refers to

they obeyed. When Caesar, subsequently, reached the rendezvous, he demanded hostages, their arms, and the fugitive slaves belonging to the Romans. While these chat-	pāruērunt. *they obeyed.*	Eō *Thither*	postquam *after that*	Caesar *Caesar*	pervēnit, *arrived,*	8
	obsidēs, *hostages,*	arma, *arms,*	servōs, *slaves,*	quī *who*	ad *to*	eōs *them*	9
	perfūgissent, *had fled,*		poposcit. *he demanded.*		Dum **While*	ea *these things*	10

Caesar, but it is an attributive of the noun *adventum*. —— **adventum**, acc. sing. of the noun *adventus*, *-ūs*, m. (ad + venīre); *adventum* is the direct obj. of the verb *exspectāre*. —— **exspectāre**, pres. inf. act. of the verb *exspectō, -āre, -āvī, -ātum*, 1 (ex + spectāre = lit. *to look out*); its subject-acc. is the pron. *eōs*, in the preceding line. Observe that *eōs . . . exspectāre* is the obj. of the verb *iūssisset*. —— **iūssisset**, 3d pers. sing. pluperf. subjunctive of the verb *iubeō, -ēre, iūssī, iūssum*, 2; *iūssisset* agrees with a pron. implied in the ending as subject-nom., referring to Caesar; it is connected by the conj. *atque* with the preceding verbs, and is under the influence of *cum*; and hence it is in the subjunctive mode.

LINE 8. **pāruērunt**, 3d pers. plur. perf. ind. act. of the verb *pāreō, -ēre, pāruī, pāritum*, 2 (*pārāre*, to bring forth, to appear); hence *pārēre* = *to appear* at one's command, *to obey*. *pāruērunt* agrees with *Helvētiī* understood as its subject-nom. The *ōrātiō rēcta* of the informal indirect discourse of lines 6 and 7, above, is as follows: *vōs*, in *hōc* locō, *quō nūnc estis, meum* adventum exspectāre *iubeō*. —— **Eō**, adv. (old dat. of the adj. pron. *is*); here = *thither*, i.e. *in eō locō*, l. 6, above. —— **postquam** (post + quam), adv.; here *post + quam* is the historical pres. ind.; here it takes the historical perf. —— **Caesar, -aris**, m., subject-nom. of *pervēnit*. —— **pervēnit**, 3d pers. sing. perf. ind. act. of the verb *perveniō, -īre, -vēnī, -ventum*, 4 (per + venīre = lit. *to come through*); *pervēnit* agrees with its subject-nom. *Caesar*.

LINE 9. **obsidēs**, acc. plur. of the noun *obses, -idis*, m. and f. (ob + sedēre, *to sit, to remain*); hence the noun = lit. *one that remains* as a pledge of conditions to be met. —— **arma, -ōrum**, or *armūm*, n. (usually derived from ἄρω, *to fit to*); hence *arma* = lit. *things fitted to the body*; then transf. *arms* for warfare both offensive and defensive. *arma* is connected by *et* understood with *obsidēs*, and is in the same grammatical construction. —— **servōs**, acc. plur. of the noun *servus, -ī*, m.; connected by *et* understood with *arma*, and in the same grammatical construction, i.e. direct obj. of *poposcit*. These slaves, of course, belonged to the Romans. Note the omission of the conj. here between these nouns (asyndeton). Consult A. & G. 208, *b*; B. 123, REM. 6; G. 474, NOTE; H. 554, 6. —— **quī**, nom. plur. m. of the rel. *quī, quae, quod*; *quī* refers to the three preceding nouns, but takes the gender of the last; it is the subject-nom. of the verb *perfūgissent*. —— **ad**, prep. with the acc. —— **eōs**, acc. plur. of the dem. pron. *is, ea, id*, used as a personal pron. of the 3d person; it is the obj. of the prep. *ad*. *eōs* refers to the Helvetians.

LINE 10. **perfūgissent**, 3d pers. plur. pluperf. subjunctive of the verb *perfugiō, -ere, -fūgī*, 3; it is in the subjunctive mode, because in a subordinate clause in informal indirect discourse. Consult A. & G. 341, and *d*; B. 235 and 245, (*b*); G. 628;

* Perspicuous English requires the following arrangement of the clauses: While these chattels were being hunted up . . ., it was ascertained that about six thousand men . . . had, in the first part of the night, left the Helvetian camp, and had gone hastily towards the Rhine and the country of the Germans; and they did so, either because they were greatly alarmed lest, . . .; or would be wholly unnoticed.

11 conquīruntur	et	cōnferuntur,		nocte	tels were being hunted up and brought together, and when the night was passed, (it was ascertained that) about six thousand men of that canton which was called Verbigenus,
are being sought	*and*	*being collected,*		*a night*	
12 intermissā,	circiter	hominum	mīlia	sex	
having passed,	*about*	*of men*	*thousands*	*six,*	
13 ēius	pāgī,	quī	Verbigēnus	appellātur,	
of that	*district,*	*which*	*Verbigenus*	*is called,*	

H. 528, 1. Observe that Caesar the historian has not the fullest confidence in Caesar the *imperātor*. —— **poposcit**, 3d pers. sing. perf. ind. act. of the verb *poscō, -ere, poposcī*, reduplicated, no supine. *poposcit* agrees with a pron. implied in the ending as subject-nom., referring to Caesar. —— **Dum**, conjunctive adv. = *while*, and it usually takes after it the pres. ind. regardless of the law of sequence of tenses. Consult A. & G. 276, *e*; B. 228, REM. 1; G. 570; H. 467, 4. *dum* is sometimes used as a restrictive particle = *provided*, and then takes the subjunctive. —— **ea**, nom. plur. n. of the dem. pron. *is, ea, id*, used substantively, and subject-nom. of the verbs *conquīruntur* and *cōnferuntur; ea* refers to *obsidēs, arma* and *servōs*, conceived of as chattels; and the pron. is in the neuter gender.

LINE 11. **conquīruntur**, 3d pers. plur. pres. ind. pass. of the verb *conquīro, -ere, -quīsīvi (-siī), -quīsītum,* 3 (con + quīrere = lit. *to search for carefully*). *conquīruntur* agrees with its subject-nom. *ea*. —— **et**, cop. conj.; it here connects the verbs *conquīruntur* and *cōnferuntur*. —— **cōnferuntur**, 3d pers. plur. pres. ind. pass. of the verb *cōnferō, -ferre, -tulī, col(n)lātum* (con + ferō); it is connected by the conj. *et* with the verb *conquīruntur*, and has the same subj., namely *ea*. —— **nocte**, abl. sing. of the noun *nox, noctis*, f. (GK. νύξ, νυκτός). *nocte* is in the abl. absolute construction with the perf. pass. participle *intermissā*.

LINE 12. **intermissā**, abl. sing. f. of the perf. pass. participle *intermissus, -a, -um* of the verb *intermittō, -ere, -mīsī, -missum,* 3 (inter + mittere) = lit. *to let go between*. *intermissā* is abl. absolute with the noun *nocte*, denoting the time. Consult A. & G. 255, *d,* 1; B. 192; G. 409, 410; H. 431, 2, (3). —— **circiter** (*circus, circum*), adv.; it modifies the adj. *sex*. —— **hominum**, gen. plur. of the noun *homō, -inis*, m. and f.; *hominum*, as a partitive gen., limits *mīlia*. As to this construction, see A. & G. 216, 2; B. 134; G. 370; H. 397, 2. —— **mīlia**, nom. plur. of *mille*, an indecl. num. adj. in the sing.; in the plur. it is regularly declined, and is used as a neuter noun. See A. & G. 94, *e*; B. 64, REM. 9; G. 293; H. 178, and NOTE. *mīlia*, as a subst., is the subject-nom. of *contendērunt*, l. 22, below. —— **sex**, cardinal num. adj. (GK. ἕξ). *sex* is an attributive of the noun *mīlia*.

LINE 13. **ēius**, gen. sing. m. of the dem. pron. *is, ea, id; ēius* is an attributive of the noun *pāgī*. —— **pāgī**, gen. sing. of the noun *pāgus, -ī,* m.; poss. gen., and limits *hominum*. —— **quī**, nom. sing. m. of the rel. *quī, quae, quod;* it refers to the noun *pāgī*, but is subject-nom. of the verb *appellātur*. —— **Verbigēnus, -ī,** m., proper noun; one of the four Helvetian clans; it is here predicate-noun. Consult A. & G. 176, *a*; B. 130, 3; G. 206; H. 362, 2, 2). —— **ap(d)pellātur**, 3d pers sing. pres. ind. pass. of the verb *appellō, -āre, -āvī, -ātum,* 1 (ad + pellere) = lit. *to drive to;* hence *to go near, to accost,* or *call,* or *name*. Synonyms: *appellāre* = *to call,* or *name* one by his title; *vocāre* = *to call* one by the utterance of his name; sometimes, *to summon;* whereas *nōmināre* = *to call* one by his name; sometimes = *to name, give a name*. But observe, these distinctions are largely etymological; often these words meaning *to call, to name,* are used without any appreciable difference in meaning.

either because they were greatly alarmed, lest, after surrendering their arms, they might be tortured; or, led by the hope of safety, they thought that, amid so great a number of prisoners, their own	sīve *whether* trāditīs *being delivered up* sīve *or* tantā *so great*	timōre *by alarm* *with punishment* spē *by the hope* multitūdine *a multitude*	perterritī *being terrified,* suppliciō salūtis *of safety* dēditīciōrum *of captives*	nē *lest, (their)* afficerentur, *they would be affected,* inductī, *being led,* suam *their*	armīs 14 *arms* 15 quod in 16 *because in* fugam 17 *flight*

LINE 14. **sīve** (sī + ve, contracted *seū*); conj. = lit. *or if*; but *sīve ... sīve* = *whether ... or*; sometimes they = *either ... or*. —— **timōre**, abl. of the noun *timor, -ōris*, m.; abl. of cause after the perf. pass. participle *perterritī*. Consult A. & G. 245, and 2; B. 165, and REM. 4; G. 408, and NOTE 2; H. 416, and NOTE 1. Synonyms: *timor* = *the fear* that results from weakness or cowardice; sometimes, however, it = *a rational fear*; whereas *metus* = *fear* as a rational emotion, arising from reflection or caution. —— **perterritī**, nom. plur. of the perf. pass. participle *perterritus, -a, -um* of the verb *perterreō, -ēre, -uī, -itum*, 2. *perterritī*, as a participle, agrees with the pron. *eī*, representing *hominum mīlia*, l. 12, above. —— **nē**, conj. = *lest*; it follows the phrase *timōre perterritī*, as if the phrase were = *veritī*; and, of course, it = *that* or *lest*; if the phrase were followed by *ut* instead of *nē*, the *ut* would = *that not*. Consult A. & G. 331, *f*; B. 200, REM. 6; G. 550, 2, and NOTE 1; H. 498, III, NOTE 1. —— **armīs**, abl. plur. of the noun *arma, -ōrum*, n. See note on *arma*, l. 9, above. *armīs* is in the abl. absolute construction with the perf. pass. participle *trāditīs*, denoting condition. See A. & G. 255, *d*, 4; B. 192; G. 409, 410; H. 431, 2, (3).

LINE 15. **trāditīs**, abl. plur. n. of the perf. pass. participle *trāditus, -a, -um* of the verb *trādō, -ere, -didī, -ditum*, 3 (trāns + dare, lit. *to give over*). *trādō* is sometimes written *trānsdō*. *trāditīs* is in the abl. absolute construction with the noun *armīs*, denoting condition. See grammatical reference to *armīs*, preceding line. —— **suppliciō**, abl. sing. of the noun *supplicium, -ī*, n. (*supplex* [sub + plicō] = *kneeling as a suppliant* or *for punishment*); hence *supplicium* = sometimes *supplication*; oftener, transf. = *punishment*. *suppliciō*, in the text, is an abl. of *means*. —— **afficerentur**, 3d pers. plur. imperf. subjunctive pass. of the verb *afficiō, -ere, -fēcī, -fectum*, 3; it agrees with *eī*, referring to *hominum mīlia*, l. 12, above, as the subject-nom.; it is a clause of *purpose* after the particle *nē*; hence in the subjunctive mode. Consult A. & G. 331, *f*; B. 200, REM. 6; G. 550, 2; H. 498, III, NOTE 1.

LINE 16. **sīve**, see note on *sīve*, l. 14, above. —— **spē**, abl. sing. of the noun *spēs, -eī*, f. (stem *spē*, vowel shortened in the gen. and dat. sing.). *spē* is an abl. of *cause* after the participle *inductī*. —— **salūtis**, gen. sing. of the noun *salūs, -ūtis*, f. (*salvus*). *salūtis* limits the noun *spē*. —— **inductī**, nom. plur. m. of the perf. pass. participle *inductus, -a, -um* of the verb *indūcō, -ere, -dūxī, -ductum*, 3 (in + dūcere = *to lead on*). *inductī*, as a participle, agrees with *eī*, referring to *hominum mīlia*, l. 12, above. —— **quod**, conj. = *because*. —— **in**, prep. with the acc. or abl.; here it takes the abl., and = *among* or *amid*.

LINE 17. **tantā**, abl. sing. f. of the adj. *tantus, -a, -um*; *tantā* is an attributive of *multitūdine*. —— **multitūdine**, abl. sing. of the noun *multitūdō, -dinis*, f. (*multus*); it is the obj. of the prep. *in*. Observe that *multitūdō*, as derived from *multus* = lit.

18 aut	occultārī	aut	omnīnō	ignorārī
either	*to be concealed*	*or*	*entirely*	*to be unobserved*
19 posse	existimārent,		prīmā	nocte
to be possible	*they thought,*		*in the first part*	*of the night,*
20 ē	castrīs	Helvētiōrum		ēgressī
from	*the camp*	*of the Helvetii*		*having gone forth*

flight would be concealed long enough to enable them to escape, or would be wholly unnoticed, had, in the first part of the night, left the Helvetian camp, and had

a *great number;* whereas *numerus, -ī,* m., from the same radical as the GK. νόμος (νέμειν, *to distribute*) = lit. *anything measured* or *distributed*, i.e. *any number.* ── **dēditīciōrum**, gen. plur. of the adj. *dēditīcius, -a, -um* (*dēdere*, to give up); hence the adj. in a pass. sense = *one given up;* as a subst. = *one surrendered*, i.e. *a prisoner;* used here substantively; it limits *multitūdine.* ── **suam**, acc. sing. f. of the poss. adj. pron. *suus, -a, -um; suam* is an attributive of the noun *fugam.* ── **fugam**, acc. sing. of the noun *fuga, -ae,* f. *fugam* is the subject-acc. of the verb *posse.*

LINE 18. **aut**, conj. = *or* (kindred with the postpositive Greek adv. αὖ = *back, again*); but *aut . . . aut = either . . . or.* These particles thus used denote that the difference is exclusive; if the difference is neither important nor exclusive, *vel . . . vel* are used. ── **occultārī**, pres. inf. pass. of the verb act. voice *occultō, -āre, -āvī, -ātum,* 1 (an intensive verb derived from *oc*[*b*]*culō,* 3). *occultārī* is a complementary inf., depending on the verb *posse.* Consult A. & G. 271; B. 181; G. 423; H. 533, I, 2. ── **aut**, see note on *aut,* immediately preceding. ── **omnīnō** (*omnis*), adv., modifies the verb *ignorārī.* ── **ignorārī**, pres. inf. pass. of the verb act. voice *ignōrō, -āre, -āvī, -ātum,* 1 (*ignōrus*, like *āgnōtus* from *gnōtus*); hence *ignōrāre* = *to be ignorant* of a thing; in the text *ignōrārī* = *to be unknown* to anybody. *ignōrārī* is also a complementary inf., depending on *posse.*

LINE 19. **posse**, pres. inf. of the intrans. verb *possum, posse, potuī* (*potis, able* + *sum*); its subject-acc. is *fugam.* Observe that the infinitive-clause is the obj. of the verb *existimārent.* ── **existimārent**, 3d pers. plur. imperf. subjunctive of the verb *existimō, -āre, -āvī, -ātum,* 1; it agrees with a pron. implied in the ending as subject-nom., referring to *hominum milia,* l. 12, above; *existimārent* is in the subjunctive mode in a *quod*-clause, because the writer suggests doubtfully; the writer is giving a suggestion, not making a statement as absolute fact. See A. & G. 341, *d*, and REM.; B. 198, (*b*); G. 541; H. 516, II. ── **prīmā**, abl. sing. f. of the adj. *prīmus, -a, -um,* superl. degree; comparative degree is *prior. prīmā* is an attributive of the noun *nocte. prīmā* with *nocte* = *the first part.* See A. & G. 193; B. 128, REM. 9; G. 291, REM. 2; H. 440, NOTE 2. ── **nocte**, abl. sing. of the noun *nox, noctis,* f. (νύξ, νυκτός); *nocte* is the abl. of *time when.* Consult A. & G. 256, 1; B. 153, REM. 2; G. 393; H. 429.

LINE 20. **ē**, prep. with the abl. (*ē* before consonants only, *ex* before vowels or consonants). ── **castrīs**, abl. plur. of the noun *castrum, -ī,* n.; in the sing. = *fort* or *castle;* in the plur. = *camp. castrīs* is the obj. of the prep. *ē.* ── **Helvētiōrum**, gen. plur. of the adj. *Helvētius, -a, -um,* used substantively. *Helvētiōrum* is a poss. gen., limiting the noun *castrīs.* As to the Helvetian clan, see note on *Helvētiī,* l. 16, Chap. I. ── **ēgressī**, nom. plur. m. of the perf. participle *ēgressus, -a, -um* of the deponent verb *ēgredior, ēgredī, ēgressus,* 3 (ē + *gradī* [*gradus*]), hence *ēgredī* = lit. *to step out;* as a participle, *ēgressī* agrees with the subject-nom. of the verb *contendērunt.*

gone hastily towards the Rhine and the country of the Germans.	ad *toward* contendērunt. *hastened.*	Rhēnum *the Rhine*	fīnēsque *territory and,*	Germānōrum *of the Germans,* 21 22
XXVIII. When Caesar discovered this movement, he gave orders to those, through whose territory the fugitives had gone,	XXVIII. quōrum *whose*	Quod ubi *Which when* per fīnēs *through, territory*	Caesar resciit, *Caesar found out,* ierant, his, *they had gone, to those,*	1 utī 2 *that*

LINE 21. **ad**, prep. with the acc.; compare GK. *eis*. —— **Rhēnum**, acc. sing. of the noun *Rhēnus, -ī*, m. *Rhēnum* is the obj. of the prep. *ad*. Really, however, *Rhēnum* is in apposition with the noun *flūmen* understood, which is the obj. of the prep. *ad*. The Rhine river is generally the boundary between Gaul and Germany. —— **fīnēsque** (fīnēs + que); *fīnēs*, acc. plur. of the noun *fīnis, -is*, f. *fīnēs* is very closely connected with *Rhēnum* by the enclitic conj. *-que*, and like *Rhēnum* is the obj. of the prep. *ad*. Observe that *fīnēs* in the sing. = *the end*; in the plur. *fīnēs* = *limits, borders, country*. —— **Germānōrum**, gen. plur. of the noun *Germānī, -ōrum*, m. (Γερμάνοι). The Germans were a people occupying the territory between the Rhine, the Danube and the Vistula. *Germānōrum*, as a gen., limits the noun *fīnēs*.

LINE 22. **contendērunt**, 3d pers. plur. perf. ind. act. of the verb *contendō, -ere, -tendī, -tentum*, 3 (con + tendere). *contendērunt* agrees with its subject-nom. *mīlia* —— adj. used as noun — l. 12, above. For different meanings of this verb, see note on *contendunt*, l. 18, Chap. I.

LINE 1. **Quod**, acc. sing. of the rel. pron. *quī, quae, quod*; it refers to the sally of the Helvetii, as related in the preceding chapter; it is the direct obj. of the verb *resciit*. *quod* at the beginning of a sentence = *et hōc*. Consult A. & G. 180, *f*; B. 129, REM. 9; G. 610; H. 453. —— **ubi** (*quo*, old dat. of *quī* + bi), adv. and conj. = lit. *in which* place; hence *where*; and then transf. = *when*. Observe that temporal clauses with *ubi, postquam*, etc., take after them the perf. ind., or the historical present. Consult A. & G. 324; B. 224; G. 551; H. 518. —— **Caesar, -aris**, m., subject-nom. of the verb *resciit*. —— **resciit**, 3d pers. sing. perf. ind. act. of the verb *rescīscō, -ere, -scīvī (-iī), -scītum*, 3 (re + sc scere); hence, as an inchoative verb = *to find out* a thing, bringing it from concealment into light again; *resciit* agrees with its subject-nom. *Caesar* expressed.

LINE 2. **quōrum**, gen. plur. m. of the rel. pron. *quī, quae, quod*; it refers to the following dem. pron. *hīs*, used as a subst.; but, as a gen., it limits *fīnēs*. Observe that, in the Latin arrangement of clauses, the relative clause often stands first. —— **per**, prep. with the acc. —— **fīnēs**, acc. plur. of the noun *fīnis, -is*, m. *fīnēs* is the obj. of the prep. *per*. Observe that *fīnis* in the sing. = *end, limit*; in the plur. *fīnēs* = *boundaries, territory*. For synonyms, see note on *agrum*, l. 12, Chap. II. —— **ierant**, 3d pers. plur. pluperf. ind. of the verb *eō, īre, īvī (iī), itum*; *ierant* is syncopated for *iverant*. Consult A. & G. 128, 2; B. 251; G. 131, 1; H. 235. —— **hīs**, dat. plur. f. of the dem. pron. *hīc, haec, hōc*, used substantively; or rather supply *gentibus*.

LINES 3-5.]   BOOK I.   209

3 conquīrerent	et	redūcerent,	sī	sibi	to hunt them up and bring them back if they wished in his eyes to be free from suspicion. And he regarded those brought back as enemies;
they should seek out	*and*	*lead back,*	*if*	*to himself*	
4 pūrgātī	esse	vellent,		imperāvit;	
free of blame	*to be*	*they wished,*		*he gave orders;*	
5 reductōs		in		hostium	
those having been brought back		*among*		*the enemy's*	

the dat. plur. of *gēns, -ntis,* f.; *hīs* is the dat. after the verb *imperāvit* — a verb of commanding. See A. & G. 227; B. 142; G. 346, 2; H. 385, I. —— utī, conj., the original form; it = *ut,* that, in order that.

LINE 3. conquīrerent, 3d pers. plur. imperf. subj. act. of the verb *conquīrō, -ere, -sīvī (-iī), -sītum,* 3 (con + quaerere); hence = lit. *to search for carefully;* it agrees with a pron. implied in the ending as subject-nom., referring to *hīs;* it is subjunctive of purpose after *utī,* i.e. this clause expresses the purpose of *imperāvit.* Supply *eōs,* i.e. *fugitīvōs* as direct obj. of *conquīrerent et redūcerent.* See A. & G. 317; B. 200; G. 543, and 3; H. 497, II. —— et, cop. conj.; connects the verbs *conquīrerent* and *redūcerent.* —— redūcerent, 3d pers. plur. imperf. subjunctive of *redūcō, -ere, -dūxī, -ductum,* 3 (re + dūcere); hence = lit. *to lead back. redūcerent* is connected by the conj. *et* with *conquīrerent,* and is, in every respect, in the same grammatical construction. —— sī, conj., conditional; obsolete form *seī,* sibilated from the GK. *eἰ.* —— sibi, dat. sing. of the reflexive pron. *suī, sibi, sē, sē* — same form in both numbers; *sibi* is here the dat. of reference. Consult A. & G. 235, *a;* B. 145; G. 352; H. 384, 4. This is the usual explanation; but I suggest that it is the dat. of the *agent* after the perf. participle *pūrgātī,* used in the adj. sense of *excused* or *pardoned.* Consult A. & G. 232, *a;* B. 148, REM. 2; G. 354; H. 388, 1.

LINE 4. pūrgātī, nom. plur., predicate after *esse,* of the participle *pūrgātus, -a, -um* of the verb *pūrgō, -āre, -āvī, -ātum,* 1. Observe that the predicate-adj. is regularly in the same case as the subject-nom. of *vellent.* —— esse, pres. inf. of the verb *sum, esse, fuī, futūrus;* here the copula. —— vellent, 3d pers. plur. imperf. subjunctive of the irr. verb *volō, velle, voluī. vellent* agrees with its subject-nom. *eī,* referring to the persons denoted by the pron. *hīs* as a subst., l. 2, above. *vellent* is in the subjunctive, because it is in protasis after *sī;* the apodosis is involved in the compound purpose-clause *utī conquīrerent et redūcerent.* —— imperāvit, 3d pers. sing. perf. ind. act. of the verb *imperō, -āre, -āvī, -ātum,* 1; it agrees with a pron. implied in the ending, referring to Caesar. The student will observe that the construction is virtual *ōrātiō oblīqua.* What Caesar said, in direct form was: *conquīrete et redūcite fugitīvōs, sī mihi pūrgātī esse vultis.* The English order of the Latin here is: *imperāvit hīs, per quōrum fīnēs ierant, utī conquīrerent,* etc.

LINE 5. reductōs, acc. plur. of the perf. pass. participle *reductus, -a, -um* of the verb *redūcō, -ere, -dūxī, -ductum,* 3 (re + dūcere). *reductōs* agrees with the pron. *eōs,* to be supplied, which latter is the direct obj. of *habuit.* —— in, prep. with the acc. or abl.; here it takes the abl., and = *among.* See note on *in,* l. 1, Chap. I. —— hostium, gen. plur. of the noun *hostis, -is,* m. and f.; as a gen. it limits the noun *numerō.* Observe its position between the prep. and *numerō; hostium* is thus made emphatic. Synonyms: *hostis* = lit. *a stranger;* as a stranger is an object of suspicion, *hostis* easily passed into the meaning of *enemy;* transf. = *a public enemy;* whereas *inimīcus* (in, *negative* + amīcus) = *a private foe.*

210   CAESAR'S GALLIC WAR   [CHAP. XXVIII.

but all the rest, after the hostages and arms and deserters had been delivered up, he allowed to surrender. He ordered the Helvetii, Tulingi and the Latovici to return to the respective territories from which they had migrat-	numerō *number*	habuit; *he held;*	reliquōs *the rest*	omnēs *all,*	obsidibus, *hostages,* 6
	armīs, *arms,*	perfugīs *deserters*	trāditīs *being delivered up*	in *into*	dēditiōnem 7 *surrender*
	accēpit. *he received.*	Helvētiōs, *The Helvetii,*	Tulingōs, *Tulingi,*	Latovīcōs *Latovici*	in 8 *into*
	fīnēs *territories*	suōs, *their own,*	unde *whence*	erant profectī, *they had set out,*	revertī 9 *to return*

LINE 6. **numerō**, abl. sing. of the noun *numerus*, *-ī*, m. *numerō* is the obj. of the prep. *in* —— **habuit**, 3d pers. sing. perf. ind. act. of the verb *habeō*, *-ēre*, *-uī*, *-itum*, 2. Observe that the Latin *habeō*, GER. *haben*, and English *have* are closely related words; they = *to have*, in the widest sense: *to have in hand = to possess; to have in mind = to think, esteem, reckon.* —— **reliquōs**, acc. plur. of the adj. *reliquus*, *-a*, *-um*, used substantively, and is the direct obj. of the verb *accēpit*. For synonyms, see note on *reliqua*, l. 7, Chap. V. —— **omnēs**, acc. plur. of the adj. *omnis*, *-e*, an *ī*-stem; abl. ends in *-ī*, gen. plur. in *-ium*. *omnēs* is an attributive of *reliquōs*, used as a noun. —— **obsidibus**, abl. plur. of the noun *obses*, *-idis*, m. and f. (ob + sedēre); hence the noun = *one who sits* or *remains against the fulfillment* of some demand. *obsidibus* is in the abl. absolute construction with the perf. pass. participle *trāditīs*.

LINE 7. **armīs**, abl. plur. of *arma*, *-ōrum*, n. plur. *armīs* is also abl. absolute with *trāditīs*. —— **perfugīs**, abl. plur. of the noun *perfuga*, *-ae*, f. (per + fugere). *perfugīs* is used here loosely for *fugitīvīs; perfugīs* is also in the abl. absolute construction with *trāditīs*. Observe the omission of the conj. here between this series of words (asyndeton). See A. & G. 208, *b*, and 346, *c*; B. 123, REM. 6; G. 474, NOTE; H. 554, 6. —— **trāditīs**, abl. plur. of the perf. pass. participle *trāditus*, *-a*, *-um* of the verb *trādō*, *-ere*, *trādidī*, *traditum*, 3; *trāditīs* is in the abl. absolute with the three preceding nouns. Consult A. & G. 255; B. 192; G. 409; H. 431. —— **in**, prep. with the acc. or abl.; here it takes the acc., and = *into*. —— **dēditiōnem**, acc. sing. of the noun *dēditiō*, *-ōnis*, f. (*dēdere*, to give up); hence *dēditiō* = lit. *a giving up* to one, surrender. *dēditiōnem* is the obj. of the prep. *in*.

LINE 8. **accēpit**, 3d pers. sing. perf. ind. act. of the verb *accipiō*, *-ere*, *-cēpī*, *-ceptum*, 3 (ad + capere); hence *accipere* = lit. *to take to one's self*. *accēpit* agrees with a pron. implied in the ending as subject-nom., referring to Caesar. —— **Helvētiōs**, acc. plur. of the adj. *Helvētius*, *-a*, *-um*, used substantively, and as such the subject-acc. of the verb *revertī*, l. 9, below. As to this clan, see note on *Helvētiī*, l. 16, Chap. I. —— **Tulingōs**, acc. plur. of the proper noun *Tulingī*, *-ōrum*, m. *Tulingōs* is also subject-acc. of the verb *revertī*. The Tulingi were a German people occupying territory immediately to the east of the Rauraci. —— **Latovīcōs**, acc. plur. of the proper noun *Latovīcī*, *-ōrum*, m. *Latovīcōs* is also a subject-acc. of the verb *revertī*. Observe in this series of words the omission of the conj. (asyndeton). The Latovici were also a German clan; they dwelt north of the Tulingi. —— **in**, prep. with the acc. or abl.; here it takes the acc.; after a verb of motion it indicates the limit of the motion.

LINE 9. **fīnēs**, acc. plur. of the noun *fīnis*, *-is*, m. *fīnēs* is the obj. of the prep. *in*. —— **suōs**, acc. plur. m. of the poss. and reflexive pron. *suus*, *-a*, *-um*. *suōs* is an

10 iūssit;	et,	quod	omnibus	frūgibus	ed; and, as all the crops were destroyed and
he ordered;	*and,*	*because,*	*all*	*the fruits*	
11 āmīssīs	domī	nihil	erat,		quō	there was nothing at home to relieve hunger,
having been lost,	*at home*	*nothing*	*was,*		*by which*	
12 famem	tolerārent,	Allobrogibus		imperāvit,	he commanded the Allobroges to
hunger	*might be borne,*	*to the Allobroges*		*he gave orders,*	

attributive of the noun *fīnēs;* it refers here not to the subj. of the leading verb, but to the subject-accusatives of the inf. *revertī.* —— **unde** (derivation dubious); as to relations of place, it = *whence;* sometimes, apart from place-reference, it denotes the source of men or things. —— **erant profectī** (*profectī erant*), 3d pers. plur. pluperf. ind. of the deponent verb *proficīscor, -cīscī, profectus. erant profectī* agrees with a pron. implied in the ending as subject-nom., referring to *Helvētiōs, Tulingōs* and *Latovīcōs.* —— **revertī,** pres. inf. of the deponent verb *revertor, -ī, -versus;* its subject-accusatives are *Helvētiōs, Tulingōs, Latovīcōs.* Observe that the act. form *revertō, -ere, -vertī* is generally used in the perf. tenses, and the deponent form in the imperfect.

LINE 10. **iūssit,** 3d pers. sing. perf. ind. act. of the verb *iubeō, -ēre, iūssī, iūssum,* 2. *iūssit* agrees with a pron. implied in the ending as subject-nom., referring to Caesar. —— **et,** cop. conj.; it connects the sentences. —— **quod,** conj. = *because.* —— **omnibus,** abl. plur. f. of the adj. *omnis, -e,* an *i*-stem; abl. *omnī;* gen. plur. *omnium. omnibus* is an attributive of the noun *frūgibus.* —— **frūgibus,** abl. plur. of the noun *frūx, frūgis* (*fruor, fructus*); abl. absolute with the perf. pass. participle *āmīssīs.* Observe that from the derivations *frūges* = *the fruits* of the earth that may be enjoyed, i.e. generally *pod-fruit;* whereas *fructus* = *tree-fruit;* and *frūmentum* = *cereal-fruit* or *grain.*

LINE 11. **āmīssīs,** abl. plur. f. of the perf. pass. participle *āmīssus, -a, -um* of the verb *āmittō, -ere, -mīsī, -mīssum,* 3 (ā + mittere, *to send away*). *āmīssīs* is in the abl. absolute construction with the noun *frūgibus.* —— **domī,** gen. sing. of the noun *domus, -ī,* f. — called by the recent grammars the locative case. Consult A. & G. 258, *d*; B. 176; G. 411, REM. 2; H. 426, 2. —— **nihil,** an indeclinable neuter noun, used only in the nom. and acc. cases, here it is subject-nom. of the verb *erat.* —— **erat,** 3d pers. sing. imperf. ind. of the intrans. verb *sum, esse, fuī, futūrus. erat* is here a verb of complete predication, and agrees with its subject-nom. *nihil.* —— **quō,** abl. n. of the rel. pron *quī, quae, quod;* it refers to the noun *nihil;* really an abl. of means = *by which;* but as this is a result-clause with the subjunctive, the *quō* is taken as = *ut eō.*

LINE 12. **famem,** acc. sing. of the noun *famis, -is,* f. *famem* is the direct obj. of the verb *tolerārent.* —— **tolerārent,** 3d pers. plur. imperf. subjunctive act. of the verb *tolerō, -āre, -āvī, -ātum,* 1 (stem strengthened from the radical *tol,* as seen in *tollo;* compare the GK. τολμάω). *tolerārent* agrees with the pron. *eī* as subject-nom., referring to the Helvetii, Tulingi and Latovici; it is the subjunctive of result after *quō,* which here = *ut eō.* Consult A. & G. 319, 2 · B. 201, (*b*); G. 631, 2; H. 500, I. —— **Allobrogibus,** dat. of the noun *Allobrogēs, -um,* m.; dat. after *imperāvit* — a verb of *commanding.* See A. & G. 227; B. 142; G. 346, 2; H. 385, I. The Allobroges were a powerful Gallic clan that occupied the territory between the Rhone and the Isere rivers. —— **imperāvit,** 3d pers. sing. perf. ind. act. of the verb *imperō, -āre, -āvī, -ātum,* 1 ; its subject-nom. is Caesar, to be supplied.

supply them with a sufficiency of grain; and he ordered the Helvetians themselves to rebuild the towns and villages which they had burned. This order he gave chiefly for these reasons:	ut *that*	eīs *for them*	frūmentī *of grain*	cōpiam *an abundance*	facerent; 13 *they should make;*
	ipsōs *themselves*	oppida *towns*	vīcōsque, *villages and,*	quōs *which*	incenderant, 14 *they had burned,*
	restituere *to rebuild*	iūssit. *he ordered.*	Id *That*	eā *for this,*	māximē 15 *especially,*

LINE 13. **ut**, conj. = lit. *that;* it introduces the purpose-clause, which is often best translated into English by the English inf. —— **eīs**, dat. plur. of the dem. pron. *is, ea, id,* used as a personal pron. of the 3d pers.; dat. of *advantage*. See A. & G. 235; B. 145; G. 346; H. 384, II, 4. —— **frūmentī**, gen. sing. of the noun *frūmentum, -ī,* n. (frugī + mentum); *frūmentī*, as a gen., limits *cōpiam*. —— **cōpiam**, acc. sing. of the noun *cōpia, -ae,* f. (con + ops). *cōpiam* is the direct obj. of *facerent*. —— **facerent**, 3d pers. plur. imperf. subjunctive of the verb *faciō, -ere, fēcī, factum,* 3; it agrees with the pron. *eī* understood as its subject-nom., referring to *Allobrogibus;* it is subjunctive of purpose after *ut.* See A. & G. 317; B. 200; G. 546, NOTE 1; H. 497, II.

LINE 14. **ipsōs**, acc. plur. m. of the intensive dem. pron. *ipse, -sa, -sum,* gen *ipsīus,* dat. *ipsī. ipsōs,* i.e. *Helvētiōs,* is subject-acc. of the inf. *restituere,* l. 15, below. —— **oppida**, acc. plur. of the noun *oppidum, -ī,* n. *oppidum* (ops, *aid* + dare, *to give*); hence *oppidum* = lit. *that which gives aid* or *shelter,* i.e. *a town* — the proper word to designate any other town than Rome; Rome is designated *urbs. oppida* is the direct obj. of *restituere,* l. 15, below. —— **vīcōsque** (vīcōs + que). *vīcōs* is the acc. plur. of the noun *vīcus, -ī,* m. (digammated from GK. οἶκος); hence it = *a row of houses* in town or country. *vīcōs* is very closely connected by the enclitic *-que* with *oppida,* and is in the same grammatical construction. *que,* enclitic conj. —— **quōs**, acc. plur. m. of the rel. pron. *quī, quae, quod;* it refers to *vīcōs,* but is the direct obj. of the verb *incenderant.* —— **incenderant**, 3d pers. plur. pluperf. ind. act. of the verb *incendō, -ere, -cendī, -cēnsum,* 3 (in, *intensive* + candēre); hence *incendere* = lit. *to set fire to. incenderant* agrees with *Helvētiī* understood as its subject-nom. Synonyms: *incendere* = strictly, *to set on fire; ūrere* = *to consume with fire;* and *cremāre* = *to destroy completely by fire, to burn to ashes.*

LINE 15. **restituere**, pres. inf. act. of *restituō, -ere, -uī, -ūtum,* 3 (re + statuere); hence = lit. *to set up again.* The subject-acc. of *restituere* is the emphatic pron. *ipsōs,* in the preceding line. The sharp student of Latin will observe that all that precedes *iūssit,* from the semi-colon, is logically the direct obj. of *iūssit;* that in a complete analysis, *ipsōs . . . restituere* is the infinitive-clause, *ipsōs* being the subject-acc. of *restituere,* which latter is modified by the direct obj. *oppida vīcōsque;* and the latter nouns are modified by the relative adjective-clause *quos incenderant.* —— **iūssit**, 3d pers. sing. perf. ind. act. of the verb *iubeō, -ēre, iūssī, iūssum,* 2. *iūssit* agrees with the noun *Caesar* understood. —— **Id**, acc. sing. n. of the dem. pron. *is, ea, id,* used substantively, and is the direct obj. of the verb *fēcit.* The pron. *id* refers to the order which Caesar gave to the Helvetii to return home. —— **eā**, abl. sing. f. of the dem. pron. *is, ea, id;* it is an attributive of *ratiōne.* —— **māximē**, adv., superl. degree of the comparative *magis. māximē* modifies the verb *fēcit.*

BOOK I. 213

16 ratiōne	fēcit,	quod	nōluit	eum	locum,	because he did not wish that such a country, as that from which the Helvetii had migrated, should be left unoccupied; and because he feared that, on account of the fertility of the fields, the Germans who dwelt across the Rhine might cross from their
reason	he did,	because	he was unwilling	that	place,	
17 unde	Helvētiī	discesserant,		vacāre;	nē	
whence	the Helvetii	had set out,		to be vacant;	lest	
18 propter		bonitātem	agrōrum		Germānī,	
on account of		the goodness	of the fields,		the Germans,	
19 quī	trāns	Rhēnum	incolunt,	ē	suīs	
who	across	the Rhine	dwell,	from	their own	

LINE 16. ratiōne, abl. sing. of the noun *ratiō, -ōnis*, f. (*rēri*, to reckon); hence *ratiō* = lit. *a reckoning*; transf., *a mode of reckoning*; hence *mode, manner*, etc. *ratiōne* is an abl. of *manner* without the prep. *cum*, as it has a modifier, *eā*. Consult A. & G. 248; B. 168; G. 399; H. 419, III. —— **fēcit**, 3d pers. sing. perf. ind. act. of the verb *faciō, -ere, fēci, factum*, 3. *fēcit* agrees with the subject-nom. *Caesar*, to be supplied. —— **quod**, conj. = *because*. —— **nōluit**, 3d pers. sing. perf. ind. act. of the irr. verb *nōlō, nōlle, nōluī* (nē + volō). *nōluit* agrees with *Caesar* understood, as its subject-nom. —— **eum**, acc. sing. m. of the dem. pron. *is, ea, id*; it is an attributive of the noun *locum*. —— **locum**, acc. sing. of the noun *locus, -ī*, m.; the plur. m. or n., i.e. *locī* or *loca*; see note on *locī*, l. 10, Chap. II. *locum* is the subject-acc. of the inf. *vacāre*.

LINE 17. **unde**, adv.; see note on this particle, l. 9, above. —— **Helvētiī**, nom. plur. of the adj. *Helvētius, -a, -um*, used substantively; subject-nom. of the verb *discesserant*. —— **discesserant**, 3d pers. plur. pluperf. ind. act. of the verb *discēdō, -ere, -cessī, -cessum*, 3 (dis + cadere); hence *discēdere* = lit. *to go apart*. *discesserant* agrees with its subject-nom. *Helvētiī*, expressed in the text. —— **vacāre**, pres. inf. of the neuter or intrans. verb *vacō, -āre, -āvī, -ātum*, 1; its subject-acc. is *locum*, in the preceding line. Note that the signification of this neuter verb is: *to be vacant, to be unoccupied, to lie waste*. —— **nē**, conj. — the particle to introduce *negative* purpose.

LINE 18. **propter** (*prope*), an adv. sometimes, and sometimes a prep.; here a prep. with the acc. —— **bonitātem**, acc. sing. of the noun *bonitās, -tātis*, f. (*bonus*). *bonitātem* is the obj. of the prep. *propter*. —— **agrōrum**, gen. plur. of *ager, agrī*, m.; as a gen. it limits the noun *bonitātem*. Observe the emphatic position of the phrase *propter bonitātem agrōrum*; this phrase is an adverbial modifier of *trānsīrent*, l. 20, below. As to synonyms, *agrī* = *the fields, the open country*, in opposition to the town; whereas *fīnēs* = *land enclosed within borders*. —— **Germānī, -ōrum**, m. (Γερμανοί), subject-nom. of the verbs *trānsīrent* and *essent*, lines 20 and 22, below. The Germans were the eastern neighbors of the Gauls, occupying the territory between the Rhine, the Danube and the Vistula.

LINE 19. **quī**, nom. plur. of the rel. pron. *quī, quae, quod*, gen. *cūius*, dat. *cui*. *quī* refers to *Germānī*, as its antecedent, but is the subject-nom. of the verb *incolunt*. —— **trāns**, prep. with the acc. —— **Rhēnum**, acc. sing. of the noun *Rhēnus, -ī*, m. *Rhēnum* is the obj. of the prep. *trāns*. This river, in Caesar's time, formed the

borders into those of the Helvetii, and become neighbors to the province of Gaul and to the Allobroges. He granted the request of the Aedui to settle the Boii	fīnibus *borders* fīnitimī *neighbors* essent. *should be.*	in *into* Galliae *to the Gallic* Bōiōs, *The Boii,*	Helvētiōrum *the Helvetian* prōvinciae *province* petentibus *asking*	fīnēs *borders* Allobrogibusque *to the Allobroges* Aeduīs, *the Aedui,*	trānsīrent *should cross,* and, quod *because*	et 20 and 21 22

boundary between Gaul and Germany. —— **incolunt**, 3d pers. plur. of the verb *incolō, -ere, -coluī,* 3 (in + colere); hence = *to live in* a place. *incolunt* agrees with its subject-nom. *quī.* —— **ē**, prep. with the abl. (*ē* before consonants only, *ex* before vowels or consonants). —— **suīs**, abl. plur. of the poss. and reflexive pron. *suus, -a, -um. suīs* refers to *Germānī,* the subj. of the subordinate clause *nē . . . Germānī . . . trānsīrent;* but *suīs* is an attributive of the noun *fīnibus.*

LINE 20. **fīnibus**, abl. plur. of *fīnis, -is,* m.; it is the obj. of the prep. *ē.* —— **in**, prep. with the acc. or abl.; here it takes the acc. after a verb of motion, and = *into.* As to the various significations of this prep., see note on *in,* l. 1, Chap. I. —— **Helvētiōrum**, gen. plur. of the adj. *Helvētius, -a, -um,* used as a subst.; as such, it limits *fīnēs.* Note the emphasis that is put on *Helvētiōrum* by its position between the prep. and its obj. —— **fīnēs**, acc. plur. of the noun *fīnis, -is,* m.; it is the obj. of the prep. *in.* As to synonyms, see note on *agrōrum,* l. 18, above. —— **trānsīrent**, 3d pers. plur. imperf. subjunctive act. of the verb *trānseō, -īre, -īvī (-iī), -itum,* 4 (trāns + īre, *to go across*). *trānsīrent* agrees with its subject-nom. *Germānī,* l. 18, above; it is the subjunctive of negative purpose after the particle *nē.* Consult A. & G. 317; B. 200; G. 545, 3; H. 497, II. —— **et**, cop. conj.; it connects the clauses.

LINE 21. **fīnitimī**, nom. plur. of the adj. *fīnitimus, -a, -um (fīnis),* used as a subst. *fīnitimī* is predicate after *essent.* —— **Galliae**, gen. sing. of the noun *Gallia, -ae,* f.; *Galliae,* as a gen., limits the noun *prōvinciae.* —— **prōvinciae**, dat. sing. of the noun *prōvincia, -ae,* f.; it is, in fact, a dat. after *fīnitimī* — an adj. of *nearness,* though *fīnitimī* here has a substantive use. As to the syntax, see A. & G. 234, *a;* B. 144; G. 359; H. 391, I. —— **Allobrogibusque** (Allobrogus + que). *Allobrogibus* is the dat. plur. of the proper noun *Allobrogēs, -um,* m. *Allobrogibus* is connected very closely with the noun *prōvinciae,* and is in the same grammatical construction. *que,* enclitic conj. = *and.*

LINE 22. **essent**, 3d pers. plur. imperf. subjunctive of the neuter or intrans. verb *sum, esse, fuī, futūrus; essent* is connected by the conj. *et,* l. 20, above, with the verb *trānsīrent,* and is in the same grammatical construction, in every respect. —— **Bōiōs**, acc. plur. of the proper noun *Bōiī, -ōrum,* m. *Bōiōs* is the direct obj. of the verb *col(n)locārent.* Observe that the noun *Bōiōs* is taken out of the clause where it naturally belongs, i.e. in the clause *ut in fīnibus suīs collocārent,* and is placed at the beginning of the sentence for emphasis. The Boii were a people of Celtic Gaul, their territory lying between the Loire and Allier rivers. A part of this clan emigrated to Germany, and a part to northern Italy. I take the construction here to be indicated by the following *ōrdō: Aeduīs petentibus, ut in fīnibus suīs Bōiōs collocārent, quod ēgregiā virtūte erant cōgnitī, concessit.* —— **petentibus**, dat. plur. of the pres. participle *petēns, -ntis* of the verb *petō, -ere, -īvī (-iī), -itum,* 3. *petentibus,* as a participle, agrees with the noun *Aeduīs,* and is followed by the pur-

23 ēgregiā	virtūte	erant	cōgnitī,	ut	in	within their own borders, because they had been known to be men of eminent valor. And the Aedui gave them fields; and, subsequent-
of distinguished	*valor*	*they had been known,*		*that*	*in*	
24 fīnibus	suīs	col(n)locārent,	concessit;		quibus	
borders	*their*	*they might locate,*	*he granted;*		*to whom*	
25 illī	agrōs	dedērunt	quōsque	posteā	in	
they	*fields*	*gave*	*whom and,*	*afterwards,*	*into*	

pose-clause *ut . . . collocārent*. —— **Aeduīs**, dat. plur. of the adj. *Aeduus, -a, -um*, used as a noun. *Aeduīs* is the indirect obj. of the — here — intrans. verb *concessit*. —— **quod**, conj. = *because*.

LINE 23. **ēgregiā**, abl. f. of the adj. *ēgregius, -a, -um* (ē + grex = *out of the herd*, i.e. *choice, eminent*). *ēgregiā* is an attributive of the noun *virtūte*. —— **virtūte**, abl. sing. of the noun *virtūs, -ūtis*, f. (*vir*, the male, man, hero). *virtūte* is an abl. of quality with the adj. *ēgregiā*. Consult A. & G. 251; B. 169; G. 400; H. 419, II. Observe that the abl. of description here is an essential part of the predicate. —— **erant cōgnitī** (*cōgnitī erant*), 3d pers. plur. pluperf. ind. pass. of the verb *cōgnoscō, -ere, -nōvī, cōgnitum*, 3. *erant cōgnitī* (*cōgnitī erant*) agrees with *eī* understood as subject-nom., referring to *Bōiōs*. —— **ut**, conj. —— **in**, prep. with the acc. or abl.; here it takes the abl.

LINE 24. **fīnibus**, abl. of the noun *fīnis, -is*, m.; see note on *fīnēs*, l. 9, above. *fīnibus* is in the abl. case after the prep. *in*. —— **suīs**, abl. sing. of the poss. and reflexive pron. *suus, -a, -um*; it refers to the Aedui; it is an attributive of *fīnibus*. —— **collocārent**, 3d pers. plur. imperf. subjunctive of the verb *col(n)locō, -āre, -āvī, -ātum*, 1. *conlocārent* agrees with the subject-nom. implied in the ending, referring to the Aedui; it is the subjunctive of purpose after the conj. *ut*, expressing the purpose of *petentibus*. Consult A. & G. 331; B. 200, REM. 2; G. 546, 1; H. 498, I. —— **concessit**, 3d pers. sing. perf. ind. act. of the verb *concēdō, -ere, -cessī, -cessum*, 3; it agrees with a pron. implied in the ending as subject-nom., referring to Caesar. It will be noticed that *concēdere* is both a neuter and an act. verb; or, in other words, it is sometimes transitive and sometimes intransitive. We regard it here as intransitive; it is often thus used. Observe also that some critics take *petentibus* as an abl. absolute with the noun *Aeduīs*; that others regard the *ut*-clause as the direct obj. of the verb *concessit*. —— **quibus**, dat. plur. m. of the rel. pron. *quī, quae, quod*; it refers to the Boii, but is the indirect obj. of *dedērunt*. Observe that *quibus*, at the beginning of a sentence = *et eīs*. Consult A. & G. 180, *f*; B. 129, REM. 9; G. 610; H. 453.

LINE 25. **illī**, nom. plur. of the dem. pron. *ille, -la, -lud*, gen. *illīus*, dat. *illī* — same form as nom. plur. *illī*, in the text = *the Aeduī;* and its use indicates that, as a clan, they were powerful and also well-known. See A. & G. 100, *a*, 101, 102, *h, f*; B. 82, 1, 84, 3, and REMS. 1, 2, 5; G. 104, III, 307, 1, 2; H. 186, III, 450, 4. *illī* is the subject-nom. of *dedērunt*. —— **agrōs**, acc. plur. of the noun *ager, agrī*, m. *agrōs* is the direct obj. of *dedērunt*. For synonyms, see note on *agrum*, l. 12, Chap. II. —— **dedērunt**, 3d pers. plur. perf. ind. act. of the verb *dedō, -ere, didī, ditum*, 3 (dē + dare, *to give over*). *dedērunt* agrees with its subject-nom. *illī* in number and person. —— **quōsque** (quōs + que). *quōs* is the acc. plur. m. of the rel. pron. *quī, quae, quod;* it refers to the Boii, but it is the direct obj. of *recēpērunt*, l. 27, below. **que**, enclitic conj.; connects the clauses. —— **posteā** (post + eā), adv.; it modifies *recēpērunt*. —— **in**, prep. with the acc. or abl.; here it takes the acc.

ly, received them into the same condition of rights and privileges as they had themselves.	parem *an equal,* atque *as*	iūris *of right* ipsī *themselves*	lībertātisque *liberty and,* erant, *were,*	condiciōnem, 26 *condition* recēpērunt. 27 *they received.*
XXIX. In the camp of the Helvetii, lists written in Greek characters were found	XXIX. In repertae sunt *were found*	In *In*	castrīs *the camp* litterīs *in letters*	Helvētiōrum tabulae 1 *of the Helvetii tablets* Graecīs cōnfectae et 2 *Greek made and*

LINE 26. **parem**, acc. sing. f. of the adj. *par, paris*. *parem* is an attributive of the noun *condic(t)iō*. —— **iūris**, gen. sing. of the noun *iūs*, *iūris*, n.; as a gen. *iūris* limits *condiciōnem*. Synonyms: *iūs* = *legal right;* whereas *fās* = *divine right*. —— **lībertātisque** (libertātis + que). *libertātis* is the gen. sing. of the noun *libertās*, *-tātis*, f. (*liber*, free). *que*, enclitic conj.; observe how closely the nouns are joined by the use of *-que*. —— **condic(t)iōnem**, acc. sing. of the noun *condiciō, -ōnis* (derived from *condere* through *condicāre*), hence = *a statement of terms, condition*, etc. *condiciōnem* is the obj. of the prep. *in*.

LINE 27. **atque** (ad + que), conj.; it usually = *and* or *and also;* but after words meaning comparison or likeness it = *than* or *as*. Consult A. & G. 156, *a*, end; B. 217; G. 643, and NOTE 3; H. 459, 2. Here *atque* after the phrase *in parem condiciōnem* = *as*. —— **ipsī**, nom. plur. m. of the intensive dem. pron. *ipse, -sa, -sum*. *ipsī* refers to the Aedui, but it is subject-nom. of the verb *erant*. —— **erant**, 3d pers. plur. imperf. ind. of the neuter or intrans. verb *sum, esse, fui, futūrus*. *erant* agrees with its subject-nom. *ipsī* expressed. —— **recēpērunt**, 3d pers. plur. pluperf. ind. act. of the verb *recipiō, -ere, -cēpī, -ceptum*, 3 (re + capere); hence *recipere* = lit. *to take back;* then transf. it = *to take to one's self*, i.e. *to receive*. *recēpērunt* is connected by the conj. *-que* very closely with *dedērunt*, and has the same subject-nom., viz. *illī*, referring to the Aedui.

LINE 1. **In**, prep. with the acc. or abl.; here it takes the abl. For difference of signification after verbs of motion and rest, see note on *in*, l. 1, Chap. I. —— **castrīs**, abl. plur. of the noun *castrum, -ī*, n.; in the sing. = *a fort;* in the plur. = *a fortified camp. castrīs* is the obj. of the prep. *in*. —— **Helvētiōrum**, gen. plur. of the adj. *Helvētius, -a, -um*, used substantively. *Helvētiōrum*, as a gen., limits the noun *castrīs*. As to the Helvetian clan, see l. 16, Chap. I. —— **tabulae**, nom. plur. of the noun *tabula, -ae*, f. *tabulae* is subject-nom. of the pass. verb *repertae sunt*. With *tabula* compare the French and English word *table*. *tabula*, in the sing. = lit. *a board;* in the plur. = *writing-boards* or *tablets* spread with wax, on which written letters were made with the *stilus* (sometimes written *stylus*, compare GK. στύλος), usually pointed and made of iron.

LINE 2. **repertae sunt**, 3d pers. plur. perf. ind. pass. of *reperiō, -īre, rep[p]erī, repertum*, 4 (re + parere = lit. *to find again*). *repertae sunt* agrees with its subject-nom. *tabulae*. The student will observe that this compound tense is made up of the perf. pass. participle and the verb *sunt;* that the participle part of it agrees in gender, number and case with its subject-nom. —— **litterīs**, abl. plur. of the noun *littera, -ae*, f. (often *lītera*). *litterīs* here is in the abl. of *manner*. See A. & G. 248; B. 166; G. 399; H. 419, III. Observe that *littera*, in the sing. = *a letter* of the

3 ad	Caesarem	relātae,	quibus	in	tabulīs	and brought to Caesar; and in these, an estimate was made in detail as to the number of those that had left home who could bear arms; and
to	*Caesar*	*brought,*	*which*	*on*	*tablets*	
4 nōminātim	ratiō	cōnfecta erat,	quī		numerus	
by name	*an estimate*	*was made,*	*what*		*number*	
5 domō	exīsset	eōrum,	quī	arma	ferre	
from home	*had gone*	*of those,*	*who*	*arms*	*to bear*	

alphabet; in the plur. = either *letters*, or an *epistle* made up of the letters of the alphabet. —— **Graecīs**, abl. plur. f. of the adj. *Graecus, -a, -um* (GK. Γραικός); *Graecīs* is an attributive of the noun *litterīs*. Observe that the phrase *litterīs Graecīs* here = *in Greek letters* — not in the Greek language. The Gauls, even in Caesar's time, had no alphabet of their own; and hence they borrowed the Greek letters from the colonists of Marseilles. —— **cōnfectae**, nom. plur. f. of the perf. pass. participle *cōnfectus, -a, -um* of the verb *cōnficio, -ere, -fēci, -fectum*, 3 (con + facere). *cōnfectae*, as a participle, agrees with the noun *tabulae*. —— *et*, cop. conj.; connects *repertae sunt* with *relatae (sunt)*.

LINE 3. **ad**, prep. with the acc.; used here with a noun after a verb of motion — *after* according to the English way of speaking. —— **Caesarem**, acc. sing. of the proper noun *Caesar, -aris*, m. *Caesarem* is the obj. of the prep. *ad*. —— **relātae (sunt)**, 3d pers. plur. perf. ind. pass. of the verb *referō, -ferre, retulī, relātum*. *relātae (sunt)* is connected by the conj. *et* with *repertae sunt*, and is in the same grammatical construction. —— **quibus**, abl. plur. f. of the rel. pron. *quī, quae, quod;* used both relatively and adjectively; as a rel. it refers to *tabulae*, l. 1, above; as an adj. it agrees with *tabulīs*. —— **in**, prep. with the acc. or abl.; here it takes the abl. But note its position between the noun and its modifier, and consult A. & G. 345, *a*; B. 58. 2; G. 413, REM. 1; H. 569, II, 1. Note also that the noun to which a relative refers is often repeated in a phrase in Latin; but that this noun need not be repeated in the English translation. Note, further, that in such construction as we have here, the rel. phrase would better be translated as a dem. phrase, i.e. instead of *in which letters*, translate *and in these letters*. Consult A. & G. 180, *f*; B. 129, REM. 9; G. 610, REM. 1; H. 453. —— **tabulīs**, abl. plur. of *tabula, -ae*, f.; obj. of the prep. *in*.

LINE 4. **nōminātim**, adv. (derived from *nōmināre* [*nōmen* for (*g*)*nōmen* from (*g*)*nōscō*, compare GK. γνόω]); hence *nōminātim* = lit. *by name*. This adv. modifies the verb *cōnfecta erat*. —— **ratiō**, nom. sing. of the noun *ratiō, -ōnis*, f. (from *rēs* through *rēī* = *to reckon*). *ratiō* is the subject-nom. of *cōnfecta erat*. —— **cōnfecta erat**, 3d pers. sing. pluperf. ind. pass. of the verb *cōnficiō, -ere, -fēcī, -fectum*, 3; it agrees with its subject-nom. *ratiō*. —— **quī**, nom. sing. m. of the interrogative pron. *quis* or *quī, quae, quid*, here used adjectively, modifying the noun *numerus*. Observe that the interrogative form of the pron. in the nom. m. sing. is either *quis* or *quī*. —— **numerus**, nom. sing. of the noun *numerus, -ī*, m. *numerus* is the subject-nom. of the verb *exīsset*.

LINE 5. **domō**, abl. sing. of the noun *domus, -ūs*, or *-ī*, f.; the form *domī* is locative. *domō* is here the abl. of *place from which* without a prep. Consult A. & G. 258, 2, *a*; B. 175; G. 390, 2; H. 412, II, 1. —— **exīsset**, 3d pers. sing. pluperf. subjunctive act. — shortened form for *exīvisset* — of *exeō, -īre, -īvī (-iī), -itum*. *exīsset* agrees with the subject-nom. *numerus;* it is in the subjunctive, because it is an indirect question. Consult A. & G. 334; B. 242; G. 467; H. 529, I. —— **eōrum**, gen. plur. m. of the dem. pron. *is, ea, id*, used here as a personal pron. of the 3d pers.;

also separately, as to the number of boys, old men, and women. The aggregate number according to all these lists was	possent, *were able,* mulierēsque. *women and.* summa *the sum*	et *and* erat *was,*	item *also* Quārum *Of which* capitum *of heads*	sēparātim *separately* omnium *all* Helvētiōrum *of the Helvetii*	puerī, *the boys,* ratiōnum *numbers* mīlia *thousands*	senēs, 6 *old men,* 7 8

as a gen. it limits the noun *numerus.* —— **quī**, nom. plur. m. of the interrogative pron. *quis, quae, quid. quī* is the subject-nom. of the intrans. verb *possent.* —— **arma**, acc. plur. of the noun *arma, -ōrum*, n. plur. *arma* is the direct obj. of the verb *ferre.* Synonyms: *arma* (from GK. ἀρειν, *to fit*) = lit. *armor fitted to the body.* Hence *arma = arms* both offensive and defensive, such as sword, ax and club; whereas *tēla = arms, missiles* used at a distance. —— **ferre**, pres. inf. act. of the irr. verb *ferō, ferre, tulī, lātum* (compare GK. φέρω). *ferre* is a complementary inf., depending on *possent.* Consult A. & G. 271; B. 181; G. 423; H. 533, I, 2.

LINE 6. **possent**, 3d pers. plur. imperf. subjunctive of the intrans. verb *possum, posse, potuī* (potis, *able* + sum); it agrees with its subject-nom. *quī*, and is in the subjunctive, because it is an *indirect question.* See grammatical references to *exīsset*, l. 5, above. —— **et**, cop. conj.; connects the clauses. —— **item**, adv. (radical *i*, whence *is* + adverbial ending tem), hence = in *that* manner, *so, also.* —— **sēparātim**, adv. (acc. of an assumed noun. in *-tis*; or rather the adv. is from a stem as seen in *sēparātus* from *sēparāre*). But see A. & G. 148, *f.* e; B. 117, 7; G. 91, 1; H. 304, I. *sēparātim*, as an adv., modifies *cōnfecta erat*, to be supplied from the preceding. Supply the *lacūna* here thus: et item sēparātim *ratio cōnfecta erat quī numerus essent* puerī, etc. —— **puerī**, nom. plur. of the noun *puer, puerī*, m.; subject-nom. of *essent* understood, of which *quī numerus* is the predicate. This construction is awkward; but about the best that we can suggest. One critic supplies here *perscrīptī erant = were enumerated*, of which *puerī, senēs, mulierēsque* are subject-nominatives. The regular construction would be genitives limiting *numerus* understood. —— **senēs**, nom. plur. of the adj. *senex, senis*, used substantively; or one may supply *hominēs. senēs* is connected by *et* understood with *puerī*, and is in the same grammatical construction.

LINE 7. **mulierēsque** (mulierēs + que). *mulierēs*, nom. plur. of the noun *mulier, mulieris*, f. *que*, enclitic conj.; it connects *mulierēs* with *senēs*, and is in the same grammatical construction. Observe that a Latin sentence, ending in an enclitic *-que*, is not to be imitated. —— **Quārum**, gen. plur. of *quī, quae, quod*, used adjectively; as such, it limits the noun *ratiōnum.* Observe that at the beginning of the sentence *quārum = et eārum.* See A. & G. 180, *f*; B. 129, REM. 9; G. 610; H. 453. —— **omnium**, gen. plur. of the adj. *omnis, -e*, an *ī*-stem, as seen in this case, and also in the dat. and abl. sing. *omnium* is an attributive of the noun *ratiōnum.* —— **ratiōnum**, gen. plur. of the noun *ratiō, -ōnis*, f.; as a gen. it limits the noun *summa.*

LINE 8. **summa**, nom. of the noun *summa, -ae*, f. (derived from the adj. *summus, -a, -um*, i.e. supply *rēs*). *summa* is the subject-nom. of the verb *erat.* —— **erat**, 3d pers. sing. imperf. ind. of the neuter or intrans. verb *sum, esse, fuī*, fut. participle *futūrus*; it agrees with its subject-nom. *summa.* —— **capitum**, gen. plur. of the noun *caput, -itis*, n. *capitum* is partitive gen. after *mīlia.* Consult A. & G. 216, 2; B. 134; G. 370; H. 397, 2. *capitum* = lit. *of heads*, i.e. *of souls.* —— **Helvētiōrum**, gen. plur. n. of the adj. *Helvētius, -a, -um. Helvētiōrum* is an attributive of the noun *capitum.* As to this clan, see note on *Helvētiī*, l. 16, Chap. I. —— **mīlia**, nom. plur.

LINES 9-12.] BOOK I. 219

9 ducenta	et	sexāgintā	tria,	Tulingōrum	two hundred and sixty-three thousand souls of the Helvetii, thirty-six thousand of the Tulingi, fourteen thousand of the Latovici, twenty-three thousand of the Raurici, thirty-two thousand of the Boii; of such
two hundred	*and*	*sixty-*	*three,*	*of the Tulingi*	
10 mīlia	trīgintā	sex,		Latovīcōrum	
thousands	*thirty-*	*six,*	*of the Latovici (thousands)*		
11 quattuordecim,		Rauricōrum		vīgintī	
fourteen,		*of the Raurici*	*(thousands)*	*twenty-*	
12 tria,	Bōiōrum		trīgintā	duo;	ex
three,	*of the Boii*	*(thousands)*	*thirty-*	*two;*	*of*

n. of the adj. *mille* = *a thousand.* *mille* in the sing. is an indecl. num. adj.; in the plur. *mīlia* or *millia* = *thousands,* and as a subst. it is declinable throughout; gen. plur. *mīlium,* dat. and abl. *mīlibus.* *mīlia* is predicate-nom. after *erat.*

LINE 9. **ducenta,** nom. plur. n. of the cardinal num. adj. *ducentī, -ae, -a.* *ducenta* is an attributive of *mīlia,* used as a noun. —— **et,** cop. conj.; it connects *ducenta* and *sexāgintā.* —— **sexāgintā** (sibilated from the GK. ἑξήκοντα); indecl. cardinal num. adj.; connected by the conj. *et* with *ducenta,* and in the same grammatical construction. —— **tria,** nom. plur. n. of the decl. num. adj. *trēs, trēs, tria.* *tria* is also an attributive of *mīlia.* Observe that the entire phrase *mīlia ducenta et sexāgintā tria* might be expressed thus: *mīlia CCLXIII,* and is thus expressed in some editions. —— **Tulingōrum,** gen. plur. of *Tulingī, -ōrum,* m.; partitive gen. after *mīlia.* See grammatical references to *capitum* in the preceding line. The Tulingi were a German clan, dwelling east of the Raurici, near the Rhine.

LINE 10. **mīlia** is here in the same grammatical construction as *mīlia* in l. 8, above, i.e. predicate-nom. after *erat.* —— **trīgintā,** indecl. cardinal num. adj.; an attributive of *mīlia.* —— **sex** (GK. ἕξ), an indecl. num. adj.; also an attributive of the noun *mīlia.* Observe that the phrase *mīlia trīgintā sex* is often expressed thus: *mīlia XXXVI.* —— **Latovīcōrum,** gen. plur. of the noun *Latovīcī, -ōrum,* m.; gen. partitive after *mīlia,* to be supplied, which *mīlia* is to be disposed of, as to its syntax, like *mīlia* in lines 8 and 10, above. The common text reads here *Latobrīgōrum* instead of *Latovīcōrum.*

LINE 11. **quattuordecim** (quattuor + decem); *quattuordecim* is an attributive of *mīlia,* used as a substantive, to be supplied. *quattuordecim* is frequently indicated by the Roman letters *XIV,* or by *XIIII.* —— **Rauricōrum,** gen. plur. of *Rauricī, -ōrum,* m.; it is sometimes spelled *Rauracōrum;* it, as a gen., limits *mīlia,* to be supplied. The Raurici were a Celtic people on the upper Rhine. —— **vīgintī,** indecl. cardinal num. adj.; it is an attributive of *mīlia* understood.

LINE 12. **tria,** nom. plur. n.; attributive of *mīlia* understood. The phrase *vīgintī tria* is sometimes indicated by the Roman letters *XXIII.* —— **Bōiōrum,** gen. plur. of the proper noun *Bōiī, -ōrum,* m.; as a gen. it limits *mīlia,* to be supplied. These people dwelt in central Gaul. A part of the clan migrated to the Hyrcanian forest, Germany; a part to northern Italy. —— **trīgintā,** an indecl. cardinal num. adj.; it modifies *mīlia* understood. —— **duo,** decl. cardinal num. adj. As to the declension of *duo,* see note on *tria,* l. 9, above. *duo* is also an attributive of the noun *mīlia.* The phrase *trīgintā duo* is indicated by the Roman letters *XXXII.* It will be observed that in the various parts of the sentence as

220   CAESAR'S GALLIC WAR   [CHAP. XXIX.

as could bear arms, there were about ninety-two thousand. The sum total of these people was about three-hundred and sixty-eight thou-	hīs, *those,*	quī *who*	arma *arms*	ferre *to bear*	possent, *were able,*	ad *about*	mīlia *thousands*	13
	nōnāgintā *ninety-*		duo. *two (were).*		Summa *The sum*	omnium *of all*	fuērunt *were*	14
	ad *about*	mīlia *thousands*		trecenta *three hundred*	et *and*	sexāgintā *sixty-*	octō. *eight.*	15

analyzed, *mīlia,* used as a noun, is to be supplied; and that in each position, as supplied, it is in the same grammatical construction as the *mīlia* in l. 8, above, i.e. they are predicates after *erat,* of which verb the subject-nom. is *summa.* —— **ex,** prep. with the abl. (*ē* before consonants only, *ex* before vowels or consonants).

LINE 13. **hīs,** abl. plur. of the dem. pron. *hīc, haec, hōc,* used substantively; obj. of the prep. *ex;* but the construction is, in fact, partitive after the noun *mīlia* in this line; *ex hīs,* as a phrase, is used instead of the gen. *hōrum.* Consult A. & G. 216, 4, *c;* B. 134, REM. 2; G. 372, REM. 2; H. 397, 3, NOTE 3. —— **quī,** nom. plur. of the rel. pron. *quī, quae, quod;* it refers to *hīs* as its antecedent, but is the subject-nom. of the verb *possent.* —— **arma,** acc. plur. of the noun *arma, -ōrum,* n. plur. *arma* is the direct obj. of the verb *ferre.* For derivation, see note on *arma,* l. 5, above. —— **ferre,** pres. inf. act. of the irr. verb *ferō, ferre, tulī, lātum. ferre* is complementary inf., depending on *possent.* Consult A. & G. 271; B. 181; G. 423; H. 533, I, 2. —— **possent,** 3d pers. plur. imperf. subjunctive of the intrans. verb *possum, posse, potuī* (potis + sum); it agrees with its subject-nom. *quī;* subjunctive in a *result* or characteristic clause. Consult A. & G. 320; B. 201, REM. 1, (*a*); G. 631; H. 503, I. —— **ad,** generally a prep., but here with numerals it = *circiter,* about; as an adv. it modifies the adj. *nōnāgintā.* —— **mīlia,** nom. plur.; subj. of *fuērunt,* to be supplied.

LINE 14. **nōnāgintā,** indecl. cardinal num. adj.; it modifies *mīlia,* used as a noun. —— **duo,** decl. cardinal num. adj.; see note on *duō,* l. 12, above. *duō* also modifies *mīlia.* The phrase *nōnāgintā duō* is sometimes indicated by the letters *XCII.* —— **Summa,** nom. sing. of the noun *summa, -ae,* f. *summa* is the subject-nom. of the verb *fuērunt* — the verb in number conforming to the predicate-nom. *mīlia.* As to *summa,* see note on this word, l. 8, above. —— **omnium,** gen. plur. of the adj. *omnis, -e,* gen. *omnis,* dat. and abl. *omnī* — an *ī*-stem. *omnium* is here used substantively, and, as a gen., limits the noun *summa;* or *numerōrum* may be supplied, and then *omnium* would be its attributive, and *numerōrum* would limit *summa.* —— **fuērunt,** 3d pers. plur. perf. ind. of the irr. verb *sum, esse, fuī,* fut. participle *futūrus;* it agrees with the plur. predicate-nom. *mīlia,* instead of the sing. subject-nom. *summa;* the construction is somewhat anomalous; but see A. & G. 204, *b;* B. 130, REM. 1; G. 211, REM. 1, EXC. (*a*); H. 462.

LINE 15. **ad,** usually a prep., but here an adv., and = *circiter;* see note on *ad,* l. 13, above. —— **mīlia,** nom. plur. n. of the adj. *mīlia, mīlium, mīlibus;* see note on *mīlia,* l. 13, above; here *mīlia* is predicate-nom. after *fuērunt.* —— **trecenta,** nom. plur. n. of the cardinal num. adj. *trecentī, -ae, -a. trecenta* is an attributive of the noun *mīlia.* Observe that the hundreds, from *ducentī* to *nōnāgentī* (200–900) inclusive, are declined like the plur. of *bonus.* —— **et,** cop. conj.; it here connects the numerals *trecenta* and *sexāgintā.* —— **sexāgintā** (sibilated from GK. ἑξήκοντα), an indecl. num. adj.; it is connected by *et* with *trecenta,* and is in the same grammatical construction. —— **octō** (GK. ὀκτώ), an indecl. cardinal num. adj.; connected by *et*

BOOK I.

16 Eōrum,	quī	domum	rediērunt,	.	cēnsū	sand. When a census was taken by Caesar's order, of those that had returned home, the number was found to be one hundred and ten thousand.
Of those,	*who*	*home*	*returned,*		*an enumeration*	
17 habitō,		ut	Caesar		imperāverat,	
having been had,		*as*	*Caesar*		*had ordered,*	
18 repertus est		numerus	mīlium		centum	
was ascertained		*the number*	*of thousands*		*a hundred*	
19 et	decem.					
and	*ten.*					

understood with *sexāgintā*, and in the same construction. The phrase *trecenta et sexāgintā octō* is often indicated in the classics by the Roman letters *CCCLXVIII*.

LINE 16. **Eōrum**, gen. plur. m. of the dem. pron. *is, ea, id*, used substantively; as a gen. it limits *cēnsū*, at the end of this line. —— **quī**, nom. plur. m. of the rel. pron. *quī, quae, quod. quī* is the subject-nom. of the verb *rediērunt*. —— **domum**, acc. sing. of the noun *domus, -ūs,* f.; *domī*, locative gen. *domum* is the locative acc. — end of motion without a prep. after the verb *rediērunt*. Consult A. & G. 258, (*b*); B. 154, REM. 1; G. 337; H. 380, II, 2, 1). —— **rediērunt**, 3d pers. plur. perf. ind. act. of the verb *redeō, -īre, -īvī (-iī), -itum,* 4 (re [red] + īre, *to go back*). *rediērunt* agrees with its subject-nom. *quī*. Observe that *rediērunt* is formed by syncope from the full form *redivērunt*. —— **cēnsū**, abl. sing. of the noun *cēnsus, -ūs,* m. (*cēnsēre*, lit. *to weigh*). *cēnsū* is in the abl. absolute with the perf. pass. participle *habitō*.

LINE 17. **habitō**, abl. sing. m. of the perf. pass. participle *habitus, -a, -um* of the verb *habeō, -ēre, -uī, -itum,* 2. *habitō* is in the abl. absolute construction with the noun *cēnsū*, denoting *time when*. Consult A. & G. 255; B. 192; G. 409, 410; H. 431. —— **ut**, adv. here, and = *as;* and so generally when used with the indicative mode. —— **Caesar**, **-aris**, m., proper noun; subject-nom. of the verb *imperāverat*. —— **imperāverat**, 3d pers. sing. pluperf. ind. act. of the verb *imperō, -āre, -āvī, -ātum,* 1; it agrees with its subject-nom. *Caesar* in number and person.

LINE 18. **repertus est**, 3d pers. sing. perf. ind. pass. of the verb *reperiō, -īre, rep(p)erī, repertum,* 4; pass. parts: *reperior, reperīrī, repertus* (re + pariō); hence = lit. *to procure* or *find again*. *repertus est* agrees with its subject-nom. *numerus*. —— **numerus, -ī**, m. (radical the same as GK. νόμος); hence = *that which is distributed, a number. numerus* is the subject-nom. of the verb *repertus est*. —— **mīlium**, gen. plur. of the adj. *mīlia, -ium,* used substantively, and as a gen. of specification, limiting the noun *numerus*. See A. & G. 214, *f·* B. 127, REM. 8; G. 361; H. 396, VI. —— **centum**, indecl. cardinal num. adj.; modifies *mīlia*.

LINE 19. **et**, cop. conj.; it connects *centum* and *decem*. —— **decem** (GK. δέκα). *decem* is connected by *et* with *centum*, and is in the same grammatical construction. The construction here is somewhat anomalous. *centum* and *decem* might be taken as predicate-adjectives after the pass. verb *repertus est*. Then *mīlium* might be taken as an adnominal gen. after *numerus;* or as the partitive after *centum et decem*. The phrase *centum et decem* is sometimes indicated by the Roman letters *C et X*. According to the account here, the Galli before the battle numbered 368,000; after the battle, 110,000. Hence 368,000 — 110,000 = 258,000 of all the clans perished. But the sum total of the Helvetii, according to the narrative, was 263,000. Hence 263,000 — 110,000 = 153,000 Helvetians perished. Ancient authorities differ as to the number slain or lost. Strabo says 400,000 Gauls perished. Plutarch makes the number 300,000. But Polyaenus makes the number of the Helvetii 80,000.

222   CAESAR'S GALLIC WAR   [CHAP. XXX.

XXX. At the close of the war with the Helvetii, envoys from almost all Gaul, the chiefs of the states came to Caesar to congratulate him. They said that they knew that, though for the Helvetians' ancient wrongs to	XXX. Bellō Helvētiōrum cōnfectō 1
	The war of the Helvetii being finished,
	tōtīus ferē Galliae lēgātī, prīncipēs 2
	of entire, almost, Gaul, the legates, chiefs
	cīvitātum, ad Caesarem grātulātum 3
	of the states, to Caesar to congratulate (him)
	convēnērunt: Intellegere sēsē, tametsī 4
	came together: To know themselves (they knew), although
	prō veteribus Helvētiōrum iniūriīs populī 5
	for old Helvetian wrongs of (to) the people

LINE 1. **Bellō**, abl. sing. of *bellum*, *-i*, n. *bellō*, abl. absolute with the perf. pass. participle *cōnfectō*, denoting *time when*. See A. & G. 255; B. 192; G. 409; H. 431. Compare also l. 15, Chap. I. —— **Helvētiōrum**, gen. plur. of *Helvētius*, *-a*, *-um*, used substantively; it limits the noun *bellō*. —— **cōnfectō**, abl. sing. n. of the perf. pass. participle *cōnfectus*, *-a*, *-um* of the verb *cōnficiō*, *-ere*, *-fēcī*, *-fectum*, 3; abl. absolute with *bellō*.
LINE 2. **tōtīus**, gen. sing. f. of the adj. *tōtus*, *-a*, *-um*, gen. *tōtīus*, dat. *tōtī*. *tōtīus* limits *Galliae*. Compare l. 7, Chap. II. —— **ferē**, adv. (*ferō*, compare l. 17, Chap. I); it modifies the adj. *tōtīus*. —— **Galliae**, gen. sing. of *Gallia*, *-ae*, f.; it limits *lēgātī*. The *Gallia* here meant is *Celtica*. —— **lēgātī**, nom. plur. of *lēgātus*, *-ī*, m. (*legere*, to despatch). *lēgātī* is subject-nom. of the verb *convēnērunt*. *lēgātus* = *any one with delegated authority*. —— **prīncipēs**, nom. plur. of the adj. *prīnceps*, *-ipis* (primus + capere), used here substantively; connected by *et* omitted with the noun *lēgātī*, and in the same grammatical construction.
LINE 3. **cīvitātum**, gen. plur. of *cīvitās*, *-ātis* (*cīvēs*); it limits *prīncipēs*. —— **ad**, prep. with the acc. —— **Caesarem**, acc. sing. of *Caesar*, *-aris;* obj. of *ad*, expressing the limit of motion after the verb *convēnērunt*. —— **grātulātum**, supine of the deponent verb *grātulor*, *-ārī*, *-ātus* (*grātus*). This supine in *-um* denotes the purpose after *convēnērunt*, a verb of motion. Consult A. & G. 302; B. 186; G. 435; H. 546. After *grātulātum* supply *eum* as its direct object.
LINE 4. **convēnērunt**, 3d pers. plur. perf. ind. act. of *conveniō*, *-īre*, *-vēnī*, *-ventum*, 3; it agrees with its subject-nominatives *lēgātī* and *prīncipēs*. —— **Intellegere**, pres. inf. act. of *intellegō* (compare l. 6, Chap. X). *Intellegere* here in indirect discourse is for *intellegimus* of direct discourse. Consult A. & G. 336, 1, and espec. 2; B. 245, 1, (*a*); G. 650; H. 523, I. —— **sēsē**, acc. plur. reduplicated 3d personal pron., for *sē*; acc. plur. of *suī*, *sibi*, *sē*, *sē* — same form in both numbers; subject-acc. of the inf. *intellegere*. *sēsē* is for *nōs* in direct discourse. —— **tametsī** (tamen + etsi), conj. = lit. *yet even if*, i.e. *although*.
LINE 5. **prō**, prep. with the abl. —— **veteribus**, abl. plur. of the adj. *vetus*, *-eris;* attributive of the noun *iniūriīs*. —— **Helvētiōrum** (*Helvētius*, *-a*, *-um*), used substantively; gen. subjective limiting the noun *iniūriīs*. —— **iniūriīs**, abl. plur. of *iniūria*, *-ae*, f. (in + iūs); obj. of the prep. *prō*. —— **populī**, gen. sing. of the noun *populus*, *-ī*, m.; objective gen. depending on the noun *iniūriīs*. Here are two genitives depending on one substantive. For the syntax of *Helvētiōrum*, see A. & G. 214; B. 131, REM. 2; G. 363, 1; H. 396, I. For syntax of *populī*, see A. & G. 217, (*b*); B. 131, REM. 2; G. 363, 2; H. 396, III. For synonyms, see note on *populī*, l. 17, Chap. III.

6 Rōmānī	ab	hīs	poenās		bellō	the Roman people, he had taken satisfaction from them in war, yet that that event had happened no less to the advantage of the Gauls than to the Roman people, because the Helvetii had left their homes when their affairs were very prosperous
Roman	*from*	*them*	*penalties*		*in war*	
7 repetīsset,		tamen	eam	rem nōn	minus	
he had demanded back,		*yet*	*that*	*thing not*	*less*	
8 ex	ūsū	terrae	Galliae	quam	populī	
for	*the use*	*of the land*	*Gaul*	*than*	*of the people*	
9 Rōmānī	accidisse;		proptereā		quod	
Roman	*to have happened;*		*for the reason*		*because*	
10 eō	cōnsiliō	flōrentissimīs			rēbus	
with this	*plan,*	*most flourishing (being)*			*the affairs,*	

LINE 6. **Rōmānī**, gen. sing. m. of *Rōmānus, -a, -um;* attributive of the noun *populī*. Mark the order of the words in this phrase. —— **ab**, prep. with the abl. —— **hīs**, abl. plur. of the dem. pron. *hīc, haec, hōc,* used as a personal pron. of the 3d pers.; obj. of *ab;* refers to *lēgātī* and *prīncipēs,* l. 2, above. —— **poenās**, acc. plur. of *poena, -ae,* f.; direct obj. of *repetīsset.* —— **bellō**, abl. sing. of *bellum, -ī,* n.; see l. 15, Chap. I. *bellō* is an abl. *of means.* Consult A. & G. 258, *f,* 1; B. 167; G. 401; H. 425, II, 1) and 2).

LINE 7. **repetīsset**, 3d pers. sing. pluperf. subjunctive of *repetō, -ere, -petīvī (-iī), -petītum,* 3 (re + petere); hence = lit. *to seek again;* agrees with Caesar understood; subjunctive after *tametsī,* concessive. See A. & G. 313, *c*; B. 211, (*b*); G. 604, 2; H. 515, 2. *repetīsset* is both a syncopated and contracted form for *repetīvisset;* see A. & G. 128, 2; B. 251; G. 131, 1; H. 235. —— **tamen**, adv. = *yet;* used in opposition to the concessive *tametsī.* —— **eam**, acc. sing. f. (*is, ea, id*); attributive of the noun *rem.* —— **rem**, acc. sing. of *rēs, reī,* f. —— **nōn**, adv.; modifies the adv. *minus.* —— **minus**, adv.; qualifies the phrase *ex ūsū* = the adj. *useful.*

LINE 8. **ex**, prep. with the abl. —— **ūsū**, abl. sing. of *ūsus, -ūs,* m.; obj. of the prep. *ex.* To see the force of *ex* in the phrase *ex ūsū,* supply and translate *eam rem nōn minus ex ūsū . . . accidisse* thus: *that this thing happened to be not less of use.* —— **terrae**, of *terra, -ae,* f.; objective gen. after *ūsū.* —— **Galliae**, gen. sing. of *Gallia, -ae,* f.; limits *terrae* as an appositive, and is = the adj. *Gallicae.* —— **quam**, conj. *quam* follows *minus,* a comparative; and in such construction = *than.* —— **populī**, gen. sing. of *populus, -ī,* m.; connected by the conj. *quam* with the noun *terrae,* and is in the same grammatical construction.

LINE 9. **Rōmānī**, gen. sing. of the adj. *Rōmānus, -a, -um;* attributive of *populī.* See note on *populī Rōmānī,* lines 5 and 6, above. —— **accidisse**, perf. inf. act. (see l. 2, Chap. XIX); its subject-acc. is the noun *rem,* l. 7, above. —— **proptereā**, adv.; herald of the following *quod*-clause, and is explained by it. —— **quod**, conj. = *because.* See note on these particles, l. 9, Chap. I.

LINE 10. **eō**, abl. sing. n. (*is, ea, id*); adnominal or attributive of *cōnsiliō.* —— **cōnsiliō** (*cōnsilium, -ī,* n.); abl. *of manner.* See A. & G. 248; B. 168; G. 399; H. 419, III. For synonyms, see l. 5, Chap. XVIII. —— **flōrentissimīs**, abl. plur. f. *flōrentissimus, -a, -um;* superl. degree; positive *flōrens,* participle of the verb *flōreō, -ēre, -uī,* 2; abl. absolute with *rēbus,* denoting *time when.* ·Consult A. & G. 255, *a*; B. 192, REM. 1; G. 409; H. 431, 4. —— **rēbus**, plur. (*rēs, reī,* f.); abl. absolute with the adj. *flōrentissimīs.*

224   CAESAR'S GALLIC WAR   [CHAP. XXX.

| with the purpose of bringing war upon all Gaul and of winning the sovereignty; and then to select from the wide domain such a place for a domicile as they judged to be the most convenient and fertile in all Gaul, | domōs *homes* tōtī *on entire* imperiōque *sovereignty and,* ex *from* ex *out* | suās *their* Galliae *Gaul* māgnā *the great* omnī *of all* | Helvētiī *the Helvetii* bellum *war* potīrentur *they might possess* cōpiā *plenty (of places)* Galliā *Gaul* | relīquissent, *had left,* inferrent *they might bring* locumque *place and,* dēligerent, *they might choose,* opportūnissimum *the most opportune* | utī 11 *that* 12 domiciliō 13 *for a home* quem 14 *which* āc 15 *and* |

LINE 11. **domōs**, acc. plur. of *domus, -ūs, -ī* locative; direct obj. of *relīquissent.* For synonyms, see note on *aedificia*, l. 7, Chap. V. *domus* is partly of the 2d, and partly of the 4th declension. —— **suās**, acc. plur. f. (*suus, -a, -um*); attributive of *domōs*. Observe that the possessives oftener than otherwise follow their nouns. —— **Helvētiī**, nom. plur. m. of *Helvētius, -a, -um*, used substantively; subject-nom. of *relīquissent*. Observe how emphatic both *Helvētiī* and the phrase *eō cōnsiliō* are made by a shift of positions. —— **relīquissent**, 3d pers. plur. pluperf. subjunctive (see l. 1, Chap. IX); agrees with its subject-nom. *Helvētiī*; subjunctive, because in a subordinate clause in *ōrātiō oblīqua*. —— **utī**, conj.

LINE 12. **tōtī**, dat. sing. f. (see l. 7, Chap. II); attributive of *Galliae*. —— **Galliae**, sing. f.; dat. after *in* in the compound verb *inferrent*. Consult A. & G. 228; B. 143; G. 347; H. 386, 1. —— **bellum**, acc. sing. of *bellum, -ī,* n.; direct obj. of *inferrent;* it is, in fact, the direct obj. of the *ferrent*-part of the compound. —— **inferrent**, 3d pers. plur. imperf. subjunctive of the irr. verb *inferō, -ferre, -tulī, il(n)lātum. inferrent* agrees with a pron. implied in the ending, referring to *Helvētiī* as subject-nom.; it is the subjunctive of purpose after the particle *utī*.

LINE 13. **imperiōque** (imperiō + que). *imperiō* is the abl. of *imperium, -ī,* n.; abl. after the verb *potīrentur*. See A. & G. 249; B. 167, 1; G. 407; H. 421, 1. *que*, enclitic conj.; connects very closely the verbs *inferrent* and *potīrentur*. Synonyms: *imperium* = military *power;* whereas *rēgnum* · (*regere*, to rule) = royal *power*. —— **potīrentur**, 3d pers. plur. imperf. subjunctive of the verb *potior, -īrī, -ītus,* 4 (*potis*, powerful). *potīrentur* is connected by *-que* with *inferrent*, and is in the subjunctive of purpose for the same reason. —— **locumque** (locum + que). *locum* is the acc. sing. (see l. 10, Chap. II); direct obj. of *dēligerent*. —— **domiciliō** (*domicilium, -iī,* n.); dat. of purpose after the verb *dēligerent*. Consult A. & G. 233, *b;* B. 147, REM. 1; G. 356, NOTE 1; H. 390, II.

LINE 14. **ex**, prep. with the abl. —— **māgnā**, abl. sing. f. of *māgnus, -a, -um;* attributive of the noun *cōpiā*. —— **cōpiā**, abl. sing. (see l. 6, Chap. II); obj. of the prep. *ex*. The phrase here = *ex māgnā locōrum cōpiā*. —— **dēligerent**, 3d pers. plur. imperf. subjunctive (see l. 12, Chap. III); connected by *-que* with *potīrentur*, and is, in every respect, in the same grammatical construction. —— **quem**, acc. sing. m. (*quī, quae, quod*); refers to *locum* as its antecedent, but is subject-acc. of *esse,* to be supplied.

LINE 15. **ex**, prep. with the abl. —— **omnī**, abl. sing. f. (*omnis, -e*), an *ī*-stem; and hence retains the *-ī* in the abl. sing.; attributive of the noun *Galliā*. —— **Galliā**, abl. sing.; obj. of *ex*. The phrase *ex omnī Galliā* is an adverbial modifier of the predicate-adjectives *opportūnissimum* and *frūctuōsissimum*. —— **opportūnissimum**,

BOOK I. 225

16	frūctuōsissimum	iūdicāssent,	reliquāsque	and hold the rest
	the most productive	*they had judged,*	*the remaining and,*	of the states as tributaries. They
17	cīvitātēs	stīpendiāriās	habērent.	Petiērunt, requested to be
	states	*as stipendiaries*	*they might hold.*	*They asked,* allowed to ap-
18	ut	sibi	concilium	tōtīus Galliae in point a council of
	that	*to themselves*	*a council*	*of entire Gaul to* all Gaul for a
19	diem	certam	indīcere	idque Caesaris certain day by
	a day	*certain*	*to proclaim,*	*this and, with Caesar's* Caesar's special

acc. sing. m. of the superl. degree; positive *opportūnus* (ob + portus); hence *opportūnus = at the port* or *harbor,* i.e. *seasonable, safe, advantageous;* comparative *-ior,* superl. *-issimus, -a, -um;* predicate-adj. after *esse,* to be supplied. —— **āc**, conj. (see *atque,* l. 10, Chap. I); connects the adjectives; its function is not, in such use, essentially different from *et.*

LINE 16. **frūctuōsissimum**, acc. sing. m. of the superl. degree; positive *frūctuōsus;* comparative *frūctuosior* (*frūctus,* fruit); connected by *āc* with *opportūnissimum,* and in the same grammatical construction. —— **iūdicāssent**, 3d pers. plur. pluperf. subjunctive act. of the verb *iūdicō, -āre, -āvī, -ātum,* 1 (iūs + dicō); hence *iūdicāre* = lit. *to examine judicially;* and then transf. from the judicial function, *to think.* For synonyms, see note on *arbitrābātur,* l. 9, Chap. XIX. *iūdicāssent* is a syncopated and contracted form for *iūdicāvissent.* *v* is syncopated, and then *ā + i* are contracted into *ā.* Consult A. & G. 128, 2; B. 251; G. 131, 1; H. 235. *iūdicāssent* agrees with a pron. implied in its ending as its subject-nom., referring to the Helvetii; subjunctive, because it stands in a subordinate clause in the *ōrātiō oblīqua.* —— **reliquāsque** (reliquās + que). *reliquās,* acc. plur. f. of *reliquus, -a, -um* (re + linquō); hence *reliquus* = lit. *that which is left behind.* *reliquās* is an attributive of *cīvitātēs.* *que,* enclitic conj.; connects very closely the verbs *dēligerent* and *habērent.*

LINE 17. **cīvitātēs**, acc. plur. of *cīvitās, -ātis,* f. (*cīvēs*); direct obj. of *habērent.* —— **stīpendiāriās**, acc. plur. f. of *stīpendiārius, -a, -um* (*stīpendium*), used as a substantive-predicate appositive of *cīvitātēs.* The *stīpendiāriī* are the vanquished who pay *stīpendium* or tribute-money. —— **habērent**, 3d pers. plur. imperf. subjunctive of *habeō, -ēre, -uī, -itum,* 2; connected by *que* with *dēligerent,* l. 14, above, and is, therefore, the subjunctive of purpose after *utī,* l. 11, above. The *ōrātiō rēcta* of lines 4–17: *Intellegimus nōs,* tametsī prō veteribus Helvētiōrum iniūriīs populī Rōmānī ab hīs poenās bellō *repetiistī* (*repetīvistī*), tamen *hanc* rem nōn minus ex ūsū terrae Galliae quam populī Rōmānī accidisse; proptereā, quod *hōc* cōnsiliō flōrentissimīs rēbus domōs suās Helvētiī *reliquērunt,* utī tōtī Galliae bellum inferrent imperiōque potīrentur locumque domiciliō ex māgnā cōpiā dēligerent, quem ex omnī Galliā opportūnissimum āc frūctuōsissimum *iūdicāvērunt,* reliquāsque cīvitātēs stīpendiāriās habērent. —— **Petiērunt**, 3d pers. plur. perf. ind. act. of *petō, -ere, -īvī, -ītum,* 3. Syncopated for the full form *petīvērunt;* agrees with *lēgātī* understood as subject-nom.

LINE 18. **ut**, telic conj. —— **sibi**, dat. plur. (*suī, sibi, sē, sē*); dat. of the indirect obj. after *licēret,* l. 20, below. —— **concilium**, acc. sing.; direct obj. of *indīcere,* of which verb *sē* is to be supplied as subject-acc. See l. 5, Chap. XVIII. —— **tōtīus**, adj., gen. sing. f.; attributive of *Galliae.* —— **Galliae**, noun, gen. sing.; limits *concilium.* —— **in**, prep.; here it takes the acc.

LINE 19. **diem**, acc. f. of *diēs, diēī,* m. or f. in the sing.; always m. in the plur. (compare l. 5, Chap. IV). *diem* here is the obj. of *in.* —— **certam**, acc. sing. f. of

226   CAESAR'S GALLIC WAR   [CHAP. XXX.

| consent. They said that they had some business as to which they wished to consult him by the common consent. Their re- | voluntāte permission habēre to have commūnī the common | facere to do, quāsdam (they have) certain cōnsēnsū consent | licēret; it might be lawful; rēs, things, ab eō of him | sēsē 20 themselves quās ex 21 which from petere vellent. 22 to ask they wished. |

certus, -a, -um; attributive of *diem.* For an explanation of this phrase, see note on the phrase *in tertiam annum,* l. 10, Chap. III, and also A. & G. 259, *b*; B. 120, 3; G. 418, 1; H. 435, I, 2. —— **indīcere,** pres. inf. act. of the verb *indīcō, -ere, -dīxī, -dictum,* 3 (in + dicere); hence *indīcere* = lit. *to speak into* a place, i.e *to speak publicly;* here it = *to appoint.* Observe that the subject-acc. of *indīcere* is *sē* understood, and that the subject-acc. is usually omitted when it precedes in the dat. case, as here in *sibi,* the indirect obj. of *licēret.* —— **idque** (id + que). *id* is the acc. sing. n. of the dem. pron. *is, ea, id,* used substantively; *id* is the direct obj. of the verb *facere;* it refers to the idea contained in *indīcere concilium.* —— **Caesaris,** gen. sing. m. of the proper noun *Caesar, -aris,* m. *Caesaris,* as a gen., limits *voluntāte.*

LINE 20. **voluntāte,** abl. sing. of *voluntās, -ātis,* f.; abl. of *in accordance with.* Consult A. & G. 253, NOTE; B. 162, REM. 3; G. 397; H. 416. For synonyms, see *voluntāte,* l. 19, Chap. VII. —— **facere,** pres. inf. of *faciō, -ere, fēcī, factum,* 3; connected by *-que* with *indīcere,* and in the same grammatical construction. —— **licēret,** 3d pers. sing. imperf. subjunctive of the impersonal verb *licet, licuit, licitum est;* subjunctive of purpose after *ut* telic. This purpose-clause as a whole is the direct obj. of *petiērunt.* Consult A. & G. 331; B. 200, REM. 2; G. 546, 1; H. 498, I, 1. The *ōrātiō rēcta* of lines 17–20: *Petimus, ut nōbīs concilium tōtīus Galliae in diem certam indīcere hōcque voluntāte tuā liceat.* It will be noted that the *lēgātī* make their requests now in the first person; that in the speech antecedent to *petiērunt,* they have been treating of the Helvetii, and their punishment for former wrongs done to the Roman people; and also of their design in migrating from home. —— **sēsē,** for *sē,* reflexive pron., plur.; subject-acc. of the verb *habēre. sēsē* is for *nōs* in direct discourse.

LINE 21. **habēre,** pres. inf. act. of *habeō, -ēre, -uī, -itum,* 2; its subject-acc. is the pron. *sēsē.* —— **quāsdam,** acc. plur. f. of the indefinite pron. *quīdam, quaedam, quoddam,* adj., or *quiddam,* subst. *quāsdam* is an attributive of the noun *rēs.* —— **rēs,** acc. plur. of *rēs, reī,* f.; direct obj. of *habēre.* —— **quās,** acc. plur. of the rel. pron. *quī, quae, quod;* refers to *rēs,* but is itself the direct obj. of *petere.* —— **ex,** prep. with the abl.

LINE 22. **commūnī,** abl. sing. m. of the adj. *commūnis, -e* (con + mūnīre, *to serve together*); hence *commūnis* = *common. commūnī* is the attributive of *cōnsēnsū.* —— **cōnsēnsū,** abl. sing. of *cōnsēnsus, -ūs,* m.; obj. of *ex.* —— **ab,** prep. with the abl. —— **eō,** abl. sing. m. (*is, ea, id*); used as a personal pron. of the 3d pers., referring to Caesar. *eō* is the obj. of *ab.* —— **petere,** pres. inf. act. of *petō, -ere, -īvī (-iī), -ītum,* 3. *petere* is a complementary inf. See A. & G. 271; B. 181; G. 423; H. 533, I, 1. Observe that many verbs of asking take two accusatives — one of the person, another of the thing; but that *petō* usually takes the acc. of the thing, and the abl. of the person with *ā* or *ab.* —— **vellent,** 3d pers. plur. of the irr. verb *volō, velle, voluī;* agrees with *lēgātī* understood; in the subjunctive, because in a dependent relative-clause in *ōrātiō oblīqua.* The *ōrātiō rēcta* of lines 20–22: *nōs habēmus quāsdam rēs, quās ex commūnī cōnsēnsū abs tē petere volumus.*

23 Eā   rē   permīssā   diem   conciliō
   This   *thing*   *being permitted,* *a day*   *for a council*

24 cōnstituērunt   et   iūreiūrandō,   nē   quis
   they appointed *and*   *by oath,*   *that not* *any one*

25 ēnūntiāret,   nisi   quibus   commūnī
   should report,   *unless*   *(they) to whom*   *in the common*

26 cōnsiliō   mandātum esset,   inter   sē   sanxērunt.
   council   *it had been assigned,* *among*   *themselves* *decreed.*

quest was granted, and they appointed a day for a council; and they mutually ratified by an oath that no one should report the proceedings except such as had an order given them by the general council.

LINE 23. **Eā**, abl. sing. (*is, ea, id*); attributive of *rē*. —— **rē**, abl. sing. (*rēs, reī*); abl. absolute with the perf. pass. participle denoting *time when*. Consult A. & G. 255, *d*, 1; B. 192; G. 409; H. 431, 2. —— **permīssā**, abl. sing. f. of the participle *permissus, -a, -um* of the verb *permittō, -ere, -mīsī, missum,* 3; *permissā* is abl. absolute with the noun *rē.* —— **diem** (see l. 19, above), direct obj. of *cōnstituērunt.* —— **conciliō**, dat. sing. of *concilium, -ī,* n.; dat. of purpose after *cōnstituērunt.* Consult A. & G. 233, *b*; B. 147, REM. 1; G. 356, NOTE 1; II. 390, II.

LINE 24. **cōnstituērunt**, 3d pers. plur. perf. ind. act. of *cōnstituō, -ere, -uī, -ūtum,* 3; agrees with the pron. implied in the ending as subject-nom., referring to *lēgātī* and to *prīncipēs cīvitātum* mentioned in lines 2 and 3, above. —— **et**, cop. conj.; connects *cōnstituērunt* and *sanxērunt,* l. 26, below. —— **iūreiūrandō**, abl. of the compound noun *iūsiūrandum, iūrisiūrandī,* n. (iūs + iūrandum); dat. *iūriiūrandō;* abl. of means. Observe that both parts of this compound noun are declined; but that the gen., dat. and abl. plur. are wanting. Consult A. & G. 77, 6, *a*; B. 45; G. 47, 5; H. 125, 126. —— **nē**, neg. particle, conj., and = *that not.* —— **quis**, indef. pron. —— *quis, quae, quid;* usually found with *sī, nē* and *num.* Sometimes written thus: *sīquis, nēquis, numquis. quis* is the subject-nom. of the verb *ēnūntiāret.*

LINE 25. **ēnūntiāret**, 3d pers. sing. imperf. subjunctive of *ēnūntiō, -āre, -āvī, -ātum,* 1; agrees with *quis;* supply *rem* as direct obj.; it is the subjunctive after the telic particle *nē* — negative purpose. —— **nisi** (nē + sī), conj. —— **quibus**, dat. plur. (*quī, quae, quod*); refers to the pron. *eī* understood, and is the indirect obj. of the pass. verb *mandātum esset* Consult A. & G. 225, *e*; B. 140; G. 345, PASSIVE FORM; H. 384, I. —— **commūnī**, abl. sing. n.; attributive of *cōnsiliō.*

LINE 26. **cōnsiliō**, abl. sing. of *cōnsilium, -ī,* n.; locative abl. considered as means. See A. & G. 258, *f*, 1, 2; B. 170, REM. 4; G. 389; H. 425, II, 1, 1). Observe that *cōnsiliō* appears to have the same sense here as *conciliō,* l. 23, above. But see note on *concilium,* l. 5, Chap. XVIII. —— **mandātum esset**, 3d pers. sing. pluperf. subjunctive pass. of *mandō, -āre, -āvī, -ātum;* pass. parts: *mandor, -āvī, mandātus.* Observe that this pluperf. subjunctive pass. is a compound tense made up of the perf. pass. participle and of the imperf. subjunctive — *esset* — of the verb *esse;* that *mandātum esset* is here used impersonally; and that it is in the subjunctive mode, because it is in a dependent relative-clause in virtual *ōrātiō oblīqua. mandātum esset,* however, might be taken personally by supplying the noun *iūs* = *legal right,* as the subject-nom. *esset,* 3d pers. sing. imperf. subjunctive of the neuter or intrans. verb *sum, esse, fuī, futūrus;* used here in the formation of the pluperf. subjunctive — *mandātum esset.* —— **inter**, prep. with the acc. —— **sē**, acc. plur.; obj. of *inter.*

XXXI. After this assembly was dismissed,	**XXXI.**	**Eō** *That*	**conciliō** *council*	**dīmissō,** *being adjourned,*		**eīdem** 1 *the same*
the same chiefs of the states, as had been to Caesar before, returned to him, and requested the favor of conferring with him apart, in a secret place, concerning	**prīncipēs** *chiefs* **Caesarem** *Caesar* **sibi** *to themselves*	**cīvitātum,** *of the states,* **revertērunt** *returned* **sēcrētō** *secretly*	**quī** *who* **in** *in*	**ante** *before* **petiēruntque,** *asked and,* **occultō** *private*	**fuerant,** *had been,* **dē** *concerning*	**ad** 2 *to* **utī** 3 *that* **suā** 4 *their,*

The phrase *inter sē* denotes a reciprocal relation. See A. & G. 196, *f*; B. 78, REM. 4; G. 221; H. 448, NOTE. —— **sanxērunt,** 3d pers. plur. perf. ind. act. of *sanciō, -īre, sānxī, sānctum,* 4; agrees with a pron. implied in its ending as its subject-nom., referring to *lēgātī* and *prīncipēs cīvitātum,* lines 2 and 3, above. From *nē quis* to *mandātum esset* inclusive the discourse is virtual *ōrātiō oblīqua,* depending on *sanxērunt*. What was thought, put in the direct form, and filling ellipses was: *Nēmō ēnūntiābit rem, nisi eī, quibus commūnī cōnsiliō mandatum fuerit.*

LINE 1. **Eō,** abl. sing. n. of the dem. pron. *is, ea, id;* attributive of the noun *conciliō*. —— **conciliō,** abl. sing. of *concilium, -iī,* n. (some critics form the gen. sing. of nouns in *-ium* or *-ius* with one *i,* e.g. *conciliī;* abl. absolute with *dīmissō,* denoting the time of the action. The council here referred to is that indicated in the preceding chapter. —— **dīmissō,** abl. sing. n. of the perf. pass. participle *dīmissus, -a, -um* of the verb *dīmittō, -ere, -mīsī, -missum,* 3; abl. absolute with *conciliō*. Consult A. & G. 255; B. 192; G. 409; H. 431. —— **eīdem,** nom. plur. m. of the iterative dem. pron. *īdem, eadem, idem;* attributive of *prīncipēs*. Observe that other forms of the nom. plur. are *iīdem* and *īdem.*

LINE 2. **prīncipēs,** nom. plur. of the adj. *prīnceps, -ipis,* used as a subst. *prīncipēs,* as a noun, is the subject-nom. of the verbs *revertērunt* and *petiērunt*. —— **cīvitātum,** gen. plur. of *cīvitās, -ātis,* f. (*cīvēs*); limits *prīncipēs*. —— **quī,** nom. plur. of the rel. pron. *quī, quae, quod;* refers to *prīncipēs* as its antecedent, and is the subject-nom. of the verb *fuerant*. —— **ante,** adv. and prep.; here an adverb, and = *before*. The sense requires the supplying of the phrase *apud eum,* i.e. *Caesarem,* immediately after the adv. *ante*. —— **fuerant,** 3d pers. plur. pluperf. ind. of the neuter or intrans. verb *sum, esse, fuī, futūrus;* agrees with its subject-nom. *quī* in number and person. —— **ad,** prep. with the acc. after a verb of motion.

LINE 3. **Caesarem,** acc. sing.; obj. of *ad*. —— **revertērunt,** 3d pers. plur. perf. ind. act. of the verb *revertō, -ere, -ī,* neuter (active forms used in the perf.), deponent *revertor, -ī, -versus* in the imperf. tenses). *revertērunt* agrees with its subject-nom. *prīncipēs*. —— **petiēruntque** (petiērunt + que). *petiērunt,* 3d pers. plur. perf. ind. act. of the verb *petō, -ere, -īvī (-iī), -ītus*. *que,* enclitic conj.; it closely connects *petiērunt* with *revertērunt,* and has the same subject-nom. —— *prīncipēs*. —— **utī,** telic conj.; *utī* is the original form, though *ut* is, in use, more common.

LINE 4. **sibi,** dat. plur. of the reflexive pron. *suī, sibi, sē, sē* (the same form in both numbers). *sibi* is dat. of the indirect obj. after the verb *licēret,* l. 6, below. —— **sēcrētō,** adv. = *privately, apart. sēcrētō* is, in fact, abl. n. of *sēcrētus, -a, -um,* participle of the verb *sēcernō, -ere, -crēvī, -crētum,* 3. —— **in,** prep.; here it takes the

[LINES 5-8.] BOOK I. 229

5 omniumque	salūte	cum	eō	agere	their own safety
of all	*and,*	*safety*	*with*	*him*	*to treat*	and the safety of all. When their
6 licēret.		Eā	rē	impetrātā	request was grant-
it may be permitted.		*This*	*thing*	*having been obtained*	ed, they all, in
7 sēsē	omnēs	flentēs	Caesarī	ad	pedēs	tears, cast them- selves at Caesar's
themselves	*all*	*weeping*	*to Caesar*	*at*	*the feet*	feet, saying that
8 prōiēcērunt:		Nōn	minus	sē	id	they strove no
they threw (saying):		*Not*	*less*	*themselves*	*for that*	less anxiously

abl. —— occultō, abl. sing. of the participle *occultus, -a, -um* of *occulō, -ere, -cului, -cultum,* 3. *occultō* is strictly an attributive of *locō* understood, which *locō* is the obj. of the prep. *in.* The phrase *in occultō*, however, may be treated as an adv. Some copies omit the phrase *in occultō*, the editors viewing it as a gloss explanatory of *sēcrētō;* but the phrase is in the MSS. Observe that *sēcrētō* indicates that the chiefs wished to confer with Caesar alone; whereas the phrase *in occultō* denotes that they wished to confer with him without the knowledge of any one. —— dē, prep. with the abl. = *from* or *concerning*. Compare note on *dē*, l. 27, Chap. XIX. —— suā, abl. sing. f. of *suus, -a, -um;* attributive of *salūte*, to be supplied from the following *salūte*.

LINE 5. omniumque (omnium + que). *omnium* is the gen. plur. of the adj. *omnis, -e,* used substantively; limits *salūte* expressed. que, enclitic conj. —— salūte, abl. sing. of the noun *salūs, salūtis,* f. *salūte* is connected by the enclitic -que with *salūte* understood, and is in the same grammatical construction, i.e. the obj. of the prep. *dē.* Observe that, with ellipsis supplied, the text is: *dē suā salūte omniumque salūte.* —— cum, prep. with the abl. —— eō, abl. sing. m. of the dem. pron. *is, ea, id,* used as a personal pron. of the 3d pers.; obj. of *cum;* refers to Caesar. —— agere, pres. inf. act. of *agō, -ere, ēgī, actum,* 3.

LINE 6. licēret, 3d pers. sing. imperf. subjunctive of the impersonal verb *licet, licuit, licitum est,* 2. Observe (1) that, though this verb is styled impersonal, yet, in fact, the phrase *cum eō agere* is its subject; (2) that *licēret* is a subjunctive of purpose after *utī;* or rather (3) the clause *utī ... licēret* expresses the purpose of *reverterunt petiēruntque.* Consult A. & G. 331; B. 200, REM. 2; G. 546, 1; H. 498, I. —— Eā, abl. sing. f.; attributive of *rē.* —— rē, abl. sing. of the noun *rēs, reī,* f.; abl. absolute with *impetrātā*. —— impetrātā, abl. sing. f. of the perf. pass. participle *impetrātus, -a, -um* of the verb *impetrō, -āre, -āvī, -ātum,* 1 (in, *intensive* + *patrāre, to procure,* especially by request); abl. absolute with the noun *rē.* See A. & G. 255; B. 192; G. 409, 410; H. 431.

LINE 7. sēsē, see l. 4, Chap. XXX; direct obj. of the verb *prōiēcērunt.* —— omnēs, nom. plur. m. of the adj. *omnis, -e,* used substantively. —— flentēs, nom. plur. of the pres. participle *flēns, -ntis* of the verb *fleō, flēre, flēvī, flētum,* 2; attributive of the subj. (*eī* understood) of the verb *prōiēcērunt.* —— Caesarī, sing.; dat. *of reference,* instead of the poss. gen. Consult A. & G. 235, *a;* B. 145; G. 350, 1; H. 384, 4, NOTE 2. —— ad, prep. with the acc. —— pedēs, acc. plur. of *pēs, pedis,* m.; obj. of *ad.* Observe that the rigidly literal translation of *Caesarī ad pedēs* is: *to Caesar at the feet.*

LINE 8. prōiēcērunt, 3d pers. plur. perf. ind. act. (compare l. 4, Chap. XXVII); agrees with a pron. implied in its ending as its subject-nom., referring to *prīncipēs*, l. 2, above. The reader will observe that the following *Nōn ... vidērent*, lines 8–14,

that what they	contendere	et	labōrāre,	nē ea, 9
said might not	*to strive*	*and*	*labor,*	*that not, those things*
be told than that they might attain their wishes; in-	quae	dīxissent,	ēnūntiārentur,	quam utī 10
	which	*they had spoken,*	*should be disclosed,*	*than that*
asmuch as they	ea,	quae	vellent,	impetrārent; 11
saw that if their	*those things,*	*which*	*they wished,*	*they might obtain;*
information were	proptereā	quod,	sī	ēnūntiātum esset, 12
bruited abroad,	*for this reason*	*because,*	*if*	*it should have been disclosed,*

is in the *ōrātiō oblīqua* or indirect discourse; and that these clauses depend on the verb *prōiēcērunt*. Perhaps it will clarify the construction to supply *et dīxērunt* immediately after *prōiēcērunt*. —— **Nōn** (nē + oe[ū]num, apocopated), adv.; it modifies the adv. *minus*. —— **minus**, adv., comparative degree of *parum* or *parvē*; superl. *minimē*. *minus* modifies *contendere et labōrāre*. —— **sē**, plur.; subject-acc. of *contendere et labōrāre*; refers to *prīncipēs*, l. 2, above. —— id, sing. n. (*is, ea, id*); cognate acc. after the verb *contendere* and *labōrāre*. See A. & G. 238, *b*; B. 150, REM. 2; G. 333, 2; H. 371, I, 2, 2); *id* is the herald, so to speak, of the following purpose-clauses, which are, in fact, appositives to *id*.

LINE 9. **contendere**, pres. inf. act. (see l. 18, Chap. I). —— **et**, cop. conj. —— **labōrāre**, pres. inf. act. of the finite verb *labōrō*, *-āre*, *-āvī*, *-ātum*, 1 (*labor*). —— **nē**, telic conj. = *that not* or *lest*. —— **ea**, nom. plur. n. (*is, ea, id*); used substantively (or supply the English word *things*) as the subject-nom. of *ēnūntiārentur*.

LINE 10. **quae**, acc. plur. n. of the rel. pron. *quī, quae, quod*; refers to *ea* as its antecedent, but is the direct obj. of *dīxissent*. —— **dīxissent**, 3d pers. plur. pluperf. subjunctive of the verb *dīcō, -ere, dīxī, dictum*, 3; in the subjunctive mode, because it is in a dependent clause in *ōrātiō oblīqua*; or, better, because *quae dīxissent* is a clause of *characteristic*. The *ōrātiō rēcta* requires the subjunctive mode in such constructions. —— **ēnūntiārentur**, 3d pers. plur. imperf. subjunctive pass. of the active *ēnūntiō, -āre, -āvī, -ātum*, 1; agrees with a pron. implied in the ending as subject-nom., referring to *prīncipēs*, l. 2, above; subjunctive of *negative purpose* after *nē*. —— **quam**, here = conj. with word of comparison, viz., the adv. *minus*, l. 8, above. —— **utī**, see note on this word, l. 3, above.

LINE 11. **ea**, acc. plur. n. (*is, ea, id*); used substantively as the direct obj. of *impetrārent*. —— **quae**, acc. plur. n. (*quī, quae, quod*); refers to *ea* as its antecedent, but is the direct obj. of *vellent*. —— **vellent**, 3d pers. plur. of the imperf. subjunctive of the irr. verb *volō, velle, voluī*; agrees with a pron. implied in its ending as subject-nom., referring to *prīncipēs*, l. 2, above. As a subjunctive it comes under the general law of a dependent clause in the *ōrātiō oblīqua*; but, better, because *quae vellent* is a *clause of characteristic*. —— **impetrārent**, see l. 7, Chap. IX. Observe that the clause *utī . . . impetrārent*, no less than the clause *nē . . . ēnūntiārentur*, depends on *contendere* and *labōrāre*.

LINE 12. **proptereā**, adv. (see l. 9, Chap. I). —— **quod**, conj. Observe that *quod*, the conj., is really an adverbial acc. n. of the rel. pron. *quī, quae, quod*, meaning, usually, *as to what, in that;* and hence = *because*. —— **sī**, conditional conj. —— **ēnūntiātum esset**, 3d pers. sing. pluperf. subjunctive pass. of the act. verb *ēnūntiō, -āre, -āvī, -ātum*, 1; *ēnūntiātum esset* is here used impersonally; or *id*, as subj., may be supplied, referring to the idea contained in *quae dīxissent*, l. 10, above.

LINES 13-17.]   BOOK I.   231

13 summum	in	cruciātum	sē		ventūrōs	they would suffer the severest punishment. Divitiacus the Aeduan spoke for them. He said that there were two factions throughout Gaul; that the Aedui were the leaders of one faction; the Arverni, of the other. After
extreme	*into,*	*torture*	*themselves*		*about to come*	
14 vidērent.	Locūtus est		prō	hīs	Divitiacus	
they saw.	*Spoke*		*for*	*them*	*Divitiacus*	
15 Aeduus:	Galliae	tōtīus	factiōnēs		esse	
the Aeduan:	*Of Gaul*	*entire,*	*parties*		*to be* (there are)	
16 duās;	hārum	alterius	prīncipātum		tenēre	
two;	*of these,*	*of one*	*the leadership*		*to hold* (hold)	
17 Aeduōs,	alterius		Arvernōs.	Hī	cum	
the Aedui;	*of the other*		*the Arverni.*	*These*	*when*	

LINE 13. **summum**, acc. sing. m. (see l. 20, Chap. XVI); attributive of *cruciātum*. —— **in**, prep. with the acc. Note its position between the adj. and noun. See A. & G. 345, *a*; B. 58. 2; G. 413, REM. 2; H. 565, 3. —— **cruciātum**, acc. sing. of *cruciātus, -ūs*, m. (from *crux* through *cruciāre*); obj. of *in*. —— **sē**, acc. plur.; subject-acc. of *ventūrōs (esse)*. —— **ventūrōs (esse)**, fut. inf. act. of the finite verb *veniō, -īre, vēnī, ventum*, 4. This infinitive-clause depends on the finite verb *vidērent*.

LINE 14. **vidērent**, 3d pers. plur. of the imperf. subjunctive act. of the verb *videō, -ēre, vīdī, vīsum*, 2; subjunctive mode, because in a dependent *quod*-clause in the *ōrātiō oblīqua*. In this sentence, given in the indirect form, the main verbs are *contendere* and *labōrāre;* all the dependent clauses either directly or indirectly are depending on these verbs. The *ōrātiō rēcta* of lines 8-14: Nōn minus *hōc contendimus* et *labōrāmus*, nē *haec*, quae *dīxerimus*, *ēnūntientur*, quam utī *haec*, quae *velīmus*, *impetrēmus*, proptereā quod, sī ēnūntiātum *erit*, summum in cruciātum *nōs* ventūrōs *esse vidēmus*. —— **Locūtus est**, 3d pers. sing. perf. ind. of the deponent verb *loquor, -ī, -cūtus*, 3; agrees with *Divitiacus*. —— **prō**, prep. with the abl. —— **hīs**, abl. plur. m. (*hīc, haec, hōc*), used as a personal pron. of the 3d pers.; obj. of *prō; prō hīs = for them*. —— **Divitiacus, -ī**, m., subject-nom. of *locūtus est*. Divitiacus was an Aeduan chief, and a friend of the Romans.

LINE 15. **Aeduus, -a, -um**, attributive of *Divitiacus*. —— **Galliae**, gen. sing., limiting *factiōnēs;* it is, however, in the predicate, connected with its noun by *esse*. Consult A. & G. 214, *c*; B. 133; G. 366; H. 401. From *Galliae* to the close of the chapter, the discourse is indirect; the words of Divitiacus — the declarative clauses — are made to take the inf. with subject-acc. construction; the subordinate clauses take the subjunctive mode. —— **tōtīus**, gen. sing. f.; attributive of *Galliae*. —— **factiōnēs**, acc. plur. of *factiō, -ōnis*, f.; subject-acc. of *esse*. —— **esse**, pres. inf.; is here a complete predicate. See A. & G. 172, end; B. 125, 4; G. 205, NOTE; H. 360.

LINE 16. **duās**, acc. plur. f. (*duo, duae, duo*); attributive of *factiōnēs*. —— **hārum**, gen. plur. f. (*hīc, haec, hōc*), used substantively; partitive gen. after *alterius*. —— **alterius**, gen. sing. (*alter, -era, -erum*); limits *prīncipātum* (compare l. 13, Chap. II). —— **prīncipātum**, acc. sing. of *prīncipātus, -ūs*, m.; direct obj. of *tenēre*. —— **tenēre**, pres. inf. act. of *teneō, -ēre, -uī, tentum*, 2.

LINE 17. **Aeduōs**, acc. plur., used substantively; subject-acc. of *tenēre*. —— **alterius**, gen. sing., limits *prīncipātum* understood. —— **Arvernōs**, acc. plur. of *Arvernī, -ōrum*, m.; subject-acc. of *tenēre*, to be supplied. The Arverni were a powerful people of Celtic Gaul. —— **Hī**, nom. plur. m. (*hīc, haec, hōc*), used as a personal pron. of the 3d pers.; expressed for emphasis; subject-nom. of *contenderent*. It becomes still more emphatic by its position before the conj. *cum*. —— **cum**, conj., temporal.

232   CAESAR'S GALLIC WAR   [CHAP. XXXI.

| these factions had been violently struggling with each other for the mastery many years, it came to pass that the Germans, as mercenaries, were called in by the Arverni and the Sequani. At first, about fifteen thousand of these people had crossed the Rhine; | tantopere *greatly* multōs *many* ab *by* arcesserentur. *were caused to come.* mīlia *thousands* | dē *for* annōs *years* Arvernīs *the Arverni* quīndecim *fifteen* | potentātū *the leadership* contenderent, *contended,* Sēquanīsque *Sequani and,* Hōrum *Of these,* Rhēnum *the Rhine* | inter *among* factum esse *it came to pass* Germānī *the Germans* prīmō *at first,* | sē 18 *themselves* utī 19 *that* mercēde 20 *for pay* circiter 21 *about* trānsīsse; 22 *to have crossed;* |

LINE 18. **tantopere** (tantus + opus), adv.; frequently written *tantō opere*, in the abl., and hence = lit. *by so much work*, i.e. adverbially, *so greatly*. —— **dē**, prep. with the abl. See note on *dē*, l. 27, Chap. XIX. —— **potentātū**, abl. of *potentātus, -ūs*, m. (*potēns*, being able); obj. of *dē*. —— **inter**, prep. with acc. —— **sē**, acc. plur.; obj. of *inter*.

LINE 19. **multōs**, acc. plur. m. of the adj. *multus, plūs, plūrimus;* attributive of the noun *annōs*. —— **annōs**, acc. plur. of *annus, -ī*, m.; acc. of *extent of time*. Consult A. & G. 256, 2; B. 153; G. 336; H. 379. —— **contenderent**, 3d pers. plur. imperf. subjunctive act.; agrees with its subject-nom. *Hī;* subjunctive mode after *cum* temporal or historic. See A. & G. 325; B. 222; G. 585; H. 521, II, 2. For different significations of *contendere*, see l. 18, Chap. I. —— **factum esse**, perf. inf. pass. of the verb *fīō, fierī, factus,* 3; this form of the verb is used as the pass. of *faciō, -ere, fēcī, factum,* 3. *factum esse* is here used impersonally, and = *it came to pass*. The clause *utī . . . arcesserentur* is its subject. —— **utī**, conj.

LINE 20. **ab**, prep. with the abl. —— **Arvernīs**, abl. plur.; obj. of *ab*, i.e. it is the abl. of the agent after the pass. verb *arcesserentur*. Consult A. & G. 246; B. 166; G. 401; H. 415, 1. —— **Sēquanīsque** (Sēquanīs + que). *Sēquanīs* is the abl. plur. of *Sēquanus, -a, -um,* used as a subst. *que*, enclitic conj.; closely connects *Sēquanīs* with *Arvernīs*. —— **Germānī, -ōrum,** m.; subject-nom. of the verb *arcesserentur*. —— **mercēde**, abl. sing. of the noun *mercēs, -cēdis,* f. (*mercēre*, to merit); abl. of means.

LINE 21. **arcesserentur**, 3d pers. plur. imperf. subjunctive pass. of *arcessō, -ere, -īvī (-iī), -ītum,* 3 (ad + cēdere); agrees with *Germānī;* it is a subjunctive of *result* after *utī* ecbatic. Consult A. & G. 332; B. 201; G. 553, 3; H. 501, I, 1. The *ōrātiō rēcta* of lines 15–21: Galliae tōtīus factiōnēs *sunt duo;* hārum alterius prīncipātum tenent *Aeduī,* alterius *Arvernī*. Hī cum tantopere dē potentātū inter sē multōs annōs contenderent, factum *est* utī ab Arvernīs Sēquanīsque Germānī mercēde arcesserentur. —— **Hōrum**, gen. plur. m. (*hīc, haec, hōc*), used substantively; limits *mīlia;* partitive construction. Consult A. & G. 216, 2; B. 134; G. 370; H. 397, 2. —— **prīmō**, adv. (*prīmus*); modifies *trānsīsse. prīmō* usually = *first* in antithesis; whereas *prīmum* = *first* in a series. *prīmō* is really an abl. m. of the adj. *prīmus, -a, -um;* supply *locō*. —— **circiter**, adv. (compare l. 19, Chap. XV); modifies the num. adj. *quīndecim*.

LINE 22. **mīlia** (compare l. 25, Chap. II), subject-acc. of *trānsīsse*. —— **quīndecim** (quīnque + decem), cardinal num. adj.; an attributive of *mīlia*. —— **Rhēnum**,

LINES 23-27.] BOOK I. 233

23 posteāquam	agrōs	et	cultum	et	and after these wild and barbarous people had acquired a fondness for the land, civilization and resources of the Gauls, more people were induced to come over; and now there were about one hundred and twenty thousand in Gaul. The
after	*that*	*the fields*	*and*	*mode of living*	*and*
24 cōpiās	Gallōrum	hominēs	ferī	āc	barbarī
abundance	*of the Gauls,*	*men*	*wild*	*and*	*barbarous*
25 adamāssent,		trāductōs	plūrēs;		nunc
had grown fond of,		*were led across*	*more;*		*now*
26 esse	in	Galliā	ad	centum	et
to be (there were)	*in*	*Gaul*	*about*	*a hundred*	*and*
27 vīgintī	mīlium		numerum.	Cum	his
twenty	*of thousands,*		*number.*	*With*	*these*

acc. sing. of *Rhēnus, -ī, m.*; direct obj. of *trānsīsse*. But as *trānsīsse* is both a trans. and a neuter verb, *Rhēnum* may be taken either as a direct object, or as an acc. depending on the prep. *trāns* in composition. —— **trānsīsse**, perf. inf. act. (compare l. 19, Chap. V); its subject-acc. is *mīlia*.

LINE 23. **posteāquam**, conjunctive adv. (*posteā* + *quam*); modifies *adamāssent*; as a conj. it connects its own clause with the infinitive-clause *trāductōs* (*esse*) *plūrēs*. —— **agrōs**, acc. plur. of *ager, agrī, m.*; direct obj. of *adamāssent*. For synonyms, see note on *agrum*, l. 12, Chap. II. —— **et**, cop. conj.; connects the substantives. —— **cultum**, acc. sing. m. (compare l. 10, Chap. I); connected by *et* with *agrōs*, and is in the same grammatical construction. —— **et**, conj.; observe its repetition in the series; the usage is repetition or exclusion. See A. & G. 208, 1 and 3, and 346, *c*; B. 123, REM. 6; G. 474, NOTE; H. 554, 6.

LINE 24. **cōpiās**, acc. plur. (compare l. 6, Chap. II). —— **Gallōrum**, gen. plur., used substantively; limits *agrōs* and *cultum* and *cōpiās*. —— **hominēs**, nom. plur. (compare l. 20, Chap. II). —— **ferī**, nom. plur. m. of *ferus, -a, -um*; modifies *hominēs*. —— **āc**, conj. —— **barbarī**, nom. plur. of *barbarus, -a, -um*; connected by *āc* with *ferī*.

LINE 25. **adamāssent** (contracted, full form *adamāvissent*), 3d pers. plur. pluperf. subjunctive of the verb *adamō, -āre, -āvī, -ātum*, 1 (*ad, intensive* + *amāre* = lit. *to love exceedingly*); agrees with its subject-nom. *hominēs*; it is in the subjunctive mode, because it is in a subordinate clause in the *ōrātiō oblīqua*. Consult A. & G. 336, 2; B. 245, (*b*); G. 650; H. 524. —— **trāductōs** (**esse**), perf. pass. inf. of *trādūcō, -ere, -dūxī, -ductum*, 3; its subject-acc. is the adj. *plūrēs*, used substantively. —— **plūrēs**, adj., acc. plur. m. of comparative degree *plūs, plūris;* positive *multus;* superl. *plūrimus*. As to the declension of *plūs*, see A. & G. 86; B. 72, 7; G. 89, REMS. 2, 3, and 90, middle; H. 165, NOTE 1. —— **nunc**, adv.; modifies *esse*. Observe that *nunc* puts the emphasis on the present; while *iam* = *now*, of any event, either present, past or future.

LINE 26. **esse**, pres. inf. (*sum, esse, fuī, futūrus*); its subject-acc. is the noun *numerum*. —— **in**, prep. with the abl. —— **Galliā**, abl. sing. f.; locative abl. with the prep. *in*. Consult A. & G. 258, 4, *c*, 1; B. 170; G. 385; H. 425, I. —— **ad**, prep. with the acc., ordinarily; but here, in use, it is an adv. = *circiter*, about. —— **centum**, cardinal num. adj.; predicate-acc. after *esse*. —— **et**, cop. conj.; connects the numerals.

LINE 27. **vīgintī**, indecl. num. adj.; connected by *et* with *centum*, and in the same grammatical construction. —— **mīlium**, gen. plur. of *mīlle*, used as subst.; may

Aedui and their dependants had repeatedly contended in arms with these people; and after the Aedui had been routed, they suffered a great calamity: they lost all their nobles, all their senate, all their cavalry. And crushed by these battles and ca-	Aeduōs *the Aedui* iterum *again* calamitātem *calamity,* omnem *all* equitātum *the cavalry*	eōrumque *their and,* armīs *in arms* nōbilitātem, *the nobility,* āmīsisse. *to have lost.*	clientēs *clients* contendisse; *to have contended,* pulsōs *having been driven out,* omnem *all* Quibus *By which*	semel *once* (*themselves*) acc̄ēpisse, *to have received,* senātum, *the senate,*	atque 28 *and* māgnam 29 *a great* 30 omnem 31 *all* proeliīs 32 *battles*

be taken as partitive gen. after *centum et vīgintī*. See A. & G. 216, 2; B. 134; G. 370; II. 397, 2. —— **numerum,** acc. sing. m.; subject-acc. of the neuter verb *esse*. The *ōrātiō rēcta* of lines 21–27: Hōrum prīmō circiter mīlia quīndecim Rhēnum *transiērunt;* posteāquam agrōs et cultum et cōpiās Gallōrum hominēs ferī āc barbarī *adamārunt (adamāverant), trādūctī sunt plūrēs;* nunc *est* in Galliā ad centum et vīgintī mīlium *numerus.* —— **Cum,** prep. with the abl. —— **hīs,** abl. plur. m., used as a personal pron. of the 3d pers. *hīs* = *Germānīs,* and is the obj. of *cum*. Observe the position of the phrase, at the beginning of the sentence; its normal Latin position would be immediately before *contendisse,* l. 29, below. Compare *cum Germānīs contenderent,* l. 19, Chap. I.

LINE 28. **Aeduōs,** acc. plur. m.; subject-acc. of *contendisse,* l. 29, below. —— **eōrumque;** *eōrum,* gen. plur. of the dem. pron. *is, ea, id,* used as a personal pron. of the 3d pers., poss. case; refers to *Aeduōs,* but, as a gen., limits *clientēs.* *que,* enclitic conj. —— **clientēs,** acc. plur. of *cliēns, -entis;* connected by *que* with *Aeduōs,* and in the same grammatical construction. The *clientēs* were the small states like the Ambarri, that were in close alliance with the Aedui. —— **semel,** num. adv.; modifies *contendisse.* —— **atque,** conj.

LINE 29. **iterum,** adv., connected by *atque* with *semel,* and also modifies *contendisse.* Synonyms: *iterum* = *again, a second time;* *rūrsus* = *again,* i.e. the reverse of something. —— **armīs,** abl. plur. (compare l. 13, Chap. IV); abl. *of means* after *contendisse.* —— **contendisse,** perf. inf. act. of *contendō,* 3; its subject-accusatives are *Aeduōs* and *clientēs.* —— **māgnam,** acc. sing. f. of *māgnus,* comparative *māior,* superl. *māximus;* attributive of *calamitātem.*

LINE 30. **calamitātem,** acc. sing. of *calamitās, -ātis,* f.; direct obj. of *accēpisse.* —— **pulsōs,** acc. plur. of the perf. pass. participle of *pellō, -ere, pepulī, pulsum,* 3; agrees with *eōs,* i.e. *Aeduōs,* to be supplied; which *eōs* is subject-acc. of *accēpisse.* —— **accēpisse,** perf. inf. act. of the finite verb *accipiō, -ere, -cēpī, -ceptum,* 3.

LINE 31. **omnem,** acc. sing. f.; attributive of *nōbilitātem*. —— **nōbilitātem,** acc. sing. of *nōbilitās, -ātis,* f.; direct obj. of *āmīsisse.* —— **omnem,** acc. sing. m.; attributive of *senātum.* —— **senātum,** acc. sing. m.; connected by *et* omitted with *nōbilitātem,* and is in the same grammatical construction, i.e. it is a direct obj. of *āmīsisse.* —— **omnem,** acc. sing. m.; attributive of *equitātum.*

LINE 32. **equitātum,** acc. sing. of *equitātus, -ūs,* m.; connected by *et* omitted with *senātum,* and is in the same grammatical construction. —— **āmīsisse,** perf. inf.

33 calamitātibusque frāctōs, quī et	lamities, although formerly
calamities and, (themselves) being crushed, who both	they had been the most power-
34 suā virtūte et populī Rōmānī hospitiō	ful people in Gaul both on ac-
by their valor and the people's Roman hospitality	count of their own valor and
35 atque amīcitiā plūrimum ante in Galliā	the hospitality and friendship
and friendship very much previously in Gaul	of the Roman people, they were
36 potuissent, coāctōs esse Sēquanīs obsidēs	forced to give to
had been able, to have been forced to the Sequani hostages	the Sequani the

act. (see l. 10, Chap. XXVIII). The subject-acc. of *āmīsisse* is *eōs*, i.e. *Aeduōs*, understood. The *ōrātiō rēcta* of lines 27–32: Cum his *Aeduī hōrum*que clientēs semel atque iterum armīs *contendĕrunt*; māgnam calamitātem *pulsī accepĕrunt*, omnem nōbilitātem, omnem senātum, omnem equitātum *amīsērunt*. —— **Quibus**, abl. plur. n. (*quī, quae, quod*); refers to the idea contained in *armīs contendisse*, l. 29, above; but is here used adjectively, and is the attributive of the noun *proeliīs*. Observe that *quibus* at the beginning of a sentence = *et eis*. See A. & G. 180, *f*; B. 129, REM. 9; G. 610; H. 453. —— **proeliīs**, abl. plur. (For etymology and synonyms, see note on *proeliīs*, l. 18, Chap. I.) *proeliīs* is an abl. *of cause* after the perf. pass. participle *frāctōs*. Consult A. & G. 245, and 2; B. 165, and REM. 4; G. 408, and NOTE 2; H. 416, and NOTE 1.

LINE 33. **calamitātibusque**; *calamitātibus*, abl. plur.; connected by *que* with *proeliīs*, and is in the same grammatical construction. *que*, enclitic conj. —— **frāctōs**, acc. plur. m. of the perf. pass. participle *frāctus, -a, -um* of the finite verb *frangō, -ere, frēgī, frāctum*, 3; agrees with *eōs*, i.e. *Aeduōs*, understood. —— **quī**, nom. plur. m. (*quī, quae, quod*); refers to *eōs*, and is the subject-nom. of *potuissent*, l. 36, below. But note that *quī* here appears to have a concessive force, and = *cum eī*, i.e. = *although they*. Consult A. & G. 320, *e*; B. 212; G. 634; H. 515, III. —— **et**, cop. conj.; followed by another *et*, as in the text, the conjunctions are a species of correlatives = *both . . . and*.

LINE 34. **suā**, abl. sing. f.; attributive of *virtūte*. —— **virtūte**, abl. sing. f.; abl. of cause. —— **et**, cop. conj. —— **populī**, gen. sing. m.; limits *hospitiō atque amīcitiā*. For synonyms, see note on *populum*, l. 17, Chap. VI. —— **Rōmānī**, gen. sing. m.; attributive of the noun *populī*. —— **hospitiō**, abl. of the noun *hospitium, -iī*, n. (*hospes*, guest); connected by *et* with *virtūte*, and is in the same gram. construction.

LINE 35. **atque**, conj. —— **amīcitiā**, abl. sing. f.; connected by *atque* with *hospitiō*; abl. of cause. —— **plūrimum**, adverbial acc. (*plūrimus, -a, -um*). —— **ante**, adv.; modifying the verb *potuissent*. —— **in**, prep. with the abl. —— **Galliā**, abl. sing.; obj. of *in*.

LINE 36. **potuissent**, 3d pers. plur. pluperf. subjunctive of the intrans. verb *possum, posse, potuī*; agrees with a pron. implied in the ending as its subject-nom., referring to the Aeduī; it is in the subjunctive, because the clause is a subordinate one in the *ōrātiō oblīqua*; but, more rigidly exact, because the relative clause expresses concession. Consult A. & G. 320, *e*; B. 210, end; G. 634; H. 515, III. —— **coāctōs esse**, perf. inf. pass. of the finite verb *cōgō, -ere, coēgī, coāctum*, 3; its subject-acc. is *eōs*, i.e. *Aeduōs*, to be supplied. —— **Sēquanīs**, plur.; dat. of the indirect obj. See

noblest of the state as hostages; and compelled on oath not to demand hostages in return, nor ask assistance from the Roman people, nor refuse to	dare to give	nōbilissimōs the noblest	cīvitātis of the state	et and	iūreiūrandō by an oath	37
	cīvitātem the state	obstringere, to bind,	sēsē themselves	neque neither	obsidēs hostages	38
	repetītūrōs about to demand back		neque nor	auxilium aid	ā populō from the people	39
	Rōmānō Roman	implōrātūrōs about to implore		neque nor	recūsātūrōs, about to refuse,	40

A. & G. 225; B. 141; G. 345; H. 384, II. As to this clan, see note on *Sēquanīs*, l. 25, Chap. I. —— **obsidēs**, acc. plur. of *obses*, *-idis*, m. and f. (ob + sedēre, *to sit*); predicate-acc. after *dare*. Consult A. & G. 239; B. 151, (*b*); G. 340; H. 373, 1. The direct obj. of *dare* is *cīvēs* understood.

LINE 37. **dare**, pres. inf. act. of the verb *dō*, *dare*, *dedī*, *datum*, 1; but note that *a* is short by exception before *re* in the pres. inf.; also that *dare* is a complementary inf., depending on *coāctōs esse*. —— **nōbilissimōs**, acc. plur. m., superl.; attributive of *cīvēs* understood. —— **cīvitātis**, gen. sing. of *cīvitās*, *-ātis*, f.; limits *cīvēs* understood. —— **et**, cop. conj.; connects *dare* and *obstringere*. —— **iūreiūrandō**, abl. sing. of *iūs-iūrandum*, a compound noun; the two nominatives unite and both are declined. For the declension of *iūs*, *iūris*, n., see A. & G. 67, *b*, end, 77, 6, *a*; B. 45; G. 60, н; and for the gender and declension of *iūrandum*, *-ī*, n., see G. 34; H. 125, 126. Observe that, if the two parts of this word be regarded not as forming a compound, but rather as two distinct words, then *iūs*, *iūris*, n., is a noun of the third declension, and *iūrandum*, *-ī*, n., is a noun of the second declension; and that the direct cases of *iūrandum*, *-ī*, n. (i.e. *iūranda*), only occur in the plur. *iūre-iūrandō* is, in our text, an abl. of means. See A. & G. 248, *c*; B. 167; G. 401; H. 420.

LINE 38. **cīvitātem**, acc. sing.; direct obj. of *obstringere*. —— **obstringere**, pres. inf. act. of the finite verb *obstringō*, *-ere*, *-strīnxī*, *-strictum*, 3 (ob, *intensive* + stringere, *to bind*); connected by *et* with *dare*, and is in the same grammatical construction. —— **sēsē**, personal pron., reduplicated, acc. plur.; subject-acc. of *repetītūrōs* (*esse*). —— **neque**, see l. 16, Chap. IV. —— **obsidēs**, acc. plur.; direct object of *repetītūrōs* (*esse*). These hostages, so often referred to by Caesar, who were given as pledges for the fulfillment of obligations, and who were released on the fulfillment of the obligations, played an important part in the intercourse of ancient nations.

LINE 39. **repetītūrōs (esse)**, fut. inf. act. of the finite verb *repetō*, *-ere*, *-īvī* (*-iī*), *-ītum*, 3 (re + petere = lit. *to fall upon again*); this verb with its subject-acc. *sēsē* depends on *obstringere*. —— **neque**, see l. 16, Chap. IV. —— **auxilium**, *-iī*, n., acc. sing.; direct obj. of *implōrātūrōs* (*esse*). —— **ā**, prep. with the abl. —— **populō**, abl. sing.; abl. *of the person* with the prep. *ā*, after a verb *of asking*. Consult A. & G. 239, *c*, NOTE 1; B. 151, REM. 2; G. 339, NOTE 2; H. 374, NOTES 3 and 4. For synonyms, see note on *populī*, l. 17, Chap. III.

LINE 40. **Rōmānō**, abl. sing. m.; attributive of *populō*. —— **implōrātūrōs (esse)**, fut. inf. act. of the finite verb *implōrō*, *-āre*, *-āvī*, *-ātum*, 1 (in [im], *intensive* + plōrāre = lit. *to ask with tears*); connected by the conj. *neque* with *repetītūrōs* (*esse*), and is in the same grammatical construction, i.e. *sēsē* for its subject-acc. —— **neque**, correlate of the *neque* in the preceding line. —— **recūsātūrōs (esse)**, fut. inf. act. of the finite verb *recūsō*, *-āre*, *-āvī*, *-ātum*, 1 (re + causā); hence *recūsāre* = lit. *to make a case back*, i.e. *object, refuse*. *recūsātūrōs (esse)* is connected by *neque* with *implōrātūrōs* (*esse*), and has the same subject-acc.

41 quōminus	perpetuō	sub	illōrum	diciōne		remain under the dominion and power of the Sequani perpetually. Diviatiacus said that he was the only person from the entire Aeduan state that could not be prevailed on to take the oath, and give his children as
by which the less	*perpetually*	*under*	*their*	*sway*		
42 atque	imperiō	essent.	Ūnum	sē	esse	
and	*command*	*they would be.*	*One*	*himself*	*to be*	
43 ex	omnī	cīvitāte	Aeduōrum,	quī	addūcī	
from	*every*	*state*	*of the Aedui,*	*who*	*to be induced*	
44 nōn	potuerit,	ut	iūrāret	aut	līberōs	
not	*was able,*	*that*	*he would swear*	*or*	*children*	

LINE 41. quōminus (quō + minus); frequently written *quō minus*; rigidly lit. *quōminus = by which the less.* —— perpetuō, adv. (*perpetuus, -a, -um*); strictly an abl. n. of the adj. used adverbially. Consult A. & G. 148, *e*; B. 117, 6, end; G. 91, 2; H. 304, II. 2. —— sub, prep. with the abl. —— illōrum, gen. plur.; refers to the Sequani, but, as a gen., limits *diciōne;* equivalent to *their* or *of them.* illōrum is more emphatic than either *eōrum* or even *hōrum.* —— diciōne, abl. sing. of *diciō, -ōnis,* f. (more commonly written *ditiō);* derived from the verb *dare;* = lit. *a giving up;* hence transf. = *dominion, sway.* *diciōne* is the obj. of *sub.*

LINE 42. atque, conj. —— imperiō, abl. sing. n.; connected by *atque* with *diciōne,* and is in the same grammatical construction. —— essent, 3d pers. plur. imperf. subjunctive; agrees with a pron. implied in its ending as subject-nom., referring to the Aedui; it is the subjunctive *of result* after *quōminus =ut eō minus.* Consult A. & G. 319, *c*; B. 200, REM. 5; G. 549; H. 499, 3, NOTE 2. The *ōrātiō rēcta* of lines 32-42: Quibus proeliīs calamitātibusque *fractī,* quī et suā virtūte et populī Rōmānī hospitiō atque amīcitiā plūrimum ante in Galliā *potuerant, coāctī sunt* Sēquanīs obsidēs dare nōbilissimōs cīvitātis et iūreiūrandō cīvitātem obstringere, *sēsē* neque obsidēs repetītūrōs neque auxilium ā populō Rōmānō implōrātūrōs neque recūsātūrōs, quōminus perpetuō sub *hōrum* diciōne atque imperiō *sint.* —— Ūnum, acc. sing. m.; predicate-acc. of *esse.* —— sē, sing. m.; subject-acc. of *esse;* refers to Diviatiacus. —— esse, pres. inf.

LINE 43. ex, prep. with the abl. here instead of the partitive gen. after *ūnum.* See A. & G. 216, *c*; B. 134, REM. 2; G. 372, REM. 2, end; H. 397, 3, NOTE 3. —— omnī, abl. sing.; attributive of *cīvitāte.* —— cīvitāte, abl. sing. f.; obj. of *ex.* —— Aeduōrum, gen. plur. of the adj., used substantively; limits *cīvitāte.* —— quī, nom. sing.; refers to Diviatiacus; it is the subject-nom. of *potuerit.* —— addūcī, pres. inf. pass.; complementary inf.; depends on *potuerit.* See A. & G. 271; B. 181; G. 423; H. 533, I, 2.

LINE 44. nōn, adv.; modifies *potuerit.* —— potuerit, 3d pers. sing. perf. subjunctive of the intrans. verb *possum, posse, potuī;* it agrees with its subject-nom. *quī;* subjunctive, because in a relative clause of *characteristic.* See A. & G. 320, *b*; B. 234, 2; G. 631, 1; H. 503, II, 1. —— ut, telic conj. = *in order that.* —— iūrāret, 3d pers. sing. imperf. subjunctive of the verb *iūrō, -āre, -āvī, -ātum,* I (*iūs*); hence *iūvāre* = lit. *to take an oath;* agrees with a pron. as subj., implied in the ending, referring to Diviatiacus; is the subjunctive *of purpose* after *ut.* See A. & G. 317, 1; B. 200; G. 545; H. 497, II. —— aut, alternative conj.; not exclusive, but emphatic. —— līberōs, acc. plur. of the noun *līberī, -ōrum,* m. See note on *līberī,* l. 9, Chap. XI. *līberōs* is the direct obj. of the verb *daret.*

hostages. For this reason, he had fled from his state, and had come to the senate at Rome to ask for help, because he alone was bound neither by an oath, nor by hostages. But a worse fate	suōs obsidēs daret. Ob eam rem 45 *his as hostages he would give. For this reason* sē ex cīvitāte profūgisse et Rōmam 46 *himself from the state to have fled and to Rome* ad senātum vēnisse auxilium postulātum, 47 *at the senate to have come aid to sue for,* quod sōlus neque iūreiūrandō neque 48 *because (he) alone neither by an oath nor* obsidibus tenerētur. Sed pēius 49 *by hostages could be held. But a worse (thing)*

LINE 45. suōs, acc. plur.; refers to Divitiacus; agrees with *līberōs*. —— obsidēs, acc. plur., m. and f.; predicate-acc. See A. & G. 239, 1; B. 151, (*b*); G. 340; H. 373, 1. —— daret, 3d pers. sing. imperf. subjunctive of the verb *dō, dare, dedī, datum*, 1; connected with *iūrāret* by *aut*; subjunctive *of purpose*. Observe that *a* is short in *dare*, the pres. inf. act., by exception. The *ōrātiō rēcta* of lines 42–45 : *Unus egō sum ex omnī cīvitāte Aeduōrum, quī addūcī nōn potuit, ut iūrārem aut līberōs meōs obsidēs darem*. —— Ob, prep. with the acc. —— eam, acc. sing. f. (*is, ea, id*); attributive of *rem*. —— rem, acc. sing. f.; obj. of *ob*, denoting the exciting cause of the emotion, instead of the abl. *of cause*. Consult A. & G. 245, *b*; B. 165, REM. 4; G. 408, NOTE 3; II. 416, I, 2). Observe that the phrase *quam ob rem = ob eam rem*, which latter is the more common.

LINE 46. sē, acc. sing.; refers to Divitiacus, and is the subject-acc. of *profūgisse*. —— ex, prep. with the abl. —— cīvitāte, abl. sing. f.; obj. of *ex*. —— profūgisse, perf. inf. act. of the finite verb *profugiō, -ere, -fūgī, -fugitum*, 3 (prō + fugiō). —— et, cop. conj.; connects *profūgisse* with *vēnisse*. —— Rōmam, acc. sing. of *Rōma, -ae*, f.; locative acc.; the name of a town as the end of motion is put in the acc. without a prep. See A. & G. 258, *b*; B. 154; G. 337; H. 380, II.

LINE 47. ad, prep. with the acc. —— senātum, acc. sing. m.; obj. of *ad*. —— vēnisse, perf. inf. act. of the finite verb *veniō, -īre, vēnī, ventum*, 4; connected by *et* with *profūgisse*, and is in the same grammatical construction. —— auxilium, acc. sing. of *auxilium, -iī*, n.; the direct object of the supine *postulātum*. Supines are followed by the same cases as their verbs. —— postulātum, supine of the finite verb *postulō, -āre, -āvī, -ātum*, 1 (*poscō*). *postulātum* denotes purpose. Consult A. & G. 302; B. 186, (A); G. 435; H. 546.

LINE 48. quod, conj. —— sōlus, adj., nom. sing. m.; modifies *is*, to be supplied as the subject-nom. of the verb *tenerētur*; the pron., of course, refers to Divitiacus. —— neque, conjunctive adv. —— iūreiūrandō, abl. n.; abl. *of means*. See note on this word, l. 37, above. —— neque, see above.

LINE 49. obsidibus, abl. plur., m. and f.; connected by *neque* with *iūreiūrandō*, and in the abl. for the same reason, namely *means*. —— tenerētur, 3d pers. sing. imperf. subjunctive pass. of the act. verb *teneō, -ēre, -uī, tentum*, 2. *tenerētur* agrees with a pron. implied in the ending as the subject-nom., referring to Divitiacus; it is in the subjunctive mode, because it is in a subordinate clause in *ōrātiō oblīqua*. The *ōrātiō rēcta* of lines 45–49: Ob *hanc* rem *egō* ex cīvitāte *profūgī* et Rōmam ad senātum *vēnī* auxilium postulātum, quod *egō* sōlus neque iūreiūrandō neque obsidibus *tenēbar*. —— Sed, conj.; the strongest of all the adversative particles. Compare with *sed, at* and *autem*, and carefully discriminate the different shades of

BOOK I.

50 victōribus	Sēquanīs	quam	Aeduīs	victīs	had befallen the victorious Sequani than the vanquished Aedui, inasmuch as Ariovistus, king of the Germans, had settled in their country, and had seized a third part of the land of the Sequani, which was the best in all Gaul;
to the victors	*the Sequani*	*than*	*to the Aedui*	*vanquished*	
51 accidisse,		proptereā	quod	Ariovistus,	
to have happened,		*for this reason*	*because*	*Ariovistus,*	
52 rēx	Germānōrum,	in	eōrum	fīnibus	
king	*of the Germans,*	*in*	*their*	*borders*	
53 cōnsēdisset	tertiamque		partem	agrī	
had settled,	*a third and,*		*part*	*of the country*	
54 Sēquanī,	quī	esset	optimus	tōtīus Galliae,	
Sequanian,	*which*	*was*	*the best*	*of all Gaul,*	

meaning. —— pēius, acc. sing. n. of the comparative adj. *pēior*, m. and f.; *pēius*, n. *pēius* is an irr. comparative of the positive *malus*, superl. *pessimus*. *pēius* may be taken substantively in the acc. n., and as such is the subject-acc. of the inf. *accidisse;* or the noun *fātum* might be supplied; or *pēius* might be taken as an adv.: positive *male*, comparative *pēius*, superl. *pessimē;* and then *accidisse* must be taken in an impersonal sense. The first explanation is preferred.

LINE 50. victōribus, dat. plur. of the noun *victor*, *-ōris*, m.; predicative appositive to *Sēquanīs*. In use here *victōribus* = an adj. See A. & G. 188, *d*; B. 127; G. 325; H. 363, 3, 2). —— Sēquanīs, adj., dat. plur.; used as a subst.; indirect obj. of *accidisse*. —— quam, conj.; in comparisons = *than*. —— Aeduīs, adj., dat. plur., used substantively; connected by *quam* with *Sēquanīs*, and is in the same grammatical construction. —— victīs, participle (see l. 32, Chap. XXV), agrees with *Aeduīs;* its force is predicative : *Aeduīs victīs* = *to the Aedui as vanquished*.

LINE 51. accidisse, perf. inf. act. of the neuter or intrans. verb *accidō*, *-ere*, *-cidī*, no supine, 3; its subject-acc. is *pēius*, used as a noun. —— proptereā, adv. —— quod, conj. —— Ariovistus, *-ī*, m., subject-nom. of the verb *cōnsēdisset*. Ariovistus was a king of the Germans, who, on being invited to come into Gaul by the Gallic chiefs to aid them in settling their disputes, vanquished the Gauls, and ruled them despotically, until he was himself vanquished by the Romans.

LINE 52. rēx, nom. sing. of *rēx*, *rēgis*, m. (*regere* = lit. *to keep straight*). Observe that the stem of *rēx* is *rēg* — a palatal; and that the nom. is formed by adding *s*: thus *rēgs* = *rēx;* in apposition with *Ariovistus*. —— Germānōrum, gen. plur. m. (see l. 14, Chap. I); limits *rēx*. —— in, prep. with the abl. with a verb denoting *rest*. See note on *in*, l. 1, Chap. I. —— eōrum, gen. plur. (*is, ea, id*), used as a personal pron. of the 3d pers. = *their* or *of them;* as a gen. it limits *fīnibus*. —— fīnibus, abl. plur. m.; obj. of the prep. *in*. For synonyms, see *agrum*, l. 12, Chap. II.

LINE 53. cōnsēdisset, 3d pers. sing. pluperf. subjunctive act. of the verb *cōnsīdō*, *-ere*, *-sēdī*, *-sessum*, 3; agrees with its subject-nom. *Ariovistus;* it is in the subjunctive, because it is in a subordinate clause in the *ōrātiō oblīqua*. —— tertiamque (tertiam + que). *tertiam*, acc. sing. f. (see l. 3, Chap. I); attributive of *partem*. *que*, enclitic conj.; closely connects *cōnsēdisset* and *occupāvisset*. —— partem, acc. sing. f.; direct obj. of *occupāvisset*. The part exacted was what is now upper Alsace. —— agrī, gen. sing. of *ager*, *agrī*, m.; limits *partem*.

LINE 54. Sēquanī, gen. sing. m.; attributive of *agrī*. —— quī, nom. sing. m.; refers to *agrī* as its antecedent; but is the subject-nom. of *esset*. —— esset, 3d pers.

240   CAESAR'S GALLIC WAR   [CHAP. XXXI.

| and now he was ordering them to withdraw from another third-part, because a few months before, twenty-four thousand people, called Harudes, | occupāvisset he had occupied, tertiā third propterēā for this reason Harūdum of the Harudes, | et and Sēquanōs the Sequani quod because mīlia thousands | nunc now dēcēdere to withdraw paucīs within a few hominum of men | dē from he was mēnsibus months vīgintī twenty- | alterā another ordering, ante before, quattuor four | parte 55 part iubēret, 56 |

sing. imperf. subjunctive; agrees with its subject-nom. *quī;* it is in the subjunctive mode, because the clause in which it occurs is a dependent relative-clause in the *ōrātiō oblīqua.* Consult A. & G. 336, 2; B. 245, (*b*); G. 650; H. 524. —— **optimus,** adj., superl. degree of *bonus;* comparative degree *melior. optimus* is the predicate-adj. after *esset.* —— **tōtīus,** adj., gen. sing. f.; attributive of *Galliae.* For synonyms, see *tōtīus,* l. 8, Chap. II. —— **Galliae,** gen. sing. f.; partitive gen. after *optimus.* See A. & G. 216, 2; B. 134; G. 372; H. 397, 3.

LINE 55. **occupāvisset,** 3d pers. sing. pluperf. subjunctive of *occupō, -āre, -āvī, -ātum;* connected by *que* with *cōnsēdisset,* and is in the same grammatical construction. —— **et,** cop. conj.; connects *occupāvisset* and *iubēret,* next line. —— **nunc,** adv. = *now,* emphatic; whereas *iam* = *now,* unemphatic, having reference to the present, past or future occurrences. —— **dē,** prep. with the abl.; for difference between *ab, dē* or *ex,* see note on *dē,* l. 27, Chap. XIX. —— **alterā,** abl. sing. f. (compare l. 13, Chap. II). —— **parte,** abl. sing. f.; obj. of the prep. *dē.*

LINE 56. **tertiā,** abl. sing. f. of *tertius, -a, -um* (*ter*); attrib. of *parte.* —— **Sēquanōs,** adj., acc. plur., used substantively; subject-acc. of *dēcēdere.* —— **dēcēdere,** pres. inf. act. of the finite verb *dēcēdō, -ere, -cessī, -cessum,* 3 (dē + cedere = lit. *to go from*). The phrase *dē alterā parte tertiā* follows, logically, the inf. *dēcēdere* with the repetition of the prep. *dē;* the usual construction with Caesar. —— **iubēret,** 3d pers. sing. imperf. subjunctive act. of the verb *iubeō, -ēre, iūssī, iūssum,* 2; connected by *et,* preceding line, with *occupāvisset,* and hence in the same grammatical construction; but with a change of tense to denote the continuation rather than the *completion* of the action.

LINE 57. **proptereā,** adv.; the herald of the following *quod*-clause. —— **quod,** conj. —— **paucīs,** abl. plur. m. of the adj. *paucus, -a, -um;* attributive of *mēnsibus.* —— **mēnsibus,** abl. plur. of the noun *mēnsis, mēnsis,* m.; abl. of *degree of difference* after the adv. *ante.* See A. & G. 250; B. 164, and REM. 3; G. 403, and NOTE 4; H. 178, and NOTE. —— **ante,** adv. The strictly literal translation of the phrase *paucīs mēnsibus ante* is: *before by a few months.* But observe that Caesar might have written: *ante paucōs mēnsēs.*

LINE 58. **Harūdum,** gen. plur. of *Harūdēs, -um,* m.; appositive of *hominum.* The Harudes were a German clan, north of the Danube. —— **mīlia,** adj., nom. plur.; used as a subst. Consult A. & G. 94, *e*; B. 64, REMS. 8 and 9; G. 293, and NOTE; H. 178, and NOTE. *mīlia,* as a subst., is the subject-nom. of *vēnissent.* —— **hominum,** gen. plur., m. and f.; partitive gen. after *mīlia.* See A. & G. 216, 2; B. 134; G. 370; H. 397, 2. —— **vīgintī,** indecl. num. adj., cardinal; modifies *mīlia.* —— **quattuor,** cardinal num. adj.; also modifies *mīlia.* Observe that, if the smaller number precedes, *et* is generally used between them; but if the smaller number follows the larger, the *et* is omitted.

59 ad	eum	vēnissent,	quibus	locus	āc	sēdēs
to	him	had come,	for whom	a place	and	seats
60 parārentur.		Futūrum	esse	paucīs		annīs,
are to be procured.		It will be about	to be	in a few		years,
61 utī	omnēs	ex	Galliae	fīnibus		pellerentur
that	all	from	Gaul's	boundaries		would be driven out
62 atque	omnēs		Germānī	Rhēnum		trānsīrent;
and	all		the Germans	the Rhine		would cross;
63 neque	enim		cōnferendum esse			Gallicum
neither	for		to be about to be compared			the Gallic (land)

had come to him, for whom a place of settlement was to be provided. The outcome would be that, in a few years, they would all be driven from the land of Gaul, and all the Germans would cross the Rhine. For the Gallic soil is so

LINE 59. **ad**, prep. with the acc. = *to* or *towards*. —— **eum**, acc. sing. m. (*is, ea, id*), used as a personal pron. of the 3d pers.; obj. of *ad*. —— **vēnissent**, verb, 3d pers. plur. pluperf. subjunctive; agrees with its subject-nom. *milia*; subjunctive, because it is in a subordinate clause in the *ōrātiō oblīqua*. —— **quibus**, dat. plur. (*quī, quae, quod*); refers to *Harūdum* as its antecedent; dat. com., or dat. of advantage. Consult A. & G. 235, and NOTE; B. 145; G. 352; H. 384, II, 1, 2). *quibus* here = *ut eīs*. —— **locus**, nom. sing. m. (see l. 10, Chap. II). *locus* is one of the nominatives of *parārentur*. —— **āc**, conj. —— **sēdēs**, nom. sing. of the noun *sēdēs, sēdis*, f. (compare *sēdēre*, to sit); the other of the nominatives of *parārentur*. *locus āc sēdēs* = *a place of abode* (hendiadys).

LINE 60. **parārentur**, 3d pers. plur. imperf. subjunctive pass. of the verb *parō, -āre, -āvī, -ātum*, 1; in the plur., because it has two nouns in the sing. as subjects. Consult A. & G. 205; B. 126, REM. 1; G. 285; H. 463, II. *parārentur* is in the subjunctive of purpose after the rel. pron. *quibus* = *ut eīs*. Consult A. & G. 317, 2; B. 233, 1; G. 630; H. 497, I. —— **Futūrum esse**, fut. inf.; used impersonally, followed by *utī* and the imperf. subjunctive for the 3d pers. plur. of the fut. ind. in the *ōrātiō rēcta*. —— **paucīs**, abl. plur. m. of *paucus, -a, -um*; attributive of *annīs*. —— **annīs**, abl. plur. of *annus, -ī*, m.; abl. of time *in which*. See A. & G. 256, 1; B. 171; G. 393; H. 429.

LINE 61. **utī**, conj. —— **omnēs**, nom. plur., used substantively, and the subject-nom. of *pellerentur*. —— **ex**, prep. with the abl. —— **Galliae**, gen. sing. f.; limits *fīnibus*. —— **fīnibus**, abl. plur. m.; obj. of *ex*. —— **pellerentur**, 3d pers. plur. imperf. subjunctive pass. of *pellō, -ere, pepulī, pulsum*, 3; agrees with its subject-nom. *omnēs*, and is in the subjunctive of *result* after *utī*. Consult A. & G. 332, 2; B. 201, REM. I, (*c*); G. 553, 3; H. 501, I, 1. Observe that the ecbatic clauses *utī . . . pellerentur atque omnēs . . . trānsīrent* are, grammatically, the subject of the impersonal *futūrum esse*.

LINE 62. **atque**, conj.; usually adds a more important notion; here connects the verbs *pellerentur* and *trānsīrent*. —— **omnēs**, nom. plur. m.; attributive of *Germānī*. —— **Germānī**, *-ōrum*, plur. m.; subject-nom. of *trānsīrent*. —— **Rhēnum**, acc. sing. m.; direct obj. of *trānsīrent*. —— **trānsīrent**, 3d pers. plur. imperf. subjunctive; agrees with *Germānī*; connected by *atque* with *pellerentur*, and is in the subjunctive mode for the same reason.

LINE 63. **neque**, conjunctive adv. —— **enim**, a conj. causal, postpositive. *enim* expresses a subjective, *nam* an objective reason. —— **cōnferendum esse**, pres. inf. 2d pass. periphrastic conjugation of *cōnferō, -ferre, -tulī, col(n)lātum*; this conjuga-

242   CAESAR'S GALLIC WAR   [CHAP. XXXI.

| superior to that of the Germans, as not to admit of comparison; and the German mode of life is so inferior to that of the Gauls, as not to admit of comparison. But, as to Ariovistus, as soon as he had defeated the forces of the Gauls in battle at Admagetobriga, he | cum *with* cōnsuētūdinem *custom* comparandam. *to be about to be compared.* semel *once* quod *which* | Germānōrum *the Germans'* victūs *of living* Gallōrum *the Gauls'* proelium *battle* | agrō, *fields,* cum *with* Ariovistum *Ariovistus,* cōpiās *troops* factum sit *was made* | neque *nor* illā *that* autem, *moreover,* proeliō *in battle* Admagetobrigae, *at Admagetobriga,* | hanc 64 *this* 65 ut 66 *when* vīcerit, 67 *he has vanquished,* 68 |

tion denotes necessity or duty; the inf. construction is here used, because the discourse is indirect; the subject-acc. of *cōnferendum esse* is *agrum*, to be supplied. —— **Gallicum**, acc. sing. m. of *Gallicus, -a, -um;* attributive of *agrum* understood.

LINE 64. **cum**, prep. with the abl. Observe that in the phrase *cum Germānōrum agrō* the same preposition — *cum* — is used as in the compound *cōn(cum)ferendum esse* which the phrase logically follows. —— **Germānōrum**, gen. plur. m.; limits *agrō*. —— **agrō**, abl. sing. m.; obj. of *cum*. —— **neque**, conj. —— **hanc**, acc. sing. f. *(hīc, haec, hōc);* attributive of *cōnsuētūdinem. hanc consuētūdinem* = the Gallic mode of living. Consult A. & G. 102, *a*, end; B. 84, 1, and REM. 1; G. 305, 2; H. 450, 2, (2).

LINE 65. **cōnsuētūdinem**, acc. sing. of the noun *cōnsuētūdō, -inis*, f. (compare *consuēscere*, to accustom); subject-acc. of *comparandam (esse)*. —— **victūs**, gen. sing. of the noun *victus, -ūs*, m. (*vīvere*, to live); hence *victus* = lit. *that on which one lives. victūs*, as a gen., limits *cōnsuētūdinem*. —— **cum**, prep. with the abl. —— **illā** *(ille, -a, -lud);* attributive of *cōnsuētūdine*, to be supplied. *illā* refers to the Germanic modus of living; the usual order in the reference of the pronouns *hīc* and *ille* is here reversed. See the grammatical references to *hanc*, preceding line.

LINE 66. **comparandam (esse)**, pres. inf. 2d pass. periphrastic conjugation of *comparō, -āre, -āvī, -ātum*, 1 (con [cum] + par); hence *comparāre* = lit. *to couple together in pairs*, i.e. *to compare. cōnsuētūdinem* is the subject-acc. As to the meaning of the 2d periphrastic conjugation, see A. & G. 109, *a*, and FOOTNOTE 3; B. 106, II, and 185; G. 251, 1; H. 234. —— **Ariovistum**, acc. sing. m.; subject-acc. of *imperāre*, l. 69, below. —— **autem**, postpositive conj.; simply marks the transition and = *moreover*. —— **ut**, an adv. here = *as* or *when;* modifies the other adv. *semel*.

LINE 67. **semel**, adv. = *once;* and the phrase *ut semel* = *when once*, or *as soon as*. —— **Gallōrum**, adj., gen. plur., used substantively; limits *cōpiās*. —— **cōpiās**, acc. plur. f.; direct obj. of *vīcerit*. —— **proeliō**, abl. sing. m.; abl. *of means*. —— **vīcerit**, 3d pers. sing. perf. subjunctive act. of *vincō, -ere, vīcī, victum*, 3; agrees with a pron. implied in the ending as subject-nom., referring to *Ariovistum;* subjunctive mode, because in a subordinate clause in *ōrātiō oblīqua*.

LINE 68. **quod**, nom. sing. n. (*quī, quae, quod*), used both relatively and adjectively; as a rel. pron. it refers to the noun *proeliō* as its antecedent; as an adj. it is an attributive of *proelium*. —— **proelium**, nom. sing. n.; subj. of *factum sit*. —— **factum sit**, 3d pers. sing. perf. subjunctive of *fīō, fierī, factus*, used as the pass. of

69 superbē	et	crūdēliter	imperāre,		began to govern
haughtily	*and*	*cruelly*	*to command (begins),*		haughtily and cruelly; he de-
70 obsidēs	nōbilissimī		cūiusque		līberōs	manded as hos-
as hostages,	*the noblest,*		*of each one,*		*the children*	tages the children of all the nob-
71 poscere		et	in	eōs	omnia	exempla	lest families, and
to demand (he demands)		*and*	*on*	*them*	*all*	*examples*	inflicted on them every species of
72 cruciātūsque	ēdere,	sī	qua	rēs	nōn	ad	cruelty if every-
tortures	*and,*	*to inflict,*	*if*	*any*	*thing*	*not*	*to*	thing was not

faciō, -ere, fēcī, factum, 3; agrees with its subject-nom. *proelium;* subjunctive, because it is in a subordinate clause in the *ōrātiō oblīqua.* —— **Admagetobrigae,** locative case of the proper noun *Admagetobriga, -ae,* f. Consult A. & G. 258, *e,* 2; B. 176; G. 411; H. 425, II. The locality referred to is in doubt; probably a village west of Vesontio, and not far from it.

LINE 69. **superbē,** adv. (*superbus,* adj.); in the formation of the adv., the final vowel of the stem of the adj. — *superbō* — is changed into *ē.* Consult A. & G. 148, *a*; B. 117, 5; G. 92, 2; H. 304, II, 2, end. —— **et,** conj.; couples the adverbs *superbē* and *crūdēliter.* —— **crūdēliter,** adv. (derived from the adj. *crūdēlis,* 3d declension). See grammatical references to *superbē,* immediately preceding. —— **imperāre,** pres. inf. act. of *imperō,* 1 (see l. 7, Chap. VII). The subject-acc. of *imperāre* is *Ariovistum,* l. 66, above.

LINE 70. **obsidēs,** acc. plur., m. and f.; predicate-acc. appositive of *līberōs,* which latter is the direct obj. of *poscere.* —— **nōbilissimī,** gen. sing. m. superl. degree; attributive of *virī,* to be supplied; which noun *virī,* as a gen., limits the noun *līberōs.* —— **cūiusque,** gen. sing. of the indef. pron. *quisque, quaeque, quidque* or *quodque;* also an attributive of the noun *virī,* to be supplied; or rather it is a modifier of the complex notion contained in *virī nobilissimī. quisque* with the superl. = *omnēs* with the positive. Consult A. & G. 93, *c*; B. 89, 7; G. 318, 2; H. 458, 1. —— **līberōs,** acc. plur. of the noun *līberī, -ōrum,* m. (*līber*); hence *līberī* = lit. *the free* members of the household. *līberōs* is the direct obj. of *poscere.*

LINE 71. **poscere,** pres. inf. of *poscō,* no supine, 3; its subject-acc. is the pron. *eum,* referring to *Ariovistum,* l. 66, above. Synonyms: *petere* and *rogāre* are the general words *for asking;* but the former denotes the *object* sought, the latter the *person* to whom application is made. *poscere* indicates an energetic request. —— et, conj.; connects *poscere* and *ēdere.* —— **in,** prep. with acc. —— **eōs,** acc. plur. (*is, ea, id*), used as a personal pron. of the 3d pers. *eōs* is the obj. of *in.* —— **omnia,** acc. plur. n.; attributive of *exempla.* —— **exempla,** acc. plur. of *exemplum, -ī,* n. (derived from *eximo,* to take out); hence the noun = that which is selected as a sample; direct obj. of *ēdere.*

LINE 72. **cruciātūsque** (cruciātūs + que). *cruciātūs,* acc. plur. of *cruciātus, -ūs,* m. *que* connects *cruciātūs* with *exempla. omnia exempla cruciātūsque* = lit. *all examples and cruelties,* i.e. *every species of cruelty;* here is an illustration of the figure hendiadys. Consult A. & G. 385, 1; B. 310, 2, (*b*); G. 698; H. 636, III, 2. —— **ēdere,** pres. inf. act. of the finite verb *ēdō, -ere, -didī, -ditum,* 3 (ē + dare, lit. *to give out*); hence transf. *ēdere* = (*a*) *to publish;* (*b*) *to cause;* (*c*) *to inflict.* —— **sī,** conditional conj.; original form *seī.* —— **qua,** nom. sing. f. (*quis, qua, quid* or *quod*), adj. Observe that the indef. *quis* is declined like the interrogative *quis,* but has *qua* instead of *quae* except in the nom. plur. f. The indef. pron. is very frequent

244   CAESAR'S GALLIC WAR   [CHAP. XXXI.

done according to his nod or wish. Divitiacus said, moreover, that the man Ariovistus was savage, wrathful, rash; that the Gauls could no longer endure his commands. Unless there were	nūtum	aut	ad	voluntātem	ēius	facta sit. 73
	the nod	or	to	the wish	of him	has been done.
	Hominem		esse	barbarum,		irācundum, 74
	The man		to be (is)	barbarous,		wrathful,
	temerārium;			nōn	posse	ēius 75
	rash;		(ourselves)	not	to be able	his
	imperia	diūtius		sustinēre.	Nisi	sī quid 76
	commands	longer		to endure.	Unless	something

with the particles *nē*, *num* and *sī*. As to the indefinites, see A. & G. 105, *d*; B. 89, 3; G. 315; H. 455, 1.   *qua* in the text has an adj. force, and is the attributive of the noun *rēs*. —— **rēs**, nom. sing. f.; subj. of *facta sit*. —— **nōn**, negative adv.; modifies *facta sit*. It is made emphatic by its position. —— **ad**, prep. with the acc.

LINE 73. **nūtum**, acc. sing. of *nūtus, -ūs*, m. (*nuere*, to nod); obj. of *ad*. —— **aut**, alternative conj. —— **ad**, prep. with the acc. Observe how the notions are kept distinct by the repetition of the prep. —— **voluntātem**, acc. sing. f.; obj. of *ad*. —— **ēius**, gen. sing. m. (*is, ea, id*), used as a personal pron. of the 3d pers.; limits *voluntātem*; refers to Ariovistus. —— **facta sit**, 3d pers. sing. perf. subjunctive of *fīō, fierī, factus*; used as the pass. of *faciō, -ere, fēcī, factum*, 3; agrees with its subject-nom. *rēs*; subjunctive in the protasis after the conditional conj. *sī*; the apodosis is in the preceding infinitive-clause. The *ōrātiō rēcta* of lines 49–73: Sed pēius victōribus Sēquanīs quam Aeduīs victīs *accidit*, proptereā quod Ariovistus, rēx Germānōrum, in eōrum fīnibus *cōnsēdit* tertiamque partem agrī Sēquanī, quī *est* optimus tōtīus Galliae, *occupāvit*, et nunc dē alterā parte tertiā Sēquanōs dēcēdere *iubet*, proptereā quod paucīs mēnsibus ante Harūdum mīlia hominum vīgintī quattuor ad eum *vēnērunt*, quibus locus āc sēdēs *parantur*. Paucīs annīs omnēs ex Galliae fīnibus *pellentur* atque omnēs Germānī Rhēnum *trānsībunt*; neque enim *cōnferendus est Gallicus* cum Germānōrum agrō, neque *haec cōnsuētūdō* vīctūs cum illā *comparanda*. Ariovistus autem, ut semel Gallōrum cōpiās proeliō *vīcit*, quod proelium factum *est* Admagetobrigae, superbē et crūdēliter *imperat*, obsidēs nōbilissimī cūiusque līberōs *pōscit* et in *hōs* omnia exempla cruciātūsque *ēdit*, sī qua rēs nōn ad nūtum aut ad voluntātem *hūius* facta sit.

LINE 74. **Hominem**, acc. sing., m. and f.; subject-acc. of *esse*. —— **esse**, pres. inf.; its function here is simply that of a copula. —— **barbarum**, acc. sing. m.; predicate-adj. after *esse*. —— **Irācundum**, acc. sing. m. of the adj. *īrācundus, -a, -um* (*īra, wrath* + *cundus*); predicate-adj. after *esse*; in the same construction as *barbarum, et* being omitted (asyndeton). As to the force of the ending -*cundus*, see A. & G. 164, *p*; G. 182, 2; H. 333, 1.

LINE 75. **temerārium**, acc. sing. m. of the adj. *temerārius, -a, -um* (temere through *temerāre* + the ending -*ārius*); also predicate-adj. after *esse, et* being omitted. As to the omission of the conj., see A. & G. 208, *b*, 1, and 3, and 346, *c*; B. 123, REM. 6; G. 474, NOTE; H. 554, 6. —— **nōn**, negative adv.; modifies **posse**, pres. inf.; supply as the subject-acc. of *posse nōs* or *Gallōs*. —— **ēius**, gen. sing. m. (*is, ea, id*), used as a personal pron. of the 3d pers.; limits the noun *imperia*; refers to Ariovistus.

LINE 76. **imperia**, acc. plur. n.; direct obj. of *sustinēre*. —— **diūtius**, comparative degree of the adv. *diū* (*diēs*); superl. *diūtissimē*; modifies *sustinēre*. ——

BOOK I. 245

77	in	Caesare	populōque	Rōmānō	sit	auxiliī,	some help in Cae-
	in	*Caesar*	*people and,*	*Roman*	*is,*	*of aid,*	sar and the Ro- man people, all
78	omnibus	Gallīs	idem	esse faciendum,		quod	the Gauls must do the same as
	by all	*the Gauls*	*the same*	*to be about to be done,*		*which*	the Helvetii had done; namely,
79	Helvētiī	fēcerint,	ut	domō		ēmigrent,	emigrate, seek an-
	the Helvetii	*have done,*	*that from home they might go forth,*				other dwelling- place, and other
80	aliud	domicilium,	aliās	sēdēs,	remōtās	ā	settlements re-
	another	*domicile,*	*other*	*seats,*	*remote*	*from*	mote from the

sustinēre, pres. inf. act.; complementary inf., depending on *posse*. Consult A. & G. 271; B. 181; G. 423; H. 533, I, 2. —— Nisi, conj. —— sī, conj.; *nisi sī* = *except if*, i.e. *unless*. —— quid, nom. sing. n. (*quis, qua, quid*); subject-nom. of *sit*.

LINE 77. in, prep. with the abl. Consult A. & G. 152, *c*; B. 120, 3; G. 418, 1, (*b*); H. 435, NOTE 1. —— Caesare, abl. m.; obj. of *in*. —— populōque (populō + que). *populō*, abl. sing. m., *que*, conj.; connects *populō* with *Caesare*, and hence *populō* is also the obj. of the prep. *in*. —— Rōmānō, abl. sing. m.; attributive of *populō*. —— sit, 3d pers. sing. pres. subjunctive of *sum*; its subject-nom. is the pron. *quid*; subjunctive in the negative condition after *nisi sī*. See A. & G. 315, *a*; B. 204, REM. 1; G. 591, 2, (*b*), 2, REM. 2; H. 507, 3, NOTE 4. —— auxiliī, gen. sing. m.; partitive gen. after the indef. pron. *quid*. See A. & G. 216, 3; B. 134; G. 369; H. 397, 3.

LINE 78. omnibus, adj., dat. plur.; an attributive of *Gallīs*. —— Gallīs, adj., dat. plur.; used substantively; and here the *dat. of the apparent agent* after *esse faciendum* (*faciendum esse*). See A. & G. 232; B. 148; G. 215, 2; H. 388. —— idem, acc. sing. n. of the dem. iterative pron. *īdem, eadem, idem*; subject-acc. of *esse faciendum*. —— faciendum esse, pres. inf. of the 2d pass. periphrastic conjugation of *fīō*. Consult A. & G. 129; B. 106, II; G. 251; H. 234. —— quod, acc. sing. n.; refers to *idem*, but it is the direct obj. of the verb *fēcerint*.

LINE 79. Helvētiī, adj., nom. plur. m., used as a substantive; subject-nom. of *fēcerint*. —— fēcerint, 3d pers. plur. perf. subjunctive act. of *faciō*; agrees with its subject-nom. *Helvētiī*; subjunctive mode, because in a subordinate clause in the *ōrātiō oblīqua*. —— ut, ecbatic conj.; ordinarily it = the English *that;* but with the following subjunctive may be more elegantly rendered into English by the English inf. mode. —— domō, locative abl. of the noun *domus, -ūs* or -*ī*, f., after the verb *ēmigrent*. Consult A. & G. 258, I. 2, *a*; B. 175; G. 390, 2; H. 412, II, 1. —— ēmigrent, 3d pers. plur. pres. subjunctive of *ēmigrō*, 1; a neuter or intrans. verb. Observe that the *ē* in the compound is simply intensive; that *ēmigrāre, to remove* or *depart* from a place, does not differ essentially from *migrāre*. *ēmigrent* is a subjunctive *of result* after *ut*, but the clause *ut domō ēmigrent* is a noun-clause, and as such is in apposition with *idem* in the preceding line. See A. & G. 332, *f;* B. 201, REM. 1, (*b*); G. 557; H. 501, III.

LINE 80. aliud, acc. sing. n. of the adj. *alius;* attributive of *domicilium*. For declension of *alius*, see A. & G. 83; B. 56, and REM. 1; G. 76, and REM. 4; H. 151. —— domicilium, acc. sing. of *domicilium, -ī*, n. (l. 13, Chap. XXX); direct obj. of *petant*. —— aliās, acc. plur. f.; attributive of *sēdēs*. —— sēdēs, acc. plur. of *sēdēs, -is*, f.; direct obj. of *petant*. Observe the omission of the conj. between the phrases (asyndeton). Synonyms: *sēdēs* = ordinarily a place for *sitting; sedīle* = a prepared

Germans, and try whatever fortune might be allotted them. If these statements were reported to Ariovistus, Divitiacus said that he did not doubt that he would inflict the direst punishment on all the hostages that were in his power;	Germānīs, *the Germans,*	petant *they might seek*	fortūnamque, *fortune and,*	quaecumque *whatever*	81
	accidat, *may happen,*	experiantur. *they might try.*	Haec *These things*	sī *if*	ēnūntiāta *reported*	82
	Ariovistō *to Ariovistus*	sint, *are, (ourselves)*	nōn *not*	dubitāre, *to doubt*	quīn *that*	83
	dē *from*	omnibus *all*	obsidibus, *the hostages,*	quī *who*	apud *with*	eum *him*	84
	sint, *are,*	gravissimum *the severest*	supplicium *penalty*		sūmat. *he may take.*	85

seat of any sort; *sella* = frequently, a magistrate's *seat, a chair* or *throne.* —— **remōtīs,** a participial adj., acc. plur. f.; *remōtus, -a, -um* of the finite verb *removeō, -ēre, -mōvī, -mōtum,* 2; as a perf. pass. participle = *having been removed;* as a participial adj. = *remote, distant;* modifies the noun *sēdēs.* —— **ā,** prep. with the abl.

LINE 81. **Germānīs,** abl. plur. m.; obj. of the prep. *ā.* —— **petant,** 3d pers. plur. pres. subjunctive act. of *peto;* connected with *ēmigrent* by the omitted conj., and hence is in the same construction as *ēmigrent,* l. 79, above. —— **fortūnamque;** *fortūnam,* acc. sing. f.; direct obj. of *experiantur. que* connects *petant* with *experiantur.* —— **quaecumque,** nom. sing. f. of the indef. relative pron. *quīcumque, quaecumque, quodcumque;* as a rel. it refers to *fortūnam;* it is the subject-nom. of *accidat.*

LINE 82. **accidat,** 3d pers. sing. pres. subjunctive act. of *accidō, -ere, accidī,* no supine, 3 (ad + cadere = lit. *to fall toward);* subjunctive, because it is in a dependent clause in the *ōrātiō oblīqua.* —— **experiantur,** 3d pers. plur. pres. subjunctive of the deponent verb *experior, -īrī, -pertus,* 4; connected by *que* with *petant,* and thence by an omitted conj. with *ēmigrent,* l. 79, and is in the same grammatical construction. —— **Haec,** nom. plur. n. *(hīc, haec, hōc),* used substantively; or supply the English word *things* after it. Observe its emphatic position at the beginning of the sentence. *haec* is the subject-nom. of *ēnūntiāta sint.* —— **sī,** conditional conj. —— **ēnūntiāta sint,** 3d pers. plur. perf. subjunctive pass. of the verb *ēnūnt(i)ō;* agrees with its subject-nom. *haec* in number and person, and is in the subjunctive after *sī* in the protasis.

LINE 83. **Ariovistō,** dat. sing. m.; dat. of the indirect obj. after *ēnūntiāta sint.* Observe its emphatic position between the parts of the verb. —— **nōn,** adv.; modifies *dubitāre.* —— **dubitāre,** see l. 12, Chap. XVII. The subject-acc. of *dubitāre* is the reflexive pron. *sē,* referring to Divitiacus. —— **quīn,** conj.; often an adv. (see l. 27, Chap. III).

LINE 84. **dē,** prep. with the abl. —— **omnibus,** abl. plur.; attributive of *obsidibus.* —— **obsidibus,** abl. plur., m. and f.; obj. of *dē.* —— **quī,** nom. plur. m.; refers, as a relative, to *obsidibus,* and is the subject-nom. of the intrans. verb *sint.* —— **apud,** prep. with the acc. Consult A. & G. 153; B. 120; G. 416, NOTE 4. —— **eum,** dem. pron., acc. sing. m.; used as a personal pron. of the 3d pers.; refers to Ariovistus; obj. of *apud.*

LINE 85. **sint,** 3d pers. plur. pres. subjunctive of *sum;* agrees with its subject-nom. *quī;* it is in the subjunctive, because in a subordinate clause in the *ōrātiō*

86 Caesarem	vel	auctōritāte	suā	atque		but that Caesar either by his own influence
Caesar	*either*	*by authority*	*his own*	*and (that)*		
87 exercitūs	vel	recentī	victōriā	vel	nōmine	and that of his army, or by his late victory, or by the name of
of the army	*or*	*by the recent*	*victory*	*or*	*by the name*	
88 populī	Rōmānī	dēterrēre		posse,	nē	the Roman people could prevent him from bringing a larger number of Germans across the Rhine, and could
of the people	*Roman*	*to deter*		*to be able,*	*that not*	
89 māior	multitūdō	Germānōrum			Rhēnum	
a greater	*multitude*	*of Germans*			*the Rhine*	

oblīqua. —— **gravissimum**, adj., acc. sing. n. of the superl. *gravissimus, -a, -um;* attributive of *supplicium.* —— **supplicium**, acc. sing. of *supplicium, -iī,* n.; direct obj. of *sūmat.* —— **sūmat**, 3d pers. sing. pres. subjunctive act. of the verb *sumō;* agrees with a pron. implied in the ending as subject-nom., referring to Ariovistus; it is in the subjunctive *of result* after the conj. *quīn.* Consult A. & G. 332, *g*, REM.; B. 201, REM. 3; G. 555, 2; H. 504, 3, 2). The reader will observe that the literal translation of *quīn dē omnibus obsidibus . . . supplicium sūmat* is: *that he will take a penalty from all the hostages* = *that he will inflict punishment on,* etc.

LINE 86. **Caesarem**, acc. sing. m.; subject-acc. of *posse,* l. 88, below. —— **vel**, disjunctive conj. *vel . . . vel* = *either . . . or.* For synonyms, see note on *aut . . . aut,* lines 19 and 20, Chap. I; and also on *vel . . . vel,* lines 14 and 16, Chap. VI. —— **auctōritāte**, abl. sing. of the noun *auctōritās, -ātis,* f. (*auctōr* through the verb *augēre,* to increase). *auctōritāte* is an abl. of means. —— **suā**, abl. sing. f. of the poss. and reflexive pron. *suus, -a, -um. suā* is an attributive of *auctōritāte;* it refers to Caesar. —— **atque** (ad + que), conj. See note on this particle, l. 12, Chap. I. *atque* connects *auctōritāte* expressed with *auctōritāte* understood; or with the pron. *eā* that may represent *auctōritāte.*

LINE 87. **exercitūs**, gen. sing. m.; limits *auctōritāte* understood. For synonyms, see note on *exercitū,* l. 28, Chap. III. —— **vel**, see *vel,* preceding line. —— **recentī**, abl. sing. f. of the adj. *recēns, -ntis;* attributive of *victōriā.* Synonyms: *novus* = *new* — that which has not *previously* existed; while *recēns* = *new,* i.e. that which has not *long* existed. —— **victōriā**, abl. sing. f.; abl. of means. —— **vel**, see *vel,* preceding line. —— **nōmine**, abl. sing. n.; abl. of means.

LINE 88. **populī**, gen. sing. m.; limits the noun *nōmine.* —— **Rōmānī**, adj., gen. sing.; attributive of *populī.* —— **dēterrēre**, pres. inf. of *dēterreō, -ēre, -uī, -itum,* 2 (dē + terrēre = lit. *to frighten away*). *dēterrēre* is a complementary inf., depending on *posse.* See A. & G. 271; B. 181; G. 423; H. 533, I, 2. After *dēterrēre* supply *eum,* i.e. *Ariovistum,* as direct obj. —— **posse**, pres. inf. act. of the intrans. verb *possum;* its subject-acc. is the proper noun *Caesarem.* —— **nē**, conjunctive adv. = *that not.*

LINE 89. **māior**, adj., comparative degree; positive *māgnus;* attributive of *multitūdō.* —— **multitūdō**, nom. sing. f.; subject-nom. of *trādūcātur.* —— **Germānōrum**, gen. plur. m.; limits *multitūdō.* —— **Rhēnum**, acc. sing. m.; acc. after the *trāns* in the compound verb *trādūcātur.* Consult A. & G. 237, *d*; B. 152, REM. 2; G. 331; H. 372. It should be noted that the acc. after this verb in either voice depends on the prep. *trāns,* and not on the verb as such.

defend all Gaul from the outrages of Ariovistus.	trādūcātur, *may be led across,*	Galliamque *Gaul and,*	omnem *all*	ab *from*	Ariovistī 90 *Ariovistus'*
	iniūriā *wrong*	posse *to be able*	dēfendere. *to defend.*		91

XXXII. On the delivery of this speech by Divitiacus, all who were present began with	XXXII.	Hāc *This*	ōrātiōne *speech*	ab *by*	Divitiacō 1 *Divitiacus*
	habitā *having been made*	omnēs, *all,*	quī *who*	aderant, *were near,*	māgnō 2 *with great*

LINE 90. **trādūcātur**, 3d pers. sing. pres. subjunctive pass. of the act. verb *trādūcō*; agrees with its subject-nom. *multitūdō*; it is a subjective of *negative* purpose after the particle *nē*. See A. & G. 317; B. 200, (*b*); G. 548, NOTE 1; H. 497, I. —— **Galliamque**; *Galliam*, acc. sing. f.; direct obj. of *dēfendere*. *que*, enclitic conj. —— **omnem**, acc. sing. f.; attributive of the noun *Galliam*. —— **ab**, prep. with the abl. —— **Ariovistī**, gen. sing. m.; limits the noun *iniūriā*.

LINE 91. **iniūriā**, abl. of *iniūria*, *-ae*, f. (in + iūs); obj. of the prep. *ab*. See A. & G. 152, *b*; B. 120, 2; G. 417, 1; H. 434. —— **posse**, pres. inf. of the irr. intrans. verb *possum*; its subject-acc. is *eum*, i.e. *Caesarem*. —— **dēfendere**, pres. inf. act. of the finite verb *dēfendō*, 3; complementary inf., depending on *posse*. Consult A. & G. 271; B. 181; G. 423; H. 533, I, 2. The *ōrātiō rēcta* of lines 74–91: *Homō est barbarus, īrācundus, temerārius;* nōn *possumus* ēius imperia diūtius sustinēre. Nisi sī quid in *tē*, Caesare, populōque Rōmānō sit auxiliī, omnibus Gallīs idem *est* faciendum, quod Helvētiī *fēcērunt*, ut domō ēmigrent, aliud domicilium, aliās sēdēs, remōtās ā Germānīs, petant fortūnamque, quaecumque accidat, experiantur. Haec sī ēnūntiāta Ariovistō sint, *nōs* nōn *dubitāmus*, quīn dē omnibus obsidibus, quī apud eum sint, gravissimum supplicium sūmat. *Tū, Caesar,* vel auctōritāte *tuā* atque exercitūs vel recentī victōriā vel nōmine populī Rōmānī dēterrēre *potes*, nē māior multitūdō Germānōrum Rhēnum trādūcātur, Galliamque omnem ab Ariovistī iniūriā *potes* dēfendere.

LINE 1. **Hāc**, abl. sing. f. (*hīc, haec, hōc*); an attributive of the noun *ōrātiōne*. —— **ōrātiōne**, abl. sing. of *ōrātiō, -ōnis*, f.; abl. absolute with the perf. pass. participle *habitā*. Consult A. & G. 255, *d*; B. 172 and 192; G. 409, 410; H. 431, 2. Synonyms: *ōrātiō* = the premeditated and rhetorically polished *speech*; whereas *sermō* = continued conversation — *an unartistic* and *an extempore talk*. —— **ab**, prep. with the abl. (l. 5, Chap. I). —— **Divitiacō**, abl. of *Divitiacus, -ī,* m.; the agent. See A. & G. 246; B. 108, 2, and 166; G. 401; H. 388, 2, and 415, 1. For description of this man, see l. 20, Chap. III.

LINE 2. **habitā**, abl. sing. f. of the perf. pass. participle *habitus, -a, -um* of the verb *habeō*, 2; pass. parts: *habeor, -ērī, -itus;* abl. absolute with *ōrātiōne*. —— **omnēs**, nom. plur. of the adj. *omnis, -e*, an *ī*-stem, abl. *omnī;* used substantively; subject-nom. of the verb *coepērunt*. —— **quī**, nom. plur. m. (*quī, quae, quod*). *quī* refers to *omnēs;* subject-nom. of the verb *aderant*. —— **aderant**, 3d pers. plur. imperf. ind. of *adsum, adesse, affuī;* frequently written *assum;* assimilation. *aderant* agrees with its subject-nom. *quī*. —— **māgnō**, abl. sing. m. of the adj. *māgnus, -a, -um;* an attributive of the noun *flētū*.

3	flētū	auxilium	ā	Caesare	petere	coepērunt.	loud lamentation to ask Caesar for help. Caesar noticed that the Sequani alone of all made no such outcries as the rest, but sadly with bowed heads kept looking on the
	weeping	*aid*	*from*	*Caesar*	*to ask*	*began.*	
4	Animadvertit	Caesar	ūnōs	ex	omnibus		
	Observes	*Caesar*	*alone*	*of*	*all*		
5	Sēquanōs	nihil	eārum	rērum	facere,	quās	
	the Sequani	*nothing*	*of those*	*things*	*to do,*	*which*	
6	cēterī	facerent,	sed	tristēs,		capite	
	the others	*were doing,*	*but*	*sad,*		*the head*	

LINE 3. **flētū**, abl. sing. of *flētus, -ūs*, m. (*flēre*, to weep); an abl. *of manner.* See A. & G. 248; B. 168; G. 399; H. 419, III. —— **auxilium**, acc. sing. of *auxilium, -iī*, n. (*augēre*, to increase); direct obj. of the verb *petere*. —— **ā**, prep. with the abl. (l. 6, Chap. I). —— **Caesare**, abl. of *Caesar, -aris*, m.; obj. of the prep. *ā*; the usual construction after *petere*, instead of a second acc. Consult A. & G. 239, *c*, NOTE 1; B. 151, REM. 2; G. 339, REM. 1 and NOTE 2; H. 374, 2, NOTE 4. —— **petere**, pres. inf. act. of *petō, -ere, -īvī (-iī), -ītum*, 3; complementary inf. depending on *coepērunt*. See A. & G. 271; B. 181; G. 423; H. 533, I, 1. —— **coepērunt**, 3d pers. plur. perf. ind. act. of the defective *coepī, coepisse*, fut. participle *coeptūrus*; a preteritive verb. Consult A. & G. 143, *a*; B. 113; G. 175, 5; H. 297. *coepērunt* agrees with its subject-nom. *omnēs*, above.

LINE 4. **Animadvertit**, 3d pers. sing. of the perf. ind. act. of *animadvertō, -ere, -vertī, -versum*, 3 (*animus* + *ad* + *vertere* = lit. *to turn the mind to*); agrees with the subject-nom. *Caesar*, expressed. The component parts are frequently written separately. See l. 1, Chap. XXIV. —— **Caesar**, subject-nom. of the verb preceding it. Observe its emphatic position. —— **ūnōs**, acc. plur. m. of the cardinal num. adj. *ūnus* (l. 1, Chap. I); agrees with *Sēquanōs*, and is essentially predicative; and = *sōlōs* here. —— **ex**, prep. with the abl. —— **omnibus**, abl. plur. of *omnis, -e*, used substantively; obj. of the prep. *ex*. The construction is equivalent to the partitive gen. (*ūnā ex parte*, lines 10, 11, Chap. II). Consult A. & G. 216, *c*; B. 134, REM. 2; G. 372, 2; H. 397, 3, NOTE 3.

LINE 5. **Sēquanōs**, acc. plur. of *Sēquanī, -ōrum*, m.; subject-acc. of the inf. *facere* (l. 25, Chap. I). —— **nihil**, an indecl. neuter noun, used only in the nom. and acc. cases; direct obj. of *facere*. —— **eārum**, gen. plur. f. (*is, ea, id*); an attributive of *rērum*. —— **rērum**, gen. plur. (*rēs, reī*, f.); partitive gen. after *nihil*. See A. & G. 216, *a*, 1; B. 134; G. 369; H. 397, 1. The allusion here is to their entreaties and tears. —— **facere**, pres. inf. act. of *faciō*, 3; its subject-acc. is *Sēquanōs*. —— **quās**, acc. plur. f. (*quī, quae, quod*). *quās* refers to *rērum*; is the direct obj. of *facerent*.

LINE 6. **cēterī**, nom. plur. m. of the adj. *cēterus, -a, -um*; used in the text as a subst.; subject-nom. of *facerent*. Synonyms: *cēterī*, frequently written *caeterī* = *others* in opposition to those first mentioned, compare GK. οἱ ἄλλοι; whereas *aliī* = *others* as merely differential from those mentioned; and *reliquī* = *the rest, the remainder* that completes the whole. —— **facerent**, 3d pers. plur. imp. subjunctive of *faciō*, 3; its subj. is *cēterī*; in the subjunctive, because a clause *of characteristic*. See A. & G. 320; B. 234, 1; G. 631, 1; H. 503, 1. —— **sed**, adversative conj. — stronger than *autem* or *at*. —— **tristēs**, acc. plur. of *tristis, -e*, an *ī*-stem; abl. *tristī*; agrees with *eōs*, i.e. *Sēquanōs*, the omitted subject-acc. of *intuērī*. Observe that in use here *tristēs* = *tristē*, an adv. Consult A. & G. 191; B. 128, REM. 10; G. 325, 6; H. 443. —— **capite**, abl. sing. of *caput, -itis*, n.; abl. absolute with *dēmissō*, denoting *manner*.

ground. He wondered at this procedure and inquired of them personally as to the cause. The Sequani answered not at all, but silently continued in the same sad mood.	dēmīssō, *being cast down,*	terram *the earth*	intuērī. *to look on (began).*	Eius *Of this* 7
	reī *thing* quae *what*	causa *the cause*	esset, *was,*	mīrātus *wondering* ex *from* 8
	ipsīs *themselves*	quaesiit. *he sought.*	Nihil *Nothing*	Sēquanī respondēre, *the Sequani responded,* 9
	sed *but* in *in*	eādem *the same*	tristitiā *sadness*	tacitī permanēre. *silent they remained.* 10

LINE 7. **dēmīssō**, abl. sing. n. of the perf. pass. participle *dēmīssus, -a, -um* of the verb *dēmittō, -ere, -mīsī, -missum*, 3 (dē + mittere, lit. *to send down*); abl. absolute with *capite*. See A. & G. 255; B. 192; G. 409, 410; H. 431. —— **terram**, acc. sing. of *terra, -ae*, f.; direct obj. of the deponent inf. *intuērī*. Synonyms: *terra = the earth* in opposition to the sky; whereas *solum = the earth* as a solid, basilar foundation. —— **intuērī**, pres. inf. of the deponent verb *intueor, -ērī, intuitus*, 2; subject-acc. is *eōs*, i.e. *Helvētiōs* understood. —— **Eius**, gen. sing. f. (*is, ea, id*); an attributive of the noun *reī*.

LINE 8. **reī**, gen. sing. (*rēs, reī*, f.); limits, as a gen., the noun *causa*. —— **quae**, nom. sing. f. of the interrogative pron. *quis, quae, quid*; predicate-nom. after *esset*. —— **causa**, nom. sing. of *causa, -ae*, f.; subject-nom. of *esset*. —— **esset**, 3d pers. imperf. subjunctive of *sum, esse, fui*, fut. participle *futūrus*; agrees with its subject-nom. *causa*, and is in the subjunctive, because the *question is indirect*. See A. & G. 334; B. 242; G. 467; H. 529, I. —— **mīrātus**, nom. sing. of the perf. participle *mīrātus, -a, -um* of the deponent verb *mīror*, 1; as a participle it agrees with the subject *Caesar*, to be supplied. —— **ex**, prep. with the abl. (l. 11, Chap. II).

LINE 9. **ipsīs**, abl. plur. (*ipse, ipsa, ipsum*); obj. of the prep. *ex;* observe that it is here used as an emphatic pron. of the 3d pers.; consult A. & G. 195, *g;* B. 85, REM. 2; G. 311, 2; H. 448. Observe, too, that *ipsīs* is reflexive; that the phrase *ex ipsīs* is more emphatic than either *ex eīs* or *ex hīs;* and that *ex sē* here is inadmissible on account of ambiguity. —— **quaesiit**, 3d pers. sing. perf. ind. act. of *quaerō, -ere, -sīvī (-iī), -sītum*, 3; agrees with the omitted subject-nom. *Caesar*. As to the omission of *v* in the perf. without contraction, see A. & G. 128, 2; B. 251; G. 131, 2; H. 235, I. Observe that *quaerō*, as a verb of asking, takes the abl. of the person with the prepositions *ab, dē* or *ex*. See A. & G. 239, 2. *c*, NOTE 1; B. 151, REM. 2; G. 339, REM. 1; H. 374, 2, NOTE 4, end. Observe also that the indirect question *quae causa esset* is, as a noun-clause, the acc. *of the thing* after *quaesiit*. —— **Nihil**, indecl. noun, used only in the nom. and acc. cases; direct obj. of the verb *respondēre*. —— **Sēquanī**, nom. plur. of the adj. *Sēquānus, -a, -um*, used as a subst.; subject-nom. of the historical inf. *respondēre*. See note on *Sēquanīs*, l. 25, Chap. I. —— **respondēre**, pres. inf. act. of *respondeō, -ēre, -spondī, -spōnsum*, 2. Observe that the historical inf. in use = the imperf. ind., and has its subj. in the nom. case. Consult A. & G. 275; B. 182; G. 647; H. 536, 1.

LINE 10. **sed**, adversative conj.; see l. 6, above. —— **in**, prep. with acc. or abl.; here it takes the abl. —— **eādem**, abl. sing. f. of the iterative dem. pron. *īdem, eadem, idem* (is + dem); an attributive of the noun *tristitiā*. —— **tristitiā**, abl. sing. of *tristitia, -ae*, f. (*tristis*, sad); obj. of the prep. *in*. —— **tacitī**, nom. plur. m. of the perf. pass. participle *tacitus, -a, -um* of the verb *taceō*, 2; used here as an adj.; it agrees with *eī*, i.e. *Sēquanī*, the omitted subject-nom. of the historical inf. *permanēre*.

BOOK I. 251

11 Cum	ab	hīs	saepius	quaereret	neque	When Caesar had repeatedly inquired the reason, and could elicit no answer at all from them, Divitiacus the Aeduan, the same speaker as before, replied: The condition of the
When	*from*	*them*	*rather often*	*he sought*	*not and,*	
12 ūllam	omnīnō	vōcem	exprimere		posset,	
any	*at all*	*voice*	*to extort*		*was able,*	
13 īdem		Divitiacus		Aeduus	respondit:	
the same		*Divitiacus*		*the Aeduan*	*responded:*	
14 Hōc	esse	miseriōrem	et		graviōrem	
In this respect	*to be*	*more miserable*	*and*		*more grievous*	

Observe that *tacitī*, like *tristēs*, l. 6, above, is used adverbially. See grammatical references to *tristēs*. —— permanēre, pres. inf., historical, of *permaneō, -ēre, -mānsī, -mānsum,* 2 (per + manēre, lit. *to remain through*); its subject-nom. is *eī*, i.e. *Sēquanī*, understood.

LINE 11. Cum (collateral forms *quom, quum, qum* rare), conj. —— ab, prep. with the abl. —— hīs, abl. plur. m. (*hīc, haec, hōc*); used as a personal pron. of the 3d pers.; obj. of the prep. *ab*. With *ab hīs* compare *ex ipsīs*, lines 8 and 9, above. —— saepius, adv., comparative degree of positive *saepe*; superl. degree *saepissimē*. Observe that the comparative degree in the text, and often elsewhere, seems to be used in the sense of the positive. —— quaereret, 3d pers. sing. imperf. subjunctive of *quaerō, -ere, -sīvī (-iī), -sītum,* 3; agrees with its subject-nom. *Caesar* understood; in the subjunctive mode after *cum* temporal or historical. Consult A. & G. 325; B. 222; G. 585; H. 521, II, 2. But note that the *cum*-clause denotes both time and cause. —— neque (ne + que), a conjunctive adv., and = *and not*. The *que* connects the clauses; the *nē*, as an adv., modifies the adj. *ūllam*.

LINE 12. ūllam, acc. sing. f. of *ūllus, -a, -um*; gen. *ūllīus*; dat. *ūllī*. Observe that this adj. is used in negative clauses; consult A. & G. 202, *b, c*; B. 56, 4, for decl.; G. 317, 1; H. 457; an attributive of the noun *vocem*. —— omnīnō (*omnis*, all), adv.; modifies *exprimere*. —— vōcem, acc. sing. of *vōx, vōcis*, f.; direct obj. of *exprimere*. Synonyms: *vōx* = *a word* with reference to its sound or form; whereas *verbum* = *a word* with reference to its meaning or use. —— exprimere, pres. inf. act. of *exprimō, -ere, -pressī, -pressum,* 3 (ex + primere) = lit. *to press out*; hence *to express* or *extort*; complementary inf., depending on *posset*. See A. & G. 271; B. 181; G. 423; H. 533, I, 2. —— posset, 3d pers. sing. imperf. subjunctive of *possum, posse, potuī* (potis, *able* + sum); agrees with a pron. implied in the ending as its subject-nom., referring to Caesar; connected by the conj. *neque* with *quaereret*, and in the subjunctive mode for the same reason.

LINE 13. īdem, nom. sing. m. of the iterative dem. pron. *īdem, eadem, idem*; an attributive of *Divitiacus*. —— Divitiacus, nom. sing.; the subject-nom. of *respondit*. —— Aeduus, nom. sing. m. of the adj. *Aeduus, -a, -um*, used as a noun-appositive. See note on *Aeduō*, l. 20, Chap. III. —— respondit, 3d pers. sing. perf. ind. act. of *respondeō, -ēre, -spondī, -spōnsum,* 2 (re + spondere = *to promise* a thing *in return*); agrees with subject-nom. *Divitiacus*.

LINE 14. Hōc, abl. sing. n. (*hīc, haec, hōc*); gen. *hūius*; dat. *huic*; is an abl. of *degree of difference* after the comparatives. See A. & G. 250; B. 164; G. 403; H. 423, NOTE 1. *hōc* is the herald of the following *quod*-clause, and might be taken as an abl. *of cause*. —— esse, pres. inf. of *sum, esse, fuī, futūrus*; its subject-acc. is

| Sequani was more wretched and grievous than that of the rest in this respect, because they alone did not even privately dare complain, nor ask for help, | fortūnam *the fortune* quod *because* querī *to complain* | Sēquanōrum *of the Sequani* sōlī *they alone* neque *nor* | quam *than* nē *not* auxilium *assistance* | reliquōrum, 15 *of the rest,* in *in* implōrāre *implore* | occultō *secret* | quidem 16 *even* audērent; 17 *dared;* |

fortūnam. —— **miseriōrem,** acc. sing. f. of the comparative *miserior, -ius;* positive *miser;* superl. *-issimus. miseriōrem* is a predicate-acc. after *esse.* —— **et,** cop. conj.; it connects the adjectives. —— **graviōrem,** acc. sing. f. of the comparative *gravior, -ius;* connected by *et* with *miseriōrem,* and in the same construction; namely, predicate-acc. after *esse.* For the declension of adjectives in the comparative degree, see A. & G. 86; B. 69, 2; G. 89; H. 154, and FOOTNOTE 4.

LINE 15. **fortūnam,** acc. sing. of *fortūna, -ae,* f. (*fors,* chance, from *ferō*); subject-acc. of the intrans. verb *esse.* —— **Sēquanōrum,** gen. plur. of the adj. *Sēquanus, -a, -um,* used substantively; limits *fortūnam.* As to this clan, see note on *Sēquanīs,* l. 25, Chap. I. —— **quam,** conj.; it connects *fortūnam* expressed with *eam,* i.e. *fortūnam* understood. —— **reliquōrum,** gen. plur. m. of the adj. *reliquus, -a, -um,* used substantively; *reliquōrum* as a gen. limits *fortūnam* understood. Dr. Anthon reads here, according to the Oxford MSS., *prae reliquōrum.* According to this lection the pron. *eā* is to be supplied; and the English of the phrase would be: *in comparison with that of the rest.* For synonyms, see note on *cē(ae)terī,* l. 6, above.

LINE 16. **quod,** a conj. = *because.* —— **sōlī,** nom. plur. m. of the adj. *sōlus, -a, -um;* gen. *solīus;* dat. *sōlī. sōlī* as nom. plur. agrees with *eī,* i.e. *Sēquanī,* the omitted subj. of the verb *audērent,* l. 17, below. For list of adjectives declined like *sōlus,* see A. & G. 83; B. 56, 3, 4; G. 76, 1, 2; H. 151. —— **nē,** adv.; modifies *audērent.* —— **in,** prep. with the acc. or abl.; here it takes the abl. —— **occultō,** abl. sing. participle from the verb *occulō, -ere, -luī, occultum,* 3 (ob + colere = *to cover up*). Observe that *in occultō* is an adverbial phrase equivalent to an adv.; that it may be analyzed by supplying the noun *locō* as the obj. of the prep. *in;* and that the phrase stands between the particle *nē* and the restrictive particle *quidem;* but observe carefully that the included phrase is, by its position, emphatic. Consult A. & G. 345, *b,* end; B. 117, 3 (*nē* . . . *quidem*); G. 679; H. 569, III, 2. —— **quidem,** adv., emphasizes the words before it.

LINE 17. **querī,** pres. inf. of the dep. *queror, -ī, questus,* 3; complementary inf. here, depending on *audērent.* Observe that *querī,* which = *to complain,* is both trans. and intrans.; that it is sometimes followed by the dat.; sometimes is used with the prepositions *apud, cum* and *dē* with their appropriate cases; and is sometimes, as in the text, used absolutely. —— **neque** (nē + que), adv., used as a correlative to *nē* . . . *quidem;* hence = *nor.* —— **auxilium,** acc. sing. of *auxilium, -iī,* n.; direct obj. of the inf. *implōrāre.* —— **implōrāre,** pres. inf. of *implōrō,* 1 (in + plorāre); hence *implōrāre* = lit. *to call to one;* connected by the conjunctive adv. *neque* with the verb *querī,* and is in the same construction; viz. complementary inf. —— **audērent,** 3d pers. plur. imperf. subjunctive of *audeō, -ēre, ausus,* 2; neuter, pass., or semi-deponent; agrees with *Sēquanī* understood; in the subjunctive, because in a subordinate clause in the *ōrātiō oblīqua.*

18 absentisque	Ariovistī	crūdēlitātem,	velut	sī	and shuddered at the cruelty of Ariovistus when absent as if he were personally present; because, to the rest at any rate, an opportunity of flight was given; but the Sequani, who
absent and,	Ariovistus'	cruelty,	even as	if	
19 cōram	adesset,	horrērent,		proptereā	
personally	he were present,	they shuddered at,		for this reason	
20 quod	reliquīs	tamen	fugae	facultās	
because	to the rest	still	flight's	opportunity	
21 darētur,	Sēquanīs	vērō,	quī	intrā	
was given,	by the Sequani	but,	who	within	

LINE 18. absentisque (absentis + que). *absentis* is the gen. sing. m. of the adj. *absens, absentis;* properly a pres. participle of *abesse;* used, however, as a participle, agreeing with *Ariovistī.* *que,* enclitic conj.; connects the clauses very closely. —— Ariovistī, gen. sing. (*Ariovistus, -ī,* m.); a possessive gen.; limits the noun *crūdēlitātem.* —— crūdēlitātem, acc. sing. of *crūdēlitās, -ātis,* f. (*crūdēlis*); direct obj. of *horrērent.* —— velut (vel + ut), adv. =*just as;* observe that *vel* in the compound is taken in its complete sense of *or even.* —— sī, a conditional conj.; and with *velut* =*just as if.*

LINE 19. cōram, adv. (derivation dubious, possibly from *ōs, ōris,* with the prefix *con,* hence with the face, i.e. *with the person, personally*). *cōram* emphasizes the idea of nearness contained in the prep. *ad* of the compound *adesset.* —— adesset, 3d pers. sing. of *adsum, adesse, ad(af)fuī;* agrees with the subject-nom. *Ariovistus* understood; in the subjunctive after the conj. *sī* in the protasis. Consult A. & G. 304, a; B. 204, 2; G. 590; H. 507, III. Observe that the apodosis is understood. The complete condition and conclusion: *velut facerent, sī cōram adesset.* —— horrērent, 3d pers. plur. imperf. subjunctive act. of *horreō, -ēre, -uī,* no supine, 2; agrees with *Sēquanī* understood; connected by the enclitic *que* appended to *absentis* with *audērent,* and is in the subjunctive for the same reason, i.e. in a subordinate clause in the *ōrātiō oblīqua.* —— proptereā (propter + eā), adv.; the herald of the following *quod*-clause; compare *hōc,* l. 14, above.

LINE 20. quod, conj. = *because;* but see note on *quod,* l. 16, above. —— reliquīs, dat. plur. of adj. *reliquus, -a, -um,* used substantively; indirect obj. after the pass. *darētur.* Consult A. & G. 225, 3, *e;* H. 140; G. 345 *Passive Form;* H. 384, I (synonyms, see l. 6, above). —— tamen, adv.; used to oppose some concession either expressed or implied; here *tamen* = *still, at any rate.* The concession implied here may be expressed thus: *proptered quod quae cum its sint, tamen,* etc. = *because, though these things are so, yet,* etc. —— fugae, gen. sing. of *fuga, -ae,* f. (Gk. φυγή); limits *facultās.* —— facultās, nom. sing. of *facultās, -ātis,* f. (*facilis* [*facere*]); hence *facultās* = lit. *the capacity of doing anything easily;* it, in the text = *opportunity;* sometimes, transf. *facultās* = *cōpia. facultās* is the subject-nom. of *darētur.*

LINE 21. darētur, 3d pers. sing. imperf. subjunctive pass. of *dō, dare, dedī, datum,* 1; pass. parts: *dor, darī, datus;* agrees with its subject-nom. *facultās;* in the subjunctive, because in a subordinate clause in the *ōrātiō oblīqua.* Observe that *a* is short before *re,* pres. inf. act., by exception. —— Sēquanīs, dat. plur. of the adj. *Sēquanus, -a, -um,* used as a noun; dat. of the *apparent agent* after *essent perferendī* (*perferendī essent*), l. 24, below. Consult A. & G. 232; B. 148; G. 215, 2, and 355; H. 388. See note on *Sēquanīs,* l. 25, Chap. I. —— vērō (*vērus,* true), conj. = lit. *in truth;* but frequently used to mark a transition, and = *but;* not so strong

had received A-
riovistus within
their borders, all
of whose towns
were in his pow-
er, must endure
every species of
torture.

fīnēs	suōs	Ariovistum	recēpissent,	22
the territories	their,	Ariovistus	had received,	
quōrum	oppida	omnia	in potestāte	ēius 23
whose	towns	all,	in the power	of him
essent,	omnēs	cruciātūs	essent perferendī.	24
were,	all	tortures	had to be endured.	

XXXIII. On
receiving this in-
formation, Cae-

XXXIII. Hīs rēbus cōgnitīs 1
These things having been ascertained,

an adversative as *vērum*. —— **quī**, nom. plur. m. (*quī, quae, quod*); refers to *Sēquanīs*; but is subject-nom. of *recēpissent*. —— **intrā** (contracted from *interā*, supply *parte*). *intrā* is either an adv. or prep.; here it is a prep. with the acc. .

LINE 22. **fīnēs**, acc. plur. of *fīnis, fīnis*, m.; obj. of the prep. *intrā*. See synonyms on *agrum*, l. 12, Chap. II. —— **suōs**, acc. plur. of the poss. and reflexive pron. *suus, -a, -um*; an attributive of the noun *fīnēs*. Observe that *suōs* refers to the noun *Sēquanīs*, the logical, though not the grammatical, subj. of the leading proposition. Consult A. & G. 196, 2; B. 80, REM. 2; G. 309, 2, and 521, 2; H. 449, 1, 2. —— **Ariovistum**, acc. sing. of *Ariovistus, -ī*, m.; direct obj. of the verb *recēpissent*. As to this personage, see note, l. 51, Chap. XXXI. —— **recēpissent**, 3d pers. plur. pluperf. subjunctive of *recipiō, -ere, -cēpī, -ceptum*, 3; agrees with its subject-nom. *quī*; in the subjunctive mode, because in a dependent clause in the *ōrātiō oblīqua*.

LINE 23. **quōrum**, gen. plur. (*quī, quae, quod*); refers to *Sēquanīs*; as a poss. gen. it limits *oppida*. —— **oppida**, nom. plur. of *oppidum, -ī*, n.; subject-nom. of the intrans. verb *essent*. —— **omnia**, nom. plur. n. of the adj. *omnis, -e*; an attributive of *oppida*. —— **in**, prep. with either the acc. or abl.; here it takes the abl. For the different significations, see note on *in*, l. 1, Chap. I. —— **potestāte**, abl. sing. of *potestās, -ātis*, f. (*posse* [potis + esse, *to be able*]). For synonyms, see note on *potentiae*, l. 25, Chap. XVIII; obj. of the prep. *in*. —— **ēius**, gen. sing. (*is, ea, id*); used as a personal pron. of the 3d pers.; it limits *potestāte*; as a pron. it = *his*, i.e. Ariovistus'.

LINE 24. **essent**, 3d pers. plur. imperf. subjunctive of *sum, esse, fuī, futūrus*; agrees with its subject-nom. *oppida*; in the subjunctive, because in a subordinate clause in the *ōrātiō oblīqua*. —— **omnēs**, nom. plur. m. of the adj. *omnis, -e*; an *i*-stem; abl. sing. *omnī*; an attributive of *cruciātūs*. —— **cruciātūs**, nom. plur. of *cruciātus, -ūs*, m. (from *crux*, a cross, through *cruciāre*); subject-nom. of *essent perferendī* (*perferendī essent*). —— **essent perferendī** (*perferendī essent*), 3d pers. plur. imperf. subjunctive, second periphrastic conjugation, of the verb *perferō, -ferre, -tulī, -lātum* (per + ferō). *essent perferendī* is connected by the conj. *vērō* with the clause ending with *darētur*; in the subjunctive, because the statement is made on the authority not of Caesar, but of Divitiacus. The *ōrātiō rēcta* of lines 14-24: Hōc est miserior et gravior fortūna Sēquanōrum quam reliquōrum, quod sōlī nē in occultō quidem querī neque auxilium implōrāre *audent*; absentisque Ariovistī crūdēlitātem, velut sī cōram *adsit, horrent*, proptereā quod reliquīs tamen fugae facultās *datur*, Sēquanīs vērō, quī intrā fīnēs suōs Ariovistum *recēpērunt*, quōrum oppida omnia in potestāte ēius *sunt*, omnēs cruciātūs *sunt* perferendī.

LINE 1. **Hīs**, abl. plur. f. of the dem. pron. *hīc, haec, hōc*; gen. *huius*; dat. *huic*; an attributive of *rēbus*. —— **rēbus**, abl. plur. (*rēs, reī,* f.); abl. absolute with the perf. pass. participle, denoting *time*. Consult A. & G. 255; B. 192; G. 409, 410;

2 Caesar	Gallōrum	animōs	verbīs	cōnfīrmāvit		sar comforted the minds of the Gauls by his remarks, and promised to give the matter his attention; saying that he had great hopes that Ario-
Caesar	*the Gauls'*	*minds*	*with words*	*encouraged,*		
3 pollicitusque	est,	sibi	eam	rem	cūrae	
promised	*and,*	*to himself*	*this*	*thing*	*for a care*	
4 futūram;	māgnam	sē	habēre	spem,	et	
about to be;	*great*	*himself*	*to have*	*hope,*	*both*	

H. 431, 2. —— cōgnitīs, abl. plur. f. of the perf. pass. participle *cōgnitus, -a, -um* of *cōgnōscō, -ere, -nōvī, cōgnitum,* 3 (con [cum] + [g]nōscere); abl. absolute with the noun *rēbus*. Observe that in this construction the participle agrees with the noun in gender, number and case.

LINE 2. Caesar, -aris, m., subject-nom. of *cōnfīrmāvit*. —— Gallōrum, gen. plur. of the adj. *Gallus, -a, -um,* used substantively; poss. gen., limiting *animōs*. See note on *Gallī*, l. 4, Chap. I. —— animōs, acc. plur. of *animus, -ī,* m.; direct obj. of *cōnfīrmāvit*. Synonyms: *animus = the soul* as a psychological and ethical personality; *anima = the soul* as the physiological principle — the principle of animal life, compare GK. $\psi\upsilon\chi\acute{\eta}$; whereas *mēns = the soul* as the thinking faculty. *animus*, however, as the most comprehensive term = *the soul* with all its faculties. —— verbīs, abl. plur. of *verbum, -ī,* n. (compare GK. $\dot{\rho}\tilde{\eta}\mu\alpha$ = *that which is spoken*). Compare also the English *verb* and *word*; an abl. of means. Synonyms: *vocem,* l. 12, Chap. XXXII. —— cōnfīrmāvit, 3d pers. sing. perf. ind. act. of *cōnfīrmō,* 1 (con, intensive + fīrmāre (*fīrmus*); agrees with subject-nom. *Caesar* expressed.

LINE 3. pollicitusque (pollicitus + que). *pollicitus* is in form the pass. participle of the deponent verb *polliceor, -ērī, pollicitus,* 2; in fact, it is a part of the compound formation of the perf. tense *pollicitus est. que,* enclitic conj. Synonyms: *polliceantur,* l. 30, Chap. XIV. —— est, 3d pers. sing. pres. tense of *sum;* part of the form — 3d pers. sing. — perf. tense, deponent verb. —— sibi, dat. sing. of the reflexive pron. *suī, sibi, sē, sē;* refers to Caesar, and is dat. of the obj. *to which* after *futūram* (*esse*). —— eam, acc. sing. f. (*is, ea, id*); an attributive of the noun *rem*. —— rem, acc. sing. of *rēs, reī,* f.; subject-acc. of *futūram* (*esse*); *rem* refers to the hard lot of the Sequani. —— cūrae, dat. sing. of *cūra, -ae,* f. (*quaerō*); hence *cūra* = the troubling one's self about somewhat; dat. *of service* after *futūram* (*esse*). The student will observe that *futūram* (*esse*) takes two datives: *sibi* the object *to which*, and *cūrae*, the end *for which*. Consult A. & G. 233, *a;* B. 147, and REM. 2; G. 356; H. 390.

LINE 4. futūram (esse), fut. inf. of *sum, esse, fuī,* fut. participle *futūrus;* its subject-acc. is the noun *rem*. Observe that the participial part of the formation of this inf. is declined like *bonus, -a, -um;* and that the form *futūram esse* occurs, because the subject-acc. *rem* is feminine. Observe further that verbs of *hope* and *promising* and *undertaking* are generally followed by the fut. inf. —— māgnam, acc. sing. f. of the adj. *māgnus, -a, -um;* comparative degree *māior;* superl. *māximus*. *māgnam* is an attributive of the noun *spem*. —— sē, acc. sing. of the reflexive pron. *suī, sibi, sē, sē; sē* refers to Caesar; it is the subject-acc. of the verb *habēre*. —— habēre, pres. inf. act. of the verb *habeō, -ēre, -uī, -itum,* 2; *habēre* is an inf. in indirect discourse; its subject-acc. is the pron. *sē*. The direct discourse would be either *egō habeō* or *Caesar habet*. —— spem, acc. sing. of *spēs, speī,* f. (stem *spē*, but shortened in the gen. and dat. sing. of *fidēs, rēs* and *spēs; spem* is the direct obj. of the verb *habēre*. —— et ... et, here a species of correlative conjunctions = *both ... and;* let them be translated after the perf pass. participle *adductum*.

| vistus, induced by his former kindness and present influence, would desist from wrong-doing. After delivering this speech — the purport of which is only given here — he dismissed the assembly. — And indeed, after these repre- | beneficiō *by favor* Ariovistum *Ariovistus* ōrātiōne *speech* secundum *after* | suō *his own* fīnem *an end* habitā *having been had,* ea *these (things)* | et *and* iniūriīs *to his wrongs* concilium *the council* multae *many* | auctōritāte *by influence* factūrum. *about to make.* dīmīsit. *he broke up.* rēs *things* | adductum 5 *led* Hāc 6 *This* Et 7 *And* eum 8 *him* |

LINE 5. **beneficiō**, abl. sing. of *beneficium, -ī,* n. (bene + facere); hence *beneficium* = lit. *well-doing;* an abl. of cause after the participle *adductum*. Consult A. & G. 245, and 2, *b*; B. 165, and REM. 4; G. 408, and NOTE 2; II. 416, and NOTE 1. —— **suō**, abl. sing. n. (*suus, -a, -um*); an attributive of the neuter noun *beneficiō*, but refers to Caesar. —— **et**, see note on *et*, preceding line. —— **auctōritāte**, abl. sing. of *auctōritās, -ātis,* f. (from the verb *augēre,* to increase, through the noun *auctor*); connected by the conj. *et* with the noun *beneficiō*, and is also an abl. of cause. —— **adductum**, acc. sing. m. of the perf. pass. participle *adductus, -a, -um* of *addūcō, -ere, -dūxī, -ductum,* 3; agrees with *Ariovistum.*

LINE 6. **Ariovistum**, acc. sing. of *Ariovistus, -ī,* m.; subject-acc. of the inf. *factūrum* (*esse*). —— **fīnem**, acc. sing. of *fīnis, -is,* m.; direct obj. of the inf. *factūrum* (*esse*). —— **iniūriīs**, dat. plur. of *iniūria, -ae,* f. (in, *negative* + *iūs*); dat. of the indirect object. Consult A. & G. 225; B. 141; G. 345; II. 384, II. —— **factūrum (esse)**, fut. inf. act. of *faciō*, 3; its subject-acc. is *Ariovistum;* hence the acc. m. form of the participle is part of this fut. inf. The *ōrātiō rēcta* of lines 4-6: **māgnam egō habeō spem, et beneficiō meō et auctōritāte adductum Ariovistum fīnem iniūriīs factūrum esse**. —— **Hāc**, abl. sing. f. (*hīc, haec, hōc*); gen. *hūius;* dat. *huic;* an attributive of the noun *ōrātiōne.*

LINE 7. **ōrātiōne**, abl. sing. of *ōrātiō, -ōnis,* f.; abl. absolute with the perf. pass. participle *habitā*. Synonyms: *ōrātiōne,* l. 1, Chap. XXII. —— **habitā**, abl. sing. f. of the perf. pass. participle *habitus, -a, -um* of the finite verb *habeō*, 2; abl. absolute with *ōrātiōne,* denoting *time when.* See A. & G. 255, *d.* 1; B. 192; G. 409, 410; II. 431. —— **concilium**, acc. sing. of *concilium, -iī,* n.; direct obj. of *dīmīsit.* Synonyms: *concilium*, l. 5, Chap. XVIII. —— **dīmīsit**, 3d pers. sing. perf. ind. act. of *dīmittō, -ere, -mīsī, -missum,* 5 (dis, an inseparable particle + mittere); hence *dīmittere* = lit. *to send apart;* agrees with *Caesar* understood. —— **Et**, conj.; here it connects the sentences. This use of *et*, standing at the head of the sentence, is not very frequent.

LINE 8. **secundum**, prep. with the acc. (from *sequī,* through the gerundive *secundus* in the participial sense of *following, second, after*). See *secundum,* A. & G. 153; B. 120, 1; G. 416, 24; II. 433. —— **ea**, acc. plur. n. (*is, ea, id*), used substantively; obj. of the prep. *secundum.* Observe that *ea* refers to the arguments of Divitiacus. —— **multae**, nom. plur. f. of the adj. *multus, -a, -um; multae* is an attributive of *rēs.* —— **rēs**, nom. plur. of *rēs, reī,* f. *rēs* is the subject-nom. of the verb *hortābantur.* The phrase *multae rēs* is explained by the *quod*-clause below. ——

BOOK I.

9 hortābantur,	quārē	sibi	eam	rem	sentations, many considerations led him to think that he ought to deliberate on these matters carefully, and undertake their adjustment; especially as he saw that the Aedui, who had often been called brothers and kinsmen by the senate,
urged,	*why*	*by himself*	*this*	*thing*	
10 cōgitandam	et	suscipiendam		putāret;	
to be cogitated	*and*	*to be undertaken*		*he thought;*	
11 imprīmīs,	quod	Aeduōs,		frātrēs	
first of all,	*because*	*the Aedui,*		*brothers*	
12 cōnsanguineōsque		saepenumerō	ā	senātū	
kinsmen and,		*oftentimes*	*by*	*the senate*	

eum, acc. sing. m. (*hīc, haec, hōc*), used substantively, i.e. as a personal pron. of the 3d pers.; refers to Caesar; direct obj. of the deponent verb *hortābantur*.

LINE 9. hortābantur, 3d pers. plur. imperf. ind. of the deponent verb *hortor*, 1; agrees with its subject-nom. *rēs*. —— quārē, adv. (quā + rē); often written *quā rē*, and = *because of which thing*, i.e. *wherefore*. But *quārē* may be taken as equivalent to *ut* here. —— sibi, dat. sing. (*suī, sibi, sē, sē*); dat. of the apparent agent after the gerundives *cōgitandam* and *suscipiendam*. Consult A. & G. 232; B. 148; G. 355; H. 388. —— eam, acc. sing. f. (*is, ea, id*); an attributive of *rem*. —— rem, acc. sing. of *rēs, reī*, f.; subject-acc. of *cōgitandam* (*esse*) and *suscipiendam* (*esse*). The thing referred to is Divitiacus' report of the tyranny of Ariovistus in Gaul.

LINE 10. cōgitandam (esse), pres. inf. of the second periphrastic conjugation, from *cōgitō*, 1 (con + agitāre); hence *cōgitāre* = *to pursue* something quickly with the mind. —— et, cop. conj. (see l. 7, Chap. I). —— suscipiendam (esse), pres. inf. of the pass. periphrastic conjugation, from the act. verb *suscipiō, -ere, -cēpī, -ceptum*, 3 (sub + capere); hence *suscipere* = lit. *to take from beneath*. —— putāret, 3d pers. sing. imperf. subjunctive of *putō*, 1; agrees with *Caesar* understood; subjunctive, because an *indirect question*; A. & G. 334; B. 242; G. 467; H. 529, I; or, perhaps, better as a purpose-clause after *quārē* = *ut*. Consult A. & G. 331; B. 200, REM. 2; G. 546; H. 498, I. Observe that *hortor* is usually followed by *ut* and the subjunctive, or by the acc. with the inf. The construction with *quārē* and the subjunctive is rare.

LINE 11. imprīmīs, adv. (in + the abl. *prīmīs*); hence *imprīmīs* = lit. *among the first things*, i.e. *in the first place, especially;* modifies a verb, to be supplied; possibly *putāvit* in *sibi eam rem suscipiendam putāvit*, which must be conceived as filling a lacuna here in the thought. —— quod, conj. = *because*. —— Aeduōs, acc. plur. of the adj. *Aeduus, -a, -um*, used substantively; subject-acc. of the inf. *tenērī*, l. 14, below. See *Aeduō*, l. 20, Chap. III. —— frātrēs, acc. plur. of *frāter, frātris*, m.; predicate-acc. of the perf. pass. participle *appellātōs*.

LINE 12. cōnsanguineōsque (cōnsanguineōs + que). cōnsanguineōs is the acc. plur. of the adj. *cōnsanguineus, -a, -um* (con + sanguineus); hence the adj. = *with the same blood*. *cōnsanguineōs* is used as a noun, connected closely with the noun *frātrēs* by the enclitic *que*; and in the same grammatical construction. que, enclitic conj. —— saepenumerō (saepe + numerō), adv.; the word might be written thus: *saepe numerō; numerō*, abl. of specification. —— ā, prep. with the abl. *ā* or *ab* usually = *from;* but before the agent after a pass. verb, *ab* = *by*. Synonyms: *dē*,

were held in servitude and kept under the sway of the Germans, and learned that their hostages were with Ariovistus and the Sequani — a condition of things which he thought to be very disgraceful to him—	appellātōs, *having been called,*	in *in*	servitūte *servitude*	atque *and*	in *in*	13
	diciōne *the sway,*	vidēbat *he saw,*	Germānōrum *of the Germans,*		tenērī, *to be held,*	14
	eōrumque *of them and,*	obsidēs *the hostages*	esse *to be*	apud *with*	Ariovistum *Ariovistus*	15
	āc *and*	Sēquanōs *the Sequani*	intellegēbat; *he was aware;*	quod *which*	in *(thing) in*	16

l. 27, Chap. XIX. —— senātū, abl. sing. of *senātus, -ūs*, m. (*senex*, an old man); the obj. of the prep. *ā*. Observe that by the phrase *ā senātū* is meant: by the *persons* comprising the senate.

LINE 13. appellātōs, acc. plur. m. of the perf. pass. participle *ap(d)pellātus, -a, -um*, from *appellō*, 1. Observe that this participle is essentially predicative here in informal indirect discourse, and does not differ essentially from the perf. inf. pass. —— in, prep. with the acc. or abl.; here it takes the abl. See *in*, l. 1, Chap. I. —— servitūte, abl. sing. of *servitūs, -ūtis*, f. (*servus*, a slave); obj. of the prep. *in*. —— atque (ad + que), conj. (l. 10, Chap. I). —— in, note the repetition of the prepositions; repeated, to keep the notions distinct.

LINE 14. diciōne, abl. sing. of *diciō, -ōnis*, f. (often written *ditiō*); derived from *dare*; hence *ditiō* = lit. *a giving up*; obj. of the prep. *in*. Observe that the phrase *in diciōne* = lit. *in the authority*; but in the English idiom the phrase = *under the authority* or *sway*. —— vidēbat, 3d pers. sing. imperf. ind. act. of *videō, -ēre, vīdī, vīsum*, 2; its subject-nom. is *Caesar* understood. Synonyms: *vidēre* = lit. *to see* with the eyes; sometimes, metaphorically = *to perceive* with the understanding, *to consider*; while *intellegere* (*intelligere*) = *to perceive* with the intellect, rarely by the senses. —— Germānōrum, gen. plur. of *Germānī, -ōrum*, m.; limits *servitūte* and *diciōne*. See *Germānīs*, l. 19, Chap. I. —— tenērī, pres. inf. pass. of *teneō, -ēre, -uī, tentum*, 2; subject-acc. is *Aeduōs*, l. 11, above.

LINE 15. eōrumque (eōrum + que). *eōrum*, gen. plur. (*is, ea, id*), used as a personal pron. of the 3d pers. — English poss. case — *their*; limits *obsidēs*. *que*, enclitic conj. —— obsidēs, acc. plur. of *obses, -idis*, m. and f.; subject-acc. of the intrans. verb *esse*. —— esse, pres. inf. of *sum, esse, fuī*, fut. participle *futūrus*; its subject-acc. is the noun *obsidēs*. Observe that *esse* here is not the copula, but a verb of complete predication = *existed* or *lived*. —— apud, prep. with the acc. Observe that, when the object of this prep. is a person, *apud* = *with*, or *at the house of*, etc. —— Ariovistum, acc. sing. of *Ariovistus, -ī*, m.; obj. of the prep. *apud*.

LINE 16. ac, conj.; see *atque*, l. 10, Chap. I. —— Sēquanōs, acc. plur. of the adj. *Sēquanus, -a, -um*, used as a subst.; connected by the conj. *āc* with the noun *Ariovistum*, and in the same grammatical construction. —— intellegēbat, 3d pers. sing. imperf. ind. act. of *intelle(i)gō, -ere, -lēxī, -lectum*, 3; connected by the enclitic conj. *que* with *vidēbat*, and here the same subject-nom., namely *Caesar*, understood. —— quod, acc. sing. n. of *quī, quae, quod*; its antecedent is the idea contained in the preceding accusative-clauses; subject-acc. of the inf. *esse*, l. 18, below. Observe that the relative, when referring to an idea, generally takes *id* before it; but sometimes we find *quod* alone, as in the text. Consult A. & G. 200, *e*, and NOTE; B. 129,

17 tantō	imperiō	populī	Rōmānī	turpissimum		self and to the republic, in so great an empire as that of the Roman people. Moreover, he saw that it was perilous to the Roman people for the Germans to become accustomed gradually to cross the Rhine, and for a
so great	*a dominion*	*of the people*	*Roman*	*most disgraceful*		
18 sibi	et	reī-pūblicae	esse	arbitrābātur.		
to himself	*and*	*to the republic*	*to be*	*he considered.*		
19 Paulātim	autem	Germānōs		cōnsuēscere		
Little by little	*but,*	*the Germans*		*to be accustomed*		
20 Rhēnum	trānsīre	et	in	Galliam	māgnam	
the Rhine	*to cross*	*and*	*into*	*Gaul*	*a great*	

REM. 8; G. 614, 2; H. 445, 7. —— in, prep. with the acc. or abl.; here it takes the abl.; see *in*, l. 1, Chap. I.

LINE 17. **tantō**, abl. sing. n. of the adj. *tantus, -a, -um*; an attributive of the noun *imperiō*. —— **imperiō**, abl. sing. of *imperium, -iī*, n.; obj. of the prep. *in*. Observe that the complete thought may be thus expressed: *in tantō imperiō, quantō in imperiō populī Rōmānī*. —— **populī**, gen. sing. of *populus, -ī*, m.; limits *eō* used substantively or *imperiō* understood. Synonyms: l. 17, Chap. VI. —— **Rōmānī**, gen. sing. m. of *Rōmānus, -a, -um (Rōma)*; an attributive of the noun *populī*. —— **turpissimum**, acc. sing. n. of *turpissimus, -a, -um*; positive degree *turpis*, comp. *-ior*, superl. *-issimus*; predicate-adj. after *esse*.

LINE 18. **sibi**, dat. sing. (*suī, sibi, sē, sē*); dat. of the obj. *to which* after the adj. *turpissimum*. Consult A. & G. 234; B. 144; G. 359; H. 391, I. —— **et**, cop. conj. —— **reī-pūblicae**, dat. sing. of *rēs-pūblica, reī-pūblicae*; connected by the conj. *et* with the pron. *sibi*, and is in the same grammatical construction. Observe that *rēs-pūblica* is a compound noun in which both parts of it are declined. Some treat *rēs* by itself as a noun of the fifth declension; and the latter part of the word as an adj. —— *publicus, -a, -um* —— in agreement with the proper case of the noun. See A. & G. 72; B. 49, REM. 6; G. 63; H. 125, 126. But only B. and H. treat the noun as a compound. —— **esse**, pres. inf. *sum, esse, fuī, futūrus*; its subject-acc. is *quod*, used substantively, l. 16, above. —— **arbitrābātur**, 3d pers. sing. imperf. ind. of the deponent *arbitror*, 1. *arbitrābātur* agrees with a pron. implied in the ending, referring to Caesar. Synonyms: l. 9, Chap. XIX.

LINE 19. **Paulātim**, adv. (*paulum*, a little). Observe that this adv. is formed by changing *o* of the stem to *a*, and adding the adverbial ending *-tim*, which = the English ending *-ly* or *-like*; hence *paulātim* = a *little-like*, or *little by little*. —— **autem**, conj., postpositive; usually adds a different notion without contradiction. —— **Germānōs**, acc. plur. of the proper noun *Germānī, -ōrum*, m.; subject-acc. of the inf. *cōnsuēscere*. See *Germānīs*, l. 19, Chap. I. —— **cōnsuēscere**, pres. inf. act. of *cōnsuēscō, -ere, suēvī, -suētum*, 3 (con [cum], *intensive* + suēscere, *to accustom one's self*); its subject-acc. is *Germānōs*.

LINE 20. **Rhēnum**, acc. sing. of *Rhēnus, -ī*, m.; direct obj. of the inf. *trānsīre*; strictly, however, *flūmen* is the direct obj., and *Rhēnum* is an appositive. See *Rhēnum*, l. 15, Chap. I. —— **trānsīre**, pres. inf. act. of *trānseō, -īre, -īvī (-iī), -itum* (trāns + īre = lit. *to go across*); complementary inf., depending on *cōnsuēscere*. See A. & G. 271; B. 181; G. 423; H. 533, I, 2. —— **et**, cop. conj. —— **in**, prep. with the acc. or abl.; here it takes the acc. —— **Galliam**, acc. sing. of *Gallia, -ae*, f.;

260   CAESAR'S GALLIC WAR   [CHAP. XXXIII.

| large number of them to come into Gaul; and he thought that men wild and barbarous would not restrain themselves, after seizing Gaul, from migrating into the province, and thence hastening | eōrum multitūdinem venīre populō Rōmānō 21 *of them   multitude   to come, to the people   Roman* perīculōsum vidēbat; neque sibi hominēs 22 *dangerous (to be) he saw;   nor on themselves   men* ferōs āc barbarōs temperātūrōs exīstimābat, 23 *wild   and   savage   about to put the curb did he think,* quĭn, cum omnem Galliam occupāvissent, 24 *but that, when   all   Gaul   they had seized,* |

obj. of the prep. *in*. See *Gallia*, l. 1, Chap. I. Observe that the phrase *in Galliam* denotes the end of motion after the verb *venīre*, and that the phrase is an adverb-phrase modifying *venīre*. —— **māgnam**, acc. sing. f. of the adj. *māgnus, -a, -um*; an attributive of the noun *multitūdinem*.

LINE 21. **eōrum**, gen. plur. (*is, ea, id*), used as a personal pron. of the 3d pers.; refers to the Germans; limits the noun *multitūdinem*. —— **multitūdinem**, acc. sing. of *multitūdō, -inis*, f. (*multus*); subject-acc. of the inf. *venīre*. —— **venīre**, pres. inf. act. of *veniō*, 4. Observe that the two accusative and infinitive-clauses — *Germānōs cōnsuēscere Rhēnum trānsīre*, and *in Galliam eōrum multitūdinem venīre* — are themselves, as noun-clauses, the compound subject-accusatives of the verb *esse*, to be supplied. —— **populō**, dat. sing. of *populus, -ī,* m.; dat. *to which* after the adj. *perīculōsum*. See A. & G. 234; B. 144; G. 359; H. 391, I. See *populum*, l. 17, Chap. VI. —— **Rōmānō**, dat. sing. m. of the adj. *Rōmānus, -a, -um (Rōma)*; an attributive of the noun *populō*.

LINE 22. **perīculōsum**, acc. sing. n. of the adj. *perīculōsus, -a, -um (perīculum)*; predicate-adj. after *esse*, to be supplied. Observe that adjectives ending in *-ōsus* denote *fulness*. —— **vidēbat**, 3d pers. sing. imperf. ind. act. of *videō, -ēre, -vīdī, -vīsum*, 2; agrees with *Caesar* understood. See note on *vidēbat*, l. 14, above. —— **neque** (nē + que), conjunctive adv.; English *and not*; but *neque . . . neque*, as correlates = *neither . . . nor*. —— **sibi**, dat. plur. (*suī, sibi, sē, sē*); refers to *hominēs*; in the dat. after the fut. inf. *temperātūrōs (esse)* — a verb signifying here *to command*. A. & G. 227; B. 142; G. 346; H. 385, II, 1. —— **hominēs**, acc. plur. of *homō, -inis*, m. and f.; subject-acc. of the fut. inf. *temperātūrōs (esse)*. See *hominēs*, l. 20, Chap. II.

LINE 23. **ferōs**, acc. plur. m. of adj. *ferus, -a, -um*; limits *hominēs*, but is an essential part of the predicate = *men who are wild*. —— **āc**, conj. See *atque*, l. 10, Chap. I. —— **barbarōs**, acc. plur. m. of adj. *barbarus, -a, -um*; connected by *āc* with *ferōs*, and in the same grammatical construction. The *barbarī*, GK. βάρβαροι, were, originally, those not Hellenes. Even the Romans were so called by others and by themselves in contrast with the Greeks. But from the Augustan age, the Romans applied the epithet to all nations except themselves and the Greeks. —— **temperātūrōs (esse)**, fut. inf. act. of *temperō*, 1 (*tempus*); its subject-acc. is *hominēs*. Observe that *temperāre* with the acc. usually = *to rule*; with the dat., *to refrain from*. —— **existimābat**, 3d pers. sing. imperf. ind. act. of *exīstimō*, 1; it agrees with *Caesar* understood. Synonyms: l. 9, Chap. XIX.

LINE 24. **quĭn** (quī + nē), conj.; after a negative it = *that, but that*. In such constructions the English idiom requires the prep. *from* with the pres. participle. —— **cum**, temporal conj. —— **omnem**, acc. sing. f. of the adj. *omnis, -e*; an attribu-

25 ut	ante	Cimbrī	Teutonīque	fēcissent,	in	into Italy, as the Cimbri and Teutoni had done before, especially as only the Rhone river separated the Sequani from our province; accordingly, he thought that he ought to be prepared to meet these contingences as speed-
as	*before*	*the Cimbri*	*Teutoni and,*	*had done,*	*into*	
26 prōvinciam		exīrent	atque	inde	in	
the province		*they would go forth*	*and*	*thence*	*into*	
27 Italiam		contenderent,		praesertim	cum	
Italy		*they would hasten,*		*especially*	*since*	
28 Sēquanōs	ā	prōvinciā		nostrā	Rhodanus	
the Sequani	*from*	*the province*		*our,*	*the Rhone*	
29 dīvideret;	quibus	rēbus		quam	mātūrrimē	
separated;	*which*	*things*		*as much as*	*the quickest*	

tive of *Galliam*. —— **Galliam**, acc. sing. of *Gallia, -ae*, f.; the direct obj. of *occupāvissent*. —— **occupāvissent**, 3d pers. plur. pluperf. subjunctive of *occupō, -āre, -āvī, -ātum*, 1; it agrees with *Germānī* understood; in the subjunctive after *cum* temporal. See A. & G. 325; B. 222; G. 585; H. 521, II, 2.

LINE 25. **ut**, conj. or adv.; here, an adv., and = *as*. —— **ānte**, prep. or adv.; here an adv. —— **Cimbrī, -ōrum**, m.; the Jutlanders, a German people once inhabiting the Cimbric Chersonese, now Jutland. *Cimbrī* is the subject-nom. of *fēcissent*. The Cimbri and Teutoni overran Transalpine Gaul. Marius defeated the Teutoni at Aquae Sextiae (Aix), in Narbonnensis B.C. 102; and the Cimbri and remnants of the Teutoni were utterly routed by Marius, near Verona, B.C. 101. —— **Teutonīque** (Teutonī + que). *Teutonī, -ōrum*, m. *que*, enclitic conj.; connects *Teutonī* with *Cimbrī*; hence both nouns are in the same construction. —— **fēcissent**, 3d pers. plur. pluperf. subjunctive of *faciō*, 3; agrees with *Cimbrī Teutonīque;* in the subjunctive by attraction. See A. & G. 342; B. 245, (*b*); G. 663; H. 529, II, 1). —— **in**, prep. with the acc. or abl.; here it takes the acc.

LINE 26. **prōvinciam**, acc. of *prōvincia, -ae;* obj. of the prep. *in*. —— **exīrent**, 3d pers. plur. imperf. subjunctive of *exeō, -īre, -īvī (-iī), -itum;* agrees with the pron. *eī*, i.e. *Germānī*, understood; subjunctive of *result* after *quīn*. See *quīn*, l. 27, Chap. III. —— **atque** (ad + que), cop. conj. (l. 10, Chap. I). —— **inde**, adv. (is + de = lit. *from that place*). —— **in**, prep. with acc. or abl.; here it takes the acc.

LINE 27. **Italiam**, acc. sing. of *Italia, -ae*, f.; obj. of the prep. *in*. Observe that the prep. is required before names of countries, after a verb of motion. Consult A. & G. 258, 2, and NOTE 2; B. 154, REM. 3; G. 337, REM. 1; H. 380, I. —— **contenderent**, 3d pers. plur. imperf. subjunctive of *contendō, -ere, contendī, contentum*, 3; connected by the conj. *atque* with *exīrent*, and in the same grammatical construction. See note on *contendunt*, l. 19, Chap. I. —— **praesertim**, adv. (prae + serere = *to join before;* hence = *especially*); modifies *fēcērunt*, or something similar understood. —— **cum**, conj.

LINE 28. **Sēquanōs**, acc. plur. of *Sēquanī, -ōrum*, m.; direct obj. of *dīvideret*. See l. 25, Chap I. —— **ā**, prep with the abl. —— **prōvinciā**, abl. sing. of *prōvincia, -ae*, f.; after the prep. *ā*. —— **nostrā**, abl. sing. f. of the poss. adj. pron. *noster, -tra, -trum;* an attributive of *prōvinciā*. —— **Rhodanus, -ī**, m.; subject-nom. of *dīvideret*. The meaning is that the Rhone only was a very slight barrier against invasion.

LINE 29. **dīvideret**, 3d pers. sing. imperf. subjunctive act. of *dīvidō, -ere, -vīsī, -vīsum*, 3; agrees with *Rhodanus*, and is in the subjunctive after *cum* causal. See

262   CAESAR'S GALLIC WAR   [CHAP. XXXIV.

| ily as possible. Moreover, Ariovistus himself had put on such haughty airs, and had assumed such arrogance that he seemed to be insufferable. | occurrendum *it ought to be hastened to meet,* autem Ariovistus *moreover, Ariovistus* tantam arrogantiam *so great arrogance* nōn vidērētur. *not seemed.* | putābat. *he thought.* tantōs sibi *so great to himself* sūmpserat, *had assumed,* | Ipse 30 *Himself,* spīritūs, 31 *spirits,* ut ferendus 32 *that to be borne* 33 |

A. & G. 326; B. 223; G. 586; H. 517. —— **quibus,** dat. plur. f. (*quī, quae, quod*), used adjectively; it modifies *rēbus.* —— **rēbus,** dat plur. of *rēs, reī,* f.; dat. after the compound *occurrendum (esse).* See A. & G. 228; B. 143; G. 347; H. 386. —— **quam,** adv. = *as.* —— **mātūrrimē,** adv., superl. degree; positive *mātūrē;* comparative *mātūrius;* another form of superl., *mātūrissimē.* Observe that *quam* is a correlative to *tam.* The text fully written would be: *quibus rēbus tam mātūrē quam mātūrrimē sibi occurrendum esse putābat.*

LINE 30. **occurrendum (esse),** pres. inf. of the second periphrastic conjugation. The gerundive of *occurrō, -ere, -currī,* rarely *cucurrī, -cursum,* 3 (ob + currerre = lit. *to run against*) + *esse;* is used impersonally only in the pass. voice; an intrans. verb; the dat. of the agent is understood. Consult A. & G. 146, *d;* B. 115, III; G. 208, 2; H. 301, I. —— **putābat,** 3d pers. sing. imperf. ind. act. of *putō,* 1. *putābat* agrees with *Caesar* understood. Synonyms: l. 9, Chap. XIX. —— **Ipse,** intensive dem. pron., expressed for emphasis. Consult A. & G. 102, *e,* and NOTE; B. 85; G. 311; H. 452.

LINE 31. **autem,** postpositive conj.; here it = *moreover.* —— **Ariovistus, -ī,** m.; subject-nom. of *sūmpserat.* As to this person, see note l. 51, Chap. XXXI. —— **tantōs,** acc. plur. m. of the adj. *tantus, -a, -um;* an attributive of the noun *spīritūs.* —— **sibi,** dat. sing. of the reflexive pron. *suī;* refers to *Ariovistus;* is the indirect obj. after *sūmpserat.* —— **spīritūs,** acc. plur. of *spīritus, -ūs,* m. (*spīrāre,* to breathe); a direct obj. of *sūmpserat.*

LINE 32. **tantam,** acc. sing. f. of the adj. *tantus, -a, -um;* an attributive of the noun *arrogantiam.* —— **arrogantiam,** acc. sing. of *arrogantia, -ae,* f. (from participle *ar(d)rogāns* [ad + rogāre] = *asking for something* not belonging to one); connected with *spīritūs* by *et* understood, and also a direct obj. of *sūmpserat.* —— **sūmpserat,** 3d pers. sing. pluperf. ind. act. of *sūmō, -ere, sūmpsī, sumptum,* 3; agrees with its subject-nom. *Ariovistus* expressed. —— **ut,** ecbatic conj. —— **ferendus (esse),** fut. inf. of the second periphrastic conjugation; the gerundive form is the same as the fut. pass. participle of *ferō, ferre, tulī, lātum* + *esse;* the fut. inf. is complementary, depending on *vidērētur.*

LINE 33. **nōn,** negative adv.; modifies *ferendus (esse).* —— **vidērētur,** 3d pers. sing. imperf. subjunctive pass. of *videor, vidērī, vīsus,* 2. Observe that the pass. *vidērī* = *to be looked on, regarded* in any way; hence = *seem, appear,* like GK. δοκεῖν. This verb in this sense, when used personally, takes often the complementary inf.; when used impersonally, it is followed by the inf. with the acc. *vidērētur* is subjunctive of *result* after *ut.* Consult A. & G. 319, 1, and REM.; B. 201, and REM. 1, (*a*); G. 552; H. 500, II.

1 XXXIV.	Quam-ob-rem		placuit	eī,	ut
	What for, thing		*it pleased*	*him,*	*that*
2 ad	Ariovistum	lēgātōs	mitteret,	quī	ab
to	*Ariovistus*	*legates*	*he should send,*	*who*	*from*
3 eō	postulārent,	utī	aliquem	locum	medium
him	*might demand,*	*that*	*some*	*place*	*middle*
4 utrīusque	colloquiō		dēligeret;		velle
of both	*for a colloquy*		*he should select;*		*to wish*
5 sēsē	dē	rē	pūblicā	et	summīs
himself	*concerning*	*welfare*	*public*	*and*	*supreme*

XXXIV. Wherefore Caesar was determined to send ambassadors to Ariovistus to request him to select some place midway between them for a conference, saying that he wished to confer with him concerning public interests, and matters of

LINE 1. **Quam-ob-rem**, adv., lit. *on account of which thing;* frequently written *Quam ob rem* = *wherefore, therefore,* i.e. that Caesar might have some pretext for subjugating Gaul. —— **placuit**, 3d pers. sing. perf. ind. act. of *placeō, -ēre, -uī, -itum,* 2; impers. —— **eī**, dat. of the dem. pron. *is,* used as a personal pron.; *placuit* is a verb signifying *to please.* A. & G. 227; B. 142; G. 346; H. 385, I. —— **ut**, telic conj. = lit. *that.*

LINE 2. **ad**, prep. with the acc. —— **Ariovistum**, acc. sing. of *Ariovistus, -ī,* m.; obj. of the prep. *ad.* The location of Ariovistus at this juncture was on the Rhine, near the modern Strasburg. —— **lēgātōs**, acc. plur. of *lēgātus, -ī,* m.; direct obj. of *mitteret.* —— **mitteret**, 3d pers. sing. imperf. subjunctive of *mittō,* 3; subjunctive *of purpose* after *ut.* Observe that *ut . . . mitteret,* as a noun-clause, is the subj. of *placuit.* —— **quī**, nom. plur. m. (*quī, quae, quod*); subj. of *postulārent.* —— **ab**, prep. with the abl.

LINE 3. **eō**, abl. sing. m. (*is, ea, id*); used as a pron. of the 3d person. *eō* is the obj. of the prep. *ab.* For *ab eō* after *postulō,* see A. & G. 239, *c,* NOTE 1; B. 151, REM. 2; G. 339, REM. 1, and NOTE 2; H. 374, NOTE 4. —— **postulārent**, 3d pers. plur. imperf. subjunctive of *postulō,* 1; agrees with *eī* as subject-nom., referring to *lēgātōs;* subjunctive *of purpose* after the rel. *quī.* —— **utī**, original form of *ut.* —— **aliquem**, acc. sing. m. of indef. pron. *aliquis, -qua, -quod,* adj., but *aliquis, -quid,* subst.; an attributive of *locum.* —— **locum**, acc. sing. of *locus,* m.; direct obj. of *dēligeret;* but see *locī,* l. 10, Chap. II. —— **medium**, acc. sing. m. of adj. *medius, -a, -um;* it, too, is an attributive of *locum;* but see note on *mediō,* l. 5, Chap. XXIV.

LINE 4. **utrīusque**, gen. sing. of the pron. *uterque, utraque, utrumque;* partitive gen. after *medium.* A. & G. 216, 3; B. 134, REM. 1; G. 369; H. 397, 3. Observe that *uterque* = *one of two* or *both.* —— **col(n)loquiō**, dat. *of purpose* of *col(n)loquium, -ī,* n. A. & G. 233, *b;* B. 147, REM. 1; G. 356, NOTE 1; H. 390, II. —— **dēligeret**, 3d pers. sing. imperf. subjunctive of *dēligō, -ere, -lēgī, -lectum,* 3; subjunctive *of purpose* after *utī.* —— **velle**, pres. inf. act. of *volō, voluī,* irr. The reader will note that the form of discourse in this sentence is indirect.

LINE 5. **sēsē**, reduplicated for *sē,* acc. sing. of *suī;* and subject-acc. of inf. *velle.* —— **dē**, prep. with the abl. Synonyms: l. 27, Chap. XIX. —— **rē**, abl. f. (*rēs, reī*); obj. of the prep. *dē.* —— **pūblicā**, abl. sing. f. of adj. *pūblicus, -a, -um;* an attributive of *rē.* —— **et**, cop. conj.; connects *rē* and *rēbus.* —— **summīs**, abl. plur. f. of *summus, -a, -um* (see *summō,* l. 20, Chap. XVI); *summīs* modifies *rēbus.*

264   CAESAR'S GALLIC WAR   [CHAP. XXXIV.

the greatest im-	utrīusque	rēbus	cum	eō	agere.	Eī	6
portance to both.	*to both,*	*affairs*	*with*	*him*	*to treat.*	*To this*	
To these ambas-	lēgātiōnī	Ariovistus	respondit:		Sī	quid	7
sadors Ariovis-	*legation*	*Ariovistus*	*responded:*		*If*	*anything*	
tus replied, say-							
ing that if he							
had needed any-	ipsī	ā	Caesare	opus	esset,	sēsē ad	8
thing of Caesar,	*to himself*	*from*	*Caesar*	*need*	*was,*	*himself to*	
he would have							
gone to him; if	eum	ventūrum	fuisse;		sī	quid ille	9
Caesar needed	*him*	*to have been about to come;*		*if*	*anything he*	
anything of him,							
he ought to	sē	velit,	illum	ad	sē	venīre	10
come to him.	*from himself*	*wishes,*	*him*	*to*	*himself*	*to come,*	

LINE 6. **utrīusque** (see l. 4, above); here an objective gen., limiting *rēbus.* —— **rēbus,** abl. plur. of *rēs, reī,* f.; connected by *et* with *rē,* and in the same construction. —— **cum,** prep. with abl. —— **eō,** abl. sing. m. (*is, ea, id*); used as a pron. of the 3d pers.; refers to Ariovistus; obj. of prep. *cum.* —— **agere,** pres. inf. act. of *agō, -ere, ēgī, actum,* 3; complementary of *velle,* l. 4, above. A. & G. 271; B. 181; G. 423; H. 533, I, 1. The *ōrātiō rēcta* of lines 4-6: *Vult Caesar dē rē pūblicā et summīs utrīusque rēbus tēcum agere.* —— **Eī,** dat. of the dem. pron. *is;* modifies *lēgātiōnī.*

LINE 7. **lēgātiōnī,** dat. of the indirect obj. of *lēgātiō, -ōnis,* f. —— **Ariovistus, -ī,** m., subject-nom. of *respondit.* —— **respondit,** 3d pers. sing. perf. ind. act. of *respondeō,* 2. —— **Sī,** conditional conj. —— **quid,** nom. sing. n. of the indef. pron. *quis, quae, quid;* used as a subst., and subject-nom. of *esset;* as an adj. it is declined *quī, quae, quod;* the most common combinations of indefinites are *aliquis, sīquis,* and *num quis.*

LINE 8. **ipsī,** dat. sing. of *ipse, -sa, -sum;* used here as an indirect reflexive pron., referring to Ariovistus. A. & G. 195, *k,* and 196, 2; B. 85, REM. 2; G. 520, 521; H. 452, 5. *ipsī* is dat. of possessor after *esset.* A. & G. 231; B. 146; G. 349; H. 387. —— **ā,** prep. with the abl. —— **Caesare,** abl. of *Caesar, -aris,* m.; obj. of the prep. *ā.* —— **opus,** indecl. neuter noun; predicate after *esset.* A. & G. 243, *e,* REM.; B. 167, 2, REM. 1; G. 406; H. 414, NOTE 4, 1). —— **esset,** 3d pers. sing. imperf. subjunctive of *sum, esse, fuī;* agrees with its subject-nom. *quid;* subjunctive, because in *the condition* after *sī* — *contrary to fact.* —— **sēsē,** reduplicate reflexive pron. for *sē,* referring to Ariovistus; subject-acc. of *ventūrum fuisse.* —— **ad,** prep. with acc.

LINE 9. **eum,** acc. sing. (*is, ea, id*) as a pron. of the 3d pers.; refers to Caesar; obj. of the prep. *ad.* —— **ventūrum fuisse,** perf. inf. of the first periphrastic conjugation, from *veniō, -īre, vēnī, ventum,* 4. As to this form of the inf. in the apodosis of indirect discourse, see A. & G. 337, *b,* 2; B. 244, 4, (3); G. 656, 2; H. 527, III. —— **sī,** see *sī,* l. 7, above. —— **quid,** see *quid,* l. 7, above; direct obj. of *velit.* —— **ille,** dem. pron., refers to Caesar; expressed for emphasis; subj. of *velit.*

LINE 10. **sē,** acc. sing. of pron. *suī;* refers to Ariovistus; an acc. *of secondary object* after *velit,* like a verb *of asking.* —— **velit,** 3d pers. sing. pres. subjunctive of *volō, velle, voluī;* agrees with its subject-nom. *ille* — subjunctive *of condition* after *sī.* —— **illum,** acc. sing. of pron. *ille;* refers to Caesar; subject-acc. of *venīre.* —— **ad,** prep. with the acc. —— **sē,** acc. of *suī, sibī;* refers to Ariovistus; the obj. of the prep. *ad.* —— **venīre,** pres. inf. act. of *veniō,* 4.

11 oportēre.		Praetereā	sē	neque	sine	Besides, he neither dared to go into those parts of Gaul, which Caesar occupied, without an army, nor could he collect his army into one place without great expense and much trouble. Moreover, it seemed strange
to be (it is) *necessary.*		*Moreover,*	*himself*	*neither*	*without*	
12 exercitū	in	eās	partēs	Galliae	venīre	
an army	*into*	*those*	*parts*	*of Gaul*	*to come,*	
13 audēre,	quās	Caesar	possidēret,		neque	
to dare,	*which*	*Caesar*	*possessed,*		*nor*	
14 exercitum	sine	māgnō		commeātū	atque	
an army	*without*	*great* (money)		*supply*	*and*	
15 mōlīmentō	in	ūnum	locum		contrahere	
difficulty	*into*	*one*	*place*		*to bring together*	
16		posse.	Sibi	autem	mīrum	
	(*himself*) *to be able.*		*To himself*	*but,*	*wonderful*	

LINE 11. **oportēre**, pres. inf. of impersonal verb *oportet, -uit;* inf., because in *ōrātiō oblīqua.* Observe that the clause *illum ad sē venīre* is the real subj. of *oportēre.* —— **Praetereā** (praeter + eā), adv. —— **sē**, acc. sing. of reflexive pron. *suī;* refers to Ariovistus; subject-acc. of *audēre.* —— **neque** (nĕ + que, lit. *and not*); but *neque ... neque = neither ... nor.* —— **sine**, prep. with the abl.

LINE 12. **exercitū**, abl. of *exercitus, -ūs,* m.; obj. of prep. *sine.* Synonyms, see l. 31, Chap. III. —— **in**, prep. with acc. or abl. (*in*, l. 1, Chap. I); here *in* has the acc. —— **eās**, acc. plur. f. (*is, ea, id*); an attributive of *partēs.* —— **partēs**, acc. plur. of *pars, -tis,* f. (*partēs,* l. 1, Chap. I); obj. of the prep. *in.* —— **Galliae**, gen. sing. f.; limits *partēs.* See *Galliae,* l. 1, Chap. I. —— **venīre**, pres. inf. act. of *veniō,* 4; complementary; depends on *audēre.*

LINE 13. **audēre**, pres. inf. of *audeō, -ēre, ausus,* n. —— pass. or semi-deponent; inf., because in indirect discourse. —— **quās**, acc. plur. f. of rel. *quī;* refers to *partēs;* direct obj. of *possidēret.* —— **Caesar, -aris,** m., subject-nom. —— **possidēret**, 3d pers. sing. imperf. subjunctive of *possideō, -ēre, -sēdī, -sessum,* 2 (*potis* + *sedēre* = lit. *able to sit tight*); hence *possidēre = to have* and *to hold;* its subj. is *Caesar;* subjunctive mode, because in a subordinate clause in *ōrātiō oblīqua.* —— **neque**, see *neque,* l. 11, above.

LINE 14. **exercitum**, acc. sing. of *exercitus, -ūs,* m.; direct obj. of *contrahere,* l. 15, below. —— **sine**, prep. with the abl. —— **māgnō**, abl. sing. of adj. *māgnus, -a, -um;* it modifies *commeātū.* —— **commeātū**, abl. sing. of *commeātus, -ūs,* m.; obj. of the prep. *sine.* —— **atque**, conj. (see l. 10, Chap. I).

LINE 15. **mōlīmentō**, abl. sing. of *mōlīmentum, -ī,* n.; connected by *atque* with *commeātū,* and in the same construction. —— **in**, prep. with the acc. or abl.; here it takes the acc., and = *into.* See l. 1, Chap. I. —— **ūnum**, acc. sing. m. of the adj. *ūnus.* See l. 2, Chap. I; it modifies *locum.* —— **locum**, acc. sing. of *locus, -ī,* m. See l. 10, Chap. II; obj. of prep. *in.* —— **contrahere**, pres. inf. act. of *contraho, -ere, -trāxī, -tractum,* 3; complementary inf., depending on *posse.*

LINE 16. **posse**, pres. inf. of *possum, potuī; posse* for *possum* in direct discourse. Observe that *posse* is connected by *neque* with *audēre,* l. 13, above, and is in the same construction. —— **Sibi**, dat. sing. of the reflexive pron. *suī* —— indirect obj. after *vidērī.* —— **autem**, postpositive conj. See l. 22, Chap. II. —— **mīrum**, acc. n. of adj. *mīrus, -a, -um,* predicate after *vidērī.*

to him what business either Caesar had, or the Roman people generally had in his part of Gaul, that he had conquered in war.	vidērī,	quid	in	suā	Galliā,	quam 17
	to seem (it seems),	*what,*	*in*	*his own*	*Gaul,*	*which*
	bellō	vīcisset,		aut	Caesarī	aut 18
	by war	*he had vanquished,*		*either*	*to Caesar*	*or*
	omnīnō	populō	Rōmānō	negōtiī		esset. 19
	at all	*to the people*	*Roman,*	*of business*		(there) *was.*
XXXV. This reply having been reported to Caesar, he sent ambassadors a second time to Ario-	XXXV.	Hīs	respōnsīs	ad		Caesarem 1
		These	*replies*	*to*		*Caesar*
	relātīs		iterum	ad	eum	Caesar 2
	having been reported,		*again*	*to*	*him*	*Caesar*

LINE 17. **vidērī,** pres. inf. pass. *videor*, perf. *vīsus*, 3. The inf. is here used impersonally; really, however, the following indirect question is the subj. —— **quid,** nom. sing. n. of the interrogative pron. *quis, quae, quid;* subject of *esset,* l. 19, below; followed by partitive gen. *negōtiī,* l. 19, below. —— **in,** prep. with acc. or abl. —— **suā,** abl. sing. f. of poss. pron. *suus, -a, -um;* an attributive of *Galliā.* —— **Galliā,** abl. of *Gallia, -ae,* f.; abl. after prep. *in.* —— **quam,** acc. sing. f. of the rel. pron. *quī;* direct obj. of *vīcisset.*

LINE 18. **bellō,** abl. sing. of *bellum, -ī,* n. — *means.* —— **vīcisset,** 3d pers. sing. pluperf. subjunctive of *vincō, -ere, vīcī, victum,* 3; agrees with a pron. implied in the ending, referring to Ariovistus, as subject-nom.; subjunctive, because in a subordinate clause in *ōrātiō oblīqua.* —— **aut,** alternative conj. See l. 19, Chap. I. —— **Caesarī,** dat. of *Caesar, -aris,* m.; possessor with *esset.* A. & G. 231; B. 146; G. 349; H. 387. —— **aut,** see *aut,* immediately preceding.

LINE 19. **omnīnō** (*omnis*), adv. —— **populō,** dat. sing. of *populus, -ī,* m.; connected by *aut* with *Caesarī,* and in the same construction. Synonyms: l. 17, Chap. VI. —— **Rōmānō,** dat. sing. m. of adj. *Rōmānus, -a, -um;* an attributive of *populō.* —— **negōtiī** (nec + otium) = lit. *no leisure;* hence = *business;* gen. sing. of *negōtium, -iī,* n.; partitive gen. after the indef. pron. *quid,* l. 17, above. A. & G. 216, 3; B. 134; G. 369; H. 397, 3. Observe that the partitive gen. is thus freq. separated from the word on which it depends. Observe that nouns in *-ius* and *-ium* freq. form the gen. sing. with one *i,* i.e. *negōtī* instead of *negōtiī.* —— **esset,** 3d pers. sing. imperf. subjunctive of *sum, esse, fuī, futūrus;* it agrees with a pron. as its subject-nom., referring to Ariovistus; subjunctive mode, because the question is *indirect.* A. & G. 334; B. 242; G. 467; H. 529, I. The *ōrātiō rēcta* of lines 7-19: Sī quid *mihi* ā Caesare opus esset, *egō* ad eum *vēnissem;* sī quid *mē* vult, illum ad *mē* venīre *oportet.* Praetereā *egō* neque sine exercitū in eās partēs Galliae venīre *audeō,* quās Caesar *possidet,* neque exercitū sine māgnō commeātū atque mōlimentō in ūnum locum contrahere *possum. Mihi* autem mīrum *vidētur,* quid in *meā* Galliā, quam bellō *vīcī,* aut Caesarī aut omnīnō populō Rōmānō negōtiī *sit.*

LINE 1. **Hīs,** abl. plur. n. (*hīc, haec, hōc*); an attributive of *respōnsīs.* —— **respōnsīs,** abl. plur. of *respōnsum, -ī,* n.; abl. absolute with the participle *relātīs.* —— **ad,** prep. with the acc. —— **Caesarem,** acc. sing. of *Caesar, -aris,* m.; obj. of prep. *ad.* A. & G. 152, *a;* B. 120, 1; G. 416, and 1; H. 433.

LINE 2. **relātīs,** abl. plur. n. of the perf. pass. participle *relātus, -a, um* of the verb *referō, -ferre, -tulī, -lātum;* abl. absolute (l. 17, Chap. XXIX). —— **iterum,** adv.

[LINES 3-7.] BOOK I. 267

3 lēgātōs	cum	his	mandātīs	mittit:	Quoniam	vistus with this message: Inasmuch as he, though treated with so much consideration by Caesar and the Roman people during his consulship as to have been styled king and friend by the senate, shows such gratitude to him and the Roman people
legates	*with*	*these*	*mandates*	*sends:*	*Whereas*	
4 tantō	suō	populīque	Rōmānī	beneficiō		
with so great	*his own*	*people's and,*	*Roman,*	*kindness*		
5 affectus,		cum	in	cōnsulātū	suō	rēx
having been treated,		*since*	*in*	*consulship*	*his,*	*king*
6 atque	amīcus	ā	senātū	appellātus esset,		
and	*friend*	*by*	*the senate*	*he called had been,*		
7 hanc	sibi	populōque	Rōmānō	grātiam		
this,	*to himself,*	*to the people and,*	*Roman,*	*return*		

(GK. ἕτερον) = *a second time*; whereas *rūrsum* or *rūrsus* (*revorsus*) = *again*. *iterum* qualifies *mittit*. —— ad, see *ad*, preceding line. —— eum, acc. sing. m. (*is*, *ea*, *id*); used as a personal pron. of the 3d pers.; obj. of the prep. *ad*. Observe the emphatic position of the phrase *ad eum* — before the subject. —— Caesar, -aris, m.; subject-nom. of *mittit*.

LINE 3. lēgātōs, acc. plur. of *lēgātus*, -ī, m.; direct obj. of *mittit*. —— cum, prep. with abl. —— his, see note on *his*, l. 1, above. —— mandātīs, abl. plur. of *mandātum*, -ī, n. (manus + dare through *mandāre*, to give into one's hands); hence, *to order*. *mandātīs* is the obj. of the prep. *cum*. A. & G. 152, *b*; B. 120, 2; G. 417; H. 434. —— mittit, 3d pers. sing. of *mitto*, 3; historical pres.; it agrees with *Caesar* expressed. Observe that the remainder of this chapter is in *ōrātiō oblīqua*. Caesar's missive was read, probably, by one of the envoys to Ariovistus. —— Quoniam (*quom* [*yuum*] = cum + iam), conj. = *since*.

LINE 4. tantō, abl. sing. n. of *tantus*, adj.; an attributive of *beneficiō* understood. —— suō, abl. sing. n. of poss. pron. *suus*; an attributive also of *beneficiō*. —— populīque (populī + que). *populī*, gen. sing. of *populus*, -ī, m.; as gen. it limits *beneficiō*. *que*, enclitic conj., connects *beneficiō* understood with *beneficiō* expressed. —— Rōmānī, gen. sing. of adj. *Rōmānus*; limits *populī*. —— beneficiō, abl. sing. of *beneficium*, -ī, n. (bene + facere); hence = *well-doing*; abl. of *cause* after *affectus*. A. & G. 245; B. 165, and REM. 4; G. 408, and NOTE 2; H. 416, and NOTE 1.

LINE 5. af(d)fectus, perf. pass. participle of *afficiō*, -*ere*, -*fēcī*, -*fectum*, 3. —— cum, conj., causal. —— in, prep. with acc. or abl. (see *in*, l. 1, Chap. I). —— cōnsulātū, abl. sing. of *consulatus*, -*ūs*, m.; obj. of the prep. *in*. Caesar's consulship, 59 B.C. —— suō, abl. sing. m. of the poss. *sum*; it modifies *cōnsulātū*; refers to Caesar. —— rēx, rēgis, nom. sing. m.; predicate-nom.

LINE 6. atque, conj. (l. 10, Chap. I). —— amīcus, -ī, m. (*amāre*); also predicate-nom. —— ā, prep. with the abl. —— senātū, abl. sing. of *senātus*, -*ūs*, m. (*senex*, old); vol. agent after the prep. *ā*. A. & G. 246; B. 166; G. 401; H. 415, I. —— ap(d)pellātus esset, 3d pers. sing. pluperf. subjunctive of *appellō*, 1; subjunctive after *cum* causal. A. & G. 326; B. 223; G. 586; H. 517.

LINE 7. hanc, acc. sing. f. (*hīc*, *haec*, *hōc*); an attributive of *grātiam*. —— sibi, dat. of the reflexive pron. *suī*; indirect obj.; refers to Caesar. —— populōque (populō + que). *populō*, dat. sing. of *populus*, -ī, m.; connected by the enclitic *que*

268 CAESAR'S GALLIC WAR [CHAP. XXXV.

that, on being invited to come to a conference he feels reluctant, and does not think that he ought either to speak or inquire about matters of common interest, Caesar's demands are these: First, he must not lead	referret, *he was making,*	ut *that,*	in *to*	colloquium *a conference*	venīre *to come*	8
	invītātus *having been invited*		gravārētur *he hesitates*	neque *nor*	dē *concerning*	9
	commūnī *the common*	rē *interest (it)*	dīcendum *to be spoken*		sibi *by himself*	et *and*	10
	cōgnōscendum *to be examined*	putāret, *did he think,*		haec *these things*	esse, *to be (are)*	quae *which*	11
	ab *from*	eō *him*	postulāret: *he should demand:*	prīmum, *first,*		nē *that not,*	quam *any*	12

with *sibi,* and in the same construction. —— **Rōmānō,** dat. sing. of adj. *Rōmānus, -a, -um;* an attributive of *populō.* —— **grātiam,** acc. sing. of *grātia, -ae,* f.; direct object. Observe: *grātiam referre = to show thanks* by act; whereas *grātiās agere = to return thanks* by speech; and *grātiam* or *grātiās habēre = to feel grateful.*

LINE 8. **referret,** 3d pers. sing. imperf. subjunctive of *referō, -ferre, -tulī, -lātum;* subjunctive after *quoniam,* l. 3, above, in indirect discourse. In direct discourse *quoniam* takes the ind., unless the reason is given on another's authority. A. & G. 321; B. 198, (*a*), (*b*); G. 540, 541; H. 516, I and II. —— **ut,** conj. = *that.* —— **in,** prep. with the acc. or abl.; here it takes the acc. (see *in,* l. 1, Chap. I). —— **col(n)loquium,** acc. sing. of *col(n)loquium, -ī,* n.; obj. of the prep. *in.* —— **venīre,** pres. inf. act. of *veniō,* 4; complementary after the participle *invītātus.*

LINE 9. **invītātus,** perf. pass. participle of *invītō,* 1; it agrees with *Ariovistus* understood. —— **gravārētur,** 3d pers. sing. imperf. subjunctive of deponent *gravor, -ātī, -ātus,* 1; subjunctive *of result* after *ut,* referring to *hanc = tālem.* A. & G. 332, *f*; B. 201, REM. 1, (*a*); G. 557; H. 500, II. —— **neque** (nē + que); hence = *and not.* —— **dē,** prep. with the abl.

LINE 10. **commūnī,** abl. sing. f. of adj. *commūnis, -e;* an *i*-stem; abl., as an adj., ends in -*ī,* but the neuter, as a subst., ends in -*e.* *commūnī* is an attributive of *rē.* —— **rē,** abl. sing. of *rēs, reī,* f.; obj. of the prep. *dē.* —— **dīcendum (esse),** pres. inf. of the second periphrastic conjugation, used impersonally; the gerundive is in form the fut. pass. participle of *dīcō,* 3. —— **sibi,** dat. sing. of the reflexive pron. *suī;* apparent agent after the gerundives. A. & G. 232; B. 148; G. 355; H. 388. Observe that *sibi* here refers to Ariovistus, while in l. 7, above, it refers to Caesar,— ambiguity, which would be avoided by reading *ipsī,* dat., in l. 7, above. —— **et,** cop. conj.; connects the gerundives.

LINE 11. **cōgnōscendum (esse),** same construction as *dīcendum (esse),* preceding line; but the gerundive form is from *cōgnōscō, -ere, -nōvī, -nitum,* 3. —— **putāret,** 3d pers. sing. imperf. subjunctive of *putō,* 1; connected by *neque* with *gravārētur,* and in subjunctive for¹ same reason. —— **haec,** acc. plur. n. of dem. pron. *hīc; haec* is predicate-acc. after *esse.* —— **esse,** pres. inf. of *sum,* perf. *fuī;* its subject-acc. is the relative-clause *quae . . . postulāret.* Observe that this infinitive-clause in direct discourse becomes *haec sunt,* which is the principal clause of the sentence. —— **quae,** acc. plur. n. of the interrogative pron. *quis, quae, quid,* used substantively = *what things;* direct obj. of *postulāret.*

LINE 12. **ab,** prep. with the abl. —— **eō,** abl. sing. m. of the dem. pron. *is,* used as a personal pron. of the 3d pers.; obj. of the prep. *ab.* —— **postulāret,** 3d pers.

13 multitūdinem	hominum	amplius	trāns	further any large number of people across the Rhine; second, he must return the hostages that he held from the Aedui, and must give permission to the Sequani to restore to the Aedui the hostages
multitude	*of men*	*more*	*across*	
14 Rhēnum in	Galliam	trādūceret;	deinde	
the Rhine into	*Gaul*	*he should lead;*	*next,*	
15 obsidēs, quōs	habēret	ab	Aeduīs,	
the hostages, whom	*he held*	*from*	*the Aedui,*	
16 redderet	Sēquanīsque		permitteret,	
he should return,	*to the Sequani and,*		*he should permit,*	

sing. imperf. subjunctive act. of *postulō*, 1; its subject-nom. is a pron. understood, referring to Caesar; in the subjunctive, because an *indirect question*. A. & G. 334; B. 242; G. 467; H. 529, I. Observe that the sequence of tenses is, as if *mittit*, l. 3, above, were *mīsit*, i.e. *mittit* is an historical present. The *ōrātiō rēcta* of lines 3–12: Quoniam tantō *meō* populīque Rōmānī beneficiō af(d)fectus, cum in cōnsulātū *meō* rēx atque amīcus ā senātū ap(d)pellātus *sīs*, hanc *mihi* populōque Rōmānō grātiam *referis*, ut in col(n)loquium venīre invītātus *gravēris* neque dē commūnī rē dīcendum *tibi* et cōgnōscendum *putēs*, haec *sunt*, quae *abs tē postulō*:—— **prīmum**, adv., introduces the first in a series, followed by *deinde*, l. 14, below. *prīmō* usually denotes first in a contrast; but the Latin adj. *prīmus* is freq. used for the English adv. —— **nē**, conj. = *that not*. —— **quam**, acc. sing. f. of the indef. pron. *quī, quae, quod*, used as an adj., and modifies *multitūdinem*.

LINE 13. **mulitūdinem**, acc. sing. of *mulitūdō, -inis*, f.; direct obj. of *trādūceret*. —— **hominum**, gen. plur. of *homō, -inis*, m. and f.; limits *multitūdinem*. —— **amplius**, adv., comparative degree; positive *ample, ampliter;* superl. *amplissimē*. —— **trāns**, prep. with the acc.

LINE 14. **Rhēnum**, acc. sing. of *Rhēnus, -ī*, m.; obj. of the prep. *trāns*. —— **in**, prep. with the acc. or abl.; here it takes the acc. = *into*. See in, l. 1, Chap. I. —— **Galliam**, acc. sing. of *Gallia, -ae*, f.; obj. of the prep. *in*. —— **trādūceret**, 3d pers. sing. imperf. subjunctive of *trādūcō*, 3; subjunctive for the imperative; or *nē* with the perf. subjunctive *trāduxeris* for the imperative, in direct discourse. A. & G. 339, and NOTE 2; B. 245, 2; G. 652; H. 523, III. —— **deinde** (dē + inde = *from thence*), adv.; here it introduces the second of the series, and = *then* or *next*.

LINE 15. **obsidēs**, acc. plur. of *obses, -idis*, m. and f.; direct obj. of *redderet*. —— **quōs**, acc. plur. m. of rel. *quī;* refers to *obsidēs*, but is the direct obj. of *habēret*. —— **habēret**, 3d pers. sing. imperf. subjunctive of *habeō*, 2; subjunctive, because in a subordinate clause in *ōrātiō oblīqua*. —— **ab**, prep. with the abl. —— **Aeduīs**, abl. plur. of *Aeduī, -ōrum;* obj. of the prep. *ab* (l. 20, Chap. III). Another form is *Haeduī* (GK. Ἐδουεῖς or Αἴδουοι).

LINE 16. **redderet**, 3d pers. sing. imperf. subjunctive of *reddō, -ere, reddidī, redditum*, 3 (re + dare = *to give back);* subjunctive after *ut*, to be supplied. *ut* is freq. omitted, in indirect discourse, after verbs of *commanding, demanding,* etc. A. & G. 331,*f*, REM.; B. 200, REM. 3; G. 546, REM. 2; H. 499, 2. But observe that this construction is for the imperative in direct discourse, and see grammatical references to *trādūceret*, l. 14, above. —— **Sēquanīsque** (Sēquanīs + que). *Sēquanīs*, dat. plur. of *Sēquanī, -ōrum*, m.; indirect obj. after *permitteret* (l. 25, Chap. I).

that they held;	ut,	quōs	illī	habērent,	· voluntāte	17
he must not	that	(those) whom	they	held,	with permission	
wrongfully har-						
ass the Aedui,	ēius	reddere	illīs	licēret;	nēve	18
nor bring war	his,	to return	to them	it should be allowed;	neither	
upon them or	Aeduōs	iniūriā	lacēsseret,	nēve		hīs 19
their allies.	the Aedui	by outrage	should he provoke,	nor	upon them	
If Ariovistus						
should thus act,	sociīsque	eōrum	bellum	īnferret.	Sī	id 20
he would secure	allies and,	of them	war	should he bring.	If	this

---

que, enclitic conj. —— **permitteret**, 3d pers. sing. imperf. subjunctive of *permittō*, 3 (per + mittere); its subject-nom. is a personal pron., referring to Ariovistus; connected by *que* with *redderet*, and in the subjunctive for the same reason.

LINE 17. **ut**, conj. (original form *utī*) = *that*. —— **quōs**, acc. plur. m. of the rel. pron. *quī*. *quōs* refers to *eōs* understood; *eōs* is the direct obj. of *reddere*, and *quōs* is the direct obj. of *habērent*. —— **illī**, nom. plur. of dem. pron. *ille*, *-a*, *-ud*; refers to *Sēquanīs*; is expressed for emphasis; used here as a personal pron. of the 3d pers.; subject-nom. of *habērent*. —— **habērent**, 3d pers. plur. imperf. subjunctive of *habeō*, 2; subjunctive, because in a subordinate clause in *ōrātiō oblīqua*. —— **voluntāte**, abl. sing. of *voluntās*, *-ātis*, f.; abl. of *in accordance with*. A. & G. 253, NOTE; B. 162; G. 397; H. 416. Synonyms: l. 19, Chap. VII.

LINE 18. **ēius**, gen. sing. m. of dem. pron. *is*, used as a personal pron.; refers to Ariovistus. If *suā* had been used, it would have been ambiguous; yet not more so than *sibi*, l. 7, above. The context often determines the reference. —— **reddere**, pres. inf. act. of *reddō*, 3 (l. 16, above); complementary inf.; depends on *licēret*. —— **illīs**, dat. plur. of pron. *ille*, *-a*, *-ud*, used for pron. emphatic of 3d pers.; dat. of the indirect obj. after *licēret*. The personal subj. of the action is often thus expressed with this verb; but it is oftener expressed by subject-acc. and inf. A. & G. 272, a. I, 1; B. 181, REM. 7, and 194, REM. 2, (e); G. 535, 3; H. 536, 2, 3). —— **licēret**, 3d pers. sing. of impersonal verb *licet*, *-ēre*, *licuit* and *licitum est*, 2; subjunctive of *purpose* after *ut*. Observe that this purpose-clause is, grammatically, the direct obj. of *permitteret*. —— **nēve** (nē + ve) = strictly lit. *or not*; in use = *and not*, *nor*; when repeated = *neither . . . nor*.

LINE 19. **Aeduōs**, acc. plur. of *Aeduī*, *-ōrum*, m.; direct obj. (l. 20, Chap III). —— **iniūriā** (in + iūs), adv.; strictly an abl. of manner of the noun *iniūria*, *-ae*, f. A. & G. 248, REM.; B. 168, REM. 2; G. 399, NOTE 1; H. 419, III, NOTE 2. —— **lacēsseret**, 3d pers. sing. imperf. subjunctive of *lacessō*, *-ere*, *-cessīvī*, *-cessītum*, 3; its subject-nom. is a pron. understood, referring to Ariovistus; subjunctive of negative purpose after *nēve*. Observe that *nēve* is used here as a continuative of *nē*, l. 12, above. We regard these clauses as noun-clauses explanatory of *haec*, l. 11, above. —— **nēve**, see *nēve*, preceding line. —— **hīs**, dat. plur. of dem. pron. *hīc*, used as a personal pron.; dat. after *in* in the compound *īnferret*; *hīs* refers to *Aeduōs*.

LINE 20. **sociīsque** (sociīs + que). *sociīs* is dat. plur. of *socius*, *-ī*, m.; connected with *hīs* by the enclitic *que*, and dat. for same reason. —— **eōrum**, gen. plur. m. of the dem. pron. *is*, used as a personal pron.; it limits *sociīs*. —— **bellum**, acc. sing. of *bellum*, *-ī*, n.; direct object of *īnferret* (see *bellum*, l. 15, Chap. I). —— **īnferret**, 3d pers. sing. imperf. subjunctive act. of *īnferō*, *-ferre*, *intulī*, *il(n)lātum*, irr.; subjunctive of negative purpose after *nēve*. The *ōrātiō rēcta* of lines 12-20: prīmum,

21 ita	fēcisset,	sibi	populōque	Rōmānō	the perpetual
thus	*he should do,*	*to himself*	*to the people and,*	*Roman*	friendship of Caesar and the
22 perpetuam	grātiam	atque	amīcitiam		cum	Roman people;
perpetual	*favor*	*and*	*friendship*		*with*	but if Caesar should not ob-
23 eō	futūram;	sī	nōn	impetrāret,		tain his request,
him (to be) about to be;		*if*	*not*	*he should obtain (his request),*		he, since in the consulship of
24 sēsē,	quoniam	M. Messālā,		M. Pīsōne		Marcus Messala
himself,	*since*	*Marcus Messala,*		*Marcus Piso*		and Marcus Piso,

nē quam multitūdinem hominum amplius trāns Rhēnum in Galliam *trādūxeris;* deinde obsidēs, quōs *habēs* ab Aeduīs, *redde* Sēquanīsque *permitte,* ut, quōs *hī habent,* voluntāte *suā,* reddere *hīs liceat;* nēve Aeduōs iniūriā *lacēsse,* nēve his sociīsque eōrum bellum *īnfer.* Observe that instead of *nē* ... *trādūxeris, nōlī* ... *trādūcere* might be used. —— **Sī,** conditional conj. —— **id,** acc. sing. n. of the dem. pron. *is, ea, id,* used substantively; direct obj. of *fēcisset;* the reference is to what Caesar requires of Ariovistus, as indicated by the clauses following *postulāret,* l. 12, above.

LINE 21. **ita,** adv., referring to Caesar's requirements. —— **fēcisset,** 3d pers. sing. pluperf. subjunctive of *faciō,* 3; in the condition after *sī,* for the fut. perf. ind. in direct discourse. —— **sibi,** dat. sing. of reflexive pron. *suī;* dat. of possessor after *futūrum (esse);* refers to Caesar. —— **populōque** (populō + que). *populō,* dat. sing., connected by *que* with *sibi,* and in the same construction. See explanation, l. 7, above. —— **Rōmānō,** see note, l. 7, above.

LINE 22. **perpetuam,** acc. sing. f. of adj. *perpetuus, -a, -um* (per + petere = lit. *to go through*); hence the adj. = *continuing throughout;* an attributive of *grātiam.* —— **grātiam,** acc. sing. of *grātia, -ae,* f.; subject-acc. of *futūram (esse).* —— **atque** (ad + que), conj. (l. 10, Chap. I). —— **amīcitiam,** acc. sing. of *amīcitia, -ae,* f. (*amīcus,* through *amāre*); connected with *grātiam* by the conj. *atque,* and in the same grammatical construction. —— **cum,** prep. with the abl.

LINE 23. **eō,** abl. sing. m. of the dem. pron. *is,* used as a personal pron. of the 3d pers.; obj. of the prep. *cum;* refers to Ariovistus. —— **futūram (esse),** fut. inf. of *sum, esse, fuī.* Observe that the participial part of this inf. conforms in gender with its subject-acc.; that *esse,* as in the text, is freq. omitted. —— **sī,** conditional conj. —— **nōn** (nē + ūnum); modifies *impetrāret.* —— **impetrāret,** 3d pers. sing. imperf. subjunctive of *impetrō,* 1; its subject-nom. is a pron., referring to Caesar; subjunctive in the *condition* after *sī.*

LINE 24. **sēsē,** reduplicated acc. plur. pron. for *sē,* acc. of *suī;* subject-acc. of *neglēctūrum (esse),* l. 30, below; it refers to Caesar. But note that, as the sentence is long, the subject-acc. is repeated in *sē,* l. 29, below. —— **quoniam,** conj.; see l. 3, above. —— **M. Messālā;** *M.,* abbreviation for *Marcō,* abl. of *Marcus, -ī,* m., *prae-nōmen.* The full name is *Marcus Valerius Messālā; Valerius* is the name of the *gēns; Messālā* is the *cōgnōmen;* he was consul 61 B.C. *Messālā* is abl. of *Messālā, -ae,* m.; abl. absolute with *cōnsulibus.* —— **M.** = *Marcō.* —— **Pīsōne,** abl. of *Pīsō, -ōnis,* m. The full name is *Marcus Papius Pīsō Calpurniānus. Pīsōne* is also abl. absolute with *cōnsulibus.* See notes, lines 2 and 3, Chap. II. Observe the asyndeton between the names. A. & G. 208, *b*; B. 123, REM. 6; G. 474, NOTE; H. 554, 6.

the senate had decreed that he who had the province of Gaul, in so far as he could do so in consonance with the interests of the republic, should defend the Aedui and the other friends of the Roman	cōnsulibus *(being) the consuls,* quīcumque *whoever* quod *so far* posset, *he was able,*	senātus *the senate* Galliam *Gaul* commodō *as with advantage* Aeduōs *the Aedui*	cēnsuisset, *had decreed* prōvinciam *as a province* reī-pūblicae *to the republic* cēterōsque *the other and,*	utī, 25 *that,* obtinēret, 26 *should obtain,* facere 27 (it) *to do* amīcōs populī 28 *friends of the people*

LINE 25. cōnsulibus, abl. plur. of *cōnsul, -ulis,* m.; abl. absolute; plur., because two nouns are referred to. The consuls were two magistrates, supposed to be of equal authority, elected annually by the Roman people. Messala and Piso were consuls 61 B.C. —— senātus *(senex,* old man), *-ūs,* m.; subject-nom. of *cēnsuisset.* As to the origin and powers of the Roman senate, see Smith's *Smaller History of Rome,* pages 12 and 119. —— cēnsuisset, 3d pers. sing. pluperf. subjunctive of *cēnseō, -ēre, -uī, -sum,* 2; subjunctive, because in a subordinate clause in *ōrātiō oblīqua.* Observe that *quoniam* would, in the *ōrātiō rēcta,* take the ind., unless the reason were given on another's authority. —— utī, the original form of the more common *ut = that.*

LINE 26. quīcumque (quī + cumque), indef. rel. pron.; declined like *quī, quae, quod + cumque;* the suffix = the English *ever. quīcumque* is subject-nom. of *obtinēret.* —— Galliam, acc. sing. of *Gallia, -ae,* f.; direct obj. of *obtinēret.* —— prōvinciam, acc. sing. of *prōvincia, -ae,* f.; in apposition with *Galliam.* A. & G. 184; B. 127; G. 321; H. 363. —— obtinēret, 3d pers. sing. imperf. subjunctive act. of *obtineō,* 2; subjunctive by attraction — an integral part of the sentence. Observe that *quīcumque = is quī;* that *is* is subject-nom. of *dēfenderet,* l. 29, below, and *quī* is the subj. of *obtinēret;* thus it is seen that the clause *quī Galliam prōvinciam obtinēret* is a subordinate clause, and, of course, in *ōrātiō oblīqua* takes the subjunctive.

LINE 27. quod, an adverbial acc. n. of the rel. *quī.* A. & G. 240, *a*; B. 123, 5, REM. 21; G. 334, REM. 1; H. 378, 2. The older grammars teach that *propter* or *ad* is understood before *quod.* Observe that *quod* in restrictive clauses = *quantum.* —— commodō, abl. of *commodum, -ī,* n.; abl. *of manner,* being modified by the gen. *reī-pūblicae;* perhaps better, as an abl. of *in accordance with.* —— reī-pūblicae, gen. sing. of the compound noun *rēs-pūblica, reī-pūblicae,* objective gen.; limits *commodō.* —— facere, pres. inf. act. of *faciō,* 3; complementary; supply *id,* explained by the following clause, as direct object.

LINE 28. posset, 3d pers. sing. imperf. subjunctive of *possum, posse, potuī;* subjunctive after *quod* in a restrictive clause. A. & G. 320, *d*; B. 234, REM. 2; G. 627, REM. 1; H. 503, I, NOTE 1. —— Aeduōs, acc. plur. of *Aeduī, -ōrum,* m.; direct obj. of *dēfenderet.* —— cēterōsque (cēterōs + que). *cēterōs* is acc. plur. of adj. *cē(ae)terus, -a, -um;* an attributive of *amīcōs. que,* enclitic conj.; connects the nouns. Synonyms: l. 6, Chap. XXXII. —— amīcōs, acc. plur. of *amīcus, -ī,* m.; sometimes an adj.; connected by *que* with *Aeduōs,* and in the same construction. —— populī, gen. sing. of *populus, -ī,* m.; limits *amīcōs.* Synonyms: l. 17, Chap. VI.

29 Rōmānī dēfenderet,	sē	Aeduōrum iniūriās	people — he, I say, would not overlook the wrongs of the Aedui.
Roman he should defend,	*himself*	*the Aedui's wrongs*	
30 nōn neglēctūrum.			
not (to be) about to neglect.			
1 XXXVI. Ad	haec	Ariovistus	XXXVI. To this message A-
To	*these (things)*	*Ariovistus*	riovistus replied:
2 respondit: Iūs	esse	bellī, ut,	It is the right of war for victors
responded: The right	*to be (it was)*	*of war, that*	to govern the
3 quī vīcissent,	eīs,	quōs vīcissent,	vanquished as
(they) who had conquered,	*them*	*whom they had conquered,*	

LINE 29. **Rōmānī** (*Rōma*), adj.; limits *populī*. —— **dēfenderet**, 3d pers. sing. imperf. subjunctive of *dēfendō, -ere, -endī, -ēnsum*, 3; its subject-nom. is a pron. understood, referring to Caesar; subjunctive *of purpose* after *utī*, l. 25, above. —— **sē**, repeats *sēsē*, l. 24, above, because of the length of the sentence; *sē* here is merely explanatory of *sēsē*, and in the same construction; viz. subject-acc. of *neglēctūrum* (*esse*). —— **Aeduōrum**, gen. plur. of *Aeduī, -ōrum*, m.; objective gen.; limits *iniūriās*. —— **iniūriās**, acc. plur. of *iniūria, -ae*, f.; direct obj. of *neglēctūrum* (*esse*).

LINE 30. **nōn** (nē + oe[ū]num), adv.; modifies *neglēctūrum* (*esse*). —— **neglēctūrum** (**esse**), fut. inf. act. of *neglegō, -ere, -lēxī, -lēctum*, 3; sometimes written *negligō* (nec + legere = lit. *not to pick up*, i.e. *not to heed, neglect*). Observe how the strict periodicity of the sentence is preserved by repeating the pronouns *sēsē, sē*; and thus inserting the subordinate clauses within the principal clauses. The *ōrātiō rēcta* of lines 20-30: Sī *hōc ita fēceris, mihi populōque Rōmānō perpetua grātia atque amīcitia tēcum erit;* sī nōn *impetrābō,* quoniam M. Messālā, M. Pīsōne cōnsulibus senātus *cēnsuit,* utī, quīcumque Galliam prōvinciam *obtineat,* quod commodō reīpūblicae facere *possit,* Aeduōs cēterōsque amīcos populī Rōmānī *dēfendat, egō* Aeduōrum iniūriās nōn *neglegam*.

LINE 1. **Ad**, prep. with the acc. —— **haec**, acc. plur. of the dem. pron. *hīc*; used substantively; obj. of the prep. *ad*. The *haec* = Caesar's *mandata*, preceding chapter. —— **Ariovistus, -ī**, m.; subject-nom. of *respondit*. See l. 51, Chap. XXXI.

LINE 2. **respondit**, 3d pers. sing. perf. ind. act. of *respondeō, -ēre, -dī, -spōnsum*, 3; its subject-nom. is *Ariovistus*. —— **Iūs**, acc. sing. of *iūs, iūris*, n.; predicate-acc. after *esse*; the subject-acc. is the following *ut*-clause. —— **esse**, pres. inf. of intrans. verb *sum, esse, fuī, futūrus*. Observe that from *Iūs* to the close of the chapter the discourse is indirect. —— **bellī**, gen. sing. of *bellum, -ī*, n.; it limits *iūs*. See l. 15, Chap. I. —— **ut**, conj.; introduces the clause *ut . . . imperārent*.

LINE 3. **quī**, nom. plur. of rel. pron. *quī;* it refers to *eī*, the omitted subj. of *imperārent; quī* is subject-nom. of *vīcissent*. —— **vīcissent**, 3d pers. plur. pluperf. subj. of *vincō, -ere, vīcī, victum*, 3; its subject-nom. is *quī:* subjunctive, because in a subordinate clause in *ōrātiō oblīqua*. —— **eīs**, dat. plur. of the dem. pron. *is*, used as personal pron. of the 3d pers.; dat. after *imperārent* — a word of command. A. & G. 227; B. 142; G. 346, and REM. 2; H. 385, I. —— **quōs**, acc. plur. m. of the rel. pron. *quī;* it refers to *eīs;* is the direct obj. of *vīcissent*. —— **vīcissent**, same construction as *vīcissent*, immediately preceding.

274 CAESAR'S GALLIC WAR [CHAP. XXXVI.

they wished; in this way the Roman people were wont to govern their vanquished — not according to the dictation of another, but according to their own pleasure. If he on his part should not dictate to the Roman peo-	quem-ad-modum *what in manner*	vellent, *they wished,*	imperārent; *might command;* [4]
	item populum *likewise the people*	Rōmānum *Roman*	victīs nōn *(those) vanquished, not* [5]
	ad alterīus *at another's*	praescriptum, *direction,*	sed ad suum *but at their own* [6]
	arbitrium *will*	imperāre *to command*	cōnsuēsse. Sī *to be (they are) accustomed. If* [7]
	ipse *himself*	populō *to the people*	Rōmānō nōn praescrīberet, *Roman should not prescribe,* [8]

LINE 4. **quem-ad-modum**, adv. = *as*; observe the parts of the compound, and the lit. meaning = *as to what mode*, i.e. *how, as*. The parts are sometimes written separately; *quem ad modum*; sometimes, *quemadmodum*. —— **vellent**, 3d pers. plur. imperf. subjunctive of *volō, velle, voluī*; its subject-nom. is a pron. understood; subjunctive, because in a subordinate clause in indirect discourse. —— **imperārent**, 3d pers. plur. imperf. subjunctive of *imperō*, 1; its omitted subject-nom. is *eī*; subjunctive *of result* after *ut*. Observe that this clause, as noun, is subject-acc. of *esse*, l. 2, above. A. & G. 332, FOOTNOTE; B. 201, REM. 1, (*d*); G. 557, REM.; H. 501, 2.

LINE 5. **item** (*i*, whence *is* + tem), adv. = lit. in *that* way; hence *so also*. —— **populum**, acc. sing. of *populus, -ī, m.*; subject-acc. of *cōnsuēsse*, l. 7, below. Synonyms: l. 17, Chap. VI. —— **Rōmānum**, acc. sing. m. of adj. *Rōmānus, -a, -um*; attributive of *populum*. —— **victīs**, dat. plur. of perf. pass. participle *victus, -a, -um*; pass. parts: *vincor, vincī, victus*, 3; *victīs* agrees with the pron. *eīs* understood; hence seen to be an essentially predicative participle = to a rel. clause: those *who have been vanquished*; or = a noun : *the vanquished*. Observe that *eīs* supplied is dat. after *imperāre*. See *eīs*, l. 3, above. —— **nōn** (nē + ūnum), adv.; modifies *cōnsuēsse*.

LINE 6. **ad**, prep. with the acc. —— **alterīus**, gen. sing. of the pron. *alter, -tera, -terum*; limits *praescrīptum*. Observe that *alterīus* has the ictus on the antepenult, and is generally used for *alīus*. —— **praescriptum**, acc. sing. of *praescrīptum, -ī, n.* (prae + scrībere); hence the noun = *the thing written before*, i.e. *a copy*, etc.; obj. of the prep. *ad*. —— **sed**, conj.; strong adversative. —— **ad**, prep. with the acc.; the notions are kept distinct by repetition of the prepositions. —— **suum**, acc. sing. n. of *suus, -a, -um*; an attributive of *arbitrium*.

LINE 7. **arbitrium**, acc. sing. n. of *arbitrium, -ī, n.* (*arbiter*, a judge); hence = one's subjective *decision* or *opinion*; whereas *iūdicium* (*iūdex* [*iūs*]) = judical opinion derived from objective right. *arbitrium* is the obj. of the prep. *ad*. —— **imperāre**, inf. pres. act. of *imperō*, 1; complementary, depending on *cōnsuēsse*. —— **cōnsuēsse**, perf. inf. act. of *cōnsuēscō, -ere, -suēvī, -suētum*, 3; contracted for *cōnsuēvisse — v* is syncopated, and then contraction takes place. A. & G. 128, 2 ; B. 251; G. 131, 1; H. 235. The subject-acc. is *populum Rōmānum*, l. 5, above. The *ōrātiō rēcta* of lines 2–7: Iūs *est* bellī, ut, quī *vīcerint*, eīs quōs *vīcerint*, quem-ad-modum *volunt, imperent*; item *populus Rōmānus* victīs nōn ad alterius praescriptum, sed ad suum arbitrium imperāre *cōnsuēvit*. —— **Sī**, conditional conj.; introduces the protasis.

LINE 8. **ipse**, nom. of the intensive pers. pron. = *he himself*; subject-nom. of *praescrīberet*. —— **populō**, dat. of *populus, -ī, m.*; indirect obj. Synonyms: l. 17,

9 quem-ad-modum	suō	iūre	ūterētur,	ple as to the manner in which they were to exercise their rights, he ought not to be obstructed by the Roman people in the exercise of his rights. Inasmuch as the Aedui had tried the fortunes of war, had met
what in manner	*their own*	*right*	*they should use,*	
10 nōn oportēre	sēsē	ā	populō	
not to be (it is not) necessary	*himself*	*by*	*the people*	
11 Rōmānō in suō		iūre	impedīrī.	Aeduōs
Roman in his		*own right*	*to be impeded.*	*The Aedui*
12 sibi,	quoniam	bellī	fortūnam	temptāssent
to himself,	*whereas*	*war's*	*fortune*	*they had tried*

Chap. VI. —— **Rōmānō**, dat. sing. m. of the adj. *Rōmānus, -a, -um;* an attributive of *populō.* —— **nōn**, adv.; modifies the verb. —— **praescrīberet**, 3d pers. sing. imperf. subjunctive of *praescrībō*, 3; it agrees with its subject-nom. *ipse*, referring to Ariovistus; subjunctive in the *condition* after *sī*. A. & G. 304, *a*; B. 207; G. 590; H. 507.

LINE 9. **quem-ad-modum**, see l. 4, above. —— **suō**, abl. sing., poss. adj. pron. *suus, -a, -um;* refers to *populō Rōmānō*, preceding line, and is an attributive of *iūre*. —— **iūre**, abl. sing. of *iūs, iūris*, n.; abl. after *ūterētur*. A. & G. 249; B. 167, 1; G. 407; H. 421, I. Observe that *suō* here refers to the subject of the subordinate clause, as does *sibi*, l. 7, Chap. XXXV; while in the following clause, which is the main clause of the sentence, *sēsē* and *suō* refer to Ariovistus. This confusion in the use of the reflexives indicates Caesar's haste. —— **ūterētur**, 3d pers. sing. imperf. subjunctive of the deponent *ūtor, -ī, ūsus*, 3; subjunctive, because an *indirect question*. A. & G. 334; B. 242; G. 467; H. 529, I.

LINE 10. **nōn**, modifies *oportēre*. —— **oportēre**, pres. inf. of *oportet, -ēre, -uit* (*opus*, need), impers. Observe that the inf. is here used, because the discourse is indirect; that the inf. is impersonal, as well as the 3d pers. sing. of any of the finite modes. The real subj. of *oportēre*, however, is the accusative-clause *sēsē ... impedīrī.* —— **sēsē**, reduplicate of the reflexive pron. *sē*, acc. sing. of *suī*. *sēsē* is subject-acc. of *impedīrī*. —— **ā**, prep. with the abl. See l. 7, Chap. I. —— **populō**, abl. of *populus, -ī*, m.; abl. of the agent. A. & G. 246; B. 166; G. 401; H. 415, I.

LINE 11. **Rōmānō**, abl. sing. m. of the adj. *Rōmānus, -a, -um;* an attributive of *populō.* —— **in**, prep. with the acc. or abl.; here with the abl. —— **suō**, abl. sing. n. of poss. pron. *suus, -a, -um;* modifies *iūre*, but refers to Ariovistus. —— **iūre**, abl. sing. of *iūs, iūris*, n.; obj. of the prep. *in.* —— **impedīrī**, pres. inf. pass. of *impediō*, 4 (*in* + *pēs, the foot in*), hence *impedīre* = lit. *to entangle the feet.* Observe that the infinitive-clause *sēsē ... impedīrī* is the subj. of *oportēre.* —— **Aeduōs**, acc. plur. of *Aeduī, -ōrum*, m. (see l. 20, Chap. III); subject-acc. of *esse factōs* (*factōs esse*), l. 14, below.

LINE 12. **sibi**, dat. sing. of *suī;* refers to Ariovistus; indirect obj. of *esse factōs.* —— **quoniam** (quom [quum], cum + iam), conj. —— **bellī**, gen. sing. of *bellum*, *-ī*, n.; limits *fortūnam.* —— **fortūnam**, acc. sing. of *fortūna, -ae*, f. (*fors*, chance); direct obj. of *temptāssent.* See l. 19, Chap. XI. —— **temptāssent**, 3d pers. plur. pluperf. subjunctive of *temptō*, 1; contracted from *temptāvissent* (see *cōnsuēsse*, l. 7, above); subjunctive, because in a subordinate clause in *ōrātiō oblīqua*. Observe that this verb is frequently written *tentō*, 1.

him in battle,	et	armīs	congressī	āc	superātī essent,	13
and had been defeated, they	and	in arms	had engaged	and	had been conquered,	
had become his	stīpendiāriōs		esse factōs.		Māgnam Caesarem	14
tributaries. Caesar was doing	tributaries		to have been made.		Great, Caesar,	
him a great	iniūriam		facere,	quī	suō adventū	15
wrong, since by his arrival he	wrong		to do (is doing)	who	at his coming	
was making his	vēctīgālia		sibi	dēteriōra	faceret.	16
revenues less val-	revenues		to himself	worse	he was making.	

LINE 13. **et**, cop. conj. (see l. 7, Chap. I). —— **armīs**, abl. plur. of *arma, -ōrum*, n. plur.; abl. *of the instrument*. —— **congressī** (essent), 3d pers. plur. pluperf. subjunctive of *congredior, -dī, -gressus*, 3, deponent; subject-nom. a pron., referring to *Aeduōs*; connected by *et* with *temptāssent*; in the subjunctive for the same reason. Supply *eōs* as direct obj. —— **āc**, conj. (see l. 10, Chap. I). —— **superātī essent**, 3d pers. plur. pluperf. pass. subjunctive of *superō*, 1 (*super = over*); hence *superāre = to be over, to conquer*, etc.; subjunctive for the same reason as *temptāssent*. Synonyms: *superāre = to win* a position from an opponent; *vincere = to drive* an opponent from his position. Död.

LINE 14. **stīpendiāriōs**, acc. plur. of the adj. *stīpendiārius, -a, -um* (*stipendium*, tribute); used substantively; predicate-acc. after *esse factōs* (*factōs esse*). —— **esse factōs** (*factōs esse*), perf. inf. of *fīō, fierī, factus*, 3, used as pass. of *faciō*. Observe that the participial formation is in the acc. plur., because the subject-acc. is *Aeduōs*. The *ōrātiō rēcta* of lines 7-14: Sī *egō* populō Rōmānō nōn *praescrībō*, quem-ad-modum suō iūre *ūtātur* (*ūsūrus sit*), nōn *oportet mē* ā populō Rōmānō in *meō* iūre impedīrī. *Aeduī mihi*, quoniam bellī fortūnam *temptāvērunt* (*temptārunt*) et armīs congressī āc superātī *sunt*, *stīpendiāriī sunt factī*. —— **Māgnam**, acc. sing. of adj. *māgnus, -a, -um*; an attributive of *iniūriam*. —— **Caesarem**, acc. sing. of *Caesar, -aris*, m.; subject-acc. of *facere*. Observe its position — very emphatic.

LINE 15. **iniūriam**, acc. sing. of *iniūria, -ae*, f. (in + iūs); direct obj. of *facere*. —— **facere**, pres. inf. act. of *faciō*, 3; its subject-acc. is *Caesarem*. This infinitive-clause is for the main clause in *ōrātiō rēcta*. —— **quī**, rel. pron.; nom. sing. m.; refers to *Caesarem*; but is subject-nom. of *faceret*; as the clause is causal, *quī* here = *cum is*. —— **suō**, abl. sing. m. of the poss. reflexive pron. *suus, -a, -um*; an attributive of *adventū*. —— **adventū**, abl. of *adventus, -ūs*, m.; abl. *of time at which*. A. & G. 256, 1; B. 171, REM. 3; G. 393; H. 429.

LINE 16. **vēctīgālia**, acc. plur. of *vēctīgal, -ālis*, n. (*vectus* from *vehere*, to carry); hence the noun = lit. *that which was carried* or *paid* to the state. *vēctīgālia* is subject-acc. of *esse* understood. —— **sibi**, dat. sing. of the reflexive pron. *suī*; dat. of reference. A. & G. 235; B. 145; G. 352; H. 384, II, 2). *sibi* designates Ariovistus here; but as it does not refer to the subj. of either the principal or subordinate clause, it is ambiguous; *eī* or *ipsī* would remove the ambiguity. —— **dēteriōra**, acc. plur. n. of the comparative adj. *dēterior, -ius*; predicate-acc. after *esse* understood. Observe that the positive of this adj. is wanting. A. & G. 91, *d*, 1; B. 74, 1; G. 87, REMS. 1 and 7; H. 166. Observe further that the accusative-clause *vēctīgālia esse dēteriōra* is the direct obj. of *faceret*. —— **faceret**, 3d pers. sing. imperf. subjunctive of *faciō*, 3; its subject-nom. is a pron., referring to Caesar; it is subjunctive after *quī* causal. A. & G. 320, *e*; B. 197; G. 633; H. 517.

17 Aeduīs	sē	obsidēs	redditūrum		nōn	uable. He would not return the hostages to the Aedui, nor would he wrongfully wage war against them or their allies if they would keep their promises, and pay the tribute annually;
To the Aedui	*himself,*	*hostages*	*about to return*		*not*	
18 esse,	neque	eīs	neque	eōrum	sociīs	
to be,	*neither*	*on them*	*nor*	*on their*	*allies.*	
19 iniūriā		bellum		illātūrum,	sī in	
with wrong,		*war (himself) to be about to bring,*			*if in*	
20 eō	manērent,		quod	convēnisset,		
that	*they remained,*		*which*	*had been agreed on,*		
21 stīpendiumque		quotannīs		penderent;	sī	
the tribute	*and,*	*every year*		*they would pay,*	*if*	

LINE 17. **Aeduīs**, dat. plur. of *Aeduī, -ōrum;* indirect obj. after *redditūrum esse* (see l. 20, Chap. III). —— **sē**, acc. sing. of the reflexive pron. *suī;* refers to Ariovistus; is subject-acc. of *redditūrum esse.* —— **obsidēs**, acc. plur. of *obses, -idis*, m. and f.; direct obj. of *redditūrum esse.* —— **redditūrum esse**, fut. inf. act. of *reddō, -ere, -didī, -itum,* 3 (red + dare); its subject-acc. is *sē.* —— **nōn**, negative particle; inserted between the component parts of this fut. tense for emphasis.

LINE 18. **neque** (nē + que) = *and not,* a conjunctive adv.; but *neque ... neque* = *neither ... nor.* —— **eīs**, dat. plur. m. of the dem. pron. *is;* used substantively; indirect obj. of *illātūrum (esse).* —— **neque**, see *neque,* immediately preceding. —— **eōrum**, gen. plur. of the dem. pron. *is*, used as a personal pron. of the 3d pers. = lit. *of them;* as a gen. it limits *sociīs.* —— **sociīs**, dat. plur. of *socius, -ī,* m.; connected by *neque* with *eīs,* and in dat. for the same reason.

LINE 19. **iniūriā**, adv.; but strictly an abl. of manner. A. & G. 248, REM.; B. 168, (*e*); G. 399, NOTE 1; H. 419, III, NOTE 2. —— **bellum**, acc. sing. of *bellum, -ī*, n.; direct obj. of *il(n)lātūrum (esse).* —— **il(n)lātūrum (esse)**, fut. inf. act. of *īnferō, -ferre, intulī, il(n)lātum,* irr.; its subject-acc. is *sē,* l. 17, above. Observe that in the compound forms, especially in the fut. inf. and also in the inf. of the second periphrastic conjugation and in the perf. pass. inf., *esse* is oftener omitted than expressed. —— **sī**, conditional conj.; sibilated from GK. *el.* —— **in**, prep. with the acc. or abl.; here abl.

LINE 20. **eō**, abl. sing. n. of the dem. pron. *is;* used here with the prep. *in* without supplement; but we may supply *locō.* —— **manērent**, 3d pers. plur. imperf. subjunctive of *maneō, -ēre, mānsī, mānsum,* 2; the subject-nom. is *eī,* referring to the Aedui; the mode is subjunctive after *sī* in the protasis; the apodosis is in the preceding infinitive-clause. As to fut. condition in indirect discourse, see A. & G. 337, 2. *a,* 3; B. 245, 4; G. 656; H. 527, II. —— **quod**, nom. sing. n. of the rel. pron. *quī;* subj. of *convēnisset.* —— **convēnisset**, 3d pers. sing. pluperf. subjunctive of *conveniō,* 4 (con + venīre) = lit. *to come together;* hence in personal and impersonal construction = *what is agreed on,* or *fit.*

LINE 21. **stīpendiumque** (stīpendium + que). *stīpendium* is acc. sing. of *stīpendium, -iī*, n. (stīps + pendere = lit. *to weigh out a gift);* hence the noun = *a tax paid in money;* whereas *vectīgal* = *a tax paid in kind.* *stīpendium* is direct obj. of *penderent.* —— **quotannīs** (quot, *every* + annus, *year*), adv. —— **penderent**, 3d pers. plur. imperf. subjunctive of *pendō, -ere, pependī, pēnsum,* 3; connected by the enclitic *que* with *manērent,* and in the same grammatical construction both as to subj. and subjunctive. —— **sī**, see note on this particle, l. 19, above.

278   CAESAR'S GALLIC WAR   [CHAP. XXXVI.

| but if they would not do thus, the title "brothers" given them by the Roman people would afford them no aid. As to Caesar's threat that he would not overlook the wrongs of the Aedui, (he would say) that no one had ever fought with A- | id nōn fēcissent, longē eīs frāternum 22 *this not they should have done, far for them the fraternal* nōmen populī Rōmānī āfutūrum. 23 *name of the people Roman to be about to be distant.* Quod sibi Caesar dēnūntiāret, sē 24 *As to what himself, Caesar threatened, — himself* Aeduōrum iniūriās nōn neglēctūrum, 25 *the Aedui's wrongs not to be about to neglect, —* nēminem sēcum sine suā perniciē 26 *no one himself with, without his own destruction,* |

LINE 22. **id**, acc. sing. n. of the dem. pron. *is*; direct obj. of *fēcissent*. *id* refers to the payment of tribute. —— **nōn**, negative particle; modifies *fēcissent*. —— **fēcissent**, 3d pers. plur. pluperf. subjunctive of *faciō*, 3; it agrees with a subj. implied in the ending, referring to the Aedui; subjunctive in condition after *sī*. Observe that the pluperf. subjunctive in indirect discourse stands for the fut. perf. ind. in direct. —— **longē** (*longus*), adv.; modifies *āfutūrum* (*esse*). —— **eīs**, abl. plur. of the dem. *is*, used as a personal pron. of the 3d pers.; abl. *of separation* after *āfutūrum* (*esse*). Observe that the compounds of *esse* take the dat., except *abesse* and *posse*. —— **frāternum**, acc. sing. n. of the adj. *frāternus, -a, -um* (*frāter*); an attributive of *nōmen*.

LINE 23. **nōmen**, acc. sing. of *nōmen, -inis*, n.; subject-acc. of *āfutūrum* (*esse*). —— **populī**, gen. sing. of *populus, -ī*, m.; limits *nōmen*. Synonyms: l. 17, Chap. VI. —— **Rōmānī**, gen. sing. m. of adj. *Rōmānus, -a, -um*; an attributive of *populī*. —— **āfutūrum** (**esse**), fut. inf. of *absum, abesse, āfuī, ab(ā)futūrus*. The *ōrātiō rēcta* of lines 14–23: Māgnam *tū, Caesar*, iniūriam *facis*, quī *tuō* adventū vectīgālia *mihi* dēteriōra *facīās*. Aeduīs *egō* obsidēs nōn *reddam*, neque eōrum sociīs iniūriā bellum *īnferam*, sī in eō *manēbunt* quod *convēnērunt*, stīpendiumque quotannīs *pendent*; sī id nōn *fēcerint*, longē eīs frāternum nōmen populī Rōmānī *aberit*.

LINE 24. **Quod**, an acc. of specification of the rel. *quī* = *whereas*. A. & G. 333, *a*; B. 123, REM. 21, and 198; G. 525, 2; 516, NOTE, end. —— **sibi**, dat. sing. of the reflexive pron. *suī*; dat. of the indirect obj. after *dēnūntiāret*. Observe that the direct obj. is the sentence: *sē . . . neglēctūrum* (*esse*). —— **Caesar, -aris**, m.; subject-nom. of *dēnūntiāret*. —— **dēnūntiāret**, 3d pers. sing. imperf. subjunctive act. of *dēnūntiō* (*-ciō*), 1 (dē, *intensive* + nuntiō); subjunctive, because a subordinate clause in *ōrātiō oblīqua*. A. & G. 341, *d*; B. 198, (*b*); G. 541; II. 516, II. —— **sē**, acc. sing., reflexive pron. *suī*; subject-acc. of *neglēctūrum* (*esse*). Observe the confusion in the reference of this pron. *sibi*, immediately preceding, refers to Ariovistus; whereas *sē* refers to Caesar.

LINE 25. **Aeduōrum**, gen. plur. of *Aeduī, -ōrum*, m.; limits *iniūriās* (see l. 20, Chap. III). —— **iniūriās**, acc. plur. of *iniūria, -ae*, f. (in + iūs); direct obj. of *neglēctūrum* (*esse*). —— **nōn**, negative particle — normally placed — immediately before the word modified. —— **neglēctūrum** (**esse**), fut. inf. act. of *negle(i)gō, -ere, -lēxī, -lēctum*, 3 (nec + legere = lit. *not to deserve*); its subject-acc. is *sē*.

LINE 26. **nēminem**, acc. sing. of *nēmō* (nē + homō), *-inis*, m. and f.; subject-acc. of *contendisse*. Observe that *nūllīus* and *nūllō* are used instead of *nēminis* and

LINES 27-31.]   BOOK I.   279

27 contendisse.	Cum	vellet,	congrederētur;	riovistus without his own ruin. He might fight when he pleased; he would learn what the invincible Germans, who were most thoroughly trained in arms and who had not lived in a house for fourteen years, could accomplish by their valor.
to have contended.	*When*	*he wished,*	*he might meet (him);*	
28 intellectūrum,		quid	invīctī	
to be about to learn (he will learn),		*what*	*the unconquerable*	
29 Germānī,	exercitātissimī	in	armīs,	quī
Germans.	*most practised*	*in*	*arms,*	*who*
30 inter	annōs	quattuordecim	tēctum	nōn
during	*years*	*fourteen*	*a roof*	*not*
31 subīssent,	virtūte	possent.		
had gone under,	*by valor*	*were able.*		

nēmine; but *nēmine* is sometimes used with a pass. participle. —— **sēcum** (sē + cum). *sē,* abl. sing. of the reflexive pron. *suī, sibi, sē, sē. sē* is obj. of the enclitic prep. *cum.* A. & G. 99, *e*; B. 79, 2; G. 413, REM. 1; H. 184, 6. —— **sine,** prep. with the abl. (archaic *sē* or *sēd* [sē + nē with loss of negative force] = *by itself, apart, without*). —— **suā,** abl. sing.; attributive of *perniciē.* Observe the ambiguity in the use of the pronouns *sē* in *sēcum* and in *suā;* the former refers to Ariovistus, the latter to *nēmine n.* —— **perniciē,** abl. sing. of *perniciēs, -ēī,* f.; obj. of the prep. *sine.*

LINE 27. **contendisse,** perf. inf. act. of *contendō, -ere, -tendī, -tentum,* 3; its subject-acc. is *nēminem.* —— **Cum,** conjunctive adv. —— **vellet,** 3d pers. sing. imperf. subjunctive of *volō, velle, voluī,* irr.; its subject-nom. is a pron., referring to Caesar; subjunctive after *cum* temporal. —— **congrederētur,** 3d pers. sing. imperf. subjunctive of deponent *congredior, -gredī, -gressus,* 3; hortatory or optative subjunctive in indirect discourse for the imperative in direct discourse. A. & G. 339; B. 245, 2; G. 652; H. 523, III.

LINE 28. **intellectūrum (esse),** fut. inf. act. of *intelle(i)gō, -ere, -lexī, -lectum,* 3; its subject-acc. is the pron. *sē,* referring to Caesar. —— **quid,** acc. of interrogative pron. *quis, quae, quid;* an adverbial acc. after *possent,* l. 28, below. A. & G. 238, *b*; B. 150, REM. 2; G. 333, REM. 2; H. 378, 2. This acc. is sometimes termed cognate acc. and sometimes acc. of specification. —— **invīctī,** nom. plur. of adj. *invīctus, -a, -um* (in + victus = lit. *not conquered);* an attributive of *Germānī.*

LINE 29. **Germānī,** nom. plur. of *Germānī, -ōrum,* m.; subj. of *possent,* l. 31, below. See l. 14, Chap. I. —— **exercitātissimī,** nom. plur. of the adj., superl. degree; positive *exercitātus;* comparative *-tātior;* agrees with *Germānī,* but is essentially predicative = *who were most skillful.* Observe that *exercitātus* is properly a perf. pass. participle of *exercitāre,* which = *to exercise, train.* —— **in,** prep. with the acc. or abl.; here abl. —— **armīs,** abl. plur. of *arma, -ōrum,* n. See l. 13, Chap. IV. —— **quī,** nom. plur. of the rel. *quī, quae, quod;* refers to *Germānī;* subject-nom. of *subīssent.*

LINE 30. **inter,** prep. with the acc. = lit. *between;* but with expressions of time = *during.* The more common phrase is *per annōs.* —— **annōs,** acc. plur. m.; obj. of *inter.* —— **quattuordecim** (quattuor, *four* + decim, *ten),* num. adj., attributive of *annōs;* frequently represented by *XIV.* —— **tēctum,** acc. sing. of *tēctum, -ī,* n. (*tegere,* to cover); direct obj. of *subīsset.* —— **nōn,** negative adv. (nē + unum).

LINE 31. **subīssent,** 3d pers. plur. pluperf. subjunctive of *subeō, -īre, -īvī, (-iī), -itum;* it agrees with the subject-nom. *quī;* subjunctive, because in a subordinate

280   CAESAR'S GALLIC WAR   [CHAP. XXXVII.

XXXVII. At the same time that this message was brought to Caesar, envoys from the Aedui and the Treveri came: the Aedui, to complain that the Harudes, who had been lately brought

XXXVII. Haec eōdem tempore Caesarī 1
These,   at the same   time,   to Caesar,
mandāta referēbantur, et lēgātī ab 2
mandates   were brought back,   both   legates   from
Aeduīs et ā Trēverīs veniēbant: Aeduī 3
the Aedui   and from the Treveri   came: The Aedui
questum, quod Harūdēs, quī nūper in 4
to complain,   because   the Harudes,   who   lately   into

clause in *ōrātiō oblīqua.* Observe that this verb is used both transitively and intransitively, but in a different sense. See the lexicons. —— **virtūte**, abl. sing. of *virtūs, -tūtis,* f. (*vir*); abl. of specification. A. & G. 253; B. 162; G. 397; H. 424. —— **possent,** 3d pers. plur. imperf. subjunctive of *possum, posse, potuī* (*potis, able* + *sum*); it agrees with its subject-nom. *Germānī*; subjunctive, because an indirect question; the question is introduced by *quid.* A. & G. 334; B. 242; G. 467; H. 529, I. The *ōrātiō rēcta* of lines 24–31 : Quod *tū,* Caesar, *mihi dēnūntiās, tē* Aeduōrum iniūriās nōn neglēctūrum (*esse*), *nēmō mēcum* sine suā perniciē *contendit.* Cum *vīs, congredere; intellegēs,* quid invictī Germānī exercitātissimī in armīs, quī inter annōs quattuordecim tēctum nōn *subiērunt,* virtūte *possint.*

LINE 1. **Haec,** nom. plur. n. of dem. pron. *hīc;* an attributive of *mandāta.* —— **eōdem,** abl. sing. n. of the iterative pron. *īdem, eadem, idem;* an attributive of *tempore.* —— **tempore,** abl. sing. of *tempus, -oris,* n.; time at which. A. & G. 256, 1; B. 171; G. 393; H. 429. —— **Caesarī,** dat. of *Caesar, -aris,* m.; indirect obj.

LINE 2. **mandāta,** nom. plur. of *mandātum, -ī,* n.; subj. of *referēbantur.*—— **referēbantur,** 3d pers. plur. imperf. ind. pass. of act. *referō, -ferre, -tulī, -lātum;* pass. *referor, -ferrī, -lātus;* its subject-nom. is *mandāta.* —— **et,** cop. conj. = *and;* but *et . . . et* = *both . . . and.* In translating here, and often elsewhere, omit the equivalent of the first *et.* —— **lēgātī,** nom. plur. of *lēgātus, -ī,* m.; subject-nom. of *veniēbant.* —— **ab,** prep. with the abl. See l. 6, Chap. I.

LINE 3. **Aeduīs,** abl. plur. of *Aeduī, -ōrum,* m.; obj. of prep. *ab.* See *Aeduō,* l. 20, Chap. III. —— **et,** see *et,* preceding line. —— **ā,** prep. with abl.; observe that the notions are kept distinct by the repetition of the prep. —— **Trēverīs,** abl. plur. of *Trēverī, -ōrum,* m.; obj. of prep. *ā.* Sometimes *Trēvir, -irī,* m. sing., is used, and = *one* of the *Trēverī.* The Treveri were a people of Gallia Belgica, dwelling not far from modern Treves. —— **veniēbant,** 3d pers. plur. imperf. ind. act. of *veniō,* 4; it agrees with subject-nom. *lēgātī.* The imperf. here is not essentially different in signification from the perf. ind. A. & G. 277, NOTE; B. 95, II.; G. 231; H. 469, I. —— **Aeduī,** nom. plur., subj. of *veniēbant,* to be supplied.

LINE 4. **questum,** supine of *queror, -ī, questus,* deponent; expresses the *purpose* of the coming. A. & G. 302; B. 186, (A.); G. 435; H. 546. —— **quod,** conj. —— **Harūdēs,** -um, nom. plur. m., and subj. of *populārentur.* The Harudes were a people of Germany, north of the Danube. Some say from Jutland, i.e. the Chersonēus Cimbrica. —— **quī,** nom. plur. of rel. pron. *quī;* subject-nom. of *trānsportātī essent.* —— **nūper,** adv. (for *novīper* [*novus*]); hence = lit. *newly.* —— **in,** prep. with acc. or abl.; here it has the acc. See *in,* l. 1, Chap. I.

LINES 5-9.]   BOOK I.   281

5 Galliam	trānsportātī essent,		fīnēs	eōrum	over the Rhine into Gaul, were devastating their territories; and they said that they could not, even by giving hostages, procure peace from Ariovistus. Moreover, the Treveri came saying that the people of a hundred Suevian villages had encamped near the bank of the
Gaul	*had been brought,*		*borders*	*their,*	
6 populārentur;	sēsē	nē	obsidibus	quidem	
were laying waste;	*themselves*	*not*	*hostages*	*even*	
7 datīs	pācem		Ariovistī	redimere	
having been given,	*the peace*		*of Ariovistus*	*to purchase*	
8 potuisse;		Trēverī	autem,	pāgōs	
to have been able;		*the Treveri,*	*moreover,*	*cantons*	
9 centum	Suēvōrum	ad	rīpam	Rhēnī	
a hundred	*of the Suevi*	*at*	*the bank*	*of the Rhine*	

LINE 5. **Galliam**, acc. sing.; obj. of prep. *in*. See *in*, l. 1, Chap. I. —— **trānsportātī essent**, 3d pers. plur. pluperf. subjunctive pass. of *trānsportō*, 1; subjunctive, because in a subordinate clause in *ōrātiā oblīqua*. —— **fīnēs**, acc. plur. of *fīnis*, *-is*, m.; direct obj. of the deponent *populārentur*. Synonyms: l. 12, Chap. II. —— **eōrum**, gen. plur. of the dem. pron. *is, ea, id*, used as a pers. pron. of the 3d pers. = English poss. case *their;* refers to the *Aeduī*, l. 3, above.

LINE 6. **populārentur**, 3d pers. plur. imperf. subjunctive of deponent *populor*, 1; subject-nom. is *Harūdēs;* subjunctive, because the statement is made on another's authority. A. & G. 341, *d*; B. 198, (*b*); G. 628; H. 516, II. —— **sēsē**, reduplication of *sē*, acc. plur. of reflexive pron. *suī;* subject-acc. of *potuisse*. —— **nē**, conjunctive adv. = *that not*. Observe how the particle is separated from the restrictive *quidem* with the emphatic word between the particles. —— **obsidibus**, abl. plur. of *obses*, *-idis*, m. and f.; abl. absolute with *datīs*. —— **quidem**, adv.; with *nē* = *not even*.

LINE 7. **datīs**, perf. pass. participle of *dō*, 1, act.; pass. *dor, darī, datus* (*a* short before *re*, pres. inf. act. by exception); abl. absolute with *obsidibus*, denoting condition. A. & G. 255, *d*, 4; B. 192; G. 410; H. 431. —— **pācem**, acc. sing. of *pāx, pācis*, f.; direct obj. of *redimere*. —— **Ariovistī**, gen. sing. of *Ariovistus, -ī*, m.; gen. poss., limits *pācem*. —— **redimere**, pres. inf. of *redimō, -ere, -ēmī, -ēmptum*, 3 (red + emere = *to buy back*); inf. complementary; depends on *potuisse*.

LINE 8. **potuisse**, perf. inf. of *possum* (potis + sum); subject-acc. is *sēsē*, l. 6, above. What the Aeduī said, lines 4-8, in direct form was: Harūdēs, quī nūper in Galliam trānsportātī *sunt*, fīnēs nostrōs populantur; nōs nē obsidibus quidem datīs pācem Ariovistī redimere *possumus*. —— **Trēverī, -ōrum**, m., subj. of *veniēbant*, to be supplied from the preceding. See *Trēverīs*, l. 3, above. The full lacūna is *veniēbant questum*. —— **autem**, adversative conj.; postpositive. —— **pāgōs**, acc. plur. of *pāgus, -ī*, m.; subject-acc. of *cōnsēdisse*. Observe that the *cantons* are put by metonymy for the *people* of the cantons.

LINE 9. **centum**, num. adj. cardinal; modifies *pāgōs*. —— **Suēvōrum**, gen. plur. of *Suēvī, -ōrum*, m.; limits *pāgōs*. The Suevi were a people of central Germany. The name is sometimes written *Suēbī* (GK. Σούηβοι). But the paraphrast has Σουεύων, gen. plur. of Σούενοι. —— **ad**, prep. with the acc. = *near* or *at*. A. & G. 258, *c*, NOTE 1; B. 120, 1; G. 386, 2; H. 433, I. —— **rīpam**, acc. sing. of *rīpa, -ae*, f.; obj of prep. *ad*. —— **Rhēnī**, gen. sing. of *Rhēnus, -ī*, m.; limits *rīpam*.

282 CAESAR'S GALLIC WAR [CHAP. XXXVII.

Rhine, and were cōnsēdisse, quī Rhēnum trānsīre 10
attempting to *to have encamped,* *who* *the Rhine* *to cross over*
cross that river;
and that the cōnārentur; hīs praeësse Nasuam et 11
brothers Nasua
and Cimberius *were attempting;* *these,* *to be over,* *Nasua* *and*
were their lead-
ers. Now Cae- Cimberium frātrēs. Quibus rēbus Caesar 12
sar was greatly *Cimberius* *brothers.* *By which* *things* *Caesar*
alarmed at these
reports, and vehementer commōtus mātūrandum sibi 13
thought that he
ought to make *exceedingly* *having been moved (it) to be hastened* *by himself*
haste lest, should
this new band existimāvit, nē, sī nova manus Suēvōrum 14
of the Suevi *thought,* *lest,* *if* *the new* *band* *of the Suevi*

LINE 10. cōnsēdisse, perf. inf. act. of cōnsīdo, -ere, -sēdī, -sessum, 3 (con + sīdere
= *to sit together*); subject-acc. is *pāgōs.* —— quī, nom. plur. of rel. pron. *quī;* refers
to *Suēvōrum;* subject-nom. of *cōnārentur.* —— Rhēnum, acc. sing. of *Rhēnus, -ī,* m.;
direct obj. of *trānsīre.* —— trānsīre, pres. inf. act. of *trānseō, -īre, -īvī (-iī), -itum*
(trāns + īre); inf. complementary.

LINE 11. cōnārentur, 3d pers. plur. imperf. subjunctive of deponent *cōnor,* 1;
subjunctive, because in a subordinate clause in virtual *ōrātiō oblīqua.* —— hīs, dat.
plur. of the dem. pron. *hīc,* used as a pers. pron. of 3d pers.; dat. after *prae* in compound *praeësse.* A. & G. 228; B. 143; G. 347; H. 386. —— praeësse, pres. inf. of
praesum (prae + sum) = lit. *to be before* or *over.* —— Nasuam, acc. sing. of *Nasua,
-ae,* m.; subject-acc. of *praeësse.* Observe the gender from the *signification* rather
than the *form* of the word. —— et, cop. conj.; connects the nouns.

LINE 12. Cimberium, acc. sing. of *Cimberius, -ī,* m.; also subject-acc. of *praeësse.* These brothers were chiefs of the Aedui. —— frātrēs, acc. plur. of *frāter,
-tris,* m.; an appositive of two nouns; hence in the plur. A. & G. 184, *a;* B. 127,
REM. 3; G. 321; H. 363. What the Treveri said, lines 8-12, in direct form was:
Pāgī centum Suēvōrum ad rīpam Rhēnī *cōnsēdērunt,* quī Rhēnum trānsīre *cōnantur;*
his *praesunt Nasua* et *Cimberius* frātrēs. —— Quibus, abl. plur. of the pron. *quī;* it
refers to the preceding statements; but is here used adjectively, and is an attributive
of *rēbus.* At the beginning of a sentence it = *hīs.* —— rēbus, abl. plur. of *rēs, reī,* f.;
abl. of cause after *commōtus.* A. & G. 245, and 2, *b;* B. 165, and REM. 4; G. 408,
and NOTE 2; H. 416, and NOTE 1. —— Caesar, -aris, m.; subj. of *existimāvit.*

LINE 13. vehementer, adv.; modifies *commōtus;* stronger than either *magnopere*
or *graviter.* —— commōtus, perf. pass. participle of *commoveō,* 2; it agrees with
Caesar expressed. —— mātūrandum (esse), pres. inf. of second periphrastic conjugation of *mātūrō,* 1; intrans.; hence used impersonally in the pass. voice. A. & G.
146, *d;* B. 115, III; G. 217; H. 301, 2. —— sibi, dat. of the personal and reflexive
pron. *suī;* dat. of the agent after the gerundive, or pass. periphrastic conjugation.
A. & G. 232; B. 148; G. 355; H. 388.

LINE 14. existimāvit, 3d pers. sing. perf. ind. act. of *existimō,* 1 (ex, *intensive* +
aestimāre = *to compute thoroughly);* it agrees with the subject-nom. *Caesar.* —— nē,
conj. = *that not,* or *lest.* —— sī, conditional particle; = *if.* —— nova, nom. sing. f.
of adj. *novus, -a, -um* (GK. *νέος);* an attributive of *manus.* —— manus, -ūs, f. by

15 cum	veteribus	cōpiīs	Ariovistī	sēsē	unite with the old forces of Ariovistus, they might be less easily opposed. Accordingly, after procuring as speedily as possible a supply of grain, he hastened by forced marches toward Ariovistus.
with	*the old*	*forces*	*of Ariovistus*	*itself*	
16 cōniūnxisset,	minus	facile		resistī	
should have joined,	*less*	*easily*		*to be resisted*	
17 posset.	Itaque	rē		frūmentāriā	
it might be able.	*Therefore*	*the thing*		*frumentary,*	
18 quam	celerrimē	potuit		comparātā	
as much	*as most speedily*	*he was able,*		*being collected,*	
19 magnīs	itineribus ad		Ariovistum	contendit.	
with great	*marches toward*		*Ariovistus*	*he hastened.*	

exception. A. & G. 69; B. 48, REM. 4, EXC. 1; G. 62, EXC.; H. 118, EXC. Observe that *manus* = lit. *a hand;* but transf., in military language = a company of hands — a military corps. —— **Suēvōrum**, gen. plur.; limits *manus.* See *Suēvōrum*, l. 9, above.

LINE 15. **cum**, prep. with the abl. —— **veteribus**, abl. plur. of the adj. *vetus*, stem *veter* (from GK. *ἔτος*, digammated); an attributive of *cōpiīs.* —— **cōpiīs**, abl. plur. of *cōpia*, *-ae*, f.; obj. of the prep. *cum.* —— **Ariovistī**, gen. sing. poss. of *Ariovistus*, *-ī*, m.; it limits *cōpiīs.* —— **sēsē**, reduplicated; acc. for *sē*, but more emphatic; acc. of direct obj., referring to *manus.*

LINE 16. **cōniūnxisset**, 3d pers. sing. pluperf. subjunctive of *coniungō*, *-ere*, *-iūnxī*, *-iūnctum*, 3 (con + iungere); agrees with *manus* as subject-nom.; subjunctive in the condition after *sī.* —— **minus**, adv., comparative degree; irr. positive *parum;* superl. *minimē; minus* modifies *facile.* —— **facile**, adv.; modifies *resistī posset.* —— **resistī**, pres. pass. inf. of *resistō*, *-ere*, *-stitī*, *-stitum*, 3; used impersonally, as are all intransitives in the pass. voice. A. & G. 230; B. 115, III; G. 217; H. 384, 5.

LINE 17. **posset**, 3d pers. sing. imperf. subjunctive of *possum;* subjunctive after *nē*, l. 14, above — negative purpose. Observe that when *potest* is followed by the inf. of an impersonal verb, it too is impersonal. Supply *eīs* as dat. of the indirect obj. after *resistī.* But *eī*, i.e. *Ariovistō*, might be supplied, and then the clause = *he might be less easily resisted.* —— **Itaque**, adv. (ita + que = lit. *and so).* —— **rē**, abl. sing. of *rēs*, *reī*, f.; abl. absolute with *comparātā.* —— **frūmentāriā**, abl. sing. f. of the adj. *frūmentārius*, *-a*, *-um* (*frūmentum);* an attributive of *rē.*

LINE 18. **quam**, adv.; modifies *celerrimē.* —— **celerrimē**, adv., superl. degree; positive *celeriter;* comparative *celerius.* —— **potuit**, 3d pers. sing. perf. ind. of *possum, posse.* Supply ellipsis thus: *tam celeriter quam celerumē potuit* = *so speedily as most speedily he was able,* i.e. *as speedily as possible.* —— **comparātā**, abl. f. of the perf. pass. participle *comparātus*, *-a*, *-um* of the verb *comparō*, 1; abl. absolute with *rē*, l. 17, above.

LINE 19. **magnīs**, abl. plur. n. of the adj. *magnus*, *-a*, *-um;* an attributive of *itineribus.* —— **itineribus**, abl. plur. of *iter, itineris*, n.; abl. of manner. A. & G. 248; B. 168; G. 399; H. 419, III. —— **ad**, prep. with the acc., after a verb of motion = *to* or *toward.* The usual day's-march of Roman soldiers was twenty Roman miles. —— **Ariovistum**, acc. sing. of *Ariovistus*, *-ī*, m.; obj. of the prep. *ad.* A. & G. 258; B. 154, REM. 3; G. 416, 1; H. 380, I. —— **contendit**, 3d pers. sing. perf. ind. act. of *contendō*, *-ere*, *-tendī*, *-tentum*, 3; its subject-nom. is *Caesar* understood. See *contendunt*, l. 18, Chap. I.

XXXVIII. When Caesar had advanced a three-days' journey, it was reported to him that Ariovistus with all his forces was hastening to seize Vesontio, which was the largest town of the Sequani; and had advanced a three-days' journey from his own borders.	XXXVIII. *When*	Cum *a three-days'*	trĭduī *march*	viam 1
	prōcessisset, *he had proceeded,*	nūntiātum est *it was announced*	eī, *to him,*	Ariovistum 2 *Ariovistus,*
	cum *with* suīs *his*	omnibus *all*	cōpiīs *forces*	ad *for,*	occupandum 3 *to be occupied*
	Vesontiōnem, *Vesontio,*	quod *which*	est *is*	oppidum *town*	māximum 4 *the greatest*
	Sēquanōrum, *of the Sequani,*	contendere, *to be pushing forward,*		trĭduīque 5 *a three-days' and,*
	viam *march*	ā *from*	suīs *his own*	fīnibus *borders*	prōfēcisse. 6 *to have made progress.*

LINE 1. **Cum**, conj., temporal. —— **trĭduī**, gen. sing. of *trĭduum, -ī*, n. (trēs + diēs) = lit. *of three days;* it limits *viam.* —— **viam**, acc. sing. of *via, -ae,* f.; *space over which.* A. & G. 257, and NOTE; B. 153; G. 335; H. 379. Synonyms: l. 2, Chap. IX.

LINE 2. **prōcessisset**, 3d pers. sing. pluperf. subjunctive of *prōcēdō, -ere, -cessī, -cessum,* 3; its subj. is Caesar understood; subjunctive after *cum* temporal. —— **nūntiātum est**, 3d pers. sing. perf. ind. pass. of *nūntiō (-ciō),* 1; impersonal; or, better, the following accusative-clauses as noun-clauses are the subject-nominatives. —— **eī**, dat. sing. of the dem. pron. *is,* used as a personal pron. of the 3d pers.; indirect obj. —— **Ariovistum**, acc. sing. of *Ariovistus, -ī,* m.; subject-acc. of *contendere* and *prōfēcisse,* lines 5 and 6, below.

LINE 3. **cum**, prep., followed by abl. —— **suīs**, abl. plur. f. of the poss. pron. *suus, -a, -um;* an attributive of *cōpiīs.* —— **omnibus**, abl. plur. of the adj. *omnis, -e;* it modifies the phrase *suīs cōpiīs.* —— **cōpiīs**, abl. plur. of *cōpia, -ae,* f.; abl. *of accompaniment* with the prep. *cum.* A. & G. 248, *a;* B. 168, REM. 4; G. 392, and REM. 1; H. 419, I. —— **ad**, prep. with the acc. —— **occupandum**, acc. sing. m. of *occupandus, -a, -um,* gerundive of *occupō,* 1; it agrees with *Vesontiōnem.*

LINE 4. **Vesontiōnem**, acc. sing. of *Vesontiō, -ōnis,* m.; obj. of the prep. *ad.* Observe that the gerundive construction with *ad* denotes *purpose.* A. & G. 300; B. 184, REM. 4, III; G. 432; H. 542, III. Vesontio was the principal town of the Sequani, the modern Besançon. —— **quod**, nom. sing. n. of the rel. *quī;* refers to Vesontio, but is attracted into the gender of *oppidum* — predicate. *quod* is the subject-nom. of *est.* As to this construction, see A. & G. 199; B. 129, REM. 1, (*a*); G. 616, 2; H. 445, 9. —— **est**, 3d pers. sing. of *sum, esse, fuī.* —— **oppidum**, nom. of *oppidum, -ī,* n.; predicate after *est.* —— **māximum**, acc. sing. n. of superl. degree of positive *māgnus,* comparative *māior;* an attributive of *oppidum.*

LINE 5. **Sēquanōrum**, gen. plur. of *Sēquanī, -ōrum,* m.; limits *oppidum.* See l. 25, Chap. I. —— **contendere**, pres. inf. act. of *contendō, -ere, -dī, -tentum,* 3 (l. 19, Chap. I); its subject-acc. is *Ariovistum.* —— **trĭduīque** (trĭduī + que). *trĭduī* is gen. of *trĭduum, -ī,* n. (see l. 1, above). *que,* enclitic; connects the clauses.

LINE 6. **viam**, acc. sing. of *via, -ae* (see l. 1, above). —— **ā**, prep. with abl. —— **suīs**, abl. plur. m. of poss. pron. *suus, -a, -um;* an attributive of *fīnibus;* it refers to

BOOK I. 285

7 Id	nē	accideret,	māgnopere		sibi	That this might not happen. Caesar thought that he ought to be especially on guard. And the more, for there was in that town the greatest abundance of everything useful in war; and it was so protected by the nature of its
That	*lest*	*should happen,*	*greatly*		*by himself*	
8 praecavendum		Caesar	exīstimābat.		Namque	
(it) to be guarded against		*Caesar*	*thought.*		*For truly,*	
9 omnium	rērum,	quae	ad	bellum	ūsuī	
of all	*things,*	*which*	*in respect to*	*war*	*for use*	
10 erant,	summa	erat	in	eō oppidō	facultās;	
were,	*the greatest*	*was*	*in*	*that town,*	*abundance;*	
11 idque	nātūrā	locī	sīc	mūniēbātur,	ut	
it and,	*by nature*	*of the place*	*so*	*fortified was,*	*that*	

Ariovistus. —— finibus, abl. plur. of *finis, -is*, m.; obj. of the prep. *d*. Synonyms: l. 20, Chap. I. —— prōfēcisse, perf. inf. act. of *prŏficiō*, 3; connected by *que* with *contendere*, and has the same subject-acc. — *Ariovistum*, l. 2, above. Craner's text reads *prōcessisse*; probably because *prōficere* in the literary sense is rare; *prōfĕcisse* is the usual lection.

LINE 7. Id, nom. sing. n. of the dem. pron. *is;* used substantively; subject-nom. of *accideret*; refers to the possibility of Ariovistus' seizing Vesontio. —— nē, conj. = *that not* or *lest*. —— accideret, 3d pers. sing. imperf. subjunctive of *accidō*, 3 (ad + cadere = *to fall to*, hence *to happen*); subjunctive of negative *purpose* after *nē*. —— māgnopere, adv. (māgnō + opere) = lit. *with great labor;* hence as an adv. = *greatly;* sometimes written: *mâgnō opere*. —— sibi, dat. of reflexive pron. *suī;* agent, referring to Caesar.

LINE 8. praecavendum (esse), pres. inf. of second periphrastic conjugation of *praecaveō*, 2; used impersonally. Observe that the pass. periphrastic conjugation denotes *necessity* or *duty*. —— Caesar, -aris, m., subject-nom. of *exīstimābat*. —— exīstimābat, 3d pers. sing. imperf. ind. act. of *exīstimō*, 1 (ex + aestimāre) = lit. *to reckon accurately*. —— Namque (nam + que), conj.; more emphatic than *nam;* = GK. καὶ γάρ; = *and I say truly for*.

LINE 9. omnium, gen. plur. f. of adj. *omnis, -e;* an attributive of *rērum*. —— rērum, gen. plur. of *rēs, reī*, f.; limits *facultās*, l. 10, below. —— quae, nom. plur. f. of rel. pron. *quī;* refers to *rērum;* subject-nom. of *erant*. —— ad, prep. with the acc. —— bellum, acc. sing. of *bellum, -ī*, n.; obj. of the prep. *ad*. —— ūsuī, dat. sing. of *ūsus, -ūs*, m.; dat. of service after *erant*. A. & G. 233, *a;* B. 147, REM. 1, end; G. 356, and NOTE 1; H. 390 NOTE 2.

LINE 10. erant, 3d pers. plur. imperf. ind. of *sum, esse, fuī;* agrees with the subject-nom. *quae*. —— summa, nom. sing. f. of adj. *summus, -a, -um;* superl. degree of *superus, -ior, -prēmus* or *summus; summa* is an attributive of *facultās*. —— erat, 3d pers. sing. imperf. ind. of *sum;* its subject-nom. is *facultās*. —— in, prep. with the acc. or abl.; here it takes the abl. See l. 1, Chap. I. —— eō, abl. sing. n. of the dem. pron. *is;* an attributive of *oppidō*. —— oppidō, abl. sing. of *oppidum, -ī*, n.; obj. of the prep. *in*. —— facultās, nom. sing. of *facultās, -ātis*, f.; subj. of *erat*. Observe that *erat* here is a verb of complete predication = *exists;* and also that *facultās* is derived from *facilis;* hence = *facility of resources — abundance*.

LINE 11. idque (id + que). *id*, nom. n. of the dem. pron. *is*, used substantively = *oppidum;* subject-nom. of *mūniēbātur*. *que*, enclitic conj.; connects the sentences.

position as to afford great facilities for protracting the war, because the river Doubs almost encircled the entire town as if circumscribed by compasses. The rest of the space, which is not more than sixteen hundred feet, where the	māgnam *a great,*	ad *for,*	dūcendum *to be protracted*	bellum *the war*	daret 12 *it gave*
	facultātem, *opportunity,*	proptereā *for this reason,*	quod *because*	flūmen *the river*	Dūbis 13 *Doubs*
	ut *as*	circinō *by a pair of compasses*		circumductum 14 *having been drawn around*	
	paene *almost*	tōtum *the whole*	oppidum *town*	cingit; *encircles;*	reliquum 15 *the remaining*
	spatium, *space,*	quod *which*	est *is*	nōn *not*	amplius *more,*	pedum 16 *of feet*

—— **nātūrā**, abl. of means of *nātūra*, *-ae*, f. —— **locī**, gen. sing. of *locus*, *-ī*, m.; limits *nātūrā*. See l. 10, Chap. II. —— **sīc**, adv., correlative of the following *ut*. —— **mūniēbātur**, 3d pers. sing. imperf. ind. pass. of *mūniō*, 4. —— **ut**, ecbatic conj.

LINE 12. **māgnam**, acc. sing. f. of adj. *māgnus*, *-a*, *-um*; an attributive of *facultātem*, l. 13, below. —— **ad**, prep. with the acc. of the gerundive construction. —— **dūcendum**, acc. sing. n. of the gerundive *dūcendus*, *-a*, *-um* of the verb *dūcō*, 3; agrees with *bellum*. —— **bellum**, acc. sing. of *bellum*, *-ī*, n.; obj. of the prep. *ad*. Observe that the phrase *ad dūcendum bellum* = lit. *for the war to be put off*, i.e. *for protracting the war*. Compare *diem dūcere*, lines 12, 13, Chap. XVI. —— **daret**, 3d pers. sing. imperf. subjunctive of *dō*, 1; subjunctive of result after *ut*, referring to *sīc*.

LINE 13. **facultātem**, acc. sing. of *facultās*, *-tātis*, f.; direct obj. of *daret*. Observe that this word has here its literal, and not transf. meaning, as in *facultās*, l. 10, above. —— **proptereā** (propter + eā), adv., the herald of the following *quod*-clause. —— **quod**, conj. = *because*. See l. 9, Chap. I. —— **flūmen**, nom. sing. of *flūmen*, *-inis*, n.; subject-nom. of *cingit*, l. 15, below. —— **Dūbis**, nom. sing. of *Dūbis*, *-is*, m.; an appositive; the modern Doubs.

LINE 14. **ut**, adv. = *as if*; compare GK. ὡς with circumstantial participle. —— **circinō**, abl. of *circinus*, *-ī*, m.; abl. of means. —— **circumductum**, acc. sing. n. of the perf. pass. participle of *circumdō*, 1; agrees with *oppidum*.

LINE 15. **paene**, adv., modifies adj. *tōtum*. —— **tōtum**, acc. sing. n. of *tōtus*, gen. *tōtīus*; an attributive of *oppidum*. —— **oppidum**, acc. sing. of *oppidum*, *-ī*, n.; direct obj. of *cingit*. —— **cingit**, 3d pers. sing. pres. ind. of *cingō*, *-ere*, *cinxī*, *cinctum*, 3. —— **reliquum**, acc. sing. n. of adj. *reliquus*, *-a*, *-um*; an attributive of *spatium*. Synonyms: l. 7, Chap. V. Observe that the adj. denotes the *part* of the obj. A. & G. 193; B. 128, REM. 9; G. 291, REM. 2; H. 440, NOTE 2.

LINE 16. **spatium**, acc. of *spatium*, *-ī*, n.; direct obj. of *continet*, l. 18, below. —— **quod**, nom. sing. n. of the rel. pron. *quī*; subj. of *est*. —— **est**, 3d pers. sing. pres. ind. of *sum*. —— **nōn**, negative particle; modifies adj. —— **amplius**, adv., comparative degree of *amplē* or *ampliter*. *amplius* is here a species of an appositive. A. & G. 247, *c*, and NOTE; B. 163, REM. 4; G. 296, REM. 4; H. 417, NOTE 2. —— **pedum**, gen. plur. of *pēs*, *pedis*, m.; gen. *of measure*, depending on *spatium*. A. & G. 215, *b*; B. 132; G. 365, REM. 2; H. 396, 5.

LINES 17-21.]   BOOK I.   287

17 mille	sexcentōrum,	quā	flūmen	intermittit,	river ceases its
thousand	(and) six-hundred,	where	the river	intermits,	circular course, a mountain of
18 mōns	continet	māgnā	altitūdine,	ita ut	great height occupies, so that
a mountain	contains,	of great	altitude,	so that	the margins of
19 rādīcēs	montis	ex	utrāque	parte	rīpae	the river touch the lower slopes
the roots	of the mountain	on	each	side	the banks	of the mountain on either side.
20 flūminis	contingant.		Hunc		mūrus	A wall having
of the river	touch.		This (mountain),		a wall	been extended around it makes
21 circumdatus		arcem	efficit	et	cum	the mountain
having been put around,		a citadel	makes	and	with	a citadel, and

LINE 17. **mille,** an indecl. adj. in the sing.; it is here the gen. plur. and an attributive of *pedum*. —— **sex(s)centōrum,** gen. plur. of *sex(s)centī, -ae, -a*; cardinal num. adj.; modifies *pedum* (note the asyndeton between the numerals). Observe (*a*) that the rigidly literal translation of *quod ... sexcentōrum* is: *which is not more of feet thousand six hundred;* (*b*) that *mille* is an insertion of the later critics. The common reading is *pedum DC*. As the base of the mountain measures about 1600 feet, the later critics write *MDC*. Dr. Anthon supposes, however, that Caesar means here by *foot*, the pace of 2½ feet. —— **quā,** adv.; or supply *vid*, and the phrase = *in what way, where*. —— **flūmen,** nom. sing. of *flūmen, -inis,* n.; subj. of *intermittit*. —— **intermittit,** 3d pers. sing. pres. ind. act. of *intermittō*, 3; the verb is used here intrans., and = *ceases* to flow around the place in a circular course.

LINE 18. **mōns, montis,** m.; subj. of *continet*. —— **continet,** 3d pers. sing. pres. ind. act. of *contineō*, 2 (con + tenere) = lit. *to hold together;* here = *occupies*, i.e. *fills up.* —— **māgnā,** abl. sing. f. of the adj. *māgnus, -a, -um;* an attributive of *altitūdine*. —— **altitūdine,** abl. sing. of *altitūdō, -inis,* f.; abl. of quality with adj. *māgnā*. A. & G. 251, *a*; B. 169; G. 400, and REM. 1; II. 419, II, and NOTE. —— **ita,** adv., correlative of the conj. *ut*. —— **ut,** ecbatic conj.

LINE 19. **rādīcēs,** acc. plur. of *rādīx, -īcis,* f.; direct obj. of *contingant*. —— **montis,** gen. sing. of *mōns, montis,* m.; limits *rādīcēs*. —— **ex,** prep. with the abl. —— **utrāque,** abl. sing. f. of the pron. *uterque, utraque, utrumque;* gen. *utrīusque;* dat. *utrīque. utrāque* is an attributive of *parte*. Observe that *que*, appended to *uter*, gives a notion of universality. Then *uter = which of two; uterque = either of two* or *both*. —— **parte,** abl. of *pars, partis,* f.; obj. of the prep. *ex*. —— **rīpae,** nom. plur. of *rīpa, -ae,* f.; subject-nom. of *contingant*. Observe that some critics take *rādīcēs* as subject-nom. of *contingant*, and *rīpae* as dat. after the same verb; others still take *rīpae* as a gen., limiting *parte*, and supply *eam*, i.e. *rīpam* as the direct object.

LINE 20. **flūminis,** gen. sing. of *flūmen, -inis,* n.; limits *rīpae*. —— **contingant,** 3d pers. plur. pres. subjunctive of *contingo, -ere, -tigī, -tactum,* 3; agrees with the subject-nom. *rīpae;* subjunctive of *result* after *ut*. —— **Hunc,** acc. sing. m. of dem. pron. *hīc;* an attributive of *montem* understood; which latter is the direct obj. of *efficit*. —— **mūrus, -ī,** m.; subject-nom. of *efficit*. Synonyms: l. 7, Chap. VIII.

LINE 21. **circumdatus,** perf. pass. participle of *circumdō*, 1; agrees with *mūrus*. —— **arcem,** acc. sing. of *arx, arcis,* m.; predicate-acc. after *efficit*. A. & G. 239, I, *a*;

unites it with the town. Hither Caesar hastened by forced marches day and night; and, having seized the town, stationed a garrison there.	oppidō *the town* nocturnīs *nightly* occupātōque *having been seized and,* collocat. *he establishes.*	coniungit. *connects.* diurnīsque *daily and,*	Hūc *Hither* itineribus *marches* oppidō, *the town,*	Caesar *Caesar* ibi *there*	māgnīs 22 *by great* contendit, 23 *hastens,* praesidium 24 *a garrison* 25

XXXIX. While Caesar was tarrying a few days near Vesontio

XXXIX. Dum paucōs diēs ad Vesontiōnem 1
While   a few   days   at   Vesontio

B. 151, (*b*); G. 340, (*b*); H. 373, 1. —— efficit, 3d pers. sing. pres. ind. act. of *efficiō*, 3 (ex + facere = lit. *to do completely*); agrees with subject-nom. *mūrus*. —— et, cop. conj. See l. 7, Chap. I. —— cum, prep., takes the abl.

LINE 22. **oppidō**, abl. sing. of *oppidum*, *-ī*, n.; obj. of the prep. *cum*. Synonyms: *oppidum* = any *town* except Rome; the latter usually *urbs*; often *oppidum* = a *castle*, but is not to be confounded with *arx*, GK. ἀκρόπολις, a *citadel*. —— **coniungit**, 3d pers. sing. pres. ind. act. of *coniungō*, 3; connected by *et* with *efficit*, and in the same construction. —— **Hūc**, adv. (archaic form of *hōc* = lit. *to this place*). —— **Caesar, -aris**, m.; subject-nom. of *contendit*. —— **māgnīs**, abl. plur. n. of the adj. *māgnus, -a, -um*; an attributive of *itineribus*.

LINE 23. **nocturnīs**, abl. plur. n. of the adj. *nocturnus, -a, -um* (*nox*); also an attributive of *itineribus*. —— **diurnīsque** (diurnus + que). *diurnīs*, abl. plur. of the adj. *diurnus, -a, -um* (*diēs*); connected by *que* with *nocturnīs*, and in the same construction. —— **itineribus**, abl. plur. of *iter, itineris*, n.; abl. of manner. The great or forced marches were more than 20 miles a day. —— **contendit**, 3d pers. sing. pres. ind. act. of *contendō*, 3; agrees with the subject-nom. *Caesar*. See l. 18, Chap. I.

LINE 24. **occupātōque** (occupātō + que). *occupātō*, abl. sing. n. of the perf. pass. participle *occupātus, -a, -um* of *occupō*, 1; abl. absolute with *oppidō*. *que*, enclitic conj.; connects the clauses. —— **oppidō**, abl. sing. of *oppidum, -ī*, n.; absolute with *occupātō*. —— **ibi**, adv. = *there*, i.e. in the town. —— **praesidium**, acc. sing. of *praesidium, -ī*, n. (*praeses*, a guard); direct obj. of *collocat*.

LINE 25. **col(n)locat**, 3d pers. sing. pres. ind. act. of *col(n)loco*, 1 (con + locāre = lit. *to place together*); connected by the conj. *que* with *contendit*, and in the same grammatical construction.

LINE 1. **Dum**, conj.; denotes real time — relation of two actions to each other· —— **paucōs**, acc. plur. m. of the adj. *paucus, -a, -um*; an attributive of *diēs*. —— **diēs**, acc. plur. of *diēs, diēī*, m.; acc. of *duration of time*. A. & G. 256, 2; B. 153; G. 336; H. 379. Observe that *diēs* is m. and f. in sing., but always m. in the plur. —— **ad**, prep. with the acc.; here *ad* = *in the vicinity of*. —— **Vesontiōnem**, acc. sing. of *Vesontiō, -ōnis*, f.; obj. of the prep. *ad*. Vesontio was the principal town of the Sequani — the site of modern Besançon.

2 reī	frūmentāriae	commeātūsque		causā
of the thing	*frumentary*	*of (other) supplies and,*		*for the sake,*
3 morātur,	ex	percontātiōne	nostrōrum	vōcibusque
he delays,	*from*	*the inquiry*	*of our (men)*	*words and,*
4 Gallōrum	ăc	mercātōrum,	quī	ingentī
of the Gauls	*and*	*of the traders,*	*who*	*of huge*
5 māgnitūdine	corporum	Germānōs,		incrēdibilī
size	*of bodies*	*the Germans,*		*of incredible*
6 virtūte	atque	exercitātiōne	in	armīs esse
valor	*and*	*exercise*	*in*	*arms to be,*

for the sake of securing grain and other supplies, from the inquiries of our men and the remarks of the Gauls and the sutlers who asserted that the Germans had bodies of abnormal size and were also well-trained in the use of arms —

LINE 2. **reī**, gen sing. of *rēs, reī*, f.; gen. after *causā*, which latter has here a prepositional force and follows the noun or nouns it governs. —— **frūmentāriae**, gen. sing. of adj. *frūmentārius, -a, -um* (*frūmentum*, grain); attributive of *reī*. —— **commeātūsque** (*commeātūs + que*). *commeātūs*, gen. sing. of *commeātus, -ūs*, m.; connected by enclitic *que*, with *frūmentāriae*, and in the same grammatical construction. —— **causā**, strictly an abl. of cause of *causa, -ae*, f.; but has here a prepositional force with the gen. preceding. A. & G. 223, *e*, 245, *c*; B. 165, REM. 3; G. 373; H. page 221, FOOTNOTE 2.

LINE 3. **morātur**, 3d pers. sing. pres. ind. act. of deponent *moror*, 1 (*mora*, delay); it agrees with *Caesar* understood. Observe that *dum*, while, regularly, takes the pres. ind., whatever may be the tense in the main clause. A. & G. 276, *e*; B. 228, REM. 1; G. 229, REM.; H. 467, 4. —— **ex**, prep. with the abl.; here = *from*, i.e. *in consequence of*. —— **percontātiōne**, abl. sing. of *percontātiō, -ōnis*, f.; obj. of the prep. *ex*. Observe that *percontātiō* is often written *percunctātiō*. —— **nostrōrum**, gen. plur. m. of *noster, -tra, -trum*; used substantively; or supply *virōrum*; as a gen. it limits *percontātiōne*. —— **vōcibusque** (*vōcibus + que*). *vōcibus*, abl. plur. of *vōx, vōcis*, f.; connected by the enclitic *que* with *percontātiōne*, and in the same construction.

LINE 4. **Gallōrum**, gen. plur. of *Gallī, -ōrum*, m.; limits *vōcibus*. See l. 4, Chap. I. —— **ăc**, conj. See l. 10, Chap. I. —— **mercātōrum**, gen. plur. of *mercātor, -ōris*, m.; connected by *ăc* with *Gallōrum*, and, as a gen., limits *vōcibus*. —— **quī**, nom. plur. m. of the rel. pron. *quī*; it refers to *Gallōrum ăc mercātōrum*; *quī* is subject-nom. of *praedicābant*, l. 7, below. —— **ingentī**, abl. sing. f. of the adj. *ingēns, -entis* (in + *gēns*); an attributive of *māgnitūdine*.

LINE 5. **māgnitūdine**, abl. sing. of *māgnitūdō, -inis*, f.; abl. of quality with adj. *ingentī*. A. & G. 251; B. 169; G. 400; H. 419, II. —— **corporum**, gen. plur. of *corpus, -oris*, n.; depends on *māgnitūdine*. Observe that the usual order of adj., gen., subst., is not here followed. —— **Germānōs**, acc. plur. of *Germānī, -ōrum*, m.; subject-acc. of *esse*, l. 6, below. —— **incrēdibilī**, abl. sing. f. of adj. *incrēdibilis, -e* (in + crēdibilis) = *not credible*; an attributive of *virtūte*.

LINE 6. **virtūte**, abl. sing. of *virtūs, -tūtis*, f. (*vir*, man); hence = *manliness*; abl. of quality with the adj. *incrēdibilī*. —— **atque**, conj.; connects the nouns. See l. 10, Chap. I. —— **exercitātiōne**, abl. sing. of *exercitātiō, -ōnis*, f.; connected by *atque* with *virtūte*, and abl. for the same reason. Observe that these ablatives of quality are essential parts of the predicate after *esse*. —— **in**, prep. with

290   CAESAR'S GALLIC WAR   [CHAP. XXXIX.

that they, having very often met them, could not bear even their looks and the fierceness of their eyes — suddenly so great alarm seized the entire army as to disturb greatly the minds and feelings of	praedicābant, *they boasted,*	— *—*	saepenumerō *oftentimes*	sēsē *themselves*	cum *with*	hīs *them*	7
	congressōs *having met*	nē *not*	vultum *countenance*	quidem *even*	atque *and*	aciem *sharpness*	8
	oculōrum *of eyes,*	dīcēbant *they said*	ferre *to bear*	potuisse, *to have been able,*	— *—*	tantus *so great*	9
	subitō *suddenly,*	timor *fear*	omnem *all*	exercitum *the army*		occupāvit, *seized,*	10
	ut *that*	nōn *not*	mediocriter *moderately,*		omnium *of all,*	mentēs *the minds*	11

the acc. or abl.; here it takes the abl., denoting *the being* in a certain state. —— **armīs**, abl. plur. of *arma, -ōrum*, n.; plur.; obj. of the prep. *in*. See l. 11, Chap. IV. —— **esse**, pres. inf. of *sum, esse, fuī*, fut. participle *futūrus*; infinitive, because in informal indirect discourse; subject-acc. is *Germānōs*, l. 5, above.

LINE 7. **praedicābant**, 3d pers. plur. imperf. ind. act. of *praedicō*, 1 = lit. *to speak before*. Originally *dicāre = dīcere*; but in later use *dicāre = to consecrate*, and *dīcere = to speak*; but the compound *praedicāre = praedīcere*; yet note the difference both as to conjugation and length of vowels in the penults and antepenults. —— **saepenumerō**, adv. = *oftentimes*. Often written: *saepe numerō*; in such lection *numerō* is abl. of specification. A. & G. 253; B. 162; G. 397; H. 424. —— **sēsē**, reduplicated *sē*; acc. plur.; subject-acc. of *potuisse*, l. 9, below. —— **cum**, prep. with the abl. —— **hīs**, abl. plur. m. of the dem. pron. *hīc*, used as a personal pron. of the 3d pers.; obj. of the prep. *cum*.

LINE 8. **congressōs**, acc. plur. m. of deponent participle *congressus, -a, -um* of deponent *congredior, -ī, -gressus*, 3; agrees with the pron. *sēsē*. —— **nē**, adv.; here = *not*. —— **vultum**, acc. sing. of *vultus, -ūs*, m.; direct obj. of *ferre*, l. 9, below. —— **quidem**, adv.; preceded by *nē*, and encloses the emphatic word. —— **atque** (ad + que), conj. See l. 10, Chap. I. —— **aciem**, acc. sing. of *aciēs, -ēī*, f. (kindred with *ācer*, sharp); hence = lit. *the sharp edge*; transf. = *the glance* of the eye. As straight glances suggest *straight lines, aciēs* by metonymy often = *a line* of battle. Observe that the context is often the criterion by which the meaning of a Latin word is ascertained.

LINE 9. **oculōrum**, gen. plur. of *oculus, -ī*, m.; limits *aciem*. —— **dīcēbant**, 3d pers. plur. imperf. ind. act. of *dīcō*, 3; connected with *praedicābant*, l. 7, above, by an omitted conj., and is in the same grammatical construction, i.e. agrees with *quī*, l. 4, above, as subject-nom. Observe that the iterative imperf. = *they kept saying*. —— **ferre**, pres. inf. act. of *ferō, ferre, tulī, latum*; complementary inf.; depends on *potuisse*. —— **potuisse**, perf. inf. of intrans. verb *possum, posse* (potis + sum); its subject-acc. is *sēsē*, l. 7, above. —— **tantus**, adj.; an attributive of *timor*.

LINE 10. **subitō**, adv. (*subitus* [sub + ire, *to go under*, i.e. *secretly*]; hence adv. = *suddenly*); modifies *occupāvit*. —— **timor, -ōris**, f. (*timēre*, to fear); subject-nom. of *occupāvit*. Synonyms: l. 14, Chap. XXVII. —— **omnem**, acc. sing. of adj. *omnis, -e*; an attributive of *exercitum*. Synonyms: l. 7, Chap. II. —— **exercitum**, acc. sing. of *exercitus, -ūs*, m.; direct obj. of *occupāvit*. —— **occupāvit**, 3d pers. sing. perf. ind. act. of *occupō*, 1 (ob + capere, *to seize on*); agrees with the subject-nom. *timor*.

LINE 11. **ut**, ecbatic conj. —— **nōn** (nē + oe[ū]num), negative particle; if the construction were telic, *nē* would be in place of *ut nōn*. —— **mediocriter**, adv.;

LINES 12-14.] BOOK I. 291

12 animōsque	perturbāret.	Hīc		prīmum
feelings and,	*it disturbed.*	*This (fear)*		*first*
13 ortus est	ā	tribūnīs	mīlitum,	praefectīs
arose	*from*	*the tribunes*	*of the soldiers,*	*prefects*
14 reliquīsque,	quī	ex	urbe	amīcitiae
remaining and,	*who*	*from*	*the city,*	*of friendship*

all. This alarm first started from the tribunes of the soldiers, and the other commanders who followed Caesar from the city of Rome out of friendship,

modifies *perturbāret*. Observe that *nōn mediocriter* = lit. *not moderately*, i.e. *greatly*; litotes — expresses a notion by denying the contrary. —— omnium, gen. plur. m. of the adj. *omnis, -e*, used substantively; limits both *mentēs* and *animōs*. —— mentēs, acc. plur. of *mēns, mentis*, f.; direct obj. of the verb *perturbāret*. Synonyms: l. 2, Chap. XXXIII.

LINE 12. animōsque (animōs + que). *animōs*, acc. plur. of *animus, -ī*, m.; connected by *que* with *mentēs*, and in the same construction. With *animus* compare *anima*, GK. ψυχή, *the animal spirit; animus*, GK. θυμός = *the rational spirit. Ipse animus ab anima ductus est.* Cicero. —— perturbāret, 3d pers. sing. imperf. subjunctive act. of *perturbō*, I; its subject-nom. is a pron. implied in the ending, referring to *timor*; subjunctive of result after *ut*, referring to *tantus*. A. & G. 319, 1; B. 201, REM. 1, (a); G. 552, 2 and 3; H. 500, II. This long sentence, commencing with l. 1, and ending with *perturbāret*, may be analyzed as follows: The principal clause is *tantus subitō timor omnem exercitum occupāvit*; the principal clause is modified by the time-clause *dum . . . mordātur*; it is modified by the causal phrases *ex percontātiōne . . . mercātōrum*; which latter phrases are modified by the relative, i.e. adjective-clauses *quī . . . praedicābant*, and *quī* understood *saepenumerō . . . dīcēbant*, with the infinitive-clauses as direct object of these verbs of saying; and, moreover, the principal clause is modified by the *ut . . . perturbāret*, as an adverbial clause of result. As to the omission of the rel. *quī* in the second clause, see II. 453, 2, (2). —— Hīc, nom. sing. m. of the dem. pron.; an attributive of *timor*, to be supplied, which latter is subject-nom. of *ortus est*. —— prīmum, adv.; usually = *first* in a series.

LINE 13. ortus est, 3d pers. sing. perf. ind. of deponent *orior, orīrī, ortus*, 4; agrees with *timor* understood. —— ā, prep. with the abl. See l. 6, Chap. I. —— tribūnīs, abl. plur. of *tribūnus, -ī*, m.; abl. of the source after the prep. *ā*. A. & G. 244; B. 120, 2; G. 408, 3; H. 413. Each legion had six tribunes, a species of staff-officers, appointed by the commander from the equestrian order. —— mīlitum, gen. plur. of *mīles, -itis*, m.; limits *tribūnīs*. —— praefectīs, abl. plur. of *praefectus, -ī*, m.; connected by an enclitic with *tribūnīs*, and abl. for the same reason. The *praefectī* were commanders of the horse, and had duties to perform similar to the *tribūnī* in the infantry. The *praefectī equitum* were largely cavalry officers recruited from the Gauls.

LINE 14. reliquīsque (reliquīs + que). *reliquīs*, abl. plur. m. of the adj. *reliquus, -a, -um*; an attributive of *praefectīs*. *que*, enclitic conj.; here to the second of the two words connected. —— quī, nom. plur. m. of the rel. pron. *quī*; refers to both the tribunes and prefects; subject-nom. of *habēbant*, l. 16, below. —— ex, prep. with the abl. —— urbe, abl. sing. of *urbs, urbis*, f.; obj. of the prep. *ex*; refers to Rome. —— amīcitiae, gen. sing. of *amīcitia, -ae*, f.; depends on *causā*. See l. 2, above.

and who had	causā	Caesarem	secūtī	nōn	māgnum 15
no great ex-perience in mil-itary affairs.	for the sake	Caesar	having followed	not	great,
And each one of these offer-	in	rē	mīlitārī	ūsum	habēbant;	quōrum 16
	in	the thing	military,	use	had;	of whom
ing a different excuse, which,	alius	aliā	causā	il(n)lātā,	quam 17
as he said, made	another,	another	reason	being presented,	which
it necessary for him to go, beg-	sibi	ad	proficīscendum	necessāriam	esse 18
ged to be al-	to himself	for	setting out	necessary	to be,
lowed to with-draw. Some in-	dīceret,	petēbat,	ut	ēius	voluntāte	discēdere 19
	he said,	sought,	that	by his	will	to depart

LINE 15. causā, abl. of *causa, -ae,* f. See l. 2, above. —— Caesarem, acc. sing. of *Caesar, -aris,* m.; direct obj. of deponent participle *secūtī.* —— secūtī, nom. plur. m. of the perf. participle of the deponent *sequor, -ī, secūtum,* 3; agrees with the rel. pron. *quī.* —— nōn, adv.; modifies *māgnum.* —— māgnum, acc. sing. m. of the adj. *māgnus, -a, -um;* an attributive of *ūsum.*

LINE 16. in, prep. with the acc. and abl.; here it has the abl. See l. 1, Chap. I. —— rē, abl. sing. of *rēs, reī,* f.; obj. of the prep. *in.* —— mīlitārī, abl. sing. f. of the adj. *mīlitāris, -re;* an *i*-stem; *mīlitārī* is an attributive of *rē.* —— ūsum, acc. sing. of *ūsus, -ūs,* m. (*ūtī,* to use); direct obj. of *habēbant.* —— habēbant, 3d pers. plur. imperf. ind. act. of *habeō,* 2; agrees with the subject-nom. *quī,* l. 14, above. —— quōrum, gen. plur. m. of the rel. pron. *quī;* partitive after *alius.* A. & G. 216, 2; B. 134; G. 371; H. 397, 3.

LINE 17. alius, nom. sing. of the adj. pron. *alius, -ia, -iud,* gen. *alīus,* dat. *alī;* subject-nom. of *petēbat.* Observe that *alius* repeated in another case expresses only the second part of the statement, but implies the other part. A. & G. 203, *c*; B. 56, REM. 2; G. 221, REM. 1; H. 459, 1). —— aliā, abl. sing. f. of *alius;* an attributive of *causā.* —— causā, abl. sing. of *causa, -ae,* f.; abl. absolute with *il(n)lātā.* —— il(n)lātā, abl. sing. f. of the perf. pass. participle *illātus, -a, -um* of *inferō, -ferre, -tulī, illātum;* abl. absolute with *causā,* denoting *circumstance attendant.* —— quam, acc. sing. f. of rel. pron. *quī;* refers to *causā;* is subject-acc. of *esse.*

LINE 18. sibi, dat. sing. of reflexive pron. *suī;* dat. *of reference.* A. & G. 235; B. 118, 2, and 145; G. 352; H. 384, II, 2). —— ad, prep. with the acc. —— proficīs-cendum, acc. sing. of the gerund of the deponent *proficīscor,* 3; acc. *of purpose* after the prep. *ad.* —— necessāriam, acc. sing. f. of the adj. *necessārius, -a, -um;* predicate-adj. after *esse.* —— esse, pres. inf. of the intrans. *sum, esse, fuī, futūrus;* its subject-acc. is *quam.* Observe that the infinitive-clause *quam . . . necessāriam esse* is the direct obj. of *dīceret.*

LINE 19. dīceret, 3d pers. sing. imperf. subjunctive act. of *dīcō,* 3; agrees with a pron. implied in the ending as subject-nom., referring to *alius;* subjunctive by proxy instead of the subjunctive of the verb in the clause which depends on *dīceret,* i.e. the sentiment of another is expressed by *dīceret* with a dependent infinitive-clause instead of the subjunctive of the verb in the clause. The natural Latin form would be: *quae sibi ad proficīscendum necessāria esset.* A. & G. 341, *d,* and REM.; B. 198, (*b*), and REM. 1; G. 628; H. 516, II, 1, NOTE. Observe that the reciprocal relation denoted by *alius aliā causā* is inferred rather than expressed. *If another was pre-senting another reason,* the inference is that *one was presenting one reason;* or which

LINES 20-24.] BOOK I. 293

20 licēret;	nōnnūllī	pudōre	adductī,	fluenced by a sense of shame remained, in order to escape the suspicion of cowardice. These could neither control their countenances, nor sometimes restrain their tears; but skulking in their tents lamented their own fate,
it might be lawful;	*some*	*by shame*	*being led,*	
21 ut	timōris	suspīciōnem	vitārent,	
in order that,	*of alarm*	*the suspicion*	*they might shun,*	
22 remanēbant.	Hī neque	vultum	fingere	
remained.	*These neither*	*the countenance*	*to fashion,*	
23 neque interdum	lacrimās	tenēre	poterant;	
nor sometimes	*the tears*	*to keep back*	*were able;*	
24 abditī	in tabernāculīs	aut	suum	
hiding (themselves) in	*tents*	*either*	*their own*	

is the same: *one was presenting one reason, another another.* —— **petēbat**, 3d pers. sing. imperf. ind. act. of *petō*, 3; agrees with subject-nom. *alius*, l. 17, above. —— **ut**, telic conj. —— **ēius**, gen. sing. m. of the dem. pron., used as a personal pron. of the 3d pers.; refers to Caesar; limits *voluntāte*. —— **voluntāte**, abl. sing. of *voluntās, -ātis*, f.; abl. of *specification* or *cause*. Synonyms: l. 19, Chap. VII. —— **discēdere**, pres. inf. act. of *discedō, -ere, -cessi, -cessum*, 3; supply *sibi* before the inf., after *licēret*.

LINE 20. **licēret**, 3d pers. sing. imperf. subjunctive of impersonal verb *licet*, 2; subjunctive *of purpose* after *ut*. Observe that the clause is the direct obj. of *petēbat*. —— **nōnnūllī**, nom. plur. m. of the adj. *nōnnūllus, -a, -um* (nōn + nūllus); used substantively, and = *some*; subject-nom. of *remanēbant*. —— **pudōre**, abl. sing. of *pudor, -ōris*, m. (*pudet*, it shames); abl. of *subjective cause*. —— **adductī**, nom. plur. m. of the perf. pass. participle *adductus* of the verb *addūcō*, 3; it agrees with *nōnnūllī*.

LINE 21. **ut**, telic conj. —— **timōris**, gen. sing. of *timor, -ōris*, f.; limits *suspīciōnem*. Synonyms: l. 13, Chap. XXIII. —— **suspīciōnem**, acc. sing. of *suspīciō, -ōnis*, f.; direct obj. of *vitārent*. —— **vitārent**, 3d pers. plur. imperf. subjunctive of *vitō*, 1; agrees with a pronoun implied in the ending as subject-nom., referring to *nōnnūllī*; subjunctive after *ut*, telic. Observe that *vitāre* is used both transitive and intransitive.

LINE 22. **remanēbant**, 3d pers. plur. imperf. ind. act. of *remaneō, -ēre, -mānsī, -mānsum*, 2 (re + manēre = *to stay behind*); agrees with its subject-nom. *nōnnūllī*. —— **Hī**, nom. plur. m. of the dem. pron. *hīc*; used as a personal pron. of the 3d pers.; refers to *nōnnūllī*; subject-nom. of *poterant*. —— **neque**, conjunctive adv. = lit. *and not;* but *neque . . . neque = neither . . . nor*. —— **vultum**, acc. sing. of *vultus, -ūs*, m.; direct obj. of *fingere*. —— **fingere**, pres. inf. act. of *fingō, -ere, finxī, fictum*, 3; complementary inf., depending on *poterant*.

LINE 23. **neque**, see *neque*, preceding line. —— **interdum** (inter + dum), adv. —— **lacrimās**, acc. plur. of *lacrima, -ae*, f.; direct obj. of *tenēre*. —— **tenēre**, pres. inf. act. of *teneō*, 2; connected by *neque* with *fingere*, and hence complementary inf. —— **poterant**, 3d pers. plur. imperf. ind. of *possum, posse, potuī;* agrees with subject-nom. *hī*.

LINE 24. **abditī**, nom. plur. of perf. pass. participle *abditus, -a, -um* of *abdō, -dere, -didī, -ditum*, 3 (ab + dare) = lit. *to give* or *put away;* *abditī* agrees with the omitted subj. of *querēbantur*, i.e. with *hī* understood. —— **in**, prep. with the acc. or abl.; here it takes the abl. —— **tabernāculīs**, abl. plur. of *tabernāculum, -ī*, n. (taberna, *booth* + diminutive ending -culum); obj. of the prep. *in*. —— **aut**, conj. = *or*. *aut . . . aut*

or bewailed the common danger with their intimate friends. Wills, as a general thing, were made throughout the camp. From the talk and alarm of these persons, even those who had much experience in camp-life, the soldiers and centurions	fātum *fate* suīs *their,* Volgō *Generally,* obsīgnābantur. *were sealed.* paulātim *little by little* castrīs *camp*	querēbantur *they were lamenting,* commūne *the common* tōtīs *through the whole* Hōrum *By their* etiam *even* ūsum *experience*	aut *or* perīculum *peril* castrīs *camp* vōcibus *speeches* eī, *those,* habēbant, *had,*	cum *with* tēstāmenta *wills* ac *and* quī *who* mīlitēs *soldiers*	familiāribus 25 *friends* miserābantur. 26 *they were bewailing.* testāmenta 27 *wills* timōre 28 *alarm* magnum in 29 *great in* centuriōnēs- 30 *centurions*

= *either . . . or.* See l. 19, Chap. I. —— **suum**, acc. sing. n. of poss. pron. *suus, -a, -um;* an attributive of *fātum;* refers to the subj. of proposition; hence = *their.*

LINE 25. **fātum**, acc. sing. of *fātum, -ī,* n. (*fārī,* to speak); hence *fātum* = that which is spoken — ordained; direct obj. of *querēbantur.* —— **querēbantur**, 3d pers. plur. imperf. ind. of deponent *queror, -ī, questus,* 3; agrees with a pron. implied in the ending, referring to *nōnnūllī.* —— **aut**, see *aut,* preceding line. —— **cum**, prep. with the abl. —— **familiāribus**, abl. plur. m. of the adj. *familiāris, -e* (*familia,* household); freq. used as subst., as here; abl. *of accompaniment* with the prep. *cum.*

LINE 26. **suīs**, abl. plur. m. of poss. pron. *suus, -a, -um;* attributive of *familiāribus.* —— **commūne**, acc. sing. n. of the adj. *commūnis, -e;* a modifier of *perīculum.* —— **perīculum**, acc. sing. of *perīculum, -ī,* n.; direct obj. of deponent *miserābantur.* —— **miserābantur**, 3d pers. plur. imperf. ind. of deponent *miseror, -ārī, -ātus,* 1; agrees with *hī* understood as subject-nom.

LINE 27. **Volgō**, adv. (digammated from GK. ὄχλοι); also written *vulgō;* modifies *obsīgnābantur.* —— **tōtīs**, abl. plur. n. of the adj. *tōtus, -a, -um;* an attributive of *castrīs.* —— **castrīs**, abl. plur. of *castrum, -ī,* n.; abl. *of place* without prep.; the prep. is omitted when the noun is modified by *tōtus.* A. & G. 258, *f,* 2; B. 170, REM. 2; G. 388; II. 425, 2. Observe that *castrum* = *a fort; castra* = *a camp.* —— **testāmenta**, nom. plur. n. of *testāmentum, -ī,* n.; subject-nom. of *obsīgnābantur.*

LINE 28. **obsīgnābantur**, 3d pers. plur. imperf. pass. of *obsīgnō,* 1; agrees with the subject-nom. *testāmenta.* —— **Hōrum**, gen. plur. m. of the dem. pron. *hīc,* used substantively; or supply *hominum;* limits, as a gen., *vōcibus ac timōre.* —— **vōcibus**, abl. plur. of *vōx, vōcis,* f.; abl. *of cause.* Synonyms: l. 12, Chap. XXXII. —— **ac**, conj.; connects the nouns. See l. 10, Chap. I. —— **timōre**, abl. sing. of *timor, -ōris,* m.; same construction as *vōcibus.* Synonyms: l. 14, Chap. XXVII.

LINE 29. **paulātim** (paulum, *a little* + tim), adv.; modifies *perturbābantur,* l. 32, below. —— **etiam** (et + iam) = *even* here, and hence an adv. —— **eī**, nom. plur. m. of the dem. *is;* used as pron. of the 3d pers. = *they* or *those;* subject-nom. of *perturbābantur.* —— **quī**, nom. plur. m. of rel. pron. *quī;* refers to *eī,* but is subject-nom. of *habēbant.* —— **magnum**, acc. sing. m. of the adj. *magnus, -a, -um;* an attributive of *ūsum.* —— **in**, prep. with the acc. or abl.; here it takes the abl.

LINE 30. **castrīs**, abl. plur. of *castrum, -ī* (see l. 27, above); obj. of the prep. *in.* Observe the position of the phrase — between the noun and its modifier. —— **ūsum**,

LINES 31-35.] BOOK I. 295

				and the com-
31 que	quīque	equitātuī	praeërant,	manders of cavalry, were great-
and,	who and,	the cavalry	over were,	ly disturbed;
32 perturbābantur.	Quī	sē	ex his minus	and such of them as wished
were perturbed.	Who,	themselves,	of these less	to be thought
33 timidōs	exīstimārī	volēbant,	nōn sē	less timid than the camp-follow-
timid	to be regarded	wished,	not themselves	ers said that
34 hostem	verērī,	sed	angustiās itineris	they did not fear the enemy,
the enemy	to dread,	but	the narrow passes of the route	but the narrow-
35 et	māgnitūdinem	silvārum,	quae intercēderent	ness of the road and the magni-
and	the magnitude	of the woods,	which intervened	tude of the for-

acc. sing. of *ūsus, usūs*, m.; direct obj. of *habēbant*. —— **habēbant**, 3d pers. sing. imperf. ind. act. of *habeō*, 2; agrees with its subject-nom. *quī*. —— **mīlitēs**, nom. plur. of *mīles, -itis*, m.; in apposition with the pron. *eī*, preceding line. —— **centuriōnēsque** (centuriōnēs + que). *centuriōnēs*, nom. plur. of *centuriō, -ōnis*, m. *que*, conj.; connects *centuriōnēs* with *mīlitēs*, and is in the same grammatical construction. The centurion was the commander of the sixtieth part of a legion.

LINE 31. **quīque** (quī + que). *quī*, nom. plur. of the rel. pron. *quī;* refers to *eī*, i.e. *decuriōnēs* understood; subject-nom. of *praeërat*. *que* connects the clauses. —— **equitātuī**, dat. sing. of *equitātus, -ūs*, m.; dat. after *prae* in *praeërant*. —— **praeërant**, 3d pers. plur. imperf. ind. of *praesum, -esse, -fuī;* agrees with the subject-nom. *quī*.

LINE 32. **perturbābantur**, 3d pers. plur. imperf. pass. of *perturbō*, 1; agrees with *eī*, l. 29, above. —— **Quī**, nom. plur. of the rel. pron. *quī;* refers to *eī* understood, which latter is subject-nom. of *dīcēbant*, l. 39, below; *quī* is subject-nom. of *volēbant*. —— **sē**, acc. plur. of the reflexive pron. *suī;* subject-acc. of *exīstimārī*. —— **ex**, prep. with the abl. —— **his**, abl. plur. of the dem. pron. *hic*, used as a personal pron. of the 3d pers.; obj. of the prep. *ex*. Observe that the phrase *ex his* is used for the partitive gen. *hōrum* after *eī*, the omitted subj. of *dīcēbant*, l. 39, below. A. & G. 216, *b, c;* B. 134, REM. 2; G. 372, 2; H. 397, 3, NOTE 3. —— **minus**, adv.; comparative of irr. positive *parum;* superl. *minimē;* modifies *timidōs*.

LINE 33. **timidōs**, acc. plur. of the adj. *timidus, -a, -um* (*timēre*, to fear); predicate-acc. after *exīstimārī;* cop. verb. Consult A. & G. 176, *a* and *b;* B. 130, 3, and REM. 2; G. 205, 206; H. 362, 2, 2), and 373, NOTE 2. —— **exīstimārī**, pres. inf. pass. of act. *exīstimō*, 1; subject-acc. is *sē*. —— **volēbant**, 3d pers. plur. imperf. ind. act. of *volō, velle, voluī*, irr.; agrees with the subject-nom. *quī*. —— **nōn**, adv.; modifies *verērī*. —— **sē**, acc. plur. of *suī;* subject-acc. of *verērī*.

LINE 34. **hostem**, acc. sing. of *hostis, -is*, m. and f.; direct obj. of deponent *verērī*. Synonyms: l. 15, Chap. XI. —— **verērī**, pres. inf. of deponent *vereor, verērī, veritus,* 2. Observe that the infinitive-clause *se hostem verērī* is direct obj. of *dīcēbant*, l. 39, below. —— **sed**, adversative conj. —— **angustiās**, acc. plur. of *angustiae, -ārum*, f. — rare in sing.; direct obj. of *timēre*, l. 38, below. —— **itineris**, gen. sing. of *iter, itineris*, n.; limits *angustiās*. Synonyms: l. 1, Chap. XXXVIII.

LINE 35. **et**, cop. conj.; connects *angustiās* and *māgnitūdinem*. —— **māgnitūdinem**, acc. sing. of *māgnitūdō, -inis*, f. (*māgnus*); connected by *et* with *angustiās*,

| ests that lay between them and Ariovistus; and that a supply of grain could not be easily furnished. Some even had told Caesar that, when he ordered the camp broken up and the | inter *between* rem *the thing* supportārī *to be supplied,* dīcēbant. *they said.* | ipsōs *themselves* frūmentāriam, *frumentary,* Nōnnūllī *Some* | atque *and* ut *that* posset, *it might be able* etiam *even* | Ariovistum, *Ariovistum,* satis *not enough* (themselves) Caesarī *to Caesar* | aut *or (as to)* commodē *easily* timēre *to fear* nūntiārant, *had declared,* | 36 37 38 39 |

and in the same construction. —— **silvārum**, gen. plur. of *silva, -ae,* f. (sibilated from GK. ὕλη); limits *māgnitūdinem.* —— **quae,** nom. plur. f. of the rel. pron. *quī;* refers to *silvārum,* and is subject-nom. of *intercēderent.* —— **intercēderent,** 3d pers. plur. imperf. subjunctive of *intercēdō,* 3 (inter + cēdere = lit. *to go between);* subjunctive, because in a subordinate clause in virtual *ōrātiō oblīqua.*

LINE 36. **inter,** prep. with the acc. Observe that it follows a verb compounded with *inter,* and that the prep. is often thus repeated. —— **ipsōs,** acc. plur. of the dem. pron. *ipse, -a, -um ;* used here as an emphatic indirect reflexive. A. & G. 196, 2, and NOTE; B. 85, REM. 2; G. 311, 2; H. 452, 5; *ipsōs* is the obj. of the prep. *inter.* —— **atque** (ad + que) = *and* or *and also.* See l. 10, Chap. I. —— **Ariovistum,** acc. sing. of *Ariovistus, -ī,* m.; connected by *atque* with *ipsōs,* and in the same grammatical construction. Ariovistus was chief of the German clan Suevi. —— **aut,** conj. alternative. See l. 19, Chap. I.

LINE 37. **rem,** acc. sing. of *rēs, reī,* f.; also direct obj. of *timēre.* Observe that the construction is a species styled *antiptōsis* or *prolēpsis* for *ut rēs frūmentāria satis commodē supportārī posset.* A. & G. 334, *c,* and 385, I; B. 310, 3, (*c*); G. 468; H. 636, IV, 3. —— **frūmentāriam,** acc. sing. f. of adj. *frūmentārius, -a, -um ;* attributive of *rem.* —— **ut,** telic conj. here = *that not* after *timēre,* a verb of fearing. —— **satis,** adv.; modifies the adv. *commodē.* —— **commodē,** adv. (*commodus,* adj. = *advantageous);* modifies *supportārī ;* as *ut* = *ut nōn* here, the phrase *ut satis commodē* = lit. *not enough advantageously,* i.e. *not very readily.*

LINE 38. **supportārī,** pres. inf. pass. of *sup(b)portō,* 1 (*sub* + *portāre* = lit. *to carry from beneath ;* hence *to convey to, to furnish;* complementary inf., depending on *posset.* —— **posset,** 3d pers. sing. imperf. subjunctive of *possum, posse, potuī;* subjunctive *of purpose* after *ut.* A. & G. 331, *f;* B. 200, REM. 6; G. 550, 2; H. 498, III, and NOTE 1. Observe that *ut* equivalent to *ut nōn* is used in this sense only after *metuō, paveō, timeō,* and especially the deponent *vereor.* —— **timēre,** pres. inf. act. of *timeō,* 2; supply subject-acc. *sē.* Synonyms: l. 12, Chap. XIV.

LINE 39. **dīcēbant,** 3d pers. plur. imperf. ind. act. of *dīcō,* 3; agrees with pron. *eī* understood, referring to the soldiers, centurions and prefects alluded to above. The *ōrātiō rēcta* of lines 33-38: nōn *nōs* hostem *verēmur,* sed angustiās itineris et māgnitūdinem silvārum, quae *intercēdunt* inter *nōs* atque Ariovistum, aut rem frūmentāriam, ut satis commodē supportārī *possit, timēmus.* —— **Nōnnūllī** (nōn + nūllus). See l. 20, above; subject-nom. of *nūntiārant.* —— **etiam** (et + iam), a conjunctive adv.; here = *even* or *also.* —— **Caesarī,** dat. of *Caesar, -aris,* m.; indirect obj. —— **nūntiārant,** 3d pers. plur. pluperf. ind. act. of *nūntiō,* 1; for full form *nūntiāverant* (syncopated and contracted); agrees with subject-nom. *nōnnūllī.*

LINE 1.]   BOOK I.   297

40 cum	castra	movērī	āc	sīgna	standards advanced, the soldiers would not obey; that, on account of their alarm, they would not march.
when	*the camp*	*to be moved*	*and*	*the standards*	
41 ferrī		iūssisset,		nōn	
to be borne forward		*he should have ordered,*		*not*	
42 fore	dictō		audientēs	mīlitēs	
to be about to be	*to the order*		*obedient*	*the soldiers,*	
43 neque	propter		timōrem	sīgna	
nor	*because of*		*alarm*	*the standards*	
44 lātūrōs.					
to be about to carry forward.					

1 XL.	Haec		cum	animadvertisset,	XL. Having observed this panic, Caesar called
	These	*(things)*	*when*	*he had perceived,*	

LINE 40. **cum**, conj., temporal. —— **castra**, acc. plur. of *castrum, -ī,* n.; sing. = *castle*; plur. = *camp*; subject-acc. of *movērī*. —— **movērī**, pres. inf. pass. of *moveō,* 2. —— **āc**, conj., shortened form of *atque*. See l. 10, Chap. I. —— **sīgna**, acc. plur. of *sīgnum, -ī,* n. (kindred with GK. εἰκών), *sīgnum* = lit. *a sign*; but in military use = *the sign of a cohort, a standard* borne by the *sīgnifer*; hence *sīgna ferre* = *to bear the standards*, i.e. *to break up the camp*. *sīgna* is here subject-acc. of *ferrī*.

LINE 41. **ferrī**, pres. inf. pass. of *ferō, ferre, tulī, lātum.* See *conversa,* l. 31, Chap. XXV. —— **iūssisset**, 3d pers. sing. pluperf. subjunctive of *iubeō, -ēre, -iūssī, -iūssum,* 2; subjunctive after *cum* temporal. Observe that the pluperf. subjunctive is for the fut. perf. in *ōrātiō rēcta*. —— **nōn**, adv.; modifies *fore audientēs*.

LINE 42. **fore**, fut. inf., archaic for *futūrōs esse* here; and generally *fore* = *futūrus esse*. —— **dictō**, dat. sing. of *dictum, -ī,* n.; dat. after *audientēs* — a word of obedience. A. & G. 227; B. 142; G. 346, and especially NOTE 5; H. 385, II, and especially 390, NOTE 3. —— **audientēs**, acc. plur. of *audiēns*, pres. participle of *audiō*, 4, with the adj. force of *obedient*. Observe that *fore audientēs* (*audientēs fore*) = *audientēs futūrōs esse* — the fut. inf. of *sum* with a predicate-adj. —— **mīlitēs**, acc. plur. of *mīles, -itis,* m.; subject-acc. of *fore*.

LINE 43. **neque** (nē + que) = *and not*, a conj. adv. —— **propter**, prep. with acc. —— **timōrem**, acc. sing. of *timor, -ōris,* m.; obj. of the prep. *propter*. Observe that the phrase expresses the cause. A. & G. 245, *b*; B. 165, REM. 4; G. 408, NOTE 3; H. 416, I, 2. Synonyms: l. 15, XXIII. —— **sīgna**, acc. plur. of *sīgnum, -ī,* n.; direct obj. of *lātūrōs* (*esse*).

LINE 44. **lātūrōs** (esse), fut. inf. act. of *ferō*; see l. 41, above; subject-acc. is *eōs*, i.e. *mīlitēs*. The *ōrātiō rēcta* of lines 40-44: cum castra movērī āc sīgna ferrī iūsseris, nōn erunt dictō audientēs mīlitēs, neque propter timōrem sīgna *ferent*.

LINE 1. **Haec**, acc. plur. n. of the dem. pron. *hīc*; direct obj. of *animadvertisset*; refers to the state of things — the panic mentioned in the last chapter. —— **cum**, conj. —— **animadvertisset**, 3d pers. sing. pluperf. subjunctive of *animadvertō, -ere, -tī, -versum,* 3 (animum + ad + vertere = lit. *to turn the mind to*); agrees with *Caesar* understood; subjunctive after *cum* historical.

298   CAESAR'S GALLIC WAR   [CHAP. XL.

a council; and, summoning to it the centuries of all the classes, he censured them severely: in the first place for thinking that they ought to inquire or consider either in what direction they were being led, or with	convocātō *having been called*	cōnsiliō *a council*	omniumque *of all and,*	ōrdinum *the centuries*	2
	ad id *to that*	cōnsilium *council*	adhibitīs *having been admitted*	centuriōnibus, *the centurions,*	3
	vehementer *exceedingly*	eōs *them*	incūsāvit: *he blamed:*	prīmum *first,*	quod, *because,* 4
	aut quam *either what*	in *in*	partem *direction*	aut quō *or with what*	cōnsiliō *purpose* 5
	dūcerentur, *they might be led,*	sibi *by themselves (it)*	quaerendum *to be sought ought*		aut 6 *or*

LINE 2. **convocātō**, abl. sing. n. of the perf. pass. participle *convocātus*, *-a*, *-um* of *convocō*, 1; abl. absolute with *cōnsiliō*, denoting *time when*. —— **cōnsiliō**, abl. sing. of *cōnsilium*, *-ī*, n.; absolute with the participle. —— **omniumque** (omnium + que). *omnium*, gen. plur. m. of the adj. *omnis*, *-e;* an attributive of *ōrdinum*. See l. 1, Chap. I. —— *que*, enclitic conj.; closely connects the phrases. —— **ōrdinum**, gen. plur. of *ōrdō*, *-inis*, m.; limits *centuriōnibus*. The *ōrdō* in military language = *centuria* — the century. There were two centuries in each maniple; six in each cohort; and sixty in each legion.

LINE 3. **ad**, prep. with the acc. —— **id**, acc. sing. n. of the dem. pron. *is;* an attributive of *cōnsilium*. —— **cōnsilium**, acc. sing. of *cōnsilium*, *-ī*, n.; obj. of the prep. *ad*. Synonyms: l. 5, Chap. XVIII. —— **adhibitīs**, abl. plur. m. of the perf. pass. participle *adhibitus*, *-a*, *-um* of *adhibeō*, 2 (ad + habēre); abl. absolute with *centuriōnibus*. —— **centuriōnibus**, abl. plur. of *centuriō*, *-ōnis*, m. (*centum*, hundred); abl. absolute with *adhibitīs*.

LINE 4. **vehementer** (adj. *vehemēns*, violent), adv. —— **eōs**, acc. plur. m. of the dem. pron. *is;* used as a personal pron. of the 3d pers.; direct obj. of *incūsāvit*. —— **incūsāvit**, 3d pers. sing. perf. ind. act. of *incūsō*, 1 (in + causa). Synonyms: *incūsāre* = *to entangle* one in a case — to blame him anywhere; whereas *accūsāre* = *to call one publicly to account*. —— **prīmum**, adv. = *the first* in a series. Observe that from *prīmum* to *futūram*, l. 77, below, the form of discourse is indirect. —— **quod**, conj., causal.

LINE 5. **aut**, correlative conj. *aut . . . aut* = *either . . . or*. See l. 19, Chap. I. —— **quam**, acc. sing. f. of the interrogative adj. pron. *quis*, *quae*, *quid* or *quī*, *quae*, *quod;* it modifies *partem*. —— **in**, prep. with the acc. or abl.; here it takes the acc. Position: l. 16, Chap. I. —— **partem**, acc. sing. of *pars*, *partis*, f.; obj. of the prep. *in*. —— **aut**, see *aut*, immediately preceding. —— **quō**, abl. sing. n. of interrogative adj. pron. *quis* or *quī;* modifies *cōnsiliō*. —— **cōnsiliō**, abl. sing. of *cōnsilium*, *-ī*, n.; abl. *of manner* or *cause*, i.e. *in accordance with*.

LINE 6. **dūcerentur**, 3d pers. plur. imperf. subjunctive pass. of *dūcō*, 3; its subject-nom. is the pron. *eī* understood, referring to the centurions; subjunctive, because in a subordinate clause in *ōrātiō oblīqua;* or better, an *indirect question;* the subjunctive is required here in direct discourse. —— **sibi**, dat. plur. of the reflexive pron. *suī;* dat. of the agent after the gerundives. —— **quaerendum** (esse), pres. inf. of pass. periphrastic conjugation — gerundive form — of *quaerō*, *-ere*, *-sīvī*, *-sītum*, 3; used impersonally. —— **aut**, see *aut*, preceding line.

7 cōgitandum	putārent.	Ariovistum,	sē
to be thought ought,	*they supposed.*	*Ariovistus,*	*himself*
8 cōnsule,	cupidissimē	populī	Rōmānī
(being) consul,	*most eagerly*	*of the people*	*Roman*
9 amīcitiam	appetīsse;	cūr	hunc tam
the friendship	*to have sought to gain;*	*why*	*him so*
10 temerē	quisquam ab	officiō	discessūrum
unreasonably	*any one from*	*duty (to be)*	*about to fall away*
11 iūdicāret?	Sibi	quidem	persuādērī,
should judge?	*To himself*	*certainly*	*to be persuaded,*

what design. He said that Ariovistus in Caesar's consulship had most eagerly sought an alliance with the Roman people; why should any one think that he would so rashly renounce his fidelity? Caesar certainly was convinced

LINE 7. **cōgitandum (esse)**, pres. inf. of pass. periphrastic conjugation of *cōgitō*, 1 (con [cum] + agitāre); hence *cōgitāre* = to agitate something in the mind intensely, i.e. *think, reflect*. *cōgitandum* is used impersonally like *quaerendum*. These gerundive forms denote *necessity* or *duty*. —— **putārent**, 3d pers. plur. imperf. subjunctive of *putō*, 1; subjunctive, because in a *quod*-clause in *ōrātiō oblīqua*. The *ōrātiō rēcta* of lines 4–7: (*Vōs inclūsō*,) prīmum quod, aut quam in partem aut quō cōnsiliō *dūcāminī*, *vōbīs* quaerendum aut cōgitandum *putātis*. —— **Ariovistum**, acc. sing. of *Ariovistus, -ī*, m.; subject-acc. of *appetīsse*, l. 9, below. —— **sē**, abl. sing. of reflexive pron. *suī*, referring to Caesar; abl. absolute with *cōnsule*, denoting the *time when*. Observe that two nouns or a noun and a pron. may be in the abl. absolute construction. Caesar was consul 59 B.C.; his colleague was M. Calpurnius Bibulus.

LINE 8. **cōnsule**, abl. sing. of *cōnsul, -ulis*, m.; absolute. —— **cupidissimē**, adv., superl. of positive *cupidē*, comparative *cupidius*; qualifies *appetīsse*. —— **populī**, gen. sing. of *populus, -ī*, m.; limits *amīcitiam*. Synonyms: l. 17, Chap. VI. —— **Rōmānī**, gen. sing. of adj. *Rōmānus, -a, -um*; an attributive of *populī*.

LINE 9. **amīcitiam**, acc. sing. of *amīcitia, -ae*, f.; direct obj. of *appetīsse*. —— **appetīsse**, perf. inf. act. of *ap(d)petō*, 3; for *appetīvisse*. —— **cūr**, adv. (*quor*, contracted from *quārē*, but some make it from cui + rē = *for what reason*). —— **hunc**, acc. sing. m. of the dem. pron. *hīc*, used as a personal pron. of the 3d pers.; subject-acc. of *discessūrum (esse)*; *eum* would be the better form for the pron. in indirect discourse. But Caesar uses the demonstratives for personal pronouns with great freedom. —— **tam**, adv.; modifies *temerē*.

LINE 10. **temerē**, adv.; anteclassic form *temeriter*; modifies *discessūrum (esse)*. —— **quisquam** (quis + quam), indef. pron., used in negative sentences; subject-nom. of *iūdicāret*. —— **ab**, prep. with the abl. —— **officiō**, abl. sing. of *officium, -ī*, n. (ob + facere = lit. *to do for another*); obj. of the prep. *ab*. —— **discessūrum (esse)**, pres. inf. act., first periphrastic conjugation, of *discēssō*, 3; its subject-acc. is *hunc*.

LINE 11. **iūdicāret**, 3d pers. sing. imperf. subjunctive act. of *iūdicō*, 1; its subject-nom. is a pron., referring to Ariovistus; in the subjunctive, because a *real* question in indirect discourse. A. & G. 338; B. 245, 3; G. 651; H. 523, II, 1. This might be taken as deliberative subjunctive in direct discourse, *cūr iūdicet*. A. & G. 268 and 338, *a*; B. 245, 3, REM. 2, near end; G. 651, REM. 2; H. 484, V, and 523, II, and NOTE. The *ōrātiō rēcta* of lines 7–11: *Ariovistus mē* cōnsule cupidissimē populī Rōmānī amīcitiam *appetīvit*; cūr hunc tam temerē quisquam ab officiō discessūrum *iūdicat?* —— **Sibi**, dat. sing.; indirect obj. after *persuādērī*; *sibi* refers to Caesar.

that, when his demands were known and the justice of his claims were clearly seen, he (Ariovistus) would neither reject his favor, nor that of the Roman people. But if, impelled by rage and folly, he should bring war upon them,	cōgnitīs suīs postulātīs atque aequitāte 12 *being known his demands and the equity* condiciōnum perspectā eum neque 13 *of the conditions being clearly perceived him neither* suam neque populī Rōmānī grātiam 14 *his nor the people's Roman favor* repudiātūrum. Quod sī furōre atque 15 *(to be) about to repudiate. As to which if by fury and* āmentiā impulsus bellum intulisset, 16 *madness being driven, war he should have brought on,*

——— **quidem**, adv.; emphasizes *sibi*. ——— **persuādērī**, pres. inf. pass. of *persuādeō, -ēre, -suāsī, -suāsum*, 2 (per + suādēre = lit. *to advise prevailingly*); *persuādērī* is here used impersonally; strictly, the following accusative-clause *eum ... repudiātūrum (esse)* is the subject.

LINE 12. **cōgnitīs**, abl. plur. of the perf. pass. participle *cōgnitus, -a, -um* of *cōgnōscō, -ere, -nōvī, -nitum*, 3; abl. absolute with *postulātīs*. ——— **suīs**, abl. plur. n. of the poss. pron. *suus, -a, -um;* an attributive of *postulātīs*. ——— **postulātīs**, abl. plur. of *postulātum, -ī*, n.; abl. absolute with participle *cōgnitīs*, denoting *time when*. ——— **atque** (ad + que), conj. See l. 10, Chap. I. ——— **aequitāte**, abl. sing. of *aequitās, -ātis*, f. (*aequus*, equal); abl. absolute with the perf. pass. participle *perspectā*.

LINE 13. **condiciōnum**, gen. plur. of *condic(t)iō, -ōnis*, f.; as gen. limits *aequitāte*. ——— **perspectā**, abl. sing. f. of the perf. pass. participle *perspectus, -a, -um* of *perspiciō, -ere, -spexī, -spectum*, 3; abl. absolute with *aequitāte*. ——— **eum**, acc. sing. m. of the dem. pron. *is*, used as a personal pron. of the 3d pers.; subject-acc. of *repudiātūrum (esse)*; it refers to Ariovistus. ——— **neque** (nē + que), conj.; *neque ... neque*, correlates = *neither ... nor*.

LINE 14. **suam**, acc. sing. f. of the poss. pron. *suus, -a, -um;* an attributive of *grātiam* understood; refers to Caesar. ——— **neque**, see *neque*, preceding line. ——— **populī**, gen. sing. of *populus, -ī*, m.; limits *grātiam*. Synonyms: l. 17, Chap. VI. ——— **Rōmānī**, gen. sing. m. of the adj. *Rōmānus, -a, -um;* an attributive of *populī*. ——— **grātiam**, acc. sing. of *grātia, -ae*, f. (*grātus*, pleasing); direct obj. of *repudiātūrum (esse)*.

LINE 15. **repudiātūrum (esse)**, pres. inf. of first periphrastic conjugation formed from *repudiō*, 1; its subject-acc. is *eum*, l. 13, above. ——— **Quod**, strictly an adverbial acc. = *as to which;* but in this position before *sī* it = *and* or *but*. ——— **sī**, conditional conj. ——— **furōre**, abl. sing. of *furor, -ōris*, m. (*furere*, to rage; compare GK. θύειν); abl. *of cause* after *impulsus*. ——— **atque** (ad + que), conj.; adds a more emphatic notion.

LINE 16. **āmentiā**, abl. sing. of *amentia, -ae*, f. (ā + mente = *far from one's mind*); connected by *atque* with *furōre*, and in the same grammatical construction. ——— **impulsus**, perf. pass. participle of *impellō, -ere, -pulī, -pulsum*, 3 (in + pelere = lit. *to drive on*); agrees with the subj. of *intulisset*, i.e. Ariovistus. ——— **bellum**, acc. sing. of *bellum, -ī*, n.; indirect obj. of *intulisset;* *eīs*, as indirect obj., is understood. See l. 15, Chap. I. ——— **intulisset**, 3d pers. sing. pluperf. subjunctive of *īnferō*,

[LINES 17-21.] BOOK I. 301

17 quid	tandem	verērentur?	aut	cūr	dē	what, pray, had they to fear? or why should
what	then	should they fear?	or	why	of	
18 suā	virtūte	aut	dē	ipsīus	dīligentiā	they despair of their own valor or his watchfulness? A trial
their	valor	or	of	his	diligence	
19 dēspērārent?		Factum		ēius	hostis	of that enemy had been made in the memory
should they despair?		To have been made		of that	enemy	
20 perīculum	patrum	nostrōrum		memoriā,	cum	of our fathers when, on the repulse of the Cimbri and Teutoni by Caius Marius, the
a trial	in fathers'	our,		memory,	when.	
21 Cimbrīs	et	Teutonīs		ā	C. Mariō	
the Cimbri	and	the Teutoni		by	Caius Marius	

-ferre, -tulī, il(n)lātum, irr.; subject-nom. is *Ariovistus* understood; subjunctive, because in a conditional clause in indirect discourse for the fut. perf. in direct.

LINE 17. **quid**, acc. sing. n. of the interrogative pron. *quis;* direct obj. of deponent *verērentur.* —— **tandem**, adv. (tam + dem) = lit. *just so far;* hence *so long, at length;* in interrogative clauses = *then, pray.* —— **verērentur**, 3d pers. plur. imperf. subjunctive of *vereor,* 2; subjunctive, because a *real* question in indirect discourse. For references, see l. 11, above. —— **aut**, conj., alternative. See l. 19, Chap. I. —— **cūr**, adv. See l. 9, above. —— **dē**, prep. with the abl. See l. 27, Chap. XIX.

LINE 18. **suā**, abl. sing. of the poss. pron. *suus, -a, -um;* an attributive of *virtūte.* —— **virtūte**, abl. sing. of *virtūs, -ūtis,* f. *(vir,* man); obj. of the prep. *dē.* —— **aut**, see *aut,* preceding line. —— **dē**, prep. with the abl. —— **ipsīus**, gen. sing. m. of the dem. pron. *ipse, -sa, -sum;* used as a personal pron. of the 3d pers.; it limits *dīligentiā;* used also for the indirect reflexive to avoid ambiguity. A. & G. 196, *i;* B. 85, REM. 2; G. 311, 2; H. 452, 5. Observe that *ipsīus* refers to Caesar, and *suā* before *virtūte* refers to the panic-stricken camp-followers. —— **dīligentiā**, abl. sing. of *dīligentia, -ae,* f.; obj. of the prep. *dē.*

LINE 19. **dēspērārent**, 3d pers. plur. imperf. subjunctive act. of *dēspērō,* 1 (dē + spērāre = lit. *to be without hope);* subjunctive, because a *real* question in indirect discourse. Compare the references to *iūdicāret,* l. 11, above. The *ōrātiō rēcta* of lines 11-19: *Mihi* quidem *persuādētur,* cōgnitīs *meīs* postulātīs atque aequitāte condiciōnum perspectā *hunc* neque *meam* neque populī Rōmānī grātiam repudiātūrum. Quod sī furōre atque āmentiā impulsus bellum *intulerit,* quid tandem *verēminī?* aut cūr dē *vestrā* virtūte aut dē *med* dīligentiā *dēspērātis?* —— **Factum (esse)**, perf. inf. of *fīō, fierī, factus,* used as pass. of *faciō,* 3; its subject-acc. is *perīculum.* —— **ēius**, gen. sing. m. of the dem. pron. *is;* an attributive of *hostis.* —— **hostis**, gen. sing. of *hostis, -is,* m. and f.; as a gen. it limits *perīculum.*

LINE 20. **perīculum**, acc. sing. of *perīculum, -ī,* n.; subject-acc. of *factum (esse).* —— **patrum**, gen. plur. of *pater, patris,* m.; it limits *memoriā.* —— **nostrōrum**, gen. plur. m. of poss. pron. *noster, -tra, -trum;* an attributive of *patrum.* —— **memoriā**, abl. sing. of *memoria, -ae,* f.; abl. *of time.* A. & G. 256, 1; B. 171, and REM. 4; G. 393; H. 429. —— **cum**, conj., temporal.

LINE 21. **Cimbrīs**, abl. plur. of *Cimbrī, -ōrum,* m. (GK. Κίμβροι); abl. absolute with the perf. pass. participle *pulsīs.* The Cimbri were a German people inhabiting Holstein, Schleswic and Jutland. The Cimbri and Teutoni invaded northern Italy,

army seemed to deserve no less praise than the commander himself; a trial of the enemy had also been made lately in Italy, in an insurrection of slaves (and though originally without discipline), yet	pulsis *having been routed,*	nōn *not*	minōrem *less*	laudem *praise*	exercitus *the army*	22
	quam *than*	ipse *the very*	imperātor *commander*	meritus *to have merited,*	vidēbātur; *seemed;*	23
	factum *a trial*	etiam *even*	nūper *recently*	in *in*	Italiā Italy	servīlī *in a servile*	24
	tumultū, *tumult,*	quōs *whom*	tamen *yet*	aliquid *in some degree*	ūsus *the experience*	25

and were defeated by Caius Marius, near Verona, B.C. 101. —— **et**, cop. conj. —— **Teutonis**, abl. plur. of *Teutonī, -ōrum,* m. (*Teutonēs, -um*); connected by *et* with *Cimbrīs*, and in the same construction. The Teutons were a German people, who inhabited Zealand and the islands at the entrance of the Baltic Sea. —— **ā**, prep. with the abl. —— **C.** = *Caiō*, abl. of *Caius, -ī,* m.; praenōmen. —— **Mariō**, abl. of *Marius, -ī,* m.; abl. *of the agent* after the prep. *ā.* A. & G. 246; B. 166; G. 401; H. 415, I. *Marius* is a name of Roman *gēns.* Caius Marius was seven times elected consul, was conqueror of Jugurtha, and was a friend of the popular party.

LINE 22. **pulsīs**, abl. plur. m. of the perf. pass. participle *pulsus, -a, -um* of the verb *pellō, -ere, pepulī, pulsum,* 3; abl. absolute with *Cimbrīs* et *Teutonīs.* —— **nōn**, adv.; modifies the adj. *minōrem.* —— **minōrem**, acc. sing. f. of the adj. *minor, -ōris* — *parvus, minor, minimus. minōrem* is an attributive of *laudem.* —— **laudem**, acc. sing. of *laus, laudis,* f.; direct obj. of the deponent *meritus (esse).* —— **exercitus**, nom. sing. of *exercitus, -ūs,* m.; subj. of *vidēbātur.* Synonyms: l. 31, Chap. III.

LINE 23. **quam**, here a conj. = *than.* —— **ipse**, an intensive pron. = *himself;* in apposition with *imperātor.* A. & G. 195, *f*; B. 85, REM. 1; G. 311, 1; H. 452, 1. —— **imperātor**, -ōris, nom. sing. m.; subject-nom. of *vidēbātur* understood. The text with ellipses supplied is: *nōn minōrem laudem exercitus meritus esse vidēbātur quam ipse imperātor meritus esse vidēbātur.* —— **meritus (esse)**, perf. inf. of deponent *mereor, -ērī, -itus,* 2; complementary inf. —— **vidēbātur**, 3d pers. sing. imperf. ind. of *videor, -ērī, vīsus,* 2; pass. of *video;* in the pass. *vidērī* = *to be looked on,* or *regarded* in any way; hence = *to seem.* As *cum . . . vidēbātur* is a subordinate clause in *ōrātiō oblīqua,* we should expect *vidērētur* here. But Caesar uses the indicative to emphasize a fact. A. & G. 336 (2. *Subordinate Clauses*), *d*; B. 245, REM. 2; G. 628, REM. (*a*); H. 529, II, NOTE 1, 2).

LINE 24. **factum (esse)**, perf. pass. inf. of *fīō, fierī, factus* (see *factum,* l. 19, above); supply *ēius hostis perīculum* from lines 19 and 20; of which *perīculum* is subject-acc. of *factum (esse).* —— **etiam** (et + iam = lit. *and now*), adv. —— **nūper** (*noviper,* from *novus*); modifies *factum (esse).* —— **in**, prep. with the acc. or abl.; here it takes the abl. locative. A. & G. 258, *c*; B. 170; G. 385; H. 425, I. —— **Italiā**, abl.; obj. of the prep. *in.* —— **servīlī**, abl. sing. m. of *servīlis, -e* (*servus,* a slave); attributive of *tumultū.*

LINE 25. **tumultū**, abl. of *tumultus, -ūs,* m. (*tumēre,* to swell); abl. *of time when.* For grammatical references, see *memoriā,* l. 20, above. The allusion is to the revolt of the gladiators under Spartacus, B.C. 73-71. Synonyms: *tumultus* = *civil broils; sēditiō* = political commotions; whereas *bellum* = *an armed contest between nations* or *states.* —— **quōs**, acc. plur. of the rel. pron. *quī;* it refers to *servīlī* as if it were

26 āc	dīsciplīnā,	quam	ā	nōbīs	accēpissent,	the experience and training which they had received from us assisted them somewhat. And from this can be judged how much advantage there is in courage; for those whom they had
and	*discipline*	*which*	*from*	*us*	*they had received,*	
27 sublēvārent.	Ex	quō	iūdicārī		posse,	
assisted.	*From*	*which*	*to be judged*		*to be possible,*	
28 quantum	habēret	in	sē	bonī	cōnstantiā,	
how much	*might have*	*in*	*itself,*	*of good,*	*resolution,*	
29 proptereā	quod,	quōs	aliquamdiū		inermōs	
for this reason	*because,*	*whom*	*for a time*		*unarmed*	

servōrum — synesis. A. & G. 199, (*b*); B. 129, REM. 7; G. 614, 3, (*a*); H. 445, 5. *quōs* is direct obj. of *sublēvārent*, l. 27, below. —— *tamen*, adv. = *yet;* used to express contrast. —— *aliquid*, acc. sing. n. of the indef. pron. *aliquis, aliquid;* acc. of specification. A. & G. 240, *a*; B. 150, REM. 2; G. 333; H. 378, 2. —— *ūsus, -ūs*, m.; subject-nom. of *sublēvārent*, l. 27, below.

LINE 26. **āc**, conj.; connects the nouns. See *atque*, l. 10, Chap. I. —— **dīsciplīna, -ae**, f.; connected by *āc* with *ūsus*, and in the same construction. —— **quam**, acc. sing. f. of the rel. pron. *quī;* refers to the nearest noun, and understood with *ūsus;* direct obj. of *accēpissent.* —— **ā**, prep. with the abl. —— **nōbīs**, abl. plur. of the personal pron. *egō;* obj. of the prep. *ā.* —— **accēpissent**, 3d pers. plur. pluperf. subjunctive of *accipiō, -ere, -cēpī, -ceptum*, 3 (ad + capere); agrees with *hostēs* understood as subject-nom.; subjunctive *by attraction.*

LINE 27. **sublēvārent**, 3d pers. plur. imperf. subjunctive of *sublēvō*, 1; agrees with *ūsus* and *dīsciplīna* as subject-nominatives; subjunctive, because in a dependent clause in *ōrātiō oblīqua.* The *ōrātiō rēcta* of lines 19–27: Factum ēius hostīs perīculum patrum nostrōrum memoriā, cum Cimbrīs et Teutonīs ā C. Mariō pulsīs nōn minōrem laudem exercitus quam ipse imperātor meritus vidēbātur; factum etiam nūper in Ītaliā servīlī tumultū, quōs tamen aliquid ūsus āc dīsciplīna, quam ā nōbīs *accēperunt sublevābant.* —— **Ex**, prep. with the abl. —— **quō**, abl. sing. n. of the rel. pron. *quī;* used substantively; refers to *perīculum*, as indicated in the previous sentences; and is also the herald of the following *quod*-clause. At the beginning of a sentence *ex quō* = *et ex hōc.* —— **iūdicārī**, pres. inf. pass. of *iūdicō*, 1; complementary inf.; depends on *posse.* —— **posse**, pres. inf. of the intrans. *possum, potuī;* used here impersonally; in strictness, the following clause *quantum habēret . . . cōnstantia* is the subject.

LINE 28. **quantum**, acc. sing. n. of the interrogative adj. *quantus, -a, -um;* used as a subst.; direct obj. of *habēret.* —— **habēret**, 3d pers. sing. imperf. subjunctive of *habeō*, 2; its subject-nom. is *cōnstantia;* subjunctive, because an indirect question. —— **in**, prep. with the acc. or abl.; here it takes the abl. —— **sē**, abl. sing. of the reflexive pron. *suī;* obj. of the prep. *in;* it refers to *cōnstantia.* —— **bonī**, gen. sing. n. of the adj. *bonus, -a, -um*, used as a noun; partitive gen. after *quantum.* A. & G. 216, 3; B. 134, REM. 1; G. 369; H. 397, 3. Observe that *quantum bonī* = lit. *how much of good.* —— **cōnstantia, -ae**, f.; subject-nom. of *habēret.* Note the emphasis as indicated by the order of the words.

LINE 29. **proptereā** (propter + eā), adv. —— **quod**, conj. See l. 9, Chap. I. —— **quōs**, acc. plur. of the rel. pron. *quī;* its antecedent is *hōs*, following line. *quōs* is direct obj. of *timuissent.* Observe that the relative clause precedes the antecedent clause — a not unusual arrangement. —— **aliquamdiū** (aliquam + diū) = *somewhat*

unreasonably feared for a time when unarmed, subsequently they vanquished when armed and flushed with the pride of victory. In short, these were the same parties with whom the Helvetii often fought not only	sine *without* armātōs *armed* Dēnique *In fine,* saepenumerō *oftentimes*	causā *reason* āc *and* hōs *these* Helvētiī *the Helvetii*	timuissent, *they had feared,* (whilom) esse *to be* congressī *having met*	hōs *these* victōrēs *victors* eōsdem *the same* nōn *not*	posteā 30 *afterwards* superāssent. 31 *they had defeated.* quibuscum 32 *whom with,* sōlum 33 *only*

long, for a while. The parts of the word are sometimes written separately; this adv. modifies *timuissent.* —— **inermōs,** acc. plur. m. of the adj. *inermus, -a, -um* (in, *negative* + arma); the adj. agrees with *quōs.*

LINE 30. **sine,** prep. with the abl. —— **causā,** abl. of *causa, -ae,* f.; obj. of the prep. *sine.* —— **timuissent,** 3d pers. plur. of *timeō, -ere, -uī,* 2; it agrees with a pron. implied in the ending as subject-nom., referring to the Roman soldiers; subjunctive, because in a subordinate clause in *ōrātiō oblīqua.* —— **hōs,** acc. plur. m. of the dem. pron. *hīc,* used as a personal pron. of the 3d pers.; direct obj. of *superāssent. hōs* alludes to the gladiators. —— **posteā** (post + eā), adv.

LINE 31. **armātōs,** acc. plur. m. of the perf. pass. participle *armātus, -a, -um* of *armō;* used as an adj. = *armed;* it agrees with *hōs.* —— **āc,** conj. See *atque,* l. 10, Chap. I. —— **victōrēs,** acc. plur. of *victor, -ōris,* m. (*vincere,* to conquer); used as an appositive of *hōs;* but in connection with *armātōs* it has an adj. force. A. & G. 188, *d;* B. 127, REM. 1; G. 325, and REM. 2; H. 363, 2, 2). —— **superāssent,** 3d pers. plur. pluperf. subjunctive of *superō,* 1; its subject-nom. is a pron., referring to Roman soldiers; subjunctive, because in a *quod*-clause in *ōrātiō oblīqua.* Observe that *superāssent* is the contracted form for *superāvissent.*

LINE 32. **Dēnique** (dein + que = lit. *and then);* here a *time* particle, corresponding with *prīmum,* l. 4, above. —— **hōs,** acc. plur. m. of the dem. pron. *hīc;* used as a personal pron. of the 3d pers.; subject-acc. of *esse. hōs* here refers to the Germans under Ariovistus. —— **esse,** pres. inf. of *sum,* perf. *fuī.* —— **eōsdem,** acc. plur. m. of the iterative dem. pron. *idem, eadem, idem;* predicate-acc. after *esse.* —— **quibuscum** (quibus + cum). *quibus,* abl. plur. of the rel. *quī;* obj. of the enclitic prep. *cum.* Observe that *cum* is thus appended to all the forms of the abl. of the rel. pronoun. Observe the anacoluthon, *quibuscum* follows *congressī,* but *superārent* requires *quōs.*

LINE 33. **saepenumerō** (saepe + numerō), adv.; sometimes *saepe numerō;* in this lection, *numerō* is an abl. of respect. —— **Helvētiī,** nom. plur. m. of the adj. *Helvētius, -a, -um,* used as a noun; subj. of *superārint,* l. 35, below. See l. 16, Chap. I. —— **congressī,** nom. plur. m. of the perf. participle *congressus, -a, -um* of *congredior, -gredī, -gressus,* 3, deponent; agrees with *Helvētiī;* but translate as if *sunt* were expressed with *congressī.* —— **nōn,** adv.; modifies *sōlum* (adj. *sōlus).* Observe (1) that the particles *nōn sōlum* are used in contrast with *sed etiam* to indicate the passing to something more important; frequently *nōn modō, nōn tantum* . . . *vērum etiam,* or *sed* alone are thus used; (2) that these particles express by antithesis what two copulatives *et* . . . *et, que* . . . *que, cum* . . . *tum* express by direct affirmation. —— **sōlum,** adv. *(sōlus,* only).

34 in	suīs,	sed	etiam	in	illōrum	fīnibus	in their own bor-
in	*their own,*	*but*	*also*	*in*	*their,*	*territory*	ders, but even in the German coun-
35 plērumque		superārint,		quī	tamen	parēs	try, and had usu- ally gained the
generally		*have conquered,*		*who*	*yet*	*equal*	victory overthem;
36 esse	nostrō	exercituī		nōn	potuerint.	Sī	and yet they had proved no match
to be	*to our*	*army*		*not*	*were able.*	*If*	for our army. If
37 quōs	adversum	proelium	et		fuga	Gallōrum	the unfavorable skirmish and
any,	*the adverse*	*battle*	*and*		*flight*	*of the Gauls*	flight of the Gauls

LINE 34. **in**, prep. with the acc. or abl.; here it takes the abl. —— **suīs**, abl. plur. m. of the poss. and reflexive pron. *suus, -a, -um;* an attributive of *fīnibus* understood; refers to *Helvētiī.* —— **sed etiam**, see note on *nōn sōlum,* preceding line. —— **in**, note the repetition of the prep. by which the notions are kept distinct. —— **illōrum**, gen. plur. m. of the dem. pron. *ille, -la, -lud;* used as a personal pron. of the 3d pers.; limits *fīnibus;* refers to the Germans. —— **fīnibus**, abl. plur. of *fīnis, -is,* m.; obj. of the prep. *in.* Synonyms: l. 12, Chap. II.

LINE 35. **plērumque** (plērum + que), adv. (plērus [*plūs*] + que) = *the greater part.* Observe that *que* is merely intensive. The adv. modifies *superārint.* —— **superārint**, 3d pers. plur. perf. subjunctive of *superō,* 1 (contracted for *superāverint);* agrees with the subject-nom. *Helvētiī;* supply *quōs* as direct obj.; subjunctive, because in a subordinate clause in *ōrātiō oblīqua.* —— **quī**, nom. plur. m. of the rel. pron. *quī;* refers to *Helvētiī;* subject-nom. of *potuerint.* —— **tamen**, adv. = *yet,* i.e. here it expresses the antithesis to an implied concession. —— **parēs**, nom. plur. m. of the adj. *pār, paris; parēs* is predicate-acc. after *esse.*

LINE 36. **esse**, pres. inf. of *sum, fuī, futūrus;* complementary inf.; depends on *potuerint.* —— **nostrō**, dat. sing. m. of the poss. pron. *noster, -tra, -trum;* an attributive of *exercituī.* —— **exercituī**, dat. sing. of *exercitus, -ūs,* m.; dat. after the adj. *parēs,* equal. A. & G. 234, *a;* B. 144; G. 359, REM. 1; H. 391, I. —— **nōn** (nē + ūnum), adv. —— **potuerint**, 3d pers. plur. perf. subjunctive of *possum, posse, potuī;* agrees with *Helvētiī* understood as subject-nom.; subjunctive, because in a dependent clause in *ōrātiō oblīqua.* The *ōrātiō rēcta* of lines 27–36: Ex quō iūdicārī *potest,* quantum *habeat* in sē bonī cōnstantia, proptereā quod, quōs aliquamdiū inermōs sine causā *timuērunt,* hōs posteā armātōs āc victōrēs *superārunt* (*superāvērunt*). Dēnique hī *sunt īdem* quibuscum saepenumerō Helvētiī congressī nōn sōlum in suīs, sed etiam in illōrum fīnibus plērumque *superārunt* (*superāvērunt*), quī tamen parēs esse nostrō exercituī nōn *potuerant.* —— **Sī** (original form *seī,* sibilated from GK. *eī*), conditional conj.

LINE 37. **quōs**, acc. plur. of the indef. pron. *quis, quae, quid;* direct object of *commovēret.* —— **adversum**, nom. sing. n. of the adj. *adversus, -a, -um* (ad + versus); an attributive of *proelium.* —— **proelium**, -ī, n.; subject-nom. of *commovēret.* Synonyms: l. 18, Chap. I. For account of this battle, see Chaps. XV and XIX, end. —— **et**, cop. conj. —— **fuga**, -ae, f. (GK. φυγή); connected by *et* with *proelium,* and in the same construction. We should expect a plur. verb; but the battle and flight are conceived as a single conception. A. & G. 205, *b;* B. 126, REM. 2; G. 211, REM. 1; H. 463, I. —— **Gallōrum**, gen. plur. m. of the adj. *Gallus, -a, -um,* used as a noun; limits *proelium* and *fuga.* Observe that Caesar here makes no distinction between the Helvetii and the other Gallic clans.

had disturbed	commovēret,	hōs,	sī	quaererent,	reperīre 38
any, they on in-	*should disturb,*	*these,*	*if*	*they should seek,*	*to find out,*
vestigation might					
discover that,	posse,	diūternitāte	bellī		dēfatīgātīs 39
when the Gauls	*to be able,*	*by the length*	*of the war*	*having been wearied out*	
were wearied					
with a protract-	Gallīs	Ariovistum,	cum	multōs	mēnsēs 40
ed war, Ariovis-	*the Gauls,*	*Ariovistus,*	*when*	*for many*	*months*
tus, after keep-					
ing himself in	castrīs	sē	āc	palūdibus	tenuisset	neque 41
camp and in	*in camp,*	*himself,*	*and*	*in swamps,*	*he had held,*	*nor*
marshes many					
months, and giv-					
ing no opportu-	suī	potestātem	fēcisset,		dēspērantēs 42
nity of meeting	*of himself*	*an opportunity*	*had made, (the Gauls) despairing*		

LINE 38. **commovēret**, 3d pers. sing. imperf. subjunctive of *commoveō*, 2; sub-junctive, because in a condition after *sī*. —— **hōs**, acc. plur. m. of the dem. pron. *hīc*; used as a personal pron. of the 3d pers.; explanatory of indef. pron. *quōs;* but is subject-acc. of *posse*. —— **sī**, conditional conj. —— **quaererent**, 3d pers. sing. imperf. subjunctive of *quaerō, -ere, -sīvī (-iī), -sītum,* 3; subjunctive after *sī*, in *the condition*. —— **reperīre**, pres. inf. act. of *reperiō, -īre, re(p)perī, repertum,* 4; complementary inf.; depends on *posse.*

LINE 39. **posse**, pres. inf. of *possum*, perf. *potuī;* its subject-acc. is the pron. *hōs*. —— **diūternitāte**, abl. sing. of *diūternitās, -ātis,* f.; abl. *of cause.* —— **bellī**, gen. sing. of *bellum, -ī,* n.; limits *diūternitāte.* —— **dēfatīgātīs**, abl. plur. m. of the perf. pass. participle *dēfatīgātus, -a, -um* of *dēfatīgō,* 1; abl. absolute with *Gallīs,* denoting *time when.*

LINE 40. **Gallīs**, abl. plur. of *Gallī, -ōrum;* absolute with *dēfatīgātīs*. —— **Ariovistum**, acc. sing. of *Ariovistus, -ī,* m.; subject-acc. of *vīcisse,* l. 45, below. Observe that this accusative-clause depends on *hōs reperīre posse,* lines 38 and 39, above. —— **cum**, conj. = *when* or *after.* —— **multōs**, acc. plur. m. of the adj. *multus, -a, -um;* attributive of *mēnsēs.* —— **mēnsēs**, acc. plur. of *mēnsis, -sis,* m.; acc. *of duration of time.* A. & G. 256, 2; B. 153; G. 336; H. 379.

LINE 41. **castrīs**, abl. plur. of *castrum, -ī,* n.; in sing. = *fort, castle;* in plur. = *camp;* abl. *locative* without a prep.; a rigid construction would make this an abl. of means. A. & G. 258,*f.* 1; B. 170, REM. 4; G. 389; H. 425, II, 1, 1). —— **sē**, acc. sing. of reflexive pron. *suī;* refers to Ariovistus; direct obj. of *tenuisset.* —— **āc**, conj. See l. 10, Chap. I. —— **palūdibus**, abl. plur. of *palūs, -ūdis,* f.; connected by *āc* with *castrīs,* and as the same grammatical construction, i.e. abl. *locative.* —— **tenuisset**, 3d pers. sing. pluperf. subjunctive of *teneō,* 2; its subject-nom. is a pron., referring to Ariovistus; subjunctive after *cum* temporal. —— **neque** (nē + que), conjunctive adv. = *and not.*

LINE 42. **suī**, gen. sing. m., objective, referring to Ariovistus; limits *potestātem.* —— **potestātem**, acc. sing. of *potestās, -ātis,* f.; direct obj. of *fēcisset.* —— **fēcisset**, 3d pers. sing., pluperf. subjunctive of *faciō,* 3; connected by *neque* with *tenuisset,* and subjunctive for same reason. The lit. translation of *suī potest. fēcisset* is: *he had not made an opportunity of himself.* Compare this Lat. idiom with English *he had not made a fool of himself*. —— **dēspērantēs**, acc. plur. of pres. participle of *dēspērō,* 1; agrees with *eōs*, i.e *Gallōs* understood, as direct obj. of deponent participle *adortum.*

[LINES 43-46.]   BOOK I.   307

43 iam	dē	pūgnā	et	dispersōs	subitō	him, had sudden-
already	*of*	*a fight*	*and*	*scattered,*	*suddenly*	ly attacked them already despair-
44 adortum		magis	ratiōne	et	cōnsiliō	ing of a battle and scattered abroad,
having attacked,		*more*	*by planning*	*and*	*design*	and had conquered them more by
45 quam	virtūte		vīcisse.		Cui ratiōnī	cunning and craft than by valor.
than	*by valor*		*to have conquered.*		*For which method*	Not even Ariovistus himself ex-
46 contrā	hominēs	barbarōs	atque		imperītōs	pected that an army could be
against	*men*	*barbarous*	*and*		*inexperienced*	

LINE 43. **iam**, adv. = *already*; often of past or future time; while *nunc* puts the emphasis on the present. —— **dē**, prep. with the abl. Synonyms: l. 27, Chap. XIX. —— **pūgnā**, abl. sing. of *pūgna, -ae*, f.; obj. of the prep. *dē*. Synonyms: l. 15, Chap. I. —— **et**, cop. conj.; couples *dēspērantēs* and *dispersōs*. —— **dispersōs**, acc. plur. of perf. pass. participle *dispergō, -ere, -spersi, -spersum*, 3; agrees with *eōs* or *Gallōs*, to be supplied. —— **subitō**, adv. (*subitus* [sub + īre], *to come under*, i.e. *secretly*); hence adv. = *secretly*; modifies *adortum*.

LINE 44. **adortum**, acc. sing. m. of *adortus, -a, -um*, perf. participle of deponent *adorior, -iri, -ortus*, 4; agrees with *Ariovistum*, l. 40, above. —— **magis**, adv., comparative degree; superl. *māximē*; modifies *vīcisse*. —— **ratiōne**, abl. sing. of *ratiō, -ōnis*, f. (*reri*, to reckon); abl. *of means*. —— **et**, cop. conj. —— **cōnsiliō**, abl. sing. of *cōnsilium, -ī*, n.; connected by *et* with *ratiōne*, and in the same construction. Observe that here both *ratiō* and *cōnsilium* express subjective conceptions, i.e. = *reason* and *judgment*; as compared with *virtūs* (*vir*), they were conceived by Caesar as very inferior means of winning victories.

LINE 45. **quam**, here = *than*, conj. —— **virtūte**, abl. sing. of *virtūs, -ūtis*, f.; abl. *of means*. —— **vīcisse**, perf. inf. act. of *vincō, -ere, vīcī, victum*, 3; its subjectacc. is *Ariovistum*, l. 40, above. The *ōrātiō rēcta* of lines 36-45: Sī quōs adversum proelium et fuga Gallōrum *commovet, hī,* sī *quaerunt*, reperīre *possunt,** diūturnitāte bellī dēfatīgātīs Gallīs, Ariovistum, cum multōs mēnsēs castrīs sē ac palūdibus *tenuit* neque sui potestātem *fēcit, Gallōs* dēspērantēs iam dē pūgnā et dispersōs subitō adortum, magis ratiōne et cōnsiliō quam virtūte vīcisse. —— **Cui**, dat. sing. of the rel. pron. *qui*; used here adjectively; an attributive of *ratiōnī*; yet really refers to *ratiōne*, to be supplied with *hāc*, in the following line. Such incorporation of the antecedent in the relative clause is common. A. & G. 200, *b*, especially the last example; B. 129, REM. 1, (*a*); G. 616; H. 445, 9. —— **ratiōnī**, dat. sing. of *ratiō, -ōnis*, f.; dat. poss. with *fuisset*.

LINE 46. **contrā**, adv. and prep.; here a prep. with acc. —— **hominēs**, acc. plur. of *homō, -inis*, m. and f.; obj. of the prep. *contrā*. —— **barbarōs**, acc. plur. m. of adj. *barbarus, -a, -um;* an attributive of *hominēs*. —— **atque** (ad + que), conj. See *atque*, l. 10, Chap. I. —— **imperītōs**, acc. plur. m. of the adj. *imperītus* (in, *negative* + perītus); an attributive of *hominēs*.

* The pres. subjunctive (*a*) might be used in both protasis and apodosis; or (*b*) the fut. ind., or (*c*) as it may be conceived to be a general condition, the perf. ind. in protasis and pres. ind. in apodosis. Thus (*a*) Sī ... *commoveat* ... *hī quaerant* ... *reperīre possint;* or (*b*) Sī ... *commovēbit* ... *hī quaerent* ... *reperient;* or (*c*) Sī ... *commōvit* ... *reperīre possunt*.

captured by this method, for which there might be room in conflicts with barbarous and unskillful men. Those who attributed their fear to a pretense of anxiety as to the grain supply and the narrowness of the road acted presumptuously, since they appeared either to despair of their commander's do-	locus *room*	fuisset, *might have been,*	hāc *by this,*	nē *not*	ipsum 47 *(Ariovistus) himself*
	quidem *even,*	spērāre *to hope*	nostrōs *our*	exercitūs *armies*	capī 48 *to be captured,*
	posse. *to be able.*	Quī *Who,*	suum *their*	timōrem *fear*	in rei 49 *to, of the thing*
	frūmentāriae *frumentary*		simulātiōnem *the pretense*		angustiāsque 50 *narrowness and,*
	itineris *of the road,*	cōnferrent *have attributed,*		facere *(these) to act*	arroganter, 51 *arrogantly,*
	cum *since,*	aut *either*	dē *of*	officiō *the service*	imperūtōris 52 *of the commander,*

LINE 47. **locus**, subject-nom. of *fuisset*. See *locī*, l. 10, Chap. II. —— **fuisset**, 3d pers. sing. pluperf. subjunctive of *sum*, *esse*, *fui*; subjunctive, because in a subordinate clause in *ōrātiō oblīqua*. —— **hāc**, abl. sing. f. (*hīc, haec, hōc*); an attributive of *ratiōne*, to be supplied; which latter is abl. of means. —— **nē**, adv. here = *not*. —— **ipsum**, acc. sing. m. (*ipse, -sa, -sum*); refers to Ariovistus; subject-acc. of *spērāre*.

LINE 48. **quidem**, adv., restrictive; emphasizes preceding word. —— **spērāre** (*spēs*, hope); pres. inf. of *sperō*, 1. —— **nostrōs**, acc. plur. m. (*noster, -tra, -trum*); limits *exercitūs*. —— **exercitūs, -ūs**, m., acc. plur.; subj. of *posse*. Synonyms: l. 31, Chap. III. —— **capī**, pres. inf. pass. of *capiō*, 3; complementary, depends on *posse*.

LINE 49. **posse**, pres. inf. (*possum*); subject-acc. is *exercitūs*. —— **Quī**, nom. plur. m. (*quī, quae, quod*); refers to *eōs*, omitted subject-acc. of *facere*, l. 51, below; and is subject-nom. of *cōnferrent*. —— **suum**, acc. sing. (*suus, -a, -um*); agrees with *timōrem*. —— **timōrem**, acc. sing. m. (*timor, -ōris*); direct obj. of *cōnferrent*. —— **in**, prep. with the acc. or abl.; here with the acc. —— **reī**, gen. sing. f. (*rēs, reī*); limits *simulātiōnem*.

LINE 50. **frūmentāriae**, adj., gen. sing. f.; limits *reī*. See l. 37, Chap. XXXIX; observe the position of the adj., and see A. & G. 344, *g*; B. 43; G. 413, REM. 3, and 678, REM. 4; H. 569, II, 3. —— **simulātiōnem**, acc. sing. f. (*simulā, -tiō, -tiōnis*, f.); obj. of the prep. *in*. —— **angustiāsque** (angustiās + que). *angustiās*, acc. plur. f. (*angustiae, -ārum*). *que*, enclitic conj.; connects *angustiās* with *simulātiōnem*, and is in the same construction. See l. 3, Chap. IX.

LINE 51. **itineris**, gen. sing. n. (*iter, itineris*); limits *angustiās*. Synonyms: see *via*, l. 2, Chap. IX. —— **cōnferrent**, 3d pers. sing. imperf. subjunctive of *cōnferō*, *-ferre, -tulī, col(n)lātum*; agrees with the subject-nom. *quī*; subjunctive, because in a dependent clause in *ōrātiō oblīqua*. —— **facere**, pres. inf. of *faciō*, 3; its subject-acc. is *eōs* understood. —— **arroganter**, adv. (derived from *ar(d)rogāns* [ad + rogāre] = *to appropriate another's traits*); modifies *facere*.

LINE 52. **cum**, conj., causal. —— **aut**, alternative conj. See l. 19, Chap. I. —— **dē**, prep. with the abl. See l. 27, Chap. XIX. —— **officiō**, abl. n. (*officium, -ī*); obj. of the prep. *dē*. —— **imperātōris**, gen. sing. m. (*imperātor, -tōris*); limits *officiō*.

53 dēspērāre	aut	praescrībere		vidērentur.	ing his duty,
to despair	*or*	*to prescribe*	*(to him)*	*they seemed.*	or to be dictating to him.
54 Haec	sibi	esse	cūrae:	frūmentum	The following matters were engaging his attention: the Sequani, Leuci and Lingones were to furnish the grain, and the grain was already ripe in the fields; as to the roads, they
These (things)	*to himself*	*to be*	*for a care:*	*the grain*	
55 Sēquanōs,	Leucōs,	Lingonēs		subministrāre,	
the Sequani,	*Leuci,*	*the Lingones*		*to furnish,*	
56 iamque	esse	in	agrīs	frūmenta	mātūra;
already, and	*to be*	*in*	*the fields*	*the harvests*	*ripe;*
57 dē	itinere	ipsōs	brevī	tempore	
concerning	*the road*	*themselves*	*in a short*	*time*	

LINE 53. dēspērāre, pres. inf. of *dēspērō*, 1; complementary; depends on *vidērentur*. —— aut, see *aut*, preceding line. —— praescrībere, pres. inf. act. of *praescrībō*, 3; connected by *aut* with *dēspērāre*, and in the same construction; supply *eī* as indirect obj. —— vidērentur, 3d pers. plur. imperf. pass. subjunctive of *videor -ērī, -vīsus*, 2 (see l. 23, above); subjunctive after *cum* causal. The *ōrātiō rēcta* of lines 45-53: Cui ratiōnī contrā hominēs barbarōs atque imperītōs locus *fuit*, hāc nē *Ariovistus ipse* quidem *spērābat* nostrōs exercitūs capī posse. Qui *vestrum* timōrem in reī frūmentāriae simulātiōnem angustiāsque itineris *cōnferēbātis, fēcistis* arroganter, cum aut dē officiō imperātōris dēspērāre aut praescribere *vidērēminī*.

LINE 54. Haec, acc. plur. n. (*hīc, haec, hōc*); used substantively; subject-acc. of *esse*. —— sibi, dat. of *object to which* of pron. *suī*; refers to Caesar. —— esse, pres. inf. of *sum, fuī, futūrus*. —— cūrae, dat. sing. (*cura, -ae*, f.); dat. of the *end for which*. A. & G. 233; B. 147; G. 356, and REM. 3; H. 390, NOTE 1, 1). —— frūmentum, acc. sing. n. (*frūmentum, -ī*); direct obj. of *subministrāre*. Observe that the accusative-clauses are appositives of *haec*, immediately preceding. Compare *frūmentum* and *frūmenta*, lines 2 and 5, Chap. XVI.

LINE 55. Sēquanōs, acc. plur. m. (*Sēquanī, -ōrum*); subject-acc. of *subministrāre*. See *Sēquanīs*, l. 25, Chap. I. —— Leucōs, acc. plur. m. (*Leucī, -ōrum*); same construction as *Sēquanōs*; note asyndeton. The Leuci were a people of Belgic Gaul. —— Lingonēs, acc. plur. m. (*Lingonēs, -um*); same construction as *Leucōs*. The Lingones dwelt near the sources of the Marne, not far from the Vosges Mountains. —— sub(m)ministrāre, pres. inf. act. (sub + ministrō, 1). Observe that *b* in *sub* is freq. assimilated. A. & G. 11, *f*; G. 9. 3; H. 34, 3.

LINE 56. iamque (iam + que). *iam* adv. Synonyms: l. 4, Chap. V. *que*, enclitic conj. —— esse, pres. inf. (*sum*); its subject-acc. is *frūmenta*, immediately below. —— in, prep. with the acc. or abl.; here with the abl. —— agrīs, abl. plur. m. (*ager, agrī*, m.); obj. of the prep. *in*. Synonyms: see *agrum*, l. 12, Chap. II. —— frūmenta, acc. plur.; subj. of *esse*. See lines 2 and 5, Chap. XVI. —— mātūra, acc. plur. n. (*mātūrus*, adj.); predicate after *esse*.

LINE 57. dē, prep. with the abl. —— itinere, abl. sing. n. (*iter*); obj. of the prep. *dē*. Synonyms: l. 2, Chap. IX. —— ipsōs, acc. plur. m. (*ipse, -a, -um*); subject-acc. of *iūdicātūrōs* (*esse*). See A. & G. 102, *e*; B. 85, REM. 1; G. 311, and 2; H. 452, 1. —— brevī, adj., abl. sing. n. (*brevis, -e*); an attributive of *tempore*. —— tempore, abl. sing. n. (*tempus, -oris*); *time in which*. A. & G. 256, 1; B. 171; G. 393; H. 429.

310   CAESAR'S GALLIC WAR   [CHAP. XL.

themselves could judge in a short time. As to the report that the soldiers would not obey his orders, and would not march, he was in no respect agitated by that matter. For he knew that, if an army would not obey orders, either	iūdicātūrōs. *(to be) about to judge.*	Quod *As to the fact that,*	nōn *not*	fore 58 *to be about to be*
	dictō *to the command*	audientēs *obedient,*	neque *nor*	sīgna 59 *the standards*
	lātūrī *to be about to bear*	dīcantur, *they are said,*	nihil *nothing*	sē eā 60 *himself, by that*
	rē commovērī; *thing to be moved;*	scīre *to know*	enim, *for,*	quibuscumque 61 *to whomsoever*
	exercitus dictō *an army to command*	audiēns *obedient*	nōn *not*	fuerit, aut 62 *has been, either*

LINE 58. iūdicātūrōs (esse), fut. inf. act. of *iūdicō*, 1; its subject-acc. is the pron. *ipsōs*. Synonyms: l. 9, Chap. XIX. The *ōrātiō rēcta* of lines 54-58: Haec mihi sunt cūrae: frūmentum *Sēquanī, Leucī,* Lingonēs *subministrant,* iamque *sunt* in agrīs frūmenta mātūra; dē itinere (*vōs*) *ipsī* brevī tempore *iūdicābitis.* —— Quod, acc. of specification of *quī* = *whereas*. See A. & G. 333, *a*; B. 123, REM. 21; G. 525, 2 and 3; H. 516, II, and NOTE. —— nōn, adv. (nē + ūnum); qualifies *fore audientēs.* —— fore, fut. inf. — rare form for *futūrī esse.*
LINE 59. dictō, dat. sing. n. (*dictum, -ī*); after *audientēs*. A. & G. 234; B. 144; G. 359; H. 391. —— audientēs, nom. plur. of pres. participle *audiēns, -ntis* of *audiō*, 4; as predicate after *fore;* yet in agreement with the subject of *dīcantur.* —— neque, conjunctive adv. = *and not*, continues the negation introduced by *nōn.* —— sīgna, acc. plur. n. (*sīgnum*); direct obj. of *lātūrī (esse).*
LINE 60. lātūrī (esse), fut. inf. act. of *ferō, ferre, tulī, lātum.* Observe that the participle part of this inf. is declinable; and is nom. plur. m., agreeing in number and gender with the subject-nom. of the pass. *dīcantur.* —— dīcantur, 3d pers. plur. pres. subjunctive pass. of *dīcō,* 3. Observe that the personal construction is used here; and consult A. & G. 330, *b*, 1; B. 194, REM. 1, (*a*); G. 528, 1; H. 534, 1, NOTE 1, (2). Observe that the sentiments are declared to be the sentiments of another; and that the verb used is in the subjunctive, while the verbs dependent upon it should properly be in that mode. See A. & G. 341, *d*, and REM.; B. 198, REM. 1; G. 525, 2 and 3; H. 516, II, and NOTE. —— nihil, neuter noun; acc. of specification. A. & G. 238, *b*; B. 150, REM. 3; G. 333, REM. 2, and 442, NOTE 2; H. 378, 2. —— sē, acc. sing. (*suī, sibi, sē, sē*); subj. of *commovērī.* —— eā, abl. sing. f. (*is, ea, id*); an attributive of *rē.*
LINE 61. rē, abl. sing. f. (*rēs, reī*); abl. *of cause.* A. & G. 245, and 2, *b*; B. 165, and REM. 4; G. 408, and NOTE 2; H. 416, NOTE 1. —— commovērī, pres. inf. pass. of *commoveō*, 2; its subject-acc. is *sē.* —— scīre, pres. inf. act. of *sciō scīre, scīvī (sciī), scītum,* 4; supply *sē* as subject-acc., referring to Caesar. Synonyms: see *scīre,* l. 4, Chap. XX. —— enim, conj. = subjective cause. —— quibuscumque, dat. plur. m. (*quīcumque, quaecumque, quodcumque*); dat. after the phrase *dictō audiēns* = *obediēns.* A. & G. 227, FOOTNOTE, end; B. 142; G. 346, NOTE 5; H. 385, I.
LINE 62. exercitus, -ūs, m.; subject-nom. of *fuerit.* —— dictō, dat. (*dictum, -ī*, n.); after *audiēns;* and this phrase in sense of *obediēns* takes the dat. after it. A. & G. 234; B. 144; G. 359; H. 391. —— audiēns, in form a pres. participle, in use an adj.; predicate after *fuerit.* —— nōn, adv. —— fuerit, 3d pers. sing. perf.

63 male	rē	gestā	fortūnam		dēfuisse
badly	*a thing*	*being done,*	*fortune*	*to have failed (them)*	
64 aut	aliquō	facinore	compertō		avāritiam
or	*some*	*crime*	*being discovered,*		*covetousness*
65 esse convictam.			Suam		innocentiam
to have been proved (against them).			*His own*		*integrity*
66 perpetuā	vītā,	fēlicitātem	Helvētiōrum		bellō
in an entire	*life,*	*good-fortune*	*in the Helvetians'*		*war*
67 esse perspectam.		Itaque	sē,	quod	in
to have been clearly seen.		*Therefore*	*himself,*	*what*	*to*

good-fortune had failed its commanders as shown by want of success, or avarice had been proved against them by the discovery of some crime. His own integrity throughout life had been clearly seen, and his good-fortune in the Helvetian war. According-

subjunctive (*sum, esse, fuī*); subjunctive, because in a dependent clause in *ōrātiō oblīqua.* —— aut, alternative conj. Synonyms: lines 19 and 20, Chap. I.

LINE 63. male, adv., positive; comparative *pēius;* superl. *pessimē;* modifies *gestā.* —— rē, abl. sing. f. (*rēs, reī*); absolute with perf. pass. *gestā,* denoting *cause.* A. & G. 255, *d.* 2; B. 192; G. 410; H. 431, 2, (3). —— gestā, abl. sing f. of perf. pass. *gestus, -a, -um* of *gerō, -ere, -gessī, -gestum,* 3; absolute with the noun *rē.* —— fortūnam, acc. sing. f. (*fortūna, -ae*); subject-acc. of *dēfuisse.* —— dēfuisse, perf. inf. of *dēsum* (dē + sum).

LINE 64. aut, see *aut,* immediately preceding. —— aliquō, abl. sing. m. (*aliquis, -qua, -quod* or *-quid*); indef. pron.; an attributive of *facinore.* —— facinore, abl. sing. n. (*facinus, facinoris*); abl. absolute with perf. pass. *compertō.* Synonyms: *facinus* (*facere*) = *any bold wicked deed; flāgitium* = *a crime against one's self;* while *scelus* = *an offense against others.* —— compertō, abl. sing. n. of perf. pass. participle *compertus, -a, -um* of *comperiō, -īre, -perī, -pertum,* 4; absolute with *facinore.* —— avāritiam, acc. sing. f. (*avāritia, -ae*); subject-acc. of *esse convictam* (*convictam esse*).

LINE 65. esse convictam, perf. inf. pass. of *convinco, -ere, -vīcī, -victum,* 3. Observe that Dr. Anthon's text reads *esse coniunctam* = *has been fastened;* whereas *esse convictam* = *has been proved.* —— Suam, acc. sing. f., poss. pron. (*suus*); an attributive of *innocentiam;* refers to Caesar. —— innocentiam, acc. sing. of *innocentia, -ae,* f.; subject-acc. of *esse perspectam.*

LINE 66. perpetuā, abl. sing. f. (adj. *perpetuus*); an attributive of *vītā.* —— vītā, abl. sing. f. (*vīta, -ae*); *duration of time.* A. & G. 256, 2, *b;* B. 153, REM. 2; G. 393, REM. 2; H. 379, 1. —— fēlicitātem, acc. sing. f. (*fēlicitās, -ātis*); subject-acc. of *esse perspectam.* Note the asyndeton between the accusative-clauses. Synonyms: *fēlicitās* (*fēlix,* happy) = *good fortune; fortūna* (*fors*) = *chance fortune.* —— Helvētiōrum, gen. plur. m. (*Helvētiī, -ōrum*); limits *bellō.* See l. 15, Chap. I. —— bellō, abl. sing. n. (*bellum, -ī*); locative; the notion of place is figurative. A. & G. 258, *f,* 1, end; B. 170, REM. 4; G. 389; H. 425, II, 1, 1) and 2).

LINE 67. esse perspectam (*perspectam esse*), perf. inf. pass. of *perspicio, -ere,* = *-spēxī, -spectum,* 3. The *ōrātiō rēcta* of lines 58-67: Quod nōn fore dictō audientēs neque signa lātūrī *dīcuntur;* — or: quod (*mīlitēs*) nōn dictō *audient,* neque signa *ferent, ut dīcitur,* — nihil *egō hāc rē commoveor;* sciō enim, quibuscumque exercitus dictō audiēns nōn *fuit,* aut male rē gestā fortūnam (*eīs*) dēfuisse aut aliquō facinore

ly, he would do at once what he had purposed to defer to a more distant day:—break up the camp the next night during the fourth watch, that he might know as soon as possible whether among them a sense of shame and duty,	longiōrem *a more distant* repraesentātūrum *(to be) about to do at once,* dē *in the course of* mōtūrum, *(to be) about to move,* posset, *he might be able,*	diem *day* quartā *the fourth* ut *that,* utrum *whether*	collātūrus *about to postpone* et *and* vigiliā *watch* quam *how* apud *with*	fuisset, 68 *he had been,* proximā *on the following* prīmum *the first* eōs *them*	nocte 69 *night* castra 70 *the camp* intellegere 71 *to know* pudor atque 72 *shame and*

compertō avāritiam esse convictam. *Mea innocentia* perpetuā vītā, *fēlīcitās* Helvētiōrum bellō *est perspecta.* —— Itaque (ita + que), conjunctive adv. = *and so.* —— sē, acc. sing. (*suī, sibi, sē, sē*); refers to Caesar; subject-acc. of *repraesentātūrum* (*esse*). —— quod, rel. pron. acc. n. (*quī, quae, quod*); direct obj. of *collātūrus fuisset;* refers to idea expressed in *sē . . . castra mōtūrum* (*esse*); freq. *id* is inserted before *quod.* A. & G. 200, *e,* and NOTE; B. 129, REM. 8; G. 614, REM. 2; H. 445, 7. —— in, prep. with the acc. or abl.; here the acc.

LINE 68. longiōrem, acc. sing. f. (*longior, -ius*); comparative of adj. *longus;* superl. *-issimus;* an attributive of *diem.* —— diem, acc. sing. m. and f. (see l. 5, Chap. IV); obj. of the prep. *in.* —— col(n)lātūrus fuisset, 3d pers. sing. pluperf. subjunctive, first periphrastic conjugation, formed from *cōnferō, -ferre, -tulī, -lātum;* subject-nom. is Caesar understood; in the subjunctive, because in a subordinate clause in *ōrātiō oblīqua.*

LINE 69. repraesentātūrum (esse), fut. inf. act. of *repraesentō,* 1; its subject-acc. is *sē.* —— et, cop. conj. —— proximā, abl. sing. f. (*proximus, -a, -um,* superl. of *propior*); an attributive of *nocte.* —— nocte, abl. sing. f. (*nox, noctis*); *time when.* A. & G. 256, 1; B. 171; G. 393; H. 429.

LINE 70. dē, prep. with the abl. Synonyms: l. 27, Chap. XIX. See also note on *dē,* l. 19, Chap. XII. —— quartā, abl. sing. f. (*quartus, -a, -um*); ord. adj. —— vigiliā, abl. sing. f. (*vigilia, -ae*). See l. 11, Chap. XII. *vigiliā* is obj. of the prep. *dē.* —— castra, acc. plur. n. (*castrum, -ī*); direct obj. of *mōtūrum* (*esse*). See l. 12, Chap. XII.

LINE 71. mōtūrum (esse), fut. inf. act. of *moveō,* 2; connected by *et* with *repraesentātūrum,* and in same construction. —— ut, telic conj. —— quam, adv.; modifies *prīmum.* —— prīmum, adv. (*prīmus*); with preceding *quam,* with or without *possum* = *as soon as possible;* the two words are sometimes written *quamprīmum.* —— intellegere (see l. 6, Chap. X); complementary inf., depending on *posset.*

LINE 72. posset, 3d pers. sing. imperf. subjunctive of *possum; purpose* after *ut.* —— utrum, adv.; in indirect questions = *whether;* in direct, it is untranslatable; followed by an alternative *an,* as seen in the text. Questions thus introduced express the alternation of a double question; whereas *sīve . . . sīve* express the alternation by single words or phrases rather than by complete clauses. —— apud, prep. with the acc. = *at, by, among,* etc. —— eōs, acc. plur. m. (*is, ea, id*); as personal pron. of the 3d pers.; obj. of the prep. *apud.* —— pudor, -ōris, m.; subject-nom. of *valēret.* —— atque, conj. See l. 10, Chap. I.

73 officium,	an	timor	plūs	valēret.	Quod	or cowardice was the more influential. But if no one else would follow him, he would yet go with the tenth legion alone, concerning which he had no misgivings; and it should be his body-guard.
duty,	or	fear	more	prevailed.	As to which	
74 sī	praetereā	nēmō	sequātur,	tamen	sē	
if	beside	no one	should follow,	yet	himself	
75 cum	sōlā	decimā	legiōne		itūrum,	
with	only	the tenth	legion		(to be) about to go,	
76 dē		quā	nōn	dubitāret,	sibique	
concerning		which	not	did he doubt,	to himself and,	
77 eam		praetōriam	cohortem		futūram.	
that (legion)		a pretorian	cohort		(to be) about to be.	

LINE 73. officium, -ī, n.; subject-nom. of valēret. —— an, alternative conj.; see note on utrum. —— timor, -ōris, m.; also subject-nom. of valēret. Synonyms: l. 14, Chap. XXVII. —— plūs, adv., or adverbial acc.; modifies valēret. Consult A. & G. 240, a; B. 123, 5, REM. 21; G. 334, REM. 1; H. 378, 2. —— valēret, 3d pers. sing. imperf. subjunctive of valeō, -ere, -uī, -itum, 2; subjunctive, because an indirect question. A. & G. 334; B. 242; G. 467; H. 529, I. The ōrātiō rēcta of lines 67-73: Itaque egō, quod in longiōrem diem collātūrus fuī, repraesentābō et proximā nocte dē quartā vigiliā castra movēbō, ut quam prīmum intellegere possim, utrum apud vōs pudor atque officium, an timor plūs valeat. —— Quod, for its force, see A. & G. 180, f; B. 129, REM. 9; G. 610; H. 453.

LINE 74. sī, conditional conj. —— praetereā (praeter + eā), adv. —— nēmō, -inis, m. (nē + homō); used in nom. and acc.; for other cases, nūllīus, nūllī and nūllō; subject-nom. of sequātur. —— sequātur, 3d pers. sing. pres. subjunctive of sequor, 3; subject-nom. nēmō; subjunctive in condition after sī. A. & G. 337, 1; B. 245, 4, (a); G. 590; H. 507, II. Observe that now the point of view of the speaker prevails —repraesentātiō. —— tamen, adv., opposed to concession denoted by sī. —— sē, acc. sing. (suī, sibi, sē, sē); subject-acc. of itūrum (esse).

LINE 75. cum, prep. with the abl. —— sōlā, abl. sing. f. (solus, -a, -um); limits legiōne. —— decimā, abl. sing. f. of ord. adj. (decimus, -a, -um). —— legiōne, abl. sing. f. (legiō, -ōnis); obj. of the prep. cum — abl. of accompaniment. Observe that the Roman legions were called first, second, etc., up to the tenth, according to the order in which they were levied. —— itūrum (esse), fut. inf. act. of -eō, -īre, -īvī (-iī), -itum; its subject-acc. is pron. sē.

LINE 76. dē, prep. with the abl. —— quā, abl. sing. f. (quī, quae, quod); used substantively; or supply legiōne; obj. of the prep. dē. —— nōn, adv. —— dubitāret, 3d pers. sing. imperf. subjunctive of dubitō, 1; subjunctive, because in a subordinate clause in ōrātiō oblīqua. —— sibique (sibi + que). sibi, dat. sing. (suī, sibi, sē, sē); possessor after futūram (esse). A. & G. 231; B. 146; G. 349; H. 387. que, enclitic conjunction.

LINE 77. eam, acc. sing. f. (is, ea, id); an attributive of legiōnem understood; which latter is subject-acc. of futūrum (esse). —— praetōriam, acc. sing. f. of the adj. praetorius, -a, -um; an attributive of cohortem. —— cohortem, acc. sing. f. (cohors, -hortis); predicate after futūram (esse). The cohort usually means the tenth part of a legion; but here, as modified by praetōriam, it = the general's body-guard. —— futūram (esse), fut. inf. of sum, esse, fuī. Observe that with futūram ends the ōrātiō oblīqua of the chapter. The ōrātiō rēcta of lines 73-77: Quod sī

Caesar had especially favored this legion, and had put the greatest confidence in it because of its valor.	Huic legiōnī Caesar et indulserat 78 *To this legion Caesar both had been indulgent* praecipuē et propter virtūtem 79 *particularly and on account of its valor* cōnfīdēbat māximē. 80 *was wont to trust in the highest degree.*		

XLI. After the delivery of this speech, the minds of all were changed in a wonderful manner, and intense eagerness and enthusiasm arose	XLI. Hāc ōrātiōne habitā, mīrum 1 *This oration having been held, wonderful* in modum conversae sunt omnium mentēs 2 *in, measure changed were of all the minds,* summaque alacritās et cupiditās bellī 3 *the highest and, ardor and eagerness of (for) the war*		

---

praetereā nēmō *sequĕtur*, tamen *egō* cum sōlā decimā legiōne *ībō*, dē quā nōn *dubitō, mihique haec praetōria cohors erit.*

LINE 78. **Huic**, dat. sing. f. (*hīc, haec, hōc*); an attributive of *legiōnī*. —— **legiōnī**, dat. sing. f. (*legiō, -ōnis*); after *indulserat* — a verb of *favoring*. A. & G. 227; B. 142; G. 346, and REM. 2; H. 385, II. —— **Caesar, -aris**, m.; subject-nom. of *indulserat*. —— **et** . . . **et** =*both* . . . *and*. —— **indulserat**, 3d pers. sing. pluperf. ind. of *indulgeo, -ĕre, -dulsī, -dultum*, 2 (in + dulcis); hence *indulgēre* = lit. *to be sweet* — *complaisant.*

LINE 79. **praecipuē**, adv.; qualifies *indulserat*. —— **et**, see *et*, immediately preceding. —— **propter**, prep. with the acc. —— **virtūtem**, acc. sing. f. of *virtūs, -tūtis* (*vir*); obj. of the prep. *propter*, expressing *objective cause*. A. & G. 245, *b*; B. 165, REM. 4; G. 408, NOTE 3; H. 416, I, 2).

LINE 80. **cōnfīdēbat**, 3d pers. sing. imperf. ind. of *cōnfīdō, -ĕre, -fīsus*, 3; connected by *et* with *indulserat*, and in the same construction. —— **māximē**, adv.; superl. of *multum (multō, māgis)*; gives prominence to the idea expressed by the verb, and = *especially*.

LINE 1. **Hāc**, abl. sing. f. (*hīc haec, hōc*); an attributive of *ōrātiōne*. —— **ōrātiōne**, abl. sing. f. (*ōrātiō, -ōnis*); absolute with the perf. pass. participle *habitā*. Synonyms: 1. 1, Chap. XXXII. —— **habitā**, abl. sing. f. of *habitus, -a, -um*, perf. pass. participle of *habeō*, 2; absolute with *ōrātiōne*. A. & G. 255; B. 192; G. 409; H. 431. —— **mīrum**, acc. sing. m. (adj. *mīrus, -a, -um*); an attributive of *modum*.

LINE 2. **in**, prep. with the acc. or abl.; here with the acc.; for position, see A. & G. 345, *a*, 2; B. 58. 2; G. 413, REM. 2; H. 565, 3. —— **modum**, acc. sing. m. (*modus, -ī*); obj. of the prep. *in*. —— **conversae sunt**, 3d pers. plur. perf. ind. pass. (*convĕrtō, -ĕre, -tī, -sum*, 3); agrees with the subject-nom. *mentēs*. —— **omnium**, gen. plur. m. (*omnis, -ĕ*), used substantively; limits *mentēs*. —— **mentēs**, nom. plur. of *mēns, mentis*, f.

LINE 3. **summaque** (summa + que). *summa*, adj., superl. *summus, -a, -um*; comparative *superior*; superl. *suprēmus* or *summus*; an attributive of *alacritās*. *que*, enclitic conj.; unites the clauses. —— **alacritās, -tātis**, f. (*alacer*, brisk); sub-

4 gerendī	innāta est;		princepsque		decima	for waging the war; and the tenth legion was the first to return thanks to him through the military tribunes for the very high opinion he had expressed concerning it, and affirmed that every member of it was most resolute for prosecuting the war.
to be waged	*sprang up;*		*as foremost and,*		*the tenth*	
5 legiō	per	tribūnōs		mīlitum	eī	
legion	*through*	*the tribunes*		*of the soldiers*	*to him*	
6 grātiās	ēgit,	quod	dē	sē	optimum	
thanks	*moved,*	*because*	*concerning*	*itself*	*a most excellent*	
7 iūdicium	fēcisset,		sēque	esse	ad	
opinion	*he had formed,*		*themselves and*	*to be*	*for*	
8 bellum	gerendum		parātissimam		cōnfīrmāvit.	
the war	*to be waged*		*most prepared,*		*he affirmed.*	

ject-nom. of *innāta est.* —— et, cop. conj. —— cupiditās, -tātis, f. (*cupidus*, desire); connected by *et* with *alacritās*, and in the same construction. —— bellī, gen. sing. n. (*bellum, -ī*); limits *cupiditās.*

LINE 4. gerendī, gen. sing. n. of the gerundive *gerendus, -a -um* of the verb *gerō*, 3; it agrees with the noun *bellī.* Consult A. & G. 298; B. 184, REM. 4, 1; G. 428; H. 543. Observe that the phrase is objective gen. —— innāta est, 3d pers. sing. perf. indicative of deponent *innāscor, -nāscī, -nātus,* 3 (in + nāscī = lit. *to be born into*); agrees with the two nouns conceived as a single whole. A. & G. 205, *b*; B. 126, REM. 2; G. 285, EXCS. 1 and 2; H. 463, II, 3. Supply after *innāta est: in eōrum mentēs,* to complete the meaning. —— princepsque (princeps + que). *princeps,* adj. with adverbial force = *prīmum.* A. & G. 191; B. 128, REM. 10; G. 325, REM. 6; H. 443. See *prīnceps*, l. 21, Chap. XII. *que,* enclitic conj. —— decima, nom. sing. f., num. adj. (*decimus*); an attributive of *legiō.*

LINE 5. legiō, nom. f.; subj. of *ēgit.* —— per, prep. with the acc. —— tribūnōs, acc. plur. m. (*tribūnus, -ī*); agent as means after *per.* A. & G. 246, *b*; B. 166, REM. 1; G. 401; H. 416, I, 2. See *propter*, l. 39, Chap. XXXIX. —— mīlitum, gen. plur. m. (*mīles, -itis*); limits *tribūnōs.* —— eī, dat. sing. m. (*is, ea, id*), as a personal pron. of the 3d pers.; indirect obj. after *ēgit.*

LINE 6. grātiās, acc. plur. f. (*grātia, -ae*); direct obj. of *ēgit.* —— ēgit, 3d pers. sing. perf. ind. act. of *agō, -ere, ēgī, actum,* 3; agrees with subject-nom. *legiō.* Synonyms: l. 6, Chap. XXXV. —— quod, conj. —— dē, prep. with the abl. —— sē, abl. sing.; obj. of the prep. *dē; sē* refers to *legiō.* —— optimum, acc. sing. n. (*optimus*); superl. of *bonus;* comparative *melior;* an attributive of *iūdicium.*

LINE 7. iūdicium, acc. sing. n. (*iūdicium, -ī*); direct obj. —— fēcisset, 3d pers. sing. pluperf. subjunctive (*faciō,* 3); agrees with the subject-nom. *Caesar* to be supplied; subjunctive, because the statement is made on another's authority. A. & G. 321, 2; B. 197 (*b*); G. 541; H. 516, II. Besides, the discourse is virtually indirect. —— sēque (sē + que). *sē,* acc. sing. (*suī, sibī, sē, sē*); subject-acc. of *esse;* refers to *legiōn. que,* enclitic conj.; connects *ēgit* and *cōnfīrmāvit.* —— esse, pres. inf. of *sum.* —— ad, prep. with the acc.

LINE 8. bellum, acc. sing. n. (*bellum, -ī*); obj. of the prep. *ad.* —— gerendum, acc. sing. n. of gerundive *gerendus, -a, -um* of the verb *gerō,* 3; agrees with *bellum;* the gerundive phrase expresses purpose. A. & G. 300; B. 184, REM. 4, III; G. 432; H. 542, III, and 544, NOTE 2. —— parātissimam, acc. sing. f., superl. adj. *parātis-*

Then the remaining legions with the tribunes of the soldiers and the centurions of the first centuries endeavored to apologize to Caesar, saying that they had never doubted or feared or thought that decision as to the management of the war belonged	Deinde *Then* mīlitum *of the soldiers* ēgērunt, *treated* neque *neither* neque *nor*	reliquae *the remaining* et *and* utī *that* umquam *ever* dē *respecting*	legiōnēs *legions* prīmōrum *of the first* Caesarī *to Caesar* dubitāsse *to have doubted* summā *the management*	cum *with* ōrdinum *classes,* satisfacerent; *they might apologize;* neque *nor* bellī *of the war*	tribūnīs 9 *the tribunes* centuriōnibus 10 *the centurions* sē 11 *themselves* timuisse, 12 *to have feared* suum 13 *their own*

simus, -a, -um; positive *parātus;* comparative *-tior;* predicate after *esse;* feminine, because *sē,* subject-acc., stands for *legiōnem.* Observe that *parātus* is a participle from *parō,* 1. —— cōnfirmāvit, 3d pers. sing. perf. ind. act. of *cōnfīrmō,* 1; connected by *que* with *ēgit,* and has the same subject-nom.

LINE 9. Deinde (dē + inde = lit. *from thence*), adv.; here denotes a continuation of the series, of which *prīnceps* introduces *the first.* —— reliquae, nom. plur. f. (*reliquus*); attributive of *legiōnēs.* Synonyms: l. 6, Chap. XXXII. —— legiōnēs, nom. plur. f. (*legiō*); subj. of *ēgērunt,* l. 11, below. —— cum, prep. with the abl. —— tribūnīs, abl. *of accompaniment* after *cum.* A. & G. 248, *a;* B. 168; G. 392; H. 419, I. The text in some editions is: per tribūnōs *et centuriōnēs* = *through the tribunes,* etc.

LINE 10. mīlitum, gen. plur. m. (*mīles, -itis*); limits *tribūnīs.* See l. 13, Chap. XXXIX. —— et, cop. conj. —— prīmōrum, gen. plur. m. (*prīmus*); an attributive of *ōrdinum.* —— ōrdinum, gen. plur. m. (*ōrdō, -inis*); limits *centuriōnibus.* —— centuriōnibus, abl. plur. m. (*centuriō, -ōnis*); connected by *et* with *tribūnīs,* and in the abl. after the prep. *cum.* Observe that *cum* . . . *prīmōrum ōrdinum centuriōnibus* = *with* . . . *the centurions of the first classes or companies,* i.e. with the six centurions of the first cohort. See note on *ōrdinum,* l. 2, Chap. XL.

LINE 11. ēgērunt, 3d pers. plur. perf. ind. (*ago, -ere, ēgī, actum,* 2). —— utī, conj. = *ut.* —— Caesarī, dat. sing. after *satisfacerent;* verbs compounded of *bene, male* and *satis* take the dat. —— satisfacerent, 3d pers. plur. imperf. subjunctive of *satisfaciō,* 3; subjunctive *of result* after *utī.* Observe that this result-clause is the obj. of *ēgērunt.* See A. & G. 332; B. 201, REM. 1 (*b*); G. 553, 1; H. 501, II, 1. —— sē, acc. plur. (*suī, sibi, sē, sē*); subject-acc. of *dubitāsse.*

LINE 12. neque, conj. See l. 16, Chap. IV. —— um(n)quam (unum + quam), adv. —— dubitāsse, perf. inf. of *dubitō,* 1 (*duo,* compare GER. *zweifeln* from *zwei*); hence *dubitāre* = to vibrate in two directions; in opinion = *to waver.* Observe that *dubitāsse* is syncopated and contracted for *dubitāvisse.* A. & G. 128, 2; B. 251; G. 131, 1; H. 235. —— neque, see *neque* immediately preceding. —— timuisse, perf. inf. act. of *timeo,* 2.

LINE 13. neque, see preceding line. —— dē, prep. with the abl. Synonyms: l. 27, Chap. XIX. —— summā, abl. sing. of the noun *summa, -ae* f. (from adj. *summus*); sc. *rēs* = lit. *the highest thing,* i.e. *control, management.* —— bellī, gen. sing. (*bellum, -ī,* n.); limits *summā.* See l. 15, Chap. I. —— suum, acc. sing. n. of

14 iūdicium,	sed	imperātōris	esse	to them; but thought it belonged to the commander.
judgment	*(to be), but*	*of the commander*	*to be,*	
15 exīstimāvisse.	Eōrum	satisfactiōne	acceptā	Having accepted their apologies, and having reconnoitred the route through the agency of Divitiacus — because of all the other Gauls he had the greatest confidence in him — and finding it to be such as to con-
to have supposed.	*Their*	*apology having been accepted*		
16 et	itinere	exquīsītō	per	
and	*the route*	*having been inquired into*	*through*	
17 Divitiacum,	quod ex	aliīs	eī māximam	
Divitiacus,	*because of*	*others*	*to (in) him the greatest*	
18 fidem	habēbat, ut	mīlium	amplius	
faith	*he had, that,*	*of thousands*	*(of paces) more than*	

poss. pron. (*suus, -a, -um*); predicate after *esse*; refers to the tribunes as the speakers. Observe that the poss. adj. is used for the genitive of the personal pron.

LINE 14. iūdicium, acc. sing. (*iūdicium, -iī*, n.); subject-acc. of *esse*. —— sed, adversative conj. —— imperātōris, gen. sing. m. (*imperātor, -ōris*); predicate gen. after *esse*. A. & G. 214, *c*; B. 133; G. 366; H. 401. —— esse, pres. inf. of *sum*.

LINE 15. exīstimāvisse, perf. inf. act. (*exīstimō*, 1). —— Eōrum, gen. plur. m. (*is, ea, id*); used as a personal pron. The *ōrātiō rēcta* of lines 11–15: *Nōs* neque umquam *dubitāvimus* neque *timuimus*, neque dē summā bellī *nostrum* iūdicium, sed imperātōris esse *exīstimāvimus*. —— satisfactiōne, abl. sing. of *satisfactiō, -ōnis*, f: (satis + facere = *to give satisfaction*); hence the noun = *excuse*; abl. absolute with *acceptā*. —— acceptā, abl. sing. of the perf. pass. participle *acceptus, -a, -um* of *ac(d)cipiō, -ere, -cēpī, -ceptum*, 3; absolute with *satisfactiōne*.

LINE 16. et, cop. conj. —— itinere, abl. sing. n. (*iter, itineris*); abl. absolute with *exquīsītō*. Synonyms: see *via*, l. 2, Chap. IX. —— exquīsītō, abl. sing. n. of the perf. pass. participle *exquīsītus, -a, -um* of *exquīrō, -ere, -sīvī, -sītum*, 3; abl. absolute with *itinere* denoting *time when*. —— per, prep. with the acc.

LINE 17. Divitiacum, obj. of the prep. *per*, denoting agent as means. A. & G. 246, *b*; B. 166, REM. 1; G. 401; H. 415, I, 1, NOTE 1. —— quod, conj. = *because*. —— ex, prep. with the abl. —— aliīs, abl. plur. m.; obj. of the prep. *ex*. Observe that *ex aliīs* = lit. *of the others*, i.e. *the other Gauls*. Some editions read *ex Gallīs*; others *ex aliīs Gallīs* here. The phrase seems to be a substitute for the partitive construction after the superl. See A. & G. 216, *c*; B. 134, REM. 2; G. 372, REM. 2; H. 397, 3, NOTE 3. —— eī, dat. sing. m. (*is, ea, id*); as a personal pron.; indirect obj. of *habēbat*. —— māximam, acc. sing. f. (*magnus, maior, maximus*); an attributive of *fidem*.

LINE 18. fidem, acc. sing. f. (*fidēs, -eī*); direct obj. of *habēbat*. —— habēbat, 3d pers. sing. imperf. ind. act. (*habeō*, 2); agrees with a pron. implied in the ending, referring to Caesar. —— ut, ecbatic conj. —— mīlium, gen. plur. n. (*mīlia, -ium*); gen. of measure; supply as partitive gen. *passuum*. —— amplius, adv. = *and more* — a species of appositive. A. & G. 247, *c*, and NOTE; B. 163, REM. 4; G. 296, REM. 4; H. 417, NOTE 2.

duct the army through an open country by a circuit of more than fifty miles, Caesar, in the fourth watch, as he had said, set the legions in motion. On the seventh day, while still en route, he was informed by scouts that the forces of Ario-	quīnquāgintā *fifty,* exercitum *the army* vigiliā, *watch,* diē, *day,* explōrātōribus *scouts*	circuitū *by a circuit* dūceret, *he might lead,* ut *as* cum *when* certior *more certain*	locīs *in the places* dē *in the course of* dīxerat, *he had said,* iter *the march* factus est, *he was made,*	apertīs 19 *open* quartā 20 *the fourth* profectus est. *he set forth.* nōn *not*	Septimō 21 *On the seventh* intermitteret, *he did stop,* Ariovistī 23 *Ariovistus'*
				ab 22 *by*	

LINE 19. quīnquāgintā, indecl. num. adj.; modifies *mīlium* used substantively. —— circuitū, abl. of *circuitus, -ūs,* m. (circum + īre); abl. *of means.* —— locīs, abl. of *locus, -ī,* m. (see *locī,* l. 10, Chap. II); locative abl. A. & G. 258, *f.* 2; B. 170, REM. 5; G. 385, NOTE 1; H. 425, 2. —— apertīs, abl. sing. m. of adj. *apertus, -a, -um* (see l. 26, Chap. XXV); an attributive of *locīs.*

LINE 20. exercitum, acc. sing. m. (*exercitus, -ūs*); direct obj. Synonyms: l. 31, Chap. III. —— dūceret, 3d pers. sing. imperf. subjunctive of *dūcō,* 3; agrees with a pron. as subject-nom., referring to *itinere,* l. 16, above; subjunctive *of result* after *ut.* Observe that of this loosely constructed sentence, *profectus est* is the main clause; that *ut . . . dūceret* depends on the participle phrase *itinere exquīsītō.* —— dē, prep. with the abl. —— quartā, ordinal adj., abl. sing. f. (*quartus*); limits *vigiliā.*

LINE 21. vigiliā, abl. sing. f.; obj. of the prep. *dē.* —— See l. 70, Chap. XL. —— ut, adv. = *as.* —— dīxerat, 3d pers. sing. pluperf. ind. act. (*dīcō,* 3). See l. 60, Chap. XL. —— profectus est, 3d pers. sing. perf. ind. of *proficīscor, -ī, profectus,* 3; agrees with a pron. understood, referring to Caesar. —— Septimō, abl. sing. m. of ordinal num. adj. *septimus, -a, -um;* an attributive of *diē.*

LINE 22. diē, abl. sing. of *diēs, -ēī,* m. and f. in sing.; m. in plur.; abl. *of time when.* A. & G. 256, 1; B. 171; G. 393; H. 429. —— cum, temporal conj. —— iter, acc. sing. n. (*iter, itineris*); direct obj. of *intermitteret.* —— nōn, adv. (nē + ūnum). —— intermitteret, 3d pers. sing. imperf. subjunctive of *intermittō,* 3; subjunctive after *cum* temporal. A. & G. 325; B. 222; G. 585; H. 521, 2. Observe that *intermitteret* might be here construed as a neuter verb with *iter* as subject-nom.; but the sense favors the syntax given above. —— ab, prep. with the abl.

LINE 23. explōrātōribus, abl. plur. of *explōrātor, -ōris,* m.; abl. *of the agent* after *ab.* A. & G. 246; B. 166; G. 401; H. 415, I. Synonyms: l. 7, Chap. XII. —— certior, comparative degree of *certus* (see l. 11, Chap. VII); predicate adj. after *factus est.* —— factus est, perf. pass. of *fīō, fierī, factus,* 3. Observe that *fīō* is used as the pass. of *faciō;* that most compounds with prepositions change short *a* to short *i* in the present-stem; while other compounds retain the short *a,* and have *fīō* in the pass. —— Ariovistī, gen. sing., limiting *cōpiās.*

LINES 1-4.]   BOOK I.   319

| 24 cōpiās | ā | nostrīs | mīlibus | passuum | quattuor | vistus were twen-
| forces | from | ours | by thousands | of paces | four | ty-four miles dis-
| | | | | | | tant from ours.
| 25 et | vīgintī | abesse. | | | |
| and | twenty | to be distant. | | | |

| 1 XLII. | Cōgnitō | Caesaris | adventū | Ariovistus | XLII. Ariovis-
| | Being known | Caesar's | arrival | Ariovistus | tus on learning
| | | | | | of Caesar's ap-
| 2 lēgātōs | ad | eum | mittit: | quod | anteā | proach sent en-
| legates | to | him | sends: (saying) | what | before | voys to him to
| | | | | | | say that his
| | | | | | | former request
| 3 dē | colloquiō | postulāsset, | id | per | as to a confer-
| concerning | a conference | he had requested, | that | through | ence might be
| | | | | | granted so far as
| 4 sē | fierī | licēre, | quoniam | propius | he was concern-
| himself | to be done | to be allowed, | since | nearer | ed, since Caesar

LINE 24. **cōpiās**, acc. plur. f. (*copia, -ae*); subject-acc. of *abesse*. —— **ā**, prep. with the abl. —— **nostrīs**, abl. plur. m. (*noster, -tra, -trum*); an attributive of *mīlitibus* understood; obj. of the prep. *ā*. —— **mīlibus**, abl. plur. of the adj. *mīlia, -ium*, used substantively; abl. *of degree of difference*. A. & G. 257, *b*; B. 164, REM. 3; G. 335, REM. 2; H. 379, 2. —— **passuum**, gen. plur. m. (*passus, -ūs*); partitive after *mīlibus*. A. & G. 216, 2; B. 134; G. 370; H. 397, 2. —— **quattuor**, cardinal num. adj.; an attributive of *mīlibus*.

LINE 25. **et**, conj. —— **vīgintī**, cardinal num. adj.; connected by *et* with *quattuor*, and is in the same construction. —— **abesse**, pres. inf. of *absum, -esse, ab(ā)fuī, ab(ā)futūrus*; the subject-acc. is *cōpiās*.

LINE 1. **Cōgnitō**, abl. sing. m. of the perf. pass. participle *cōgnitus*, from *cōgnōscō, -ere, -nōvī, -nitum*, 3; abl. absolute with *adventū*. —— **Caesaris**, gen. sing. (*Caesar, -aris*, m.); limits *adventū*. —— **adventū**, abl. sing. m. (*adventus, -ūs*); absolute with the participle *cōgnitō*. —— **Ariovistus, -ī**, m.; subj. of *mittit*.

LINE 2. **lēgātōs**, acc. plur. m. (*lēgātus, -ī*); direct obj. of *mittit*. —— **ad**, prep. with the acc. —— **eum**, acc. sing. m. (*is, ea, id*); as personal pron.; obj. of the prep. *ad*. —— **mittit**, 3d pers. sing. pres. ind. act. (*mittō*, 3); historical pres.; hence admits of either primary or secondary sequence. —— **quod**, acc. sing. n. (*quī, quae, quod*); refers to *id*; is direct obj. of *postulāsset*. —— **anteā** (ante + eā), adv.

LINE 3. **dē**, prep. with the abl. —— **col(n)loquiō**, abl. sing. n. (*colloquium, -ī*); obj. of the prep. *dē*. —— **postulāsset**, 3d pers. sing. pluperf. subjunctive of *postulō*, 1; for *postulāvisset*. A. & G. 128, 2; B. 251; G. 131, 1; H. 235. In subjunctive, because in a subordinate clause in *ōrātiō oblīqua*. —— **id**, acc. sing. n. (*is, ea, id*); subject-acc. of *fierī*. —— **per**, prep. with the acc.

LINE 4. **sē**, acc. sing. m. (*suī, sibi, sē, sē*); obj. of the prep. *per*. Observe that the prepositional phrase here denotes cause = lit. *through himself*, i.e. *so far as concerned himself*. —— **fierī**, pres. inf. of *fīō*, 3; used as pass. of *faciō*. —— **licēre**, pres. inf. of the impersonal *licet, -cuit, -citum est*, 2. —— **quoniam**, conj. (qom + iam) = lit. *when now*. —— **propius**, adv., comparative; superl. *proximē*.

had come nearer, and he thought he might attend it without danger. Caesar did not reject the overture, and thought that Ariovistus was now returning to his senses, because he conceded of his own accord that which to Caesar's request he had previous-	accessisset, *he had approached,* facere posse *to do to be able,* condiciōnem *the condition* sānitātem revertī *sanity to return* quod anteā *which before (to him)*	sēque *himself and,* exīstimāre. *to think* Caesar *Caesar,* arbitrābātur, *he was thinking* petentī *seeking*	id *that* (he thought). iamque *already and,* he	sine *without* Not eum *him* cum *when* ad denegāsset, *had denied,*	perīculō 5 *danger* respuit 6 *did reject* ad 7 *to* id, 8 *that* ultrō 9 *voluntarily*

LINE 5. **accessisset**, 3d pers. sing. pluperf. subjunctive of *accēdō, -ere, -essī, -essum,* 3 (ad + cēdere); its subject-nom. is a pron. understood, referring to Caesar; subjunctive after *quoniam,* causal — reason on another's authority. A. & G. 321, 2; B. 198, *b*; G. 541; H. 516, II. —— **sēque** (sē + que). *sē,* acc. sing. m. (*suī*); subject-acc. of *exīstimāre.* —— *que,* enclitic, connects the infinitive-clause *id . . . licēre* with *sē . . . exīstimāre.* —— **id**, acc. sing. n. (*is, ea, id*); direct object of *facere.* —— **sine**, prep. with the abl. —— **perīculō**, abl. sing. n. (*perīculum, -ī*); obj. of the prep. *sine.*

LINE 6. **facere**, pres. inf. (*faciō,* 3); complementary; depends on *posse.* —— **posse**, pres. inf. (*possum, potuī*); subject-acc. is *sē* understood. —— **exīstimāre**, pres. inf. act. (*exīstimō,* 1). The *ōrātiō rēcta* of lines 2–5: quod anteā dē colloquiō postulā-vistī, id per mē fierī *licet,* quoniam propius *accessistī, egōque hōc* sine perīculō facere posse *exīstimō.* —— **Nōn**, adv. (nē + ūnum, apocopated). —— **respuit**, 3d pers. sing. perf. ind. act. of *respuō, -ere, -puī,* 3 (re + spuere = lit. *to spit back* or *out*); agrees with *Caesar* expressed. Observe the emphāsis by the order of pred., obj., subj.

LINE 7. **condic(t)iōnem**, acc. sing. f. of *condiciō, -ōnis*; direct obj. —— **Caesar**, subject-nom. —— **iamque** (iam + que), conjunctive adv.; modifies *revertī. que,* enclitic; connects the clauses. —— **eum**, acc. sing. m. (*is, ea, id*); as personal pron. of the 3d pers.; subject-acc. of *revertī.* —— **ad**, prep. with the acc.

LINE 8. **sānitātem**, acc. sing. f. (*sānitas, -ātis*); obj. of the prep. *ad.* —— **revertī**, pres. inf. of deponent *revertor, -ī, -sum,* 3; subject-acc. is pron. *eum.* —— **arbitrā-bātur**, 3d pers. sing. imperf. ind. (*arbitror,* 1), deponent; agrees with the subj. implied in the ending, referring to Caesar. Synonyms: l. 9, Chap. XIX. —— **cum**, conj. —— **id**, acc. sing. n. (*is, ea, id*); direct obj. of *pollicērētur.*

LINE 9. **quod**, acc. sing. n. (*quī, quae, quod*); direct obj. of *dēnegāsset.* —— **anteā** (ante + eā), adv. —— **petentī**, dat. sing. m. pres. participle (*petēns, -ntis*) of *petō,* 3; agrees with *eī* understood, dat. sing. (*is, ea, id*), used as a personal pron.; indirect obj. of *dēnegāsset.* Observe that the participle with the pron. = *to him requesting it,* i.e. *when he requested it;* a circumstantial use of the participle denoting *time when.* —— **dēnegāsset**, 3d pers. sing. pluperf. subjunctive of *dēnegō,* 1 (dē, intensive + alō = nē + alō); subjunctive, because an *essential part* of the sentence. A. & G. 342; H. 235, REM. 1; G. 629; H. 529, II, NOTE 1, 1). —— **ultrō**, adv. (*ulterius,* further) = an action performed in an over-ready manner. Synonyms: see *sponte,* l. 4, Chap. IX.

LINES 10-14.]　　　　　　　BOOK I.　　　　　　　321

10 pollicērētur;　　māgnamque　　in　　spem　　veniēbat,　　ly refused; and
　　he promised;　　*great　　and,　　in　　hope　　he was coming*　　was beginning to
　　　　　　　　　　　　　　　　　　　　　　　　　　　　　　　　indulge a large
11 prō　　suīs　　tantīs　　populīque　　Rōmānī　　in　　hope that, in view
　　for　　his　　so great,　　of the people and,　　Roman　　to　　of his own kind-
　　　　　　　　　　　　　　　　　　　　　　　　　　　　　　　　ness and that of
12 eum　　beneficiīs,　　cōgnitīs　　suīs　　postulātīs　　the Roman peo-
　　him,　　kindnesses,　　being known　　his　　demands　　ple towards him,
　　　　　　　　　　　　　　　　　　　　　　　　　　　　　　　　he would desist
13 fore,　　　　utī　　pertināciā　　dēsisteret.　　from his obsti-
　　it to be about to be　　that　　from pertinacity　　he would desist.　　nacy when cog-
　　　　　　　　　　　　　　　　　　　　　　　　　　　　　　　　nizant of his de-
　　　　　　　　　　　　　　　　　　　　　　　　　　　　　　　　mands. The fifth
14 Diēs　　colloquiō　　dictus est　　ex　　eō　　day after this par-
　　The day　　for the conference　　was appointed　　from　　that　　ley was fixed on

LINE 10. pollicērētur, 3d pers. sing. imperf. subjunctive of deponent *polliceor*, 3; subjunctive after *cum* causal. A. & G. 326; B. 198, (*c*); G. 586; H. 517. —— māgnamque (māgnam + que). *māgnam*, acc. sing. f. (*māgnus*); an attributive of *spem*. *que*, enclitic conj. —— in, prep. with the acc. and abl.; here it has the acc. See note on *dē*, l. 16, Chap. I. —— spem, acc. sing. f. (*spēs*, *-eī*); obj. of the prep. *in*. —— veniēbat, 3d pers. sing. imperf. ind. (*veniō*, 4); agrees with the pron. understood, referring to Caesar.

LINE 11. prō, prep. with the abl. —— suīs, abl. plur. n. (*suus*, *-a*, *-um*); agrees with *beneficiīs* understood; refers to Caesar. —— tantīs, abl. plur. n. (*tantus*, *-a*, *-um*); also agrees with *beneficiīs* understood; which latter is the obj. of the prep. *prō*. —— populīque (populī + que). *populī*, gen. sing.; limits *beneficiīs* expressed. Synonyms: see l. 17, Chap. VI. *que*, enclitic conj.; connects *beneficiīs* understood with *beneficiīs* expressed. —— Rōmānī, adj., gen. sing.; attributive of *populī*. —— in, prep. with the acc. or abl.; here it has the acc.

LINE 12. eum, acc. sing. m. (*is*, *ea*, *id*); used as personal pron. of the 3d pers.; obj. of the prep. *in*. Observe that *in eum* is a prepositional phrase modifying *beneficiīs*, instead of objective gen. —— beneficiīs, abl. plur. n. (*beneficium*, *-ī*); connected by the enclitic *que* with *beneficiīs* understood, and in the same construction; viz., obj. of the prep. *prō*. —— cōgnitīs, abl. plur. n. of the perf. pass. participle *cōgnitus*, *-a*, *-um* (*cōgnōscō*, 3); abl. absolute with *postulātīs*. —— suīs (see l. 11, above); an attributive of *postulāns*. —— postulātīs, abl. plur. n. (*postulātum*); absolute with *cōgnitīs*.

LINE 13. fore, fut. inf. for *futūrum esse;* used impersonally. —— utī, the original form of *ut = that*. —— pertināciā, abl. sing. after the prep. *dē* in *dēsisteret*. A. & G. 243, *b*; B. 160; G. 390, NOTE 3; H. 413. —— dēsisteret, 3d pers. sing. imperf. subjunctive of *dēsistō*, *-ere*, *-stitī*, *-stitum*, 3; its subject is a pron. implied in the ending, referring to Ariovistus; subjunctive after *ut — result-clause* as subj. A. & G. 332, *a*, 2; B. 201, REM. 1. (*c*); G. 553, 3; H. 501, I, 1. It will be observed that *fore utī dēsisteret* is a periphrase for *sē dēstitūrum esse;* and also, that in the periphrase the result-clause is grammatically the subj. of *fore*. Consult A. & G. 288, *f*; B. page 291, middle; G. page 334, middle; H. 537, 3.

LINE 14. Diēs, *-ēī*, m.; subject-nom. of *dictus est*. —— col(n)loquiō, dat. sing. n. (*colloquium*, *-ī*); dat. of purpose. A. & G. 233, *a*; B. 147; G. 356; H. 384, II, 1, 3). —— dictus est, 3d pers. sing. perf. ind. pass. (*dīcō*, 3). —— ex, prep. with the abl. —— eō, abl. sing. m. (*is*, *ea*, *id*); an attributive of *diē*.

322   CAESAR'S GALLIC WAR   [CHAP. XLII.

for the conference. Meantime, as the envoys were often passing to and fro between them, Ariovistus demanded that Caesar should bring no infantry to the conference, saying that he was afraid that he might be treacherously ensnared by him; both should be attended by cavalry;	diē quīntus. *day the fifth.*	Interim saepe *Meanwhile often*	ūltrō *hither*	citrōque 15 *yon and,*
	cum lēgātī *when the legates*	inter eōs *between them*		mitterentur, 16 *were sent,*
	Ariovistus postulāvit *Ariovistus demanded*	nē quem *that not any*		peditem 17 *infantry*
	ad colloquīum Caesar addūceret: *to the conference Caesar should bring:*			verērī 18 *to fear* (he feared)
	sē, nē per *himself that through*	insidiās ab *ambuscades by*		eō 19 *him*
	circumvenīrētur; *he might be circumvented;*	uterque *each*	cum *with*	equitātū 20 *the cavalry*

LINE 15. diē, abl. sing.; obj. of the prep. *ex*. —— quīntus, ordinal num. adj.; an attributive of *diēs*. —— Interim (inter + im for *eum*), adv. = *intereā*. —— saepe, adv. —— ūltrō, adv. See l. 9, above. —— citrōque (citrō + que). Observe that the phrase *ūltrō citrōque* = lit. *beyond and this side*, i.e. *hither and yon; to and fro.*

LINE 16. cum, temporal conj. —— lēgātī, nom. plur. m. (*lēgātus, -ī*); subj. of *mitterentur*. —— inter, prep. with the acc. —— eōs, acc. plur. m. (*is, ea, id*); used as a personal pron. of the 3d pers.; obj. of the prep. *inter*. —— mitterentur, 3d pers. plur. imperf. subjunctive pass. of *mittō*, 3; agrees with the subject-nom. *lēgātī*; subjunctive after *cum* temporal.

LINE 17. Ariovistus, -ī, m.; subject-nom. of *postulāvit*. —— postulāvit, 3d pers. sing. perf. ind. act. of *postulō*, 1; agrees with the subject-nom. *Ariovistus*. Synonyms: l. 3, Chap. XVI. —— nē, conjunctive adv.; used with following indef. pron. *quem*. —— quem, acc. sing. m. (*quī, quae, quod* or *quid*); indef. pron., used as adj.; an attributive of *peditem*. —— peditem, acc. sing. m. of *pedes, -itis* (*pēs*, foot); hence properly *foot-soldiering*; direct obj. of *addūceret*.

LINE 18. ad, prep. with the acc. —— col(n)loquīum, acc. sing. n. (*colloquium, -ī*); obj. of the prep. *ad*. —— Caesar, -aris, m.; subject-nom. —— addūceret, 3d pers. sing. imperf. subjunctive act. (*addūcō*, 3); subjunctive after *nē* = *negative purpose*. A. & G. 317, 1; B. 200, (*b*); G. 548; H. 498, I. —— verērī, pres. inf. of *vereor, -ērī, veritus*, 3. Synonyms: l. 12, Chap. XIV.

LINE 19. sē, subject-acc. —— nē, conj.; after verb of fearing = *that*. Consult A. & G. 331, *f*; B. 200, REM. 6; G. 550, 2; H. 498, III, NOTE 1, and FOOTNOTE 4. —— per, prep. with the acc., denoting means. —— insidiās, acc. plur. (*insidiae, -ārum*, f. plur.); obj. of the prep. *per*. —— ab, prep. with the abl. —— eō, abl. sing. m. (*is, ea, id*); as pron. of the 3d pers.; refers to Caesar; obj. of the prep. *ab* — abl. of the agent. A. & G. 246; B. 166; G. 401; H. 415, I.

LINE 20. circumvenīrētur, 3d pers. sing. imperf. subjunctive pass. of circum + veniō, 4; agrees with a pron. referring to Ariovistus; subjunctive after *nē*. —— uterque, distributive pron. (*uterque, -traque, -trumque*) = *either of two*, or *both*. A. & G. 202, *d*; B. 89; G. 108; H. 397, NOTE 2; subject-nom. of *venīret*. —— cum, prep. with the abl. —— equitātū, abl. sing. m. (*equitātus, -ūs*); accompaniment. A. & G. 248, *a*; B. 168, REM. 4; G. 392; H. 419, I.

BOOK I.   323

21 venīret;	aliā	ratiōne	sēsē	nōn	he would not come on other terms. Caesar, as he did not wish the conference prevented by the interposition of any pretext, and did not dare commit his own safety to the cavalry of the Gauls, decided that the best plan was, to take all the horses from the Gallic caval-
should come;	*in another*	*manner*	*himself*	*not*	
22 esse ventūrum.		Caesar,	quod	neque	
to be about to come.		*Caesar,*	*because*	*neither*	
23 colloquium		interpositā	causā	tollī	
the conference,		*being interposed*	*an excuse,*	*to be put off*	
24 volēbat,	neque	salūtem	suam	Gallōrum	
he was wishing,	*nor*	*safety*	*his*	*to the Gallic*	
25 equitātuī	committere	audēbat,	commodissimum		
cavalry	*to commit*	*did he dare,*	*most advantageous*		
26 esse	statuit,	omnibus	equīs	Gallīs	
to be	*he determined,*	*all*	*horses*	*from the Gallic*	

LINE 21. venīret, 3d pers. sing. imperf. subjunctive (*veniō*, 4); hortatory subjunctive. A. & G. 266, *e*; B. 189, I, *b*; G. 263, 3; H. 484, II. Of course, the present subjunctive would be the hortatory form in direct discourse. A. & G. 339, and REM.; B. 245, 2; G. 652; H. 523, III, and FOOTNOTE 4. —— aliā, abl. sing. f. (*alius, -a, -ud*); an attributive of *ratiōne*. —— ratiōne, abl. sing. f. (*ratiō, -ōnis*); means. —— sēsē, subject-acc. of *esse ventūrum* (*ventūrum esse*). See l. 4, Chap. XXX. —— nōn, adv.

LINE 22. esse ventūrum (*ventūrum esse*), fut. inf. act. of *veniō*, 4; subject-acc. is the pron. *sēsē*. —— Caesar, -aris, m.; subject-nom. of *statuit*, l. 26, below. —— quod, conj. —— neque, see l. 16, Chap. IV.

LINE 23. col(n)loquium, -ī, acc. sing. n.; subject-acc. of *tollī*. —— interpositā, abl. f. of the perf. pass. participle *interpositus, -a, -um* of *interpōnō, -pōnere, -posuī, -positum*, 3; abl. absolute with *causā*, denoting *the means*. —— causā, -ae, f.; abl. absolute. —— tollī, pres. inf. pass. of *tollō, -ere, sustulī, sublātum*; subject-acc. is *colloquium*.

LINE 24. volēbat, 3d pers. sing. imperf. ind. (*volō, velle, voluī*); agrees with a pron. implied in the ending, referring to Caesar. —— neque, see *neque*, l. 22, above. —— salūtem, acc. sing. f. (*salūs, -ūtis*); direct obj. of *committere*. —— suam, acc. sing. f. (*suus, -a, -um*); an attributive of *salūtem*. —— Gallōrum, gen. plur. m. (*Gallī, -ōrum*); limits *equitātuī*. Caesar's cavalry was made up of Gauls whom he distrusted.

LINE 25. equitātuī, dat. sing. m. (*equitātus, -ūs*); indirect obj. after *committere*. —— committere, pres. inf. act. (*committō*, 3); complementary. A. & G. 271; B. 181; G. 423; H. 533, I, 1. —— audēbat, 3d pers. sing. imperf. ind. of *audeō, -ēre, ausus*, 2; neuter pass. or semi-deponent; the subj. is a pron. implied in the ending, referring to Caesar. —— commodissimum, acc. sing. n., superl. of the positive *commodus*; predicate-acc. after *esse*.

LINE 26. esse, pres. inf. of *sum*, perf. *fuī*, fut. participle *futūrus*; used here impersonally; or rather, *impōnere* with its modifiers is subj. of *esse*. —— statuit, 3d pers. sing. perf. ind. act. (*statuō*, 3); its subject-nom. is *Caesar*, l. 22, above. —— omnibus, abl. plur. m. (*omnis, -e*); an attributive of *equīs*. —— equīs, abl. plur. m. (*equus, -ī*); abl. absolute with *dētrāctīs*. —— Gallīs, dat. plur. m. of the adj. *Gallus, -a, -um*; an attributive of *equitibus*.

ry, and to mount upon them the soldiers of the tenth legion, in which he had the greatest confidence, in order to have as friendly a guard as possible, should there be any need for action. When this was done, one of the soldiers of the tenth	equitibus *cavalry*	dētrāctīs, *being taken away,*	eō *thither*	legiōnāriōs *the legionary*	27
	mīlitēs *soldiers*	legiōnis *of the legion*	decimae, *tenth,*	cui *to (in) which*	quam *as much as*	28
	māximē *the greatest*	cōnfīdēbat, *did he confide,*	impōnere, *to mount,*	ut *that*	praesidium *a guard*	29
	quam *as much as*	amīcissimum, *the most friendly,*	sī *if,*	quid *in any repect,*	opus *need*	30
	factō *of action*	esset, *there were,*	habēret. *he might have.*	Quod *Which*	cum *when*	31

LINE 27. **equitibus**, dat. plur. m. of *eques, -itis*; dat. after the participle *dētrāctīs*. See A. & G. 229; B. 143, REM. 3; G. 345, REM. 1; H. 386, 2. Observe that *eques* = both *a horseman*, and later, as serving on horseback, *a knight* — a species of aristocrat next to senators in rank. —— **dētrāctīs**, perf. pass. participle of *dētrahō, -ere, -trāxī, -tractum*, 3; abl. absolute with *equīs*. —— **eō**, adv. = lit. *thither*, i.e. *on the horses;* modifies *impōnere*. Observe that a dem. adv. often = a pron. with prep. See A. & G. 207, *a*; B. 129, REM. 10; G. 611, REM. 1; H. 304, II, 3, NOTE. —— **legiōnāriōs**, acc. plur. m. (adj. *legiōnārius, -a, -um*); an attributive of *mīlitēs*. Observe that this epithet is used to distinguish the regulars from the *vēlitēs* or skirmishers.
    LINE 28. **mīlitēs**, acc. plur. m.; direct obj. of *impōnere*. —— **legiōnis**, gen. sing. f. (*legiō, -ōnis*); limits *mīlitēs*. —— **decimae**, gen. sing. f., ordinal adj. *decimus, -a, -um;* an attributive of *legiōnis*. —— **cui**, dat. sing. f. (*quī, quae, quod*); refers to *legiōnis;* is dat. after *cōnfīdēbat*. A. & G. 227, *c*, NOTE; B. 142, and REM. 3; G. 346, REM. 2; H. 385, II. Observe that *fīdō* and *cōnfīdō* usually take the abl.; but here the dat. —— **quam**, adv.; it strengthens the superl. See A. & G. 93, *b*; G. 303; H. 170, 2, (2).
    LINE 29. **māximē**, adv., superl. of *magis;* modifies *cōnfīdēbat*. —— **cōnfīdēbat**, 3d pers. sing. imperf. ind. act. of *cōnfīdō, -ere, cōnfīsus, 3;* agrees with a subj. implied in the ending, referring to Caesar. —— **impōnere**, pres. inf. act. of *impōno, 3* (in + pōnere = lit. *to place on*). —— **ut**, telic conj. —— **praesidium**, acc. sing. n. (*praesidium, -ī*); direct obj. of *habēret*.
    LINE 30. **quam**, adv.; see l. 28, above. —— **amīcissimum**, acc. sing. n. (adj. *amīcus*); agrees with *praesidium*. —— **sī**, conditional conj. —— **quid**, acc. sing. n. (*quis, quae, quid*); indef. pron., used substantively; acc. of specification. A. & G. 240, *a*; B. 123, 5, REM. 21; G. 334, REM. 1; H. 378, 2. —— **opus**, indecl. neuter noun; subj. of *esset*.
    LINE 31. **factō**, perf. pass. participle of *fīō, fierī, factus, 3;* abl. after *opus*. A. & G. 243, *e*, NOTE; B. 167, 2, REM. 2; G. 437, NOTE 2; H. 414, IV, NOTE 3. —— **esset**, 3d pers. sing. imperf. subjunctive (*sum*); in protasis after *sī*. —— **habēret**, 3d pers. sing. imperf. subjunctive of *habeō*, 2; *purpose* after *ut*. Observe that in this purpose-clause the apodosis of the conditional clause is contained. —— **Quod**, nom. sing. n. (*quī, quae, quod*); refers to the idea contained in the previous sentence; is the subject-nom. of *fieret*. Observe that *quod* = *et id*. See A. & G. 180, *f*; B. 129, REM. 9; G. 610; H. 453. —— **cum**, temporal conj.

LINES 32–37.] BOOK I. 325

32 fieret,	nōn	irrīdiculē	quīdam		ex
was done	*not*	*without humor*	*a certain one*		*of*
33 mīlitibus	decimae	legiōnis	dīxit,		plūs
the soldiers	*of the tenth*	*legion*	*said,*		*more*
34 quam	pollicitus esset	Caesarem			facere:
than	*he had promised*	*Caesar*		*to do* (*was doing*):	
35 pollicitum	sē	in	cohortis		praetōriae
to have promised	*himself*	*in*	*the cohorts*		*praetorian*
36 locō	decimam	legiōnem		habitūrum,	ad
place	*the tenth*	*legion*		(*to be*) *about to have,*	(*it*) *to*
37 equum		rescrībere.			
horse		*to transfer* (he is transferring it).			

legion wittily said: Caesar has done more than he promised. He promised to regard the tenth legion as his bodyguard; he has enrolled the members thereof as knights.

LINE 32. **fieret,** 3d pers. sing. imperf. subjunctive (*fīō*); agrees with the subj. *quod;* subjunctive after *cum.* —— **nōn,** adv.; modifies *irrīdiculē.* —— **irrīdiculē** (in, *negative* + rīdiculē = *not unwittily*, i.e. *wittily*), adv., litotes; modifies *dīxit.* —— **quīdam,** nom. sing. m. indef. pron. (*quīdam, quaedam, quoddam*); subject-nom. of *dīxit.* Observe that *quīdam* generally takes the abl. with *ē* or *ex*, instead of the partitive gen. —— **ex,** prep. with the abl.

LINE 33. **mīlitibus,** abl. plur. m. (*mīles, -itis*); obj. of the prep. *ex*. See A. & G. 216, *c*; B. 134, REM. 2; G. 372, REM. 2.; H. 397, 3, NOTE 3. —— **decimae,** gen. sing. f. (*decimus, -a, -um*); see l. 28, above. —— **legiōnis,** gen. sing. f. (*legiō*); limits *mīlitibus*; see l. 28, above. —— **dīxit,** 3d pers. sing. perf. ind. act. (*dīcō,* 3); agrees with *quīdam.* —— **plūs,** adv.; comparative of *multum;* modifies *facere.*

LINE 34. **quam,** conj.; with comparative = *than*; connects *facere* with *pollicitus esset.* —— **pollicitus esset,** 3d pers. sing. pluperf. subjunctive of deponent *polliceor, -ērī, -licitus,* 2; subjunctive, because in a subordinate clause in virtual *ōrātiō oblīqua* — an integral part. See A. & G. 342; B. 245, 1, (*b*); G. 650; H. 529, II, NOTE 1, 1). —— **Caesarem,** acc. sing. m. (*Caesar, -aris*); subject-acc. of *facere.* —— **facere,** pres. inf. act. (*faciō,* 3). Observe that some editions read *eī,* i.e. *legiōnī,* between *Caesarem* and *facere.*

LINE 35. **pollicitum** (esse), perf. inf. of *polliceor,* 2; its subject-acc. is the pron. *sē.* —— **sē,** acc. sing. (*suī, sibi, sē, sē*). —— **in,** prep. with the acc. or abl.; here it takes the abl. —— **cohortis,** gen. sing. f. (*cohors*); limits *locō.* —— **praetōriae,** gen. sing. f. (adj. *praetōrius, -a, -um*); attributive of *cohortis*. See l. 77, Chap. XL.

LINE 36. **locō,** abl. sing. m. (*locus, -ī*); obj. of the prep. *in.* See note on *locī,* l. 10, Chap. II. Observe also the words that precede the obj. of the prep. here, and consult A. & G. 344, *g*; B. 43; G. 413, REM. 3, and 678, REM. 4; H. 569, II, 3. —— **decimam,** acc. sing. f.; an attributive of *legiōnem.* —— **legiōnem,** acc. sing. f. (*legiō, -ōnis*); direct obj. of *habitūrum* (*esse*). —— **habitūrum** (esse), fut. inf. act. (*habeō,* 2); its subject-acc. is *sē* understood, referring to Caesar. Observe that the phrase *habēre in locō* = *to regard as.* —— **ad,** prep. with the acc.

LINE 37. **equum,** acc. sing. m. of *equus, -ī* = *equitēs* by metonymy; obj. of the prep. *ad.* —— **rescrībere,** pres. inf. act. of *rescrībō,* 3; its subject-acc. is *sē,* i.e. *Caesarem,* understood; supply *eam,* i.e. *legiōnem,* as direct obj.; and note the omission

XLIII. There was a large plain and in it a plateau of considerable extent. This place was almost equidistant from the camps of Ariovistus and Caesar. To it, as it	XLIII. Plānitiēs erat māgna et in 1 *A plain there was great, and in* eā tumulus terrēnus satis grandis. Hīc 2 *it a mound of earth sufficiently large. This* locus aequō ferē spatiō ab castrīs 3 *place by an equal almost space from the camp* Ariovistī et Caesaris aberat. Eō, 4 *of Ariovistus and Caesar was distant. Thither,*

of the conj. between the clauses (asyndeton). The pleasantry lies in the application of the phrase *ad equum,* i.e. by metonymy *ad equitēs, now* to the cavalry, and *now* to the Roman knights. *ad equum rescrībere* = (*a*) *to transfer to the cavalry* — a degradation, as the cavalry were, for the most part, Gauls; (*b*) *to raise to the rank of knights* — an aristocratic order. The *ōrātiō rēcta* of lines 33–37: *Caesar facit* plūs quam *pollicitus est: pollicitus est* sē in cohortis praetōriae locō decimam legiōnem habitūrum (esse), ad equum *rescrībit* (historical pres.).

LINE 1. **Plānitiēs, -ēī,** f. (*plānus,* flat); subject-nom. of *erat;* sometimes spelled *plānīciēs*. —— **erat,** 3d pers. sing. (*sum, esse, fuī*); here, and often, a verb of complete predication. —— **māgna,** nom. sing. f. (*māgnus, -a, -um*): an attributive of *plānitiēs*. —— **et,** cop. conj.; connects *plānitiēs* and *tumulus.* —— **in,** prep. with the acc. or abl.; here it takes the abl.

LINE 2. **eā,** abl. sing. f. (*is, ea, id*); used as a pron. of the 3d pers.; or supply *plānitiē;* obj. of the prep. *in*. —— **tumulus, -ī,** m. (*tumēre,* to swell); connected by *et* with *plānitiēs,* and in the same construction. —— **terrēnus** (*terra,* earth), adj., nom. sing. m.; an attributive of *tumulus*. —— **satis,** adv., comparative *satius;* modifies adj. *grandis*. —— **grandis,** adj., nom. sing. m. (*grandis, -e*); an *ī*-stem; abl. *grandī;* an attributive, also, of *tumulus*. —— **Hīc,** nom. sing. m. (*hīc, haec, hōc*); an attributive of *locus*.

LINE 3. **locus,** nom. sing. m.; subject of *aberat*. See *locī,* l. 10, Chap. II. —— **aequō,** adj., abl. sing. n. (*aequus, -a, -um*); modifies *spatiō*. —— **ferē,** adv. (*ferō;* hence the adv. = *that brought near, within a little, almost*); modifies the adj. *aequō;* but note its position; usually thus between the noun and the adj. which modifies the noun. —— **spatiō,** abl. sing. n. (*spatium, -ī*); *measure* or *degree of difference*. See A. & G. 257, *b*; B. 153, REM. 3; G. 403, NOTE 1; H. 379, 2. —— **ab,** prep. with abl.; often thus repeated after a compound verb containing the same prep. —— **castrīs,** abl. plur. n. (*castrum, -ī*); obj. of the prep. *ab*. See *castrīs,* l. 12, Chap. XII.

LINE 4. **Ariovistī,** poss. gen.; limits *castrīs*. As to Ariovistus, see l. 51, Chap. XXXI. Observe that instead of *Ariovistī et Caesaris,* some editions read the abl. *utrīsque,* or the gen. *utrīusque,* which = either: *from both camps,* or *from the camps of each*. —— **et,** conj.; connects the proper names. —— **Caesaris,** gen. sing. m.; connected by *et* with *Ariovistī,* and in the same construction. —— **aberat,** 3d pers. sing. imperf. ind. of *absum, abesse,* ab(ā)*fuī,* ab(ā)*futūrus;* agrees with *locus* as subject-nom. —— **Eō,** adv. (in fact abl. sing. m. of the dem. *is, ea, id;* agreeing with *locō* understood).

5 ut erat dictum,	ad	colloquium	vēnērunt.
as it had been appointed,	*to*	*the conference*	*they came.*
6 Legiōnem Caesar,	quam equīs	dēvēxerat,
The legion, Caesar,	*which by horses*	*he had conveyed,*
7 passibus ducentīs	ab eō tumulō	cōnstituit.
by paces two hundred	*from that mound,*	*posted.*
8 Item equitēs	Ariovistī	parī intervāllō
Likewise the cavalry	*of Ariovistus*	*at an equal interval*
9 cōnstitērunt. Ariovistus,	ex equīs	ut
halted. Ariovistus,	*from horses*	*that*
10 colloquerentur et praeter	sē	dēnōs ut
they should confer and besides	*themselves*	*ten each that*

had been arranged, they came for the conference. Caesar stationed the legion that he had brought along on horseback two hundred paces from the plateau. The cavalry of Ariovistus also halted at a like distance. Ariovistus demanded that they should confer on horseback, and that

LINE 5. **ut,** adv. = *as.* —— **erat dictum** (*dictum erat*), 3d pers. sing. pluperf. ind. pass. in form, but *dictum* may be taken as a participle, and *dictum erat* with *ut* = *as it had been fixed;* used impersonally; supply *ab illīs,* abl. *of the agent.* —— **ad,** prep. with the acc. —— **col(n)loquium,** acc. sing. n. (*colloquium, -ī*); obj. of the prep. *ad.* —— **vēnērunt,** 3d pers. plur. perf. ind. act. (*veniō,* 4); agrees with *eī* understood, referring to Ariovistus and Caesar.

LINE 6. **Legiōnem,** acc. sing. f. (*legio, -ōnis*); direct obj. of *cōnstituit.* —— **Caesar, -aris,** m.; subject-nom. of *cōnstituit.* —— **quam,** acc. sing. f. (*quī, quae, quod*); direct obj. of *dēvēxerat.* —— **equīs,** abl. plur. m. (*equus, -ī*); abl. *of means.* —— **dēvēxerat,** 3d pers. sing. pluperf. ind. of *dēvehō, -ere, -vēxī, -vēctum,* 3 (*dē, over* + *vehere* = lit. *to convey over the distance*). Some copies read *rēxerat.*

LINE 7. **passibus,** abl. *of distance* or *measure* (*passus, -ūs,* m.). A. & G. 257, *b;* B. 153, REM. 3; G. 403, NOTE 1; H. 379, 2. —— **ducentīs,** abl. plur. m. (*ducentī, -ae, -a*); an attributive of *passibus. passibus ducentīs* = *at the distance of two hundred paces.* —— **ab,** prep. with the abl. —— **eō,** abl. sing. m. (*is, ea, id*); an attributive of *tumulō.* —— **tumulō,** abl. sing. m. (*tumulus, -ī*); place *from which* with the prep. *ab.* A. & G. 258; B. 173, 2; G. 390, 1; H. 427, II. —— **cōnstituit,** 3d pers. sing. perf. ind. act. of *cōnstituō,* 3; agrees with the subject-nom. *Caesar* expressed.

LINE 8. **Item,** adv. (*is*) = after *this* manner, *also;* whereas *etiam* (et + iam) denotes the addition of a more important notion. —— **equitēs,** nom. plur. m. (*eques, -itis*); subj. of *cōnstitērunt.* Synonyms: l. 2, Chap. XV. —— **Ariovistī,** gen. sing. m.; poss. gen.; limits *equitēs.* —— **parī,** abl. sing. n. (adj. *pār, paris*); liquid stem; but having the form of an *ī*-stem in abl. sing. and gen. plur.; an attributive of *intervāllō.* —— **intervāllō,** abl. *of distance* or *measure.* See grammatical references to *passibus,* l. 7, above (*intervāllum, -ī,* n.).

LINE 9. **cōnstitērunt,** 3d pers. plur. perf. ind. act. of *cōnstituō, -āre, -stitī, -stātum,* 1, irr. in perf. stem; agrees with subj. *equitēs.* —— **Ariovistus, -ī,** m., subj. of *postulāvit,* l. 11, below. —— **ex,** prep. with the abl. —— **equīs,** abl. plur. m. (*equus, -ī*); obj. of the prep. *ex. ex equīs* = lit. *from the horses,* i.e. *on horseback.* Of course, in the plur. when written or spoken of more than one rider. —— **ut,** telic conj.

LINE 10. **col(n)loquerentur,** 3d pers. plur. imperf. subjunctive of the deponent *colloquor, -quī, -catus,* 3; purpose after *ut.* Observe that this clause and the next

| each party should bring ten attendants to the conference. On coming to the place, Caesar began a speech; he recounted his own kindnesses and those of the senate toward him; he stated that he had been called king and friend by the senate; that pres- | ad colloquium adducerent, postulāvit. Ubi 11 *to the conference they should bring, demanded. When* eō ventum est, Caesar initiō ōrātiōnis 12 *thither it was come, Caesar, at the beginning of (his) speech,* sua senātūsque in eum beneficia 13 *his own the senate's and, to him, kindnesses* commemorāvit, quod rēx appellātus esset ā 14 *mentioned, in that king he had been called by* senātū, quod amīcus, quod mūnera 15 *the senate, in that a friend, in that gifts* |

are direct objects of *postulāvit.* See A. & G. 331; B. 200, REM. 2; G. 546, I; H. 498, I. —— **et**, cop. conj. —— **praeter**, adv. or prep.; here prep. with the acc. —— **sē**, acc. plur. (*suī, sibi, sē, sē*); obj. of the prep. *praeter.* —— **dēnōs**, acc. plur., distributive num. adj. (*dēnī, -ae, -a*); derived from *decem*; = *ten each*; used substantively; direct obj. of *adducerent.* —— **ut**, telic conj.

LINE 11. **ad**, prep. with the acc. as the limit of motion. —— **col(n)loquium, -ī**, n.; acc.; obj. of the prep. *ad.* —— **adducerent**, 3d pers. plur. imperf. subjunctive; subjunctive of purpose after *ut.* —— **postulāvit**, 3d pers. sing. perf. ind. act. (*postulō,* 1); agrees with the subject-nom. *Ariovistus*, l. 9, above. —— **Ubi** (quō + bi) = lit. *in which place;* compare correlative *ibi.*

LINE 12. **eō**, adv. (see *eō*, l. 4, above). —— **ventum est**, 3d pers. sing. perf. ind. pass. impersonal of *veniō*, 4; supply *ab eīs*, as abl. *of the agent;* = lit. *it was come by them*, i.e. = *vēnērunt.* —— **Caesar, -aris**, m.; subject-nom. of *commemorāvit.* —— **initiō**, abl. sing. n. (*initium, -ī*); *time when.* A. & G. 256; B. 171; G. 393; H. 429. —— **ōrātiōnis**, gen. sing. f. (*ōrātiō, -ōnis*); limits *initiō.* Synonyms: l. 1, Chap. XVII.

LINE 13. **sua**, acc. plur. n. (*suus, -a, -um*); an attributive of *beneficia.* —— **senātūsque** (senātūs + que). *senātūs*, gen. sing. m. (*senātus, -ūs*); limits *beneficia.* **que**, enclitic conj. —— **in**, prep. with the acc. or abl.; here it takes the acc. See *in,* l. 1, Chap. I. —— **eum**, acc. sing. m. (*is, ea, id*); used as a personal pron.; obj. of the prep. *in.* —— **beneficia**, acc. plur. n. (*beneficium, -ī*); direct obj. of *commemorāvit.*

LINE 14. **commemorāvit**, 3d pers. sing. perf. ind. act. (*commemorō,* 1); agrees with *Caesar* expressed as subject-nom. —— **quod**, conj. = *because.* Observe that the following *quod*-clauses are explanatory of *beneficia,* and in apposition with it. —— **rēx, rēgis**, m.; predicate nom. —— **appellātus esset**, 3d pers. sing. pluperf. subjunctive pass. (*ap[d]pellō,* 1); agrees with a pron., referring to Ariovistus; subjunctive, because in a subordinate clause in virtual *ōrātiō oblīqua.* See A. & G. 341, *d;* B. 198, (*b*), and REM. 1; G. 628; H. 516, II, 1, NOTE. —— **ā**, prep. with the abl. See l. 6, Chap. I.

LINE 15. **senātū**, abl. sing. m. (*senātus, -ūs*); abl. *of the agent* after *ā.* Consult A. & G. 246; B. 166; G. 401; H. 415, I. Observe that by metonymy *senātū* = *senātōribus.* —— **quod**, conj. —— **amīcus**, predicate-nom. after *appellātus esset,* to be supplied. —— **quod**, same construction as *quod* preceding. —— **mūnera**, nom. plur

16 amplissimē	mīssa;		quam	rem	et	ents had been very generously sent him; that such favors were the portion of but few, and were usually conferred in return for great personal services; and that he, though without sufficient merit and without just ground for making a claim, had
most amply	*sent (to have been);*		*which*	*thing*	*both*	
17 paucīs	contigisse	et	prō	māgnīs	hominum	
to few	*to have happened*	*and*	*for*	*great*	*men's*	
18 officiīs	cōnsuēsse			tribuī	docēbat;	
offices	*to have been accustomed*		*to be bestowed,*		*he showed;*	
19 illum,	cum	neque	aditum	neque	causam	
him,	*when*	*neither*	*access*	*nor*	*cause*	
20 postulandī	iūstam	habēret,		beneficiō	āc	
of demanding,	*just*	*he had,*		*through favor*	*and*	

n. (*mūnus, -eris*); subj. of *mīssa* (*essent*). The reference is to presents suitable for those whom the Roman senate had honored with title of king, such as a golden crown, an ivory staff, etc. See Livy, XXX. 15.

LINE 16. **amplissimē**, adv., superl. degree; positive *amplē;* comparative *amplius.* —— **mīssa** (**essent**), 3d pers. plur. pluperf. subjunctive (*mittō*, 3); subjunctive for the same reason as *appellātus esset.* The *ōrātiō rēcta* of lines 13-16: *mea senātūsque in tē beneficia commemorō: quod rēx appellātus es ā senātū, quod amīcus, quod mūnera amplissimē mīssa* (*sunt*). The reader, of course, is aware that the discourse of Caesar here, which we have changed into the direct, is in the text *informal* indirect discourse. —— **quam**, acc. sing. f. (*quī, quae, quod*); used here adjectively as an attributive of *rem;* it refers to the idea in the preceding clause. Observe that *id quod* might have been used. Consult A. & G. 200, *e*; B. 129, REM. 8; G. 614, REM. 2; H. 445, 7. —— **rem**, acc. sing. f. (*rēs, reī*); subject-acc. of *contigisse* and *cōnsuēsse.* —— **et** . . . **et** = lit. *both* . . . *and;* but suppress the first *et* in the English translation.

LINE 17. **paucīs**, dat. plur. m. (adj. *paucus, -a, -um*); used substantively = *a few;* indirect obj. —— **contigisse**, perf. inf. act. of *contingō, -ere, -tigī, -tactum,* 3 (con + tangere); *rem* is subject-acc. —— **et**, see *et* . . . *et,* preceding line. —— **prō**, prep. with the abl. —— **māgnīs**, abl. plur. n. (*māgnus, -a, -um*); an attributive of *officiīs.* —— **hominum**, gen. plur. m. and f. (*homō, -inis*); limits *officiīs.*

LINE 18. **officiīs**, abl. plur. n. (*officium, -ī*); obj. of the prep. *prō.* Observe the natural Latin order here: adj., gen., subst. —— **cōnsuēsse**, syncopated and contracted perf. inf. act. for *cōnsuēvisse,* of *cōnsuēscō, -ere, -suēvī, -suētum,* 3; subject-acc. is *rem.* —— **tribuī**, pres. inf. pass. of *tribuō,* 3 — complementary inf. —— **docēbat,** 3d pers. sing. imperf. ind. act. of *doceō,* 2; supply *eum* as direct obj.; the acc. and inf. clauses preceding are secondary objects.

LINE 19. **illum,** acc. sing. m. (*ille, -la, -lud*); refers to Ariovistus; more emphatic than *eum;* subject-acc. of *cōnsecūtum* (*esse*). —— **cum**, concessive conj. = *though.* —— **neque** . . . **neque** = *neither* . . . *nor.* See L 16, Chap. IV. —— **aditum**, acc. sing. m. (*aditus, -ūs*); direct obj. of *habēret.* —— **neque**, see *neque* immediately above. —— **causam**, acc. sing. f. (*causa, -ae*); direct obj. of *habēret;* same construction as *aditum.*

LINE 20. **postulandī,** gen. of the gerund (*postulō,* 1); limits *causam.* A. & G. 298; B. 184, REM. 4, 1; G. 428; H. 542, I. —— **iūstam**, acc. sing. f. of adj. *iūstus, -a, -um*

| attained these honors through the kindness and generosity of himself and the senate. He informed him also how ancient and just were the reasons for the alliance that existed between the Romans and the Aedui, what de- | līberālitāte *liberality* cōnsecūtum. *to have attained.* quamque· *how and,* ipsīs *to themselves* | suā *his own* Docēbat *He showed* iūstae *just* cum *with* | ăc *and* etiam, *also,* causae *causes* Aeduīs *the Aedui* | senātūs *the senate's,* quam *how* intercēderent, *existed,* | ea *those* veterēs *the ancient* necessitūdinis *of relationship* quae *what* | praemia 21 *rewards,* 22 23 24 |

(*iūs*); an attributive of *causam*. —— **habēret**, 3d pers. sing. imperf. subjunctive (*habeō*, 2); subjunctive after *cum* concessive. A. & G. 326, REM.; B. 210; G. 587; H. 515, III. —— **beneficiō**, abl. sing. n. (*beneficium*, -*ī*); *cause*. A. & G. 245; B. 165; G. 408; H. 416. —— **ăc**, see note on *atque*, l. 10, Chap. I.

LINE 21. **līberālitāte**, abl. sing of *līberalitās, -tātis*, f. (*līber*, free); connected by *ăc* with *beneficiō*, and in the same construction. —— **suā**, abl. sing. f. (*suus*, *-a*, *-um*); an attributive of *līberālitāte*; refers to Caesar. —— **ăc**, see *ăc*, preceding line. —— **senātūs** (*senex*, old man), gen. sing. m. (*senātus, -ūs*); limits *ed*, i.e. *līberālitāte* understood. —— **ea**, acc. plur. n. (*is, ea, id*); an attributive of *praemia*. —— **praemia**, acc. plur. n. (*praemium, -ī*); direct obj. of the deponent *cōnsecūtum* (*esse*).

LINE 22. **cōnsecūtum** (**esse**), perf. inf. of the deponent *cōnsequor, -quī, -secutus*, 3; its subject-acc. is *illum*. The *ōrātiō rēcta* of lines 16-22: quam rem et paucīs contingere et prō māgnīs hominum officiīs cōnsuēscere tribuī tē, cum neque aditum neque causam postulandī iūstam *habēs*, beneficiō ăc līberālitāte *med* ăc senātūs ea praemia cōnsecūtum *esse*, *doceō*. —— **Docēbat**, for parts, see l. 18, above. —— **etiam** (et + iam), conjunctive adv.; adds a notion = *even, also*. —— **quam**, adv. = *how*. —— **veterēs**, adj., nom. plur. (*vetus, -eris*); stem *veter*, orig. an *s*-stem; abl. -*e* or -*ī*; an attributive of *causae*. Synonyms: see l. 37, Chap. XVIII.

LINE 23. **quamque** (quam + que). *quam*, adv.; modifies adj. *iūstae*. *que*, enclitic; connects *veterēs* and *iūstae*. —— **iūstae**, nom. plur. f. (adj. *iūstus, -a, -um*); an attributive of *causae*. —— **causae**, nom. plur. f. (*causa, -ae*); subject of *intercēderent*. —— **necessitūdinis**, gen. sing. f. (*necessitūdō, -inis*); limits *causae*. Observe that this word = lit. *necessity*; transf. a *necessary* relation between persons; hence *friendship*, etc.

LINE 24. **ipsīs**, dat. plur. m. (*ipse, -sa, -sum*); follows the compound *intercēderent*. A. & G. 228; B. 143; G. 347; H. 386. Observe that *ipsīs* = *Romānīs*, and is more emphatic than *eīs*. —— **cum**, prep. with the abl. —— **Aeduīs**, abl. plur. m. (*Aeduī, -ōrum*); obj. of the prep. *cum*. See l. 20, Chap. III. —— **intercēderent**, 3d pers. plur. imperf. subjunctive of *intercēdō, -ere, -cessī, -cessum*, 3 (inter + cedere = lit. *to go between*); subjunctive, because an indirect question, introduced by interrogative adv. *quam*. A. & G. 334; B. 242; G. 467; H. 529, I. Observe difference of idiom: English = existed between them *and* the Aedui; Lat. *ipsīs cum Aeduīs intercēderent* = *existed to them* WITH *the Aedui*. —— **quae**, nom. plur. n. (interrogative *quis, quae, quid*); used adjectively, modifying *cōnsulta*.

					crees of the sen-
25 senātūs	cōnsulta,		quotiēns	quamque	ate, how often
senate's	*decrees,*		*how often*	*how and,*	and how honor-
26 honōrifica	in	eōs	facta essent,	ut omnī	able, had been
honorable	*on*	*them*	*had been made,*	*how at every*	enacted in their
					interest; how the
27 tempore	tōtīus	Galliae	prīncipātum	Aeduī	Aedui from time
time	*of entire*	*Gaul*	*the principate*	*the Aedui*	immemorial had
					held the ruling
28 tenuissent	prius	etiam	quam	nostram	position in all
had held	*before*	*even,*	*that,*	*our*	Gaul, even be-
					fore they had
29 amīcitiam	appetissent.		Populī Rōmānī	hanc	sought our alli-
friendship	*they had sought.*		*Of the people Roman*	*this*	ance. Moreover,

LINE 25. senātūs, gen. sing. m. (*senātus, -ūs*); limits *cōnsulta.* —— cōnsulta, nom. plur. n. (*cōnsultum, -ī*); subject-nom. of *facta essent.* —— quotiēns, adv. (*quoi,* how many); often written *quotiēs.* —— quamque (quam + que), see note, 1. 23, above; *quam* modifies *honōrifica.*

LINE 26. honōrifica, nom. plur. n. (adj. *honōrificus, -a, -um*); predicate-adj. after *facta essent.* —— in, prep. with the acc. or abl.; here it takes the acc., and = *toward.* —— eōs, acc. plur. m. (*is, ea, id*), personal pron.; obj. of the prep. *in;* refers to the Aedui. —— facta essent, 3d pers. plur. pluperf. subjunctive of *fīō, fierī, factus,* 3; used as pass. of *faciō;* subjunctive, because the question is *indirect.* See grammatical references to *intercēderent,* l. 24, above. —— ut, interrogative adv. = *how.* Observe that its meaning can only be determined by the context; we observe that it is used in connection with *quam,* and the inference is drawn at once that *ut* like *quam* introduces an indirect question, and must have a similar meaning. —— omnī, abl. sing. n. (*omnis, -e*); an attributive of *tempore.*

LINE 27. tempore, abl. sing. n. (*tempus, -oris*); *time when.* A. & G. 256, 1; B. 171; G. 393; H. 429. —— tōtīus, gen. sing. f. (*tōtus, -a, -um*); modifies *Galliae.* See l. 7, Chap. II. —— Galliae, gen. sing.; limits *prīncipātum.* —— prīncipātum, acc. sing. m. (*prīncipātus, -ūs*); direct obj. of *tenuissent.* See l. 21, Chap. III. —— Aeduī, -ōrum, m.; subject-nom. of *tenuissent.*

LINE 28. tenuissent, 3d pers. plur. imperf. subjunctive (*teneō,* 2); subjunctive, because in an indirect question. —— prius, adv. (from adj. *prior,* former). —— etiam, adv. = *even;* modifies *prius.* —— quam, conj.; lit. = *than* with comparatives; as a part of the adv. *prius* = *that;* sometimes the two words are written as one: *priusquam.* —— nostram, acc. sing. f. (*noster, -tra, -trum*); an attributive of *amīcitiam.*

LINE 29. amīcitiam, acc. sing. f. of *amīcitia, -ae* (*amīcus*); direct obj. of *appetissent.* —— appetissent, 3d pers. plur. pluperf. subjunctive of *appetō, -ere, -īvī (-iī), -ītum,* 3; agrees with a pron. implied in the ending as subject-nom., referring to the Aedui; subjunctive, because in a subordinate clause in virtual *ōrātiō oblīqua.* The *ōrātiō rēcta* of lines 22-29: *Deceō* ('*ē*) etiam, quam veterēs quamque īnstae causae necessitūdinis *nōbīs* cum Aeduis *intercēdant,* quae senātūs cōnsulta, quotiēns quamque honōrifica in *hōs* facta *sint,* ut omnī tempore tōtīus Galliae prīncipātum Aeduī *tenuerint* prius etiam quam nostram amīcitiam *appetīerunt.* —— Populī, gen. sing. m. (*populus, -ī*); limits *cōnsuētūdinem.* —— Rōmānī (*Rōma*), an attributive of *populī.* —— hanc, acc. sing. f. (*hīc, haec, hōc*); predicate after *esse;* herald of the following *ut*-clause.

Caesar informed him that the customs of the Roman people were such that they desired that their allies and friends might not only lose nothing of their own dignity, but might rather be advanced in influence, worthiness and honor. Who then could have bear to have them robbed of that which they	esse *to be* (is) amīcōs *friends* sed *but* velit *they* (the Roman people) *wish* amīcitiam *the friendship*	cōnsuētūdinem, *the practice,* nōn *not* grātiā, *by grace,* populī *of the people*	ut *that* modo *only* dignitāte, *dignity,* esse; *to be;* Rōmānī *Roman*	sociōs *the allies* suī *of their own* honōre (and) honor quod *which* attulissent, *they had brought,*	atque *and* nihil *nothing* auctiōrēs *more increased* vērō *but*	30 31 32 ad 33 to 34
dēperdere, *to forfeit,*					

LINE 30. **esse**, pres. inf. of *sum*, perf. *fuī*, fut. participle *futūrus*. —— **cōnsuētūdinem**, acc. sing. f. (*cōnsuētūdō, -inis*); subject-acc. of *esse*. —— **ut**, ecbatic conj. = *that*; refers to *hanc* = *such*. —— **sociōs**, acc. plur. m. (*socius, -ī*); subject-acc. of *dēperdere*. —— **atque**, conj. See *atque*, l. 10, Chap. I.

LINE 31. **amīcōs**, acc. plur. of *amīcus, -ī*, m.; connected by *atque* with *sociōs*, and in the same construction. —— **nōn modo ... sed**, conjunctives, but when thus used a rising to something more important in the second clause is denoted. See Madvig, § 461. —— **suī**, gen. sing. n. of the poss. pron. *suus, -a, -um*; used substantively = *of their own property*; limits *nihil*. —— **nihil**, acc. sing.; indecl. noun, used only in nom. and acc.; direct obj. of *dēperdere*. —— **dēperdere**, pres. inf. act. of *dēperdō, 3*; subject-accusatives are *sociōs* and *amīcōs*; but note that the inf. clauses depend on *velit*.

LINE 32. **sed**, adversative conj. —— **grātiā**, abl. *of specification*. A. & G. 253; B. 162; G. 397; H. 424. —— **dignitāte**, abl. sing. f. of *dignitās, -ātis* (*dignus*, worthy); same construction as *grātiā*. —— **honōre**, abl. sing. m. (*honor* or *honos*); same construction as *dignitāte*. Observe the asyndeton. See note on *legibus*, l. 5, Chap. I. —— **auctiōrēs**, acc. plur. m. of comparative adj. *auctior, -ius*; positive *auctus*, participle (*augēre*, to increase); predicate after *esse*.

LINE 33. **velit**, 3d pers. sing. pres. subjunctive (*volō, velle, voluī*); agrees with *populus Rōmānus* understood; subjunctive of *result* after *ut*, l. 30, above. —— **esse**, pres. inf. (*sum, esse, fuī*); subject-acc. is *eōs*, to be supplied, referring to *sociōs*, etc. —— **quod**, acc. sing. n. (*quī, quae, quod*); refers to *id*, l. 35, below, but is the direct obj. of *attulissent*. —— **vērō**, adversative conj.; weaker than *vērum* or *sed*, but stronger than *autem*. —— **ad**, prep. with the acc.

LINE 34. **amīcitiam**, acc. sing. f. of *amīcitia, -ae* (*amīcus* from *amō*); obj. of the prep. *ad*. —— **populī Rōmānī**, see l. 29, above. —— **attulissent**, 3d pers. plur. pluperf. subjunctive of *af(d)ferō, -ferre, attulī, allātum*; agrees with *Aeduī* understood; subjunctive, because an *integral part* of the sentence; broadly, because in a subordinate clause in *ōrātiō oblīqua*.

35 id	eīs	ēripī	quis	patī	posset?	had brought with them at their alliance with the Roman people? Thereupon he made the same demands that he had instructed the envoys to make: he should not bring war upon the Aedui nor upon their allies; he should return the hostages; if he could not send back
that	*from them*	*to be snatched,*	*who*	*to endure*	*was able?*	
36 Postulāvit	deinde	eadem		quae	lēgātīs	
He demanded	*then*	*the same (things)*		*which*	*to the legates*	
37 in	mandātīs	dederat:	nē	aut	Aeduīs	
in	*orders*	*he had given:*	*not*	*either*	*on the Aedui*	
38 aut	eōrum	sociīs	bellum	īnferret;		obsidēs
or	*their*	*allies*	*war*	*he should bring;*		*hostages*
39 redderet;	sī	nūllam	partem	Germānōrum		
he should restore;	*if*	*no*	*part*	*of the Germans*		

LINE 35. **id**, acc. sing. n. (*is, ea, id*); subject-acc. of *ēripī*. —— **eīs**, dat. plur. m. (*is, ea, id*); used substantively as a personal pron. Consult A. & G. 229; B. 143, REM. 3; G. 345, REM. 1; H. 385, II, 2. Observe that the clause *id eīs ēripī* is the obj. of *patī*; and consult A. & G. 331, *c*; B. 194, REM. 2, (*a*); G. 546, REM. 1; H. 535, II. —— **quis**, interrogative pron. (*quis, quae, quid*); subject-nom. of *posset*. —— **patī**, pres. inf. of the deponent *patior, patī, passus*, 3; complementary; depends on *posset*. —— **posset**, 3d pers. sing. imperf. subjunctive (*possum, posse, potuī*); agrees with the subject-nom. *quis*; a real question. A. & G. 338; B. 245, 3; G. 651; H. 523, II, 1. Compare note on *iūdicāret*, l. 10, Chap. XL.

LINE 36. **Postulāvit**, 3d pers. sing. perf. ind. act. (*postulō*, 1); agrees with *Caesar* understood. Synonyms: l. 3, Chap. XVI. —— **deinde** (dē + inde = lit. *from thence*), adv.; often used as a sequent to *prīmum* expressed or understood. —— **eadem**, acc. plur. n. (*īdem, eadem, idem*); used substantively; direct obj. of *postulāvit*. —— **quae**, acc. plur. n. (*quī, quae, quod*); direct obj. of *dederat*. —— **lēgātīs**, dat. plur. m. (*lēgātus, -ī*); indirect obj.

LINE 37. **in**, prep. with the acc. or abl.; here it takes the abl. —— **mandātīs**, abl. plur. n. (*mandātum, -ī*); obj. of the prep. *in*. —— **dederat**, 3d pers. sing. pluperf. ind. act. of *dō, dare, dedī, datum*, 1 (a short before *re*, pres. inf.); agrees with a pron. implied in the ending, referring to Caesar. —— **nē**, adv. —— **aut** . . . **aut** = *either* . . . *or*. See l. 19, Chap. I. —— **Aeduīs**, dat. plur. m. of *Aeduī, -ōrum*; after *in* in *īnferret*. See *Aeduō*, l. 20, Chap. III.

LINE 38. **aut**, see *aut*, preceding line. —— **eōrum**, gen. plur. m. (*is, ea, id*); used as a personal pron.; limits *sociīs*. —— **sociīs**, dat. plur. m. (*socius, -ī*); connected by *aut* with *Aeduīs*, and in the same construction. —— **bellum**, acc. sing. n. of *bellum, -ī*; direct obj. of *īnferret*. See note, l. 15, Chap. I. —— **īnferret**, 3d pers. sing. imperf. subjunctive of *īnferō, -ferre, -tulī, il(n)lātum*; its subject is a pron., referring to Ariovistus; subjunctive for imperative in direct discourse. A. & G. 339; B. 245, 2; G. 652; H. 523, III. —— **obsidēs**, acc. plur. m. (*obses, -idis*); direct obj. of *redderet*.

LINE 39. **redderet**, 3d pers. sing. imperf. subjunctive of *reddō, -ere, -didī, -ditum*, 3; subjunctive for imperative in direct discourse. —— **sī**, conditional conj.

| home any part of the Germans, he, at least, should not permit any more to cross the Rhine. | domum *home* | remittere *to send back* | posset, *he was able,* | at *at any rate,* | nē *not* | 40 |
| | quōs *any* | amplius *more* | Rhēnum *the Rhine* | trānsīre *to cross* | paterētur. *he should allow.* | 41 |

| XLIV. Ariovistus replying briefly to Caesar's demands, and boasting much as to his | XLIV. | Ariovistus *Ariovistus* | | ad *to* | postulāta *the demands* | Caesaris *of Caesar* | 1 |
| | pauca *a few (things)* | | respondit; *replied;* | dē *concerning* | suīs *his own* | virtūtibus *merits* | 2 |

—— **nūllam**, acc. sing. f. of the adj. *nūllus, -a, -um* (nē + ūllus); an attributive of *partem*. —— **partem**, acc. f. (*pars, -tis*); direct obj. of *remittere*. —— **Germānōrum**, gen. plur. m. (*Germānī, -ōrum*); limits *partem*. See l. 18, Chap. I.

LINE 40. **domum**, acc. sing. (*domus, -ūs,* or *-ī*, locative); denotes place *to which* after a verb of motion. A. & G. 258, *b*; B. 174; G. 337; H. 380, II. 2, 1). —— **remittere**, pres. inf. act. of *remittō, -ere, -mīsī, -missum*, 3 (re + mittere = *to send back*); complementary inf. —— **posset**, 3d pers. sing. imperf. subjunctive (*possum*); subjunctive in condition after *sī*. —— **at**, conj.; another form is *ast* = GK. ἀτάρ; it adds a different but not directly opposite notion like *sed;* it often follows conditional propositions, as in text, in sense of *at least*. —— **nē**, see *nē*, l. 37, above.

LINE 41. **quōs**, acc. plur. m., indef. pron. (*quis, quae, quid*); subject-acc. of *trānsīre*. —— **amplius**, adv., comparative degree; positive *amplē;* superl. *amplissimē;* modifies *trānsīre*. —— **Rhēnum**, acc. m. (*Rhēnus, -ī*); direct obj. of *trānsīre*. —— **trānsīre**, pres. inf. act. of *trānseō, -īre, -īvī (-iī), -itum,* 4. —— **paterētur**, 3d pers. sing. imperf. subjunctive of the deponent *patior,* 3; subjunctive in indirect, for imperative in direct discourse. The *ōrātiō rēcta* of lines 29–41: Populī Rōmānī *haec est cōnsuētūdō*, ut sociōs atque amīcōs nōn modo suī nihil dēperdere, sed grātiā, dīgnitāte, honōre auctiōrēs velit esse; quod vērō ad amīcitiam populī Rōmānī *attulērunt*, id eīs ēripī quis patī *potest? Postulō* deinde eadem quae lēgātīs in mandātīs *dedī:* nē aut Aeduīs aut eōrum sociīs bellum *intuleris* (or *nōlī īnferre*); obsidēs *redde;* sī nūllam partem Germānōrum domum remittere *possīs,* at nē quōs amplius Rhēnum trānsīre *passus sīs* (*nōlī patī*). Of course, if *nōlī patī* is read, *nē passus sīs* must be deleted; so, too, if *nōlī īnferre* is read instead of *nē intuleris,* the latter must be suppressed.

LINE 1. **Ariovistus, -ī**, m.; subj. of *respondit.* See l. 51, Chap. XXXI. —— **ad**, prep. with the acc. —— **postulāta**, acc. plur. n. of *postulātum, -ī* (*postulāre,* to demand); obj. of the prep. *ad.* —— **Caesaris**, gen. (*Caesar*); limits *postulāta.*

LINE 2. **pauca**, adj., acc. plur. n. (*paucus, -a, -um*) = *a few things;* direct obj. of *respondit;* elegantly translated as an adv. —— **respondit**, 3d pers. sing. perf. ind. act. of *respondeō, -ēre, -dī, -ōnsum,* 2 (re + spondēre = lit. *to promise in return*); hence = *to answer.* —— **dē**, prep. with the abl. Synonyms: see *dē,* l. 27, Chap. XIX. —— **suīs**, abl. plur. f. (*suus, -a, -um*); attributive of *virtūtibus.* —— **virtūtibus**, abl. plur. f. of *virtūs, -ūtis* (*vir*); obj. of the prep. *dē.*

LINES 3-7.] BOOK I. 335

3 multa	praedicāvit:	Trānsīsse	Rhēnum	own merits said:
many (things)	he boasted:	To have crossed	the Rhine	He had crossed the Rhine not of
4 sēsē	nōn suā	sponte,	sed rogātum	his own accord, but at the request and call of
himself	not by his own	will,	but being asked	the Gauls; he had not left home
5 et arcessītum	ā Gallīs;	nōn sine	māgnā	and relatives without a large
and invited	by the Gauls;	not without	great	hope of rich rewards; he had
6 spē	māgnīsque praemiīs	domum	propīnquōs-	settlements in
hope	great and, rewards	home	relations	Gaul granted by
7 que reliquisse;	sēdēs	habēre	in Galliā	the Gauls them-
and, to have left;	seats	to have	in Gaul	

LINE 3. **multa**, acc. plur. n. (*multus, plūs, plūrimus*); used substantively; direct obj. of *praedicāvit*. —— **praedicāvit**, 3d pers. sing. perf. ind. act. (prae + dīcō, 1); agrees with a pron. implied in the ending, referring to Ariovistus. The student will beware of confounding *dīcō*, 1, with *dūcō*, 3. —— **Trānsīsse**, perf. inf. act. of *trānseō, -īre, -īvī (-iī), -itum*; subject-acc. is the pron. *sēsē*. Observe that from this point to the close of the chapter Ariovistus' speech is given in the indirect form. —— **Rhēnum**, acc. sing. m. (*Rhēnus, -ī*); direct obj. of *trānsīsse*.

LINE 4. **sēsē**, acc. sing.; refers to Ariovistus (see l. 4, Chap. XXX); subj. of *trānsīsse*. —— **nōn**, adv.; modifies *trānsīsse*. —— **suā**, abl. sing. f. (*suus, -a, -um*); an attributive of *sponte*. —— **sponte**, abl. sing. f. of an assumed theme *spōns, spontis*, f.; *in accordance with*. A. & G. 253, NOTE; B. 162, and REM. 3; G. 397; H. 416. Synonyms: l. 19, Chap. VII. —— **sed**, adversative conj. —— **rogātum**, acc. sing. m. of pass. participle *rogātus* of verb *rogō*, 1; agrees with the pron. *sēsē*.

LINE 5. **et**, cop. conj.; connects the participles. —— **arcessītum**, acc. sing. m. of the perf. pass. participle of *arcessō, -ere* or *-īre, -sīvī, -sītum*, 3 or 4; connected by *et* with *rogātum*, and in the same grammatical construction. —— **ā**, prep. with the abl. —— **Gallīs**, abl. plur. m. (*Gallī, -ōrum*); agent after the prep. *ā*. A. & G. 246; B. 166; G. 401; H. 415, I. —— **nōn**, negative adv.; modifies *reliquisse*. —— **sine**, prep. with the abl. —— **māgnā**, abl. sing. of the adj. *māgnus*; an attributive of *spē*.

LINE 6. **spē**, abl. sing. f. (*spēs, -eī*); obj. of the prep. *sine*. —— **māgnīsque** (magnīs + que). *māgnīs*, abl. plur. n.; an attributive of *praemiīs*. *que*, enclitic conj.; connects the phrases closely. —— **praemiīs**, connected by *que* with *spē*, and in the same construction. Observe hendiadys for *nōn sine māgnā spē māgnōrum praemiōrum*. See A. & G. 385; B. 310, 2, (*b*); G. 698; H. 636, III, 2. —— **domum**, acc. sing. f. of *domus, -ūs*, or loc. *-ī*; direct obj. of *reliquisse*. —— **propīnquōsque** (propīnquōs + que). *propīnquōs*, acc. plur. m. (adj. *propīnquus*); used as noun; direct obj. of *reliquisse*.

LINE 7. **reliquisse**, perf. inf. act. of *relinquō, -ere, -līquī, -lictum*, 3; supply *sē* as subject-acc., referring to Ariovistus. —— **sēdēs**, acc. plur. f. (*sēdēs, -is*); direct obj. of *habēre*. —— **habēre**, pres. inf. act. of *habeō*, 2; subject-acc. *sē* or *sēsē*, to be supplied. —— **in**, prep. with the acc. or abl.; here it takes the abl. See note on *in*, l. 1, Chap. I. —— **Galliā**, abl.; obj. of the prep. *in*.

selves, and hostages given by their own free-will; he had taken tribute in accordance with the rights of war, which victors were wont to impose on the vanquished. He had not waged war against the Gauls, but the Gauls had waged war	ab *by* ipsīs *themselves* voluntāte *will* iūre *according to the right* victīs *on the vanquished* Gallīs, *on the Gauls,*	concessās, *conceded,* datōs; *given;* bellī, *of war,* impōnere *to put* sed *but*	obsidēs *hostages* stīpendium *tribute* quod *which* cōnsuērint. *were wont.* Gallōs *the Gauls*	ipsōrum 8 *by their own* capere 9 *to take* victōrēs 10 *victors* Nōn sēsē 11 *Not himself* sibi bellum 12 *on him war*

LINE 8. **ab**, prep. with the abl. See l. 6, Chap. I. —— **ipsīs**, abl. plur. m. (*ipse, -sa, -sum*); reflexive pron.; refers to the Gauls; obj. of the prep. *ab*. Consult A. & G. 246; B. 166; G. 401; H. 415, I. For facts, see l. 40 ff., Chap. XXXI. —— **concessās**, acc. plur. f. of perf. pass. participle of *concēdō, -ere, -cessī, -cessum*, 3; agrees with the noun *sēdēs*. On the use of *habeō* with the perf. participle, see A. & G. 292, *e*; B. 191, 3, (*d*); G. 238; H. 388, 1, NOTE. —— **obsidēs**, acc. plur. m. and f. (*obses, -idis*); in the same construction as *sēdēs*; in other words, supply (*sē*) *habēre* from the preceding clause. —— **ipsōrum**, gen. plur. (*ipse*); limits *voluntāte*; refers to the Gauls.

LINE 9. **voluntāte**, abl. (*voluntās, -tātis,* f.); *in accordance with*. Synonyms: l. 4, Chap. IX. —— **datōs**, perf. pass. participle (*dō, dare, dedī, datum*); agrees with *obsidēs*. —— **stīpendium**, -ī, n.; acc. sing.; direct obj. of *capere*. —— **capere**, pres. inf. (*capiō*, 3); subject-acc. *sē*, to be supplied.

LINE 10. **iūre**, abl. sing. n. (*iūs, iūris*); *in accordance with*. See grammatical references to *sponte*, l. 4, above. —— **bellī**, gen. sing. n. (*bellum, -ī*); limits *iūre*. —— **quod**, acc. sing. n. (*quī, quae, quod*); direct obj. of *impōnere*. —— **victōrēs**, nom. plur. of *victor, -ōris,* m. (*vincere*); subj. of *cōnsuērint*.

LINE 11. **victīs**, dat. plur. m. of the perf. pass. participle *victus, -a, -um* of *vincō, -ere, vīcī, victum*, 3; used substantively; or supply *virīs*; dat. after *in* in *impōnere*. A. & G. 228; B. 143; G. 347; H. 386, 1. —— **impōnere** (in + pōnere, *to place on*), pres. inf. act. of *impōnō*, 3; complementary; depends on *cōnsuērint*. A. & G. 271; B. 181; G. 423; H. 533, I, 2. —— **cōnsuērint**, 3d pers. plur. perf. subjunctive act. of *cōnsuēscō, -ere, -suēvī, -suētum,* 3; preteritive verb. See A. & G. 279, *e*; B. 113, REM. 2, end; G. 175, 5, end; H. 297, I, 2; syncopated and contracted from *cōnsuēverint*. A. & G. 128, 2; B. 251; G. 131, 1; H. 235; subjunctive, because in a subordinate clause in *ōrātiō oblīqua*. The *ōrātiō rēcta* of lines 3–11: Trānsiī Rhēnum *egō* nōn *meā* sponte, sed *rogātus* et *arcessītus* ā Gallīs; nōn sine māgnā spē māgnīsque praemiīs domum propīnquōsque *relīquī*; sēdēs *habeō* in Galliā ab ipsīs concessās, obsidēs ipsōrum voluntāte datōs; stīpendium *capiō* iūre bellī, quod victōrēs victīs impōnere *cōnsuērunt*. —— **Nōn**, adv.; modifies *intulisse*; made emphatic by standing at the beginning of the sentence. —— **sēsē**, acc. sing.; subj. of *intulisse*, to be supplied. See *sēsē*, l. 4, above.

LINE 12. **Gallīs**, dat. plur. m. (*Gallī, -ōrum*); after prep. *in* in *intulisse* understood. See grammatical references to *victīs*, preceding line. —— **sed**, adversative

13 intulisse;	omnēs	Galliae	cīvitātēs	ad	against him; all the states of Gaul had come to assail him, and had encamped over against him; but all these forces had been routed and vanquished by him in a single battle. If they wished to try again, he was
to have brought;	all,	of Gaul,	the states,	to	
14 sē	oppūgnandum	vēnisse	āc	contrā	
himself	to be fought against	to have come,	and	opposite to	
15 sē	castra	habuisse;	• eās	omnēs	cōpiās
him	a camp	to have had;	these	all	forces
16 ā	sē	ūnō	proeliō	pulsās	āc
by	himself	in one	battle	to have been routed	and
17 superātās esse.	Sī	iterum	experīrī	velint,	
to have been overcome.	If	again	to try	they wish,	

conj. —— Gallōs, acc. plur. m. (*Gallī, -ōrum*); subject-acc. of *intulisse*. —— sibi, dat. sing. (*suī, sibi, sē, sē*); dat. after *in* in *intulisse*; refers to Ariovistus. —— bellum, acc. sing. n. (*bellum, -ī*); direct obj. of *intulisse*.

LINE 13. intulisse, perf. inf. act. of *īnferō, īnferre, intulī, il(n)lātum*. —— omnēs, acc. plur. f. (*omnis, -e*); an attributive of *cīvitātēs*. See l. 1, Chap. I. —— Galliae, gen. sing. f. (*Gallia, -ae*); limits *cīvitātēs*. —— cīvitātēs, acc. plur. f. of *cīvitās, -tātis* (*cīvēs*, citizen); subject-acc. of *vēnisse*. Observe that *cīvitātēs* here, by metonymy = *cīvēs*. —— ad, prep. with the acc.

LINE 14. sē, acc. sing.; obj. of the prep. *ad*; refers to Ariovistus. —— oppūgnandum, acc. sing. m. of gerundive *oppūgnandus, -a, -um* of *oppūgnō*, 1 (ob + pūgnāre, *to fight against*). Observe that this gerundive construction with *ad* denotes purpose. See A. & G. 300; B. 184, REM. 4, III; G. 432; H. 542, III, and 544. Observe further the gerundive agrees with the pron. *sē*; and finally, we know this to be the gerundive construction, and not the gerund with a direct obj., because the acc. of the gerund *with a preposition* does not, as a rule, take the direct obj. —— vēnisse, perf. inf. act. of *veniō*, 4; subject-acc. is *cīvitātēs*. —— āc, conj. See *atque*, l. 10, Chap. I. —— contrā, adv. and prep.; here a prep. with the acc.

LINE 15. sē, acc. sing.; obj. of the prep. *contrā*; refers to Ariovistus. —— castra, acc. plur. (*castrum, -ī*, n.); direct obj. of *habuisse*. See *castrīs*, l. 12, Chap. XII. —— habuisse, perf. inf. act. of *habeō*, 2; connected by *āc* with *vēnisse*, and has the same grammatical construction. —— eās, acc. plur. f. (*is, ea, id*); an attributive of *cōpiās*. —— omnēs, acc. plur. f. (*omnis, -e*); attributive of complex notion involved in *eās cōpiās*. —— cōpiās, acc. plur. f. of *cōpia, -ae*; subj. of *pulsās* (*esse*) and *superātās* (*esse*). See *cōpiīs*, l. 6, Chap. II.

LINE 16. ā, prep. with the abl. —— sē, abl. of the agent after the prep. *ā*; refers to Ariovistus. Consult A. & G. 246; B. 166; G. 401; H. 415, I. —— ūnō, abl. sing. n. (*ūnus, -a, -um*); modifies *proeliō*. See *ūnam*, l. 2, Chap. I. —— proeliō, abl. *of manner* (*proelium, -ī*, n.). A. & G. 248; B. 168; G. 399; H. 419, III. Possibly the allusion is to the battle fought near Admagetobriga. —— pulsās (esse), perf. inf. pass. of *pellō, -ere, pepulī, pulsum*, 3; subject-acc. is *cōpiās*. —— āc, see *āc*, l. 14, above.

LINE 17. superātās esse, perf. inf. pass. of *superō*, 1 (*super*, over); compare GER. *über*, and GK. ὑπέρ; hence *superāre* = lit. *to be over*. Observe that the participial forms of this compound inf. in gender and number conform with the gender and number of the subject-acc. *cōpiās*. The *ōrātiō rēcta* of lines 11-17: Nōn egō Gallīs (*intulī*), sed Gallī mihi bellum *intulērunt*; omnēs Galliae cīvitātēs ad *me* oppūgnan-

ready to fight again; if they wished to enjoy peace, it were unjust to refuse to pay the tribute, which they had paid of their own accord up to this time. The friendship of the Roman people ought to be to him an honor and pro-	sē *himself* pāce *peace* stīpendiō *the tribute* ad *up to* populī *of the people*	iterum *again* ūtī *to enjoy* recūsāre, *to refuse,* id *that* Rōmānī *Roman*	parātum *prepared* velint, *they wish,* quod *what* tempus *time* sibi *to him*	esse *to be* inīquum *unjust* suā *by their own* pependerint. *they had paid.* ōrnāmentō *for an ornament*	dēcertāre; *to fight;* esse *to be (it is)* voluntāte *will* Amīcitiam *The friendship* et *and*	sī 18 *if* dē 19 *concerning* 20 21 22

dum *venērunt* āc contrā *mē* castra *habuērunt*; *eae* omnēs *cōpiae* ā *mē* ūnō proeliō *pulsae* āc *superātae sunt.* —— **Sī**, conditional conj. —— **iterum**, adv.; modifies *experīrī.* Synonyms: l. 29, Chap. XXXI. —— **experīrī**, pres. inf. of deponent *experior, -rīrī, -pertus,* 4; complementary; supply *eum* as direct obj.; or the inf. may be taken absolutely. —— **velint**, 3d pers. plur. pres. subjunctive (*volō, velle, voluī*); subjunctive in the protasis after *sī*.

LINE 18. **sē**, acc. sing. (*suī, sibi, sē, sē*); subj. of *parātum esse.* —— **iterum**, see *iterum*, preceding line. —— **parātum esse**, perf. inf. pass. of *parō*, 1; pass. parts: *paror, -rārī, -rātus;* subject-acc. is *sē.* —— **dēcertāre**, pres. inf. act. of *dēcernō*, 1 (dē + certāre) = lit. *to fight through;* a neuter verb, often followed by an abl. of manner or means. —— **sī**, see *Sī*, l. 17, above.

LINE 19. **pāce**, abl. of *pāx, pācis,* f.; after *ūtī.* A. & G. 249; B. 167, 1; G. 407; H. 421, I. —— **ūtī**, pres. inf. of *ūtor, ūtī, ūsus,* deponent, 3; complementary. —— **velint**, see *velint*, l. 17, above. —— **inīquum**, acc. sing. n. of the adj. *inīquus* (in + aequus = lit. *not just*); predicate after *esse.* —— **esse**, pres. inf. (*sum, fuī, futūrus*); used here impersonally; or, strictly, the inf. *recūsāre* is subject-acc. —— **dē**, prep. with the abl. Synonyms: l. 27, Chap. XIX.

LINE 20. **stīpendiō**, abl. sing. n. (*stīpendium, -ī*); obj. of the prep. *dē*. Observe that this word is contracted from *stipipendum* (stipem, *gift* + pendēre, *to weigh*); hence the noun = lit. *weighed gift.* —— **recūsāre**, pres. inf. act. of *recūsō*, 1 (re + causā); hence *recūsāre* = lit. *to make a case against,* i.e. *refuse.* —— **quod**, acc. sing. n. (*quī, quae, quod*); refers to *stīpendiō;* direct obj. of *pependerint.* —— **suā**, abl. sing. f. (*suus, -a, -um*); an attributive of *voluntāte.* —— **voluntāte**, abl. sing. f. (*voluntās, -tātis*). See *voluntāte*, l. 9, above.

LINE 21. **ad**, prep. with the acc. = *to* or *towards;* here = *up to* or *until.* —— **id**, acc. sing. n. (*is, ea, id*); an attributive of *tempus.* —— **tempus**, acc. sing. n. (*tempus, -oris*); obj. of the prep. *ad.* See *tempore*, l. 21, Chap. III. —— **pependerint**, 3d pers. plur. perf. subjunctive of *pendō, -ere, pependī, pēnsum,* 3; agrees with *Gallī* understood. The *ōrātiō rēcta* of lines 17–21 : Sī iterum experīrī *volunt, egō* iterum *parātus sum* dēcertāre; sī pāce ūtī *volunt*, inīquum *est* dē stīpendiō recūsāre, quod suā voluntāte ad *hōc* tempus *pependērunt.* —— **Amīcitiam**, acc. sing. f. of *amīcitia, -ae (amīcus);* subject-acc. of *esse*, l. 23, below.

LINE 22. **populī**, gen. sing. m. (*populus, -ī*); limits *Amīcitiam.* Synonyms: see *populum*, l. 17, Chap. VI. —— **Rōmānī**, gen. sing. m.; an attributive of *populī.* ——

						tection, not a

23 praesidiō,   nōn   dētrīmentō   esse   oportēre, | tection, not a
  guard,   *not*   *for detriment* *to be (it)* *ought*, | detriment, and
24 idque   sē   eā   spē   petīsse. | he had sought it
  that and, *himself* *with this* *hope*   *to have sought*. | with this expectation. If, through
25 Sī   per   populum   Rōmānum   stīpendium | the influence of
  If *through* *the people*   *Roman*   *the tribute* | the Roman people, the tribute
26 remittātur   et   dēditiciī   subtrahantur, | was to be withheld, and his
  should be stopped *and (his)* *subjects* *were taken away*, | tributaries were
27 nōn   minus   libenter   sēsē   recūsātūrum | to be taken from
  not *less*   *gladly*   *himself (to be) about to reject* | him, he would renounce the

sibi, dat. of the *object to which* after *esse*; refers to Ariovistus. —— ōrnāmentō (*ōrnāmentum, -ī*, n.); dat. of the *end for which*. Consult A. & G. 233, *a*; B. 147, REM. 2; G. 356; H. 390, I. —— et, cop. conj.; connects the nouns.

LINE 23. praesidiō, dat. (*praesidium, -ī*) connected by *et* with *ōrnāmentō*, and in the same grammatical construction. —— nōn, adv.; qualifies *esse*. —— dētrīmentō, dat. of *dētrīmentum, -ī*, n. (*dētrī* as seen in *dētrītus*, pass. participle of dēterō + mentum); hence the noun = lit. *a wearing out*, i.e. *disaster, damage*, etc.; connected with *praesidiō* by *et* understood, and in the same construction. —— esse, pres. inf. of *sum*; depends on *oportēre*. —— oportēre, pres. inf. impersonal (*oportet, oportuit*, 2). Observe that *oportēre* stands for *oportet* in *ōrātiō rēcta*; and that *oportēre* is no less impersonal than *oportet*; and that here, strictly, its grammatical subj. is the accusative-clause *Amīcitiam . . . esse*.

LINE 24. idque (id + que). *id*, acc. sing. n. (*is, ea, id*); dem. pron.; used substantively; direct obj. of *petīsse*. Observe that *id* refers to idea involved in *Amīcitiam populī Rōmānī*. —— sē, acc. sing. of the reflexive pron. *suī, sibi, sē, sē*; refers to Ariovistus; subject-acc. of *petīsse*. —— eā, abl. sing. f. (*is*); an attributive of *spē*. —— spē, abl. sing. f. (*spēs, -ēī*); *manner*. A. & G. 248; B. 168; G. 399; H. 419, III. —— petīsse, perf. inf. act. *peto, -ere, -īvī (-iī), -ītum*, 3; syncopated and contracted for *petīvisse*. A. & G. 128. 2; B. 251; G. 131, 1; H. 235; subject-acc. is *sē*. Synonyms: l. 71, Chap. XXXI.

LINE 25. Sī, conditional conj. —— per, prep. with the acc. —— populum, acc. sing. (*populus, -ī*, m.); obj. of the prep. *per*; acc. *as means*; see A. & G. 246, *b*; B. 166, REM. 1; G. 401; H. 415, 1, NOTE 1. Synonyms: l. 17, Chap. VI. —— Rōmānum (*Rōma*), adj.; an attributive of *populī*. —— stīpendium, nom. sing. n.; subj. of *remittātur*. See *stīpendium*, l. 9, above.

LINE 26. remittātur, 3d pers. sing. pres. subjunctive pass. of *remittō, -ere, -mīsī, -missum*, 3 (re + mittere = lit. *to send back*); subjunctive in the condition after *sī*. —— et, cop. conj. —— dēditiciī, nom. plur. m. of the adj. *dēditic(i)ius*, used as substantive; subject-nom. of *subtrahantur*. —— subtrahantur, 3d pers. plur. pres. subjunctive pass. of *subtrahō, -ere, -trāxī, -trāctum*, 3 (sub + trahere = lit. *to draw under*); connected by *et* with *remittātur*, and in the subjunctive for the same reason.

LINE 27. nōn, adv.; modifies *minus*. —— minus, adv., comparative degree; positive *parum*; superl. *minimē*; qualifies *libenter*. —— libenter, adv. (*libēns*); modifies *recūsātūrum (esse)*. —— sēsē, reflexive pron., acc. sing.; subj. of *recūsātūrum (esse)*. See *sēsē*, l. 4, Chap. XXX. —— recūsātūrum (esse), fut. inf. act. of

friendship of the Roman people with no less pleasure than he had sought it. As to his leading a great number of Germans into Gaul, he did this with a view of his own defense, not with that of assault-	populī *the people's,*	Rōmānī *Roman,*	amīcitiam, *friendship*	quam *than*	appetierit. 28 *he sought (it).*
	Quod *As to the fact that*		multitūdinem *a multitude*	Germānōrum *of Germans*	in 29 *into*
	Galliam *Gaul*		trādūcat, *he is leading,*	id *this*	sē *himself,* sui 30 *of himself*
	mūniendī, *defending,*		nōn *not*	Galliae *of Gaul*	impūgnandae 31 *to be attacked,*

recūsō, 1 (see *recūsāre,* l. 20, above); subject-acc. is *sēsē.* Observe that the apodosis is involved in this inf. See A. & G. 337, 2, *a*; B. 245, 4, (2); G. 656, 2; H. 527, II.

LINE 28. **populī Rōmānī,** the phrase as gen. depends on *amīcitiam.* As to these words, see note, l. 22, above. —— **amīcitiam,** acc. sing. f. (*amīcitia, -ae* [*amīcus, amāre*]); direct obj. of *recūsātūrum (esse).* —— **quam,** conj.; with compounds = *than;* connects the infinitive-clause with *appetierit.* —— **appetierit,** 3d pers. sing. perf. subjunctive of *appetō, -ere, -īvī (-iī), -ītum,* 3 (ad + petere = lit. *to seek for*); subjunctive, because in a subordinate clause in indirect discourse. The *ōrātiō rēcta* of lines 21-28: Amīcitiam populī Rōmānī *mihi* ōrnāmentō et praesidiō, nōn dētrīmentō esse *oportet,* idque *egō* eā spē *petiī.* Sī per populī Rōmānī stīpendium *remittātur* et dēditīciī *subtrahentur,* nōn minus libenter *egō recūsābō* populī Rōmānī amīcitiam, quam *appetiī.*

LINE 29. **Quod,** acc. *of specification* = *whereas, as to the fact that.* See A. & G. 333, *a,* and 341, *a* and *d,* and REM.; B. 123, REM. 21, and 198, REM. 1; G. 525, 2 and 3; H. 516, II, and especially the NOTE. —— **multitūdinem,** acc. sing. of *multitūdō, -inis,* f. (*multus*); direct obj. of *trādūcat.* —— **Germānōrum,** gen. plur. m. (*Germānī, -ōrum*); limits *multitūdinem.* See note on *Germānīs,* l. 14, Chap. I. —— **in,** prep. with the acc. or abl.; here it has the acc. See *in,* l. 1, Chap. I.

LINE 30. **Galliam,** obj. of the prep. *in.* See *Gallia,* l. 1, Chap. I. —— **trādūcat,** 3d pers. sing. pres. subjunctive act. of *trādūcō,* 3; agrees with Ariovistus as subject; in subjunctive, because expressing the sentiments of another. See grammatical references to *Quod,* preceding line. Observe that this clause is an adverbial modifier of the predicate of the main clause. —— **id,** acc. sing. n. (*is, ea, id*); used substantively; direct obj. of *facere;* refers to the idea contained in the clause *Quod ... trādūcat.* —— **sē,** acc. sing. of the pron. *suī, sibi, sē, sē;* subject-acc. of *facere.* —— **suī,** objective gen. of the reflexive pron. with the gen. of the gerund instead of the direct object.

LINE 31. **mūniendī,** gen. of the gerund of *mūniō,* 4; limits *causā.* Consult A. & G. 298, *a* and *c*; B. 184, REM. 4. I, (*a*); G. 428, REMS. 1 and 2; H. 542, NOTES 1 and 2. Observe that the gerund construction here after *causā* denotes *purpose.* —— **nōn,** adv.; modifies *facere;* made emphatic by its position. —— **Galliae,** gen sing., and, with the gerundive, limits *causā.* —— **impūgnandae,** gen. of gerundive *impūgnandus, -a, -um* of *impūgnō,* 1 (in + pūgnāre = lit. *to fight against*); see grammatical references to *mūniendī.*

BOOK I.

32	causā	facere;	ēius	reī	testimōnium	ing Gaul. The evidence as to this purpose was that he did not come without an invitation, and that he had not waged war, but prevented it. He had come into Gaul before the Roman people. Never before this
	*for the sake,**	*to do* (is doing);	*of this*	*thing*	*a proof*	
33	esse	quod	nisi	rogātus	nōn	vēnerit
	to be (is)	*that*	*unless*	*being asked*	*not*	*would he come,*
34	et	quod	bellum	nōn	intulerit,	sed
	and	*that*	*war*	*not*	*he has brought in,*	*but*
35	dēfenderit.	Sē	prius	in	Galliam	vēnisse
	warded off.	*Himself*	*sooner*	*into*	*Gaul*	*to have come*
36	quam	populum	Rōmānum.		Numquam	ante
	than	*the people*	*Roman.*		*Never*	*before*

LINE 32. causā, a prep. here; but strictly a noun—abl. *of cause*. A. & G. 245, *c*; B. 165, REM. 3, 186, B, NOTE (*a*); G. 373; H. page 221, FOOTNOTE 2. —— facere, pres. inf. act. (*faciō*, 3); agrees with its subject-acc. *sē*. —— ēius, gen. sing. f. (*is, ea, id*); an attributive of *reī*. —— reī, gen. sing. f. (*rēs, reī*); limits *testimōnium*; the allusion is to his purpose of self-defense. —— testimōnium, acc. sing. n.; predicate after *esse*.

LINE 33. esse, pres. inf. (*sum, esse, fuī, futūrus*); its subject-acc. are the following *quod*-clauses. —— quod, conj. = *that*. —— nisi (nē + sī), conjunctive adv. = lit. *if not*, i.e. *unless;* used with the perf. pass. participle *rogātus* = *rogātus sit*, a protasis, of which the apodosis is *vēnerit*. —— rogātus, perf. pass. participle of *rogō*, 1. —— nōn, negative adv.; modifies *vēnerit*. —— vēnerit, 3d pers. sing. perf. subjunctive (*veniō*, 4); its subject-nom. is a pron. understood, referring to Ariovistus; subjunctive, because the statement is made on authority of another. A. & G. 341, *d*; B. 198, (*b*); G. 628; H. 516, II, 1, NOTE.

LINE 34. et, cop. conj.; connects the *quod*-clauses. —— quod, see *quod*, preceding line. —— bellum, acc. sing. n.; direct obj. of *intulerit;* supply *eīs*, as dat. after *in* in the compound *intulerit*. —— nōn, adv. —— intulerit, 3d pers. sing. perf. subjunctive act. of *īnferō, -ferre, -tulī, il(n)lātum;* subjunctive for the same reason as *vēnerit*. —— sed, strong adversative conj.

LINE 35. dēfenderit, 3d pers. sing. perf. subjunctive act. of *dēfendō, -ere, -fendī, -fēnsum*, 3; supply *bellum* as direct obj.; or *id* referring to *bellum;* subjunctive for the same reason as *intulerit*. The *ōrātiō rēcta* of lines 29–35 is as follows: Quod multitūdinem Germānōrum in Galliam *egō trādūcō, hōc egō meī* mūniendī, nōn Galliae impūgnandae causā *faciō; huīus* reī testimōnium *est* quod nisi rogātus nōn *vēnī* et quod bellum nōn *intulī*, sed *dēfendī*. The reader will observe that from *Sī iterum* to *dēfenderit* (lines 17–35) the sequence of tenses has been primary. —— Sē, acc. sing. of reflexive pron. *suī;* subj. of *vēnisse*. —— prius, adv. (*prior, prīmus*); might be taken as a part of the compound *priusquam* — parts separated (tmēsis). —— in, prep. with the acc. or abl.; here after a verb of motion it takes the acc. See note on *in*, l. 1, Chap. I. —— Galliam, acc. sing. f.; obj. of the prep. *in*. —— vēnisse, perf. inf. act. of *veniō*, 4; its subject-acc. is *sē*.

LINE 36. quam, see note on *prius*, preceding line; but it might be taken as a conjunction = *than; prius . . . quam = sooner . . . than*. —— populum, acc. sing. m. (*populus, -ī*); subj. of *vēnisse*, to be supplied. Synonyms: l. 17, Chap. VI. —— Rōmānum, acc.; an attributive of *populum*. —— Numquam, adv. (nē + umquam [contracted from ūnum + quam]) = lit. *not ever*. —— ante, prep. with the acc.

* The *of* in *causā = for the sake of*—appears in the last word of l. 30. These gerunds and gerundive phrases are difficult to render literally. The above is the best we can do with them.

time had an army of the Roman people gone beyond the border of their province. What did he mean? Why had he come into his possessions? This part of Gaul was his province, as that was ours. As there ought	hōc *this* prōvinciae *the province's* vellet? *should he wish?* venīret? *should he come?* Galliam, *Gaul*	tempus *time* fīnibus *borders* Cūr *Why* Prōvinciam *The province* sīcut *as*	exercitum *an army* ēgressum. *to have gone forth.* in *into* suam *his* illam *that*	populī *of the people* Quid *What* suās *his* hanc *this* nostram. *ours.*	Rōmānī *Roman* sibi *for himself* possessiōnēs *possessions* esse *to be* Ut *As*	37 38 39 40 ipsī *to himself* 41

LINE 37. **hōc**, acc. sing. n. (*hīc, haec, hōc*); an attributive of *tempus*. —— **tempus**, acc. sing. n. (*tempus, -oris*); obj. of the prep. *ante*. See *tempore*, l. 21, Chap. III. —— **exercitum**, acc. sing. m. (*exercitus, -ūs*); subject-acc. of *ēgressum* (*esse*). Synonyms: l. 28, Chap. III. —— **populī Rōmānī**, see note on these words, l. 22, above; the phrase as gen. limits *exercitum*.

LINE 38. **prōvinciae**, gen. sing. f. (*provincia, -ae*); limits *fīnibus*. The allusion is to the Roman province in the south-eastern part of *omnis Gallia*. —— **fīnibus**, abl. plur. m. (*fīnis, -is*); abl. *of separation* after *ēgressum* (*esse*). A. & G. 243; B. 160; G. 390, NOTE 3; H. 413. Synonyms: l. 12, Chap. II. —— **ēgressum** (esse), perf. inf. of the deponent *ēgredior, -ī, -gressus*, 3 (ē + gradī = lit. *to step out*); its subject-acc. is *exercitum*. —— **Quid**, acc. sing. n. of the interrogative pron. *quis, quae, quid*; direct obj. of *vellet*. —— **sibi**, dat. sing. (*suī, sibi, sē, sē*); ethical dat. A. & G. 236; B. 145, REM. 1; G. 351, and NOTE 2; H. 389.

LINE 39. **vellet**, 3d pers. sing. imperf. subjunctive of *volō, velle, voluī*; subjunctive, because a *real* question in indirect discourse. A. & G. 338; B. 245, 3; G. 651; H. 523, II. 1. —— **Cūr**, adv., contracted from *quāre*, old orthography *quor*. —— **in**, prep. with the acc. or abl.; here, after verb of motion, it takes the acc. —— **suās**, acc. plur. of the poss. adj. pron. *suus, -a, -um*; an attributive of *possessiōnēs*, but refers to Ariovistus. —— **possessiōnēs**, acc. plur. f. (*possessiō, -ōnis* [*possidēre*]); obj. of the prep. *in*.

LINE 40. **venīret**, 3d pers. sing. imperf. subjunctive of *veniō*, 4; subjunctive for the same reason as *vellet*, preceding line. —— **Prōvinciam**, acc. sing. f. (*provincia, -ae*); predicate after *esse*. —— **suam**, acc. sing. f. (*suus, -a, um*); an attributive of *Prōvinciam*; refers to Ariovistus. —— **hanc**, acc. sing. f. (*hīc, haec, hōc*); an attributive of *Galliam*. —— **esse**, pres. inf. of *sum*.

LINE 41. **Galliam**, acc. sing. f. (*Gallia, -ae*); subj. of *esse*. See *Gallia*, l. 1, Chap. I. Observe that *hanc Galliam* = the part of Gaul conceived to be near the speaker. —— **sīcut**, adv. (sīc + ut = lit. *so as*). —— **illam**, acc. sing. f. (*ille, illa, illud*); gen. *illīus*; dat. *illī*; agrees with *Galliam*, to be supplied; and this *Galliam* understood is the subject-acc. of *esse* understood. Observe the contrast indicated by the pronouns *hanc* and *illam*. —— **nostram** (i.e. *Rōmānam*), acc. sing. f. (*noster, -tra, -trum*); an attributive of *prōvinciam* understood. The *ōrātiō rēcta* of lines 35-41: *Ego* prius in Galliam *vēnī* quam *populus Rōmānus*. Numquam ante hōc tempus *exercitus* populī Rōmānī prōvinciae fīnibus *ēgressus* (*est*). Quid tibi vīs? Cūr in *meīs* possessiōnēs *venīs?* Prōvincia mea haec est Gallia, sīcut *illa vestra* (*Rōmāna*). —— **Ut**, adv. = *ac*; correlative with *sīc*. —— **ipsī**, dat. of intensive pron. *ipse, -sa, -sum*; more emphatic than *sibi*; dat. of the indirect obj. after *concēdī*.

42 concēdī	nōn	oportēret,	sī	in	nostrōs	to be no concessions to him, in case he made an
to be conceded	not	it ought,	if	on	our	
43 fīnēs	impetum	faceret,	sīc	item	nōs	attack on our territory, so, too, we were unjust,
borders	an attack	he should make,	so	also	us	
44 esse	inīquōs,	quod	in	suō	iūre	in that we interrupted him in the exercise of
to be (we are)	unjust,	because	in	his	right	
45 sē	interpellārēmus.		Quod	frātrēs	ā	his rights. As to his saying that the Aedui
himself	we disturbed.		As to the fact that	brothers	by	
46 senātū	Aeduōs		appellātōs		dīceret,	had been called "brothers" by the senate, he
the senate	the Aedui		(to have) been called		(as) he said,	was not so barbarous, nor so
47 nōn	sē	tam	barbarum	neque	tam	
not	himself	so	savage	nor	so	

LINE 42. concēdī, pres. inf. pass. of *concēdō*, -*ere*, -*cessī*, -*cessum*, 3 (con, *intensive* + cēdere = lit. *to go away*); complementary inf. —— nōn, negative particle. —— oportēret, 3d pers. sing. imperf. subjunctive of the impersonal *oportet*, -*ēre*, -*uit*, 2; subjunctive in the apodosis. —— sī, conditional conj., introducing the protasis. —— in, prep. with the acc. or abl.; here it takes the acc. —— nostrōs, acc. plur. m. (*noster*, -*tra*, -*trum*); an attributive of *fīnēs*; but in sense = *Rōmānōs*.

LINE 43. fīnēs, acc. plur. m. (*fīnis*, -*is*); obj. of the prep. *in*. —— impetum, acc. sing. m. (*impetus*, -*ūs*); direct obj. of *faceret*. —— faceret, 3d pers. sing. imperf. subjunctive of *faciō*, 3; in the protasis after *sī*. —— sīc, adv. (sī + ce, apocopated); modifies *item*. —— item, adv. (i [is] + tem) = lit. *in this manner;* hence *also*. —— nōs, acc. plur. of the pers. pron. *egō; = Rōmānōs;* subject-acc. of *esse*.

LINE 44. esse, pres. inf. of *sum*. —— inīquōs, acc. plur. m. (adj. *inīquus*, -*a*, -*um* [in, *un* + aequus, *just*]); predicate adj. after *esse*. —— quod, conj. = *because*. —— in, prep. with the acc. or abl.; here it takes the abl. —— suō, abl. sing. n. (*suus*, -*a*, -*um*); an attributive of *iūre;* but refers to Ariovistus. —— iūre, abl. sing. n. (*iūs*, *iūris*); obj. of the prep. *in*.

LINE 45. sē, acc. sing. (*suī*, *sibi*, *sē*, *sē*); direct obj. of *interpellārēmus*. —— interpellārēmus, 1st pers. plur. imperf. subjunctive act. of *interpellō*, 1; subjunctive, because in a subordinate clause in *ōrātiō oblīqua*. The *ōrātiō rēcta* of lines 41-45: Ut *mihi* concēdī nōn *oportet*, sī in *vestrōs* (i.e. *Rōmānōs*) fīnēs impetum *faciō*, sīc item *vōs* (*Rōmānī*) estis inīquī, quod in *meō* iūre *mē* interpellātis. —— Quod, conjunctive adv. = *in that*. —— frātrēs, acc. plur. m. (*frāter*, -*tris*); predicate after *appellātōs* (*esse*). —— ā, prep. with the abl. See *ab*, l. 6, Chap. I.

LINE 46. senātū, abl. sing. m. (*senātus*, -*ūs*); abl. *of the agent* after the prep. *ā*. A. & G. 246; B. 108, 2, and 166; G. 401; H. 388, 2, and 415, I. —— Aeduōs, acc. plur. m. (*Aeduī*, -*ōrum*); subject-acc. of *appellātōs* (*esse*). As to the clan, see l. 20, Chap. III. —— ap(d)pellātōs (esse), perf. inf. pass. of *ap*(*d*)*pellō*, 1. Synonyms: l. 30, Chap. XX. —— dīceret, 3d pers. sing. imperf. subjunctive act. of *dīcō*, 3; its subj. is Caesar understood; subjunctive, because the statement is made on another's authority. A. & G. 321, and 341, *d*; B. 198, (*b*), REM. 1; G. 628; H. 516, 2, 1, NOTE.

LINE 47. nōn, adv.; modifies the adv. *tam*. —— sē, acc. sing. (*suī*, *sibi*, *sē*, *sē*); subj. of *esse*. —— tam, adv.; modifies the adj. *barbarum*. —— barbarum, acc. sing.

inexperienced in affairs as not to know that neither in the last war with the Allobroges had the Aedui brought aid to the Romans, nor had they availed themselves of the aid of the Roman people in those contentions which the Aedui	imperītum *ignorant*	esse *to be*	rērum, *of affairs*	ut *that*	nōn *not*	scīret, *he did know* 48
	neque *neither*	bellō *in war,*	Allobrogum *of the Allobroges,*	proximō *last*		Aeduōs *the Aedui* 49
	Rōmānīs *to the Romans*	auxilium *aid*	tulisse, *to have brought,*	neque *nor*		ipsōs *themselves* 50
	in *in*	his *these*	contentiōnibus, *quarrels*	quās *which*	Aeduī *the Aedui*	sēcum *himself with* 51
	et *and*	cum *with*	Sēquanīs *the Sequani*	habuissent, *had had,*		auxiliō *the aid* 52

m. (*barbarus, -a, -um*); predicate after *esse*. —— neque (nĕ + que), conjunctive adv. = lit. *and not.* —— tam, adv.; modifies the adj. *imperītum.*

LINE 48. imperītum, acc. sing. m. of the adj. *imperītus, -a, -um* (in + *perītus*); connected by *neque* with *barbarum*, and in the same grammatical construction. —— esse, pres. inf. of *sum*; its subject-acc. is *sē*. —— rērum, gen. plur. f. (*rēs, reī*); gen. after adj. *imperītum.* A. & G. 218, *a*; B. 135, (*a*); G. 374; H. 399. 2. —— ut, ecbatic conj. —— nōn, adv.; modifies *scīret.* —— scīret, 3d pers. sing. imperf. subjunctive act. of *sciō, -īre, scīvī (-iī), scītum,* 4; subjunctive of result after *ut*, referring to *tam*. Synonyms: see *scīre*, l. 4, Chap. XX.

LINE 49. neque . . . neque = *neither . . . nor.* —— bellō, abl. n. (*bellum, -ī*); *time in which.* A. & G. 256, 1; B. 171; G. 393; H. 429. The time of this war was B.C. 62. —— Allobrogum, gen. plur. m. (*Allobrogēs, -um*); limits *bellō.* —— proximō, abl. sing. n. of adj. *proximus, -a, -um;* superl. degree; comparative *propior;* no positive; an attributive of *bellō.* Observe (1) that *proximus* = *nearest, next;* of time = next *preceding* or *following;* the precise meaning to be determined by the context; (2) that in English, as an abbreviation, *prox.* points to the following. —— Aeduōs, acc. plur.; subj. of *tulisse.* See *Aeduōs*, l. 46, above.

LINE 50. Rōmānīs, dat. plur. m. (*Rōmānus, -a, -um,* adj.); used as a noun; indirect obj. after *tulisse.* —— auxilium, acc. sing. n. (*auxilium, -ī*); direct obj. of *tulisse.* —— tulisse, perf. inf. act. of *ferō, ferre, tulī, lātum;* the subject-acc. is *Aeduōs.* —— neque, correlative of *neque*, preceding line. —— ipsōs, acc. plur. m. (*ipse, -a, -um*); refers to the Aedui; is the subject-acc. of *ūsōs esse*, l. 53, below.

LINE 51. in, prep. with the acc. or abl.; here it takes the abl. —— hīs, abl. plur. f. (*hīc, haec, hōc*); an attributive of *contentiōnibus.* —— contentiōnibus, abl. plur. (*contentiō, -ōnis*); obj. of the prep. *in.* —— quās, acc. plur. f (*quī, quae, quod*); refers to *contentiōnibus;* direct obj. of *habuissent.* —— Aeduī, subject-nom. m. of *habuissent.* See *Aeduō*, l. 20, Chap. III. —— sēcum (sē + cum). *sē*, abl. sing. (*suī, sibi, sē, sē*); obj. of the enclitic prep. *cum.* Consult A. & G. 99, *e*; B. 79, 2; G. 413, REM. 1; H. 184, 6.

LINE 52. et, cop. conj.; connects *sēcum* and *cum Sēquanīs.* —— cum, prep. with the abl. —— Sēquanīs, abl. plur. (*Sēquanī, -ōrum*); obj. of the prep. *cum.* See *Sēquanīs,* l. 25, Chap. I. —— habuissent, 3d pers. plur., pluperf. subjunctive of *habeō,* 2; agrees with subject-nom. *Aeduī;* in subjunctive, because in a subordinate clause in *ōrātiō oblīqua.* —— auxiliō, abl. sing. n. (*auxilium, -ī*); after *ūsōs esse.* A. & G. 249; B. 167, 1; G. 407; H. 421, I.

53 populī	Rōmānī	ūsōs esse.		Dēbēre
of the people	*Roman*	*to have used (received).*		*To have*
54 sē		suspicārī	simulātā	Caesarem
from himself	*(he ought)*	*to suspect*	*being feigned,*	*Caesar,*
55 amīcitiā,	quod	exercitum	in Galliā	habeat,
the friendship	*because*	*an army*	*in Gaul*	*he has,*
56 suī	opprimendī	causā	habēre.	Quī
of himself	*to be crushed*	*for the sake,*	*to have (it).*	*Who*
57 nisi	dēcēdat	atque	exercitum	dēdūcat ex
unless	*departs,*	*and*	*the army*	*withdraws from*

had had with himself and the Sequani. He ought to be suspicious, accordingly, that Caesar while pretending friendship, in that he had an army in Gaul, had it there for the sake of crushing him. Now unless he departs, and withdraws his army

LINE 53. **populī Rōmānī**, see note on these words, l. 22, above; the phrase as such is gen., and limits *auxiliō*. —— **ūsōs esse**, perf. inf. of deponent *ūtor, ūtī, ūsus*, 3; its subject-acc. is *ipsōs*, l. 50, above. —— **Dēbēre**, pres. inf. act. of *dēbeō, -ēre, -uī, -itum*, 2 (dē + habēre, lit. *to have from one;* hence = *to owe*). Synonyms: *oportet* denotes a moral claim; *dēbēre*, the moral obligation of a person to meet the claim.

LINE 54. **sē**, acc. sing. (*suī, sibi, sē, sē*); subject-acc. of *dēbēre*. —— **suspicārī**, pres. inf. of *suspicor*, 1, deponent; complementary. A. & G. 271; B. 181; G. 423; H. 533, 2. —— **simulātā**, abl. sing. f. of perf. pass. participle of *simulō*, 1 (*similis*); abl. absolute with *amīcitiā*. —— **Caesarem**, subject-acc. of *habēre* (*Caesar, -aris*, m.).

LINE 55. **amīcitiā**, abl. absolute with *simulātā*. See A. & G. 255; B. 192; G. 409; H. 431. —— **quod**, a conj. = *because*. —— **exercitum**, acc. sing. m. (*exercitus, -ūs*); direct obj. of *habeat*. —— **in**, prep.; here with the abl. —— **Galliā**, abl. sing. f. (*Gallia, -ae*); obj. of the prep. *in*. See l. 1, Chap. I. —— **habeat**, 3d pers. sing. pres. subjunctive of *habeō*, 2; subjunctive, because in a subordinate clause in *ōrātiō oblīqua*.

LINE 56. **suī**, objective gen. instead of the direct obj. of the gerund. —— **opprimendī**, gen. of the gerund of *opprimō, -ere, -pressī, -pressum*, 3. For the gerund construction with *suī*, see grammatical references to *suī* in phrase *suī mūniendī*, lines 30 and 31, above; for the gen. construction, limiting *causā*, see *causā*, l. 32, above. —— **habēre**, pres. inf. of *habeō*, 2; subject-acc. is *Caesarem*; its direct obj. is *eum*, i.e. *exercitum*, to be supplied. The *ōrātiō rēcta* of lines 45–56: Quod frātrēs ā senātū Aeduī appellātī sunt, ut dūcis,* nōn ego tam barbarus neque tam imperītus sum rērum, ut nōn egō sciam, neque bellō Allobrogum proximō Aeduōs Rōmānīs auxilium tulisse, neque ipsōs in hīs contentiōnibus, quās Aeduī mēcum et cum Sēquanīs habuērunt, auxiliō populī Rōmānī ūsōs esse. *Dēbeō egō* suspicārī simulātā Caesaris amīcitiā, quod exercitum in Galliā *habet, meī* opprimendī causā habēre. —— **Quī**, rel. pron. m. refers to Caesar; subject-nom. of *dēcēdat*; the relative standing first in a sentence = *et is*. A. & G. 130,*f*; B. 129, REM. 9; G. 610; H. 453.

LINE 57. **nisi**, conj. (nē + sē = lit. *not if*). —— **dēcēdat**, 3d pers. sing. pres. subjunctive act. (*dēcēdō*, 3) — dis + cēdere = *to go apart;* subjunctive in the condition after *nisi*. —— **atque**, conj. See l. 10, Chap. I. —— **exercitum**, acc. sing. m.

* Might take this form: Quod frātrēs ā Senātū Aeduōs appellātōs *dīcas*. See H. 516, II. 1, and NOTE.

from these re-	hīs	regiōnibus,	sēsē	illum	nōn	prō	amīco,	58
gions, Ariovistus will regard him	these	regions,	himself	him	not	for	a friend,	
not as a friend,	sed	prō	hoste	habitūrum.			Quod	59
but as an enemy. But if he should	but	for	an enemy (to be)	about to have.		As to which (But)		
kill him, he would be doing	sī	eum	interfēcerit,	multīs	sēsē	nōbilibus	60
a pleasing thing	if	him	he should slay,	to many,	himself,	nobles	
to many nobles and chiefs of the	prīncipibusque		populī	Rōmānī	grātum		esse	61
Roman people;	chiefs	and,	of the people	Roman	pleasing		to be	
he had learned this from them	factūrum;		id	sē	ab	ipsīs		per	62
through their en-	about to do;		that	himself	from	themselves		through	

(*exercitus, -ūs,* m.); direct obj. of *dēdūcat.* See l. 31, Chap. III. —— **dēdūcat,** 3d pers. sing. pres. subjunctive of *dēdūcō, -ere, -dūxī, -ductum,* 3; connected by *atque* with *dēcēdat,* and in subjunctive for the same reason. —— **ex,** prep. with the abl.

LINE 58. **hīs,** abl. plur. f. (*hīc, haec, hōc*); an attributive of *regiōnibus.* —— **regiōnibus,** abl. plur. f. (*regiō, -ōnis*); obj. of the prep. *ex.* —— **sēsē,** reduplication of *sē;* acc. of the reflexive pron. *suī;* subject-acc. of *habitūrum (esse);* refers to Ariovistus. See l. 4, Chap. XXX. —— **illum,** acc. sing. m. (*ille, -la, -lud*); direct obj. of *habitūrum (esse);* refers to Caesar. —— **nōn,** adv. (nē + ūnum); modifies *habitūrum (esse).* —— **prō,** prep. with the abl. —— **amīcō,** abl. m. (*amīcus, -ī*); obj. of the prep. *prō.*

LINE 59. **sed,** strong adversative conj. —— **prō,** see *prō,* preceding line; by repetition notions are kept distinct. —— **hoste,** abl. sing. m. and f. (*hostis, -is*); obj. of the prep. *prō.* —— **habitūrum (esse),** fut. inf. act. of *habeō,* 2; subject-acc. is pron. *sēsē.* The *ōrātiō rēcta* of lines 56–59: *Et tū* nisi *dēcēdēs,* atque exercitum *dēdūcēs* ex hīs regiōnibus, *egō tē* nōn prō amīcō, sed prō hoste *habēbō.* —— **Quod,** an adverbial acc. of *quī, quae, quod* = lit. *as to which.* A. & G. 240, *b;* B. 123, 5, REM. 21; G. 334, REM. 1; H. 378, 2. But as a transitional word with *sī* = *but if* or *and if.*

LINE 60. **sī,** conditional particle. —— **eum,** acc. sing. m. (*is, ea, id*); used as a pron. of the 3d pers.; refers to Caesar; direct obj. of *interfēcerit.* —— **interfēcerit,** 3d pers. sing. perf. subjunctive of *interficiō,* 3 (inter + facere) = lit. *to make or put between — to interrupt,* i.e. *life;* hence = *to slay;* subjunctive in the protasis after *sī.* —— **multīs,** abl. plur. m. (adj. *multus, -a, -um*); an attributive of *nōbilibus* which latter is used as a noun. —— **sēsē,** see *sēsē,* l. 58, above. —— **nōbilibus,** dat. plur. of *nōbilis, -e;* indirect obj.

LINE 61. **prīncipibusque** (prīncipibus + que). *prīncipibus,* dat. plur. m. of *prīnceps, -ipis. que,* enclitic, connects *prīncipibusque* with *nōbilibus;* hence in the same construction. —— **populī Rōmānī,** see note on the phrase, l. 22, above; as gen., the phrase limits *nōbilibus prīncipibusque.* —— **grātum,** acc. sing. n. (adj. *grātus, -a, -um*); used substantively; direct obj. of *esse factūrum.* —— **esse factūrum** (*factūrum esse*), fut. inf. act. of *faciō,* 3; subject-acc. is pron. *sēsē;* the apodosis in indirect discourse of the protasis *sī interfēcerit.*

LINE 62. **id,** acc. sing. n. (*is, ea, id*); refers to the idea contained in the preceding sentence; direct obj. of *habēre.* —— **sē,** acc. sing. of *suī;* refers to Ariovistus; subject-acc. of *habēre.* —— **ab,** prep. with the abl. —— **ipsīs,** abl. plur. (*ipse, -sa,*

[LINES 63-67.] BOOK I. 347

63 eōrum	nūntiōs	compertum	habēre,	quōrum	voys, and he could secure the favor and friendship of all of them by Caesar's death. But if he would go away and give over to him the free possession of Gaul, he would reward him richly, and whatever wars he might
their	*messengers*	*having ascertained,*	*to have,*	*of whom*	
64 omnium	grātiam	atque	amīcitiam	ēius	
all,	*the favor*	*and*	*friendship*	*by his*	
65 morte	redimere	posset.	Quod	sī	
death	*to purchase*	*he was able.*	*As to which* (But)	*if*	
66 discessisset		et	līberam	possessiōnem	
he should have withdrawn,		*and*	*the free*	*possession*	
67 Galliae	sibi	trādidisset,		māgnō	
of Gaul	*to himself*	*should have delivered,*		*with a great,*	

-sum); intensive pron.; refers to the Romans; obj. of the prep. *ab.* —— **per,** prep. with the acc.

LINE 63. **eōrum,** gen. plur. m. (*is, ea, id*); used as a personal pron. of the 3d pers.; limits *nūntiōs.* —— **nūntiōs,** acc. plur. m. (*nūntius, -ī*); obj. of the prep. *per* — *agency* as *means.* A. & G. 246, *b*; B. 166, REM. 1; G. 401; H. 415, I, 1, NOTE 1. —— **compertum,** perf. pass. participle of *comperiō, -īre, -perī, -pertum,* 4; agrees with *id.* —— **habēre,** perf. inf. act. (*habeō,* 2); subject-acc. is *sē.* Observe that *habēre* with certain perf. pass. participles forms a periphrase about = to the required tense ind. or inf. act. Here the phrase = *comperīsse,* nearly. See A. & G. 292, *c*; B. 191, 3, (*d*); G. 238; H. 388, I, NOTE. —— **quōrum,** gen. plur. m. (*quī, quae, quod*); refers to Roman nobles and chiefs; as a gen. it limits *grātiam.*

LINE 64. **omnium,** gen. plur. m. (*omnis, -e*); used substantively; explanatory modifier of *quōrum* — an appositive. Observe that *quōrum* is not a partitive gen. after *omnium*; it = the same number as *omnium*; in our idiom, however, the phrase may be rendered: *all of whom.* See *omnēs,* l. 5, Chap. I. —— **grātiam,** acc. sing. f. (*grātia, -ae*); direct obj. of *redimere.* Synonyms: *grātia* = objective favor; whereas *favor* = subjective regard. —— **atque,** conj. See l. 10, Chap. I. —— **amīcitiam,** acc. sing. of *amīcitia, -ae,* f. (*amīcus*); connected by *atque* with *grātiam,* and in the same grammatical construction. —— **ēius,** gen. sing. m. (*is, ea, id*); used as a personal pron.; limits *morte*; refers to Caesar.

LINE 65. **morte,** abl. sing. f. (*mors, mortis*); means. A. & G. 248, *c*; B. 167; G. 401; H. 420. —— **redimere,** pres. inf. act. of *redimō, -ere, -ēmī, -ēmptum,* 3 (red + ēmere) = lit. *to buy back;* complementary inf.; depends on *posset.* —— **posset,** 3d pers. sing. imperf. subjunctive (*possum, posse, potuī*); subjunctive, because in a subordinate clause in *ōrātiō oblīqua.* The *ōrātiō rēcta* of lines 59-65: Quod sī *tē interfīcerō,* multīs *egō* nōbilibus prīncipibusque populī Rōmānī grātum *fēcerō; hōc egō* ab ipsīs per eōrum nūntiōs compertum *habeō,* quōrum omnium grātiam atque amīcitiam *tuā* morte redimere *possum.* —— **Quod sī,** see note on these particles, lines 59 and 60, above.

LINE 66. **discessisset,** 3d pers. sing. pluperf. subjunctive of *discēdō, -ere, -cessī, -cessum,* 3; subjunctive in the protasis after *sī.* Observe that from this point the sequence is again secondary. —— **et,** cop. conj. —— **līberam,** adj., acc. sing. f. (*līber, -era, -erum*); an attributive of *possessiōnem.* —— **possessiōnem,** acc. sing. f. (*possessiō, -ōnis*); direct obj. of *trādidisset.*

LINE 67. **Galliae,** gen. sing. f. (*Gallia, -ae*); limits *possessiōnem.* For description, see l. 1, Chap. I. —— **sibi,** dat. of the reflexive pron. *suī*; indirect obj. of

wish to be waged, he would wage them to the finish without any labor or danger on Caesar's part.	sē *himself,*	illum *him,*	praemiō *reward*	remūnerātūrum *to be about to remunerate*		et 68 *and*
	quaecumque *whatever*	bella *wars*	gerī *to be waged*	vellet, *he wished,*		sine 69 *without*
	ūllō *any,*	ēius *of his,*	labōre *labor*	et *and*		perīculō 70 *peril,*
	cōnfectūrum. *(to be) about to accomplish.*					71
XLV. Caesar replying made many statements	XLV.	Multa *Many (things)*	ab *by*	Caesare *Caesar*	in *to*	eam 1 *this*

trādidisset; refers to Ariovistus. —— **trādidisset,** 3d pers. sing. pluperf. subjunctive of *trādō, -ere, -didī, -ditum,* 3 (trāns + dare); connected by *et* with *discessisset,* and in the subjunctive for the same reason. —— **māgnō,** abl. sing. n. (*māgnus, -a, -um*); an attributive of *praemiō.*

LINE 68. **sē,** acc. sing. (*suī, sibi, sē, sē*); subject of *remūnerātūrum (esse)*. —— **illum,** acc. sing. m. (*ille, -la, -lud*); refers to Caesar; direct obj. of *remūnerātūrum (esse)*. —— **praemiō,** abl. *of manner (praemium, -ī);* has a modifier *māgnō;* otherwise it would require the prep. *cum.* —— **remūnerātūrum (esse),** fut. inf. act. of the deponent *remūneror, -ārī, -ātus,* 1. Observe that the fut. infinitives of the deponents are always in the active form. A. & G. 135, *c*; B. 109, 2; G. 220, NOTE 2; H. 231, 3. —— **et,** cop. conj.

LINE 69. **quaecumque,** acc. plur. n. (*quīcumque, quaecumque, quodcumque*); indef. rel. pron.; used here adjectively; an attributive of *bella.* —— **bella,** acc. plur. n. (*bellum, -ī*); subject-acc. of *gerī.* —— **gerī,** pres. inf. pass. (*gerō, -ere, gessī, gestum,* 3). —— **vellet,** 3d pers. sing. imperf. subjunctive of *volō, velle, voluī;* agrees with Caesar understood; subjunctive, because in a subordinate clause in *ōrātiō oblīqua.* —— **sine,** prep. with the abl.

LINE 70. **ūllō,** abl. sing. m. of the adj. *ūllus, -la, -lum;* an attributive of *labōre.* —— **ēius,** gen. sing. m. (*is, ea, id*); refers to Caesar; limits *labōre.* —— **labōre,** abl. sing. m. (*labor, -ōris*); obj. of the prep. *sine.* —— **et,** cop. conj. —— **perīculō,** abl. sing. n. (*perīculum, -ī*); connected by *et* with *labōre,* and in the same grammatical construction.

LINE 71. **cōnfectūrum (esse),** fut. inf. act. of *cōnficiō, -ere, -fēcī, -fectum,* 3 (con + facere); subject-acc. is *sē,* l. 68, above. Observe that the indef. rel. clause: *quīcumque bella gerī vellet* — is the direct obj. of *cōnfectūrum (esse).* The *ōrātiō rēcta* of lines 65-71: Quod sī *discesseris,* et līberam possessiōnem Galliae *mihi trādideris,* māgnō *egō tē* praemiō *remūnerābō* et quaecumque bella gerī *volēs,* sine ūllō *tuō* labōre et perīculō *cōnficiam.*

LINE 1. **Multa,** nom. plur. n. (adj. *multus*); used substantively; subject of *dicta sunt.* —— **ab,** prep. with the abl. —— **Caesare,** abl. (*Caesar, -aris,* m.); obj. of the prep. *ab* — agent. —— **in,** prep. with the acc. or abl.; here it takes the acc. —— **eam,** acc. sing. f. (*is, ea, id*); an attributive of *sententiam.*

						with the purpose
2 sententiam	dicta	sunt,	quārē		negōtiō	of explaining
purport	*said*	*were,*	*why*	*from the business*		why he could
3 dēsistere	nōn	posset;	neque	suam	neque	not abandon his undertaking. He
to desist	*not*	*he was able;*	*neither*	*his own*	*nor*	said that neither
4 populī	Rōmānī	cōnsuētūdinem			patī,	his own usage nor that of the
the people's	*Roman*		*custom*	*to permit* (permitted),		Roman people
5 utī	optimē	merentēs	sociōs		dēsereret,	admitted of his leaving most
that	*the best*	*meriting*	*allies*	*he should abandon,*		meritorious allies in the lurch;
6 neque	sē	iūdicāre	Galliam	potius	esse	nor did he think that Gaul belong-
nor	*himself*	*to judge*	*Gaul*	*rather*	*to be*	ed to Ariovistus
7 Ariovistī	quam	populī	Rōmānī.		Bellō	rather than to
Ariovistus'	*than*	*the people's*	*Roman.*		*By war*	the Roman peo-

LINE 2. **sententiam**, acc. sing. f. (*sententia, -ae*); obj. of the prep. *in*. —— **dicta sunt**, 3d pers. plur. perf. ind. pass. of *dīcō*, 3; its subject-nom. is *multa*, used as a noun. —— **quārē** (quā + rē), adv.; sometimes written *quā rē*. —— **negōtiō**, abl. sing. n. (*negōtium, -ī*); abl. *of separation* after *dēsistere*.

LINE 3. **dēsistere**, pres. inf. act. of *dēsistō, -ere, -stitī, -stitum*, 3; complementary; depends on *posset*. —— **nōn** (nē + ūnum), adv. —— **posset**, 3d pers. sing. imperf. subjunctive; agrees with a pron. understood, referring to Caesar; subjunctive, because an *indirect question*. Observe that the clause *quārē . . . posset* is explanatory of, and in apposition with *sententiam*, preceding line. —— **neque** (nē + que), conj. See *neque*, l. 16, Chap. IV. —— **suam**, acc. sing. f. (*suus, -a, -um*); refers to Caesar; an attributive of *cōnsuētūdinem* understood. —— **neque**, see *neque*, immediately preceding.

LINE 4. **populī**, gen. sing. (*populus, -ī,* m.); limits *cōnsuētūdinem*. Synonyms: see *populī*, l. 17, Chap. III. —— **Rōmānī**, gen. sing. m.; an attributive of *populī*. —— **cōnsuētūdinem**, acc. sing. f. (*cōnsuētūdō, -inis*); subject-acc. of *patī*. —— **patī**, pres. inf. of the deponent *patior, patī, passus,* 3.

LINE 5. **utī**, conj. = *ut*, that. —— **optimē**, adv., superl. degree (*bene, melius, optimē*); modifies *merentēs*. —— **merentēs**, acc. plur. m. pres. participle of deponent *mereor, -ērī, -itus,* 2; an attributive of *sociōs*. Observe the deponents have the participles of both voices. —— **sociōs**, acc. plur. m. (*socius*); direct obj. of *dēsereret*. —— **dēsereret**, 3d pers. sing. imperf. subjunctive of *dēserō, -ere, -uī, -sertum,* 3; telic subjunctive after *utī*. Observe that *patī, regularly*, takes the inf. with subject-acc. after it.

LINE 6. **neque**, see *neque*, l. 3, above. —— **sē**, acc. sing. (*suī, sibi, sē, sē*); refers to Caesar; subject-acc. of *iūdicāre*. —— **iūdicāre**, pres. inf. act. of *iūdicō,* 1 (compare *iūdex*, judge). —— **Galliam**, acc. sing. f. (*Gallia, -ae*); subject-acc. of *esse*. —— **potius**, adv.; strictly an acc. n. of the adj. *potior, -us*, comparative of *potis*. —— **esse**, pres. inf. (*sum*, perf. *fuī*, fut. participle *futūrus*).

LINE 7. **Ariovistī**, predicate-gen. of *Ariovistus, -ī,* m. — after *esse*. A. & G. 214, *c*; B. 133; G. 366; H. 401, 402. —— **quam**, conj.; with comparatives = *than*. —— **populī Rōmānī**, gen.; the phrase is connected by *quam* with *Ariovistī*, and is

350   CAESAR'S GALLIC WAR   [CHAP. XLV.

ple. The Arverni and the Ruteni were conquered in war by Quintus Fabius Maximus; but the Roman people had pardoned them, and had not reduced them to a province, nor had they imposed tribute upon them.	superātōs esse *to have been conquered* Q. Fabiō Māximō, *Quintus Fabius Maximus,* ignōvisset, *had pardoned,* redēgisset, *had they reduced (them),*	Arvernōs *the Arverni* quibus *whom* neque *nor* neque *nor*	et *and* populus *the people* in *into* stīpendium *tribute*	Rutēnōs ab *the Ruteni by* Rōmānus *Roman* prōvinciam *a province* imposuisset. *had they imposed.*	8 9 10 11

in the same grammatical construction. See l. 4, above. —— Bellō, abl. of *bellum, -ī*, n.; means. See *bellum*, l. 15, Chap. I.

LINE 8. superātōs esse, perf. inf. pass. of *superō*, 1 (*super*); its subject-accusatives are *Arvernōs* and *Rutēnōs*. —— Arvernōs, acc. plur. m. (*Arvernī, -ōrum*); a clan living north of the Ruteni. —— et, cop. conj.; connects the nouns. —— Rutēnōs, acc. plur. m. (*Rutēnī, -ōrum*); connected by *et* with *Arvernōs*, and in the same grammatical construction. The Ruteni were a clan bordering on the province. The clans here mentioned were defeated by the Romans 121 B.C. Ariovistus entered Gaul 71 B.C. — a rather late comer. But Ariovistus says in Chap. XLIV: *Sē prius in Galliam venisse, quam populum Rōmānum.* —— ab, prep. with the abl.

LINE 9. Q. Fabiō Māximō, abl. *of the agent* after the pres. *ab*. Observe that the person here alluded to was Quintus Fabius Maximus (Allobrogicus); that *Quīntus* (quīnque + tus, orig. *the fifth-born*) is the *praenōmen;* that *Fabius* is the name of the *gēns*, and *Māximus* is the *cōgnōmen*, and that *Allobrogicus* is the *āgnōmen*. —— quibus, dat. plur. (*quī, quae, quod*) after *ignōvisset;* refers to *Arvernōs* and *Rutēnōs*. —— populus, -ī, m., subject-nom. of *ignōvisset*. —— Rōmānus, adj.; an attributive of *populus*.

LINE 10. ignōvisset, 3d pers. sing. pluperf. subjunctive act. of *ignōscō, -ere, -nōvī, -nōtum*, 3; subjunctive, because in a subordinate clause in indirect discourse. —— neque, see *neque*, l. 3, above. —— in, prep. with the acc. or abl.; here it takes the acc. —— prōvinciam, acc. sing. f. (*prōvincia, -ae*); obj. of the prep. *in*.

LINE 11. redēgisset, 3d pers. sing. pluperf. subjunctive of *redigō, -ere, -ēgī, -āctum*, 3; connected by the conj. *neque* with *ignōvisset*, and in the subjunctive for the same reason. —— neque, see *neque*, l. 3, above. —— stīpendium, acc. sing. n. (*stīpendium*); direct obj. of *imposuisset*. Observe that, as *redēgisset* is trans., it takes *eōs* understood as direct obj.; but that *imposuisset* takes here the direct obj. expressed, and a dat. *eīs* understood, depending on the prep. *in* in the compound *im(n)posuisset*. —— imposuisset, 3d pers. sing. pluperf. subjunctive of *pōnō, pōnere, posuī, positum*, 3; connected by the conj. with *ignōvisset*, and in the subjunctive for the same reason. The *ōrātiō rēcta* of lines 3–11: neque *mea* neque populī Rōmānī *cōnsuētūdō patitur*, utī optimē merentēs sociōs *dēseram*, neque *egō iūdicō* Galliam potius esse Ariovistī quam populī Rōmānī. Bellō *superātī sunt Arvernī* et *Rutēnī* ab Q. Fabiō Māximō, quibus populus Rōmānus *ignōvit*, neque in prōvinciam *redēgit*, neque stīpendium *imposuit*.

LINES 12-18.] BOOK I. 351

12 Quod	sī	antīquissimum	quodque	tempus	Moreover, if the remotest antiquity should be regarded, the supremacy of the Roman people in Gaul was most just; if the judicial opinion of the senate should be heeded, Gaul ought to be free; for though the country had been conquered in war, the senate had decreed that its people might make use of their own laws.
As to which (But)	*if*	*most ancient*		*every*	*time*
13 spectārī		oportēret,	populī	Rōmānī	
to be considered		*it behooved,*	*of the people*	*Roman*	
14 iūstissimum	esse	in	Galliā	imperium;	sī
most just	*to be*	*in*	*Gaul,*	*the ruling power;*	*if*
15 iūdicium	senātūs		observārī	oportēret,	
the judgment	*of the senate*		*to be regarded*	*it behooved,*	
16 līberam	dēbēre		esse	Galliam,	quam
free,	*to be bound* (ought),		*to be,*	*Gaul,*	*which*
17 bellō		victam,		suīs	lēgibus	ūtī
by war		*having been vanquished,*		*its own*	*law*	*to use*
18		voluisset.				
		(the senate) had wished.				

LINE 12. **Quod**, strictly, an adverbial acc.; but before *sē*, at the beginning of a sentence = *but* or *and.* —— **sī**, conditional conj. —— **antīquissimum**, acc. sing. n., adj., superl. of *antīquus, -ior;* an attributive of *tempus.* For Synonyms, see l. 37, Chap. XVIII. —— **quodque**, acc. sing. n., indef. pron. (*quisque, quaeque, quidque* or *quodque*); an attributive also of *tempus.* Observe that *quisque* with the superl. = *omnis* with the positive. —— **tempus**, acc. sing. n. (*tempus, -oris*); subj. of *spectārī.*

LINE 13. **spectārī**, pres. inf. pass. of *specto*, 1. —— **oportēret**, 3d pers. sing. imperf. subjunctive (*oportet*); impersonal verb; strictly, the conditional clause is its subj. See l. 11, Chap. XI. —— **populī**, gen. sing. m. (*populus, -ī*); limits *imperium.* Synonyms: *populum*, l. 17, Chap. VI. —— **Rōmānī**, adj.; an attributive of *populī.*

LINE 14. **iūstissimum**, acc. sing. n. of superl. *iūstissimus, -a, -um;* positive *iūstus (iūs);* predicate-acc. after *esse.* —— **esse**, pres inf. of *sum;* here the copula. —— **in**, prep. with the acc. or abl.; here it takes the abl. —— **Galliā**, abl. sing. f. (*Gallia, -ae*); obj. of the prep. *in.* —— **imperium**, acc. sing. n. (*imperium, -ī*, n.); subj. of *esse.* —— **sī**, conditional conj.

LINE 15. **iūdicium**, acc. sing. n.; subject-acc. of *observārī.* —— **senātūs**, gen. sing. m. (*senātus, -ūs*); limits *iūdicium.* —— **observārī**, pres. inf. pass. of *observō*, 1. —— **oportēret**, see l. 13, above.

LINE 16. **līberam**, acc. sing. f. (*līber, -era, -erum*); predicate-acc. after *esse.* —— **dēbēre**, pres. inf. act. of *dēbeō*, 2; its subject-acc. is *Galliam.* Synonyms: l. 5, Chap. IV. —— **esse**, pres. inf. of *sum;* complementary of *dēbēre.* —— **Galliam**, subject-acc. of *dēbēre.* —— **quam**, acc. sing. f. (*quī, quae, quod*); refers to *Galliam;* subject-acc. of *ūtī.*

LINE 17. **bellō**, abl. sing. n. (*bellum, -ī*); means. —— **victam**, acc. sing. f. of perf. pass. participle *victus, -a, -um,* from *vincō, -ere, vīcī, victum*, 3; agrees with the pron. *quam,* and has here a concessive force. —— **suīs**, abl. plur. f. (*suus, -a, -um*); an attributive of *lēgibus.* —— **lēgibus**, abl. plur. f. (*lēx, lēgis*); abl. after *ūtī.* —— **ūtī**, pres. inf. of deponent *ūtor, ūtī, ūsus*, 3; subject-acc. is *quam.*

LINE 18. **voluisset**, 3d pers. sing. pluperf. subjunctive (*volō, velle, voluī*); agrees with *populus Rōmānus* understood; subjunctive, because in a subordinate clause in

XLVI. While this discussion was going on at the conference, Caesar was informed that the cavalry of Ariovistus were approaching nearer the mound and were riding towards our men, and were hurling stones and javelins at them. Caesar ceased speaking, and	XLVI. Dum *While* geruntur, *are being carried on,* equitēs *the cavalry* accēdere *to be approaching* lapidēs *(and) stones* Caesar *Caesar*	haec *these (things)* Ariovistī *of Ariovistus* et *and* tēlaque *weapons and,* loquendī *of speaking*	in *in* Caesarī *to Caesar* propius *nearer* ad *toward* in *against* fīnem *an end*	colloquiō 1 *the conference* nūntiātum est 2 *it was reported* tumulum 3 *to the hill* nostrōs *ours* nostrōs *ours* fēcit *makes*	adequitāre, 4 *to be riding* cōnicere. 5 *to be throwing.* sēque ad 6 *himself and, to*

ōrātiō oblīqua. The *ōrātiō rēcta* of lines 12-18: Quod sī antīquissimum quodque tempus spectārī *oportet,* populī Rōmānī iūstissimum *est* in Galliā imperium; sī iūdicium senātūs observārī *oportet, lībera dēbet* esse *Gallia,* quam bellō vīctam, suīs lēgibus ūtī (senātus) *voluit.*

LINE 1. **Dum,** conj.; here = *while;* and used with the pres. ind. act., whatever the tense of the main clause. See A. & G. 276, *e;* B. 228, REM. 1; G. 229, REM., and 570; H. 467, 4. —— **haec,** nom. plur. n. *(hīc, haec, hōc);* subject-nom. of *geruntur;* the reference is to the *many* things spoken by Caesar in Chap. XLV. —— **in,** prep. with the acc. or abl.; here it takes the abl. —— **col(n)loquiō,** abl. *(colloquium, -ī,* n.); obj. of the prep. *in.*

LINE 2. **geruntur,** 3d pers. plur. pres. ind. pass. of *gerō, -ere, gessī, gestum,* 3; agrees with the subject-nom. *haec.* —— **Caesarī,** dat. sing. m. *(Caesar, -aris);* indirect object. —— **nūntiātum est,** 3d pers. sing. perf. ind. pass. of *(nūntiō,* 1); impersonal; strictly, the following acc. and inf. clause is the subj.

LINE 3. **equitēs,** acc. plur. m. *(eques, -itis);* subject-acc. of *accēdere.* —— **Ariovistī,** gen. sing. m. *(Ariovistus, -ī);* limits *equitēs.* —— **propius** *(prope,* near), adv., comparative degree; here used as prep. —— **tumulum** *(tumēre,* to swell); acc. sing. *(tumulus, -ī,* m.); obj. of the adv. *propius,* used as prep. Consult A. & G. 234, *e,* 261, *a,* and NOTE; B. 144, REM. 4; G. 359, NOTE 1; H. 391, II, 2.

LINE 4. **accēdere,** pres. inf. act. *(accēdō,* 3 [ad+cēdere]). —— **et,** cop. conj. —— **ad,** prep. with the acc. —— **nostrōs,** acc. plur. *(noster, -tra, -trum [nōs]),* used substantively; or supply *mīlitēs;* obj. of the prep. *ad.* —— **adequitāre,** pres. inf. act. of *equitō,* 1 (ad + equus); connected by *et* with *accēdere,* and in the same construction.

LINE 5. **lapidēs,** acc. plur. m. *(lapis, -idis);* direct obj. of *cōnicere.* —— **tēlaque** (tēla + que). *tēla,* acc. plur. n. *(tēlum, -ī). que,* enclitic conj.; here connects *tēla* with *lapidēs;* hence in the same construction. Observe the omission of *et* between the inf. clauses (asyndeton). —— **in,** prep. with the acc. or abl.; here it takes the acc. —— **nostrōs,** acc. plur.; used substantively; obj. of the prep. *in;* see *nostrōs,* preceding line. —— **cōnicere,** pres. inf. act. of *cōniceō* (con + iacere), 3; pres. inf. act.; its subject-acc. is *eōs,* i.e. *equitēs,* understood.

LINE 6. **Caesar, -aris,** m.; subject-nom. of *fēcit.* —— **loquendī,** gen. of the gerund *(loquor, -ī, -cutus,* 3); limits *fīnem.* —— **fīnem,** acc. sing. m. *(fīnis, -is);*

7 suōs	recēpit	suīsque		imperāvit	nē
his own	*he betakes,*	*to his own and,*		*he commanded*	*that not*
8 quod	omnīnō	tēlum	in·		hostēs
any	*at all*	*weapon*	*against*		*the enemy*
9 rēicerent.		Nam etsī	sine	ūllō	perīculō
they might return.		*For although*	*without*	*any*	*peril*
10 legiōnis	dēlectae	cum	equitātū		proelium
of (to) the legion	*chosen*	*with*	*the cavalry*		*a fight*
11 fore	vidēbat,	tamen			committendum
to be about to be	*he saw,*	*yet*	*(it)*		*to be caused*

withdrew to his friends, giving them orders not to hurl back a single weapon at the enemy. For though he saw that a skirmish with the enemy's cavalry would be without any hazard to his chosen legion, yet he did not think

---

direct obj. of *fēcit.* —— **fēcit**, 3d pers. sing. perf. ind. act. of *faciō*, 3; agrees with the subject-nom. *Caesar.* Some editions have *facit* instead of *fēcit.* —— **sēque** (sē + que). *sē*, acc. sing., reflexive pron. *(suī, sibi, sē, sē)*; refers to Caesar; direct obj. of *recēpit.* *que*, enclitic conj.; connects *fēcit* and *recēpit.* —— **ad**, prep. with the acc.

LINE 7. **suōs**, acc. plur., poss. adj. pron. *(suus, -a, -um)*; used substantively; or might be taken as an attributive of *amīcōs*, to be supplied. —— **recēpit**, 3d pers. sing. perf. ind. act. of *recipiō, -ere, -cēpī, -ceptum*, 3; agrees with a pron. implied in the ending, referring to *Caesar.* —— **suīsque** (suīs + que). *suīs*, dat. plur. — indirect obj. *(suus)*; used substantively; or supply *mīlitibus. que*, enclitic conj.; closely connects the clauses. —— **imperāvit**, 3d pers. sing. perf. ind. act. *(imperō,* 1); agrees with a pron. implied in the ending, referring to Caesar. —— **nē**, negative telic conj.

LINE 8. **quod**, acc. sing. n. of the indef. pron. *quis* or *quī, quae, quod* or *quid*; used adjectively; an attributive of *tēlum.* —— **omnīnō** *(omnis)*, adv. = lit. *wholly*; but with a negative, freq. = *not at all.* —— **tēlum**, acc. sing. n. *(tēlum, -ī)*; direct obj. of *rēicerant.* —— **in**, prep. with the acc. or abl.; here it has the acc. See note on *in*, l. 1, Chap. I. —— **hostēs**, acc. plur. of *hostis, -is*, m. and f.; obj. of the prep. *in.*

LINE 9. **rēicerent**, 3d pers. plur. imperf. subjunctive of *rēiciō, -ere, -iēcī, -iēctum*, 3 (re + iacere, *to hurl back*); agrees with a pron. implied in the ending, referring to Caesar's soldiers; subjunctive of purpose after *nē.* —— **Nam**, conj. = *for*; introduces a confirmation of a preceding statement. —— **etsī** (et + sī) = lit. *and if*; in use, a concessive conj. = *although.* —— **sine**, prep. with the abl. —— **ūllō**, abl. sing. n. of the adj. *ūllus*, gen. *ūllīus*; an attributive of *perīculō.* —— **perīculō**, abl. sing. n. *(perīculum, -ī)*; obj. of the prep. *sine.*

LINE 10. **legiōnis**, gen. sing. f. *(legiō, -ōnis)*; objective gen.; limits *perīculō.* Consult A. & G. 217; B. 131, REM. 2; G. 363, 2; H. 396, III. —— **dēlectae**, gen. sing. f. of participle *dēlectus, -a, -um* *(dēligō*, 3); an attributive of *legiōnis.* —— **cum**, prep. with the abl. —— **equitātū**, abl. sing. m. *(equitātus, -ūs)*; obj. of the prep. *cum.* —— **proelium**, acc. sing. n. *(proelium, -ī)*; subject-acc. of *fore.* Synonyms: l. 18, Chap. I.

LINE 11. **fore**, fut. inf. for *futūrum esse*; fut. inf. of *sum*; a somewhat rare form. —— **vidēbat**, 3d pers. sing. imperf. ind. act. of *videō*, 2; agrees with a pron. understood, referring to Caesar; ind. after *etsī*, representing a supposition as a *fact.* Synonyms: l. 14, Chap. XXX. —— **tamen**, adv.; complement of the conj. *etsī*; = *yet.* —— **committendum** (esse), pres. inf. pass. periphrastic conjugation; denoting necessity *(committō,* 3); used impersonally; supply *sibi*, i.e. *Caesarī*, as dat. *of the agent.*

| that he ought to so act, that it might be said that, in case the enemy should be routed, they had been treacherously circumvented by him at the conference. After it was generally known to the soldiers with what insolence Ariovistus at the conference had interdicted the Romans from all | nōn putābat ut, pulsīs hostibus, 12
(by himself) not did think that, being routed the enemy,

dīcī posset eōs ab sē per 13
to be said it might be them by him through

fidem in. colloquiō circumventōs. 14
faith (in him) at the conference to have been defrauded.

Posteāquam in vulgus mīlitum ēlātum est, 15
After that to the mass of the soldiers it was reported,

quā arrogantiā in colloquiō Ariovistus 16
what arrogance at the conference Ariovistus

ūsus omnī Galliā Rōmānīs interdīxisset, 17
using, all Gaul to the Romans he had forbidden, |
|---|---|

LINE 12. **nōn** (nē + oe[ū]num, apocopated); modifies *putābat*. —— **putābat**, 3d pers. sing. imperf. ind. of *putō*, 1; agrees with a pron. understood, referring to Caesar. Synonyms: l. 9, Chap. XIX. —— **ut**, ecbatic conj. —— **pulsīs**, abl. plur. m. of the perf. pass. participle *pulsus, -a, -um* of *pellō, -ere, pepulī, pulsum*, 3; absolute with *hostibus*. —— **hostibus**, abl. of *hostis, -is*, m. and f.; agrees with *pulsīs*, i.e. abl. absolute.

LINE 13. **dīcī**, pres. inf. pass. (*dīcō*, 3); pass. parts: *dīcor, dīcī, dictus*; complementary inf. —— **posset**, 3d pers. sing.; used impersonally; subjunctive of result after *ut*. A. & G. 332, *e*; B. 201; G. 553, 2; H. 501, I. —— **eōs**, acc. plur. m. (*is, ea, id*); used as a personal pron.; refers to the enemy; subject-acc. of *circumventōs* (*esse*). —— **ab**, prep. with the abl. —— **sē**, abl. sing., reflexive pron. (*suī, sibī, sē, sē*); refers to Caesar; abl. *of the agent* after the prep. *ab*. —— **per**, prep. with the acc.

LINE 14. **fidem**, acc. sing. f. (*fidēs, -eī*); obj. of the prep. *per*; supply *ēius*, i.e. *Caesaris*, as objective gen. —— **in**, prep. with the acc. or abl.; here it takes the abl. —— **col(n)loquiō**, abl. sing. n. (*colloquium, -ī*); locative abl. with the prep. *in*. —— **circumventōs** (esse), perf. inf. pass. (*circumveniō*, 4); subject-acc. is *eōs*. Note how frequently *esse* is omitted in the formation in the fut. act., and also in the perf. pass. infinitive.

LINE 15. **Posteāquam** (posteā + quam), adv.; usually takes the ind. —— **in**, prep.; here with the acc. —— **vulgus**, frequently written *volgus, -ī*, n.; but m. in Verg. A. 2: 99; acc., obj. of the prep. *in*. Note that the phrase *in vulgus* here = *in multitūdinem*. —— **mīlitum**, gen. plur. m. (*mīles, mīlitis*); limits *vulgus*. —— **ēlātum est**, 3d pers. sing. perf. ind. pass. of *efferō, -ferre, extulī, ēlātum* (ex + ferō, *bring out*); hence *efferre = to report*. *ēlātum est* is used here impersonally; or, strictly, the following clauses from *quā* to *dirēmisset* are the subject.

LINE 16. **quā**, abl. sing. f. of the interrogative pron. *quis, quae, quid*; used adjectively; an attributive of *arrogantiā*. —— **ar(d)rogantiā**, abl. sing. f. (*arrogantia, -ae*); abl. after *ūsus*. A. & G. 249; B. 167, 1; G. 407; H. 421, I. —— **in colloquiō**, see this phrase, l. 14, above. —— **Ariovistus, -ī**, m.; subject-nom. of *interdīxisset*.

LINE 17. **ūsus**, perf. participle of deponent *ūtor, ūtī, ūsus*, 3; agrees with Ariovistus. Compare this use of *ūsus* with that of the GK. ἔχων = English *with*. ——

LINES 18-21.] BOOK I. 355

18 impetumque	in	nostrōs	ēius	equitēs	Gaul and his cavalry had made an attack on our men and how this incident had interrupted the conference, a much greater degree of energy and zeal for fighting was infused into the army.
an attack and,	on	ours	his	cavalry	
19 fēcissent,	eaque	rēs	colloquium	ut	
had made,	this and,	thing	the conference	how	
20 dirēmisset,	multō	māior	alacritās	studiumque	
had broken off,	much	greater	alacrity	zeal and	
21 pūgnandī	māius	exercituī	iniectum est.		
of fighting	greater,	to the army	was infused.		

omnī, abl. sing. f. (*omnis, -e*); an *ī*-stem; abl. in *-ī*; an attributive of *Galliā*. —— Galliā, abl. (*Gallia, -ae*, f.); *separation* after *interdīxisset.* See A. & G. 243; B. 160; G. 390, 2, and NOTE 2; H. 413. —— Rōmānīs, dat. plur., adj. *Rōmānus, -a, -um*, used substantively; indirect obj. A. & G. 228; B. 143; G. 347; H. 386. —— interdīxisset, 3d pers. sing. pluperf. subjunctive of *interdīcō*, 3; agrees with *Ariovistus*; subjunctive, because an *indirect* question.

LINE 18. impetumque (impetum + que). *impetum*, acc. sing. m. (*impetus, -ūs*); direct obj. of *fēcisset. que*, enclitic conj., closely connecting the clauses. —— in, prep. with the acc. or abl.; here it takes the acc. See *in*, l. 1, Chap. I. —— nostrōs, acc. plur. (*noster, -tra, -trum*), used substantively; or supply *milites*; obj. of the prep. *in.* —— ēius, gen. sing. m. (*is, ea, id*), used as a personal pron.; refers to Ariovistus; limits *equitēs.* —— equitēs, nom. plur. of *eques, -itis*, m.; subject-nom. of *fēcissent.*

LINE 19. fēcissent, 3d pers. plur. pluperf. subjunctive of *faciō, -ere, fēcī, factum*, 3; connected by the enclitic conj. *que* with *interdīxisset*, and in the subjunctive for the same reason. —— eaque (ea + que). *ea*, nom. sing. f. (*is, ea, id*); an attributive of *rēs. que*, enclitic conj.; connects the clauses. —— rēs, nom. sing. f. (*rēs, reī*); subj. of *dirēmisset.* Note that *rēs* = the attack of cavalry. —— col(n)loquium, acc. sing. n. (*colloquium, -ī*); direct obj. of *dirēmisset.* —— ut, adv. here = *quam*, how; very emphatic, as shown by its unusual position.

LINE 20. dirēmisset, 3d pers. sing. pluperf. subjunctive of *dirimō, -ere, -ēmī, -ēmptum*, 3; agrees with the subject-nom. *rēs*; subjunctive, because an *indirect* question. —— multō, abl. *of degree of difference* of *multus* — after the comparative *māior*; might be taken as an adv. —— māior, adj., comparative degree (*māgnus*); modifies *alacritās.* —— alacritās, -ātis, f.; subject-nom. —— studiumque (studium + que). *studium, -ī*, nom. sing. n.; subject of *iniectum est. que*, enclitic conj.; connects the subjects.

LINE 21. pūgnandī, gen. of the gerund (*pūgnō*, 1); limits *alacritās* and *studium.* Consult A. & G. 298; B. 184, REM. 4, I; G. 428; H. 542, I. —— māius, nom. sing. n., adj., comparative degree; *māior*, m. and f., *māius*, n.; positive *māgnus*; an attributive of *studium.* —— exercituī, dat. sing. (*exercitus, -ūs*, m.); indirect obj. after *iniectum est.* Synonyms: see *exercitū*, l. 31, Chap. III. —— iniectum est, 3d pers. sing. perf. ind. pass. of *iniciō, -ere, -iēcī, -iectum*, 3; agrees with the nearer noun *studium* as subject-nom. both in number and in *the case* of the participial part of the perf. pass.

356   CAESAR'S GALLIC WAR   [CHAP. XLVII.

| XLVII. Two days after the incidents alluded to above, Ariovistus sent envoys to Caesar, to say that he wished to treat with him about those matters which they had begun to discuss, but had not finished; and to request him either again to appoint a day for a conference; | XLVII.
Caesarem
Caesar

dē hīs rēbus,
about these things

coeptae neque
began not and,

eō; utī
him; that | Bīduō
Two days
lēgātōs
envoys

quae inter
which between

perfectae essent,
had been concluded,

aut iterum
either again | post
after
mittit:
sends:

eōs
them

agere
to treat

colloquiō
for a conference | Ariovistus ad
Ariovistus to
Velle sē
To wish himself

agī
to be treated

cum
with

diem
a day |

LINE 1. **Bĭduō**, abl. sing. of the noun *bīduum, -ī*, n. (bis, *twice* + diēs); distance as *degree of difference* after the adv. *post*. See A. & G. 250; B. 164, REM. 3; G. 403, NOTE 4, (*a*), (*b*); H. 423, and NOTE 2. Hence *bīduō post* = lit. AFTER *by the space of two days.* —— **post**, adv.; modifies *mittit*. —— **Ariovistus**, -ī, m.; subj. of *mittit*. —— **ad**, prep. with the acc.

LINE 2. **Caesarem**, acc. sing. m. (*Caesar, -aris*); obj. of prep. *ad*. —— **lēgātōs**, acc. plur. of *lēgātus, -i*, m.; direct obj. of *mittit*. —— **mittit**, 3d pers. sing. — historical — of *mittō, -ere, mīsī, mīssum*, 3; agrees with *Ariovistus* as subject-nom. —— **Velle**, pres. inf. of *volō, velle, voluī*, irr. Observe that the inf. construction here in the indirect discourse depends on *dīxit*, to be supplied, i.e. we may thus conceive it to be understood; but really it depends on the historic pres. *mittit*. —— **sē**, acc. sing. of the reflexive pron. *suī, sibi, sē, sē*; refers to Ariovistus; subject-acc. of *velle*.

LINE 3. **dē**, prep. with the abl. —— **hīs**, abl. plur. f. (*hic, haec, hōc*); attributive of *rēbus*. —— **rēbus**, abl. plur. of *rēs, reī*, f.; obj. of the prep. *dē*. —— **quae**, nom. plur. f. (*quī, quae, quod*); subj. of *coeptae* (*essent*) and *perfectae essent*. —— **inter**, prep. with the acc. —— **eōs**, acc. plur. of the dem. pron. *is*; used substantively; obj. of the prep. *inter*. —— **agī**, pres. inf. pass. of *agō, -ere, ēgī, actum*, 3; pass. *agor, agī, actus; agī* is complementary inf.

LINE 4. **coeptae** (**essent**), 3d pers. plur. pluperf. subjunctive pass. of the defective verb *coepī, coepisse*, fut. participle *coeptūrus*, pass. participle *coeptus*; agrees with the subj. *quae*; subjunctive, because in a subordinate clause in indirect discourse; pass., because the pass. is used with pass. infinitives. —— **neque** (nē + que). —— **perfectae essent**, 3d pers. plur. pluperf. subjunctive pass. of *perficiō*, 3; connected by *neque* with *coeptae essent*, and in the subjunctive for the same reason. —— **agere**, pres. inf. act. of *agō*, 3; see *agī*, preceding line; complementary inf. of *Velle*, l. 2, above. —— **cum**, prep. with the abl.

LINE 5. **eō**, abl. sing. m. (*is, ea, id*); used as personal pron., 3d pers.; refers to Caesar; is the obj. of the prep. *cum*. —— **utī**, orig. form; = *ut*; here telic conj. Supply *rogāvit* before this telic clause. —— **aut**, alternative conj. = *or*; but *aut* ... *aut* = *either* ... *or*. —— **iterum**, adv.; modifies *cōnstitueret*. —— **col(n)loquiō**, dat. of purpose (*colloquium, -ī*, n.). See note, l. 4, Chap. XXXIV. —— **diem**, acc. sing. m. or f. (*diēs, -ēī*); direct obj. of *cōnstitueret*; always m. in plur.

BOOK I. 357

6 cōnstitueret,	aut,	sī	id	minus	vellet,	or, if he did not wish to do that, to send to him some one of his friends as his envoy. Caesar did not think there was any case for discussion; and the more so, as the day before the Germans could not be restrained
he would constitute,	*or,*	*if*	*that*	*less*	*he wished,*	
7 ē	suīs	lēgātum	aliquem	ad	sē	mitteret.
of	*his,*	*as envoy*	*some one*	*to*	*him*	*he would send.*
8 Colloquendī		Caesarī	causa		vīsa	nōn
Of conferring		*to Caesar*	*the reason*		*looked upon*	*not*
9 est;	et	eō	magis,	quod	prīdiē	ēius
is;	*and*	*by this*	*the more,*	*because*	*before-day*	*of this*
10 diēī		Germānī	retinērī		nōn	poterant,
day		*the Germans*	*to be hindered*		*not*	*were able,*

LINE 6. cōnstitueret, 3d pers. sing. imperf. subjunctive act. of *cōnstituō*, 3; agrees with a pron. understood, referring to Caesar; subjunctive *of purpose* after *uū*. Consult A. & G. 331, *b*; B. 200, REM. 2; G. 546, NOTE 1; H. 498, I. —— aut, see *aut*, preceding line. —— sī, conditional conj. —— id, acc. sing. n. (*is, ea, id*); used substantively; refers to motive of holding a conference; direct obj. *vellet*; or *facere* may be supplied. —— minus, adv. = lit. *less*; transf. = *not, not at all* = an emphatic negative. Observe that the positive *parvē* is rare; that the superl. has two forms: *parvissimē*, and, classic, *minimē*. —— vellet, 3d pers. sing. imperf. subjunctive of *volō, vellē, voluī*; subject-nom. is *Caesar*, to be supplied; subjunctive after *sī* in the protasis.

LINE 7. ē, prep. with the abl. —— suīs, abl. plur. (*suus, -a, -um*), used substantively; or supply *mīlitibus*; obj. of the prep. *ē*. *ē suīs*, the phrase limits *aliquem* instead of partitive gen. —— lēgātum, acc. sing. m. (*lēgātus, -ī*); in apposition with *aliquem*. —— aliquem, acc. sing. m. of the indef. pron. *aliquis, aliquid* — subst.; direct obj. of *mitteret*. —— ad, prep. with the acc. —— sē, acc. sing. (*suī, sibi, sē, sē*); refers to Ariovistus; obj. of the prep. *ad*. —— mitteret, 3d pers. sing. imperf. subjunctive of *mittō*, 3; agrees with a pron. understood, referring to Caesar; subjunctive, because connected by *aut cōnstitueret*, and thus is under the influence of *uū*, i.e. subjunctive *of purpose*. The *ōrātiō rēcta* of lines 2–7: *Volō egō dē hīs rēbus, quae inter nōs agī coeptae neque perfectae sunt agere tēcum*; *utī aut iterum colloquiō diem cōnstituās, aut, sī hōc minus velīs, ē tuīs lēgātum aliquem ad mē mittās.*

LINE 8. Colloquendī, gen. of the gerund of *col(n)loquor, -ī, -locūtus*, 3, deponent; as gen. limits *causa*. Observe that deponent verbs have the fut. inf., the participles, gerund and supine of the act. voice. —— Caesarī, dat. of *Caesar, -aris*, m.; indirect object. —— causa, -ae, f.; subject-nom. of *vīsa est*. —— vīsa, nom. sing. f. of the participial part of the perf. pass. ind. *vīsa est*; f., because *causa* is f. The parts of verb are *videor, -ērī, vīsus*, 2. —— nōn, adv. (*nē + ūnum*). Observe its position between the parts of a compound tense formation.

LINE 9. est, 3d pers. sing. of *sum*; but part of *vīsa est*; perf. ind. pass.; agrees with *causa*. —— et, cop. conj.; connects the clauses. —— eō, abl. n.; *cause* (*is, ea, id*); herald of the following *quod*-clause. —— magis, adv., comparative degree; superl. *māximē*. For complete analysis, supply *haec vīsa est* from the preceding. —— quod, conj. = *because*. —— prīdiē (pri [prior] + diēs), adv. —— ēius, gen. sing. (*is, ea, id*); an attributive of *diēī*.

LINE 10. diēī, gen. sing., m. and f. in sing. (*diēs, -ēī*); gen. after the adv. *prīdiē*. Observe that *prīdiē ēius diēī* = lit. *the day before that day*. —— Germānī, -ōrum,

from hurling weapons at our men. He thought that to send one of his Roman friends as his envoy would be attended with great risk, and would expose him to savage men. It seemed, accordingly, most suitable to send to him Ca-	quīn *but that*	in *against*	nostrōs *our (men)*	tēla *weapons*	cōnicerent. 11 *they would throw.*
	Lēgātum *An envoy*	ē *of*	suīs *his (men)*	sēsē *himself*	magnō cum 12 *great with*
	perīculō *danger*	ad *to*	eum *him*	mīssūrum *(to be) about to send*	et 13 *and*
	hominibus *to men*	ferīs *wild*	obiectūrum *(to be) about to expose,*		exīstimābat. 14 *he thought.*
	Commodissimum *Most fitting*		vīsum est *it seemed*	Cāium *Caius*	Valerium 15 *Valerius*

nom. plur. m.; subj. of *poterant*. —— retinērī, pres. inf. pass. (*retineō*, 2); complementary; depends on *poterant*. A. & G. 271; B. 181; G. 423; H. 533, I, 2. —— nōn, adv.; modifies *poterant*. —— poterant, 3d pers. plur. imperf. ind. of *possum* (potis + sum); agrees with *Germānī*.

LINE 11. quīn (quī + nē), conj.; after negatives = lit. *that* or *but that*. —— in, prep. with the acc. or abl.; here it takes the acc. —— nostrōs, acc. plur. m. of poss. pron. *noster, -tra, -trum*; used substantively; obj. of the prep. *in*. —— tēla, acc. plur. n. (*tēlum, -ī*); direct obj. of *cōnicerent*. —— cōnicerent, 3d pers. plur. imperf. subjunctive of *cōniciō, -ere, -iēcī, -iectum*, 3; agrees with a pron. understood, referring to the Germans; subjunctive of result after *quīn*. Consult A. & G. 319, *d*; B. 201, REM. 3; G. 554; H. 504, 4.

LINE 12. Lēgātum, acc. sing. m. (*lēgātus, -ī*); direct obj. of *mīssūrum* (*esse*), l. 13, below. —— ē, prep. with the abl. —— suīs, abl. plur. m. (*suus, -a, -um*); used substantively; or supply *virīs*; obj. of the prep. *ē*. *ē suīs*, the phrase limits *lēgātum*, instead of the gen. — rare construction. —— sēsē, reduplicate pron. acc. sing. (*suī*); subject-acc. of *mīssūrum* (*esse*). —— magnō, abl. sing. n. of the adj. *magnus, -a, -um*; an attributive of *perīculō*. —— cum, prep. with the abl. Observe its position.

LINE 13. perīculō, abl. sing. n. of *perīculum, -ī*; obj. of the prep. *cum*. —— ad, prep. with the acc. —— eum, acc. sing. m. (*is, ea, id*); used as personal pron.; obj. of the prep. *ad*. —— mīssūrum (esse), fut. inf. act. of *mittō*, 3 (see l. 2, above); subject-acc. is *Lēgātum*, preceding line. —— et, cop. conj.; connects *mīssūrum* and *obiectūrum*.

LINE 14. hominibus, dat. of the indirect obj. of *homō, hominis*, m. and f.; the dat. in fact depends on *ob* in the compound *obiectūrum*. —— ferīs, dat. plur. m. of *ferus, -a, -um*; an attributive of *hominibus*. —— obiectūrum (esse), fut. inf. act. of *obiciō, -ere, -iēcī, -iectum*, 3; connected by *et* with *mīssūrum*, and in the same grammatical construction. What Caesar thought in direct form in lines 12-14 may thus be expressed: Lēgātum ē *meīs egō* magnō cum perīculō ad *hunc mittam* et hominibus ferīs *obiectam*. Observe that these lines, in the text, are *informal* indirect discourse; while lines 2-7 are *formal* indirect discourse. —— exīstimābat, 3d pers. sing. imperf. ind. act. (*exīstimō*, 1); as subject-nom. is a pron. understood, referring to Caesar. Observe that the infinitive-clause in this sentence depends on *exīstimābat*.

LINE 15. Commodissimum, nom. sing. n. — predicate-adj.; superl. of *commodus* (con, *intensive* + modus = *full measure*). —— vīsum est, 3d pers. sing. perf. ind. pass. of *videor, -ērī, vīsus*, 2; used impersonally; but, strictly, *mittere*, l. 24, below, is

16 Procillum,   C. Valerī Cabūrī   fīlium,   summā | ius Valerius Procillus, the son of Caius Valerius Caburus, a young man of very great merit and refinement, whose father had been presented with the rights of citizenship by Caius Valerius Flaccus, both because of his fidelity and be-
Procillus,   *of Caius Valerius Caburus,   the son,   of very great*

17 virtūte   et   hūmānitāte   adulēscentem,   cūius
merit   *and*   *humanity*   *a young man,*   *whose*

18 pater   ā   Cāiō Valeriō Flaccō   cīvitāte
father   *by*   *Caius Valerius Flaccus*   *with citizenship*

19 dōnātus   erat,   et   propter   fidem   et
presented   *was,*   *and*   *on account of (his) fidelity*   *and*

the grammatical subject, and the entire sentence following *vīsum est* is the logical subject. Observe that *vidērī* is pass. of act. *vidēre*; and that, in the pass., it = *to be looked upon*, or *regarded*, in any manner; hence = *to seem*. —— **Cāium**, acc. sing. m. (*Cāius, -ī*), *praenōmen*; sometimes in imitation of the GK. written *Gāius* (Γάϊος). —— **Valerium**, acc. sing. m. (*Valerius, -ī*), *nōmen*.

LINE 16. **Procillum**, acc. sing. m. (*Procillus, -ī*), *cōgnōmen*. These names as a complex proper noun are the direct obj. of *mittere*, l. 24. Observe that, though *Procillus* was a Roman family name, it is, in the text, the name of a Gaul sent by Caesar to Ariovistus. —— **C.**, abbreviation for *Cāiī*, gen. sing. m. (*Cāius, -ī*). —— **Valerī**, gen. sing. m. (*Valerius, -ī*). —— **Cabūrī**, gen. sing. m. (*Cabūrus, -ī*). These names form a complex proper noun in the gen., limiting *fīlium*. Caburus was a Celt who was honored with Roman citizenship. —— **fīlium**, acc. sing. m. (*fīlius, -ī*); in apposition with *Procillum*. —— **summā**, abl. sing. f., *superus, -ior, suprēmus* or *summus;* an attributive of *virtūte*.

LINE 17. **virtūte**, abl. sing. of *virtūs, -ūtis*, f. (*vir*, man); abl. *of quality*. A. & G. 251; B. 169; G. 400; H. 419, II. —— **et**, cop. conj.; connects the nouns. —— **hūmānitāte**, abl. sing. f. — *hūmānitās, -tātis* (*hūmānus* [*homō*]); connected by *et* with *virtūte*, and in the same construction. —— **adulēscentem**, acc. sing. of *adulēscēns, -centis*, m. and f.; an appositive of *fīlium*. Observe that *adulēscēns* = *a man* or *woman from 17 to 40 years old*. —— **cūius**, gen. sing. m. (*quī, quae, quod*); limits *pater*.

LINE 18. **pater**, nom. sing. m. of *pater, -tris* (GK. πατήρ); subj. of *dōnātus erat*. —— **ā**, prep. with the abl.; here the abl. *of the agent*, and = *by*. —— **Cāiō**, abl. sing. m. (*Cāius, -ī*). —— **Valeriō**, abl. sing. m. (*Valerius, -ī*). —— **Flaccō**, abl. sing. m. (*Flaccus, -ī*). These names as a complex noun are abl. *of agent* after the prep. *ā*. Note that C. V. Flaccus was governor of Gaul B.C. 83. —— **cīvitāte**, abl. sing. of *cīvitās, -tātis*, f. (*cīvēs*); *means* after *dōnātus erat*. Observe that *dōnāre* in the act. admits of (*a*) the dat. of the person and acc. of the thing; or (*b*) the acc. of the person and abl. of the thing; and that (*c*) in the pass. the acc. of the thing becomes the nom., and the abl. of the thing remains. A. & G. 225, *d*; B. 167; G. 348; H. 384, II. 2).

LINE 19. **dōnātus erat**, 3d pers. sing. pluperf. ind. pass. of *dōnō*, I; agrees with the subject-nom. *pater*. —— **et**, cop. conj.; connects the clauses. —— **propter**, adv. or prep.; here a prep. with the acc. —— **fidem**, acc. sing. f. (*fidēs, -eī*); obj. of the prep. *propter*. —— **et**, conj.; connects the phrases.

cause of his knowledge of the Gallic language, which Ariovistus from long practice now spoke fluently; also because in his case the Germans had no motive for inflicting personal injury;—and to send with him Marcus Mettius

propter	linguae	Gallicae	scientiam, 20
on account of (his)	*tongue's*	*Gallic*	*knowledge,*
quā multā	iam	Ariovistus	longinquā 21
which much	*already*	*Ariovistus*	*by long*
cōnsuētūdine	ūtēbātur,	et quod	in eō 22
habit	*used,*	*and because*	*in him*
peccandī	Germānīs	causa nōn esset,	ad 23
of doing wrong	*to the Germans*	*cause not was,*	*to*
eum mittere,	et	Marcum Mēttium,	quī 24
him to send,	*and*	*Marcus Mettius,*	*who*

LINE 20. **propter,** see *propter,* preceding line. Observe the repetition of the prepositions, thus keeping the notions distinct. —— **linguae,** gen. sing. f. (*lingua, -ae*); limits *scientiam.* Observe that, as the tongue is the principal organ of speech, *lingua,* by metonymy, often = *language.* —— **Gallicae,** gen. sing. f. of the adj. *Gallicus, -a, -um (Gallia)*; an attributive of *linguae.* —— **scientiam,** acc. sing. of *scientia, -ae,* f. (*scīre*); obj. of the prep. *propter.*

LINE 21. **quā,** abl. sing. f. (*quī, quae, quod*); refers to *linguae,* but is an attributive of *linguā,* to be supplied; abl. after *ūtēbātur.* —— **multā,** abl. sing. f. (*multus, -a, -um*); also a modifier of the understood *linguā;* but would better be translated as an adv., i.e. *fluently.* —— **iam,** adv. = *now,* of the pres., past, or fut.; whereas *nunc* emphasizes the present. —— **Ariovistus, -ī,** m.; subject-nom. of *ūtēbātur.* —— **longinquā,** abl. sing. f. of *longinquus, -a, -um (longus,* long); an attributive of *cōnsuētūdine.*

LINE 22. **cōnsuētūdine,** abl. sing. f. (*cōnsuētūdō, -inis*); manner. —— **ūtēbātur,** 3d pers. sing. imperf. ind. of the deponent *ūtor, -ī, ūsus,* 3; agrees with the subject-nom. *Ariovistus* expressed. —— **et,** conj.; correlative to *et . . . et,* l. 19, above. —— **quod,** conj. = *because.* —— **in,** prep. with the acc. or abl.; here the abl. —— **eō,** abl. sing. m. (*is, ea, id*); used as a pron. of the 3d pers.; obj. of the prep. *in;* refers to *C. V. Procillum,* lines 15 and 16, above.

LINE 23. **peccandī,** gen. of the gerund of *peccō,* 1; limits *causa.* —— **Germānīs,** dat. plur. m. (*Germānī, -ōrum*); possessor after *esset.* A. & G. 231; B. 146; G. 349; H. 387. —— **causa, -ae,** f., subject-nom. of *esset.* —— **nōn,** negative particle; modifies *esset.* —— **esset,** 3d pers. sing. imperf. subjunctive of *sum;* agrees with *causa;* is subjunctive, because the clause is informal indirect discourse. Caesar as historian quotes Caesar the diplomat. See A. & G. 341, *d,* REM.; B. 198, (*b*); G. 628; H. 528, 1. —— **ad,** prep. with the acc.

LINE 24. **eum,** acc. sing. m. (*is, ea, id*); used as a personal pron.; obj. of the prep. *ad;* refers to Ariovistus. —— **mittere,** pres. inf. act. of *mittō,* 3; grammatically, the subject-nom. of *vīsum est,* l. 15, above. —— **et,** conj.; connects *mittere* expressed with *mittere* understood. —— **Marcum,** acc. sing. m. of *Marcus, -ī.* —— **Mēttium,** acc. sing. m. of *Mēttium, -ī. M. Mēttium* is direct obj. of *mittere* understood. This name is sometimes printed *M. Mētius.* Observe that the complete lacuna is: *commodissimum vīsum est M. Mēttium ad eum mittere.* —— **quī,** nom. sing. m. (*quī, quae, quod*); refers to *Mēttium;* but is subj. of *ūtēbātur.*

BOOK I.

25 hospitiō	Ariovistī	ūtēbātur.	Hīs	who was a guest-friend of Ariovistus. Caesar directed them to ascertain what Ariovistus said, and report to him. Now when Ariovistus saw them in his camp before him, he shouted in the presence of his army: Why were they come to him? was it then
the hospitality	*of Ariovistus*	*enjoyed.*	*To them*	
26 mandāvit,	ut, quae	dīceret	Ariovistus,	
he gave orders	*that what (things)*	*said*	*Ariovistus,*	
27 cōgnōscerent	et ad sē	referrent.	Quōs	
they should learn	*and to him*	*should report.*	*Whom*	
28 cum apud	sē in	castrīs	Ariovistus	
when before	*him in*	*the camp*	*Ariovistus*	
29 cōnspexisset,	exercitū	suō	praesente,	
had seen,	*army*	*his*	*being present,*	
30 conclāmāvit:	Quid ad	sē	venīrent?	
he cried aloud:	*Why to*	*him*	*should they come?*	

LINE 25. **hospitiō**, abl. sing. n. of *hospitium*, *-ī* (*hospēs*, m. and f. = *host* or *guest*); abl. after *ūtēbātur*. —— **Ariovistī**, gen. sing. m. of *Ariovistus*, *-ī*; limits *hospitiō*. —— **ūtēbātur**, 3d pers. sing. imperf. ind. of *ūtor*, 3, deponent; agrees with the subject-nom. *quī*. —— **Hīs**, dat. plur. (*hīc*, *haec*, *hōc*), used substantively; indirect obj. of *mandāvit*; refers to C. V. Procillus and M. Mettius.

LINE 26. **mandāvit**, 3d pers. sing. perf. ind. act. of *mandō*, 1 (*manus* + *dō*); agrees with *Caesar* understood as subject-nom. —— **ut**, telic conj. —— **quae**, acc. plur. n. of the interrogative pron. *quis*, *quae*, *quid*; direct obj. of *dīceret*. —— **dīceret**, 3d pers. sing. imperf. subjunctive of *dīcō*, 3; agrees with *Ariovistus* expressed; subjunctive, because an indirect question; or *ea* might be supplied, and *quae* taken as a rel., and the subjunctive explained as *characteristic*. —— **Ariovistus, -ī**, m.; subj. of *dīceret*.

LINE 27. **cōgnōscerent**, 3d pers. plur. imperf. subjunctive of *cōgnōscō*, *-ere*, *-nōvī*, *-nitum*, 3; agrees with the pron. *eī* as subject-nom., referring to *C. V. Procillum* and *M. Mettium*; subjunctive *of purpose* after *ut*. —— **et**, conj.; connects the clauses. —— **ad**, prep. with the acc. —— **sē**, acc. sing. (*suī*, *sibi*, *sē*, *sē*); obj. of the prep. *ad*; refers to Caesar. —— **referrent**, 3d pers. plur. imperf. subjunctive of *referō*, *-ferre*, *-tulī*, *-lātum*; connected by the conj. *et* with *cōgnōscerent*, and in the subjunctive for the same reason. —— **Quōs**, acc. plur. m. (*quī*, *quae*, *quod*); refers to Procillus and Mettius; direct obj. of *cōnspexisset*.

LINE 28. **cum**, conj. *temporal* or *historical*. A. & G. 325; B. 222; G. 585; H. 521, II, 2. —— **apud**, prep. with the acc. = *before*, *with*, *in the presence of*, *at the house of*. —— **sē**, acc. sing. of *suī*; refers to Ariovistus; obj. of the prep. *apud*. —— **in**, prep. —— **castrīs**, abl. plur. n. (*castrum*, *-ī*); obj. of the prep. *in*. —— **Ariovistus, -ī**, m., subject-nom.

LINE 29. **cōnspexisset**, 3d pers. sing. pluperf. subjunctive act. of *cōnspiciō*, *-ere*, *-spexī*, *-spectum*, 3; agrees with the subject-nom. *Ariovistus*; subjunctive after *cum* temporal. —— **exercitū**, abl. sing. m. (*exercitus*, *-ūs*); absolute with the participle *praesente*. Synonyms: l. 31, Chap. III. —— **suō**, abl. sing. m. (*suus*, *-a*, *-um*); an attributive of *exercitū*. —— **praesente**, abl. sing. m. (*praesēns*, *-entis*); pres. participle of *praesum*, used as an adj.; absolute with *exercitū*, denoting *attendant circumstance*. Observe that the form *praesente* is generally used of persons; *praesentī*, of things.

LINE 30. **conclāmāvit**, 3d pers. sing. perf. ind. act. of *conclāmō*, 1 (*con*, *intensive* + *clāmō* = *shout aloud*); agrees with a pron. as subj., referring to Ariovistus. ——

to act as spies?
As they tried to speak, he interrupted them, and threw them into chains.

an	speculandī	causā?		Cōnantēs	31
or	of spying	for the sake?		(Them) attempting	
dīcere	prohibuit	et in	catēnās	cōniēcit.	32
to speak	he prohibited	and into	chains	threw.	

XLVIII. The same day as that on which the incidents narrated above occurred, Ariovistus moved forward his camp and halted, at

XLVIII. Eōdem diē castra prōmōvit 1
On the same day the camp he moved forward,

et mīlibus passuum sex ā Caesaris 2
and by thousands of paces six from Caesar's

Quid, adverbial acc. (*quis, quae, quid*) = *as to what? why?* —— **ad**, prep. with the acc. —— **sē**, acc. sing. of *suī*; refers to Ariovistus; obj of the prep. *ad*. —— **venīrent**, 3d pers. plur. imperf. subjunctive of *veniō*, 4; a *real question* in indirect discourse is usually in the subjunctive. A. & G. 338; B. 245, 3; G. 651; H. 523, II, 1.

LINE 31. **an**, conjunctive particle; usually introduces the second of a double question; in a single question, *an* often indicates indignation or surprise = *then*. —— **speculandī**, gerund of deponent *speculor*, 1; limits *causā*. A. & G. 298; B. 184, REM. 4, I, (*a*); G. 428, REM. 2; H. 542, I. —— **causā**, abl. of *causa*, -*ae*, f. — an abl. *of cause* with prepositional force = *for the sake of*. —— **Cōnantēs**, acc. plur. of the pres. participle of *cōnor*, 1; agrees with *eōs* understood.

LINE 32. **dīcere**, pres. inf. act. of *dīcō*, 3. —— **prohibuit**, 3d pers. sing. perf. ind. act. of *prohibeō*, 2; agrees with a pron. understood, referring to Ariovistus. —— **et**, cop. conj.; connects the verbs. —— **in**, prep. with the acc. or abl.; here it takes the acc. See *in*, l. 1, Chap. I. —— **catēnās**, acc. plur. f. (*catēna, -ae*); obj. of the prep. *in*. —— **cōniēcit**, 3d pers. sing. perf. ind. act. of *cōniciō*, *-ere*, *-iēcī*, *-iectum*, 3; connected by *et* with *prohibuit*, and in the same grammatical construction. The *ōrātiō rēcta* of lines 30 and 31: Quid ad *mē venītis?* an speculandī causā (*venītis*)? Observe that the full purport of the last interrogative may be thus given: *utrum pācificandī an speculandī causā venītis?*

LINE 1. **Eōdem**, abl. sing. m. of the dem. pron. *īdem, eadem, idem*; an attributive of *diē*. —— **diē**, abl. sing. of *diēs, -ēī*, m. and f. in sing.; always m. in plur.; *time when*. A. & G. 256, 1; B. 171; G. 393; H. 429. —— **castra**, acc. plur. n. (*castrum, -ī*); direct obj. of *prōmōvit*. See *castrīs*, l. 12, Chap. XII. —— **prōmōvit**, 3d pers. sing. perf. ind. act. of *prōmoveō, -ēre, -mōvī, -mōtum*, 2; agrees with Ariovistus understood.

LINE 2. **et**, cop. conj.; connects the clauses. —— **mīlibus**, abl. plur. of the adj. *mīlia*, used as substantive; sing. *mīlle*, indecl.; abl. *of degree of difference*. A. & G. 257, *b*; B. 153, REM. 3; G. 403, NOTE 1; H. 423, NOTE 2. —— **passuum**, gen. plur. m. (*passus, -ūs*); partitive after *mīlibus*. A. & G. 216, 2; B. 134; G. 370; H. 397, 2. —— **sex**, card. num. adj. (GK. ἕξ); an attributive of *mīlibus*. —— **ā** (*ab*), prep. with the abl. —— **Caesaris**, poss. gen. (*Caesar, -aris*, m.); limits *castrīs*.

3 castrīs	sub	monte	cōnsēdit.		Postrīdiē	the foot of a mountain, six miles from Caesar's camp. The next day, he led his troops past Caesar's camp, and encamped two miles beyond him. He did this with a view of cutting off Caesar from grain and other supplies that were being brought up from the country of
camp	*under*	*a mountain*	*he encamped.*		*The day after*	
4 ēius	diēī	praeter	castra	Caesaris	suās	
that	*day*	*beyond*	*the camp*	*of Caesar*	*his own*	
5 cōpiās	trādūxit	et	mīlibus		passuum	
forces	*he led across,*	*and*	*by thousands*		*of paces*	
6 duōbus	ūltrā	eum	castra	fēcit,	eō	
two,	*beyond*	*him*	*a camp*	*he made,*	*with this*	
7 cōnsiliō,	utī	frūmentō	commeātūque,		quī	
design,	*that*	*from grain*	*supplies and,*		*which*	

LINE 3. **castrīs**, abl. plur.; obj. of the prep. *ā*. See *castra*, l. 1, above. —— **sub**, prep. with the acc. or abl.; here it takes the abl. —— **monte**, abl. sing. m. (*mōns, montis*); obj. of the prep. *sub*. The *mōns* referred to is the Vosges. —— **cōnsēdit**, 3d pers. sing. perf. ind. act. of *cōnsīdō, -ere, -sēdī, -sessum*, 3 (con + sidere = lit. *to sit together*); connected by *et* with *prōmōvit*, and in the same grammatical construction. —— **Postrīdiē** (postem + diēs), adv.

LINE 4. **ēius**, gen. sing. (*is, ea, id*); an attributive of *diēī*. —— **diēī**, gen. sing. of *diēs, -ēī*, m. and f. in sing.; always m. in plur.; gen. after the adverb *postrīdiē*. See l. 1, Chap. XXIII. —— **praeter**, prep. with the acc. —— **castra**, acc. plur.; obj. of *praeter*. See *castra*, l. 1, above. —— **Caesaris**, poss. gen.; limits *castra*. —— **suās**, acc. plur. f., poss. pron. (*suus, -a, -um*); an attributive of *cōpiās*.

LINE 5. **cōpiās**, acc. plur. f. (*cōpia, -ae*); direct obj. of *trādūxit*. See *cōpiīs*, l. 6, Chap. II. —— **trādūxit**, 3d pers. sing. perf. ind. act. of *trādūcō*, 3 (trāns + dūcō); agrees with Ariovistus understood. —— **et**, conj.; connects the clauses. —— **mīlibus**, see *mīlibus*, l. 2, above. —— **passuum**, see note on this word, l. 2, above.

LINE 6. **duōbus**, abl. plur. n. of card. num. adj. *duo, duae, duo*; an attributive of *mīlibus*. For declension of *duo*, see A. & G. 94, *b*; B. 64, REM. 2; G. 95; H. 175. —— **ūltrā**, prep. with the acc. —— **eum**, acc. sing. m. (*is, ea, id*); used as personal pron.; obj. of the prep. *ūltrā*. —— **castra**, acc. plur.; direct obj. of *fēcit*. —— **fēcit**, 3d pers. sing. perf. ind. act. of *faciō, -ere, fēcī, factum*, 3; agrees with a pronoun understood, referring to Ariovistus. —— **eō**, sing. n. of *is*; an attributive of *cōnsiliō*.

LINE 7. **cōnsiliō**, abl. sing. n. (*cōnsilium, -ī*); *manner.* A. & G. 248; B. 168; G. 399; H. 419, III. Synonyms: l. 5, Chap. XVIII. —— **utī**, orig. form of conj. *ut*. —— **frūmentō**, abl. sing. n. of *frūmentum, -ī*; abl. *of separation* after *interclūderet*. Consult A. & G. 243, *a*; B. 160; G. 390, 2, NOTE 3; H. 414, I. —— **commeātūque** (commeātū + que). *commeātū*, abl. sing. of *commeātus, -ūs*, m.; connected by *que* with *frūmentō*, and in the same construction. *que*, enclitic conj. —— **quī**, nom. sing. m., rel. pron.; agrees with the nearest noun as antecedent; it is the subj. of *supportārētur*.

the Sequani and the Aedui. From this day for five successive days, Caesar led out his troops in front of his camp, and kept them drawn up in battle array, that, if Ariovistus desired to fight, he might have an opportunity. Ariovistus, during all this time, kept

ex Sēquanīs et Aeduīs supportārētur, 8
from the Sequani and the Aedui were being furnished,
Caesarem interclūderet. Ex eō diē diēs 9
Caesar he might hinder. From that day days
continuōs quīnque Caesar prō castrīs 10
continuous five Caesar before the camp
suās cōpiās prōdūxit et aciem īnstrūctam 11
his own troops led out, and the line drawn up
habuit, ut, sī vellet Ariovistus proeliō 12
he held, that, if wished Ariovistus in battle
contendere, eī potestās nōn deësset. 13
to contend, to him an opportunity not might be lacking.

LINE 8. **ex** (*ē*), prep. with the abl. —— **Sēquanīs**, abl. plur. (*Sēquanī, -ōrum*); obj. of the prep. *ex*. See l. 25, Chap. I. —— **et**, cop. conj. —— **Aeduīs**, abl. plur. m. (*Aeduī, -ōrum*); connected by *et* with *Sēquanīs*, and in the same construction. See *Aeduō*, l. 20, Chap. I. —— **supportārētur**, 3d pers. sing. imperf. subjunctive pass. of *supportō*, 1 (sub + portāre = lit. *to bring up from below*); agrees with the subject-nom. *quī*; subjunctive by attraction.

LINE 9. **Caesarem**, acc. sing. m. (*Caesar, -aris*); direct obj. of *interclūderet*. —— **interclūderet**, 3d pers. sing. imperf. subjunctive act. of *interclūdō*, 3; agrees with a pron. understood, referring to Ariovistus; subjunctive *of purpose* after *uñ*, l. 7, above. Observe that this telic clause explains the phrase *eō cōnsiliō*, and is in apposition with it. —— **Ex** (*ē*), prep. with the abl. —— **eō**, abl. sing. m. (*is, ea, id*); an attributive of *diē*. —— **diē**, abl. sing. m. of *diēs*; obj. of the prep. *ex*. —— **diēs**, acc. plur. m.; *extent of time*. A. & G. 256, 2; B. 153; G. 336; H. 379.

LINE 10. **continuōs**, acc. plur. m. of the adj. *continuus, -a, -um* (con + tenēre = lit. *to hold together*); hence the adj. = *uninterrupted, continuous*; an attributive of *diēs*. —— **quīnque**, indecl. num. adj.; an attributive of *diēs*. —— **Caesar**, subject nom. —— **prō**, prep. with the abl. —— **castrīs**, abl. plur. n. (*castrum, -ī*); obj. of the prep. *prō*. See l. 12, Chap. XII.

LINE 11. **suās**, acc. plur. f. (*suus, -a, -um*); an attributive of *cōpiās*, referring to Caesar. —— **cōpiās**, acc. plur. f. (*cōpia, -ae*); direct obj. of *prōdūxit*. See *copiīs*, l. 6, Chap. II. —— **prōdūxit**, 3d pers. sing. perf. ind. act. of *prōdūco, -ere, -dūxī, ductum*, 3; agrees with *Caesar* expressed. —— **et**, cop. conj.; couples the clauses. —— **aciem**, acc. sing. f. (*aciēs, -ēī*); direct obj. of *habuit*. See *aciem*, l. 12, Chap. XXII. —— **īnstrūctam**, acc. sing. f. of the perf. pass. participle of *īnstruō, -ere, -strūxī, -strūctum*, 3; agrees with *aciem*, but with *habuit* = *īnstrūxit*, nearly. See A. & G. 292, *e*; B. 191, 3, (*d*); G. 238; H. 388, 1, NOTE.

LINE 12. **habuit**, 3d pers. sing. perf. ind. act. of *habeō*, 2, —— **ut**, telic conj. —— **sī**, conditional conj. —— **vellet**, 3d pers. sing. imperf. subjunctive of *volō, velle, voluī*; subjunctive in the protasis after *sī*. —— **Ariovistus, -ī**, m.; subject-nom. of *vellet*. —— **proeliō**, abl. sing. n. (*proelium, -ī*); *means*. For synonyms, see *proeliīs*, l. 18, Chap. I.

LINE 13. **contendere**, pres. inf. act. of *contendō*, 3; complementary; depends on *vellet*. See *contendunt*, l. 18, Chap. I. —— **eī**, dat. sing. m. (*is, ea, id*); used as a

14 Ariovistus   hīs   omnibus   diēbus   exercitum
   Ariovistus *in these* *all*   *days*   *(his) army*
15 castrīs   continuit; equestrī proeliō cotīdiē
   within the camp *held;* *in cavalry* *skirmish* *daily*
16 contendit.   Genus   hōc   erat   pūgnae,   quō
   he contended. *The kind,* *this* *was* *of fight,* *in which*
17 sē   Germānī exercuerant.   Equitum
   themselves *the Germans* *had trained.* *Of horsemen*
18 mīlia   erant   sex;   totidem   numerō
   thousands   *(there) were* *six;* *the same* *in number*

his army in camp, but engaged daily in cavalry skirmishes. The species of fight in which the Germans had trained themselves was this: There were six thousand cavalry, and the same number of very

pers. pron.; indirect obj. —— **potestās**, nom. sing. f.; subject-acc. of *deësset*. For synonyms, see *potentia*, l. 25, Chap. XVIII. —— **nōn**, negative adv. —— **deësset**, 3d pers. sing. imperf. subjunctive of *dēsum, deësse, dēfuī*; agrees with *potestās* as subject; subjunctive after *ut*, preceding line, —*purpose*. Observe (*a*) that this telic clause is also the apodosis; and (*b*) that *dē* in *dēsum* is shortened as to its vowel in the infinitive by the law: a vowel before another vowel is short.

LINE 14. **Ariovistus**, subject-nom. of *continuit*. —— **hīs**, abl. plur. m. (*hīc, haec, hōc*); an attributive of *diēbus*. —— **omnibus**, abl. plur. m. (*omnis, -e*); modifies the phrase *hīs omnibus*. —— **diēbus**, abl. plur. m. (*diēs, -ēī*); *duration of time*. See A. & G. 256, 2, *b*; B. 153, REM. 2; G. 393, REM. 4; H. 379, 1. —— **exercitum**, acc. sing. m. (*exercitus, -ūs*); direct obj. of *continuit*. For synonyms, see *exercitū*, l. 31, Chap. III.

LINE 15. **castrīs**, abl. plur. n. (*castrum, -ī*); place *in which*, without a prep. See A. & G. 258, *f*, 1; B. 170, REM. 4; G. 389; H. 425, II. 1, 1). —— **continuit**, 3d pers. sing. perf. ind. act. of *contineō, -ēre, -uī, -tentum*, 2; agrees with *Ariovistus* expressed. —— **equestrī**, abl. sing. n. of the adj. *equester, -tris, -tre* (*eques*); an attributive of *proeliō*. —— **proeliō**, abl. sing. n. (*proelium, -ī*); *manner*. For synonyms, see l. 18, Chap. I. —— **cotīdiē**, adv. (quot + diēs).

LINE 16. **contendit**, 3d pers. sing. perf. ind. act. of *contendō, -ere, -tendī, -tentum*, 3; connected by *et* understood, at the beginning of the clause, with *continuit*, and agrees with *Ariovistus* expressed. See *contendunt*, l. 18, Chap. I. Observe that the connection of this verb with *continuit* determines the tense. So far as forms go, it might be pres. ind. —— **Genus**, nom. sing. n. (*genus, generis*); subj. of *erat*. —— **hōc**, nom. sing. n. (*hīc, haec, hōc*); predicate. *hōc* points to the following. —— **pūgnae**, gen. sing. f. (*pūgna, -ae*); limits *Genus*. For synonyms, see l. 18, Chap. I. —— **quō**, abl. sing. n. (*quī, quae, quod*); refers to *Genus*; agrees with *generō*, to be supplied from *Genus*; abl. *of manner*.

LINE 17. **sē**, acc. plur. of the reflexive pron. *suī*; direct obj. of *exercuerant*. —— **Germānī**, nom. plur.; subject. —— **exercuerant**, 3d pers. plur. pluperf. act. of *exerceō, -ēre, -uī, -itum*, 2; agrees with *Germānī*. —— **Equitum**, gen. plur. of *eques, -itis*, m.; partitive gen. after *mīlia*. A. & G. 216, 2; B. 134; G. 370; H. 397, 2.

LINE 18. **mīlia**, nom. plur. n. (*mille*); indecl. in sing.; subj. of *erant*. See *mīlibus*, l. 2, above. —— **erant**, 3d pers. plur. imperf. ind. of *sum, esse, fuī*; here a verb of complete predication. —— **sex** (sibilated from GK. *ἕξ*), card. num. adj.; an attributive of *mīlia*. —— **totidem**, adv. (tot + idem). —— **numerō**, abl. sing. m. (*numerus, -ī*); abl. *of specification*.

fleet and very brave foot-soldiers; whom from the whole number, each cavalryman had selected one foot-soldier for his own protection. In company with them they were wont to engage in battles; the cavalrymen retreated to them; if anything was rather difficult,	peditēs *foot-soldiers* ex omnī *from all* salūtis *safety* proeliīs *battles* equitēs *the horsemen*	vēlōcissimī *most swift* cōpiā *the supply* causā *for the sake of,* versābantur. *they were engaged.* recipiēbant; *retreated;*	āc *and* singulī *individuals,* dēlēgerant; *had chosen;** Ad To hī, *they,*	fortissimī ; *most brave;* singulōs *individuals* cum *with* eōs *them,* sī *if*	quōs 19 *whom* suae 20 *their own* his in 21 *them in* sē 22 *themselves,* quid erat 23 *anything was*

LINE 19. **peditēs**, nom. plur. m. of *pedes, -itis* (*pēs*): subject-nom. of *erant*, to be supplied. —— **vēlōcissimī**, nom. plur. m. of the adj. *vēlōcissimus, -a, -um;* superl. of positive *vēlōx, -ōcis;* comparative *vēlōcior;* agrees with *peditēs*. —— **āc**, conj. See *atque*, l. 10, Chap. I. —— **fortissimī**, adj., superl. degree, nom. plur. m.; positive *fortis;* comparative *fortior;* connected by *āc* with *vēlōcissimī*, and in the same construction. —— **quōs**, acc. plur. m. of rel. pron. *quī, quae, quod;* refers to *peditēs;* it is the direct obj. of *dēlēgerant.*

LINE 20. **ex** (*ē*), prep. with the abl. —— **omnī**, abl. sing. f. (*omnis, -e*); an attributive of *cōpiā.* —— **cōpiā**, abl. sing. f. (*copia, -ae*); obj. of the prep. *ex*. —— **singulī**, nom. plur. m. of the adj. *singulus, -a, -um;* most commonly in the plur.; used substantively; subject-nom. of *dēlēgerant.* —— **singulōs**, acc. plur. m., in agreement with *quōs*. —— **suae**, gen. sing. f. of the reflexive pron. *suus;* an attributive of *salūtis.*

LINE 21. **salūtis**, gen. sing. of *salūs, -ūtis*, f.; gen. after *causā*. —— **causā**, abl. of *causa, -ae*, f.; abl. *of cause;* here it has a prepositional force and governs the gen. Consult A. & G. 223, *e*; B. 165, REM. 4; G. 373; H. 416, and FOOTNOTE 2. —— **dēlēgerant**, 3d pers. plur. pluperf. ind. act. of *dēligō, -ere, -lēgī, -lēctum,* 3 (dē + legere = lit. *to choose from*); agrees with the subject-nom. *singulī.* —— **cum**, prep. with the abl. —— **hīs**, abl. plur. m. of the dem. pron. *hīc;* used as a personal pron.; obj. of the prep. *cum.* —— **in**, prep.; here with the abl.

LINE 22. **proeliīs**, abl. plur. n. (*proelium, -ī*); obj. of the prep. *in*. Synonyms: l. 18, Chap. I. —— **versābantur**, 3d pers. plur. imperf. ind. of *versor,* 1, middle voice = *to busy* oneself with; hence *to be engaged;* agrees with a pron. understood, referring to the cavalry. *versō* (*vertō*), act. voice = *turn*, or *wheel about.* —— **Ad**, prep. with the acc. —— **eōs**, acc. plur. m. (*is, ea, id*); used as personal pron., referring to the infantry; obj. of the prep. *ad.* —— **sē**, acc. plur. of *suī;* direct reflexive; direct obj. of *recipiēbant.*

LINE 23. **equitēs**, nom. plur. m. (*eques, -itis*); subj. of *recipiēbant.* —— **recipiēbant**, 3d pers. plur. imperf. ind. of *recipiō*, 3; agrees with the subject-nom. *equitēs.* —— **hī**, nom. plur. m. (*hīc, haec, hōc*); used as a personal pron. of the 3d pers.;

* *quōs ... singulī singulōs ... dēlēgerant*, more freely = *whom they had selected individually, every man, one.*

24 dūrius,	concurrēbant;	sī	quī,	graviōre	they ran to help them; if any one on receiving
too hard,	ran up;	if	any one,	a severer	
25 vulnere	acceptō,		equō	dēciderat,	a rather severe wound fell from his horse, they
wound	having been received,		from a horse	should fall,	
26 circumsistēbant;		sī	quō	erat	longius	rallied around him; if they must advance
they stood around (him);		if	anywhere	it was	farther	
27 prōdeundum	aut	celerius	recipiendum,	tanta	to any point somewhat distant, or retreat
to be advanced	or	more speedily	to be retreated,	so great	
28 erat	hōrum	exercitātiōne	celeritās,	ut	rather swiftly, so great, from practice, was
was,	of these	from training,	the celerity	that,	

refers to *peditēs*; expressed for emphasis; subject-nom. of *concurrēbant*. —— **sī**, conditional conj. (sibilated from GK. *ei*). —— **quid**, nom. sing. n. of the indef. pron. *quis, quae, quid*; subj. of *erat*. —— **erat**, 3d pers. sing. imperf. ind. (*sum, esse, fuī*); agrees with the subject-nom. *quid*; ind. — simple condition, nothing implied.

LINE 24. **dūrius**, nom. sing. n. of comparative adj. *durior, -ius*; positive *dūrus*; superl. *dūrissimus*. Observe that the adj. is predicate, and that it = *rather difficult*. See A. & G. 93, *a*; B. 163, REM. 6; G. 297, 2; H. 444, 1. —— **concurrēbant**, 3d pers. plur. imperf. ind. act. of *concurrō*, 3; agrees with the subject-nom. *hī*. —— **sī**, conditional conj. —— **quī**, nom. sing. m. of the indef. pron. *quis* or *quī, quae, quid*; subject-nom. of *dēciderat*. Observe that the usual form of the indef. pron. used as noun is *quis*; but here *quī* as substantive is used. See A. & G. 104, *a*, NOTE; B. 89. 4; G. 107, NOTE 1; H. 454, 1. —— **graviōre**, abl. sing. n. of the comparative adj. *gravior, -ius*; positive *gravis*; an attributive of *vulnere*. See l. 3, Chap. XX.

LINE 25. **vulnere**, abl. sing. of *vulnus, -eris*, n.; sometimes written *volnus*; abl. absolute with *acceptō*. —— **acceptō**, abl. sing. n. of the perf. pass. participle *acceptus, -a, -um* of *accipiō*, 3; absolute with *vulnere*. —— **equō**, abl. sing. m. (*equus, -ī*); abl. after *dē* in *dēciderat*. —— **dēciderat**, 3d pers. sing. pres. subjunctive of *dēcidō, -ere, -cidī*, 3 (dē + cadere, *to fall*).

LINE 26. **circumsistēbant**, 3d pers. plur. imperf. ind. act. of *circumsistō, -ere, -stitī*, 3 (circum + sistō); agrees with *hī* understood as subject-nom.; supply *eum* as direct obj. —— **sī**, see *sī*, l. 24, above. —— **quō**, adv. = *to any place*. —— **erat**, 3d pers. sing. imperf. ind. of *sum*; used impersonally with the gerundive. —— **longius**, adv., comparative degree; positive *longē*; superl. *longissimē*. See grammatical references to *dūrius*, l. 24, above.

LINE 27. **prōdeundum**, nom. sing. n. of the gerundive *prōdeundus, -a, -um* of *prōdeō, -ire, -īvī (-iī), -itum*; supply *sibi*; plur. as dat. *of the agent*. Observe (*a*) that *prō* with *eō* retains an original *d* between the parts of the compound; (*b*) that verbs of the fourth conjugation freq. have the gerund and gerundive ending -*undum* and -*undus* instead of -*endum* and -*endus*. —— **aut**, conj. = *or*. Synonyms: l. 16, Chap. VI. —— **celerius**, adv., comparative degree; positive *celeriter* (*celer*, swift); superl. *celerrimē*; see grammatical references to *dūrius*, l. 24, above. —— **recipiendum**, gerundive (*recipiō*, 3); connected by *aut* with *prōdeundum*, and in the same construction. —— **tanta**, nom. sing. f. of the adj. *tantus, -a, -um*; an attributive of *celeritās*.

LINE 28. **erat**, see *erat*, l. 26, above; but note that here *erat* is a verb of complete predication. —— **hōrum**, gen. plur. of the dem. pron. *hīc, haec, hōc*; used as a

368   CAESAR'S GALLIC WAR   [CHAP. XLIX.

| their swiftness that, clinging to the horses' manes, they kept up with them at full speed. | iubīs *by the manes* adaequārent. *they equalled.* | equōrum *of the horses* | sublevātī *being supported,* | cursum 29 *(their) speed* 30 |

| XLIX. When Caesar perceived that Ariovistus kept himself in camp, that Caesar himself might not be kept too long from supplies, | XLIX. Ubi *When* Caesar *Caesar* prohibērētur, *he might be kept,* | eum *him* intellēxit, *perceived,* ūltrā *beyond* | castrīs *in the camp* nē *that not* eum *that* | sē *himself* diūtius *longer* locum, *place* | tenēre. 1 *to hold* commeātū 2 *from supplies* quō in locō 3 *which in, place* |

personal pron.; limits *celeritās.* —— exercitātiōne, abl. sing. f. of *exercitātiō, -ōnis;* abl. *of cause.* —— celeritās, -tātis (*celer,* swift), nom. sing. f.; subj. of *erat.* —— ut, ecbatic conj.; refers to the adj. *tanta.*

LINE 29. iubīs, abl. plur. of *iuba, -ae,* f.; abl. *of means.* —— equōrum, gen. plur. m. (*equus, -ī*); limits *iubīs.* —— sublevātī, nom. plur. m. of the perf. pass. participle *sublevātus, -a, -um* of *tollō, -ere, sustulī, sublātum;* agrees with a pron. understood, referring to *peditēs.* —— cursum, acc. sing. of *cursus, -ūs,* m. (*currō,* run); direct obj. of *adaequārent.*

LINE 30. adaequārent, 3d pers. plur. imperf. subjunctive act. of *adaequō,* 1; agrees with *peditēs* understood as subject-nom.; subjunctive *of result* after *ut.* · Consult A. & G. 319, 1, and REM.; B. 201, (*b*), and REM. 1, (*a*); G. 552; H. 500, II. Observe that *adaequāre* (ad + aequō [*aequus,* GK. εἶκός] = *to make equal*); that, in use it is both trans. and intrans.; that it is sometimes followed by *cum,* and sometimes takes the dat. Compare the text with *his oppidī moenibus adaequātīs,* Chap. XII, middle, Book 3.

LINE 1. Ubi (quō + bi), adv. = (*a*) *where;* (*b*) transf. of time = *when.* —— eum, acc. sing. m. (*is, ea, id*); used as a personal pron.; refers to Ariovistus; subject-acc. of *tenēre.* —— castrīs, abl. plur. n. (*castrum, -ī*); locative abl. See A. & G. 258, *f,* 1; B. 176, REM. 2, NOTE 1; G. 389; H. 425, II, 1, 1). —— sē, acc. sing. (*suī, sibi, sē, sē*); direct obj. of *tenēre.* —— tenēre, pres. inf. act. of *teneō,* 2.

LINE 2. Caesar, -aris, m.; subject-nom. of *intellēxit.* —— intellēxit, 3d pers. sing. perf. ind. act. of *intellegō, -ere, -lēxī, -lēctum,* 3; agrees with *Caesar.* See l. 6, Chap. X. —— nē, conjunctive adv. = *that not.* —— diūtius, adv., comparative degree of the adv. *diū (diēs);* superl. *diūtissimē.* —— commeātū, abl. m. of *commeātus, -ūs; separation.* A. & G. 243; B. 160; G. 390, 2, NOTE 3; H. 414.

LINE 3. prohibērētur, 3d pers. sing. imperf. subjunctive pass. of *prohibeō,* 2; agrees with a pron. understood, referring to Caesar; subjunctive *of purpose* after *nē.* —— ūltrā, prep. with the acc. —— eum, acc. sing. m. (*is, ea, id*); an attributive of *locum.* —— locum, acc. sing. m. of *locus, -ī.* See *locī,* l. 10, Chap. II. —— quō, abl. sing. m. (*quī, quae, quod*); an attributive of *locō.* —— in, prep., here with the abl.; observe its position. —— locō, abl.; obj. of the prep. *in.* Observe that such redundancy is common in Caesar.

4 Germānī	cōnsēderant,	circiter	passūs	he chose a suitable place for a camp beyond the place at which the Germans had halted, and rather more than half a mile from them, and marched to it with his army drawn up in three lines. He ordered the first and second lines to remain under arms and the third line to
the Germans	*had encamped,*	*about*	*paces*	
5 sexcentōs	ab eīs,	castrīs	idōneum	locum
six-hundred	*from them,*	*for a camp*	*a convenient*	*place*
6 dēlēgit	aciēque	triplicī	īnstrūctā	ad
he selected	*line and,*	*three-fold*	*having been arranged*	*to*
7 eum	locum	vēnit.	Prīmam	et secundam
that	*place*	*he came.*	*The first*	*and second*
8 aciem	in	armīs	esse,	tertiam castra
line	*in*	*arms*	*to be,*	*the third the camp*

LINE 4. **Germānī, -ōrum,** m.; subject-nom. of *cōnsēderant.* —— **cōnsēderant,** 3d pers. plur. pluperf. ind. act. of *cōnsīdō, -ere, -sēdī, -sessum,* 3; agrees with *Germānī.* —— **circiter,** adv. and prep.; here a prep. with the acc. —— **passūs,** acc. plur. m. (*passus, -ūs*); obj. of the prep. *circiter.*

LINE 5. **sexcentōs,** acc. plur. of the card. num. adj. *sexcentī, -ae, -a* (sex + centum); an attributive of *passūs.* Observe that 600 Roman paces = ⅔ of a Roman mile; or a little more than ½ mile. —— **ab** (*ā*), prep. with the abl. —— **eīs,** abl. plur. m. (*is, ea, id*); used as a personal pron.; obj. of the prep. *ab.* —— **castrīs,** dat. plur. n. (*castrum, -ī*); dat. *of purpose.* See A. & G. 233, *b*; B. 147; G. 356; H. 384, II, 1, 3). *castrīs* might be taken as dat. *for which* after the adj. *idōneum.* —— **idōneum,** acc. sing. m. of the adj. *idōneus, -a, -um;* agrees with *locum.* —— **locum,** acc. sing. m. of *locus, -ī.* See *locī,* l. 10, Chap. II.

LINE 6. **dēlēgit,** 3d pers. sing. perf. ind. act. of *dēligō, -ere, -lēgī, -lēctum,* 3; agrees with a pron., referring to Caesar. —— **aciēque** (aciē + que). *aciē,* abl. sing. f. (*aciēs, -ēī*); abl. absolute with *īnstrūctā.* *que,* enclitic conj.; connects the clauses. —— **triplicī,** abl. sing. f. of the adj. *triplex, -icis* (trēs + plicō); an attributive of *aciē.* See l. 5, Chap. XXIV. The three lines consisted of the *hastātī,* the *prīncipēs,* and the *triāriī.* —— **īnstrūctā,** abl. sing. f. of the perf. pass. participle *īnstrūctus, -a, -um* of *īnstruō,* 3; absolute with the noun *aciē.* —— **ad,** prep. with the acc.

LINE 7. **eum,** acc. sing. m. (*is, ea, id*); an attributive of *locum.* —— **locum,** see *locum,* l. 5, above; obj. of the prep. *ad.* —— **vēnit,** 3d pers. sing. perf. ind. act. of *veniō,* 4; agrees with a pron. understood, referring to Caesar. —— **Prīmam,** acc. sing. f. of the adj. *prīmus, -a, -um;* an attributive of *aciem.* —— **et,** cop. conj. —— **secundam,** acc. sing. f. of the adj. *secundus, -a, -um;* also an attributive of *aciem.* Observe that *secundus,* as a participle of *sequor,* 3 = lit. *following,* i.e. *the next, the second.*

LINE 8. **aciem,** acc. sing. of *aciēs, -ēī,* f.; subject-acc. of *esse.* See *aciem,* l. 12, Chap. XXII. —— **in,** prep. with the acc. or abl.; here with the abl. —— **armīs,** abl. plur. n. (*arma, -ōrum*); obj. of the prep. *in.* Synonyms: l. 13, Chap. IV. —— **esse,** pres. inf. of *sum.* —— **tertiam,** acc. sing. f. of the ord. num. adj. *tertius, -a, -um* (*ter,* thrice); agrees with *aciem* understood; which latter is subject-acc. of *mūnīre.* —— **castra,** acc. plur.; direct obj. of *mūnīre.*

fortify the camp.	mūnīre	iūssit.	Hīc	locus	ab	hoste	9
This place, as we have said,	*to fortify*	*he ordered.*	*This*	*place*	*from*	*the enemy*	
was rather more than half a mile distant from the enemy. To the	circiter	passūs	sexcentōs,	utī	dictum est,		10
	about	*paces*	*six-hundred,*	*as*	*has been said,*		
	aberat.	Eō	circiter	hominum		numerō	11
same place Ariovistus sent about sixteen thousand	*was distant.*	*Thither*	*about*	*of men*		*n number*	
	sēdecim	mīlia	expedīta	cum	omnī	equitātū	12
light-armed troops with all	*sixteen*	*thousands*	*light-armed*	*with*	*all*	*the cavalry*	
his cavalry, to terrify our men	Ariovistus	mīsit,	quae	cōpiae		nostrōs	13
	Ariovistus	*sent,*	*which*	*forces*		*ours*	
and keep them from fortifying the camp. Nev-	perterrērent	et		mūnitiōne		prohibērent.	14
	should terrify	*and*		*from fortifying*		*should prohibit.*	

LINE 9. **mūnīre**, pres. inf. act. of *mūniō*, 4. —— **iūssit**, 3d pers. sing. perf. ind. act. of *iubeō, -ēre, iūssī, iūssum*, 2; agrees with a pron. understood, referring to Caesar. —— **Hīc**, dem. pron.; an attributive of *locus*. —— **locus**, nom. sing.; subj. of *aberat*. —— **ab** (*ā*), prep. with the abl. Observe that this phrase *ab hoste* follows *aberat*, the prep. being repeated. —— **hoste**, abl. sing. m. (*hostis, -is*); obj. of the prep. *ab*. Synonyms: see *hostium*, l. 15, Chap. XI.

LINE 10. **circiter**, adv.; see *circiter*, l. 4, above. —— **passūs**, acc. plur.; obj. of *circiter*. See *passūs*, l. 4, above. —— **sex(s)centōs**, see l. 5, above. —— **utī**, adv.; here = *as*. —— **dictum est**, 3d pers. sing. perf. ind. pass. of *dīcō*, 3; used impersonally; but supply *ā nōbīs*, as abl. *of the agent*. See l. 5, above.

LINE 11. **aberat**, 3d pers. sing. imperf. ind. of *absum, abesse, ab(ā)fuī, ab(ā)futūrus*; agrees with the subject-nom. *locus*. —— **Eō**, adv. (*is*). —— **circiter**, an adv. here; modifies the adj. *sēdecim*. —— **hominum**, i.e. *peditum*; partitive gen. after *mīlia*. A. & G. 216, 2; B. 134; G. 370; H. 397, 2 —— **numerō**, abl. sing. m. (*numerus, -ī*); *specification*.

LINE 12. **sēdecim** (sex + decem); also written *sexdecim*; sometimes separately *decem et sex*; modifies *mīlia*. —— **mīlia**, acc. plur.; direct obj. of *mīsit*. See *mīlia*, l. 25, Chap. II. —— **expedīta**, acc. plur. of the participle *expedītus, -a, -um* from *expediō*, 4 (ex + pēs); agrees with *mīlia*, used as a noun. The student will observe that *hominum mīlia expedīta = hominum mīlia expedītōrum*. —— **cum**, prep. with the abl. —— **omnī**, abl. sing. m. of the adj. *omnis, -e*; an attributive of *equitātū*. —— **equitātū**, abl. sing. m. (*equitātus, -ūs*); obj. of the prep. *cum*.

LINE 13. **Ariovistus, -ī**, m.; subject-nom. of *mīsit*. —— **mīsit**, 3d pers. sing. perf. ind. act. of *mittō*, 3. —— **quae**, nom. plur. f. (*quī, quae, quod*); used adjectively; an attributive of *cōpiae*. —— **cōpiae**, nom. plur. f. (*cōpia, -ae*); subject-nom. of the two following verbs. —— **nostrōs**, acc. plur. of the poss. pron. *noster, -tra, -trum*; used substantively; or supply *mīlitēs*; direct object.

LINE 14. **perterrērent**, 3d pers. plur. imperf. subjunctive of *perterreō*, 2 (per, *intensive* + terreō); subjunctive *of purpose* after *quae cōpiae = ut eae cōpiae*. Consult A. & G. 317, 2, and NOTE; B. 200, (*b*), and 233, 1; G. 630; H. 497, I. —— **et**, cop. conj. —— **mūnitiōne**, abl. f. (*mūnitiō, -ōnis*); *separation*. See grammatical references to *commeātū*, l. 2, above. —— **prohibērent**, 3d pers. plur. imperf. subjunctive act. of *prohibeō*, 2; connected by *et* with *perterrērent*, and in the same grammatical construction.

15 Nihilō sēcius Caesar, ut ante	ertheless Caesar, as he had previously planned, ordered the two lines to ward off the enemy, the third line to finish the work. When the camp had been fortified, Caesar left in it two legions and some of the auxiliaries, but led back to the larger camp the other four legions.
In nothing the less Caesar, as before	
16 cōnstituerat, duās aciēs hostem prōpulsāre,	
he had determined, two lines the enemy to drive off,	
17 tertiam opus perficere iūssit.	
the third the work to complete he ordered.	
18 Mūnītīs castrīs, duās ibi legiōnēs	
Having been fortified the camp, two, there, legions	
19 relīquit et partem auxiliōrum, quattuor	
he left and part of the auxiliaries, the four	
20 reliquās in castra māiōra redūxit.	
remaining into camp the greater he led back.	

LINE 15. Nihilō, abl. of *nihilum, -ī*, n.; abl. *of specification*; might be taken as adv. —— sēcius, adv.; comparative degree; positive *secus*; = *less*; with *nihilō* = *none the less, nevertheless*. —— Caesar, *-aris*, m.; subj. of *iūssit*, l. 17, below. —— ut, adv. = *as*. —— ante, an adv. here; oftener a prep.

LINE 16. cōnstituerat, 3d pers. pluperf. ind. act. of *cōnstituō*, 3; agrees with a pron. implied in the ending, referring to Caesar. —— duās, acc. plur., num. adj. (*duo, duae, duo*); an attributive of *aciēs*. —— aciēs, acc. plur.; subject-acc. of *prōpulsāre*. See *aciem*, l. 8, above. —— hostem, acc. sing. (*hostis, -is*); direct obj. of *prōpulsāre*. See *hoste*, l. 9, above. —— prōpulsāre, pres. inf. act. of *prōpulsō*, 1.

LINE 17. tertiam, acc. sing. f. of the ord. num. adj. *tertius, -a, -um*; an attributive of *aciem*, to be supplied; which latter is subject-acc. of *perficere*. —— opus, acc. sing. n. (*opus, -eris*); direct obj. of *perficere*. —— perficere, pres. inf. act. of *perficiō*, 3 (per + *faciō*). —— iūssit, 3d pers. sing. perf. ind. act. of *iubeō*, 2; agrees with Caesar expressed.

LINE 18. Mūnītīs, abl. plur. perf. pass. participle *mūnītus, -a, -um* of *mūniō*, 4; abl. absolute with *castrīs*; the phrase denotes *time when*. —— castrīs, see note on *castrīs*, l. 12, Chap. XII. —— duās, acc. plur. f.; agrees with *legiōnēs*. See *duās*, l. 16, above. —— ibi, adv. —— legiōnēs, acc. plur. f. (*legiō, -ōnis*); direct obj. of *relīquit*.

LINE 19. relīquit, 3d pers. sing. perf. ind. act. of *relinquō, -ere, -līquī, -lictum*, 3. —— et, cop. conj. —— partem, acc. sing. of *pars, partis*, f.; connected by *et* with *legiōnēs*, and in the same construction. —— auxiliōrum, gen. plur. of *auxilium, -ī*, n.; limits *partem*. Observe that in the plur. — *abstractum prō concrētō* — *auxilium* = *auxiliary troops*, i.e. troops sent by foreign nations to serve in the Roman armies. —— quattuor, card. num. adj., indecl.; an attributive of *legiōnēs*, to be supplied.

LINE 20. reliquās, acc. plur. of the adj. *reliquus, -a, -um*; also an attributive of *legiōnēs* understood. —— in, prep.; hence with the acc. after verb of motion = *into*. —— castra, acc. plur. n. (*castrum, -ī*); obj. of the prep. *in*. —— māiōra, acc. plur. n. of the comparative adj. *māior, -ius*; for declension of *māior*, see A. & G. 86; B. 69, 2; G. 89; H. 154. —— redūxit, 3d pers. sing. perf. ind. act. of *redūcō*, 3; connected by *et* understood at the beginning of the clause with *relīquit*, and in the same grammatical construction. As to this asyndeton, see A. & G. 208, *b*, 346, *c*; B. 123, REM. 6, 310, 1, (*a*); G. 473, REM., 474, NOTE, and 492; H. 636, I, 1.

L. The next day, Caesar, according to his custom, led out his troops from both camps, and advancing a little from the larger camp, drew up his line in battle array, and gave to the enemy an opportunity of fighting. When he saw that they would not even	L. Proximō diē īnstitūtō suō Caesar 1 *On the following day by practice his own Caesar* ē castrīs utrīsque cōpiās suās ēdūxit 2 *from camps both forces his he led out,* paulumque ā māiōribus castrīs prōgressus 3 *a little and, from the larger camp having advanced* aciem īnstrūxit, hostibus pūgnandī 4 *the line of battle he drew up, to the enemy of fighting* potestātem fēcit. Ubi nē tum quidem 5 *an opportunity he made. When not then even* eōs prōdīre intellēxit, circiter merīdiem 6 *them to come forth he perceived, about midday*

LINE 1. **Proximō**, abl. sing. m. of *proximus, -a, -um;* superl. of comparative *propior* (*prope*, near); no positive; an attributive of *diē*. —— **diē**, abl. sing. m. of *diēs, -ēī; time when*. —— **īnstitūtō**, abl. sing. of *īnstitūtum, -ī*, n. (in + statuere, *to set up, establish*); abl. of *in accordance with*. A. & G. 245; B. 162; G. 397; H. 416. But see also A. & G. 253, and NOTE; and note that A. & G., B., and G. make the construction an abl. of specification. —— **suō**, abl. sing. n. (*suus, -a, -um*); an attributive of *īnstitūtō*. —— **Caesar, -aris**, m.; subject-nom. of *ēdūxit*.

LINE 2. **ē** (*ex*), prep. with the abl. —— **castrīs**, abl. plur. n. (*castrum, -ī*); obj. of the prep. *ē*. See *castrīs*, l. 12, Chap. XII. —— **utrīsque**, abl. plur. of the adjective pron. *uterque, utraque, utrumque* = which of two, *each, both;* an attributive of *castrīs*. The *larger* camp had capacity for the six legions and the auxiliaries; the *smaller* for the two legions mentioned in the preceding chapter. —— **cōpiās**, acc. plur. f. (*cōpia, -ae*); direct obj. of *ēdūxit*. See *cōpiīs*, l. 6, Chap. II. —— **suās**, see note on *suās*, l. 11, Chap. XLVIII. —— **ēdūxit**, 3d pers. sing. perf. ind. act. of *ēdūcō, 3;* agrees with *Caesar* expressed.

LINE 3. **paulumque** (paulum + que). *paulum* may be taken here as subst., acc. *of extent of space;* or as an adv. *que*, enclitic conj. —— **ā** (*ab*), prep. with the abl. —— **māiōribus**, abl. plur. n. of the adj. comparative degree *māior, māius;* positive *māgnus;* superl. *māximus;* an attributive of *castrīs*. Observe that some texts omit *castrīs*. —— **castrīs**, see *castrīs*, l. 12, Chap. XII. —— **prōgressus**, perf. participle of the deponent *prōgredior, -ī, -essus;* agrees with a pron. understood, referring to Caesar.

LINE 4. **aciem**, acc. sing. f. of *aciēs, -ēī;* direct obj. of *īnstrūxit*. See l. 12, Chap. XXII. —— **īnstrūxit**, 3d pers. sing. perf. ind. act. of *īnstruō, 3;* connected by *que* with *ēdūxit;* and in the same grammatical construction. See *īnstruit*, l. 13, Chap. XXII. —— **hostibus**, dat. plur. (*hostis, -is*, m. and f.); indirect object. —— **pūgnandī**, gerund of *pūgnō, 1;* limits *potestātem*. Consult A. & G. 298; B. 184, REM. 4, I, (*a*); G. 428; H. 542, I.

LINE 5. **potestātem**, acc. sing. of *potestās, -ātis*, f.; direct obj. of *fēcit*. Synonyms: l. 25, Chap. XVIII. —— **fēcit**, 3d pers. sing. perf. ind. act. of *faciō, 3;* agrees with a pron. understood, referring to Caesar. —— **Ubi** (quō + bi), adv.; of place = *where;* transf. of time = *when*. —— **nē**, adv.; modifies *quidem*. —— **tum**, adv. = *then;* modifies *prōdīre*. Observe that *quidem* emphasizes *tum*. —— **quidem** adv. See *quidem*, l. 7, Chap. XVI.

LINE 6. **eōs**, acc. plur. (*is, ea, id*); used as a personal pron. of the 3d pers.; subject-acc. of *prōdīre*. *eōs* refers to the forces of Ariovistus. —— **prōdīre**, pres. inf.

LINES 7-12.]   BOOK I.   373

7 exercitum	in	castra	redūxit.	Tum	dēmum	then come out,
(his) army	into	camp	he led back.	Then	at length	he led his army back into camp
8 Ariovistus	partem	suārum	cōpiārum,		quae	about noon. Finally, Ariovistus
Ariovistus	a part	of his	forces,		which	sent some of his
9 castra	minōra	oppūgnāret	misit.		Acriter	troops to attack the smaller
camp	the less	should attack,	he sent.		Sharply	camp. Even till
10 utrimque	ūsque	ad vesperum	pūgnātum est.			evening, the battle raged fiercely
on both sides	even	to (till) evening	it was fought.			on both sides.
11 Sōlis	occāsū	suās	cōpiās	Ariovistus		At sunset, Ariovistus led his
At the sun's	setting	his	forces	Ariovistus		troops back to
12 multīs	et	illātīs	et	acceptīs		their camp, after
many	both	being inflicted	and	being received		receiving and

act. of *prōdeō*, 4. See note on *prōdeundum*, l. 27, Chap. XLVIII. Observe that the infinitive-clause is the direct obj. of *intellēxit*. —— **intellēxit**, 3d pers. sing. perf. ind. act. of *intellegō*, 3; agrees with Caesar understood. See note on *intellegēbat*, l. 6, Chap. X. —— **circiter**, adv. and prep.; here prep. with the acc. —— **merīdiem**, acc. sing. of *merīdiēs, -ēī*, m. (medius + diēs); obj. of the prep. *circiter*.

LINE 7. **exercitum**, acc. sing. m.; direct obj. of *redūxit*. See *exercitū*, l. 31, Chap. III. —— **in**, prep. with the abl. or acc.; here the acc., and = *into* with a verb of motion. —— **castra**, see note on *castra*, l. 20, Chap. XLIX. —— **redūxit**, 3d pers. sing. perf. ind. act. of *redūcō*, 3; agrees with a pron. understood, referring to Caesar. See l. 3, Chap. XXVIII. —— **Tum**, see this particle, l. 5, above. —— **dēmum**, adv.; lengthened form of *dem*, as seen in *idem* (i + dem); compare GK. δή.

LINE 8. **Ariovistus, -ī,** m.; subject-nom. of *mīsit*. —— **partem**, acc. sing. f. (*pars, partis*); direct obj. of *mīsit*. —— **suārum**, gen. plur. f. (*suus, -a, -um*); an attributive of *cōpiārum*. —— **cōpiārum**, gen. plur.; limits *partem*. See *cōpiās*, l. 2, above. —— **quae**, nom. sing. f. (*quī, quae, quod*); refers to *partem*; subject-nom. of *oppūgnāret*.

LINE 9. **castra**, acc. plur.; direct obj. of *oppūgnāret*. See *castrīs*, l. 2, above. —— **minōra**, acc. plur. n. of comparative adj. *minor*; positive *parvus*; superl. *minimus*; an attributive of *castra*. See note on *castrīs*, l. 2, above. —— **oppūgnāret**, 3d pers. sing. imperf. subjunctive of *oppūgnō*, 1; subjunctive after *quae* = *ut ea* — an adjective purpose-clause. Consult A. & G. 317, 2, and NOTE; B. 200, (*b*); G. 630; H. 497, I. —— **misit**, 3d pers. sing. perf. ind. act. (*mittō*, 3); agrees with Ariovistus expressed. —— **Acriter**, adv. (*ācer*, sharp); modifies *pūgnātum est*.

LINE 10. **utrimque**, adv. (*uterque* = *each* of two, *both*); modifies *pūgnātum est*. —— **ūsque**, adv. (*ubi*, when). —— **ad**, prep. with the acc. —— **vesperum**, acc. sing. of *vesper, -erī*, m.; obj. of the prep. *ad*. See l. 8, Chap. XXVI. —— **pūgnātum est**, 3d pers. sing. perf. ind. pass. of *pūgnō*, 1; used impersonally. See l. 2, Chap. XXVI.

LINE 11. **Sōlis**, gen. sing. m. of *sōl*; limits *occāsū*. See *sōlem*, l. 29, Chap. I. —— **occāsū**, abl. sing. m. of *occāsus, -ūs*; abl. *of time at which*. —— **suās**, acc. plur. f. (*suus, -a, -um*); an attributive of *cōpiās*. —— **cōpiās**, acc. plur.; direct obj. of *redūxit*. See l. 6, Chap. II. —— **Ariovistus, -ī,** m.; subject-nom. of *redūxit*.

LINE 12. **multīs**, abl. plur. n. of the adj. *multus, -a, -um*; an attributive of *vulneribus*. —— **et**, cop. conj. *et . . . et* = *both . . . and*; but omit the first *et* in trans-

inflicting many wounds. When Caesar inquired of his prisoners why Ariovistus did not decide the issue by a battle, he found the reason to be this: it was the custom among the Germans for their matrons to declare by lots and vaticinations whether or not it would be expedient to en-	vulneribus *wounds* captīvīs *the captives* Ariovistus *Ariovistus* reperiēbat *he ascertained* ea *this* familiae *of the family*	in *into* quaereret *sought* proeliō *by battle* causam, *the cause,* cōnsuētūdō *the custom* eōrum *of them*	castra *camp* Caesar, *Caesar,* nōn *not* quod *that* esset, *was,* sortibus *by lots*	redūxit. *led back.* quam-ob-rem *what for thing* dēcertāret, *did fight out,* apud *among* ut *that* et *and*	Cum ex 13 *When from* 14 Caesar, 15 hanc *this* Germānōs 16 *the Germans* mātrēs 17 *the mistresses* vāticinātiōnibus 18 *by soothsayings*

lating here. —— il(n)lātīs, perf. pass. participle of *īnferō, īnferre, intulī, il(n)lātum*; abl. absolute with *vulneribus*. —— et, see *et*, immediately preceding. —— acceptīs, abl. plur. n. of the perf. pass. participle *acceptus, -a, -um* of *accipiō*, 3; connected by *et* with *illātīs*, and in the same grammatical construction.

LINE 13. vul(vol)neribus, abl. plur. n. of *vulnus, -eris*; absolute with the participles. —— in, prep.; here with the acc. —— castra, acc. plur.; obj. of the prep. *in*. See *castra*, l. 7, above. —— redūxit, see l. 7, above. —— Cum, temporal conj. —— ex (ē), prep. with the abl.

LINE 14. captīvīs, abl. plur. of *captīvus, -ī*, m. (*capere*, to take); obj. of the prep. *ex*. —— quaereret, 3d pers. sing. imperf. subjunctive act. of *quaerō*, 3; subjunctive after *cum* temporal. —— Caesar, -aris, m.; subject-nom. of *quaereret*. Observe the emphatic position. The unemphatic position would be immediately after *cum*. —— quam-ob-rem, interrogative adv.; often written *quam ob rem*; but see l. 1, Chap. XXXIV.

LINE 15. Ariovistus, -ī, m.; subject-nom. of *dēcertāret*. —— proeliō, abl. sing. n. (*proelium, -ī*); *means*. —— nōn, negative particle; in its normal Latin position. —— dēcertāret, 3d pers. sing. imperf. subjunctive act. of *dēcertō*, 1; subjunctive — indirect question. —— hanc, acc. sing. f. (*hīc, haec, hōc*); prep. after *esse* understood.

LINE 16. reperiēbat, 3d pers. sing. imperf. ind. act. of *reperiō*, 4; agrees with a pron. understood, referring to Caesar. —— causam, acc. sing. f. (*causa, -ae*); subject-acc. of *esse* understood. —— quod, conj.; introducing a clause explanatory of the herald *hanc*. —— apud, prep. with the acc. —— Germānōs, acc. plur. m. (*Germānī, -ōrum*); obj. of the prep. *apud*.

LINE 17. ea, nom. sing. f.; predicate-nom. after *esset*. —— cōnsuētūdō, -inis, f.; subject-nom. of *esset*. —— esset, 3d pers. sing. imperf. subjunctive of *sum*. —— ut, ecbatic conj. —— mātrēs, nom. plur. of *māter, -tris*, f.; compare GK. μήτηρ; subj. of *dēclārārent*.

LINE 18. familiae, gen. sing. of *familia, -ae*, f.; limits *mātrēs*. —— eōrum, gen. plur. m. (*is, ea, id*); used as a personal pron. of the 3d pers.; limits *familiae*. Observe that *familia* after *māter* and *pater* sometimes forms its gen. in *-ās*; that some

BOOK I.

19 dēclārārent, utrum proelium committī ex | gage in battle;
  declared,   *whether* *a battle* *to be engaged in,* *of* | and they thus declared: It is
                                                                   not the divine
20 ūsū   esset necne ; eōs ita dīcere : | will that the
  advantage *it was* *or not;* *these* *thus* *to say* (these | Germans should
                                                                   conquer, if they
21   nōn esse fās Germānōs superāre, | should engage in
  thus said): *not* *to be* *divine law* *the Germans* *to conquer,* | battle before the
                                                                   new moon.
22 sī ante novam lūnam proeliō
  if *before* *the new* *moon* *in battle*

23 contendissent.
  they should have contended.

---

editors write the two words, even in the plur., as a compound, thus: *mātrēsfamiliae*.
—— **sortibus**, abl. plur. of *sors, sortis*, f.; *means*. Consult A. & G. 248, *c*; B. 167; G. 401; H. 418. —— **et**, cop. conj. —— **vāticinātiōnibus**, abl. plur. of *vāticinātiō, -ōnis*, f. (*vātēs*, a prophet, through *vāticinor*); abl. *of means*.

LINE 19. **dēclārārent**, 3d pers. plur. imperf. subjunctive of *dēclārō*, 1; agrees with *mātrēs*; subjunctive of result after *ut*. —— **utrum** (*uter*), conj.; followed by *an* or *necne* in alternatives; in questions both direct and indirect; but it is untranslatable in direct questions. Consult A. & G. 211, and *d*; B. 241 and 242, OBS. (1); G. 458, 460; H. 353, ff. —— **proelium**, acc. sing. n. (*proelium, -ī*); subject-acc. of *committī*. Synonyms: l. 18, Chap. I. —— **committī**, pres. inf. pass. of *committō*, 3. —— **ex** (*ē*), prep. with the abl.

LINE 20. **ūsū**, abl. sing. m. (*ūsus, -ūs*); obj. of the prep. *ex;* the phrase is adjectival here, and = *advantageous;* and, moreover, it has the force of a predicate-adj. after *esset*. See *ex ūsū*, l. 8, Chap. XXX. —— **esset**, 3d pers. sing. imperf. subjunctive of *sum, esse, fuī;* used impersonally; in fact, however, *proelium committī* as noun-phrase is the subj.; subjunctive, because an indirect question. A. & G. 334; B. 242; G. 467; H. 529, I. —— **necne** (nec + ne) = *or not;* alternative of *utrum*. —— **eās**, acc. plur. f. (*is, ea, id*); used as a personal pron. of the 3d pers.; subject-acc. of *dīcere*. —— **ita**, adv. —— **dīcere**, pres. inf. act. of *dīcō*, 3; subject-acc. is the pron. *eās*.

LINE 21. **nōn**, negative adv. —— **esse**, pres. inf. of *sum*. —— **fās**, an indecl. neuter noun, but in use here it is subject-acc. of *esse*. *fās* = *divine law*, in contrast with *iūs* which = *human law*. —— **Germānōs**, acc. plur. m. (*Germānī, -ōrum*); subject-acc. of *superāre*. —— **superāre**, pres. inf. act. of *superō*, 1 (*super*, over).

LINE 22. **sī**, conditional conj. —— **ante**, prep. with the acc. —— **novam**, acc. sing. f. of the adj. *novus, -a, -um;* an attributive of *lūnam*. —— **lūnam**, acc. sing. f. of *lūna, -ae* (*lūcēre*, to give light); obj. of the prep. *ante*. —— **proeliō**, abl. sing. n. (*proelium, -ī*); *means*.

LINE 23. **contendissent**, 3d pers. plur. pluperf. subjunctive of *contendō*, 3; agrees with a pron. understood, referring to the Germans; subjunctive in the condition after *sī*. The *ōrātiō rēcta* of lines 20–23: *Nōs ita dīcimus*: nōn est fās (*vōs*) Germānōs superāre, sī ante novam lūnam proeliō *contenderitis*.

LI.

LI. Postrīdiē	ēius	diēī	Caesar	1
The day after	*that*	*day*	*Caesar*	
praesidium utrīsque	castrīs,	quod satis	esse	2
a garrison for both	*camps,*	*which enough*	*to be*	
vīsum est, relīquit,	omnēs		ālāriōs	3
seemed, left,	*all the allied troops on the wings*			
in cōnspectū	hostium	prō castrīs	minōribus	4
in sight	*of the enemy*	*before the camp*	*smaller*	
cōnstituit, quod	minus	multitūdine	mīlitum	5
he stationed, because	*less*	*in the multitude*	*of soldiers*	
legiōnāriōrum	prō	hostium	numerō	6
legionary	*in comparison with*	*the enemy's*	*number*	

LI. The following day, Caesar left what seemed to be a sufficient guard for both camps; but marshalled before the smaller camp in sight of the enemy, all the auxiliaries, that he might use them to keep up appearances, inasmuch as he was less powerful in the number of

LINE 1. **Postrīdiē ēius diēī**, see this phrase explained, l. 1, Chap. XXIII. — **Caesar, -aris,** m.; subject-nom. of *relīquit*, l. 3, below.

LINE 2. **praesidium,** acc. sing. n. (*praesidium, -ī*); direct obj. of *relīquit*. — **utrīsque castrīs,** see explanation, l. 2, Chap. L. *castrīs* is a dat. *of reference* or *advantage.* See A. & G. 235; B. 118. 2; G. 356; H. 384, II, 1, 2). — **quod,** nom. sing. n. (*quī, quae, quod*); refers to *praesidium;* subject-nom. of *vīsum est.* Observe that *quod* might be taken here as = *quantum;* and the clause made an adverbial modifier of *relīquit,* instead of an adjectival modifier of *praesidium.* — **satis,** adj.; predicate-nom. after *esse.* — **esse,** pres. inf. of *sum.*

LINE 3. **vīsum est,** 3d pers. sing. perf. ind. of *videor, -ērī, vīsum,* 2; pass. of *videō;* and as such = *seem,* or *seem best;* agrees with the subj. *quod.* — **relīquit,** 3d pers. sing. perf. ind. act. of *relinquō, -ere, -līquī, -lictum,* 3; agrees with *Caesar* expressed as nom. — **omnēs,** acc. plur. m. of the adj. *omnis, -e;* an attributive of *ālāriōs.* — **ālāriōs,** acc. plur. m. of the adj. *ālārius, -a, -um;* used as a noun; direct obj. of *cōnstituit.* Note that the adj. = *belonging to the wings* (*āla*); as the allies held the wings, the plur. = *the auxiliaries.* Note also the omission of the conjunctions before the clauses (asyndeton).

LINE 4. **in,** prep.; here with the abl. — **cōnspectū,** abl. of *cōnspectus, -ūs,* m.; obj. of the prep. *in.* Synonyms: see l. 9, Chap. XI. — **hostium,** gen. plur. (*hostis, -is,* m. and f.); limits *cōnspectū.* Synonyms: l. 15, Chap. XI. — **prō,** prep. with the abl. — **castrīs,** abl. plur.; obj. of the prep. *prō.* See l. 12, Chap. XII. — **minōribus,** abl. plur. n. of the comparative adj. *minor;* an attributive of *castrīs.* See *castrīs,* l. 2, Chap. L.

LINE 5. **cōnstituit,** 3d pers. sing. perf. ind. act. of *cōnstituō,* 3; connected by a conj. understood with *relīquit,* and in the same construction. — **quod,** conj. = *because.* — **minus,** adv.; modifies *valēbat.* — **multitūdine,** abl. *of specification* of *multitūdō, -inis,* f. (*multus*). Consult A. & G. 253; B. 162; G. 397; H. 424. — **mīlitum,** gen. plur. m. of *mīles, -itis;* limits *multitūdine.*

LINE 6. **legiōnāriōrum,** gen. plur. m. of the adj. *legiōnārius, -a, -um;* an attributive of *mīlitum.* — **prō,** prep. with the abl.; here *in comparison with.* — **hostium,** see *hostium,* l. 4, above; limits *numerō.* — **numerō,** abl. sing. m. (*numerus, -ī*); obj. of the prep. *prō.*

7 valēbat,	ut	ad	speciem	ālāriīs	legionary soldiers than the enemy; while personally, after drawing up his army in three lines, he advanced even to the enemy's camp. Then at last, the Germans of necessity led out their troops from their camp, and stationed the Harudes, the Marcom-
he was strong,	*that*	*for*	*show*	*the allies on the wings*	
8 ūterētur;	ipse,		triplicī	īnstrūctā	
he might use;	*he himself*		*in a threefold*	*having been drawn up*	
9 aciē,	usque	ad	castra	hostium	accessit.
line,	*even*	*to*	*the camp*	*of the enemy*	*approached.*
10 Tum	dēmum	necessāriō		Germānī	suās
Then	*at length*	*necessarily*		*the Germans*	*their*
11 cōpiās	castrīs	ēdūxērunt			generātimque
forces	*from the camp*	*led out*			*tribe by tribe and,*
12 cōnstituērunt	paribus		intervāllīs,		Harūdēs,
they arranged	*at equal*		*intervals,*		*the Harudes,*

LINE 7. **valēbat**, 3d pers. sing. imperf. ind. of *valeō, -ēre, -uī, -itum,* 2, intrans. —— **ut**, telic conj. —— **ad**, prep. with the acc. —— **speciem**, acc. sing. of *speciēs, -ēī,* f. *(specere,* to see); obj. of the prep. *ad.* —— **ālāriīs**, abl. plur. of the adj. *ālārius, -a, -um,* used as noun; obj. of *ūterētur.* A. & G. 249; B. 167, 1; G. 407; H. 421, I.

LINE 8. **ūterētur**, 3d pers. sing. imperf. subjunctive of the deponent *ūtor, -ī, ūsus,* 3; subjunctive *of purpose* after *ut.* —— **ipse**, intensive pron.; refers to Caesar; subject-nom. of *accessit.* —— **triplicī īnstrūctā aciē**, see the phrase explained, l. 6, Chap. XLIX; and observe that the abl. absolute denotes *time when.*

LINE 9. **usque** (ubi + que), adv. —— **ad**, prep. with the acc. —— **castra**, obj. of the prep. *ad.* See l. 12, Chap. XII. —— **hostium**, see *hostium,* l. 6, above; it here limits *castra.* —— **accessit**, 3d pers. sing. perf. ind. act. of *accēdō,* 3 (ad + cēdere, *to go to);* agrees with a pron., referring to Caesar.

LINE 10. **Tum dēmum**, see note on these particles, l. 7, Chap. L. —— **necessāriō**, adv. (adj. *necessarius).* Observe that the Germans were not intrenched; hence they were compelled at length to come out and fight. —— **Germānī, -ōrum**, m.; subj. of *ēdūxērunt.* —— **suās**, acc. plur. f. *(suus, -a, -um);* an attributive of *cōpiās.*

LINE 11. **cōpiās**, acc. plur. *(cōpia, -ae);* direct obj. —— **castrīs**, abl. plur. n. *(castrum, -ī);* abl. after the compound *ēdūxērunt.* Consult A. & G. 243, *a*; B. 160; G. 390, and 2; H. 413. But observe that Caesar oftener repeats the prep. after *ēdūcere.* —— **ēdūxērunt**, 3d pers. plur. perf. ind. act. of *ēdūcō,* 3; agrees with *Germānī.* —— **generātimque** (generātim + que). *generātim (gēns,* race); adv. = *by clans* or *by tribes. que,* enclitic conj.; connects the clauses.

LINE 12. **cōnstituērunt**, 3d pers. plur. perf. ind. act. of *cōnstituō,* 3; connected by *que* with *ēdūxērunt,* and in the same construction. —— **paribus**, abl. plur. n. of the adj. *par, paris;* an attributive of *intervāllīs.* —— **intervāllīs**, abl. plur. of *intervāllum, -ī,* n.; abl. *of manner.* A. & G. 248; B. 168; G. 399; H. 419, III. See l. 25, Chap. XXII. —— **Harūdēs**, acc. plur. *(Harūdēs, -um);* direct obj. of *cōnstituērunt;* and so the following nouns to, and inclusive of, *Suēvōs.* These clans in origin were all Germans.

mani, the Tri-	Marcommanōs,	Tribocēs,	Vangiōnēs,	Nemētēs, 13
boces, the Van-	the Marcommani,	the Triboces,	the Vangiones,	the Nemetes,
giones, the Ne-				
metes, the Sedu-	Sedūsiōs,	Suēvōs,	omnemque	aciem suam 14
sii, the Suevi,	the Sedusii,	the Suevi,	all and,	the line their own
clan by clan, at				
equal distances,				
and surrounded	rēdīs	et carrīs	circumdedērunt,	nē 15
their entire army	with chariots	and wagons	they surrounded,	that not
with their wag-				
ons and carts,	qua spēs	in fugā	relinquerētur.	Eō 16
that no hope in	any hope	in flight	might be left.	Thither
flight might re-				
main. On these	mulierēs	imposuērunt,	quae in	proelium 17
they placed their	the women	they placed,	who into	battle
women who, in				
tears, with out-				
stretched hands,		proficīscentēs	passīs	manibus 18
as their men	(the soldiers)	going forth,	being stretched out	the hands,

LINE 13. **Marcommanōs**, acc. plur. (*Marcommanī, -ōrum*). —— **Tribocēs**, acc. plur. of *Tribocēs, -um*, m. (*-ī, -ōrum*). —— **Vangiōnēs, -um**, m. —— **Nemētēs, -um**, m.; the Greek paraphrast reads Νημίται.

LINE 14. **Sedūsiōs**, acc. plur. (*Sedusii, -ōrum*); the Greek paraphrast is Σηδού-σιους; hence we have marked the antepenult long. —— **Suēvōs**, acc. plur. (*Suēvī, -ōrum*); written in some copies *Suēbos*, acc. plur. of *Suēbī* (GK. Σούηβοι or Σόηβοι)· But the paraphrast is Σουεύους. —— **omnemque** (omnem + que). *omnem*, acc. sing. f. (*omnis, -e*); an attributive of *aciem*. —— **aciem**, acc. sing. f. (*aciēs, -ēī*); direct obj· —— **suam**, acc. sing. f. (*suus, -a, -um*); an attributive of *aciem*.

LINE 15. **rēdīs** (*rhēdīs*), abl. sing. of *rēda, -ae*, f.; *means*. The *rhēda* was a four-wheeled carriage. —— **et**, cop. conj. —— **carrīs**, abl. plur.; connected by *et* with *rēdīs*, and in the same construction. See *carrōrum*, l. 4, Chap. III. —— **circumdedērunt**, 3d pers. plur. perf. ind. act. of *circumdō*, 1 (circum + dō); connected by *que* with *cōnstituērunt*, and in the same construction. —— **nē**, adv.; introduces the negative *purpose*.

LINE 16. **qua**, nom. sing. f. of the indef. pron. *quis* or *quī*, *quae* or *qua*, *quid* or *quod*; an attributive of *spēs*. —— **spēs, -ēī**, f.; subject-nom. —— **in**, prep., here with the abl. —— **fugā**, abl. sing. f. (*fuga, -ae*); obj. of the prep. *in*. —— **relinquerētur**, 3d pers. sing. imperf. subjunctive pass. of *relinquō*, 3; agrees with the subject-nom. *spēs*. —— **Eō**, adv. (*is*) = lit. *thither;* but here it = *in eīs*, i.e. on the wagons and carts.

LINE 17. **mulierēs**, acc. plur. of *mulier, -eris*, f.; direct object. Observe that *mulier*, as if *mollier*, is derived from *mollitiēs* (*mollis*, tender). —— **imposuērunt**, 3d pers. plur. perf. ind. act. of *impōnō*; agrees with a pron. understood, referring to the Germans. —— **quae**, nom. plur. f. (*quī, quae, quod*); refers to *mulierēs*, but is subject-nom. of *implōrābant*. —— **in**, prep., here with the acc. —— **proelium**, acc. sing.; obj. of the prep. *in*.

LINE 18. **proficīscentēs**, acc. plur. of the pres. participle of the deponent verb *proficīscor*, 3; agrees with *eōs* understood, the direct obj. of *implōrābant*. —— **passīs**, perf. pass. participle of *pandō, -ere, pandī, passum*, 3; abl. absolute with *manibus*. Observe that, so far as the form is concerned, the participle might be that of *patior*,

19 flentēs	implōrābant,	nē	sē		in	were going forth to battle, implored them not to deliver them over into slavery to the Romans.
weeping	*they besought,*	*that not*	*themselves*		*into*	
20 servitūtem	Rōmānīs		trāderent.			
slavery	*to the Romans*		*they might be delivered.*			

1 LII. Caesar		singulīs	legiōnibus		singulōs	LII. Caesar placed in command of each legion a lieutenant and a questor, that every one might have them as witnesses of his valor;
Caesar		*over single*	*legions*		*single*	
2 lēgātōs	et	quaestōrem	praefēcit,	utī	eōs	
lieutenants	*and*	*a quaestor*	*placed,*	*that*	*them*	
3 testēs	suae	quisque	virtūtis		habēret;	
as witnesses	*of his,*	*each one,*	*valor,*		*might have;*	

-*ī, passus*, 3; but the meaning does not meet the sense required by the context. Dr. Anthon reads *crīnibus* instead of *manibus*, giving a good sense — *with disheveled hair* — but a reading without sufficient MS.-authority. —— **manibus**, abl. plur. of *manus, -ūs*, f.; absolute with the perf. pass. participle.

LINE 19. **flentēs**, nom. plur. f. of the pres. participle *flēns* of *fleō, flēre, flēvī, flētum*, 2; agrees with the rel. pron. *quae*. —— **implōrābant**, 3d pers. plur. imperf. ind. act. of *implōrō*, 1; agrees with the subject-nom. *quae*. —— **nē**, adv. —— **sē**, acc. plur. of *suī*; direct obj. of *trāderent*; refers to the women. —— **in**, prep., here with the acc.

LINE 20. **servitūtem**, acc. sing. of *servitūs, -ūtis*, f. (*servus*); direct obj. of the prep. *in*. —— **Rōmānīs**, dat. plur. of *Rōmānī, -ōrum*, m.; indirect object. —— **trāderent**, 3d pers. plur. imperf. subjunctive of *trādō*, 3 (trāns + dō); subjunctive *of purpose* after *nē*. Consult A. & G. 331; B. 200, (*b*), and REM. 2; G. 546, and 2; H. 498, I.

LINE 1. **Caesar, -aris**, m.; subject-nom. of *praefēcit*. —— **singulīs**, dat. plur. f. of the distributive num. adj. *singulī, -ae, -a* (sing. is rare and post classic); an attributive of *legiōnibus*. —— **legiōnibus**, dat. plur. of *legiō, -ōnis*, f.; dat. after *prae* in the compound *praefēcit*. Consult A. & G. 228, and NOTE, end; B. 143; G. 347, and 3; H. 386, and 1. A roman legion of soldiers consisted of ten cohorts. See any encyclopedia. —— **singulōs**, acc. plur. of *singulī*; an attributive of *lēgātōs*.

LINE 2. **lēgātōs**, acc. plur. of *lēgātus, -ī*, m.; direct obj. of *praefēcit*. See preceding grammatical references. —— **et**, cop. conj —— **quaestōrem**, acc. sing. of *quaestor, -ōris*, m.; connected by *et* with *lēgātōs*, and in the same construction. *quaestor* usually = a Roman *magistrate* in charge of the finances; here a paymaster of Caesar's forces, but in an emergency appointed to act as *lēgātus*. —— **praefēcit**, 3d pers. sing. perf. ind. act. of *praefīciō*, 3 (prae + facere); agrees with the subject *Caesar* expressed. —— **utī**, telic conj. —— **eōs**, acc. plur. of *is, ea, id*; used as a personal pron. of the 3d pers.; here = *lēgātōs et quaestōrem*; direct obj. of *habēret*.

LINE 3. **testēs**, acc. plur. (*testis, -is*, m. and f.); appositive with *eōs*. —— **suae**, gen. sing. f. (*suus, -a, -um*); an attributive of *virtūtis*. —— **quisque**, indef. pron., universal (*quisque, quaeque, quidque*); subj. of *habēret*. —— **virtūtis**, gen. sing. of *virtūs, -tūtis*, f. (*vir*); limits *testēs*. —— **habēret**, 3d pers. sing. imperf. subjunctive act. of *habeō*, 2; agrees with *quisque*; subjunctive *of purpose* after *utī*.

while he personally began the battle from his right wing, as he had observed that the division of the enemy opposite to it was the weakest. Accordingly, our troops, on the signal being given, attacked the enemy fiercely; but the ene-	ipse *he himself* partem *part* animadverterat, *he had perceived,* nostrī *our men* datō *being given,*	ā *from* minimē *least* ācriter *spiritedly* impetum *an attack*	dextrō *the right* fīrmam *strong* proelium *the battle* in *against* fēcērunt, *made*	cornū, *wing,* hostium *of the enemy* commīsit. *began.* hostēs *the enemy,* itaque *so and,*	quod *because* esse *to be,* Ita *Thus* sīgnō *the signal* hostēs *the enemy*	eam 4 *that* 5 6 7 8

LINE 4. **ipse,** intensive pron. (*ipse, -sa, -sum*); refers to Caesar; is subject-nom. of *commīsit*. —— **ā,** prep. with the abl. See note on *ā,* l. 7, Chap. I. —— **dextrō,** abl. sing. n. of the adj. *dexter, -tra, -trum,* or *-tera, -terum;* an attributive of *cornū.* —— **cornū,** abl. sing. of *cornū, -ūs,* n.; obj. of the prep. *ā.* Observe that *cornū* = lit. *a horn;* that, in imitation of the GK. κέρας, the side of an army in form of a horn, or as a symbol of strength in the bullock, is denoted by *cornū;* but that the proper Roman figure to indicate the notion is derived from the *wing* (*āla*) of the bird of prey; and that the figure *wing* of an army has come down to us as the fittest survival. —— **quod,** conj. = *because.* —— **eam,** acc. sing. f. of the dem. pron. *is, ea, id;* an attributive of *partem.*

LINE 5. **partem,** acc. sing. of *pars, partis,* f.; subject-acc. of *esse.* Observe that the phrase *eam partem* designates the left wing of the Germans. —— **minimē,** adv., superl. degree; comparative *minus;* modifies the adj. *fīrmam.* —— **fīrmam,** acc. sing. f. (*fīrmus, -a, -um*); predicate-adj. after *esse.* —— **hostium,** gen plur. m. and f. (*hostis, -is*); partitive after *fīrmam.* See A. & G. 216, 2; B. 134; G. 370; H. 397, 2. —— **esse,** pres. inf. of *sum;* subject-acc. is *partem.*

LINE 6. **animadverterat,** 3d pers. sing. pluperf. ind. act. of *animadvertō;* agrees with a pron. understood, referring to Caesar. See l. 10, Chap. XIX. —— **proelium,** acc. sing. n. (*proelium, -ī*); direct obj. of *commīsit.* See *proeliīs,* l. 18, Chap. 1. —— **commīsit,** 3d pers. sing. perf. ind. act. of *committō, -ere, -mīsī, -mīssum,* 3 (com + mittere = *to send together*); hence = *to bring together, to join.* —— **Ita,** adv.

LINE 7. **nostrī,** nom. plur. m. of the poss. pron. *noster, -tra, -trum* (*nōs*); used substantively; subj. of *fēcērunt.* —— **ācriter,** adv. (*ācer,* sharp). See *ācriter,* l. 2, Chap. XXVI. —— **in,** prep. with the acc. or abl.; here with the acc. See *in,* l. 1, Chap. I. —— **hostēs,** acc. plur. (*hostis, -is*); obj. of the prep. *in.* —— **sīgnō,** abl. sing. of *sīgnum, -ī,* n.; absolute with *datō.*

LINE 8. **datō,** perf. pass. participle of *dō,* 1; absolute construction with *sīgnō,* denoting *time when.* A. & G. 255; B. 192; G. 409, 410; H. 431. Observe that *sīgnum* is a word of wide meaning, only to be determined by the context; that the signal for battle was usually given by the trumpet. Compare *sīgnum tubā dandum,* Chap. XX, Book 2. —— **impetum,** acc. sing. m. (*impetus, -ūs*); direct obj. of *fēcērunt.* —— **fēcērunt,** 3d pers. plur. perf. ind. act. of *faciō,* 3; agrees with the subject-nom. *nostrī.* —— **itaque** (ita + que) = *et ita.* Observe that *ita* is the correlate of the following conj. *ut.* —— **hostēs,** nom. plur. (*hostis, -is*); subj. of *prōcurrērunt.*

9 repente	celeriterque	prōcurrērunt,	ut	spatium	my ran forward so unexpectedly and swiftly, that no time was given for hurling javelins at them. Throwing aside the javelins, our men fought the battle hand to hand with swords. But the Germans, speedily forming a phalanx, according to their custom received the swords' onsets.
suddenly	*quickly and,*	*ran forward*	*that*	*room*	
10 pīla	in	hostēs	cōniciendī	nōn	
the javelins	*against*	*the enemy*	*of (for) hurling*	*not*	
11 darētur.	Rēiectīs		pīlīs,	comminus	
was given.	*Having thrown away*		*the javelins,*	*hand to hand*	
12 gladiīs	pūgnātum est.	At	Germānī	celeriter	
with swords	*it was fought.*	*But*	*the Germans*	*quickly,*	
13 ex	cōnsuētūdine	suā	phalange	factā	
according to	*custom*	*their*	*a phalanx*	*being made,*	
14 impetūs	gladiōrem	excēpērunt.		Repertī sunt	
the attacks	*of the swords*	*received.*		*Were found*	

LINE 9. **repente,** adv. (adj. *repēns,* sudden, etymology dubious). —— **celeriterque** (celeriter + que). *celeriter,* adv. (*celer,* swift). *que,* enclitic conj.; connects the adverbs. —— **prōcurrērunt,** 3d pers. plur. perf. ind. act. of *prōcurrō, -ere, -currī, -cursum,* 3 (prō + curro) agrees with *hostēs.* —— **ut,** ecbatic conj. —— **spatium,** nom. sing. n.; subj. of *darētur;* a broad word, applicable to either *space* or *time*

LINE 10. **pīla,** acc. plur. of *pīlum, -ī,* n.; direct obj. of the gerund *cōniciendī.* See *pīlīs,* l. 6, Chap. XXV. —— **in,** prep., here with the acc., and = *against.* —— **hostēs,** acc. plur.; obj. of the prep. *in.* —— **cōniciendī,** gen. of the gerund of *cōniciō, -ere, -iēcī, -iectum,* 3 (con + iacere) as gen. it limits *spatium.* A. & G. 298; B. 184, REM. 4, I, (*a*); G. 428; H 542, I. —— **nōn,** negative particle; in its normal position, immediately before the verb.

LINE 11. **darētur,** 3d pers. sing. imperf. subjunctive pass. of *dō,* 1; agrees with its subj. *spatium:* subjunctive of *result* after *ut,* referring to *ita.* —— **Rēiectīs,** abl. plur. n. of the perf. pass. participle *rēiectus, -a, -um* of *rēiciō,* 3; absolute with *pīlīs.* —— **pīlīs,** abl. plur. n. (*pīlum, -ī*); absolute with the perf. pass. participle; the phrase denotes *time when.* See *pīla,* preceding line. —— **comminus,** adv. (com + manus) = lit. *with hands,* i.e. *hand to hand* contest; oppositive to *ēminus,* away from the hand, i.e. *not hand to hand.*

LINE 12. **gladiīs,** abl. plur. of *gladius, -ī,* m.; abl. *of means.* Synonyms: see *gladiī*, l. 8, Chap. XXV. —— **pūgnātum est,** 3d pers. sing. perf. ind. pass. of *pūgnō,* 1; here a verb of complete predication. See l. 2, Chap. XXVI. —— **At,** conj.; expresses a contrast. —— **Germānī, -ōrum,** m.; subject-nom. of *excēpērunt.* —— **celeriter,** adv.; see l. 9, above.

LINE 13. **ex,** prep. with the abl. —— **cōnsuētūdine,** abl. of *cōnsuētūdō, -inis,* f.; obj. of the prep *ex.* —— **suā,** abl. sing. (*suus, -a, -um*); an attributive of *cōnsuētūdine.* —— **phalange,** abl. sing. of *phalanx, -ngis,* f. (GK. φάλαγξ); absolute with *factā.* The German phalanx appears to have been in the form of the Roman *testūdō* or covered column. —— **factā,** perf. pass. participle of *fīō, fierī, factus,* 3; abl. absolute with *phalange,* denoting the *time when.*

LINE 14. **impetūs,** acc. plur. m. (*impetus, -ūs*); direct obj. of *excēpērunt.* —— **gladiōrum,** gen. plur. of *gladius, -iī,* m.; limits, as a gen., *impetūs.* —— **excēpērunt,**

Very many of our soldiers were found, who leaped upon the phalanxes and tore away the shields with their hands and inflicted wounds from above. Although the enemy's line on the left wing was routed and put to flight, the	complūrēs *very many* īnsilīrent *leaped* et *and* hostium *the enemy's* atque *and*	nostrī *our* et *and* dēsuper *from above* aciēs *line* in *into*	mīlitēs, *soldiers,* scūta *the shields* vulnerārent. *wounded* ā *on* fugam *flight*	quī *who* manibus *with (their)* (the enemy). sinistrō *the left* conversa *turned*	in *on* hands cornū *wing* esset, *was,*	phalangas *the phalanxes* revellerent *pulled away* Cum Though pulsa *routed* ā dextrō *on the right*	15 16 17 18 19

3d pers. plur. perf. ind. act. of *excipiō, -ere, -cēpī, -ceptum*, 3 (ex + capere) = lit. *to take out;* then, *to take* somewhat from some position to one's self; hence, *to receive*. —— **Repertī sunt**, 3d pers. plur. perf. ind. pass. of *reperiō, -īre, rep(p)erī, repertum*, 4; agrees with the subject-nom. *mīlitēs*.

LINE 15. **complūrēs**, nom. plur. m. of the adj. *complūrēs, -a* (con + plus, *more*); an attributive of *mīlitēs*. —— **nostrī**, nom. plur. m. of the poss. personal pron. *noster, -tra, -trum;* also an attributive of *mīlitēs*. —— **mīlitēs**, nom. plur. m. (*miles, -itis*); subj. of *repertī sunt*. Observe that we have cases in agreement instead of the partitive gen., i.e. the construction of the text instead of *complūrēs nostrūm mīlitum*. —— **quī**, nom. plur. m. (*quī, quae, quod*); refers to *mīlitēs;* is subject-nom. of *īnsilīrent*. —— **in**, prep. with the acc. or abl.; here repeated after a compound containing it. —— **phalangas**, Greek acc. plur. f. of *phalanx, -ngis;* obj. of the prep. *in*. Consult A. & G. 64; B. 248; G. 66, NOTE 4; H. 68, and 1, (1). Observe that the vowel of the Greek acc. plur. *-as* is short, while the Latin ending *-ēs* is long. See note on *phalangem*, l. 7, Chap. XXV.

LINE 16. **īnsilīrent**, 3d pers. plur. imperf. subjunctive of *īnsiliō, -īre, -uī*, 4 (in + saliō); agrees with the subject-nom. *quī;* subjunctive *of characteristic* — a relative clause after an indefinite expression. See A. & G. 320, *a*, NOTE; B. 201, REM. I, (*e*); G. 631, and 2; H. 503, I. —— **et**, cop. conj. —— **scūta**, acc. plur. n. (*scūtum, -ī*); direct object. Synonyms: see *scūtīs*, l. 11, Chap. XXV. —— **manibus**, abl. plur. f. (*manus, -ūs*); means. —— **revellerent**, 3d pers. plur. imperf. subjunctive of *revellō, -ere, -vellī, -vul(vol)sum*, 3 (re + vellō); connected by *et* with *īnsilīrent*, and in the same grammatical construction.

LINE 17. **et**, conj. —— **dēsuper**, adv. (dē + super). —— **vulnerārent**, 3d pers. plur. imperf. subjunctive of *vulnerō*, 1 (*vulnus*); sometimes written *volnerō;* connected by *et* with the immediately preceding verb, and in the same construction. Supply *hostēs* as direct obj. —— **Cum**, concessive conj. = *though*.

LINE 18. **hostium**, gen. plur: m. and f. (*hostis, -is*); limits *aciēs*. —— **aciēs**, nom. sing. f.; subj. of *pulsa* (*esset*). —— **ā** (*ab*), prep. with the abl. —— **sinistrō**, abl. sing. n. of the adj. *sinister, -tra, -trum;* comparative *sinisterior;* superl. *sinistimus;* an attributive of *cornū*. —— **cornū**, abl. sing. n.; see *cornū*, l. 4, above; obj. of the prep. *ā*. —— **pulsa**, nom. sing. f. of the participle *pulsus, -a, -um* of *pellō, -ere, pepulī, pulsum*, 3; predicate after *esset*, to be supplied.

LINE 19. **atque**, conj. (ad + que) = *and also*. —— **in**, prep., here with the acc. —— **fugam**, acc. sing. f. (*fuga, -ae*); obj. of the prep. *in*. —— **conversa**, nom. sing.

20 cornū	vehementer	multitūdine		suōrum
wing	*vigorously*	*with the multitude*		*of their (men)*
21 nostram	aciem	premēbant.	Id	cum
our	*line*	*they pressed.*	*This*	*when*
22 animadvertisset	Pūblius	Crassus	adulēscēns,	
had noticed	*Publius*	*Crassus,*	*a young man,*	
23 quī	equitātuī	praeërat,	quod	expedītior
who	*the cavalry*	*was over,*	*because*	*more disengaged*
24 erat	quam	eī, quī	inter aciem	versābantur,
was he	*than*	*those who*	*amid the battle*	*were occupied,*

enemy pressed our line furiously on the right wing with their vast numbers. On observing this, Pūblius Crassus, a young man, who was in command of the cavalry, as he was "freer to act" than those who were in the midst of the

f. of the participle *conversus, -a, -um* of *convertō*, 3; predicate after *esset*. —— **esset**, 3d pers. sing. imperf. subjunctive of *sum, esse, fuī*; agrees with the subject-nom. *aciēs*; subjunctive after *cum* concessive. A. & G. 326; B. 210; G. 587; H. 515, III. —— **ā dextrō cornū**, see the phrase explained, l. 4, above. The reference is to Caesar's right wing.

LINE 20. **vehementer**, adv. (*vehemēns*, furious). —— **multitūdine**, abl. of *multitūdō, -inis*, f. (*multus*); *means*. —— **suōrum**, gen. plur. of the poss. adj. pron. *suus, -a, -um*; used substantively; or supply *mīlitum*; limits *multitūdine*.

LINE 21. **nostram**, acc. sing. f. (*noster, -tra, -trum*); an attributive of *aciem*. —— **aciem**, acc. sing. of *aciēs, -ēī*, f.; direct obj. See l. 12, Chap. XXII. ——.**premēbant**, 3d pers. plur. imperf. ind. act. of *premō*, 3; agrees with *hostēs* understood. —— **Id**, acc. sing. n. (*is, ea, id*); direct obj.; refers to the Germans' onset on Caesar's right wing. —— **cum**, conj., temporal.

LINE 22. **animadvertisset**, 3d pers. sing. pluperf. subjunctive act. of *animadvertō, -ere, -tī, -sum*, 3 (see l. 6, above); subjunctive after *cum, temporal* or *historical*. A. & G. 325; B. 222; G. 585; H. 521, II, 2. —— **Pūblius**, *praenōmen*; abbreviated *P*. —— **Crassus, -ī**, m., the *cōgnōmen* or family name of the *gēns Licinia*. Observe that *Publius Crassus* as a complex proper noun is in apposition with *adulēscēns*. —— **adulēscēns, -ntis**, subst.; subj. of *animadvertisset*. Observe that the *adu(o)lēscēns*, m. and f. = *a young person* between fifteen and forty years of age. The Crassus of the text is thus designated to distinguish him from his father M. Licinius Crassus, the triumvir.

LINE 23. **quī**, nom. sing. m.; subj. of *praeërat*. —— **equitātuī**, dat. sing. m. (*equitātus, -ūs*); dat. after *prae* in the compound — in *praeërat*. See grammatical references to *legiōnibus*, l. 1, above. Some copies have here *equītātīī*, an archaic form of the dat. —— **praeërat**, 3d pers. sing. imperf. ind. of *praesum, -esse, -fuī*; agrees with the subject-nom. *quī*. —— **quod**, conj. = *because*. —— **expedītior**, comparative degree of the participle *expedītus* of *expediō*, 4 (ex + pēs); predicate-adj. after *erat*. See *expedītius*, l. 9, Chap. VI. Observe that Crassus was *more disengaged*, because he was a cavalry officer, and was not engaged in the infantry charge.

LINE 24. **erat**, 3d pers. sing. imperf. ind. of *sum*; agrees with a pron., referring to Crassus. —— **quam**, conj. —— **eī**, nom. plur. m. (*is, ea, id*); used as a personal pron. of the 3d pers.; subject-nom. of *erant* understood. —— **quī**, nom. plur. m. (*quī, quae, quod*); subj. of *versābantur*. —— **inter**, adv. or prep.; here prep. with the acc.

fight, sent the third line to aid our men who were in distress.	tertiam *the third*	aciem *line,*	labōrantibus *to the struggling*	nostrīs *ours,*	subsidiō 25 *for assistance,*
	mīsit. *he sent.*				26
LIII. In this way, the battle was re-established, and all the enemy fled, and they did not cease to flee until they reached the Rhine river, a-	LIII.	Ita *Thus*	proelium *the battle*	restitūtum est *restored was,*	atque 1 *and*
	omnēs *all*	hostēs *the enemy*	terga *(their) backs*	vertērunt *turned,*	neque 2 *not and,*
	prius *before*	fugere *to flee*	dēstitērunt, *they stopped*	quam ad *that to*	flūmen 3 *the river*

—— **aciem**, acc. sing. f. (*aciēs, -ēī*); obj. of the prep. *inter*. Observe that *inter aciem* here = *inter pūgnam*. —— **versābantur**, 3d pers. plur. imperf. ind. of middle form *versor, -ārī, -atus*, 1; agrees with the subj. *quī*. But see *versō*, Andrew's Lex. II.

LINE 25. **tertiam**, acc. sing. f. of the ord. num. adj. *tertius, -a, -um;* an attributive of *aciem*. —— **aciem**, acc. sing. f. (*aciēs, -ēī*); direct obj. of *mīsit*. Observe that the third line constituted the military reserve. —— **labōrantibus**, dat. plur. m. of the pres. participle *labōrāns, -ntis* of *labōrō*, 1 (*labor*); dat. *of the object to which*. Observe that this participle is attributive, modifying *mīlitibus* understood; that *nostrīs* has a similar function, i.e. modifies *mīlitibus* understood; and that the rigidly literal translation is: *to our toiling soldiers*. Such construction is best rendered by a relative and finite verb. —— **nostrīs**, dat. plur. m. of the poss. adj. pron. *noster, -tra, -trum*. —— **subsidiō**, dat. sing. of *subsidium, -ī*, n.; dat. *of the end for which* — predicative. Consult A. & G. 233, *a*; B. 147; G. 356; H. 390, II.

LINE 26. **mīsit**, 3d pers. sing. perf. ind. act. of *mittō, -ere, mīsī, missum*, 3; agrees with a pron. implied in the ending as subject-nom., referring to Crassus.

LINE 1. **Ita** (radical *i*, whence *is* + ta), adv. = *thus*, i.e. because the hard-pressed were reinforced. —— **proelium**, nom. sing. n.; subject of *restitūtum est*. —— **restitūtum est**, 3d pers. sing. perf. ind. pass. of *restituō*, 3 (re + statuere, *to set up again*). —— **atque** (ad + que), conj. See l. 10, Chap. I.

LINE 2. **omnēs**, nom. plur. m. (*omnis, -e*); an attributive of *hostēs*. —— **hostēs**, nom. plur. m. and f. (*hostis, -is*); subj. of *vertērunt*. —— **terga**, acc. plur. n. (*tergum, -ī*); direct obj. —— **vertērunt**, 3d pers. plur. perf. ind. act. of *vertō*, 3; agrees with the subject-nom. *hostēs*. —— **neque** (nē + que), conjunctive adv.; here = *et nōn*.

LINE 3. **prius**, adv. (adj. *prior*, former); separated from the following *quam* by tmēsis. A. & G. 385; B. 310, 4, (*d*); G. 726; H. 636, V, 3. —— **fugere**, pres. inf. act. of *fugiō*, 3; complementary; depends on *dēstitērunt*. —— **dēstitērunt**, 3d pers. plur. perf. ind. act. of *dēsistō, -ere, -stitī, -stitum*, 3; connected by *neque* with *vertērunt*, and in the same construction. —— **quam**, conj. = *than*. As part of *priusquam*, its force will appear if we translate the former part of the compound *sooner*. —— **ad**, prep. with the acc. —— **flūmen**, acc. sing. n. (*flūmen, -inis*); obj. of the prep. *ad*.

4 Rhēnum	mīlia	passuum	ex	eō	locō	circiter
Rhine	*thousands*	*of paces*	*from*	*that*	*place*	*about*
5 quīnque	pervēnērunt.		Ibi	perpaucī		aut
five	*they arrived.*		*There*	*very few*		*either*
6 vīribus	cōnfīsī	trānāre		contendērunt,		aut
on strength	*relying*	*to swim over*		*they hastened,*		*or*
7 lintribus	inventīs		sibi			salūtem
boats	*having lighted on*		*for themselves*			*safety*
8 reppererunt.	In		hīs	fuit	Ariovistus,	quī
they found.	*Among*		*them*	*was*	*Ariovistus,*	*who,*

bout five miles from the place of conflict. At the river, a very few, relying on their strength, either tried to swim across, or lighting on some skiffs found safety. Among them was Ariovistus who, having

LINE 4. **Rhēnum**, acc. sing. m. (*Rhēnus, -ī*); an appositive. —— **mīlia**, acc. plur. — *extent of space*. A. & G. 257; B. 153; G. 335; H. 379. —— **passuum**, gen. plur. m. (*passus, -ūs*); partitive after *mīlia*. A. & G. 216, 2; B. 134; G. 370; H. 397, 2. —— **ex**, prep. with the abl. —— **eō**, abl. sing. m. (*is, ea, id*); an attributive of *locō*. —— **locō**, abl. of *locus, -ī,* m.; obj. of the prep. *ex*. See *locī*, l. 10, Chap. II. —— **circiter**, adv.; modifies *quīnque*.

LINE 5. **quīnque**, card. num. adj.; an attributive of *mīlia*. There is MS.-authority for the reading *quīnquāgintā*. But the Greek paraphrase reads : τετταράκοντα στάδια — 24,000 Greek feet. *quīnque* is, therefore, the better lection. —— **pervēnērunt**, 3d pers. plur. perf. ind. act. of *perveniō*, 4; agrees with a pron. implied in the ending, referring to the enemy. —— **Ibi**, adv. (radical *i*, whence *is* + bi) = lit. in *that* place. —— **perpaucī, -ae, -a** (per, *intensive* + paucus); used substantively; subj. of *contendērunt*. —— **aut** . . . **aut**, see *aut*, l. 19, Chap. I.

LINE 6. **vīribus**, dat. or abl. plur. of *vīs, vīs,* f.; plur. *vīrēs,* gen. *vīrium;* depends on *cōnfīsī;* might be taken as dat. of indirect obj., or abl. *locative,* in a figurative sense. A. & G. 254, *b*; B. 142, REM. 3; G. 346, REM. 2, and NOTE 2, and 401, NOTE 6; H. 425, II. 1, 1), NOTE. —— **cōnfīsī**, nom. plur. m. of the perf. participle of *cōnfīdō, -ere, -fīsus,* 3; neuter pass. or semi-deponent; as a participle it agrees with *perpaucī,* used as a noun. —— **trānāre**, pres. inf. act. of *trānō* (*trānsnō*), 1 (trāns + nō); complementary inf. —— **contendērunt**, 3d pers. plur. perf. ind. act. of *contendō,* 3; agrees with the subj. *perpaucī*. See *contendunt*, l. 18, Chap. I. —— **aut**, see *aut*, preceding line.

LINE 7. **lintribus**, abl. plur. of *linter, lintris,* m. and f. — generally f.; absolute with *inventīs*. —— **inventīs**, abl. plur. of the perf. pass. participle *inventus, -a, -um* of *inveniō,* 4; absolute with *lintribus,* denoting *time when*. —— **sibi**, dat. plur. of the reflexive pron. *suī;* dat. *of reference* or *advantage*. —— **salūtem**, acc. sing. f. (*salūs, -ūtis*); direct object.

LINE 8. **reppererunt**, 3d pers. plur. perf. ind. act. of *reperiō, -īre, repperī* or *repperī, repertum,* 4; connected by the conj. *aut* with *contendērunt,* and has the same subj. —— **In**, prep., here with the abl., and = *among;* but see *in*, l. 1, Chap. I. —— **hīs**, abl. plur. m. of the dem. pron. *hic, haec, hōc;* used as a personal pron. of the 3d pers.; obj. of the prep. *in*. —— **fuit**, 3d pers. sing. perf. ind. of *sum, esse,* fut. participle *futūrus;* agrees with the subject-nom. *Ariovistus*. —— **Ariovistus, -ī,** m.; king of the Germans; died, soon after this battle, in Germany, either from wounds or chagrin at his defeat. See Chap. XXIX, Book 5. —— **quī**, rel. pron.; refers to Ariovistus; subj. of *profūgit*.

found a skiff tied to the bank, escaped in it; our men pursued with cavalry all the rest, and slew them. Ariovistus had two wives, one a Suevan by nation, whom he had brought with him from home; the other a Norican, a sister of	nāviculam *a canoe*	dēligātam *being fastened*	ad *to*	rīpam *the bank*	nactus *having found,*	9
	eā *with this*	profūgit; *he escaped;*	reliquōs *the rest*	omnēs *all*	equitātū *with cavalry*	10
	cōnsecūtī *having pursued*	nostrī *our men*	interfēcērunt. *put to death.*		Duae *Two*	11
	fuērunt *were*	Ariovistī *Ariovistus'*	uxōrēs, *wives,*	ūna *one*	Suēva *a Suevan*	12
	nātiōne, *in nation,*	quam *whom*	domō *from home*	sēcum *himself with,*	dūxerat, *he had led,*	13

LINE 9. nāviculam, acc. sing. of *nāvicula, -ae,* f. (*nāvis*); diminutive = *a canoe,* or *skiff;* direct obj. of the deponent participle *nactus.* —— dēligātam, acc. sing. f. of the perf. pass. participle of *dēligō,* 1; agrees with *nāviculam,* but is essentially predicative = *which was fastened.* —— ad, prep. with the acc. —— rīpam, acc. sing. f. (*rīpa, -ae*); obj. of the prep. *ad.* —— nactus, perf. participle of the deponent *nancīscor, -ī, nactus* or *nanctus,* 3; agrees with the subj. of the relative clause.

LINE 10. eā, abl. sing. f. (*is, ea, id*); used as a pron. of the 3d pers., referring to *nāviculum;* or supply *nāviculā;* abl. *of means.* —— profūgit, 3d pers. sing. perf. ind. act. of *profugiō, -ere, -fūgī,* 3; agrees with the subj. *quī.* —— reliquōs, acc. plur. m. of the adj. *reliquus, -a, -um;* used substantively; direct obj. of *cōnsecūtī.* —— omnēs, acc. plur. m. (*omnis, -e*); an attributive of *reliquōs.* —— equitātū, abl. sing. m. (*equitātus, -ūs*); *accompaniment* without *cum,* which is sometimes omitted.

LINE 11. cōnsecūtī, nom. plur. m. of the deponent participle *cōnsecūtus, -a, -um* of *cōnsequor, -uī, -cūtus,* 3; agrees with the subj. *nostrī.* —— nostrī, nom. plur. m. of the personal poss. pron. *noster, -tra, -trum;* subj. of *interfēcērunt.* —— interfēcērunt, 3d pers. plur. perf. ind. of *interficiō,* 3; agrees with *nostrī* as subject; supply *eōs,* i.e. *reliquōs,* as direct object. —— Duae, nom. plur. of the num. adj. *duo, duae, duo;* compare GK. δύο. For declension, see A. & G. 94, *b;* B. 64, REM. 2; G. 73, REM., and 95; H. 175. *duae* is an attributive of *uxōrēs.*

LINE 12. fuērunt, 3d pers. plur. perf. ind. of *sum, esse, fuī;* agrees with the subject-nom. *uxōrēs.* —— Ariovistī, gen. sing. (*Ariovistus, -ī*); predicate-gen. A. & G. 214, *c, d;* B. 133; G. 366; H. 401, 402. —— uxōrēs, nom. plur. of *uxor, -ōris,* f.; subject-nom. of *fuērunt.* —— ūna, nom. sing. f. (*ūnus, -a, -um*); an attributive of *uxor,* to be supplied; which latter is subject of *fuit* understood. —— Suēva, nom. sing. f. of the adj. *Suēvus, -a, -um;* predicate after *fuit* understood.

LINE 13. nātiōne, abl. *of specification* (*nātiō, -ōnis,* f.). Synonyms: both *gēns* and *nātiō* = *race, nation;* but sometimes the one is used in a more restricted sense than the other; sometimes they are used as precisely similar in meaning. —— quam, acc. sing. f. of the rel. pron. *quī, quae, quod;* refers to *uxor* understood, and is the direct object of *dūxerat.* —— domō, abl. of place *from which* without a prep. A. & G. 258, 2, *a;* B. 175; G. 390, 2; H. 412, II, 1. —— sēcum (sē + cum), *sē,* abl. of the reflexive pron. *suī, sibi, sē, sē;* obj. of the enclitic prep. *cum.* —— dūxerat, 3d pers. sing. pluperf. ind. act. of *dūcō, dūcere, dūxī, ductum,* 3; supply in *mātrimōnium,* and see l. 12, Chap. IX; agrees with a pronoun understood, referring to Ariovistus.

[LINES 14-19.]   BOOK I.   387

14	altera	Nōrica,	rēgis	Vocciōnis	soror,	quam	king Voccio, whom, as she had been sent into Gaul by her brother, Ariovistus had married there. Both perished in this flight. Ariovistus had two daughters: one of these was slain; the other was captured. Caius Valerius Procillus, as he was dragged by the guards in the flight, bound
	another	a Norican,	king	Voccio's	sister,	whom	
15	in	Galliā	dūxerat	ā	frātre	mīssam;	
	in	Gaul	he had led	by	brother	having been sent;	
16	utraeque	in	eā	fugā	periērunt.	Duae	
	both	in	this	flight	perished.	Two	
17	fīliae,		hārum	altera	occīsa,	altera	
	daughters (were his),		of these	one (was)	slain,	the other	
18	capta est.	Cāius	Valerius	Procillus,	cum	ā	
	captured was.	Caius	Valerius	Procillus,	when	by	
19	cūstōdibus	in	fugā	trinīs	catēnīs		
	the keepers	in	the flight	with a triple	chain		

LINE 14. altera, nom. sing. f. of *alter, -tera, -terum* = here *secunda*; an attributive of *uxor*, to be supplied. —— Nōrica, nom. sing. f. of the adj. *Nōricus, -a, -um*; predicate after *fuit* understood. —— rēgis, gen. sing. m. (*rēx, rēgis*); limits *soror*. —— Vocciōnis, gen. sing. m. (*Vocciō, -ōnis*); an appositive. —— soror, nom. sing. f. (*soror, -ōris*); an appositive with *altera uxor*. —— quam, f., rel. pron. (*quī, quae, quod*); refers to *soror*; but is the direct obj. of *dūxerat*.

LINE 15. in, prep., here with the abl. —— Galliā, abl.; obj. of the prep. *in*. —— dūxerat, see *dūxerat*, l. 13. —— ā (*ab*), prep. with the abl. —— frātre, abl. sing. of *frāter, frātris*, m.; obj. of the prep. *ā*; abl. *of the agent* after *missam*. —— missam, acc. sing. f. of the perf. pass. participle of *mittō*, 3; agrees in gender, number and case with *quam*.

LINE 16. utraeque, nom. plur. f. of the adj. pron. *uterque, utraque, utrumque*; subj. of *periērunt*. —— in, prep. with the abl. —— eā, abl. sing. f. (*is, ea, id*); an attributive of *fugā*. —— fugā, abl.; obj. of the prep. *in*. —— periērunt, 3d pers. plur. perf. ind. act. of *pereō, -īre, -īvī (-iī), -itum*; agrees with *utraeque*. For syncopation, see A. & G. 128, 2; B. 251; G. 131, 1; H. 235. —— Duae, nom. plur. f. (*duo, duae, duo*); an attributive of *fīliae*.

LINE 17. fīliae, nom. plur. f. of *fīlia, -ae*; subj. of *fuērunt*, to be supplied; supply also *Ariovistī* as prepositional gen. —— hārum, gen. plur. f. (*hīc, haec, hōc*); used substantively; partitive after *altera*; refers to the daughters; some regard *hārum* as referring to the wives, and put the comma after *hārum* instead of *fīliae*; *hārum* might then be the predicate-gen. —— altera, nom. sing. f. (*alter, -tera, -terum*); subj. of *occīsa* (*est*). —— occīsa (est), 3d pers. sing. perf. ind. pass. of *occīdō*, 3. See l. 21, Chap. VII. —— altera, observe the reciprocal use of the pronouns: *the one, the other*; subj. of *capta est*.

LINE 18. capta est, 3d pers. sing. perf. ind. pass. of *capiō*, 3. —— Cāius, -ī, m.; *praenōmen*. —— Valerius, *nōmen*. —— Procillus, *cōgnōmen*. *Cāius Valerius Procillus*, as a complex proper noun, is subject-nom. of *incidit*, l. 22, below. See l. 14, Chap. XLVII. —— cum, conj., temporal. —— ā (*ab*), prep. with the abl.

LINE 19. cūstōdibus, abl. plur. of *custōs, -ōdis*, m. and f.; obj. of the prep. *ā*; abl. *of the agent*. A. & G. 246; B. 166; G. 401 · H. 415, I. —— in, prep., here with

with a triple chain, fell in with Caesar himself who was pursuing the enemy with cavalry. And this incident indeed afforded Caesar no less pleasure than the victory itself; because he saw the most worthy man in	vinctus *being bound* Caesarem *Caesar* incidit. *fell.* minōrem *less* attulit, *brought,*	traherētur, *he was being dragged,* hostēs *the enemy,* Quae *Which* quam *than* quod *because*	in *on* equitātū *with cavalry* quidem *indeed* ipsa *the very* hominem *a man*	ipsum 20 *the very* persequentem 21 *pursuing,* rēs Caesarī nōn 22 *thing to Caesar not* victōria voluptātem 23 *victory pleasure* honestissimum 24 *the most respected*

the abl. —— fugā, abl. sing.; obj. of the prep. *in*. —— trīnīs, abl. plur. f. of the distributive num. adj. *trīnī, -ae, -a;* an attributive of *catēnīs*. —— catēnīs, abl. plur. of *catēna, -ae*, f.; abl. *of manner;* observe that *catēnīs*, though plur. in form, is sing. in meaning; hence the distributive *trīnīs* rather than *tribus;* compare *bīna castra* = *two camps.*

LINE 20. **vinctus**, nom. sing. m. of the perf. pass. participle from *vinciō, -īre, vinxī, vinctum,* 4; as a participle it agrees with a pron. understood, the subject-nom. of *traherētur*. —— **traherētur**, 3d pers. sing. imperf. subjunctive pass. of *traho, -ere, trāxī, tractum,* 3; agrees with a pron. understood, referring to *Procillus;* subjunctive after *cum* temporal. A. & G. 325; B. 222; G. 585; H. 521, II, 2. —— **in**, prep. with the acc. —— **ipsum**, acc. sing. m. of the intensive pron. *ipse, -sa, -sum;* belongs to *Caesarem*, and adds emphasis.

LINE 21. **Caesarem**, acc. sing. m. (*Caesar, -aris*); obj. of the prep. *in*. —— **hostēs**, acc. plur. m. and f. (*hostis, -is*); direct obj. of the participle *persequentem*. —— **equitātū**, abl. sing. after *cum* omitted. See l. 10, above. —— **persequentem**, acc. sing. m. of the pres. participle *persequēns, -ntis* of *persequor,* 3, deponent; deponents have the participles of both voices; as a participle it agrees with *Caesarem.*

LINE 22. **incidit**, 3d pers. sing. perf. ind. act. of *incidō, -ere, -cidī* (in + cadere, *to fall*); not to be confounded with *incīdō* (in + caedere, *to cut*); agrees with the subject-nom. C. V. Procillus. —— **Quae**, nom. sing. f. (*quī, quae, quod*); used adjectively; an attributive of *rēs*. But see A. & G. 180, *f;* B. 129, REM. 9; G. 610; H. 453. —— **quidem**, adv.; usually puts emphasis on the word before it; here its proper place is after *rēs;* but is attracted to *quae*, because the initial consonants are cognate; similar words in Latin like to be near each other. —— **rēs**, nom. sing. f. (*rēs, reī*): subj. of *attulit*. —— **Caesarī**, dat. m. (*Caesar, -aris*); dat. of the indirect obj. after *a(d)tulit*. A. & G. 228, and NOTE 1; B. 143; G. 347; H. 386. —— **nōn**, negative particle; modifies the adj. *minōrem*.

LINE 23. **minōrem**, acc. sing. f. of the comparative adj. *minor, -ōris;* an attributive of *voluptātem;* positive *parvus;* superl. *minimus*. —— **quam**, conj. = *than*. —— **ipsa**, nom. sing. f. (*ipse, -sa, -sum*); belongs to *victōria*. —— **victōria**, nom. sing. f.; subj. of *attulit* understood. —— **voluptātem**, acc. sing. of *voluptās, -tātis,* f. (*volō* through *volupe*); direct object.

LINE 24. **at(d)tulit**, 3d pers. sing. perf. ind. act. of *a(d)ferō, -ferre, attulī, allātum;* agrees with the subject-nom. *rēs*. —— **quod**, conj. = *because*. —— **hominem**,

25 prōvinciae	Galliae,	suum	familiārem	et
of the province	*of Gaul,*	*his own*	*familiar friend*	*and*
26 hospitem,	ēreptum	ē	manibus	hostium
guest,	*having been rescued*	*from*	*the hands*	*of the enemy*
27 sibi	restitūtum	vidēbat;	neque	ēius
to himself	*to have been restored*	*he saw;*	*not and,*	*by his*
28 calamitāte	dē	tantā	voluptāte et	grātulātiōne
ruin	*from*	*so great*	*pleasure and*	*rejoicing*
29 quidquam	fortūna	dēminuerat.	Is	sē
anything	*fortune*	*had lessened.*	*He,*	*himself*

the province of Gaul, his own friend and guest, snatched from the hands of the enemy, and restored to him; and that fortune had not, by his destruction, diminished aught from his great pleasure and joy. Procillus said

acc. sing. of *homō, -inis,* m. and f.; subject-acc. of *restitūtum (esse),* l. 27, below. —— honestissimum, acc. sing. m. of the superlative degree; positive *honestus;* comparative *honestior;* an attributive of *hominem.*

LINE 25. prŏvinciae, gen. sing. f. (*prŏvincia, -ae*); limits *hominem.* —— Galliae, gen. sing. of *Gallia, -ae,* f.; limits *prōvinciae.* —— suum, acc. sing. m.; refers to Caesar; an attributive of *familiārem,* used as noun. —— familiārem, acc. sing. m. of the adj. *familiāris, -e,* used as subst.; an appositive with *hominem.* —— et, cop. conj.

LINE 26. hospitem, acc. sing. m. or f. of *hospĕs, -itis;* connected by *et* with *familiārem,* and in the same construction. —— ēreptum, acc. sing. m. of the perf. pass. participle *ēreptus, -a, -um* of the verb *ēripiō,* 3; as a participle it agrees with *hominem.* —— ē, prep. with the abl. —— manibus, abl. plur. of *manus, -ūs,* f.; obj. of the prep. *ē.* —— hostium, gen. plur. m. and f. (*hostis, -is*); limits *manibus.*

LINE 27. sibi, dat. sing. of the reflexive pron. *suī;* refers to Caesar; indirect obj. of *restitūtum.* —— restitūtum (esse), perf. inf. pass. of *restituō,* 3; its subject-acc. is *hominem,* l. 24, above. Observe that the infinitive-clause is the direct object of *vidēbat.* —— vidēbat, 3d pers. sing. imperf. ind. act. of *video,* 2; observe that the clause *quod . . . vidēbat* is explanatory of, and in apposition with, *res,* l. 22, above. —— neque (nĕ + que) = *et nōn;* containing the negative. —— ēius, gen. sing. m. (*is, ea, id*); used as personal pron. of the 3d pers.; as a gen. it limits *calamitāte.*

LINE 28. calamitāte, abl. sing. of *calamitās, -tātis,* f.; abl. *of means,* or *instrument.* —— dē, prep. with the abl. —— tantā, abl. sing. f. (adj. *tantus, -a, -um*); an attributive of *voluptāte.* —— voluptāte, abl. sing. f. (*voluptās, -tātis*); obj. of the prep. *dē.* —— et, cop. conj.; connects the words as of equal importance. —— grātulātiōne, abl. sing. f. of *grātulātiō, -ōnis,* f. (*grātus* through *gratulor*); connected by *et* with *voluptāte,* and in the same grammatical construction.

LINE 29. quid(c)quam, acc. sing. n. of *quisquam, quaequam, quidquam;* indef. pron.; used chiefly in negative sentences; direct obj. of *dēminuerat.* —— fortūna, nom. sing. f.; subj. of *dēminuerat.* —— dēminuerat, 3d pers. sing. pluperf. ind. act. of *dēminuō,* 3 (dē, *intensive* + minuere, *to lessen*); agrees with the subj. *fortūna.* —— Is, dem. pron., used as a personal pron.; expressed for emphasis; refers to Procillus; subj. of *dīcēbat.* —— sē, abl. sing. of the reflexive pron. *suī;* abl. absolute with the adj. *praesente,* denoting and attendant circumstance; refers to Procillus; in the abl. absolute contrary to the rule that the pron. must denote a different person from that in the leading clause.

that the lots had been consulted thrice in his own presence, whether he should be immediately put to death with fire, or be reserved for another time; that by the favor of the lots he was saved. Marcus Mettius was also found and restored to Caesar.					
	praesente	dē	sē	ter	sortibus 30
	being present,	*with respect*	*to himself*	*thrice*	*by the lots*
	cōnsultum	dīcēbat,	utrum	īgnī	statim 31
	to have been consulted	*said,*	*whether*	*with fire*	*at once*
	necārētur,		an	in aliud	tempus 32
	he should be put to death		*or*	*to another*	*time*
	reservārētur;		sortium	beneficiō	sē esse 33
	he should be reserved;		*by the lots'*	*kindness*	*himself to be*
	incolumem.	Item	Marcus	Mēttius	repertus 34
	unharmed.	*Also*	*Marcus*	*Mettius*	*(was) found*
	et	ad	eum	reductus est.	35
	and	*to*	*him*	*brought back.*	

LINE 30. praesente, abl. sing. m. of the participle *praesēns, -ntis;* really a pres. participle of *praesum;* absolute with *sē.* —— dē, prep. with the abl. —— sē, abl. sing.; refers to Procillus; obj. of the prep. *dē.* —— ter, adv., numeral. —— sortibus, abl. plur. of *sors, sortis,* f.; *means.*

LINE 31. cōnsultum (esse), perf. inf. pass. of *cōnsulō, -ere, -uī, cōnsultum,* 3; used impersonally; supply *ab illīs* as abl. *of the agent.* —— dīcēbat, 3d pers. sing. imperf. ind. act. of *dīcō,* 3; agrees with the pron. *Is* expressed. —— utrum, conj.; introduces an indirect question. —— īgnī, abl. sing. of *īgnis, -is,* m.; *means.* —— statim, adv. (*stāre,* to stand); hence adv. = as one stands — *immediately, at once.*

LINE 32. necārētur, 3d pers. sing. imperf. subjunctive pass. of *necō,* 1 (*nex,* death); agrees with a pron. as subj., referring to Procillus; subjunctive, because an *indirect question.* —— an, conj.; correlate of *utrum.* —— in, prep., here with the acc. —— aliud, acc. sing. n. (*alius, -a, -ud*); an attributive of *tempus.* —— tempus, acc. sing. n.; obj. of the prep. *in.*

LINE 33. reservārētur, 3d pers. sing. imperf. subjunctive pass. of *reservō,* 1; connected by *an* with *necārētur,* and in the same grammatical construction. —— sortium, gen. plur. (*sors, sortis*); limits *beneficiō.* —— beneficiō, abl. sing. n. (*beneficium, -ī*); *cause.* —— sē, acc. sing. of the reflexive pron. *suī;* subject-acc. of *esse.* —— esse, pres. inf. of *sum, fuī, futūrus.*

LINE 34. incolumem, acc. sing. of the adj. *incolumis, -e;* predicate after *esse.* What Procillus said in direct form, was: *Mē* praesente dē *mē* ter sortibus cōnsultum *est,* utrum īgnī statim *necārer,* an in aliud tempus *reservārer;* sortium beneficiō *egō sum incolumis.* —— Item, adv. —— **Marcus Mēttius**, subject-nom. See Chap. XLVII. —— repertus (est), 3d pers. sing. perf. ind. pass. of *reperiō, -īre, rep(p)erī, repertum,* 4.

LINE 35. et, cop. conj. —— ad, prep. with the acc. —— eum, acc. sing. m. of the dem. pron. *is, ea, id;* used as a pers. pron. of the 3d pers.; obj. of the prep. *ad.* —— reductus est, 3d pers. sing. perf. ind. pass. of *redūcō, -ere, -dūxī, -ductum,* 3; agrees with the subject-nom. *Marcus Mēttius.*

1 LIV.	Hōc	proeliō	trāns	Rhēnum	LIV. When this battle was reported across the Rhine, the Suevi, who had come to the river's banks, began to return home; and the Ubii, who dwelt next to the Rhine, followed them, and slew a large number of them while panic-stricken.
	This	*battle*	*across*	*the Rhine*	
2 nūntiātō		Suēvī,	quī	ad	rīpās
having been announced		*the Suevi,*	*who*	*near*	*the banks*
3 Rhēnī	vēnerant,	domum	revertī	coepērunt;	
of the Rhine	*had come,*	*home*	*to return*	*began;*	
4 quōs	Ubiī,	quī	proximī	Rhēnum	incolunt,
whom	*the Ubii,*	*who*	*next*	*to the Rhine*	*dwell,*
5 perterritōs		īnsecūtī	magnam	ex	his
thoroughly terrified,		*having pursued,*	*a great,*	*of*	*them,*

LINE 1. **Hōc**, abl. sing. n. (*hīc, haec, hōc*); an attributive of *proeliō*. —— **proeliō**, abl. sing. n. of *proelium, -ī*; abl. absolute with *nūntiātō*, denoting *time when*. A. & G. 255; B. 192; G. 409, 410; H. 431. Synonyms: see *proeliīs*, l. 18, Chap. I. The battle referred to is the rout of the Germans mentioned in the preceding chapter. —— **trāns**, prep. with the acc. —— **Rhēnum**, acc. sing. m. (*Rhēnus, -ī*); an appositive with *flūmen* understood; which latter is the direct obj. of *trāns*.

LINE 2. **nūntiātō**, abl. sing. n. of the perf. pass. participle *nūntiātus, -a, -um* of the verb *nūntiō* (*nūntius*); abl. absolute with the noun *proeliō*. —— **Suēvī** (GK. Σούηβοι), nom. plur. m.; subj. of *coepērunt*. —— **quī**, nom. plur. m. (*quī, quae, quod*); subj. of *vēnerant*. —— **ad**, prep. with the acc. = *to, near, in the vicinity of.* —— **rīpās**, acc. plur. f. of *rīpa, -ae;* obj. of the prep. *ad*.

LINE 3. **Rhēnī**, gen. sing. m. (*Rhenis, -ī*); limits *rīpās*. —— **vēnerant**, 3d pers. plur. pluperf. ind. act. of *veniō*, 4; agrees with the subj. *quī*. —— **domum**, acc. sing. f. of *domus, -ūs;* locative *domī;* the limit of motion. A. & G. 258, 2. *b*; B. 154, REM. 1; G. 337; H. 380, II, 2, 1). —— **revertī**, pres. inf. of *revertor, -ī, -sus*, deponent; complementary inf. A. & G. 271; B. 181; G. 423; H. 533, I. 1. —— **coepērunt**, 3d pers. plur. perf. ind. act. of the preteritive verb *coepī, coepisse, coeptus*, with pass. inf. in the same sense as act.; agrees with the subject-nom. *Suēvī*.

LINE 4. **quōs**, acc. plur. of *quī;* refers to the Suevi, but is the direct obj. of the deponent participle *īnsecūtī*. —— **Ubiī, -ōrum**, nom. plur. m.; subj. of *occīdērunt*. These were a German clan on the east of the Rhine. —— **quī**, nom. plur. m.; subj. of *incolunt*. —— **proximī**, nom. plur. of the adj. *proximus, -a, -um;* superl.; comparative *propior;* no positive; agrees with the pron. *quī* in gender and number. —— **Rhēnum**, acc. sing. m.; obj. of the adj. *proximī*, as if it were a prep. A. & G. 234, *e*; B. 144, REM. 4; G. 359, NOTE 1; H. 391, II, 2. —— **incolunt**, 3d pers. plur. pres. ind. act. (*incolō*, 3).

LINE 5. **perterritōs**, acc. plur. m. of the perf. pass. participle *perterritus, -a, -um* of *perterreō*, 2; agrees with the rel. pron. *quōs* in gender, number, and case. —— **īnsecūtī**, nom. plur. m. of the participle *īnsecūtus, -a, -um* of *īnsequor, -ī, -cūtus*, deponent; agrees with *Ubiī* in gender, number and case. —— **magnam**, acc. sing. f. of the adj. *magnus, -a, -um;* an attributive of *numerum*. —— **ex**, prep. with the abl. —— **hīs**, abl. plur. (*hīc, haec, hōc*); used as a pron. of the 3d pers.; obj. of the prep. *ex*.

Caesar, having finished two very important wars in a single campaign, led his army into winter-quarters among the Sequani, a little earlier than the season of the year required; he put Labienus in command of the winter-quarters; while he in person set out	numerum *number* duōbus *two* paulō *by a little* hīberna *winter-quarters* dēdūxit; *withdrew;*	occīdērunt. *slew.* māximīs *of the greatest* quam *than* in *among*	Caesar, *Caesar,* bellīs *wars* tempus *the time*	ūnā *in one* cōnfectīs, *having been finished,* annī · *of the year* Sēquanōs *the Sequani* hībernīs *over the winter-quarters*	aestāte *summer* mātūrius *sooner* postulābat, *demanded,* exercitum *the army* Labiēnum *Labienus*	6 7 in 8 *into* 9 10

LINE 6. **numerum**, acc. sing. m. (*numerus, -ī*); direct obj. of *occīdērunt.* —— **occīdērunt**, 3d pers. plur. perf. ind. act. of *occīdō, -ere, -cīdī, -cīsum*, 3 (ob + caedō); agrees with the subject *Ubii.* —— **Caesar, -aris**, m.; subject-nom. of *dēdūxit*, l. 10, below. —— **ūnā**, abl. sing. f. of the adj. *ūnus, -a, -um;* an attributive of *aestāte.* —— **aestāte**, abl. sing. f. of *aestas, -ātis* (from *acvum* through *aevitās*); abl. *of time at which.* A. & G. 256, 1; B. 171; G. 393; H. 429.

LINE 7. **duōbus**, abl. plur. n. of the num. adj. *duo, duae, duo;* an attributive of *bellīs.* —— **māximīs**, abl. plur. n. of *maximus, -a, -um;* superl. of the adj. *māgnus;* comparative *māior;* also modifies *bellīs.* —— **bellīs**, abl. plur. n. (*bellum, -ī*); absolute with *cōnfectīs.* —— **cōnfectīs**, abl. plur. n. of the perf. pass. participle *cōnfectus, -a, -um* of *cōnficiō*, 3; absolute with the noun *bellīs.* —— **mātūrius**, adv., comparative degree; positive *mātūrē;* superl. *mātūrissimē* or *mātūrrimē.*

LINE 8. **paulō**, adv.; might be taken as an abl. *of degree of difference.* —— **quam**, conj. = *than.* —— **tempus**, nom. sing. n.; subj. of *postulābat.* —— **annī**, gen. sing. m. (*annus, -ī*); limits *tempus.* —— **postulābat**, 3d pers. sing. imperf. ind. act. of *postulō*, 1; agrees with *tempus.* Synonyms: see *poscere*, l. 71, Chap. XXXI. —— **in**, prep., here with the acc.

LINE 9. **hīberna**, acc. plur. n. of the adj. *hībernus, -a, -um;* used as a noun; or supply *castra;* obj. of the prep. *in.* —— **in**, prep., here also with the acc. —— **Sēquanōs**, acc. plur. of *Sēquanī, -ōrum;* obj. of the prep. *in*, which here = *among.* Observe that the people are here put for the country. —— **exercitum**, acc. sing. m. (*exercitus, -ūs*); direct obj. of *dēdūxit.* Synonyms: *exercitū*, l. 31, Chap. III.

LINE 10. **dēdūxit**, 3d pers. sing. perf. ind. act. of *dēdūcō*, 3 (dē + dūcō); agrees with a pron. understood, referring to Caesar. —— **hībernīs**, dat. plur. n. (*hīberna*); dat. after *prae* in the compound *praeposuit.* —— **Labiēnum**, acc. sing. m. (*Labiēnus, -ī*); direct obj. of *praeposuit.* The allusion is to Titus Attius Labienus, Caesar's most trusted lieutenant.

11 praeposuit;	ipse	in	citeriōrem	Galliam	for Hither Gaul to hold the proconsular courts.
he placed;	*he himself,*	*into*	*citerior*	*Gaul*	
12 ad	conventūs	agendōs	profectus est.		
to	*the assizes*	*to be held,*	*set forth.*		

LINE 11. **praeposuit**, 3d pers. sing. perf. ind. act. of *praepōnō, -ere, -posui, -positum*, 3 (prae + pōnere, *to put before*); agrees with a pron. understood, referring to Caesar. —— **ipse**, intensive pron.; refers to Caesar, and is the subj. of *profectus est*. —— **in**, prep., here with the acc. after a verb of motion. —— **citeriōrem**, acc. sing. of the adj. *citerior, -ius;* superl. *citimus;* positive wanting; an attributive of *Galliam*. —— **Galliam**, acc. sing. f. (*Gallia, -ae*); obj. of the prep. *in*. The Gaul referred to is Cisalpina, lying on the south side of the Alps.

LINE 12. **ad**, prep. with the acc. —— **conventūs**, acc. plur. m. of *conventus, -ūs* (con + venīre); hence the noun = *coming together;* obj. of the prep. *ad*. —— **agendōs**, acc. plur. m. of the gerundive *agendus -a, -um* of *ago, -ere, ēgī, actum;* agrees with *conventūs*, and the construction denotes the purpose of *profectus est*. A. & G. 300, and NOTE; B. 184, REM. 4, III; G. 432; H. 542, III, FOOTNOTE 5. These conventions or proconsular courts were within Caesar's jurisdiction as pro-consul. —— **profectus est**, 3d pers. sing. perf. ind. of the deponent *proficīscor, -ī, -fectus*, 3; agrees with a pron. implied in the ending, referring to Caesar.

Handy Literal Translations. Cloth, *pocket.* **50 cents** per vol.
Eighty-seven volumes, viz.: (*See also "Tutorial Translations."*)

Cæsar's Gallic War. *The Seven Books.*
Cæsar's *Civil* War.
Catullus.
Cicero's Brutus.
Cicero's Defence of Roscius.
Cicero De Officiis.
Cicero On Old Age and Friendship.
Cicero On Oratory.
Cicero On The Nature of the Gods.
Cicero's Orations. *Four vs. Catiline; and others. Enlarged edition.*
Cicero's Select Letters.
Cicero's Tusculan Disputations.
Cornelius Nepos, *complete.*
Eutropius.
Horace, *complete.*
Juvenal's Satires, *complete.*
Livy, Books I and II.
Livy, Books XXI and XXII.
Lucretius, *in preparation.*
Ovid's Metamorphoses, *complete in 2 volumes.*
Phædrus' Fables.
Plautus' Captivi, and Mostellaria.
Plautus' Pseudolus, and Miles Gloriosus.
Plautus' Trinummus, and Menæchmi.
Pliny's Select Letters, *complete in 2 volumes.*
Quintilian, Books X and XII.
Roman Life in Latin Prose and Verse.
Sallust's Catiline, and The Jugurthine War.
Seneca On Benefits.
Tacitus' Annals. *The 1st Six Books.*
Tacitus' Germany and Agricola.
Tacitus On Oratory.
Terence: Andria, Adelphi, and Phormio
Terence: Heautontimorumenos.
Virgil's Æneid, *the 1st Six Books.*
Virgil's Eclogues and Georgics.
Viri Romæ.

Æschines Against Ctesiphon.
Æschylus' Prometheus Bound; Seven Against Thebes.
Æschylus' Agamemnon.
Aristophanes' Clouds.
Aristophanes' Birds, and Frogs.
Demosthenes On the Crown.
Demosthenes' Olynthiacs and Philippics.
Euripides' Alcestis, and Electra.
Euripides' Bacchantes, and Hercules Furens.
Euripides' Hecuba, and Andromache.
Euripides' Iphigenia In Aulis, In Tauris.
Euripides' Medea.
Herodotus, Books VI and VII.
Herodotus, Book VIII.
Homer's Iliad, *the 1st Six Books.*
Homer's Odyssey, *the 1st Twelve Books.*
Isocrates' Panegyric, *in preparation.*
Lucian's Select Dialogues. *2 volumes.*
Lysias' Orations. *The only Translation extant.*

Handy Literal Translations, continued next page.

Handy Literal Translations (*Continued.*)
Plato's Apology, Crito, and Phædo.
Plato's Gorgias.
Plato's Laches (*paper*).
Plato's Protagoras, and Euthyphron.
Plato's Republic.
Sophocles' Œdipus Tyrannus, Electra, and Antigone.
Sophocles' Œdipus Coloneus.
Thucydides, *complete in 2 volumes.*
Xenophon's Anabasis, *the 1st Four Books.*
Xenophon's Cyropædia, *complete in 2 volumes.*
Xenophon's Hellénica, and Symposium (The Banquet).
Xenophon's Memorabilia, *complete.*

Freytag's Die Journalisten (*paper*).
Goethe's Egmont.
Goethe's Faust.
Goethe's Hermann and Dorothea.
Goethe's Iphigenia In Tauris.
Lessing's Minna von Barnhelm.
Lessing's Nathan the Wise.
Lessing's Emilia Galotti.
Schiller's Ballads.
Schiller's Der Neffe als Onkel.
Schiller's Maid of Orleans.
Schiller's Maria Stuart.
Schiller's Wallenstein's Death.
Schiller's William Tell.
Corneille's The Cid.
Feuillet's Romance of a Poor Young Man.
Racine's Athalie.

Interlinear Translations. Classic Series. Cloth. $1.50 per vol.
Cæsar.
Cicero's Orations, *Enlarged Edition.*
Cicero On Old Age and Friendship.
Cornelius Nepos.
Horace, *complete.*
Livy. Books XXI and XXII.
Ovid's Metamorphoses, *complete.*
Sallust's Catiline, and Jugurthine War.
Virgil's Æneid, *First Six Books, Revised.*
Virgil's Æneid, *complete, the Twelve Books.*
Virgil's Eclogues, Georgics, *and Last Six Books Æneid.*
Xenophon's Anabasis.
Xenophon's Memorabilia.
Homer's Iliad. *First Six Books, Revised.*
Demosthenes On the Crown.
New Testament, *Without Notes.*

Completely Parsed Cæsar, Book I. Each page bears *interlin-ar* translation, *literal* translation, parsing, grammatical references. *All at a glance without turning a leaf.* $1.50.

New Testament, with Notes, and Lexicon. *Interlinear Greek-English, with King James Version in the margins.* New edition, with finely discriminating presentation of the Synonyms of the Greek Testament. *Cloth,* $4.00; *half-leath.,* $5.00; *Divinity Circuit,* $6.00.

Old Testament, Vol. I. Genesis and Exodus. *Interlinear Hebrew-English, with Notes; King James Version and Revised Version in the margins; and with the Hebrew alphabet and Tables of the Hebrew verb.* Cloth, $4.00; half-leath., $5.00; Divinity Circuit, $6.00.

Tutorial Literal Translations, 41 vols. (*See Tutorial Texts.*)
Cicero Ad Atticum, Book IV., *with Test Papers.* 50 cents.
Cicero De Finibus, Bk.I., Bk II., *with Test Papers, each* 50 cents.
Cicero's Philippic, II., 50 cents.
Cicero Pro Balbo, 50 cents.
Cicero Pro Cluentio, 50 cents.
Cicero Pro Plancio, 50 cents.
Livy, Book III., Book V., Book VI., Book IX., *each* 50 cents.
Ovid's Fasti, Books III.-IV., 50 cents.
Ovid's Heroïdes, 1-2-3-5-7-12, 50 cents.
Ovid's Tristia, Book I., Book III., *each* 50 cents.
Tacitus' History, Book I., 50 cents.
Tacitus' History, Book III., *with Test Papers,* 60 cents.
Vergil's Æneid, Books VII., VIII., IX., X., XI., XII., *each* 50 cts.
Vergil's Æneid, Books VII.-X , 50 cents.
Æschylus' Eumenides, *with Test Papers,* 50 cents.
Æschylus' Persae, 50 cents.
Andocides De Mysteriis, $1.00.
Aristophanes' Vespae, *with Test Papers,* 50 cents.
Demosthenes' Adversus Leptinem, *with Test Papers,* 50 cents.
Demosthenes' Androtion, 50 cents.
Demosthenes' Meidias, 75 cents.
Euripides' Heraclidæ, 50 cents.
Euripides' Hippolytus, 50 cents.
Herodotus, Book III., 50 cents.
Homer's Iliad, Book XXIV, 50 cents.
Homer's Odyssey, Books IX.-XIV., *with Test Papers,* 60 cents.
Homer's Odyssey, Book XVII. 50 cents.
Sophocles' Ajax, *with Test Papers,* 50 cents.
Sophocles' Philoctetes, 50 cents.
Xenophon's Anabasis, Book VII., 50 cents.
Xenophon's Oeconomicus, 50 cents.
"*Teachers' Editions*" also contain *Test Papers* (below).

Tutorial Latin, and Greek Texts, Teachers' Editions, etc.

A most helpful feature of the **TEACHERS' EDITIONS** is that, besides the Text, the Notes, and the Translation, they contain also sets of Test Papers facilitating examinations, and Vocabularies with the correct inflections and renderings of all words occurring in the text that because of peculiar significance or difficult construction, suggest special guidance Moreover, the Test Papers and the Vocabularies are interleaved.

Æschylus' Persae, Text and Notes, Price, 75 cents.
   Same, Teachers' Edition, with Translation, $1.00.
Æschylus' Prometheus Vinctus, Text and Notes, Price, 60 cents.
   See "Handy Literal Translation." 50 cents.
Æschylus' Septem Contra Thebas, Text and Notes, 75 cents.
   See "Handy Literal Translation," 50 cents.
Aristophanes' Ranæ, Text and Notes, 75 cents.
   See "Handy Literal Translation," 50 cents.
Cæsar's Gallic War, **Book I.**, Text and Notes, 40 cents.
   Same, Teachers' Edition, with Translation, 70 cents.
Cæsar's Gallic War, **Book II.**, Text and Notes, 40 cents.
   Same, Teachers' Edition, with Translation, 70 cents.
Cæsar's Gallic War, **Book III.**, Text and Notes, 40 cents.
   Same, Teachers' Edition, with Translation, 70 cents.
Cæsar's Gallic War, **Book IV.**, Text and Notes, 40 cents.
   Same, Teacher's Edition, with Translation, $1.20.
Cæsar's Gallic War **Book V.**, Text and Notes, 40 cents.
   Same, Teachers' Edition with Translation, 70 cents.
Cæsar's Gallic War, **Book VI.**, Text and Notes, 40 cents.
   Same, Teachers' Edition, with Translation, 70 cents.

Tutorial Classic Texts and Teachers' Editions—(*Continued.*)

Cæsar's Gallic War, **Book VII.**, Text and Notes, 60 cents.
  Same, Teachers' Edition, with Translation, $1.00.
Cicero Ad Atticum, **Book IV.**, Text and Notes, 60 cents.
  Literal Translation, with Test Papers, 50 cents.
Cicero de Amicitia, Text and Notes, 40 cents.
  Same, with Test Papers, and the Vocabularies, 60 cents.
  Same, Teachers' Edition, with Translation, 70 cents.
Cicero De Finibus, **Book I.**, Text and Notes, 60 cents.
  Same, Teachers' Edition, with Translation, 80 cents.
Cicero De Finibus, **Book II.**, Text and Notes, 75 cents.
  Literal Translation, with Test Papers, 50 cents.
Cicero De Officiis, **Book III**, Text and Notes, 75 cents.
  Same, Teachers' Edition, with Translation, $1.20.
Cicero De Senectute, Text and Notes, 40 cents.
  Same, Teachers' Edition, with Translation, 70 cents.
Cicero In Catilinam **Book I.**, Text and Notes, 40 cents.
  Same, Teachers' Edition, with Translation, 70 cents.
Cicero Pro Archia, Text and Notes, 40 cents.
  Same, Teachers' Edition, with Translation, 70 cents.
Cicero Pro Balbo, Text and Notes, 40 cents.
  Same, Teachers' Edition, with Translation, 70 cents.
Cicero Pro Cluentio, Text and Notes, 75 cents.
  Same, Teachers' Edition, with Translation, $1.20.
Cicero Pro Marcello, Text and Notes, 40 cents.
  Same, Teachers' Edition, with Translation, 70 cents.
Cicero Pro Milone, Text and Notes, 75 cents.
  Same, Teachers' Edition, with Translation, $1.20.
Cicero Pro Plancio, Text and Notes, 60 cents.
Cornelius Nepos, Text and Notes, 25 cents.
  See Handy Literal Translation, 50 cts.; *Interlinear*, $1.50.
Demosthenes' Androtion, Text and Notes, $1.00.
  Literal Translation, 50 cents.
Demosthenes' Meidias, Text and Notes, $1.30.
  Literal Translation, 75 cents.
Euripides' Alcestis, Text and Notes, 70 cents.
  Same, Teachers' Edition, with Translation, $1.00.
Euripides' Andromache, Text and Notes, 70 cents.
  Same, Teachers' Edition, with Translation, $1.00.
Euripides' Bacchæ, Text and Notes, 75 cents.
  Same, Teachers' Edition, with Translation, $1.20.
Euripides' Hecuba, Text and Notes, $1.00.
  Same, Teachers' Edition, with Translation, $1.20.
Euripides' Hippolytus, Text and Notes, 75 cents.
  Same, Teachers' Edition, with Translation, $1.20.
Herodotus, **Book III.**, Text and Notes, $1.00.
  Same, Teachers' Edition, with Translation, $1.40.
Herodotus, **Book VI.**, Text and Notes, 60 cents.
  Same, Teachers' Edition, with Translation, $1.00.
Herodotus, **Book VIII.**, Text and Notes, 60 cents.
  See, "Handy Literal Translation," 50 cents.
Homer's Iliad, **Book VI.**, Text and Notes, 40 cents.
Homer's Iliad, **Book XXIV.**, Text and Notes, 75 cents.
Homer's Odyssey, **Books IX.-X.**, Text and Notes, 60 cents.
Homer's Odyssey, **Books XI.-XII.**, Text and Notes, 60 cents.
Homer's Odyssey, **Books XIII.-XIV.**, Text and Notes, 60 cents.
  Literal Trans., Books IX.-XIV., with Test Papers, 60 cents.
Homer's Odyssey, **Book XVII.**, Text and Notes, 40 cents.
Horace's Epodes, Text and Notes, 40 cents.
  See "Handy Literal Translation," 50 cts.; "*Interlinear*," $1.50.
Horace's Odes, **Book I.**, Text and Notes, 40 cents.
  Same, Teachers' Edition, with Translation, 70 cents.

Tutorial Classic Texts and Teachers' Editions—*(Continued.)*

Horace's Odes, **Book II.**, Text and Notes, 40 cents.
    Same, Teachers' Edition, with Translation, 70 cents.
Horace's Odes, **Book III.**, Text and Notes, 40 cents.
    Same, Teachers' Edition, with Translation, 70 cents.
Horace's Odes, **Book IV.**, Text and Notes, 40 cents.
    Same, Teachers' Edition, with Translation, 70 cents.
Horace's Odes, **Books I., II., III., IV.**, Text and Notes, $1.00.
    See "*Handy Translation,*" 50 cents. "*Interlinear,*" $1.50.
Horace's Satires, Text and Notes, 80 cents.
    See "*Handy Translation,*" 50 cents; "*Interlinear,*" $1.50.
Horace's Epistles, Text and Notes, 80 cents.
    Same, Teachers' Edition, with Translation, $1.20.
Juvenal's Satires, **I., III., IV.**, Text and Notes, 80 cents.
Juvenal's Satires, **VIII., X., XIII.**, Text and Notes, 60 cents.
Juvenal's Satires, **XI., XIII., XIV.**, Text and Notes, 75 cents.
    See "*Handy Literal Translation,*" 50 cents.
Livy, **Book I.**, Text and Notes, 60 cents.
    Same, Teachers' Edition, with Translation, $1.00.
Livy, **Book III.**, Text and Notes, 60 cents.
    Same, Teachers' Edition, with Translation, $1.00.
Livy, **Book V.**, Text and Notes, 60 cents.
    Same, Teachers' Edition, with Translation, $1.00.
Livy, **Book VI.**, Text and Notes, 60 cents.
    Same, Teachers' Edition, with Translation, $1.00.
Livy, **Book IX.**, Text and Notes, 75 cents.
    Same, Teachers' Edition, with Translation, $1.20.
Livy, **Book XXI.**, Text and Notes, 60 cents.
    Same, Teachers' Edition, with Translation, $1.00.
Livy, **Book XXII.**, Chapters 1 to 51, Text and Notes, 60 cents.
    Same, Teachers' Edition, with Translation, $1.00.
Ovid's Fasti, **Books III., IV.**, Text and Notes, 60 cents.
    Same, Teachers' Edition, with Translation, $1.00.
Ovid's Heroides, **Books I., V., XII.**, Text and Notes, 40 cents.
    Literal Translation of same, 50 cents.
Ovid's Heroides, 1, 2, 3, 5, 7, 12, Text and Notes, 70 cents.
    Same, Teachers' Edition, with Translation, $1.20.
Ovid's Metamorphoses, **Book XI.**, Text and Notes, 40 cents.
    Same, Teachers' Edition, with Translation, 70 cents.
Ovid's Metamorphoses, **Book XIII.**, Text and Notes, 40 cents.
    Same, Teachers' Edition, with Translation, 70 cents.
Ovid's Metamorphoses, **Book XIV.**, Text and Notes, 40 cents.
    Same, Teachers' Edition, with Translation, 70 cents.
Ovid's Tristia, **Book I.**, Text and Notes, 40 cents.
    Same, Teachers' Edition, with Translation, 70 cents.
Ovid's Tristia, **Book III.**, Text and Notes, 40 cents.
    Same, Teachers' Edition, with Translation, 70 cents.
Plato's Laches, Text and Notes, 75 cents.
    Same, Teachers' Edition, with Translation, $1.20.
Plato's Apology, Text and Notes, $1.00.
    See "*Handy Literal Translation,*" 50 cents.
Plato's Phaedo, Text and Notes, 80 cents.
    See "*Handy Literal Translation,*" 50 cents.
Sallust's Catiline, Text and Notes, 60 cents.
    Same, Teachers' Edition, with Translation, 90 cents.
Sophocles' Ajax, Text and Notes, 75 cents.
    Literal Translation, with Test Papers, 50 cents.
Sophocles' Antigone, Text and Notes, 40 cents.
    Same, Teachers' Edition, with Translation, 70 cents.
Sophocles' Electra, Text and Notes, 80 cents.
    Same, Teachers' Edition, with Translation, $1.20.

Tutorial Classic Texts and Teachers' Editions—*(Continued.)*

Tacitus' Annals, **Book I.**, Text and Notes, 60 cents.
Tacitus' Annals, **Book II.**, Text and Notes, 60 cents.
  See "Handy Literal Translation," 50 cents.
Tacitus' Histories, **Book I.**, Text and Notes, 60 cents.
  Same, Teachers' Edition, with Translation, $1.00.
Terence's Adelphi, Text and Notes, 75 cents.
  See "Handy Literal Translation," 50 cents.
Thucydides, **Book I.**, Notes and Test Papers only, 40 cents
Thucydides, **Book VII.**, Text and Notes, 60 cents.
  See "Handy Literal Translation," 50 cents.
Vergil's Eclogues, Text and Notes, 75 cents.
  Same, Teachers' Edition, with Translation, $1.20.
Vergil's Georgics, **Books I., II.**, Text and Notes, 75 cents.
  Same, Teachers' Edition, with Translation, $1.20.
Vergil's Aeneid, **Book I.**, Text and Notes, 40 cents.
  Same, Teachers' Edition, with Translation, 70 cents.
  See "Handy" Translation, 50 cents; *"Interlinear,"* $1.50.
Vergil's Aeneid, **Book II.**, Text and Notes, 40 cents.
  Same, Teachers' Edition, with Translation, 70 cents.
Vergil's Aeneid, **Book III.**, Text and Notes, 40 cents.
  Same, Teachers' Edition, with Translation, 70 cents.
Vergil's Aeneid, **Book IV.**, Text and Notes, 40 cents.
  Literal Translation, 50 cents.
Vergil's Aeneid, **Book V.**, Text and Notes, 40 cents.
  Same, Teachers' Edition, with Translation, 70 cents.
Vergil's Aeneid, **Book VI.**, Text and Notes, 40 cents.
  Same, Teachers' Edition, with Translation, 70 cents.
Vergil's Aeneid, **Book VII.**, Text and Notes, 40 cents.
  Same, Teachers' Edition, with Translation, 70 cents.
Vergil's Aeneid, **Book VIII.**, Text and Notes, 40 cents.
  Same, Teachers' Edition, with Translation, 70 cents.
Vergil's Aeneid, **Book IX.**, Text and Notes, 40 cents.
Vergil's Aeneid, **Book X.**, Text and Notes, 40 cents.
  Literal Translation, Books IX-X, 50 cents.
Vergil's Aeneid, **Book XI.**, Text and Notes, 40 cents.
  Literal Translation, 50 cents.
Vergil's Aeneid, **Book XII.**, Text and Notes, 40 cents.
  Literal Translation, 50 cents.
Xenophon's Anabasis, **Book I.**, Text and Notes, 40 cents.
  Same, Teachers' Edition, with Translation, 70 cents.
Xenophon's Anabasis, **Book IV.**, Text and Notes, 75 cents.
  See "Handy Literal Translation," 50 cents.
Xenophon's Cyropaedeia, **Book I.**, Text and Notes, 75 cents.
  See "Handy Literal Translation," 50 cents.
Xenophon's Hellenica, **Book III.**, Text and Notes, 80 cents.
  Same, Teachers' Edition, with Translation, $1.00.
Xenophon's Hellenica, **Book IV.**, Text and Notes, 80 cents.
  See "Handy Literal Translation," 50 cents.
Xenophon's Oeconomicus, Text and Notes, $1.00.
  Same, Teachers' Edition, with Translation, $1.40.

UNIVERSITY TUTORIAL SERIES.

Latin and Greek Texts. See above.
Latin and Greek Grammars and Readers.
  Latin Grammar, The Tutorial. 80 cents.
    Exercises to same, 40 cents. *Key to Exercises,* 70 cents.
  Latin Comp. and Syntax, *with Vocabularies,* 60 cts. *Key,* 60 cts.
  Preceptors' Latin Course, 70 cents. *Key to same,* 70 cents.

In the First Greek Lessons the author has drawn largely from the Bible for illustrative sentences, so that after going through the Lessons the student will have little difficulty in reading the New Testament in the Greek.

Brooks' Classics

Historia Sacra, with 1st Latin Lessons. Revised, *with Vocabulary.* **Price 50 cents.** This justly popular volume, besides the Epitome Historiæ Sacræ, the Notes, and the Lexicon, contains 100 pages of elementary Latin Lessons so arranged as to form a practical course in Latin for the beginner, making it practicable for the teacher, without recourse to any other book, to carry the pupil quickly and in easy steps, over the ground preparatory to a profitable reading of the Epitome Historiæ Sacræ. **Price 50 cents.**

First Lessons in Greek, *with Lexicon.* Revised Edition. Prepared on the same plan as the author's First Latin Lessons. Tables giving derivations of the parts of speech. Tables showing the formation of the tenses. **Price 50 cents.**

Virgil's Æneid, *with Lexicon.* Illustrated and revised Edition. Notes, Critical, Historical and Mythological. Metrical Index and Map, and numerous engravings of Antique Statues, Arms, Gems, Coins and Medals. Also Questions for Examinations. **Price reduced to $1.50.**

SAYS DR. SHELTON MACKENZIE:—"It is the most beautiful edition of Virgil's Æneid yet published. As an illustrated school book it has never been even approached."

Ovid's Metamorphoses, *with Lexicon.* Illustrated and Revised Edition. Expurgated and adapted for Mixed Classes. Elucidated by an Analysis and Explanation of each Table. With English Notes, Historical, Mythological and Critical, and Questions for Examinations. **Price reduced to $1.50.**

SAYS DR. NEWELL:—"It bears the impress alike of the accurate scholar and the experienced teacher. He has added a body of explanatory notes, which for fullness, variety and appropriateness, will compare with any similar work, and gain by the comparison."

Hinds & Noble, Publishers

4 Cooper Institute   New York City

Idioms of Caesar
Cicero's Idioms

Complete, with English equivalents. Alphabetically arranged for ready reference, or for serial memorizing ♣ ♣ ♣ ♣ ♣

EACH—Price 25 cents—PAPER

By JOACHIM C. MUELLER
PROF. OF LATIN, CALVIN COLLEGE, CLEVELAND, OHIO

The two pamphlets cover, respectively, the GALLIC WAR, and the 4 ORATIONS *vs.* CATILINE; and besides the Latin idioms done into correct English, each pamphlet also contains an English-Latin index to help the pupil put English idioms into classical Latin.

These handy books are published in the belief that nothing in the study of the Latin is harder for the average beginner than to render the idioms accurately and well.

The suggestion offered by the compiler of these exceedingly convenient lists, is that the teacher assign say ten idioms for each recitation, and that the pupils memorize them and also form sentences illustrating the idioms—developing a surprising facility in sensing the drift of the text.

This plan has been so successfully employed by the compiler in his own classes beginning Latin, for whom these lists were prepared, that he has in preparation similar lists of the idioms of other classic Latin writers.

HINDS & NOBLE, Publishers of

Completely Parsed Cæsar, BOOK I, $1.50
Shortest Road to Cæsar. For beginners. 75 cents
Interlinear Translation of Cæsar, $1.50
Literal Translation Cæsar, 50 cents

4-5-6-12-13-14 Cooper Institute,   New York City
Schoolbooks of all publishers at one store

College Girls' Three-minute Readings

$1.00—CLOTH, 500 PAGES, WITH INDEX—$1.00

Here is a volume for American girls by American women—an ideal long in demand, now realized for the first time. In this book patriotism is the keynote dominating a series of new, fresh, *speakable* selections, pathetic, humorous, descriptive, oratorical; running, in fact, the gamut of the emotions. A book for the American girl and the American young woman in the college, the high school, the academy, and *the home*.

This new book is new in every sense of the word, but particularly in voicing the golden thoughts of scores of the *living* representative women of America—women educators, women philanthropists, women reformers.

Here is a *partial* list of the contributors:

Mrs. A. Giddings Park	"Susan Coolidge"
Eva Lovett Cameron (*Brooklyn Eagle*)	Agnes E. Mitchell
Edith M. Thomas	Rev. Anna H. Shaw
Emma Lazarus	Margaret Junkin Preston
Adelaide Procter	Amelia Barr
Celia Thaxter	Norah Perry
Christina Rossetti	Alice Cary
Anna Robertson Lindsay	Adeline Whitney
J. Ellen Foster	Emily Warren
Margaret E. Sangster	Lucy Larcom
Clara Barton	Ella Wheeler Wilcox
Frances E. Willard	Harriet Beecher Stowe
Kate Douglas Wiggin	Mary Mapes Dodge
Isabel A. Mallon (*Ladies' Home Journal*)	"Gail Hamilton"

and there are many others.

A brief note, happily worded, conveying information not to be found elsewhere, regarding the author or the occasion, accompanies most of the selections.

Teachers will find selections appropriate to Memorial Day, Arbor Day, Washington's Birthday, and all other patriotic occasions. And from the pages of this book speak the voices of many of our presidents, from Washington to McKinley.

Besides a perspicuous list of contents, the volume contains a complete general index by titles and authors; and also a separate index of authors, thus enabling one who remembers only the title to find readily the author, or who recalls only the author to find just as readily all of her selections.

Like the companion volume, College Men's Declamations, this work contains many "pieces" suitable both for girls and boys, and the two books may well stand side by side upon the shelf of every student and every teacher, ever ready with some selection that is sure to please, and exactly suited to the speaker and to the occasion.

HINDS & NOBLE, Publishers
4-5-13-14 Cooper Institute   New York City

College Men's 3-minute Declamations

$1.00—CLOTH, 381 PAGES, WITH INDEX—$1.00

Here at last is a volume containing just what college students have been calling for time out of mind, but never could find—something besides the old selections, which, though once inspiring, now fail to thrill the audience, because declaimed to death! Live topics presented by live men! Full of vitality for prize speaking.

Such is the matter with which this volume abounds. To mention a few names—each speaking in his well-known style and characteristic vein:

Chauncey M. Depew	President Eliot (*Harvard*)
Abram S. Hewitt	George Parsons Lathrop
Carl Schurz	Bishop Potter
William E. Gladstone	Sir Charles Russell
Edward J. Phelps	President Carter (*Williams*)
Benjamin Harrison	T. De Witt Talmage
Grover Cleveland	Ex-Pres. White (*Cornell*)
General Horace Porter	Rev. Newman Smyth
Doctor Storrs	Emilio Castelar

Here, too, sound the familiar voices of George William Curtis, Lowell, Blaine, Phillips Brooks, Beecher, Garfield, Disraeli, Bryant, Grady, and Choate. Poets also:—Longfellow, Holmes, Tennyson, Byron, Whittier, Schiller, Shelley, Hood, and others.

More than a hundred other authors besides! We have not space to enumerate. But the selections from them are all just the thing. And all the selections are brief.

In addition to a perspicuous list of contents, the volume contains a complete general index by titles and authors; and also a separate index of authors, thus enabling one who remembers only the title to find readily the author, or who recalls only the author to find just as readily all of his selections.

Another invaluable feature:—Preceding each selection are given, so far as ascertainable, the vocation, the residence, and the dates of birth and death of the author; and the occasion to which we owe the oration, or address, or poem.

Like the companion volume, College Girls' Readings, this work contains many "pieces" suitable both for girls and boys, and the two books may well stand side by side upon the shelf of every student and every teacher ever ready with some selection that is sure to please, and exactly suited to the speaker and to the occasion.

HINDS & NOBLE

4-5-13-14 Cooper Institute　　　　　　New York City

Schoolbooks of all publishers at one store

You don't like to be worsted
In an Argument

Do you? Whenever and wherever thinking men assemble, almost every topic of conversation discovers differences of opinion precipitating argument and discussion. In your own school—are there not pupils who are ambitious to become expert fencers in argument? Have you a debating society looking for new ideas newly put? Is there a lyceum that needs enlivening? a lodge where dullness needs to be replaced by bright discussion on a variety of up-to-date topics? Would your club have a livelier go if your meetings had more sparkle? And your own home circle!—will it be the brighter for clever conversation on the many subjects that are in the public mind? Then you need "PROS AND CONS," a book that we have just published, that is full of the very material—new, practical, up-to-date—for accomplishing any or all of these objects.

The book begins with instructions for organizing a society, giving a sample set of by-laws and a constitution, and the rules governing debate. In a concise and succinct style twenty-one important and live subjects are fully treated, each one by several speakers, affirmative and negative, the final speakers summing up the arguments for their respective sides. These topics are:

Single Gold Standard
Annexation of Cuba
Punishment vs. Reward
Penny Postage
High License
Government Ownership of Railroads
Hawaiian Annexation
Woman Suffrage
Navigation vs. Railroads
Nicaragua Canal
Protective Tariff
Expensive Social Entertainment
Hypocrite vs. Liar
Government and Telegraphs
Opportunities for Financial Success
Immigration
Department Stores
Greenbacks
Taxation
Direct Vote vs. Elec'l College
Postal Savings

After this thorough drilling in actual debate the author presents a skeleton argument for each one of a series of questions—both sides, for and against—enabling the disputant to find a basis for his argument on which he may enlarge at will. Here we have such questions as

> Government Control of Mines
> Trusts and Monopolies
> Municipal Ownership of Franchises
> Modern System of Education
> National Banks
> Bimetallism vs. Protection, etc.

By these easy stages the debater reaches a level where he may stand alone, and, while cutting loose from the set models of the earlier chapters of the book, may yet follow the *form* of the preceding debates, choosing his *subject* from a well-selected list of 250 questions of human interest.

In addition to the numerous set debates, *and following the* debates-in-outline, *the author has interspersed a variety of separate orations and essays, illustrating the salutatory, the valedictory, and the form of address for other special occasions.*

PROS AND CONS

BY A. H. CRAIG, author of "The Common-school Question and Answer Book," *now in its 182d thousand.*

CLOTH—$1.50 Postpaid—472 PAGES

HiNDS & NOBLE, Publishers
4-5-13-14 Cooper Institute   New York City
Schoolbooks of all publishers at one store

Character Building. Inspiring suggestions. $1.00.
Mistakes of Teachers corrected by common sense (the famous *Preston Papers*). Solves difficulties not explained in text-books which daily perplex the conscientious teacher. $1.00.
Best Methods of Teaching in Country Schools(Lind's), $1.25.
Page's Theory and Practice of Teaching. *With Questions and Answers.* Paper, 50 cts. Cloth, $1.00.
Psychology Simplified for Teachers. Gordy's well-known "New Psychology." Familiar talks to teachers and parents on how to observe the child-mind, and on the value of child-study in the successful teaching and rearing of the young. *With Questions* on each Lesson. $1.25. *Twenty-sixth thousand!*
The Perceptionalist. Hamilton's Mental Science, rev. ed. $2.
Smith's New Class Register. The best of record books. 50 cts.
Likes and Opposites. Synonyms and their Opposites. 50 cts.
Letter Writing. New handy rules for correct correspondence. 75c.
Punctuation. Hinds & Noble's new Manual. Paper, 25 cts.
New Speller. Hinds & Noble's new graded lists of 5000 words which one *must* know how to spell. 25 cts.
Craig's COMMON SCHOOL Questions *with Answers.* $1.50.
Henry's HIGH SCHOOL Questions *with Answers.* $1.50.
Sherrill's New Normal Questions *with Answers.* $1.50.
Quizzism and its Key (Southwick). $1.00.
Moritz' 1000 Questions. For the Entrance Examinations to the New York High Schools, the New York Normal College, the College of the City of New York, St. Francis Xavier's College, West Point, Annapolis, and the Civil Service. **30 cents.**
Answers to same. 50 cents.
Recent Entrance Examination Questions. For the New York Normal College, the College of the City of New York, St. Francis Xavier's College, Columbia College, the High Schools, Regents' Exam's, West Point, Annapolis, and the Civil Service. **30 cents.**
Answers to same. 50 cents.
How to Prepare for a Civil Service Examination, with recent *Examination Questions and the Answers.* 560 pages, $2.00. Abridged Edition, **without** *questions and answers*, 50 cents.
How to Become Quick at Figures. Enlarged Edition. $1.00.
Bad English. Humiliating "Breaks" corrected. 30 cts.
Composition Writing Made Easy. *Very successful.* Five Grades, viz.: A, B, C, D, E. 20 cts. each. *All five for 75 cts.*
1000 Composition Subjects. 25 cents.
U. S. Constitution in German, French, and English, *parallel columns*, with explanatory marginal Notes. Cloth, 50c.; paper, 25c.
Bookkeeping Blanks at 30 cts. per set. Five Blank-Books to the set. Adapted for use with any text-book — Elementary, Practical, or Common School. *Used everywhere.*—Price, 30 cts. per set.
Object Lesson Cards (Oliver and Boyd). 48 Cards, 13 x 20 inches. $28.00.
Lessons on Morals (Dewey) 75 cents. *In preparation.*
Lessons on Manners (Dewey) 75 cents. *In preparation.*

Commencement Parts. "Efforts" for all occasions. Orations, addresses, valedictories, salutatories, class poems, class mottoes, after-dinner speeches, flag days, national holidays, class-day exercises. *Models* for every possible occasion in high-school and college career, every one of the "efforts" being what some fellow has *stood on his feet* and actually delivered on a similar occasion—not what the compiler *would* say if *he* should happen to be called on for an ivy song or a response to a toast, or what not; but what the fellow himself, when his turn came, *did say!* $1.50.

New Dialogues and Plays. Life-like episodes from popular authors like Stevenson, Crawford, Mark Twain, Dickens, Scott, in the form of simple plays, with every detail explained as to dress, make-up, utensils, furniture, etc., for school-room or parlor. $1.50.

College Men's 3-Minute Declamations.
Up-to-date selections from live men like Chauncey Depew, Hewitt, Gladstone, Cleveland, President Eliot (Harvard) and Carter (Williams) and others. New material with vitality in it for prize speaking. *Very popular.* $1.00.

College Maids' 3-Minute Readings. Up-to-date recitations from living men and women. On the plan of the popular College Men's Declamations, and on the same high plane. $1.00.

Pieces for Prize Speaking Contests. $1.00. *Nearly ready.*

Acme Declamation Book. *Single pieces and dialogues.* For boys and girls of all ages; all occasions. Paper, 30 cts.; cloth, 50 cts.

Handy Pieces to Speak. *Single pieces and dialogues.* Primary, 20 cts.; Intermediate, 20 cts.; Advanced, 20 cts. *All three for 50 cts.*

Pros and Cons. Complete debates of the affirmative and negative of the stirring questions of the day. *A decided hit.* This is another book invaluable not only to high-school and college students, but also to every other person who aspires to converse engagingly on the topics of the day. Our foreign policy, the currency, the tariff, immigration, high license, woman suffrage, penny postage, transportation, trusts, department stores, municipal ownership of franchises, government control of telegraph. *Both sides* of these and *many other questions* completely debated. Directions for *organizing* and *conducting* a debating society, with *by-laws* and *parliamentary rules.* $1.50.

New Parliamentary Manual. By H. C. Davis, compiler of "Commencement Parts." 75 cents. *Nearly Ready.*

Ten Weeks Course in Elocution (Normal Reader). With numerous and varied selections for illustration and practice. $1.25.

www.ingramcontent.com/pod-product-compliance
Lightning Source LLC
Chambersburg PA
CBHW032144010526
44111CB00035B/1101